William Johnson's Natchez

William Johnson's Natchez

The Ante-Bellum Diary
of a
Free Negro

Edited by

William Ransom Hogan

and

Edwin Adams Davis

With a New Introduction by
William L. Andrews

LOUISIANA STATE UNIVERSITY PRESS
Baton Rouge and London

Contents

Illustrations

Introduction to the 1993 Edition

WILLIAM L. ANDREWS

*W*ILLIAM JOHNSON'S diary, which he kept for almost sixteen years, from 1835 until his death in 1851, is the lengthiest and most detailed personal narrative authored by an African American during the antebellum era in the United States. Out of ordinary account books in which he tallied the daily expenditures and income of his early business ventures, Johnson's diary evolved into an extraordinary record of social, economic, and political life in his hometown of Natchez, Mississippi, as seen through the eyes of a free man of color. Everything from the mundane—Johnson's search for a lost cow—to the momentous—former president Andrew Jackson's visit to Natchez—whetted the diarist's voracious pen. He writes at times as though he were a self-appointed local historian. On other occasions he turns private annalist intent on documenting what he has done to deserve the attention of a local history. Underlying it all is the distinctive perspective that informs the tone and temper of Johnson's personal annals: the point of view of both a participant and an observer, an outsider who courts a place on the inside, a southern man of property who knows that as a Negro in a slave society he was born to *be* a southern man's property.

Nothing like William Johnson's diary exists in the history of antebellum southern or African-American letters. Yet this truly singular experiment in the history of African-American life writing is hardly known today outside that circle of scholars acquainted with the edition of Johnson's diary published by the Louisiana State University Press in 1951. The reissuing of Johnson's diary is designed to revive this unique text of nineteenth-century American diary literature by putting it into the hands of readers who now more than ever before are prepared to appreciate its significance.

To William Ransom Hogan and Edwin Adams Davis, the Louisiana historians whose painstaking research did so much to bring this diary to light and situate it in its peculiar time and place,

William Johnson's narrative made an excellent inaugural contribution to the Source Studies in Southern History series. In the pre-civil rights era in which the diary first appeared, it no doubt seemed appropriate to present this African-American narrative foremost as a source book of local history, the intimate biography of a town—William Johnson's Natchez—rather than as the private autobiography of a black man. In 1993, however, following a period of unprecedented interest in African-American expressive culture, not to mention two decades of heightening attention to the diverse forms of American life writing, the diary prominent among them, it seems just as appropriate now to emphasize the subtitle of 1951—*The Ante-Bellum Diary of a Free Negro*—so that Johnson as personal annalist, not just local historian, may be recognized and reckoned with. Johnson still deserves a reader's admiration for his indefatigable and scrupulous rendering of the daily flow of events in Natchez. But what is perhaps even more remarkable is the fact that without precedents, models, encouragement, or an immediate audience, this Mississippi free man of color dedicated himself to recording what it was like to live, as W. E. B. Du Bois would have put it, "within the veil" of color and caste segregation in the antebellum South.

While William Johnson quietly penned his daily reflections in handsome leather-bound volumes intended for his eyes only, the autobiographies of other blacks from the South, most notably Frederick Douglass and William Wells Brown, were making international headlines and selling widely in paperback editions that made the American slave narrative popular reading throughout Europe and the United States. Like the famous fugitives Douglass and Brown, William Johnson had been born into human bondage, the product of an unsanctioned union between a slaveholder and his slave. But the white man who was both William's father and his owner manumitted him in 1820 when he was about eleven years old, thereby enlisting William in the class of free people of color whose unheralded struggles for opportunity and respect in the South would remain largely ignored in favor of the much more thrilling examples of resistance and flight to the North embodied in the likes of Douglass, Brown, and Harriet Jacobs.

If William Johnson read the stories of a Douglass or a Brown (and if he did he never confided the fact to his diary), it is doubtful that he would have been attracted to the roles of reformer and race leader that Douglass' and Brown's narratives extol as the special mission of the liberated slave. The kind of freedom that

Johnson worked to achieve and maintain in the South depended, obviously enough, on his reaching some sort of accommodation with the economic and political institutions of his region. By contrast, the dominant form of African-American autobiography in the antebellum era, the fugitive slave narrative, predicated a black man's freedom on his uncompromising refusal to countenance slavery in the South or to excuse its corrupting influence on such northern institutions as the church and the laissez-faire economy. This ideal of freedom as the reward of heroic resistance to all that constrains one's individuality, however much it may have appealed to the cultural values of antislavery activists and freethinkers in the antebellum North, could have little efficacy for a man of color in the slaveholding South, particularly one who had invested as much as William Johnson had in the southern status quo.

It may be that Johnson's personal experience of racism and discrimination was sufficiently infrequent that it did not arouse in him that sense of intolerable humiliation and outraged manhood that impelled Douglass to risk all to escape the South. Or it may be that even when confronted with such humiliations, as in the case of his wife's being refused a stateroom on a steamboat bound for New Orleans in the summer of 1842, Johnson believed he could find a way around such problems, as he seems to have done on that occasion by bribing the vessel's captain. The diary gives enough indications of Johnson's ability to maneuver around and sometimes exert power over whites, especially those who owed him money (evidently a large number), that he may have found it possible to take a philosophical view of his situation, finding the ledger of his dealings with the dominant caste balanced in favor of rather than against the preservation of his personal pride. Still, diary entries such as the following from June 2, 1838, leave one wondering about how comfortable Johnson was with the accommodations he made: "I saw a Young man by the name of Horton Kick a Young man by the name of Brown On the Back Side and made him run out of the House and he did not resent it On that a man Can stand some things is most true."

If William Johnson had to stand some things that a Frederick Douglass would have taken a stand against, a reading of Johnson's diary suggests that the free man of color tried to use his position in the community, marginal as it was, to do what he could to help particular slaves and apprenticed free blacks advance ever closer to freedom and independence. In 1841 the barber notes that he gave one of his slaves "several Lessons on the slate of Cyphering," adding approvingly, "he did very well indeed." In the next year Johnson comments on his hearing "The Boys . . . say thier Books again," and admonishes himself about being consistent in their education. These lessons in writing and arithmetic were not clandestine or illegal, of course. Johnson's "boys" were often free men of color apprenticed to him for training until such time as they could go out on their own as self-supporting barbers. As a middleman between apprenticed slaves and their masters, however, Johnson had a good deal to say about who was making progress and who wasn't, who merited increased freedom and opportunity and who didn't. The case of the young slave William Winston, who came to work for Johnson in 1836, illustrates the role the latter played in the process of one slave's emancipation. Johnson saw in Winston's master a white man who felt a slave should be given enough training to learn to keep his accounts in preparation for the time when he would be allowed to go out on his own. But the white man did not think that Winston should be paid wages for his work while in training because "wages was and Injury to a Boy, . . . it would give them Bad Habits." Ever the diplomat, Johnson did not challenge outright this plainly racist notion. He simply made sure that his conversations with Winston's master ended with the clear understanding "that Winston was a very smart Boy and that I Liked him very much indeed." Having heard the slaveholder speak conditionally of Winston's future—"*if* he conducted himself well that he would give him a start some day" (emphasis added)—Johnson's unequivocal endorsement of Winston was skillfully timed to give maximum benefit to a slave whose prospects very much depended on the good offices of a black man whom whites had learned to rely on.

Johnson's praiseworthy willingness to train and encourage slaves and free blacks in his own barbering business cannot be divorced, however, from his participation in the slave trade. The free black barber not only trained other people's slaves; he bought and sold his own. Scarcely a week goes by that Johnson does not mention in his diary the behavior of his slaves or the free black apprentices under his authority and his manner of managing them. Johnson seems to have been neither a great deal better nor conspicuously worse than many other slave owners in Natchez. He fraternized with his slaves at times and granted them occasional privileges, such as passes to go to the circus or religious gatherings. But he never ponders in his diary the morality of slavery as an institution, nor does he pause to consider the ironies of his own role in it. Like most men of his region and era, Johnson seems to have taken slavery for granted, reflecting as little on its inherent injustice as on the brutal code by which it was enforced. Rarely does he give a second thought to the whipping of those who tested his command or broke his rules. An 1841 entry testifies, "I Gave Lucinday a Good Flogging this Evening for her Conduct on yesterday." Her transgression, for which she earned her master's epithet "the Little Strumpet," consisted of making a private assignation when she should have been at church.

Nothing Johnson might have written about his struggles for dignity as a black man in a slave society can palliate the moral and social contradiction, so blatant in our eyes today, of a former slave's choosing to become a slaveholder. Among free blacks in the antebellum South slaveholding was not common, but it was certainly not unheard of either. Amy Johnson, the diarist's mother, owned slaves, and it is probable that other well-to-do men and women of color of Johnson's acquaintance retained slaves as well. In *Black Masters: A Free Family of Color in the Old South*, the remarkable history of the Ellison clan of Charleston, South Carolina, Michael P. Johnson and James L. Roark point out that by 1860 more than fifty free men and women of color of that city possessed slaves. For free African Americans in Charleston, and perhaps for William Johnson as well, owning slaves may have been in part a status symbol, a sign of one's membership in the free Negro elite. Still it is worth remembering that a black entrepreneur like Johnson, who needed labor to expand his business, could not have hired white men to work for him, and the supply of free blacks willing and able to become serviceable employees was never great. Comparatively few slaves worked in Johnson's barbershop, and those who did seem to have received a modicum of reward, as well as training, for their efforts. In the last years of his life Johnson's desire to become a small-time planter led him to put an increasing number of his slaves to work clearing, ploughing, and harvesting crops on his land. These slaves have little identity in the diary, an indication that Johnson thought little about them or their welfare.

For a free black man living and operating in the antebellum South, it was undoubtedly more politic and perhaps even more beneficial to black people within the sphere of his influence to identify himself publicly as a patron of slaves and free colored men who wished to improve their lot in accordance with the laws and mores of the social order. Johnson's attitude toward his slaves, and probably toward enslaved blacks in general, might best be characterized as fundamentally paternalistic. He had his favorites among the slaves he dealt with, such as William Winston, and he seems to have done his best for them as long as they did not transgress his code of behavior. But when Winston broke his rules—"Winston I find has after the best admonitions that I have been able to give, will disobey my orders—I find him to day with a Pistol in his Pocket"—Johnson's reaction was not one of empathy for a young slave trying to assert his inchoate sense of manhood (one thinks of Richard Wright's classic short story, "The Man Who Was Almost a Man"). Instead Johnson gave himself up to self-pity: "Oh if I could only find some honest Person that I could trust in." The mix of exasperation, condescension, and occasional sympathy that Johnson registers in his private narrative when speaking of his slaves' condition and behavior provides an intriguing early indication of the kinds of class and caste prejudices among African Americans that surface only much later in the public genres of black American autobiography.

The complexity of William Johnson's situation as an economically prosperous but socially and politically marginalized man of color in the South must have made his undertaking any form of autobiography other than a diary extremely problematic. When Johnson began his diary on October 12, 1835, he had plenty of reason to see himself as a candidate for a great American success story. Though only twenty-six years old and not quite six months married, he had managed to establish himself as a businessman and property owner whose ready cash and reputation for largesse made more than a few white gentlemen of Natchez his willing debtors. Johnson could easily have prided himself as one of those energetic "natural" men of the expansionist Jacksonian era to whom getting and spending, speculation and self-promotion defined what America was all about. But William Johnson was black, and a free man of color who trumpeted his successes to the world would have struck his southern readers (and probably many in the North too) as dangerously egotistical and therefore suspect. A free Negro who wished to hold on to what he had earned would do well to keep his good fortune to himself and conduct himself in such a way as not to tempt envious whites eager for an excuse to take him down a peg.

Although it would appear that an understandable sense of accomplishment and self-consequence must have spurred Johnson to begin his diary, he did not launch it with the sort of self-conscious invocation or announcement of large purpose that often prefaces well-known nineteenth-century American diaries. His younger contemporary, Charlotte Forten, daughter of one of the most influential and affluent black abolitionists in the North, undertook a journal in 1854 because she believed it would be "a pleasant and profitable employment of my leisure hours, and will afford me much pleasure in other years, by recalling to my mind . . . much-loved friends . . . interesting books . . . and the different people, places, and things that I am permitted to see." Johnson's journal, by contrast, gets down to business from the start; it opens directly, almost abruptly, with an unadorned statement of his purchase of a large tract of land bought at auction from the estate of a white man. Choosing this deal as the beginning entry of his diary was probably not accidental, however. It may very well be that with this land purchase Johnson felt he was crossing a threshold in his life's design, which he hoped would elevate him from a town businessman to a country gentleman.

Most likely this free black man had long since learned to keep his own council about such presumably outsized ambitions. Johnson's undemonstrative matter-of-factness in recording the first of several major land purchases in his life strongly hints at a guardedness long ingrained by his experience on the margins of the color line in the South. This guardedness, this refusal to confide sometimes even to his diary the deeper personal significance of an event, pervades Johnson's diary. The tendency to mask his responses to incidents or to write in a kind of emotional code implies that Johnson's training in the etiquette of the color line taught him a degree of self-censorship that effectively barred him from exploring the more outspoken forms of autobiographical discourse available to a man of Johnson's economic class in the South or the North.

The least socially threatening form of public autobiographical expression for African Americans in the antebellum era was the conversion account and the narrative of ministerial labors. Two of the earliest African-American diaries to be published were recorded by the Methodist ministers John Marrant and Daniel Coker, each of whom clearly expected his story to be used to further the work of the Lord. In the 1850s southern whites proved they were not averse to sponsoring the publication of the conversion stories of two slave preachers, Thomas Anderson and Noah Davis, whose marvelous piety exemplified the sort of inoffensive otherworldliness that slaveholders liked to see in black Christians. William Johnson, however, seems to have felt the promptings of religion very rarely, and then only when a crisis reminded him of the transience of life. The unexpected death of his sister in January of 1848 led him to pray uncharacteristically in his diary, "Oh Mercifull Father Have Mercy on me." A few days later Johnson upbraided himself for sins of "ungovernable temper" and "angry words," which he pledged to atone for, at least in part, "by a strict adhesan to duty" and "by endeavoring to become more amiable." "By striving thus to Emulate the good," he concluded that he might "at last enjoy at least a semillance of that Joy and contentment which they Say only the good can enjoy." Whether Johnson came to enjoy "that Joy and contentment" that are the reward of "the good" is impossible to decide, however, because after his return from the funeral Johnson's life and diary re-entered their former patterns without further reflection on abstract moral or religious matters.

The state of his business, not the condition of his soul, preoccupied William Johnson when he reflected on the important events of each day. Although in his more philosophical moods he may have entertained the notion that "striving to emulate the good" would bring him "joy and contentment," Johnson's diary makes clear that he devoted himself day to day to amassing the goods of this world. It may not have been contentment he was after so much as a sense of invulnerability to the caprices of fate that affected people of color, both enslaved and free, in the world Johnson knew all too well. Once in a great while this worldly man mentions attending a religious camp meeting or reading the Bible, but the long-term effect of these fairly perfunctory religious exercises on his thought and action is hard to discern. From time to time Johnson thanked the deity for good health and prosperity; one finds infrequent petitions to God to restore a sick child or to grant that "I may be Lucky Enogh to make some good Investments." But these acknowledgments of God's attention to the human realm are balanced by more resigned, sometimes cynical, observations about the world as intrinsically amoral or operating according to its own steely brand of justice. Such comments as "What Ever is, is right," "Such is the way of the worl," and "Such is the nature of Mankind" punctuate occurrences that Johnson wrote off as ridiculous, frustrating, or deplorable, implicitly admitting that they were also beyond a black's man's control.

A careful student of the ways of white folks, Johnson courted the good opinion of those Natchez aristocrats who presided over his situation with indirect but godlike power. Yet Johnson's diary betrays much ambivalence about the harsh standards of a world in which it seemed that whatever is white is right. Johnson could savor instances of that world's pitiless judgment on those who failed its Darwinian demands, such as the white lawyer who once had the power and money to be "a sworn persecutor of the Poor Friendless Colord" but whose financial losses ultimately forced him to beg small change from Johnson himself. But when a Mississippi magistrate found in favor of a white man who had robbed a free woman of her freedom, Johnson could only sputter impotently, "Great God, what a Country." The black barber might invoke God's pity and mercy for a local slave abused by his or her master, but he would never go so far as to call for God's purifying wrath on the institution itself.

Still, owning and employing slaves, in particular doomed, recalcitrant ones like Steven, brought out conflicts in the diary between Johnson the hard-nosed businessman, to whom profit is the guiding principle, and Johnson the racial paternalist, from whom the plight of a man like Steven elicits more empathetic attachment than a worldly man, and especially a black entrepreneur in the South, could afford to feel. When Johnson decided to sell Steven after repeated warnings and whippings had failed to cure him of his chronic drunkenness, malingering, and running away, it was not the tough-minded man of the world who wrote on the eve of Steven's sale: "And what is the Cause of my parting with him, why it is nothing but Liquor, Liquor, His fondness for it. Nothing more, Poor Fellow. There are many worse fellows than poor Steven is, God Bless Him." Although the diary generally portrays Johnson as an unsentimental man, on the "very Sad Day" of Steven's sale, the master admits that "many tears was in my Eyes to day On acct. of my Selling poor Steven." From the image of Steven given in the diary, his character and behavior would seem to have been diametrically opposed to everything that Johnson wanted to represent and attain. Yet Johnson's attachment to Steven evinces a conscientiousness in Johnson, a sense of obligation to a black man doubly enslaved by color and by alcoholism, that softens the hard edges of the freeman's proud self-portrait in the diary. Although there can be little doubt that Johnson regarded most of his slaves and black apprentices as his social inferiors—"Low minded Creatures. I Look on them as Soft," he wrote in 1839—the freeman's struggle to soothe his guilty conscience over his disposition of Steven provides a glimpse into the heart of a man who sometimes found it very hard to resolve his own conflicting identifications with the exploiters and the exploited in his own society.

William Johnson's decision to write about his life in an intensely private form that required neither literary precedent nor preparation, not even a stated social, moral, or religious mission, stands as literary testimony to the isolation and insularity of the free people of color in the antebellum South. Though we are learning more about the poets and belletristic communities that developed among the near-white Creoles of early nineteenth-century New Orleans, scholars have yet to find much indication that public autobiographical expression was practiced or even thought desirable among free African Americans in the South. Only two men from the antebellum South's propertied class of free African Americans undertook personal narratives comparable to that of Johnson. In 1842 curious and liberal-minded northern readers responded favorably to *The Narrative of Lunsford Lane*, which was published by Lane's Boston antislavery supporters. Like Johnson, Lane was a hardworking black man who dedicated himself to business success, acknowledging in his autobiography the pride he took in building a lucrative enterprise as a tobacconist in Raleigh, North Carolina. The crucial difference between Lane's story and Johnson's lies in the fact that the former treats his removal to the North and ultimate alliance with abolitionists as the climax of the southern freeman's efforts to achieve independence and dignity. Willis Augustus Hodges, the only other southern freeman of Johnson's class who wrote an autobiography in the antebellum era (but did not see it through to publication), concurred with Lane in arguing that economic opportunity for free blacks in the South was paltry compensation for the persistent oppression of their civil and human rights.

In contrast to the stories of Lane and Hodges, William Johnson's diary does not reveal that its author thought about even visiting the North, much less moving there to live. As Johnson built his estate, his fortune, and his family, he seems to have felt it wisest to stay close and keep a watchful eye on them all. "I Shall be a match for any Set of Rascals that may make me unhappy," Johnson asserted confidently early in his diary, as if to confirm his determination to make a place for himself in the land of his birth regardless of whether that suited envious whites. Having established by 1841 one of the most elegant barbershops in downtown Natchez, replete with a bathhouse and a hair-curling salon for women, Johnson's investments, ambitions, and family responsibilities all militated against his abandoning the tangible rewards of his labors in the name of an abstract freedom in the North. We may still wonder, however, how a free man of color, even one so well-established and evidently respected as William Johnson, managed to negotiate his situation on the South's color line day to day. How did a black man in constant contact with whites remember his place and keep from overstepping his bounds, so as to avoid reprisal from white southern men notorious for their grudge-prone, hair-trigger tempers? At the same time how did this black man resist submitting routinely and tamely to white privilege, so as not to disqualify himself from the reputation of self-respecting manhood and personal honor that were prerequisites to a southern male's social and economic ascent in the antebellum era?

In its report of Johnson's violent death in 1851, the Natchez *Courier* paid tribute to the victim's "peaceable character" and "excellent standing" in local society, which made his example "one well worthy of imitation by all of his class." One member of Johnson's class who did not imitate him, however, was his murderer, who as William Hogan and Edwin Davis discovered in their research, was able to escape prosecution ultimately by claiming he was a white man. The irony that the murderer went unpunished, despite Johnson's "excellent standing" in the community, accentuates the fatal flaw in his life's design. All Johnson's efforts to circumvent and surmount white racism by building business alliances with and social and economic respectability among powerful white men could not withstand the assault of a lone, unconnected man of color who could take refuge in the most potent of all unearned privileges, whiteness itself. In the end, the unpredictable violence of southern life, exacerbated exponentially for a man of color, blindsided William Johnson, as if to remind even the most seemingly inviolable of black men of the insecurity of their faith in reason, mutual trust, and enlightened self-interest against the fury of prejudice.

Johnson's diary is full of descriptions of fistfights, beatings, shootings, and duels, not to mention more than a handful of entries recounting the whippings he administered to his own slaves and black apprentices. These almost daily altercations Johnson accepted as a natural part of life, but he had too much sense to involve himself in the quarrels and brawls of whites or to seek revenge in the ways they were given to. If necessary he would hire a white man to collect his debts from other whites, and he was willing to go to court to recoup what a white tenant owed him. But he used his diary to record his judgments of those whites whom he could not afford, socially or economically, to confront publicly with their misdeeds. The diary came to serve a therapeutic function, providing Johnson the opportunity to let off steam about "rascally" whites who took advantage of blacks with impunity because of color.

A Frenchman whose dalliance with "Every Negro wench that he can possibly have any talk with" provoked a notable outburst in 1837: "I would give One hundred Dollars if Some Gentleman would only Cetch the Low minded Dog and Cow hyde him well Out of there yards—it would do me so much good." As a man of color Johnson was, of course, powerless to take a horsewhip to the Frenchman himself. But through his diary he could register his frustration with his social situation and express his suppressed sense of injustice. The diary may have helped Johnson maintain his equanimity, therefore, when faced with instances of white rascality that cried out for denunciation. The diary could become a kind of alternative, even subversive, history of what whites did not want to come to light, as in the case of the murder of a slave named Arthur in August, 1844. In contrast to his generally casual attention to stories of the deaths of enslaved blacks, Johnson focused on the death of Arthur and the sham of an inquest that followed it, perhaps because the episode represented a particularly egregious example of the manner in which whites could cover up even the most heinous crime committed against a powerless black. "Thus it was and thus it is, &c.," Johnson concludes in a bitterly cynical reiteration of the routine and banal officialese in which he expected the public account of the proceedings would be couched. Only in the diary could Johnson speak freely of what he would pretend the next day he did not know. Yet it is a measure of Johnson's own weary resignation to such outrages that his judgment, even in the privacy of his own diary, is limited to "Thus it was and thus it is, &c."

Commenting in *Incidents in the Life of a Slave Girl* (1861) on the situation of the free blacks she left behind when she escaped slavery in North Carolina, Harriet Jacobs represents the South as almost as intolerant of the desire for freedom among the so-called free Negroes as among the slaves. Instead of accepting the proposal of a young North Carolina free man of color with whom she had fallen in love while she was a slave, Jacobs recalls urging him instead to move to the North, "where his tongue would not be tied, and where his intelligence would be of more avail to him." One reason for the evolution of Johnson's diary from account books and simple day books in the late 1820s and early 1830s to the more expansive annals of personal and public life we find in the 1840s may be attributed to this black writer's desire for a forum in which he could give vent to his intelligence and judgments. Unquestionably Johnson had multiple motives for keeping his diary, most more practical than psychological. Nevertheless, to the extent that the black man saw the diary as an opportunity for his alienated voice to speak beyond the veil of color and perhaps beyond even time itself, Johnson's private narrative makes a claim on us today. That claim, in its mutedness and deliberate ambiguity, speaks profoundly of and to the condition of free black people in the slaveholding South. When Johnson acidly announces to his diary that he will list "the names of some of the Leading Parties or Head Dogs in the Bone Yard" of the Natchez Colonization Society, and then fails to enter a single name, that failure to deliver gives today's reader more to contemplate about the consequences of a lack of privacy and personal autonomy for a man of Johnson's caste and class than anything Johnson might have tried to write about that subject. In the midst of the dreaded "Inquisition" of 1841 in Natchez, when a concerted effort was under way to intimidate and drive out unwanted free men and women of color, Johnson's tense and furtive entries, punctuated by such cryptic asides as "I know what I Know," dramatize better than any other means yet available the central contradiction motivating this singular black autobiography from the antebellum South—the heroic desire to articulate "what I Know" matched against the fearful awareness that knowing must never be acknowledged.

BIBLIOGRAPHY

Anderson, Thomas. *Interesting Account of Thomas Anderson, A Slave, Taken from His Own Lips.* Edited by J. P. Clark. Virginia, 1854.

Andrews, William L. *To Tell a Free Story: The First Century of Afro-American Autobiography, 1760–1865.* Urbana, 1986.

Brown, William Wells. *From Fugitive Slave to Free Man: The Narratives of William Wells Brown.* Edited by William L. Andrews. New York, 1993.

Coker, Daniel. *Journal of Daniel Coker, A Descendant of Africa.* Baltimore, 1820.

Davis, Edwin Adams, and William Ransom Hogan. *The Barber of Natchez.* Baton Rouge, 1954.

Davis, Noah. *A Narrative of the Life of Rev. Noah Davis, A Coloured Man.* Baltimore, 1859.

Douglass, Frederick. *Narrative of the Life of Frederick Douglass, an American Slave.* Edited by Houston A. Baker, Jr., New York, 1982.

Grimké, Charlotte Forten. *The Journals of Charlotte Forten Grimké*. Edited by Brenda Stevenson. New York, 1988.

Hodges, Willis Augustus. *Free Man of Color: The Autobiography of Willis Augustus Hodges*. Edited by Willard B. Gatewood, Jr. Knoxville, Tenn., 1982.

Jackson, Blyden. *The Long Beginning, 1746–1895*. Baton Rouge, 1989. Vol I. of *A History of Afro-American Literature*. 4 Vols. projected.

Jacobs, Harriet A. *Incidents in the Life of a Slave Girl, Written by Herself*. Edited by Jean Fagan Yellin. Cambridge, Mass., 1987.

Johnson, Michael P., and James L. Roark. *Black Masters: A Free Family of Color in the Old South*. New York, 1984.

Kagle, Steven E. *Early Nineteenth-Century American Diary Literature*. Boston, 1986.

Lane, Lunsford. *The Narrative of Lunsford Lane, Formerly of Raleigh, N.C.* Boston, 1842.

Marrant, John. *Journal of Rev. John Marrant*. London, 1790.

Walker, Juliet E. K. *Free Frank: A Black Pioneer on the Antebellum Frontier*. Lexington, Ky., 1983.

Weiss, Richard. *The American Myth of Success*. Urbana, 1969.

Preface

*T*HE DISCOVERY of the diary and other personal papers of William Johnson, a free Negro of ante-bellum Natchez, Mississippi, in a Natchez attic in 1938 was one of the most important Southern historical discoveries in recent years.

Mrs. Edith Wyatt Moore, Natchez newspaper woman and local authority on the history of the Natchez area, was the intermediary through whom the general editor of this series, at that time head of the Department of Archives, Louisiana State University, contacted the widow of Dr. William R. Johnston, the grandson of the diarist. She accompanied him to Mrs. Johnston's home, made the introduction, and offered her personal recommendation. For some months he made irregular visits to Natchez. At first Mrs. Johnston held the various volumes and other papers that he might see them; later he was permitted to hold and read them in her presence; and finally she left the room or even the house during his visits.

Mrs. Johnston was acutely aware of the historical value of her papers for she is an educated, intelligent woman, and she is justly proud of the hundred-and-twenty-five year record of her husband's family. She had long cherished the hope that William Johnson's diary would eventually be edited and published. In the end, it was proposed that the Department of Archives purchase the entire manuscript collection. An agreement was also made stipulating that the collection would be inventoried, that a paper concerning the career of William Johnson would be written and read at a meeting of the Southern Historical Association, that the diary would be edited without prejudice and in conformance with accepted rules of historical scholarship, and that it would be published. The purchase of the collection was then concluded. With the publication of this volume the last of the stipulations will have been kept.

The original purchase contract did not include the Johnson library (typical in most respects of libraries of ante-bellum planters) totaling several hundred well-chosen volumes. It comprised books of history and travel, atlases, and sets of the standard American and English writers, as well as bound volumes and unbound issues of contemporary journals and magazines. Some of the rarer items have since been sold and have found their way into private collections or university libraries.

There were several gaps in the diary. In 1948 two of the missing volumes were discovered in an old house near Natchitoches, Louisiana, by Paul Veith, a prominent rare-book seller of New Orleans. These volumes, it seems, had been borrowed several years before the purchase of the collection and had not been returned. Efforts by Mr. Veith, Dr. William R. Hogan, and Virgil L. Bedsole, who had become head of the Department of Archives, to recover them failed. Some time later, however, they mysteriously appeared one afternoon on Mrs. Moore's front porch in Natchez and were subsequently purchased.

The research and editing process was begun in 1939 in collaboration with Dr. Hogan, then a colleague in the Department of Archives, was discontinued during the war years and begun again with the war's end. The editors have attempted to make an honest and unprejudiced presentation of William Johnson and his diary.

The collection is an extensive one, totaling 1,310 items. There are 62 bound volumes (the majority of them in full leather), which include the 14-volume diary; cashbooks; daybooks; ledgers; bankbooks; notebooks; seven volumes of music; two volumes of Natchez newspapers; and a one-volume diary probably kept by Katharine Johnson, the diarist's daughter, covering the years 1864 to 1874. The unbound material includes personal letters of William Johnson and other members of the family; business correspondence; various business papers, including tax receipts, deeds, bills, invoices, contracts, inventories; photographs of the family (but none of the diarist); scattered Natchez newspaper issues; and over fifty items of contemporary sheet music. The collection spans the years 1793 to 1937, with the major concentration covering the period from 1830 to 1870.

The 14 diary volumes range in size from small notebooks (bound in boards) approximately 6 x 7½ inches to large leather-bound tomes 8 x 13 or 6 x 16 inches and several hundred pages in thickness. They are in fairly sound physical condition except that several have loose or broken hinges. The leather has dried with the passage of years, and it scales and peels when handled. The corners of most of the volumes are bent and worn; the interior pages are dog-eared, some of them loose (only the loving care of a family proud of its heritage has preserved them) and many of them torn. It is obvious that the diary has been read and re-read by successive generations of the Johnson family. But the writing, with the exception of comparatively few pages, is still as clear and distinct as when the Negro barber and businessman painstakingly—or hurriedly—penned the pages (sometimes with a homemade quill pen) over a hundred years ago.

Born in slavery and later freed by his master, William Johnson not only won a modest fortune by his own efforts before his assassination in 1851 but, and of considerably more consequence, gained the respect of his Natchez white and free colored neighbors. He was one of that usually inarticulate, and economically, socially, and culturally complex group of free Negroes not understood by contemporary writers nor as yet fully interpreted by present-day historians. His diary is significant in that it reveals certain important phases of general ante-bellum Southern life; free-Negro–white relations; an intimate picture of life in an ante-bellum Southern town; and the economic and social position of one free Negro, as well as his daily activities, attitudes toward the slavery regime, and thoughts and opinions concerning local, state, and even national and international affairs.

EDWIN ADAMS DAVIS

William Johnson's Natchez

Introduction

*D*URING THE hurrying, materialistic 1830's and 1840's, a time when "getting ahead" epitomized the American spirit, free Negro William Johnson rose from lowly beginnings to become a respected businessman of Natchez.* The incidents of this rise form a major theme of his diary, one of the most remarkable documents in American historiography. Even more valuable are the diary recordings of his private observations of Natchez citizenry and contemporary events. These observations, drawn from the perspective of his unusual social and business position, reveal much of the flesh and the spirit of ante-bellum Natchez life with a candor that is sometimes naïve but more often acutely perceptive.

Numerous nineteenth-century Americans kept diaries, many of them written by men in public life with a solicitude for the enlightenment of posterity equaled only by meticulous attention to self-justification. The keeping of a diary was often a badge of distinction as well as an accompaniment of gentility. Diarist William Johnson, leading Natchez barber as well as a landlord, moneylender, slaveowner, and small farmer, possessed the gentility that resulted from sustained effort for self-improvement and the distinction of limited affluence.

His journal is an unconscious but vitally expressive self-portrait of a free Negro—a type of historical record altogether too rare. For the most part, the life stories of ante-bellum small planters, farmers, poor whites, and free men of color have been lost in a haze of historical uncertainty, relieved only by statistical and legal data which too often lack humanizing touches.

The historical collection of which the diary is the principal exhibit

* The editors are under especial obligation in the preparation of this study to La Verna Rowe Davis, who generously made a substantial contribution to the tasks of checking and proofreading the diary and doing research for its editing, and to Professor Wendell Holmes Stephenson of Tulane University for counsel and technical criticism.

The research was partially conducted under a Rosenwald Foundation grant.

For their assistance in preparing the manuscript for publication, the editors also wish to acknowledge: John C. L. Andreassen, Mary Barker, V. L. Bedsole, Charlotte Capers, Paul Eakin, Sue Lyles Eakin, John Hope Franklin, A. J. Hanna, Laura D. S. Harrell, Alice H. Lerch, Gordon Nelson, William D. McCain, Virginia Ott, Vivian Wintz.

1

was discovered in 1938 in the attic of a three-story house erected by the diarist in 1840-41 and still standing in Natchez less than a block from the Adams County courthouse. The personal and business diary, comprising more than 2,000 manuscript pages abounding in graphic detail, was written by the free Negro barber between 1835 and 1851. This chronicle is supplemented by several hundred pages of legal and financial documents, a few score letters, sixteen volumes of account books, four bound volumes of rare newspapers (two of which are not listed elsewhere), more than four hundred pieces of nineteenth-century sheet music, and miscellaneous family papers extending to 1937. The whole collection was purchased by the Department of Archives of Louisiana State University from the widow of a grandson of the diarist.[1]

A careful study of this collection, and particularly the diary, will go far to correct the accidental misinterpretation or deliberate distortion that has characterized most literary and quasi-historical writing about the town of Natchez and its immediate vicinity. This area has long been identified with the familiar literary stereotype of the ante-bellum South—large holdings in land and slaves, colonnaded mansions, imported furniture, and the rest of the plantation legend, all fused into a picture of an opulent, leisurely, and cultured way of life. The Natchez-under-the-Hill river front has likewise been celebrated as the wildest hell-spot on the pre-Civil War Mississippi River, and even in the entire South.

These two aspects of Natchez life have provided the patterned descriptive phraseology and basic elements of many intriguing stories: below the crest of "the Bluff" overlooking the Mississippi were the bawdy glories of vice—"squalor on the steaming mud flats"; above, "the tranquil streets—the elegance of the wind-swept

---

[1] The editors are greatly indebted to Mrs. W. R. Johnston, widow of the diarist's grandson, for her generous co-operation in making this publication possible. They are also obligated to Mrs. Edith Wyatt Moore of Natchez and Paul F. Veith of New Orleans for aiding in the acquisition of the diary.

A detailed description of the William Johnson Papers, 1793–1937, containing 1,304 pieces and 60 bound volumes, will be found in William R. Hogan (ed.), *Guide to Manuscript Collections in the Department of Archives, Louisiana State University* (University, La., 1940), 33–35.

The best bibliography of publications dealing with ante-bellum free Negroes is found in John Hope Franklin, *From Slavery to Freedom* (New York, 1947), 604–605. See also Franklin, "James Boon, Free Negro Artisan," *Journal of Negro History*, XXX (1945), 150–80, for a study which corroborates some of the conclusions reached in this Introduction. Professor Franklin has written, however, that he has "never encountered a document similar to the Johnson manuscript." Professor Ray A. Billington is in the process of preparing for publication a diary of a northern free Negro, tentatively entitled "The Journals of Charlotte Forten."

heights." The whole effect, according to this conventional version, was that of a town with "a split personality." [2]

The chief defects of this type of analysis in black-and-white are that, like many good stories, it lacks the pedestrian virtues of accuracy and completeness. One objection is that the two extremes of the Natchez past were not in full glory at the same time. By the mid-1830's the reputation of Natchez-under-the-Hill was beginning to be partially replaced by one emphasizing its busy commercial water front, where river steamboats docked daily, where European goods were received directly from ocean-going vessels that had been towed up the Mississippi and cotton was often prepared for direct shipment to Liverpool. The day of the Under-the-Hill gambler and hell-raising flatboatman had not completely passed in the 1830's, but it had undoubtedly begun to wane,[3] whereas the plantation system reached its period of greatest prosperity in the 1850's.

Life in Natchez had many other facets apart from the luxuriant living of the aristocrats. Even patricians or would-be patricians occasionally participated in the frequent street fights that gave the "tranquil streets" a definite frontier flavor, and not all the houses of ill fame were below the Bluff. An unmistakable cosmopolitan tone was added by the town's Spanish background and by the presence of substantial groups of foreign-born persons—Irish, English, German, Italian, and French. The records of the census of 1850, partly unpublished, reveal that well over one fourth of the 4,680 residents of the town proper had been born in foreign countries, nearly 800 were Yankee in origin, more than 200 were free Negroes, and about one third were slaves.[4]

Social and economic groups so overlapped in the Natchez region as to challenge glib analysis. A recent authoritative study of Mississippi agriculturists in the 1850's concedes that the plantation system reached "its zenith in Mississippi, and perhaps in the entire

[2] The quotations are from Harnett T. Kane, *Natchez on the Mississippi* (New York, 1947), 8, the latest version of this type of interpretation.

[3] Virginia Park Matthias, "Natchez-under-the-Hill as It Developed Under the Influence of the Mississippi River and the Natchez Trace," *Journal of Mississippi History,* VII (1945), 215–21.

[4] Herbert Weaver, *Mississippi Farmers, 1850–1860* (Nashville, 1945), 30, 32; *The Seventh Census of the United States: 1850* (Washington, 1853), 448. The population of Natchez, largest town in Mississippi, rose from 2,034 in 1818 to 6,612 in 1860. In the same period the total population of Adams County, of which Natchez was county seat, rose from 10,600 (including 6,709 slaves and 125 free Negroes) to 20,165 (including 14,292 slaves and 225 free Negroes). Secretary of State's Records, Census of 1818, Adams County, Series F, No. 101 (Mississippi Department of Archives and History, Jackson, Miss.); *Population of the United States in 1860* (Washington, 1864), 270–71.

South" around Natchez, thereby implying that the plantation legend may have had a partial foundation in fact in this area where cotton capitalism produced nearly a dozen millionaires before the Civil War. But the same study immediately adds that these "very wealthy planters represented such a small minority" even in the river counties "that their plantations cannot be accepted as typical of the planter class."[5] In Adams County the houses of the numerous small planters and farmers were much less pretentious than those of the large planters,[6] and their lands often intermingled; and the business interests of plantation owners, professional men, bankers, shipowners, and commission merchants were inextricably bound together—often in the person of a single individual. Not a few of the big-planter class of the 1850's were individuals who had pushed their way up by law or medical practice, advantageous marriages, or ambitious expansion of landholdings and slaveholdings, just as some small planters had risen from small farmers, overseers, and even squatters. Adams County society was by no means static or immobile.

In 1835, when William Johnson began his diary, Natchez was visited by "an accomplished gentleman of the British court," Charles Augustus Murray, who subsequently published his impressions of the town:

> In the evening we reached Natchez: the view on approaching it from the north is very fine, and the bold bluffs, on which stands the upper town, were all tinged with the golden beams of a setting sun. . . . There are two towns, Upper and Lower Natchez; of which the former is by far the largest and the most respectable. The lower town, containing little more than the buildings which necessarily grow up in the neighborhood of a harbour where much shipping business is done, was considered, a few years ago, as the most abandoned sink of iniquity in the whole western country. It was the resort of the lowest and most profligate wretches of both sexes; and gambling, drinking, robbery, and murder, were the daily occupations of its population. But the respectable inhabitants of the upper town assembled last summer in full force, and, under the authority of Judge Lynch . . . compelled some hundreds of the most notorious characters to leave the place at a few hours notice. Their memory

[5] Weaver, *Mississippi Farmers*, 47. [6] *Ibid.*, 55.

4

is not yet dead, nor has the lower town, though much improved, been able yet to acquire a very respectable name. . . .

We toiled our way up the most miserable road that I ever beheld, towards the top of the bluffs. Numerous drays were ascending and descending, most of which were up to or over the axle-tree, in the pure, unadulterated clay, of which the road is composed. . . .

The upper town of Natchez is pleasantly situated upon an elevated platform, commanding a fine view of the serpentine course of the river; it contains several handsome buildings, and some streets well laid out. The inhabitants have had the good taste to leave many rows of trees standing. . . . There are many handsome, well-supplied shops; but the streets are in much the same condition, in regard to pavement, as those of the other western cities: that is to say, if you choose to walk after dark, you must . . . take your chance of spraining your ancle, in holes and broken places a foot deep, or of stepping up to your knees into a gutter, or some equally agreeable receptacle of mud. The principal, if not the only, article of trade in Natchez, is cotton; and many of the wealthier merchants reside at villas, prettily situated on the undulating slopes by which the town is surrounded.[7]

One of the contemporary accounts that expand various details of Murray's picture contains the following description of the exterior view of the near-by plantation homes and their gardens:

The most beautiful sight around Natchez is the gardens and fine residences of many Planters. Their houses are generally large and spacious, galleries supported by large and Massy Colums showing heavy Architecture. The gardens or yards are generally planted with a great many different plants and shrubs; the ground plat is laid out & tastefully arrainged with a great number of walks and Bowers; the sides of the walks are planted with flowring shrubs all shorn and trimed to their proper height; some present a hedge so thick that a man could nearly walk over the top; roses, jessamines, Hyacynths, Pinks, and a great variety of flowering plants and shrubs not known in the North; numbers of evergreens give the gardens quite a pleasant appearance, even in winter.[8]

[7] *Travels in North America During the Years 1834, 1835, & 1836*, 2 vols. (London, 1839), II, 176–79.

[8] Thomas Maitland Marshall (ed.), "The Journal of Henry B. Miller," *Missouri Historical Society Collections*, VI (1931), 283. Additional contemporary descrip-

Such accounts represent the external descriptions of persons who never fully entered into the daily life of the town, whereas William Johnson's diary provides an internal, day-by-day account that illuminates the whole of the Natchez scene. He was fascinated by the entire range of Natchez life; his interests ran from murder and sober business transactions to tomfoolery and social functions of all classes. Few happenings escaped him: births, deaths, weddings, family quarrels, lodge functions, conventions, political campaigns, departures of young men for Texas or California and of the well-to-do for resorts and for Europe, holiday celebrations, militia musters, parades, horse races, cockfights, theatrical and circus performances, concerts, balls, trials, jail breaks, the opening of a section of a new railroad, steamboat arrivals and explosions, the terror of the yellow-fever epidemics of 1837 and 1839, the cholera epidemic of 1849, and the ravages of that "Demon of Destruction," fire. In many of these events, as Johnson recorded them, the names of obscure foreign-born tradesmen, free Negroes, and other "little people" commingled with better-known names.

The barber presented this spectacle in the phraseology, often colloquial and phonetic, of a man who was largely self-taught. Words and phrases that have passed out of common use, such as "sloped off" and "in a horn," appear here and there in his sentences. The cumulative effect is obviously not that of a literary masterwork, but rather that of a unique bundle of historical raw materials which are now very readable, now commonplace, now monotonous in flavor.

The impact of the depression that followed the Panic of 1837 can be incisively traced in Johnson's day-by-day recordings of the gradual though irregular transition from bustling fortune-making to successive money crises, auctions, foreclosures, imprisonments for debt, and bankruptcies. Many businesses, including Johnson's barbershop, suffered severely during the money crisis of 1837, but late in that year experienced a recovery that lasted until early in 1840, when the depression hit in full force. This reflected the curious reluctance of the lower Mississippi Valley and Texas to

---

tions of Natchez and vicinity in the 1830's are found in Tyrone Power, *Impressions of America; During the Years 1833, 1834, and 1835*, 2 vols. (Philadelphia, 1836), II, 119–31; A. A. Parker, *Trip to the West and Texas* (Concord, 1835), 95–96; [Joseph Holt Ingraham], *The South-West. By a Yankee*, 2 vols. (New York, 1835), II, *passim*; J. E. Alexander, *Transatlantic Sketches*, 2 vols. (London, 1833), II, 61–63; J. S. Buckingham, *The Slave States of America*, 2 vols. (London, c. 1842), I, 447–60; [Lorenzo A.] *Besancon's Annual Register of the State of Mississippi for the Year 1838* (Natchez, 1838), 117–21, 229.

abandon the fever of speculation that marked the late 1830's, even in the face of admitted and widespread monetary tightness.[9]

The flavor of Mississippi politics, and particularly of what Johnson called "all the Pomp of Nonsense and Splendid Foolishness" of political rallies, appears in many of the diary entries. Beginning in 1836 he faithfully recorded presidential elections, as well as other events on the national and even the international scene, until his death in 1851. He was particularly interested in the local excitement of the campaign of 1840, during which the Whigs built log cabins and rolled a giant ball through the streets as means of arousing party fervor. Such antics stirred him to mild disapprobation, chiefly because he hoped for a Democratic victory.

By 1844 his personal concern in the outcome of party strife had lessened, but still it greatly interested him as one manifestation of the human comedy. In July he attended political meetings, and was present on the twenty-fifth at Pine Ridge where "the party was pleasent indeed very, no One Drunk." On August 9 the barber noted that "the Excitement is fast Commencing about the Election. I care very Little who is Elected, Natchez Guards at there Armory had a meeting and a marching and wound up thare meeting with a fight. In the first place Shanks and the Capt. Page has a quarrell, [and] After a Little Capt Page and W W W. Woods has a fight   Page caught him around the necke and choked Him wonderfully: untill he was Seperated. Great times, we have them." Six days later he wrote: "To day is the day of the Democratic Barbacue   At an Early Hour the[y] assembled on the Bluff and marched up the Street and I think it was the Larges[t] procession that I have Ever Seen in this City on any Ocasion. . . . I wrode Out in the afternoon and took a Look at them. Oh they were a great many indeed about I think 2000 persons — it all passed off in Beautifull Stile and so pleasent   Did not see a realy Drunkin man on the ground   Dempsey P. Jackson came near geting in a fight by offering to Bet rarther too Loud." The final notation of the campaign reads: "To day the Election Commences, and it will be a warm affair, for they are Challenging a greate many Fouriegners, making them Show there papers —go it. It is what I like to see."[10]

---

[9] In addition to the entries in Johnson's diary, see Joseph Miller Free, "The Ante-Bellum Theatre of the Old Natchez Region," *Journal of Mississippi History,* V (1943), 25; Matthias, "Natchez-under-the-Hill," *loc. cit.,* 216; Buckingham, *The Slave States of America,* I, 456; William R. Hogan, *The Texas Republic: A Social and Economic History* (Norman, 1946), 82–94; Frederick Jackson Turner, *The United States, 1830–1850: The Nation and Its Sections* (New York, 1935), 229, 465.

[10] Direct quotations from the diary, used in this Introduction for illustrative purposes, are not footnoted.

7

Johnson kept his ear to the ground for off-color news about both white and black people. On September 4, 1842, he noted that "a party of Persons Shelverdereed [chivareed] Mr John Williamson Last night — They were Finally Stoped by the Shirriff and Police offircers — They have never had a chance at him since He married before and this they Gave him because he had made use of some Language that some men did not Like when Mr Patterson was married — They were dressed in all maner of Shapes   One was Dressed . . . Like his wife with a behind as Large as they Could well make it to Look   The thing went of[f] well I am told." He also recorded runaway marriages; the talk about town that a painter should be lynched for running off with a doctor's daughter; the attitude of an old gentleman toward his wife and her "Big whiskered" lover who had escaped together; and the rumor of the seduction of a free Negro girl by a free Negro man with a family. And occasionally he did not hesitate to repeat even more intimate facts and gossip.

The town's newspapers presented conventional versions of many incidents, but Johnson often recounted conflicting beliefs or gave additional information, even in reporting social functions. Both the Natchez *Courier* and the Natchez *Free Trader* carried official accounts of the meetings of the Anti-Gambling Society in 1835; but Johnson related what subsequent steps the association actually took: "The Citizens went Out to the Race track in search of the Gamblers; [among others] the[y] Brought in Elick Piper from Mr Mardice's place — Had a meeting at the Court House for the purpose of trying him — Gridley [the sheriff] took him from them and put him to Jail — Twas their Intention to have whipd him." And the historian of horse racing will find much of value in Johnson's entries concerning occurrences at the race track, entries that reflect horse-racing atmosphere in a manner that never reached the pages of reports in contemporary newspapers and sporting journals.

The newspapers, often silent about unlawful conduct of groups of citizens that the Negro noted, completely ignored the actions of a mob that tore a balloon to shreds when it failed to leave the ground in keeping with the advertised promises of the balloonist. The newspapers said nothing about an occurrence of March 17, 1837, concerning which Johnson wrote: "To night there were a parcel of Irishmen Collected together near the market house and Every person that past they were striking at them with their Sticks or Something Else   Dr Denny was Returning from Mr Ranos Dinner when the Irishmen Knocked him down and Beat him Like the mischief   They cut his head and nose pretty seviere . . .

they struck the sherriff also,   The Fencibles [a militia organiza-
tion] turned Out, put 2 or three of the Irish in jail." And the newspaper accounts of the firemen's procession at the Washington's
Birthday celebration in 1845 failed entirely to mention the several
fights noted by the barber.

More than a hundred accounts of street fights between individuals, some of them related in great detail and in racy language, not
only enliven the barber's diary but re-emphasize the persistence of
the frontier spirit even in the town that was the acknowledged
social and cultural center of Mississippi. The Natchez newspapers
of the period contain very few references to cutting and shooting
scrapes and to duels, one editor explaining the omission by stating
that it would require the services of a full-time assistant if all of
the frequent brawls were accurately reported.[11] It is also likely that
political and personal affiliations as well as considerations of bodily
safety impelled editors to omit newsworthy stories of fights. But
William Johnson had no such inhibitions in his writings. He enjoyed
setting down the particulars of raucous brawls and deadly affrays,
sometimes in a quietly humorous style.

Fights began, according to Johnson, for a wide variety of causes.
Horse races and politics often provided the background, but quarrels
might also originate over a twenty-cent hat or a refusal to take a
drink. The impressive list of weapons recorded by the diarist included chairs, iron bars and sticks, bricks, umbrellas, hatchets,
sword canes, whips, bowie knives, dirks, and pistols. And in addition to using fists, several combatants resorted to gouging and biting.
The barber was interested in the anatomical details of personal
encounters, as when he wrote in 1843 that "Guinea John" had
stabbed an Italian "Just below the navle, Tis supposed that the nife
has Cut a Gut."

He either saw the fights or heard firsthand accounts from customers awaiting their turns under the razor. When a couple of
Irishmen became playful on November 22, 1835, for example, their
doings were dutifully related: "Two Irishman commenced boxing in
fun and then began to fight. The one kicked the other in such a
seviere maner that he broke his gaul. His Head was bruised also —
He Died in 8 or ten hours after the fight."

Many of the encounters were between prominent citizens, most
of whom apparently preferred a brawl to the comparatively infrequent duel. A lively pen sketch illustrated Johnson's two-page ac-

---

[11] Natchez *Daily Courier*, March 10, 1842. The various editions of this newspaper
and of the *Mississippi Free Trader and Natchez Gazette* are hereafter cited as
Natchez *Courier* and Natchez *Free Trader*.

count of an encounter in 1836 involving several spirited young men. Some of them were already well established in the town's business and professional life, and one was to become a Confederate general. The entry began, "To Day we had Bloody work for a while in the streets up at Throckmortons Corner," and ended, "It was one of the gamest fights that we have Ever had in Our City." On September 9, 1837, the barber reported: "An Election Came On to day for Major General of 2d Division of Malitia of this State, Judge [John A.] Quitman & Mr Besancon [editor of the *Free Trader*] has a fight.   Mr Besancon made a thrust at him that would have killed him had not a piece of Silver in the Pocket of the Judge arrested the Progress of the sword, They were seperated by the Sherriff or some other Gentleman." And on October 7, 1843: "Mr Postlethwaite and Potter has a fight   Elick Postlethwaite was the first to make the attack, and I am told that if they had not been Seperated that Potter would have whipped him, and as far as the fight went Potter got the best of it for he gave P. a Black Eye and Scratched his face and neck prety smart. Postlethwaite bit Potters finger a Little — The fight was about the Settlement of Some Estate in which they acuse Each other of Swindling the Estate. They Said a good many Hard things of Each other."

Accounts of several of the bloodiest fights, as well as scores of horse races and a number of other events, were illustrated by the diarist with small, crude sketches which add considerable verve to his comments. A few of his best drawings are reproduced in this volume.

Were William Johnson's pen sketches accurate? Though they contain suggestive detail, they were obviously impressionistic. But the related question—to what extent was he a reliable reporter in his writings?—requires a more extended and considered answer.

Judged as a source of information concerning the contemporary scene, Johnson's diary is uneven, but its merits far outweigh its very human deficiencies. It was written by a man who was intelligent, observant, curious about many things, and largely unimaginative—all characteristics of a good witness. His occasional flashes of temper were usually acknowledged, his mild prejudices self-evident, and his whole narrative amply corroborated by other contemporary data and often distinguished by an overtone of anxiety to set down the truth. When he wrote from hearsay, he occasionally showed a skepticism that enabled him to reconcile conflicting details or to write a correction in a later entry, and he often labeled mere gossip as "talk" or "sly talk." (Gossip, like folklore, must be correctly labeled and used with care by the historian, but neither can properly be ignored.) When he relayed news from newspapers, as he sometimes did, his reports could have been no more reliable than his sources. Though his position on the social scale obviously barred him from taking direct part in many social events, he was present as a fairly detached observer in a surprising number of situations from which a person of his mixed blood would be banned today.

Johnson was less detached but even better informed in his recording of the activities and attitudes of free Negroes. His diary presents impressive evidence that the free Negro population in Natchez and Adams County existed in widely varying economic circumstances and maintained distinct social levels within the group. The free people of color had their own aristocracy—the Johnsons, the McCarys, the Barlands, the Fitzgeralds, and the family of George Winn. Three of these upper-class families had received legacies of land or town property from white men, and all of them were slaveowners. Usually the tax rolls and census records listed them as holding five to twenty slaves (in comparison with the one or two slaves held by the other ten or twelve free Negro slaveowners). Socially and culturally, they were several notches above other Negroes. Their marriages were officially recorded, and they would have been indignant had anyone suggested that they attend any of the numerous Natchez "darkey parties," functions that were marked by intermingling of slave servants and lower-class free Negroes.

At a lower level were free Negroes with less prospect of advancement, such as journeymen barbers, young free mulatto apprentices, stewards and barbers on steamboats, and a hack driver or two. Still lower on the economic scale was the mass of the independent free people of color, including peddlers, hotel employees, draymen, day laborers, and small farmers—some hopelessly poor.

Another free Negro group consisted of those who were attached to white households. The unpublished census records for 1840, the census year in which the free Negro population in Adams County and Mississippi reached its maximum, indicate that more than one fourth of the 283 free colored persons in Adams County belonged in this dependent category. About two fifths of the white families to which free Negroes were attached owned no slaves, and in a few instances free Negroes were listed as the entire dependent connection of the unmarried white male who was named as the family head.

Under Mississippi law, the property-holding right of free Negroes was their chief civil advantage over slaves. Members of both groups were prohibited from voting, serving on a jury, testifying in a case in which a white person was a party, or speaking insolently to a white person. Slaves were prohibited from carrying weapons of any kind, and free Negroes were allowed to own them only if they secured licenses. These and a number of additional prohibitions and regulations were designed to circumscribe the conduct of the entire Negro population.[12] But in actual practice, as William Johnson's diary amply demonstrates, individual slaves in Natchez were sometimes allowed a status approaching that of freedom,[13] and some of the laws regulating free Negroes were never strictly enforced against those with considerable property.

In the 1840's, however, white slaveowners in the river counties of Mississippi manifested a growing fear that free Negroes as a class constituted a grave cause of potential unrest among slaves. Demands that laws regulating the conduct of both slaves and free Negroes be rigidly enforced became more frequent. In particular, it was pointed out that a substantial segment of the free Negro population of the river towns had immigrated into the state in express violation of the law.[14]

In 1841 the alleged abolitionist activities of free Negroes living in Natchez contrary to law caused what Johnson termed the "Inquisition." At a general meeting of the citizens, committees of vigilance and safety were appointed to ascertain whether free persons of color were conforming to existing laws, particularly the provisions requiring individuals to prove, before the county board of police, that they were of good character and entitled to remain in Mississippi or leave the state. A typical communication to the Natchez *Free Trader* urged the people of Natchez to act promptly, "to strike a severe blow against the practices of the rogue, the incendiary, and the abolitionist," by regulating slave conduct and by "the immediate removal of every free negro, who has intruded upon our society." [15]

---

[12] Charles S. Sydnor, "The Free Negro in Mississippi Before the Civil War," *American Historical Review*, XXXII (1927), 771, and *passim*. This article is a very competent analysis of the status of free Negroes in Mississippi as reflected chiefly in state laws, Supreme Court decisions, and published census summaries.

[13] See especially the long statement about *"privileged* slaves" in Natchez *Free Trader*, August 7, 1841.

[14] Sydnor, "The Free Negro in Mississippi," *loc. cit.*, 779, has this statement concerning the origins of the free Negro group: "By way of summary the free negro element in Mississippi could be legally recruited by emancipation within the state in the way provided by act of the legislature, by the birth of a child to free [Negro] parents, by the lapse of the term of servitude of a slave coming from another state, or occasionally under other conditions when legalized by special act of the legislature. The class could be illegally augmented by a master freeing his slave without going through the procedure required by law, and by the immigration of free negroes into the state—whether *bona fide* free negroes, or Mississippi slaves who had been taken to a free state, there manumitted and then returned to the state."

[15] Natchez *Free Trader*, August 7, 1841. See also *ibid.*, August 10, 12, 14, 1841, and Natchez *Courier*, August 4, 28, 1841. The *Free Trader* of August 10 reprinted a

The "Horrows of the Inquisition"—to use William Johnson's phraseology—aroused his sense of injustice. While Johnson's own position in the community was relatively secure, he nevertheless expressed his gratification that "One of Our noble, Generous and Gentlemanly young men" offered his assistance. His white friends signed petitions in behalf of his free Negro apprentices, and he boasted that "Those Names are Enough to make any Common man Proud — Those Names are an Ornament to Any Paper — Those are Gentlemen of the 1st Order of Talents and Standing." But some of the free Negroes were deported, and the anxiety and tension of the group as a whole deeply concerned the diarist. Said he: "Poor Andrew Leeper was, I understand, ordered off to day, and so was Dembo and Maryan Gibson They are as far as I Know inocent and Harmless People And Have never done a Crime . . . Oh what a Country we Live in."

The spirit of the "Inquisition" persisted through the next two decades. After 1840 the files of the petitions and memorials to the legislature contain comparatively few by white men for permission to manumit slaves, and very few Negroes were freed by law. Nearly a hundred emancipation papers were officially recorded in the Adams County deed records in the previous decade, and fewer than ten between 1840 and 1850. The statistical result was that the census of 1850 was the first to show a decline in the total free Negro population in Adams County and in the state as a whole.

Meanwhile, on the pages of William Johnson's diary, both free and slave Negroes appeared with such wide range of personalities and attitudes as to defy generalization. In the Natchez area some slaves and free Negroes were publicly humiliated and even clubbed to death by whites, just as a few whites were attacked and even killed by slaves. But slaves and free Negroes also risked their lives to save white masters and friends, and there were instances of friendship and respect between whites and blacks that must present striking exceptions to any cherished stereotypes of patronizing affection by one group or abject humility by the other. Among both whites and blacks, there were the sober element and the drunkards, the honest and the thievish, the thrifty and the spendthrift, the intelligent and the moronic, the proud and the meek, the strait-laced and the promiscuous.

---

long article from a New Orleans newspaper emphasizing this theme: *"Drive them from us. It is our only means of salvation. If we do not take away their present privileges, as sure as we live a race will spring up, between the slave and the white man, and their sympathies will be roused for their brethren in bondage, and the issue, it does not require a prophet to foretell."*

Any attempt to label all slaves as devoid of pride and discrimination in mating must explain away the evidence that one of Johnson's young slaves, Jim by name, "Seperated" from a prospective slave wife when he became convinced that a former judge of Mississippi's highest court had recently been given "1st chances." As for Jim's master, he stated more than once that either a slave or free Negro disgraced himself if he "married" a girl generally known to be "a buster" instead of one whose favors had not been bestowed indiscriminately.

While Johnson never stated *why* he wrote his diary, certain aspects of his situation and character suggest a tentative solution of this arresting problem. Precision as to dates and money transactions was necessary if the free Negro businessman expected good will and prompt payment by whites with whom he had constant business dealings. Hence he used his diary, in part, as a means of keeping certain business records, some of which were later transferred in more formal fashion to his account books. This practice naturally led him to record information and conversations about contemplated purchases of land and town property and to note prices and sales of diverse sorts. An even more compelling stimulus to keep a journal arose from his position at the top of his class, in one sense an almost isolated position in which he dared completely unbosom himself to no one except one or two free Negro cronies. His diary, therefore, served as an outlet for secret expression of suppressed moods and thoughts that most white men would not have found necessary to stifle in public. On the other hand, his broad range of interest in the various aspects of his home environment was equaled by none of the numerous nineteenth-century southern diarists. His overwhelming curiosity was at least faintly reminiscent of Pepys and Boswell. The barber would have understood, and perhaps shared, Boswell's feeling that the making of a record was "the most meaningful portion of life itself."

Whatever Johnson's motivation for composing his journal, its unimpeachable testimony concerning the writer is one of its distinctive elements. Some detectives consider that often they can "make a better catch" by studying only a suspect's written records, without the sight of his face or the sound of his voice to confuse rather than clarify the issue of guilt or innocence. Certainly the person who wants detailed knowledge of the barber of Natchez has the best means in his diary, written with his intense passion for noting facts intended primarily for his own information and pleasure.

A biographer with a Freudian bent might bewail the barber's lack of introspection, but in another sense this renders easier the problem of analyzing the diarist and his writings about himself. By no means an unusually imaginative man, he did not distort his personal record by fanciful additions. Instead, he set down many personal things of an intimate, simple type that in total effect evoke at least a substantial shadow of his personality.

Here, in his pages, we can see him in motion. Occasionally we can look through his eyes. To the extent that he came to understand himself and other men and wrote his findings, we can learn with him. All of which foreshadows the fundamental questions concerning this diarist who was born a slave, accumulated a substantial estate, and earned the heartfelt respect of his community before an enemy struck him down from ambush: What were the circumstances in which he gained freedom and grew to manhood? What manner of man was he?

THE DIARIST: EARLY LIFE

The series of events that was to liberate the slave William from bondage began in 1814 when he was about five years of age.[16] In that year his white master, William Johnson of Adams County, crossed the Mississippi River to Vidalia, parish seat of Concordia Parish, Louisiana, and gave notice to the parish judge that he intended to free "his female slave Amy" (mother of the slave William). In accordance with Louisiana law, the notice of intention to emancipate Amy was publicly posted for forty days, and on March 20, William Johnson made it a matter of legal record that, "for divers good causes and considerations me thereunto moving," he thereby "released from Slavery, liberated, manumitted, and set free my Negro woman Amy." He further certified that she was able to support herself by her own labor, and that for the past four years she had been honest, had not attempted to escape, and had committed no crimes. He obligated himself to maintain her should she "be in want owing to sickness, old age, insanity, or any other proven infirmity."[17]

16 William Johnson's tombstone in the cemetery of the Natchez Cemetery Association bears this statement: "Born 1809 in Natchez, Miss." The Natchez *Courier*, June 20, 1851, stated that he was "born and raised in Natchez." These two statements are partially substantiated by a variety of additional evidence.

Johnson very infrequently spelled his name William T. Johnson, and once wrote "William Tiler Johnson" in the middle of scrawling in an account book, but he used William Johnson as his customary signature.

17 Concordia Parish Conveyance Records, B, 389–91 (Concordia Parish courthouse, Vidalia, La.). See also copy of same record in Adams County Deed Records, I, 243–45. (All Adams County public records cited in this study are in Adams County courthouse, Natchez, Miss.) Between 1814 and 1831 several Adams County slaveowners accomplished emancipation of slaves in Concordia Parish.

The emancipation of William's mother was followed four years later by the freeing of his sister, described as "a mulatto girl named Delia aged about thirteen years." In 1818, William Johnson sent her to Philadelphia with his designated agent, George Ralston of Natchez. With the written authority of Delia's owner, Ralston arranged for her liberation in the northern city.[18]

Two years afterward, in 1820, William Johnson addressed a petition to the Legislature of Mississippi (then in session at Natchez) asking that body to free Amy's child, William. He pointed out that as a reward for "her good conduct and fidelity" he had already emancipated Amy according to the laws of Louisiana, but that those laws had also prevented him from carrying out his intention of manumitting "her child named William" because he was too young. The petitioner further stated that he had long resided in Mississippi, that he had established a permanent residence in the state, and that he was not indebted to anyone. Then came this eloquent appeal: "Your Petitioner humbly prays your Honorable Body to permit him to make that disposition of his property most agreeable to his feelings & consonant to humanity . . . [to give] that Liberty to a human being which all are entitled to as a Birthright, & extend the hand of humanity to a rational Creature, on whom unfortunately Complexion Custom & even Law in This Land of freedom, has conspired to rivet the fetters of Slavery."[19] On January 22, 1820, Lewis Winston, an Adams County member of the lower house of the legislature, presented this petition to the House of Representatives. The petition was referred to a special committee headed by Winston, which produced a report consisting of a bill providing for William's emancipation. Both the lower house and the Senate amended it, and on February 10 the bill was sent to Governor George Poindexter, who approved it the same day.[20]

[18] Adams County Deed Records, K, 223–24. A "mulatto" as used in contemporary court records meant any Negro who possessed a proportion of white blood, although state law defined a mulatto as any person of one-fourth or more Negro blood. "Probably the key to the condition of the free negro and mulatto can be found in the assumption that all colored persons were considered slaves unless the contrary could be proved. This principle was most clearly stated at various times by the Supreme Court of Mississippi." Sydnor, "The Free Negro in Mississippi," *loc. cit.*, 769.

[19] Petition of William Johnson, January 21, 1820, Petitions and Memorials to the Legislature, Series I, No. 93 (Petitions and Memorials to both Territorial Assembly and State Legislature in Mississippi Department of Archives and History).

[20] *Journal of the House of Representatives, State of Mississippi*, 3 Sess. (Natchez, 1820), 73, 107, 141, 162, 163, 169, 172.

Here is the text of the act:

AN ACT TO EMANCIPATE WILLIAM, A PERSON OF COLOR

Sec. 1. *Be it enacted by the Senate and House of Represen-tatives of the state of Mississippi, in general assembly convened,* That the mulatto boy named William, son of Amy, a free woman of color, and the slave of William Johnson of Adams County, be, and he is hereby emancipated and set free from slavery, saving however the rights of creditors, and on the express condition that the said William Johnson, enter into bond and security in the sum of one thousand dollars, to be filed in the office of secretary of state, and made payable to the governor for the time being, and his successors in office, conditioned that the said boy William, shall never become a public charge, and that the said William Johnson shall educate and maintain said child, according to the provisions of the second section of this act.

Sec. 2. *And be it further enacted,* That the said William Johnson shall educate, or cause to be educated, and maintain or caused [*sic*] to be maintained, said child until he arrive at the age of twenty-one years.

E. TURNER,
Speaker of the House of Representatives.
JAMES PATTON,
Lieutenant-Governor and President of the Senate.

Approved, February 10, 1820
GEO. POINDEXTER [*Governor*].[21]

Who was this William Johnson who arranged for the emancipation of "the mulatto boy named William," his mother, and his sister in three different states? The little that is known of him does not shed even oblique light on his real character and unadvertised activities; and, singularly enough, the imprint he made in the public records was less distinct than that of any of the three slaves to whom he gave freedom. Even the heart-moving petition he addressed to the state legislature in behalf of his slave William might well have been written by a lawyer employed for that purpose.

The established facts concerning William Johnson can be quickly summarized. Although he was not important enough to be named as the head of a family in the state censuses of 1816 or 1818 or the

---

[21] *Laws of the State of Mississippi, Passed by the General Assembly,* 3 Sess. (Natchez, 1820), 38. See also Natchez *Mississippi State Gazette,* February 12, 1820.

United States census of 1820, he was listed as a "white poll" in the tax rolls of 1818, 1820, 1821, and 1823, which also showed that his taxable slaveholdings rose from none in 1818 to eight in 1823.[22] In 1822 "William Johnson of the County of Adams" also appeared in a deed record as the individual who was the owner of "one negroe man slave named Braxton aged about nineteen years and twenty thousand weight of Seed Cotton now on the plantation occupied by said William Johnson in the said County of Adams." [23] Finally, between 1820 and 1825 William Johnson was engaged in more than a dozen civil suits, either as defendant or plaintiff. These suits were mostly actions for the collection of promissory notes, ranging in size from $90 to $522, and such records of judgments as have been preserved indicate that Johnson usually was a defendant who was being forced to pay.[24]

Meantime, this shadowy William Johnson's illiterate former slave Amy—described in a court record as a mulatto about five feet in height—had established her household in Natchez. Under the name Amy Johnson, she was listed as the head of a free Negro family in censuses taken in 1816, 1818, and 1820. In 1819 she was issued a license "to retail in Natchez," probably as a peddler. And between 1816 and 1822 her name appeared in several court suits. In one case she was successfully sued for $10.77½ and costs, and in another she sued a barber, Arthur Mitchum, for assault. The assault case was tried slightly more than three years after the incident occurred in May, 1819. Counsel for Amy charged that the barber had spit in her face, "greatly squeezed" and pulled her nose, had pulled out large quantities of her hair, had hit her with a brickbat and pounded her whole body with his fists, and had torn and caused $50 worth of damage to her "gown dress Petticoats shift and bonnett." As a result, counsel averred, she had been unable to work for a long

[22] Auditor's Records, Tax Rolls, 1818, 1820, 1821, 1823, Adams County. (All Auditor's Records, Tax Rolls, cited in this study are in Mississippi Department of Archives and History.) His name does not appear on the tax rolls of 1824. A "William Johnston" and a "William Johnson" appear in two earlier (1803, 1811–12) records, but identification of these individuals as the man under discussion is impossible. See Adams County Court Minutes, 1802–1804, p. 169; Adams County Deed Records, G, 184–86.

[23] Adams County Deed Records, M, 352–53. See also an 1819 transaction to which William Johnson was a party, ibid., 197; and his name as an entry in a Natchez inn day book, 1822, pp. 32, 59, William Johnson Papers (Louisiana State University Department of Archives, Baton Rouge, La.).

[24] Adams County Circuit Court Record of Judgments (Civil), 1820–21, p. 339; ibid., 1821–22, pp. 117–18, 396–98; ibid., 1822–23, pp. 484–86; ibid., 1824–25, pp. 624–26. See also Adams County Court Case Docket Index, 1802–27, three entries, 1820–22, and seven entries, 1824–27; Adams County Criminal Court Minutes, 1823–28, January, 1825, pp. 142–43.

time. Plaintiff therefore asked that she be awarded damages in the amount of $500. But the court judged that she was entitled to $27.50 and costs.[25] The record did not show what Amy was doing or saying while her altercation with the barber was in progress, but in view of her children's testimony as to her quarrelsome disposition, it is highly probable that Mitchum did not emerge from the fight without knowledge of what she thought about his character and antecedents.

In 1820 Amy Johnson was witness to two important events in the lives of her children. Her fifteen-year-old daughter Adelia married twenty-year-old, Philadelphia-born free Negro James Miller, who was to remain in business in Natchez until 1830;[26] and her eleven-year-old son William was freed by the state legislature. Thereafter the boy took the name of the man who freed him.

During the early 1820's the young free Negro, William Johnson, was being initiated into the barber business in the Natchez shop of his brother-in-law, James Miller. The apprentice system of learning barbering was in vogue among free Negroes in all of the river towns, and young relatives often went through the same process. Many of the leading barbershops in the principal cities of Mississippi and Louisiana were operated by free Negroes, and in this decade James Miller became the most widely patronized barber in Natchez. Miller not only was Johnson's brother-in-law and business mentor, but also later sold him his business, moved to another city, and entered into a correspondence with Johnson which is a basic source of information concerning him.

By 1827 James Miller was well established and highly respected in Natchez. In that year forty-four prominent men of the community—including Dr. Ayres P. Merrill, Dr. Stephen Duncan, James Wilkins, James Stockman, Lemuel Gustine, Alvarez Fisk, and members of the city council—petitioned the state legislature

---

[25] This paragraph to this point is based chiefly on the following: Governor's Territorial Records, Census of 1816, Adams County, Series A, No. 23 (Mississippi Department of Archives and History) ; Secretary of State's Records, Census of 1818, Adams County, Series F, No. 101; United States Census Reports, 1820, MSS, Schedule I (Free Inhabitants), Adams County, Mississippi, 17 (National Archives, Washington, D. C.) ; Adams County License Record, 1818–26, entry for July 20, 1819; Adams County Court Case Docket Index, 1802–27, two entries, 1816–20; Adams County Court Minutes, 1818–22, April, 1820, p. 40; and (for Mitchum case) Adams County Circuit Court Record of Judgments (Civil) , 1821–22, pp. 111–13. For Mitchum's advertisement as a barber whose shop was equipped with razors, "clean Napkins," soaps, and "double tooth brushes," see Natchez *Mississippi Republican*, January 14, 1818.

[26] Adams County Marriage Records, II, 54. Amy Johnson made her mark as co-bondsman with James Miller.

asking for the removal of all of his civil disabilities as a free man of color, except those which excluded him from voting and militia and jury service. The petition stated that Miller had resided in Natchez for nine years and had acquired property "by honest industry," and that he "affords & has invariably afforded a good example to his brethren & that his conduct & demeanor are highly praiseworthy." The legislature failed to remove all his civil disabilities, but it did strengthen his position by passing an act permitting him to remain in the State, "any law to the contrary notwithstanding." [27]

By early 1829, however, Miller began to contemplate a move to New Orleans, despite the fact that his economic position was as strong as that of any free Negro in Mississippi. Not only had a law been passed for his especial benefit, but he had a thriving business in Natchez, owned four slaves, and had $3,750 "loaned at interest." [28] Nevertheless on October 14, 1830, Miller sold the unexpired portion of the lease of his Main Street barbershop "and other adjoining Houses" and the furniture therein to William Johnson, his young brother-in-law, for $300. Johnson's first purchases for the new shop were a dozen razors, for which he paid $3.00, a razor strap, and two bottles of "bear's oil" (or bear fat), then widely used on men's hair. [29]

At the time William Johnson established himself as a businessman in Natchez he was twenty-one years of age, but this was not his first independent venture as a barber. For nearly two years he had operated a shop at Port Gibson, Mississippi, in the second county to the north. His account books for the period 1828–30 show that he kept a record of seven trips to Natchez and of his daily collections, which he summarized in an entry in September, 1830: "The amount taken in During my Stay in Port Gibson which was twenty two months was one thousand and ninety four Dollars and fifty cents, This was by Hair Cutting and Shaving alone." [30]

---

[27] Petition of forty-four citizens of Adams County in behalf of James Miller, Natchez, December 22, 1827, Petitions and Memorials, Series I, No. 95; *Laws of Mississippi*, 11 Sess. (1828), 48–49.

[28] Auditor's Records, Tax Rolls, 1829, Adams County. For discussion of the possibility of "old Jim" Miller's "Letting you have the shop," see Washington Sterns to [William Johnson], March 6, 1829, Johnson Papers.

[29] Cash Book, 1830–38, Johnson Papers.

[30] Day Book, 1828–34, entry for September, 1830, *ibid.* Another free Negro barber, Elisha Miller, was in Claiborne County (of which Port Gibson was the leading town) in 1827 and 1828. Auditor's Records, Tax Rolls, 1827, 1828, Claiborne County. Johnson possibly succeeded Elisha Miller in his Port Gibson shop. In any event, about 1829, Elisha Miller moved to Vicksburg, where he was a barber until the middle 1840's. Both James and Elisha Miller were from Philadelphia and

During the five years of the young barber's Natchez residence prior to 1835—the year in which he married and began to keep a diary—he recorded even the smallest of his daily expenditures. Occasionally he entered them in two or three different account books. All of this is helpful, for a study of the complete financial records of any man reveals much concerning his character and habits.

In the case of William Johnson, his accounts show that in the early 1830's the barber undoubtedly was a young-man-about-town in his own sphere. He drank beer, and he frequently bought whisky and occasionally other stimulants—cider, ale, gin, brandy, Madeira, and champagne. During the summer he drank a soda water almost daily. He played dominoes, checkers, and billiards; he attended the circus; and he often escorted one to four free women of color to theatrical performances, where they saw some of the leading figures of the American stage—Tyrone Power, James H. Hackett, Clara Fisher, and the Ravels. He regularly gambled small amounts, particularly at roulette and faro, and in buying lottery tickets. Purchases of packs of cards were frequent entries in his account books. He backed his skill at shooting with bets and on one occasion lost twenty-five cents in a fence-jumping contest. He lost wagers ranging from twelve and a half cents to $14 at horse races—beginning a twenty-year period of singularly bad luck in picking winners. In 1831 he made a trip to New Orleans; in the following year he spent several days in St. Francisville, Louisiana; and in 1833 he sojourned between two and three months in Philadelphia and New York. His account-book entries for his eastern trip were meager, but they do show that he paid $63.65 for "perfumery" (for his barbershop), $30.00 for a violin, and $5.00 for two canary birds; his Philadelphia-to-New Orleans passage aboard the ship *Archer* cost him $45.00 and his New Orleans-to-Natchez passage $8.00. During this whole period he was courting three or four girls, and he was also occasionally noting expenditures of fifty cents each for "Sensuality" or "Sensual Pleasure." Other items were reasonably priced, too. In 1831 he recorded the purchases of a barrel of flour for seventy-five cents, and "beef" and steaks for twelve and a half

perhaps were brothers. Elisha Miller apparently did not possess the money-making talent possessed by Johnson and James Miller.

The Claiborne County tax rolls for 1824, 1825, and 1828 also list a white farmer named William Johnson. He may or may not have been the William Johnson who had freed the young Negro who took his former master's name, but he is the editors' choice among the half dozen or more white William Johnsons and William Johnstons living in four Mississippi counties along the Mississippi River between 1824 and 1828.

cents. On the whole, the young bachelor evidently was too busy to be introspective and was glad to be alive.[31]

Johnson's trips to New Orleans and St. Francisville are revealed by his expenditure records to have been chiefly pleasure jaunts. On July 14, 1831, he paid $10.00 for steamboat passage to New Orleans, where he remained almost a month. There he made numerous purchases of clothes, soda water, lottery tickets, and fruit. On July 19 he hired two carriages for $12.00 and drove "the Ladys" to "the Lake," where he paid $3.00 for dinner and also purchased whisky and two watermelons. On July 23 he played billiards. The next day he hired a gig, played billiards, purchased liquor, soda water, and oranges, and paid a "bathing" fee. Two days later he again played billiards, hired a carriage, and noted an expenditure of $3.00 for dinner at "the Lake." He once varied this routine by the purchase of a French-and-English spelling book. On August 5 he spent $1.25 for a handkerchief for "Miss Mary Gatewood." Six days later he crossed the Mississippi with "the Ladys," presented them a music box for which he had paid $9.50, played billiards, and purchased both whisky and wine. On August 13 he took a steamboat back to Natchez, and noted that he paid $2.00 for a "hack or Carriage up the hill" from the wharf at Natchez Landing and fifty cents to a drayman for hauling his trunk. His month in New Orleans had cost him exactly $135.87½.[32]

His trip to St. Francisville in 1832 was for the purpose of meeting "Miss Mary Gatewood," probably a free woman of color. For almost a year she had been writing to him from New Orleans, but on July 5 he received a letter written by her at St. Francisville. Two weeks later he hired a horse for three days and rode southward to the Louisiana town. There he "gave" her $100 in "U. S. paper," bought beer at "Madam Scott's," and tipped the Madam for "attention to us." The records fail to state the circumstances which prompted him to give Mary such a large sum. Johnson returned to Natchez on July 22, and during the next six months "Miss Gatewood" wrote to him even more frequently.[33]

But the woman he was to marry was a resident of Natchez. Since 1831, Johnson had been escorting a young free mulatto girl named

---

[31] All of the items in this paragraph have been selected or summarized from entries for 1830–35 from the following account books kept by William Johnson: Cash Book, 1830–38; Cash Book, 1830–44; Day Book, 1828–34; Day Book, 1830–40; Day Book, 1830–44; Ledger, 1833–37, Johnson Papers.

[32] Cash Book, 1830–38; Cash Book, 1830–44, *ibid.*

[33] Cash Book, 1830–38; Cash Book, 1830–44, *ibid.* Johnson's Ledger, 1833–37, p. 39, contains this cryptic remark: "Francisville Francisville good good."

Ann Battles to the theater and had been giving her presents, including guitar strings and a silk dress. Occasionally Ann and her suitor were accompanied to the theater by her free mulatto mother, Harriet Battles, but most of Johnson's accounts concerning the mother indicate that she did his "washing" at $4.00 per week. Finally, in March, 1835, he recorded that he paid $48.87½ to a local tailor for a wedding coat. On April 21, 1835, William Johnson and Ann Battles were married.[34]

Twenty-year-old Ann had managed to ensnare the most eligible bachelor in her class in Natchez. Her husband was the hard-working, hard-playing, twenty-six-year-old owner of the town's most popular barbershop, building property worth at least $2,700, and four slaves. Moreover, like many small men—his height was slightly less than Ann's five feet, seven inches, and his weight usually 135 or 140 pounds—he was meticulous in his dress. He also wore rings, carried an expensive gold watch, and paid a boy fifty cents a month to blacken his shoes. Concerning his other qualifications, Ann presently was to be informed. Their sixteen-year union was to be blessed (in the phrase and thought of the times) with ten children, the last of whom arrived a month before the husband's death in 1851.

During the weeks immediately before and after his wedding, William Johnson neglected his accounts. Within a few months, however, he had recovered his itch to make records of his activities, and he then not only revived his accounting system, but began to write the diary which constitutes the bulk of this volume.

THE DIARIST: BUSINESS CAREER

William Johnson's business career centered around his barber business. He was always ready to find profits in other enterprises—such as moneylending and house and room rentals—but shaving and haircutting services furnished to townsmen and transients provided his basic source of revenue. He was fortunate enough to acquire his town property just before the boom of the mid-1830's and to consolidate his position as the leading barber in Natchez in the same period. Thereafter he was able to ride out the baleful effects of depression years that followed in the wake of the Panic of 1837 and to acquire a considerable estate by the time of his death in 1851. His record clearly stamped him as a businessman who was energetic, shrewd, and sometimes opportunistic.

[34] Adams County Marriage Records, V, 542; diary entry, April 21, 1836; marriage license in Johnson Papers. For intimation of courtship between the two as early as 1829, see Washington Sterns to [William Johnson], March 6, 1829, *ibid.*

Johnson's barber business in Natchez was conducted entirely by blacks working under his direct supervision, and catered exclusively to whites. In the first three years (beginning in mid-October, 1830), this business was carried on in an old brick building on Main Street rented by Johnson; but by the fall of 1833 he had accumulated sufficient capital to acquire the property, with a down payment of half the purchase price of $2,750 and a twelve-month note for the remainder.[35] The barber's accounts indicate that his total expenses, including rent and wages paid to his employees, for his first year in Natchez were $1,362.06¼, for his second year more than $1,500.00, and for his third year more than $1,600.00.[36] While his record of income for these early years in Natchez is not complete, it is sufficiently detailed to indicate that it must have been at least $2,500 annually.

A shave cost a cash customer twelve and a half cents and a haircut twice as much, but much of Johnson's barber business was done on credit. His account books for 1834–40 indicate that he usually had about ninety credit customers, many of them leaders in the community's business and professional life. The standard rate for shaving by the month was $1.50, and while some customers paid regularly, others let as much as two years elapse before they settled their accounts. But practically all of them eventually paid.

As Johnson's business grew better, he made improvements in the physical aspects of his shop. As early as March, 1831, he paid $26 "for painting my sign," he periodically had the floor repaired and walls repapered or whitewashed, and from time to time he bought new furniture and pictures for his establishment. In 1837 he installed nearly fifty "shaving boxes," which he rented to customers at twenty-five cents per month, payable in advance. By 1839 he dressed his barbers in linen coats. At the time of his death in 1851 his Main Street shop contained two "Sophas," six barber chairs, four mirrors, thirty-one framed pictures, two washstands, a coat

[35] Adams County Deed Records, W, 133–35; receipt for Johnson's down payment, signed by Jacob Eiler, agent for owners Samuel M. Neill and wife, October 15, 1833, Johnson Papers. This property had a frontage of 68¾ feet, and included the greater part of the modern site of the Eola Hotel parking lot and 20 feet of the modern United States Post Office property. At the time of purchase, it also included at least one frame building.

[36] See monthly summary for October, 1830–March, 1833, in three pages inserted in middle of Day Book, 1840–43, Johnson Papers. The total for March, 1833–October, 1833, has been pieced together from a variety of sources, including Cash Book, 1830–38, and Cash Book, 1830–44, *ibid.*

rack, a hatrack, a small writing desk, a table, a "small stand," "Razors Scissors &c," and a "showcase and perfumery." [37]

Johnson had available for his fastidious customers a variety of "perfumery," hair oils, and fancy soaps. These included cologne, "lavender water," bay rum, "lemon scent," several types of "essences," "Pomade Cosmetique," "Creme de Perse," Macassar oil, and "rose soap." And "rectified bear's oil" was always at hand for application to the hair of the less squeamish.

In Johnson's barbershop, customers could get their personal razors set or sharpened at the proprietor's honing table. They could also purchase razors and shaving brushes, as well as toothbrushes, cigars, and suspenders. And a plasterer could buy surplus hair at $1.50 per bushel.

Moreover, the shop always opened early and closed late. Sunday morning found the proprietor and at least one of his barbers on duty behind the chairs, and sometimes work went on as usual even on Christmas Day.

Johnson also performed special tonsorial services. Infrequently he shaved both male and female heads, measured them and installed wigs thereon, and sold hair powder to the wig wearers. He often rode horseback to near-by plantation homes to cut children's hair, and in 1841 he was paid $1.00 for curling the hair of a young lady. Late in 1836 he charged former Governor George Poindexter $6.00 for twelve shaves in his room "at the tavern." He collected $1.00 for shaving a sick man, even during a yellow-fever epidemic, and $5.00 for shaving a corpse.

The barber eventually expanded his business to include a bathhouse and two smaller barbershops. His bathhouse, erected in the summer of 1834 at a cost of $170, included four "tubbs" valued at $15 each, and a device for using water that had been hauled to the establishment in barrels. The bathhouse season began in April or May and ended in September, but a few customers were usually waited upon in the colder months, except December. Cold baths were fifty cents, and hot ones seventy-five. Total receipts for the most profitable year—April, 1836, through March, 1837—were almost $500, about one seventh of which was entered on charge accounts.[38]

The bathing concern was in operation at least ten years, but Johnson's accounts are much more complete for the first three. He

---

[37] "Appraisal of Wm Johnson's Stock farming Utensils, Negroes &c," October 10, 1851, in "Estate of William Johnson," Adams County Probate Records, File 136.

[38] Ledger, 1833–37, pp. 88–125, Johnson Papers.

not only listed a number of prominent citizens in his bathhouse record as customers, but also gave whimsical designations to individuals whose names were unknown to the proprietor. These appellations included "Mr. Negro Trader," "Mr. Thermometer," "Mr. Sick Man," "Col. Troublesome," "Little Low Man," "Mr. Red Face," "Mr. Long Nose," "Mr. Frock Coat," "Mr. Silver Smith," "Mr. Italian Singer," and "Mr. from Texas." In 1840, Johnson noted in his diary the unusual circumstance that "the French Lady" took a bath in this establishment.

Johnson opened two small one-man barbershops in addition to his principal establishment. One of these—located in the Tremont House, on Wall Street, just around the corner from his Main Street shop—was in operation from early 1840 through 1843. The Natchez-under-the-Hill business was begun in 1838 and continued in different locations there until 1851. Both shops were rented by Johnson and were operated by free Negro employees, or by Charles, a slave.[39]

In William Johnson's diary, one result of the depression that followed the Panic of 1837 was apparent in entries concerning his own business. The Natchez male tended to spend more of his ready cash in barbershops in times of prosperity, to spend less during the depression period.

In 1835 and 1836, the beginning years of the diary, Johnson's daily receipts frequently totaled $15 to $20 in cash, and occasionally between $20 and $30. At the end of the second week of February, 1836, he recorded that his gross income for the week was $117.87½ and that his expenses were $50.94—both figures being not far from his average for this period.

Johnson's barber business was exceedingly poor for several months following the Natchez bank crisis of May, 1837. By mid-July a diary entry of this sort was typical: "Buisness as usual very dull." In the first week in August he wrote to his sister: "Buisness is so dull that tis hardly worth Keeping shop open for what one can make, if I had Rent to pay it would Burst me wide open. 6 shops on the hill and two or three under the hill." On September 25 he wrote again: "there is nothing doing here now — 1.50 is a big days work here now — I never herd of such times in my Life — I don't actually make my Expenses now — and have not for the last 12 days in my

[39] Ledger, 1837–41, p. 207; Day Book, 1840–43, entries for February, 1840, *ibid.* See Natchez *Courier*, November 27, 1837, for announcement of the opening of the Tremont House, "the large new brick building on the corner of Main and Wall streets, known as Mr. Silas Lillard's Blue Block." *Besancon's Annual Register*, 118, listed the Tremont House as one of the town's minor hotels.

shop — tis the Case with all us in the trade." [40] On October 12 he recorded that the past month had been the "dullest times for Buisness" he had seen in his seven years in business in Natchez, and four days later he took in only thirty-seven and a half cents — "the dullest of all days that I Ever saw in Natchez. . . . Now dont that beat Nature."

Such was the impact of the money crisis of 1837 on the barbershop business in Natchez. But if that business was a reasonable criterion, the town experienced temporary recovery late in 1837 (after the fall yellow-fever epidemic had run its course). Johnson's business continued "good" throughout most of 1838 and 1839, but became very "dull" early in 1840 and continued so until the end of 1843. At one point in 1842 income from his barbershop was so low that he considered changing his means of livelihood. Recovery began early in 1844, and the barbershop proprietor thereafter was better satisfied with his daily returns, which, however, never approached the boom days of 1835 and 1836. After early 1844 he considered $5.00 to $10.00 a "tolerable fair" day's cash business for his principal shop, and $12.00 or $13.00 exceptional.

William Johnson's barbers were all free Negroes or neat-handed, trustworthy slaves, most of whom learned the trade as boys in his shop. His younger barbers were selected from a number of applicants, and on more than one occasion the shop master refused to take prospective apprentices. The free boys he agreed to train were placed in the shop by their parents or white protectors when they were between ten and fifteen years of age. Until they were eighteen they served as apprentices or would-be apprentices, subject to the barbershop owner's discipline and control. In return for their labor services, he taught them the barber trade, gave them a rudimentary education, and fed and in some instances clothed them. At the age of eighteen the apprentices were usually released to make their own wage agreements with him or some other proprietor. In the 1840's Johnson habitually paid $100 to $150 per year to his former apprentices who had graduated into the journeyman class.[41]

Johnson carried out his part of the apprenticeship agreements in good conscience. He disciplined his boys when he thought they

---

40 Johnson to Mrs. James Miller, August 6, September 25, 1837 (copies), Johnson Papers.

41 Similar apprenticeship contracts were made for poor white children or orphans who were bound out to learn "the art, trade, and mystery" of printing, the seamstress trade, bricklaying, and merchandising. See Adams County Deed Records, I, 351, 437–38, L, 66–67, M, 81, N, 182–83, KK, 182. For free Negro orphans apprenticed as "mechanics" to white masters, see *ibid.*, I, 354, 355. For a law regulating apprenticeship of orphans, see *Laws of Mississippi*, 29 Sess. (1846), 194–97.

needed it: he did not hesitate to flog them for being impudent, for "being so careless and passionate, whilst shaving," for smoking his cigars, or for taking absence without leave. He also regretted it when he caught two of them fondling a black slave wench. "Oh what Puppys," he wrote in his diary. "Fondling — beneath a Levell, Low minded Creatures. I look on them as Soft." On the other hand, he was pleased when they did well in their studies, paid them small amounts regularly and made special awards for good work, and allowed them to attend "darkey parties," theatrical and circus performances, races, and church meetings. And when they finally had become journeymen and departed to set up their own shops in a neighboring town or on a steamboat, he was apparently sincere in his hopes that the young men he had trained would "do well."

Johnson's free apprentices included William Winston, William Nix, "French William," Edward Hoggatt, and various members of the Burns family.

Of all of these apprentices, Johnson was more firmly attached by ties of affection, mutual interests, and long business association to William Winston, whom he called "Bill" or "Winston." When Bill came to work for Johnson in 1836 "to Lern the Barbers trade," he was about twelve years of age and still a slave. But his master, former Lieutenant Governor Fountain Winston, had made provision in his will for the freeing of Bill's mother, Rachel, and had added several provisions in behalf of the boy: "Believing Bill or William the son of Rachel too white to be continued in Slavery," he had directed that he remain with his mother until he was old enough to be bound as an apprentice to "some reputable mechanic." When he was twenty-one, he was to be freed. Fountain Winston further directed that his furniture should go to Rachel; $500 should be set aside to support Rachel and Bill (during the latter's minority); and all of his property (amounting to $3,000 plus land in Tennessee), except his library, should be held in trust for the boy—provided only that his habits should be good. Bill Winston worked for Johnson most of the time from 1836 until the master barber's death in 1851, and thereafter for the Johnson family. By way of postscript, it can be added that Bill and his mother were listed as free Negroes in the United States census of 1850; that a special law authorizing him to remain in Mississippi was passed by the legislature in 1854, a most unusual concession to a free Negro in the 1850's; and that the pastor of the white Presbyterian Church made this entry in his diary on Tuesday, March 17, 1863: "Married at Chapel — night — William F. Winston to Anna M. Lieper — free colord persons — after wh. attend prayer meets of negroes and spoke."[42] If Winston's old master had lived to be present that night, he would unquestionably have been proud of his former apprentice.

Johnson also employed two older free Negro barbers, Wellington West and Washington Sterns, for brief periods. West, who also worked for Johnson's brother-in-law in New Orleans, was a satisfactory employee, but Sterns drank too much to suit the shop proprietor and it was not altogether safe to allow him free access to the shop till.[43]

William Johnson tried to teach several slaves the barber trade, but found only two of them satisfactory. A slave named Charles proved to be one of his best employees. He paid a "Major Young" $150 per year (less the cost of clothing) for Charles's services, an arrangement that benefited both parties. During most of the 1840's Johnson allowed him to run his Natchez-under-the-Hill shop with comparatively little supervision. Charles brought in his receipts every two weeks, and Johnson often gave him one tenth to one fifth of the proceeds. The slave also selected his own clothing, made trips to his Jefferson County "home," and in most respects was as free as any of Johnson's journeymen.[44] The master barber believed that Charles disgraced himself when he took as a wife a servant girl who was known to be "a Buster," just as he intimated that his former journeyman, free Negro Bill Nix, had made a mistake in marrying a black girl who had once been "made use of" by a white man. Early in April, 1851, Charles was withdrawn from the "lower" shop, apparently because Major Young had decided to free him,

[42] Adams County Will Books, II, 81–83; "Estate of Fountain Winston," Adams County Probate Records, File 69; U. S. Census Reports, 1850, Schedule I, Adams County, 31; *Laws of Mississippi*, 35 Sess. (1854), 295; Diary of Rev. Joseph B. Stratton, 1843–1903 (Louisiana State University Department of Archives); Adams County Marriage Records, VIII, 143. Fountain Winston bequeathed his library to his white nephew. See also Rachel Winston to William Johnson, June 27, 1837 (copy), Johnson Papers, in which she asked the barbershop proprietor to send her "the sum of two Dollars for the making of two shirts for William Winston, being as I am not able to pay for it myself."

[43] For the careers of Sterns and West, see Johnson's diary entries for December 26, 1835; November 9, 1836; May 6, 1837; August 18, 1839; July 24, 1840; August 24, 1841; and footnotes to these entries.

[44] An undated memorandum of Johnson's original agreement with Major Young concerning Charles (in Johnson Papers) contains virtually the same provisions that the barber usually made concerning free Negro apprentices. Charles's clothing expenditures were to be at Major Young's expense, and Johnson was "to Learn him the trade" and "to Learn him his Books—&c &c Learn him to write also." This agreement obviously was made in the period 1836–40, when Charles was under Johnson's supervision. On May 24, 1842, Johnson agreed to pay $15 per month for Charles's services, but on September 2, 1842, and thereafter, the rate stipulated was $150 per year.

and Johnson's twenty-five-year-old slave Jim was installed in his place. In the two and a half months that remained before the master barber was killed, Jim proved himself a capable successor.

A number of Johnson's barbershop customers borrowed money from him, for one of his business sidelines was that of acting as moneylender and broker. In his first three years in Natchez he made a few loans, some of which were to other free Negroes, but by 1834 his business of lending to whites was in full swing and in 1836–37 reached its period of maximum operation. An analysis of his loans from March 31, 1836, through March 30, 1837, shows that in that year he lent nearly $4,700, and that on February 16, 1837, at least $2,100 was still outstanding. By September 12, 1839, the amount of his loaned money outstanding had been reduced to about $925. In the following year his lending activities dwindled even more; in 1844 the total of his loans was about $580; and in the late 1840's his lending consisted of only a few small loans each year.[45]

The operation of a lending business, even on a modest scale, made it necessary that the barber keep well informed concerning the confusing variety of money then in circulation. This he did, and he often made a small profit in changing one type of money into another. This brokerage fee supplemented the profit which he made from interest on loans. His interest rates varied from 5 per cent per month to 6 per cent per year. But it is doubtful that his profit from both sources exceeded $300 in any one year.

Johnson's largest single loan was $1,000 to the firm of Gemmell & Taylor. He also made others ranging in size from $660 down to $100 to such firms and business and professional men as Elijah Bell (a hotel proprietor), McAlister, Watson & Co., Barlow & Taylor, A. Spielman, John B. Nevitt, Dr. John M. Hubbard, a Dr. Benbrook, Dr. Reed Potts, and former Governor George Poindexter. But most of his loans were smaller than $100 and very frequently for short periods. The prevailing money tightness was reflected in a number of loans for periods of one to fourteen days and the bor-

---

[45] The summary of Johnson's lending and brokerage business in this and the succeeding paragraphs is based on a detailed analysis of fifteen of his account books in the Johnson Papers and of his diary, many of which both supplement and overlap each other. But for the totals for 1836–37 and 1844, see particularly his Cash Book, 1830–38; Day Book, 1843–44; and Day Book, 1844–45. For his lending accounts receivable on September 12, 1839, see Ledger, 1837–41, p. 116; the $925 receivable on September 12, 1839, does not include $250 owed Johnson by his mother.

rowing of small amounts by individuals supposedly well-to-do or rich.

Johnson rarely failed to collect money that was due him—partly because he was careful to make most of his loans to responsible individuals, partly because he was capable of being extremely persistent in his collections, even to the point of going to court in rare instances. One expedient that he used in difficult cases was to transfer a note to some white man who could bring stronger pressure to bear on the signer of the note.

One semiliterate man once wrote a detailed explanation of the circumstances which had prevented him from paying a debt due the barber. But he promised to pay very shortly, and added, "Nead Sesity Drive a Man to Doe Sometimes to Doe things that he Does not wish to Doe and So it was the Case with me and I hope you will not think hard of me for so doing. . . . But I shal Be up soon and it will Be all Right with you." [46]

The barber-moneylender—never one to neglect any possible method of making an honest dollar—also augmented his income by canny buying and selling and by a variety of small enterprises. In 1830–31 he conducted a toyshop in one of his vacant rooms; a decade later he was making small sales of wallpaper. In 1834–35 he made between $20 and $30 per month by having two of his slaves haul coal and sand and water barrels (for watering the streets) in horse-drawn carts which he had purchased. At one time he had at least seven street-watering customers, including two banks. For several weeks he also received half the profits (about $8.00 or $9.00 per week) from the operation of a dray by one Henry Melin; Johnson apparently furnished the horse and dray, and Melin did the work.[47] Later he sold some of the carts and rented others. Moreover, one of his four or five horses was sometimes rented for a stipulated amount; for example, in 1838 a local businessman paid $50 for "five months use of" Kitty Fisher, a horse which had cost Johnson $97 in the previous year. In 1849 Johnson purchased a buggy for $25.00, and soon rented it for $6.00 per month to two men to transport fish nine or ten miles to the Natchez market. He also sold

---

[46] Jeremiah Waller to Johnson, August 17, 1845, Johnson Papers.

[47] For records of Johnson's toyshop, wallpaper, and dray enterprises, see (for toyshop) Day Book, 1830–44, pp. 71, 85–87, accounts from October 30, 1830, to June 4, 1831; (for wallpaper sales) Day Book, 1840–43, accounts for 1841–42, *passim;* (for dray business) Day Book, 1830–44, page headed "Watering Book . . . ," and Ledger, 1833–37, pp. 20–21, 24–25, 34–35, 69, Johnson Papers. See also receipts for payments for "watering the street" in front of "U. S. Bank," 1835, signed "W. Johnson," Commercial Bank of Natchez Papers (Louisiana State University Department of Archives).

some of his large number of canary birds—and always at a profit. On most of these enterprises Johnson kept accounts which recorded his original investments, costs, and profits.

Johnson also made three profitable speculations in land and city property and bank stock, but his profits in these transactions were wiped out in a subsequent venture in buying railroad stock. In 1835 he purchased a 162.31-acre tract of land for $4.12½ per acre, and in less than six weeks realized a profit of $628.00; and in 1836 he bought a city lot for $1,300.00 and sold it later for $2,000.00.[48] He also made a profit in a purchase and quick resale of Commercial Bank of Natchez stock in March, 1836. But his investment of $2,000 in stock of the Mississippi Rail Road Company, a Natchez corporation that eventually built 25 miles of a planned 125 miles to the northeast before it went into bankruptcy, does not show on his books to have yielded dividends.[49]

The barber, meanwhile, had begun to acquire a small but steady income from real-estate rentals. Even in the early 1830's, when he was paying $12.00 per month rent for his Main Street property, he was subletting various rooms for $5.00 to $6.00 per month each. By 1835–37 he was the owner of the property and had made substantial improvements, and in those boom years he received rents which sometimes ran as high as $50 per month per room. But few of his tenants remained for long periods, and his total income for a single year from rentals (as computed from his account books and diary for the period March 31, 1836, through March 30, 1837) did not exceed $600. His tenants in the mid-1830's were two doctors and several small tradesmen, including Adolph Flecheux (also called Flecho), a jeweler and engraver; a storekeeper whom the barber called "Mons LaVigne"; and a stationer.

In 1836–38 William Johnson erected several new buildings and thereby increased his income from rentals. The first, constructed under contract by Thomas Rose in the latter part of 1836 and the first half of 1837, was built on a lot on the south side of State Street (a half block from the courthouse). This property was owned by

48 For these two transactions, see Adams County Deed Records, W, 362, Y, 209. BB, 206, CC, 271, and Johnson's diary entries for October 12, 20, November 23, 26, 1835; May 17, 1839.

49 See Johnson's diary entries for March 14, 15, 1836, and entries for same dates in Cash Book, 1830–38, Johnson Papers, for his purchase and resale of the bank stock. On May 31, 1836, he recorded his payment of the first installment on his railroad stock, for which he eventually received a paid-up certificate, dated June 22, 1839, also in Johnson Papers.

Johnson's mother-in-law, Harriet Battles,[50] but managed by him. The two-story, five-room frame building cost Johnson $2,952; and it brought in more than $1,500 in rent payments before it burned in late September, 1839. Johnson had insured it for $2,000, however, and when payment on his policy was secured, erected another building on the same property in 1840–41. The chief tenants prior to the devastation of the first structure by fire had been P. McGetterick, who operated therein "a coffee house" called "The Southern Exchange," and a business firm called Green & Blake.[51]

In 1838–39 Johnson also constructed a new three-story brick building on his Main Street property at a total cost of nearly $3,400.[52] From the rent of what Johnson called his "Fancy Store on Main Street," which was located in part of the brick building, he received at least $2,500 in two and a half years. But an analysis of his rents for the years 1844 and 1845 indicates that his two buildings on Main Street, one brick and one frame, brought him no more than $600 per year (above maintenance costs), and his income from this source continued at about this figure until his death in 1851. His Main Street tenants in the 1840's included Colonel D. F. Waymouth, a storekeeper; J. N. Staples, another storekeeper; Dr. A. A. Jones, who operated a "botanic" drugstore; Jones's successor, Dr. J. R. Applewhite; Arthur Kenney, a "boot maker"; "Mr. Bunting," who operated a tenpin alley; and several fruit-store proprietors, including Antonio Lynch and Joseph Meshio.

The last large building erected by the Natchez barber was constructed on the site of the State Street frame house which had been destroyed by fire in late September, 1839. This three-story brick house, which now stands at 210 State Street, was built under Johnson's immediate supervision between August, 1840, and November, 1841, and some conception of the process of its construction can be gained by consulting his diary for that period. His slaves performed

50 This lot, now 210 State Street, was purchased in 1829 by Harriet Battles. Gabriel Tichenor, prominent businessman who had freed her in 1822, sold it to her for $2. Adams County Deed Records, O, 36, R, 489–90.

51 For the cost, occupancy, and burning of this building, see Johnson's diary entries for March 9, May 11, 1837; September 25, 1839; and footnotes to these entries. McGetterick's Southern Exchange should not be confused with William Parker's Mississippi Hotel, also called "The Southern Exchange," which stood directly across State Street, on the north side.

52 See Day Book, 1830–40, entries from August 12, 1838, to January 16, 1839; Cash Book, 1830–44, entries in January, February, 1839, and periodic entries, mostly under name of George Weldon, contractor, to September 9, 1839; Ledger, 1837–41, pp. 161, 205, Johnson Papers.

some of the rough labor, and the carpentry, bricklaying, and plastering were done by local white artisans, but William Johnson acted as his own chief contractor. Aside from a dancing master named Joseph Barbiere, who occupied a room or two in the building in late 1841 and 1842, Johnson's records do not indicate that tenants occupied any part of it. It has been the family home for more than a century.

Just before Johnson's death in 1851, he purchased a lot immediately adjacent to the State Street property on which he had constructed the family home. It was located on the corner of State and Canal streets, extending 162 feet along the south side of State and 101 feet along Canal.[53]

Johnson received small returns from hiring out his slaves for periods ranging from one day to five or six months. He was paid as much as $20.00 to $28.00 per month for a strong Negro man's services in 1836, and $5.00 to $10.00 for a slave woman's services in the early 1840's. In all, he hired out nine slaves in the twenty years he was a slaveowner, but the income from this source was never more than $100 in a single year, and usually much less. On the debit side of his ledgers, there were sometimes entries showing that he himself paid out money for slave hire.

In the middle 1830's the tax rolls showed that he was the owner of four or five slaves (usually two or three men, and a woman or two), that his mother owned five (all women and children), and that his mother-in-law was the owner of one female slave. By the middle 1840's Johnson's slaveholdings rose to eight or nine slaves. When his mother died in 1849, Johnson succeeded to the ownership of her group. At the time of his death two years later he was thus the owner of fifteen slaves, listed (with evaluations) in his estate appraisal as follows:

[53] Adams County Deed Records, HH, 526–27; and receipt for final payment, November 1, 1851, Johnson Papers. This lot is now occupied by the Mississippi Central Railroad Co. and was originally granted by Spanish Governor Manuel Gayoso de Lemos to Don Andres Gil, resident doctor of the Royal Hospital, which was immediately adjacent. See Gayoso to Gil, May 29, 1793 (in Spanish), Johnson Papers. Subsequent transfers of the property can be traced in two deeds, 1802–1803, Johnson Papers, and Adams County Deed Records, P, 214–16, X, 77–78, HH, 525–26. Payment on this purchase was completed after Johnson's death by the Johnson estate, which also completed purchase on two other cheap town lots to which Johnson had acquired partial title in 1844. See *ibid.*, EE, 314, 394, KK, 246–47.

Old Man Ned	$ 100	Old Phillip	$ 250
Missiny	150	Sarah	700
Peggy	300	Lucinda	600
Mary	350	John	200
Silvy or Sylvia	500	Celia	300
Anderson	850	Mary Jane	250
Sam	500	Old Rose	25
Jim	1,000		

Total . . . . $6,075[54]

These fifteen slaves (six or seven of whom had been acquired from Amy Johnson's estate) were the residue of thirty-one who had been owned at various times by Johnson in the twenty years since he had bought his first in 1832. Available records indicate that at least three had been sold (at a profit in each instance), six had died, and one—Walker, who was genial but weak-minded—had escaped or had been stolen. Among the fifteen remaining in 1851, Lucinda and Sarah had long been house servants, while Sylvia (a cook), Phil, Anderson, and Jim had seen considerable service in the last project of Johnson's life, his farm.

Before William Johnson embarked in the middle 1840's on what was for a man of his means an extensive land-acquisition program, he had long canvassed the possibilities of acquiring a farm or small plantation. As early as 1835 he bought a tract of slightly more than 160 acres, but could not resist quickly disposing of it when an opportunity to almost double his investment appeared. Thereafter he watched land sales very closely but not necessarily with a gleam of speculation in his eye. Like many other contemporary Americans who believed that ownership of land constituted "the key to happiness," he developed a longing to feel his own ground under his feet. He knew that many other Natchez businessmen owned land; in the middle 1830's he first experienced a certain pride of ownership in horses he had purchased as well as a measure of success in disposing of some of them at a profit; and his frequent hunting trips acquainted him with swampy terrain in riding distance to the southwest, which greatly interested him because of its cheapness and possible profitableness. These were some of the factors in his decision to buy lands in and near the area he called "the Swamp,"

[54] "Appraisal of Wm Johnson's Stock farming Utensils, Negroes, &c," October 10, 1851, in "Estate of William Johnson," Adams County Probate Records, File 136.

35

a partially wooded area containing a number of shallow lakes and located about six to eight miles southwest of Natchez.

Johnson's initial land acquisition in his move to become a part-time farmer was a tract supposedly containing 120 acres and situated on the Mississippi River, to the immediate west of the southern end of the Swamp. This tract, for which he paid $600 in August, 1845, was called "Hard Scrabble," and most of it was on slightly higher ground than the swampy sector away from the river. Thirteen months later Johnson paid $3,000 to William Mosbey for 242.14 acres of similar land which adjoined the first tract on the north and also lay along the river. According to a resurvey he had actually acquired about 345.5 acres in these two purchases.[55] This was the land on which Johnson did his farming, but some of it was so low and swampy that it was valuable only for its timber. Before the end of 1846 Johnson also acquired a ninety-nine-year lease of 403.1 acres of school land, located a section away from the river and split by a long, shallow lake. For this portion of the Swamp he paid slightly more than $500.[56] Since Johnson was awarded $146 by a court because his first tract was found to contain less than 120 acres, Johnson had become a landowner at an expenditure of about $3,950. From the summer of 1845 to his death six years later, much of his time and energy was to be devoted to an attempt to make his farming and timber venture pay and to protect his timber rights against what he regarded as illegal encroachments by two of his neighbors.

Since the barber could not devote all his time to his farm, one of his first problems was to secure adequate supervision of his labor force. To this end, he usually contrived to have on his place a white man who was expected to act as a combination of tenant, overseer, and chief laborer. Early in 1847 he made an agreement with W. H. Stump, who had been living on a near-by farm: Stump was to have a third of "what is made on the ground" at Hard Scrabble, and a third of "the Proffit that may arise from wood that may be cut" on both

---

[55] The first tract was purchased from Winslow Winn, and the second from William Mosbey (sometimes spelled "Moseby" or "Mosebey") and wife. The land was all in Sections 5 and 9, Township 6, Range 4, West. Adams County Deed Records, FF, 81–82, 452–53, GG, 543; and see also Cash Book, 1844–47, entries under names of Winn; and Mosbey between January 8, 1845, and September 22, 1846, Johnson Papers. Winslow Winn and Mosbey's wife were children of George Winn, a free Negro who had been the owner of both tracts when he died in 1831. "Estate of George Winn," Adams County Probate Records, File 65. See also Johnson's diary entries for December 10, 1837; November 23, 1839; February 27, December 2, 1840; and footnotes to these entries.

[56] Adams County Deed Records, II, 427.

tracts by three of Johnson's slaves; and the white man was to "find" his family, Johnson to "find" his "force." In 1848 Johnson paid Stump $15 per month to farm both of his tracts and furnished housing and food for him and his wife. Early in January, 1849, the barber expressed a measure of dissatisfaction with Stump's services: "I find there is Scarcly anything down thare done when I am not thare, I found Mr Stump and Little [Winslow] Winn going down the Road." Shortly afterward, however, Johnson had an end-of-the-year settlement with Stump, but found that he was unwilling to remain on the farm a third year.

In 1849 Johnson hired a succession of white men to work on his farm. On March 1, Samuel Clark was employed to perform general farm labor for $12 per month, but apparently he spent most of the next three months cutting timber. Clark received $98 for cutting 109 cords of wood, a compensation Johnson considered exorbitant, but he paid it rather than argue with a "prety Smart Rascal." In the spring of 1849 a "Mr. Strong" also assisted in the farm work. Then on June 20, H. Burke agreed to act as overseer for a stipend of $15 per month, in addition to housing and food. Burke proved even less satisfactory than his predecessors. During his sixteen months of overseeing, he did much fishing, hunting, and drinking—all of which caused Johnson to berate him, in his diary at least, for his "Rascally Conduct"—but the free Negro noted on more than one occasion that the overseer was able to do a fairly good day's work while partially drunk. "Old Man Langford" also lived on Johnson's farm for several months, but he was usually drunk or sick, and he and Johnson parted company with no regret on the Negro's part.

The first rule on Johnson's farm, not always successfully enforced in the owner's absence, was that everybody worked. This applied first to the resident labor force, which included the chief white tenant or overseer, an occasional white laborer employed at $10 to $12 per month and provisions, one free Negro who was paid $150 per year, and five to six slaves—most of them Johnson's. During one year Johnson also paid $140 for the services of two slaves, a man and a woman. In addition, the barber was able to augment his labor force temporarily in harvesting periods, and occasionally his sons, one or two of his barbers, his relatives from New Orleans, and two or three of his free Negro friends worked a few days. And when Johnson was at the farm, he himself often arose before daybreak and paced his hands in two or three hours labor before breakfast.

The yearly routine on Johnson's farm naturally evolved from its productions—corn, vegetables, fruit, timber, wool, and cattle. The first few weeks of the year were sometimes devoted to enlarging the planting acreage by clearing; in one year about sixty-five peach trees and potatoes and onions were planted in the third week in February, and between February 25 and March 3 plowing of the cornfields began. Much labor was expended on his four corn-and-fodder fields—the "Upper Field" and the "Lower Field" in his northern tract, and the "Front Ridge" and the "Back Ridge" at Hard Scrabble (the southern and smaller tract)—although he came to the conclusion that four plows could "go over" the whole of the Upper Field and Lower Field in three days. In 1847, a very wet year, corn planting was only half completed by April 1, though usually it had been finished two weeks earlier. During the next few weeks, the force was engaged in planting such vegetables as peas, potatoes, pumpkins, watermelons, and cabbages. Fences were repaired, and occasionally there was ditching to be done and replanting of corn if the stand was poor. June found the force digging potatoes and cultivating corn; in July and August corn was shucked and fodder pulled. In late August and September turnips were planted, grass was cut, and more corn pulled. At the end of October and the beginning of November, corn was shelled and sacked, potatoes were dug, and pumpkins were hauled to town. Then late corn was pulled and the stalks were cut. By the end of 1848 Johnson's hands were using a "machine" which he thought could easily shell fifty bushels of corn per day.

Other productions enabled the owner and his overseer to keep the force busy in slack times. There were about seventy-five sheep to be sheared in May or early June. There were hogs to be marked, because they ran wild in the Swamp and some of the neighbors were not overly scrupulous in determining original ownership before they killed or placed evidence of ownership on unmarked pigs. The farm's force also had to spend some time in care of the score or more of cattle, three or four mules, two to four oxen, and twenty to thirty horses and colts.

But the farm's chief subsidiary product was timber, some of which was cut by Johnson's force, some by contract with white wood choppers or a white owner of a small gang of slave wood choppers. When the wood was cut under contract, Johnson paid between fifty-five cents and $1.00 per cord, and then had his force transport it to the river bank. There it was sold at $2.00 to $2.50 per cord to steamboats. During 1850 this business reached such proportions that Johnson's overseer sold about 450 cords.

Was Johnson's farm a profitable enterprise? An exact cost-and-profit answer is impossible, but it is certain that the expenses of feeding the considerable number of persons in his town household were substantially reduced by the use of produce raised on the farm. Vegetables, corn, eggs, and butter were often delivered to his town kitchen. His sheep brought a minute annual profit, and his timber business from $50 to $750 annually. In 1847 he rented the improved portion of his northern, or Mosbey, tract for $100, and a house on the place for $50; in 1849 he rented Hard Scrabble, his smallest tract, for $50, which was a reasonable return on an original investment of $454. In his six years of farming he probably made $700 above costs in sales of cattle and horses. In 1848 and 1849 he received not more than $250 annually from sales of corn and potatoes. But near the end of 1849, Johnson's inferior potato crop caused him to remark, "Oh I have had bad Luck this year in the way of Croping, very indeed." And at the end of 1850, he wrote, "Things Looks bad and I have a Strong Notion not to Cultivate the place the Coming year." Yet in spite of this pessimistic outlook and his firm conviction that his force often loafed when he was not present, Johnson continued farming in 1851. Shortly before he was killed in June, he even purchased nearly 800 acres of additional swampland in scattered tracts near his farm.[57]

Regardless of whether William Johnson's farming and timber operations had been reasonably profitable, his landed investment brought a substantial return to his widow. On July 1, 1853, she sold the lands and lease which had cost her husband slightly less than $4,300 to planter James Surget for $7,812.50.[58]

Thus, by 1851, William Johnson had made long economic strides since 1828–30, when his barbershop at Port Gibson had yielded an annual income of about $600. By 1851 his slaves were valued at more than $6,000, his land at nearly $8,000, his farm tools and stock at almost $1,600, and two Main Street houses at about $7,500. A conservative estimate of the value of his estate would have been $25,000, not including the good will attached to his barbershop business. He had been successful as a barbershop proprietor, landlord, and moneylender, and his farm had not been a wholly unre-

[57] Adams County Deed Records, HH, 342, II, 428. All of this land was in Sections 4, 6, 7, and 8 of Township 6, Range 4, West, and Sections 22 and 32 of Township 6, Range 3, West. The instruments cited above gave Johnson one-third interest of nearly 2,400 acres. Another deed record (*ibid.*, GG, 480) recorded his purchase of the other two thirds for $10, but apparently title to the two-thirds interest was defective. See *ibid.*, II, 597, KK, 127, HHH, 720. Copies of Johnson's three deeds are in the Johnson Papers.

[58] Adams County Probate Real Estate Records, II, 232–39; Natchez *Courier*, June 1, 8, 15, 1853.

munerative venture. His business career had provided a notable example of free Negro business enterprise.

Johnson's position as the most prominent Negro businessman in Natchez was further reflected in a number of contributions he made to philanthropic and organizational activities. These included small donations to promote several militia and fire company celebrations, to a fund for the "Distressed Passengers" of a steamboat that had blown up, and for the firing of a cannon on the Bluff to celebrate the annexation of Texas. And not infrequently he gave small amounts to destitute persons.

These and other aspects of his career gave him a solidly entrenched position in Natchez life. He was regarded as a reasonably public-spirited man of substance who was entitled to the maximum respect attainable by a person of his mixed blood.

THE DIARIST: PERSONAL LIFE

Boredom rarely afflicted William Johnson. Disgust and disappointment came to him, as to all men, but his life was too full of profitable work and spirited play to allow him to become stricken with ennui. Much of his time and energy was devoted to the supervision of his barbershop and other business undertakings, but he had many additional interests. Among them was an eager absorption in all manner of sports, an enthusiasm he shared with his closest friend, free Negro Robert McCary. And a continual correspondence and pleasant exchange of visits with his sister Adelia and her husband, James Miller of New Orleans, were a part of a pattern of a multiform family life.

The observations in Johnson's diary obviously were made by a man with an alert mind who was unreservedly occupied in the daily round of activities and participated in many of them. His own words were: "I am always ready for Anything." This was no exaggeration, particularly where recreation was concerned. He bought tickets in lotteries and raffles, and he found amusement in playing shuffleboard and checkers, pitching quoits and dollars, and playing marbles and cards. On one occasion he and three friends played cards all night. Johnson enjoyed winning in any type of competition, usually recorded whether he was winner or loser, and in one instance referred to himself as "the old Shark" in the matter of a toy-boat-sailing contest with Robert McCary and their children.

After April, 1836, his attendance at the theater was not as regular as before. A disturbance in the gallery which slaves and free Negroes occupied together caused him to write that "I made up my mind not to go up there any more untill there was some Regulations made up stairs." Three years later he saw a few performances at the theater, including that of Ellen Tree in *The Lady of Lyons*,[59] but his theater attendance was never again as regular as it had been in the early 1830's, when he had found it an effective adjunct to courtship. Johnson also saw an occasional circus, animal show, fireworks display, and balloon ascension, but his interest in such spectacles dwindled considerably in the 1840's.

The barber's chief sports were hunting, shooting at targets, and fishing. In the midst of the yellow-fever epidemic of 1837, he wrote to his sister that there was little work to do in his shop, and that "if it was not from fear of making myself sick I would go out a hunting Every day." [60] The countryside near Natchez tempted hunters with a variety of game, including ducks, snipe, quail, pigeons, coons, squirrels, rabbits, wild hogs, alligators, and deer. Johnson owned a number of different types of guns, and was proud of his expertness at handling them, both in shooting wild animals and in competitive firing at targets. "I always Beat the crowd that I go with," he wrote in reporting a hunt, "and no mistake."

William Johnson also was avidly interested in horse racing. He saw a great many races in Natchez and some in New Orleans, and he recorded the results of many of the major races regardless of whether he had actually been among the spectators. The barber's zeal in entering race results in his diary arose in part from his admiration of Colonel Adam L. Bingaman, owner of a racing stable that made his name widely recognized in turf circles. Bingaman owned a number of nationally known horses, including Ruffin and "the Champion of the South West, the renowned Sarah Bladen," while his chief Adams County rival, planter William J. Minor, owned a string imported from Great Britain, and also its offspring.[61] Johnson not only reported races entered by members of the Bingaman and Minor stables, but also dozens of others. And he was especially careful to note arguments and brawls that arose at the track.

As a willing bettor on the horse races and occasionally a paid-up subscriber to the Adams County Jockey Club,[62] Johnson attended the races when he pleased and even enjoyed a limited use of the

---

[59] Cash Book, 1830–44, entry for March 12, 1839, Johnson Papers. This was omitted from his diary.

[60] Johnson to Mrs. James Miller, October 4, 1837 (copy), *ibid.*

[61] See footnotes 10 and 59, pp. 67 and 81.

[62] See, for example, the record of his $10 subscription in Cash Book, 1830–44, entry for February 26, 1842, Johnson Papers.

facilities of the track for his own horses. His horses ran there for small stakes against those of such white friends as St. Clair, a carpenter, and John Jacquemine, or less often against nags owned by other free Negroes. These contests, always for stakes of less than $50, were not a part of the official racing schedule and were not to be compared with match races on which the Adams County aristocracy wagered as much as $500 to $10,000. Johnson's horses always ran after the regularly scheduled races had been completed or on some other day. None of his horses had cost him more than $200, and they and their opponents were not pedigreed stock.

In common with many of his fellow citizens, Johnson took keen delight in betting on the races and other events of a varying nature. He had a curious caution, however, for a man who was addicted to gambling, and sometimes hedged his bets or paid small sums to withdraw wagers. Besides risking money, he bet boots, bricks, cigars, or "a month of shaving," and more often lost than won. In one year he lost more than $250 in wagers on the races and won less than half that amount,[63] and he lost $105 in four days in November, 1847. Usually he bore his losses with equanimity, as he thought a gentleman should, except when he suspected that the outcome had been framed in advance. After he recorded in his accounts that he had lost seven bets totaling $35 in one day in 1850, he stated in his diary: "I am under the impression that There is Something done in the way of Swindling out there at times."

The free Negro placed wagers on his judgment and prowess in many activities other than racing. He made small bets on cockfights and steamboat races and in nearly all the games which he played, including "cards." He was especially fond of backing himself in a target-shooting match. One of his favorite opponents in shooting contests was John Jacquemine, whom Johnson often called "John the Greek." Jacquemine was the proprietor of an amusement center about two miles from town, where he held shooting matches, operated a tenpin alley, and sold fruits and lemonade.[64] Apparently "John the Greek" had little race prejudice, for he frequently appeared in public with the barber. In 1844 Johnson recorded this bet: "I bet Mr Jaqamine to day 1 pr shoes that his young heiffer from the Cow that I won of him would not have a calf in year from this date and I bet him 1 pr shoes that my Horse would out walk his &c." The

---

63 His Ledger, 1835–39, pp. 78, 96, Johnson Papers, contains a complete itemization of his winnings and losses in race bets for the period December 1, 1836–March 1, 1837. Each list is headed "Mr. R. Tract." His losses for the period totaled approximately $157 (including two dozen cigars) and his winnings $76.50.

64 Natchez *Courier*, April 30, 1842.

barber paid his overseer Burke "One Hundred Dollars in Brandon money that he won from me on corn Shucking," and he also lost $14 in election bets to W. H. Stump, one of his illiterate white farm tenants.

A constant companion in after-work pastime and pleasure was his mulatto friend, Robert McCary, whom he called "Mc" or "Old Mc." McCary, born a slave, had been freed in 1815 as the result of the will of his deceased owner, James McCary, a Natchez cabinet-maker. The will of the cabinetmaker had commended his "Soul unto Almighty God"; directed that the minor slave "Bob" and Bob's mother and sister be freed; left most of his property to Bob and his sister, with a special bequest of $1,000 to Bob; and admonished his executor that Bob and his sister should be "educated and brought up in the fear of God, and in the principles and practice of true religion and morality." [65] At least some of these Presbyterian-sounding admonitions were observed in the rearing of Robert McCary. He came into considerable property from his benefactor's estate, and he was sufficiently educated to undertake the teaching of free Negro children other than his own in the middle 1840's. Moreover, McCary was a fairly successful barber with tastes and interests very similar to Johnson's, and it was only natural that a close friendship should spring up between them. Inasmuch as they were almost alone in the top bracket of the free Negro group in Natchez, they had little choice in selecting intimates but, aside from the inevitability of the situation, genuine affection flowed between them.

McCary and Johnson supported each other in business deals by endorsing notes, and Johnson occasionally lent McCary money. But, in addition, they were continually together—at the race track, at hunting, in card games, in Sunday walks on the Bluff, in long talks in their shops after they had been closed, and in memorable sessions at the dinner table. Johnson recorded several of their meals, but one in 1836 was perhaps the best: "Mc and myself had a tolerable good Dinner," he wrote. "We had as follows — Mc had 2 Bottles of Medoc Clarlet, 1 Bottle of Champagne wine, Buiscuit Egg Bread, P. pork, 1 Broiled Chicken & Beef Stake, I had a pice of good Bacon, wheat Bread, Oysters in Flitters, one Large Bottle of

---

[65] For Robert McCary's early history, see Adams County Will Books, I, 88–90; "Estate of James McCary," Adams County Probate Records, File 27; Petition of Walter Irvine, November 22, 1814, Petitions and Memorials, Series D, No. 38; Adams County Deed Records, K, 146, P, 659, Q, 177, R, 164, 280, S, 115, 116, 200, T, 318, U, 127. Some of these documents use the spelling "McCarey."

Anneset, one Dozen Orenges, ı small Bottle of Muscat wine . . . Mc had a Bottle of Brandy & honey."

Johnson was fond of his ten children. He helped nurse them in sickness, allowed them small sums of weekly spending money, took them on walks and taught them to sail boats, and usually was tolerant of their childish misdemeanors. When he was forced to give a severe whipping to his eldest, William, Jr., "for his bad Conduct, Throwing Brick and so forth," he had to reassure himself that his action was correct. He taught William, Jr., Richard, and Byron to hunt, fish, and ride horses, and he gave them their first lessons in the barber trade at a very early age. The daughters of the house were given music lessons, and at least one of them was sent to school in New Orleans. All of the children were regularly instructed in elementary subjects.[66]

Johnson did not often mention his wife in his diary. Apparently she handled the household affairs to his satisfaction and left him time to concentrate on business. In only one entry in his diary did he cast himself in the role of aggrieved husband: "I had Last night and this morning together several Quarrels with my wife   She Commenced it of course   I did not have a great deal to say — all amounts to nothing any how for I Cant say that I said anything to Her to Hurt her feelings that I believd myself whilst I was talking. I only did it in a Spirrit of Retalation — that [is] all so Help me."

The most galling irritant in the home life of the free man of color was the conduct of his illiterate free mulatto mother, Amy Johnson. In his attitude toward her, there was devotion and perhaps love, but no sentimental ascription of virtues she did not possess. He was quite willing to assume financial obligations for her: he lent her money to purchase such slaves as Dinah and Sharlot and for other purposes. In fact, Johnson often found it necessary to pay her bills in order that the family financial standing should not be impaired. But he could not prevent her from spreading false reports concerning him and other members of the family. Neither could he restrain "the old woman," as he unflatteringly referred to her, from brawling in the streets. After all, she was free, part white, and much more than twenty-one.

---

[66] A list of Johnson's children and the dates of their births follows: William, Jr. (January 24, 1836); Richard (October 11, 1837); Byron (June 22, 1839); Anna L. (March 25, 1841); Katharine G. (December 20, 1842); Phillip (died soon after birth in 1844); Eugenia (January 2, 1845); Alice (probably born in late 1846 or 1847); Josephine (July 29, 1849); Clarence (May 16, 1851). See eight baptismal certificates (some with incorrect dates) in Johnson Papers, and U. S. Census Reports, 1850, Schedule I, Adams County, 14.

Amy Johnson's most embarrassing conduct occurred in the summer of 1837. On the last morning in June, she "Commenced as usual to quarrell with Everything and Every body," and her son gave her a few flicks with a whip as "the quickest way to stop it." She thereupon advanced upon him and dared him to strike her, which, he said, he "would not do for anthing in the world." During the next six weeks Amy was often in a terrible temper, and on one occasion threw salt all over the floor at the front entrance of the Johnson home. Until August 12 she and her son spoke not one word to each other. Partial reconciliation was effected through the good offices of Johnson's brother-in-law, James Miller, who was visiting him. On September 25, Johnson wrote to his sister: "tell Mr. Miller that Mother does a great deal Better than I expected she would — She has quit running out in the streets to complete her quarrells — now she does pretty well — about 3 quarrells or three fusses a week will satisfy her very well — and before he came up here she used to have the bigest Kind of a fuss Every morning." [67] But on November 23, he noted in his diary that "The old woman is on a regular spree for quarrelling to day all day — oh Lord, was any One on this Earth So perpetually tormented as I am."

Despite all such unfavorable remarks concerning his mother, Johnson saw to it that, at her death in 1849, she received a burial befitting a parent of the town's leading barber. He rented seven or eight "hacks," or carriages, for the funeral procession, and her remains were interred in a plot purchased in the white section of the town's leading cemetery. The son made this entry in his diary: "To day has been a [day] of Great trouble to me and all of my Family. The Remains of My Poor Mother was Burried, oh my God. My Loss is too Greate. Oh my Poor Belovd Mother is Losst to me forever in this world."

Aside from his contacts with his immediate family and Robert McCary, Johnson's closest personal relationship was with his sister, Adelia, and her husband, James Miller. The Millers moved to New Orleans in 1830 and there accumulated an estate which thirty-five years later was appraised at more than $21,000.[68] The Millers and

[67] Johnson to Mrs. James Miller, October 4, 1837 (copy), Johnson Papers. See also Johnson to Mrs. James Miller, August 6, 1837 (copy), *ibid.* For Johnson's accounts with his mother, see Cash Book, 1830–38, *passim;* Day Book, 1830–40, *passim;* Ledger, 1833–37, pp. 46–50, 64; Ledger, 1835–39, pp. 28, 50; Ledger, 1837–41, p. 99; Cash Book, 1844–47, *passim, ibid.*

[68] Petition of Jefferson Hoggatt, October 6, 1865, "Succession of James Miller," Orleans Parish Succession Records, Second District Court, No. 25,534 (Orleans Parish civil courthouse, New Orleans, La.). The New Orleans *Daily Delta*, June 19, 1847, referred to him as "old Miller, the wealthy colored barber in Common

the Johnsons and their children frequently visited each other and constantly corresponded. In 1842, after Miller arrived in Natchez early one morning, he and Johnson spent nearly all day in conversation, eating, playing the violin, playing shuffleboard, and riding. During the next few days, they took a steamboat trip to Vicksburg and went hunting several times. Or when Mrs. Miller and several of her children arrived, the two families and a few friends usually had a party, and sometimes Johnson arranged for two carriages to take a dozen or more of them to his farm for an outing. In addition to such holidays spent together, the families often made business arrangements for each other. Johnson and his wife furnished the Millers with produce from the Natchez area, and Miller purchased barber supplies for his Natchez brother-in-law and in the late 1840's handled the New Orleans sale of corn and potatoes from Johnson's farm.[69]

The Miller-Johnson correspondence was a major interest of both families for at least thirty years. James Miller was primarily a materialist and his views concerning monetary matters, often expressed with a wry twist, undoubtedly influenced his Natchez relatives. In 1848 he wrote to Johnson: "I Have no News of Enny a Count to send you tho we Have a town fool of Peaple they are such as has Come to Look for that Main thing Money so it dos Not Make Money Circulate as they are All Looking for it." And after his brother-in-law's death, Miller once wrote to his widow: "Mrs Johnson there is some members in My family that Has very Little regard for my whelfair More than for what they Make of Me &c People that wait for ded Mens shose gose a Long time Barefooted some times you no."[70]

Letters from Johnson's sister, Adelia Miller, were concerned with complaints about the conduct of his free Negro apprentices, requests that the Johnsons send various kinds of food, news about her children, and gossip. Yet a tone of forcefulness runs through all of her letters, an impression that is reinforced by a contemporary newspaper account of an examining trial in New Orleans in which she was accused of assaulting a Dutch dyer, with whom she previously had had a minor lawsuit. According to a newspaper report, the

---

street." For his property acquisitions, see Orleans Parish Conveyance Records, VII, 288–89; XI, 337–38; XIII, 736; XVI, 145; XXI, 145, 471; XXIII, 170; XXV, 25 (Orleans Parish civil courthouse). Like Johnson, Miller owned a number of houses which he rented.

[69] Miller to Johnson, November 25, 1848; August 14, 1849, Johnson Papers.

[70] Miller to Johnson, December 9, 1848; Miller to Mrs. William Johnson, August 19, 1853, *ibid.*

Dutchman had been informed that Mrs. Miller's slaves were beating his daughter. When he had rushed out of his dyehouse to save his child, he had been confronted by Adelia, who had told him, he testified, "dat he vos a shdinking Dutch devil, and knowed nothing about the matter." He had replied "dat she had petter as been to work in the field, dan insulting one of de American bobulation." The free woman of color had thereupon "committed an assault" consisting of shaking her fist in the dyer's face. Despite the testimony of several character witnesses that she was orderly and respectable in every way, the judge required her to give bond for a later trial on the charge of having insulted a white person.[71]

Mrs. Miller was also capable of humor and moral indignation. In one letter to her brother she commented on the coincidence that she and her sister-in-law were both pregnant: "You must tell Ann that she is growing quite fruitful   thats right   misery Likes company." In the same letter she stated that there had been "a greate to do" about a widow, presumably a free Negro, openly consorting with "a white man a merchant . . . as bold in it as if she was married to him." And she added, "I have often thought that she was a goate in sheeps clothing — now I am convinced." [72]

William Johnson agreed in most instances with his sister's condemnation of persons who deviated from a strict moral code. He condemned, for example, promiscuous crossing of the color line by whites. In 1837 he bitterly castigated a Frenchman who was chasing slave wenches: "Oh the Rascal   I would give One hundred Dollars if Some Gentleman would only Cetch the Low minded Dog and Cow hyde him well . . . it would do me so much good." Four years later his comment on a report that two white men had been "caught in bed" with two black women was "Hard times indeed, when Such things Ocur." But apparently the promiscuity involved in such cases was the cause of his indignation, because he wrote not one line of condemnation of certain prominent white planters, well known to him and all of Adams County, who were rearing mulatto families that they had fathered. One of these planters eventually chose to live his last years with his colored family in New Orleans, and to bequeath all his property to his colored offspring. And before he died, both he and members of his mulatto family entered into correspondence with William Johnson's widow and sons, indicating that the two families were bound together by ties of intimate friendship.

71 New Orleans *Daily Delta*, June 19, 1847.

72 Mrs. James Miller to Johnson, June 20, 1837, Johnson Papers. See also her letters to Johnson, January 2, 1844; February 16, 1844; November 6, 1846; and her letter to Mrs. William Johnson, October 2, 1847, *ibid.*

On the other hand, Johnson's feeling of superiority to some of the ill-favored characters who lived near his farm in the Swamp was partly based on his contempt of their morals, as well as their general way of life. When it was reported that one of them was "keeping" the wife of another, the free Negro commented: "They are an awfull Set down thare." When a number of "Swampers" were tried for stealing timber and were acquitted, he insisted that they were "not honest." He was derisive when a "Very Green" Swamper, his wife, and two or three of their neighbors came to Natchez to see a traveling menagerie; they walked with arms locked and "were a Show themselves." In regard to one of the bitter controversies over land lines in the Swamp, Johnson quoted one of the disputants as having said that the wife of his opponent, who had pulled down buildings standing on disputed land, was "a Damed old Rip" who "had Came out thare with a Gun and she being a woman he Left, but Said that she had not Better Come out thare again." He further described a fight that arose because two of the brothers-in-law of a woman who had married a Swamper alleged to have Negro blood were incensed; one of them had said "that any man that would take the part of a Colord Man Marying a white woman was a Damed Rascal." In other cases, Johnson simply stated that a man who had cut a companion in a Natchez barroom brawl had escaped to the Swamp, or that one of the inhabitants had chained his daughter to prevent her from marrying a wood chopper. On the whole, the side glances, in his diary, at the denizens of the area presented a composite picture of a group of illiterate whites—one of whom once threatened to give him "a real niger Beating"—and a few free Negroes who eked out a bleak existence by raising a little corn and cotton, fishing, shooting hogs with little regard to ownership, and cutting timber. And this very near the famed plantation homes which were the residences of the First Families of Mississippi.

In his own sphere, William Johnson was himself something of an aristocrat. His home contained furniture that was by no means inexpensive and included a large sofa, mahogany chairs, large mirrors, pier glasses, and bookcases; the floors were frequently recarpeted; and the pictures on the walls included a painting that cost $25. Among the musical instruments in the house were a piano, a guitar, a flute, and violins; and in 1838 the barber paid $30 for a music box. He purchased whisky, cider, ale, gin, and a number of different wines. He subscribed to five or six Mississippi and New Orleans newspapers, as well as one New York newspaper, the *Saturday Evening Post*, the *New Yorker*, the *New York Mirror*, and the *Spirit of the Times*; and he bought books, including French and

Spanish grammars and dictionaries, a few novels and historical works, and a volume of Shakespeare. Johnson's efforts to improve his cultural standing sometimes failed, but behind them there was an urge that deserved respect—the impulse toward civilized gesture and aspiration, the impulse to give the life of every day a certain purpose and dignity.

William Johnson spent time each week in reading, some of which was critical, but he was by no means an intellectual. Possessed of a lively intelligence that demanded occupation, he depended first upon work and then upon play and family life for stimulus. Perhaps his healthy nature, with an instinct for equilibrium, felt the necessity for opposing the strict discipline of a busy existence to the disquieting attraction of the inner life of the intellect that so often brought unhappiness to mixed-bloods or persons with diverse cultural backgrounds. In any event, after work he usually turned to people rather than to ideas.

Accordingly, he rarely concerned himself with issues that did not directly affect him. Neither did he give vent to long philosophical or religious outbursts. While in his early twenties, he once wrote that "This world is nothing but Vanity and vexation of Sperritt and that is all." [73] In 1846 he recorded that he was beginning to read the Bible through again. He sometimes thanked "our Maker" for good health; and on such occasions as his sister's death in 1848, his diary entries reflected his belief in immortality and an attitude of prayerful supplication to a "Mercifull Father." But such statements were rare.

Johnson rarely probed the depths of melancholy into which everyone inevitably descends, at least briefly. His darkest period came in the week in which his sister died in New Orleans. He arrived there soon after her death, and in the course of his visit allowed himself to become extremely angry. At the end of the week he wrote:

> Oh how sad, how very sad I feel to night. The future seems all dark. No ray of light illumins its dark unpenetrable gloom   Truly most truly, Sin brings its own reward, that of anguish, and remorse. And I have sined most grevously, by giving vent to a passionate temper, In allowing my Lips to give utterence to angry words. O, the misery that is entailed on one by an ungovernable temper. Would that I could blot out from memory the past week, which has indeed been one of Unhap-

[73] Day Book, 1830–44, p. 146, *ibid.* This statement was signed "William Johnson Natchez Feb. 23d, 1831."

49

piness to me. But alas it is folly to mourn over the past, the relentless past, which all my sighs can never recall. On the future lies my only hope of happiness. In the future I may at least, in part atone for the past by a strict adhesan to duty, by endevoring to become more amiable, And by striving thus to Emulate the good I may at last enjoy at least a semillance of that Joy and contentment which they Say only the good can enjoy, But can I hope to attain that degree [of] excellence and goodness that will insure happiness   I can but try, and if I fail — *try again.*

Although William Johnson probably was as religious as the ordinary individual of his day, it is doubtful that he would have classified himself as subscribing to the tenets of any single sect. He once paid a substantial sum for Masses for a deceased Negro's soul; he subscribed $5.00 to the local Catholic church in 1839; and he had his children baptized in a Catholic cathedral in New Orleans. But none of these actions meant that he was a Catholic or leaned toward Catholicism in his beliefs. The baptism of his children, for example, could be explained on the grounds that it furnished a means of recording the legitimacy of their birth and their free status—both matters of importance to persons of their uncertain legal position. Moreover, Johnson spent half of most Sundays in work and the other half in recreation; he once subscribed to a Methodist religious publication, and he was buried by a white Methodist minister; and one of his most pointed religious comments bears the stamp of Calvinism. In 1843 he remarked on an epidemic in New Orleans: "The yellow fever [is] a terable mallady: but if it is Gods will, why not? Slay Slay them." It thus appears that Johnson was a religious eclectic, perhaps an inevitable result of his anomalous situation. Certainly he would have never considered joining the Negro churches conducted in Natchez by the Baptists and Methodists in the 1840's, and neither would he have relished occupying a seat among slaves in the back gallery of Trinity Church.

Though he seldom mentioned religion, the free Negro's philosophy was at least workable, his personality reasonably well adjusted, and his understanding of people penetrative. In fact, he was sharply sensitive to the whole of life immediately about him. He was concerned with politics because a number of the town's arresting personalities were running for office, making speeches, and talking about political issues; he was not allowed to vote, but that did not prevent him from frequently expressing sympathy for the Democratic party in his diary, except when his Whig friend, Colonel

Bingaman, was seeking office. Occasionally his eminently practical talent for ignoring what he could not help failed him, but his spirit was resilient, and he usually had little patience with either whites or blacks who did not enjoy living and would not allow others to do so. Yet, most of all, he took pleasure in his acquaintances, and his brief notes on individuals frequently were acute observations.

The free Negro's artless remarks regarding the foibles of the whites were at once pointed and slyly humorous. He undoubtedly relished reporting that a prominent lawyer made very fast time in running from an opponent who had been besting him in a fight. In another diary entry he wrote: "Judge Crawford Presides in Court To Day. [Judge Cage, the regular judge, was busy elsewhere.] Capt Cotten, not Knowing that Judge Crawford was inn, asked Mr Van Hosen [Hoesen, a lawyer,] How the Judge would do. He replyed that he would do very well if he would Keep sober. The Judge replied that he would try and do that — They were all of Course surprised & confused." And when redheaded Mr. Fox married a red-haired girl, Johnson's comment was that "all the Little Foxes will be Red of Course."

The diarist seldom laughed at himself, though he once recalled that he had "taken 4 Pills Last night and they Sortr took me Just as it was Raining hard. I Recollect that fact because I had to take of my Draw[er]s." In public, he doubtless confessed to jokes on himself, but in the privacy of his diary, he felt more inclined to give expression to the long-suppressed feeling that made him declare, "I Shall be a match for any Set of Rascals that may make me unhappy."

William Johnson's position as a free person of color was that of a man who had reached the top in his class but who possessed elements of two conflicting cultures in his heritage—that of the slave and that of the planter. In his mental habits he tended to associate himself with the gentry. Since it was a point of conventional elegance to spice one's English with a bit of French, he occasionally concluded an entry in his diary with an inaccurate French phrase. When a member of a militia organization allowed his opponent in a fight to chase him into some "French Ladies Room," Johnson commented, "He is a member of the Natchez Guards and to run in that maner does not become him." Whether he read all of the numerous magazines and papers to which he subscribed is problematical, but the fact that he subscribed was an attempt to identify himself with this group. His interest in music, horse racing, and politics, and his abiding respect for influential whites were also indicative of his tendency to follow the cultural pattern of what he called "the most wealthy and inteligent part of this Community."

His Negro blood did not deter him from using severe measures in disciplining his slaves, but neither was he among the masters who were despotically brutal. In this connection it should be noted that not only was whipping slaves generally thought to be indispensable for the maintenance of order, but also that flogging was a common mode of discipline of groups of whites, such as apprentices, criminals, schoolboys, and soldiers and sailors. In the case of William Johnson, he felt it necessary that reasonable labor returns should be secured from his slave investments, and his position as a prominent free Negro businessman made it imperative that his slaves behave themselves.

He therefore demanded seemly conduct, while at times he also manifested a paternalistic sympathy. In accordance with the policy followed by more enlightened and humane masters, he never disrupted any of his slave families by the sale of one member; he fed his slaves well; and he allowed them to attend church meetings, "darkey parties," and circuses. The whippings he administered were always for misconduct or carelessness in the handling of property, but never for laziness. He punished Lucinda, for example, because she secured permission to attend church but instead "went off in some private Room, the Little Strumpet"; and several years later he again whipped her for hitting her husband in the street.

But he flogged the irrepressible Steven more than all his other slaves combined. He whipped him for stealing and for keeping forbidden rendezvous with Negro girls, but mostly for drinking and running off and hiding. In spite of laws prescribing strict penalties for the sale or gift of intoxicants to slaves, Steven had no difficulty in securing liquor. Its consumption always caused him to perform some act which inevitably brought him a severe thrashing, a stay in the guardhouse, or confinement in handcuffs or chains. Steven was not unintelligent—he once cleared himself of a charge of stealing before a jury in a minute's testimony in his own behalf—and his master felt a secret sympathy for him. As Johnson made arrangements to sell the slave at the end of 1843 because of "Liquor, Liquor, His fondness for it," he declared that "there are many worse fellows than poor Steven is, God Bless Him." The next day he shed tears because he had been forced to make arrangements to sell this slave who had been his property for nearly twelve years. When finally he delivered Steven to his new master, he gave him presents and shook hands with him.

The Natchez barber was allowed a considerable degree of latitude—at some points—in his relationships with white people. He rented rooms and buildings to whites; he lent them money; he sued them in court; he employed whites to erect buildings for him and to work on his farm. Several times white men helped him in business difficulties where his color ordinarily would have been a handicap. One of them once requested him not to express an opinion about an election "for a greate many would think that what I would say would have a greate Effect." On more than one occasion he had long man-to-man conversations with whites; one night in his shop he conversed at length with a white friend on the subjects of banks, moneylending, insolvent people, the prospects of war, England and the English, slavery, and Texas and Mexico. He had many friends among the whites, some of whom were in the upper reaches of Natchez society. Johnson exchanged several small gifts with Dr. Luke P. Blackburn, later governor of Kentucky. And no less a figure than General John A. Quitman once brought a letter to the barber from Jackson, the state capital. The barber's comment on this event in his life was, "He did me proud, He did me proud."

Johnson's chief sympathizer among the aristocratic whites was Colonel Adam L. Bingaman, scion of a rich Adams County planting family, top-ranking scholar of the Harvard class of 1812, leading Whig politician and orator, and nationally known turfman. Johnson gave a detailed account of Bingaman's activities; lent him a music box, a pamphlet, and a seine; and made him a gift of "a pair of Large Candle sticks with a Glass vase over Each." On the other hand, Bingaman allowed him to use his pastures for his cattle and his studhorses for breeding purposes. This is only a small part of the evidence that points to a relationship of mutual respect and understanding between a former slave and a man who had graduated as the "First Scholar" at Harvard.

The line that limited Johnson's range of action in his contacts with white people was sometimes obscure and tenuous. On the whole, he was granted something approaching equality in business and financial matters, but he labored under parts of the unwritten code of social restrictions that applied to all persons of color. As Johnson understood only too well, that code contained a provision that prohibited interracial participation, under formal and public conditions, in the rites of eating and drinking, but even this provision was occasionally violated. The barber participated in the raffle of a gold watch at Rowland's Coffee House, and, upon winning half the prize, treated the assembled company to champagne. And his account books show that this was by no means the only time that he purchased wine or liquor for a member of the "master race." Moreover, Johnson and the white men of the Swamp often ate together. Two white men who came to see him and his family at his town residence and stayed until after the dinner hour declined to join him in eating—but Johnson and his friend, McCary, went hunting with white townsmen and ate with them in the field. Johnson also once entertained a Natchez dentist and a white friend, who had been hunting with him, at a meal served in his farmhouse.

One of the most ironical incidents in the barber's life began one morning with a message he received from a white man who asked if the free Negro would be "Kind Enough to Come up, Saying that he was unwell or he would come down." That night when Johnson knocked at the man's residence door, his wife ushered the barber into the man's bedroom, awakened him, and "told him that a Gentleman had came to see him." The man then arose, shook hands, invited his visitor to be seated, offered him a drink, talked about "One thing or other," and "after awhile came to the Point — he wanted to Borrow a hundred and fifty Dollars." The barber stated that he did not have "the Surplus" and the visit ended.

In other instances, the color line was more sharply drawn. Johnson attended the theater, but he sat in the Negro balcony. He heard the Reverend John Newland Maffitt, famed Methodist pulpit orator, preach, but he stood outside the church. He was permitted to give financial support to the Jockey Club and make bets with white men, some of whom were prominent professional men, but his horses never ran in regularly scheduled races. And in 1842 his wife was allowed to travel to New Orleans in a steamboat stateroom only after considerable difficulty on Johnson's part. His account of an interview with the captain of the *Maid of Arkansas* is enlightening: "I asked him if [he] could not spare a State Room and he told me . . . that it was against the Rules of His Boat . . . and Spoke of Prejudice of the Southern people, it was damd Foolish &c, and that he was doing a Buisness for other people and was Compelld to adopt those Rules — I did not prevail by no means — He then said that I Could Have a State Room on Conditions which I told him would answer." [74]

[74] William Johnson and James Miller were on friendly terms with a number of Mississippi River steamboat captains and their crews and secured special accommodation concessions on more than one occasion, but for the difficulties encountered by "three coloured females," apparently free and well-to-do, in traveling in 1839 by steamboat on an Alabama river, see Buckingham, *The Slave States*, I, 479–80. They remained in the ladies' cabin during the day, but slept on the floor at night

In his writings Johnson literally damned white men as "infernal rascals" or "scoundrels" for "shaving" him in financial deals, but in public he walked and talked softly. The William Johnson of the 1830's was flattered by the chance attentions of the aristocracy, but after 1845 he recorded no such elation. As he grew older, as he gradually exhausted the scraps of privilege that he could catch from the abundance of the planter aristocrats, he may have become a trifle bitter. The Johnson of the earlier diaries was hardly the preoccupied, sometimes complaining Johnson of the last four or five years before his death in 1851.

That his murder was avenged by the law no more than if he had been a common slave was the final irony.

THE WINN-JOHNSON DISPUTE

In the late 1840's William Johnson became involved in a prolonged quarrel with a man named Baylor Winn concerning a boundary between their lands in the Swamp. The dispute led to his death. On June 16, 1851, as Johnson was returning from his farm, he was shot down from ambush. He died the next morning, but not before he had recovered consciousness and named Winn as his assassin. Winn was arrested, but after a series of trials that aroused public interest for more than two years, was finally released from custody.

The chief point at issue in the first two trials was whether the defendant was a free Negro; this the prosecution failed to establish legally to the satisfaction of juries in two different counties. The defense was thereby placed in an unassailable position in the third trial, in which Winn was finally tried for murder. Since the only witnesses to the killing were two free Negroes and a slave, and under Mississippi law therefore not eligible to testify against Winn as long as he must be presumed to be white, the prosecution reluctantly abandoned the case against the defendant in the midst of the third trial.

William Johnson had long known Baylor Winn, who was about twelve years older than the barber. His account books recorded the purchase of turkeys from Winn as early as 1831, and they had other small financial transactions in later years. They also had casual friendly contacts in other ways. They sometimes rode and hunted together; and a few days after Winn helped Johnson tend a sick horse, the barber presented him with a new razor and

---

and ate their meals standing in the pantry, apart from both the white tables and the Negro servants' table.

soap. The Swamper went out of his way to persuade Johnson that he should buy the land which ultimately became the best of his two farming tracts.

Meanwhile, Johnson had become well acquainted with another group of Winns. These were the children of George Winn, a free Negro planter who had died in 1831, leaving an estate of fifteen slaves and nearly 1,200 acres in Adams County as well as land elsewhere. George Winn had bequeathed this property to three children acknowledged as his legal heirs: Winslow; Polly, or Mary, who married overseer William Mosbey; and Helen, or Ellen, who married Washington Ford.[75] All of the George Winn estate was on or near the Mississippi, and parts of it became Johnson's two farming tracts, purchased in 1845 and 1846 from Winslow Winn and Mosbey and his wife. These and subsequent purchases of swampland away from the river made Johnson a neighbor of Baylor Winn.

In 1847 and 1848 Johnson began to hear disquieting rumors concerning Baylor Winn. His children were in revolt against his harsh domination. His hands were cutting timber on Johnson's land and rafting it to New Orleans. But the two men were still on moderately friendly terms. They exchanged visits at their farmhouses, they met in the road and had long talks on such subjects as politics, Winn's children, and "Love &c."

The break between the two men did not come until the spring of 1849, after Winn and Benjamin Wade, a Natchez banker and businessman, had jointly purchased more swampland adjacent to Johnson's.[76] Johnson learned that Winn was continuing to cut timber with flagrant disregard of boundary lines and posted him

---

[75] "Estate of George Winn," Adams County Probate Records, File 65; Adams County Marriage Records, V, 493. For listings of George Winn as a free Negro, see Auditor's Records, Tax Rolls, 1810, 1820, 1823, 1829, 1831, Adams County; U. S. Census Reports, 1830, Schedule I, Adams County, 23. The state census of 1816 listed the following under the name of George Winn: three free people of color, no white males, one white female above twenty-one years of age, and ten slaves. Governor's Territorial Records, Census of 1816, Adams County, Series A, No. 23. But by 1850 at least one of the children of George Winn had crossed the color line as far as the United States census was concerned, for the wife of Washington Ford was listed as white. U. S. Census Reports, 1850, Schedule I, Adams County, 37. In 1877, William T. Martin, prominent attorney and former Confederate general, testified that Washington Ford had "married a mulatto woman and had no social position at all." Frank W. Klingberg, "The Case of the Minors: A Unionist Family within the Confederacy," *Journal of Southern History*, XIII (1947), 40.

[76] For Winn-Wade acquisitions, see Adams County Deed Records, GG, 15, 17, 19, 424–25, II, 521; Natchez *Courier*, June 2, 1848. As early as 1836 Winn had some of his slaves on "Benj. Wade's place." Auditor's Records, Tax Rolls, 1836, Adams County.

in his diary as "not an Honerable Man." Winn and Wade agreed to a resurvey of the line that was the chief point at issue, but Winn changed his mind and refused to allow the survey to be made. Following the advice of lawyers, Johnson thereupon wrote Winn a letter requesting him to stop timber-cutting in the disputed area until a survey could be made. "Now the truth of the Buisness," he wrote, "is that old man Winn is an overbearring old Colord Gentleman, and it will be found out So before Long if he fools much with me, for I Know him too well." He also wrote to William Mosbey, who had departed for Indiana, and the reply he received confirmed his suspicions concerning Winn. Mosbey answered that he suspected the earlier survey had been incorrect, but that he had decided to sell out and leave the state rather than enter into contention with Winn. "Every honest man," he added, "knows B. Winn to be a black hearted wretch & those in co[mpany] with him no better." [77]

On more than one occasion Winn brandished firearms when surveyors appeared. He also threatened Johnson's life, cursed him, and "tore around at a wonderfull rate." All this Johnson bore with patience, but he continued to insist that the survey be made. Eventually he succeeded in securing two surveys, the last by court order. And after he found that Wade's teams were "haulling away my wood" that his hands had cut, he sued Wade and Winn for trespass on his property. But on May 2, 1851, before the case could come to final trial, he wrote a letter to the defendants proposing a compromise. Under the terms of Johnson's offer, the line as certified by the court surveyor would be adhered to by both parties; each side would pay their own witnesses; and Wade and Winn would pay the fees of the court officers and for twelve or fifteen cords of wood cut by Johnson and hauled off by them. Since Winn and Wade previously had cut timber on land that the court surveyor certified was Johnson's, this was a generous proposal. The defendants signed the agreement, and Johnson's lawyers dismissed his suit.

During the next six weeks Johnson relaxed from the strain of the controversy which he thought had ended. He paid his lawyers, made various small purchases, took his children on berry-picking trips, and visited his farm. He recorded in his diary that his tenth child had been born, and noted the death of a slave child to whom he and his family were strongly attached. But on June 14 he wrote, "I Cannot find two of my Horses to day. . . . Something

[77] Mosbey to Johnson, November 28, 1849, Johnson Papers.

wrong I think." Two days later, as he was returning from his farm, he was ambushed and fatally wounded. The buckshot had slain a man whose short life had been full scale in its abundance of joy and sincerity mixed with occasional sorrow and error, whose struggle to attain harmony of spirit had led him to write a candid chronicle that made him "one of the most remarkable and interesting of American diarists." [78]

The murder of William Johnson and the subsequent trials of Baylor Winn provided headline news for the Natchez press for more than two years. The initial account in the *Courier* included a striking tribute to Johnson:

SHOCKING MURDER

Our city was very much excited on Tuesday morning, by hearing that what could only be deemed a horrible and deliberate murder had been committed upon an excellent and most inoffensive man. It was ascertained that William Johnson, a free man of color, born and raised in Natchez, and holding a respected position on account of his character, intelligence and deportment, had been shot, together with a young mulatto boy, about three miles below town, as they were returning home just before sunset on Monday evening last, in company with a son of Johnson and one of his negro slaves. From the testimony elicited before the Coroner's Jury, we learn the following facts. The party had been down the river a few miles, and in returning had stopped for Johnson to light a segar, at the house of a young man named Wynn, with whose father (Baylor Wynn) Johnson had had a legal dispute relative to the boundary of their plantations, which adjoined each other. The dispute had been decided in favor of Johnson, who for the sake of peace had dismissed the suit, settling it at less than his legal rights. While sitting upon their horses near this house, Baylor Wynn entered. Having lighted his segar, Johnson with his party rode off. About three or four miles from this place they were much astonished to see Wynn riding near them, and leaving the road to go into the bushes. Shortly after, Johnson saw him again in another direction going behind some bushes a short distance from the road. A few minutes after a gun was fired from the bushes, three buckshot therefrom striking Johnson, one entering his lungs and going through him, one passing through him along

[78] Allan Nevins, *Ordeal of the Union*, 2 vols. (New York, 1947), I, 528.

the lower part of his back, and one going through his arm. His horse was also wounded. The mulatto boy with him was also badly wounded by a shot entering his back, and lodging under the skin immediately over the abdomen. Johnson fell from his horse within a few yards from where he was struck, while the mulatto boy had strength enough, wounded as he was, to ride to town after assistance. Johnson died at two o'clock, that night. His dying declarations were taken in form, charging upon Baylor Wynn the commission of the crime. The boy still lies in great danger, and it is very doubtful whether he can recover.

Wynn was arrested that same night and committed to jail. Very strong circumstantial testimony points to him as guilty of the deed. The tracks of the horse where he went behind the bushes were all measured, and identified beyond question as those of Wynn's horse. His negro slaves declare that shortly after sunset he came in riding that horse, and ordered it rubbed down and taken care of. He had previously been repeatedly heard to threaten Johnson's life, and to say that the settlement of the suit was not the end of their difficulty. The Coroner's Jury which sat on Tuesday morning returned a verdict that Johnson came to his death by a wound or wounds inflicted by Baylor Wynn. Wynn is to be brought up for examination on Saturday (tomorrow) morning, when the whole case will be thoroughly investigated. Wynn, we understand, claims to be a white man, and has voted and given testimony as such. On this point will depend the admissibility of much of the testimony against him.

This murder has created a great deal of excitement, as well from its atrocity, as from the peaceable character of Johnson and his excellent standing. His funeral services were conducted by the Rev. Mr. Watkins, who paid a just tribute to his memory, holding up his example as one well worthy of imitation by all of his class. We observed very many of our most respected citizens at his funeral. Johnson left a wife, nine children, and quite a handsome property; probably twenty to thirty thousand dollars.[79]

[79] Natchez *Courier*, June 20, 1851. The Natchez *Free Trader*, June 18, 1851, in its shorter account, identified the wounded mulatto boy as Edward Hoggatt, one of Johnson's free Negro apprentices. A manuscript account in the Johnson Papers identifies "the Rev. Watkins" as pastor of the Methodist church, and the doctor to whom he made his dying statement as Dr. Luke P. Blackburn. See also Wood-ville (Miss.) *Republican*, June 24, 1851. The graves of William Johnson, his

Baylor Winn's various trials in connection with the murder of William Johnson kept him in jail more than two years, but eventually he was released. In preliminary examination immediately after Johnson's death in June, 1851, he was committed to jail without bail on a charge of willful murder. The prosecution was careful in both the preliminary charge and in the grand jury indictment in the succeeding January to designate that the charge was directed against Baylor Winn, free man of color. His preliminary plea was that he was not a mulatto but was of mixed white and Indian blood. Decision on this plea was vital to both prosecution and defense, for unless Winn could be proved to be a free Negro, Mississippi law barred the prosecution's Negro witnesses from testifying against him.

Winn's first and second trials, therefore, were not upon the murder charge, but to determine whether he was a mulatto. His attorneys produced two witnesses from Virginia, the state of his birth, who testified that he was of white and Indian blood, one of them stating that "the admixture of Indian blood in Winn was from an Indian tribe in Virginia, called Pamunky, or Pamunkies, while the other named the remnant of the tribe as being the Mattaponi, or some similar name." [80] The jury had no means of knowing that both the Pamunkey and Mattapony Indians of Virginia had a substantial intermixture of Negro blood,[81] and that back in King William County, Virginia, where the Pamunkeys lived, all persons named Winn had long been registered as free Negroes. The jury was unable to reach a decision, being divided six to six, and a mistrial was ordered. Winn's counsel thereupon moved for a change of venue. Since public opinion in Natchez and Adams County was inflamed against the prisoner, the court granted the motion.[82]

In the latter part of April, 1852, Baylor Winn's second trial took place at a session of the circuit court held at Jefferson, in neigh-

---

mother, and one of his daughters are in the cemetery of the Natchez Cemetery Association. According to the custodian, they are the only Negro graves in the white section.

[80] Natchez *Free Trader*, January 28, 1852.

[81] John H. Russell, *The Free Negro in Virginia, 1619–1865* (Baltimore, 1913), 129; John G. Pollard, *The Pamunkey Indians of Virginia* (Washington, 1894), 9–10; James H. Johnston, "Documentary Evidence of the Relations of Negroes and Indians," *Journal of Negro History*, XIV (1929), 29; Thomas Jefferson, *Notes on Virginia* (Washington, 1907; reprint of 1800 edition), 133. See also Arthur H. Estabrook and Ivan E. McDongle, *Mongrel Virginians: The Win Tribe* (Baltimore, 1926).

[82] Natchez *Courier*, January 21, 28, 1852; Adams County Circuit Court Minutes, 1849–53, January 19–May 7, 1852.

boring Fayette County. It was described as "the great and exciting trial of the session." Court sessions in Mississippi towns were always times of high excitement, not alone because men's lives were often at stake, but because the contests of eloquence and legal skill between opposing counsel were always appreciated. In the Winn case, a battery of four of the ablest criminal lawyers in the state—headed by J. S. B. Thacher of Natchez, formerly a judge of the High Court of Errors and Appeals—was assembled for the defense, while the district attorney was aided in the prosecution by a brilliant young attorney, Will T. Martin, who had been one of Johnson's lawyers in his suit against Wade and Winn and later was to become a Confederate general. The case was before the jury more than a week, a great number of witnesses were called, and Martin summed up the state's case in a long-remembered three-hour speech; but in the end, the state failed to place Baylor Winn within the reach of Negro testimony by proving that he had Negro blood.[83]

The burden of proof in these two cases was on the state. Although a number of people, including Johnson, thought that Winn had Negro blood, he had voted and given court testimony as a white man, he had served as a road overseer, he was listed in censuses as a white man, and he had married at least one white woman. The Johnson family paid a representative to travel to Virginia to secure evidence concerning the Winns of King William County, but apparently a legal technicality prevented the introduction into the case of documents he brought back, documents which bore the official certification of the State of Virginia and local recording officials that all of the Winns of King William County were free Negroes.[84]

[83] Natchez *Free Trader*, May 5, 1852; Jefferson County Circuit Court Minutes, 1848–54, pp. 432–38 (Jefferson County courthouse, Fayette, Miss.). In its issue of April 28, 1852, the Natchez *Courier* stated that the Jefferson County jury had returned a verdict "which establishes the fact of Winn being part Indian." The *Courier*'s issue of May 5 corrected this statement and pointed out that the verdict had merely been that the prosecution had failed to establish to the satisfaction of the jury that Baylor Winn was a free Negro.

[84] Three documents listing Winns of King William County, Virginia, 1802–52, certifying that all were registered as free Negroes and giving testimony of recording officials that to the best of their knowledge they were "the same and only family of Winns which ever resided in this county," signed by Deputy County Clerk James O. Pollard, March 24, 25, 1852, and by Commissioner of Revenue Samuel Robinson, March 26, 1852, all in Johnson Papers; receipts signed by Will T. Martin and R. W. Samuels for $136.54 for "balance . . . due R. W. Samuels for trip to Virginia," May 31, October 23, 1852, *ibid.*
The Natchez *Courier*, October 20, 1852, stated that Baylor Winn was still in jail.

After the Jefferson County jury voted that the state had failed in its attempt to prove Winn a free Negro, the prisoner was remanded to jail in Adams County and a new indictment was drawn up. Another change of venue was granted, so that Baylor Winn's final trial was held in Woodville in June, 1853, after two postponements resulting from the absence of witnesses. The prosecution finally went into court after two days of examining witnesses and asked for a nolle prosequi on the grounds that the law debarred the use of the only conclusive evidence that could be brought against the prisoner, the evidence of Negro eyewitnesses. Exactly two years after William Johnson died, the person whom he had designated as his murderer walked out of the Woodville courtroom a free man.[85]

Eight days afterward, on June 25, one of Johnson's sons made a sworn affidavit against Baylor Winn as a free mulatto for the same murder. Upon this representation Winn was again arrested, but this time he remained in jail only three days. On June 28, at his preliminary examination, the defense attorneys made a motion to quash the affidavit, arrest the warrant, and grant the prisoner his discharge. The grounds of the defense motion were that the affidavit was made by an incompetent person; that the question of Winn's blood had already been adjudicated; and that the prisoner had once been in jeopardy for the same offense, and hence not liable to be tried again. The examining justice sustained the motion, and Winn was discharged. The last attempt to convict Baylor Winn had failed.[86]

But memories of the murder and trials lingered in the minds of men a long time. When William Johnson's son, Byron, was killed by another Negro in 1872, a Natchez newspaper devoted two columns to recounting the shooting affray and to lauding Byron Johnson; and the newspaper account contained this additional statement: "His father before him (a free man of color) had by a long life of probity and rectitude won a high place in the estimation of this community, and, about twenty years ago, died much lamented at the hands of an assassin. Byron emulated the example of his father, in whose worthy memory he ever felt a just degree

[85] Woodville *Republican*, June 21, 1853; Wilkinson County Circuit Court Minutes, 1851–56, pp. 60, 77, 78, 108, 109, 163, 164, 192 (Wilkinson County courthouse, Woodville, Miss.). See also Natchez *Courier*, May 12, June 23, December 22, 1852; Natchez *Free Trader*, May 12, June 23, 1852.

[86] The Natchez *Free Trader*, July 2, 1853, described the abortive attempt to convict Winn and also responded to community interest in the case by printing a three-quarter-column résumé of the whole series of trials.

of pride." [87] Nearly fifty years after the Winn trials, a juror published a three-page résumé of the Winn-Johnson affair. This author had been a member of the Jefferson County jury that had been forced to declare that the evidence before it did not show Winn to be a free Negro, but he remembered prosecutor Will T. Martin's speech in summation as "one of the ablest I ever heard," and his account of the case was clearly sympathetic toward Johnson, "a barber that every one liked." [88] And even today, people still live who clearly recall General Martin discussing the Winn trials of nearly a century ago.

After William Johnson's death, his widow was the head of the family for fifteen years. Tutors were hired for the children in the 1850's, and at least two of the boys were sent to New Orleans for additional schooling. [89] In 1854 she contracted for the construction of a new brick business building on her Main Street property, and it was in this building that her sons and employees continued the barbershop through the Civil War and afterward. She died in 1866, shortly after her eldest son, William, Jr., was confined in an insane asylum in New Orleans. But the beneficent shadow of her deceased husband's fast friendship with Colonel Adam L. Bingaman, the former "Napoleon of the Southern Turf," still lay over the Negro family; for the elderly colonel took the responsibility of making certain that the mentally deranged boy was properly cared for in New Orleans, of comforting the family in their double affliction, and of assisting in the administration of the estate. [90]

Young Byron Johnson thereupon became the mainstay of the family. Before his death in 1872, he had become a successful barber and planter. Afterward his sister, Anna L. Johnston, for many years a well-known schoolteacher in Adams County, succeeded to the family leadership. Before her death in 1922, she was ably assisted by Clarence M. Johnston, the diarist's youngest son and a blacksmith, and a grandson, Dr. W. R. Johnston. [91]

---

[87] Natchez *Democrat*, January 16, 1872. General William T. Martin was engaged for the prosecution in this case, just as he had been for the Winn trials. In the 1840's and 1850's, Martin used the signature "Will T. Martin."

[88] Frank A. Montgomery, *Reminiscences of a Mississippian in Peace and War* (Cincinnati, 1901), 50–52.

[89] See, for examples, Lawrence W. Minor to Mrs. William Johnson, March 12, 1853; William Johnson, Jr., to Mrs. William Johnson, May 14, 1853; receipt for tuition of two children, April 3, 1853, signed by N. Morton, Johnson Papers.

[90] Bingaman to Byron Johnson, May 12, September 22, 1866; Bingaman to Anna L. Johnson, September 18, December 16, 1868, Johnson Papers. See also "Estate of Anna Johnson," Adams County Probate Records, File 184.

[91] The family name had been changed to Johnston.

Dr. Johnston, a liberal-arts graduate of Wilberforce College and a medical graduate of Howard University, was the leading physician of his race in Natchez at the time of his death in 1938. A newspaper obituary recognizing his devotion to his profession and his "worthy example of citizenship" made him the third male of three successive generations to be thus lauded by the Natchez press. But one of the most noteworthy actions he performed before his death was to make preliminary arrangements for the publication of his grandfather's diary, hereinafter brought to the printed page.

The Diary of
William Johnson

1835

*O*CTOBER 12   Bought at Auction 162 acres of Land
at $4.12½ per acre Belonging to the Estate of Mr Lewis
— Loaned Mr T. Gilbert at the auction Room $50.00*
13   Hyred Ben of Mr. Barlow[1] to water the streets
14   Mr. J. Potts Returned from The North — Mc[2] has a new
Door made — Settles with Mr Ivin for D Johnsons — pays him
Eighty One cents Cash — I Bought this Book of Little Fox   Paid
him for it 1.50
15   I payed Messrs. Sprague & Howell[3] $579.18¾ for Mr.

* The editors have attempted to reproduce William Johnson's diary as nearly
as possible in the form in which it was originally written. Only such minor changes
as will materially assist the reader have been made. Long, unpunctuated sections
have been divided into phrases and sentences by the insertion of commas and
blank spaces. Some subject matter has been generally omitted: weather observations
usually found at the beginning of each entry; daily market purchases which the
diarist noted during irregular intervals; and a considerable number of unintellig-
ible, undecipherable, incomplete, or repeated words, phrases, or sentences. Incorrect and inconsistent spellings have been carefully retained, and no effort has been
made to audit or rectify mathematical figures, sums, or discrepancies, nor to correct
misstatements of fact. A few proper names have been capitalized, and a few personal names have been replaced by dashes.

1 Noah Barlow was a member of the merchandising firm of Barlow & [John G.]
Taylor, formerly N. Barlow & Co. He had been a customer of Johnson's barbershop
since 1830, and in 1836–38 the barber made a number of loans to him or to his firm.
The firm was dissolved on January 1, 1839. See advertisement in Natchez *Courier*,
February 25, 1839.
2 William Johnson usually referred to his closest friend, free mulatto Robert
McCary, as "Mc." McCary owned his own barbershop. For his emancipation, see
Adams County Will Books, I, 88–90; Adams County Deed Records, P, 659. In 1835
he was about twenty-eight or twenty-nine years of age, and his free mulatto wife,
Mary, was twenty-six or twenty-seven. The tax rolls listed him as the owner of one
lot, valued at $2,500, but no slaves. Adams County Court and Police Board Minutes,
1832–45, March, 1832; Auditor's Records, Tax Rolls, 1836, Adams County.
3 A merchandising firm, located on Commerce Street, which held irregular auction
sales. In an advertisement, Natchez *Courier*, October 22, 1838, William B. Howell,
surviving partner of the firm, announced its dissolution as a result of the death of
Sturges Sprague (formerly a law partner of George Winchester). In addition to the
merchandising and auction aspects of the business, a deed record filed in 1838
showed that it was a large speculative concern which owed more than $100,000 but
had assets including western lands and town property, slaves, and shares in railroad,

Lewis & I also paid five Dollars for Drawing off the Deed of said Land — I paid Mr Soria[4] $18 for 12 Mahogna Chairs & two Dollars 25 cents for a Small Stove — Also Beat Mc shooting my new Rifle in the pasterure

16   McCary & myself went into the Swamp Hunting & we Killed about thirty Aligaters between the three of us. Mr Barland killed 4 Ducks & one squerrell & Mc Killed two Ducks & one Loon and I Killed One pelican, One Large Duck & two Black squeirrells and a Loon — We were Late geting Home — First I shot with the Rifle was the Black Squrrell, wounded the pelican and then the Loon, Aligators and the Duck

17   I paid Col Woods' Little son 1.75 for Recording the Deed for my Land   I Bought at Mr Gains[5] store one Round Jacket & pantaloons for Stephen[6] Amounting to 3.75 Eeach, all on a credit — $7.50 — also One Rondabout[7] for myself — creddit — $5.50 — Dr Potts returns from Woodville. Col Throckmorton[8] re-

---

banking, and steamboat companies. Adams County Deed Records, AA, 355–58; Natchez *Courier*, February 25, 1839.

[4] Jacob Soria was the proprietor of a general merchandising business and auction room at the corner of Main and Pearl streets. He participated in various auction activities, sold slaves, and traded in town lots both in Natchez and distant Texas. In October, 1836, he entered into a partnership with his brother, Isaac, for conducting an "Auction, General Agency, and Commission" business. For the announcement of this partnership, see Natchez *Free Trader*, October 13, 1836. For the dissolution of the partnership and continuance of the business under its old name, Jacob Soria & Co., see Natchez *Courier*, December 19, 1840.

[5] This was A. L. Gaines & Co., operated by A. L. Gaines and R. M. Gaines after the withdrawal of James M. Gaines on April 3, 1835, and specializing in the sale of clothing and fabrics. Natchez *Courier*, September 11, 1835.

[6] Steven, or Stephen, was a slave of the diarist, who unsuccessfully attempted to teach him to become a barber and eventually sold him because of his fondness for liquor. Johnson purchased him in 1832 for $455 and sold him in 1844 for $600. See Cash Book, 1830–44, entry for April 3, 1832, Johnson Papers, and this diary, entry for January 1, 1844. At this time Johnson also owned slaves named Lewis, Sarah, and Walker.

[7] A short coat or jacket. Also called a "roundabout."

[8] From as early as 1827 through 1834, Colonel Robert L. Throckmorton had operated a store in Natchez. He reported that his merchandise sales for 1830 were $22,141. In 1835 he became identified with the merchandising firm of Throckmorton & Patterson, which also owned Natchez Island (374-acre island in the Mississippi River, four or five miles below Natchez) in 1839–40. During the first half of the 1830's, Johnson's records show that he made small purchases of clothing and shoes from the Throckmorton establishment, and that its proprietor was one of his regular barbershop customers. Natchez *Ariel*, March 30, 1827; Auditor's Records, Tax Rolls, 1831, Adams County; Adams County Deed Records, BB, 597; and Cash Book, 1830–44, Cash Book, 1830–38, and Day Book, 1830–44, all unpaged entries, Johnson Papers. The U. S. census of 1830 listed two white males in his

turns from his plantation. Buys Out Mr Rowans part of the plantation — Mr Vernon Commences to shave himself

18 Mr Thomas Ellis Returns from the North. I gave French[9] $2.00 Mr Thomas pays me fifteen Dollars that he Borrowed from me a few Days before — Loaned Mr. C Wilkins my Horse to go to Col. Bingamans[10] Late in the Evening

19 I paid Mr. Barlow five Dollars for the hyre of Ben four Days — also one Dollar for a powder Horn — Bought a game Bag from Col Throckmorton' Store Cash $3.00 Also 1.50 cents for a Razor from a Gentleman — Mc Bought a Double Barrell shot gun from Louis David, price forty five Dollars

20 I Received of Mr. Hera, No. 2011, Receivers office, Washinton, Miss.,[11] 11th December, 1833. DUPLICATE Re-

---

family, no white females, and eight free Negroes. U. S. Census Reports, 1830, Schedule I, Adams County, 9.

Throckmorton had long been a resident of Adams County. As early as 1815 he signed a petition for the erection of bridges over St. Catherine's Creek. See Petition of W. Turpin and others, November, 1815, Petitions and Memorials, Series D, No. 38.

9 "French" (also called "William," "French William," "Old French," and "French William Johnson") was a free Negro barber employed by the diarist from 1831 to 1839. During the last two years of this period he was in charge of the diarist's Natchez-under-the-Hill shop. He was the son of the individual, not completely identified by the editors, known as "Capt. Johnson." See James Miller to [William Johnson], May 30, 1838 (copy); [Johnson] to [Miller], June 8, 1838 (copy); [Johnson] to [Miller], July 6, 1838 (copy), all in Johnson Papers, to be read in conjunction with entries in this diary, June 4, 11, July 18, 1838. William Johnson, the barber-diarist, showed "French William Johnson" special consideration at the same time that he chastised him and spoke contemptuously of him. They probably had a blood relationship of some sort.

William Johnson's other barbers in 1835–36 included free Negro William Nix and a group of younger Negro boys who were learning the trade, such as William Winston, William Wilson (probably free), and Charles, a slave.

10 Adam L. Bingaman was an important Adams County planter and Whig party leader in Mississippi. He was also widely known both in the South and East for his interest in horse racing. He and William J. Minor were the most prominent Natchez turfmen, and at this time Bingaman was a co-owner (with James Surget) of the racecourse near Natchez (see Adams County Deed Records, P, 436, Q, 373–76, AA, 530–31, BB, 11–12), and in the 1840's he gave his name to the Bingaman Race Course, at Algiers (across the Mississippi River from New Orleans). Bingaman "was graduated B.A." from Harvard "as the First Scholar of the Class of 1812"; served in the lower house of the state legislature, 1823–26, and as speaker of that body, 1834–36; and was president of the state Senate, 1838–40. He was an unsuccessful candidate for both houses of the United States Congress, 1838–41. The relationship between Bingaman and the free Negro barber, William Johnson, was one of peculiarly close understanding.

11 A town about six miles east of Natchez. Formerly the capital of the territory and state, Washington's population had declined from about 1,000 in 1815 to about 500 in 1835. About half the population were Negroes, and most of the whites were plantation owners or were connected with Jefferson College or with the

ceived from Thomas Lewis of Adams County, Missi. The sum of two hundred & two Dollars and Eighty Eight cents being in full for the north west quarter of Sextion No six in Township No. three of Range No. four west Containing 162 31/100 acres at the Rate of One Dollars & 25 cents per acre   Cash   202.88   Thos. Lewis   Received   I paid Messrs Barlow & Taylor three dollars & 94 cents freight on my Box of perfumery from New York

    21   I Loaned Dr. Hubbard[12] One hundred and fifty Dollars — Rail Road[13] & Texas Meeting[14] held at the Court House[15] — Mc-Dowell the Taylor Died

    22   I paid Phill five Dollars & 50 cents for geting water seven Days from the pond under the Hill[16] — Mr Newcomb quit shaving by the month 25th Septem

    23   William & John[17] Stayed Out untill after ten Oclock   I

---

land office, the only public office remaining in Washington in 1835. In that year the town was "distinguished solely for its quiet beauty and the 'sabbath-like repose of its streets.' " Charles S. Sydnor, *A Gentleman of the Old Natchez Region: Benjamin L. C. Wailes* (Durham, 1938) , 41, 80; *Besancon's Annual Register,* 121.

12 During the next nine months Dr. John M. Hubbard borrowed $865 from Johnson and, by March 11, 1837, repaid about two thirds of his indebtedness, partly by professional services. On March 11, 1840, Dr. Hubbard squared his accounts, including long shaving bills, with the barber and moneylender. Ledger, 1835–39, pp. 61–62; Ledger, 1837–41, p. 39, Johnson Papers. Hubbard evidently was fairly well-to-do, for in 1836–37 he sold ten slaves, city lots, and personal property (including furniture, carriage, physician's instruments, and books) to Lester S. Hubbard of Sandusky, Ohio, for $33,099. Adams County Deed Records, Y, 115, Z, 70, 426. His office was at the corner of Franklin and Pearl streets, and he was City Health Officer in 1839.

13 This was one of a series of railroad meetings held in Natchez in the period 1834–36. At least five Natchez railroad projects reached the stage of preliminary organization, but the only one that began active operation of trains was the Mississippi Rail Road Company, incorporated by the state legislature early in 1836. This railroad, frequently mentioned in this diary, began operations of trains in April, 1837. It eventually extended its tracks about twenty-five miles to the northeast, first to the town of Washington and later into Franklin County. William Johnson was a stockholder in the Mississippi Rail Road Company.

14 The first skirmish of the Texas Revolution against Mexico had taken place near Gonzales on October 2, 1835. As early as October 26 the provisional government of Texas addressed an impassioned appeal for aid by the citizens of the United States. The lower Mississippi Valley gave immediate response. In all of the river towns from New Orleans to Cincinnati, friends of the Texas colonists held meetings to raise money and volunteers.

15 For a good description of the courthouse and the courthouse square about this time, see [Ingraham], *The South-West,* II, 41–42.

16 Like most Natchez citizens, Johnson usually depended upon cisterns for his drinking-water supply. The water from the pond was probably intended for his livestock.

17 In 1835–36 two Negro boys named "John" worked for William Johnson. The John mentioned here was a slave who died near the end of June, 1836, and was given a respectable burial by his master. The second John, a free Negro, began to

Beat them Both with my stick when they Came home   They were both doun at Mr. Parkers kitchen[18]   Reid striks at Young Abby with the bar of the Door   Abby got out of his way   No fight

24   A Public Dinner given at Mr Bells[19] for Mr Poindexter[20]   There was no music on the Ocasion — Two gentlemen took a Bath in the Evening — Mr. Page pd me 1.50 cts   I Bot Bill Nix[21] a Blue Cloth Roundabout   Paid seven Dollars for it to Owen & Fortune[22] — I Bot 6 pair woolen socks from an Irish pedler   Gave him 1.75 for them   Toot Larjon. $88.[0]6¼[23]

25   Elias Burns returned To Natchez from up the River — Bill Nix Beat John shaveing — 56 cent salery. I gave French $2.00   I went into the Swamp.[24] Made some very bad shots.

---

learn the barber trade from Johnson on January 23, 1836, but he was never legally apprenticed to the shop owner. Most of Johnson's diary references to "John" were to the free Negro.

[18] Apparently this was a reference to the kitchen of the Mississippi Hotel, also called "Parker's Hotel" or "The Southern Exchange." Johnson usually handled his apprentices and employees with a tight rein.

[19] Until June, 1836, Elijah Bell was the proprietor of the Mansion House, one of the more important Natchez hotels. For a brief description of the hotel, see [Ingraham], *The South-West*, II, 43.

[20] George Poindexter, native of Virginia, came to Natchez in 1802. In the Mississippi Territory he served as attorney general, member of the territorial legislature, territorial delegate to Congress, territorial judge, and member of the constitutional convention of 1817. After Mississippi became a state, he served as congressman, 1817–19, as governor, 1820–22, and as United States senator, 1830–35. As a Whig opponent of Jacksonianism, he was defeated for re-election to the Senate.

[21] William (or Bill) Nix (or Nicks) was a free man of color who worked in Johnson's barbershop from 1835 to 1844 (and possibly later), except for periods when he acted as body servant for various well-to-do individuals on their trips to meetings of the state legislature at Jackson or to the New Orleans races. At the time he began work he was perhaps fifteen years of age and an apprentice, or had the status of an apprentice. Hence he was subject to his master's discipline. In 1841 he was described as being of "light complexion . . . five feet six inches in height." See Cash Book, 1830–38, *passim*, Cash Book, 1830–44, *passim*, and Ledger, 1833–37, pp. 153–61, Johnson Papers; Adams County Court and Police Board Minutes, 1832–45, September, 1841; U. S. Census Reports, 1850, Schedule I, Adams County, 7.

[22] On May 8, 1835, Miles Owen and J. R. Fortune announced that they had purchased the interest of R. Abbey in the New York Clothing Store and would operate it under the firm name of Owen & Fortune. Natchez *Courier*, September 11, 1835.

[23] Johnson occasionally closed an entry with this phrase, or a variation, followed by an entry of money. It was probably a corruption of the French phrase meaning "all the money" and the figures might possibly have represented his total receipts for that day. With only a few exceptions, Johnson's infrequent "French" phrases have hereafter been deleted.

[24] Johnson referred to a swampy, wooded area which contained a number of shallow lakes and was located about six to eight miles southwest of Natchez, between the old bed of St. Catherine's Creek and a narrow, higher area along the Mississippi River. All of the Swamp lay within Township 6, Ranges 3 and 4, West. Johnson

Killed three squirrels — Got home at 7 Oclock — Bills[25] came Out in the morning Ordering the Gamblers to Leave the City in 24 Hours[26] — T. Gilbert paid me $50.00 that he Borrowed on Monday the 12th day of October

26 Messrs Bush, Marshall & Dr Merrill returned Home from the North — Nelson Gelespie Died Late in the night   To day I herd of the seduction [of] Geogeana Cary by [from] the old negro Elick   The charge was made against Emery Willson[27] — Merrit Williams returned with Negros for sale

27 Mrs Battles[28] Left for New Orleans on the Bunker Hill — Mr. Oakly on same Boat — Commencd watering street by Stephen   Mr Rowes hyere my Horse   I Loaned Mr. Newman

---

made many hunting and fishing trips into this area, and between 1845 and 1851 purchased land there and along the river, immediately to the west.

25 Johnson probably referred to handbills or broadsides.

26 During the summer of 1835 a group of professional gamblers committed a number of depredations in Vicksburg, which was already agitated by the disclosures of the slave-rebellion plans of John Murrel and his confederates. A public meeting decided that they should be forced to leave the city and a committee was appointed to notify them to depart within twenty-four hours. The gamblers refused and barricaded themselves in their headquarters. The citizens' committee marched against them, and in the ensuing fight Dr. Hugh Bodley was killed. As a result of his death several of the leaders were hanged. See Vicksburg *Register*, July 9, 1835; H. S. Fulkerson, *Random Recollections of Early Days in Mississippi* (Baton Rouge, 1937; reprint of the Vicksburg, 1885, edition), 95–97; Dunbar Rowland, *Encyclopedia of Mississippi History, Comprising Sketches of Counties, Towns, Events, Institutions and Persons*, 2 vols. (Madison, 1907), II, 860–61. Following this episode a great many of the gambling fraternity moved their headquarters to Natchez, where the press began to urge their removal from the city. See Natchez *Courier*, September 11, 1835. The action of the citizens on October 25 was a result of this agitation and the bold actions of the gamblers.

27 Georgeana Cary, known as Georgeana Coleman in 1840, was a free woman of color, probably one of the six children of Milford and Sally Cary, free people of color. Georgeana, Milford, and Sally were unable to write their names. See Adams County Deed Records, K, 162, BB, 218–19, CC, 170; Adams County Court and Police Board Minutes, 1832–45, March, 1832; U. S. Census Reports, 1820, Schedule I, Adams County, 17; *ibid.*, 1830, Schedule I, Adams County, 18.

In the summer of 1835 a Natchez Negro named Emory Wilson had been manumitted in Cincinnati. Adams County Deed Records, W, 222–23. See also Robert Bradley's petition to legislature to manumit his slave Emory Wilson. Petition dated January 20, 1834, Petitions and Memorials, Series I, No. 95.

28 Harriet Battles, mother-in-law of the diarist, had been freed by Gabriel Tichenor of Natchez in 1822. In 1832 she had been described as "a free mulatto woman about thirty five years old five feet six inches high." She died in 1874 in Natchez. See Adams County Deed Records, O, 36; Adams County Court and Police Board Minutes, 1832–45, March, 1832; Adams County Will Books, IV, 63–64; Adams County Probate Records, No. 512, File 47.

Harriet Battles was the daughter of the free woman of color Jane (commonly called Jenny) Bush, who had been freed in Concordia Parish, Louisiana, about 1819 and lived in Natchez thereafter until 1840. See certificates signed by J. Robitaille, June 11, 1840, and by Horace Gridley, June 26, 1840, Johnson Papers.

$5.00 Mr McAlister moved Down to the store House — Jail[29] was broke & all get Out

28 Mother[30] Received the sick woman from Mr Merrit Williams On Conditions that if she got well he was to have half for what she would sell for or it was optional with Mother wheather she gave him any part of what she might sell for, the child included — Mr. Porter Came back to Natchez — Shimon takes Down the old Bed and moves the Cloths press — I paid Mr Seviere $2.00 for a Cask & pd Paterson & Wiswall 1.00 for a Fossit for Barrell — Hyred Ben of Mr Barlow to water the streets

29 I bet Mr McFadden a years shaving agains ten Bushell of Oats. I took Red Mariah against Fanny Kemble — Wm Stokes returned from Louisville — S. B. Iberia — Dr Welding returned to Natchez — A Mr Jeorge Welding gets married to a Miss Walker Down at Mr Van Campens — Mr Green & Mr. Easton arives from Newyork Fourteen Days passage, 11 by sea, One in Orleans

30 Race between Fanny Kemble & Redd Mariah — 2 Miles and Repeate — $2000 aside — Redd Mariah made 4 or five very bad starts — When they did start F. K. was held up No start Mariah ran two miles Out The 2d start they had Mariah Jumped the fence and threw the Boy — she did not Run for it. The money was given up to Fanny Kemble — My opinion was that Red Mariah would have won the Money[31] — Rouland & a Mr Lupton fights Luton Bruised him very much and had him Down for a ½ minute. Rouland Resiled with him & threw him & the fall Broke his Leg in someway or other

31 I Loaned Dr. Benbrook $3.00 I went to the Race track First Race between Mr. Rich. Harrisons Little Black Rachel Jackson & a grey mare of Mr Hocket Woods. Bets were all in favor of Rachel Jackson — Single Dash of a mile. The grey or

29 The Natchez jail was located on the south side of State Street about the middle of the block directly opposite the courthouse. It was described by Ingraham as "a handsome two story brick building, resembling, save in its grated tier of windows in the upper story, a gentleman's private dwelling." *The South-West*, II, 41–42.

30 Johnson's mother, Amy Johnson, was a free mulatto woman, about forty-eight years of age in 1835. She had been freed in 1814; she died in 1849. For her emancipation, see Adams County Deed Records, I, 243-45. Johnson recorded her purchase of several slaves, including Dinah, Mary and her child Moses, and Sharlot. As late as 1843, Amy Johnson was the owner of five slaves.

31 Fanny Kemble, owned by Adam L. Bingaman, and Red Maria, owned by John G. Perry, were horses well known in sporting circles. The Natchez *Free Trader*, November 3, 1835, reported: "The great match race between Red Maria and Fanny Kemble was run yesterday. Red Maria bolted and Fanny Kemble took the purse." Perry protested the decision of the judges in a letter to the Natchez *Free Trader*, which published it in the January 29, 1836, issue.

Mary won the Race with perfect Ease beating the other about 60 or 80 feet — Second Race Mr. H. Woods bay Colt & Big Indian, 2 miles Out   Won by big Indian about 40 or fifty yards — I did bet one Dollar on Rachel Jackson with a Stranger & I bet one on the bay Colt against Indian — also with the Stranger, & ten Dollars with Mr Saml. Gosien — Lost all — A Mr Simington Died at the Forks of the Road.[32] He was a Negro trader. I paid Mr Barlow $3.75 for the Hyre 3 days of Ben

November 1   Mr. Lipincot pd. me $20 Stakes that he held for G Lancaster & myself on the Race — I went Hunting after Dinner   met P. Baker. We had a talk about Lycening [licensing] guns &c — I Shot a sap sucker, One Lark upon the wing & One on a tree and a small Sparrow — Mc Shot an owl, 2 Larks setting and one upon the wing — also one yellow Hammer & sparrow hawk — I gave French $2, John 62½, Bill 12½, Walker 1.00[33]   Mr Hutcheons and old Mr Bomans Leaves this place for Texas to fight the Spaniards, Got a Letter from E Miller[34] dated 12th from Philadelphia. He was to have been married on the 15th of October — Young Men for Texes — W. A. Moore, Dr. Jas. D. Jennings, John W. Allen, Jno H. Roberts, Wm B. Dameron, W. C. W. Baker, Geo. W. Thayer, Jno W. Tilden, Jno M. White, H. M. Pittman, David Shelby, Tho. B. Cook & McClanden.[35]

2   The Election Came on for all The officers in the State &

32 "Forks of the Road" was the name given to the area around the intersection of the Washington road and a road leading to the plantations north of Natchez. The intersection, located about a mile east of the city, was sometimes called "Niggerville" because it was the most important slave-trading center of the Natchez area. See the advertisement in Natchez *Free Trader*, February 26, 1836; and also Frederic Bancroft, *Slave-Trading in the Old South* (Baltimore, 1931), 301; Wendell Holmes Stephenson, *Isaac Franklin: Slave Trader and Planter of the Old South* (University, La., 1938), 57–60. It was described as a "cluster of rough wooden buildings, in the angle of two roads," having slave "pens" in which "several hundred slaves of all ages, colors and conditions, of both sexes, were exposed for sale." [Ingraham], *The South-West*, II, 192, 201.

33 Walker was a slave, about thirty-seven years of age in 1835, and purchased for $55 by Johnson at an auction in the previous year. Johnson described him as a very black man who smiled broadly and was usually confused when addressed. Cash Book, 1830–44, entry for May 6, 1834; Johnson to O. L. Bemis, July 24, 1837 (copy), Johnson Papers.

34 Elisha Miller was a free Negro barber at Vicksburg. Johnson and Elisha Miller exchanged letters and visits, and Johnson occasionally lent him money.

35 These were among the first volunteers to leave Mississippi to participate in the Texas Revolution. A Texas historian points out that "for most of these valiant young Americans [from the southern states] fate held a tragic ending." The Texan forces that sustained overwhelming defeats by the invading Mexicans in the spring of 1836 were largely composed of newcomers. Rupert N. Richardson, *Texas, The Lone Star State* (New York, 1943), 140.

County — Got a Letter from E Miller to Day instead of yesterday[36] — Mechanics Meeting in the Court House for the purpose of Making the Editor of the Free Trader[37] give the author of the article Signed to the Mechanicks

3   Mr. Hough Leaves this place for New Orleans on S. B. Chester, I sent a Dayly paper & a Letter to Jas Miller — He Directs me to Collect the money that he Owes me from his partner Mr Skeggs — Mr Bledsoe Orders a wig to be made   very Light Hair — Finds William at Mr Parkers Kitchen with his Girls   Struck him with the whip 1st and then with the stick   He ran home and I followed him there and whiped him well for it, having often told him about going Down there — He then Comes Out on Bill Nix and Seys that he Bought five finger Rings &c.

4   I took Bill Nix and gave him a whiping. He then Confessed that he had taken the Key of Side Bourd which unlocked Mothers trunk and that he had got money frequently to the amount of Eight or ten Dollars   He had bought a finger Ring of Cockarill & Surie, cost $3.00, a whip from Mr Spielmans Zack, cost 1.00, a pair of Boots from Middleton, cost $2.50   He paid John for a pair of Pantaloons   His Mother was greatly Hurt at the Conduct of Her Degraded Son — Mr Bledsoe teling Mr. Bradley that Capt Myres after having Settled with the owners of the Boat and given them a Receit in full for the money that they Owed him he went to New Orleans and Collected money to the amount of a thousand Dollars and kept it by saying the Boat owed Him

5   The Dayly Paper anoncees the Result of the Election   Col Bingaman & Mr McMurran, Representatives, Mr Chambers, Shreriff.[38]   Miss Sarai Newman gets married to a Mr Foster of Woodville, a merchant — I paid Phill $3.00 for water Out of the pond for seven Days — Mr Duolon paid me for two months shaving $2.00   I paid Mr Mellen five Dollars for One years Subscription to the Weekly Courier & Journal for Mr Jas Miller[39] —

---

[36] This mistake is explained by the fact that Johnson frequently delayed a few days before making entries in his diary, then caught up with his entry-making at a single sitting.

[37] Lorenzo A. Besancon was the editor of the Natchez *Free Trader*, the city's leading Democratic organ.

[38] The complete election returns were published in Natchez *Free Trader*, November 3, 1835.

[39] Johnson was here arranging for a subscription to a Natchez newspaper, edited by William P. Mellen, for his free Negro brother-in-law, James Miller of New Orleans. Miller had lived in Natchez for a number of years prior to 1830, when Johnson took over his barbershop. The relationship between Miller and Johnson was very close, both personally and in business.

Mr Smith paid me for One months Shaving 1.50   I paid Mr Bledsoes Boy $11 for 2 Gunea pigs

6   I paid $2.50 for a Bundle of Shingles. The Citizens went Out to the Race track in search of the Gamblers; the[y] Brought in Elick Piper from Mr Mardice's place — Had a meeting at the Court House for the purpose of trying him — Gridley took him from them and put him to Jail — Twas their Intention to have whipd him[40] — Mr Bray puts up his new sign. His men all got Drunk   Made a great noise

7   Col Bingaman & Mr Chambers gives a Dinner at Mr Parkers.[41] Underwood & John Mason fights. Underwood whiped him very Easy — I paid Mr S. Cotten $27.00 the amount Due to Dr Hunt, Deceased. I Loaned Mr Whiting $8.00   pd   Mr Harrison Black mare runs a mile against Sorril mare Called the Sumpter Filly — Black M. won the Race very Easy, by 30 yards — Cryzers horse ran against the one Eyed Sorrel mare   The mare won the race by Eleven feet. They ran 750 yards

8   The Fencibles[42] Left Here for Vicksburg on Bourd of the Steam Boat Ponchartrain. They Left here about 1 Oclock in the

---

[40] The Adams County Anti-Gambling Society had previously elected a Committee of Vigilance to wait upon the professional gamblers and order them to leave town. Several members of the committee soon visited the St. Catherine Race Course and ordered two gamblers, Brice and Cobler, to leave town immediately, and Ellick Piper to depart within four days. The gamblers informed the group, "in terms of insulting triumph," that they would remain. See Natchez *Free Trader*, November 3, 1835.

Cobler may have been the "Cabler" who had been whipped and tarred and feathered in Vicksburg, and ordered to leave town immediately. See Vicksburg *Register*, July 9, 1835.

[41] The three-story Mississippi Hotel, operated by William Parker who had been eighteen years in the hotel business in Natchez (by his own account), was located on the north side of State Street, between Wall and Canal streets. William Johnson managed a piece of property which was directly across State Street and was owned by his free Negro mother-in-law, Harriet Battles. For a long description of the Mississippi Hotel, see Natchez *Free Trader*, March 11, 1836; see also Samuel B. Olden, Jr., "Hotels, Inns and Taverns in Mississippi, 1830–60," *Journal of Mississippi History*, V (1943), 172–74, 176, 183. Olden concludes that the Mississippi Hotel "probably offered the best accomodations to be had in the Mississippi of that era." The "central portion" of the hotel was destroyed in a fire in late September, 1839, and the remainder in a tornado in the next spring. See Natchez *Free Trader*, October 7, 1839, May 11, 1840; Natchez *Courier*, December 11, 1840, December 28, 1841.

[42] The most noted Mississippi volunteer militia companies were formed at Natchez and Vicksburg. The Natchez Fencibles had been organized in 1824, under the command of John A. Quitman, who was still listed as captain sixteen years later. Ingraham thought the organization "the best disciplined and finest looking body of men west of the Alleghanies." *The South-West*, II, 259. At the beginning of 1841 the Natchez organizations included the Fencibles, Hussars, Guards, and Adams Light Guards. The Natchez Rifle Corps had voted to dissolve in December, 1840.

Evening — 31 in Number — Gave William $2.00   Stephen pd me
$12.00

9   I Commenced to pull Down the part of the Stable to
Rebuild it up again — Paid $10.00 for 2000 Shingles — The Jone
Left here at Night taking 4 or 5 more of the Fencibles to Vicks-
burg   Mr Massy Came to buy my Land for Mr Flecheo — Mr
Newman pays me $5.00 that he Borrowed Tuesday 27th day of
October   I Loaned Dr Benbrook $2.00

10   Mrs. Merricks House on Main street Sold at Auction and
was Bought by Abby for five thousand & Eighty Dollars — Hyred
[blank]⁴³ To Drive for me — 1.50 per Day — Receid a Letter by
Greenburg Wade for [from] Orleans. Mrs Miller⁴⁴ wishes me to
purchase a house & Lot Down there at $3500. Mr F. Rowland
pays me $50.00 the ballance of the money Due me from Mr Rob-
ert for house Rent. I stoped Stephen in to work for Mr Rowes
from 9 Oclock untill Night, tho he did not work any.

11   Maj. Miller⁴⁵ Came to Natchez. Mr Harden took my
Letter to Mrs Miller   I sent $15 to get a wig for Mr Bledsoe —
My mule ranaway   I sent John & Stephen down to Ragleys place
for him. They Could not find him   Mr Rowes has my old Roan
Horse all Day — I gave Mr Jackson Five Dollars. He commenced
work after Dinner, worked untill night — Mr Whiting paid me
$8.00 that he Borrowed on Saturday November 7th

12   Mc & myself went out to Parson Connelly Sale to Look
at his Cows. They were all Dry — Stephen & John went to Rayley
place for my mule   Came home with him at 11 A. M. Oclock   Mr
M. Williams sends his sick Boy to Bourd until he returns from Red
River   I made Maj Dunbar a present of 2 guinea pigs

13   Bought a Sorrel Horse — Rob. Roy — at Auction for
$106 cash — I thought Mc would take him when I Bought him and
when he came up I asked him if wanted to buy a Horse and he told
no, that food was too high — I then told him to take him to his
stable and keep him to ride for his feed — He then said as above
stated that corn was too high — I then proposed for him [to] ride
him on Sunday — He said no that he was agoing to ride Mr

---

⁴³ The word "blank" enclosed in brackets signifies that Johnson had omitted a
word or words.

⁴⁴ This was the diarist's free Negro sister, Adelia, who had married James
Miller, another free Negro barber, in Natchez in 1820. In 1830 the Millers had
moved to New Orleans.

⁴⁵ No evidence has been found which tends to connect Major Miller, occasionally
mentioned by Johnson, with either James Miller or Elisha Miller, the free Negro
barbers in New Orleans and Vicksburg.

Browns Horse to try him — Mr Gilbert auditer &c. came down from Jackson — Fencibles Returned from Vicksburg They Looked very well. Higly pleased with the citizens of that place [who] would not suffer them to pay for anything what every — Mr Barber Returned from the North — Mother Buys Mary and her Child from Mr Murcherson for $800.00

14 I pd Mr Jackson $5 for his work on the stable Mr McAlister has his ware house done & engages 25 Barrels of Pittsburgh coal

15 I took a wride on my New Horse — went Out as far as Mr Wilkins Garden fence. I gave French $2.00 Dr Hubbard pd me $40.00, part of a $150.00 that I Loaned him. Mr Sweney pd me $3.00 for One Months Shaving

16 Mr Turner Leaves Natchez he pays me $6.00 Mr Rose Sent my carts home after Breakfast — Stephen came also — Mr Chambers Buys a Bay Horse, $250 I met Col Throckmorton with 20 Darkeys I Expect he bought them — yes he Bot them of Collier. Dr Hubard pays me $110.00 that he Borrowed of me Loaned Mr Whiting five Dollars — Parsons came with theatrical company[46]

17 I paid Jackson $15.00 for working on stable He is a mean man. Enough said — Pollow & Spring[47] fights Pollow got hurt very much. I Rubed it with opedildoc[48] Poindexter brings

---

[46] This was in preparation for the opening of the second of four theatrical seasons, beginning in the fall of 1834, in which deep-voiced tragedian Charles Booth Parsons managed the Natchez theater with striking success. Many of the leading personages of the theatrical world, as well as lesser stars who made their headquarters in New Orleans, played brief engagements in Natchez in the period 1835–39. Free, "The Ante-Bellum Theatre of the Old Natchez Region," *loc. cit.*, 22–23; Nellie Smither, "A History of the English Theatre at New Orleans, 1806–1842," *Louisiana Historical Quarterly*, XXVIII (1945), 214–15, 217, 225–27.

Between 1828 and 1840 the Natchez theater building was on the south side of Main Street, between what are now Pine and Rankin streets. Charles Augustus Murray, the English traveler, thought the Natchez playhouse compared favorably with the best "county theatres in England." Although it was "not remarkable for elegance of decoration," it had two tiers of boxes and a gallery, with a capacity of perhaps 700. Its tax valuation in 1840, the year in which it was destroyed by a tornado, was $15,000. Murray, *Travels in North America*, II, 179–81; Free, "The Ante-Bellum Theatre of the Old Natchez Region," *loc. cit.*, 20, 26; *Laws of Mississippi*, 11 Sess. (1828), 89–90; [Ingraham], *The South-West*, II, 40; Power, *Impressions of America*, II, 121–23; Natchez *Free Trader*, December 16, 1836; Auditor's Records, Tax Rolls, 1840, Adams County.

[47] Two of Johnson's dogs.

[48] Opodeldoc was a solution of soap in alcohol to which camphor and other oils had been added. It was sometimes called "soap-liniment."

news from the Election returns that Linch is Elected[49] — Col Wilkins, Mr Vick, Poindexter & others has a wine Drinking at Bells   I got the pair of shoes that I won of Young Reed at Masons store

18   Parson and one of his actors by the name of Chipp has a fight. Parson takes him by the hair of his head and throws him Down and Choakes him. I made a small Loft in the stable   Mr Dolbear has a box of soap opened for himself   I bot 4 pair socks of the old frenchman on a credit, 1.00   Mr Whiting pays me $5.00 that he Borrowed on Monday 16th inst — Mr R J. Walker[50] returns to Natchez & Mr Becket Returns also — also Young Snodgrass

19   Dr Benbrook pays me $15.00, money that I Loaned him some time ago — I Loaned Harden 1.00   Performance the 1st time to night, the Comedy of Town & Country or which is best. Reuben Glenroy by Mr Parson, Roselie Somers by Miss Petre. Farce, Irish tutor[51]

20   Dr Benbrook pays me $4.50, money that he Borrowed of me   A mistake   This money was pd on Saturday 21st   The play to night, Romeo & Juliet — Merciusio by Parson, Juliet by Miss Clark — Farce, turn Out &c. Mr Emerson is in town   I rode to the Landing and paid for in all 31 Barrels of Coal — also pays for 30 Barrels for Mc   He gave me the money to pay for his. Mr Burns Leaves his Boy Milton with me — Mc Buys a Horse from Mr Brown for One Hundred & 35 Dollars

21   Mrs Battles arrives from Orleans on the Walk in the Water — Harden was the steward of the Boat. I Loaned Mr Lighter $4.00. I Received a wig from New Orleans for Mr Bledsoe order — Mr J. Potts has his Head shaved. The Play to night is

---

[49] Charles Lynch, who had been acting governor in 1833 and president of the state Senate from 1833 to 1834, was elected governor of Mississippi as a Whig (Poindexter faction) in 1835 in a race against the Democratic incumbent, Hiram G. Runnels. Lynch served as governor, 1836–38.

[50] Robert J. Walker, native of Pennsylvania, came to Natchez in 1826. There he practiced law, acquired an interest in Louisiana plantations and Natchez property, and speculated in Texas lands (see Adams County Deed Records, Z, 164–67); he then served as United States senator, 1836–45, and later as secretary of the treasury and territorial governor of Kansas.

[51] The Natchez *Free Trader* of November 20 announced: "Mr. Parsons has again returned among us with an excellent stock company, and commenced the season last evening with the comedy of 'Town and Country' and the farce of the 'Irish Tutor.' Mr. Parsons as Reuben Glenroy, and Miss Petrie as Rosalie Somers fully sustained the high reputation they have acquired, and were ably supported by the company. Shakespeare's tragedy of 'Romeo and Juliet,' with the afterpiece of 'The Turn Out' will be presented this evening."

Virginius   V by Parson & Virginia, Miss Clark — My Drayman only pd me $6.00   The Land adjoining my Land was sold at auction, 322 acres & 30 hundreds of an acre — It was Bought by Messrs Phil. Harrisson & Mr Bledsoe at $3.75 per acre   The people was hourly Expecting inteligence of the Governors Election   Mr. [blank] commences by the month, 1.50 pays in advance

    22   I gave old French $2.00   I did not see old Mc the whole day. Two Irishman commenced boxing in fun and then began to fight. The one kicked the other in such a seviere maner that he broke his gaul. His Head was bruised also — He Died in 8 or ten hours after the fight   His name was Russell   He was Killed by [blank]. He was put in Jail on Monday 23d inst

    23   Mr Bledsoe gets the wig that I sent to Orleans for   He pays me $15.00 for it. Tis what it cost me — I Loaned Mr. Whiting $10   I told Mr Flecheo that he could take my Land at 8 dollars per acre. I Loaned Mr Gilbert my Horse to wride out to Col Bingamans — Northern mail arrived. Brings News to Gilbert that Linch was Elected by small majority — Old Fletcheo Gets Drunk and came in the shop   Play, Tour de Nesle or the Chamber of Death   Margariett of Bergundy, Mrs Lyons   Farce, dead Shot.

    24   I Loaned Dr Hubbard One hundred and 75 dollars — Mr Baynton arrives here. The Little Dwarf arrives here. The play is Hunch Back. Master Walter by Mr Parsons — A Bear belonging [to] Mr Phiffs Killed a Little Yellow Child Down at Mr Parkers Hotel   They had to shoot him Dead to Loose him — Mc takes his horse home to his own stable — Mr Pulling and Milne has a sort of a fight about the moving of some coal. Mr P. threw a Hatchet at Mr M. and it mist him   Mr M attempted to get a gun Down to shoot

    25   Dr Hubbard paid me One Hundred & 75 Dollars, money that he Borrowed yesterday the 24th   Mc gets $13.00 worth of Hay & Oats for his Horse, I herd Mr Prentice[52] gets some glass in his throat by Biting a wine glass. He was then very ill — Maj. Miller Leaves this place for some other place above

---

[52] Seargent S. Prentiss was a lawyer, leader of the Whig party in Mississippi, and a famous orator. He served in the lower house of the state legislature, 1836, and in the United States House of Representatives, 1838-39. "He was to Mississippi, in her youth, what Jenny Lind is to the musical world, or what Charles Fox, whom he resembled in many things, was to the whig party of England in his day." Joseph G. Baldwin, *The Flush Times of Alabama and Mississippi, A Series of Sketches* (Americus, Ga., 1843), 197.

26 Mr Bledsoe & Mr P Harrison returns from Looking at the Land they were about purchasing of Mr Flecheux — At the Same time Mr Flecheux was contracking to purchase my tract of Land Down there, Containing One hundred & 62 and 31 hundreths acres — He got my Land at 8 dollars per acre and sold it again for 15 dollars per Acre to Mr Bledsoe and Harrison. I must add that he Cheated all of us a Little. He pd me $300.00 when we made the Contract,[53] I herd by a Gentleman that Crenshaw that was shot in the Woodvill[54] Jail by Dr Webb had Died and that [the] man Hunter that was put in for stealing a Negro from Dr Carmicle was taken Out of Jail by 5 or 6 persons and was shot 3 times and then hung on a tree — Mc gets six yards of carpeting at Sorias to Cover his Horse with   He pd [blank] per yard for it — I had to Beat William about being so careless and passionate, whilst shaving   It was to Day that I herd that Maj A Dunbar gives Mr O. Enos forty thousand Dollars for his share of the Plantation — To night there was a Ball at Mr Bells New House for the first time — Mr J Steele pd me $5 for the hyre of my carts

27 Mr Ried, Mr Pulling and Mc & myself were to go in the swamp to hunt but I did not get through selling my Land nor Sterns did not come to stay in Mcs shop and it also rained early in the morning so we did not go — Mr Dunbar sends the Guinea pig in for me to swap it for a male pig but I could not. I went to Mr McMurrans office to transfer a Deed to Flecheux but did not finish it

28 I made the transfer to Flecheux of my tract of Land Containing One hundred and 62 and 31/100 acres in Section No 6 and in township No. 3, Range 4 West — I pd Esq Carson One Dollar to write the Acknowledgement. S. Boat Walk in The Water Leaves this [place] for New Orleans   Takes a way the Shipp

---

53 Johnson never liked to be deprived of profits. Nevertheless, both he and Adolph Flecheux made substantial profits in buying and selling the land in question. In the previous month Johnson had purchased the 162.31-acre tract for $4.12½ per acre, and, as stated above, sold it for $8.00 per acre. Adams County Deed Records, W, 362, CC, 271.

Between August 1, 1835, and near the end of 1836, Flecheux was a tenant of one and then two rooms in one of Johnson's store buildings. Advertising under the name of "M. Flecho," he directed attention to his work as "Engraver, Copper-plate printer, and Jeweller." Johnson had more trouble collecting rent from him than from any of his other tenants, and eventually lost a court suit, on a technicality, for $180 unpaid rent. Natchez *Free Trader*, July 29, 1836; Day Book, 1830–40, unpaged entry under Flecheux's name, and Ledger, 1835–39, p. 44, Johnson Papers.

54 Woodville was the seat of government of Wilkinson County, the adjoining county south of Adams County.

Florence, Heavy Laden with cotton[55]   I wrote to Mrs Miller by Harden and sent two Dollars for to get Cannary Seed with   This is the first week that Stephen worked Out by the Day

    29   Mc and myself wrode Out as far as St Catharine Bridge[56]   We met Campbell and another young man. They had been out a hunting and had killed 4 geese, One of Brays Journeman Haters forged his name and got $80 worth of Clothing. The[y] were first agoing to whip him but afterwards concluded to put him to Jail which they Did — I gave old French $2.00   My Bird still very sick. Mr Lighter pays me 4 Dollars that he Borrowed from me on Saturday 21st inst

    30   I gave Mr F. Taylor for collection my account against Mr Stokes for $64. Due 7th of November. Andrew the Drayman pd me $4 due me for his Draying — Hyred Stephen & Walker with ther carts to haul dirt from Watts Building — Loaned Cary my Dray — Mr Wm Minor returned from France, Ingland and a great many places. Mc swaps his violin for a better one

    December 1   Steven & Walker still working for Messrs Neibut & Gemmell — Pollo & McAlisters Dog has a fight, He was too strong for Pollo but did not whip him   It was a stand off.

    2   The Association[57] Races Commences   Hard Heart walked around and took the money, purse $1000. Mr Donnoi pd me $3.00 up to 1st of December. I loaned Mr Boyer 1 Dollar   I sent the old piano to the Masonic Hall[58] to be Repaired by Mr Maury.

    3   Bought a Black Horse at the sale of Mr N. Gelespies

55 Ocean-sailing vessels were towed up the Mississippi River to Natchez, loaded with cotton, and towed back to New Orleans, whence they sailed for foreign ports. See article entitled "Rail Roads" in Natchez *Courier,* September 11, 1835.

56 St. Catherine's Creek, east and south of Natchez, emptied into the Mississippi River a few miles below the city. Johnson probably referred to a bridge on the "lower" or "river" road.

57 In the first half of the 1830's the winter horse races of the Mississippi Association for Improving the Breed of Horses were usually held before the meets of the Adams County Jockey Club. Both began in December and were run on the Natchez track, usually known in the 1830's as St. Catherine's Course and later as Pharsalia Course.

In 1830 both names for the track were used (see Natchez *The Natchez,* October 23, December 4, 1830, January 22, 1831), but thereafter St. Catherine (or St. Catharine) was the common designation until late 1835, when Pharsalia became the accepted name. The earliest notices of the Mississippi Association for Improving the Breed of Horses that have come to the attention of the editors appeared in the Natchez *Newspaper and Public Advertiser,* October 25, 1826, and Natchez *Ariel,* December 1, 1826, September 21, November 24, 1827.

58 For descriptions of the building, see [Ingraham], *The South-West,* II, 38–39; Marshall (ed.), "Journal of Henry B. Miller," *loc. cit.,* 281.

property for the sum of $30, Six months Credit — Also pd cash for a pair of Saddle Bags and a powder horn — Fanny Kemble galloped around three miles heats with out opposition — took the money

4   McCary and myself went in the swamp a hunting. Mc Killed six squirrels and I killed six and the Dogs caught One which made 7 for me, I also Killed 3 Birds — Mr William Minor[59] Returns home his six imported Horses also   Came on the same Boat, They were Led up main street by six white men, They were imported too. Chuckfihily takes the purse, no opposition. I Received a Letter from N Orleans. It mentioned the death of Mr Woods — He Died of the Liver Complaint.

5   There was a race between two Horses belonging to overseers. The Sorrel Horse won the race beating the Bay mare 30 or 40 yards — A two mile race of Rushlows Horse Arabb and a Little Bay mare belonging to an Old Gentleman from Kentucky   The Horse won the Race very Easy wining very near all the money the old man had. They had won a Race the Day before from him   Hester Comings[60] Bought her sister Hanah and her child

---

[59] William J. Minor's imported racing stock included Britannia and Doncaster, both of which were later used for breeding purposes. He had been one of the officers of the Mississippi Association for Improving the Breed of Horses, which was reorganized in Adams County in 1832, and his papers reflect his continued interest in the subject. In Johnson's diary, Minor figured chiefly as the owner of "Minor's Pasture" (usually called "Minor's Grove" by the newspapers), where many militia meetings and holiday celebrations were held, and as the owner of horses that were racing on the Natchez and New Orleans tracks. He was unquestionably one of the South's leading turfmen during the period covered by this diary. As the son of Stephen Minor, who had been an extremely prominent figure in the Natchez area during the Spanish regime, he also carried forward the family tradition in fields other than horse racing. He was president of the Agricultural Bank at Natchez, captain of the Natchez Hussars, and a large-scale planter. By 1860 his family landholdings included the family residence at Concord plantation, near Natchez, and three Louisiana plantations valued at more than a million dollars. When he died on September 18, 1869, one of his sons added this notation to his diary: "Mississippi has lost her noblest son." See *American Turf Register and Sporting Magazine*, IV (1833), 361, and X (1839)–XV (1844), in practically all entries reporting Natchez and New Orleans races; "Stock Farm" and "Breeding Stud & Training Stable" accounts, 1837–55, in Ledger, 1834–83, Minor–Thomas J. Wells correspondence, 1854–62, and Plantation Diary, 1869, in William J. Minor Papers (Louisiana State University Department of Archives); J. Carlyle Sitterson, "The William J. Minor Plantations," *Journal of Southern History*, IX (1943), 59–74; Weaver, *Mississippi Farmers*, 109–10; Hogan (ed.), *Guide to the Manuscript Collections in the Department of Archives, Louisiana State University*, 47–49. See also William J. Minor, *Short Rules for Training Two Year Olds* (New Orleans, 1854), and *Constitution of the Adams County, Mississippi, Jockey Club* (Natchez, 1854), Minor Papers.

[60] Hester Cummings, who was about twenty-five years of age in 1835, was a free woman of color in whom William Johnson took a friendly interest. She performed several neighborly services for his family, and occasionally he held money for her.

for $1000. I wrote to John Clay for Walker[61]   Steven and Walker worked the whole week with there carts for Mr Gemmell & Neibut[62] — 6 Days

6   Nothing new what Ever. I rode out to Scotts old Field in the afternoon   Sold old Wharpen my old Black Horse for $40. He paid me $10 in advance.

7   My carts both working for Mr Gemmell   Old Warpen returns the Horse and I made him give me $4. to take him back again. I paid Mr McMurran $5.00 for Drawing the assignment on a Deed from me to Flecheo.

8   I pd Mr Geo. Lancaster my State & County tax for 1835 Amounting to $19.50   I pd $7.12½ for a Bale of Hay — The Hatters commences to Bourd. Maj. Miller is in town — I gave Mr F Taylor my Account against the state for $4.50 to collect   I also gave him my Account against Mr Tho. Steel for $30.00 for Collection   Steam Boat Walk in the Water was Burned up. She took fire about 8 Oclock at night — The Charleston caught on fire also but they succeeded in puting Out the fire, The Cotten that was Burned on the Walk Amounted to 1200 Bales. The amount of boat and Cotten was Estimated a[t] one Hundred and ten thousand Dollars — There was a runaway Boy Burned up and a pet Bear, also Harden the Bar Keeper, Capt Glover commanded the Boat.[63] Mr Jos Lapiece Returns from the North. He came down the River — Mr. Whiting pays me $10 that He Borrowed from me on Monday 23d of November — Col Bingaman takes Mr Rushlows[64] Negros for debts. Rushlow would not pay Him

9   I gave my note To The Estate of Nelson Gellespie for

and arranged for the payment of her taxes. She lived in Natchez throughout the 1830's and 1840's, and the census of 1840 listed her as the owner of two slaves.

61 Johnson was here writing a letter, in behalf of his slave Walker, to John Clay, Bourbon County, Kentucky, who owned a slave whom Walker considered his wife.

62 See Neibert & Gemmell advertisement in Natchez *Courier*, September 11, 1835. Their store, which stood about in the middle of property now occupied by the United States Post Office building, was immediately adjacent, on the west side, to William Johnson's Main Street barbershop. Before May 6, 1836, Peter Gemmell and John G. Taylor erected a three-story building on the property, which was owned by them. Adams County Deed Records, X, 164–65, CC, 471–73.

63 The Natchez *Free Trader*, December 11, 1835, carried an account of the disaster.

64 The man called "Rushlow" by Johnson was Joseph Rocheleau, who ran several horses on the Natchez racecourse in 1833–35. Thereafter he was in financial difficulties. He not only lost possession of his slaves, but also of his horses (including Hard Heart, the most consistent winner on the Natchez track in the mid–1830's). In 1840 he was twice indicted for professional gambling. See *American Turf Register and Sporting Magazine*, V (1834), 635–37; *ibid.*, VI (1835), 479, 521; Adams County Deed Records, V, 423–24; Adams County Circuit Court Minutes, Spring, 1840, pp. 159, 213.

$30, payable on the 3d Day of June, 1836 — Endorsed by Mr Wm Harris   Anderson Maxwell is in this place

10   My teams came home — ½ a Day   Col Bingaman Buys Milton From Elias Burns, cash $800   Mr Skeggs pays me Mr Houghs Shaving Bill ammounting to $16.50   Flecheux came to me and offered me Mr Bledsoes Note for Money that he Owed me, I would not take it for it had a year to run — Mr Bledsoe called to see if it was true that Flecheux had paid me — Mr Joseph Lapiece commences by the Month to get shaved

11   I Excepted Messrs Bledsoe and P. Harrisons note for $1750.00 from Adolph Flecheux in payment of a $1000.00 that he owed me for the Land he Bought from me,   I gave him my note Endorsed by R. McCary, payable in the Agricultural Bank[65] for $624.00 on the 15th Day of January, 1836 — I Inquired of the Bank what she would ask to Discount the note at 12 months, and her price was 125 Dollars   I made the Discount, a Loss to Flecheux, before I gave him my note — I went Out at 4 Oclock. I shot 1 partridge, 1 thrush, and I Broke the wing of a trush — Yesterday Stephen and Walker worked out.

12   I Bought a pair of Boots from Carroll & Buttler, paid them cash for them, $6.25   I then Bought of Col. Throckmorton and Paterson a pair of corded Pantaloons which I paid them $16.00 for — I also Bot a pair of slipers cash 1 dollar — Count O. Enos is in town — He said that Mr Dunbar, Harriet, and Mr Chas. Wilkins arrived at the Plantation at night and he Left before Day in the morning and came up here — Young Gent at P. office pd for a months shaving   Little Bon[66] pays me 12 Dollars that he Borrowed from me a Long time ago

---

[65] For a description of the Agricultural Bank building in 1835, see [Ingraham], *The South-West*, II, 37–38. Marshall (ed.), "Journal of Henry B. Miller," *loc. cit.*, 282, gives this brief description of three Natchez banks in 1838: "The Planters Bank of Natchez with a capital of 4,000,000 of dollars; it has seven branches; the Banking house is located on Main between Pearl & Wall streets; the house makes but a very ordinary appearance, being an old rusty building. The Agricultural Bank with a capital of $2,000,000; the Banking House is on the west Corner of Main & Commerce streets, and is quite a fine Brick Building with a portico on Main street supported by 6 Doric Columns; the Portico & Columns are Plastered in imitation of stone work. The Commercial Bank with a capital of $2,000,000; the new Banking House is situated on Main opposite the City Hotel and is quite a splendid building, with a fine marble Front and Portico; the Portico is supported by four Ionic columns, fluted; the banking room is large and spacious with Cornice and a very fine centre."

[66] "Little Bon," frequently mentioned in this diary, was S. M. Bon, who advertised that he sold "ready made clothing," stationery, and Havana cigars in his Main Street shop, and would serve as "Tailor and Draper, Renovator, &c."

13   I took my two Horses Out and Gave them a Race to
gether. John rode the sorrell Horse and Bill Nix wrode the Bay
horse, Paginini — They won two heats a piece — Old Mr Hutcheons
returns from Texas   Mr Vernon Came with Him — George Gal-
breth was Knocked off of the Steam Boat Bravo and Drowened.
The windlass on the Boat struck him   I Loaned Mr Newman
$10 for a few Days—Mr Bell has some of his Boys in his stable
whiping them about stealing from the Boarders

14   The Brick Layers Finished the Building and took Down
the Front scaffolds — Tom Jones Digs the Foundation for the
Brick wall or kitchen   Mc Buys The old Frenchmans Birds —
pays $15 for the pair — Tosspott arrives here on his way to
Orleans from above, I herd that E. Millers shop was sold for
$5000 and that Bony Goins had Bought it — Mr Newman pays
me $10 that he Borrowed of me yesterday the 13th   I got
my coat mended by Mr Dolland — I Received a Notice from the
Agricultural Bank to pay my note for $154.75 with old Mc as
indorser on it — Dick McCrary comes in the shop prety Drunk,
has his hair cut, does not pay for it. I Borrowed about two pounds
of Canay Seed from McCary   Mrs Drake takes Her Benifit —
Mrs Mandeville Died.[67]   Maj Miller Leaves this place

15   Mr Andeau paid me $10.00   I sold Mr Wm R. Cam-
mell One Female Canary Bird for $8.00 I Requested Mr Cammell
if there was any payment to make on that property of E Millers
in Vicksburg to Let me know it and I would remit the amount to
Madison or to himself so that the payment would be made   He
promised to Let me know   Mc sells the 2 Birds that he got from
the old frenchman to Mr Dumax for $25.00   Mr Thomas com-
mences kitchen for the Big House. Walker & Stephen Finished
work for Mr Gemmell about 3 Oclock in the Evening   The Circus
Company Arrived in Natchez from Above[68]

16   Parson Potts's Residence[69] is sold at auction and was
Bought by Col Sessions for $32,500   The Performers Played for

67 Johnson probably referred to the wife of Henry D. Mandeville, newly appointed
cashier of the Planters' Bank, Natchez. The family papers, 1815–1925, are in the
Louisiana State University Department of Archives.

68 Johnson probably referred to Brown and Company's New Orleans Circus.

69 This is a reference to a sale of The Elms, a large Natchez ante-bellum resi-
dance. The Reverend George Potts, longtime Presbyterian minister, acquired The
Elms by marriage to a daughter of Samuel Postlethwaite. See Edith Wyatt Moore's
article on The Elms in Natchez *Democrat*, Pilgrimages Edition, 1943. In 1832–33
he had been one of the leaders of the prosecution in a famous theological trial,
concluded in Adams County, in which the Reverend Theodore Clapp of the First

the Express Benefit of the Texians, $596.25   Mr Lilliard has his Boys sold at Auction   They were sold very high — Old Mr Brustee offers a Little Yellow Boy at Auction. Tryed to get $650.00 for him But he could not. He was not sold   I shaved Mrs Leonards Head

17   I Loaned Dr Reed Potts $380.00   The Circus Performs to night for the 1st time. Gov Reynols[70] is in town   Not more than 20 persons in the theatre to night   A Mr John King of Wilkerson County was Robbed of $1700.00 by Some body in the Circus

18   A Race between Mr Reichleaus Arabb and Mr Jack Perrys Grey mare, The Arabb Horse won the Race with Ease, time 1 m. 55½   Bets were 2 to one in favor of the mare, purse $500 aside. The mare ran again in the Evening against Mr [blank] Horse and the horse beat her. My Horse ranaway with me. Started at Mr Watts Conner and ran to Mrs Richards Conner and threw me on a pile of Plank and sprained my ancle. Mr Chambers Lost on the above Race $50.00, Col Bingaman about $250.00, Mr Gocian $75.00   Gerge Smyly came up from below, told me that he had Bought a Plantation a Little above Orleans   Mr Sweyney pays $2.00 for 1 months shaving   Mr Downs from Woodville was Knocked Down and Robbed of about $100.00 & a watch and other papers by some robber or other   William and John went Down to shave his wounds that was on his Head,   Mr Gridley Buys The Dulon Coffee House owned by Mr Byers. It sold for $100   Mr Mellen & Mr Bessancon Came very near fighting in the Market House Early in the morning[71]

Presbyterian Church of New Orleans was ousted from the Presbyterian ministry. Frances A. Cabaniss and James A. Cabaniss, "Religion in Ante-Bellum Mississippi," *Journal of Mississippi History*, VI (1944), 215–16. According to Johnson, "Parson Potts" and family left Natchez on April 19, 1836.

70 Johnson undoubtedly referred to former Governor Hiram G. Runnels.

71 In the fall of 1835 William P. Mellen, onetime (1831) publisher of the weekly *Natchez*, was editor of the Natchez *Courier and Journal*, the town's Whig journal. From 1835 to 1839, Lorenzo A. Besancon was editor of the Natchez *Mississippi Free Trader and Natchez Gazette*, the Democratic organ. Both newspapers were issued weekly in 1835, but by the beginning of 1838 both were being published in daily, triweekly, and weekly editions. Besancon was often involved in altercations in print, which sometimes led to personal encounters and at least one challenge to a duel. In the entry of May 30, 1837, in this diary, Besancon was still threatening "to whale Mr Mellen." Besancon was the compiler and publisher of *Besancon's Annual Register of the State of Mississippi for the Year 1838*, and served in the state legislature, as quartermaster general of the Mississippi militia in 1838, and as state bank com-

19   Mr Emerson sells his Property at Auction, 50-odd feet on Franklin street and 160 feet on Perl street. It was Bought by Dr Hubbard for $11,050. Old Cashill Bid against him, It was sold on One 2 & 3 & 4 and five years credit with 8 per cent interest   I Bought 2 Baskets of Champain wine, 50 cts a Bottle   Bunker Hill came up Last night. Fitchew as steward with a Letter and a Barrel of Oysters to Mother and 2 Dollars worth of Cannary seed to myself   Dick McCrary and Dr Wood came in to get shaved, both of them Drunk — Big Dutchman Down from Vicksburg wanted to Hear from E. Miller, and if I had herd or knew where he was — Col Fall from Jackson is or was afraid to wride my Horse and John gets on him and the Horse ran away and threw him

20   I gave Mother $7.00 that I sold her cannary Bird for To Mr Campbell of Vicksburg — Mother makes me a present of 2 Cannary Birds — I gave old French $2.00   I loaned Mother $5.

21   A Race between Arabb and a mare of Mr Crows or Mr Claibournes. Bets in favor of the mare   The Horse Beat her with Ease, Distance a Single Dash of a mile. I saw the Col Loose $75 with Rushlow and I won $15.00 from Mr S. Gosien   I bet him $20.00 to his $15.00   Mother Bought Dinah from Mr Merrit Williams and I Endorsed Her note payable on the first Day of June, 1836 to him for $100. That was all he was to get for Her — Mc & myself went to the Circus to hear the song of Billy Barlow — I pd Mr Linde for Mr Soria & Co. $12 for 2 doz of Champain — Circuit Court Commences. Judge Irish Judge[72] Jack Perry abusees Col Bingaman for Every thing but a gentleman   The[y] come very near Fighting

22   I paid Mr Maury $15 for repairing my Piano Forte and gave him orders to sell it for the Best price He Could get for

---

missioner, 1837–39. In 1843 he was editor of a New Orleans newspaper. During the Mexican War he was a captain in the Louisiana Mounted Volunteers. After the war he joined the Gold Rush to California, then returned to New Orleans where he again became a newspaper editor, and in 1853 died of cholera on a Mississippi River steamboat. *Mississippi Newspapers, 1805–1940* (Jackson, 1942), 175; *Besancon's Annual Register*, 106; Besancon to A. G. McNutt, January 10, 1839, Governor's Records, Series E, No. 33 (Mississippi Department of Archives and History); *Louisiana Newspapers, 1794–1940* (Baton Rouge, 1941), 142; Francis B. Heitman, *Historical Register and Dictionary of the United States Army, from its Organization, September 29, 1789, to March 2, 1903*, 2 vols. (Washington, 1903), II, 45; Natchez *Free Trader*, July 14, 1837; Natchez *Courier*, January 25, 1853.

[72] George Irish was the judge of the First District Circuit Court from 1835 to 1837. Dunbar Rowland (ed.), *The Official and Statistical Register of the State of Mississippi, 1924–1928* (New York, n.d.), 38.

it But that he must not sell it for Less than $70. The Boys found 6 Dead Rats under the floor in the centre of the Shop — Mr Turner came Home 6 or 7 Days ago

    23   I rode to the River and Bot a Bale of Hay. I Hyred my cart to Nelson at 50 cts per day

    24   Mr F. Taylor paid me $40 that he collected from Mr Stokes & Bray for House Rent. I rote a pass for John & William to the Theatre and for Lewis and Steven for the Circus — Old Middleton pays me his wages, $3.75

    25   A Race between Mr Rushlows Arabb horse and Mr Claibournes Sorrel mare Antelope   Twas won by Antelope by about a quarter of a mile   Col B. won about $1600 from 2 men, 15.00 from Mr Beasly & one hundred from Elias Burns — I worked untill 11 Oclock and made $7.37½, then gave the Boys all they could make untill night. John & William made $8.50   The Presidents Message[73] was Received in town Last Evening and was struck off to Day. Mr Mellens office — Mc got on his Horse to ride out to the tract and his Horse ran Down the Hill by his House and threw him and broke his Left Arm. He was caught by a Boy who got on him and the Horse threw him Amediately. One of Mr Bells Boys was shot with a musket Ball threw the Left shoulder by Floyd the Black smith. He was ordered to stop and he would not stop so Floyd and Mr Carpenter both shot at him. Carpenter had his gun Loadened with Buck shot[74] Mr McAlister sells his Brick store, now ocupied as a ware house, 27 feet front, to Messrs. Patterson and Wiswall for $20,000.[75]

    26   I Bought the following Articles and put the[m] up for John to take up to Jackson

Eight Razors	$5.37½	2 Shaving Brushes	.50
One Razor Strap	.75	1 Metalic Shaving Box &	
2 pair of sissors	1.50	soap	1.00
1 Box Powder & Puff	1.25	1 Flesh Brush	1.25
2 Bottles Lavender water	.50	1 Comb	12½
1 Razor Hone Loaned	00	3 Cakes of fine Soap	1.25
		1 Flesh Brush Large	.75

73 See James D. Richardson (ed.), *A Compilation of the Messages and Papers of the Presidents, 1789–1897*, 10 vols. (Washington, 1896–99), III, 147–77.

74 Floyd and Carpenter were probably members of the volunteer night patrol.

75 On March 27, 1835, Samuel T. McAlister informed the public that he had sold the entire stock of his merchandise business to L. M. Patterson and Samuel Wiswall, Jr. For Patterson & Wiswall advertisements, see Natchez *Courier*, September 11, 1835, February 25, April 18, 1839, December 28, 1841. In 1837 the firm established a branch in the town of Washington.

I went to the track but there was no race and I came Home quick   Sterns[76] begins to work for Mc   The New Building Commences to give away on the Front Pillars — I sent a Letter to Mrs Miller on the Bunker Hill. I sent a Barrell of Pork to the Boat & She was too full to take it so it was returned.

27   I went up in the Evening to see Mc and I staid up there about an hour. Came home to super. William & John & Bill Nix staid out untill ½ 10 O'clock at night. When the[y] came they knocked so Loud at the Door and made so much noise that I came Out with my stick and pounded both of the Williams and J.   John ran Out of the Yard and was caught by the Padroll, Mr McConnell and Reynolds. I made Mr McConnell give him 12 or 15 Lashes with his Jacket off[77] — Loaned Mrs Benbrook 1.00

28   Hard Heart was put up at Auction was not sold, $2000 Bid on him   Mr Thomas Ellis Bought Little Billy, $805. Col Bingaman takes John Home to go with him to Jackson — Neibut & Gemell props up the New Building for fear of its falling   Mr Rowes tells me about my carts, how long they worked &c   Mr Roberson casted Mr R English in court, gained the girl Nancy and $600 Damages

29   Col Throckmorton returns from his plantation   Mr Hale From Wilkerson County also — I Loaned Mr Jones some Corn to feed his Horses with at 12 Oclock in the Day — I went [to] Mr Rowans to shave Mrs Leonards Head, But did not   She was Dressed to ride Out.

30   I Received a Bank Notice from the Agricultural Bank To pay a note of mine Drawn in favor of Flecheux for $624.43, Endorsed by Mc, payable the notice stated, on the 7 & 18th of

---

[76] Washington Sterns (also spelled Stearns and Sterne) was a free Negro barber who occasionally worked for both Robert McCary and William Johnson. His brother, Walter, was also a barber.

[77] At this time Natchez had a volunteer night patrol, although there was considerable agitation for a tax-supported system. On January 15, 1836, the editor of the Natchez *Free Trader* urged: "We cannot but observe with regret the want of a proper 'night watch.' We have now a *volunteer watch*, numerous, active and faithful, but still not a *proper* watch. It may be the best for the present moment, but it is too heavy a tax upon our business men, and destructive to their health. Can we not have a 'watch' organized in the same effective manner as in other cities, to be paid by the city? Would it not be better than the present mode? All would then be taxed according to the property at stake; whereas, now, some who have the most at stake, may be prevented by delicate health from turning out at all, thus making it bear more heavily upon others." A paid "City Guard," armed with "short swords," was finally created in March, 1838, by an ordinance of the board of selectmen. Natchez *Free Trader*, March 29, 1838.

January, 1836, tho when I gave the note I thought it was payable on the 15th of January instead of the 7th   I herd from the steward of [the] Lady Washington that E Miller had came Home. I wrode up to see Mc   Found him seting in his arm chair and ageting Better. I Received a Letter from E Miller. He had Just got Home. Complained a good Deal about how badly Madison treated him — I wrote to E Miller by the same mail   I Received a Bank Notice for Mother, a note of Her's Due J Soria payable 1s./4th of January, 1836 — Endorsed by S. A. McAlister payable in the Planters Bank — Col Bingaman Leaves here for Jackson Legislature[78] — I Received the First number of the Mississipian, printed at Jackson. Printed and Edited by Col Fall and His Brother

31   A Weding at Mr McAlister   Miss Nancy Roundtree gets married to a Mr [blank]   They were married by Esqr. Carson — The Furniture of the Reverned Geo. Potts was sold at Soria's Auction Room. I Bot four Blankets at $2 per Blanket — I Bot a Duch Barbers Chair   Pd $6.00 for it

1836

January 1   I Loaned Capt. Longcope my Horse to wride out to Mr Turners. He came Back very much pleased with Him, told me that he would prehaps take him at my price which was $200.

2   Just before Day this morning I herd the cry of fire   I jumped up almost Naked and ran over to Mr Bells with a Bucket of water   The fire was then Burning in Mr Harris's ware or cotton yard, I worked at Mr Bells untill after Day Light. I then went over to the City Hotel & worked there with the water at the pump untill 12 Oclock and then the Engine quit work.[1] I then

---

[78] Bingaman was speaker of the lower house from 1834 to 1836.

[1] The fire gutted the block bounded by Franklin, Wall, Main, and Canal streets, and caused a loss estimated at over $50,000, of which only $10,000 was recoverable through insurance. The damage to the Mansion House, at the corner of Franklin and Wall streets, was estimated at $7,000, while nearly one half of the City Hotel, about the center of the block on Main Street, was ruined. For a complete report on the fire, see Natchez *Free Trader*, January 8, 1836.

came Home to my shop and worked until night — I took Steven in the shop to work at the trade

3   A man was arrested and taken to Jail on suspicion of having set fire to the Cotten Yard of Mr Harris — He had offered to bet $50 with a man that there would be a fire at the time the above fire took place and I herd that he also offerd to [bet] that there would be a Larger fire in two weeks than the fire that tooke place yesterday night — On the strength of those Bets he was taken up and put in Jail — Rode up to Mcs in the Evening   Found him siting by the Bed side in a Chair   We talked about a half Hour &c

4   I took up my Note in the Agricultural Bank, payable 1st/4th inst. for $154.75 Drawned in Favor of R. McCary. Endorsed on the Back P M. Lapiece, S. T McAlister. It was given for Property that I Bought of Mr Lapiece. I also took up a note of my Mothers Drawed in favor of J Soria and Indorsed by S. T McAlister for $100.00 given for a sick girl   Dr Welding wants to Borrow $22 for a Day or two. I told him I could not stand it   I made in cash to Day $21.62½ in the Shop shaving and Cuting Hair. I cut Parson Potts hair   Sterns wants to know what I thought of his taking that Fellow Berry to work with him in Mcs shop. I told him that I did not know anything about him — I cut Little Miss Howells hair. She gave me wrong directions about it — afterwards went to Old Sterns to have it Cut Over — Loaned Mother $100 to Pay Mr Murcheson for the woman Mary & her child Moses[2] — William went to shave Mr Vanison   He had shot his Hand

5   I shaved Mrs Leonards Head the 2d time   Cut a young girls hair at Mrs Masons — Cash by shaving and Hair Cuting, $17.12½   The[y] Commited the man Frilly to Jail by the Magistrate to awaite his tryal. I sent by Mr Monroe Robetile a Barrell of Pork to Mrs Miller   Cut Mr Chambers hair   He told me of Wms bringing him an impertinent answer

6   Buisness very Brisk — Mr Dolbear & Mr Valleau returns from New Orleans. Mr Page pd me 1.50 for a months

---

[2] Johnson made a number of loans to his mother, Amy Johnson, for slave purchases. In this case, his mother was paying an installment on the total purchase price of $800 for Mary and Moses. The slaves were purchased from Simon Murchison of the general merchandise firm of Murchison & Doyal. For announcement of Murchison taking Harrison Doyal into partnership in his firm, April 10, 1835, see Natchez *Courier*, September 10, 1835. In 1839 the firm reported total sales amounting to $20,000, which placed it among the larger Natchez firms. Auditor's Records, Tax Rolls, 1840, Adams County. For announcement of dissolution of the firm on April 25, 1840, see Natchez *Courier*, December 19, 1840.

shaving — Mr Harris sends in his Account for the Bacon that we Bot of him in the Summer — the Ammount $17.60   Cash by Hair Cuting & shaving $20.12½   The weding was to day or to night of the widow Minor to Mr Howell

7   I pd. Mr W. Harris $17.60 for Bacon that we Bought some time ago. Went up to see old Mc   Found him on the mend.   Made in cash $17.37½, also sold a Razor for $2.00   Mr Garnet Howell gets married very privately to Mrs Minor, the widow of Mr Steven Minor Deceased — Some One attempted to set Mrs Cornells House on fire[3]

8   Cash in the shop $15.75   I sold a pair of Razors to Mr Chaille for $5.00   Made a bargain with Mr Reaton to set his Razors for One year for 3 Dollars per year   I Loaned him one of my Razors — Old Sterns Cetches Dick stealing money from the draw[er] — Dick ranaway carrying with him the Days work $5 and what he himself had, making in all about $10. — Steven went Out — The patroll caught him and whiped him and I whiped him myself in the morning afterward

9   News from Jackson that Mr Vannorman is Elected President of the Senate. Mr Irvin Elected Speaker of the House of Representatives[4]   Dr Griffin arrived from New Orleans — Mr Phipps arrived also from Red River   William shaves Mr Boynton at Mr Bells   Sick   Old Middleton pd me $3.75   Walker pd me $6.00   Cash by Shop 14.50

10   Went up to see Mc   We talked together a Little while — I then came home, had my Horse saddled and wrode out as far as Mr Nevits Plantation.[5]   I shot a Bird with my pistol — Between 8 and 9 Oclock to night the fire Broke Out in a House the next door below the Barber shop ocupied by John Williams, Barber — He was taken and his wife and children and put in Jail. I worked very hard at the fire, tore my coat all to pieces in the Back, spoiled my Boots also — The town full of Gards the same

---

3 The building was saved through the prompt work of several citizens, led by Van Winkle, the editor of the Natchez *Courier.* In reporting the fire the Natchez *Free Trader,* January 8, 1836, urged: "The recent loss of property, probably caused by some villian, in connection with this attempt, is sufficient to induce a general call upon the City Council to adopt such measures as will insure the organization of an energetic police or *night watch,* so that our citizens may sleep under strong assurance of safety."

4 Johnson referred to William Van Norman and John L. Irvin.

5 Johnson referred to Captain John B. Nevitt's Clermont plantation, a short distance up the Mississippi River from Natchez.

night. I Came home about ½ after ten Oclock. Loaded my Gun and garded my yard untill ½ after 2 Oclock[6]

11   Sterns did not work at the shop for he had been Burnt out yesterday Night — I sent Bill Nix to work in his place — He made $4.37½. Mc gave him 1 Dollar   Mrs Dunns Servants taken up by the Padroll   A white man taken up that Left there the same Evening — Mr Stantons Cotten Yard was set on fire or there was an attempt to set it on fire, in the Noon Day time by Some Dareing Ras[c]al or other — Mr Wells Stable was found with fire in some part of it in the daytime also — I went out about 9 Oclock at night and Garded my yard untill 12 Oclock — The padroll took up 12 or 15 persons about the streets — Col Throckmorton returns from Jackson Late at night — Big town Meeting

12   I Loaned Dr Welding $15 for 4 Days Only — The Commity Examined John Williams & Family, two other Blacks, also the white man that was taken up at Mrs Cornells, also her Servants. They were all acquited and Discharged. It was thought that the fire was the Effect of Accident   I was Out on Gard in my Yard untill 10 Oclock precisely. It then Commenced raining and I went to bed. The Frenchman Robatile came along the street drunk making a noise. The guard threatened to put him in the Guard House. He then cooled off & promised to go home peaceably   I Bot a Razor Hone for Mr Fleming, price $1.50   I gave a gold piece worth $10.66 away to some One through a mistake for 50 cents

13   Mr Bray and his Journeman by the name of Rontz had a quarrell — Rontz accused Nathaniel of stealing his knife— Bray Discharged him. The[y] both abused Each other. Bray had a Sword Cane and Rontz had a Brick Bat — Mr T. Evans came Down from his plantation Last week — Milton takes the measles and is sick   Mr Perkins on Padroll came very near having a fight with a Mr [blank] in front of Mr Barlows store — Perkins cocked his pistol at the other man   Mr Parker Keeps open house for three Days in consequence of the news arriveing of the Election of Mr Walkers being Elected Senitor with a ma-

---

[6] The Natchez *Free Trader*, January 15, 1836, reported that twenty-eight houses were burned at the landing of Natchez-under-the-Hill, resulting in a total loss of $110,000. "The state of things on Sunday night beggars description:—The citizens of the upper town upon the first impulse rushed towards the Landing. Then the startling cries of 'Its a plot to burn us up,' 'Don't leave the upper town,' 'Guard the banks,' 'Take care of your own property,' were wildly vociferated by a hundred voices. Every man turned out, almost every one with fire-arms, and regular patrols were established. Every square was guarded during the whole night, and every stranger stopped. Several persons were apprehended and lodged in jail."

jority of six votes, 2d balloting[7] — Mr Vernon Buys out the Interest of Lyons in the firm of Lyons & Metcalf

14   I Bought a Lantern to hang in the street   I pd Mr Vancampen $3 for it   I subscribed for Mr Maffits Christian Herrald[8] — Mr Sweney was arrested and put under gard at the Gard House   He was supposed to have Either set fire to Mrs Dunns House or Else he knew something about it — The fire was Discovered in the Room of Mrs Dunn — The Gard took Nancy Latimore[9] and Cut her all over her Back, whiped her very much. She went through the Market the next morning with her cloathes hanging all off at Each Shoulder. Her back was very much whiped   It was thought Dr. Lattimore made her walk in the Streets in that way

15   The Black Boy Jeff Belonging to the Miss Joys that Killed Collins the Overseerer for Mrs Minors Plantation was Hung — I herd To Day that Governor Quitman had killed a Gentleman by the name of Connelly in a Duel at Jackson — Col. S. Guinn and Mr Caldwell had a fight and they had Each of them 3 Pistols and they fired and advanced on Each other. The 3d shot Col Guinn shot Mr Calwell and killed Him — Mr Sweney was tryed and Discharged by the Committee — He came to shave to night with his pockets full of Pistols[10] — Messrs Holton and Bell and

7 Johnson referred to the election of Robert J. Walker to the United States Senate. He defeated the incumbent, George Poindexter, and served until 1845.

8 The *Mississippi Christian Herald* was published weekly at Natchez in 1835–36 as the official organ of the Mississippi Conference of the Methodist Episcopal Church. It was edited by the Reverend John Newland Maffitt, Irish-born Methodist clergyman who considered Natchez his home while he was editing the *Herald.* Maffitt gained contemporary fame by oratorical skill exhibited in sermons and lectures delivered in many sections of the United States. He first visited Natchez in his capacity as a revivalist in 1834, and during the next four years delivered several series of sermons and addresses there. See John G. Jones, *A Complete History of Methodism as Connected with the Mississippi Conference of the Methodist Episcopal Church, South,* 2 vols. (Nashville, 1908), II, 322, 331, 345, 348, 367, 387, 390–92; *Minutes of the Annual Conferences of the Methodist Episcopal Church, for the Years, 1829–1839* (New York, 1840), 368, 436, 518; W. C. Black, "A Centennial Retrospect; or, Methodism in Natchez, Miss., from 1799 to 1884," in Henry G. Hawkins, *Methodism in Natchez* (Jackson, 1937), 64–66; *Appleton's Cyclopaedia of American Biography,* IV (New York, 1888), 172.

9 Nancy Lattimore was a free woman of color, licensed to remain in the state in 1832. Evidently she was still under control of Dr. David Lattimore. See Adams County Court and Police Board Minutes, 1832–45, March, 1832; Adams County Deed Records, CC, 46.

10 The Natchez *Free Trader,* December 8, 1836, in deprecating the "many sad consequences resulting from wearing weapons," stated that the practice "has become almost a passion throughout the whole south and south-west." The same article quoted the Memphis *Enquirer*: "It is almost a strange sight in this section of the country, to see a man whose bosom heaves not under a ponderous butcher knife,

Harris and Hunt were all making fun of Rabby — they thought him too smart Entirely

16   Dr Benbrook Came over to night to Borrow $20 but I Could not Loane it, so I told him — Bill Nix shaves Little Bills Head and he puts on a wig — I Sold Mr John Pottses wig to Mr Bennit for $16.00. I offered him the money for it but he told me that I could keep it and pay myself what he owed me Out of it and pay the ballance over to him — The report concer[n]ing Gov. Quitman of yesterday is not true

17   Last night there was another Attempt to fire Mrs Cornells House — There [was a] gard out side and inside of the House and yet they could not Discover how it Commenced. Mr Arlet was on Gard at the time that the fire took place. It is my Candid Opinion that Mrs Dunn must have done it Herself or had it done — public sentiment is very much against her — I wrode Out as far as Capt. Nevits old field to tame my Horse. When I got Out there I shot at the mark with my Pistol — made some prety good shots — made in cash in the Shop $15.62½ and Mr E G. Howell paid me $6.00.

18   I took up my note Drawn in favor of J Duval and Endorsed by R. McCary payable in the Agricultural Bank for $624.43. The old Coulerd Gentleman from up Coumberland River in Tennessee Came Down with his Flat Boat. He had Cows, Hogs, Sheep, Geese, Turkeys, Ducks, and chickens — His Brother in Law Named Moore came with him — I presented my Account against Fletcheo for 5 months Rent to the 1st of January, 1836, Ammounting to $70.00 — He only paid me $28.00   Mr Hustons Furniture is sold at Auction at Messrs Sprague and Howells store — I wrode Down to the Oil mill to see the cows in the Flat Boat — Mr Ballard Buys Out Mr D Stantons store and goods — pd for the House alone $25,000.

19   I Loaned Mother $20 to pay Selser the Butcher with. Mr Newman pd me $5.00 that he Borrowed from me Last week — I wrode Out to old Mrs Mahams to see what she [would] charge me a month for my Horses to run in Her cane pastore   The old Lady said that the fence were all Broken Down &c. We Bought two cows from the Flat Boat at $25 a cow — Mother Bot 47 geese from same Boat at 75 cts per goose   Mr

---

brace of pistols, or glittering dirk . . . How many have fallen innocent victims to this desperate vice!" See also David L. Cohn, *The Good Old Days* (New York, 1940), 431.

Cashion Hankerson Died. William shaved him — William went to shave Mr Baynton at the tavern

20   The Fencibles Buried Mr Hankerson out at Gov'ner Quitmans Place[11] — I paid $50.00 to Moore of the Flat Boat for 2 Cows — I Loaned Mother to pay for her geese at the same time $6.25   Mrs Gellespie Died Late this Evening — Stokes came down the River

21   Dr Griffin paid me $15 for shaving & hair cuting up to this Date — I sent Mr Miller five months wages up to the 24th of January — Except One week for Christmas — the whole Amount of wages up to Date was $71.25   I then took out 22 dollars for Pork that was sent down and also $27.75 for 3 Pictures or En- gravens and 3.75 cents for the week he did not pay me, making my Account against Him $53.50, Leaving a Ballance in his favor of this amount, $17.75, by Mr Tosspott. Stokes and another man by the name of Faning has a fight in the street. He snaps a pistol at Stokes — Baker took them Both up   Articles That I Bought From John Williams at the Landing on account of his going up the River —

2 Dozen of Winships Camphor Soap	1 old Thermometer
4 Papers of Coate Plaster, new	2 old Hair Brushes
7 Tooth Brushes — new	1 Hat Brush
10 Shaving Brushes — new	3 old Razors Straps
14 Shaving Razors	3 pair sissors & 1 Broken pair
2 Bran new Razors	2 Little Small Looking Glasses
16 old Razors, no good	1 tin Box with powder and puff
4 Emty cases	2 glass Jars, 1 Large the other Small
12 fine tooth combs, new	
1 small Table with a draw[er]	1 Barbers chair — Broke at the Back
9 Roller towels	
15 Small hand Towels	

Mr Isaih Bray gets married to Miss Caroline Polkinghorn the Plas- terers Daughter

22   I went up the street to see Mr. Lyons about geting John for he had told me the Day before that I could get him if I wanted Him

23   John Came to stay with me To Lern the trade — I Bot a stove from Mr Marsh for $12. He paid $10 for it — I Bot 4

[11] For an excellent journalistic account of the history of the plantation, see Edith Wyatt Moore's article in Natchez *Democrat*, Pilgrimages Edition, 1943.

vests at Auction at Sorias at 1.37 per vest — I bot John a pair of pantaloons and a Roundabout and vest at Mr Barlows and Taylors, cash $6.56   I also got Milton a pair pantaloons, vest and Round Jacket at Mr Barlows, the[y] amounted [to] $7.25 or 7.75 I do not recollect which — They were Charged to Col Bingaman by orders from Mr Lewis Bingaman — I went arround to the Court House to see if Tom Steel had sued or not before Esqr Cook for I paid the cost myself — Tom Steele came around and paid me the $30.00 that he Borrowed from me on the 20th day of July, 1835. He promised to pay it in three Days after he got it from me — About 9 Oclock I went up To Mrs Thomsons to get Her to come to Ann — Commenced Raining about 10 Oclock and rained all night or very near it   About 12 Oclock William was Borned[12]

   24   I rode up to McCarys in the afternoon—we talked about a greate many things. Sterns Brought my Old Dream Book home 3 days ago — To day he had all the Boys in Mcs Shop Cuting Shines — I gave Bill Nix a pair of Boots, also John a pair of boots — Milton Bot his Boots for $3. Little Bill Bot a pair shoes at 1.25   At one Oclock to night sent for Dr Hogg to see the Baby

   25   I Bot 5 dozen of wash Ball soap from Sorias Auction, 87½ cts per   Mr Dolbear pays me up to the present date $3.00   Mr Phipps pays me to present date $4.00   Mr Elick Stewart came home from up the River — Mr Hough returns from N Orleans — Went [to] Mrs Howels to cut young Miss S. Minors hair   I got a Bottle of Castor Oil at Dashiels & Potts — I sent Mrs Miller the money a day or two ago which pd Middletons wages up to this very day the 24th, to yesterday I ment

   26   Dr Hogg[13] came to get shaved. I requested him to walk up and see the Baby — he did so and prescribed some Powders. The[y] were in 3 seperate papers — they were to be given in a Little Sugar or Molasses — To repeat One Every third hour untill they were all taken — continued takeing the Sperrits of Nitre until the Child makes Dilleau — This medicine was not taken, we thought it too strong — Middleton pays his weeks wages, Last weeks wages — Mrs Lieper goes down to Maj Dunbars to see Harriet Mitchel who is and was very sick — Mr Lewis Bingaman gets a pair of Razars for the Col. He said had sent to Him from

---

[12] This was William Johnson, Jr. (later known as William R. Johnson), the eldest of the diarist's ten children. In later years January 24 was regarded as the proper birthday of William, Jr. The infrequent references to the mother in this diary usually designated her as "my wife" or "Ann."

[13] This was Dr. Samuel Hogg, who several times administered to Johnson's family. His office was on Main Street, and he lived in the Mansion House hotel.

Jackson to get him a pair — Dr. $4.00   A Mr Donelson Commen[c]es by the month to shave   I gave Mrs Bennet $25 for her attention &c. to my wife   Patty Dobbins sucks the tit for the Child — also does Lucy Barret   Mrs Thomson was down to see the Baby to day — Mr Walker puts up my stove and pipe

27   Was a report that Gov. Reynols and Judge Quitman was agoing to fight a Duell in a few days, tho not generally believed — I herd of the Indians killing A greate many people at Tampee Bay, Killing all at one fort[14] — All the Soldiers from Baton Rougu had gone after the Indians. The Citizeens Left alone to gard the Barracks and the Town — Last night Walker Came Home Drunk and sliped off again. I then went under the Hill to Look for him — I intended to mall him well but I could not find him and to night he Came home the Same way — I did not strike him but came very near it — A Mr Donnelson Commences by the month to Shave   The Rail Road Delegation Leaves this place for Jackson. Mr R Gains was One of them. The[y] Left 2 or 3 days ago — Pd for marketing a week $6.00

28   The Bunker Hill arrives from New Orleans — I Received 2 News papers and One Letter   The Letter Acknowledges the receipt of the money that I sent to Mr Miller, up to the 24th of January, 1836 — Mr Wm Henry very sick,   Also states that Warner was playing the fife in Orleans for a recruiting Party for Florida against the Indians   The Captain refered to Mr Miller for his character and Mr Miller would not say nothing for Him nor against Him so the[y] took him any How — Col. Throckmorton returns from his Plantation at midnight Last night — Mr W. Harris Leaves here to night for Jackson, Miss. I Bot a Bale of Hay, wt. 435 lbs, cash $7.75 — I spoke for a box in the Post office — Hester Commings sat up Together with Mrs Battles with the child.

29   Louis Winsborough[15] sends me over a Pitcher of Coffee — very good coffee   The old Black man pd me for 4 days hyre of my mule 1.50 — I pd. for ten Barrells of Coal and the Hauling in all $7.50   A Mr Hunter I think gets his hair cut a few days

---

14 Johnson probably referred to the depredations of the Seminole Indians in the vicinity of Tampa Bay.

15 The census of 1840 listed one L. D. Winsborough as a white resident of Natchez with one free person of color in his family, and in the same year he ran a "Natchez Landing" advertisement in a local newspaper. U. S. Census Reports, 1840, Schedule I, Adams County, 26; Natchez *Courier*, August 22, 1840. Perhaps "Louis Winsborough" was the free Negro.

ago and has it charged to the Herald office, also Mr T. J. Finny gets a bottlee of Bears Oil, to same office, price 37½   The Calf Eats of[f] a part of my Horses Tale in the Stable yesterday morning — Last night Hester told Mrs B and myself that ————— ————— widow was in the Family way by her Overseer, ————— —————, who married one of the Miss ————— — She stated that Mrs ————— was a going to Kentucky before Long To have the Child I presume   She said that one of Mrs ————— girls told her [mother] how Bad it Looked because her Overseer was a married man — She answered — What if he was!   She did not care for he was only married to a Negro — I subscribed to a Periodical and Geografical work to day to be delivered in April, Cost $10 or will be $10 when it comes

  30   I paid Walker the tinner $7.50 for stove pipe.   I got a note from Young Bill Haden[16] for $10, which sum I Loaned him, by the hand of the Black man that came for it — I went after Dr Hogg to get him to Come to the Baby — He did so and prescribed Borax and Castor Oil — Three Races to day but it Rained so Hard that I did not go out

  31   Mc Came Down to my shop in the Evening.   I Cut his hair and I Read Governer McDuffee[17] speech to him — on Slavery and Abolition — We both got tyred of it before I had finished it — I wrode Out in the Evening as far as the Race track and ran my horse in the old field against Pollow & Oscar — Mother gets a Cow from Mr Whiting price $15 — Aunt Jinna came to see the Baby — Big Larence came to Blow upon it to cure it of the thrush   Gave my Boys and people altogether in all to day $3.87½

  February 1   I wrode Out to the Race tract — A 2 mile Race and repeat between Mr O. S. Clabourne's Bay Mare Energy and Mr Harmons Grey mare Naked Truth   Energy got Distanced. I Lost $5 with Mr Woods that stays out at Harmons — St Clair Lost His Little Bay Horse — Mr Gocian won him   He Bet $250 against him. Mr Tom Cemp & Jocian has a quarrell   Mr Cemp

  [16] "Young Bill Haden" (or "Haden's Boy") was the son of a Negro barber named William Haden, who had been freed in Kentucky in 1824. The elder Haden had come to Natchez in the same year, and had been granted permission to remain in the state by a special act of the legislature in 1828 and by the Adams County Police Board in 1832. Adams County Deed Records, O, 480; Petitions of William Haden, undated, Petitions and Memorials, Series I, No. 100, No. 101; *Laws of Mississippi*, 11 Sess. (1828), 48–49; Auditor's Records, Tax Rolls, 1829, 1834, Adams County; Adams County Court and Police Board Minutes, 1832–45, March, 1832.
  [17] Governor George McDuffie of South Carolina.

told him that he thought him beneath his notice and Gocian Cursed him — the thing was hushed up — I hyred my Horse and Cart to Mr Noyes at 1.50 per day — The Bunker Hill Left here to day for New Orleans — I wrote a Letter to Mrs Miller but had not a chance to send it — the Boat Left

2   I had to whip Little Bill & John for fighting in the shop — I shaved Mr Arlets Head To night — He pd me $2 for a months Shaving — Yesterday a Boat Brought News that the Florida Indians had Taken Talahasa and Apalashacola Both — but To day the S B Jone Came up, C Giles Clerk — he stated that the news that was Received yesterday Respecting the Indians is not true — that it was false, unfounded   I Received a Letter from the Capt and he wanted to know if he could hyre young Bill Haden — he offered to give $20 per month to have him work with him

3   A Race one mile out for $500 a side Between Mr Crysers Robbin angainst Mr O Clabournes Bay mare Jennee — she won the Race very Easy — Dr Welding pd me $16.50 for $15 that he Borrowed from me on Tuesday, January 13th inst — Press Brice knocks a man down at the Race track and Beats Him — Nickols made him stop Beating him — I Loaned Mr Whiting $50 to be paid in a week to me again

4   I Bot three Coats at Auction at Sorias — 1 Black close Bodied price $17 and 1 frock green $19.50 and one dito $19, for the three I paid him $55.50   I sent John to carry a Red Bird with the cage to Mrs Howells Little Daugter Stevania   Mr Kane ran his Grey Horse against an unkept Bay mare One mile Out for $50 — She won the race very Easy — Little Bon has Haydens Black woman offered at Auction but she was not sold to day — Mr [blank] at Skeggs & Hougs pd me $3.75 and Left this place   Mr Page pd me $1.50 for one months shaving

5   Little Bon sells Hadens woman at Auction for $810 To S. T McAlister   Old Mr Berthe Died this morning — I Loaned my horse to Mr Gubert to go to the Funeral — Mr Taylor and myself repaird my Big Glass Frame

6   I lost $2.50 beting with H Cobler on J Steels Horse agains J Holdens horse   Holdens Horse won the Race — Mr Noyes sent me $7.50 for the hyre of my Horse & Cart for 5 days, Ending to day — Little Bill takes around the Herrald News paper and the generous man gave him 25 cents after his walking about three hours with the papers

7   The Boys, 3 of them, went Out to the Race track in the

afternoon on my work Horses — Mc came up to see my Little Son. I gave old French $2.00 — Some infernal Rascal tyed a tin spout to my Bay Horses tail, also a piece to my Grey Horse's tail — If only knew who it was I wont say here what I would do — The white Haired young Fellow that Drives the Hack Drove up to Mr Parkers door to night and Mr Cary from Woodville was in it — He had Lost his hat and cap and he was chaseing the Hack Driver around the Hack to whip him — so the fellow to save himself from whiping he ran off and Left his Hack — His friend that works at Lankershires Came up and Cary cursed him and would not permit him take the Hack away so the fellow ran off to get a pair of Pistols — He came back again and the man Cary Gave him a wonderfull kick — The fellow ran Back and drew his Pistol But the friends of the drunking man took him in the Tavern

8   Some infernal Rascal tyed a tin [blank] to my Paganinnis tail and he ran up the street in that fix — I hyred my Horse and Cart to day about 11 Oclock to Mr Noyes

9   Mr. Maffitt gets his hair cut, 25 cts, and a Bottle of Bears Oil, 37½, and a cake of soap, 37½   The Irishman has my Horse and cart all day to day — Mr Keaton gets Razors that I set for him

10   The Irishman got my Horse to day 3 or four Hours — I Loaned Dr Benbrook $3. He pd it to night — I put the Note that I Received from C Dart Ammounting to $350 in the Planters Bank for Collection, Indorsed by Mr Steadman — I took the note in part pay for a Lot that I sold him in August Last. Elick Barland Bot a Bay mare at auction for $170 at 12 months credit — Mr McIntosh Williams and Dr Smith Bot Each one of them a nag a piece — Yes, Barland Bot another Brown mare also — Same Credit — Dr Griffin gets his Razors, set of them, and a pot of soap at 50 cents — Mr J. Potts came down from his plantation — Dr Cartwright pd 1.25 — Mr Geoge Lancaster Bot a 3 year old sorril filly, price $145 — credit — I loaned Mr Carroll $10 to be returned in the morning

11   Mr James Caradine gets married to Miss Mary I. A. Sample a Grand Daughter of old Mr Hendersons   I told Wiswall that Mother sold Mr Gridley a turkey as he thought but it was a Chicken — Mr Rowes sends my new honeing table home — Wellington Leaves here on the Bunker Hill for New Orleans   I Loaned Dr Benbrook $6 to be returned in the morning — paid I presume   A Mr Smith from Lake Washington was robbed of $250.00 at Mr Bells by one of his servants — they whiped 2 of them — They got $150 of the money — Mc shaved Soria 1st time since his arm was Broke

12 I paid my account at Messrs Wiswall & Pattersons store amounting to $20.62½ Mr [blank] pd me $18 which pays up his account to the first of March, 1836 — Mr Whiting pays me $50 that He Borrow from me on Wednesday the 3d inst — Mr Carroll pd me $10 that I Loaned him Wednesday 10th inst — Mrs Mellen has a Little Boy child named [blank]

13 Cut Mr Finnys hair 25 cts — St Clair runs his grey Horse that he Bot the other day against Mr Mardices mare for $50. She won very Easy — Milton & John Broke my cart — I took in in all this week $117.87½ My Expenses this week was $50.94 — Clear proffit $87.00 Capt. Nevit and Mr Thom Ellis gets Back to night from Jackson

14 Mr Lohe Died up at Mr J Fergusons — Mc and myself went under the Hill — Saw good many people Drunk — I gave Wm $2. Mr R M Gains returns from Jackson this Evenining — Mrs Gains has a Little Daughter Born to night

15 Mr. Lohe was Buried this Evening at 3 Oclock — Mr Gains hair cut & shave 37½ F T. Griffith also — I made a Bet with Mr Mardice to day that Red Mariah would Beat Hard Heart the Race provided she did not Bolt — the Race to be run next Saturday

16 The martins were flying about — I Loaned Dr Reed Potts $250.00 — Mr R. J. Walkers old Furniture was sold at Auction I wrote to Capt E Miller by a Mr Green — Young Bill Haden Left here to day for Vicksburg He promised to pay E. Miller $10 that I Loaned him

17 I Sold Capt. Nevit five work Horses and a mule — there names as follows & prices —

Big Bay Horse, Fiddler.................. $80.00
Black Horse, Black Hawk............... $35.00
Black Horse, Gelespie.................. $35.00
Old Ball.............................. $25.00
Grey Horse, John...................... $50.00
Little Dan, the Mule.................. $40.00

Mr Spielman wants to Buy 2 feet of Land from me on the uper side of my Lot — offerd me $200 for two feet — I weighed 140 weight, old Mc weiged me — Col Throckmorton returns from his plantation

18 Lade has a calf in the stable this Evening — McCray

gets married to Miss Galbrath — They were married up at old Mrs McGuyere's house up starers — The Boys Eats old Frenchs Cake & Miltons   Old French for pay was about to steal 2 Bits from the draw[er] — Messrs Holtons and Barlows sells Out there old Furniture that was saved from the fire — Mr J. Perry has a fight with Mr Crow and knocks him down with a chair and hurt him on the very much

19   The old woman[18] Buys a good many Birds — doves, Red Birds &c. The Bunker Hill came   I got a paper by her

20   The Race to day between Red Mariah & Cassandra was won fairly by R. Mariah But after the judges once gave it in favor of R. Mariah they afterwards turned and made it a Dead Heat — Old Dr Branch & A Stranger & Mr John P. Smith were the judges   Mr Ja. Perry was perfectly wronged in the race and he told them so — abused Mr Lee Clabourn for all sorts of D—— rascals & Dm thieves, rouges and Every thing else that he Could Lay his tounge to — He shoved Mr Os Clabourne Back 3 times and struck him Once — They were all armed and it was thought that they would fight but neither of the Clabournes would strike — Old Mc won $10 from Love on his ½ mile Race with the other Butcher   I Lost on Cassandra $5 with Burton & I Lost $5 on a Brown Horse that Ran 1 mile with Mr Mardice, and I Lost $10 with a Butcher on Lancasters Roan horse — I gave old Bob Larrence $2. Exppences and charges against me this week is $52.

21   I wrode out to the tract and there was a Quarter Race between Wakefields [horse] and a Long tail old grey Horse. I won $2.50 from Minet and he paid it. I Bet him 2 to one — Wakefields horse won the Race very Easy — Messrs Elliot, Bush, and Emerson and Mr Rowan came up in the Shakespeare from New Orleans — Little Robt McCary was taken very sick, had to send for Dr Hog. Two Oclock in the night the child took a fit also — My Little son taken sick also this Evening

22   Mr F. Taylor paid me in cash $25 and a Hat that I got which was $5 was charged to me also making in all which he settled for to day $30. This money is some that is due me from Messrs Stokes & Bray — The amount of there Account for the up stairs part of the House is in all to the 7th day of February $118. From this amount Mr Taylor has paid me in this $70 which Leaves them still in my Debt up to the 7th of Feb. $48 — I sold Louis Winsborough a Frock Coat that I Bot at Auction for $19.50 on a Credit until he could Raise the money — To day it was that Mr Minet

---

18 Amy Johnson, the diarist's mother.

whom I won the $2.50 from yesterday Claimed the money and said that he won it — We drew the money for I knew he had no kind of right to it what Ever — A Race for $500 to day between Mr J Perrys Lucilla and Mr Rochleaus Horse Laquett by Arab. Lucilla won the Race very Easy — 1 mile heats

23   I bot a Bale of Hay to day and had to pay $2 a hundred for it. I had the Lampus Burned out from my ho[r]se — I had to Beat Steven this morning for taking the shop key away and was not ready to open the Shop

24   A Race To Day between those Horses Sally Hope owned by F. Ruth, Chuckfohila by Col. A L. Bingaman, Betsy Smith by Mr J Smith or Peyton, Long tale Blue by Mr Claybourne   Those Horses came out just as they are Entered on this Book — 4 mile heats — There were a Bet of One thousand Dollars between the Last 2 named Nags — L. T. Blew Lost the Race by runing over a Little Black Boy belonging to Col. Bingaman   Mc was out with me   I won on the Race $5 from Mr Whiting And $5 from Mr Floyd, this on a credit — pd — Capt. John B. Nevit paid me $250.00 for five Horses and one mule that he Bot from me on Wednesday the 17th inst — Dr Reed Potts paid me $50.00, a part of $250.00 that I Loaned him on the 16th inst — The Bunker Hill Left here to Day — I sent for a wig in a Letter to Mrs Miller for Dr Harden and to know if Mr Miller would take a Boy of Maj Youngs   A Race between Lukes Horse & Winns Horse One mile Out   The Judges Decided that it was a Dead Heat, a Draw Race. Nat. Woods & Miss Nixon, She is a Grand Daughter of Mrs Hankerson, were to slip off together and get married privately But they were stoped — Mr T. Henderson is Her Agent — I herd that when he was a talking to her about marrying so young &c. that she sat with her Back to him singing And when he Left the door of the Room she made a noise with her mouth in the tone of a Buster — Our old Dog Venus Died of Dropsey Late at Night

25   I Loaned Mr Spieelmand $300.00   I told Mr F. Taylor in presence of Mr Bray that I thought about 4 months Rent was due me at $6 per month for the worke shop in the yard which would be $24.00   It was agreed on instantly by Mr. Bray — Mr Whiting paid $5 that I won from him yesterday on Sally Hope VS Chuckfohila. I herd to Day that Miss Mary Gatewood had got married to a Mr [blank] — I went for Dr Hogg to come and see the Baby — His perscription was some kind of Powders Every other hour, 3 powders — A gentleman from Wilkerson County Came in the Shop drunk — he gave Bill Nix $2

   26   A Race to day between Naked Truth and Betsy Evans — Naked Truth won the race very Easy — 3 mile heats — I Came off winr to day $13   I won $5 worth of cold from Mr McFadgin & I won $5 in cash from old Mc & I won $2 from Mardice & I won $2 from St. Clair & $5 from St Claire on another race and I Lost $6 with H. Cobler

   27   A Race between Antelope (Clabourne) James Polk (H. Smith)   She won the race, 2 mile heats — tho the Horse won the second Heat she won the 2 Best in three — Mr Gocian was thrown from his Horse Naty Cetcher and got his rib Broke. The Porter man Mr McGetrick, his horse ran away with the cart and threw him out and knocked him speachless, cut his Head — He fell in the Byou[19] at McFaddins Landing — Mr J Spielman paid me $300.00 that I Loaned him on Thursday the 25th inst — Myself & Mc won from Little John, the Race rider, $10. He bet that Jim Polk would not win a heat. I Bet Louis Winsborough a pair of fine Morrocks boots that Hard Heart would beat Red Mariah, the Boots not to cost Less than $7. I got 8 Barrels of coal from Mr McFadin to day, $5 worth of it I won from him — I Loaned Shimond $100.00 to make up Her Even $500.

   28   Mr Nat Woods & Miss Nixon runs away together to get Married — Mr Louis Miller gets a musket and is runing about in search of them — She ran off about dinner time — McGetrick died at 10 Oclock — he was thrown out of his cart yesterday under the hill

   29   I called in Dr Hogg this Evening to see the child   He came in and wrote a perscription — it was Hive Syrup — Mr Donoi pd $3. I herd that Mrs Miller would be up this week about Saturday — The Jone & North Alibama came up this Evening. One of them had on Bourd McClain, the man that ran away with Mr Nights Money, $7980 — Nat Woods was married to day in Fayette to Miss Nixon   Js. Collier, Clerk of C &c.

March 1   The race between Red Mariah & Hard Heart took place to day, 4 mile Heats.[20] They ran the first 4 miles and She Beat him very Badly — This was conciderd no Heat — Mr Minor was perswaded to go and try to pay the forfeit But the Judges would not permit it for the stakes was up So they started again and She Beat

---

[19] Johnson used variant spellings of "bayou," as well as of numerous other words. In practically all cases they will be recognized without difficulty.

[20] This was the outstanding match race of the early 1836 season at Natchez. John G. Perry's Red Maria (which had been involved in two controversial races on November 2, 1835, and February 20, 1836) defeated William J. Minor's Hard

him very near a quarter of a mile   My Bets were as Follows —
1st I Bet Mr Mardice $10 that Red Mariah would win the race
— this I won, 2d I Lost on Hard Heart with Louis Winsborough
2 pair of Boots, cost $14 — Lost with Mr Wiswall a pair of Boots,
cost $7, the amount he took out in shaving — Myself and Mr G
Lancaster took a Bet of $50. I gave him one dollar to Let me in
for half — we Lost of course and my part was $26 — Mr Randolph
of S Carlina won it — The Balloon was to have gone up to day but
the weather was too Bad it could not[21] — It is the opinion of a great
many persons that Hard Heart was hurt in some way — Mr
McMurran & Col. Bingaman came in to night from Jackson Legislature — Mr La Vigne pd me for 5 months Rent $100 and I pd him
his account which was $24. It Left a Ballance in my favor $76
— Mr Underwood ranaway from this place.

2   The Balloon with a Mr Clayton in it assended this Evening at 5 Oclock — It was the most Beautiful & Splendid sight
Ever seen in this place before   A race took place to day that was
made Last night at the theatre, between Cassandra And a mare of
Mr Shelby & Jack Smith   Cassandra won the first heat, only by
a foot or Less and the 2d mile or 2d heat Mr Smiths mare took
the cramp at the start and was distanced, tho I did not see the
Race

Heart for a $5,000 bet. Rain and snow fell during the race, which was run on
a track fetlock deep in mud and water. The match had been announced several
months in advance. See *American Turf Register and Sporting Magazine*, VIII
(1836) , 90; *Spirit of the Times*, V (1835) , 8.

But Minor soon got revenge. Before the April meeting of the St. Francisville
(Louisiana) Jockey Club, Perry addressed a challenge "To the world in general,
and Mississippi in particular," offering to run his Red Maria against any horse in
the world in either two- or four-mile heats for bets up to $10,000. In answer to
this challenge, two of William J. Minor's entries, Betsey Malone (which he had
recently purchased for $3,000) and Linnet (owned by Thomas J. Wells, but
running under the Minor colors) defeated Red Maria in races in which Minor
won side bets totaling $5,000. *American Turf Register and Sporting Magazine*,
VII (1836) , 473–74, 567.

21 On February 19 the Natchez *Free Trader* carried the following notice: "On
the first of March Mr. Clayton will make an ascension from this city. He is the
same bold Aeronaut who in April last made a voyage from Cincinnati to the
Alleghany mountains, three hundred and fifty miles, in nine and a half hours.
The people of half the union have already witnessed his success, and the opportunity is now offered to the citizens of Natchez and its vicinity." His "aerial
vessel" was called *Star of the West*. The price of admission to see the inflation
and launching was $1.00, with half price for children. Clayton wrote an article
for the March 4 issue of the *Free Trader* in which he told of the sights and
sensations of his ascension. He landed about fifteen miles east of Natchez.

3   Property Entered on Mr Coles List, the assessor, 1836

my house & Lot at............... $4000
Steven at........................ $ 800
Sarah at......................... $ 500
Louis at......................... $ 300
Walker do........................ $ 55

Col Bingaman Sold His Boy Milton to Col Os Claibourne For Fifteen Hundred and Fifty Dollars.   He gave his note payable in 60 Days for the $1500 and he gave me the $50 for Learning the Boy to shave. Mr Chs. Wilkins Returned from New Orleans. He Brought me a Letter from Mr J Miller. He wished to know the particulars about the Boy of Maj Youngs and about the wig that I wrote for — Col. Gordon & Mr Farrar returned from Jackson, Miss   Mr Clayton came in town about 8 Oclock this morning — He Landed in his Balloon out at Mrs Millers place, 14 or 15 miles from town   Mr Mardice pd. me $2 that I won from him about a week ago

4   I made out my Account against Mr A. Flecho for House Rent and gave it to Mr F. Taylor for Collection   It was for five months Rent, Commencing on the 1st of November, 1835 up to the 1st of March, 1836, at $14 per month, $70.00   I also stated at the botom of the Note that after the first day of April Mr Flecho must pay me $20 per month if he kept the House   Mr Tom Steele sells his Lot at Auction. It was Bot by Mr. Gridley for $1760.00, one 3d cash and one 3d in 6 and the other in 12 months — The Lot joins Peter Little Property — Pollo and Mr McAlister dog has a fight — he wips Pollo. Mr Floyd pd me $5 that I won from him Wednesday 24th Feb., 1836 on the race between Sally Hope and Chuckfohila — Mrs Evans has a fine son at 3 or 4 Oclock this morning — To Day a note given by C Dart & Endorsed by Mr Stedman — Drawned in my Favor — payable in the Planters Bank was not paid — It was due 1st & 4th of March, 1836 — The above note was Protested

5   A race between Betsy Recheuleau and Casandra, 2 miles Out for $1000 — Betsy R. Beat Cassandra about 30 yards, Easy, 1s mile in 1.56s, the 2 miles in 3.56s   Mr F Taylor and my-self Compairs the Stokes & Bray Accounts — remainder in my favor $80 — to the 7th of Febuary, 1836 — I pd Mr F Taylor $5 for the Hyre of Sharlote as a nu[r]se. I Let Mr Wilkins have my Horse to go out to Maj Dunbars at night — I got a Letter from Mrs Miller to day

6   I wrote a Long Letter to Mr Miller by The Bunker Hill, in care of Fitzchew — Old Mc wrides out on old Pagg — C Wilkins had my Horse and I could not go

7 Miss Blevens [VS.] full sister to Fanny Kemble Mile Heats for $2000 a side — 1st heat 1.56 sec, the other 1.59½ Track very mudy — Miss Blevins won the Race by 20 or 25 yards — Last Heat Mr F Taylor pd me $20 cash that he Collected from Mr. Flecho which Leaves Mr Flecho $50 in my Debt to the 1st of March 1836 — Dr Pollard wrode in from Mr Dunbars on my Horse that I Let Mr Wilkins have to ride out there with on Saturday night the 5th inst

8 I went Down to get Mr Dart to pay me the $350 that he owed me, which fell Due on 1st and 4th inst in the Planters Bank and was Protested I paid Mr Soria $16.50 for 2 pair pants and 7 pocket Hank kerchiefs, silk — Col. Bingaman gets by John 1 Botile of Antiqu oil, 1 Cake of Soap — price of Both $1.12½

9 A Race was to have taken place to Day between Alice Grey & Mr Minors Diana for $5000. Just before the Horses Came Out Both parties were Betting very Freely untill it was time for the stakes to be put up when Mr Minor Came up and paid the forfeit which was $2500.00 Mr St. Clair paid me 1 dollar that I won from him sometime ago—Loaned Mc 25 cents to go in at the gate with — Mother misslaid or Lost A Receipt for $400 that she paid Mr Murcherson for Mary.

11 A Race between Splendid and Marger Greerer for $1000. Mile Heats, A good Deal of Betting on both sides — Splendid won the race very Easy. Time 1.55 seconds — 2d heat same time — I subscribed to paper called The Sperrits of Times. Pd cash for it $5.00 Big dinner at Mr Bells Tavern given to Our Representatives and for the pasage of R Road Charter A[t] night the City was Lit up in the most splendid stile.[22] I sent two of my Carts Down to get repaired at Mr Cryzers & Alisons Shop

12 I bouht five Lottery tickets from Mr Britton, cost $42.50 There nobrs were as follows: (11-16-18), (4-15-41), (45-54-67), (7-63-68), (8-49-50) I subscribed $5 to a paper that Mr R Bledsoe had to make up a sum for the preperations for the Vicksburgh Citizens and Company — El Excelenta.

13 Old Mc and myself took a ride Out towards Mr Scotts old Field We met a Greate many persons Comming into Natchez to get Bank Stock, They were from Woodville — Old Esdra has his Little Black Boy Buried — he Died the day before yesterday I presume

22 See Natchez *Free Trader,* March 11, 1836.

14   The Bank Stock of The Commercial Bank was Drawn for to Day — There was the Greatest Rush made for it by the people that was Ever Known in this place before   A very Greate many Persons did not get any shairs. The tickets that was under No 400 had the priviledge of taking 50 shaires and all tickets that drew a nomber higher than 400 was not Conciderd worth anything — Mr E. Polete Drew a Number   It was No 376. I gave him $50 for it — He was to make me the transfer on tomorrow in the Bank which He did in the office of Mr F Taylor, who was a witness to the same — Mr Dalhgreen & Mr Dillon has a fight at Mr Bells Tavern about Bank Stock   Dalhgreen gave Dillon a Black Eye. Mother Sends for Dr Hogg to see Mosses. He came and prescribed some powders to be taken at night and in the morning — My Horse is quite Lame   I had a stiffe shoe put on him

15   To Day Mr Hypolete Joannis made me the Transfer for 50 Shares of Commercial Bank Stock or he gave me, in the first place, the folowing Lines written and witnessed by Mr F Taylor as follows — This is to Certify that William Johnson is authorised to subscribe fifty Shairs of Commercial Bank Stock for me   Natchez, March 14th, 1836.   Witness   F Taylor   Hypolete Joaunnis   I gave Mr Hypolete Joannis $1000 to get the Certificate for the 50 Shairs to his Number, He went in in due time, paid the money and Transferd his certificate to me, The Certificate Read as Follows,   Received of Hypollita Joannis, One Thousand Dollars being the first Installment of Twenty Dollars on Fifty Shares of Stock in the Commercial Bank of Natchez.   B. Wade   The with in stock I do this day Transfer To William Johnson — Natchez, March 15th, 1836.   This was writen on the Back of the Certificate.   This was also writen by Mr F Taylor and signed by Mr Hypolete Joannis — Mr Bledsoe Called on me to know if I had the Scrip of the Land that I sold to Flecheux. I told him I had not it.   A Race To Day between Lauderdale & Piano, 2 miles heats for $2000 aside.   Lauderdale won the Race very Easy, Odds was in favor of Piano — She had to carry too much weight. Mr Morris Boyles wrode her.[23]

---

[23] This race was reported in *American Turf Register and Sporting Magazine*, VIII (1836), 91. M. E. Boyles entered and rode Piano in this race. A number of horses were run under Boyles's name, both at Natchez and St. Francisville, but apparently he was not the owner of all of them. He soon gave up riding and began training horses. In 1837 he became the trainer for William R. and Bennet H. Barrow of West Feliciana Parish, Louisiana. See Edwin Adams Davis, *Plantation Life in the Florida Parishes of Louisiana, 1836–1846, as Reflected in the Diary of Bennet H. Barrow* (New York, 1943), 58, 87, 113.

16 To Day I went to Mr Bells Tavern with a Mr William H. Bowers to make Him a Transfer for my fifty shares of Commercial Bank Stock which I purchased of Mr Hypolete Joannis. I made the transfer to Mr Wm H. Bowers and I Received from him for the above Stock $1000 which was the first Installment that was required by the Bank Directors being money that I gave Mr Joannis to pay for the Certificate yesterday. And I Received also $225.00 premium on the Stock from said Mr William H. Bowers, in all $1225.00   I Received of Col Marchalk an Account of his against a Mr John Murrel for $36, payable One day after Date. Said Murrel Lives in Orleans. I was to send the account Down to Mr Jas. Miller to Collect for Col Marschalk[24] by the 1st Boat or Chance of doing so — I gave my Receit to the Col stating that I had Recevd the above Account of him to Send to Mr Miller for Collection   Bank Stock is worth a Premium of $4 or $500 to day   Mr Perry offers to sell Betsy Rushlow at public sale with her Engagement to run a Race

17 I got Mr Hypolet Joannis to sign an article to Mr W H. Bowers which Entitled him to vote for Directors in the Commercial Bank — Old Hypolete was very much Disposed to be contrary about it untill Mr A Flecho Explained to him what was nessary for him to do   He then signed it, The Bunker Hill arrived to day   I Received a Letter From Mrs Miller stating that Mr William Henry had died of dropsey — Mr Francis Roach gets married to Miss [blank] out at Washington

18 This Day was of all this season the Dullest Day for Buisness that I have Had — To day the Ellection came for The Offircers of the Bank, I mean the Commercial Bank. I Loaned

---

24 Andrew Marschalk did the first printing in Mississippi in the late 1790's and between 1802 and the early 1830's was a newspaper editor. Charles S. Sydnor, "The Beginning of Printing in Mississippi," *Journal of Southern History,* I (1935), 49–55; *Mississippi Newspapers, 1805–1940,* pp. 176, 182, 248. Newspapers were in the forefront of political controversy, and the issuance of the third number of his Natchez *Mississippi Herald* in 1802 caused him to be indicted by a politically minded grand jury as being "a malicious and seditious man of depraved mind and wicked and diabolical disposition and also deceitfully wickedly and maliciously contriving against the members of the Honble House of Representatives of Mississippi Territory" by representing them as "Corrupt dishonest contemptible and dishonorable persons." Adams District Superior Court Minutes, 1802–10, pp. 68–70. For more of the same, see *ibid.,* 70–77; and for later evidences of political controversy in which he became involved as a result of his "positive genius for sarcasm and invective," see Mack Swearingen, *The Early Life of George Poindexter* (New Orleans, 1934), 58, 64, 126–39, and *Journal of House of Representatives, Mississippi,* 3 Sess. (1820), 72. But by 1836 this "remarkable as well as venerable man" had retired, and he died on August 10, 1838, at his home at Washington, Adams County. Natchez *Free Trader,* August 11, 1838.

Mr Newman $5 to be Returned in a few Days — Mr Agry has his store broken open, his clerk shot at the thief, and Drew Blood, but could not Cetch him

19   Rained all day — no buisness doing worth speaking of   I Loaned Mr Whiting $100 To be paid on next Tuesday to me again — It was a post note on the Pheonix Bank of New York. Mr J. Potts wanted me To Take a man of his to Learn him how to shave   It was One that he had Just Bought — I Told him that I could not take him. Mr L. R. Marshall[25] was Elected President of the Commercial Bank — I Received from Mr Brittin $17 Out of $42.50 that I paid him for five Lottery tickets   I paid Col Fall $5 cash for one year subcription to his paper The Mississipian. Cut Mr Finnys hair and shave 37½ also a comb 37½ and B of Oil 75   Mr Neibut wants to Buy my Property. I refused to sell at any price.

20   Bill Nix and John & myself wrode Out   Drove up Leckeahana. We found her out near Capt. Nevits. I gave old French $2.00

21   Full sister to Fany Gemmel[26] ran or were to have run; but the forfeit was paid by one of them   I sold Mr Tom Jones one of my carts without the Body for $30. He paid cash $20 — To pay the other $10 this week   To day the Boys went after the Red Cow and Calf and Brought her up — To day Mr Kanes grey horse and Mr Lancaster Bay Horse ran a mile   Mr Canes horse won the Race,   Mc he Lost $5 on the Bay horse

22   Mr Tarb and Mr Joseph Lapice Has a fight on the pavement. They were soon separated   Tarb pulls off Mr Lapieces Stock and tears his Coat. I Bot a Keg of White Lead — Bill Nix & John Paints the Back part of the House. Mc went across the River to see old Madam Victora to get Her Little Boy to Lern the

[25] Levin R. Marshall was a prominent banker and planter who resided at Richmond, about a mile south of Natchez. For a detailed report on five of his plantations, located in Arkansas, Louisiana, and Mississippi, in 1836, see Theodora B. Marshall and Gladys C. Evans (eds.), "Plantation Report from the Papers of Levin R. Marshall, of 'Richmond,' Natchez, Mississippi," *Journal of Mississippi History*, III (1941), 45–55. By 1860 his Adams County agricultural holdings totaled 2,500 acres (1,700 improved) worked by 188 slaves, while his extensive Louisiana plantations were valued at more than $380,000. See Weaver, *Mississippi Farmers*, 109; U. S. Census Reports, 1860, Schedule IV, Adams County, 7 (Mississippi Department of Archives and History); Adams County Will Books, III, 60–61. The state tax rolls for 1860 gave his Adams County slave total as 192, of which 30 were at his residence and 162 at Poplar Grove. Auditor's Records, Tax Rolls, 1860, Adams County.

[26] Johnson probably referred to the horse Fanny Kemble, owned by Colonel Adam L. Bingaman.

trade   He was not there, but she promised to send him over for Mc to Look at on Sunday next by old Antony   I paid up my note to day in the Agricultural Bank for $154.66½ Drawn in favor of the Quigless Estate and Indorsed by S. T McAlister — This Evening Mr Jones sent, got the Cart that I sold him yesterday — To Day I Hyred two Carts to Mr Mills to work on the Rail Road with, at 37½ per day for Each Cart. He sent and got them this Evening

 23 A Race for the Jocky Clubb purse 2 miles Heats. Three Horses started, Hard Heart, Prince Talerand & Naked Truth   Hard Heart won The First Heat. The Second Heat. Naked Truth won the Second Heat, Princ Talerand close to her heals, H. H. behind Both. Third Heat Naked Truth won beating P. Talerand a Little or about a Length   H. H. was still behind. He made a Run on them Coming Down the stretch and if they had have run one Yards farther he would have won the Race very Easy   It was a very unexpected Run and suprized Every person present.[27] My Horse Rob. Roy Ran a Quarter agains St. Clairs grey Horse. Rob Roy won the Race very very easy — it was for $20 only

 24 A race To Day between Lauderdale & Chuckfahila — 3 mile Heats. Lauderdale won the Race with Ease — Bets were in his favor from the first — I made Several Bets To day and they set as follows — I Bet $5 Even with L. Winsborought & I bet $15 to five & took Lauderdale with St Clair & I Bet $100 against 4000 Bricks with Wm Thomas and $4 to one on Robersons mare agains St Clairs Horse, ½ mile   I Bet $4 to 1 on the mare — She won the Race very Easy. I won the first $5 of to day from Louis and St Clair   Both Bets on a credit — Tis paid

 25 A Race To Day between the following Horses, Mile Heats — Jocky Clubb purse. Betsy Melone, Fanny Jarman, Piano — that is the way they Came Out the First Heate But the Second Heate the[y] Came Out in this way — Betsy Malone 1st, Piano 2d, Fanny Jarman 3d

 26 A Race To Day, three Best in five, between the Following Nags   Cassandra & Hard Heart & Fanny Jarman   To Day

---

[27] This race was the first of the five-day spring meeting of the " (New) Natchez (Miss.) Jockey Club." Colonel Adam L. Bingaman's Naked Truth was the winner. The Natchez Jockey Club had previously held a four-day meet, beginning February 24, but apparently a reorganization occurred and a second spring meeting was held. These two meets, added to an unusually large number of match races and other less important races recorded by William Johnson, point to early 1836 as a season of intense enthusiasm for racing in Adams County. See *American Turf Register and Sporting Magazine*, VIII (1836), 89–92; *Spirit of the Times*, V (1835), 8.

Mr Whiting paid me $100 that he Borrowed from me on Saturday, March the 19th inst   He gave me $2.50 for the Loan of the above money — I Loaned Dr Welding $2 to day at the Race Track — Stokes Ranaway a day or two ago

27   To day or, night I mean, my Cow (Lade) was knocked in the Head by someone as She Lay Down the Hill, where she had fallen and Broke her Back.

28   I wrode Out To Maj Chotard to Cut the Childrens Hair. I cut 4 heads of Hair — To Day the Drumb was agoing around town beating with a Flagg with a paper containing the Rail Road paper for the purpose of getting the R. Road Stock subscribed for   I paid Mr James Surget $21 for a Riffle that was sold at Auction from the Estate of Mr Car

29   Mr Sweyney paid me $3.00   Old Mc paid $25 for five shairs of Rail Road Stock — All sorts of Rail Road meetings at present.

30   To Day I subscribed for 26 Shairs of the Rail Road stock, I in the First place put my name for One thousand Dollars But Mr McAlister told me if it [was] two much for me that he would take One thousand dollars of it. I then put my name Down for $2000.00   We were all Down to night at Mrs Battles   Tis the first time that Ann has been to her Mothers since the Birth of Little William   Rail Road Meeting This Evening — There were several speeches made by Different Persons Stating the Greate Masacree of Buoie, Kit Parker and others, I herd this Evening that Mr Parker Received a Letter from McNiel stating that his son, I mean the son of Mr Parker, was Killed by the Spaniards[28]   Tis generally believed   Skeggs and Houg has Mr Bray put in Jail for Debt

31   Mr Arlett paid me $10. He still owes me $5.00 yet — Mcs woman, that he hyred Ranaway and went home to her Mistress. A man shot himself To day at Mr Kings Tavern under the Hill, did not kill himself but very Badley wounded

April 1   Mr Wiswall Leaves here To Day For the North — Mr Joseph Lapiece pd me $3 for two months Shaving. Mr John Tayler arrived from New Orleans in the Bunker Hill

2   I Loaned Mr F. Taylor $100 To be paid over To me again on Wednesday next, To Day it was that [I] went up to settle my carpenters Bill with Mesrs Neibert & Gemmell, but we did not Settle on Account of the Book Keepers Loosing my Account. I

---

28 The Alamo had fallen on March 6.

Bot a stock[29] To Day for $2.25. Mr Becket Commenced by the Month To be shaved   Mr Doland moved Down to The Frame House belonging to Mr Mellen on Main street

3   Mc And myself wrode out as far as Capt Nevits old Field. We caught a squrrell upon a tree and we had some fun Out of the old Fellow before he got away from us. Snap and Pollow has a fight. Snap whiped Pollow, made him Run

4   I made a Bet To day with Mr Whiting of $10 that Lauderdale would Beat a Race while he was at St Francisville, or that he would Beat the Race that he Runs provided there Does not start more than One nag — I also made a Bet with Mr Mardice that Red Mariah would Beat Betsy Malone if they Run together[30]

5   The Volenteers to Texas Left here. The Following are all that I Recollect of — Capt John A Quitman — Mr Strickland out of the Store of M. Izod — Mr Arlet, store of E Lewis — Mr Sweney, store of Messrs Smith & Co — Mr Rayley, store of Messrs Stanton & Buckner — You[ng] Joseph Munce — Young Coffin — Young Jim Boman — Mr Wm Parker, Mississipii Hotell[31]

6   My Little mare Teckahand was found this morning, where She was Either thrown off or Else ran off of the Bluff — I think

[29] Johnson probably referred to a close-fitting band or cravat for the neck.

[30] Johnson lost both of these bets made on St. Francisville races, which were held later in this month.

Several Adams County racing stables, including those of Colonel Adam L. Bingaman and William J. Minor, entered the meets of the St. Francisville (Louisiana) Jockey Club in 1835 and 1836. During the succeeding years, Louisiana plantation owners William R. Barrow, Bennet H. Barrow, Daniel Turnbull, Alexander Barrow, and others, developed strong racing stables in the St. Francisville area, and occasionally some of them were entered in Natchez and New Orleans race meets. See West Feliciana Parish Notarial Records, I, 192–97 (West Feliciana Parish courthouse, St. Francisville, La.) ; *American Turf Register and Sporting Magazine*, VI (1835) , 576–78; VII (1836) , 472–75, 566; Davis, *Plantation Life in the Florida Parishes of Louisiana, 1836–1846*, 57–60.

[31] Compare with incomplete muster in James H. McLendon, "John A. Quitman in the Texas Revolution," *Southwestern Historical Quarterly*, LII (1948) , 167, n. 15. Both John A. Quitman and Felix Huston of Natchez led contingents of Mississippi volunteers to Texas, but both arrived too late to fight the Mexicans. The April 8 issue of the Natchez *Free Trader* carried an explanation of the circumstances surrounding Quitman's and Huston's expeditions. The issue of April 15 stated that Mississippi would send between 300 and 400 men to the Texan war and that Adams County had subscribed about $2,000 for the aid of the Texan volunteers from Mississippi. Although Felix Huston did not arrive in Texas until July, 1836, before the end of the year he was in command of the army of the Republic of Texas, in which position he distinguished himself by his flamboyant and foolhardy demands that he be allowed to march against Mexico and by nearly killing the future Confederate general Albert Sidney Johnston in a duel. Hogan, *The Texas Republic*, 281–82.

that Bill Nix and John must have ran Her over the Bluff, She was so Badly hurt that I Despaired of her

7   It was to day and not yesterday that I had to Have the Little mare Shot, and I paid Bill Hazard $2.00 to haul her to the River and put there in. She fell off near Mr Mickeys House, Dwelling House. To night I sent up and had my old Piano Brought Home from Mr Maurys

8   To day Rbt Lieper Commenced to water the street on our Square, and Armstead Commenced To water on the uper Square at [blank] per Day — I settled to Day with Mr Koontz for Messrs Neibert & Gemmell — his Bill against me was $104.36 and my Bill against him was $174.50   I took his Due Bill for the Ballance which was $70.14

9   I pd Mr F Taylor $5 for the hyre of his girl Sharlott — I had a Dog Collar made and put full of nails. It was made for Pollo — Mr F Taylor pd $100 by a check on the Agricultural Bank for the money, it was money that I Loaned him on Saturday, April 2d, 1836. I paid Messrs Soria & Co. $12.75 for a willow Cradle and 7 yards of Carpeting   A Race to day between Robersons mare & Flaggs Bay Horse   A half Mile Race. The mare won the Race very Easy. Mr McAlister sold his house Last week for $35,000 to Mr D. Mickie in a horn.[32]

10   I turned Out my Horses this Evening To Grass and they Both Ranaway — To day A man belonging to Mr Plummer & John got in a Quarrell and the Fellow Knocked John down   John at Last Saw Mr Lawrence, went to take The Boy and he made Battle with him, so before he could take him he had to Knock him down once or twice, He then put him in Jail to be Tryed To Morrow

12   Mc and myself went to see the Benefit of Mr Rice[33]   He had a very good House   I made up my mind not to go up there any more untill there was some Regulations made up stairs. Mr John T. Butler gets married to Miss Celia Ann Browder. She is a grand daughter of Old Mr Hendersons. They were married by Parson Potts

---

[32] The phrase meant that the transaction had been completed. In this case, that McAlister had already been paid and had the money in hand.

[33] Johnson referred to the benefit performance of "Daddy" Rice or "Jim Crow" Rice, to whom properly belongs the title "father of American minstrelsy." Thomas D. Rice's "Jim Crow" role had already become famous, and in this same year (1836) he appeared with sensational success in London, Dublin, and Cork. Carl Wittke, *Tambo and Bones; A History of the American Minstrel Stage* (Durham, 1930), 20–29; William B. Gates, "The Theatre in Natchez," *Journal of Mississippi History*, III (1941), 92, 94.

13   I Bot two Double Barrel Guns at Mr Sorias & C, pd him
$60 for them, $30 Eeach. I Sent my gun up to Auction to be Sold
to the hyest Bidder, Mr F Taylor pd me $100 that I Loaned him
on the 2d Day of April — I Loaned my horse to Mr Tuomy to
Wride in the Country a mile or two — he got on the horse and then
got Frightend, and got off and Sent the horse home again — I
Loaned Mr Whiting $100 to be paid in One month from this date
at 4 per cent per month   I gave Mr Taylor $7 to give to Mr
Samuel Atkerson of the Evening Post.

14   I gave Mr Whiting an Account against Mr Thomas Jones
for $10, Balance Due me on a Cart. I Bot To Day a cart from Mr
Kane for which I paid him $30.00   To day Mr Flecheo and Mr
Taylor were Looking over there Accounts to Settle Mr Flecheos
Bill against me   Was $7 & Some Cents tho do not know how
many

15   The watering cart watered the Streets to day. A Race
To Day for $2000 a side between the Little Sorril Horse Splendid
and Waxy, Late from Vicksburgh, 2 miles Out   Splendid won the
Race very Eeasy — There was a 500 yards Race between Tom Noes
Grey Horse and Puss, belonging to Waller. The Grey Horse won
the race very Easy — This is a Race that I made a Bet of $13
to $10. I then got affraid and gave Mr Mardice $4 to Draw the
money — This was a Race between Isorah and a Grey mare belonging To Lee Clabourne, One mile Out, Isorah won the Race
tho it was a very Close Race. I Lost six Dollars on it. A Race
between A Bay Horse & a Grey Horse belonging to Lemuel Wilkerson — The Grey Horse won the Race very Easy — We got a Letter
from Mrs Miller and a present of 200 Orenges and 3 or 4 pine
aples

16   I paid Mr Rowes $18 for geting the Draught of my in-
tended House drawn, it was done by Deadsmore the Carpenter,[34] I
went up to Mr Fisks to cut the Hair of three Young Miss
Wilkinss. Dr Reed Potts gave me a check on the Planters Bank
for $200 that I Loaned him some time ago and I went and got the
money with it

---

[34] This was for a house which was to be constructed for William Johnson and
Harriet Battles, his free Negro mother-in-law, on a lot on State Street then owned
by Harriet Battles. Gabriel Tichenor had sold the property to her in 1829 for $2.00.
Adams County Deed Records, R, 489–90. This property, 210 State Street, is now
owned and occupied by Mrs. W. R. Johnston, widow of William Johnson's grandson.
   For the advertisement of J. C. Deadmore, "practical architect, and linear and
prospective draftsman," see Natchez *Free Trader*, March 11, 1836.

17   I wrode down as far as Colliers place trying to get into the Swamp but could not on account of the water being so High. I then went up the Bluff with my Horse and wrode to the Scotts old field, Killed 3 small Birds and 2 wood Peckers and found a wild Turkeys nest with elevin Eggs in it   I took them and Brought them home with me. Bill Nix was with me. I had my new shot gun.

18   I sold my Little Cart to day To Mr Mills for $20 and he paid me $5 for the hyre of it. News to day from Dr McQuitter and Mr C. Wilkins, Direct from Texas, that Gen Houston was surrounded by the Mexicans and was thought to bee in Greate Danger of being Cut to pieces by them, also that 15 hundred Indians had Joined the Mexicans[35]

19   Recevd of Mr F Taylor $45 in Cash and I took a Hat at $5 which made it aquivelent to $50. It now Leaves the Account in my favor $60, tho I have yet to take Out the Back Shop from the Sixty Dollars. Mc Buys a Little Sorril Horse from Mr Brown for $60. He also Bought provender to the Ammount $12.37½ this Evening — To day and yesterday A Family was moving up stairs in the old House. Hester Commings Came to me to try and Borrow $4 or $500 to finish paying for her sister to Mrs Postlethwait. Parson Potts Leaves this place for the North To Live there, He took his Family with him

20   Becket from Philad. was up to see me, I sent a Letter to E Miller by him. Fencibles from Vicksburgh Came down here with Ladys to atend a Grand Ball at Parkers Hotell   To day Little Bon and Bruce, that man that Jack Perry shot, Came to me to Borrow $300 but sure enoughf they did not get it

21   Greate perade day with the Vicksburgh and Our Company together — Mr John Beaslin gets married to Miss Gates   She is a sister to Mr Wells Wades wife, That is all I know of Her — This Day One Year ago I was married — I made in Cash to day $26.25   To Day I Loaned Mr Becket in cash for Mr E. Bell $50 to be Returned on Saturday the 23d inst

22   The Fencibles Came by quanties to get shave and Bathed. I made an agreament with Mr Thatcher to give him fourteen Baths for his Bathing tub   Fifteen or sixteen Volunteers from Vicksburgh Bathed here to day — I Bot a Bay Horse at auction

---

[35] Four days later the Natchez *Free Trader* stated: "The reports for the past week from Texas have been various and contradictory; but all accounts agree that Santa Anna is still waging a war of extermination, and that hundreds of the chivalrous and brave are rallying to the rescue."

To Day for $56. He did belong to old Dr Branch — To day I
Received $8.44 net money for my old shot gun. She sold for $9.

 23 To day about 12 Oclock The Vicksburgh Volunteers Left
this place for Vicksburgh[36] To day I put my new Horse to hauling of watter — he works very well indeed

 24 To day after 12 Oclock the Boys, Mc and myself went
Out to St Catharine Creek to fish, 8 of us in number and we only
caught only 5 Fish in all — I caught 2, Mc 1, French 1, John 1 I
Bot a Large Quantity of News papers from Dr Wren at or for $10
for the Lump

 25 Col Bingaman Returns from St. Francisville Races. Mr
Minor and all the Party in fact came up, Some by Land and some
by water — I Bot Some Children Books to day at auction. Some
good Ones among them St Francisville Races — 4 miles Heats:
Betsy Malone Vs Red Mariah Scarlet Beet Lauderdale, and
Liynet Beet Betsy Rushlow very Easy — indeed no kind of a
Race. I paid Mr Mardice $10 that he won from me on the Race
between Red Mariah and Betsy Malone — S Gocian Returns from
up the River.

 26 I wrote to Mrs Miller by old Mr Brustee and I sent that
note or an account against a Mr Murrel for $36 and some cents, I
paid Mr Whiting $10 that he won from me On a Race between
Red Mariah & Betsy Malone — no, it was a Race between Lauderdale and Scarlet. A man by the name of Finley I believe after
having just Finished a Large Building for Mr Brown[37] near the
Saw Mill took a Chisell and cut his throat with it — To day I made
Out account against the Natchez Fencibles for moneys due me
from Vicksburg Volunteers It was $10

---

[36] The Vicksburg Volunteers came to Natchez to visit the Natchez Fencibles.
The Volunteers, under Captain Guion, formed "a splendid corps, and their commander may well be proud of them and they of him. They partook of a public
dinner at the Mansion House on Thursday, and attended the Theatre in company
with the Fencibles in the evening." Natchez *Free Trader*, April 22, 1836. In Johnson's entries of April 20–23, he is in error in referring to the militia group from
Vicksburg as both "Fencibles" and "Volunteers"; the Vicksburg organization was
the Volunteers, the Natchez host company was the Fencibles.

[37] In the 1820's Andrew Brown, a Scotsman, purchased this lumber mill from
Peter Little, who had acquired the site from the Stephen Minor estate. The mill
has been in constant operation since that time and is still in possession of the
family, the present owner being Andrew Brown Learned. The mill is located under
the Bluff overlooking the Mississippi River. For a full column description of a
cricket match held under the Bluff, "near Mrs. Brown's beautiful villa," and a
dinner celebrating the anniversary of "England's Patron Saint," St. George, held
in "the splendid grape arbor of Andrew Brown, Esq.," see Natchez *Courier*, April
27, 1842. For a brief description of the area, see Charles Lyell, *A Second Visit to
the United States of North America*, 2 vols. (New York, 1849), II, 153.

27 I Bot $10 worth of News papers from Dr Wren at the Post Office. Post Office just moving Down To Mr Darts property

28 Mc & myself and John went into the Swamp to Hunt, He had his Double Barrel shot gun and I took my Rifle and Double B. gun also One of Mr Barlands Hounds followed us up to town and then Left and went off, Mc Killed 1 King Fisher, 1 Owl, 1 Little Swaller, and the Dogs caught a Rabit — I killed 1 Squerrel, 1 wood pecker, 1 wood Cock, 1 Little fat Bird.

29 I loaned Mr Spielman $300 To be Returned in One week

30 Buisness Dull — I Loaned Mr Taylor the Painter $20 To be returned shortly — Mrs Ware The Mother of Mr Thos Ellis Died She died out at His Residence[38]

May 1 Nothing of any interest to day or Buisness of any Account.

2 Mr. Henry Turner sold 524 84/100 of acre; it sold for $24 an acre It was Bought by Mr Saml. Justine, The terms are one & two years Credit, notes payable in Bank Stephen is Out to hunt for Pagg. Run him but could not get him home

3 To day I wrote to Mrs Miller, Greate news from Texas, that they had captured St Anna and killed 500 of his men and had taken about six hundred of them as prisoners of war[39] — Steven went Out to day to Look for Pagg but could not find him, Old Mr Becket Staid all night at Our house.

4 I Loaned Dr Hubbard $40 to day — To day we were all very busy in geting Brick in the yard from Mr Bells yard. Steven went Over to help haul them

5 Mr Ed Stanton called and assessed my property. I gave him the same List that I gave to Mr R Cole, I and all the Boys

[38] Mrs. Ware was the wife of Nathaniel Ware, who came to Mississippi Territory about 1811. There he became a prominent territorial official and made a fortune in land speculation. In 1814 he married Mrs. Sarah (Percy) Ellis, widow of a well-known planter, John Ellis. At the birth of the Wares's second daughter in 1820, Mrs. Ware lost her mind. Thomas G. Ellis, a son by her first marriage, lived at Routhlands (later Dunleith), which he had acquired through marriage in 1828 to Mary Routh, heiress daughter of Job Routh. See William Diamond, "Nathaniel A. Ware, National Economist," *Journal of Southern History*, V (1939), 504; Natchez *Ariel*, May 17, 1828; Adams County Deed Records, B, 1; Adams County Marriage Records, I, 290; V, 134; Edith Wyatt Moore, "Dunleith" and "Richmond," Natchez *Democrat*, Pilgrimages Edition, 1943. For a notice concerning administration of the estate of Thomas G. Ellis, deceased, see Natchez *Courier*, November 28, 1838. See also W. A. Evans, "Sarah Ann Ellis Dorsey, Donor of Beauvoir," *Journal of Mississippi History*, VI (1944), 89–102.

[39] The battle of San Jacinto was fought on April 21. Natchez received the news with enthusiasm; the Natchez *Free Trader*, May 6, 1836, headed its article, "Glorious News from Texas."

were all at work with Brick in the yard. Mr Finny the man that cut his throat the other Day Died to Day and was buried

6   I paid Mr Baker $58.27 For City Tax. I thought it very strange for my tax last year was only $17.50   The Collector told me that the City would not Receive the Last List which was Taken by the City assessor   Old Sterns went Out to Fishen   Caught 7 doz Fish so I Understood. Mr Gemmell Sells his House to Messrs Beaumont & Williams for $20,000 for 31 feet 9 Inches — A few Days ago Beaumont & Williams Sold Out there Stock on hand to Mr Pearce.

7   To day about 12 or 1 Oclock the Volunteers went Down the River Commanded by Gen Felix Huston — I do not know the Exact amount but I think must have been about [blank] in Number, among the Rest that Little puppy, tryfling Little Puppy that was Learning a trade with the Dixes Saddlers — I hope they will give him a center pop   To Day Mr Bells man stop hauling Brick in my yard.

8   I went in the afternoon Out to hunt for Old Pagg and Bill Nix went with me, After we get Out into an old Field, Barlands old Field, when my horse got scared at Something and ran of[f] with Bill Nix and threw him, his Leg got fast in the stirrups   The Horse ran 15 or 20 feet with him before he got Loose from that cituation, the horse fell down and kicked a ½ minute before he Could Rise, he ran off then and Jumped a Large buyo, thrugh bryars &c. I had my Pistol with me and I shot a Large Black Snake and killed One with a Stick Out at that pond near the Fitzgerald place

9   The Hatters are moving from up stairs, Mr Jno T. Griffith paid me $7.25   Mr Ross and Mr Nickols has a few Blows at Mr Bells Hotell, Mr Nickols said something against Gen Huston and Mr Ross took it up as he was not present, Report to night says that they have challenged Each other, I paid Mr Mitchell to day $100 for Mother, it was a note that she owed to Mr Merrit Williams for Dinah. I was the Indorser on the Note, It fell or was to have become due on the first of June, 1836

10   The Dispute which arrose between Mr Ross & Mr Nickols was made up to day at 11 Oclock — Mr Nickols withdrew the Challenge and Mr Ross apologised to him and the thing was settled and no more was said about it — To day I went to auction and Bought ten pair of pantaloons at 1.12½ and a white linnen coate

11   Mr Ried, Mc and myself & Bill Nix went over to the

Grassy Lake to fish   We had a tedious time of it tho we caught a fine mess of Fish

12   Buisness getting dull very fast   To Day Mc was Telling about Sterns — Yesterday whilst we were a Fishing On the other side of the River Sterns got Drunk and went Out into the yard to Sleep and he fell off of the chair that he was setting On. Made water in his pantaloons, That I think is a Little a head of anything that I have herd of Lately — To Day Mr J Spielman paid me $150 being a part of $300 that I Loaned him on Fryday, April 29th, 1836 — I paid to The Gentleman that Brought me the Large Book or History, geography &c. $10 in cash

13   To Day Mr Spielmen paid me $150.00 which was the remaing part of the three hundred Dollars that I Loaned him on the 29th of April. I Bought from Mesrs Soria & Co 12 shirts for the Boys at $10.50 for the dozen

14   I settled my account against Mr A L Gaines. My account against him was to the present Date, $33.50 and his account against me was $23. Left a Ballance in my favor of $10.50 which was paid to me by Mr W. A. Miller for the firm — Loaned Mr J. Spillman $150.00 — Mr Taylor the Painter paid me $20 that he Borrowed from me on Saturday, April 30, 1836

15   Buisness quite Brisk — Mc and Myself wrode Out in the Evening near Col Bingamans Plantation and Came around again, after having Geatherd some fine Mulberrys, into the same Road that we first went Out in

16   To day I gave Mr C Dart or his partner Mr Steadman their Note in my favor for $350 payable first of March, and I gave them in cash $349 Making in all $701 and the protest included, for a Note of theirs against Mr Walworth payable in 90 Days for $720 Indorsed by Murcherson & Doyal — Mr Bell Sold His Tavern to Mr West from Woodville for $140,000 payable in six years, the First Payment to be made the first of January, 1837, of $20,000

17   There is some talk about a Duel that is Brewing between Maj Shield & Maj. Potts — Judge Cage, Mr Fielding Davis & Family all Left here on the Steam Boat. Mother paid me $50, part of some money that I Loaned Her. I Received a Letter to day from Mrs Miller   She tells of Her having to Bind Geogana & Margarett Gatewood over to keep there peace, the[y] insulted Her &c. She tells me that they Received the Note that I sent them belonging to Col Marschalk.

18   Several Families Leaving this Place to Day on different boats. The difficulty between Mr J C Potts and Maj Shields was settled

19 The Volunteers from Madison County Left here for Texas. To Day it was that I Found Old Pagg. in possession of a Black man belonging [to] Mr Barber. The Boys name was Patrick, I Brought him Out of his yard with the Saddle, Bridle, Martingale and all on the Horse. I got on him and rode home on him, After having showed the Horse to his master he promised me that he would pay any Damage that I seen proper to Charge him for the Horse

20 Mr Barber sells the Black man Patrick that stoled my Horse, he Sold him on that account alone. To Day the Old Gentleman that Lost his Wife by her Runing away with a Big whiskered man by the name of Clayton, the old man swears that he will kill Clayton on the first site   Mr Patterson paid me $10 that was due me from the Vicksburgh Volunteers — To day I Bot at Sorias Auction 12 pair of Pantaloons at 94 cents per pair. I gave John 1 pair, Charles[40] 1 pair, Bill Nix 1 pair, Steven 1 pair, Louis 1 pair

21 Mr J Spielman paid me $150 that he borrowed from me on Saturday, the 14th inst. I paid Mr Smith for Messrs Soria & C. $11.25 for 12 pair pantaloons that I Bot at their Auction Room, I paid Mr Walker for a Bath Tub for William — I Received a Notice from the Planters Bank to take up my Note Due 28th & 31st inst, Indorsed by Mr S. T. McAlister, being the First installment on my Rail Road Stock

22 Mc and Myself Took a small Ride Out at the Race track — Peter Kelly, St. Clair & Patt. ran their Horses 1000 yards. P. and St. Clair was to give Kelly 50 feet in the Out Come, and Peet Kellys Horse won the Race Easy

23 The Messrs and Miss Eveans's Came Down from there place, the other Day — Ann & Bill Nix takes a wride out on the Woodville Road.

24 I Sold my Little Gun to Day for $35 cash. Mr Thomas Ellis and Mr Frank Routh with Ladys went to the North.

25 I Received a Note from Col Marchalk. He wished to know if I had herd any thing of the Note that I sent to Mr Miller for collection &c. I then wrote him word that yes I had herd in a

---

[40] Charles (also referred to as Charles C. Young in one of Johnson's account books) was a slave who eventually became one of Johnson's most trustworthy employees. After learning the barber business under Johnson's supervision, he was in charge of one or the other of Johnson's two subordinate barbershops during most of the period 1840–51. He was the property of a Major Young and frequently made trips to his Jefferson County "home."

Letter from Mr Miller that he had Received the Letter and the Note also But Could not find the man that the Note was against, Mr Rowes pays me $100 that He Borrowed from me on Saturday, May 7th

26　　I Bot to Day of L. B. Hanchett 25 Doz of Cologne water at 1 Dollar per Doz

27　　Governor Quitman return from Texas in fine Health — To Day the Insurance office Bot the property that Beaty, Mc & Roberson Lived in on Perl Street for $12,500 in cash　　Took up Mothers acct. at Mr Murchersons for $33.37½

28　　Mr Dick McCrary Returns from Texas full of good Health and Sperrits, He said that he saw Alison & Foster over in Texas,　Mrs Bell left To Day on the S. B Persian for the uper Country — Maj Miller on the Same Boat　　Mr ——— attempted to suck Mr ———s El panio and the people were about to Lynch him, He had to sell Out and Leave the place amediately. He was a partner of Mr ——— ——— in the ——— ——— Tavern down thair.

29　　To day is precisely One week since old French got his hand cut by John

30　　Buissness Tolerable only. Dr Hog Lanced Williams Hand, To night Mr Rafner &c. and Mrs De Rush moved Out of the up stairs part of my House　　Their month will be Out on the 7th of June

31　　Dr Hog Dressed Williams Hand — greate quantity of Corruption Came Out of it. Young Mr Cooper strikes Lame Robert and the Pistol went off that he had in his hand and came very near killing him. They followed him up the hill and stoped him — I tell you he was mighty bad scared for a Little while for there were severall men that wanted to whip him for it — To day Mr Cryser sends me up ten Barrells of Coal at 87½ cts per Barrell — To day I took up my note for one hundred and 1.43 cents Indorsed by Mr S T McAlister dra[w]n in favor of Mr Petree, the enginieer of the Rail Road, The Brigg or Ship Janus arrived　　Brought 6 Bull Terriers to Alfred Cockran　　Wood & Penticost shiped four Bath tubs to Elisha Miller, Vicksburg

June 1　　I pd Mr Cryzer for ten Barrels of Coal $8.75　　I pd Mr S. M. Bon for One barrell of potatoes 1.75　　A Race to day between Flaggs Little Bay Horse and a Horse by the name of Tom Hinds — Brown run him, Flags horse won the money　　They [ran] 1000 yards　　A Race between Whitings mare and Boyers mare — Whitings mare won the Race very Easy — A Race between

Hocket Woods sorrill mare and a Bay mare belonging to a Mr Jannary — the Sorrill won the Race very Easy — I won $5 from Mr Mardice on Flaggs Horse & I won $5 from Mr J Soria on H Woods sorril mare — I took $5 and gave it to my Little William. St. Clair Denies Oweing five Dollars that I won from him some time ago.

2   Mc Tells me that Dr Denny, after having promised him the White office for a shop, tells him to day that Mr Vanison that Ocupies the ajoining Room, objected to Mcs having the Room and promised to get him a tenant at $30 per month, Mr Parker sells Out his Tavern To Mr Gildart of Woodville for Eighty Thousand in a Horn

3   I Bot Moses from a man by the name of William Good, at Least I Bot him at auction under the Hammer for four Hundred Dollars cash — I Bot also 2 Boxes of wine at 2.87½ per Box and 5 small Boxes of shaving soap, 43 cents per Box   Mr Samuel Davis sells his Family Residence to Mr Gildart for twenty thousand Dollars. No Sail   I Bot of Mr Chew all the Birds that Mr Grayson Left here and their Cages also for ten Dollars Cash.

4   Old La Vine and a Little Frenchman by the name of Surie has a Street fight, the one with a shovell, the other with a stick   Surie made La Viene back clear Back from Mr Murchersons store to his own   It was very Laughable, News that Dr Silas Potts is much worse, not Expected to Live, I Loaned Dr Reed Potts fifty Dollars — I Loaned S M Bon five Dollars to be paid on Monday next, This has been paid by Bon

5   Maj Shotard and Family Left to day on a Steam Boat for the North — Mr Bell, Mr Bush, Mr Elliot all went on the Same Boat. Louis Winsborough went up to waight on them, I saw Little Bons Clerk selling Oysters and snacks of one kind or other at a Table under the Hill, His name is Hendrickus

6   News in town Respecting the Death of Mr Gilbert in Jackson   He was Killed   I paid a Mr Pollock to day three Dollars for subscription to the Saturday Evening Post, Tis what I have already paid once before, I Took up my Note that I gave to Mr Gellespies Estate for $30 Indorsed by Mr Wm Harris   It was given for a Black Horse that I Bot at the sale six months ago. The Miss Evanses withdrew their sale of the Lot of ground to [the] Insurence office. They wanted to Reserve 10 feet for the Benifit of their other property & then the office would not take it

7   Maj Miller and Mr Cox came to Natchez

8   I bot one of the Patent pumps but did not Receive [it]

to day — Steven, Belonging to Mr Nickols came to me and asked my permission to Let him have Sarah, which I agreed to if he would always behave himself properly in my yard.

9 Buisness Tolerable fair, ten Baths to day — Mr Maxent Sells Out his Store on Main Street at auction. His stock Sold very high — Ten Baths to day

10 Maxent Selling Out at Auction, Sold His Fencibles Retreat, It Rented for $44 per month, Walker is sick Does not work to day — I Bot 9 Bottles muskettele wine, .56 per bott — One Childs chair ¾

11 Buisness geting very Dull Owing to so many many persons having gone to the North. Mr Wm Nickols was about to be married to Miss Routh & her Father came Down and put a stop to it.

12 Roads very Dusty, Mc and myself wrode Out as far as the Race track Mr Cryzer, Koontz & Lancaster has a Race, a ½ mile Race, Cryzer won it very Easy, Koontz and Mr Lancaster had One of the titest kind of a Race tho the grey horse won it, I think about a foot & a half — I Received a Letter from Mrs Miller and One from John A Desclow at Vicksburg — Old Mr Vanison I am told is Courting Mrs Purnell.

13 I Bot Mr Maxent pair of cannay Birds for $15.00 To Day at 2 Oclock I Hyred my Horse Pagg to Mr [blank] at Profilits to go into the country I Rented Mr Flecheo the up stairs part of the Old House for $20 per month. He is to pay me more in the winter for it. I put Moses with Dr P. Dally for One month

14 Little Bon pays me $5.00 that I Loaned him on Saturday, June 4th, 1836. I wrote E Miller To Day Dunning him for money. Italian Concert to night at Parkers hotell

15 Louis & Steven Both Taken sick, we gave them both medicine, Messrs Spraigue & Howell sells Mr C Darts Land at Auction There were 9688 acres sold or offered. It was to pay a debt Due the Bank, Sold under a Deed of Trust.

16 The Boys Finished the Bricking of the yard & not a single Bath During the whole day — Bill Nix shaves Mr Watson after his Death He was sent for by Mr Soria

17 I Received a Letter from E Miller to day which contained $60 to pay for the Bath Tubs that I sent Him — I went around to Walker & Collins and paid over the $60 to them for their Bath tubs

18 Late Last night Mrs Spielman has a Daughter. Old

Mrs Bennit presided ore the Cean [scene]   Mr Andeau Died this morning very Early — Peter Kelly Runs his sorril Horse against St Clairs sorrill mare for $200, five hundred yards   Peters horse won by 3 feet — Dr. ———s Daughter ran of[f] with Some One   I have not herd who with yet — Yes, it was with Mr ——— ———, the painter, They went up to Rodney and was there walking about in the woods together so seys Mr Murder and the Citizens came very near Lynching him — the[y] did not get married

19   Mc and myself wrode Out beyond the Race track and Looked at the Rail Road — My Horse was quite Sick, so I wrode my old Bay Horse   Mc wrides his Little Bob tail poney

20   Maj. Dunbar arrived from New Orleans   Brings me a Letter from Mrs Miller of New Orleans. I cut Miss Dinah Postlethwaits hair to day — I Shave Judge Guion at Parkers Hotell. I had my Cistern pump put up and a new Top for it which I paid Mr Seaton $12 in cash, The Man did not act the fair thing with him so I made it up by paying the two Dollars over — Italian opera at Mr Parkers Hotell to night

21   Bill Nix paints three of my Bath Tubbs — John is sick with a pain in the Ear — Brought on from Eating Ice Cream.

22   Buisness only Tolerably Brisk, Mr McGetrick makes a Bet with Mr Cobler to day of $25 that his Brown Horse would beat Mr Mardices Little Bay mare a ½ mile Race   They gave me the $50 to hold as there stakes   The winner was to have the fifty Dollars — I Loaned Dr Hubbard $400 to be paid on Monday; Some Talk about town of Lynching ——— ——— the Painter for taking off Dr ———s Daughter.

23   Dr Hubbard pd me $100, that being a part of Four Hundred that I Loaned him yesterday — He prescribed for John 20 grs of Calamal & 5 grs of James Powders   News to day that fifteen thousand Mexicans were Marching towards Texas and that six hundred thousand Dollars were subscribed by the Mexicans in One Single Day[41]

24   Roberson and Dr Hogg has a kind of a fight, old Dr Hogg made him Travell prety fast. Particulars are those, Roberson Owed the Dr 12 dollars for Medical Services. The Dr gave

---

[41] Following Santa Anna's defeat at San Jacinto, another invasion of Texas supposedly threatened by the Mexicans failed to materialize. But the provisional Texas government gave some credence to the reports and began to prepare to resist the new invasion. See William C. Binkley, "The Activities of the Texas Revolutionary Army After San Jacinto," *Journal of Southern History*, VI (1940), 342–43.

his account to Whiting to Collect for him so he presented the Acct. to Roberson & R. said that he was not the man, so Dr suied on it, & Robs. Came to his office to abuse him about it, and the old Dr told him to Leave his office. The Dr and him came to Blowes, and the Dr struck him with a chair & R. ran in the Street and struck him in the Breast with a Brick, then ran up Street as Hard as he could split and the old Dr after him   So Roberson run throuh Thistles Stable and came out at the Back side of the Stable and went Home   The Dr & Maj Miller went around to Robs House   Dr went in & struck him with his cane and R. caught the stick and the sword came out, and the Dr would have killed him if his arm had not been caught by Mr Ross — Roberson then Broke and run as hard as he could split to the Jail, and went in for Safe Keeping — In time of the fight Robs Brother Struck Maj Miller on the head with a Brick Bat and then Run and the old Maj after him as hard as he could split   The Maj stumbled and fell and as he fell he made a cut at Robison and Cut him in the Butt   Mr ——— ——— gave Dr ——— the plain Talk about His Daughter &c.

    26   Mc and myself wrode Out as far as the Race track. Good many young men from town were Out there Drunk   Mr Debins, Mr Abona, Mr [blank], Mr S Davis, Mr Hyram Hanchet and a good many Others

    July 2   Tarlton Brings my mule

    4   Big marching about town   The Huzars turned Out for the first time in the streets on parade — the Fencibles and the Mechanicks also — Big Dinner at Mr West tavern[42] — Mr Calmes Died this morning Early after having been to Market, He Broke a Blood vessell and Died before Dr Hogg could get to see him

    5   Mr Calmes, the Jailer, was Buried to Day by the Masons, Large procession — I sent my mule up to Spraigue & Howell to be sold but they did not sell her   There were no purchasers   Little William Winston[43] came to stay with me to Lern the Barbers trade. I gave young Marschalk the note be-

---

[42] A lengthy account of the festivities was carried in the Natchez *Free Trader*, July 8, 1836.

[43] William Winston worked for William Johnson, usually in his principal barbershop, during most of the time from this date until 1851, the year of Johnson's death. In 1836 he was still a slave, but the will of Fountain Winston (who had died in 1834) had provided that he should be emancipated when he was twenty-one years of age. At this time he was about twelve years of age. His mother was Rachel Winston, whose emancipation was directed by the same will. See Adams County Will Books, II, 81–83.

longing to his father that I Received to day from Mr Miller by young Ferriday

6 I sold Mr Thoms Barnard my mule on acct untill the first of January for fifty Dollars — He gave his due Bill for the amount and it Read in this way — Due W Johnson in the month of January, 1837, fifty Dollars for a dark mule — $50.00 I pd Messrs Spraigue & Howell $2 for trying to sell my mule at auction, Loaned Mother $10.

7 To day I had a Settlement with Mr F Taylor, and here is the full statement of the Settlement of The Stokes & Bray Account — For The up stairs part of the Shop $154.00. For The Ground Rent of the back Work Shop, 5 months at $6 per month 30.00, $184.00

9 Nothing New to Day Several Small Races this Evening. I was out to see them

10 Mc and myself went Out Towards Moores place. We had a very pleasent Ride, Jim Tooly wrode my Horse to try and see his gates, Returned him saying that he was Lame and hurt in the Back, by some way in the Back or Loins — A Hard Lye, he told it

11 I Loaned Mr Lighter $2.00 which I am never to get this side of the grave — Sure enough I never am to get it for He is now Dead [added later]

12 I loaned Mr Cryzer $25.00

13 The mice Eat up Both of my Cannary Birds

14 I Finished my Painting of my Bath Rooms

15 I was quite unwell, Kept my Bed all Day — Mr Burleigh sells his Land at Auction — The Bullet Buyo — 312 acres, it was Bot by Mr McFaddin for $10.25 per acre, Dr Gustine Claimed the Land and was at the auction Room spreading Out his Claims &c.

16 Peggy Torrence & her child Died a[t] Dick Ellises — To Day it was that I Loaned Mother One hundred Dollars to pay Mr Murcherson for the woman Mary. She paid Mr Doyal to day $130.00 and it Left a Ballance Due Mr Murcherson of $170.

17 The Boys worked in the Shop by them selves — I was unwell and did [not] work yesterday Either They took in with Baths &c. $22.00 and to Day they took in with Dito $9.37½ — Mrs Spielman is very sick and has been for a week and more — Mrs Denny Suckolds the child, Fencible meeting took place and they Expelled ——— the painter, and at night which was Last

Night they had a sort of a fight or scuffle, and Peet Larrence says that they choaked and kicked Mr McGinnis very much, so I do not know how true it is

18 I put a note in Bank to Day for Collection   It was the note that I got from Mr C Dart in payment of the money that He Owed me   The amount of the note is $720.00 and it will be Due on the 10th & 13th of August — The Bell was Rang Last Night for the purpose [of] attracking the attention of a Croud of anti Linch party that had [incomplete entry]

19 Mr Sweyney Returned from Texas. I made a Bet to day with Mr Mardice of a pair of fine Boots on his Race, I Bet him that McGetricks horse would Beat his mare the Six Hundred yard place, Mr Rushleau Takes the sorril Filly that he Lost some time ago from the Pock-marked Butcher and the Butcher said that he Bot her from Mr Griffiths Jack — The nag belonged to Maj. Young of Jefferson County — Mr Pitcher Buys Bons Glandered Horse at auction   Price $36 cash

20 I sent by the white Boy that worked with Elisha Miller on Bourd of a Steam Boat to day four young Mocking Birds and a Letter To Mrs Miller

21 I Loaned Mr E. Thomas $100 payable in sixty Days or sooner if Convenient To him, Mc has pair of Pantaloons Cut Out & To be made by Skeggs & Hough

22 Mr McGinis pretends to [be] very crazy, I bought To Day at Auction 18 Bottles Lime Juice, 9 Bottles of London Mustard, 2 Bottles of Lemmon Syrrup. My Horses were turned Out Late in the night of this Day by someone as yet unknown and my Bay Horse was found by Himself in the Byyou up near the Residence of Mr Louis Millers. The Ballance of the Horses had Left Him.

23 I Found my fine Bay horse this morning in a Byio with his Left hind Leg or hip knocked out of place and very much Bruised, indeed. I then on the strength of having Lost so fine a Horse Took old Pagg out-& swaped him away to the meanest and most Low Life Rascally Butcher that Ever has Lived in this town, His name is Louie or Some Such Name, He is a pock marked Butcher and a most infernal Rascal, He put a young horse on me and told me that if he did not work that he would take him Back again & that he was not Blind and promised me very faithfully that if the horse did not answer my purpose that it would be no trade, Well a Day or two afterwards I tryed his horse, and I found him to be no kind of a work Horse, and blind in One Eye, and the other very near Blind — I took him back to the Rascall and he had swaped my horse away and could not he said take Back his Horse.

24 Nothing new of any consequence. Mc and myself wrode out in the Scotts old Field, the Road very Dusty.

25 I took the Blind Horse Back to the Butchers and he refused to take him Back for he had Just Swaped Pagg of[f] for another Horse He gave 7.50 difference and got another Horse To day I was as mad as the very Old Harry — in the first place I was in a passion about the Rascally Butchers Horse — in the next place Mother & old French had some Difference. Frence he Left and Ranaway & L. W. Winstons mother was making some arrangment or quarrelling about her sons having Bought a Bed from One of the other Boys at 37½ cents Oh the Deel could not be in more passion than I was

26 I took a horse Down to day to see if he would work, But he would not worke atall so I sent him Back to him again

27 I Loaned Mr Skeggs $100 The old grey horse that I was about to swap for or did swap for with Littleton Commings yesterday would not suite me so we swaped Back again

28 It was To Day Henry Melvin Returned my Little Brown Horse to me stating that he was affraid that he would go Blind. He had swaped or given me an Old Sorrill Horse for the Brown Horse and I gave him five Dollars to Boot, Senitor Walker arrived Here this Evening about 6 Oclock in a s. Boat

29 I Loaned Dr Hubbard One Hundred Dollars I Bot four Barreles of Flower to day at $4.12 a Barrel, also six pair of pantaloons $2.50 per pair — Mother paid me ten Dollars on the Butchers account — She takes the three Barrels of Flower at $10 which is on a Credit

30 I paid Mr Stanton to day $6 for One years subscription to the Free Trader, and I took his Receipt for the same I Lost on a Race to day between McGetricks Tom and Mr Mardices mare One pair of fine Boots and ten $ and I Lost on a Race between St Clairs mare and Hocket Woods Stud horse $6 — the horse won the Race very Easy by 20 or 30 yards I Borrowed from Ann to Day $10 which I Lost on the Races, & I have Loaned out this week $200 and my Expenses and Losses this week is $101.87½ A Mr Hueis Killed a Mr Thatcher Cotten by Shooting him

31 To Day we sent' to New Orleans by James One pound Cake for the children, four Dozen peaches and two or three Jars

of preserves, and One Dog puppy for Mrs Miller, I stoped home all Day

August 1   This man Hews was tryed to day for the murder of Thatcher Cotten, and was acquited and Discharged — There were a general shout when he was Discharged — Tis strange how men will act. This man Cotten has been in this place for three or four years and there was not ten men in the place that knew him for in the Day time he was always hid and at night he would Come out and be all over town

      3   I went to the Billiard Table To hunt for Mr Whiting to try and Collect One hundred dollars that he Borrowed from me   I found him playing Back gammon — I could not get the money from him.

      4   I went up to old Whitings house to Collect my money from him But could not, he promised to pay me to morrow. Mr Ganson gets married to Miss [blank] at Sorias Dwelling — Mr Ru[s]hleau Comes to Borrow Monday [money] from me to Day But I did not have it to spare.

      5   To Day at 10 Oclock Mrs Butler was Buried — the wife of Young Butler the Merchant

      6   Mr S. M. Bon takes my account against Mr J Whiting for $100. He was to have the use of the money for three weeks if he Could Collect it, I paid Mr Reid $6 for a pair of Boots that I lost with Mr Mardice on a Race. William wrode up to shave Dr Pollard at the Hospital and my horse got a way and ran home and Lost the saddle for an hour or two, then Wm went after it and found it, Bill Nix Commences in the Spelling Book to Read for he fail[ed] in Reading in the Introduction

      7   Dr R. Potts tells Mr Harris about St Clairs taking hold of him in the street and wanted to fight him — the Dr had a Black man in Custody for making a noise in the street, and St Clair made him Let the man alone and Leave him   Mc and myself wrode Out as far as the Bridge at St Catharine   To Day the Boys made in their Bath Department or made during the week $4.12: Charles Received 62½ cents more than any of the[m] for his good Conduct During the week   Steven paid me $8 for this weeks work. Last Evening he worked at Mr Spraigues & Howells Auction Rooms, To day the Boys were spelling and Bill Nix was the foot of the Class

      8   To day I was out to Dr Duncans to cut the Childrens hair — I cut three Heads of children hair. I cut Miss Charlottes hair very close   To day the new Ingine was hauled up the street and it did not perform well.[44] To day it was that Dr Potts was whiping a Black man and St Clair[45] walked up and took him by the Collar and Choked him and Slung him around and then Told him to get on his Horse and Clear Out, which he did do very soon

9 No news to day of any importance. And very warm

11 I Bot to day 71 yards of white Cotton and a Lot of shoes. The whole amount of the Bill was $13.37½. Bill Nix is Discharged from the Bath Concern from improper Conduct — 1.75 in the firm up to the time of his Discharge.

12 I Bot of Messrs Soria & Co. One Barrell of Havanah Sugar — weight 215 pound at 17¼ cts, $34.94 To Day Mr Skeggs paid me $30, it being part of One Hundred Dollars that he Borrowed from me on Wednesday July 27th, 1836

13 To day I went Down to the Commercial Bank and Drew Out the money that was paid by Mr Walworth on a note that he gave Mr C Dart and I traded with Mr C Dart for the above note It was for $720. To day a Mr George McGraw was Buried & Mr Chaile died — William shaves him Ann gave me $28.75 as Middletons wages — he Lost Last weeks wages for he says that he was sick

14 A pascel of young men very drunk at Mr West Tavern. Tom Munce, Capt Pomp, Carpenter and others — They acted very much Like Fools — I wrode out as far as the old Field by myself tho I took my 2 Dogs with me and took a seat and Read a newspaper I must confess that I was much pleased with my Evenings Employment. Mr Chaile was Buried to day at 10 Oclock. Large Funeral

15 Wellington Left here for New Orleans. I sent by Wellington $33.50 to Mr Miller which pd up for Middletons wages up to the 24th of July[46]

[44] Johnson probably referred to a fire engine.

[45] In 1835–36, Johnson had made loans of $380, $50, and $250 to Dr. Reed Potts. The doctor repaid them promptly, but subsequently was accused of a serious financial irregularity, not involving the diarist, and left town. Prior to his departure, Potts and another physician had formed the firm of Dashiell & Potts, which sold medicines, drugs, paint, trees, vines, shrubbery, and window glass.

St. Clair was a white carpenter who did some work for Johnson, raced horses against him, bet on horse races with the Negro, and borrowed money from him.

[46] Middleton was an old Negro slave who belonged to James Miller of New Orleans but was allowed to work for various persons in Natchez under Johnson's general supervision. On August 6, 1837, Johnson wrote his sister, Mrs. Miller, that Middleton was usually sick or drunk and wanted the Millers to take him to New Orleans "to take care of him." Copy of letter in Johnson Papers. But in November,

16   Mr Gilbert Died on the River — To day Mother sends Mary with a paper to get a master — The Boys commenced this Evening to dig out the stable — Dr R P stops shaving to this date

17   I was puting a Loft in my stable To Day — Jenny Bang the weaver Runs away. Col. Throckmorton Returns Home from the North   Col Wilkins very very low indeed. Messrs Lyle, Carrol, Profilet, Dr Davis arrived from the north, To day the Boys were at work at the stable.

19   Young Mr Alfred and John T Gellespie got Drowned in Second Creek at Mr Calvin Smiths plantation — they were in a swiming with Mr John Rouths son

20   Little Samuel Gwinn died   To Day the Boys & myself Finished the stable that I was at work on for Mr Dumax — I Loaned Messrs Carroll & Butler $225, paid in cash to be paid on Tuesday, 23d inst — this is paid paid

21   My Horse ran away from Town and I hyred a Little Filly from the stable to hunt him, But he was found by Mr Bouyers so I took the Filly and Ann & myself wrode Out to the Old Field. Old Mc he took the wrong way and went Out by Capt Nevits plantation

22   Mr Dumax Takes my stable at five Dollars per month, the other two gentlemen Brought their Horses at the same time

23   It was to day that those gentlemen took the stable — I was in treaty for a swap to day with Mr Bouyer, for a Little mare that he has, He offered her to me for One hundred and Thirty Dollars. That is he said that if I would give him thirty Dollars in Cash that he would take a Due Bill that I had against Mr Jno Whiting. But I was to stand good for the payment. But I would not agree to stand good for the payment for the Due Bill But if he would take the Bill for Better or for worse that I would give him $35 in cash and he would not take it, tho he said he would if I would give him $40.00   So we did not trade, i.e. to day

24   To day Mr Bouyer and myself made a Trade, the conditions are those; He Took a Due Bill against Mr Whiting for $100. This he took for good and all and if it was not paid by Mr Whiting why it was to be his Loss and not mine, and I was to give him $40 in Cash which I did for a Little Sorril mare which warrented sound Except One Eye that was hurt & I told him I

1841, Middleton was repaying Johnson for a small loan the barber had made him "in part Payment of a Home."

thought she had the Big Head But he garanteed that she had nothing Like the Big Head — upon those condition we closed our trade — that he was to take the Bill for Better or worse and to have no Recourse on me hereafter   The Ship St. Louis came up. Capt Story in Command of her

25   I hyred my horse to a carpenter to go to a funeral and the horse fell in a grave or partly into it and hurt his Leg — To Day Mr Lawrrence whiped K and her son James prety severee — the[re] were a motion made to prosecute him I believe

26   Mr Cannon and Mr Esdra Returns from the North — and a mean Fellow he is, in my Humble Opimon

27   To Day I Loaned Mr Spencer for the use of Barlow & Taylor $100.00   Mr Sheling gets married To Miss Ela Hinson — She is the sister of Mrs Dumax — This is the first wedding that Ever took place in the new Building[47] Belonging to Mr McAlister on Main St

28   I wrode Out with Mc as far as Mr Williams Plantation   I wrode my Little Sorril Mare for the purpose of trying her and to see whether she stumbled so much as was Reported, I found she did not Stumble as much as I thought

29   I herd to day that Last Saturday when the Bunker Hill Left here that there was on Bourd of her 100 men Bound for Texas Comanded by a Capt Williams — The Boat Landed at Peter Littles place to wood & those men went on shore and Robbed his Hen Roos and then whiped his Negro Boy — The old man his self then Came Out and they partly knocked him Down and then pouned him pretty severely — they then Left and went on Bourd of the Steam Boat taking with them all the old Fellows Chickens & Turkeys — To Day a Boy belonging to Mr S. Davis was hung on the other side of the River   His name was Nim Rod — He was Hung for Killing the overseer by the name of Levels I believe, Early this Evening Mr Vannerson gets married to old Mrs Purnell

30   To day is the first wride that Mr Bon Takes — that is by the month, He is to pay me $20.00 per month for wriding the nag — Mardmaduke Davis was Buried   Old Rowland Cham-

---

[47] Johnson may have referred to the New Hotel. The Natchez *Free Trader*, April 15, 1836, had carried the following notice: "The New Hotel adjoining the theatre on Main street is now open for the reception of boarders, under the directions and charge of Mr. McFadden. This Hotel is just finished, and is handsomely furnished with entirely new furniture, beds, bedding, etc. The rooms are neat and airy, and the accommodations excellent. The bar is supplied with the best of liquors."

bers sells the property of David Miles at auction   It was Bot by James Steele at $6000 So I herd

31   Capt Cotten arrived from the North with his Family — Mr Taylor Takes his girl Sharlot home

September 1   Mr Spielman puts up the first piece or side of the new kitchen in his yard

2   At a Raffle this Evening at Rowlands Coffee House for a gold watch valued at $150.00 I won it by throwing 41. The number was 16, taken by L. S. M. Bon. Therefore it was to be divided between us — I had two other chances and I got Mr Pulling to throw for me and he threw Low numbers   I then threw for Mr Muchaster and threw 37. Mr Walker threw 40   After wining the watch I called for a Basket of Champane wine. The Company Drank Eight Bottles which amounted to $20. I made Bon pay the half of the Expences   P. McGraw & Ried Returns from the North — Sterns wife Left Him a week or two ago — Backed him Out

3   I settled with Mr Bon for his part of the watch that we won & I paid him in cash $35 and in horse hyre $20 which is up to the 30th of this month — To Day I Loaned Mr Spencer for use of Barlow and Taylor, $200 and took his Due Bill for $300 in full, for I Loaned him for the House $100 Last Saturday, 27th ultm   To [it] makes precisly three weeks since I Received any wages from Steven. I found Out this Evening by whiping prety severely that he had Received his wages from Messrs Spraigue & Howell, and had made away with the whole of it, on the Back of which old Mr Christopher Miller comes and complained of Seven Coming Out to his House after his girl &c.

4   Last night at 2 Oclock Mr James McAlister Died with Congestive Fever   Dr Dally was the phician, He was taken on Thursday Evening Last and Buried this Evening amidst a Heavy shower of Rain at 4 Oclock   The procession was small Owing to the Bad weather   Messrs Spraigue & Co. paid me yesterday $26 and some cents being the ammount Due me for the sale of two Drays that I had sold at their Auction Room — the Drays sold for $28, a mere nothing

5   Mrs Miller came up from New Orleans on the Steam Boat Jone. She Brought up her Family   Consists of Mrs Adelia Miller and her Daughter Katharine Miller & William Miller & James Miller & Emer Miller and Lisar, and Mary, a servant[48] Mr S. M. Bon wrides my horse Out and my horse threw him and Ran off He was Out in the neighbourhood of Mr Lillards place. To Day I hyred Steven to Mr Geo. Snider for $28 per month.

6 I Loaned my Little Sorril mare to Mr Mellen to wride Out to his Dwelling House or Plantation This Evening I went Out to the Race track, and there was a Race between Peter Kelly and St Clair, this I did not see, then there was a Race between Janny Ranes mair and John Holdens Sorril Horse, The mare won the Race very Easy. It was 3 quarters of a mile that they Run & I Lost $3.50 with Hendrickus and 4 Dollars with McGettrick. Louis Winsborough Came Down the River.

7 I took supper Down at Mrs Battles, so did Mrs Miller & C. To day for the first time I herd from Mc that Dr R Potts had Collected Something Like $350 for McGlohern and had not paid it over to him, and that the people was much hurt at the thought of such conduct for he Denied having collected the money.

8 Nothing more worth writing down to day

9 The Steam Boat Jone Came Down from Manchester — Mrs Miller Sends a Letter to Mr Miller and One Barrell of Quinces To day Bill Wilson[49] & Bill Winston has a fight in the Back Room. Winston has the Best of the fight tho. I Parted them Both and made a greate Deal of fun of Winston. Second Fight took place in the Back of the Yard and Bill Winston whiped him Fairly and he hollowed to have Bill Winston taken off of him. Winston had him Down flat on the ground — I Loaned Mr Skilling my horse to wride this morning — Mr Lawrence has Mrs Corns Charles, Taking him before the Esqr for Robing Dr Pollard at the Hospital

10 I wrode Out as far as the Track I there saw a Race between St Clairs mare and Peter Kellys Horse, ½ mile Race — The horse won the Race very Easy I thought — There was a Race also between H Coblers horse and Tho. Loves Horse and Loves horse won the Race very Easy — I saw a Fight To Day in the Old Field Back of Holdens Fence, One of them was named Meligen He was a Silver Smith. The other man whiped him —

---

[48] This was one of a number of visits made to Natchez by Johnson's free Negro sister, Mrs. James Miller of New Orleans. The children accompanying her on this trip were Katharine, William, James, Emma, and Anna Eliza.

[49] William Wilson was a Negro boy, probably free, who worked for the diarist, 1836–37, but was never legally bound to him as an apprentice. For Johnson's record of accounts with Wilson, see Ledger, 1835–39, p. 104, Johnson Papers.

they had Two Ronds — they were both Knocked Down the first Blow — Mr Wm Chambers came home from the North

11   Old Dad and his wife went Down to Woodville   Left Big Waller, Little Clabourne, Jeorgan to mind the House. Wm wrides out there and comes home very soon — Some what hurt at the sight of things &c — Waller had him perfectly straight

12   Mr Wiswall Returned From the North and Mr Doland by the Same Boat.

13   Dr. Reed Potts Fled the City or Left it a few Days ago — I forget when it was that I hyred Moses to Dr Dally, But I think this Entry is very near right

14   Mr Wiswall Commenced by the month & Mr Walker also — Mr Wm Harris paid me $18.00 for One years shaving, the year Ended a month or two ago   My Horses Broke the stable Last night in Fighting and Rob Roy hurt himself very much with nails against one thing or other — I had old Jinnys stall made for her the other Day — Mr Kale Hurst Drives some of the Best Looking Beeves through the town that I have seen for a many a day — he intends to slaugter them himself So I am Told

18   French wrides Out at Carys Dwelling House in the Country — She Tells French that he must not Blame her, But she understood that his Father did not want him to come out there anymore, French he herd no more — he then Bursted Wide open   Col Bingaman Lost a fine animal to day with the cholic

20   Janson Backed Out from the trade with Mc for his House & Lot, the terms were $7000 payable in three years, 3 instalments — 1st, 2d, & 3d years — Mrs Battles has a Small Dinner — Mrs Miller & Ann were present.

22   Mr F. Taylor Takes his girl Katharine home. Mr Spielman Finishes his kitchen and Back house & stable.

23   I subscribed for a chance in a gold watch to be thrown for a[t] Mr Rowlands Coffe house Shortly — Mr Spielman came to me to Rent the up stairs part of my House that is now Ocupied [by] Flecho — The watch I spoke of above I threw and Lost it   I only threw 28 — Mr Owen and lady came home

24   A Race To Day between a sorril stud and Mr Mardices Little mare. One mile Out, The mare won the Race very Easy — There were also a Race between H Coblers Little Black horse and Mr Cryzer Bay Horse, 3 Hundred yard Race, The Little Black Horse won the Race Easy   I won ten Dollars From Mr Ge Lancaster   I got one Bale of Hay from Mr Cryzer to day, wt. 420 at 1.50 per hundred, $6.20, in part pay of $25 that I Loaned him

25 Mc and myself wrode Out beyond Col. Wilkins Residence and got a few walnuts, Mr S Plummer arrived on the S. B. Mogull — This Boat Brought News of the death of Louis Phillipe who was shot by some unknowned person   All false [later entry]

26 Judge F Guion Came To Town and to day was the first day of the Criminal Court

27 I Loaned Mr Spielman two hundred to be paid when Ever Called for by me. Mrs McGuires goods were sold to day at Public Auction by Jacob Soria & Co

28 Mc takes a chance for Mr Moselys Horse, the chance was $20. I was in with Mc   He only threw 26. The Horse was put up at $260. He was won by Mr Mellen at 41. Mary is on tryal to day at Mr McAlister, to Cook for him. Mr A. L. Gains Returns from the North, Peter Lawrence got clear of the charge of whiping Kity McCary[50] — there was no Bill found against him. Rascally. Rascally — Mr Waller paid me ten Dolars that I Loaned him a week or two ago

29 I gave Mr Piper to day 2 pistols to have them fixed up. Mr Bons month up to day for wriding my Little Soril mare.

30 Mr McAlisters agrees to take Mary at twelve Hundred Dollars at four months credit — Mr Murcherson & Mr R. M. Gains Returns from Kentucky. They Bring news of the Louisville Races   Thar Angorah was beaten in the first 4 mile by [blank] upwards of three hundred yards

October 1 I Loaned Mr Paterson for use of the store 200.00 To be paid on Monday next, 3d instant   Armat Came home from the North.

2 Myself and William Took Little William & James Miller Out as far as Capt. Nevits Old Field a wriding.

3 Mr Piper sends my Pistols home this morning — News came to day statining or confirming the Death of young Mr Lyons, the son of Jos B Lyons   He Died at Louisville

4 The Camp Meeting Broke up this morning — Jos Snider & Earl Clapp Brings Steven Down from the Camp Ground — Col Throckmorton Returns from his plantation   Col. A. L. Bingaman, Messrs R. & T. Evans, Mr Elliot, and the Miss Evanses Came Down from Louisville — Earl Clapp has Steven

---

[50] Kitty McCary (or McCarey) was the free mulatto sister of Robert McCary, Johnson's close friend.

streched Out whiping Him for Runing away   He gave him a
genteel whiping for me

5   The Bunker Hill Brought up the Ship Powatan & the
shipp Tremount for Vicksburg — Mr Lillard came home from the
North

6   Mr D Barlow Received some goods in his new store for
the First time and is opening them this Evening — I hyred my
Little Sorril mare to Mr Jno Knight for fifteen Dollars per month
— I Endorsed a note to day for Mc due in six months for $46
given for a Riffle — to Calames Estate — John Wren Came Home
from Colledge as a Dr   Mr. Simms Returned from the North
— I got a Barrel of sweet potatoes from Mrs Cary, price
$3.00   They were for Mrs Miller

7   Mr Knight Returns my nag stating that he had Received
a nag from the Country — Mr Williams has two Large Windows
made in front of his store, Louis Broke my Cart under the Hill
to day

8   Mardice Filly, Kanes mare, Brannens Filly — ½ half mile
Race this Evening. Mr Mardices mare won the Race very Easy,
Mardices S Horse, St. Clairs Lt horse, Mile & Repeat. The big
horse Distanced the other Horse   Dick Ellis R. Horse, Rober-
sons Blk mare, 1 quarter of a mile. Old horse won the Race very
Easy — Old Sterns Commences to work for Mc   Mr Whiskers
and Mr McGetricks horse Ran a Race   The Bay Horse won the
Race — I won From McGetrick 1.00   Paid, From Waller $6.00,
From Raby 12 weeks shaving $4.50, From Mr McFadgin $5.00

9   A beautiful day and the streets were never more dusty.
Mc and myself wrode Out beyond Col Wilkinses and I Took my
Pistols along — We shot at the tree several times   Mc he missed
the tree and he shot three times with my Riffle Barrell Pistol

10   Mrs Miller Leaves to day on the Steam Boat Danial
O'Connell. She took Lavenia, William and James & Emer Miller,
also Lisar with her to New Orleans — I gave as a present to Her
a Barrel of potatoes [and] a Barrel of Corned Beef   I wanted
her to give Cap Johnson a part of the Beef and Madam Hanah
Johnson a part. To day Mr F. Taylor Came Down to Mr
Flecheos and Took Out of his Establishment just by way of
secureing Rent, the Following articles to the amount of $80 or
a Little upwards. He gave me to take care of the Following, 3
Feather Brooms and one Finger Ring — the Ring were put down
at $4 and the Brooms were put at $2.75 per Broom

11   The streets were very dusty   Skeggs & Houg opening new goods. They intend keeping a Clothing Store Here after, Mr Wiswall sends his horse over to my Stable, Mr Jewet Came and informed me that 4 of the watches belonging to Flecheo or that were in Flechos Belonged to him and that he had put them there to have them Sold for him   If [I] mistake not they were taken to secure my account against Flecho — Mrs Glover sells her house & Lot at auction, it sold for four thousand five hundred Dollars, Mr Furnum Bot it   The Lot just behind it sold for $350 and was Bot by Mr Bledsoe — all on a credit

   12   Old Gridley has his property sold at auction, The Billiard Table Room sold for ten thousand Seven Hundred Dollars — It sold for the want of money only — Tyler the Butcher Bot it — I sold my cart to Mr Toburn for $28 payable in thirty Days from Date, He also Left his wagon here to be mine if he did not pay me at the Expiration of the thirty Days. Mr Britton has a new front put in his house   My Little Will has two teeth Just making there appearace — Mr Greene arrived here   He has a hair Brush, shaving Cake of Soap, Shaving Brush, amounting 1.37½   Mr Hendrickus commencd by the month

   13   I Sent Steven Out to Col Bingamans to work in the Cotton Field. To day Mr Conly Strikes Mr Fulton with a Stick in the first place, then a Blow or two past and then Mr Conly stabbed him in the thy — they then took Mr Conly to Jail for about an hour, he was then tryed and was held to Bail in the sum of five thousand Dollars

   14   I made out my account to day against Mr Adolph Flecheo. The amount of which was for the Lower Room up to the First of Oct. $111.00, and For the uper Dwelling and Lodging Rooms up to 13th Oct, 80.00   Myself and Mr Taylor went around to Mr Perdues Esqr to get an atachment out to take the goods and chattles of Mr F[l]echos things, which we did. Mr Izod was deputy offircer — and on the same Evening Mr McAlister did the same

   15   Mr Flecheo Returns from New Orleans on the Hellen Douglas and he came to Explain the Reason why he made so Long a stay in Orleans — Mr Spielman paid me $250. Tis money that I Loaned him Some time ago

   16   Mc and myself walked Down to the Bluff Late this Evening.[51]

51 For a number of years prior to 1827, title to the open space along the Mississippi River bluff at Natchez (long used as a city common or esplanade) had been disputed in the courts by the corporation and Jefferson College. A compro-

17   I and Mr F. Taylor had a Settlement in this way   My account against Mr Flecheo was $191 and I took Out the atachement for this amount and we had considerable talk on the Subject. I then took out his deducted Bill, which we thought was about $20 and then I agreed to pay half of the Expense of the attachments Fees which was about $6 or Something like it   He gave his note payable on the First of January, 1837, for $180, with Mr Seureau as security — I Loaned Mother to day $100 in cash to pay Mr Murcherson for the woman Mary and her child Moses. This Leaves a Ballance Due Mr Murcherson of $70

18   Buisness Tolerable Brisk; Mr Izod Called on me to day to know if I or Mr Flecheo was to settle the amount of Cost on the atachments that I got out on Mr Flecheos goods and Chattles, the amount of cost was $12.50   I told him that I would pay it or half of it — which he was very willing for me to do it, I went down this Evening to Messrs Case & Barbers to get one Dozen Razors that he was to Bring me from the North. He gave me one Dozen thin Bladed Ratlers, very diferent from what was to have Brought me, I then Bought One Dozen of Magnum Bonums Razors for which I paid him $9 in cash — Dr Dally sends Moses home Sick, much worse than he was when he first went to Live with him, I Received a Letter from Mrs Miller stating that they were all well

19   My Cart Broke its axeltree to day and I sent it Down to Mr Cryzers to be mended and whilst I was there I paid him for mending the shaft of the same cart that Broke two weeks ago, the amount of this Bill was $5.50 and he has now to put in a new axeltree for which he agrees to do for $6. To day Mr Soria Sells at his auction Room a House and Lot that belongs to Emery Wilson. The Lot Lies on the Pine Ridge Road — Fronts that street 150 feet and Runs back 150 ft. deep — it was foremaly the Property of Mr Bledsoe, It sold for four Thousand Dollars, one third payable in six months, and the Ballance in One and two years without interest. It was Bot by a Mr N. L. Carpenter — I took my riffle and cleaned her up in order to take a hunt on

---

mise split the disputed area between the litigants so that the area between a new street, called Broadway, and the verge of the bluff was henceforth to be used as a "Promenade or pleasure ground." This city park is the area called "the Bluff" by William Johnson and still so called today. See Adams County Deed Records, P, 676–79; "Report of Committee of Trustees of Jefferson College," *South-Western Journal,* I (1838), 33; William B. Hamilton, "Jefferson College, and Education in Mississippi, 1798–1817," *Journal of Mississippi History,* III (1941), 268-71.

Fryday if the weather was good, in my native old hunting ground the swamp

20   Young Mr Helm gets married to Miss Biggs. I Bought to day from Mr Wiswall one Dress patron of shalla,[52] price $2 a yard, 11 yards, and I Bought One dress patron of Calico, price $5.50   I gave Ann $20 also — I got a pair of spurs to day at Mr Spielmans, they were charged to me, price One Dollar — Mrs Lieper has her Litle Daugter this morning

21   To day Mc and myself wrode Down in the Swamp a hunting, we went Down after Breakfast — Mc took his Riffle and I took my Little Shot Gun. Mc Killed one squirrell and wounded a Crow, This I seen myself. He Reports that he killed 2 ducks in the Lake and one crane — this I don't know so much about, I Killed 7 wood cock, 1 sparrow, and one owl, this I Brought home. I Broke the thy of a Large Eagle, But did not get a hold on him, he flew across the Lake after he was shot   Mcs Poney got away and went to Barlands fence   His wif sent Out and had him caught. Kept till old Mc came there. I came to town to Look for him and then went Back as far as the Clabourne plantation before I met him, To day Mr La Vigne paid me for seven months Rent up the 19th of Septm at $20 per month, $140.00   I also settled with him for my store account, $24.

22   Mr Patterson paid me to Day $100, being a part of two hundred Dollars that I Loaned him a week or two ago — he still Owes me One hundred Dollars

23   The Boys went into the swamp to get pecons — Mc and myself went down also, we got a Tolerable good chance of them. Mr John Lacrose and Black Lewis, belonging to Mr Reid, went into the swamp and they said that they killed Seven Ducks; and the Black Fellow Lewis, in shooting off his gun, shot Reids fine Dog by accident

24   Mr Spielman very much in want of a Little Money   I told him I had none, Mr L. R. Marshal arrived, Mr Cockran also

25   Mr Bush and Preston W Farrar came home from the North, I wrote a Letter to Mrs Miller to day. Mother paid Mr Murcherson to Day Seventy Dollars, being the Last part of the Eight Hundred Dollars that she was to pay for the Black woman Mary and her Child Moses. Mr Murcherson gave her the Bill of Sale to Day of Mary and her child Moses — Miss Katharine Evans and Mr Sidney Smith went up to the Plantation this morn-

---

[52] Johnson probably referred to challis, a soft woolen-and-silk dress fabric.

ing — I Let the Little Horrits have my Horse to wride Out this
Evening — I think it will be his Last wride on him — he is too
Smart, too Smart. Mr Lyle and Mr P. Baker makes a pass or
two at each other up at Profilets Corner — Baker insulted Mrs
Lyle — was the cause of the fight. I got a Bale of hay to day
from Mr Cryzer, wt. 450. I gave him credit for it at 1.50 per
hundred

 26 I Paid Mr Izod to day in cash $12 Cost on the atach-
ment that I got Out against Mr Flechos goods — the understanding was that Each of us was to pay half of the Expense, To day
Louis Let the grey mare Back over in the Buyo with the Cart
and Broke of[f] One of the shafves and did not hurt the mare
but very Little, I took the whip for the first time since I have
had him and whiped him with it Kean has a Concert at the
Masonic Hall to night

 27 I Bot to day at Mr Sprague & Howells two Thousand
Segars, at $12.75 per thousand

 28 Mr McCary and Mr Reid and myself went in the woods
a hunting We went in the swamp. Mr Barland was Out a
hunting at the same time. Old Mc killed one Duck and one squirrel Mr Reid did not kill anything that he got, he said that he
killed two Ducks, but did not get them, I killed 7 Large snipe
and five Small Ones, two Large Squirrels, One Duck, two Loons,
one yellow Hammer and One very Large alligator, I Shot him
with a riffle, I found him out on the Dry Land Down at the
Cypress Buyio. Mr Barland killed three squirrels — I Beet the
Croud by a Large Deal, Mr T. G. Ellis arrived to day from the
North

 29 Mr J. C. Potts arrived from the North with his Lady.
He came by sea

 30 I Let the young man, a man at Messrs Wiswalls and
Pattersons wride out this Evening on my Little mare, Count O.
Enos returns from the North

 31 The property of Misse Evans at the Sorias conner
Extending Down to Spielmans Saddler Store, this was Bot by
Mr Cammell & Griffin at forty thousand Dollars, Tis generally
believed that it was purchased by those Gentlemen for the
purpose of having an Exchange Built upon it, To day the
Mr Lillard starts some Irish workman to Dig Out the Foundation of the Dunbar Lot that he Bot the other week

 November 1 The young Evans Sells there property to
Day at Auction. The Lots were those Lying between Bank alley

and the market House   It Sold for twelve thousand and ten
Dollars and was Struck of[f] to Mr Picther. Tis thought that
he made the purchase for a Company to Build an Insurance
office on it the Lot. There were also three Lotts sold out near
the Forks of the Road. It was the property of John Whitings
and was Sold for Debt. The first two Lotts Contained 42 ft Front
and runing back both together 410 feet — they sold for $410 per
Lot. Mr Baity Bot the 1st two and the other Sold for two
hundred and something, I dont Recollect Exactly, Bons Lot
Fronts the Rail Road and it tis a very poor piece of Property,
I do asure the Reader   Mr Manchaster pd me his Shaving Bill
to day and it amounted to forty Dollars — he pd me the Cash,
Elick Piper came To Natchez this morning

    2   I Let Mr Horrits have my Little mare to wride Out
this Evening — Mr Elick came home   Mr Elick Stewart and
Mr R. Herd came home, Mr Ballad Told me to day that Legee
wanted to charge $250 for the musick on Bourd of the Ship and
he told me that they were not agoing to have him at all

    3   There were to night on Bourd of the Ship Pohatan a
Large Ball   She was Lying up at or above the uper Oil Mill,
The Party or Ball was given by Mr Lillar & the Captain, I am
told they were at Least three or four hundred pursons, Mrs
Dunbars Carriage turned over and it Broke her wrist and Bruised
her head or face a Little, Mr Clays Carriage upset also but did
not hurt any One   Mr A. L. Gains and Mr Lawyer Baker had
a quarrell. Dr Hog Said Something in behalf of Gains for which
Mr Baker got offended and Drew his Dirk on the Dr   He was
held by Some of the gentlemen or Else the old Dr and him would
Have been to gether for the Dr told them not to hold him — to
lett him go as he was not at all affraid of him[53]

    4   The Steam Boat Jone came up yesterday about 11
Oclock, took in a Load of coten at this place and Left again for
New Orleans This night at about 8 Oclock — I wrote a Letter by
her to Mrs Miller, Mr A L Gains and Mr Baker makes up or
makes Friends, Mr N Barlow paid me to Day $300, money that
I Loaned him a short time ago

---

[53] Johnson occasionally reported details of Natchez social affairs which the local
press omitted from its columns. The Natchez *Free Trader*, November 5, 1836, reported the ball held on the ship *Powhatan* in glowing general terms: "Among
the crowd of gentlemen we discovered planters, merchants, mechanics, and poli-
ticians—Whigs and Democrats, all joining joyously in the general melee, as though
pleasure was their only business. Nothing occurred to mar the festivity of the
occasion."

5   Mc and myself went out to the Race track and we saw several pretty Sharp Little Races, St Clair carried 100 pounds to 80, 1 mile out. Coon Mardices & St Clair   The Mardice Filly won the Race very Easy & there was also a thousand yard Race between Young Kings Sorril horse and Lem Wilkersons Sorril mare   The mare won the Race, very tight Race   A Race between Rabys Sorril Stud and a grey Horse belonging to a Stranger, a mile Out   The sorril Stud won the Race very Easy by a hundred yards — A Race between L. Clabourn and Raby — the mare beat Rabys Sorril Stud about 40 ft — A Race Between John Holden & St. Clair, 1 Mile Out. John Holdens horse won the Race Easy, I am told about 40 or 50 feet — Mr Gocian and Col Bingaman has a Dispute, Mr Gocian Left the Col. and Came to town, Judge Quitman returned from the tour he took Electioneering way up in the Chickasaw and Choctaw Counties,[54] Brought home a greate many circulars and handbills that were put in circulation to his greate Injury[55]

6   Mc and myself went out or wrode Out as far [as] Wilkins old Field

7   To Day is the First Day of the Election. Judge Quitman Delivered an adress To the people of This place at the Court House   It was a meeting oposed to the Election of Martin Van Buren. He was a giving his views on the Subject of Nuification, and at the same time stateing to the public how Basely the oposite party had Circulated hand Bills way up in the Eastern and Northern part of the State and to Day there were a hand Bill sent out Stateing that to day the votes for Presidential Ellection were to be handed in an[d] that to morrow there would be none taken   Skeggs & Devan Strikes a Blow or two at Each other in a fight

8   Mr Ellic Henderson told me to Day that Last week his gin was Burnt, with about 80 or 90 Bales of Cotten in it, it occured by Friction in the Engine — I Bot to Day at auction 1 shot gun Double Barrell price at $3.50, I also Bot a Spanish Saddle price at $20.00   The Judges Reversed their opinions of

---

54 John A. Quitman, Mississippi lawyer, soldier, and champion of state rights, was at this time a candidate for election to the United States House of Representatives to fill the vacancy caused by the death of David Dickson. His opponent was Samuel Jameson Gholson, a member of the state legislature.

55 Johnson did not record in his diary that on this day a Mr. Atkinson had announced in the Natchez *Free Trader* the opening of his "NEW AND FASHIONABLE HAIR CUTTING ESTABLISHMENT." The barber business was often a transient one in Natchez, and during this era many shops opened, remained in business for varying periods, and then sold out or closed.

yesterdays Ellection. They to Day permited them to vote for the President — Bill Nix wrorde out with a note to Washing[ton] to see old Mr Whales[56] to get him to Come to town and Survey a Lot of ground opposite of Mr. Parkers Hottell   I got to day ½ a Cord of wood from Mr McFadden under the hill   He owes me now $5 and a ½ a cord of wood

9   Dr Braselman Sells his Dwelling House at Sorias Auction, Dr Davis Bot it at Eight thousand Dollars and he paid the Selling of the Property, terms 6, 12 and 24 months with Out interest. Mr McRae has his property Sold at Sorias Auction To Day — terms were One Fourth cash, the Ballance in 4 months. It was Bot by Mr [blank]   It was a small Lot 25 feet Front and 50 ft Deep — I Loaned Mother twenty Dollars to pay the Butcher — Mrs Cary Sent in to Day a Small Box of Hicory nuts and a Box of Crabb apples to be Sent to New Orleans, the crabb apples to Mrs Miller and the H. Nuts to Wellington,[57] Mother gets a Bag full from the country also for Adelia

10   There were nothing much worth Relating to Day

11   Thare were to Day Several of us went into the Swamp a Duck hunting. We went way Down to the Cypress Buyio. Our game was as follows. Mc got One Duck, one squerrill, 1 wood cock, 1 King Fisher, 1 Pelican — Mr Minet Killed 1 Duck & wounded a Brant, so he told me — and I Killed 6 Ducks, 1 squerrel, 1 Loon, 1 wood Cock, 1 King Fisher   Mr Hanchet got 3 Ducks, 1 squerril   Mr Harrison got 2 Ducks, 1 squerril. Maj Miller came to Natchez — I forgot to mention that when we were a coming Home that Mr Minet got thrown twice by that Little Sorrill mare of mine, the way that he was first trowned was by McCarys Shooting off his gun behind the Horses. Mr Hanchet was thown at the Same time — Mc and myself had a tolerable good Dinner — We had as follows — Mc had 2 Bottles of Medoc Clarlet, 1 Bottle of Champagne wine, Buiscuit Egg Bread, P. pork, 1 Broiled Chicken & Beef Stake, I had a pice of good Bacon, wheat Bread, Oysters in Flitters, one Large Bottle of Anneset, one Dozen Orenges, 1 small Bottle of Muscat wine   Minet

---

[56] Johnson undoubtedly referred to B. L. C. Wailes, register of the land office at Washington from 1826 to 1835, official of Jefferson College, geologist and naturalist, planter, and promoter of agricultural improvement.

[57] Wellington West was a free Negro who later worked for Johnson for brief periods but was more often in New Orleans, where he lived in the home of James Miller and probably worked in his barbershop. See Mrs. James (Adelia) Miller to Johnson, June 20, 1837, Johnson Papers.

Brought a pint of whiskey or Brandy, I cant know which, but he Drank it up himself — Mc had a Bottle of Brandy & honey

12   Nothing much a Doing — Gov. Poindexter, on hearing that Franklin County had given a majority of 300 to Van Buren, He Said that if he was a going to Sellect One hundred Fools in the United States that he would make the Draw for them on Franklin County in this state — It was Gen. Harring that I herd stateing it after hearing him say so — I Sent to Day on the Steam Boat Carrolton by James 1 Large Bag of Crabb apples and a Brak for making Buiscuit[58]   Mrs Cary Sent a part of the apples — She Sent I think a bout 1 Peck and a Box of Hicory Nuts which was Sent altogether in the Bag

13   I Remained home all Day. I wrote During the afternoon two Letters, One to E. Miller and one to Kentucky. Buisness is tolerable Brisk, Mc came down in the afternoon and we sat and talked for an hour or two about Ellections &c   Mother went up to see Kitty McCary. She found her very Low indeed, not Expected to Live more than a Day

14   Nothing new. Dr Brasselman Brought his account to day against me for Cleaning and Drawing Teeth — nineteen Dollars & some cents and I compaired our accounts and he was in my Debt $6

15   Gov. Poindexter Last night in going to his Bed Room, mistook his way and Fell out of the End of Mr West Tavern   He fell about 14 feet and Broke his Leg and one thy and sprained his ancle[59]   Here is a small statement of the Election Returns [blank]

16   Nothing new in the Political way — K McCary Died Last night and was buried this morning   Dr Brown, the Steam Dr, Died Last night[60] — Capt Nevit has his gin Burnt Last night

---

[58] A brake was used for kneading dough.

[59] As J. F. H. Claiborne recorded former Governor George Poindexter's accident: "In November, 1836, he was boarding at the Mansion House, Natchez, and passed his nights for the most part at the gambling table. One night after he had lost heavily, and was somewhat fuddled, he set out for his room, and opening a door, which he supposed opened on a gallery, he was precipitated some twenty feet to the brick banquette below, breaking the bone of his right leg in two places, dislocating both ankles, fracturing the left leg above the knee, and receiving severe contusions in various parts. . . . The day after it happened, a reverend gentleman called to tender religious consolations, and seeing him so badly crushed, said, 'Governor, what did you fall against?' 'By G——d, sir, I fell against my will!' " *Mississippi, as a Province, Territory and State, with Biographical Notices of Eminent Citizens* (Jackson, 1880), 413–14.

[60] "Steam doctors" was the term commonly applied to physicians who prescribed vapor baths, or steaming, in connection with the "botanic system" of medical

by Some unknown scoundrell[61] — I had a Bet of twenty dollars on Mr Gholson against Gov Quitmans Election   I was some what affraid of Loosing my $20 so I Let Mr Lancaster have the Bet.

17 Mr Taylor collected To Day from Mr Flecho Fifty Dollars, being the amount Due for Rent to the 16th inst, which money was paid over to me — I went around To Mcs to Day and He had taken Little James, his Sisters Son, To Lern the trade

18 I cut Jud[g]e Quitmans hair this Evening — there came in a Drunking man from Franklin County and he was cursing the Nulifiyers   He gave some or made pretty Isolent Remarks to the Jud[g]e Respecting his party.

19 We had four Baths this Evening, the first Baths we have had for some time   I Loaned Mr McGetrick To Day fifty Dollars — Mr Spielman paid me $100. This was money that I gave him an Order on Mr Patterson for it   Mr Turner Came back to Natchez — Louis Winsborough arrived from the uper Country   Dr Welding was in town this afternoon — he Came from Louisville Down here

20 I went around to Old Mc and I found him Talking with Dr Dally   We talked awhile then Left   Mr Baker Commenced to shave by the month, Every Day   Louis Winsboroug Came yesterday and Left to day for New Orleans with Poultry &c — This is a mistake [later]   Mc and myself wrode Out in the afternoon as far [as the] Duke of Lankershires — Little Young Calvin Ferriday Died a few days ago with Dysintary, attended by Dr Davis — Mc and myself Drinks a Bottle of Champaigne wine and then wrode Out

21 Messrs Haris & Lumm Sells there Lotts to Day at Auction On One, two & three years Credit with 8 per cent interest

---

practice, which had been "discovered" by Samuel A. Thomson. The Thomsonians held that vegetable remedies provided the great health secret. This medical sect flourished until after the Civil War. See, for example, the extended "Medical Notice" of Doctors Harden and Lawrence in the Natchez *Free Trader*, June 3, 1836. In his *Forty Years of American Life, 1821–1861* (New York, 1937; reprint of 1874 edition of volume first published in 1864), 43, Thomas Low Nichols wrote: "The spread of hydropathy was another example of the readiness of Americans to accept anything new. The system of Priessnitz [Priesnitz] had scarcely been heard of before several large water-cure establishments were opened in America, and in a few years five or six water-cure journals were published, medical schools of hydropathy opened, and numerous practitioners, male and female, were dispensing packs and douches, with much desirable cleanliness, and much sanitary improvement also, to the American public."

[61] The Natchez *Free Trader*, November 18, 1836, reported: "This is the fourth time this calamity has befallen the same gentleman. His saw mill was also burnt about 18 months since."

— I became the purchaser of the First Lot that was offered, Lot No 9 and a corner Lot amediately opposite the Dwelling of Mr Covington — it was Knocked off at my Bid being the hyest Bid for it, thirteen Hundred and ten Dollars — They fought to Day on the other side of the River with Pistols   It apears that they fell Out Last Night about a Barrell of oysters and in the Dispute Esdra Struck him with his fist and the other fellow Challenged him and they fought this morning on the Sand Bar   They fired two Rounds and Esdra shot him just below the Knee in the Leg and so it Ended[62]

     22   Considerable Bustle about town in the way of Buisness — To Day Mrs Battles commences to move Out of Her House to have another put up in the place of the old One, Yester at 10 Oclock Mrs Profilet was Buried — She Died in Orleans on the 17th inst and was Brot up here to Natchez to be Buried — Mc and myself Drank a Bottle of Champaegne wine Last night in my Shop

     23   Nothing that I Know of worth relating.

     24   Bill, Mc and myself went in to the Swamp on a hunt and a very Dry hunt we made of it   We went Down as far as the Cypress Byo and Mc he Killed One Duck and I Killed 4 Rice Birds, 1 yellow Hamer, one Large crane, 2 small Birds and one squirrel — and the Little Rascally Bill Lost all my Birds after we got to town, and the way I whiped him was the Right way

     25   Buisness quite Brisk — Nothing new only that there is a Report in town that Chancelor Quitman is Elected and that the White Ticket has got a majority in this state   This news came in a Letter to Judge or Col Wilkins[63] — I went up to auction

---

[62] The Natchez press reported the duel briefly: "We understand a duel was fought in Concordia, La., by two gentlemen of this city. The principals are said to have acted with great calmness and deliberation; the first fire proved harmless. The second shot, one of the parties received the ball of his antagonist in the calf of his leg, and the parties all went off *perfectly satisfied!!*" Natchez *Free Trader*, November 25, 1836. In 1838, Adolphe (or Adolphus) Esdra—considered "a mean Fellow" by Johnson—became half owner of a saloon and billiard hall known as the Commercial Exchange, situated at the corner of Main and Commerce streets, about one and one-half blocks from Johnson's Main Street property. According to the tax rolls of 1840, he was a white man and his merchandise sales for 1839 were only $700. Adams County Deed Records, AA, 13–14; Auditor's Records, Tax Rolls, 1840, Adams County. Late in December, 1841, he announced that he was selling his jewelry stock at his store opposite the Planters' Bank. Natchez *Courier*, December 28, 1841.

[63] The rumor was false, for Gholson defeated Quitman. In 1839 he was appointed judge of the United States district court of Mississippi, and served until Mississippi seceded from the Union in 1861.

to Day and Bought four Tables for the shop — I put the[m]
up and took Down the Ballance   I pd. $2.87½ per Table

   26   A Race this Evening one mile out for 2 or 3 hundred
Dollars a Side — It was Lemuel Wilkerson grey horse and Mr
E Clabournes Bay mare — She Beat him the first ½ mile But
then he won the Race

   27   I got up this morning before Day and took my gun
Out to Scotts old Field and put her under a Log and Came
home   I got back to town at Day Break — I Rode Out in the
afternoon, took my gun from under the Log and commenced
Shooting Crows. I Killed 2 crows at One Shot and I Killed four
at four other Single Shots, making in all Six and I Shot 1 Rice
Bird, 1 gold Finch & 1 Tom Tit — Bill Nix & Simpson was with
me, I then when [went] in the old Field, made the Boys Take
a Race   Charles wrode my Little mare & Bill Nix wrde my
Sorrill Horse Rob Roy — the Horse could Out Run her very
Easy — I did not get in untill night

   28   To Day we had Bloody work for a while in the streets
up at Throckmortons Corner. Last night up at Mrs Rowans
Bourding House several gentlemen were in conversation about a
Duel that was fought in South Carolina. When Mr Charles
Stewart stated that those Gentlement that fought actually fought
with Bullits, Mr Dalhgreen Said that they must [have] fought
with paper Bullits — Mr C. Stewart then Said if any man would
say that they fought with paper Bullits that he is a Damed Lyar
and a Dd Scoundrel & a Dmd Coward — this was at the Supper
Table   Mr Dalhgreen Jumped up and Slaped Mr C. Stewarts
Cheek one very hard slapp   They were then parted so young
Stewart told him that they would settle it in the morning — So
this morning young Stewart took a Stand up at Carpenters Drug
Store for the purpose of making the attackt upon Dalhgreen
as he would be going to the Bank — Dr Hubbard at the Request
of his Brother went up to Carpenters with young Stewart to see
him Out in the affair   Elick Stewart said that he would not take
any part in the affair and he took a stand over on Sorias Corner
— and as Dalhgreen past the Door Stewart steped up to him and
told him that now was [the time] to Settle therr Dispute and
at the Same time Struck Mr Dalhgreen with his stick, Mr D
then Struck him Back with an umberralla — Stewart Struck him
with the Stick again — Mr D. then steped Back and Drew a
Pistol and Fired at Mr S. and missed Him — Mr S. then Drew
and Fired and the Ball Lodged under the arm in the Left Side of

Mr Dalhgreen, Mr D. then steped in at Throckmortons Store   S steped in at the Door but finding that D. had another Pistol he steped Back and stood in the caseing of the Door   D. then advanced on him, shot Him on Left Side of the face on the Temple or uper hinge of the Jaw Bone and the instant the Ball took Effect he Droped on his Knees and Fell over on the pavement as Dead, so Dead that he Barely Breathed. At the instant he fell Mr Elick Stewart ran up and struck D. with his fist   D then advanced on him with an Empty Pistol and in doing so Dr Hubbard shoved Him Back, E. S. Drew a Bouye Knife and commenced cuting at him — Mr D. had no weapon at this time and was fighting with his naked hands and Mr E. S. with the Knife — It was one of the gamest fights that we have Ever had in Our City before — E. S cut him twice over the Head and cut his Little finger nearly off and split his hand pretty Bad[64]   Mr R. Bledsoe and Mr Hewit has a small fist fight. After a Blow or two past, Mr Bledsoe went and got his Pistols. I am told as Soon as Mr Hewit saw the pistol he Said whoorer and ran Down the street and got in a Store and Mr Bledsoe made him retract what he had Said in writing before he would Let him go — this he did from fear

   29   To Day I went up to the Agricultural Bank and Received in cash Seventeen Hundred and Fifty Dollars being the amount of a note that I Received from Flecheaux given him by Mr R. Bledsoe for Land that I sold to Flecheaux which Said Flecheaux Sold to Mr R. Bledsoe — I went to day around to Dr Hubbards office to shave young Mr Stewarts head, he was quite ill — I then went on up to Mrs Rowans to Shave Dr Dalhgreens Beard off — he was very Comfortably Situated and in a thriving condition   I made a mistake in this. Col. Bingaman Sent Steven in town to me to day and instead of Coming in he went under the Hill and got Drunk I Supose; I found him on a Dray and I sent Dr Hogg to see what was the mater with him and the Dr pronounced him Drunk at first site

   30   It was yesterday that Mr Rowse Bot a horse at auc-

---

[64] The Natchez *Free Trader*, December 2, 1836, reported the affair with its usual reticence in a paragraph headed "A Rencontre": "We shall not pretend to relate the particulars, but merely record the fact that such an affray took place, that blood was shed and probably loss of life will follow, and at the same time declare that such a disaster could never have occurred but for the abominable practice of carrying arms." For a more lengthy account of the "Public Meeting" which the affair prompted, see Natchez *Free Trader*, December 9, 1836.

tion — To day it was that I went up to Shave those Young Gentleman and not yesterday, as I have stated above there

December 1 I went around to day at Mr Dupyees To shave Mrs Sarah Dunbars Head, which I did, William went to shave Mr Poindexters face — I Loaned Mr Spielman $25 to be paid on Saturday next, Little Will was sick Last night and I had to send for Dr Hogg — He came and prescribed 4 grains of Calimal, tho we did not give [it] to him for he said that if he got worse to give it and if he got Better not to give it to him — So he got Better — thanks to the Greate I Am

2 A Race to day at the Track. It was a $500 purse given by Mr Selfe Self — Mr Harmons Naked Truth, Oldersons Gentility, Hodens Double Head — Naked T. won the Race, 3 mile Heats — Holdens Horse Let Down in Both fore Legs[65] — I Shaved Mr C F Stewarts Head to Day — Mc Bot a Coatee at Micheals & Montgomerys to day, $26 and He Bot an Over Coat at Young Reeds Store at $32 — Michell Bot a Boat Load of Coal and Runs around and Sells it to the people, 1.50 per Barrell — Mc takes ten Barrells, I took 3 Barrells

3 One mile and Repeat between Mr Minors imported Colt Brittania and Mr Clabourns Little Bay mare, 2 year Olds. Brittania won the Race very Easy indeed Beating the other about 60 or 70 yards — Col Bingaman had One to Run. She got Lame and He paid the forfeit — Poor young Stewart is worse to Day — Dick Ellis Runs a young Colt 1 mile against McKennys Bay Horse — The Bay Horse won the Race very Easy indeed — Mc Buys 2 Large Peer Glasses, on a credit of 12 months, is to pay $320 for them   He got them from Mr T. Ellis

4 I Staid at Home all of this Day — Mc Came around at night and sat a while, I sent Down the street and Bot 3 doz oysters and Mc and myself Eat them

5 I Loaned Mr Barlow & Taylor five Hundred Dollars to be paid when Called for at anytime — I gave him a check on the Commercial Bank for the money. And it was only to day that I made the Deposit in the Bank of three thousand three hundred Dollars   To Day Mr Rowes Raises the new Frame of the House hireer [higher] — it was said to be too Low — To day Mr Mitchel Sent me Down ten Barrels of coal. Mc He Engaged it without my Leaf — I paid $15 for ten Barrels and 1.25 for hauling it up

---

65 The races of December 2–3, 1836, over the Pharsalia Course at Natchez were duly reported in *Spirit of the Times*, VI (1837), 390. But Naked Truth, winner on December 2, was listed as the entry of Colonel Adam L. Bingaman.

—I had Engaged 50 Barrells of coal from Proctor But finding that I had to pay 1 Dollar a Barrell to pay for it I told him that I would only take 40 Barrells — Mc gets his Large glasses in from Mr T. Ellises, Sent One to the House and kept the other at the shop — Col Bingaman sends his Horses to Vicksburg about a week ago and He went up this morning Himself, H Cobler and Mr Mardice, to attend the Vicksburg Races — I Subscribed this Evening for the Buliten Paper of New Orleans,[66] I pd for six months in advance

6   Mr Skeggs pays me $20, being The Last of One Hundred Dollars that I Loaned him some time ago — I ment to have said he has paid me all the whole amount of the Hundred Dollars — Charles & Bill Nix goes to the Circus to night, and they dont go any more to Browns Circus this Season, nor French Dont go this week[67] — I have been for two Days Trying to [get] my Present Tenants, La Vigne & Flecho, To move Out and Let me have my House to Rent to two other tenants, the Firm of Mr Down & Paine, I Bot two pair of Pantaloons to day at the Auction of Soria & Co and I paid $4.87½ per pair

7   I was called on this morning by those Gentlemen from New York to Know when they could get Either of my Houses. I Sent word to the old Frenchman that if He was willing to give up his apartment that those Gent would pay his present months Rent, and that he might Remain in the House until he could sell out at auction — At Least they would not charge him anything for the use of the Back Room   This the old man Declind and said that He would stay in the store as Long as he pleased and he could pay as much as any one   I Receivd word from him Stating that he would not Leave the House if they were to give him $200. This Esdra put him up to say and he told him that I could not Raise the Rent more than one third of the Rent that I was geting at present from him, I then wrote him this note   Mr La Vigne, if you Remain in my House Longer then the present month, you must pay seventy five Dollars per month for it — I Loaned Mr E. Bell Six Hundred Dollars to Day payable in the Course of a week or three Days

8   To Day about Dinner they had had a Learg quantity

---

[66] Johnson probably referred to the New Orleans *Commercial Bulletin*, which had been established in 1832.

[67] The Natchez *Free Trader*, December 9, 1836, made the following comment on the circus: "The Equestrian corps of Messrs. Brown & Co. have been doing wonders for a week past in the way of astonishing the people with their daring feats."

of Gentlemen were on the Bluff to See the car Start, They had put Down about 40 feet of Rails and had put on a Car, and they were a Runing it Backwards and fowards on the Small Road that they had constructed,[68] There were present Gov. Quitman, Mr Vanison, W. P. Mellon, R. Fields, T. Jones, W Chambers, Rice, Holton, Capt Cotten and a greate many more   To Day I Bot the improvements that Flecho put on my House, that is the window and Several other things and the Counter also — He is to Leave the House on the 16th of this month without Fail — Wheathers Bot the House that he Lives in at auction to Day, It Sold for 17 hundred Dollars   I had to whip Bill Winston and Bix Nix for fighting in the shop to night when gentleman was in the Shop. I had to give it to them Both.

9   I Received of Mr Proctor to Day thirty Barrels of coal, price 1 Dollar per Barrell   Mc He got 20 Barrells of the same man, I gave the Carpenters to day $2 to Buy Liquor with, The[y] commenced puting on the weather Bourding to day for the first. I had to give William a few cracks this Evening for insolent Language whilst Cutting a gentlemans Hair, it was at dinner time

10   I hyreed Mr Bon my Little mare this Evening to wride, I Loaned Mr Rowes my Large grey mare to work for this Day Only   To Day Mr Bell was to have Brought me or paid me $600 that I Loaned him a few Days ago — Mr Hale had his Horse stolen from him this night after Supper

11   Mc and myself wrode Out in the afternoon, and we Saw the Boiler or Ingine belonging to Our Rail Road. It was Hauled up the Hill this Day at 12 Oclock from the Ship — Greate many Persons were present — it was Hauled up by the Oxen

12   Col Bingaman gets Down from Vicksburg Last night about 10 or 11 Oclock — He Ran his Horse the 4 mile Heat against Mr O. Clayboures Suzan Yandel, 2 to One in favor of the Horse, The mare won the Race Easy

13   I Bot to day at the auction store of Mr Soria & Co. twenty two Cases of fine Razors at ten Bits per Case, Those Razors were Sent from Ingland to Mr Alfred Cochran. They were Damagd in Some way and Mr C. would not Receive them, But sent them to Auction to be Sold to the Hyest Bidder — I

---

[68] According to the Natchez *Free Trader*, December 16, 1836, the first cars did not actually run until December 14. In an article headed "The Rail-Road," the newspaper stated: "Day before yesterday the first rails were laid, and a car caused to move upon the Natchez end of the rail-road."

Paid Mr Proctor $30 to day for 30 Barrells of Coal — Mr Rowes agrees to make three sash doors for $80.

14   Buisness very Brisk and Simpson Sick — I took the measure of Mr Charles Stewarts Head to day for to have him a wig got and I at the Same time took the measue of Mr Stanfords head for the same purpose — Mr Poindexter sends me a Note Requesting me to Let his nephew have my Horse to go to Woodvile — He took the Horse and was only gone a few hours and Came Back, He arranged the Buisness without having to go down there   I pd Mr Soria 29.84 for 22 cases of Razors and a doz Razors straps

15   To Day I paid in two Hundred Dollars which is ten cent on twenty Shares of Rail Road Stock   Mc paid in fifty Dollars, ten per cent on five shares Rail Road Stock[69]   I indorsed a note for Mc in favor of Mr Thoms Ellis for three Hundred and twenty Dollars for two peer Looking Glasses. The note is payable in twelve months — Gen. Santa Anna pass[ed] up this morning On the Steam Boat Tennesiean — Gen Almonta was with him   They were on there way to Washington City[70]

16   Hendrickus[71] Sells Out at Auction, he was Compelled to do so for Cullen had him inditeed for Selling Liquor without Licenses and he had to Leave the House

---

[69] Both William Johnson and his free Negro friend, Robert McCary, were stockholders in the Mississippi Rail Road Company. Johnson's certificate for twenty shares, paid up in the amount of $2,000, and dated June 22, 1839, is in the Johnson Papers.

[70] At the battle of San Jacinto on April 21, 1836, General Santa Anna, president of Mexico and commander in chief of the invading Mexican army, was captured by the Texans. After prolonged controversy as to what disposition should be made of the prisoner, Sam Houston, president of the Republic of Texas, allowed him to proceed with an escort to Washington, where he was to lay before President Jackson a proposal to sell Texas to the United States. According to the diary of Colonel (not General, as stated above) Juan N. Almonte, Mexican officer who accompanied Santa Anna, the journey began on November 26. The party proceeded to Plaquemine, Louisiana, where Santa Anna and company boarded the Mississippi River steamboat *Tennessee* on December 12, and reached Natchez on December 13. Richardson, *Texas, The Lone Star State*, 144, 150; John V. Haggard (tr.), "Almonte Diary, 1836–1837" (both original and translation in University of Texas Library Archives, Austin, Texas).

Santa Anna's brief stopover at the Natchez wharf may have prompted the article which appeared in the Natchez *Free Trader*, December 16, 1836, headed "Aid for Texas." The article called upon the citizens of Natchez to make contributions to the moral welfare of this "interesting people" by depositing any kind of religious literature at a central point where it could be collected by an officer of the "Texian" army, who was also "a member of the church." The object was to distribute religious information among the "chivalrous, but morally destitute" people of Texas.

[71] Perhaps this was J. N. Henriques. His announcement of the opening of an auction business appeared in the Natchez *Free Trader*, November 25, 1837.

17 To Day I got the First number of the Bullitin, Published in New Orleans, try weekly Flecho offers his stock of Jewelry at auction, But does not Sell much — the Sail was stoped Mons La Vigne pays me for three months Store Rent up [to] the 19th inst — I Settled my Bill of Eight Dollars and Mothers Bill of 9.87½ with him So he paid in cash 42.64. Mr Hall Horn Brot me the Presidents Message, struck of[f] this Evening at the Courier & Journals office[72] — The Circus Company Left here to night after the performance was over for the Evening — They Left here very sudenly indeed

18 Mc and myself Took a walk over the Bluffs and we Saw an Owl Shot Down from of[f] a tree in Mr Michees yard

19 Mons. La Vigne Handed me my key this morning of the store that he Rented of me Mr Rose makes a Finish of shingleing the new House and commences on the Kitchen — Mr Newcomb Brought me his account to day of Black Smithing for 1834, the amount of it was $11. I did not pay it for I thought and am sure that I paid it before [Drawing of horse] Ingraham for the purpose of trying Her & if she suited him he said that he would give me One Hundred and twenty five Dollars for Her, and that he would Return her to morrow and if she suited him it should be a trade and if not he would pay me two Dollars for the use of Her, on to morrow

20 Yesterday in the afternoon I Let Mr Ingraham have my Little Sorrill mare on tryal to wride out home, and He promised me to Send Her in Early in the morning and it is now night and she has not been Sent in yet, I am beginning to think that He has made off with Her — I Sold Mr R. Evans a pair of hansome Razors to day on a Credit for $6 and I also Sold a pair to Mr John Coleman of Jefferson County, very hansome Ones for five Dollars Cash — I wrode out this Evening by the Oil Mill and there I saw a Large Fox Squirrill on a tree quite close to the House — Col Bingaman Closed a Race to be Ran ten Days before the Jocky Clubb Races — He runs a Sorrill mare that He calls the Lavender Girl against Naked Truth, 4 miles heats — He made the Race with Mr Lee Claibourne, This mare that the Col Runs is the one that Jumped over Bourd off the Steam Boat

21 I gave Mr Rose a check on the Bank for five Hundred

---

72 The entire text of the speech was published in the Natchez *Free Trader,* December 23, 1836.

Dollars this morning on the Commercial Bank — Mr Barlow paid me five Hundred Dollars that I Loaned him on the 5th inst

22   I wrode under the Hill this Evening to the Public Sale of Mr Wm McRae, He Sold Out his Stock at Auction — My Legings that I Lost in the Swamp Some time ago was Brought home by a Black man

23   Mr Gubert Came to hyre my House for a Barber from New Orleans — I could not Stand it. I was Called on by a Lady to See the Same Room. I went up in the Evening to See Her. The utmost Politness prevaild during my Short visit. Mr Taylor the merchant was Leaving his new store of Mr Lillards New Building — The Brick Layers commenced Laying the Pillars of the Mechanical Societys Building — To day I made 1 dollar by changing two Hundred Dollars Bankable money, ½ per cent

24   I paid Mr Thos Rose to Day One thousand Dollars in part pay for Buil[d]ing Mrs Battles House, I gave a check for $200 on the Commercial Bank — the Ballance I paid him cash[73]   Old Esdra Buys the Brick Store Formily Ocupied by A Spielman as a Saddlery Establishment, $8000. Two of old Mrs Thomass [Negroes] perswaded a Black man belonging to Mr James the merchant of this place to go with them to a turky Roost to Steal Turkeys — So they told him, but they Seen him have $15. There object was to get him Down in the hollow and Robb him — So he went with them and as Soon as he got Down in the Hollow or Byio one of the[m] plunged a knife in to his Breast with the full intention of Murdering him and then to Robb him —. the poor Fellow ran off to the nearest house and Fell Down and to[ld] them the above tale

25   I wrode Out half way to Washington this Evening — I Race horse in Exercise — To Day I Saw fully 20 Drunken men, the most of wich were Dutch men and belonged to the Rail Road — I Saw about the same quantity at work in the St. Catharine Creek making the Bridge for the Rail Road — This was quite a Dull Christmast — I went Down to Bon Store and I bought some figs and a Dollars worth of Cake

26   Auction up at Spielmans old Store. They were Selling Glass of Every Discription — I wrode out this Evening and took Bill Winston with me and I shot 1 Duck in the pond belonging to Mr Waymoth and I Killed 1 Lark in the old Field oposite Capt Nevitts Residence

---

[73] Johnson's accounts show that Thomas Rose constructed the house on his mother-in-law's State Street property between December 7, 1836, and July 8, 1837.

27   This morning a man by the name of Miller from Verginia got in a fight with Mr Allen, the clerk of Mr Knight, and I herd that Allen was too hard for him — Then Mr Knight commencd on him with a Horse whip and gave him a Severe whiping and the man made no kind of Resistance — he is the man that posted Mr Knight as a Scoundrel and a Coward &c. the other day in the Public Taverns

28   Those two young Thomass that was arrsted for the murder of Mr Jamess Black man was Bailed Out of Jail by there Mother. They were held to Bail in the sum of fifteen Hundred Dollars for there appeara[n]ce to the Criminal Court.

29   Mr Ben Harmand Died To Day about 9 Oclock — Leaves Col A L. Bingaman & Mr Fedrick Stanton to arrange His Estate   I wrote a Letter to Jackson this Evening To a Samuell Watts in answer to a Letter that I Recevid from Gen. Mathew Patton — He mearly wanted to Know if he could get a Journaman Barber.

30   The Big Jawed Barber opened Shop in the front of Mr Bells Mansion House

31   Mr A Flecho moves Out of my Store To the House that He Rents from Mr Sisloff away up town — I called at Dr Hoggs This Evening and paid him ninety five Dollars for medical Services — There were three Bills included in this amount — Mothers, my sisters, Williams & my Own — I put up a number of Boxes for my Customers   Dr. Hogg paid me to day $21 for seven months Shaving & Hair Cuting.

1837

January 1   I got up very Early this morning and Took my gun Out in the woods and Left in order to Take a Hunt after Dinner — I made in cash $11.75 to day.

2   Buisness quite Brisk. I made in Cash to day $22.50 and I Collected 3.50 of Mr C W Green

3   I went under the Hill to Buy Some plank To make a fence on Mrs Battles Lot — They asked for 1½ stuff $30 a thousand, I did not get any to day

4   I walked under the Hill this Evening and Bot Some Plank for Fenceing

5   I Sold a pair of Razors to Gov Quitman and a pair To young Mr Hutcheons — A Mr Scanlan Commences To Open His goods in my Store. I made in cash to day $17.57½ by work

6   Buisness is quite Brisk, Elleck Bell and Severe and Young Francis Marchalk Returns from Texes. Bell was Sickly. Looked Bad and was Lousesy — He got Shaved, hair cut &c. A Frenchman Gentleman move[d] into my Lower Store. He has Dry goods — I Bot a Doubled Barrell Shot Gun to day and paid twenty five Dollars for it — She is cheap if She is good — I made in cash to day 18.25 and Sold 1 pair Razors for five [dollars] making in all $23.25

7   To Day The Fencibles shot at the Target and a Mr Bemis won the Star, I Took in cash To Day $18.50 and $2.50 by collection, in all $21 — very good, very good indeed.

8   I cashed To day $12.25 and Collected $6 from Walker making in all $18.25

9   This morning Mr Adolph Flecho moves the Last of His things from up stairs in my House, I Spoke to a Mr Wells the Painter to paint the front of my House which He is to Commence to morrow. Mr Scanlin moves up stairs where Flecho Came Out of with Family   I Took in cash to day $13.37½ — I went up to day to Mr Sorias to get the notes that I was to give to Mr Harris & Lumm for a Lot that I Bot from them and I got the notes and had them Indorsed by the Following Gentlemen, Mr P Gemmell and Mr E. Bell & Mr John G Taylor, and when I came to find Out instead of the Lot being 90 feet deep and 50 front, it was 50 feet front and 76 feet deep

10   I saw Mr Lumm this morning at the Auction Room and I asked him how it hapend that the Lot I Bot of him and Mr Harris Came To be so much Less than what it sold at auction and he told me that Mr Soria did not sell it for any [blank]

11   I hyred Lewis to day To Mr Thom Jones to work with his cart and Horse at Esdras to Take Out Dirt at $3 per Day

12   Buisness of Every Discription was Dull. In fact I know of nothing of any Importance going on Except The wedding of Mr Thomas Winn To Young Miss Lyons of this place

13   Gen Harring & E. Bell has bought the old Quigless Plantation in Partnership for a stock Farm — Mrs Cornells old Frame House was Discovered To be on Fire this morning about [blank] Oclock   The fire commenced in the uper part of the

House and was Bursting through the Roof when I first saw it   It Burned Down To the ground.   The House was Occupied, the Principal part of it by The Courier Printing Office under the management and controll of Mr Black, and the other part by Dr Cornell as a Botanic Store,[1] To day there was a seviere piece writen in the Daily Courier the writer of which signed himself an Old Citizen, Would To God I knew the unmercifull wrech, not that I would Hurt a hair on his Boddy But Simply to have the Satisfaction of Knowing the midnight assassin

14   Mr Harris Sent for me this morning by Young Harrison, I went up to this Counting Room and there was Mr Soria in the Room, Mr Harris made him say yes to Several things that he seemed very Reluctant to agree to, In One instance He said that he called Out or Explaind to the People that there was a mistake in the square that I Bot a Lot in, This I know was not the case, He then Said (this is Mr Harris) that He could not make any allowance for it was Sold under a mistake. I made in cash $20.

15   This day I was at home the whole day & had no company Exept that of my Own Family

16   William went down to shave Mr Joseph Fray. He Died at Sisloffs under the Hill — I Bought To Day at auction from Mr Soria twelve pair of Shoes or ankle Boots & I Bought of Mr OFarrell & Becket a trunk of French perfumery. I gave him 28 Dollars for the trunk

17   I Sold Dr Hogg a pair of Ankle Boots for $2.50.

18   I gave my note to Mr [blank] to day and it Reads in this manner precisely

> $268   NATCHEZ MISS. Novr. 21 1836
> Twelve Months after date I promise to pay to the order of [blank]
> Four Hundred & Sixty Eight Dollars
> Value Received Negotiable & payable at the Commercial Bank in the City of Natchez
> No._____
> Due_____   William Johnson
> Indorsed on the Back by Mr Peter Gemmell, E Bell, John G Taylor

> $502.67   Natchez Miss. November 21 1836
> Two years after date I promise to pay to the order

---

[1] The Natchez *Free Trader* of January 20, 1837, reported the fire.

ˌof [blank] Five Hundred & 2.67/100 Dollars
Value Received Negotiable and payable at the Com-
mercial Bank in the City of Natchez
No 22
Due 21/24 Novem 1838　　　　　　　　W.

This is a coppy of the third note that I gave to Mes Harris &
Lumm.　Three years after date I promise to pay [to] the Order
of [blank] five Hundred & thirty Seven [dollars], 34 cents, value
Receied Negoteable and payable in Commercial Bank in the City
of Natchez　　Due 21/24 Nove 1839, indorsed on the Back by
Peter Gemmel, E Bell, John G. Taylor.　Those notes are given in
payment of a Lot of ground Situated up opposite the Residence
of Mr Covington — It was to have been 50 feet front on theˈ
Street Canal and 90 feet Deep instead of which it was only 76
feet Deep and 50 front　　Some Considerable mistake about it in
Some way — I gave the Following notes up to day on the following conditions, that if Mr Harris made any allowance with any
One that he would make it with me, deduction is what I mean In
regard to the Deficent feet in the Lot.

Cologne

40 Drops of The Oil of Lemon
40　do　　　do　　Lavender
40　do　　　do　　Bergumont
　　To 1 quart of alkahall & 1 or 2 drops of Oil of Rose
　　22　　Mc goes out to hunt in the afternoon with Mr Izod　Mc
Killed five Larks, Mr Izod three
　　23　　Sterns and myself went a guning, we went over in the
neighbourhood of Capt Nevits plantation, Sterns Killed 3 Rice
Birds, 3 yellow Hamers, 1 Partridge, 1 Lark, 1 thrush, 1 Sparrow,
1 Rabbit & 1 Squirrell, in all 12 and I Killed 1 Lark, One spotted
Breast, 2 yellow Hammers, 4 thrush, 3 Sap Suckers, 3 Rice Birds,
3 Bull Finches, in all 17.
　　24　　To day was a very Dull Day. I Bot Some Merinco
for Curtains To make a Reading Room[2]　I Sent up to the
Courrier and Journal office to get Some papers which was sent
to me by Mr Black　He Sent me 8 or ten of them
　　25　　Mr Joseph B. Lyons was Taken with an appoplectic
Fit and Died in a few moments　I made a mistake in Saying
it was yesterday that I Sent for those papers, for it was to Day.

---

[2] Johnson may have referred to moreen (moirine), a heavy woolen or cotton-
and-woolen fabric. See also "Morieno," in entry for March 31, 1837.

26   Mr Lyons was Buried To Day. Col Bingaman Came to town to day, he has just Returned from Jackson, Miss — Mr William H Pearce gets married this morning To Miss Gillet   Mr Louis Miller pd me five Dollars to place to his Credit for Shaving

27   Buisness Only tolerable Brisk, Mrs Andrew Brown Died Late Last night at Her Residence at the Saw Mill.

28   A Race To day between Mr O. Clabournes Sorril mare Antilope & Hard Hart.

31   This morning a Big Negro Belonging to the Miss Evanss undertook to take away a Horse & Cart from Milford Cary for a Debt Due to Mrs Overraker

February 1   I went To Dr Hubbards office To Day and paid Him my account, which was twenty three Dollars   The Account was from Sept 5th, 1834, To the present Date   I also paid Him the Account that He had against my Sister Mrs Miller for advice, Cuping &c., Amount $20.00   The account Commenced 14th April, 1835, to 28th inst, same month — The Dr Owed me Five Hundred Dollars and He paid me Some time back $160 and the amount of the two accounts being $43 made his account two Hundred and 13 against me, Deducting His Bill from mine Left Him in my Debt $297 which he gave me His Due Bill for — Ganson Ranaway from Natchez To Day. He Sold Out his Liece [lease] & groceries the other day To Henderson the Carriage maker for $3500   He got the cash in hand for what He Sold & then Fled the City — Left his wife behind him in a particular situation

2   Nothing transpired To Day that is Hardly worth Recording.

3   Not much Buisness a Doing of any Kind, I Saw Dr Hubbard To Day and Told Him of the mistake that I made the day before yesterday when we had a Settlement, and He acted in true Gentlemans Stile, gave me his Due Bill for three Hundred & forty 2 Dollars, being the amount Due me on Settlement   Mr N L. Williams called To Get me to signe an article of writing or to subscribe to the opening of an alley at the Back of Our Respective yards — He told me that it would Cost Each of us about $150 a piece. I then Signed it — Mr Spielman had also Signed it. He also Told me that he would See Mr Gemmell about this particcan wall. Mr. W Harris Returns from Jackson.

4   A Race To day four mile heats, between John Minor and Sally Hope or Allice Riggs   The Bets were two to One in favor of the mare and the Race was a Beautifull One   The Horse took the Lead from the Start and Kept it Beating the mare Out about 20 yards. The mare found She could not win it and she fell Back. It was the Same Case in the Second Heat, after she found she Could not win she fell Back and got Beat about 80 yards — The Boy wrode Her very Bad I thought   I Lost a years Shaving with Mr J Session and One with Mr Arlette and One [with] Mr Howell on the Race   There was a Rascally Race to Day between this man Clark and a man on Pine Ridge Clark wrode his Little Bay Studd and was a head and his Horse ran up towards the fence and the other past him and won the Race   I Lost $18 on it — Torrice won it from me — I had a talk with Mr N L. Williams and I thought from His talk that He wanted to have me pay Him for the particean wall instead of Mr Gemmell who purchased the wall from [blank]

5   In the afternoon McCary and myself wrode Out to Mrs Scotts Old Field — Mc wrode His new Horse That he Bought from Mr Emerson   My Horse Rob Roy could walk and did walk much faster than did his Horse.

6   To night they will perform the play of Cherry & Fair Star and I Let the Boys go to See the performance, French, Charles, Bill Nix & Bill Winston, Mr Seviere Called this Evening to me about Mr R. Bradleys account and I told him that I did not have it made Out But that I would have it Ready for him in a few days — The following Horses arrive and past through the Town Last night, Dick Chin, Exsho & Linnet. They were Brought over by Mr Watson To Run in the Jocky Clubb Races   There is one of them has a Race for ten thousand Dollars to be Ran in March next against Susen Gendele[3] — I called and got the deed of my Lot from Mr Wm Harriss counpting Room and had the date Recorded at the clerks office. I had Taken it to the office before But did not Discover that Mr Harris had not put the date on the deed. I paid Mr Wood $2 to put it on Record — Mons. Toilioire Moves Out of the Store next Door To me, To Day there were papers Sent around stating the resignation of Col Bingaman of his Seat in the Legislature of this State[4]

7   Adolph M. Flecho Ran off from this place To Day — I

---

3 Johnson meant Susan Glendale.

4 Bingaman was the only representative from the older, river counties who had voted to admit the recently organized counties to representation. He resigned as a result of the criticism he received and went before the people to explain his vote, but was defeated. He was elected to the state Senate the following year.

hold a note of His that He gave me for Rent that was Due to me for $180.00 Drawn Some time in October Last and payable the first of Jan. 1837 with Mr Seureau indorser on it   The note is past Due and was not protes[t]ed — I How Ever took the note this Evening and gave it to Lawyer G Baker To Collect the money if He could possibly do So and I told him could [he] collect it that I would give him $40 of the money

8   Mr [blank] moves in next Door with Goods   He Took the Room that Mons Toloire moved Out of the other Day — I Sent my account to Gov Poindexter for Shaving and He paid it, $6.00   I Sent under the Hill & collected from Dr Thoms G. Shroyer, 3.00

9   I sent & collected $4.00 from Mr R North for Baths &c.   Several strangers came in this Evening To Rent my two stores, I told them that I would give them an answer in the morning. To Day Charles's Brother came to town To Learn the Black Smiths trade   He Came Down to See Charles. Sterns came Down to night and cleaned Both of my Shot Guns

10   I made Out Mr E. P. Fourniquets account this Evening and In intended to Send it to Him to morrow if all is right. Mr Walter Guion Returns to Natchez with mustoshes and whiskers on his face, Judge Winchester Returns from Jackson and Seys that if the people of Adams County Does reelect Col. Bingaman again to the Legislature that he [will] Resign his Seat   We Received a Letter from New Orleans from Mrs Miller and 2 papers also   I Borrowed Mr G Lancasters violin to day. It was open and in Bad fix

11   Mr Spielman has the old gate post Taken up which had Our Land mark on it. He had a new gate made and put up — Lewis hauled for Mr D. Barlow to day — all Day

12   Nothing new in town, and after 12 Oclock in the afternoon I took Out a Couple of Boys that is Bill Nix and Bill Winston, and Sterns and myself took a Hunt. We went all around by the Quigless plantation   Sterns had my Little Shot Gun and I had my Rifle   We took it a foot and was very tyred in Deed   Sterns Killed 4 Larks and One Crow, and I Killed three Birds Only — Mr Wm Reid went in the Swamp to day and Brought 2 Large teeth from an alligator that I Killed in the swamp on the 28th day of October, 1836. He gave one of the teeth to Mc

13   F Rouland commences to Sell Out his stock at auction of Liquors, the House &c. I Bot 9 Bottles of Aniseed, 68 cents per Bottle, and 5 glass jars at 56¼ cents per Jar — This was all that I Bot durring the whole of the Sale   The House Sold for $24,000 and was Bot by Messrs Murcherson & Doyal.

   14   I wrode out to Mr T. G. Elliss to Shave him and I did so. He had a Little Son there that was asking him all sorts of questions, then next came a Daughter of his, a very hansome Black Eyed Little Girl   She was older than the Boy. She stood there Looking on at me Shave her farther   All at Wonce she Broke wind — I was fit to Burst with Laughter

   15   Very Little Buisness Doing to day — Dr Ross came to me to day to know if he could Liece the spot of ground on which my gate stands   I promised him the Refusal of the Same, Mr F. Taylor told me this Evening that he had got Mons Sereau to accknoledge his indorsing Flechos note to me for $180, he then took the note back to Mr Baker, and gave it to him for Collection — Mr Baker a[s]k nothing more

   16   I Have at this present time in my Pocket Book the Following paper, Dr John M. Hubbards Due Bill Drawn in my favor For Three Hundred and Forty two Dollars, Dated February 1st, 1837   I Loaned him the money — Also A Due Bill Dran in my favor dated July the 21st, 1836 for One Hundred Dollars payable in Sixty Days after date, Signed E Thomas. This was money that I Loaned Him — Also A Due Bill of Messrs Neibut & Gemmell Drawn in my favor, Dated April 8th 1837 for the Sum of Seventy Dollars, 19 cents, due on a Settlemt with the firm by there clerk Wm Koontz — Received Payment. Also A Due [bill] of Messrs Neibut & Gemmell drawn in my favor for the Sum of One thousand Dollars dated 4 of March, 1836   This was money that I Loaned the Firm. Also A Due Bill given me by Mr Eligah Bell for Money Loaned, dated December 7th, 1836 — the amount is Six Hundred Dollars   Mr W. Vernons account which Dr D. Stanton promised To pay — $18.50   Also Mr E. P. Fourniquets for $23.50   I gave Mr Tho. Rose To day seven Hundred and fifty Dollars   This amount aded To fifteen Hundred Dollars that I paid him before makes twenty two Hundred and fifty Dollars that I have paid Him

   17   Mr D P. Scanlin Left this place, gave me my Keys. He moved Down to New Orleans & he gave me a note of James B. Woodworth for the Sum of $22.50 and a note of W D. Woodworth for $13. He told me that if I could get 25 Dollars for both of the notes to take it. I Bot 2000 Segars at $14.50 per thousand   I Sent Mrs Miller To Day $20 being the Sum due To

Her for Middletons wages up to the 8th or 10th of March, next month — This Settlement is for five months up to the 9th of next month Leaving Out two weeks that He Lost, the amount of which is $72. I Took Out $52 for Doctors Bills that I paid out of the money — $32 to Dr Hogg & 20 Dollars to Dr Hubbard — deducting Both of there Bills Leaves a Ballance in her favor of twenty Dollars, which I sent to Her as I Stated above by Mr Tosspott

18   I Saw Mr Hay this morning and we closed a contract as follows, that after or on the 9th day of March next, I am to give him possession of my two uper Stores with the present fixtures in it for the sum of One Hundred Dollars per month, payable quarterly and that He would Repair and take Down the flour, counter & shelve the same in complete order   Mr Koontz paid me $74.88, being the amount Due me from the firm of Neibut & Gemmell Last year, for which I took there due Bill — I gave Mr Doland ten Dollars for a pair [of] pantaloons in cash, & am to give him ten more in work

19   Mc and myself took a wride in the afternoon. We went in the direction of the Race track but turned about and Came home.

20   Louis is quite Sick   I Sent for Dr Hogg. He came and bled him, then gave in a powder 10 grs of ipacak and 12 of Calamell   To take flax seed tea if it purged him, and to take warm water if it vomited Him. I Loaned James B Woodsworth $2 this Evenig which I am not apt to get I think   To day The confesion of a man by the name of John Washburn was published in the Courrier and Journal — The Fellow was hung in Cincinnatti   It was a Terrible tale that he told of his self if true.

21   Woodworth the carpenter moved Out to Mr Fords   He Left here without paying the Notes that was Left in my Hands for collection by Mr D. P. Scanlin Against Woodworth & Brother. We had News to Day from Vicksburg stating that Eleven Persons had got Drownd from the Steam Boat Ben Sherrod by accident

23   To day The Race came of[f] between Angorah vs Exito, pronounced Exsho, two mile out Heat for $2000 a Side   Angorah won the Race Beating the other about 18 feet, time 4 m 2 seconds. I lost between Messrs Gocian, Love & St Clair, $11. Mc Lost $14. This was doing a Loose Buisness   The man that Mr Baker Bot The other day Ranaway Last night

24   I Bot Some Knives, lancets & Shot pouches to day at

Mr Spraugue & Howell auction Room, Cash. I herd to day that Elisha had got in Some fuss.

    25   I walked under the Hill this Evening to try and collect the Sum of One Hundred from Mr E. Thomas   I found him at Last in a Flat Boat. He gave me an Order on Mr Quertomas for the amount   I took the order and presented it. He promised the pay in the morning

    26   There were a Splendid Race to day at the Tract which I did not see for I was not Out to day   This was between Mr Os Claibournes Van Buren and a mare from Ohio Called the Buck Iye Lass — The Horse won the Race by four feet, they Ran a mile Out

    27   Mr Quertomas came in this morning and paid me One Hundred Dollars, this being money that I Loaned Ever Since the 21st July, 1836 to Mr E Tomas. He gave me an Order on Mr Quertomas for the money which he excepted and paid,   I call him a Gentleman, who Disputes it? I wrote to the Capt this Evening by mail, Mr Ingraham sent me in a pair of Razors that I sold to him Some time ago   After he has had them set three or four times he concludes not to take them and sends for the money that he paid for them   I sent it out — It was $5 but I think if he comes a Bothering me any more I will be very apt to — Never mind

    28   I paid a Mr Leaf five Dollars which pays for the Sperrits of the Times up to the 20th of Feb., 1838.

    March 1   Jocky Club Races, 2 Mile Heats   Angorah (Col. B), Exito (Wells), Havoc Filly (Col. Claibourn) — The first Heat Angorah came in first, Havoc Filly & Exito, time 4 m. — 2d Heat, time 3 min. 52 s., Angorah 1st, Exito next, the Filly distanced

    2   Splendid three mile Race To day, 4 Horses Entererd   I will write the names of the nags as they came Out the second Heat, Kathleen, Jim Polk, Antelope & Naked Truth, I pd. Mr Patterson & Wiswall for you $50   Twenty five Dollars of the money I Loaned Her and the Ballance was your own money[5]

    3   A Race to day, 4 Mile Heats   Here is the name of the nags as they came Out the First Heat. Fanny Wright, Linit & Danl. O'Connel, 4 m. 40   Suzen Yandle, She was Distanced and withdrawn, 2nd heat, Danl. O'Connell Distanced — Fanny Wright won the Race, min 8, 22 seconds   I Received a Letter

---

[5] Johnson probably referred to his mother.

from Mrs Miller and a Letter or Rail Road notice to pay two Hundred on the 15th inst

4 To day was to have been the 3 best in 5, but there was no nag Entered against Angorah — She Loaped around Once and took the money Antelope was Entered but did [not] Run. There was an old Fellow from Misouri that won Several Races this Evening

5 Ann & myself took a ride out in the Neighbourhood of Capt. Nevits Plantation, then after we came home we took of[f] the Saddles and I took Kitty and wrode Out to Carys and Brought in Little Will His Grand Mother had taken him Out there

6 Col A L. Bingaman Received a challenge from Col Osburn Claibourne To fight. The Col. Came in very Early this morning and got shaved He seemed to be wraped up in thought, he had nothing to say — The Roumer Says that they are to fight with Riffles — I am very Sorry to heare that they are agoing to fight — I only wish that they may be preventd from fighting for I Like them Both — Col. Clabourne has 40 of his Slaves put up to be Sold at auction, Report Seys they are sold for debt Lawyer Baker[6] has old Armstead[7] in Jail and gave him to day One Hundred & fifty Lashes He Seys that he stoled four Hundred Dollars from him — Mr Duffield was put in Jail Last night for debt

7 This Day at Woo[d]ville in Wilkerson County Mr W. Hale formily a member of Congress Died[8]

9 No News of any greate Importance, There are Strong talk about the Duell that they Expecd I paid Mr T Rose four hundred Dollars, and took his Receipt for the whole of the Bui[l]ding — this makes Twenty Six Hundred and Seventy-five Dollars that I have paid him, and tis the Last Dollar that I

---

[6] Grafton Baker was a lawyer to whom Johnson occasionally made loans in the late 1830's.

[7] Armstead was a free Negro. He doubtless was the Armstead Carter who had been freed by Cyrus Marsh of Natchez in June, 1834. As late as 1850 his name appeared on the U. S. census rolls as a free Negro drayman, born in Virginia and aged forty-seven, with a total of six free persons of color in his family. See U. S. Census Reports, 1840, Schedule I, Adams County, 12; *ibid.*, 1850, Schedule I, Adams County, 29; Auditor's Records, Tax Rolls, 1843, Adams County; Adams County Deed Records, V, 258; Natchez *Free Trader*, November 22, 1859.

[8] William Haile of Woodville served at various times in the lower house of the state legislature, where his chief service was his assistance to the Choctaw and Chickasaw Indians, and portions of two terms in the lower house of the United States Congress.

owed Him on the House[9] — The firm of Woods, Cropper & Koontz was Dissolved by mutual consent. They were in partnership about 2 Days, The Difficulty that was to have taken place to Day was very Hansomely arranged, the matter was Left to a Committee of Honor — I was never more glad than to hear it, Sterns was Siting in my Little Room when a couple of girls came for him to go after old Mrs Williams, the midwife. They Said his wife was in nead of the Midwife. Sterns was at the time playing five up with Mc, Sterns was two and Mc 3. Sterns threw down his cards, put out.

10   News in town of the failure of Severall Commission Houses Failing in New Orleans, The House of Briggs Lacost in [and] Company failed or Stoped payment to day. I paid Mr Charles Greaves To Day One hundred and Eighty three Dollars and fifty Cents for the Building of two Chimneys, the One for the House and the other for the Kitchen. Very tight very tight I think, A Mr Green pd me $5 in advance for shaving   Mr E. P. Fourniquet Resigns his office as Cashier in the Planters Bank, The circumstance aluding to Sterns is a mistake for instead of being yesternight it [is] to night the 10th inst, Old John Williams came Back to Natchez and Set Shop under the Hill

11   I gave Mrs Herd $4 To pay for One weeks Bourd for Mosses. I went around To Dr Hubbards office To try and Collect Some money, and I made out to collect $100 from Him which Leaves him in my Debt Two Hundred & 42 Dollars — I tryed to collect Some money from Mr Bell but I faild — Mrs Battles paid me this Evening $80.00   To day Col Bingaman and a Large party of gentlemen Left this place for New Orleans to see the Races   Mr Lee Claibourne takes down Antilope & two other nags   I paid Mr R Bradley $19.44 and He paid me my account of $47.50   To Day I went up to Mr N. Woods and got the pair of Boots that I won from Him on the Race & a pair that I won of Mr Rooks. They were Charged to Mr Rooks — I Rented a House to a Mr Green to day for the sum of One Hundred and 25 Dollars per month

12   Nothing transpired of any moment to day.

[9] Johnson's accounts indicate that between March 9 and July 8, 1837, he also paid Thomas Rose (or his representative) additional sums amounting to $275 for the construction of chimneys and a brick pavement in front of the house on State Street which was constructed for William Johnson and his mother-in-law. This resulted in a total of $2,950. Ledger, 1835-39, pp. 84, 112, Johnson Papers. The two-story frame building had two rooms on each floor and a one-story kitchen "in the rear." Each room had a fireplace. From May, 1837, to September, 1839, it was called "The Southern Exchange."

13 I Took the Remaining part of the pictures that I got from M Linde over to his House, which was ten in number

15 I know of Nothing worth writing about, I paid in on my Rail Road stock To Day two hundred Dollars

16 I Received a Lease to day that I got Mr Baker to draw out for me, I took a coppy of the Same and gave the coppy to Mr A Greene & George W. Blake   I Leased Mrs Battles House to them for the term of One year from the eleventh day of March

17 To night there were a parcel of Irishmen Collected together near the market house and Every person that past they were striking at them with their Sticks or Something Else   Dr Denny was Returning from Mr Ranos Dinner when the Irishmen Knocked him down and Beat him Like the mischief   They cut his head and nose pretty seviere — They cut his coat also, and they struck the sherriff also, The Fencibles turned Out, put 2 or three of the Irish in jail

18 I Loaned Mr A Spielman $300 payable in thirty Days after date at 5 per Cent per month, pretty tough pretty tough — They Let Out the man that struck the Sherriff yesterday — He gave Bale for his appearance to Court, The Frenchman moved Out of the Store to day

19 I took a wride Out on my Horse this Evening   I wrode out beyond the Bridge. Stoped a few minutes at the Race tract on my Return, no sport or amusements going On what Ever   Mcs Little Robert quite sick

20 Buisness very dull, I herd to day from New Orleans that Angorah had won the first Days Race very Easy indeed

21 Buisness Quite Lively, Mr Thom Evans Came up to my shop to tell French William that he must not Let him find Him coming about his primices again. French had been peeping through his fence at One of his Girls on Sunday Last, Big Madison West & a Black Fellow by the name of Lewis Wyley gave a party at Robt Liepers[10]   French was invited and I would not Let him Go.

22 I and the Boys were Repairing the Stable &c. I Rented Mr Dolbeare my store, the next door above me, for $50 per month, I Loaned Mr Grafton Baker fifty Dollars — Mr A. L. Gains Came from New Orleans

---

10 Madison West, Lewis Wiley, and Robert Lieper were free Negroes. See Adams County Deed Records, P, 485, T, 34; U. S. Census Reports, 1840, Schedule I, Adams County, 12; Auditor's Records, Tax Rolls, 1843, Adams County. All the Liepers mentioned in this diary were free Negroes.

   23   I went to the landing this Evening and Bot 1 Bale
of Hay, 4 Sacks of Oats   I also Bot a game Cock   I payed five
Dollars for him, thus it is ten Dollars for Provender & five for
the chicken — I put him down in the yard and the Frizeling
chicken whiped him So I find he is not much   To day Mr James
in a small Dispute with Mr Stanford Struck Him with his fist
twice, Stanford drew a Dirk and Mr James ran into his store
and got a Hatchet — Shortly after that young Rayley and Mr
James Came to gether and Mr James struck him also with his
fist. Rayley drew his dirk And Mr James drew a Pistol and
Cocked it at him, so that put an End to the fight
   24   Col Bingaman Returns from New Orleans to day,
Came up on the Jone   He won Every day that he Entered a
horse in New Orleans   Angorah won the 2 mile day, Naked
Truth the 3 mile day, and Fanny Wright the 4 mile day, then
Angorah won the 3 best in five — Linnet won a day and Antelope
a Day[11] — Mr Brown Died to day at the hospital with the Small
Pox
   25   Mr Thom. Redman died in the night Last night, he was
found Dead in his Bed this morning, Mr Maxents Little daughter
died to day. The corpse of Mary Mercer arrived in a Steam Boat,
it came by Sea   Mr Mardice & Son came up from New Orleans to
day   The Boat Brought news of the Failure of Mesrs Brander,
McKenna & Wright, Mr Wm Harris [is] there agent in this
place   They failed for 4 Million and a half of Dollars   I paid
One of the Sniders to day the sum of ten Dollars for part pay for
making Brick Pavement, He first took the job in this way, that
he would take his Brother for the amount of what He Owed me,
and this Evening when I met him he askt me for ten Dollars which
I gave Him

11 Colonel Adam L. Bingaman's stable (including Angora, Naked Truth, and
Fanny Wright) won five of eight New Orleans races held over the recently constructed Eclipse Course, at Carrollton, March 17–22, 1837. A New Orleans newspaper reported that "the lucky Col. B. . . . has been highly successful with his
stable. . . . The gentleman has won, we believe, when not only his friends but
he himself thought he must inevitably lose." These races, two of which were held
before crowds estimated at 10,000 to 12,000 persons, are historically important
because they marked the beginning of the rise of New Orleans as a racing center.
Racing crowds reached Carrollton, now a part of New Orleans but then outside
the city limits, by a new short-line railroad, steamboats and other water trans-
portation, or highway. The receipts on opening day, March 17, when Angora
won the principal race, were three and one-half barrels of dollars. New Orleans
Picayune, March 7, 11, 15, 17–23, 1837; New Orleans *True American*, March 8–15,
1837; *Spirit of the Times*, VI (1836), 365; VII (1837), 61. (The editors are indebted to Professor Charles E. Smith of Louisiana State University for research on
this footnote.)

26 Sterns and myself and the old man wrode Out near Mrs Mahans plantation — We Shot with Pistols at a mark and I Beat him and won 5 Dozen Segars from him, The Flat Boat man that sold me the chicken the other [day] was put in jail for attempting to Steal Negores

27 I Shaved young Mr Stanfords Head this Evening — Streets very dusty. Mr W Harris Came up from New Orleans, he Left New Orleans On the Steam Boat Faney and She got Burned up on her way up the River, Passengers was all Saved Except One Black servant girl who was drowned — To day News Came that Little R. J. Walker was killed in a Duell with Mr Benton at the City of Washington, District of Columbia.[12]

28 Jeff commences to water the street, Dr Dunn and another Gentleman took a Bath.

29 I went to Sprague & Howells Auction Room To day and Bot 9 pair of Pantaloons at 6½ Bits per pair Dr Lloyd Receives his Bedding, Bed and &c.

30 I went over to the Auction Store of Sprague & Howell and Bot 98 yds of Curtain Calico, 15 cts per yd, and 44 yds of Diaper at 21 cts per yard, 11 pair Stockings 25 cts per pair I Bot Several other triffling things among which were a Case of writing instruments I had some new Towells cut out this Evening and I marked 14 of them

31 I Bot at auction to day 58 & 1 qrt yards of Morieno at the store of Messrs Sprague & Howell. I paid 14 cents per yard for it

April 1 I made a Settlement to day with Mr Snider for Laying the Pavement in front of Mrs Battles House in State Street, his bill was Seventy 5 Dollars and 50 cents I Deducted what his Brother owed me which was 28 Doll[ar]s from the amount of his account, and paid him the Ballance Due him, He charged me very near two prices — William Goes up to night to shave Mr Campbell over the Store of Mr Sorias & Co.

2 Mc & Sterns & myself went Out to day thru Mr Bells place

3 To Day the City Hotell opened for the First Day. They Kept open House for Every Boddy to Day.[13] Mr F. Taylor

---

12 Robert J. Walker was at this time a United States senator from Mississippi. The report was unfounded.

13 This was the new City Hotel, which had been built upon the site (on the north side of Main Street, about midway between Canal and Wall streets) occupied by the old hotel of the same name. The old hotel had burned on January 2,

moves in my House the next door above, $50 per month.

   4   Nothing new of any importance   I Received a Letter from Mrs Miller to day which had been Lying in the Store of Wood Pentecost & C. for severl weeks and had been Broken Opend and Read by Some One

   5   Mr E P. Fourniquet came up to day from New Orleans

   6   I Bot a Bale of hay to day and paid $11 for it, 50 cents for hauling of it, I herd to day that there had been a sale of 700 Bales of Cotten sold in New Orleans for 8 cent per pound

   7   I Changed 150 Dollars to day with Mr Hunter for which he gave me $3.50 premium

   8   I Bought Lucinda to day from Mr L A Besancon for the Sum of five Hundred and fifty 5 Dollars   He at the Same time pd me forty five Dollars for his Bill of Shaving &c. To day the Fencibles and the Natchez Guards turned Out together, Tis the first time that the Guards has turned out in the public streets since the Company First organized — I pd mother to day for Bourd $18 cash to this date, I changed $250 Ban[k]able money for Branch paper with Mr Hunter. He gave me 3 per cent, cash $7.50, Premium

   9   Mc and myself took a walk on the Bluff and then went under the hill to see a Steam Boat, it was the Columbus — She had in tow the Steam Boat Tobaco Plant

   10   I hyred Lucinda to Mr Spielman to day for five Dollars per month

   11   I was to day at the Landing and bought a Small Lot of plank that was Saved from the wreck of a Flat Boat, I gave $2.25 for the Lot. I then had to boat it to Shore for it was on a Raft. Bill Nix and Stephen helped get it Out

   12   Mr Elias Byrne paid me the amount of his account up to this date which was $7 in full. In the mean time Mr. Green tells me that it is not convenient to pay his Rent at present. Mr English Speaking of a Dr [blank] Stated that if he came in his way he would put him into Eternity and he said also that if Mr

---

1836. The Natchez *Free Trader*, April 7, 1837, carried a complete account of the "open house": "The hotel is three stories high, fronts upon Main street 150 feet, is 60 feet deep, with a wing running back 160 feet, the whole length of the lower floor of which is occupied by the dining room, a beautiful area enclosed by the buildings for a yard to be improved with walks, beyond which a large two story house for servants. The hotel contains upwards of 120 rooms, capable of accommodating nearly 400 persons, and in point of architectural beauty, arrangement for convenience and comfort, may vie with the Astor House, New York." Holton and Barlow were the owners.

Parker came in his way that he would trim his Ears for him   Mr Parker had went the Drs Bale and the Dr had ranaway, it was for 41 Dollars Borrowed money

13   Election Came on to day for Representatives an[d] Senate, Mr T. Ellis was anounced for the Lower House but he Declined Runing — Col. Bingaman was anounced for the Senate in yesterdays paper, But was Contradicted in to days paper, He was anounced as a candidate for the Lower House, But he went in the Court house and stuck up his Declineation, also sent out the Same to Washington   Mr Armatt or his friends has sent Out several pieces to day puffing up his intentions &c. I went under the hill to day and had the plank hauled up that I Bot the other day

14   Mr Armatt was Elected over Col. Bingaman for Representative from this County [14]

15   To day the paper anounced the Election of Mr. Armatt as Representative, I sent William to day after Mr Oakly to Collect $5 that he has owed me for Some time and he paid it

16   We took a walk around town, Mc and myself and at night we took another walk, Ann and her Mother was a Long with us

17   Went over the River and Took a hunt, and Killed twelve Ducks

18   I had my horse Rob Roy sold at Auction   He was sold for 66 Dollars and was bought by Mr Woodlief. I Bought a cart & harness for $20

19   I wrote a note to Mr Bell stating that I wanted him to pay me what he owed me   He Sent me word that he would call and see me but he never appeard

20   Nothing new   I Sent a Letter by mail to Mrs Miller. I Bot 28 yards of twilled Calico at the Auction Room of Mesrs Sprague & Howell — I pd him 27 cents

21   I went under the Hill to day and Bought a Large Grey Horse for which I gave the man Ninety Seven Dollars for him — He warrented the horse to be sound. The Guards and Fencibles turned Out and went out into the paster of Mr Minor and took a Dinner [15]

22   I gave seven Baths to day. The Horse I bought yester-

---

[14] Thomas Armat was elected over Adam L. Bingaman by a vote of 369 to 64. Colonel Bingaman had previously declared that he would not be a candidate for re-election. See Natchez *Free Trader*, April 24, 1837.

[15] The occasion was the thirteenth anniversary of the founding of the Natchez Fencibles. See Natchez *Free Trader*, April 28, 1837.

day, I commenced hauling water with him this Evening   I
found out yesterday Evening that the Horse was wind broken —
Big Gim Michel Jumped over Bourd and Dround himself in a
fit.

23   I wrode Out in the afternoon on my Little mare and I
took Bill Nix with me on the Grey Horse, and we Lete the
horses Eate grass for a while

24   To day the Cars at the Rail Road commences to Run
at 12 Oclock, precisely at 12 Oclock[16]   L. David Received
an notice to attend to tryal of Flechos Note due me for
$180.00   Mr Ellix Stewart Gave Mrs Battles an Order on Dr
Hubbard for $20. The Dr Excepted the Order and promised to
pay it [in] ten Days   I sent down my 2 horses to Mr Cryzers
to have them Shod   I had the Large horse Shod all around and
the Filly Shod before only

25   Nothing new that I have herd of to day

26   My Lewis was buried Early this morning — I paid Mr
R. Stewart ten Dollars for funeral Expenses &c. The Firm of
Watt Burk & Co. Failed for 6 millions of dollars — Mc and
myself were piching Dollars to night and he won Eight Segars
from me — Capt. Dawson asked me this morning if I would permit
him to pass through my yard into Mr Bells yard, that is to have
a gate way untill Mr Bell would tear the old house down. I Consented to Let him have a passage through for a Short time.

27   Mr S Gocian Leaves this place for Tennessee to procure
Race Horses for the Col — I won 2 Cegars from Mc this Evening piching Dollars — The Boys Commencd this Evening to
ceal there Room — I Loaned Dr Lloyd my Little Mare   I
Loaned him the Little mare the other day

28   Myself and the boys were Cealing the Room where
they sleep and Bill Winston were a white washing the same   Mr
Wiswall told me this morning if I would Send over to his yard he
would give me the water Out of his Cistern, as he wanted to have
it plastered   It Leeked in his Cellar — I sent over the Horse
and Cart and a Coupple of the Boys and they took Out a good

---

16 According to the Natchez *Free Trader*, April 28, 1837, the railroad ran its
first train on April 27. "Notwithstanding the numerous predictions of the utter
failure of our railroad, yesterday a locomotive with a full train of cars filled with
citizens, left the *depot* at one o'clock, and moved gallantly off, a few miles, a full
band of music enlivening the scene. Our railroad was one of the *last chartered*
but is *the first in operation*; and although it is only completed a short distance,
yet the fact of its progressing at all under the pecuniary embarrassments which
weigh down the whole community, argues well for its speedy completion."

deal of it — To day I had a Suit in Court and I Lost it   I had
Sued the Little Frenchman Sereau for $180, a note which he
Indorsed for the Frenchman Flecheo that ran away from this
place for debt. I Lost the money by not having the note protested when it fell due, Mr Baker was my Lawyer and Mr F
Taylor wittness — L David was wittness in behalf of him, Sereau
— He had herd me say that I Expected to loose the money for
I had neglected to have the note protested when it fell due — He
acknoledged the promise of Paying the debt if it Could not be
made Out of Flecho, but my having but the One witness and the
law requirrs that there shall be two witnesses in such cases   To
day Mother and Little Will Buckes went Out and took a wride on
the Rail Road &c.

29   Nothing going on that I know of Except that Murcheson and Mr Collier has a fight

30   I hyred a gig to day from Mr Lancershire

May 1   I was at the Landing To day, and I bought two
Large Chickens   There was a Flat boat Sold to day that was
Sunk   She Layed up at the uper Landing and was Laden with
Hay — Mr S. Davis bought the Hay at $20 per ton   There were
75 Bales of it and there were about 40 more that was in the
water which Sold for 20 Dollars and was bought by a Mr Mitchell
and the Boat Sold for only Six Dollars, good Boat. And as I
Came up the Hill I Drove up the cow Rose with a young
Calf about 3 Days old

2   Auction to Day at Mesrs Soria & C. It was a mar[s]hal
Sale of thirteen Slaves belonging to Mr. Whitney   They were
Sold for a $9000 Debt of Mr C Dart in which Mr C. Dart got Mr
Whitney to indorse for and that is the way in which he was
Brought to this Situation   They Sold Cheap — A Mr Bean the
clerk of D Barlow knocked Mr John Fletcher Down with a Stick
at Parkers Hotell, and they were Seperated, The Clerk Drew his
dirk and a Pistol & Flecher he broke and run and in about a
half hour after he was met by this man and he beat Flecher with
a stick and Flecher he ran again

3   Buisness very dull indeed, Southern Exchange was closed
this morning by Mr Withers for debt Due the State   It was for
about $250

4   Agricultural Bank made a Sudin Stop of Specie payment
to Day and there were a Large Meeting of the Dirrectors of the
Planters Bank to night and they Resolved to stop specie payment on tomorrow   I took Mr Bells Due Bill for Six hundred

Dollars and traded it away for a Note of Mothers which she owed Mr Taylor for a Sick Girl   The amount of it was $660.00 including the interest of ten per cent   I paid him the interest which was 60 Dollars

5   Planters Bank Stoped Specie payment, Tis a Dreadfull State of things we have now. The Agricultural Bank Issues three and two Dollar Bills   The first I saw was in Mcs hands [17]

6   Col Bingaman Sends his Horses up To Vicksburg for to be there in time for the Races — he takes his best horses up with him on the Steam Boat Hail Columbia, Eus Sterns was on her   He had just came up for the first time since he Ranaway from this place for being found with a watch that had been Stollen together with Some other things from an Irishman on the Bluff   The Negro that was Concern[ed] with him belonged to Mr Saturly — Poor Mosses Died to day at Mrs Herds — he is better off I hope

7   The times are Gloomy and sad to day   Money is no money — Our City Banks have Stoped and Our Branches are doing the Same and I have now about 800 Dollars of Branch money that I do not Know what I shall do with — tis strongly believed that the United States Bank will stop payment in 90 Days — and I believe it. I know not what will become of us. Dave Miller came to see us this Evening   He was on the Steam Boat and on his way to New Orleans and said that he would be agoing up in a few Days to work for Elisha

8   Mr Arlette that Died this morning was buried this Evening at ½ past 5 Oclock this Evening — The Fencibles and Guards both turned Out — very Large and respectable procession — I Received a Letter to day from Mr Miller and a Spanish pup from Tampeco as a present   Mr Nathaniel A Green of New York Leaves this place for the North — Mr Manderville paid me his account by order of Mr Green

9   Steam Boat Ben Sherrod was burned up this morning near Fort Adams and a Greate many Lives Lost on her. She was Discoverd to be On fire this morning about 4 Oclock [18] — The

---

[17] See Natchez *Free Trader*, May 5, 1837. The Planters' and Agricultural banks of Mississippi were among the first in the United States to suspend specie payment.

[18] The steamboat *Ben Sherrod*, engaged in a race with the *Prairie*, burst its boilers and caught fire at night, and sank several miles below Natchez. About 60 of approximately 210 persons aboard were rescued, mostly by other passing steamboats. See Natchez *Free Trader*, May 12, 1837, for an extended account which blames the captain of the *Ben Sherrod* for persisting in the race after his vessel had twice caught fire and for refusing to allow the deck hands and passengers to lower the yawl until it was too late. See also *Lloyd's Steamboat and Railroad*

Branches of Our Banks have all Fail[ed] — terrible times, not Exactly failed tho they have stoped spiecie payment [19]

10 No Buisness going On of any account to day — Old Mrs Herd sent Barnet the Constable with an account in two Bills making in all the sum of $18.00 To day Mr Bennet & Barnet Came to see me about the Counter in the Southern Exchange They had Bought the Counter from Mr McGaughlin and Blake and the[y] had Conditionally sold it to Mr McGetrick

11 I Sold $50 of Vicksburg Commercial money to day for $53 of Agricultural money — I gave Mr McGetrick the keys to day of the Southern Exchange [20] — I wrode out near Mrs Lintons Residence and there I Caught a young thrush

12 Nothing new transpired

13 Nothing of any interest transpired To day

14 There were a number of us went Out to St Catherine to fish Mc Caught 8 Small fish, Sterns One and I Caught One None of the Boys caught a single One and there were 7 of them in number I made them Run Races for meat and Bread I had a good many Races out of them

15 A very dull day indeed, I went under the Hill to day and tryed at Every Corn Boat to get them to Take our paper money at par but non would. They asked 10 Bits in Spicie and 12 Bits a Barrell in Our paper money. I gave them paper and paid the Difference — I went around to Mcs Shop this Evening and took some marbles and we played. Mc won 30 games and I won 17 games, Sterns 6

16 French William went Down to the City Hotell To see Dr Williams, the Oculast. The Dr poured Something in his Eyes

Directory, and Disasters on the Western Waters (Philadelphia, 1856), 95-101. On May 16, 1837, William Johnson contributed $2.00 to a fund being raised in Natchez for "The Distressed Passengers of the Ben Sherrod." Cash Book, 1830–38, Johnson Papers.

[19] On May 12, 1837, the Natchez *Free Trader* carried a long article on the general banking situation.

[20] P. McGetterick rented the two-story frame building erected by Johnson on his mother-in-law's State Street property for $79 per month for at least a year. Mc-Getterick ran "a coffee house" in the building and called his establishment "The Southern Exchange," which should not be confused with William Parker's Mississippi Hotel, also called "The Southern Exchange"—directly across State Street, on the north side. See description of Johnson's Southern Exchange in Ledger, 1833–37, p. 150, Johnson Papers; Natchez *Courier*, February 25, April 18, 1839. For two months prior to McGetterick's occupancy, Johnson had rented the building to the firm of Green & Blake for $125 per month; and from October 1, 1838, to near the end of September, 1839 (when it burned), he rented it to Carroll & Evans for $50 per month. See Day Book, 1830–40, March 11, 1837–September 5, 1839, Johnson Papers.

that Burned him for a Little while, it Smelled something Like Sasafras — Dr John Humbug, M-D   James Tooley has a Large placard up this morning on the wall about Dr Williams the Oculist. Dick went Out to fish to day and Caught Only One Doz Fish.

17   I went under the Hill this morning and Bought thirty five Barrells of Corn at 1.25 per barrell and it was the Only Boat that was Selling at that price   The Ballance were Selling at 12 Bits spicie and $2 in our paper. I also Bought One Hundred and 2 pounds of Bacon at 10 cents per pound and One Barrell of flower at Eight Dollars — The Bacon and flour I pd for in Agricultural money but Corn I paid for in Gold & Silver. Sterns went up to the Long Lake to fish

18   Buisness Dull, We were all Cleaning and washing all the Glasses and Fixing of the Cases &c. To day   Mr Spielman Owes me $330

19   Buisness very Lively in the Bath way

20   Eleven Gents Baths to day

21   I went Out to St Catharine to fish this Evening and took Charles and Bill Nix with me and was to have met Mc on the Banks of the Creek but did not see [him]   I went too Low Down on the Creek for Him, Col. Bingaman Returns from Vicksburg after wining all his Races.

22   Commercial Bank Stoped Specie payment this morning

25   I arose very Early in the morning and took Bill Nix and Bill Winston and mounted Our horses and crossed the River and went a Fishing in the Concordia and Cocodria Lake — Mc, J. Lacrose and G. Butler went along at the Same time and when we got Over to the Lake we found Messrs Levi Harrison, Pond, Rufner, Cambell, Stevenson, Noyes and Some Darkeys and after a short time young Bell and H Austin Came Down. Young Bell got Drunk and Lye down and went to sleep and Caught no fish of course tho all the persons that were over there caught a Greate many. My two and myself Caught 4 Doz and 4 fish   Mc Caught as many or more prehaps than we three did — I Left Mc at the Lake a fishing   We Reached town quite Early in the Evening and got home in time to have Our fish Dressed for Supper — Mc and Mr Rufner, Harrison and a good many more Left Late in the evening and did not Get home until about 10 Oclock   They treeed a Coon on there way home   Mc he took an active part in Killing the Coon   He was Shot Down by Rufner and Mc he

Drew his Bucher Knife and was a spledgeing it about in Greate stile over the Coon

27 Charles started Home this morning Early He Wrode on my Little mare

28 A very dull day in town Mr Grafton Baker got pretty high — got into Several difficultys The one at the City Hotell I dont know anything about, but the One at the Mansion House He attempted to pull Dr Branders nose for refuseing to drink with him — When he made the attempt to pull his nose the Dr Knockd him Down with his stick, he struck him on Jaw or side of the face Mr Baker Recoved and struck him with his fist which Knocked the Dr Down

29 A Challenge passed To Day between Mr Armatt and Mr Besancon Mr Armatt Sent the Challenge, and Mr Besancon Accepted the Challenge and they were to have fought three feet a part Tis too Close I dont think they will fight, Mr B. it appears accused Mr Armatt of having been the author of Some piece that apeared in the Courrier and Journal office — this is said to have been the origin of it. To day Mother paid me Sixty Dollars and She now owes me $600 towards the Girl Sharlot

30 To Day I Sent the Little Red Cow Down to New Orleans On the Steam Boat, Hail Columbia — the Cow and Calf was for Mrs Miller — The Boat was to have gone at 10 Oclock but did not get away untill 3 Oclock this Evening She had On Bourd Some of the finest Cattle that I have Ever Seen — Harden was On the Boat and as Bar Keeper and Fitzchue was on her also — I Sent a Letter by Harden and One by Louis Winsborough both to Mrs Miller — Whilst I was Down at the Landing to day I was told that those Gentleman that had Crossed the River was then about to fight a Duel. It was thot to be Besancon & Armatt that had gone across but it was a mistake for they had not gone over — I got in a Skifft and crossed the River but neither of the parties had gone over so I came directly back again — Mr Besancon told me this morning that he had been very much abusesd by the other party, and that he would fight the whole Concern of them, but what, he would be Satisfied or Revenged He Seemed to have a good Strong Disposition to whale Mr Mellen if he met him any where and said also that Mr Black would get a fall through the course of the day

31 Nothing New that I know of To Day

June 1 Myself with Charles and Bill Crossed the River in Company with Mc To go over the River To fish We went

179

over to the Concordia Lake and we caught a Greate many fish   I had when I Got home ten Dozen and 4 fish and I had gave away and Lost about 2 Dozen   Mr Eleck Bell hooked them from me   Mc he Caught 7 Doz or near about it   We did not get over until Sun Down or night and we had to pay Double ferryage — there were 7 horses & 8 or ten men Came over at the same time in the Boat.

3   In to days Free Trader we had a full Statement of all the corespondence between Mr Armat and Mr Besancon   It was a Lengthy coresponace Quite so indeed but all Ended in peace[21]   There were Seventeen persons Bathed to day in my Bath House. This Day I owe Mother $40 which Sum added to Sixty Dollars that She paid me on 29th of May is One Hundred Dollars that she has paid me on the money that I paid Mr Taylor for Her — She now owes me five Hundred and Sixty Dollars

4   Nothing has transpired that is worth a Comment. I gave French $2.25 to day and the Boys $3 both for Bath Buisness

5   Mr William H. Chambers Died Last night about 9 Oclock — Mrs Rebecka Bingham Died this evening   Mr Chambers was buried out at the Family Burial Ground

10   I bought of young Mr Harris to day $10 Rail Road Scrip for Seven & ½ of our paper Currency

12   A Fight took place this morning between Mr George Lancaster and Big Frank Little in the Market House, Frank Little it appears whiped Mary Lattimore[22] as she terms herself, for being at the Bench Drinking Coffee   She was Left in charge of Mr Lancaster and as soon as he herd that F Little had whiped her he went into market and commenced On F. Little as hard as he could with his fist   They had a pretty sharp fight but was at Last Seperated by the bystanders, I herd Mr P. Gemmell walk past my Shop door Cursing N. L. Williams   He was about to Flake him and did attempt to Jump the counter after him and

---

[21] The Natchez *Free Trader*, June 3, 9, 1837, carried accounts of the affair. Lorenzo A. Besancon was the editor of the *Free Trader*, and Thomas Armat was a local lawyer and politician. The June 9 issue contains four and one-half columns of correspondence regarding the proposed duel, and illustrates how duels were often averted by the intervention of friends who made a settlement satisfactory to both sides. The cause of the difficulty between the two men was political controversy. The distance between the parties in this proposed duel was to be thirty feet, and not three feet, as stated by Johnson in his May 29 entry.

[22] Mary Lattimore was a slave, the property of Dr. David Lattimore. On September 8, 1838, he swapped "a Mulatto woman named Mary," aged about twenty-one, to "Nancy [Lattimore] a free person of color" in exchange for another female slave, aged about eighteen, and $1.00. Adams County Deed Records, DD, 46.

was prevented by Mr Neibut. He cursed him for a d——d scoundrell and a greate many more things.[23]

13   Nothing new worth recording — Mr Walker Gets the
Girl that ran away from him some time ago

14   Mr Woodville P. Ward, the Post Master at Vicksburg,
Died to day with Small pox — Extracted from N. Paper

15   To day Mr Melton, Scocth Meleene and William Reid in
settling there accounts Disputes and had very near a fight   Mr
Meleene Let Reid jab him in the abdomen with a gun seveal times
and made no Resistance whatever — Sterns goes across the River
to fish this Evening and intends fishing all day to morrow

16   The carpenters Commenced To repair the gallery the
next Door at Capt Dossens, and very Glad I am to have thet
place Stoped up. I Received a Letter from Captain Miller to day
from Vicksburgh [24]

18   Mr A. Spielman owes me to this date the sum of three
hundred Dollars

21   To day Mr N. L. Williams Came To me To know if I
had made any arrangement with Mr Gemmell. I told him that
I had not but was waiting for a tittle for the wall from Mr
Gemmell, and he Said Mr Gemmell Cannot give you a title for
the wall, for he has treated me very shabbyly Lately, and I will
not do anything To oblige him in any way. He would Sooner put
his head in the River and hold it there a half hour than ask me to
Sign a deed for it   You had better Seys he, waight untill I get
back from the North, and then we will have the buisness fixed
for He Cannot give you a tittle and I have not passed my deed
to Captain Dossen yet but will do it when I return from the
North. He gave me to understand that he would sell me the wall
for the Same Sum that I was to pay Mr Gemmell for it.

22   To Days paper Announces the Ellction of Mr Izod to
the Office of Sherriff — He had a majority of three hundred and
fifty two over Col Woods — To Day Mr McGetrick paid me One
months rent that was due on the 15th ins — the Amount of Rent
was $79.00   I took 59 Dollars in Branch paper and $20 in

---

[23] On May 6, 1836, Nathaniel L. Williams had purchased the three-story brick
store building, occupied by the firm of Neibert & Gemmell and owned by Peter
Gemmell and John G. Taylor. William Johnson's barbershop was immediately
adjacent. Adams County Deed Records, X, 164-65. In 1837, Williams opened a
new "Book and Drug Store," probably in the building he owned. Natchez *Courier,*
November 27, 1837.

[24] Johnson occasionally referred to Elisha Miller, the free Negro barber in Vicksburg, as "Captain Miller."

Rail Road Scrip — He Left One hundred Dollars in Scrip — After taking Out the $20 it Leaves a Ballance of Eighty Dollars in Scrip in his favor of which I am to take Out Every month twenty Dollars as Long as it will Last   To day I herd Mr Paterson Driving Mr Abonette from his Store, saying go off! Go off — and I herd that they had takin him by the Collar and Led him to the door — Mr Bell had him put in Jail this Evening for debt

 23   I Received a Letter this Morning by the Steam Boat Bunker Hill — The Letter Came from Mrs Miller, Mr Wiswall and Mr N L. Williams Leaves this place for the North.

 24   To day I paid Mr Mark Breden & Spielman & Co. the Sum of One Hundred and fifty three Dollars for Building a Bake Oven — very high price   Mother paid me twelve Dollars on the above Amount, This will Leave a Ballance of One hundred and forty One Dollars — I Loaned Mr McFadden $50 to be paid On Tuesday next, 27th instant

 25   Buisness unusually dull, I wrode out and took Bill Winston with me To get Black Berrys. We got a greate many in a short time, Capt Pomp, or Mr Strickland is appointed Deputy Sherriff — Aunt F. McCary Stayd all night at our house

 26   I Read a pretty tight burlesque to day in the Jackson paper of the Duel that was to have Taken place between Mr Armatt & Besancon   It apeared to be a Burlesque on Mr Armatt alone

 27   Judge Rawlins called To Know Something Respecting my whishing to have a petition for a reduction of taxes on my Property — To Day we had a first rate fight between Bill Rushelow & Bill Winston — They made a Stand of[f] — Neither whiped

 28   I herd this morning of the Dreadfull attack of Mr Rogers of Manchester on a Dr Reigna of the Same place, what the fight Grew Out of I have not herd, but appears that Mr Rogers Saw Dr Reigna on his gallery and was in Company with his family, ie, his wife and Children   Mr Rogers drew a pistol and fired on him then Jumped To him, Knocked him down and stabed him clear through the body and screwed it around in his Dead Boddy — Latest accounts that he was put in Irons — to stand his tryal, Mr. R. Parker came in this Evening to Know how many Slaves I had about my yard as my property   I told him that I had five and that I had Several Boys and they were not mine and they were not Bound to me yet.

 29   I Caught old Mary to night with a Basket with 7 or 8 unbaked Buiscuit — I have reason to believe that she got them at the City Hotell, and the way I cursed her was the wright way and if Ever I can hear of her doing the Like again I will whip her untill I make her faint

30   This morning M[other] Commenced as usual to quarrell with Everything and Every body, I, Knowing perfectly well what it Grew Out of, I thought I would take the quickest way to stop it, and I accordingly took a whip and gave her a few Cuts; As soon as that was done M. commenced to quarrell and abuse me Saying that I done it to oblige Sarah and advancing on me at the same time Dareing me to strike, which I would not do for anthing in the world. I shoved her back from me three times

The Basis of Our Free Instition

No Priviledged orders — Liberty of Speech — Freedom of the press — The rights of conscience — Strict Construction of the federal Constitution — Universal Sufferage — Responsibility to the people — No Imprisonment for debt — And a general Diffusion of Knoledge among all Classes of the People

Richard M. Johnson
By William T. Johnson

July 4   To day was the most splendid day I have Ever witnessed on the fourth of July.

7   To day I paid Mr P. Baker for my Taxes for the City During this year which amounted to One hundred and $5.62½, Good Lord, what a Tax

8   To day Bill Nix & Charles & myself Finished my Bird House that we Commenced yesterday Evening — I put the Birds in this Evening, Brown & Davis Ranaway to Day and stole Negroes belonging to the Rail Road.

9   Mc and myself and Bill Winston wrode Out towards Capt Nevits road. Myself and Bill got a tin Bucketfull of Blacke Berrys — To day there were Several gone after those Rascals Brown & Davis. Capt Quitman, Thom Munce and Young Rayley.

10   To day the Sherriff takes Louis Millers Furniture and sells it at the Court House Door for Debt. It was taken. I am told his wife and children & sisters Crying very much when they were taken,[25] Captain Quitman returned and Brought back all

---

[25] In the previous month William Johnson's sister, Mrs. James Miller, had written in outraged tone from New Orleans that Louis Miller had there claimed to be James Miller's brother-in-law. James Miller had denied any kinship. Mrs. Miller to Johnson, June 20, 1837, Johnson Papers. He was not the Louis Miller listed as white in the U. S. census of 1830.

183

the Slaves belonging to the Rail Road that had been taken away by Brown & Davis — there were 38 in number I herd

12   To Day they were a party of men went in Search of Brown, the Rail Road Contractor whom report Seys has ran-away

13   I herd Mr Brown, the Contractor of the Rail Road, Laughing very much how those Gentlemen were Deceived that had Started Out yesterday morning in search of Him   There were the following Gentlemen went in persuit of Him, Mr T. Ellis, Mr S. Gocian, Rufner, Mr Woodlief & Dunlap, and several others   Old Mr Gridley also — The report was that Brown had Left and had took with him 9 of the Slaves belonging to the Rail Road Company

14   The Boys finished there Small Building at the Bake oven this Evening   Dr Denny Died with a fit On him   He was not sick at all as far as I have herd

15   To day Mr McGetrick paid the months Rent up to this date precisely   He is good pay — Dr Denny was Buried to day Out at the Family Burial Ground of Mrs Lintotts   There were but very few attended the funerall

16   Mc and myself wrode out as far as the Old Scott field   Mc wrode his New horse that he had Just swaped for with Mr Woodlief, He was a good horse   He cheated him bad, I think

17   To day the Election for Congressmen commenced. Mr Spielman paid me fifty Dollars, being a part of some moneys that I Loaned him Some time ago — He owes me now two hundred and fifty Dollars yet.

18   Dr Griffin paid me to day Sixty five Dollars that I Loaned him on the 3d of May, 1837. Tosspott was here to day and Brought a Letter to Mother from New Orleans, tho none for me

19   Buisness as usual very dull. Mc Moved up in his New Shop oposite or ajoining the Commercial Coffee house   To day a Mr [blank] has Just oppened a new Shop where the Spaniard moved from on Market Street, I Took a wride this Evening and took my Little Will with me, We had a pleasant trip or wride, quite So

20   Je Zava treant Quart peas, a twa ca — Carly — I was up at Auction to day and bought 13 yds of Calico. It was a[t] Dolbears & Presho's   I gave 10 cents per yard for it.

21   Mrs Battles paid me two dollars that I Loaned her a

week ago — There were Some Stir this Evening or to night by Some One's hallowing fire, False alarm, I presume

22 Buisness very dull indeed Nothing new worth takeing notice of What a poor Devel this Frenchman is. To night a Black Girl of Capt Dawsons Sends him word to Come after awhile and get his hankerchiefs — the fact is he has Got a few Lace or fringed hanks and the infernal fool has given [them] to wash to Every Negro wench that he can possibly have any talk with Oh the Rascal I would give One hundred Dollars if Some Gentleman would only Cetch the Low minded Dog and Cow hyde him well Out of there yards — it would do me so much good

23 I herd to day that my Negro man Waker had ran away On Bourd of Some Steam Bourd [boat] that Left here on Friday Evening, 21st inst There were three Boats Left here on that day, namely the st. Boat Claibourne & Wyoming & Oceana, the Last name[d] Boat was Bound for St. Louis.

24 I was full of Buisness — and all Buisness I was writing and Flying around as Buisy as you please in sea[r]ch of Waker, that ranaway from me I Sent a Letter by Mr Birk to be handed to the Sherrif of Louisville with a Discription of the thief and the Negro — And I also Sent an advertizement to the office of the Courrier to [be] published in the daily One week and to be published in the weekly untill forbid [26] — Ann wrote two Letters this Evening and I Sent them by mail to Mr Miller for Mrs Miller, I paid the Postage on them both witch I am affraid she wont Like so well

25 I Sent Mr F Taylor his account to day and he Disputed the Bill and promised to Call and see me On to morrow, and have a settlement in full. Dr Dallys Little daughter was Buried Tis the first death that Ever has been in the City Hotell.

26 Dr Hogg Came home from Bay of St Louis

27 Buisness was very dull. The boys are painting the Bath Tubs and Bath Rooms — To day Mr Taylor paid me for 2 months & a half Rent, He paid me $90.50 I at the same time handed him his note for $30 which had run One year, the 8th inst He paid me the Principal But would not pay the interest

29 Buisness very dull in my proffession tho very Brisk in

---

[26] About two weeks later the diarist wrote to his sister, Adelia: "I suppose you have herd that my old Negro Walker has ranaway and *gone*—he was stolen by a Fellow—under the hill—I never Expect to see him any more." Johnson to Mrs. James Miller, August 6, 1837 (copy), Johnson Papers.

the Bath Line, 17 persons had Baths To day — To day Mr Amassa Smith was put in Jail for debt. Judge Montgomery has our Division fence pulled down and the Foundation of a house Laid out on the Line of the fence.

30 Mc and myself went down to Andy Gobeaus Steam Ferry Boat and went across the River and staid a few minutes and came back, We went across in 4 minutes, and we were seven minutes & ½ in Coming back

31 To day was oh the dullest day I have had for years. I think the Whigs are convincd that they are beaten, from the returns that came to day — Mr Grafton Baker is anounced in the paper of to day a Candidate for the office of Judge in the 1st Judicial Destrict and Judge Maury runs for the same office — Joseph Smith was put in Jail To day for debt, Took the Oath of Insolvency and Came Out. He remained in about 12 hours

August 1 Buisness as usual, very dull, I had to Curse William this morning the first thing, and Came very near giving him a drubing — He met old Dr Harden Coming in the shop this morning as he was on his [way] Out to market, and he said G—— darn it, I cant never get to go to market, Gentlemen keeps coming in, What a Bad Fellow. To day Mr Rice of the Landing left this place to go up the river, to stay about two months. And to day Mr Christopher pd me his account for Shaving which was $5.25 Mr Rice pd me $2.00

3 To day I Received from Mr McGettrick his Rent which will be due on the 15th inst of Seventy nine Dollars — I Bought 19 Dozen of Lavender from Mesrs Patterson [&] Wiswall at two at two Dollars per Dozen, and paid them in Brandon money and I Bot One hundred weight of Bacon from Messrs A L. Gains & Co. at 12 cent per pound, This I paid them for in Mississippi Paper.

4 Buisness very dull, Natchez is getting worse and worse

5 There were three Deaths in town Last Night, the One was a Mr Patterson, a Cosen of Pattersons across the way — the other a Mr Murphy and Joe Walker the Carpenter, To day I had ocasion to go to the stable and whilst I was there I Descoverd something Shaking the Loft and I Steped to the troft and Loked up and there I found Little ——— ——— with a Muscovia Duck in the act of [blank] He was frightend very much — I took him and gave him a Genteel whiping and I intend to whip him again about it. This Evening myself and the Boys made a Bath Sign and put it up at the door.

6   I took my nag and wrode out as far as the Scott old Field, Dismounted from my Horse and Took Out a Small Book from my pocket and Read untill it grew Late, I arived in town about Super time, I herd to night the noise of Cetch him, hold him, Cetch him, hold him, &c. and after a while I herd that it was Mr Knox that was runing   He ran from Parkers Hotell in his shirt tail and dogs after him. He was Caught at the City Hotell

7   The old woman gets in one of way; threw Salt all on the floor at the door, Quarrells and makes all maner of fuss for nothing at all, I made Sharlot her Girl go and scour it up but would not Say a word to the Old Lady about it — To Day Mr Joseph Reichleaus property was put up and Sold at the Court House by the Sherriff for debt, They Sold very high I thought   I Bot 4 Pictures & a table there — a number of things that sold very high — They sold Every thing that he had in the way of House Furniture,   This Evening the old woman Commences and makes a Terrible Quarrelling and abuses me a good deal for giving Moses a Small flaking for runing and hallowing in the Street before the Door, I whiped Bill too as he was One of the Party   Hanchet and a young man by the name of Colson has a fight

8   Nothing good in the way of Buisness, oh I never saw such times in all my Life.

9   Mr Spielman Commences to make a fence On the Back part of Our Lot, the Division fence, He has the Corner of Said Lot underpined with Brick by his Brother, Mr Miller came up from New Orleans on Bourd of the Steam Boat Moravian — He arrived about 1 Oclock to day — After we took dinner we took a wride Out as far as the old Field beyond Col. Wilkins's.

11   I was Out untill Late this Evening untill night hunting for my horse, and when I came home behold the horse was in the Stable — Safe

12   No Kind of Buisness — Brisk. I made Out the account against the Estate of Mr John Carroll — I must have it Probateed. To day Mr Spielman wanted to pay me One hundred dollars in Brandon or Alabama money and I would not Except it but told him to try and get it changed and he said he would try and do so. The article of corn is selling to day or retailing at One Dollars per Barrell, in Spiecie   To day Mother and myself Spoke together and it is the first time Since the first of July Last   This was done throug[h] the interfereance of Mr Miller

13   To day has been very dull, Last night there were a

parcell of vagabonds, I may say, for I cannot call them Gentlemen, for the[y] were hallowing and hooping through the Streets, One of the Black Gards Broke Several paines of Glass Out of the uper End of my house, ocupied by Dr Loyd, I do not Know the names of any of them yet Except Mr Pincterton, he was One of the partee, He I think is making rarther a poor show, for a Gentlemen. Report seys that he got a severe Drubing by a gent from the same County in which he is Cashier — It was up there that he got it.

14 Large Auction down at Messrs Spraugue & Howells auction Room, I Bot nothing at auction, I went Down to the Black Smith Shop To pay for my Horse's having the Lampus Burned Out.[27] I gave it to a Black Boy for Mr Allison and Came Away — Jo [blank] belonging to Mr Bunce was Buried He Died Last night

15 Mr Miller from New Orleans, Mc and myself went into the Swamp hunting and fishing We did not find much Game.

16 Nothing New Buisness as usual, very dull.

17 I herd to day thrugh Mr Spencer that My Negro man Walker that ran away from me 21st of July was in Jail up at Paduca.

18 Buisness quite dull. We had yesterday an Election for a Selectman, to fill the vancansy Ocasiond by the Resignation of Judge Rawlings, Mr Spielman paid me thirty Dollars To day. He now Ows me two hundred and twenty on Borrowed money, without the Interest I was up yesterday to See Mr Soria to get a Bill of Sale for Walker or a Certificate for the Same, for I had Lost the Orinishal One

19 Nothing new to day. A Mr Lounds & Berry Rents my Store the next door above my Shop, the Rent to Commence from Monday, 21st instant, at the monthly Rent of fifty Dollars — To day I receivd A Letter From the hands of Capt Saturly Directed to Capt Willson at Padducah

30 I was this morning at Grand Gulph. Buisness was very Dull there, and the place Reported unhealthy, We came on passed Rodney — which Looked Like there was no people in the town, Evry thing apeard so dull, And we Came on Down within 6 or 8 miles of Natchez, and a Deck passenger that was sick and came On at Vicksburgh, Jumped over Bourd tis supposed and was Drown'd — He had, in the pocket of a vest that was found on the Boat belonging to him, the Sum of five Dollars and 62½ cts

[27] The lampas was a congestion of the mucous membrane of the hard palate.

— The money was taken and put into the Clerks office To give to
the owner or Relation if they Could find any — We arrived at
Natchez Just at Supper time, Mr W. Walton, Mr Grace who was
the clerk of the Boat, and a Mr Barron, who by trade is a
Carpenter, he was Robbed on the Boat he said of $150. He had
no money to pay his passage with and I Loaned him $30 to pay
it with, I wrote a Letter to day on the Boat and Sent it to Mr
James Miller by the Boat, stating that I had got safe at home
and the Disappointment of my trip, and that they were all well,
&c. I find that I have been away ten Days and the Boys during
that time has taken in $54.87½ — that will do very well I think

September 1 There was an Auction to day at Dolbears &
Preshos — they were Selling the Effects of the Late Mr Wm A.
Arlette — I Bot a Breast Pin for which I paid Mr Pressho $16
in cash His cloathes sold for One Hundred Dollars and [were]
purchased by his Brother, & his Horse Sold for $215, I think, bid
of[f] by Mr Milene on a credit of Six months — A Mr Spruce
Died Last Night at Mr Parkers Hotell, and was Burried to day —
he resided at the Grand Gulph and was a Merchant of that place
— To day the Miss Mandevilles came home from [blank]

2 Several Races to day — One between a Sorrill Filly of
Mr Minors and one [of] Mr Mardices — 600 yd Race The
Same two had to run a mile Race in 15 minutes after the first
Race wich they did and Both Races were won with Great Ease
by Elizar Jones — and there was another Race between a Sory
Filly belonging to J Routh and a Brown Filly belonging to Mr
Minor — imported Stock Mile heats Mr Rouths nag won both
heats with greate Ease, Mr Jas Rayly won a good Deal of money
On that Race To Day Mr D B. Barron came and paid me the
thirty One Dollars that I Loaned him On Bourd of the Steam
Boat Pittsburgh to pay his passage Down the River — Mr John
G. Taylor paid me three Dollars for two months Shaving

3 I remaind at home all day but took a walk Late in the
afternoon with Mc around town. This Evening Mother was Seting
up on the Porch asleep and tumbled right over, and fell Clear
down to the Bottom of the steps — She hurt her Eye very much
and Bruised her face a good deal, George, a Black Boy at Mr
Mandevilles, fell Down to night from the Planters Bank window
and is very much hurt

4 It [rain] caught me Out at the Race tract. I was Out to
see a race between Mr Mardices Mare and Arabb — ½ mile
race They made a Bad Start and there was no Race. To day

at the Court House was sold One Iron Safe or chest belonging to C. Dart — it was for a Debt of Burke Watt & Co. Mr Mitchell Bot it for 74 Dollars — The Sherriff also sold some goods and Effects of Elidia Tuomy — they Sold very high

5   I went up to Mess[rs] Sorias and Cossins and Bot 2 Casks of Bacon Hams at 7¾ cents per pound — The One wieghed 400 lbs and the other 394 lbs — 794 lbs   Pd Cash for Same $61.53, I Sold to Riddle 58 lbs at 10 [cents], to Hazard 62 at 10 cents, $6.20, To S M Bon 54 lbs, $5.40

6   Poor Old Mr Saml Patterson Died this Morning — I was at Auction to day and Bot a wire safe at Mesrs Dolbears & Preshos at $8.25 and had it Charged to me, This with something Else that I got there about a month ago makes in all about $15 and some cents — I sent an old Broken Sho Case to them to sell and they only got 62½ cents for it and we are to Let it Stand untill we get Even or have a settlement   To night Mr [blank], I believe, took my pole and Carried it around to the Little Frenchmans & took his pole and put it up at Mr McAlisters door   He Came Out and threw it Down and cut it up — I herd him then saying to Mr Grabbo — I Don't thank any One, Sir for it, I dont thank you Sir for it nor no other man, to play such tricks — I never played such a trick with you nor any One Else and no One Shall play them with me, Mr Grabbo Commenced Excuseing himself but in so Low a voice that I Could not hear him where I stood — I paid Mesrs Becket & OFarrel $4.50 for 4 cases of Razors & a Curry Comb that was got from there store a short time ago — To Day I Sold to Granger Butler One hundred weight of Bacon hams at 10 cents per pd — he paid Cash $10. I also Sold Mrs Lieper 54 lbs amounting to $5.40 on a Creddit,   I Loaned Mother $10 To day to pay for 2 cannary

7   I was up to Auction To Day and Bot of Messrs Dolbears & Presho 5 Gallons of Brandy @ 1.87 per gl and One Silver Gard Chain at $4. I Bot of Mr William Miller 2 fifty dollars Bills or Rail Road Scrip — B. No 78, the other No 80, Dated 18th & 25th of June, 1837, as well as I can Recollect — I gave him $75 for the hundred. Wil Hazard paid me $5 To Day for Some Bacon hams, 62 pounds — he still Owes me 1.20 cents yet, Old Mr Sm. Patterson was Burried this morning — he had a very Large funeral

8   Buisness was very dull   Nothing New that I know of   Capt Dawson is sick   He came home a few Days ago, himself and Lady — I was awaken this morning by a Boy Knocking at the door, He said he had Some thing for Wm Johnson — It

was a Bit of an old Letter that French William Johnson had Left
there   It was from a Negro wench up at Mr Barnards
    9   I got up from Bed very Early this morning and took my
Horse and gun and went in to the swamp to Make young Winn a
present of my Little Spanish Gip²⁸ — I went Down as Low as
Winns Lowest fiel[d] — Made a very poor hunt — Stoped at his
house and gave him the Gip and told him that the Tax Collector
in Franklin County was about to sell his Land for taxes due on it,
I shot one sparrow hawk and one Large hawk, a crow and one
squirrell — When I Came up to Mr Bells place I Left my gun and
munition there and came to town and was very sick with a head
ache,   An Election Came On to day for Major General of 2d
Division of Malitia of this State, Judge Quitman & Mr Besancon has a fight. Mr Besancon made a thrust at him that would
have killed him had not a piece of Silver in the Pocket of the
Judge arrested the Progress of the sword, They were seperated
by the Sherriff or some other Gentleman or two²⁹ — Dr Benbrook
and Mr Rivers has a fight   The Dr Struck Rivers first with a
stick, then Rivers struck him with a Large walking Cane with
Both hands a hold of it which Knocked the Dr as flat [as] a
flounder, and Struck him twice after that whilst he was down, As
soon as he Came to his sinseses he hallowed Murder Like a man
that was getting murderd
    10   Nothing transpired of any interest
    12   To day an article appeared in the Free Trader giving
an account of the attact that was made on Mr Besancon by Judge
Quitman, He a[l]so gave in to days paper a Revolutionary Anecdote from the pen of Mr Bensancon which Beats all Natur³⁰ — I
was out at Mr Bells plantation this Evening — I went Out there
for my Gun that I Left there Last Saturday — I got her and came
through by Mrs Scotts old field, I saw nothing but a owl and
Shot at it but did not Kill it, I came home about supper time — I
met Mr ———— & Mrs ———— wriding out together — it was Late
Late this Evening — it dont Look — Enough Said   I have been

---

²⁸ Johnson had a Spanish pony named Gipsy.

²⁹ The Natchez *Free Trader*, September 12, 1837, carried an account of the affair.

³⁰ Editor Besancon's article, entitled "Revolutionary Anecdote," is an excellent
example of the satirical writing popular at that time. It related the story of
"Major Furioso," a "blustering, flourishing and bragging" individual who marched
off to the Revolution to aid Washington, but at the Battle of Germantown he
hurried from the field in order to protect, as he said, the women and children.
Besancon concluded his article: "After the war was over, in recounting the hair
breadth escapes, etc, it was ascertained that the *fighting* major had no intention of
fighting, but marched out for the purpose of speculating in lots."

Expecting to see or hear of a Fight all day between Mr Quitman & Besancon

13 The Presidents Message was printed to day at the office of the Free Trader [31] — quite a Lengthy article — I hyred my grey horse to Mr Rose with the cart for $3.50 per day

14 Last night about 3 Oclock I was awakened by the cry of fire & the Ringing of the Bells — I arose and Discovered the Direction of the fire, and ran Down to where it was, It was the rear work Shop at Walkers, the tinners   It Burned the whole of his shop, Dicks Shop of saddlery, & Hastings upholstering Shop or store — it Burned all the Rear Buildings of all those Stores — It Burned a ware house of Messrs Sprague & Howells and a two story brick of Mr Parkers in the shape [of] an L, ocupied as a wash House [32]

15 Buisness as usual very dull — Mr John M. Ross died this night with the yellow feaver,[33] so I herd this morning. Dr Lloyd was his Phiscician   The Dr Cryed Like a child when Mr Ross Died. He will be Buried to morrow morning at 9 Oclock Out at Mrs Dangerfields

16 Mr McGetrick paid me his Rent This Evening, which was 79 Dollars — Mr Eligah Bell Died at Pensacola to day, so seys the Daily Courrier of the 28th & 29th inst [34]

17 Mr Thacher Died Last night with some ver[y] strong Simtoms of yelow fever — He was in Orleans a few days ago and some think that he caught the feaver there

18 Mr W. H. Perkins Sent for me to day Stating that he wanted to see me in the afternoon, and if I would be Kind Enough to Come up, Saying that he was unwell or he would come down, I promised him to come up. I went up to day to Mr Pitcher to get my House Insured. I Left a Discription of the Property and

---

[31] Johnson referred to Van Buren's message to the special session of Congress, September 1, 1837. See Richardson (ed.), *Messages and Papers of the Presidents*, III, 324-46. The Natchez *Free Trader* published its account of the message on September 14, 1837.

[32] For the account of the fire in the Natchez *Free Trader*, see issue of September 16, 1837.

[33] The disease did not reach epidemic proportions until after the middle of September. On August 31, 1837, the Natchez *Free Trader* had reported: "We were much pleased yesterday to see the runaway negroes and the city force busy in sweeping and purifying the streets of our city. Thus far the health of Natchez has been astonishingly good; but as the yellow fever is prevailing to an alarming extent in New Orleans, and congestive fevers are rife and fatal above this at Vicksburg and other places, it is certainly a matter of prudence to observe the strictest regard to cleanliness in the streets and private yards of our city."

[34] This sentence was probably inserted later.

came away. He promised me to act on it & Let me Know the rates, After Dinner I walked up to See Mr Perkins, I Knocked at the door, it was opened by his Miss, She showed me in to his bed Room where he Lay asleep   She Commencd Calling him by saying, Willy, Willy. He at Length awoke and she told him that a Gentleman had came to see him   He saw me, shook hands together, he then got up, invited me to take a seate, I did so, wanted me to drink, I refused, We then talked about One thing or other   In the mean time the Miss walked up Stairs   He after awhile came to the Point — he wanted to Borrow a hundred and fifty Dollars from me, I told him that I had not the Surplus about me and that I could not

    19   Mr Boyd, a young Man Living at Mr Ballads, Died to night ½ after seven Oclock with the yellow Fever — He was a good deel beliked by those who new him — Shaved by Bill Nix on a Creddit   This morning Little Hastings was making some remarks in the presence of several gentleman about Mrs Horn or the Miss Edmondsons and it hapened that Mr Horn was present and Hastings did not know him — he Just Caught Hastings by the nose and pulled his nose for him then Kicked his back sides — so says report current this morning — I am told too that the way he ran was the right way

    20   Mr Boyd was Enterred to day   There was a Large Procession followed. Both Companies Fencibles & Gards [35] — amediately after the procession passed Mr Horn Knockes a Mr Mitchell Down in the Street — he hallowed, oh gentleman help &c   He was taken over on a Box under the shed at Mess[r]s Spraugue & Howells — There he Lay on the Box pretending to faint — I Saw him and Said at wonce that he was using Deception for the purpose of geting off without Some more of the Same — I Signed an article this Evening for the insurance office — It was in the hands of Mr Pitcher. Mr Horn beat that man with his stick because he had Said Something Disrespectfull of his faimily — I bot to day One Barrell of Sugar, 221 pounds @ 7½ cent[s]   The sugar will Cost me about $17.72   I got it at Mr Dolbeares & Preshos — I had it charged to me for they owe me now, I then went under the hill this Evening and Bot 4 Barrels of Coal at 1.50 per Barrell, This was Charged to me as Mr Sisloff was in my debt   Mr Dulaneos young man called & paid

---

[35] Boyd, a native of New York City, was a member of the Natchez Fencibles, the town's leading militia organization. See Natchez *Free Trader*, September 23, 1837.

me $3, money that he forgot to pay before he Left this place

21 The Editor of the Free Trader Came Out and Burlesqued the Statement of Mr G. Baker, Mr Dunlap, F Stanton, and P. Postlethwaite in regard to his fight with Judge Quitman in the court yard[36]

22 Mr Horn was Sued and went to tryal before Justice Tooley for fighting in the street the other day — The mater was Explained and was settled in short order. It was made up — To day Dr Grimes gave Mother his Pol. Parrot — Dr Johnson Came from the other side of the River and reports Mr E. Howell as getting much Better

23 I Sold Mr Horn my Cage and two Cannary Birds for $12, payable when he Comes to town again — Mrs West wrides out on Kitty-Fisher this Evening in Company with Mr Ayres. Mr Besancon Left here for Vicksburg

24 My buisness I find quite Dull, I wrode out in Mr Minors pasture this Evening and there I found Mc and Minet and Scotch Cammell and severall others shooting at the mark I did not shoot untill they Left, I then took several shots with Mc, 25 yards — we shot about 4 times and I made the Best shot on the paper — None were very good however

25 Capt. Dawson Commenced moving his furniture to the Landing to put them up untill a Boat Comes along — I sent Bill Nix out to day [to] Shave Mr Antony Cammell who was very sick at his residence on Pine Ridge — Mr A Cammell Died to day or Late this Evening — Capt. Dawson gave Bill Nix a Guitar & a Larg glass frame

26 Free Masons went Out to the Country and buryed the remains of Mr A. Cammell this Evening — It was a very respectable turn out — I Bot at auction to day Eight small aprons — Tis a Strange idea, we have news in Town this Evening that Elijah Bell is Dead and that he Died at Pencecola — Every body believes it

27 No kind of buisness of any account going on A Mr Blackford Died yesterday & was Buried to day by the Rifleman

---

[36] This referred to a fight between John A. Quitman and Lorenzo A. Besancon, editor of the Natchez *Free Trader*, that took place on a militia election day. Besancon explained his side of the controversy in the September 12 issue, and in the issue of September 21 gave considerable space to statements by Quitman and his witnesses—H. P. Postlethwaite, Frederick Stanton, James Dunlap, and Grafton Baker. Quitman, particularly, resented Besancon's published reference to him as a "noted political demagogue."

for he was a member of that corpse [corps] — Corn is selling at 2 Dols a Barrell in Silver

28   To day Mother Paid me Forty Dollars on the borrowed [money] I Loaned her some time ago — I Loaned Mr Sisloff $30.00 To be paid very soon — paid — Mr Besancon arrived this Evening Late from Vicksburg — Mr F. Taylor takes ten of Mr Bells Boys for a Debt Due to Robins & Painter

29   I paid Mr Jeff Beaumont to day One hundred Dollars on my Rail Road stock, I paid it in Rail Road money — The No of the bill was No 25, date 25th May, 1837, payable to Dunlap & Jemison &c   I bid off a Riffle to day at 36 Dolls at Mr Sorias Auction Room, it was the sale of Mr Perrys Estate, on a creddit of Six months.

30   Good Deal of Sickness in town to day — Conner Died To day with fever, William shaved Mr Murcherson   He was sick & Mr Jemerson dito & Mr Conner do — To day it was that I gave my note to W W. Wilkins for 36 Dollars payable in Six Months after date — McCary was the Endorser on the note, It was given for a Riffle that I bot of the Estate of D Perry — I Sold Mr. William Hale a Riffle for the Sum of forty One Dollars. Conditions are those   He was to pay me five Dollars in Cash and he gave me his note for $36. He gave me his note with Mr Becket as indorser but did not give me the five yet awhile   He promised to pay the five on Monday

October 1   To day or this Evening I wrode Out to Mr Kale Hersts new house. I had my Riffle along. I got a shot at a Jay Bird & I took of[f] his head — I then got a shot at a Squirrel & I missed him Clear Enough — I then saw Mr Lee, the partner of some of the Sniders, who had a Shot gun, I invited him to take a shot or so and he & myself went at it, 25 yards Distance, and we shot untill night and I made the Best Shot — The Remains of Mr Joseph Neibert was buried — He had Died on Thursday night Last and was broght down in a Skift — The Corpse Smelt so bad that the people could not follow him to the grave — they went Out a Small Distance, then stoped there

2   I was under the hill a good part of the day geting Some Oats from A Mr Summers — I bought 67 Bushels of Oats at 37½ cent per Bushell   I paid him in gold $25½ — I also bought a Barrell a Meal from the same Boat — Capt Dawson & Family Left here on the Cinderrela to night for there Residence up Arkensas (Pine Bluffs)   They took with them a Little Free Boy

by the name of Lewis — He is a son of Carolins that Lived on the other side of the river

3 Old Mrs Coffin Died and was Buried this Evening — She died this morning — Greate many persons sick in town at present   I took in Cash to day $4.12½

4 Mrs McGettrick Died Last Night at the Southern Exchange — She was the first person that Ever Died under that Roof in this world — Times are Still uncomonly dull [37]

5 To day Mr William Ney Died of Yellow Fever — sick 3 days [38] — I Took my nag & gun this morning Early and went into the swamp — I had Charles along too wriding on the Big Grey Horse — In passing through the Old Quigless place I saw a very large Fox, the Larges[t] I Ever saw in my Life — I had no chance of a shot at him for he soon ran out of Sight — We then went on down to Mr Winns plantation & young Winn went with us Straight Down to the aligator Lake — There we saw Some 40 or prehaps fifty aligators but they were so far off that we could not Kill or hit them tho we shot at them several times without Effect — I Shortly after quiting that Lake came back and took down the Long Lake — I here got a shot at a Fish hawk with my rifle — I broke his neck — We went on then a Little farther   I then got a shot at an Owl and Killed him dead — It was a Center Shot — Winn he Left here and went to his men to fish — I went on down to Cypres Byou and I wounded a young aligator — we then went to Mudy Lake — He[re] I found four raccoons upon One tree — The first I Shot with the Shot gun — the other three I Killed with my rifle Shooting Each of them through the head — I had a few minutes before I Saw the Coons — Shot a small Beckeroach — I was then going back to find Winn but mistook my way and got Lost between Dock or Cypres Byou Lake and

---

[37] On this date Johnson wrote to his sister, Mrs. James Miller, who lived in New Orleans: "We are all in hopes you will write shortly—for we are uneasy about yourself and family—in that Sickly place   I wish you had some healthy place to go to . . . to day is the 4th of October   I commenced this Letter a week ago— and now I finish it—we have had a greate many casses of yellow fever in this place and we have Lost a good many persons out of town   tho none that you Know— Except Mr Neibut—He died Last week at his plantation and was Brought down & Burried here." Copy in Johnson Papers.

[38] A tribute to the Natchez doctors appeared in the October 5 issue of the Natchez *Free Trader*: "Our community cannot but have a grateful sense of the self-devotion and zeal with which the gentlemen of the medical faculty in this city have met the present crisis." The Reverend David C. Page (rector of the Protestant Episcopal Trinity Church, 1836–45) was also praised for "both his ministrations upon the sick, and his attendance upon those last sad rites when dust is rendered back to dust."

Muddy Lake — There I and Charles were both roving about between the 2 Lakes without Knowing where we were — I Saw a Deer in the mean time   I was Lost — Charles he shot a Sap Sucker

6   Mr B. Openiser was Burried. He was a member of the Riflemen Comp[39] — Mrs O Ryley Died at the Southern Exchange

7   A Mr Deming Died this morning at the City Hotell — He was a Book Keeper in Bank Commercial   Mr Saml. Turner Died Last night — He was a member of the Guards — Mrs Lecand Died to day also   To day Mr William Manning paid his Rent up to the 25th of Sept., $20.

8   No change in Buisness, being very dull as usual — I Remained home all this day or untill quite Late in the afternoon, I then wrode out as far as Mr W. Minors pasture — then came Down Main St. home   Mc went across the River this Evening to See Mr Pulling who is sick on the other Side at Arlettes' house

9   P. Wade was buried to day — He belonged to the Rifleman Core — they turned out. Mr Stanton Lost one of his Black men to day, William shaved him and got $5 for it. To day I sold Capt. Nevit $3 in silver for $3.50 in paper money — Mr Ach Dunbar sends his Boy to get 2.25 in silver for Mr Simms and I sent it to him and in a short time he sent back for One more dollar in silver which I sent, making in all $3.25 that I Loaned him — I wrode this Evening as far as the old fort

10   Mr Cris died this morning.[40] Buiness is quite dull indeed — Mr M Breden sets a grate for me in Dr Lloyds office — price seven Dollars — He told me to place the amount to his account

11   My Second Son was born this morning between 1 and two Oclock.[41] Mrs Seis was the attendant — I found her after an half hours hunt for her down at Dr Davis's — Himself and wife was both in Bed Sick — very Sick

12   To [day] is Just seven years since I Bot Out this Shop from Mr James Miller, that is now and has been Ever Since a Resident of N Orleans   This is now, and has been for the Last month, the dullest times for Buisness that I Ever saw in this place

[39] This was the Natchez Rifle Corps, formed in 1835 and dissolved in 1840.

[40] The Natchez *Free Trader*, October 10, 1837, reported that there had been sixteen deaths during the preceding three days.

[41] This was Richard Johnson (baptized Clement Richard Johnson), the diarist's second child.

— Lots of Sickness in Every quarter of the town,[42] and no business — Mr A W Becket Died this morning at Selsertown,[43] will
be Buried to morrow at 6 Oclock or after — Mr Melne Died this
Evening Late

13   Little Bill Winston was taken sick this morning and
this morning about 9 oclock Our fine cow fell off the Bluff and
was instantly killed by the fall   Dr Grimes is taken sick this
morning — I loaned Mr Mark Breeden fifty Dollars to be paid
in nine days from date — I wrode out to the old Field this
Evening Late, took my gun with me, and only shot One Bird — a
Sap Sucker — Mrs Battles's Cow fell off the Bluff this morning
as I before stated — I gave the cow to Mr John Fletcher, he had
her dressed and tryed to give her away but could not — He had
a greate deal of trouble with it   Maj Young sends for Charles to
come home — He is affraid of the Sickness — very good idea

14   Mr Cammell Died under the hill Last night and so did
his Brother in Law, Mr Senax   Mr Soloman Died Last night
also — Sickness is on the increase I think,[44] Charles and his
Brother Left here for home in a hack — Maj. Young ·Sent for
them yesterday   Mr Horn paid me for the Cannary Birds that
he Bot from me some time ago — $12. Mr H. C. Ashe died to
night ½ past 10 Oclock — he was Shaved by Bill Nix — A Mr.
Wood Died, was shaved by same — Mr Young died, Lived on the
Bluff — Ship Amelia arived to day

15   Greate many Processions to day [45] — Mr Ashes Funeral
procession was a very Large One. (Fencible)   Mr T. Steel
Died   Mr Carnehan Died to night — Several deaths that I dont
Recolect now   I was Out this Evening, Out as far [as] the old
field by Cap Nevit. I Killed One squirel and Sap Sucker — I
Went on horse Back — Mr Eastern Died at Mansion House

16   Mr Wiswalls furniture came up — Piano &c. To day

---

[42] On October 12, 1837, the Natchez *Free Trader* stated: "There is evidently
more sickness among the colored people, who have thus far been almost exempt
from the fever. The Fencibles and the Rifles were both out yesterday to perform
the burial service to comrades." Thirty-nine deaths were reported for the preceding
week.

[43] Selsertown was a small settlement about six miles northeast of Washington.

[44] On October 14, 1837, the Natchez *Free Trader* admitted that the epidemic had
not begun to abate and that five of the city's doctors were ill or too weak to work.
"We long for frosty weather—for thunder—or any other disinfecting agent."

[45] Two days later Alfred Cochran, chairman of the health committee, wrote to
his father: "The fever does not abate, it is worse. The number of deaths last week
is greater than before; our fair little city, formerly the seat of health, life, and
profitable business at this season, seems now but the abode of sorrow and death."
He died about two weeks later. Natchez *Courier*, November 27, 1837.

was the dullest of all days that I Ever saw in Natchez — I only took in, ie in the shop, 37½ cents — Now dont that beat Nature

17   Buisness quite Dull as usual — Never, never in all my Life, did I Ever see such times in Natchez before — What in the world is the town Coming to. Mr. George McIntosh from New Orleans was up to See me   Tis the first time that I have seen him in 7 or 8 years — He Looks very well — He informed me that my friends were all very well, He is now on the way to Red River to work at his trade, i. e. Carpentering — From what he tells me about George Britton I shall always Suspect G. Britton as being a profound Rascal

18   Mr. Dodge Died this Evening at his Store, was followed to the grave by 3 persons — Miss Edmondson Died Last night, Mr Crisst Died this mornining. French shaved Him   Dr Loyd gets another horse to day — Now he has two

19   Nothing New — McIntosh Left here today

20   Nothing new that I know of

21   I got up this morning at a few minuets after 4 Oclock and started into the Swamp, and I took Winston with me, I went down to Mr Winns plantation. Dave Barland has a wonderfull Black Eye — Mr Moxby & Mr McKenny & myself went into the Swam[p] very near to the mouth of St Cathrine to hunt

22   No buisness adoing in the town, I Remained home all day and Mc took Super with me in the shop

23   Mr P. McGetrick pd his rent, $79.00, and fifty Dollars of it was Rail Road Money, No 25, date 25 May, 1837, payable to Dunlap & Jamison — I took it at par and I wont take any more in that way — Dr Dally has been drunk for the Last two days and nights and is Drunk this Evening — Dr Lyle Took him home this Evening and put him to Bed — I Loaned Mr McFaden a Bath Tub to day — Miss Stedman Gets married to Mr [blank]

24   Mr Wm Ramsey Died to day under the hill at McFadins Landing — Shave dr $5. To day I saw Capron so Drunk that he could not walk — Veni Vidi — Patterson across the street Started to Port Gibson this Evening — Mr Bertly Came home this Evening from the North; Tosspott was here this Evening on his way up the River — they were all well below

25   John McGlocklin Died Last night — he was a member of the Rifleman Company & Masons

26   Mr A Cochran Died this morning — Mc was to have gone into the swamp with me this morning but said it was too cold, so we did not go

27   I got up from my Bed this morning a[t] day Break and Took Winston with me and wrode into the swamp — I Killed One Summer Duck, One Mallard, dito, 3 Large Snipe, 3 Squirrels, two of them was Black, 1 Sap Sucker, 1 yellow hammer, and One white Crane, in all 11 Head   Mr A. Massy Died to day

28   Nothing new took place   No news in the city. I paid R Herst $3 that I gave Mother to pay him 6 months ago for some show Beef

29   There is no one in town Scarcely — Mr Maurice Hicky Died Last Night & 3 at the Hospital and seveal others about town that I dont know   I sent Out my Big grey Horse to Mr R Hearset place to Eat grass — I saw Dr Cartwright this morning   He has Just returned from the North, I Slaped Will Buck Last night with my hand twice, 1st in my Life

30   Mr Dalton Died at the Mansion House — Dr Cornell Died and several others that I dont know — Mr Sweney was to night a hunting for some one to write for him and I told him that Mr Abona was doing nothing and would Like such a situation and I sent for him up to the Jefferson Hotell — When he Came I introduce[d] him to Mr Sweney and he then told him that he herd that he was out of Business and Mr S. gave him Something to do

31   Buisness is quite Dull — I Bot 10 Sacks of Oats at 1 Dollar a sack

November 1   No news Worth talking about. Mr Cegwin pd me to day 12 dollars in part pay of 25 Dollars that He owes me

2   Mc & myself Left Town this morning by ½ past 4 Oclock. He wrode my Big Grey Horse & I my Little mare — Mc Killed 2 ducks, 4 squirrels & 1 owl, & I Killed 4 Squirrells, 1 Sap Sucker, 1 yellow Hammer, 1 Small Snipe, 1 King Fisher & 1 Black Bird

3   This morning Mr Noyes went up to the Lake on the other side of the River & Killed three wild Geese. He Said he Killed them all at One Shot — This morning between 10 & 11 Oclok the remains of Mr P Gemmell was Entered in the Grav[e]yard   It was a Large Procession that Followed Him

4   I wrode out to Col Bingamans to get a Cow. I got there after they had been turned Out, Consequently I got none

5   I got up very Early this Morning and wrode Out to Col Bingamins to get a Milch Cow. I got Out about 8 Oclock in the Morning & found the Col. Out in the Lane among the

Stock   Mr Pryor was with him. Mr Pryor shot a Small duck in the Pond — I Came home with the Cow tho I had a greate deal of trouble in Driving her in — Mr D. Barlow & S Wiswall is in town to day

6   Being the first day of the Election, there were a greate many Persons in town. I Loaned Mr Caleb Herst to day $100 To be paid in a few Days — I have Lost Out of my Pocket between 20 & 40 Dollars in some way or other

7   The second day of the Election — and Last day of the Election. I Loaned Mr J M. Stockton $10 To have been paid this Evening — Mr Louis Miller walked up behind Mr Ruffner and Struck him Over the Head with a pi[e]ce of Iron and Knocked him very near to the ground. R recoverd and struck him with a Brick Bat and then ran up and Knocked him down, tho he was pulled of[f] before he had a Chance of hurting him

8   Young Sisloff came to borrow $30 to day, and I did not have it to Loan at the time in Pocket, So he did not get it, Mr Vanerson & Lady Came home to day — Mr A. Fisk & Miss Wilkins Came home, Jim Dolland Came also. I was to day in the Swamp. I went Down from town at 12 Oclock. I Shot with the Riffle and had but three Balls, I then had to use Buck Shot, I Shot a number of times and only got one duck — it was a summer Duck — I am very much Disgusted with my Riffle for I Cant Shoot her

9   Nothing of any Interest transpired to day in town, Dr Wren moves the Post office up to the Masonic Hall

10   Greate many Strangers in town. Mr Lamdin arrived Last night from the North Mr J. M. Stockton paid me $10 that he Borrowed from me yesterday or the day before — Mr Jim Doland came home from Ohio — Last night he arrived. Mr Williamson & N. L. Williams came also — P. McGetrick is Elected Ranger   I got two Boxes of Caps from Mr L. David on a Credit — ½ Boxes [46]

11   I went in the Swamp to day — Left town very Early in the morning & took Little Bill Winston with me — and when we got into the Swamp Young Winn went with me and we had a fine hunt, He Killed 4 Ducks, 3 of them were duck of malla[r]d and One of the[m] Summer Duck and he Killed One Large Blue Crane, & I killed 1 Becke roach, very Large One, 2 Ducks of Mallard, 1 wounded Pelican   We took Our Dinner Down at the

[46] Johnson included with this entry an incomplete report of state and local election returns, which the editors have deleted.

Cyprus Buyo — I Broght the Right foot and Claws of an Eagle that was Killed by Winn in the Swamp — Election for Selectman to fill the vancancy in the Bourd took place to day — Mr Gridley, Mr Walworth, R Patterson, Thoms Conner, & W W. Wilkins. Conner & Wilkins was Ellected[47]

12 Buisness Somewhat Better than has been for Some time past. Nothing new to day. Mc and myself walked down to the Bluff this Evening Late to Look at the ships

13 Our Streets are full of Dust and it is very Disagreable indeed.

14 Our Streets nothing but dust, quite Disagreable — A Duel took place on the other side of the River between two of our Citizens — Mr Akin and Mr Marshall. The Latter was Killed Dead. He was shot below the Heart & Died instantly, They fought 30 paces with Riffles — The origin was about Some of Levine Michels Cattle, The[y] fought two Rounds — the first did not take Effect, I Bot a Little old Black horse to day at Spraigue & Howells a[u]ction, Sold by Mr G Lancaster   I Gave 11 Dollars for him

15 To day Mr Kennedy & Dr Marshall Called to see me about those Portraits of Mrs Dunnam & Mrs Gemmell — Mr Kennedy Promised to pay me by the first of January. I then agreed to Let them go, The Dr would not agree to make himself at all Responsible for his Brothers debts

16 I Bot a half bag of Shot at Cannon & Nickols Store to night at 2 Dollars — I pd Enough for them, I Bot two Mean Razors at Murchersons   I pd 2.50 for them, Mr Doniphan gets married to Miss Sarah H. Cartwright   They got married up at Dr Wrens — Steven came home from working out at Mr Ringolds this Morning Early

17 Mc and myself went into the swamp to hunt this morning and when we got as Low as Mr Winns plantation Young Winn went into the Swamp with us. He wrode my old Black Horse, I wrode K Fisher, Mc wrode my Big Grey Horse, Mc Killed 3 Ducks, 2 King Fisher, 1 Sap Sucker, 1 Robbin & there were a Squirrel up a tree in which we both Shot & both have Strong Claims on it, tho Mc got it, Mr Winn Killed 1 Duck and 1 Squirrel & I Killed 2 Squirrels and 1 King Fisher   Mr Winn Gave me his Game   Pollo Gets Lost in the swamp. I Left my Black horse in the swamp with Winn

---

[47] The election had been called to fill the vacancies caused by the yellow-fever deaths of Cochran and Gemmell. Natchez *Free Trader*, November 11, 1837.

18   Greate many persons in town from the Country, Mr Winn Came up from his Plantation. He Brought me 2 Dozens Chickens that I Bought from his Sister a week or 2 ago. Pollo Came home this morning a Little after Breakfast   I Received a Letter this morning, a Letter from Smithland with an advertiseme[n]t of a Runaway Negro who had been put in the Paduca Jail Supposed to be mine, All a mistake — Winn took Dinner with me. I Sent Steven with the Cart Down to Winns place to get 2 Dozen Chickens & when he got there they [had been] brought here by Winn So they had [to] come back again without them.

19   To day was quite a Lively day in town, and there were Several New Cases of Sickness which has Caused Some alarm, that and Seve[r]al Deaths that we had to day — Mr Pedigrue Died Last Night about 1 Oclock up at the Residence of Mrs A. Glasscocks   They were to have been married this week on Thursday night next   I loaned my Big Grey Horse to young Winn to go into Franklin County to See about a tract of Land that he has in that County

20   Dr Grimes Died Last Night about 11 oclock with Yellow fever   Mr A. Cox, Maj Miller, Judge Montgomery went out to Col Bingamans to Dinner, A Lieper wanted to Borrow my Gun, I refused to Loan it & gave him my Reason

21   I made Steven take the old Black horse this Evening to haul from the Landing 6½ Bushels of Oats in a Cart frome the Flat Boat. Some of the Aniconda party poisoned the Cow that I got from Col Bingaman — oh what a Rascally thing — good Heavens

22   Sterns wanted to Borrow my Gun to go a hunting and I refused To Loan her to him, I wrote a Letter to Mrs Miller to day and Sent it by Mr Tosspott, Bill Winston paints a chair or two   Bill Nix makes a wood horse

23   I took a wride Early this morning and I saw Ice for the first time this season in a pond out by Snyders Brick Yard, I Shaved Col B. to day and I told him that his cow that he Loaned me was about to dye, that she had Eaten Something that had poisoned her I thought, The old woman is on a regular spree for quarrelling to day all day — oh Lord, was any One on this Earth So perpetually tormented as I am. To day the Grand Carravan of Animals arrived in town, the Musicians was on the back of the Elephant as they past through the Streets,[48]   Mr P. McGettrick

---

[48] The Waring, Raymond & Company circus carried a museum as well as a menagerie. The Natchez *Free Trader*, November 28, 1837, commented upon one of

pd me seventy nine Dollars for One months Rent of Southern Exchange Due on the fifteenth of this month, I was to day or late this Evening in the woods and I Killed 2 Bull finches, 1 Sap Sucker, and one Red Bird — 4 heads　　I received a Letter from Capt. Miller — he told me in it that his Brother John had Died in Liverpool of the Cancer

24　　To day has been a brisk & stiring Day in town　　I Took up my note to day in the Planters Bank Due to Harris and Lumm, for the consideration of Four Hundred and Sixty Eight Dollars — Indorsed by Elijah Bell, Peter Gemmell, & John G. Taylor　　This note I gave to Mesrs Harris & Lumm in part payment for a Lot of Ground near the Rail Road that I purchased of them Last year. Mr M. Breden paid me $50 that I Loaned him on 13th of October, Last. To day I gave Mr Johnson $5 being the amount over his account in Settling with me a few Days ago　　He paid me too much — I Had a Conversation to day with Cap[t] Dawson for or about the wall between Our Property and told him the particulars about it

25　　To day has been a very Brisk day in the way of Buisness, I made out my account to day against Dr. N. Lloyd[49] — The amount of which was [blank]　　That was at the rate of 50 Dollars per Month　　He then Said that I promised to Let him have the House at the Same price that Mr Taylor got his part. I then made Out the account at $45 per month and presented it to him. He put it in his Pocket and walked off — promised to Look over it and Settle it — Capt Dawson Came in this morning and Brought an article of writing which was in the Shape of a Deed for the wall between Our Property. I Told him that I would prefer defering the Buisness untill I fully understood how I was situated in regard to the Neibut & Gemmell Estate, He agreed very willingly. Winn and Gregory Came back from Franklin County to day about 12 Oclock.

26　　Mc Came Down Late in the Evening — we walked Out On the Bluff and Cam[e] back and Took Our Supper in the Shop

---

their performances: "There have been many establishments of the kind in this city, having individual performers of a superior class to any who have appeared in the present company; yet we cannot but give our hearty applause to many of the performers in Waring and Raymond's company. On Saturday evening last Carrol performed 'The Indian' particularly well. He turned twenty-eight back somersets in succession—a feat which we have never seen done before for such a length of time and through such a number of evolutions."

49 See advertisement of Dr. H. Nelson Lloyd, "late of Woodville," in Natchez *Courier*, November 27, 1837.

27 A good deal of Buisness agoing on in town — I went up to the Animal Show to day and took Little Will Buckes with me and the old man & Bill Nix — Mr Fields paid me $2.50 for a Bird Cage that I Sold him a Long time ago

28 I Engaged One hundred Barrells of Coal to day from a Mr Moore at the Landing

29 I was under the Hill a good part of This Day getting Out Coal from a Flat Boat opposite the old Rail Road, I hauld out a greate quantity for a One Horse Cart, 11 loads I think — I Contracted for One Hundred Barrells of Coal — I saw Mr Thomas & Barnet, I think, have a hold of Mr McGettrick, taking him up to Jail. It was on account of his taking some things that belonged to the Estate of O. Riley — The Officers had taken a greate Deal of Furniture out of the House

30 To day I finished Hauling my coal from the Land-ing I made a Bet to day with Mr Mardice of five Dollars that Tishamingo would not win his race when he run in Orleans, that is, provided he did run Dr Lloyd moved out of my house to night after Supper

December 1 Greate Bustle in the Street in the way of Buis-ness — The new firm of Thomson & Breed is now Opening there New goods this morning in the Store formally Ocupied by Pat-terson & Wiswall — Dolbeare Has an auction up at his store to day and tis the first One he has had since the sickness — I Got this Book from Him and he charged me three Dollars for it — He gave me Creddit for it because he owes me — I Had the Boys puting away coal in the ware or Smoke house — They put it all in this Evening — Mrs. Amy Johnson paid this Evening twenty five Dollars on, or in part pay, money that I Loaned her — Dr. N. Lloyd moved out from my House Last night and sent me my Key — I walked over to see the Dr to get the money from him that He owes me, but did not see him at all — I made a firm Bargain with Bill Hazard and he was to Haul my Coal from the Landing at 15 Barrels for ten Bits in Silver — Well I set his Cart to work and after he hauled up 70 Barrells of it, I told him to Come and get his money and when he came He said that He did not recollect of making such a contract — I told him very well that it made no Difference that I would pay him Just what he charged and so I did — I gave him $8.75 for hauling 70 Barrells But if Ever I give him Another Chance to Gull me in that way I hope to Burst wide open — I paid Mr John Brown To day for One [hun-dred] Barrells of Pittsburgh Stone Coal that I got from him yesterday — I took his Receipt for 100 Dollars Tho I got the Coal at 62½ per Barrell.

2 Young Mr. Howard West of Woodville and Miss Dunbar was married Last night   It was a ru[n]away match — I Receeved a Letter from Mrs Miller This Evening by Mr. Tosspott. I saw Welch the Constable Selling a horse at auction that was taken from Mr Macomber for debt. He told for $65 and was Bot by a Big Irishman by the name of Mc Something or other.

3 I sent Bill Nix up to Jefferson county to day after Charles. Charles has been up there During the Sickness, Bill got up there in about three hours

4 I went to Day around to Messrs. Armats & Rawlings to probate my account against The Firm of Neibut & Gemmell — We could not recollect whether Mr Smith was in the firm or not, So I Came of[f] untill I could find Out, Loucinda came home to day from Mr Spielmans and I hyred Sarah to Mr. J. M. Stockton at twelve Dollars a month — Mr Stockton is Just agoing to House Keeping & has Rented the house belonging to Daniel Holland at Forty Dollars per month — Charles got home to day at 12 Oclock precisely from Jefferson County   To Day Mc gets in his coal   He got 40 Barrells at 87½ cents per Barrell.

5 To day I was up to Dr. Lloyds office to get some money that He owes me for House Rent, The amount of which was $449. The Dr. paid me in Brandon money One hundred Dollars, which Leaves a Ballance in my favor of three hundred and Forty nine Dollars, which he still owes me — I gave him a receipt on the back of my Account for the One hundred Dollars that he paid me — A Question then arrose between us whether I was Entitled to the account or himself — I Contended that it was undoubte[d]ly my right to hold the account and he offered to bet me the full Amount of the Account that it was his right to Keep it. I refused to bet and came of[f] and Left the account in his hand I came home and stated the substance of the question to Mr. M. Breden who at wonce agreed that I was in the right and told me that I aught to have Closed the Bet with him. I went up to Mr Blacks Printing office this morning to See One of his Newspapers files — It was to find out when Mr Smith went into Copartnership with Messrs Neibut & Gemmell — I found One or two papers which contained the advertisement and was dated January 9th, 1836   I presume that they went in to Copartnership On the [9th] of January — I then went to Messrs Armatts & Rawlings to probate my account against the Estate of Messrs Neibut &

Gemmell, the amount of which was One Thousand Dollars   I did not get it probated because we were not sure whether Mr. Smith was in the firm or not at that time or not. We wanted to ascertain that fact fully before we would probate the account — I was at the Landing this Evening and it was very mudy — Mr. R. Gains had just arrived on the Steam Boat Chilacothe and I Loaned him my Big Grey Horse to wride up the hill on, To Day Mc paid in twenty five Dollars on his R. Road Stock, I got two Linnen Shirts from Messrs Lounds & Berry at five Dollars Each and had them Charged to me, as they are oueing me for Rent.

6   I made Out an account this morning against Mr William Manning for two months Rent up to the 25th of November at 20 Dollars per month — I Sent it in and he paid me ten Dollars on the amount, which Leaves him in my debt thirty Dollars up to the 25th of November — I also made out an account against the firm of Lounds & Berry for One Months Rent Due the 21st of September Last at $50 per month, Mr. Dalhgreen and a Mr. Hagan from New Orleans Crossed The river last night for to fight a Duel Early this morning but the parties interfeared and the mater was Settled and they both Came Over this Morning with out having a fight, I am truly Glad it Ended in that way — To day Mr F. Taylor Told me that there was to be a tryal on Saturday next at The Court House and the Question was to be this — That himself and Dr Guinn and Mr. McAlister had signed a paper in behalf of Robert Smiths[50] having a right to stay in Natchez and he said if the people of Natchez would not Let Smith stay here that he intended to prosecute the Ballance and that none should remain in the place — He also said that He believed Robt. Smith to be an Honest and as correct a Colourd Man as there was in Natchez — I then told him that I Knew R. Smith Better than he did and I knew that at this present time he was run off from New Orleans for Buying Goods from a Slave Negro and that when he came off he Left five hundred Dollars in Mr. Johnsons hands to pay his Bale for Johnson went his Bale — He confessed that he had herd some thing of it and I

---

50 Robert Smith (also known as Robert D. Smith), born in Maryland and about thirty years of age in 1837, was a free Negro whose right to remain in the state was finally granted by action of the state legislature and the Adams County Board of Police. He became a "hackman" in the 1840's, the father of eight children by 1850, and the owner of a slave by 1854. See *Laws of Mississippi*, 27 Sess. (1843), 109–10; Adams County Court and Police Board Minutes, 1832–45, August, 1843; U. S. Census Reports, Schedule I, Adams County, 29; Auditor's Records, Tax Rolls, 1854, Adams County. In 1849, William Johnson rented seven or eight hacks for his mother's funeral, at $2.00 per hack, from Smith.

told him that he was wrong I thought in trying to make others suffer because he Could not gain his point.

7   Mr. Charles E. Wilkins Died To day — poor young man   He was a Harmless young Gentleman and one I Loved, Mrs. Fox was buried this afternoon. Her Corps was Brought up from below on a Steam Boat. We have herd to day that Mr Sparrow has had his Cotten Gin burned and upwards of One hundred Bales of Cotten in it   Tis a greate Loss, tho we have not herd whether it was by friction that it Caught or not, It was not Insured so I herd — We have herd to day that the Ship Amelia is Lost with a full Cargo of Coton Bound for Liverpool — She was Insured and all her Cotten — I Loaned Mr John G. Taylor & Barlow to day One Hundred Dollars in paper money — good as Cash — A Mr. John F. Mosby gets married to Mrs Francis B. Babbit by the Reverned Benjamin Chase

8   Business has been Middling fair — Tho this has been a Day of Trouble with me, I have been in a good many Small passions in my times but I have never felt so much Like Dieing as I have this day — I was arround to Mess[r]s. Armat & Rawlings office this afternoon To get them to probate my Note that I had against the Estate of Peter Gemmel & Company, tho I did not have it done on account of my or there not Knowing who was Charged with the settlement of the Business after the Desolution of Partnership between Neibut & Gemmell — & To day Mr E P Stuart paid me $20 that being the amount that himself and his Brother Owed me for shaving and hair cutting for some time back — I Rented my uper Stoore To Mr [blank] for forty Dollars per month or at that rate, for he thought that he would not want it Longer than two weeks — Mr Green gets the Back Room from the Gentleman to put his Desk in the same.

9   There was to have been a meeting to day according to the statement of F Taylor [51] concerning Robert Smith and the free people of Couler Generally — The day has past and Gone and I have heard nothing of said Tryal — To day Mr Kegwin paid me ten Dollars being the remain[in]g part of twenty five Dollars that he Owed me — This day Mr. Sweeney paid me $20 for the hyre

[51] F. Taylor was a white man who rented an office in a Main Street building owned by Johnson and occasionally collected debts owed Johnson on a commission basis. For example, in 1836, Johnson recorded in an account book that he had paid Taylor $2.50 for collecting $30.00 from "T. Steele." See Cash Book, 1830–38, entry for January 23, 1836, and *passim*, Johnson Papers. See also Day Book, 1830–40, entry for May 3, 1837, *ibid.*, for an example of Taylor's collecting a $600 account due the barber.

of Stephen, it was due on the 16th of Last month, The alarm of
fire was Given to night soon after Church Commenced and it
produced a Considerable scatering among the people Generally —
It was a Chimney Caught On fire up at Smiths Kitchen, the Carpenter, and was soon put out

10 Young Winn[52] was up this morning — Took Breakfast
with us — He Brought me a fine mess of fish from the swamp
That he Caught in his Cein — Winn is a poor young man that
[could] have been much above his present Circumstances if he
had only Justice done him

11 I was in the Oyster house this morning and I accidently Let Drop Out of my pocket $143 which went down to the
Bottom, I Sent Winston down and he got it Out, I saw Mr Smith
this Evening and he told me that he was not Bound for the debts
of the firm & that Mr. Neibut & Gemmell had given him a Bond
of Discharge from any Responsibility. To night about 11 or ½
Oclock Col Bingaman and partee arrived on the Steam Boat
Sultana from the New Orleans Races. He Lost the three first
Days Racing and won the three Last days Races — His winning
nags were Angorah [and] Fanny Wright, 4 mil[e]s and repeat,
& Mogul

12 More Company in town than I have seen in for some
Considerable time   The Following are a few that I Recollect of
seeing to day on the streets —[53]

Gov. McNutt   Col. Bingaman
Gov Reynolds   Capt. T. G. Ellis
W. B. Gov Dr. Morgan   Brigadeer Gen Quitman
Maj A Miller   Capt W. B. Minor
Mr. Ventress   Judge P. Ellis

[52] "Young Winn," or "Little Winn," as Johnson sometimes called Winslow Winn,
was the son of George Winn, a free Negro who had died in 1831. George Winn
had been in Natchez as early as 1799, and in the year of his death owned 1,192
acres of land about five or six miles below Natchez on the Mississippi River, fifteen
slaves, and a tract of land in Lawrence County. In his will (1831) George Winn
acknowledged the following children as his legal heirs: Winslow; Polly, or Mary,
who married overseer William Mosbey in 1834 or 1835; and Helen, who later married Washington Ford. (Winslow Winn, Mosbey, and Ford are frequently mentioned in this diary.) Helen was given preferential treatment in the will's be-
quests, and Winslow was accorded the least consideration. See "Estate of George
Winn," Adams County Probate Records, File 65; Auditor's Records, Tax Rolls,
1831, Adams County. The U. S. census of 1830 and the tax rolls, 1810–31, con-
sistently listed George Winn as a free man of color, and the state census of 1816
further listed in his family one white female above twenty-one years of age, no
white males, three people of color, and ten slaves.
[53] The names were listed in four columns in the diary.

Mr. A Cox	Maj. Jas Surget
Cap Frank Surget	Capt. J. B. Nevitt
Maj. Shotard	Mr. Sml. Davis
Pres E. B. Marshal	Mr. J F. Gelespie
Col. Harris	Judge Guion
Maj Shields	Mr. J. Turnbull
Maj Young	Dr. Gwinn
M S. Elliott	Mr. Reynolds of Orleans
Dr. S. Gustine	Mr. L. Bingaman
Dr. S. Duncan	

Those are the most wealthy and inteligent part of this Community   I herd that Col Bingaman spit in Mr. Morgans face and cursed him and then threw a chew of tobacko in his face, On account of his Sueing the Col. in New Orleans [54] — Mr. Eligh Smith just return from the north — nearly all Locks [long hair]

13   Very Little business going On in town. To day was the day which the big Frenchman Sold Out his goods at auction — I Bot a pair of Large Candlesticks price 7.50 for the pair and I Loaned Mr. Bean $5 to help him pay his Bill, pd   To Day Maj. S. Young Gave Charles a Suit of Cloaths Down at Mr. Barlows Store — *good* — Mr. Bean paid me the five that he Borrowd of me to day — Dr. Hogg arrived this Evening, Mr. David Knox from Philadelphia arrived this Evening in Natchez. Looks very well indeed

14   The Presidents Message was Carried arround town by Robert Smith Selling at 1 Bit per coppy [55] — I Bot One, To Day I gave Col Bingaman a pair of Large Candle sticks with a Glass vase over Each — To day I Shaved and trimed Maj Dunbars   I got for the same two Dollars — he gave it to me — I Bot a Brush and Comb to day for Dr. Hogg and Sent it arround by his Boy, I gave 1.97½ for them — Dr. Lloyds Sorril Horse Came home to my stable

15   I had a Settlement To day with Mr Dolbeare and I was of the Opinion That he was in my debt at Least 25 or 30 Dollars and when his account was made Out it amounted to 49.70 and

---

[54] There was probably a connection between this incident and the action of the Adams County Circuit Court on July 11, 1838, in awarding a judgment of $3,-395.62 to Gilbert Morgan against Adam L. Bingaman. No details were given in the court minutes; the court was sustaining a judgment previously rendered. Adams County Circuit Court Minutes, Special Term, July, 1838.

[55] Van Buren's message was issued on December 5, 1837. See Richardson (ed.), *Messages and Papers of the Presidents*, III, 373–95. The Natchez *Free Trader*, December 14, 1837, carried the complete text.

my account against him was $50 so there was Only 30 cents Coming to me, so we passed Receipts and all was Settled — my Bill against him was for One months house Rent, due 22d of April 1837. I Shaved Gov. McNutt this morning — I Bot from C. Celly To day 2 wash Bowls at 37 cent per Bowl — I Bot a Load [of] wood from Col B.['s] Boy, pd him Six Dollars for the Load — I measured it and it was about 3 quarters of a Cord

    16   Greate Bustle in the streets to day — I Bot to day at auction at Mr. Dolbeares 16 forks and 22 Knives, 2 Dishes, with Covers, and a market Basket and One Doz pairs of Scissors — I paid him for scisors 1.12½, for Coverd Dishes 1.50, for Knives and forlks 2.25, and for Market Basket 37½ cents in Brandon Money — This Week Expenses has been $44.25. The week is from Sunday morning untill Saturday night, This morning Young W Winn Brought me a fine Shoate, as a present, they Killed yesterday   Old Dr Johnson was with them when they were hunting — Mr. Ellick Stewart was tryed for his street fight and was acquited, It was oweing, this affair, all together to his Brothers fight

    17   I Took my Little mare this afternoon and wrode Out as far as the St. Catharine Race track by the way of the Rail Road. The Bridge was not finished and there were fifty two Brick pillars under the Bridge

    18   A Good deal of Buisness in town. Old Esdra came down and had a Small fuss with the old woman about her Girl Sharlot. The old woman took her way two days or three before her month was Out and The old fellow Came Down and showed his Receipt and the old Fellow wer perfectly right in his Calculations — Her month was up on the 20th and she took her away to day. Mr. Spielman offered me Mr McRaes note Indorsed by Mr R. Bledsoe and payable in April for my Girl Lucinda — the amount of the note was 700 Dollars and he was to give me the Ballance $50 in cash and I refused to trade

    19   The Fencibles and Gauards Turned out. They Looked Better than I Ever have seen them look yet   It was to Celebrate the aniversary of the Guards — They then had a Splendid Ball Down at the City Hotel,[56] Mr Ringold Left here to day for New Orleans to remain all winter, I collected from Mr. Ringold 19.50 and made in cash 14.62½ — Very good

[56] The occasion was the anniversary of the Natchez Guards. The Natchez Fencibles participated, by invitation, in the morning parade, the afternoon shooting match, and the evening ball at the City Hotel. See Natchez *Free Trader*, December 21, 1837.

20   The first important thing that I have done this morning was to go arround to Messrs Armat and Rawlings and get A Note that I Left there for Collection against the Estate of Messrs. Neibut and Gemmell — I got the note and took it arround to Esqr Cooks and had the note probated — I was to day down at McGettricks to collect Some money but did not get it   Mr Phelps Came to Natchez from above

21   I Took my account that I had against Mr Ashe Estate, had it Probated before Justice Perdue — I then sent it to Mr Coyle, the administrator, and he said that it would be a year before it would be paid

22   I went to the Landing and Bot some wood from a man by the name of Isack N Miller and I found him to be One of the meanest Lying Scoundrells that I have met with for some time   He in the first place agreed to throw it Out on the Bank of the River

23   I was the whole of this day very near getting my wood Out from the flat Boat that I Bot my wood in — The infernal Rascal that I Bot my wood from was to have thrown it Out of the Boat after I paid him and instead of his doing it this morning he got upon the Steam Boat Livingston and put out and Left me the wood to throw Out myself which I did with the assistance of one or two of the Boys and it Rained, Hailed and Snowed to day and I was in it, I went up at Dobeares auction Room to night and Bot 4 Shirts, Cotton Boddies and Linnen finish — 1.87½ per Shirt

24   I was on the Eve of going a Hunting down in the swamp — was rarther sore and gave it Out

25   I worked Something harder than I Ever worked On a Christmas before in my Life. I was geting Some wood that I had Bot. I got it all hauld up Just before Dinner — Col. Bingaman Left Natchez for Jackson, Miss. He belongs to the Senate, I Bot to day ½ Barrell of Flour under the Hill for which I paid five Dollars — I Bot it on a Flat Boat

26   To day I and the Boys finished puting up the wood that I Bot under the Hill. There were 14 Cords and three quarters of it, Mother got One Cord of it — She Paid me the Barrell of Flour to day that I Lett her have Some time ago — She Bot it at Mr Stockmans   I was under the Hill to day and I Bot four Barrells of Corn and One sack of Oats   Corn is worth 1 Dollar now, something Cheaper than I have seen it for some time — To day a man came in and wanted to [see] me, He inquired if

I had Lost a Negro man, and I told him I had   He wanted to Know how much I would give for the apprehension of him and I told him fifty Dollars and all Expenses paid by me. He Laughed and Said it would Cost $300 and Expenses paid — I Told him to Call and I would see him again about the Buisness and he promised me, Mr Gridley, Mr. Jas. Sessions and a Gentleman from Philadelphia was present at the time   Mr P. McGettrick paid me One months Rent of Southern Exchange, $79 in full, due 15th inst. The following Gent. are candidates for city Selectmen for the year 1838 —

Henry Tooley	Cyrus Marsh Beat
Andrew Brown	Jacob Soria — Beat
Wm. W. Wilkins	James Stockman — Beat
John P. Walworth — declined	James Lyle
Robert Patterson	James R. Cane — Beat
Orlando Lane — Beat	William Cannan — Beat
Levin M. Patterson — Beate	E H Dashiel — Beat
Rhasa Parker	Tho. C. Conner — Elected

27   I had a Settlement to day with Mr. Manning and He now Owes me up to the twenty first of December Just $24 and is now good to me for five Rooms in the house at $7 per month. I Then Took from his account $13 which Mr Edward Smith owed him, I took Mr Smiths wood for the debt. So Mr. Smith now owes me $13 up to the 21st of December   I Bot at auction to day six pair of shoes for Winston — A Mr. [blank] and myself is about making a trade for my man Walker, He wanted me to give him three Hundred Dollars and pay his Expenses and he would get him for me   I told him that I would give him three hundred Dollars for the Delivery of Walker to me, Or that I would take three Hundred Dollars for him Just as he stood, We did not Close the trade, he said he would see me again.

28   Buisness Quite Brisk in the streets. I find it not so brisk as it was a few days ago with me, Steam Boat Black Hawk Bursted her Boiler and Killed about [blank]   To day Mr Izod offerd the property of Dr. David Lattimores old Burned Billings [buildings] at the highest Bidder — it was sold on account of Debt, due Mr. Lustot or Some Such a name — I saw the Drays a hauling the Specie from the Landing which was on the Blak Hawk when she bursted, Last night,[57] I wrote a Letter to day to

[57] The bursting of the boilers of the steamboat *Blackhawk* occurred on the Mississippi River below Natchez, between 11 P. M. and midnight of December 27,

Mr. E. Miller of Vicksburgh — by mail[58] — I Saw Dick Elliss To day and he told me that He would mak about One hundred Bales of Cotten this year.   That is pretty Strong for him I think,   Mr Newman paid me $10 that I Loaned him yesterday — he gave me a Tom Bigby Bill.[59]   I dont Like that so much, Last night about ½ after 11 Oclock Mr. Gellett Came and awoke me to get the Loan of my bath tubb for his Brother who was very ill with a Cramp in his Stumache.   I got up and assisted him in taking it up to his house   Neither of us had a hat on at the time — I Bot to day from Mr. Bledsoe ½ Dozen Razors for two Dollars   To night the young men gives a Concert at the City Hotell, Mr. Simms, Mr Taylor, Mr MacMicheal performs

   29   I got up this morning very Early and Took my Horse, Dog & Gun, and went into the swamp to hunt, I Took no One with me, and I wrode very slow, I Killed 3 squirrells, 3 Yellow hammers, 2 wood Cocks, One Large duck of Mallad and two Rice Birds,   Mr Mossby had been Out the day before and Killed 7 wild hogs and he gave me four spare Ribbs   They were very nice indeed   They were all very well down thare, Mrs B. gave away her Black Dog To a Boy belonging to Dr. Ogdon to take up the River to his plantation

   30   Buisness has been very dull I think for a Saturday,   I understand this morning that Emery Wilson ran off Last night and Took with him his Family, he from what I can Lern is considerably in debt, [to] Mr William Stanton.

1837. She was racing to reach Natchitoches, Louisiana, ahead of another steamboat. It was estimated that more than fifty persons, or about half of her passengers and crew, were killed or drowned, but the *Blackhawk* was towed to a sand bar by a passing steamer. The specie noted in the diary entry referred to nearly $200,000 of United States Army funds that were being sent to the Indian country; all of this money was saved except about $9,500. See *Lloyd's Steamboat Directory*, 87–89; Natchez *Free Trader*, December 30, 1837; and MSS. calendared in Grace E. Heilman and Bernard S. Levin (eds.), *Calendar of Joel R. Poinsett Papers in the Henry D. Gilpin Collection* (Philadelphia, 1941), 68–70, 78, 147.

58 Johnson made a summary of this letter: "This is a Letter that I wrote to day to Elisha Miller or the substance of one, it was that I was well and Family. And That the times were very dull.   Times were hard and money was scarce, & that I wanted the money that I had Loaned him, &c." Johnson Papers. The summary was dated December 29, 1837, but it obviously concerned the letter he wrote on the previous day. This letter was in answer to one written by Miller in Vicksburg, December 3, 1837. Copy in *ibid*.

59 Johnson probably referred to an Alabama state-bank note.

1838

January 1 ⁂ Buisness has been very Lively and a very greate Quantity of persons in town to day — Mr. Edward Thomas paid me to day fifty Dollars. It was a debt that Mr Marshall, the portraite Painter, Owed me for House rent and he gave me an Order on the Estate of Mr William Arllettes   To day it was paid me by Mr. Arllette.   Messrs Barlow & Taylor paid me To day One Hundred Dollars, money that I Loaned him a short time ago.   They also paid me $15 that I Loaned them a good while ago — Mr John P. Smith Took Charge of the Mansion House,   To night I Let all the Boys go to the theatre or Circus

2   To day Dr. Davis & Mr Brazier moves in the House next Door Owned by Capt Dawson, They pay One thousand Dollars Rent per year for it, I Bot at Mr Sorias 2 fine cut glass Tumblers @ 62½ per glass — To day Mr Stockton promised to pay me ten Dollars and sure Enough he did not do it, Mc is quite troublesome to Dr. Hubbard Just at this time for he is in greate want of the money Just at this time, to pay a note of his that is due the 1st & 4th inst

3   I was at the Auction Room to day and Bot 19 Candlesticks and 1½ Doz of Cosmetique Perfumery and One Doz of Hair Oil of some Kind or other.   Dr Davis gave me to day 11.25 to send my Boy for Corn for him which I did and I got ten Barrells of Corn at 1 Dollar per Barrell, I Bot at Auction To night 6 China Boles and 4 pair of Low Quarterd Shoes

4   Dr Loyd Takes his Horse Home and Dr Davis Sends in his Horses

5   Times are getting something Better   I handed the Change To Day To Dr. Davis after Buying his Corn, it was a One and 25 cents.

6   Buisness not very Brisk for a Saturday, To day Mother Bot a Cow at Messr Howell & Spraigues auction Room   The price was 26 Dollars — Today Mother sent four Turkeys to New Orleans in Care of Mr. Napoleon Goings from Vicksburgh, To Mrs. Miller of Gravier Street

7   I remained Home all day, Except a few minutes that I took to wride down to Mrs. Liepers to Get William. The streets were quite Muddy — Mc Came Down and took supper with me in my shop

9   All manner of auctions in town To day. Sale to day a[t]

Dolbeares[1] and a[t] Sorias — and at old Cashells, We have all Kind of Night Auctions too   A Frenchman opened a Lot of Goods direct from France   He had as much as he Coud do and more to waite on the people, He got Peter Boisseau to asist him, He had a Lot of sattin stocks, Owen & Fortune Bot them and they Bot all his Boot[s] Except a few pair that he sold before they saw him, I got one pair of Boots at 7 Dollars and I got 2 Stocks, one plain and one sattin — The Concern Cost me $19.50. I bot a pair of Pantaloons also that is included in the bill

10   Auctions to day at Sprague & Howells and at Dolbeares and at Sorias To day, the things belonging to the Estate of Mr. Sml Mason — I bot a pair [of] and Irons, tongs and poker, One spider[2] and one Oven   The Concern only cost 1.50. Very Cheap — Dr Samuel Hogg paid me to day $19.50 for his shaving bill up to this date and I paid him Eleven dollars that I owed him for Medical Services up to this date — $7 of the amount was for Mother

11   Business not very brisk

12   I made out Mr Lambdins account To day for 20 months shaving to the First of January, 1838. The bill was $40 and he paid it, then gave the Boys $5.00   Mr. Christopher paid me His bill which was $10.00

13   I was up at auction to day several Times and they were selling the Furniture of Mr Mason that Died with sickness — I then took my nag and wrode out to the Race Track and I saw a Race or two, a race for a saddle One mile Out. The following nags started and came out as they are severally named here, Mr. Mardices Eliza Jones, Pat Obriens Little bay mare, Mr. Roberson bay mare and a Sorrill mare from Kentucky. I Lost One uncollected five Dollar bet on the above Race and then won five Dollars in Cash from a man on Old Isack VS. a Sorrill Horse wrode by Mr Gocian — H. Cobbler wrode Isack. I then Came to town and went under the Hill and bot a Kegg of Lard, wt. 46 lbs net, cost 4.12½

14   I remained home all day untill Late in the after noon — I then wrode Out near the R. tract. Bot a Mocking Bird from an Indian, 25 cents — Young Winn sent me up four fine pieces of spare Ribs   He Came up himself as far as the Landing but was unwell and did not Come up on the Hill — I sent him down

---

[1] F. H. Dolbeare & Co. conducted an auction–merchandise business located on Main Street. Natchez *Courier*, August 13, 1838.

[2] A spider was a frying pan or skillet, usually with legs.

a Lethern Bottle to hunt with, and I gave the Boy a ½ Dol-
lar   He also Brought me a puppy, One of the first Litter from
Francis   Mc went under the Hill this Evening and Bot a quarter
Box of Segars

15   To day I was up at the Frenchmans Store a[nd] Bot
a Frock Coat — gave Him thirty Eight Dollars for it and then
gave him twelve Dollars for a suite of cloaths for my Little
William which is not two years old untill the 24th inst.

16   I Loaned William to day ten Dollars to buy him a coat
from the Frenchman — To day the man that Rented my uper
Room is repairing it by Lathes &c

17   An Ellection was held for Health Officer to day and
after the 4 or 5th Balloting Dr. Hugh Lyle was Elected. Himself and Dr. Davis was a tie the Last Balloting and Old Dr.
Tooley gave the Casting vote in favor of Dr. Lyle leaving out Dr
[blank], Dr. Dally, Dr. Davis, and Mr. Withers was apointed
Harber Master in place of Mr Wells   To day They passed Some
of the meanest Kind of Laws Resspecting grocers, fruit and
so forth [3]

19   To day buisness was very dull I think, To night I
sent my piano to the Duchman to repair and play on it   I
Loaned it to him, F Taylor told me to day that he herd that
Abona got a Cow hideing around at Smiths Hotel by a Large man
around there

20   Several auctions to day and one on the Bluff Selling
the Planters Hotell out. I Bot a water Boiler and a wash
stand   They both Cost 2.62½   It was all that I Bot

22   There were some three or four Auction Sales in town,
Mr Edward Smith paid me to day Eight Dollars, being the remaining part of a months Rent that was due me a month ago
yesterday. He now owes me still one month do yesterday

23   Mr Fedrick Taylor paid me $5 for shaving & hair
Cuting to this date   Mr P. McGettrick paid me one months Rent
of the Southern Exchange Due on the 15 inst — He gave $63
and had paid for the setting of 3 grates which he said was $16
making in all 79.00   I Bot at Auction to night 2 vest, cost 4/0,
and four pair of Suspenders, 2½, making in all $2.38, and 1 Book,
Life in London, 3/., per vol 75 cents — I Bot from a Frenchman
5 stocks, Gave him 7 Dollars

[3] The city ordinance required licenses for such businesses as grocery stores, taverns, oyster houses, and fruit stands.

24   My Little William is Just two years old this day, 24th January, 1838.

25   Mr. Sisloff paid me to day $10 that I Loaned him a few days ago — Mr Ballard paid me five Dollars for shaving Mr. John Boyd on Sept 20th, 1837. To day Mr Ballard paid me $7 for shaving whilst sick at Mrs. Dupys — Wm went to shave Mr Caleb Herst who is now sick Mrs. Herst Mother died Last Night.

26   The Lady that intends occuping my uper Store Room Came to Get permission to Cook in my Shop, boys Room where they Sleep — I Told her she Could do so

27   I wrode Out to the Race tract to day and saw a race, a Kentucky mare against Mr. Mardices Lizar Jones, 1 Mile Out, odds in favor of the Kentucky mare and the other won the Race Easy — To day I wrote a Letter to E. Miller and it was a Dun — I sent it by Mr Stockman, no, Stockton, the merchant Taylor

28   I remained in town all day. McCary and myself Took a walk Down to the Bluff, up the Bluff to the Saw mill Road, then back again to the place we started and Down to the old Bluff Road, then on the Peter Little Bluff, then up the back street up to Pine Street and then down or up Said Street to the head of Main Street and then down to McCarys Shop and then down home again

29   I was up to day at the Sale of Mr P. Gemmell & Neibuts Sale. The[y] Sold a Greate Quantity of Lumber and all the utensils belonging to the firm — the[y] allso Sold Six Slaves that belonged to them, There was one of them that Sold for $2400.00, a Carpenter by a trade

31   The remains of Mr Thomas G. Ellis was brought down on the Steam Boat Tuskena, Capt Bradley. He was broat down by Mr John Routh, Dr Ogden and several others. I went Out at night to shave him and after I shaved him I assisted Mr Lee Cand & Yandel to take a Cast of his face. Mr. Bush and a Young Mr Ogdon was thare all assisting with it. The process is this. After the face was shaved and the hair all removed from the face, Eye Brows, and so forth, they then took a Brush and Oiled the face all over, puting dough in the Lips and in the nose, then Bandaged up the Face in such a manner as to prevent the plaster a parris from runing down the neck They then poured in the plaster which they mixed in a pitcher with warm water untill it becomes higher than his nose. It was suffered to remain on the face about 20 minutes, it was then taken off and it presented a fine Likeness of Him

February 1 To day the remains of Mr T G Ellis was Enterred in his home Gray yard. The Fencibles and Guards of which Company he was the Captain, the Masons went Out also — Quite a Large procession.

4 I remained at Home all day. The Ground is still frozed, Ever since Friday night

5 I was at several Auctions to day and I Bot some plank at Blackfords' sale, $14, six months creddit, tho I preferd to pay the money to giving my note.

6 I took a walk to Pedigrues sale which took place down at Mr Vancampen House

7 I made Out my account Yesterday against Mr Friderick Miller for One months Rent of One of my stores which, according to agreement was 40 Dollars, Tho I made Out the acct. for Only Thirty Dollars on acct. of his having done some Repairs to the store I was to have met him down at Mrs. Varrelmans Boarding house at 5 Oclock I went there a Little before the time and did not find him. I put the paper in Mr Walsh Hands, and he Collected the money and paid it over to me to day which was thirty Dollars. I gave him three Dollars for Collecting it. I took my bill to Mr Spielman for four months and three weeks hire of my Girl Lucinda up to the 4th of December 1837, which Bill He paid me, $24 I pd him his Bill for saddlery which was $12.75

8 Nothing New that I Know of To day the Man Dedrick Miller that Rented my House Sent me the Key, tho he paid the Rent several days ago He thought he would try to prevent me from Renting it to any One Else

9 I dont recolect much of anything that Occured to day.

10 I went up at Auction To night and bought some shaving soap &c., 6 Boxes of soap @ 50 cts per Box and 6 Boxs or Bottles of Indelable Ink 18¾ per Box and One Musick Box at $30. I Rented a French gentleman my uper store Room to day He Rented it for One week at the rates of $40 per month.

11 To day I went Out into the woods with my Gun and I Killed 10 Robbins, 2 Rice Birds, and 4 yellow Hammers, and I Only went Out at 1 Oclock. Mc went Out too, some w[h]ere in the nighboughhood of Minors pasture and Only Killed 4 Birds. Mr Armat Returns from Jackson and brings with him a Black Eye. He said it was hurt by a Dr Aiken or Hagan. The[y] had a small fight at the States House steps in Jackson. He sead that he Knocked the Fellow Down flat. Mr. Armatt paid me five Dollars to day on his acct. for hair cuting &c.

12   I was up the street to day and met Cegwin and Loaned him $50 to be paid next Saturday without fail, at the Rate of 5 per cent per month, To day we received News that Prentess & Wood had got their seats in Congress and that Claibourne & Golson had Received their Discharge [4]

15   I wrode out and took my Gun Late in the afternoon and Killed 1 Little wheat Bird, 1 Black do, 1 sparrow & 1 Robbin   It was too cold and too Late

16   Plenty Robbins about in all Quarters of the town, Mr Izods Kitchen Caught on fire and Burned up Just about 12 Oclock in A M. To day I Went out with my Little Gun, Killed 2 Black Birds, 1 Sap Sucker, 7 yellow Hammers and 48 Robbins

17   Cegwin paid me $50 that I Loaned him Last Monday morning — Buck Williams and Holton had something of a fight To day   Holton Knocked him Down and Blacked his Eye. They were settleing there accts when Mr. Williams Called Him a puppy and as soon as he did that H. Knocked him down. So says Report of to day — I Let Mr Rufner have One of the frames belonging to the Estate of Mr. Marshall   He promised me that it should be all right when I told him that I had no right or power to Dispose of the things belonging to said Estate

18   I remain home all day to day   Mc He went Out with his Gun in the afternoon and Killed 18 Robbins. There is at this time a Greate quantity of them in all parts of the woods.

22   This has been a Greate day with the military men of the City   The Guards and Rifflemen turned out in the forenoon and Fencibles in the afternoon [5]

23   To day Mr Louis Bingaman Sent my Little mare Home   He has had Her all day or for the Last three or [blank] Days and upwards, To day I Sent under the Hill to see if I Could

[4] For detailed information concerning the disputed election, see Dallas C. Dickey, *Seargent S. Prentiss: Whig Orator of the Old South* (Baton Rouge, 1945), Chap. V, "The Disputed Mississippi Election." See also Dallas C. Dickey, "The Disputed Mississippi Election of 1837–1838," *Journal of Mississippi History,* I (1939), 217–34; *Biographical Directory of the American Congress, 1774–1927* (Washington, 1928), 180. Prentiss and Word were not officially seated until May 30, 1838.

[5] The occasion was the celebration of Washington's Birthday. The Natchez *Free Trader,* February 23, 1838, reported that Mr. Mandeville (Henry D. Mandeville, Jr., a young lawyer who had political ambitions) made the principal address. "It was commendably brief, finely written, flowery as become the age of the speaker, free from hacknied, time-worn eulogium, and delivered with a graceful unembarrassed air." A file of letters, 1832–72, to and from Mandeville are in the Mandeville Papers.

Rent a shop to put William in down there and He returned Saying that 45 Dollars per month was what the[y] asked for it, ie the Shop that the Spainard moved Out of

24   Mr Cegwin pd me $30 to day. It was Monday that I Loaned him the money — He still Owes me $30 that I Loaned him

26   I wrode under the Hill to day and Rented a shop To put William in, I paid him, I mean the man Mr [blank] the sum of forty Dollars for the first month in advance, I sent William Down to day and some things to work with

27   I sent some things down To William under the Hill and I understood that He Came very near Burning the Shop Out by the neglect of a stove pipe that went through the top of the House

28   Taxes Taxes   I gave in my Tax List To day and it reads as follows

My two Lots value	$10,000	
My Three Slaves	2,000	
	12,000	12,000
Mother, three women and two children Slaves		1,650
Mrs Battles House & Lot 4,500 and Slave women		4,750

March 1   Nothing new That I Know of   P. McGraw advertises the Deslolution of Partnership between Him and G Pulling without the consent of Mr Pulling   We may soon Calculate on a fuss between them — McGraw went to the Country after the piece Came Out and did not return untill Late this Evening

2   To day Robt. Smith from New Orleans Came to me and wanted me to take a Boy that He Has in New Orleans which is a son of J——— S———   He wanted me to take the Boy and Keep Him as Long as they were in this place which He supposed they would be Here about three Years — He said the Boy was not treated wright by Mr. S——— and for that Reason he wanted him away from thare — I agreed to take him on the above terms and He promised to write for him — To day I had to Curse Mr. Braziers Boy Norman about Thowing at my Chickens in his yard and for Sundry other offences — I had the promise from his master that if he misbehaved again that he would Correct him sevierly — To day, soon after G Pullings advertisement came Out, P. H. McGraw served an injunction Bill on Him and had him removed from his store   He had to Give Bond for His appearance at Court in the Sum of ten thousand Dollars for his appearance   To day there were a Greate many Executions Out against the property

of Mr. Gridley and it is now advertised to be sold by the sherriff to the Highest Bidder — poor old Fellow. I Loaned my music Box to Col Bingaman to day — I sent it Out by John

    3   I spent a portion of this Rainy day in making nest for the Hens, &c. Myself and Winston did the work. Dr Daly Celler got full of Rain and so did Several others. The suer was full I am told, to the Top — I walked around To Dr. Guinns and Cut Mrs. Guinn Hair,   To day there were a Race between Col Bingamans Colt, Capt. McHeath and Col B Smiths mare, single dash of a mile. The Horse won the Race Easy

    4   I was up to the Rail Road this Evening and The Sewer had fallen in, in about ½ Doz places to a Considerable Extent, I saw thos Gent walking about up there, Old Esqr Tooley, Rot. Patterson, A L Gains and R Parker — They were Looking at the Sewer

    8   Mr Braziers Boy Norman was caught up in a tree I understand stealing of Chickens Last night   They took him to Jail and Kept him there untill Late to day and whiped him and then turned him Out

    10   To day there was a Race Out at the tract and I went Out to see it. The Nags belonged to Col Bingaman, Col Smith and Mr Minor. Capt McHeath won the first heat very Easy and in coming up to the stand His wrider dismounted and The Blankets was thrown on him and when Mr Minor saw that he spoke of it to Mr Prior [6] and Mr [blank] returned him a very impertinent answer and told him that he was too Damed Smart and To mind his Own Business, &c. This made Mr Minor Mad and he Left the matter for the judges to Decide On and they Decided that Col Bingaman should not Start his Horse again, that He was Ruled off or out of the Race — The Col then stated that it was a Damed Rascally Decission and there followed a Greate deal of abuse to the judges   Those were the Judges, Mr Jno Steel, Mr Lief, Mr Gift. They proclaimed it Out that Col. Bingaman Could

---

    [6] Capt. McHeath was a horse belonging to the Adam L. Bingaman stable, which was trained by J. Benjamin Prior. In 1843, Prior's name headed the list of young trainers who were the subject of a long laudatory statement by the editor of the *American Turf Register and Sporting Magazine*, XIV (1843), 105: "As a class these young trainers sustain a very high character for integrity and faithfulness as well as ability. Most of them are of gentlemanly bearing and address, while nearly all are intelligent to a degree that would command respect and insure success in any walk of life. Not a few of them are the habitual and worthy associates of gentlemen." Prior was long associated with Natchez racing; the tax rolls of 1849 and 1854 listed him as the owner of the Natchez race track. Auditor's Records, Tax Rolls, 1849, 1854, Adams County.

not start according to Rule   He swore that He would start his Horse. With that Mr. Minor sent his nag Home   Mr Smith ran his mare slowly around, but the Horse ran pretty fast, Doubled Distanced her, for she did not Run — Mr Pror abused Mr Minor a good Deal — it was Laughable to see the following men Cursing the Judges — Col B., Young B, Mr Sam Gocian, Mr Prior, Mr Joseph Smith. First One and then the other was at it. I am very sorry it Occured indeed   There was no Decission on the Subject, it was Left to be Decided between parties at a meeting of the Jocky Clubb — Mr A Spielman pd me fifty Dollars that I Loaned him 24th of Feb., 1838, I think

11   I remained home all this day   Mc Came down and tis the first time He has been Down since his wife Took so sick. Mr Prentess arrived at Vicksburgh this afternoon — they Gave him very warm Reseption

12   The town full of strangers to see the Races   To day I Took my acct to Mr Spielman which was, Interest included, $319.50   I took a saddle at 40 and a Briddle & martingale $7, which still Leaves him in my debt $272.50   Mr N Barlow pd me $20. He said that He owed me for two years shaving up to the 1st of Sept. Last. He still Owes me a Balance of $10 yet, up to the date, 12th of March, 1838

13   To day The Large Race between Linnet and Angorah Came off for ten thousand Dollars a side, It was a very pretty Race, for the first two miles and a Half, Angorah in the Lead and all at wonce the Boy fell off Directly after Linnet passed Her   She ran on out [7]

14   To day the race Came of[f] between Exito and Fanny Wright, four mile Heats for $5000 a side — Bets were two to one in favor of Fanny Wright and there was a greate deal Bet. Fanny got Beat pretty Easy — I think — The time in the first Heat was 8 m 14 seconds, the 2d Heat time 8 minutes 8 seconds [8]

17   Buisness tolerable Good. Greate many strangers in town, principally sportsman

18   I remained at Home all day untill very Late in the afternoon   Mc and myself then took a walk over the old fort and viewed the River &c.

19   Buisness not very good. Steven got drunk Last night

[7] Angora was owned by Adam L. Bingaman; Linnet by Thomas J. Wells of Louisiana. The Natchez *Free Trader,* March 14, 1838, stated that Linnet won the race because Angora's saddle slipped and she lost her rider.

[8] Fanny Wright was owned by Adam L. Bingaman; Exito by Thomas J. Wells. The Natchez *Free Trader,* March 15, 1838, gave a good account of the race.

and went of[f] and remained all night and was not Here this morning to go to Market. I sent Bill Nix to the Jail to see if He was there and He was not there. I then sent Him out to Dr Ogdons and in going there He found Him and brought Him Down and Left Him in the gate and he Jumped over the Fence and went threw in Judge Montgomerys yard. Bill He ran around the Corner and found him and brought Him in, I Kept him [in] the shop a Little while and then sent him to Help Mrs Lieper to move from the old House Down to the House belonging to Bill Hazard   He ran off 4 times in about three hours and Bill Nix Caught Him Every time, so He Brought Him Home after a while and I went to the stable and gave him a pretty sefveere thrashing with the Cow hide — then he was perfectly Calm and Quite and could then do his work. Tis singular how much good it does some people to get whiped   Mr. Kenney paid me $40.00 for One months House rent due to day, the 19th inst   I then told him here after He could have the Room for $35 per month

 20   I was up to auction to day and Mr Soria was selling off the Furniture of Dr James Denny — Sold on a credit of six months from Date

 21   Mr S. S. Prentiss Dellivered a fine speech at the Court House in presence of a very Large Congregation [9] — I was Out to day

 22   I wrote the following Lines and gave them to Mr Umphrys   Ranaway from the subscriber in Natchez on the 21st July 1837, a negro man by the name of Walker. He is about forty years of age — very Black Complection, smiles when spoken to and shows his teeth which are very sound and white tho he chews tobacco to Excess — Walker is about six feet High, raw Boned and muscular. He was brought to this Country by Mr Merret Williams and Granville Smith and was sold by them to Dr Duncan & Preston and was by them returned to Williams and Smith and was sold at Sorias Auction Room where I purchased him as an unsound Slave — Mr. John Clay of Bourbon County Ky. now owns a wife of Walkers and I presume he is now in that neighbourhood   He has a full head of hair and a heavy Beard, tho no grey hairs in his head that I Know of   I think that he is inclined to stoop or Lean to one side when walking. His feet is pretty Large — He I am told professes to belong to the Babtiste Church   I know of no marks on his person — If he is taken up

---

[9] The Natchez *Free Trader*, March 22, 1838, reported: "It was not one of his happiest efforts—we have heard him make a far better one."

in Ky I will Give a reward of two hundred Dollars when [he] is Delivered to me in Natchez or if he is in Ohio I will Give three hundred Dollars for his safe Delivery to me in Natchez or I will Take three Hundred Dollars for the Chance of Him William Johnson [10]

24 It is the Last day of the Jocky Clubb Races Here and it was the most Splendid days Raceing that I Ever saw on this tract I think

25 I remained Home all day — Nothing New to day that I know of Except there are a greate many persons that are now awaiting a Boat To go to The New Orleans Races.

26 A good many Citizens Left Here for New Orleans Col Bingaman Left about 2 Oclock this morning On Bourd of the st Boat St. Louis — He took several other Horses down besides what he had already Down. William made in the shop this week about $30, This has been Quite a buisness day, good Deal of Hair Cutting this Evening, Bond opened his Dancing School To day at the City Hotell [11]

27 Steven ran off Last night and God Only Knows where he has gone to, for I dont, tho if I should have the Good Luck to Get Him again I will be very apt to Hurt his Feelings — This is the second time he has ranaway in a week.

29 To day it was that I paid Mr W W. Wilkins a note that He held against me for thirty six Dollars due the Estate of Mr Perry. R McCary was the Indorser on it — To day I took one of the bigest Kind of a hunt for Steven But could not find the Rascal at all

31 I got on my Horse Early this morning and wrode Out to Washington in search of Steven but Could not find Him at all I also went Out again in the afternoon to Becon Landing but could not hear of Him. During the time that I was in sea[r]ch of him He sent me word that if I would Only Let him off without whiping him that he would never runaway again Durring His Life

April 1 I remained home all day until Late in the Evening, then Mc and myself took a small walk

---

[10] Since Johnson's announcement was not published in the local press, it was probably issued in the form of a handbill.

[11] J. C. Bond had advertised a dancing school in Natchez as early as 1819, and he was still advertising as late as 1845. See Natchez *Mississippi Republican*, February 25, 1820; Natchez *Free Trader*, April 8, 1845. But apparently he was not continuously in the town throughout the twenty-five-year period.

2   To day was the day that Mr. Gridleys Property was to have been sold by the Sherriff for Debt but it was not sold. There was no bid On it — Mr F Stantons warehouse was to have been sold also tho it was not offerd at all

4   I was a good part of this day afixing my water Barrells for Bathing.

5   Buisness Quite dull. I got my Barrells to give Baths to day for the First time and Mr Ayres Called and took a Bath — The First this Season and paid the Cash for it   I to day Saw a Man up at the auction Room and he wanted to buy my Girl Sarah. I told him he could have her for twelve Hundred Dollars in cash. I intend to see about it To morrow and if I can find out about him I will do something   Peter Boisaw Open to day in the new Coffee House and to day was the day the Collinizationest had a Large meeting and here is the names of some of the Leading Parties or Head Dogs in the Bone Yard — Tis a pitty that they [are] not doing something Else better for there Country   [names omitted by diarist] [12]

6   I have made a Little mistake in my saying that I saw the man yesterday at auction for it was to day   News by a Boat to day from New Orleans that Col Bingamans Horses was poisoned in Orleans and they would not Eat and that was the Reason that they could not run and that the Col and Mr Prior had Fell Out and Prior had Left the Col [13] — To day I paid Dr Wren my

---

[12] Johnson was here expressing his opposition to the Mississippi Colonization Society, organized at Natchez in 1831 as an auxiliary of the American Colonization Society. The Mississippi organization had as its objective the removal of free Negroes from the state, preferably by sending them to Liberia. If Johnson had named some of the "Leading Parties or Head Dogs in the Bone Yard," he would have listed the officials of the society, which included wealthy and prominent Dr. Stephen Duncan of Natchez and a long list of individuals prominent in educational, religious, business, and political life. The total number of Mississippi Negroes sent to Africa before 1860 was between 550 and 600, but probably at least 500 of these were slaves freed by their owners with the specific object of colonization. Most of the established group of free Negroes probably shared Johnson's attitude of opposition. A summary of the activities of the Mississippi Colonization Society is in Charles S. Sydnor, *Slavery in Mississippi* (New York, 1933), 203-38.

[13] On April 4, 1838, at the New Orleans races, Colonel Adam L. Bingaman "publicly announced that Mad Anthony was suddenly amiss, and his suspicions that he had been tampered with in his stable." He therefore canceled the entry of the horse in a race, which was won by William J. Minor's Britannia. Nevertheless, Bingaman's stable won six out of eleven races entered, and afterward he became reconciled with his trainer, J. Benjamin Prior, and re-employed him. See *Spirit of the Times*, VIII (1838), 77; New Orleans *Picayune*, March 29–April 12, 1838. (The editors are indebted to Professor Charles E. Smith for research on this footnote.)

newspaper postage in specie, 98 cents, which pays up to the First of July next for Box rent and all   I Received a Letter this Evening by Mr J C Bond from Elisha Miller at Vicksburg with One Hundred Dollars in it   He now Owes me $50 more that he Borrowed from me a good while ago

7   I felt a degree of Suspicion about a man that I thought from his Generall apearance, would if he Could, do me a Damage, that is, I thought He wanted to steal my Girl Sarah.

8   I remained all day at home Except about a half Hour that I was away at Mr. A Kenneys To see Him about this man Dr McAlvaney   We sat, Talked awhile, then I Left and Came Home — We were talking altogether about that Dr McAlvenee. Poor Fellow He was in a monstrous Scrape — He sent Mr Boyer to see me in the first place who stated that he knew the Dr very well and for many years and that he was a very respectable man and had a very Respectable Family and that he was very sorry for what had happened and was Drunk or he never would have Gone inside of Mr Stocktons yard in the world

9   Buisness was Quite dull and nothing new that I Know of

10   I was up at the auction Room to day and there I bought two Counting House stools, paid thirteen Bits a piece for them   To day about 9 Oclock Mr Caulwell the Carpenter Got married to Miss Beatie — Yesterday Mr J. C. Bond got my Horse Kitty To go Out as far a[s] Mr Dunbars to teach Dancing He wants to get Her to wride Out on 2 or 3 times a week — I Loaned H. A. Cegwin to day $30 to be paid this week — good

11   I was up To day at the Auction Room of Dolbeare and bought One Keg of butter at 15 cents per pound   It weighed net 39 pounds, $5.85   Warner was to see me to day and during his short stay he told a greate many Toughf Lyes about England &c.

12   To day was spent in Talk about the Duell that was to have Taken place this Evening between Col. Nickolds and Dr Booye   They were to have fought between 4 and 5 Oclock this Evening — There was a Greate many Person assembled to see the Expected fight   Crowds were On the Other Side and a Greate many were on this side trying to see and after all, those that remained seen as much as we that Crossed the River for shortly after we Got Over Dr Ker He got up on the Levee and there commenced a Long Harangue of Stuff which was seconded by the Elustrious Abby and The Hon. R. Patterson who is at this time One of the Bourd of Selectmen   A Committee was appointed. The following Composed the Com — Abby, Patterson & Lucas —

They were Dispached fourth with to the Parties to state the Resolutions that Had been passed by the speaker and Crowd — 1st, that they Had resolved to follow those Gentleman and prevent there fighting on any part of the Ground — Well the time had passed when they were to have fought and still there was no preperations made that I could see for the fight when at last Here Came the Sherriff of La and stoped the Consern. They were held to bale in the sum of One Hundred Dollars to Keep the peace   Col Nickolds were on the River Bank and the Dr was on the other side of the Road in the woods on a Log

13   The Large Town Meeting that was to have Taken place to day on the Subject of Dueling appears to have been Neglected by the partees as there was no meeting at all. No person To Open the meeting. Tis well Enoughf

14   Not much buisness a doing of any Kind. I went under The Hill This Evening and Bot One Barrell of Flower $7, N. O paper and One Keg of Lard at 7 cents per pound and One Kegg that I paid 10 cents for and I paid 40 cent per Bushell for 11 Bushells of Oats   I Bot them from a man from Indiana

15   I remained home all day to day ie untill Late this Evening — Then Mc came Down and we Tok a walk to the Bluff and back again   I wrode down to the River to see the Boatman that I had been trading with yesterday and He promised me to remain where I Left him with his Boat untill tomorrow morning as I had promised him to Buy some of his provission if he would wait

16   The people of this good place are in the dayly Expectation of seeing a fight or something Like it for there are Disputes among several gentlemen of this place — Below will be found the remarks of Dr Bowie[14] — TO THE PUBLIC — The following narrative of the Events which have transpired within the Last few days will apprize the Public of the Position I now occupy. After the Outrage that was offered to my Person, I demanded of Col Nickolds that satisfaction to which I was Entitled — in reply to my note He objected to the Language in which it was Couched — but professed his willingness to respond to the call when made in a proper form — That there might be no Evasion, I Concluded to waive all objections and modified the Language of my second

---

[14] The Natchez *Free Trader*, April 27, 1838, contained Allen T. Bowie's denunciation of Colonel Nichols for having evaded a duel with him. Bowie's statement, dated April 16, 1838, was substantially as Johnson here quoted it, except for misspellings and alterations in punctuation.

call as he had desired. The meeting was prevented by circumstances (causes) beyond the Controll of Either Party, My Friend, Mr E. H. Ogden, waited on Col. N. on Friday morning and after informing Him that Dr McWhorter had refused to Except any Communications on His, Col. N's behalf, requested him to name the time and place for a second meeting, as well as a friend who would act for him — Col Nichols replied that he was then under arrest but would take an Early oppertunity of so doing. Thus stood the affair On Saturday morning — I had then been waiting 24 hours in the Expecttation of receiving some Communications when Col. N Having accidently met my friend, informed him that he considered the affair at an End, To which my friend Mr. Ogden replied that I Considered the Challenge s[t]ill in force — that the meeting was mearly posponed and reiterating the Call of yesterday, again requested him to name a friend — To which Col. N. replied that He had obeyed the Call and Should wait untill another was made, It is Certainly difficult to understand how a response to a Call, which resulted in an inefectual meeting is a satisfaction for an Injury — yet by this Subterfuge, which in Effect amounts to a refusal to Except my Call, I am Left as I Originally Stood after the Insult offered and as it is impossible to Elevate this man to the Dignity of a Gentleman, I shal Leave him in the Situation in which by his Own Conduct He has placed himself   Alen T. Bowie

May 5   Nothing new Except that There were two Little Frenchman and a French woman that have Just Open a Barbers Shop.

17   To day was the day that Rodolph and Angorah was to have ran for five hundred Bales of Cotton, 4 miles heats and One Hundred Bales the forfiet — Rodolph was not here and the mare Angorah gallopd arround and to the Amount of Bales as the Horse Rodolph was not to be found   I Took a wride this Evening Late on my Little mare & I Took my Little William with me

18   My Girl Lucinda Came Home two or three days ago from Mr Stocktons   Mr McAlister Moves the Contents of his office to day or a part of them, I Took a wride this Evening on my Little mare. Col Bingaman Left Home this Evening for the Jefferson races.[15]

19   I Lost my fine Mocking Bird through the negligence of Winston. I would not have taken fifty Spanish Dollars Cash in

---

15 At Fayette, Jefferson County, Mississippi.

hand for him, tho what is to be will be, in Spite of me, Mr L. A Bensancon and Lady arrived this morning from New Orleans on the S B. Ellen Douglass

20   To day after Dinner I Ley down and Took a Knap of sleep and afterwards took my Horses and went Out to Shillings Lake To fish and after fishing about an hour returned and did not Catch One single fish   I took Winston with me and Dick — neither of us Caught any fish, I returned and went arround the upper side of Mrs Lintons fence to see if I could Cetch a Bird but could not

21   Mr Arther Kenney paid me his Rent which was due on the 19th inst., thirty five Dollars — Mr W. A. Britton paid me to day fifty Dollars in full for five months use of my Horse   I went arround to the Court House this Evening and Bot a Lot of things, pd five Dollars for them   I paid Mr Fox[16] to day for one years subscription to the New Yorker, three Dollars in full

26   To day I Loaned Mr John G Taylor for use of Barlow & Taylor, One hundred and fifty Dollars. I went under the Hill to day and got two Boxes (1000) of Good Segars from Mr Tossis, Segars that I won from him On a Race some time ago — I was under the Hill this Evening and paid a Mr Hamatt Eighty Dollars for two months house Rent due on the 26th of June, 1838. Six Baths today — not very good for Saturday — To day H. A. Cegwin was to have Called and paid me One Hundred Dollars Borrowed money but did not, I have a strong notion not to Loan him any more, for he dont come up to the scrach in proper time

27   There is nothing New that I know of   I went Down to the River this day about 12 Oclock and crossed over the River taking Winston and my old Grey Horse along to Concordia to fish   I caught 23 I think and Winston Caught 7. We found a good many Over there a fishing when we went   I Caught two poor Little Mocking Birds over there, and Brought them over with me

28   There has been Nothing New of Any Interest That I have herd of. H. A. Cegwin Came this morning, A Candidate for the Office of Selectman, To day Mr. Saml Gocian Came and paid me $25, being a part of 50 Dollars that I Loaned him some

16 W. H. Fox was a Main Street merchant who sold books, clothing, and drugs. Natchez *Courier*, November 27, 1837, August 13, November 28, 1838.

time ago — To day the Col.[17] Sent my music Box Home again, in Bad order — To day Mr Tracy paid me twenty Dollars — this makes $40 that He has paid in all which was due on the 4th inst., this being the First Month. He paid me in work $5. This is to Come out of the Second months Rent

29 Mr Dumax and Mr Maxent had a fight Last night, One of the hardest Kind, and they made a stand off for Neither of them got whiped

30 Mrs Adriance has a Daughter this Evening — Mrs Wiswall had a daughter the day before yesterday Mr Bandurant was married this Evening To Miss Jones, who he has Long Courted

31 Mcs little Bill Button is now ranaway from Mc and he Sent Dick after him this morning and Dick ranaway himself and I caught him this night and Took him home To Mc Mr W. Bennitt paid me twelve Dollars for four months Shaving Due the First of April, 1838.

June 1 This has been decidely the dullest day we have seen for some time, Cegwin paid me One Months Shaving Due the First inst — I went to the Methodist Church and Listened on the Out Side of it at Mr. Maffitt Preaching — He is a splendid speaker, The best I Ever herd in all my Life [18] — The heavy rain that we have had to day and yesterday has done a greate harm to the Planters in this County. Dr Duncan and Col Bingaman both has Lost a greate deal of Cotton and Labour

2 I saw a Young man by the name of Horton Kick a Young man by the name of Brown On the Back Side and made him run out of the House and he did not resent it Oh that a man Can stand some things is most true.

3 Mr H. A. Cegwin paid me to day Fifty Dollars. He Still owes me fifty Dollars more on a hundred Dollars that I Loaned him Some time ago

4 Buisness Quite Brisk To what it has been for some

---

17 Colonel Adam L. Bingaman.

18 The diarist was here referring to the Reverend John Newland Maffitt, renowned Methodist pulpit orator, who was delivering a series of sermons and addresses in Natchez. On the night of June 7 he was scheduled to deliver a lecture on "The Life of Genius," with admission tickets $1.00 each, for the purpose of raising funds to complete the work on the steeple of the Methodist church building. Natchez *Free Trader,* June 7, 1838. Later the *Free Trader* published in pamphlet form an address delivered by Maffitt on June 25 at a Natchez Masonic meeting. *Ibid.,* August 31, 1838.

time back, I gave William twenty dollars to day for his two weeks work, he brought fifty Seven Dollars and he Showed me a Letter that Mr. Miller had wrote me and the substance of the Letter was that Capt Johnson had requested Mr. Miller to write to me that he wanted me to Settle with Wm   It appears that the infernal Rascal has been writing to his Father himself

    6   Mrs Battles moves Down to Her House

    7   Fourteen Baths to day

    8   Buisness Tolerable good

    10   Good deal of Buisness in my Line, Bathing in particular   I had to turn off a good many

    11   Four Baths to day   I wrote a Letter to day and put it in the Post Office, Directed it to James Miller, No 29 Canal St., New Orleans — The substance of the Letter was about French William, Col Bingaman Left here Last night to go to Jackson

    12   Buisness Quite Dull, I thought, Only tolerable Dull, I was up at Soria Auction room to day and Bot 1 Sofa at $34, 2 Large pictire & Frames, $4.25, 2 Kitchen Hand Irons, 1 Large Carpet, $12.00   I paid Mr McFaddin $100 for filling up my Lot up by the Rail Road — Maj Shields gets married to night to Miss Surget

    13   Mr Walker Finished my Conducting Pipe that Leads water into my Baths — Price $25. To day about 11 Oclock Mr Thoms Rose Finished the frame to my arning [awning]

    19   I Loaned Mr N. Barlow to day three hundred and fifty Dollars to be paid when calld for. It was all Brandon Money

    20   To day Mother paid me one Hundred and twenty-five Dollars, which Leaves her Still in my debt Four hundred and Seventy Dollars to this date. The oven that I paid Mr Breeden for is not included in the above amount at all. It Cost me $153.00   This is mine at any time, To day or this Evening Young Bledsoe and Preacher Dixon has a sort of a fight   The Particulars I have not herd.   Bledsoe got a Bruised Eye and Dixon got nearly Knocked Down with a 4 pound w[e]ight — got his head cut a good Deal

    21   I went up to Mr Bleedens yard & got One Barrell of Lime — did not pay him for it at the time, Mother paid me twenty five Dollars more, making in all 150 within two days that she has paid me

    23   To day has been a profitable day with me in the way

of Bathing, 22 Baths   E Miller Came Down from Vicksburgh Late Last night on the S. B Monarch

24   To day the Capt Miller Left here for Vicksburgh   I went down To the River with Him, and staid untill he Left

27   I Bot of a Stranger to day 6000 Segars and paid him 28 Dollars a Thousand

28   To day Mr Thom Rose finished my Gallery and Steps, Commenced on them yesterday in the day — To day Dr. V. Metcalf paid Mother $10.00 for One months Bourd of His Boy

30   I was up at Auction this morning or to day and Bot some articles, the Following are a part, 1 tin pan and a Lot of brushes, To day Mr. John G. Taylor paid me One hundred and fifty Dollars Borrowed money, all in Brandon Money too, Mr. A. Spielman paid me two hundred and ninty Dollars — This was money that I Loaned him   He paid me in Brandon. The amount that I Loaned him was $272. To day Dr Hubbard paid me Eighty Dollars in money and fifty seven [dollars and] 77 cts by a note on Mr F Beaumont

July 1   Nothing New that I have herd of to day, I wrode Out to day to the old Field beyond Col Wilkins and Took my Riffle, and spent the Evening shooting at a mark, Mc Came Out also and we shot to gether all the Evening and to take our shooting altogether I Beat him about a fut

3   William made about the above amount, $54, and I took the Rent out and Diveded by two and gave him ½ that was made in the Shop, I paying the Expense myself, which was about 4 Dollars short of the amount

6   To day the Steam Boat Diana Left here for New Orleans. She Left here this Morning and William went Down on Her

12   The Steam Boat Diana left here ie She Left here Late this Evening — Late & a Greate many person Left here on Her   Miss Lizar Evans, Mrs Sam Williams, Ruffner & Lady — I took my Riffle Late this Evening and went in the old field Back of Col Wilkins & Shot 1 jay Bird, 1 Wood pecker, 1 Partrige, 1 Buzard

13   I made Mr Spielmanan an offer to day of 9 inches of my Ground to Build a wall on provided that He would Give me the 1 ½ of his wall   There was several propersitions made which I have not time to put Down this Evening

14   Nothing of any importance transpired to day

17   A Bill put in by Mr Sisloff For the Erection of my House

3000 ft. of Flooring at 40	160.00
30 do wash Boards	12.00
1200 ft of Sheeting [at] 20	24.00
114 Joist 16½ F Long 2½ – 110 – 3916 ft [at] 30	117.
38 do 16½ to 2½ – 8 1045 [ft]	31.35
76 Rafters 12 ft L. 3 – 4 — 912 [ft]	27.36
12000 Shingles [at] 6	72.00
Hauling the above	37.00
2000 ft. Clear pine [at] $60	120.00
Hauling Same	4.00
Glazing window Light & Door Sash	60.00
Hara wase	75
Carpenter work	731.00

The Amount of Carpenters Bill in to-to $1469.19 [19]

Mr. Sisloff handed me a Bill of the Brick Layer for the bilding, the amount of which was 1600.

18   I Bot at Dolbears Auction Room to day One Large or Common size Jar, 2 Jugs & one Lantern, 3   William Came up from New Orleans this morning and brought me a Receipt for two Hundred Dollars that I Sent to his Father

August 13   I am still Buisy Diging out the Foundation to Erect my House.

14   Nothing new.

15   Nothing New that I Know of   I Loaned Mr Richard Terrell to day Two Hundred Dollars — To be paid to Mr Miller as soon as He arrives in New Orleans

16   Mr. S Davis pd me up to the First of Sept 1838 — To Day I sued this man Hery Woodruff before Esqr Cook and the old man told him that he would have to pay the money in five Days or else take it to Court, That [was] what he told him

17   The Steam Ship arrived this Morning from Vicksburg — She had a greate number of our Citizens

18   Nothing New that I Know of   Ther was a Shooting match to Day I understood at the Race tract and a Great number of Persons were thare   Jo. Lancaster vs. H Cobler;

19 Johnson's figures have not been audited.

$500 to two hundred & 50. The odds was in favor of H Cobler and the other won the money with Ease.

24 To day Mr McGettrick came to see me about Our Counter, I Told Him that I would allow him seventy nine Dollars for it — Otherwise He Could say what the Counter was Damaged and if in Reason I would pay it   He then after Talking some time said that He would make me a present of the whole Concern and walked off. That was all that passed between us — To day The man Friar That was Convicted at the Last Criminal Court was to have been Hung but from a supposed writ or Error. To day 4 or 5 Darkeys was taken up for Gambling

25 Nothing New that I Know of

26 Nothing New that I Know of. I Took a wride Out in the afternoon with Mc   We went Out to the Scotts Old Field

27 Nothing New that I Know of

30 I wrote two Letters this Evening, the One to Mr Miller, the other Mr R Terrell

31 I had a settlement to day with Mr McGettrick for the Counters that was Left in the House and He Owed me One months Rent $65 and I Gave him $20 making in all $85 for the Counter   This was a regular and satisfactory Settlement between us

September 1 I paid Mr Elam & Wright to Day one Hundred Dollars in part pay for building my House, Mr Sisloff pd me twenty five Dollars that he Borrowed from me the other day

2 I wrode Out To Day with Mc   We went Out as far [as] The Creek. We had a very agreable and pleasent wride indeed

6 To day I Bot a cow from Patrick Hurst for $27 and I paid him the money Cash and the Rascal promised to take her back if did not Like Her and when I made the offer for him to take her back he would not,   I pronounce him a Rascal

7 To day I paid Mr Geo Weldon by a note on the Estate of Neibut & Gemmell & Com. for One Thousand and Eighty Dollars,   Included interest it would have amounted To $1200 Tho he was to take it of[f] me for the above amount, which He did, and then Gave the same to Messrs Elam & Wright in part pay for Brick work Done on my house — The note was Excepted by Messrs Elam & Wright and they Gave me a

Receipt for the same instead [of] Mr Weldon, as our agreament was made in that way [20] Dr Merrill was present and saw
the document

9 I took my Gun to day at 12 Oclock and went Down
in the swamp

14 To day I went at the request of Mr Elam and took
my Due bill from the administrators of Messrs Neibut, Gemmel
& Com. and gave them back the receipt which they had gave
me, and to sho that I had traded the Due bill to Mr Elam, I
Endorsed it without Exempting myself from The Liability of
an Indorser but the understanding between The Parties and
myself was that they took the note as it stood against the Estate,
without my being Responsible for the Collection of the same

15 We have herd To day that The Steam Ship had arrived
in New York After a Passage of 9 Day[s], 11 Hours or something Like it

17 No Brick work Done to day. I and the Boys Commenced to Dig Out the shoe makers yard and to make it Level,
I turned the Gutter End for End and Put a handle in the matoc
[mattock]

18 I paid Mr Elam To Day One Hundred in part pay
for Brick work On my House in Main Street, Natchez

19 Nothing New to Day that I Know of

20 Several of Our Citizens got Home to day from the
North, A G. Carpenter, J. G. Dickerman

21 Buisness very Dull and no news that I Know of. The
workman are still at work at my new Building. I have two Mocking Birds up to this Date

22 The Brick Layers could not work on my House at
all to day — too much Rain — I bot all three of Mothers Birds to
day

23 Nothing New that I Know of

24 Mc and myself went in the Swamp to Day and took
a Hunt   We stoped at Mosebys — Mr Barland and young R.
Barland went along also. We separated Down at the uper part

---

[20] Johnson was here referring to a three-story brick building then being erected
on part of his Main Street property, which included the present-day site of part
of the Eola Hotel parking lot plus twenty feet of the modern United States Post
Office property. Johnson's accounts show that George Weldon was the principal
contractor, while Elam & Wright did the bricklaying. Immediately east of this
brick structure, Johnson owned a frame building. These two buildings housed the
diarist's principal barbershop, a large store, and several small shops which he
used for rental purposes.

of Winns Lower Field   Mc and Mr Barland & N. went together
Down in the neighbourhood of the Lakes and Mr Moseby and
myself went Down near the River throug[h] more Brush
and thickets than Ever I went through in all my Life in One
day — The fact was, that Mosbys Hounds would not Hunt and
He in order to start a Deer Hunt traveled Just where his Dogs
Should have gone   Mc and Mr Barland went in next the Lake
and I and Mr M went next the River — None of them Killed
or Shot anything Except myself and I Killed 3 Loons, 1 Large
Beceroach, 1 small dito and 1 Large Blue Crane. This Game
I Shot very Early in the morning, Mr Tim White and a
Col Milroy had a fight or fought a Duell   They took 2
Rounds   The Last Round Tim White was shot slightly through
the thigh and he fell. Fairchil & Edwards had a fight —
Edwards got the worst of it — The Journemen Quit the office
and no paper was Issued for One Day

25   Buisness was Dull, The Drs turned Out to day for
the perpose of Getting The Drugests to Sign an article Promising not to prescribe for Sick Persons — Dr Davis, Dr Dally,
Dr Young, Dr Frisby, Dr Loyd and Dr Metcalf — those were
the Gentlemen that I Saw

26   Buisness Dull   I paid Mr Hamet to day $40 House
Rent under the Hill, up to 26th of Oct — Mrs Harring Died
at Her Residence this Evening — Mrs Ballance Died also this
Evening

27   Mr Doyal and Capt. Thomas went in the Swamp with
Barland and nephew They Killed a Deer, Mr Thomas Killed
the Deer

28   My House is to Day two Storreys high — Mr Dickerman wanted to Know if I would sell him a foot or 14 inches of
Ground of[f] from the Lot of Mrs Battles — I told him no

29   Mr Weldon was to Day puting on the Joice for the
second storry but did not finish — Amy, valuable servant Belonging to the City Hotell, Died Last night — I had in my Box
to date $116 La money and $255 Brandon &c. and $400.00
Bankable — all $771

30   I took a wride out in the Direction of Mr. Minors
Plantation   We did not get back untill quite Late.

October 1   I had a match with John the Greek[21] to shoot

---

[21] "John the Greek" was John Jacquemine, often Johnson's hunting companion, with whom he frequently made small bets. In 1842, Jacquemine advertised
that he had "fitted up a very neat cottage," about two miles from town on the

25 yards with a Riffle, 3 best in five for One Qrt. Box of Segars and I Lost the Cegars — I shot afterwards with him and Mc and beat them Both — they both shot with my Riffle

2 Buisness Quite Dull — To day I Commenced to dig out the foundation or the Dirt Out of the uper Room — Mr Wellington Smith Died to day at 9 Oclock   He was thrown from his Horse yesterday Evening Out at the Plantation of Mr St J. Elliotte — The mare on which he wrode was Killed also at the same time

3 Buisness very dull   I was buisy working with the Dirt out of my uper Lower Room — Dr Gustine was in town to night and told me that he had paid the $40 that he owed me to Dr. Maxwell, and wrote me a Letter to Mrs Callender to ascertain the fact

4 Buisness very dull indeed, I bot to day of Mr Colson Glas Sash to the Amt [of] $122 and Gave my note payable in March for the amount

5 Col Sprague Died at his Plantation To day over near Texes

7 I wrode Out to the tract in the afternoon and One or two shooting matches — Chrstman & Lancaster, Col Bingaman & James Wright

8 Dull Day — I went Out in Mr Minors Pasture this Evening by myself and shot at a target. I made some very bad shots

9 On reflection it was to day I think instead of yesterday that I was Out shooting

12 Mc & John Jacumine & myself went out in Mr Minors Paster to shoot Rifles at 25 ct per Shot

13 Buisness not very good on account of the Greate Quantity of shops in town

14 I went Out in Mr Minors Pasture this Evening and took my Pistol with me and shot at the mark   I only made three good shots in the whole afternoon, those were nearly Center shots — Andrew Eveans was along but shot very badly — I had

---

Kingston road, where he sold fruits and lemonade, held Saturday shooting matches, and operated a tenpin alley. His name first appeared on the tax rolls in 1843, and by 1851 he was referred to as "Capt. John Jacquemine." Natchez *Courier*, April 30, 1842; Auditor's Office, Tax Rolls, 1843, 1851, Adams County. In 1850 he was listed in the U. S. census as a "merchant," born in Greece, whose wife had been born in South Carolina and eight children in Mississippi. U. S. Census Reports, 1850, Schedule I, Adams County, 2. According to family tradition, he became the owner of an excellent hotel on Main Street.

both of my Horses along and had some trouble in Cetching them

15 To day is the Auction Sale of Fabber & Farnsworths Goods — Marshals Sale   Steam Ship Natchez arrived to night about Supper time with a full freight from New York

16 Mr Jas. Ballard arrived this Evening and Shortly afterwards Mr & Mrs Holton arrived on the S Boat Diana — Brick work of my House not finished Yet — Only One man at work at it

17 I wrode Out this Evening and Shot a Duck   I dont think I was Out more than 20 minuets in all, I shot it Out at Mr Waymoths Garden Pond

19 I gave Mr Tweksburg an order to Vancampen & Jones for Some Lumber and to Sislocs for some also — He then went to work Plaining of Planks and made about 3 qrts of a Days work — The Rain of yesterday Caused my new House to crack very considerable, that is from the top to the Botom on the Lower Side — Lawyer Baker and Lawyer Armat has a small fight to Day at Dinner at the Mansion House, To day a number of the Free Trader Containd the Seveerest piece against the Banks that I have Ever Seen   From the pen of Mr John Hagan the article Eminated [22]

20 I paid Mr George Welding to day One Hundred Dollars in part pay for my Brick House On Main St — Mr A Kenney paid me thirty five Dols Rent   Mr Jno R Wells paid me to day $75.00 and still owes me a Ballance of $25 Borrowd Money

25 I Rented my House ie the uper frame House to Mr A Spielman at $45 per month, Commencing from to day

26 There was a General Muster at the Race Tract and it was a very Large turn Out   The Gov of the State[23] witnessed and reviewed the Regment, It was Kept up Longer than any Muster that I Ever Saw, and there likeed to have been a Small fight

27 Mr Winn Took Dinner with me to day. Capt Jno gave a Big Dinner

28 The Governor and His Miletary Staff Left Here To day and The Steam Ship Left here at the Same time and was bound for New York. She ran Down to the Ireland[24] and Stuck fast on the Sand bar.

---

22 The article was a condemnation of "wildcat" banking practices.

23 Alexander G. McNutt was governor of Mississippi from 1838 to 1842.

24 Johnson probably referred to Natchez Island, four or five miles down the Mississippi River.

29   Mr Spielman Commenced This morning to take Down His Old House on Main Street

30   Buisness is very Dull for the season

31   Buisness very Dull for the Season, Spielman has his House Tourned all Down and it pact away To day — The Irish Turned Out prety strong to Day, or this Evening, after a Fellow by the name of McCabe who tis believed Killed a man Last night and threw him over the Bluff so as to make it appear that he had fallen over the Bluff Himself. The Irish threw over the House that he Lived in and Let it fall Down the Bluff   The Guards and Fencibles had to turn Out To Keep them from Linching him

November 1   I Commenced to day to Dig the Dirt Out of my yard, and Spielman Commenced to Dig the Foundation for His new House   I paid Mr Elam & Stanford Two Hundred Dollars in part payment for my new House

2   Buisness Quite Dull

4   I remained in town until 12 Oclock and then I took my Gun and wrode Out as far as the old Scotts Field. I Killed 2 Larks, 1 sap sucker, big Lead Bird and One Black Bird, 1 throush, I found old Sterns Out in the woods and took him along with me and he Killed more game than I did, When I Came home I found out that Charles and Bill Nix had Joined the Methodist Church and Sarah also — Mr Doyal and several other Gentlemen Killed 7 Deer and they got 5 of them

5   I Paid Mr Welding to day thirty Dollars in spiecie and he Gave me a Receipt for thirty five, thus he gave five Dols premum on it.

6   I saw Mr Moseby, the Deputy Marshal for this Derstict, Selling Out A G. Carpenters Drug Store at Public Marshalls Sale to day and there was nobody to Purchase any thing   I saw several Lots of things sell for 2 Bits only and was purchased by Tim White   The whole amount of stock Only sold for $12.50   Vancampen moves from Main Street to The Frame House belonging to Estate of Bingham

7   Last night we had One of the Heaviest Kind of Rains, nearly fulled Spielmans celler with water, Thomson & Breed moves from Main Street out of the Store of Mr S T McAlister to the store of Hanchet in Commerce St.

12   Buisness Quite Dull as usual, Elam & Wright is at work on the fire walls of my new House   Wright nearly finishes The Cornice in front to day

14   Mr Weldon Commences to put on the Rafters on my

House this Evening. Mr Hyatter was married Last night to Miss Mellen

15   Mr Spielman Commences The Brick work for His House   Mr S M Boyd gets married to Miss Catharine Wilkens

16   This morning quite Early I Came Down in my shop and found that the Boys had Just been smoking some of my Cegars which they Denied   I Listened a while and was satisfied that they had stolen them   I then Boxed Bills Jaws and Kicked his Back Side and I slaped Charles along side of the Head severall times

17   The Carpenters Finished puting on the Roof of my House to day. The Brick Layers have not finished the House yet

19   Mr James Ballard Commences To do his Own Shaving   Dr Davis moves from next Door and Takes his Horses from my Stable

20   Buisness better than it has been for some time past   I Had a Settlement with Mr Elam & Stanford to Day for the Brick work of my New House   The Bill for Brick work amounted to Nineteen Hundred and fifty seven Dollars and Eighty Cents   I paid them and took a Receipt for the same

21   Buisness still Getting Better, My note falls Due to day in the Commercial Bank for $502.67, Drawn or in the Possession of Mr Isack Lumm — I am to day under the impresion that the note will not be paid, for want of the change — They Commenced to day to put Down the Floors to my new House, I saw Mr Thom Rose this Evening and mearly Out of a project asked him if he had $500 that he would Loan me and He said yes — and told me if I wanted it [to] come up at any time and he would Loan it to me, I gave him thanks and told Him should I want it I would Call with Greate pleasure &c. Parson Vaugn moves in Capt Dawson House next Door

22   I have been Quite Buisy to day to arrange a note of $500 that is Due from me to Isack Lumm — I went under the Hill and made an arrangement with Capt Cotten to take up a note of Mr Lumms for $187.49   I took up his note by giving him mine, I also took up an unsettled acct of His at Messrs Barlows & Taylors, the amount of which was $157   I am now having an Office fitted up under the Hill for Mr W A Britton and it will be Done to morrow — I took up a note of $37 against Mr Weldon to day from H. A. Cegwin to be Charged in acct &c.

23   Buisness Quite Dull. The Door Frames to Spielmans House was put up To Day. I Gave Mr Lumm the note that I took up yesterday at Capt Cottens, the Ammount of which was

187.49   Thus I have got rid of that much any how — I saw Mr Bledsoe to day and rented his House for Mrs. Michell at $33.50 per month, payable by the month

24   I Saw a race to day between Ben Aldersons bay Horse And James Bislands Black Horse, 500 yds for 500 Dollars   The Bay H. won the race by 2 ft and Some inches   I Gave my note to day to Messrs Barlow & Taylor for $84.44   It was a Debt of Isack Lums to Barlow & Taylor that I made the arrangement for in order to take up my note that Mr Lum has of mine — I was under the impression yesterday that the note was for One Hundred & 57.49 but it was for $84.44

25   I remained all Day at Home   Only took a Small walk in the afternoon with Mc

26   Buisness quite Lively — Isack Lum gave me Credit on the back of my note for $271.93

27   I have been quite buisy to day all Day in Diging Dirt out of my yard

28   Buisness getting Some what Better than was a few weeks ago

December 1   Messrs Carroll & Evans paid me one [month's] Rent of there Store in State Street to day $50

2   Buisness has been Tolerable fair for Such a Day. There were 50 men got Shaved To Day in my shop

3   Mr Sisloff paid me $50 that I Loaned Him on Saturday Last.

4   The Steam Boat Augusta was brought Down to Day by the Hail Columbia. She had Blown up Last night a few miles above this place, 49 Persons Shaved in my shop to Day

5   Fifty-six Persons shaved to Day in my shop

11   I paid in to Day One Hundrd and seventy four Dollars and 53 cents on my R. Road Stock — this makes $774.53 that I have paid in on my Stock, I moved Down to Mrs Battles This Evening

12   Nothing very Lively that I Know in the way of Buisness — I was prety buisness [busy] in Cutting out my Door in front of my House to get in my yard, I Sent a Letter to New Orleans to day by Mr Hanah to Mr Miller

13   Buisness has not been very Lively to day — I commenced this Evening to pave the Entry into my yard — Spielmans House is as high as the cornice of my House this Evening

14   I had the Last old Tree Cut Down off the pavement to

Day — Mr Spielman Takes Down The Scaffolds in front of his Building — They very near finished Ceiling my House to day

   15   Buisness was quite dull and nothing New that I Know of. There was a Town Meeting to night at the Court House for The Purpose of Nominating a Suitable Ticket for Sellect Men for the Ensueing year, The following Named persons was nominated, H. Gridley, J. Walworth, L. Picher, O Lane, H. Wood, R Parker.

   16   I was up to Mc Shop this Evening and He walked Down with me and Took Supper

   17   The Streets very mudy

   18   Mother Left for New Orleans To Day on the Bunker Hill

   19   Mr Kenney pd. me to Day his Rent to this Date, $35

1839

January 1   L. David Left off Shaving Here and so did H. A. Cegwin

   2   I went under the Hill to Day and paid Messrs Cotten & Jemison One hundred and Eighty nine Dolls and 12½, this being the amount of the debt that I asumed of Mr Isac Lum

   3   Buisness Quite Dull and nothing new. The Carpenters commenced puting up the cornice to my new store to day — I gave my note to day to Mr Hutcherson for 79 Dollars, payable in 70 Days after Date

   4   Buisness Dull, nothing new that I Know of   Dick takes Jim to night under the Hill, he has been runaway for two Days

   5   Col Bingaman, S Mucherson, Jdg Boyd and several other Gentlemen Left to day on the Steam Boat North Alibama for Jackson — Bill Nix Left on the same Boat, I paid Mr Weldon thirty five Down to Day on the Building

   6   I remained at home all Day, tho Nothing new that I know of

   7   The City Election Came of[f] To Day

   8   Nothing new that I know of Except that the Election for Mayor of the City Came of[f] To day and Mr J. A Lyle was Elected

   9   Buisness has been Tolerable Brisk   Mr Spielman moves Out of my Little Store this Evening

10   Mrs. Battles paid me one Hundred Dolls to day — I gave Mr Dyer $20 to day and ten the other Day for small nails which makes thirty Dollers that I have paid him on the plastering Bill

11   M. Rufner moves in my New Store to Day and His Rent Commences with me on the 26th inst

12   Mother Came up from New Orleans to Day and Brought Lizar with Her

14   I gave Mr Jno G. Taylor 100 in Commercial money for 100 in Branch Paper

15   Nothing new that I know of — I made an agreement with Mr Ruffner to Day to paint my new Store with three Coats of Paint for the Sum of Seventy Five Dollars And it to be taken Out in Rent

16   I had a Settlement with Mr Weldon to Day for the Brick Building that he put up for me. I paid him to day $1305 and I have paid him before $2070, which just Makes the Sum of [blank] Dollars — the full amount of our contract for Said Building — Paid Post Office Box Rent to Day $3.00

17   Quite Dull in the way of Buisness — To Day [a] Fight took place over at the Barlow Conner between Hary & Mr D. Gibson — After striking several Blows the Coward Harvy Drew Out a Large Bowie Knife and Stabbed Mr Gibson

18   I was to Day Out at the Sale that Took place at Mr Bradish, deceased, and Bot 1 Box of Burgundy wine and 1 Keg of White Lead and a young Cow Called Pidy — Her mark is Crop and under Bit on the right Ear and a Slope of the left, Ball Face, Large white place on her Hipp and another on her shoulder on the right side, white all under her Belly and on the inside of Each Leg, Small Horns and no Brand that I can see — She has had one Calf only and is young with another

19   I wrode out to day to the Braddish Plantation to try and Get the Cow that I Bot there on yesterday but did not drive her in yet   Try her on Monday next — Paid A. Marschalk for *New Yorker* up to the 11th of May Next

20   Buisness was pretty fair — Mc and Jno Jackomine and myself was Out this Evening shooting at the mark in the Minor Pasture — Mc won only 1 Bit from me and 2 from Jam and 1 Doz Segars, And I won 1.75 from Jackominee   I Beat him 2, 50 cent Matches — Oh I beat him Bad — Shure — Shore — Shuree

21   I sent Steven Out this moring Early to Drive in my Cow that I Bot a[t] the Bradish Sale and he did not get back untill Late in the After noon and I [had] to send John out for him and they

Both Came back to gether — I Let Mr Dyer have to day Seven Dollars — this makes thirty seven Dollars that I have paid him on the Plastering Job

22   Nothing new that I know of Except that I won 5 Cegars from Mc a shooting with a Blow-Gun this Evening — Mr Brown whiped Mr Jack Wright to night Down at the Conner near Dr Gwinns Residence

23   Business was Quite Dull — I was out in the Pasture this Evening shooting my Rifle and I shot very Badly   I Lost 1 Dollar shooting with John Jackomine   we shot 25 steps   He won Every Shot, 1 Bit — I could not Break in on the Paper on no part of the ground — Mc has his Rifle finished of[f] in Greate stile with silver pieces

24   My Little son William R. Johnson was Born three years ago this morning the 24 inst   He is three years Old to this Date — The Cols Boy John Came Down from Jackson to Day — Left Jackson Yesterday

25   Nothing new that I Know of   City Taxes — I Gave in my Property to day at those Rates — 2 town Lots, Value $12000 — 2 Houses, 3 Slaves — 2000 — the amount in full $14000, which is more in my Opinion than the Property would Bring at Auction in Cash — I was out this Evening to Shoot with my Pistol and I put two Balls in a Card out of nine shots

26   City Tax — I gave in Mothers 4 Slaves a[t] $1000 and Mrs Battles Property at $3000

27   Buisness was tolerable fair — I went out in the Pasture this Evening to Shoot the Rifle. Mc and John Jackomine Has a mach, 3 best in 5 or 2 best in 3, for One Dollar — And I had a Bet with Mc of 1.50 to 1 Dollar an 4Doz Cegars also, and John won with Ease

28   I paid my Rent to Day for the under the Hill Shop up to the 26th inst, [$40]   I paid Mr Bledsoe for Rent of the Mrs Mitchel House to Day up [to] the 26th inst, [$33.50]

29   To day Mr Ben Glasscock shot Col Austin that married the widow Glasscock on the other side of the River

30   To Day Mr Britton paid two months Rent of his office under the Hill, forty Dollars, up to the 26th inst — I Loaned Mr Elam fifty five Dollars to day in Good Bankable paper and silver together

31   Dr Davis paid me to Day fifty Dollars for One Years Rent of my Stable. His Bill was $37 and he paid me the Difference, 13 Dollars

February 2   Buisness not very Lively I thought   I paid Mr R. Parker To Day Eighteen Dollars 75 cents for measuring the work in my new Store, The Amount they made it was $748.87½   I paid Mr Dyer to Day ten Dollars on acct — I paid Mr Barlow 9 Dollars 30 cents for hair Powder

    3   Buisness was very Good to day untill 12 Oclock   After Dinner I went Out in the Pasture with my Riffle and there I found a number of men shooting — Floyd and Smith had a match for $50 and Smith Paid the forfeit and then shot a match for 5 Dollars and Floyd won it, 6 best in Eleven — After that I proposed for Floyd and Smith to Put up a Dollar and I would Put up one for John Jackomine, which was Done. John won it — then Mc went in — There was 4 in then — John won that   Then Mc won this one and John won the 4th Pool — Smith Backed out   Floyd won the 5th   I went in halves with John and I won $3 for my Part and he won $3 also

COPPY OF G. WELDONS CARPENTER BILL
Presented Feb. 4th, 1839

To Sundries Tarring Down of old Building	$20.
Labour on frame Building, 6 Days	20.
Lumber for &c. works	12.
Making Door frame Stuff & hanging Door	10.
To Sixty feet of Stuff for Alley	3.60
To forty four pairs but hinges, 2 Bits per pr	11.
5 Grose of Screws, 6 Bits Eash Grosse	3.75
To turning Counter Legs & hauling	5.50
One Keg of Nails	9.00
Scantling for Ceiling, 3 X 5, 340 ft.	10.20
Joist for floor Base, 3 X 10 X 80 ft 200	6.00
Stuff for Counter Legs & Crop Pieces, 100 ft	3.00
hauling the Same from Landing	1.00
Clear Cyprus plank for Shelving, Cornice &c. Ced [*sic*] 3108 ft	186.48
Sceling [ceiling] plank, 3 cts, 1500 ft.	45.00
hauling the Same	1.50

Lumber, Carpenters work on old house, building, hauling   hardware $348.03

Victorius Afer (C M) was an African and Flourished in A D. 360

    4   I Gave Mr Wel my note to day for One thousand Dollars, Payable twelve months After Date without interest   This morning I paid Mr Doyal on the Isack Lum Note $50 and he was to

Give me Credit on the back of the note   I Gave Winston a very Seviere Floging to Day for impudence and other Small offences that He Commited

5   Buisness has been Quite Dull indeed and nothing new that I Know of — I went under the Hill to Day and Got 2 Barrells of Coal and the Roads are in a very bad Condition for work — I Gave Winston & John to Day a comple[t]e Floging this morning for Going home Last night without Leave and for other small offences. Dr Hubbard sent me his Little Cannary Bird to Keep a while — with Birds   He Sent it Sunday.

6   Nothing new that I Know of   Carroll paid me his Rent, $50, to day up to the First inst

7   Buisness was very Dull indeed — M[iss] Routh Dowel was married to night to Esqr McClure

8   I paid Mr Doyal To Day fifty Dollars To be Credited on the Lum note   I paid Mr. Dyer to Day ten Dollars on his Plastering Account

9   Buisness was not brisk to Day by no means — Book Auction in Lillards New Building to Night — I paid for Coal 1.50 and for Corn the same to Day and I had it hauled up with my own Cart — The Road was in wreched bad Order

10   Shooting Match. Floyd V. S. John Jackomine, Dis 80 yds, $5, 3 Best in five. Floyd won with Ease   2d match with Pistols, 3 Entries at 2.50 Each,   John Jackomine, Mr Floyd, Mr Johnson, 2 best in 3 — I won the Mach with Ease and I then Shot a few Shots at 1 Dollar o pop with Mr. Floyd and we Broke about Even. Mc, John Jackomine and Mr Floyd Shot at a Dollar the Shot and Mc won five Dollars   Mr Weatherby pd me $3 for three months Shaving up to the first inst

11   Buisness has been Quite brisk   Josh Closed His Shop to Day   The Plasterer made a finish of Plastering to Day of my New House

12   Buisness has been very Brisk indeed on account of the Grand Parker Ball, I have had the finest Day in the way of Buisness that I have had for some time. I whiped Winston to Day again on account of his going Home to tell his Mother Lyes, &c

13   Buisness very good   I paid Mr Dyer & Brown to night fifty Dollars, also assumed a store account at Allens store for $19.50 which makes 69.50. This Deducted from the Amount I have paid Leaves a Ballance against me of Two Hundred and Forty Three and 33 Cents

14   Buisness quite brisk as yet Thank God, The Little

French Barber Opened Shop in Joshs old Stand in Wall Street. Mr Breden pd me twelve Dollars that I Loaned him a week or two ago

15   Dr Hubbard made a settlement with me To Day

16   Buisness has been very Good to Day. I went Out to the Race tract to Day and stayed nearly the whole afternoon out there. I made a greate many Bets of Different Kinds, and won in all forty One Dollars, twenty one of which was good, the other $20 of Aaberdeen Planters Bank

18   Buisness was only tolerable Brisk   Col Bingaman got Home to day from Jackson and broug[h]t Bill Down with Him — I pd Mr Doyl to Day Sixty on Account of Lum note, I also pd Mr Dyer to Day ten Dollars on acout of Plastering   William Johnson

19   I went Out in the Pasture this Evening to see the 2 matches between Mr Crossman and Mr. Conner. The one was 60 yards — Crossman won that and the other was 15 steps and Conner won that — I won 2 Dollars off Floyd with my Pistol

20   Buisness was more Brisk, Mr Winn was to see me on some Buisness to Day in regard to His sister and I told him what I thought of the Mater

21   Mr Robt. Smith Brought me His Little Boy to Day To See how I Liked Him To make a Barber Out of Him, The Late John Rex of North Carolina Died short time since and Gave fifteen thousand Dollars to Build an Infirmary for the poor sick of Reighla or Raleigh — All his Slaves, twenty in number, to be Emancipated and to be Sent, if they are willing, to Liberia Under the patronage of the Collonization Society — He has provided ample means for the purpose

22   To night is the Grand Ball at Parkers Hotel. The Manergers of the Ball are all Bigist Kind of Bugs. I pd to Day fourteen Dollars for 43 Razors to Day   I Bot them from Houghf at Sorias auction Room

23   Buisness of all Kinds very Dull. L David Paid me to Day the amount of his Shaving Bill for two years wich amounted to $42 including Box Rent, and cuting Boys hair in all made it $43.25   His Own account VS. me was $16 and I Deducted $3.25 for Lost time, which made his act 19.25, thus Left a Ballance in my favor of $24 which He paid — Enough Said

24   Bill Shooting To Day in The Pasture. I was winner to day, $15.50 on the Day

25   This was the Grand Elumination Day and Big Dinner Day

26   I pd. Mr Hamett his Rent of forty Dollars to Day for

shop under the Hill, $33.50   I paid Mr Bledsoe his Rent this morning for the House Occupied by Mrs Mitchell

27   I had three Little China trees set Out in the yard to Day

28   Buisness Tolerable fair   I wrode my old Gray Horse out to Mr Minors Pasture this Evening and to[ok] Several Shots with my Pistol and made 3 very good shots and I made four shots with McCary with Riffles and it was a stand off — He Beating and I Beating two

March 1   Buisness has been very good to Day   I paid a note to Day that I Gave Mr Pearce a Short time ago for some Glass Sash — $122.00   The note I found in the Commercial Bank and was Owned by Gilbert Morgan   I paid it and took up my Note. I Bot a pair of Pantaloons. I wrode Out in Minors Pasture this Evening. Took Several Shots with a Pistol and then we Shot for Liquor and I made a tolerable Shot. I then Shot for Mr Thayer and Caused him to Loose the Liquor, it was so Dark that I Could not see to take good Sight. It was hard to tell which it was that was the nearest to it, mine or Mr Bruins Shot

2   Buisness not very Brisk   The Boy Peter that has been with me 4 or five Days went Home and his Mother Brought Him back again an I told Her that she had better Keep him for I thought inpossible to Lern him the trade and She took Him Home again

3   Buisness was Quite Dull too for the Season — I went Out into the Minor Pasture in the afternoon   There were a greate many more from town out thare to Shoot for Thayers Gun, And I took a ½ Chance in her with Jno. Jackomine and He Lost it — The Gun was Won by a man by the name of Terrell or Therrel tho it was very Close between Floyd and Him   Wm Conner Took two chances, Mr. Floyd two Chances, and Jno Jackomine two Chances with mine and we Lost very Easy indeed

4   Business Quite Dull to Day — I made a Bargain to Day with Capt Dawson for the One half of the Party wall between us at $500 and I agreed to settle any small amount that he might be owing by way of a payment on the Same — I paid Barlow & Taylor to[o] on the Lum note, forty five Dollars and ten the other Day — I only owe them now on the note acct, $29.44

5   I have found it thus far very dull in the way of Buisness — Capt. Dawson Came to me and Said that He wished I pay Mr Dix the amount of an acct that He [had] VS Him which was $45 He thought, and also to pay Mr Clark $45 or some such amount of money and it would be credited on the wall acct between us — I saw Mr Dix and arranged the mater with him and I also saw Walsh

and agreed to pay the Clark Debt in fifteen Days — and it was all right — There was three or four old Frame Buildings Burned Down Last night over Back of Mrs Pilmores Residence and with them Her stable and Carriage House Burned also

7   I paid Mr S B Withers to Day on account of Mr Dyer the Plasterer, Forty Eight Dollars and 62½ cents. I went Out into Mr Minor Paster this Evening and Shot with Mr Lacrose, Mr Crossman, &c.

8   Buisness not very Brisk

9   Buisness was Tolerable Brisk. I Bot a good Deal of stuff at Auction to Day — Mr McAlister and Mr Williamson has a fight to night at W. store

11   I paid Mr Dicks To Day Forty five Dollars and 63 cents for Capt. Dawson — This is the first money that I have paid on the Wall — The sum that I was to give him was five Hundred Dollars for the Wall   I now Owe him Four Hundred and Fifty four Dollars and 25 cents on the wall

12   Buisness has not been very Brisk and yet I Collected from Mr Langly twelve Dollars and from Mr Gale $4.50, which pays there Bills to Date

13   To day there was a Public Dinner given to Col Wilkins at Parkers Saloon, The French Barber Broke up in the new shop in Lillards Building

14   Buisness was Quite Brisk. I paid Walsh, the officer, to day $49.41 for Clark, the Carriage maker, a debt of Capt Dawson — this and what I paid Dicks makes $95.16 that I have paid Capt Dawson on the wall

16   Buisness very Good

17   Buisness was pretty Good

18   Buisness very Good for the Season

19   Buisness good for Such times — I paid The House of E. Thomson & Co twenty nine Dollars, this being a Ballance of a note that I owed Mr Hutchison for a Lot [of] cigars that I Bot a Short time Ago for $79 and I paid Hutcherson $50 some time ago and the Ballance to Day to Thomson

20   I spent a good part of this Day at the Auction Room where the Marshall was Selling Out Mr O.Farrell and the Sherriff also, both at wonce

21   I spent a Good Part of the Day at the auction Room below at O Farrells Sale and Bot a number of things that I had have better Left alone

22 Mc and myself went Out into the Pasture to shoot with our Rifles and we made some good shooting

24 Buisness was tolerable good for the Season

25 Buisness very Good. To Day the Criminal Court Commences

26 I was this afternoon shooting out in Mr Minors Pasture with J. Lacrose, McCary and a Stranger whose name I know not

27 Buisness not so good as it was a few Days Ago — The Grand Jury finds a Bill against Mr McMikecheal for Raffling off his Characatures, he was presented by A L Gains — Mother paid me in two small payments in all $44 — She owes a Ballance of three Hundred and five Dollars

29 Buisness was not very Livily for the season

31 Buisness Quite fair, Parson Vaugn was Buried to day near 3 Oclock, very Large Procession indeed

April 1 Buisness was Tolerable fair and nothing new that I know of   Criminal Court Commenced I believe

2 I paid in the Sherriffs office to day twelve Dollars and fifty Cents, this being the Sum of Goods that I Bot at O. Farrells Sale, ie one Riffle and two Breast Pins

3 I made a mistake by saying that I pd for those yesterday, for it was to day that I paid for them Instead of yesterday — the above articles — Buisness has been Quite fair to Day. I was Out to Day, that is this Evening, in Capt Minors Pasture Shooting with my Riffle and I won Five Dollars from Mr Lacrose — We Shot 20 Steps Distance, I believe that I Can beat him, take our Shooting on an avariage, the shooting was pretty Good, what I Seen of His, tho I think mine was a Little better than His. There were Several others out

4 Buisness was Tolerable fair During the day ie for the Season

5 Buisness tolerable fair   This Evening Mr Willis and Mr Rouly Had a Small fight up at L. Davids store and about some Buisness and Mr Rowly knocked Mr Willis Down and was on him in an instant and they had to pull Him off

6 I pd Mr Izod $20 to Day on acct of Brown and Dyer, This makes One Hundred Dollars that I have paid him, this being the amount that I assumed on there acct

7 Buisness Good and Every thing Looked aright   I took a Bath in the Afternoon, then took a sleep and later in Evening wrode Out And Shot my Pistol at targets   Mr Willis sent a Challenge to Mr Rowley   Mr Rowley Excepts it, appoints the time, wepons, place, Hour &tc, Goes out and waits for Him untill some time after the Appointed time and Mr W. Did not Come and Mr R and Second Came in. Gen. Huston for Mr R. and Col Curl for Mr W

8   Buisness good in fore noon tho very Dull in the afternoon. Mc and mysefe played Sixteen Games at Marbles this Evening and He won ten Out of 16 and I have not been so tyred for some time As I am now from playing those Marbles

9   Buisness was Rarther Dull, I think, for the season

10   Buisness tolerable good — nothing new that I Know of. I pd Mr I Lum to Day ten Dollars on acct. of my note that he holds on R R Lot

12   Buisness Tolerable fair. I wrode Out this Evening and took my Pistol and shot at the mark. I did not make any Bully shooting at all, I thought

13   Buisness was very fair Early in the Day and Dull in miday   There were a Greate many Persons Left Town to Day to go out to Washington on the Cars To Dinner Prepaired for the Guards by the Ladies of Washington — This bids fair to be a very dull afternoon indeed

14   Buisness very Good. Several Baths &c   To Day I was to have Shot a match, the 6 Best in 11 for twenty Dollars, with Floyd. The Bet was made by Mr Dyer and I told him he had better pay the forfeit which was Done. I believe I then Shot a Small match, 3 best in five for Two Dollars and I Lost it

15   Mc Out practiceing with the Riffle in the Buyio as usual, and I at Home

16   Buisness tolerable good for the season   I pd. Mr I Lum to Day ten Dollars on acct. of my note. He seys that I Owe him a Ballance [of] twenty seven Dollars and some Cents. Thank Heaven have nearly pd. it all up — Arabs, I saw them last night at the Theatre for the first time

17   Buisness not so good as yesterday   To Day Mr Dykes pd. me One hundred Dollars for One months Rent of my Brick Store On Main St. and is the [first] Real money that I have got a hold of yet arising from the Rent of it. Mr Dykes moved in on the 2d of this month and has paid the Rent up to the 2d of May

18   Buisness good   The Adams Guards turned out to day for the first time with new Uniform — 3 Companies turned Out & Looked very well indeed

20   Large Sweep Stake Race to Day tho only 2 Horses Started, Capt. Minors and Col. Bingamans   Capt Minor won the Race very Easy indeed, tho 2 to 1 against the winning Horse   I paid Mr Dyer seventy nine Dollars on the Plastering Bill. This is the Last Cent I owe him on that or any other Score — I pd. Mr Isack Lum twenty Seven Dollars, it being the Last money that I owe Him on note

21 I wrode Out to Capt Minors Pasture Late in the Afternoon and I found a good many Out there Shooting John Greek Beet Floyd out of $4.50 Young Bledsoe Stabbs the Gardiner of His Brother and the Guards or Watch put him in the Guard House

22 Buisness has been very Good for the season, I cant Complain at all I walked Down in the Buyio this Evening and shot my Pistole 7 or 8 times and made very bad shooting indeed

23 Buisness has been very good indeed for the Season

24 I saw a Race to Day at the tract, 3 Entries. Capt. Minors Horse Duncaster vs. Banbox and Mr Garrisons Horse Lubber — 2 miles and repeat — They Came Out as they are named above

27 I Lost out of my Pocket about Fifty Dolls Some way or other on the tract

28 Buisness was tolerable good for the season

29 Buisness tolerable good for the season Tukesburry shot a Mr Ogg and Killed Dead Sure

30 Tukesburys trial came on to day and they were all day about it. Finelly Commited Him untill Court.

May 1 I paid on some day last week $10 to Mr Leafe for One years Subscription to the Spirrits of the time

2 Large Darkey Ball To Night a[t] Parkers Ball Room. Sportsman are Leaving here very fast on Every Boat, I Sent William the Key of the Shop under the Hill to day

3 Mr Gridley wanted me to Let him have the Bledsoe house, ie he wanted to rent it

4 Buisness was not very Brisk to day in town and I went Out to the Race tract and Saw·Several very good Little Races, Short Ones

5 Buisness geting Quite Dull Again — I remained Home all day, ie untill Late in the Afternoon I then wrode Out a Little piece in the Country

6 Greate number of Gents and Ladies went a fishing to Day on the Concordia Side — Swell H. Party given by Dr. McWilliams And Mr W. Smith

7 I went Over the River to Day Took Jno Jackomine and Winston with me

8 Buisness getting very Dull indeed. Mr. W. Britton paid me Sixty Dollars to Day, Rent of the Little office under the Hill, the

month Ending on the 26th ulto at $20 per month   Mr W. Harris pd. me to day for one years shaving Ending on the 15th inst

9   Not much Buisness a Doing of any kind — I paid Mr R Bledsoe to Day twenty Dollars for the House that I Rented from him up to Satd the 11th inst   I did Expect to have to pay him for the whole month which will End on the 26th inst., tho he did not require it of me   I pd him the 20 and Sent $13.50 to Mrs Mitchell as Her change.

10   Buisness not good for the season.

12   Buisness very Dull indeed, more so than I have Ever seen it I think.

16   I wrode Out this Evening on my old grey Horse and gave him a Brush or two after Kitty To Lern her how to start quick — I have got her in train[in]g for a Six Hundred Yard Race To Come off on Saturday next 18th inst for 20 Dollars a Side

17   Capt Course Called to see me to Day about my Lot and the Price of it   I told him $2000 and he agreed to pay my Rail Road Stock in and Give me a Ballance in two payments, ie in six and twelve months with good indorsers. I told him that I would take it and he told me that I might Consider it sold. Very well Sir said I and he walked out[1]

18   Buisness was Quite Dull for for the season. Nothing new that I Know of To Day Except that I had a Horse Race this Evening with John the Greek, 600 yds. for twenty Dollars and I Lost the Race very Easy by Bad management and bad wriding together

19   Nothing new that I Know of. I was Out to Day in the Pasture To Shoot tho did not have much fun

20   Buisness quite good for the time of year, Charles went Home to Day to see his People &c. Mr Harris sold his Lots ajoining mine   He sold five Lots for seven thousand five hundred Dollars

21   Buisness has been very good for the Season. I took in the shop to Day $17.50 by work alone I believe.

22   Buisness very Good for the Season   I Commenced to Day to Draw Out a Deed To Capt. Course for my Lot near the Rail Road and I will finish it I think to morrow

23   Buisness very Good for the Season   It was to Day that I herd Mr McFarren of Washington Telling Col Bingaman of the

---

[1] Isaac J. Course represented the Mississippi Rail Road Company. In 1836, Johnson had purchased the lot (now occupied by the Oil Well Supply Co., on the north corner of Canal and High streets) for $1,300, and he here sold it to the railroad for $2,000. Adams County Deed Records, Y, 209, BB, 206; and duplicate deeds in Johnson Papers. By 1838, Course was general agent of the railroad. Natchez *Courier*, November 28, 1838.

unmercifull treatment of Old Mrs Bellsinger To Mr B. Harmans
Little Daughter about 7 years Old — The Child is about To be Taken
away from Her now since she has treated it so badly   Here is the
Particulars as they were stated by Mr McFarren. It appeared that
the Child had missed going to School One Day and that Mrs B.
Told the School Mistress That She would Call and Take Her Home
in the afternoon and Take the Child Home and would Give Her
the worst whipping that she Ever had in her Life that night and
that in the morning she would whip her again and then send her
back to School by a Black Girl and requested the School Mistress
to whip her again. She did accordingly send the Child by the Girl
and when she arrived at the School House, the School Mss [mis-
tress] Examined the Little girl and Lo the Child was whiped and
cut from her feet up to the pole of Her neck — observed that she
Could not whip her any more for she was so badley abused — She
sent of[f] Ameediately for a Doctor and several other Gentlemen
to Come and see the Child and when they Came they Had the Old
Lady arested and the Result was that She had to give Bail for Her
appearance in the Sum of One thousand Dollars   Dempsey P Jackson went Her Bail and Col Bingaman took the children from Her.

    24   Buisness Tolerable Good for the season. Nothing new
that I Know of   Mcs in the Buyo as usual shooting at the Targets

    25   Buisness good for the Season. I dont wish [to] Grumble
by no means at the times — Mcs in the Bayou shooting as usual

    26   Buisness was very Dull indeed for a Sunday — I Took or
had my Riffle in the woods this Evening and there [were] seve[r]al
out there a shooting — Floyd, Mc, Rust, Jackomine, myself and
afterwards Easely B. Vaughn and E. C. I got to Betting on shooting and Lost One Dollar

    27   Miss Mandeville was married to Day to Oakly[2] about
1 Oclock and started in a Steam Bo[at] Directly afterwards and
started up the River   Col Bingaman went up on the same
Boat   William Broght up his Change to night and he had made
Only One Hundred and 19 Dollars

    29   Buisness not Good for the Season — I think Only 2 Baths
to Day — I Loaned young Bob. the Painter $5 and he gave me his
violin to Keep for him untill he Comes back from New York — The
Following Party was in the Bayou this Evening shooting, Mr W

---

  2 This referred to the marriage of James D. Oakley to Cornelia N. Mandeville,
daughter of Henry D. Mandeville, cashier of the Planters' Bank. Adams County
Marriage Records, VI, 334; Natchez *Free Trader*, May 30, 1839.

Howell, Mr E. Profilette, Mr J Lacrose, Mr Pinckerton, R. McCary, J. Soria, M Lindo, J Rust

30   Taxes   Taxes   Taxes   I paid Mr P. Baker To Day seventy seven and Fifty Cents for my City Tax for 1839. I paid Messrs L & Isack Lum To Day 25 Dollars for seting Grate a[nd] Laying five hearths in new building — Deed of Town Lot. I had my Deed acknoledged and signed by Mrs Johnson before Eqr. Robetile to Day and I then took it to the R. R. Bank and Left in the hands of Mr Owen, to be arranged by the Bank for me and he told me that it would be a right — (yesterday instead of to Day)

31   I paid Mr Baker to Day 8 Dollars and fifty Cents, a Tax on Charles alone — thats pretty tite   Buisness appears to Get worse instead of Better   I Cant account for it

June 2   Buisness Only Tolerable Brisk to Day   Capt E Miller Came Down Last night from Vicksburg.

3   Bill Nix went Out in the Country to get Medecine for Capt E Miller   I Took the acknoledgement of my wife to the Title of or to the Deed of the Lot that I sold to the Rail Road and then took it to the Bank and Left it with Mr Owen.

7   Buisness has been Quite Dull I Think tho nothing new that I Know of

8   Buisness Quite Dull for this Season of the Year — Particularly in the Bathing Line

10   Buisness as usual very Dull — both in shaving and Bathing

11   Buisness as usual, quite Dull and nothing New Except that I saw in a paper from New Orleans One of the Rascallys pieces that I have seen for som time Relative to the Pe of C [person of color] and a tryal of Jane Richardson who was Imprisoned for One year from 30th May — Good Lord what are things a Comming to. Mrs Dubison Died this Evening at Mrs Mellons Bourding House

12   Buisness no[t] So Good as I Could wish — Mr N Barlows Store was Closed Last Night by the Sherriff or Ma[r]shal, I dont Know which — The Dog Killer Killed poor old Spring this Evening in our yard

15   Nothing new that I know of — N. O. Picayune contains Larg account of the fire in New O the other Day, Property [lost] to the Amount of One Hundred Thousand, or more in fact, Dollars — pity, pitty

16   Buisness tolerable fair for the Season — Nothing new that I Know of

17   Buisness Quite Dull, Capt E. Miller left for Vicksburg on the Steam Boat St Louis — I noticed Mrs Prior on Bourd also with a very B. woman on Bourd him. Mr S. J. tried very hard to get on Bourd but the Boat Left him. I do not Know w[h]ere they were agoing at all — I find that if I had not been Down with the Capt. he would have missed his passage Sure, and no misstake — I Sent Mr W. Harris to Day 4 new Razors at 2 Dollars a piece and a Razors st[r]op at One Dollar, $9 in all. He did not pay me to Day no how

    18   Nothing new worth Attention — I find by being absent for a few minutes that as I returned Bill and Charles had a Black Girl at the Shop Door   Oh how they were Shaking Hands and Cutting up in Greate Friendship — Oh what Puppys. Fondling — beneath a Levell, Low minded Creatures. I Look on them as Soft

    19   Coming from Supper to night I [saw] Bill & Charles with a Big Nig Standing at the front Door as is usual when I am away — Oh what Low minded wretches   Mr W Harris Left to Day for the North

    20   Mr Lambdin Left to Day for the North

    21   Buisness has been Dull — Mr S Davis paid me $5.50 to night which pays his acct. up to the 1st of July 1839

    22   Buisness good for the Season   My third Son was Born to night near ten Oclock.[3]

    23   Nothing new that I Know of

    24   Nothing new that I know of   Jud[g]e Dunlap paid me to day five Dollars on acct.

    25   The New Store that I Built was Rented to Day by me to Col Waymoth at the Rate of One Thousand Dollars per anum, payable monthly — I Gave Him a Small instrument of writing to this Effect and wish it perfectly understood that I Rented it only for the One Year[4]

    26   I made a Bet to night that the Edward Shippen would beat the Sultana up to Lewisville ten hours in the run   The Bet was 6 months shaving against ten Dollars, made with Mr S Davis — Col Waymoth has the Carpenters at work to Day to refit the store to suite his Buisness — the work is Done by the Messrs Weldons   Mr W. Britton Leave to Day for the North

---

[3] This was Byron Johnson (baptized Benedict Biron Johnson), the diarist's third child. He died January 13, 1872. See two-column editorial on his death in Natchez *Democrat*, January 16, 1872.

[4] Colonel D. F. Waymouth (or Weymouth) occupied Johnson's new brick store on Main Street until December 16, 1840. In 1839, Waymouth reported sales of only $2,000, a very small figure compared to those reported by the large merchandising concerns of the town. Auditor's Records, Tax Rolls, 1840, Adams County.

27   Buisness Quite Dull for the Season   The Boys Commenced to Day for to Level or move the Brick in the new yard that is to be

28   Buisness not so good   The Boys was a part of the Day in puting up a fence in the yard

29   Buisness very Dull indeed. The Boys were nearly all Day puting up a fence in the next yard. Col Waymoth moves to Day in my new store on Main street

30   Buisness quite Dull indeed. About 12 Oclock to Day I started Down in to the swamp to look at the Old Grounds — I took a Riffle with me and I Killed 1 Beck Roach, 1 Blue Crane, 1 Beck Roch wing Broke, 1 Indian hen, 1 Large Aligater Badley woun[d]ed   Shot at him 7 or 8 times   Old Mrs Spruell shot her old man Harry and has ran away — Steam Cars ran over an old Black woman that belongs to Mrs Horn and mashed Both of her Legs of[f] — B. Edward Shippen beat the Steam Sult Anna [Sultana] to Louisville 17 hours in the Rund [run]. Ed. S made her trip in 5 Days, 23 hours, 40 minutes

July 1   Buisness dull — Old Man Irvin Died this Evening at his Residence

2   To Day The Sherriff was buisy in having the Goods hauld out of Mr Barlow Store for Debt — to be sold at the Court House — Old Mr Irvin was Buried to Day

3   Buisness Dull. Nothing New. The Dep. Sherriff was very much ingaged to Day in Selling of Mr N. Barlows Goods at Auction which I am very sorry to see — so much for the Practice of Indorsing for others — A Duchman by name Peter Smith Brought me a check on the Rail Road Bank for $80 to Keep for him untill morning — Given by Hicks & Arnold. I Gave the Duchman a Receipt for the Same.

4   Buisness only tolerable fair

5   Mc and myself wrode Down into the Swamp to Day to shoot Aligators and we went Down to the Alg. Lake tho we found no skift and we Came Back and found a Large Aligator in a Hole and we Killed Him   He was a very Large One indeed   I Killed 3 white Cranes, 1 Blue One, 3 Squirrells, 2 Snakes and helpt Kill the Big Aligator — Mc Killed 3 Squirrells, several Cranes, a[nd] he helpt Kill the Aligator

6   Buisness fair for the Season of the Year.

7   Mr Ruffner, Mr Whip and myself went Down into the swamp with Guns. Mr Ruffner wanted to Cetch froggs tho He Did not Get but 3 or 4 of them, they were so wild. Killed by Mr Whip, 1

Blue Indian hen, 1 white Crane, smaller One, 1 Frogg — Mr Ruffner, 1 Black Squirrel, 2 Large frogs, wounded, 1 Snake, caght 3 Aligators, Young Ones, with a Hook — I Killed 2 Squirrells, 1 white Crane, 4 or 5 young Aligators, 2 tolerable Large Snakes and 1 very Large one, water Mockersins, 1 frog. Mr Whip and myself Measured The Aligator that McCary and myself killed on Last Friday and it measured thirteen feet Long

8   Buisness has been qite Dull indeed so far. Rail Road Bank Opened this morning in the new Banking House opposite me on Main Street — Mrs McAlister has a Little Daughter. Last Night I tapt John and Winston over Heads for sticking pins in a water mellon

11   To Day has been a Remarkable Dull Day in my Line of Buisness in Particular — To Day it was that I took up my note that Mr George Weldon held — I owed Him a Ballance of Eight Hundred Dollars which I took up in this way — I Gave him a Note on the Rail Road Banking Company for three hundred and sixty four Dollars, which he took, and I Gave him a note on Messrs Wood [and] Metcalfe for Three Hundred and nineteen Dollars, which he took — I then Gave Him in Cash One Hundred and seventeen Dollars which makes the Eight Hundred Dollars which He held against me, as a Ballance on One thousand Dollars that He had my Note for. William T. Johnson

12   This has been a Dull Day in the way of Buisness — Mr V. Boyers Little Son Died Last night — I paid the sherriff thirteen Dollars and five Bits for 14 Boys Shirts, 27 pr sissors and ten Razors straps

13   Buisness is as might be Expected, very Dull — Phillips the Tavern Keeper has a fight with a Little Bar Keeper and the Little Fellow has him Down and nearly Bit a piece Out of his under Jaw or Neck and whiped him from what I can Lern — this happened the other Day — Mr Gimmy Kane reports old man Tooley for Exacting Spiecie or its Equivilent — Long article — Bill Nixs is up to this Day a pure pure Negro at Heart and in action, &c.

14   Buisness, oh very Dull indeed   I have managed it so as to Let $19.08 pass throgh my hands for One thing or other   Mother paid her Taxes to Day which was fifteen Dollars

15   Buisness has been very Dull,   I have spent the $19.08 for One thing or other which I throuh mistake put Down as yesterdays work. I Bot some plank Under the Hill the other Day and I went under the Hill this morning to get it and the Rascally Boatman Could not then spare the time to get it off

16   Buisness was pretty fair. I wrode Down to the Byou this afternoon to shoot my Pistoll and I found a Good many Citizens Down there   Mress Izod, Munce, Howell, McGowan, McCary, Harrison, Studson, Soria, Basinet, Lindo were all Down theare shooting with Riffles — Box of Segars and [a] ten Dollar pr Boots was Bet between Mr Muncie, McGowan — Munce won them Easy

17   Mr Howell and Mr Izod was to have shot a Match this Morning — a five Oclock Match, $10 forfeit, twenty five. They met and shot and Mr Howell won it

18   Nothing new that I Know of in the way [of] Buisness — nothing

19   I was in the woods the greatest part of the Day

20   Nothing New worth writing about To Day   Dull in the way of buisness

22   Buisness Quite Dull

27   Not much Buisness Going on in my line of Buisness

30   Buisness quite fair

August 1   Buisness good for the Season   We Herd that the Vicksburg volunteers would not be Down untill Tuesday next   Whig Speech to Day from Mr Reubin Davis[5] and One from Col Bingaman

2   Buisness not so good. A fight to day at Profilets Conner between Mr Barber and a Dr Ager — The Little Fellow got the Best of the fight. He stabbed the other 5 or 6 times with a Dirk

4   A Seviere wind in the afternoon tore my arning [awning] Considerably. Charles the Boy of Mr Armets Boy Came Down the River this Evening. Mrs Steuart has a Girl Baby that cannot do well — we Sent a girl to Draw her Breast. Nothing new that I Know of

6   A day of Greate Excitement in town. Vicksburg Volunteers Came Down from Vicksburg on a visit to see Our Town and people

11   Buisness Quite Fair for the Season   Catharine Lieper Died To Day or this afternoon

12   Buisness Quite Good   Catharine Lieper was buried to Day. They had a Very Large Procession Indeed

13   Buisness Dull to Day   Wm Takes Hold of the under the Hill shop to Day — Several Gentleman told me to Day about [how] Rascally and Dirty William Kept the shop below the Hill

---

[5] Reuben Davis was a lawyer, soldier, congressman, and author of *Recollections of Mississippi and Mississippians* (Boston, 1890). Not one of his more than 200 clients accused of murder went to the gallows.

and said if he Did not do better that they would run him off from Down thare

14   Buisness has been Only tolerable — Nothing new that I Know of — Little James Ker was Buried to Day — Dr Ker's Son — Young Man Murphy is now in the Hospital with Mania a portia,[6] too much Liquor Sure   I Loaned Mr Jno. G. Taylor Fifty Dollars to Day

15   Buisness was tolerable fair in the Bathing Line   Batchelor Left the Rail Road and has Opened a Grocery store Out On the Rail Road

16   Remarkable Dull in the way of Buisness   Cinta Lieper Came to town to day from Jackson, Miss

17   Buisness Tolerable Fair, Baths Tolerabl good   I Loaned Mr Jno G. Taylor Forty Dollars to day   He had just paid me fifty Dollars that I had Loaned him the day before yesterday — Crist and Mr Jno G. Taylor both came in my shop to night and they Both were Funny

18   Buisness Tolerable fair, Wellington[7] was in my Shop to day and worked untill 12 Oclock   I remained at home all Day ie untill Late in the Evening. I then took my Little Son Wm and we wrode out beyond the Briars Residence — Willington and Mrs Battles wrode Out in a Hack to the Miss Eveanss   Old Mc wrode Out on his Sick Horse to day in a Dirrection towards Dr Sam Gustines   Tis the first time that he has wrode his Horse for Eight months — the Hors has been Sick

19   Very Dull in the way of Buisness — Mr Thomas Evans wal[k]ed over to Esqr. Robertiles office to Day and made othe [oath] to Wellingtons being a free Born Boy &c.

Natchez August 16, 1839

To all who it may Concern. I do hereby Certify the Bearer of a Mullato Boy named Wellington West is a free Boy Born Free in Natchez in the year One thousand Eight hundred and Seventeen — His Mother was a woman of Black Complection named Judy West — was free and Lived in Natchez many years before her Death

William Parker

---

[6] Johnson meant *mania a potu*, madness from drinking, or delirium tremens.

[7] This was Wellington West, free mulatto, who worked intermittently in Johnson's barbershop. Son of Judy West, free woman of color, he was born in Natchez about 1817 and in 1841 was licensed by the Adams County Police Board to remain in the state. He also appears to have traveled up and down the Mississippi River with considerable freedom, probably as a barber on a steamboat.

I with pleasure Concer in the above Certificate
                                        Noah Barlow
        also do I

                                        J G Taylor
State Miss
Adams County   Personally appeared before me the under-
signed Justice of the Peace in and for the County of Thomas L.
Evans & made Oath that has Known the Bearrer of this instru-
ment of writing & certificate for many years back   Since then
I hav always Known him to be a free man of Couler and was
born here in the City of Natchez and Born a free man to the
Best of my belief and his name is Wellington West
        Sworn to & Surscribed before
        me this 19th August 1839   Thos L Evans
        L Robetaile   J P

20   Prehaps the poorest Day we have had for some time both
in the way of work and Bathing too, Old Mr Isrial Leonard Died
yesterday Out at his Residence

21   Buisness has been better, no Baths to Day. No news of
any importance to Day — The Town is perfectly Healthy up to this
date, Thanks To Heaven for it

22   Buisness Continues to be Dull in our way   Mr Noah
Barlow was announced in this morning as a Candidate for the office
of Clerk of Circuit Court — Mr Sam Wood also, the Present In-
cumbent   This man Carpenter, N L., was telling me a Long story
about his settlement with Capt Nevitt — a whole parcel of stuff —
Mr McCuller was married to night to Mrs Perkins, widow of C
Perkins Deceased   Mr R. Ayres is married to Miss McCrary,
Daughter of old Dr McCrary

23   Buisness has been so very dull, oh what are the times a
Comming to. Nothing new that I Know of To day. Old Nancy
Jerado daughter is I am told Kept by Robert S———— of this
place   Old French pays a Short and his Last visit to night — So
he Seys. God Knows how true. They are all a pack of Strump —
What I thought they was

24   Buisness as usual Quite Dull! Wellington Denies wriding
with Old Nancys Daugters in the Charterd Hack

25   Buisness not very Brisk — A Steam Boat Came Down
from Vicks Burgh, the Partrick Henry — Messrs S S Prentis, Judg
Pinkard, Mr Jones, Dr Dauson, Mr Cox and several others of
note   Wellington West Left Natchez in the same Boat for Orleans
— Armatts Charles died yesterday I am told

26   Buisness Dull as usual   Parson, the Brick Layer, whiped the Dog Killer To Day for shooting His Dog — oh he gave him a Compleate Pounding — I wrode out this Evening to the Byou and shot 11 times with my Pistol

27   Buisness was Dull as usual   Nothing New. I walked Out into the Byou this Evening and shot a match with John Greek, 6 best in Eleven, for a pair of Shoes. Cost $3.50. He was to shoot a riffle 60 yds and I a Pistol 15 yds. He won the match very Easy — He made his match in 1½ Inch and I mine in very near 4 Inches — I Lost also 25 cent worth of Cigars and 3 Bits in money, 20 Steps with his own Riffle — he shot 3 Balls through One hole and I was no where — So we Stopt at that — I Shave the Hon. Mr Prentiss to Day — The Fellow that was put in Jail for Robbing the Pole under the Hill forced by the Jailoress and ran Down into the Byou this Evening — but was followed by Mr Boyer & Rablees and the Jailors Boy — the former and the Latter Caught Him and Brought him Back — I paid my Rent to Day of the under the Hill Shop, $20, to Mr Dashutte and took his Receipt   My Red Bird was Killed by Mick Last night

28   Buisness very Dull. My Cows Calf Died Last night   Dr Davis, Yellow Feaver &c. To Day the report all through town is that we have yellow fever in town, reported by Dr Davis — One of the Cases Died at the Hosspital yesterday with Black Vomit — One or two Families Left town to day — Jdge Black for One. Mr I P. Smith is moving to day out of the Briars place

29   Buisness not worth talking about. The man that was yesterday reported to have had the yellow fever is, I am told, walking about to day — I wrode Out to the Byou this Evening and I Saw all those Gentlemen in their Shooting, Messrs. E Profilett, W. B. Howell, C Larcoste, J Soria, R McCary, L Griffin, S B Stutson, T. Munce, Juliene, I Lacrose, Young Lacoste and several others that I do not Recollect, They had good Liquor, Soda Buiskets &c.   I made a match, best 6 in 11 in about 2 inches 1 quarter, 15 Steps — I went Security for the appearance of Whip at the next October term of Court in the Sum of two hundred and ten Dollars

30   Buisness Quite Dull as usual and nothing new that I Know of Except that Kenney and Whip has a fight about their Books — Particulars as far as I have herd — Whip and Sulivan was Partners in the shoe makeing Buisness — They both, it appears, sold Out or bargained to sell Out to said Kenney for thirteen hundred Dollars, $650 Each — Well it seems that when Whip and Sulivan Commenced Buisness that S put in $400 and Whip $280   Well S. sued

Whip for the Difference which was $120 tho it appears that when
Whip sold out or pretended to sell Out that it was to get rid of
Sulivan so . that Whip and Kenney Should go into buisness to
gether   Well Whip became alarmed at being sued by Sulivan &
took the advice of Kenney, so he told me, and to prevent Sulivan
from getting a hold of his Propperty takes and makes a Bill of Sale
to said Kenney   Kenney then Came Out in the Free Trader and
states that he as an agent for Jackson of Louisville, Ky, had Bot
the Entire Interest of said Whip & Sulivan and notified the Public
to make Payment to him, Arther Kenney — Whip sees the advertisement in the Paper then Demands a settlement with Kenney
which K. refused to do, then refused to give a note — Whip then
takes the Key out of the Door and Kept it. Kenney then put around
the House and went in the back way and forced open the front
Door and took and has possession and has it yet   I as Indorsed or
was Security for Whips apearance to 2d Monday in October — I
got off by paying Sulivan Seventy Dollars for him to Dismiss the
Suit against Whip which he did — and I took a receipt from
Sulivan for the same — I then took a note from Whip for the Seventy Dollars that I paid Sulivan for him the said Whip
    31   Buisness not very Brisk — Nothing new that I Know
of   I went Down into the Byou this Evening and shot several times
with a riffle, Basanets Rifflle, and I got Beat very Easy by Jno Jackomine, 3 Shots to his 2 — half doz Cigars was the Bet and I won
them off from Mc so I quit Even at Least — I got a Letter to night
from W West of New Orleans & that he has Bot me the Razors
that I wrote for at 7 Dollars per Dozen   There was an Allarm of
Fire to night about supper time tho turn Out nothing. It was at the
Office of a Maj Street in State St — it Burned some paper or Books
or something Like that

    September 1   Buisness not very Brisk as usual — This Morn-
ing was a Greate time among the Baptist People — Old Mrs Bon-
durant & a Miss Woodfork and three of the Miss Thomases were
all Baptised in the River Just below the old Fort & in the afternoon
there were Sixteen Darkeys Baptised at the same place and by the
same man — Mr Bradley — the 16 Darkeys were all Baptised in the
time that he Baptised the 5 Ladies in the Morning
    2   Buisness dull — nothing new — Yellow fever Still very bad
in New Orleans[8] — I went this Evening in to the Buyio in Company

---

[8] For reports on the yellow-fever epidemic in Natchez and New Orleans, see
Natchez *Free Trader*, various issues in September, 1839.

with Mc & Basanett to shoot with Pistols and they had their Pistols and I Beat them all with Ease — Mc has a Large Pistol of P. Michells and I Descover in a short time that he will be very hard to Beat with it — I Reced One Letter from Mrs Miller to day — Mr A Kenney assumed the amount that Mr Whip Owed me — Seventy Dollars

3   Our town is very healthy at present and we Lern that the Sickness is much worse in Orleans instead of a change for the better — God help them for I cannot

4   Buisness Dull — I had a match to Day with Jno Greek for a pair of shoes — 3 best in five with Pistols — and I won the shoes Easy — not so Easy Either for we had to shoot a good many times more than the match — Mr Spelmaman gave his note to day for 170 dolls, 60 Days after Date

5   This Morning about 3 Oclock I was awakened by the Cry of Fire, Fire — I got up and ran with all possible Speed and found The Fire Burning on a stable up in Cotten Ally formily Kyles Ally — it then spread Out in Different Dirrections and both Sids of the Ally was on fire at the same time — I comme[nc]ed to work on the Cotton that was in the shed   With the help of others got it all out and at Least the One half Burned up afterward. It Burned Down the following Houses — Messrs Jacob Sorias, 2 Story Ware House, Messrs. Stanton, Buckner & Com 2 Story Commission & Ware house, also their Large Cotton Shed[9]

6   This morning or Last night we had the alarm of Fire Given. I got up and ran with all possible speed and found it to [be] Mrs W B Howells Dwelling House with stores underneath all on a full Blaze. I at wonce thought that my Little Effects would be Burned up without Doubt for the then Fearfull Element had the appearance of Breaking Out on Main St. I was for a time so bewilder that I Could not Commence to work at first. The Fireman of the City in this Case did perform wonders. They Extinguished the fire when for a Long time no one could have Reasonably hoped such a thing. The People are very much Jaded from the Labour Done Last night

---

9 The Natchez *Free Trader*, September 6, 1839, gave a complete account of the "Disastrous Conflagration." The fire destroyed a large number of stores and brick warehouses in the block bounded by Pearl, Franklin, Commerce, and Main streets, which was perhaps the most valuable business area in Natchez. None of the stores facing Main Street were destroyed, although many of them were on fire at various times. Included in the list of buildings burned were the "large noble brick commission store of Stanton, Buckner & Co. with cotton-shed attached" (loss about $15,000); the warehouse of Jacob Soria & Co., auctioneers (loss about $25,000); the store and family residence of John R. Stockman (loss about $12,500); and the boardinghouse of Mrs. Cornell (loss about $22,000).

by them at the other fire   Thank God I have wonce more Escaped, wonce more from Distruction[10]

7   Large Barbacue and Shooting match this Evening out at Washington on this fore noon — Greate many Persons Out theare I am told

8   Buisness good   Report Seys to night that there were 4 Deaths of *Yellow Fever* in Our Hospital to day.

9   Considerable Excitement about the Cases of Yellow Fever that occured Yesterday at the Hospitle and tis Said that there are ten or fifteen Cases of Sickness now at Different Places under the Hill — I insured my new Brick House to day at the Natchez Insureance Company in the sum of three Thousand Dollars, 1½ per Cent, in all $46.50[11] and whilst at the office I saw a map of the Swamp and on the Map the Entrys Read thus — Jeremiah Hunts Entry of 670 Acres, Now Geo Winns — Washinton Sargents Grant —

Philo Andrews	321
P Andrews	176.60
P. Andrews to F Winston then to Geo Winn	556
P Andrews	58.90
Geo Winn	280
Jno Fletcher & Stockman	188.59
Benj Farrar	[blank]

10   Nothing New that I Know of — I Saw at a Distance this Evening a Fire in the Country oft to the right of Washington — I Commenced a Letter to Day to my Sister — first for a Year I believe

11   No new Casses of Sickness to Day that I have herd of. G. Baker, Judge Dunlap, N Barlow, S Woods, Mr Izod & Doubison have all got home this Evening. They have been Electioneering in the Lower End of the County.

16   There has been Consideral talk of Yellow Fever throughout the whole City to Day — *5 Deaths*

17   Several persons or Famlies has Left the City for the Country   I wrode Out myself to the Quigless place to See how

---

[10] The second fire apparently started from the smoldering ashes of the previous one. It was extinguished with minor damage to the store of William B. Howell on Commerce Street.

[11] Natchez Insurance Company Fire Policy No. 398, September 9, 1839, certified that Johnson paid the premium on "a three story brick house situated on the North side of Main Street between Wall and Pearl Streets, Natchez, occupied by D. F. Waymouth." Johnson Papers.

it would Suit to Live out thare in Case of much Sickness in town.[12] I Gave McCary to day 200 Dollars to get small Bills for it was Rail Road money — There were *three Deaths* in the City to Day

18   Six Months Post notes are Just Due to Day and there is the Bigest Kind of a Crowd in the Office Carr[y]ing of[f] the Cash — *5 Deaths* To Day — I got J. Whip to give me and order or Draft of Mr A Kenney for the Seventy Dollars that Whip owed me on the money I paid for him in the office for Sulivan.

19   No buisness a Doing of Any Account — All sorts of a run on the Rail Road Bank both to day and Yesterday for specie.[13] The People are Leaving town very fast to Day for fear of Yellow Fever   *No Deaths* in the City to Day — Yesterday Dr Lyle was appointed Health officer, in the absence of Dr Hubbard, by the Selectmen[14]

20   The Health of Our City is Better to Day I think. Young Jams C. Wilson *Died* this Evening — Dr Hubbard arrived Last Night — has been absent 2 weeks — he is Health Officer — A Kenney pd. me his Rent to day

21   Buisness tolerable for the season — I Bot a Gun or a Rifle from Mrs Vaugn and Gave her seventeen Dollars for it. I went Out and shot her several times and made better shooting at the Commencement than I did 'afterwards — The fact is I Cannot shoot a Riffle worth a cent

22   Buisness not very Good. People all Leaving the City very fast to Day. Mr *Coddingten Died* this Morning.

23   Citizens are fast Leaving the City — I too made up my mind to Leave the City too. I sent Out a Load of small things

24   Buisness was quite lively for the times — Mrs Vaugn Left the City to day and I bot a Sadle and Bridle and Marting Gale [martingale] from her for five Dollars — I moove out to the Quigless Place to day — Henry Austing Drove the Hack with my Family and I came out on Horse back

25   I am in the Country Sound as a Dollar   It was near 9 Oclock to night that I saw from the Country a Large fire Given Light from Natchez and I mounted my horse and in a few minutes

---

12 It was a common practice for Natchez families to move to the country until a yellow-fever epidemic had passed. On December 2, 1839, the Natchez *Courier* stated that "the greater part of the population left the city" during the period from early September until the middle of November.

13 The Natchez press did not comment on the run upon the bank.

14 The Natchez *Free Trader*, September 20, 1839, carried a short note on the yellow-fever epidemic: "We shall take no responsibility by giving advice (on leaving the city) and shall still be most happy to disappoint those who would seem to be dissatisfied that we do not report 'a smart chance' of deaths every day."

was in town and found, I am Sorry to say, One of the Larges Kinds of Fires on the Hill in State Street[15]   It was Yesterday Evening that I took the First Gun to Hunt on the Qui[g]less Place and in a few minuets I found and Killed two Bacbons — in fine Order they were in

26   I was in the Country from 11 Oclock untill night — Mr Charles Sweney Died to Day in Natchez   Mr N Green *died* to Day

27   I am Still in the Country. Several of Our Citizen Died to day — Mrs Battles Came Out to Day to see us in the Country   A Lieper Came Out to Shoot Riffles with me and I beat him with all Possible Ease   He Cant Shoot at all

28   I Sent a note into Mr Izods to inform him that Mr Smith had hauled a Load of Plank from the place in the Country and had sent for another and I refused to Let it go — His Answer to me was to Let no One tresspass on the Premises what Ever &c.

29   Charles was taken sick this morning — Good many Casses of Sickness in town to Day — The woods was set on fire to day by some One and I Cannot find Out by whom

30   This has been a Dull Day. I sent for Dr Davis to See Charles to day as he was not Any Better

October 1   Dr Davis Came Out to day to see Charles and thought him a greate Deal worse than when he saw him yesterday — Mr Dan. Barlow Came over and I Cut his hair and shaved him, over at the Old Quigless Place — I shot a match to day with Mr Purnell and beat him Easy — he Complained of the Guns being Dirty — I wrote a Letter this Evening to Maj Young to inform him how dangerously ill Charles is. Several Persons out to set up with Charls to night

2   Thanks to a Kind Providence that Charles is still

---

[15] Late in September, 1839, the building formerly called "The Southern Exchange," owned by Johnson's mother-in-law and managed by him, burned. But unless the fire noted in this entry recorded the event, Johnson did not mention it in his diary. The Natchez *Free Trader*, October 7, 1839, described "the fire a week since, which consumed the square bounded by State, Canal, Washington, and Wall streets" (the block in which the house stood). Johnson was outside the city during the yellow-fever scare of this period—which may be the explanation of his failure to record his loss. In any event, the building, which had cost nearly $3,000 to construct, was covered by insurance to the extent of $2,000. On March 7, 1840, the Natchez Insurance Company paid him the full amount of the policy, and before the end of the year he began to rebuild. Natchez Insurance Company Fire Policy No. 208, September 20, 1837; William Johnson to Natchez Insurance Company, December 2, 1839 (copy); Day Book, 1830–40, entry for March 7, 1840, Johnson Papers.

alive   Dr Davis was Out to see him to day and says that his Case is a very Criticle One yet — Wm Came Out this Evening Late to See Charles

3   Nothing new that I Know of — Mc wrote me a small Letter from town — I took a wonderfull hunt to day around about the Hills and Killed nothing at all — yes one old Buzzard for amusement. I cant find any game Out here myself

6   I took Winston and John and my gun and went into the Swamp to Hunt — I Killed 1 Owl, 3 sap suckers and 6 squirrells — Winston only 1 sap sucker, 1 yellow Hamer — Mr Paine Killed 15 squirrells and Mr D Barlow 4 — I only went Down about 11 Oclock in the day

8   Mc Came Out to see us to day

9   Mr Purnell, myself and Bill Nix walked down into the swamp to day to Hunt — Mr P Killed 1 squirrel and 1 poor dove and 2 Partrigees — Bill Killed 1 poor Jay Bird and I Killed ten squirrells and 1 more that I did not get — The Best hunt I ever made in the swamp in squirrells — Mr P wounded a Large Wild Cat with small shot — I took my Little Gun and walked up the Road and the first thing I saw was a very Large Rattle Snake — I shot him and Brought him Home and skined it and saved the Oil from it and in an Hour or two after Bill and Winston went Out and Killed Another, 12 years and a ½ old, the Same Age of the other — I did him in the Like maner — Nothing new that I Know of. Late this Evening I shot a Partridge — first One I have shot since I Came out here

10   Mr Purnell, myself and Winston, Bill Nix and John walked Down into the swamp to Hunt Pukons [pecans] and Squirrells — we went Down after Breakfast — Mr Purnell Killed 7

Mr. Johnson	do	13
Winston	do	5
		—
		25

John and Bill Nix Killed 1

11   I wrode to town to Day and Staid an hour or two — Came back and took dinner, then went below [at] ½ past 3 Oclock and Killed 2 Squirrells and Mr Purnell went into the woods Early to day and Killed 13, and his Boy 1

12   Nothing New that I Know of — After Breakfast this morning Mr Purnell and myself went into the swamp to Hunt and

we had rarther Bad Luck   Mr Purnell Killed 5 and his boy Caught 1 and I Killed 3 and Winston 3 — I got a few Pecons

13   Nothing new that I Know of — Bill Nix went in town to day to work and did not come out this Evening as I thought he would. I Let my Horses both go Loose this Evening and the[y] ran off and went to town by way of the old Field

14   I arose this morning Early, took my Riffle and went in serch of my Horses   I went through to the old Field to the Main road, then Sent the Boys through town and they found them at the shop in the yard — I shot 1 Patridge and 1 Grey Squirrell

15   I have been too sick to Hunt or go about. John Jackomine, French and Winston all went into the swamp to day to Hunt and Greek Killed 1 Squirrell and 1 Partridge, French 3 Sap Suckers, Winston 1 do — they went below Winns Field of Corn — the[y] are poor marks man — Last night I took a Dose of Calomell — the first I have taken for years — thank be to God for it

16   Nothing New that I Know of — I am quite unwell my self at present and has been for seveeral Days. I walked Down in a Deep Byou to Day and read a Book, the Life of Danial, through before I Came Out again

17   I have been on the point of taking medicine to day several times, tho thank be to Heaven, I am so far able to do without it — Mrs Battles and Jane walked out this morning Early to see us

18   About dinner time to day I took Charles, Winston and Mr. Blaker and both of the Horses and went th[r]ough the thicket into the Swamp to Get Pecans — We were much bothered in the thicket an of course did not get many — I feel 50 per ct better than I did yesterday, thanks be to the Giver of all Good — Mrs B. and Jane walked back to town this morning Early

19   I, Charles and Winston went Down to the Pecon trees to day or this Evening rarther, to get Pecons tho we got very few — We got into a thicket and it plaugeed us for some time to get out

21   Mr Purnell and myself went down into the swamp to day — we started Late —We Shot nothing worth any thing. He killed several Large gars and A Crane and I Killed two also, Gars, and I Killed 2 Large Snipe in Muddy Lake and then we Could not get them

22   Several new Casses of Fever in Natchez to day — I was buisy to day Cleaning my Rifles and Shot Guns and I Oiled them with Rattle Snake Oil

24   Mr Purnell and myself went into the Swamp to hunt   We went Down to Mr Mosbys — Jno the Greek was along

too — We Killed no Deer that day tho Greek, myself and Winston say [saw] two together — Gregory was along and Killed a Large Aligator in Mudy Lake and I Cut about 30 pounds of fat Out of it — there were 5 or 6 aligators Killed by the Crowd, Composed of 6 or 7 of us

25   I remaind home all Day with the Exception of wriding Over to Mrs Smiths to Cut hair   I cut hair for Eligah Smith and for Dr McWilliams

25   I wrode over to day and cut the [hair] of Young Williams and Mr R. Patterson and another Young Williams   Dr had Killed a aligator 24 ft Long and his Brother had Killed a Hog in Our Swamp that weighed 600 pds   They Can take my Boots

27   I remained Home all Day — went no where but down to the Creek to water the Horsses — Kitty Fisher th[r]ew Buckes and came very near Hurting him   Mc, The Star Shooter, Came Out here to day and after dinner we Commenced to shoot Riffles and we Shot Eight matches and here is the way they Came off — 2 best in three   they were — Mc Only win 1, Mr Purnell 3 and myself 4 — I beat the Crowd with my old Gun   We beat him bad when he shot before   No, no, to day I mean

28   Mr Purnell made me an axel tree to my water cart and help to fill in several pieces in the wheel

29   Mr Purnell and myself went Down in the swamp to day To Kill Aligators — We Killed a Good many of them   We shot 3 in Muddy Lake and three in there or near holes. 2 of them in a Lake on the other side of Aligator Lake and 1 on Aligator Lake and a Good many in Aligator Lake. I Killed a Squirell, 2 Snipe and Winston Killed 1

30   Mr. Purnell and myself took the Boys and went down into the swamp to get the fat from out of the Aligators that we Killed yesterday   We got the fat out of three of them — We went on the Back side of Aligator Lake, also the One next to it

November 12   I wrode through Col Bingamans plantation to Day and others to see the Race and there was none — Capt Minor paid the forfeit to the Col[16] — From the tract I went to town   I

16 On November 11, 1839, the Natchez *Free Trader* carried a lengthy announcement of the races at the Pharsalia Course, lauding Colonel Bingaman as "the king of our grounds" and listing other prominent racing men, including Minor, Claiborne, Railey, Elliott, and Scott. The *American Turf Register and Sporting Magazine*, X (1839), Appendix (Racing Calendar) for 1839, 64, reported the Natchez races of November 11–16. On the first day the sweepstakes was won by

Bot a Hat and staid a short time in town, then left and Came out to Mayorka Place

    13   I remained Home all Day and was not Buissy of Course

    14   I took an Early Breakfast this morning and wrode to town and staid thare untill near 2 Oclock, then Came out. I met John and Winston with a wheel Barrow taking my Birds to town

    15   I am still out at the old Quigless Plantation

    17   To day I took the boys and went into the Swamp and I Killed one of the Largest Kind of an Aligator in the Aligator Lake . He was a Buster in any Country, I tell you — Winston and John went along

    18   I Commenced this morning to moove in from the Country to the House on Wall St owned by Mrs Richards   I moved all my things in to day safe and without any Loss or accidents

    19   I arose this morning Early and went to my Shop for the purpose of rema[in]ing all Day at Buisness and it is the first whole day that I have made in the Shop Since I went out of town for the Sickness — I found Buisness tolerable fair for the Season

    20   Buisness Fair — Nothing new that I know of

    21   Buisness fair for the Season and nothing new that I know of

    22   I went to the Commercial Bank to day, paid in a note that was due to Harris and Lum   The amt of the note was Five hundred and thirty seven dollars, 34 cts   I pd it in with several different Kinds of money, Such as Commercial, Planters Bank, New Orleans Shipping Comp, City Paper, Union Bank &c. I Left it thare on conditions that if Lum would not receive it I would settle the mater with Him, so they Gave me my note.

    23   Buisness has been quite dull   Young W Winn Came in to day to see me and tis the first time that I have seen him sinse He Came home from Philladelpha[17]   He arrived Last Week — He Looks to bee in better Health than when he Left Here

    24   Buisness Quite fair — I remained at home all day after I shut up my shop

---

a horse owned by Stephen D. Elliott in a race against a horse owned by James Railey. Colonel Bingaman's horses won on the next four days (including a $1,200 purse), and a William J. Minor entry won on the last day.

[17] The will of free Negro George Winn, father of Winslow Winn, provided that his children be educated in Ohio or an adjoining state. His daughter Helen was in Pennsylvania schools from 1835 to 1840, and apparently her brother, Winslow, was also sent to that state to continue his education. In the 1830's the estate accounts also show that, when possible, tutors were hired for the children.

25   To day was the Generaral Muster day and I presume a very unpleasent time they had of it [very cold day]

26   Nothing new that I Know of. Buisness not Good

27   Buisness has been something better to day — Thomas Pulling died Last night and Mrs P. Tuomy of Main St also — Mrs Vaughn pd me $2.50 for having 20 Barrells of Coal hauled up from Under the Hill   I pd. my Taxes for State & County to day — the amount of which was Fifty five Dollars

28   I took up to the House to day 38½ pieces of Gold — Amt $192.50   The Silver yet remains 182 dollars

29   The streets are very mudy indeed — Buisness is very dull for the season — I Let Miles Owen have One hundred and sixty dollars in Gold for the same Amount in Silver and he is to return the same at the Expiration of three weeks, if I want it

30   Buisness not very brisk — I received 2000 Cigars to day from the Hail Columbia — they are a prety fair article, tho not the best in the State by a fut. I pd. 20 cts to day for Lard — Got One Keg

December 1   I wrode Down in the swamp this Evening — Started from town [at] 1 Oclock and wrode down to the Aligator Lake and tryed to get Some teeth but Could not. I Caught 4 Possums and brought them all Home alive   I took Winston with me

2   Buisness Quite Good to day. Greate many Strangers in town to day

3   Buisness tolerable fair. The House that St. Clair Built was Burned Down Just before Day Light this morning — it Caught in a Kitchen or Stable or Something Like it   I was to Day at Cook['s] office in regard to my Policy. I inquired of Mr Rabb to Day if he Knew what Ever became of Philo Andrews and he said that he himself had been here for 20 years and that Andrews had Left here before He Came to the Country and that the records did not sho where he had Ever made any transfer of his Land to Any One Else and that his wife was Now in Philadelphia and had Married again but did not know the Present name and was Living with her aunt by the name of Greenfield — I saw an old Gent. afterwards up at Mc['s] Shop who told me that he Knew Mr Philo Andrews well and that Thom J Ford ownd all the Land that Andrews Had in the Swamp and that he had Bot it from Said Andrews before he Left this Country for N. Ingland States

4   Buisness not Brisk

5   I went under the Hill to Day and bought thirteen shoats and three Hounds, young Ones — I gave twenty nine Dollars for them all

6   Buisness was dull for this Season of the Year — I presented my Policy to Day to Mr Pitcher for payment, tho have not herd the result

7   I wrode out to the Race tract to day and I Lost $2 on a Bet that I made with Ramsey — Coon Mardice Lost his race very Easy, after winning the first Heat it was a pretty race, sure

9   To Day was Quite a Dull Day for Buisness and nothing New that I know of

12   Buisness was Quite fair to Day tho nothing new that I know of — I had to day Steven hauling Slate Stone to make a pavement in front of my New Store. Mr Duglap is to pave the way for me

13   My Pavement was finished to day and it Looks very well indeed — I had a Conversation to day with young Mr Wales of Washington about Philo Andrews and he told me that He believed that Andrews was Still aliving and was seen some where in Mobile or in Mexico and told me He Left here in Consequence of His Stealing a Negro and that he Proberly was now a Live and the Property that [he] had was Now, He thought, owend by Mr Brooks

14   I wrode out to day to the race tract and Lost Seven Dollars and Fifty cents on Mardices mare. She Cant run worth a cent, Sure and no mistake. Col Waymoth paid me Two Hundred and fifty Dollars to Rent for three months of my new Store up to the First of December 1839 — Mother paid me thirty Dollars to day on acct of Borrowed money and owes me a Ballance of two hundred twenty Dollers yet.

15   Buisness was very good in my Line   After 12 Oclock I Closed up and went into the Swamp and took with me my three young Hounds and I started a Deer and in geting off my Horse I fell flat on my side and rolle[d] over on my Back — By this time the deer ran off and I Saw it but could not get a shoot   It had ran too far before I could recover from my fall — I shot 4 crows and Winston shot one — I found a new Lake

16   Something of a Buisness day with me   Nothing New that I know of

18   Buisness has been some what dull I think. My pavements was finished Yesterday and Look very well indeed up to date

1840

January 1   I Loaned Mr Wm Mosby One Hundred Dollars to be paid when called for or Demaned. Sure and no mistake
3   I Commenced this morning again to Survey the Lot in State Street and we find that the City plat Seys that there is three Hundred and thirty three feet in the Square — We then serveyed the Square and find that there is three hundred and thirty four feet, ten inches front on State Street — We then Divide the Lot Equally which Gives to Mr Lapiece a front of One hundred and sixty seven ft, five Inches and Gives the Titchenor Lot also One Hundred and sixty seven feet, five inches — This Survey makes Mr McCullam Come On my Lot a fraction over four inches on the front on State Street — 1 foot 1½ inches from the row of Brick on the pavement which was thot to be the old Line — We then surveyed the Line in Canal Street and there the City Survey of old seys that there is three Hundred and twenty One feet. According to Our survey Last, we find that there is three Hundred and twenty six feet, nine Inches, a gain of five feet, nine inches, in the Square. I Loaned Mr George Watson Eighty Dollars to night to be returned as soon as He goes up to Grand Glph — in Louisiana Funds
4   Buisness has been very Good — I Loaned Mr Geo. Watson twenty Dollars   With Eighty that He got yesterday He now owes me One Hundred Dollars, which money He is, according to promise, to remit to me as soon as he gets to Grand Gulph — in the Funds of Louisiana — *I hope so, I do indeed*   The[r]e is nothing New to day that I have herd of. Gen Jackson is Expected Down in the morning But I dont believe that he will be here at all
5   The Bluff is covered with persons waiting to see Gen Jackson. I took my Horse and wrode Down in the swamp and took a Look at the Land as I went and found it to be pretty swampy — I then went to Mosbys and He had gone in to the Swamp to Hunt   I saw 3 of my Hounds
6   I with the rest of the Good Citizens of this City had the pleasure of seeing Genr Jackson on His way to New Orleans, He having stoped at the Landing a short time[1]

---

[1] Jackson's brief pause at the Natchez Landing was noted in the Natchez *Free Trader,* January 7, 1840. Three militia organizations—the Natchez Fencibles, the Natchez Guards, and the Adams County Light Guards—had boarded the steamboat *Edward Shippen* at Natchez and ascended the river to a point some eight miles distant where they met the *Vicksburg* and the *Clarksville,* the two boats

9   Buisness Tolerable fair — The Mesuage of the President
of the U S A was Isued from the Courrier office this morning before the Free Trader saw it. It was then Isued Late from the Free
Trader with the Mesuage from the Governor — I wrode Out this
Evening to shoot and I Killed 3 Birds and got one more and my
Kitty Fisher ran away from me and took the sadle with her — I
wonder where she is now — never mind it will all be right some day
or other

10   I walked out to Hunt my mare that runaway from me
yesterday and John Had found Her and I got on Her and then went
out a hunting but did only Kill 4 Rice Birds in all — Steven ranaway yesterday — He got Drunk as usual and then ranaway — I
hope I will be able to put Him in a Safe place yet if dont mind

11   Nothing new

12   Buisness dull. Nothing new that I Know of   I wrode out
this Evening to the Quigless plantation and shot 2 Squirrels and
wounded another and killed 2 Pigeons and Winston Killed two
squirrels and 1 sap sucker — I shot Mr Powells Gun

13   Dull in the way of Buisness — I Bot 3 Barrells Corn and
a Bale of Hay to day

14   The Military Companys all turned Out this Evening to
receive Genr. Jackson but he did not come up — Maj James Surget
Buys Mrs Williams Plantation

15   Gen Andrew Jackson Came up Last night and this morning came up to the Town and in the fineest Kind of Stile — oh
what a Splendid reception

16   Buisness was very Dull indeed

17   Buisness Dull for the Season   Nothing new that I Know
of

18   Buisness was pretty Lively for the day

19   I wrode Out to the Ivy place to day to Look for my Little
cow but could not find Her no where

20   Buisness has been rarther dull for the Season   The
Papers of this morning announces Mr. Holton as manerger of the
Mansion House   I Got Permission from Mr W Minor to fence in
and plant the vacant Ground Back of where I Live at Present ie.,
Mrs. Richards Property

February 3   To day I Bot at Jones & co 1500 Cigars @ $20
per Thousand — R Road funds $30

---

which carried the Jackson party. Jackson assured the people of Natchez that he
would spend a day with them on his return trip. He was en route to New Orleans
to visit the scene of his victory over the British in 1815.

4   To Day I went Down to E. Thompson and Bot Perfumery to the Amount of $114.00 in Rail Road funds

6   To day, I being affraid of R R. money, I Bot at E Thomson & Co 4500 Cigars At $20 per Thousand — $90.00

7   I was up to day to See Mrs Soria and I found her in her Siting Room — I told Her that I came to get my Hog that she had and she then told me that Mr Soria Bot the Hogs, and that the Hog was hers   We talked on for a quarter of an hour tho I was convinced in my own mind that she Knew it was my Hog — She promised, However, that Mr Soria Should Look over the mark and that they had the mark set down on a piece of Paper some where — Oh what a palpable snap   Poor Hog — it is Bound to be stold and even sight of its proper owner

8   Our Money of the R. Road Bank selling at 50 per cent Discount

9   To day Ends the 9th day that Bill has been under the Hill and makes Forty Six Dollars, 50 ct, And it also makes 9 Days that Charles has been in the Tremont Shop And makes 22 dollars and in the 9 days that he was under the Hill he made Fifty Dollars and fifty cents — I remained Home all day to day, did not go out Any where after I came from the shop

10   Buisness was not Lively by no means — Charles takes Charge below and Bill in the Tremont House

17   Mr L Pitcher told me this morning that my money was ready for me now at the office. I asked him what Kind of money He had to pay me in and he replied that it was Rail Road money and regreted that he had not payed me the money sooner   Did not agree to take the money at all

18   To Day Silver, Silver, Silver is Deman[d]ed by Our Profession or two for One in paper

19   Gen Quitman handed me a Letter to day that was given Him at Jackson for me. He did me proud, He did me proud. Union money and Rail Road are both on a par this morning.

20   This has been quite a Dull Day in the way of Buisness — Nothing New that I Know of — Mr Cregeer has been missen since Last night and nothing herd of him at all — A very Large town meeting to night on the Currency — Several resolutions past but I presume they will not better the Condition of the people Any

23   Buisness has been dull for the Season I think

24   This was the night in which the Bill Ball was Given at Mr

Barlows City Hotell whe[re] there never has been Just Such another Mixture[2]

25   Nothing new that I Know of to day

26   Buisness was not very good for the Season

27   Buisness has been uncommonly dull to day. Good money cannot be had. John ran away this morning and went under the Hill and cut several Shines for which I Gave him a Good whiping to night together with some advice — Mosbey, by Course [of] Law, took the Guardianship of his Sister in Law from Mr. Lapice to day in Probate Court — He will suffer some Loss by it yet for I think he has been too smart for once in his Life   Mr Lapice is a perfect Gentleman and has done a good part by them I think   Mr Mosbey paid me two Hundred Dollars that he promised me that he would give me good money for it — Such is the nature of Mankind[3]

March 2   I made an Exchange of shops to day with Antoio Pan, my Shop for His — I am only to pay as usual $20 and no moree

3   Buisness only Tolerable — I Bot 12 pieces of Paper to day and sent it under the Hill to the shop. I had two trees set Out to day in front of my Shop — Twelve dollars was the cost of my paper I Bot to day

4   I walked up the Hill and then up the Streets as far as Mr Howells Residenc with Mr R. J. Walker[4]

5   Buisness very dull   Selling Out by Auction the Store of Dr Thorn, Commerce Street

9   To day I Bot at the Auction Room of Messrs Soria 1 fine red and white Cow for fifty nine Dollars and one Bath tub at thirteen dollars

10   Buisness was dull for the Season. A Meeting was Held yesterday at the Court House, the result of which was Published to day in the Courrier, Notetifing all gamblers and Pick Pockets to Leave town in 48 Hours &c.[5]

---

[2] The ball was given by the firemen in commemoration of Washington's Birthday. The Natchez *Free Trader*, February 12, 1840, had announced the ball and that tickets could be purchased at various Natchez business houses.

[3] Peter M. Lapice was the administrator of the estate of George Winn, free man of color, who had died in 1831. William Mosbey had married one of Winn's daughters, had been appointed guardian of Winn's son, Winslow, and here had himself appointed guardian of the second daughter. Throughout the 1830's and 1840's the Winn children complained bitterly that they had not been properly treated by Lapice, who on several instances informed the probate court concerning his difficulties in administering the estate. "Estate of George Winn," Adams County Probate Records, File 65.

[4] Possibly United States Senator Robert J. Walker.

[5] The Natchez *Free Trader*, March 12, 1840, devoted an entire column to the gamblers. It proposed a resolution "that the pickpockets, gamblers and loafers who

11   Buisness has not been very Brisk   Mr Thom Wilson gets married to night to Miss Homes

12   Nothing new that I Know of   I was at work part of the day in my Late Gardin on the Hill — Dr Hubbard gets married to night to Miss King

13   Buisness has been unusually dull   Nothing new that I herd of yet. I spent all of this afternoon in my Gardin on the Hill a planting of corn and the Like

14   Buisness tolerabl Good for the Season. Nothing new that I Know of

15   To Day [was] not one of Any much Proffit to me for to day I wrode downn on the River to Look at the swamp and I found that the water was up to the Cross Roads — Sterns was with me and we went down behind the Laks and I saw some good game down thare — Our dogs ran two fine deer into the swamp across the Lake or in and was Lost in a short time by the Aligators I do Expect

16   To day has been a very dull and allmost a perfect suspension in the way of Buisness

19   Nothing new that Know of — John and Jack has a regular fist fight to night and after fighting for 8 or ten minutes they Both stoped — So goog and so good — Jack Knocked John down flat on the ground twice

20   Buisness was very dull indeed   Nothing that I Know of — Billy Towns has won the race in New Orleans — The Cows got in my Corn Pach this morning and Eat down my corn

21   One of the Dullest days that I have seen for many a Day. I cant weell account for it — Viviere the Little Frenchman has made an assignment of all his Effects to Lolabat f[o]r the perpose of Swindleing his Creditors and nothing Else I presume

22   Buisness was very Limited indeed and nothing new. Jackmine and myself wrode down in the swamp this Evening to take a Hunt and we went down as far as the Mosbey place. I Killed 5 Robbins, 1 Squirell and 1 Owl — Greek Killed 2 Robbins only

April 8   Nothing New that I Know of — Buisness is Remarkable Dull for the Season — 59 Yds of Cotten I Bot to Day @ 18 cts

9   Nothing adoing that I Know of   I walked Out to the Bayou to see some shooting. Mr. Howell, Mc and Floyd & Jacko-

---

have no ostensible mode of making a living be allowed forty-eight hours to leave the city, and all those remaining after that time may expect to receive their just dues."

mine was there and Jackomine won 2½ doz Cigars from Mc, Easy —
To day Mr Isaih Watson pd me One Hundred dollars in Grand Gulf
money, it being money that I Loaned to his Brother George Watson

    10   I was in the Bayou waiting to shoot a match with Mc and
Floyd   Floyd could not come and the other did not come Down
untill very Late in the Afternoon — too Late to Shoot at all   We
were to have shot for three Dozen Sigars. The[re] were all Kind
of money sold at Auction to day, some at a Premium and some at a
Discount

    May 2   Buisness tolerable dull. I moved my man Phil and his
wife Silvia up to my dwelling House the other day — I Bot them
the day before yesterday from Col Waymouth of Main Street.
There is nothing new that I Know of

    3   Buisness has been only tolerable   I wrode down in the
swamp to day to take a Look at the swamp and found it full of
water — I wrode down as far as Mosbeys — The water in One place
was running Over from the River into the Lake. Land was in some
places 200 yds and in other places 100 and 120 and in Some 220

    4   There has been the Largest Crowd at the Auction of the
Marshall and the Sheriff at the Court House that I have Ever Seen
— the Property of Mr Brown, of Mr Barlow, of J Smith the Carpenter, of Perkins, of Lenears, of McMurtry and of others. There
was no real good sales made — oh my Country, my Country, what
are you Coming to

    7   To Day was in the aforenoon very pleasant Day untill past
One Oclock and then we had rain, with One of the Greatest Torna-
does that Ever was Seen in this place before[6]

    8   This was a part of the time pleasent and agreable and part
of the time was warm and unpleasent   Several persons found during this Day that was Killed under the Houses   Oh what times,
no One Ever seen such times

    17   I took my Horse together with Sterns and Jno Jackomine
and went into the Swamp — We found the road in a terrible condition Indeed — trees was a Lying all over the Road in Every Direction — Maj Jno Winns Plantation Houses were all Blown over —

---

    6 For accounts of the tornado, see the extra edition of Natchez *Free Trader,*
May 8, 1840. Three days later the *Free Trader* estimated damage to buildings
at $1,260,000 and total damages at $5,000,000. It was estimated that more than
300 people were killed or drowned in the river and more than 100 wounded.
Timothy Flint, missionary and writer, was among those dug out alive from the
ruins of the Steam Boat Hotel. See also Lyell, *A Second Visit to the United States
of North America,* II, 152.

Gin and all — and the water from the River was very high and runing over for an Hundred yards or more

18   There was a man Sold a negro yesterday at Auction and stole him again Last night, and a negro Girl from Capt Barlow. The name of the Girl was Mary — Mr Sargent got off on some Boat Last night and has gone to Philadelphia where he Lives — Buisness has Been Only tolerable to day in the way of Bathing and in the way [of] shaving too

19   Nothing New that I Know of.   I made out an Account to day of three Dollars against Mr Howe for the making or rarther putting up a Division fence between myself and Him   He paid it. I Bot to Day at Auction 2 glass Cases at 2 dollars Each — they will Suit for House Perposes

20   The Courrier of to day announces to the Public that the Danger of an over flow of the River is at and End and that there is no danger of it and that all the rivers above was on the fall and we may Expect a fall Directly   Buisness has been Only tolerable fair — I past off the Greater part of the afternoon in Picking [pitching] dollars with John Jackomine and Mc and all Quit Even — Comittee from New Orleans Came up from New Orleans to night

21   Buisness has been Tolerable fair for the Season — I was to day very Buissy in Cleaning Brick in State Street. I had Steven & Phil, John & Winston — We done a fair Days work — Mr Parker is selling of[f] his Brick very fast — number of Carts are hauling from thare

22   Buisness pretty Good — The Papers of Day report the Finding of the Steam Boat Hinds with fifty One Dead persons on Bourd of her — more than any One Could have Supposed was on Her[7] — I was to Day geting Brick down at Mr Parkers. He gave me a Small Lot of them to take them away which I did with Great pleasure   Mr Louis Bingaman Came Home this Evening from Philadelphia

24   I wrote some passes Last night, One for Phillip, 1 for Sarah [and] One [for] Lucinda to Go Out to Brackets to a Preaching and neither of them Came Home at all Last Night

25   Buisness dull for the Season   I was Out of humor this morning the first thing and by way of Commencing Buisness I

---

[7] During the tornado of May 7, 1840, the steamboat *Hinds* had been blown away from the wharf at Natchez Landing and into the river and those aboard her either killed or washed overboard. Nearly two weeks later the boat was towed ashore at Baton Rouge, Louisiana, and it was reported that the bodies of fifty-one persons were still aboard. See Natchez *Free Trader*, May 23, 1840; *Lloyd's Steamboat Directory*, 169-71.

whipped Lucinda, Sarah and Steven On account of the Bracket meeting — Mr Carter paid me to day $9, the amount of his acct. to date and will proberly Leave on the first Boat for Virginia

26   Court was Commenced Yesterday   Nothing new that I Know of — I was I[n] the Bayou this Evening and was shooting and was Beat by Jno Greek and Mc. We then Commenced to Pi[t]ch and was so good and so good

27   Nothing new to day Except this, which I am Sorry to See — Planters Bank   May Term 1840
          VS   Fi-fa.
Achibald Dunbar Et-al.

       Job G Self,
          VS   Fi. fa. on bond.
Archbald Dunbar Et. al

To be Sold 5th day of June, 1840, 18 Negroes, Daniel, Bob, Aggy, Jim, Magdaleen, Lucinyd, and Elsa, Terese, Zie, Judy, Alexander, Eliza, Judy, George, Peter, Ephaim, George Bell, Quilly.

28   Nothing new that I Know of. I am in the Brick work to day altogether, no this is a mistake intirely

29   Buisness has not been very Brisk to day by no means and the town is buisy now Getting repaired.

31   Buisness has been not as good as is Common on such Days usually

June 1   Buisness has been Tolerable good for the Season — Mr Oblemis gave Mr Gibbs a Complete drubing in the marking House this morning   I dont Know particulars — I was at work a good part of day at the Brick that I Bot of Mr Parker on State St.

3   Nothing new that I Know of. Cilva Came Home this morning Quite Sick   Her month is up I think with Mr Caulwell this Day — The Boys that went Out to get some Black Barrys did not Get any worth thinking about   I wrode Out myself and Got a few and my Horse Got away and ranaway. It was Mcs Horse   Broke the Bridle and Lost it — So much for Idle time misspent

5   Nothing New that I Know of — I Got up pretty Early this morning and started to go over the River To Fish — There were in Company as Follows,   Mr McCary, Mr Lancaster, Mr Alderson, Mr Jno Jackomine, myself, and Mr Noyes and two or three Small Boys — I wated as the Rest did and tis the first time that I Ever did so — Noyes and Jackomine both Left us and went on the other side of the Lake and we Caught a Greate many fish indeed   Mc Caught 66, Mr Alderson Caught 87, I caught 94, John 24

6 Peter McGettrick was to day found Guilty of Stealing a Gold watch from a wounded man, a man that was Hurt durring the Storm

7 Nothing New that I Know of The River still on the rise and is already Higher than it was in 28 in my Humble Opinion[8] — I repaired to my Dwelling at an Early Hour and remained Home all the Evening sleeping and reading &c James O'Farrell came up this morning from New Orleans and reports that Himself and some of the Guards arrested the man that Stole Mr Barlows Black Girl Mary and that He was safe in the Jail in New Orleans

8 Nothing New that I Know of. The River is still on the Rise at Our Landing and we will have an Over Flow Certain. I was a part of the day Buisy in getting Brick from Mr Parker, the same that I gave Him fifty Dollars for in good funds — Sure and no mistake Mr Parker had a meeting of His Creditors at the Mercer House to take into Consideration the propriety of Letting Him of[f] From His Debts — I believe there was nothing done in the Case

9 Nothing New that I Know Buisness is Dull and Getting more so. Sterns went across the river to Day to Fish and Came Home old Fashion — Winston and John went into the woods to Get Black Berrys and John got the most. They Got between the two, 9 quarts

10 I no of Nothing very interesting that has transpired to day. Mr Wm Robertson Left Here this morning for Virginia

11 I Left Natchez this morning for Concordia To Fish and there were Seveal others in Company — Mc, Jno Jackomine, Mr Alderson and old Winston. I as usual Caught more than any other person in Company — I Caught 231 Fish tho they were very Small indeed — Winston Caught 122 I believe — They none of the Rest Caught as many

12 Buisness has been dull for to day — I am yet Getting Brick from Mr Parkers Hotell

14 Buisness has been quite Dull. Nothing New that I Know of. Bill Nix made Eight Dollars and Seventy five cents Less this week than Charles did Last week, I Took my old Grey Horse this afternoon and wrode out in the neighbourhood of Mr Minors to Look for my Little mare

---

[8] John W. Monette—doctor, historian, and geographer—agreed with the Natchez barber: "The elevation of the flood of 1840 was about 10 inches below that of 1828 for the whole distance from the mouth of the Ohio to the Balize, except about 190 miles next below the mouth of the Yazoo." "The Mississippi Floods," *Mississippi Historical Society Publications,* VII (1903), 451.

15   Buisness has been quite Dull and nothing new that I Know of

16   The times are all Dull, Quite So   Court is now in Session and yet Everything Dull in the way of trade

17   I Loaned John Jaqumine Fifty Dollars to pay for his Fruit

18   I Sent John Home this Evening and wrote a Note to His Mother informing her that the Boy had Got some Complaint and to Examin Him. Oh the Rascal

19   Nothing new that I Know of   Buisness has been very Dull indeed

22   Nothing New that I Know of   I was a great part of this day down at Parkers Buildings at work geting away the Brick that I Bot of Him or rarther Cleaning off the Pavement according to our agreament

23   I was to day down at Mr Parkers at work as usual, cleaning away the trask [trash] — I did a wonderfull days work

24   Nothing new that I Know of. Buisness has been Dull, Quite so indeed. The dancing master was put in Jail to day for stealing. Name, Goker or Croker or something Like it

25   I have spent a good part of the day in the sun packing up Brick on the Lot

26   Buisness has been very dull indeed   Nothing new.

27   The Buisness of the Shop has been remarkable Dull I think   I Bot a Slim Sorril Horse to Day at Auction for $30.½ in New Orleans money — The Horse was own by Mr Cockrill, the Silver[smith] on Mt Street.

28   Buisness has been Quite Good for the Season — John Left here on the Decalax for Red River in Company with [blank] from this place, He wran off — I took a wride this Evening to Col Wilkins old Fields, Mc and myself we had a fine wride — I was wr[i]ding my new Horse that I Bot at Auction

July 2   Buisness has been very Dull also — Croud, Crowd. I walked out to Capt Minors Pasture to day at 9 Oclock to see a fight that was to come off between W. Hicky and a Mr Phillips   A Fist Fight it was to be tho they did not fight — Report seys that they are to fight to morrow on the other side of the River

3   Buisness Quite Dull

4   Buisness was Quite Dull, this being the 4th of July   I did not Keep open more than half of the Day but walked out into the Pasture to see How the Citizens were Engaging themselves and I found them all in fine Humor and in good order

6 Buisness has been Dull and nothing New. Mr Vanwinkle informed me that the shop in the Tremont House was ready for me, thus I have been out of the use of said shop from the 7th of May to this date, 6th of July, 2 months, 20 days of the time Lost I pd for, ie, I pd up to 27th of May.

8 I and Mr Jaquamine went Down in to the Swamp on a Hunt. He Killed 2 Squirrells, 1 Black Bird, 3 Kildees, 1 Crow, 1 Indian Hen

9 Buisness has been dull   Mr Jno Thom. Winn[9] was shot Last night whilst at supper by some unknown person — A more Gentlemany Young man I have never seen I think, a man that the world must Love if they could but Know Him

10 Buisness as usual has been Quite Dull   I have been for the Last ten Days Sinking money.

11 Nothing of any Interest to day Except the tryal of those Pe[r]sons for the Murder of Col Jno T Winn — Suspition rest[s] very Strong on Mr Walton

12 Buisness has been Dull for the Season   After Dinner I wrode Down the Saw Mill Road to get my Horses and I found them doing well and I Left them on the Ground — The authorities of the City has gone out to Mrs Walterns to try those Persons about Col Winn[10]

13 Nothing of any Importance   The Investigation is still going on in that Case of Col. Winn — Oh that they may be able to find Out the murderer, oh the Black Hearted *wretch*

14 I Commenced to day and planted a Small Crop of Corn, Second Crop that I have Planted this Season — I Eate one very fine water melon out the Garden to Day, the first that I have tasted from there, tho some one stole 2 before

15 Buisness was Dull and nothing new that I Know of

16 Buisness Dull. Mr S. Wood paid me to Day his Shaving acct. in full to 3d instant — $10 — The officer, Young Withers, arrived to day with Bill Web, the Celebrated Horse theif, and also another man by the name of [blank] — When they Left Here they

9 Winn was lieutenant colonel of the Fourth Regiment, Mississippi Militia. The regiment held a commemorative meeting on July 11. For accounts of his assassination and funeral, see Natchez *Courier*, July 11, 14, 1840. The tax rolls show that he paid taxes on a Washington lot valued at $3,500 and twenty-three Negro slaves. Auditor's Records, Tax Rolls, 1840, Adams County.

10 The Natchez *Courier*, July 18, 1840, reported that the Negroes "who had confessed" to the murder of Colonel Winn were subsequently found to be innocent of the charge.

stole Mr Watts Big Bay Horse and one from a Mr Johnson, Brick Layer — They will all be taken Care of by the State

17   I Loaned Mr Samuel Wood thirty Dollars in Good money — To be Paid on Monday — and I have no Doubt of the fact myself. Well those are the tightest times Ever Ive seen in Natchez before   I thing nothing a Doing at all — What are we a Comming to I Cannot Presume at all — no not at all — I Bot of Mr Finney To Day the Frame ware House owned by Mr McAlister. I gave Him fifty Dollars in Agriculteral money and I am To Give Him an Order on Ruffner for twenty five Dollars more   This was Our Contract

18   I was Quite all Day at work around at Mr McAlisters ware House Haulling away the stuff &c. I got Quite wet   Steven ran off Last night and was Brought Home by Mr Hendesee after Breakfast this morning and Beg Him off from a good whiping Sure   Tremendious Wig Meeting to Day at the Court House — Log Cabbin &c in view[11] — Nothing new that I Know of

19   To Day the times are Like other past Days   Quite Dull and nothing new that I Know of

20   Buisness very Dull   Oh what times I have not Seen for a Long time   Mrs Miller arrived this morning from New Orleans bringing Emer, Delia, and Octavia — Wellington Came up also and a servant Adaline, Mother paid me to day Ninety Dollars on acct. and owes me a Ballance of Sixty Dollars yet to date

22   Nothing New that I have Herd of to Day

23   Nothing New that I Know of   Tis already thought by the Planters that the Cotton Crop will be short in consequence of so much Rains — Mrs S. Richards Gave me a Receipt for Eighty Dollars, two months Rent up to the 16th of this month, and I had to pay Her $25 In New Orleans money — She wants me to pay in future forty Dollars in New Orleans funds per month after this date which I will not do — Sure and no mistake

24   Buisness Dull — We have news that Arad Woodard was arrested in some part of Ohio — He is the man that Killed Mr Frazier of Woodville, a Gentleman, who had a Family — I had a settlement with Sterns[12] to night and told him that I could not aford

---

11 The speech of Henry D. Mandeville, Jr., delivered before the Tippecanoe Club of Adams County on this date was printed in the Natchez *Courier*, August 8, 1840. The editor commented: "The friends of the Whig Cause will be highly delighted with the flowing beauty and lofty sense of political integrity and virtue that mark every line of his speech."

12 Washington Sterns (also spelled Sterne and Stearns), free Negro barber, worked intermittently for William Johnson and Robert McCary between 1831

to Keep him any Longer and that his maner of doing buisness would never do. To be Drunk ½ of his time would never Suit me nor my Customers and I paid him twenty Dollars in good money and then He said that he would work for his vituals, that he did not care for the wages. I told him if He was Disposed to Come around in that way He Could do so, but at present I could do with out any assistance and if Buisness got Better in the fall why I might give Him a Situation, tho I was not sure

25 Buisness is Quite Dull indeed. Nothing new that I Know of — I got an Order from Mr Ruffner this morning and I am not sure that I will take it — the Order is against Mr Geo Weldon for Fifty Dollars. The Same Gent above promises to Give me an order.

26 I remain Home all Day Except a trip down to the Mill to see my mare

27 I paid Mr Crist to day $12 on his bill for Black Smithing ie or his wheel righting &c. A Log Cabin was Brought to town this morning on one of Col A Bingamans Waggons, Himself wriding Close behind with a good many more — Mr Barlow gave Sterns a regular Flogging and so did one of [the] Negro men and the old Fellow wran over the Bluff — A. Lieper Hauled him home

28 Our paper of [to] Day Contains the Late Marriage of Mr P. M. Lapieces Eldest Daughter to a Mr Pelie, of New Orleans — they were married on the 8th inst

29 Considerable Shines Cut in the way of Flags, Shines of Every Kind — I saw Mrs Richards to day and she wanted me to give in advance two months Rent — I Could not Exactly stand that by no means

---

and 1840. In this last year Johnson paid him $25 per month and fed him. Sterns was the oldest and most independent of all Johnson's barbershop employees; he had written to Johnson in terms of equality as early as 1829 and he had inherited property. He had been freed in 1827 by an executor of the will of Payton Sterne of Natchez, who had left his property to "three coloured children in my possession, Sons and Daughters of a certain woman of color named Milly." The will (probated 1819) had further enjoined the executors to arrange for the children's freedom and for their education. In 1841 the Adams County Board of Police refused to grant Washington a license to remain in the state, but his name appeared on the tax rolls two years later. As a result of a number of emancipations of members of the family arranged by Washington Sterns and his mother, the Natchez free Negro group bearing their name increased considerably in size in the 1830's and 1840's. See Adams County Will Books, I, 175; Adams County Deed Records, O, 389, R, 127, 131, 138, 665, U, 130, 131, EE, 40; Petition of David Lawson [1819], Petitions and Memorials, Series I, No. 93; Sterns to [William Johnson], March 6, 1829, Johnson Papers; Cash Book, 1830–38, entries for August 15, 1831, through March 12, 1832, and Ledger, 1837–41, pp. 172–73, Johnson Papers; Auditor's Records, Tax Rolls, 1843, Adams County; U. S. Census Reports, 1850, Schedule I, Adams County, 7.

30   To day it was that the Greate Log Cabbin was Raised on Pine Ridge.[13] There were a Greate many persons thare and among them some very Hansome women   I wrode Out thare myself in the Afternoon and in going out I met 278 Persons and among the whole number I did not see a man Drunk tho I Soon Lerned the Cause of it — they Had no Intoxicating Liquors during the day — We Learn by the Papers of to day that Mr Quackinboss had Killed a young man by the name of James Hunter

31   Nothing transpired to Day worth much attention

August 1   Nothing doing much in the way of Buisness — things not going on to suit me by no means

2   Very Little a Doing in the shop and at ½ past 10 Oclock I Left in Company with Wellington to Fish at the Concordia Lake. We got on the other Side at 11 Oclock and in twenty minuts was Down to the Fishing Lake — I Caught I think about thirty and Wellington about 25. I Know of no man that has Ever Fished over [there] that has Ever Came Home with more Fish than I for the same Length of time — I Fished about 24 Hours and no Longer. We got Home at 4 Oclock

3   Nothing new. I sent down Stephen and Phillip this morning to Commence on the House we had Burned down last year   The[y] Commenced at Breakfast time and worked all Day. Mr Brown was giving them the Instructions &c.[14]

4   Buisness has been only tolerable   Nothing New. Steven and Phill worked all Day Down at the Building and I also Hyred 2 hands and gave them 1.75 to work from 12 Oclock untill night — they belonged to the Miss Evanss — The Mr Brown Commenced to measure off the Ground Yesterdy.

5   Little or nothing doing at present and there dont appear to me that buisness will Ev[e]r revive   Oh what miserabl times. Good Hevens

6   Buisness has been Dull   Nothing new that I Know of

---

[13] Pine Ridge was a community several miles northeast of Natchez.

[14] Johnson here began to build a three-story brick building on the State Street site formerly occupied by the frame building which burned in September, 1839. By examining the diary entries regarding construction from this point until November 3, 1841, a conception of the process of construction of the building which now stands at 210 State Street can be gained. Johnson used his slaves to perform some of the rough labor, including mixing mortar and collecting bricks from the central portion of William Parker's Mississippi Hotel (which had burned in the same fire that destroyed Johnson's frame building), and sublet carpentry, bricklaying, and plastering to a number of individuals. See also Ledger, 1837–41, pp. 122, 161, 169–78, 205, 265–66, 270. George Weldon worked on both this house and Johnson's Main Street brick building.

7   No news of importance

10   Steven got Drunk to day and walked of[f] and I, after he had been Brot Home, Hand Cuffed him and Floged Him. In the first place I Knocked him Down at the Building — he then ran away, but was soon Brought Back again and when he came back he was so drunk that he Could not walk, talk or do any [thing] Else — I gave Him Late in the afternoon a tolerable severe whiping and Left him, so the First thing I know the Rascal had ranaway[15]

13   Buisness has been very dull   Mrs Miller left this place this morning on the S Boat (Batton Rouge) with her three Children — all in good Hea[l]th

14   To Day I was informed by Mr Lancashire that the Land which I sold to Mr Flecho had never been put on record. It is now in the occupancy of Mr Watt, formily the property of Mr Bledsoe

15   Buisness Dull. An acct. was presented to me to Day by Mr Potter For Mess[r]s Vannerson & G Baker for Fifty Dollars and I then by my Books find Mr Baker charged with One Hundred and Fifty dollars, 50 cents — I Left my act. with Him and I gave him Credit for the fifty, thus Mr Baker owes me $101.50 yet — I Got Mr McFaddin to day [to] tear up his old note that I held for three years, the 24th June past, for fifty dollars I Loaned him   He Gave me Another that the amt. of Interest made it sixty two dollars to the 24th of June, 1840 — I paid Mr Fox to day thirty dollars for Brick work done by him to this date $28 was the Amount due but I had no Change, He then took thirty Dollars — Mr Weldon Commenced to put on the Joice for my new House.

16   Buisness very Dull indeed — I Sent Mrs Richards the Key of her House to day which I have been for some time Living in — I have Some Reason to believe that the Old Lady is Quite Displeased at my Leaving the House

17   Buisness Still very dull and Nothing new that I Know of — The whole town is at present Ingaged in Talking Pollitics   Phill works to day at the Building and Steven works at home. Two Layers at work.

18   Buisness no better as yet. Mr Ja. A. Lyle and Petter Lawrence has several small Fig[ht]s during the afternoon   Some thing about a Dispute that originated with Tho. Mackin and Peter Lawrence — It however resulted in a Fight between the Parties already named   In the first Fight some think that Peet would

---

[15] There was considerable agitation by the citizens of Natchez at this time against the selling of intoxicants to Negroes. See letter in Natchez *Courier*, August 13, 1840.

have whiped him with Ease but they were Seperated by Persons present — Peet then took to his Heels and Lyle Caught Him and Broke the stick over his head, Knocked him Down &c. In the first place Thom Maccin Kicked Peet Lawrence Out of his house under the hill

19   Nothing new that I Know of. The Good Whig Citizens of this place is very active in Building a Log Cabbin on the Bluff this Evening, geting it ready for to morrow, for to morrow is the Grand Log Cabbin day. The town is all Excitement, oh what regoiceing

20   Of all the Pomp of Nonsence and Splendid Foolishness that I Ever have seen, this Day Exceeds all   I am sory to see the Ladys Join in the Foolery.[16] I have One wish and that is that the Democrats will Get a Large Majority in Every State, May the Good Heavenly Father of the Universe have an Loving Kindness for them — To day I went Out to the woods of Mrs Bingaman where the Speeches was Deliverd by Different Gentlemen. The First I Herd was by Mr McMurran, it was a chas[t]e and Gentlemany Speech, the Best that I have Ever Herd by a Wig. The Language was Beautifully and Every Charge he made was I thought well Explained — After walking about for some time I returned to the spot and found a Mr Gill Martin adressing — I herd Him through. His Language was of a very Elloquent Nature, pronouncitons good, His Denunciation strong and I thought him rarther an Irishman than otherwise from the accent. Quite a Flowery affair — We then had a National Song by Young Duffield, assisted by Holton and some other Genius — The Song was good Enough — The Next Called to the Chair was the Elder Duffield. He made quite a Lengthy Speech — Sir Giles over reach — Richard the third, King Leear and Several other Greate men of Ancient times was represented by Him in Part and Poor Van Buren was made Everything of: King, Lord, Master, Tyrant, Usurper, Rober, and Every thing that Could be Conceived or Imagined. I was much Disappointed in the man and I have very Little Doubt but what the argument made use [of] changed many to the opposite side — I Saw a cene Last Night that Convinced me of Human Frailty   It [was] During a Speech that Mr Martin made this night — A Poor Individual who

---

16 Whig orator Seargent S. Prentiss held a different opinion. "The array of ladies on the Whig side of politics is likened by Mr. Prentiss, of Mississippi, to the 'rainbow of hope adorning the storm cloud of political strife.'" Natchez *Courier,* August 25, 1840.

was at that time Drunk said in walking of[f] from the Crowd, its a Damed Lie, and at that instant [entry not completed][17]

   21   Nothing New that I Know of. I Herd Mr Dobins this morning State and If Mr Van Buren was recollected [re-elected] that He was willing to Shoulder his musket and wage war against Him and His Party and then asked Mr L. Pitcher if he would not be willing to do the same — Mr P. replied no, not unless He was fraudulently Elected. He might then if it was required — Mr D. in Speaking of President V, Called Him George the Third — there were then 4 or 5 present, M Collier &c. Two Dickermans and 2 Clarks both half Left the Whig Ranks and will vote for Van Buren   Disgusted at the Log Cabbin Speeches — I got the key to day from Mrs Maxwell, 1st time I have had it since the storm

   22   Nothing New worth relating to day

   23   Buisness Gets no better — I remaind Home all Day reading Enoch Crosby or the Spy Unmasked[18]

   24   Buisness Dull as usual and Nothing New that I Know of Except that our Free Trader is Out before the Public this morning under the controwl of Mr T A S Doniphan. I paid Him this morning Six Dollars for six months Subscription to it — I Made a Bargain to day with Mr Weldon. He is to Build me a Kitchen, 12 by 14, for forty Dollars, payable when it Suits me, to be Commenced to morrow And I am to find the materials — Gen. Hinds Died yesterday at His Residence in Jefferson County — He Broke a Blood vessell[19] — I paid Mr Elam twenty Dollars to [day] for Dr McPheeters and took and order for the Same on the Dr — I Loaned Mr H Cobler Fifty dollars in Currency to be paid in ten days from date — I promised to pay Mr Weldon forty Dollars for the making of a Small Kitchen worth proberly 14 Dollars   I have been doing Bad Buisness all this whole Day — I got up too Soon this morning, Entirely

   25   The Buisness of to day has been very small indeed —

[17] For a more favorable report of the "Natchez Log Cabin Raising," see Natchez *Courier*, August 22, 1840.

[18] Johnson referred to H. L. Barnum, *The Spy Unmasked; Or, Memoirs of Enoch Crosby, Alias Harvey Birch, the Hero of Mr. Cooper's Tale of the Neutral Ground; Being an Authentic Account of the Secret Services which He Rendered His Country during the Revolutionary War* (New York, 1828). A second edition of Barnum's work was published in Cincinnati in 1831 and there were subsequent cheap printings.

[19] General Thomas Hinds of Mississippi commanded Jackson's cavalry at the Battle of New Orleans, was brigadier general of the territorial militia, and upon the passage of the first state militia law in 1818 became the commander of the Mississippi militia with the rank of major general. He also served in the state legislature and in Congress.

Nothing new. I worked with dirt this Evening very hard   I was remooving it Out of the Streets opposite the State Street Building — I Received a Couple of Letters this Evening from New Orleans. I Bot some window frames this Evening, sash frames too, from Mr Elam — if they are good I got them Cheap

26   To day has been One of not much Interest to me on account of the dull times. Nothing new to day of any Importance

27   Nothing New — Buisness still Continues Dull, very indeed

28   Mr Weldon makes a finish this Evening of the Little Kitchen that he has been at work on for several Days past

29   News from North Carolina gives a Wig Majority for Mr Morehead for govenor, 6000 votes.[20] In Concequence of the news there was Small Extras Struck of[f] and a Log Cabbin Meeting on the Bluff   Speeches were made by Mr Armat, Col. Bingaman, Mr Murcerson, and Mr Mandeville — there was a Greate Burst of Eloquence in a particular point of view — Bull Rushes and Palmettoes of La was very Sublime.[21]

30   I walked down at 12 Oclock to day under the Hill and I there Crossed the River to see if Mr Elexander had sent me a Cow. I remained over the River for One hour or moore, then crossed and Came off up the Hill — Democratic Meeting to day at the Court House — I dont Know what number was present, tho I will Learn. Mr H. Smith Seys that they had the Documents to show that Mr Forbes had been in New York Prison, Sing Sing   He asked me if he was concerned in the Freetrader office — I told him that he had nothing to do with the office at all. I was Quite Buisy all Day to day taking my Brick from the yard of McMurran

September 1   Nothing new in town   The Speech that was Deliverd by Mr Claiboune yesterday is said to be very good and Eloquent,[22] the Best that has been in the Court House for many a day

[20] John Motley Morehead was elected governor of North Carolina by the Whig party in 1840. He was re-elected in 1842.

[21] The Natchez *Courier,* September 1, 1840, reported the meeting: "The Whigs of Natchez rallied at the Cabin by hundreds on Saturday night. Old Saratoga [a cannon] sent forth her best thunder, and shouts of triumph went up most cheerily. Speeches were made by Thomas Armat, Esq., H. D. Mandeville, Esq., Colonel A. L. Bingaman and Simon Murchison, Esq. Mr. Mandeville was uncommonly happy and eloquent." Bingaman was president of the Tippecanoe Club of Adams County.

[22] The pro-Whig newspaper, the Natchez *Courier,* commented on the speech in its issue of September 1, 1840: "The standing army, sub-treasury, silk-stocking spoilers held a meeting at the Courthouse yesterday, and as usual with said party, nothing was heard but villification of Gen. Harrison and a cormorant senseless cry

and tis said to be the Best that Ever has been deliverd in the Court Hous[23]

2 Buisness tolerable Good to day, better than what I Expected I Had the Tremont Shop opened this morning by Wellington

3 I wrote by the Baton Rogue to day to Mrs Miller in New Orleans — A Bet was made to day in my Shop between Mr McDanial and Mr F Taylor of ten dollars on the General Result of the Presidential Election — The Brick Layers Commenced to work to Day on my Building Again And Steven Got Drunk to Day also and walked off, tho Charles found him and Brought him Home and I have him now in Chains awaiting for better times

4 To Day has been One of the Dullest days I have yet seen I think for some time back — Nothing New. Brick Layers at work on my Building — Mr H. Cobler paid me fifty Dollars that I Loaned Him 10 days ago — I Gave Steven a tall Floging this morning and turned him Loose to work again — I Bot five Barrells Corn to day at 1 dollar per Barrell

5 Buisness no better, Nothing New The Election for Lieu. Col &c Commences to day — The people made a party Question of it Something New for this place, and it was noticed that Mr Ruff took a very active part in said Ellection, tryed to Influence a good many Persons — The Election resulted as follows — Mr Murcherson and McNiel, Both in Liquor, After playing C for some time got into a dispute and then a fight in wich Mr Murcherson got his face bruised very much and the other was not Hurt Mr Wales was Elected by thirty four Majority[24]

6 Buisness not good by no means — Nothing new of consequence — I Left town to Day about 12 Oclock with my short rifle and wrode Down into the Swamp and Shot One Indian Hen,

about bank! bank! A gentleman of taste informs us that the only decent speech delivered was that of F. L. Claiborne, a lofty thinking opponent, who said that he would not abuse General Harrison—his services deserved the gratitude of the country and he would not defame him."

[23] Johnson ignored the excursion of the Adams County Whigs to a meeting at Torry's store in Jefferson County. The Natchez *Courier*, September 1, 1840, reported: "Today there will be a large Whig gathering at Torry's store in Jefferson county. The Rail Road cars leave the city this morning at 5 o'clock for the Franklin Depot, at which point all of our citizens who choose to go will be supplied with horses to ride to the place of meeting. Gentlemen are requested to take with them saddles and bridles. A deputation of twenty members has been appointed by our Tippecanoe Club to attend this Barbecue."

[24] E. L. Wailes and William H. Dunbar were candidates for the office of lieutenant colonel of the Fourth Regiment, Mississippi Militia. See Natchez *Courier*, September 5, 1840.

One Large Blue Crane, One Owl, One very Large Whitesh Hawk, and help to Kill one Squirrell which we could not Get Out of the tree or Nest — The Pic. of Orleans of the above date states that Comanche Indians Entered the town of Linville and Shot and Scalped Mr ONeal of Pensacola and Killed Maj. H. O. Watts and took his wife Prisoner[25] — and Seys among the person[s] Killed at Victoria was Col Pinctney Calwell and a Mexican servant.

7 To Day has been a dull day and nothing new that I Know of. Wellington takes the Key of the Shop under the Hill this morning and Charles goes into the Wall Street Shop — My New Doors was put in on Saturday Evening — Mr Doyal, Mr Wrigley, Mr Wood, Mr Howell and Mr Barland were all on a Hunt to Day in the Swamp and, No I believe now that it was on the 5th inst that they were Out, and they woun[d]ed a Large Buck and Lost him — And they also Lost old Kill Buck, one of the Best Dogs in the pact

8 Buisness Something better than it was yesterday tho nothing new that I Know of — The Mechanaks at work at my House

9 At or near Breakfast thime this morning the arlarm of Fire was Given. It Prooved to be the two story Building, a Kitchen it was, and some other small Building and an old Black man and a Woman was very much Burned. She is Bound to die — I have not herd how the fire originated There were a Great many person[s] present — The Loss is Estimated at five thousand Dollars[26]

10 Capt. Isreal Barrett Died this morning near Breakfast time with Congestive fever. He is a man that is beliked by all that Knew him He was a plain, unasuming, Gentlemany man A Large Democratic Meeting was held to Day at the Court House in Honor of Perrys Victory[27]

11 Our papers of to day Said nothing of the Democratic meeting of yesterday The new ware House Just put up for Mr McAlister is by several Good mechanics pronounced a ruff job I

25 Linnville was a small port town on the Gulf coast of Texas. It was burned by the Comanches in their great raid of 1840.

26 For accounts of the fire, see the Natchez *Free Trader* and the Natchez *Courier,* September 10, 1840. A card of thanks appeared in the *Courier* over the signature of Samuel C. Risk, acting secretary of two Natchez volunteer fire companies. "The members of Fire Companies, Protection No. 3 and Relief Hose No. 2, respectfully render their sincere thanks to Messrs. O'Rielly, Thos. S. Munce, Peter P. Baker and several other gentlemen whose names were not known, for the active and valuable assistance rendered said companies at the fire of yesterday morning."

27 Johnson referred to Oliver H. Perry's victory over the British on Lake Erie in 1813. The Natchez *Free Trader,* September 10, 1840, carried a notice of the celebration.

had my old riffle repaired to Day and I will some day take Her in to the woods. I shaved Jud[g]e Rawlings this Evening and He showed me his walking stick and remarked that it was a part of a mana waw [man-of-war] and that he wanted a Hicory Stick very much and He had use for it at this time. I Knew it was for Mr Freeman

12   Nothing new that I Know of — The Courrier is moore abusive this morning than it has been for severl days. Consideral meeting at the Log Cabbin to night. The Orators on the Ocasion were Col Wood, Mr Manderville, Mr Mathewson and Mr Hewit — The Col. made in the Estimation of Every Body a Diry [dry] Speech, Mr Mandeville a very abusive one and Mr Mathewson a few stale Anecdotes and that of Mr Hewit a speech that had but Little or no bearing on the Leading Principles of Government[28]

13   There was nothing new in Our papers of Yesterday — McCary and myself took a wride this Evening   We went Out [to] the old Quigless road and came around by the Scotts old Field — Good deal of fun about the speeches that was made Last Evening in the Log Cabbin by Col. Wood and Mr Mandeville

14   Nothing New   The times are dull and the people hard run — I am still Building on State Street. The Joice of the Second Floor was partley put up this Evening

15   Nothing New that I Know of   The town Quite Healthy[29] and Buisness rarther Better to day than it has been for some time back, 6 Baths to day Including the French Lady — We finished putting on the Joice on my State St Building

16   Buisness not Quite as Good as it was yesterday — The Brick Layers commenced to work on the Building — Mr Lockheart and a Mr Bullock has a fight at the City Hotel this Evening   They fought with Chairs pretty much — Lockheart got the worst of the Battle, fell against a Door Plate and cut his Head

17   Nothing new that I Know of   Brick Layers are work

[28] The Natchez *Courier*, September 14, 1840, reported the meeting. The editor commented adversely upon Mandeville's castigation of Jackson.

[29] On September 23, 1840, the editor of the Natchez *Courier* published a letter from a subscriber commenting upon the health of the city: "After the great tornado of May last had filled our city, both on the hill and at the landing with extensive ruins, and covered the shores of the river for miles near the city with vast quantities of decaying timber, and when the subsequent inundation continued until the middle of June, many of the 'knowing ones' predicted a certain and devastating epidemic of yellow fever in the city. Some of our most prominent physicians who believe in the exclusive local origin of yellow fever, we are informed, predicted an early visitation of yellow fever in Natchez, and advised some friends to retire early from the city to escape the impending danger. It is now the 20th of September, and not a case of yellow fever has been seen in Natchez or New Orleans."

[ing] on my Building — Carpenter set two windows and one Door Frame this Evening — Lancasshire plasters his conner office — His Son Came out as an Atorney and Counsillor at Law in yesterdays Paper — the first time.   I Bot at Auction to day a Lot of Pictures and among them was a Likeness of Mr Van Buren — I got the Lot [for] nine Bits

    18   To day has been a remarkeable dull day in the way of Buisness — Brick Layers Commenced this morning but had to Leave off work by the Breakfast Bell time — I Commenced this Evening together with Winston to Clear Out Our Chimney — We did so and found a trowell in it

    19   To Day the Whigs has a Large meeting in the Court House and at night they had another at the Log Cabbin[30] — They had a Band of music and formed themselves in a procession and walked Down to the Cabbin where they were addressed by several Gentleman — 1st by Mr Smith, on a rest, 2nd by Col A L Bingaman, off hand, 3d by Mr Hewitt, and a few words by a Mr Nailer and then by a Mr McCardle from Vicksburg and during the speaking some man struck Mr Crizer — Mr Crizer talked of knocking the teeth down the throat of our old friend Mr Williamson

    20   At 12 Oclock I took my Horse and my gun and wrode down into the Swamp and Killed 2 ducks and one white Cran, wounded 2 more and Killed 4 Grey Squirrell all on my way to Mosbeys — I gave him a news paper or two and then Left for home and came from thare in One hour and ten minutes — A wonderfull wride I think

    21   Buisness very Good for the season — Collected $15 and Took in seven by work &c   I feel prety Sore from the wride I took in the Swamp yesterday

    22   Buisness Dull compaired with yesterday — thus it appears that no two days are Exetly Like in Buisness — Thare is nothing new in the way of Buisness or Politics — Mr C. Archiey came in town yesterday from P. Gibson — Mr F asked me to day if he had bin in and if he was armed &c

    23   During the whole Day nothing new of any Importance Occurd During the Political Exertion of to Day — I Commenced this afternoon at the Chimney under the Hill to Build it up — Got Out of mortar and Quit — Some Fellow has for two mornings been passing Counterfiet money in Our market — The Young Col Bingaman wants Bill to go North with Him — *Cant come it Judge*

---

[30] The meetings were described in the Natchez *Courier*, September 21, 1840.

25   To Day I made an Early start for the Swam[p] taking Winston with me. I got down to Mr Clarks and Borrowed His Gun and gave Winston mine — I then made for the woods and I Killed 3 Large Grobecs, 1 Crane, 1 Beckaroach, 1 wood Cock, and 6 squirrells and was during the Grater part of the hunt unable to get along as well as I might — I was sick with the Head ache — I went down to Mr Mosbyes and found them all well

26   To day has been One in wich I felt bad from morning untill night. It tis the Effects of my Hunt on yesterday in the Swamp — I took a Dose of Antimnial wine[31] and did not take Enough tho I hope to the Lord I will Get much Better with out taking Any medicine — Those Lines above was pened by the Quill of the Amercan Eagle and those [these] are written with the Quill of a Grobeck that was Killed 25th inst

27   Buisness Quite Dull and nothing new that I Know of   The Committee from Vicksburg arrived this Evening for Batton Rouge Expecting to find the Deligates of this place in readiness to go down with them but they had gone on yesterday night — The Delegation from this place was not Strong

28   Mr J D. Freemans Defence appeared in this morning paper VS. Judge Turner and it was One of the tallest Documents that has been before people for some time. The proof is all Clear and palpable — the facts are Stubern and Cant be overthrown. Mr Cox and Judge Montgomerys Letters are plain cases — The meeting of to Day was in part addressed by Young Mr Lancashire — I am told this Evening that it was One that did much Honor to the young Gentleman. I am much pleased to hear of his Effort

29   The Delegation that went from this place, also One from Port Gibson and Vicksburg, Raymond and La. all arrived within the Last few ½ hours from Baton Rouge. Capt. Minor received them in the Log Cabbin   He was chairman at the time and Anounced to the Delegation that the meeting requested a Speech from Mr Yerger, a General Call was made and he arrose and made a speech of an 1 hour and ½ at Least, relating many Anecdtes, some very Laughable Ones indeed — He is a man of Greate Industry   He was followed by Mr Chilton who made a very short Talk, concluded with the Turky Anecdote. The meeting then adjoured

30   Mr McA[l]ister and Watson mooves to day to the Rail Road Bank. Opens ther new Commision House — Buisness is dull,

---

[31] Johnson probably meant antimonial wine, a solution of tartar emetic in sherry wine.

very Dull — News I have none — Lies there are a planty of them in the Courrier Paper of this morning

October 1   I Took my Gun this morning and went into the Swam[p]   Winston was with me   I Killd One Becaroch, Two Loons, Five Ducks and Three Squirrells, one Large Hen Hawk — Winston Killed one Squirrell and One Snipe

2   I was Quite unwell this morning from the Cold I Caught yesterday a Hunting

3   Nothing New that I Know of Occured During the day — Big Log Cabbin Speeches made to night — I agreed to Let Bill Nix go up with Col Bingaman and the rest of the Whig Delegates from this place to Jackson — Convention of the Whigs — To Night two strangers come in my Shop to get theare hair Cut and after it was Done C [Charles] Looked at a Breast pin and the owner asked him what [he] thought it was worth, He said about $50. The owner Said yes, a hundred of them, and remarked that C. put his hand to his Bosom when he got up, After which he Said that he never saw the pin any moore and after a Long and tyresome search for it, He as good as said it was taken Out of his Bosom. C. deserves to be accused of it for puting his hand to the Mans Breast and B[Bill] for Leaving the Room when the search was agoing on. I am well Satisfied that it was not in the Room on the Floor to Night

4   Every thing Still and Dull — I walked Down to the Shop Early this morning and Enquireed of Charles if he had found the mans Breast pin yet and he told me that he had not seen it and I Looked on the floor as I Stood in front of my desk and thare Layed the Pin under my writing Desk on the Flour where it had Evidently been placed thare by Some One — It was a plain Case as Ever Came under my observation. It Leaves me to think much, very much — Oh that Butter will run, will run so   Bill Left for Jackson Last night on the Ganges as Body Servant to Col A L Bingaman — Mr Powell and myself wrode down into the Swamp this Evening and I took him down as far as the Cypress Bayou, and we met Messrs Barland, Doyal and Wrigley Comming Back with two deer that they had Killed between the Lakes — On our way down Mr Powell Killed one Hawk and one Squirrell and on our way upp He Killed one Loon, 2 Squirells and one Duck and I Killed One Squirrel and 1 yellow Hamer

5   Our town was all Excitement   The Wigs of Natchez had a Large meeting and Procession through the Streets and then Down to the Log Cabin. There were a Greate many Ladies at the meeting and I think the Greatest number of men that were in the procession at any one time was 220 some odd — I did not Count them myself but was told so by Some good authority tho the Papers of the Courrier stated that the number was about One thousand — I have my Doubts — The Democrats had a Large meeting in the Court House at the same time. They Supposed the number of Democrats to be about three Hundred and Fifty — I Still have some doubts about that — Mr Freeman was the orator for the Democrats, also Mr Van Hosen and for the Whigs Dr Bowie and Mess[r]s McMurran and Carson — all able Speeches So I am told — and a song by the renown young Mr Duffield and Holton — tune old Rosin the Bow[32]

6   This has been a very dull Day and Nothing New that I Know of   The town quiet to day Compared with yesterdays Bustle

7   To [day] has been a remarkable Dull Day and Nothing new in town. All sorts of reports about the result of the Main Election — Some times that Gov Kent is Elected by 3000 and at other that Fairfield is Elected by 2900 and so on   Another is that Kent is Elected by 345, then Contradicted and F is Elected by 85.[33] Such is the state of things at present   As for myself I dont believe Either of the reports

8   Bill and Charles went out to Camp meeting this morning, One on my Sorril Horse and the other on my Grey Horse   I very soon after wrote a Couple of passes, one for Phillip and the [other] for Stephen and Let them Go untill to morrow morning Early — The Corpse of Mr Josiah A Lyle was Brought down to day from his plantation   He was Shot yesterday morning by Hagan of New Orleans — he went up in the Baton Rogue — The Following persons went up on to the plantation with Mr Lyle, McCaffery, Hanley Forbs, Thom MacRen[34]

9   Buisness has been Dull. I had the sheeting hauled down to the Building to day. The Rafters was put on yesterday and to day — the Brick Layers this Evening at work and will Finish or nearly do so to morrow — I partly made a Bargain to Day with Mr Weldon to make me a pair of Dormer windows for Sixty Dollars — No positive News from the Mane Election yet, tho generally Believed Kent is Elected by a small and very Small

---

[32] See Natchez *Courier,* October 7, 1840.

[33] Edward Kent was elected over John Fairfield, the Democratic candidate.

[34] The Natchez *Courier,* October 8, 1840, carried a half-column account of the encounter.

majority — The public are not all surprised at Hagans Killing Mr Lyle. They are of the opinion that He was much to Blame in the first place for shooting Hagan about a year ago with the Intention to Kill Him — Camp Meeting is all the go at present   Case came off this morning B vs. D.   All no go

10   I had a settlement to day with Mr Van Winkle and the Following Credits was given to me — fifty Dollars that I pd to Dr McPheeters, Seventy One that I had paid Mr Potter and One acct of M Rufners for thirty four dollars and another vs Dr McPheeters for fourteen dollars, the work done by M Ruffner — So when those credits was made I find a Ballance of two dollars in my favor up to the 6th of the present Month   I paid Mrs Neibut thirty five dollars to day for House Rent up to [the] 10th of November — My new Brick House is very near Finished — that is the Brick work — it will be Finished on Monday if we have Good weather and nothing Happens — And article Came Out this morning in the Courrier which Explains the Origins of the Difficulty between Mesrs Lyle and R. Hagan and makes it a very ugly thing on the part of Mr Lyle &c. I walked down at the Log Cabin to night to hear the Speeches that was Said would Come of[f] to night. A Short time After I got thare Mr Mandeville was anounced. I Listened for Some time to his Discreption of the Different Conventions and Gatherings throught out the United States, then his attempt to Burlesque the article that appeard in the mornings F. Trader — about where the money Came from to pay for those assemblys &c. I Considrd them very Lame ie His remarks in regard to the whole subject[35] — Mr Andrew Brown the[n] Followed after a previous Talk by Mr Ruffner, which was not quite Eaqual to one of Mr Websters   Mr Brown did very well so I am told

11   Buisness quite dull and nothing new — I took a wride this Evening with Mc and we went Out near Col Wilkins Residence and then came Home again Seeing nothing in particular But a Large Flock of Partriges

12   The Democrats had a Large meeting to day[36] — had a fine Dinner after the Meeting was over and a Great number attended the meeting

13   Buisness tolerable for the times. Nothing new that I have herd of   I Bot a very fine Double Shot Gun to day at Mr Stock-

---

[35] For the speech of Henry D. Mandeville, Jr., see Natchez *Free Trader*, October 14, 1840. Johnson here showed his anti-Whig bias.

[36] Senator Robert J. Walker's speech was summarized in the Natchez *Free Trader*, October 14, 1840.

mans Store, Gave Forty Dollars for Her — I was to Day Induced
by The Snob, Swain, To Moove from the Shop that I had in Wall
Street, He agreed to pay me twenty five Dollars per month for
the shop. After I had moved Out from the shop He then Declines
taking the shop — They had something of A fight this morning, ie Himself and a Brother, about a yellow Girl of the Bell
Estate   They had a fight, then Desolved or talked of doing so.
Snob Cant come it over me again

14   Buisness Some what Dull this week or I mean to day — I
had new Tubes put in my Little Gun to Day — I hope she will
shoot Closer after this — Walker and Ruffner Bot Each of them
a Gun at the same place Where I Got mine the other day — They
paid Forty five dollars a piece for thers, five more than mine
Cost. To Day Young Winslow Winn[s] Brother in Law and Sister
arrived from The North and went on down to there Plantation in
the Boat

15   Greate many persons have Gone Out to Washington to the
Grand Whig Barbacue[37]   I Bot a Keg of nails to day for shingles,
paid Eight Dollars for then [them] — and got 15 lbs of other Large
nails — Mr Weldon agrees to put on the shingles at four Dollars
the square and I to find the nails. Nothing new that I Know
of   Buisness this morning was good tho in the Afternoon very
Dull

16   I took a salt Bath to day and went Home and remained
there untill after super, then Came up to the shop with Mc   Mr
Izod anounces his resignation in this mornings papers[38] — Something unexpected for only half of His time has Expired since he
Came into office — Mr Strickland has offered for the office

17   I have been Quite unwell to day. I was very much surprised at the Bill that Mr Fox presented to me to day for work done
on this Brick Building in State Street — His Bill Commenced in
this way — Mr William Johnson Natchez, Miss   Oct. 13th 1840

---

37 The Natchez *Courier*, October 15, 1840, carried the program of the meeting
and announced: "The cars will leave the Natchez Depot, on Thursday, the 15th
inst., for Washington, at 9 o'clock, A. M. and leave on their return, at 1 o'clock
P. M." Two days later, in reporting the meeting, the *Courier* stated: "When the
historian talks about the political conflicts of these times in after years, the
brightest chapter of his book will be that which records the patriotism of our
ladies."

38 Izod had resigned as sheriff of Adams County. See Natchez *Courier*, October
16, 1840.

To James C. Fox Dr

To Laying 83936 Brick and Furnishing Materials at		
$7 p m		558.55
Furnishing 2 Trimmer arches	2 each	4.00
56 ft of Cornice	1 Dol per ft	56.00
Three Doble arches	3 dollars Each	9.00
12 Single dito	1.50 each	18.00
Seting 3 window Frames	50 each	1.50
Plank in Foundation		10.00
17000 Bricks at $10 per thousand		170.00

$856.05[39]

18   Nothing new. I am Still Sick with a very Bad Cold — Mc came up and spent the Evening with me &c

19   To Day the shoe maker that Mr Kenney Left His shop in charge of was about to Leave this place and Winston saw Him Just in time to report him   I Sent word Down amediably to Mrs Kenney and to Kennys Brother to inform him of the fact and He got after the Fellow forth with — I paid James C. Fox the amount I owed Him Except fifty five Dollars which I gave Him my Due Bill for — Mr. Dalhgreen gets married to Widow Thoms Ellis[40]

20   I have not been to my Shop this day. Sick at Home — Mr Weldon nearly done putting on the Shingles on my House — State street

21   I am still on the sick List and unable to go to work   Buisness very Dull in the shop.

22   Buisness very dull for the Season. I went up to the shop to day but could not stay but a short time, too unwell. I had to come Home

23   I was up again this morning to the Shop and down to the Building and walked about too much and had to go Home Feeling bad. W. Winn walked up with me and took Dinner with me, we had Considerable talk about the manner in which he come it over Mr P. M. Lapiece &c. Mrs Cotton died to night Just after supper with an apoplectic fitt. She was very well this morning.

---

[39] Johnson's total.

[40] The marriage of Charles G. Dahlgren—former secretary to Nicholas Biddle, commission merchant, banker, and later Confederate general—and Mrs. Mary Magdalen Routh Ellis on this date is recorded in Adams County Marriage Records, VI, 427. See also Natchez *Free Trader*, October 29, 1840; Natchez *Courier*, November 3, 28, 1838, March 16, 1852. On June 16, 1845, Dahlgren paid Johnson $5.00 for having shaved the corpse of Thomas G. Ellis, his wife's first husband, in 1838. Day Book, 1844–45, Johnson Papers. See sketch of Dahlgren's life in *Biographical and Historical Memoirs of Mississippi*, 2 vols. (Chicago, 1911), I, 611–12.

24   I was Down at the Shop and walked about for some time
and then up to Mcs, then to the Streets, one place or other untill
near Dinner — then Came home very bad of[f] with the Head
ache. To day was the General Muster and we had considerabl
Miletary Doings Out at the Race tract and in town together[41] —
Buisness is very dull indeed for the Season. News from Ohio Came
to day giving Whig Majority &c.[42]
25   Buisness tolerable fair for the season   Nothing new that
I Know of. Greate deal of Excitement in the way [of] Electioneering — I remaind at Home all Day, was not well.
26   Buisness has been very Lively. City full of People. Whig
Meeting to Day and One to be holden Every night this week in
the Court House, That Party has Droped the Log Cabin, they Say
it is too Cold[43]
27   Buisness was Tolerable Good   I am Glad to find it so for
we have Long had hard times — Mr W A. Britten, Mr Adriance
and Several other Gent got Home to day and they are all I believe
that is to Come now
28   Buisness Geting Better, Nothing New To Day
29   Buisness very good   Steven ranaway soon this morning.
He got Drunk and then put off.
30   McCary, Messrs Thrift, Doyal, Stever, Mitchell all were
down in the Swamp on a Hunt, Mr Steover Killed 8 Ducks, Mr
Doyal 5, Thrift 5, Mitchel 2, Mc one and 2 Snipe   Killed a Coon,
Left him in the woods — They were Down in the Swamp yesterday — I had Steven put in the Chain Gang to day after dinner —
McCary found him on the top of wagon and took him off and
sent me word
31   Buisness very Good for the Season. Nothing very New.
Yesterday The Courrier reports a Large Wig majority in Pensylvania of 6 or 8 thousand and to Day we have a Counter report from
the Free Trader office which gives a majority for Mr Van Buren
of Ten Thousand and 216. The Courrier Late in the Afternoon
Publishs another Paper sheet making Out the F. T. a Falsehood
and seys that they have a majority or gain of Nearly 6000 votes.[44]
N B I [made a] mistake in regard to the Printing for it was done
after this date

41 The regimental muster included the Natchez Hussars and the Fourth Regiment, Mississippi Militia. See Natchez *Courier*, October 24, 1840.
42 The news was correct, since the Whigs carried Ohio.
43 The Natchez *Free Trader*, October 26, 1840, reported that the Whig meetings
at the Log Cabin had been "frozen out."
44 Harrison carried Pennsylvania, thus gaining her thirty electoral votes.

November 1   Nothing of much interest. Greate Deal of Excitement in the City about the Election that will Commence in the morning at 9 Oclock   I was under the Hill this Evening and half of the Citizens from off the hill was down Electioneering in Every dirrection;   we staid untill dark

2   Buisness has [been], oh remarkable Dull and there is such a Large Concourse of Persons in the City too — To day is one that I thought we would have a fine Days work but the Contrary is the fact and no mistake sure   To Day is the First Day of the Presidential Election and I saw at One time 163 Persons Come in at One time in the Court House yard to vote and the[y] all were at that time Followers of the Tumble Bug Ball, properly named I thing. The Ball was Rolled up and Down the Different streets, and then under the Hill, and up and there was nothing wise about the Concern that I Could See,[45] 649 were the number of votes Polled. The Ball Starts again from the Court House and then Down Town to the Log Cabin, there it was adressed by Col Bingaman for a very short time.

3   The Election is still going on   The Greate Hum Bug Ball was stollen Last night by Some One that has more sense than the man that made it, and Demolished the thing, an rolled it Down the Bluff[46]

4   Just before Day this morning we were all suprized to hear the alarm of Fire, and I went Down to the Bluff as soon as Possible and there I saw the Last remains of my shop. It was with the rest of the whole Block wraped in Flames and Every thing was Lost. Nothing was saved by me. There was a Large Amount of Property Lost by a greate many of the Citizens under the Hill,[47] I went

---

[45] One of the effective Whig methods of arousing party enthusiasm was the rolling of a gigantic ball from town to town. Trooping crowds followed singing, "Hail to the ball which in grandeur advances." One of the campaign slogans was "Harrison and two dollars a day and roast beef."

[46] The Natchez *Free Trader,* November 3, 1840, reported: "The election yesterday went off in the most peaceable and orderly manner; no fights and an abundance of good feeling."

[47] "A false alarm of Fire was given yesterday morning about 2 O'clock—the bells in the city tolled—the Firemen and most of the citizens, aroused from their beds, and were drawn to Main street by a great light, which was supposed to be a house on fire, when it proved to be only a bonfire kindled in the middle of the street, and all this noise and disturbance made 'to have a little fun.' We have not language at command, too strong to apply to the miscreants who would thus sport with the feelings of a community who have seen the fairest portions of our city swept away by this destroying element, for the sole purpose of having a drunken spree, or gratifying the fiendish joy of laughing over the horror, consternation, and alarm that seized a whole city. To make the affair worse, is the fact that in one hour after the false alarm was given the cry of fire, was again heard, and the bells were again tolled and some time elapsed before any notice was taken of

Down to the Lakes this morning and Took my new Gun, the First time that she was Every Shot — The First time I Shot the gun it was at some Ducks in a Lak right Back of Aligators Lake and I Killd two Summer Ducks with the right hand Barrel and [with] the Left I Shot 1 duck and with the right I Shot two more In six Shots I Killed 9 fine Ducks, three of them Mallads — and I Killed One owl; Winston Killed 1 duck and 1 Snipe

6 To day I Partly made a Bargain with Mr G. Welldon to Bui[l]d me a Small House down at the Landing for which I was to pay Him 110 [dollars] for and he to find Every thing Complete in the way of stuff, and I am put in for it Deep — Sure and no mistake, Mr Barbour the Gentleman that Fought yesterday on the Island, Died this morning from the wound that He received in the abdomen, He Fought on the Natchez Island with Mr McWhoter. Both of them was from the other side of the River, He was Buried this Evening — He died at the Mansion House[48]

7 Buisness Tolerable Good.

8 Buisness Just Tolerable Nothing new. Charles wrode Kity Fisher Out to Maj Youngs

9 Business Pretty Good for the Season. Mrs. R. M. Gaines was Taken very ill to day and died in a few Hours, was in a Family way. Died Just the same way in wich Mrs Cotton died — Mr Gains was up at Jackson at the time

10 I Got up very Early this morning and wrode down into the Swamp in Company with Mr Jaqumine and John. After we got Down into the Flat near Barlands House Jaqumines horse got Away and ran nearly to town. I waited untill he was caught and then we started and went down to the Lake Back of Our old place. There I got a shot at Some ducks on the wing and Killed two Large duck of Mallards I then turned of[f] and went to the Lakes Back of Aligator Lake. I there got two ducks, then went on to the foot of that Lake and turned of[f], wen[t] oh the Lower End of Aligator Lake and there I got three more duck of Mallards — which made in all 7 ducks Mr Jaqmine got one Indian Hen, that

---

it, during which time the houses of our fellow citizens under the hill, were burning like stubble. Let our city authorities see to this matter." Natchez *Free Trader*, November 5, 1840. The Natchez *Courier* of the same date stated that twenty wooden buildings were burned and estimated the loss at nearly $40,000. The *Courier* continued: "Under the hill is a fated spot. This is the third time within the last two years that this part of our city has been burned to ashes."

[48] McWhorter and Barber were both citizens of Vidalia, Louisiana, directly across the Mississippi River from Natchez. The Natchez *Courier*, November 6, 1840, mentioned the duel. They fought with pistols at ten paces.

was the Amount of his hunt. Thus you see I Killed in [all] 7 ducks, 1 Large Hawk, 1 Large Grey Plover and 1 Squirell   John Killed 2 Large Plover, 1 Small snipe, 1 Lark — I met Mr Barland, Waker, Patterson & Paine Coming Out of the Swamp. They had as Follows — Mr Paine Killed 31 ducks, Mr. Barland 23, Mr Patterson 6, Walker 4. Thus the four Killed 64 ducks — add my 7 to the Lot will make 71, then add 19 moore that I met John Gillmoore Coming to town with and it will make 90 ducks that Came out of the Swamp in one day — the Greatest Quantity that Every I herd of Coming Out of the Lakes in one day before

11   Fine Race at the tract to day.[49]   3 Entrys   Capt Minors [blank], Mr Kenners Hauri, Col Bingamans Concheter. Concheter won the first Heat and the Kenner Horse won the Race Easy I am told. I did not see it

12   Buisness Tolerable Good. I wrode out to the Race tract to day. Saw a very fine Race. The Nags was Mr Kenners Horse Grey Dock, Col Bingamans Horse John R Grimes and Capt Minors mare Britania — The first named horse won the Race tho Col Bingaman won the First Heat — Mr W Minor did not win a single heate — Mr Stutson and Thom Pain was in the Swamp to day and Killed 50 ducks, so I am told

13   Three Mile Race to day at the tract,   2 Entrys   Col Bingamans Sarah Bladen, Mr Kenners Bay Mare — She Lost the Race for old Sarah Bladen was too fast for Her Sure and no Mistake   I Lost three Dollars and a half — the Same that I Lost yesterday[50] — Nothing new that I Know of   Buisness not as good with me as it was in days of Old Lang Sine. I was at the Race tract to day and there I Saw a three mile Race. It was — Enough said   I spoke of it before

14   To day I was at the Race tract and saw several Races   The First, a Race between nag started by Col Bingaman but own[ed] by Maj James Surgett — The Surget Filly won the

49 The Natchez *Courier,* November 11, 1840, announced: "There are fine accomodations at the course for the ladies, and we hope, that this is the dawn of a renewal of the good racing for which the Pharsalia course was famous." The railroad advertised that cars would be run to the race track every day.

50 The fall race meeting of 1840 was dominated by three sportsmen: Duncan F. Kenner of Louisiana, and Adam L. Bingaman and William J. Minor of Natchez. Colonel Bingaman's Sarah Bladen won six races in Natchez and New Orleans in this year, and as late as 1841 was considered one of the six leading "four mile horses" in the United States. She was referred to by a national sporting magazine as "the Champion of the South West, the renowned Sarah Bladen." *American Turf Register and Sporting Magazine,* XIII (1842), 103; XIV (1843), 103. See also Natchez *Courier,* November 12, 13, 14, 16, 1840; Francis Brinley, *Life of William T. Porter* (New York, 1860), 140.

Race beating Mr Kenners bay mare Luda three Straight mile heats — time 1.57 and 1.54 and 1.54 — Good Race, Sure. I saw a Race between the Sam Moore Soril Horse and Thom Kenops Brown or Bay mare, the Hors won the Race very Easy — by 100 ft I Supose

15 Nothing new transpired during the whole day of any Interest Both of the Political Partees are Claiming the State of Pensylvania. We dont Know which — I wrode out in the Afternoon with Mc He wrode the Poney and I wrode Kity Fisher, and the way She paced Coming Back was Familiar to me

16 Nothing New that I Know of I Commecd this Evening to make the Fence on the Lot down in State Street — I was under the Hill too and tryed to Rent a shop but could not Come it Exactly but Came very near it Sure and no mistake

17 I was doing Some fencing and stopd work Nothing of Importance, Nothing true from Pensylvania I Am In hopes that the Democrats will carry the State

18 Nothing New that I Know of Buisness has been Just so so It was to day I believe that I went up to Auction and Bought a spoted Cow and Calf at auction for twenty Dollars. Mr Wadsworth Bot one also. His was a young Cow without a Calf. I would Call her a Dun Cow

19 Ice on the Lakes. I went Down into the Swamp this morning very Early and Took Winston with me. I took my New Gun And Gave Winston my Little old Gun — He Killed 1 duck of Mallard, 1 yellow Hamer, 2 Little Small snipes and I Killed 4 Large Duck of Mallard, 3 Smaller Ducks, 1 S[q]uirril and 2 Snipes

20 Buisness Tolerable Good I Was under the Hill to day and Bargained for a House and was Talking about Lumber &c But did not get Any. I Bot a Stove from Mr Deckard the other day and I find it will not answer and saw Him and told Him the situation of the stove and He very willingly took it Back again and I sent it to Walker and Collings where He ordered it sent and that is the Last. Mc and Capt Thrift went into the Swamp this morning very Early MC Killed 2 Small ducks and Capt Thrift Killed 3 Large D.

21 Bill and Wellington went out to shoot Birds — they got pretty wet and Killed a few Little Birds not worth nothing — Nothing New that I Know of Buisness dull on account of Rain.

22 I Left Town to day about 12 Oclock and went into the Swamp with Mr S S. Boyd I took Him down on the Back Side of Aligator Lake, Down very near the End of it And I Killed Five Ducks, 4 of them was Large Duck of Mallards and 1 of them [a]

Didaper — Mr Boyd Killed nothing at all, I Gave him 2 daucks and Him to have the Credit of Killing them &c. I Saw Several Men that was down there that same day   They Killed Nothing.

23   Nothing new   First day of Criminal Court.[51] It was this Evening I believe that Mr Doyal, Slover, Barland, Howell, Izod and others Got Back from there weeks Hunt on the other side of the River — They gave me a shoulder of a deer. Mr B. Had my Rifle over with him

24   Mr Wrigley went into the Swamp to day and did not get but one Duck

25   Col Waymouth came up the other day from New Orleans and made Young W. Leave His store, tis Said on acct. of there Being too Familiar, Jane Lang Left to

26   Yesterday Evening I Closed a Bargain with Mr Tucker for the completion of my House in State Street. Two hundred and seventy dollars was the Sum agreed on by us Both. I Bot a Cooking stove to day of Mr Simon Moses and Gave Him Thirty Eight dollars for it and took it Home

27   Buisness Looking Somthing beter — I have to day Put up my New stove and am very much pleased with it indeed   I had a Long Talk to day with Young Mr Waymouth and He in the Course of the Conversation [said] He wanted me to Go on the Back of His Paper or in other words Indorse for Him for two Thousand Dollars in the Event of his Purchasing out the stock of His Brother, I Could not Come it Sure. We had A Long talk in the Cold, telling me how He was abused and for Nothing and how he was Charged of Stealling and of *Fonication*. I told him that if I was in his place that I would make an apollogy to the Col

28   Nothing New that I Know of. Buisness has been Tolerable Good To Day. Thursday Evening Wellington oppened my new shop under the Hill — I Bott at Auction to day a very fine half Keg of Gocian Butter and gave 28 cts per pound for it. Tis a first Rate article of Butter — I Saw Young Waymouth this morning and I had a talk with Him and I find Him still proud, in the Case of His Brother and Himself   And this Evening was married and has gone I believe to New Orleans on the Princess   I was the first I believe to tell the Col. of it and He was quite mad I thought

29   Buisness was Tolerable good. Nothing New that I Know of   I took a wride in the Country, 4½ miles, in Company with Mc   we went out in the Direction of Mrs Williams   We saw Nothing Remarkable during our wride

[51] The Adams County Circuit Court.

30   Buisness has [been] very Good for a Monday. Mr Robertson paid me the Amount of His acct which was Twenty Eight Dollars to the 12th of June, 1840 — Came to hand in Good time. I wanted the money very much at present— I find out to day that my New Brick Building is about to fall down — I hope not — must have been Ocasioned by the Tornado

December 1   Buisness Has not been so Lively to day as it was yesterday. Nothing new in the way of Buisness or News. I Receved a Letter Last night from Mrs Miller by the Hand of Jaqumine   Contained a few remarks only. A new Coffee House is opened to day in Stevensons old Stand — Mr Staples wants to Get the Store now occupied by Col Waymouth. To day we did not come to Any Conclusions about it.

2   Buisness has been not so good to Day has [as] was Several Days back tho collections has been Better. Nothing new to Day Excepet that Cloea Pomet or the woman that is a sister of Mrs Mardice was put in Jail under the Gallon Law,[52] Mr Coon Mardice being the Principal witness in the case. John Breaks the Big Race Picture to night, the Effects of carelessness   Mrs Jno. P. Smith asumes the Adminstrarix of the Estate of Her Husband — Alsup & Farrish, Agents. Young Win. told me that His sister & Brother in Law had given him and Mosby the Lower place[53]

[52] Johnson referred to a liquor-regulation law which had been passed in 1839. It had been given the name "gallon law" because it prohibited the sale of liquors in smaller quantities than one gallon. Another section of the law made it unlawful "for any person to sell any vinous or spirituous liquors" to any "Negro, either slave or free, in any quantity whatsoever." *Laws of Mississippi,* 23 Sess. (1839), 28. That the law was not being rigidly enforced in the Natchez vicinity was indicated on August 13, 1840, when the Natchez *Courier* published a communicated statement to the editor headed "Dangerous Nuisances" and signed "*LAW AND JUSTICE*" protesting the sale of liquor to free and slave Negroes. The writer claimed that "hundreds of negroes are nightly drunk in consequence of the attention paid to them by the grogshops on the roads leading out of Natchez," and he protested Negroes' dashing on horseback "through the streets of Natchez at the rapid rate of 12 miles an hour." The peace and safety of the city was threatened. "The night-guard in Natchez, as now organized, is not worth a baubee. The captain of this *safeguard* marches from the foot of Main street to Commerce, with the crew of his own selection by his side, and after thumping the curb stones until the retiring hour of twelve, he makes it convenient to turn himself and comrades into some convenient place and snore out the balance of the night." See also Buckingham, *The Slave States,* I, 418–21.
[53] The brother-in-law and sister of Winslow Winn (often called "Young Winn" by Johnson) were Washington Ford and his wife, Helen. William Mosbey had married another sister, Mary (also called Polly) Winn. Apparently the transaction mentioned above was a part of the settlement of the estate of free Negro George Winn, father of Mrs. Mosbey and Mrs. Ford. Most of the land mentioned above was eventually purchased from the Mosbeys and Winslow Winn by Johnson

3   Buisness was Dull and nothing new During the whole afternoon that was of any interest. Mrs McCaffery died to day I believe   Frank Littles old Grey Horse to night aged 21 years old

4   Nothing new. Maj A. Miller has Just arrived and will return to Washington City by the first Boat — He is by some one thought to be our next Marshall of the State. Glad I am to Hear it. Lawyer Tho. Armat was sentenced by Judge Cage to Jail, there to remain 48 Hours and be fined the sum of Two Hundred Dollars, for comtempt of Court &c

5   Nothing New that I have heread. A Day of Singular Coincidences   The following Are a few of them. In the first place, my 2 Turkeys were Stollen & my 2 Cows were Left Out and Ranaway   I had 1 Calf to Die — Steven Ranaway — All of those I was pestered with   I intended to have gone a Hunting but for the fact of all those things Runing away &c I was prevented and all for the Better I hope   Yes, and I had my mare Kitty Fisher Badly Hurt by John in Looking for my Cows — I signed an article of agreement this morning with Mr Staples, Renting him my House for One thousand Dollars per year Commencing on 15th inst

6   I find Buisness not so good   This is a nother mistake for Buisness is not at all to be complained of for it is some what Lively   Considerbley so

7   I arose this morning at ½ past 3 Oclock and got in readyness for a Hunt in the Swamp. Before I got Quite Ready Mr Jaqumine wrode up   We had some Coffee prepared and then [it] was of about 4 Oclock   We got down to Maj. Tom Winns place by Day Light and the 1st Big Lak had [a] fine Lot of Large Ducks in it and J and myself had a Long step to go to them and he got ready before I was and Fired a way   Crippled 1 duck and it went down the Lake a piece and he Followed it and there he found 2 that had been shot by Somebody Else. We went on down. My Horses got away from me and Ran off for a mile I suppose — There I found Mc along side of the Lake   We all got together and had a Tolerable Hunt   We Killed 2 Alligators between us; Mr Jaqamine Killd (or got) 5 Ducks and One Squirrell, Mc Killed 1 duck Only, I Killed 4 mallard ducks, 3 Beckaroaches & 1 Squirrell   I always Beat the crowd that I go with and no mistake — I shot my new gun — Mr Crist sold out his interest in His Black Smith Shop a few days ago

8   Nothing new that I know of Except that Mr. Louis Binga-

in 1845–46. See Adams County Deed Records, CC, 383–85, 579–85, DD, 199, 659, 669, FF, 81–82, 138–39, 454–55.

man is married to a Miss A Livingston of New York. The N P.
speaks of the wedding Dress Costing $2000 And of the marriage
Contract or Settlement $100,000[54] — Not bad to take   I paid a
Flat Boatman to day Twenty Five Dollars for a Thousand feet of
Lumber, inch Stuff. I Loaned Mr Strickland this Evening twenty
Dollars to be returned in the morning

9   Nothing new of any Interest

10   Stolen Goods was found by Young Mr Wethers to day at
Betsy Greens — the Goods belonged to Mr Turner and A L. Gains,
and Sanders, the Grocer, had also a Lot of Goods found on Him — A
mistake, 11th was the Day. I paid a Mr James Duncan to day $6
for the Mississippian

11   Betsy Green, Lots of Goods that was Stollen was found at
Her House, and there was also goods found at Saunderss and at
[blank]   Young Withers was the officer

12   I was nearly all the forenoon down at the Building in State
Street Filling in dirt that was washed out from yesterdays and
Last nights Rain. I paid Mr Tucker ten Dollars to night on his
work — My cow nearly dead, the One I Bot from the Drover the
other day — 17 dollar cow

13   Buisness only Tolerable. Nothing new that I Know
off   Mc came up to my House and was prety Tight and we Talked
about Hunting &c.

14   Mc and Mr Jaqumine and myself all Got up this morning
and had our Breakfast at 4 Oclock   Taking John along with us,
went off for the swamp and we went Down Long Lake and hunted
over in several Lakes that I have never seen before. One of them
was a tremendious Large Lake full of young willows and had
greate many Ducks [on] it — Small ones — Our Hunt. I Killed
with my new Gun, 8 Black Birds, 3 Squirrels, 3 Ducks and 1 King
Fisher — 15   Mr Jaqumine Killed 6 ducks — McCary Killed 3
Ducks and 1 squirrell — 4 Heads — The ducks that were Killed
were all Little Teal Ducks — John Killed 1 duck   I Killed the
most of my duck Flying

---

54 In the previous year, 1839, Mississippi had legally recognized a married
woman's right to property, but similar recognition had not yet been made by
New York. For two interesting examples of early Adams County marriage contracts involving prominent Natchez families, see Adams County Deed Records,
O, 236–37 (John A. Quitman with Eliza Turner, 1825) and P, 6–10 (William
Ferriday with Helen C. Smith, 1826). As stated in the contract, Ferriday's agreement was signed to assign and secure to his future wife the separate use and
disposal of certain property. Three trustees were appointed in her behalf to
administer $10,000 and certain stipulated real property furnished by her parents.

Our Fare for the Day

Boil Bacon Ham	Liquors	Venison Stake
Crackers — Beef stake	Whiskey and	Sauserage — aples —
Buisket	Brandy, good water &c.	
	Segars	Sweet milk

15   Mr Louis Bingaman returns to Day with His young wife
— puts up at the Mansion House   The Col. got Shaved, went
around to see Her for the first time &c. I paid Mr McMicheal to
day Five Dollars for volume 18 of the New York Mirror — up
some time in June — I Loaned my Small Gun to Mr Gaile to Hunt
with this Evening

16   Nothing new to day — Col D F Waymouth Sells Out His
Store at auction   I Bot a Large Lot of Paper, 349 pieces, amounting To 87.50 and I paid Him Seventy Five Dollars for [a] stair
case and for a stove and I Bot a few Bonnets, Toys &c., amounting
in all $186.15 — And we had a Settlement and he paid me for
three months and 16 days Rent of the store, amounting in all to
$292.15   Mr Hewit mooves in the store at the same Rent and to be
paid monthly

17   Buisness not very Good   Col D F Waymouth Left
Natchez to day. Mr Hewit Commenced to day and mooved in the
store — I thought He Commenced yesterday But was mistaken —
did [not] Commence untill to day

18   Buisness has been very dull. I Commenced to Day to
haul Brick down from my yard to State Street to Build a Kitchen
with — Brick Layers Commenced the Foundation of the Kitchen
this Evening

19   I paid Mr Tucker to night twenty five dollars on acct of
work done on State St. Building — M Ruffner has a fight and
whiped Little Troskaliska   Troskaliska sued Him. John R. Grimes
Has won his Race in Orleans

20   I remained Home all Day. To night at an Early Hour Mr
Ruthen Isler was shot Down by a Fellow by the name of Morgan
who, it is Said, stood in the street and Shot into the Buck Head
Coffee House on Franklin Street. The Fellow then Ran — The
young man that was said to be in Company with the Murderer was
a short time ago an apprentice [of] Mr Thom Rose of
this place

21   Nothing new that I Know of   I am Quite Buisy with
Building in State Street. To Night is the Grand Ball Given by the

Guards of Natchez. It was prety well attended and given by Mr
Barlow in the City Hotell[55]

22   The Presidents Messuage is in the mornings papers. I
paid $27 for Lumber for my Building   Carpenter Commenced to
petition of[f] the Rooms this Evening — Chimney was Commenced
in the Kitchen to day. Lancasshire sends his man and taks a part of
the Pavement of Mr Lapiece. I told Mr Wiswall of the Fact.
Morgan the Murderer was commited to day for the April term,
Nothing Else new

26   No news — I paid Mr Tucker to day $60 for work done on
the Building

27   Buisness Good to day   Nothing new Except that I Herd
that a man by the name of Spencer had ran off 47 Negrows belonging to the Rail Road[56] and had [headed] towards Texas, Has been
gone a week and the Following men were to day Just going in
pursuit of them or him, ie, Mssrs Strickland, S Gocian, Jim Camell
— I Left town to day at 12 Oclock — Took my Little gun and went
down into the Swamp — got 2 Shots and Killed 3 Large Duck of
Mallard and was Home to or before Supper time.

28   Buisness has been Quite Dull. To day the Investagation
Commenced about the Murder of Mr Willford Hocket — there was
nothing done of any acount but the tryal Comes on again to morrow

1841

January 1   I remained at Home all day and went no
whare   Several of my good Democratic customers paid me up in
full

---

[55] The Natchez *Courier*, December 23, 1840, reported the ball: *"THE BALL.*
—The Ball at the City Hotel was a delightful affair. The ladies looked well,
danced well, talked well, walked well, sat down well, but did not eat anything,
of course. The men-folks danced tolerably, chatted considerably, ate furiously, and
drank discreetly. . . . We know not which displayed more *taste* about the supper,
those who *got it up,* or those who *got it down.* There were squadrons of venison,
battalions of turkeys, and whole regiments of chickens. In short there was every
thing from *bear-meat* to *blanc-mange.* The onslaught was terrific and the execution
tremendous—and the man of sensibility could not look upon the mangled corpses
of the dead, without a tear. Unlike most conquerors, the appetite of the victors
for *carnage* seemed to be appeased at the end of the attack, they sighed not for
more *Turkeys* to overcome."
[56] The Mississippi Rail Road Company.

2   Buisness has been Dull — Nothing new that I Know
of   Mr McDanial, Chain Gang man, ranaway from Natchez and
took all of His force

3   Buisness not very good — I wrode out this Evening and
came in by Mr L R. Marshals

4   Nothing new that I know of. To day the Election Came off

5   Nothing New of Much importance. I partly Engaged a man
to day to do my Plastering   He is to work for Eighty dollars per
month. Conditions agreed upon is that if He works only a week,
the said week will be paid for &c, and if He works the whol time
I pay Him, tho am not to allow Him for days that he does not
work   I made a Bargain to day with Mr A Brown for Fifteen
thousand Laths at three Dollars [and] 50 cts per thousand   He
told me to send for them. I Gave an order to Wilsons driver tho
He hauled none up to day — I sent Steven Down. He hauled up
ten Bunches of them, 100 in Each

6   Nothing new. I Hyred a Mr Barbee to day to Plaster our
House in State St at 80 dollars per month or in propotion to that
amount if He worked Last [less] time

7   Nothing new   I Hyred a Mr Evans to Plaster at 3 dollars
a day

8   Commenced to day to make up mortar for the Plasterer,
prepaired the Beds and did no more, Bill and Charles and Wellington all goes out to a Party Given by a servant of the Missis Evans
out at there Residence — Butter, Butter will run in suitable wether
— I wrote to E. Miller this Evening requesting Him to pay me
the Eighty five Dollars that I Loaned Him — I wrote by a Mr
Tucker, my Carpenter — Lime is now offerd at the Landing in Barrells at 1.25 per Barrell

9   Nothing new

11   I wrode under the Hill this morning and Bot Thirty Barrells of Lime, 1.25 per Barrel for it and had all of it hauled up to
the Building on State Street — I paid the Plasterer, Mr Evans, Six
Dollars on his work

15   Nothing new that I Know of — Mr Tucker has not Came
down from Jackson yet — has been Gone Ever since Saturday
Last. I am some what affraid that He will not return again — The
Plasterer Commencd this Evening and Plastered the Left Hand
Conner Room

16   Brick layers Commenced on the Building or the Kitchen
and it rained so they had to Leave it — the Plasterers did not work

to day but untill about Breakfast time for it Rained too Hard — I Gave Mr Evans ten dollars of Plastering money

17 Nothing new. Mr Mosbey, the man that married the widow Babbit, Killed a Mr Jones To Night — He Shot Jones with 15 Buck Shot through the Stomach — Self Defence — of Course

18 I Took my mare and Gun this Evening and wrode up to the Lake and Killed Eleven Black Birds with my new Gun — I Killd several more tho I Could not get them   Winston was up with my Little Gun and He Killed thirteen Black Birds — Mr Ruffner and another man was up thare and I dont Know How many they got. Mr Tucker Came down from Jackson Late Last night — Has been Gone a week to day — The Plasterers Could not work to day — I had our white sow Killed and cleaned to day — Mr A G Carpenter paid me $6 for Shaving &c.

19 Nothing new that I Know of — The Mechanics Could not work to day at all

20 Nothing new that I Know of. No work done to day on my Building in Consequence of the unpleasant weather — I paid the Main St. walker five Dollars on acct

21 Nothing new that I Know of Except that Mr Brown paid me twelve Dollars that He has owed me for some time back   To Day I paid Mr Potter for Dr McPheters Eighty five Dollars which pays his Rent in full to the 1st of February, 1841. The Carpenter Commenced to day to Lay the Gallery Floor — also the floor in the Dormer window

22 The plasters Commenced again to Plaster the House, the Gallery was finished this Evening

23 I have been Quite vexed nearly all Day — One thing in Particular, that is, the Agricultural Bank money. I paid Dr Mc-Pheeters the other Day 85 Dollars in Agricultural M. and Took his Receipt for the same from Mr Potter And To Day [he] sends me word that He wants to see me and I saw Him and He wanted me to take the Money Back again. I very Foollishly Took the money in my Hand and went of[f] with it and after some time sold it to Mr Adriance at a Discount of 25 per cent and got Planters Bank at 12½ per ct. I paid a difference of 6.25 on Exchanging the One for the other, I then tok that and Gave it to Mr Potter tho I Reserved 20 dollars of the Planters money and Left that Saying I could not do Any Better than that

24 Nothing new that I Know of. I Remained at Home untill Late in the Afternoon   I then Took my Little William and took Him down to the Building with me and tis the First time that He has Ever been on the inside of the Building. He is now Just Five Years Old to day, the 24th Jnry, 1841

    25   Buisness has been Tolerable Brisk. Nothing new that I Know of   I was all arround Town to day Hunting for New Oreans funds — wanted to sell Agricultural and I did so and I got for Three Hundred Dollars in Agricultural, two Hundred and twenty three Dollars and fifty cents   One Hundred and Fifty Dollars of the money was on Demand and Had Just been Endorsed, the other One Hundred & Fifty Dollars was the Post notes and one years Interest Due on it — I paid Mr Barbee thirty Dollars on Plastering Bill

    26   I made out a Bill of Rent due from Mr A Kenney up to the 19th of January, 1841, and I find that the whole Amount of His Rent Due to the 19th was One Hundred and five Dollars — I Left the Statment with Him — The 19th of July He owed me 23 dollars and the full Amount of His Rent, without the Creddits to the 19th of January, 1841, is 203. The creddits are in all 98 dollars

    27   City Tax Assessment. I gave in my Property as Follows —

Number of Lots — One value	7000.00
Number of Slaves Five — value	2200.00
	$9200.00
Mrs Battles —	
Number of Lots 1	1500.00
Number of Slaves — two	550.00
	$2050.00
Mrs Amy Johnson	
Number of Slaves — Four	1000.00
	$1000.00

I Spent the Greater part of this Day Down at the Building working a Little and Looking on a Little and so on — Came Back from the Building and found the Boys in a Contraversy. Tryed to Have an Explanation of the Affair. Winston Continued to talk after being told several times to Hush — Gave Him a slap — He Jump[ed] Out of the front Door and Runs around the Conner and up the Bank Ally — I Caught Him opposite to the Bank in the Alley — Slapped Him Like as One would in Such Casses &c.

    I Got Mr Tucker to make a Couple of Large Window frames this Evening for the Kitchen — they were made to mach the sash that Mr Weldon made for my store windows — Front windows in the Kitchen was set up this Evening and [if] the weather Continues Clear the Brick Layers will Finish this week very Easy

28 I Commenced to Day to make the Whitning for the third Coat Made a Couple of Large Barrells During the Day — The Brick Layers were nearly Done [with] One End of the Kitchen to Day

29 Nothing new that I Know of Buisness very Dull indeed — I was at the Building a good part of to day — The Brick Layers Came very near making a Finsh of the Kitchen this Evening — They will top of[f] the Job very Early in the morning — Old Mrs C Cashell Died yesterday and was Buried to day — The Roof of the Kitchen will be put on Early next week if nothing Happens Serious

30 Col. Bingaman offerd His Blooded stock to Day at Auction at the Race tract tho Did not Sell Any of them, I Set Phill and Steven to day to Geting Brick from Parkers Building They Got very few.

31 I Started Over the River in the Afternoon with Mr Jaqumine to Hunt for Game and to Get his Saddle that has been Lost for some time on the other side of the River — I saw Mr Woods, Mr Howell, Mr Wrigley and Mr Doyal All were over on a Deer Hunt and Got nothing — I Got five Black Birds — Shot Once at Black Birds — did get one shot Once a[t] Ducks a Flying, never got one — Twice at Black Birds — Jakumin said He got fifteen, tho I did not see them myself

February 1 Steven and Phill at work Getting Brick from Mr Parkers old Buildings — Commenced on Sat. 30th Janry

2 Commenced to day to Digg a Hole for Back House in State Street

3 I Commenced to day with One Labourer to do the Brick work for Back House

4 Nothing new to day. Built up a Brick Privey to day — Commenced it yesterday

5 Nothing new that I Know of. Buisness Tolerable good — I was most of the day down at the Building Knocking around doing not much of Anything — The moon in Eclipse to night

7 I herd to day that John and Winston was up about the Lake a Hunting and I took my Horse in the afternoon and wrode up thare and Caught Both of them and gave them Both a Floging and took away there Guns — I threw away Winstons as far as I could in the Mississippi

8 Buisness has been Quite Dull all day — Nothing new that

I Know of   I gave the two Mr Weldons an Order to Mr Pearce for Sixty five Dollars that is due me for Rent — I Had the team Engaged Haulling Brick from Parkers Building   Col R L. Throckmorton died on the 6th instant — apoplexy

9   Nothing new that I Know of. The Plasterers are at work to day on the Building, have just Commenced work for the first time for two weeks &c.

10   Buisness very dull. Nothing new that I Know of. I Commenced this Evening to put on the Sheating on the Kitchen

11   Nothing new that I Know of   I took my Gun this Evening Late and went Out in Company with Mr Walker and Mr Ruffner to hunt Robins — Mr Ruffner got 7, I got 4 Robins and 1 Flicker, Mr Walker Killed nothing at all — I Caught 1 Mocking Bird and Bot 1. Gave 4 dol for Bird and Cage

12   Nothing New that I Know of   I had 24 Bushells of Bran Hauled up this Evening from under the Hill and nearly the same yesterday

13   The first Commencement of the New Theatre in Main Street[1] — I Got on my Little Nag this morning and wrode out in the old Fields to Shoot Robbins and this is my Hunt with my Little Gun — 7 Sparrow, 1 Blue Bird, 6 Rice Birds, 3 Ceder Birds, 1 Partridge, 52 Robbins and Came Home soon after Dinner — Old Mr Harrison was along with me and He Killed [blank] Robbins — We Came Home together

14   Buisness Tolerable fair   I Remained at Home all day with the Exception of a Small ½ hour walk in the afternoon down to the Building &c with MC

15   Nothing new. Every thing is out Hunting Robbins — Wellington took my Little Gun out this morning and came Home this Evening at supper with 57 Robbins and said that He Killed 10 more   This I did not see

16   Nothing new that I know off   Buisness was Quite fair. Only one of the Plasterers at work To Day, the other on a spree

---

[1] The Natchez theater had been destroyed by the tornado of May 7, 1840. In January, 1841, James M. Scott leased a brick building on Main Street and fitted it up as a theater. He advertised in the Natchez *Courier,* February 13, 1841: "Mr. Scott begs leave to inform the ladies and gentlemen of Natchez, that the new Brick Theatre on Main street, designed and executed by Mr. George Tucker is now completed, and will be opened on Saturday, February 13, 1841, with an efficient Stock Company." The program was to include: Tobin's *Honeymoon,* a comic song, a hornpipe, a song, the farce *Catching an Heiress,* and also "An OPENING ADDRESS" written for the occasion by "*Phazma*" and delivered by Mrs. Silsbee. See also Natchez *Free Trader,* January 23, February 10, 12, 15, 1841; Gates, "The Theatre in Natchez," *Journal of Mississippi History,* III (1941), 115–16.

I think   I wrode out this afternoon and shot one Robbin and Came Home again

17   Both Plasterers are at work to day, Commenced white Coting — News Came To Day that the United States Bank at Philadelphia Had Suspended — Good Deal of Talk about it[2]

18   Buisness Has been dull   Nothing New — Plasterers Has been doing White coting all this Day in the Garrett of the Building

19   Buisness has been Dull or a Little so — Nothing new that I Know of. Mr W. Cullen was Burried to day — Mrs Rowley Has Left Her Husband and has gone to New Orleans for the perpose of geting a Divorce from him — so Seys report Current, Plasterers are still at work on the Building. They Finished of[f] the Large front Room to day in the second story and Commenced on the other Back Room — I Saw Fox, the Carriage maker, sewing up the Flank of a Poor Cow that Mr McAlister Boy had Extracted a Live Calf from This Evening — The Calf Looks well but the Poor Cow will die from Pain

20   Quite a fine Days work   I Bot to day four China trees and Set them Out. I Bot at Auction after that 5 augers, 3 trowells such as Plasterers use & at Present there is five auction Houses going on in Natchez, viz. E. Thom[p]son & Co, McAlister & Watson, Jones & Tainter & C[o], J. Soria and I. Hoff — Full House at the Theatre, Some Fighting &c.

21   Nothing new   I took Little Will and wrode Out on the Makon Hill and over Looked the Swamp, then Came Home Early   McCarys Dick was very Drunk and came to my Kitchen at night, John and Winston Had been with Him During the Evening, took 2 drinks with Him &c.

22   All the Different Companys belonging to town are On the Streets. They Look well and to night there is to be a Grand Ball — Firemans Ball   I presume there will be a Greate many thare to night — Mr S S. Prentice Left this Evening for Vicksburg — Laurian Fell at Fitzchene meeting this Evening — so seys report   I saw a number of Horses and negros belonging to Capt Coton for sale at the Court House and one dray with them, for Debt I presume — Mr Sam Moore Has a Pop or two at Mr Fox, the carriage maker

23   Buisness in the Shop has been Dull. Nothing new that I Know of   I have been all day nearly at work down at the Building making mortar &c. Had my Grey Horse put in the cart to day

---

[2] After remaining open for only some twenty days, the Philadelphia Bank of the United States had suspended operations for the third and last time.

and Had five or six Loads of Sand Hauled from under the Hill by Steven and John

24 I was a Part of to day very Buisy Painting up Stairs in the garret of the House, myself and Winston and John did a Little too

25 Buisness has been Dull. Nothing new that can be relyed on. Mr Brown, the Plasterer, commenced to work to day — His first days work — They got through with the work up stairs to day and has Commenced on the Large Room below — Winston has been Painting nearly all day in the Building and Finished the Garrett this Evening Late — I pd Messrs McAlister and Watson fifteen Dollars that I owed them for Cigars a few days ago — I saw Mr P. M. Lapiece to day and I mentioned that I would Like to hyre, Rent or Lease a part of His Lot in State street — He told me that He would see me again about it and that He was in a greate Hurry to attend to some Buisness — Very well sir, Said I — I put $32 in the Box to night. Mother Bot Mrs Pitchers Cow for twenty Dollars

26 Buisness Quite Dull. Three men Plastering on my Building — I and Winston and John removed the Dirt and trash from the Building this Evening and Painted the garret Stairs. I Loaned Mr Oblenis my Grey Horse to day to do some work

27 Buisness Tolerable Good — Nothing new To day — The Plasterers Finished the roughf Coating [of] the Large Room below stairs to day about One Oclock I Have been Quite Buisy all day remooving the Lime from the Base and Doors and Winston has been Painting — John was also remooving Lime. He Got in a small dispute with this Little Bad Fellow, Guss, and I went down to the Building and gave Him a Floging — He is the First individual that has Ever been whiped in the new Building and it is a Little strange that this day One year ago I had to whip Him for Something Liking runing away &c. He is a very mischeveous Boy indeed — I do not Know where to find His match at Present — I gave Mr Evans ten dollars this Evening on work I gave Mr Brown 7.50 for two ½ days Plastering. If the Floor in the Kitchen was done I would have had the Plasterers Continued on and worked at the Kitchen I Spoke to Mr Deal, Maneger for Mr Lapiece, to day to see if he Could get the Old Gentleman to agree to Let me fence in the Lot next to me belonging to Mr Lapiece He Said that He would mention it to Mr Lapiece for me — Silvy was Confined to night at a Late Hour and Her Baby [was born] about 3 Oclock in the night

28 Nothing new that I have herd of to day Report seys

that a number of young men was on a spree Last night, Small Difficuties between Capt Guion of Vicksburg and Capt Page — also between Capt. Guion and Mr Thom Kemp   Nothing of Any importance transpired — Mr Kemp was during some part of the night wriding up and down in the Dumax Confectionary Establishment &c. Mc and myself wrode out on the Woodville road, then in the Scotts Old Field, then Home in good time, Mc wrode His new Black Horse, I wrode Kity and she was very Lame

March 1   Buisness Quite Dull indeed — I spent the Greater part of this day down at the Buiding putyng up the nail holes, Winston was painting, John was doing something in the way of Cleaning off the Lime — The Plasterers, 2 of them, Came down this morning and thought the Plastering too Green to Give it a white Coate. Mr Barbee thought that it was dry Enough and Commenced to work and made a days work. The Carpenter Commenced to put a Floor in the Kitchen, The estate [of] Mr Lyle was [sold], consisting of Horses, Drays &c. and his watch — on 6 months credit — Sam Stewart Home to Day from Scool

2   Buisness only Tolerable   Steven got drunk this morning and ranaway — Bill found Him out in the Body of a Cart under the Brick shed and Brought Him Home

3   Buisness has been Quite dull. I had a Settlement with Mr Geo. M. Evans, the Plasterer, He has worked twenty Days and I through a mistake paid Him for twenty two days — thus I have Lost Six Dollars — He told me that He was agoing out to Washington to take a Job. Mr Ruffner Sent me two workman this Evening After Dinner to paint — I Sent and Got three Keggs of White Lead from Mr Lambdin To day and they were charged I presumed.

4   A Large congregation of Persons Has Asembled at the Court House to hear a Long Studied Speech from Young Mr Mathison of this place, a Laboured article. Greate Effort Doubtless made to produce Effect — To Day Gen Henry Harrison is our President, Sure   I Commenced to Day to Lath the Kitchen &c. The Painters are two of them at work on the Building

5   Plasterrer got Done Lathing the Kitchen Late this Evening and Commenced to do a Little plastering in the uper Room &c. Nothing new — Natchez Curier made its appearance for the first time to day — I Bot One Paper, 6¼ cts — Mr Edwards wants me to take the Paper and He said that He would take it out in trade

6   I have met with several Disapointments during the day — In the First place when I got up this morning I found that Steven had not fed the Horses nor gone to work — After Breakfast I found

Him in the Guard House　　Had been taken up during the night drunk and put in thare — I had him Flogged and then turned Him Out and sent Him down to work. I then walked under the Hill and saw Mr Lapiece and told Him that I would Like to get about thirty ft of His Lot and that I would fence it in and full up the Large holes in it and do some repairs on the Cistern and if He thought it worth a rent that I was willing to pay a reasonable price for it. He told me I could do so and then on the back of that sent me word by Patterson that He had received a Letter from Potter and that Potter was agoing to build the theatre on the Lot and that I Could not have it　　I told Him that it made very Little difference with me for I Could Build me a cistern very Easy in 8 or 10 days — P & W is the cause of that Letter, no doubt. I then did not make a Bargain with the Tinner as I thought I would — I was then cheated in the Perchasing of Calico & Left my Pocket Book on desk. Might have Lost money for what I Know. Paid out a Hundred dollars to day One way or other

　　　7　　I walked out on the old fort in Company with Mc and took along my new Spy-Glass and we made some few peeps throgh the Glass and then Came to the Building again — after which we walked nearly around the Town

　　　8　　I paid off Mr Barbee the Plasterer to day and the full Amount of His acct against me was 106.66½　　I had paid Him nearly all the money so I only Had to pay Him 46.66½ to day — Now I Kept a good and accurate acct of His work and I Only made it 97.51 that I owed Him and said that He Commenced work by the month at 80 Dolls per month which is a fraction over 3 dolls per day. I told Him that I did not understand it so tho I paid Him, it only made a difference of 8.50 in our accts so I paid it — Enough Said — Myself and Winston painted 5 doors this afternoon in a short time

　　　9　　To day was a very dull day in the way of Business tho I was much ingaged doing work on the Kitchen　　I did some plastering myself to day, tho it Rained we did not stop plastering　　Finished off with Rough Coating One Room in the Kitchen and nearly Finished off the other

　　　10　　Finished Roughf Coating the Kitchen this Evening — I had the wooden Cistern taken down to day to the Building this Evening.

　　　11　　Buisness in the shop uncommonly dull, I have been Quite buisy all Day — Mr Brown the Plasterer finished the Kitchen this Afternoon, and Layed One Hearth in Kitchen. Paper Hanger Com-

mencd this morning to Hang the paper in front Room   Came very
near finishing the Room to day — I Commenced to work on the
wooden Cistern to day, stoping up the cracks with tar &c   I Commenced to day to moove down some of the Furniture to the Building &c. Mr Phillips Left to day for the uper States Somewhere

12   I was to day making a Hen House. I got the Plank from
Mr V Boyer — 1400 ft @ $15 per thousand   The Paper Hangers
got done Papering this Evening

13   Buisness very dull, I think

15   Buisness Tolerable Good. President Harrisons Inaugurr
address 6 & ½ Collums Long — Mooved to day from Mrs Neibut
House, Mr Stuctman & Mason

16   Buisness Tolerable Good. I got my Cow down at the new
Building to day and made a pen for Her — A Flat Boatman Shot
another Flat Boatman to day under the Hill. The name of the man
that was shot is [blank], the man that Shot Him is named
[blank]   McFarland was thrown from His Horse this Evening in
State St and so badley Hurt that I think He will Die from it   The
Horse was scared by a Dog belonging [to] old Mr Brier

17   Buisness Has been very Dull   Nothing new to day worth
talking about. I did some Little patching of fence to day tho not
much — I Had the middle Peer Takin out of my Brick Store on
Main Street to day — I was affraid it would fall tho it did not
thanks to Him [to] whom thanks are due

18   Times are dull, quite so — I have been making a partition
in the Kitchen this Evening & did not quite finish it at night, will
do so to morrow Proberly — Mr Brick is at work on my Brick
Store making a New Pillar to it.

19   Nothing New that I know off   McFarland that was
thrown from His Horse on Tuesday Evening Died this morning and
was buried this Evening — there was also a man by the name of
Kelly that was Burried yesterday at His House — I owed Mr Benj
Waker One Note of 78 dollars, 75 cents, due 1st of May next And I
took up my note to day by giving Him One Hundred Dollars in
Agricultural Money, thus giving Him 21.25 more than the note Calls
for — The only reason I have for doing so is I find Aggr Money very
hard to get off at 27 or 30 per ct discount, ie, the notes that are payable on demand. I told Mr Staples to day that I believe I would not
take any more Agricultural money for rent and that I would take
of[f] twen[t]y five per cent of the Rent and take it in Good
Money — $150 is the money that I have paid Mr Weldon on His
work — He Looked at the same to day

20   Buisness only Tolerable — To Day Mr George Weldon brought me His acct for work Done on my Building in State Street. The acct. reads this way

March 11th 1841

William Johnson Dr —
To G. Weldon — For first floor and

3 Door frames and 3 window frames as per Contract	117.00
To framing second floor, 12 Sqr 4.	48.00
To 1 door frame & transum Light Sash	20.00
To seting 3 window frames	1.50
Framing, Raising Floor 12 Sqr.	48.00
framing 15 Sqr of Rafters	60.00
7 Sqr Collar Beames	28.00
To 15 Sqr Sheeting and Shingles	90.00
100 ft. reveal Bourd	5.00
2 Dormer Windows	75.00
12 pds nails	1.50
150 ft 2 inch pine 6 ct per	7.50
60 feet wall strip for second floor	1.80
60 feet raising floor do	1.80
60 ft. Raising plate	1.80
	———
	$506.90
Here He makes a Deduction of $3 for weather Bourding that He Kept —	3.00
	———
	503.90
Here He makes a deduction of $15 for over charge on shingling per square —	15.00
	———
	488.90
here He adds on $40 for a Kitchen Built on Main Street	40.00
	———
	528.90
Here He gives me Credit for cash $150 pd Some time ago —	150.00
	———
	378.90
Here He gives a Credit of $15 that I paid Him to day — 20th March, 1841	15.00
	———
	363.90

The account handed in by Mr Weldon is about $1.30 more than what I Expected it would be — I Paid Mr Reynolds to day twenty five Dollars in Agricultural Money which He took at $18 and I gave Him 7 dolls in New Orleans money thus making up in all $25   This is in part payment of Brick work done for me   I must here remark that Buisness has been very Good to day — Greate deal of Hair Cutting to day — I have been a good part of to Day Displeased at things, Charges Principly — I will Know Better After a while, I paid Mr Tucker Thirty Dollars on account of Building work. Mr Tucker swung the Front Gate this Evening but did not Quite finish it   I had Sylvia and Her Child Brought Down this Evening

21   Buisness was prety Good, prety fair — I remained all Day at Home and Had John up stairs at His Book untill Late in the afternoon on account of His bad Conduct during the week — Nothing new of Any importance to me

23   Mother and Mrs Mitchell Came up from New Orleans about 3 Oclock in the morning — Mr Miller sent me a Letter to day with two hundred and fifty Dollars for Hester and wanted me to take a mortgage on Hesters old woman to Secure the $250 — I Saw Hester and Gave Her the money — She took One Hundred and fifty dollars of the money and told me that she did not want any moore — that She Had made the arrangement [to] do with Less money and that I must send the One Hundred Dollars Back to Mr Miller &c.

24   To Day I have not been doing much of anything of Consequence, I to day at the request of Mr Joseph Mechio gave Him the following Lines   Natchez, March first, 1841 — I Have this day rented a House to Mr Josph Meschio for the term of one year from date at thirty Dollars per month, payable monthly   Signed   William Johnson   I promise to pay said Wm Johnson the rent monthly   J Meschio   The rent will be $25 per month until 1st of Oct., 1841 — Here is the Bill of work done by Mr Tucker for me, the full Amount of which I paid Him for this Day, 24th March, 1841

To repairing Front Doors — —	3.00
” do window sashes	2.50
To Lumber, Pine Lumber	4.00
” Caseing 3 Windows at $4 per	12.00
” Making 4 window Frames @ $4	16.00
do 2 Door Frames	70.00
Caseing 2 Doors under Stairway	9.00

Bridging Joist & putting up Pillar	5.50
2 pine Doors at $7 per	14.00
Puting up furrowing to Lath on	3.00
Geting out & puting Down Base in Closepress	
under Stairway	2.00
Making 18 Lights of Sash, 25 cts	4.50
Puting up Studing & Finishing around Dormer	
windows	8.00
Puting in framing timbers in 2 windows & making	
2 window Frames	8.00
Strateages & Darbeys for Plasterers	1.50
Framing Roof to Kitchen	8.00
do joist for 2 floors	10.00

25   To Day about [blank] Oclock my Little Daugter was Born And the Larges & Finest Child I Ever saw of its Age — Mrs Dickson was with Her, Ann was well at Dinner time[3]   I Sent in a Letter to day One Hundred Dollars to Mr Miller in Orleans. I gave the Letter to Mr Britton On Board Steam Boat Sultana, Mr Howard paid me to day $10 the Amount of His acct. in full to date — Mr Jery Thomas paid $3 on His acct.

26   To day Has been Quite a Dull [day]. I hired a man to day to Commence to Dig out the Cellar to State St. House — Little Richard by Accident pulled down the Large Picture of the Last Supper & the Glass was badly Broken by the fall — I was trying this Evening to stop the wooden Cistern from Leeking but Could not   To Night the infair takes place at the Meryland House for Mr. I Bunce & Lady — I Had Some few Loads of dirt Hauled in my yard this Evening from Mr Parkers old Ruins — Winston puts the Box on one of our trees.

27   Nothing New that I Know of. To Day Mr Julian has the News Room Contents sold at Auction to pay the Rent of the House — They went Low

28   I remained at Home all day and read a Book through

29   I find it a very dull day. I was some part of to day diging Out a Cellar under the House

30   Nothing New that I Know of   A Receipt to Produce the meal worm, by Mr W Sergent   You must take a Quantity of Flour

---

[3] This was Anna L. Johnson (christened Ann Johnson, and known as Anna L. Johnston in her later years), the diarist's eldest daughter and fourth child. She died November 25, 1922. Adams County Probate Records, No. 5,618, File 313; Adams County Will Books, VII, 306–307. In the above entry, "Ann" referred to the mother.

or meal and put it into Layers between papers say 1 qrt. of an inch thick and it will produce the worm — for Birds

31 I wrode Down in the swamp to day and made a very Poor Hunt. I Killed 1 Squirrel, 3 Black Birds, 1 Sap Sucker, 3 Sedar Birds and Winston Killed 2 yellow Hammers, 1 Sparrow Hawk, 2 Black Birds — Mr Lindo Came Down a[nd] Claimed a mocking Bird that Mother was about Buying from Jim and Got it — I was down at Mr Thom Winns place. To Day Mr Vernon Had a good Deal of wood on the Bank. Mr Ford Had up a new gin and was Inprooving Mr Gregory Had Three Hundred Cord of wood Cut on the Andrews tract, Mr Mosbey Had Seventeen Hundred Cord Cut and was still improoing. Mr N L. Williams Rented a Room from me to day at $8 per month for the Purpose of putting His things in To Keep the officers from getting a Hold on them

April 1 Nothing new — I Had a window put up in place of my old One to day by Mr Tucker — Gov. McNutt is in Natchez at Present. Came I presume to review the Malishe Muster

2 To Day the young man Phelps Came and wanted me to pay Him for catching Steven I Gave Eight Pieces of Paper for it, Such as I sell for 5 Bits a Roll, which is Just five Dollars that the Infernal Rascal has Cost me precisely — not to Include His days work.

3 The Malisha of this Beat will parade to day on the Bluff under the Command of Capt. N Barlow — Nothing New that I Know of. I am still opperating upon my Cellar — The Circus Opened to night and the Animal Show and the Theatre is open also — So Everybody can Have as much of Either as they please — I have Layed out nearly or fully twenty dollars To day And not One Cent of the Amount went Towards paying my Debts — A Fellow wants to see Mr Rawlings — His Cister at Maj. Young Want to see Him or Sends Her Best Respects to Him &c. Charles was the person wanted.

4 I Kept the Boys Home to day untill Dinner time at there Books — Nothing new that I Know of

5 Theatre and Circus and several other shows are in operation to day — Nothing new that I Know of Except that I, Bill & Charles were all down at the Animall Show and John was runaway at the same time, Agricultural Bank Bot the Capt Dawson Property to day, $12000. It was sold at the Court House.

6 I have only 3 Runaways at present, my Cow, my Big Grey Horse and Little Sorrill mare, Scot Mais and Farmer and several other persons was taken up Last night — Supposed to be Robbers

7   Charles & Winston & John all Looking for my Cow this Evening and could not find Her at all — Agricultural Bank takes Possession of the Dawson Property to day, by Dr Tolley

8   Everything Looks well tho Buisness is dull — I pd Mr Reynolds on acct. to day Fifteen Dollars — John went Out to Hunt my Cow yesterday Evening and On His return Brought Home to His mother a Tame Turkey and said that it was wild and He Caught it — I Took Him and the Turkey this Morning Early and started back where He said He got it and made Him put it down and it was one of the tamest Kind of turkeys — I then set in on Him and Gave Him a regular whiping and made Him go Home again

9   Nothing new and the day a very Dull One indeed — John Caught Mrs Montgomerys Cannary Bird and She Gave Him One Bit for it, Very Liberal Entirely

10   Nothing new that I Know of. I saw Mr L. Claibourne to day and made Him an offer of One Hundred dollars for the Brick and all the Ruins that was on Mr Parkers primises & He Said you Can take them tho you must not pull down the Houses that the people are Living in   I told Him I would not and so the Bargain was Confirmed.

11   Nothing new that I Know of. After I Shot [shut] up the shop I wrode down to the saw mill wrode and up to the Shillings Lake to fish myself and well, when I got thare I did not fish for I did not think it worth while to try

12   I Commenced this morning on the old Parkers Building and Had Steven and 2 or three other Hands, old man Brileys & young relations — We took Down, I expect, about 4 or five thousand Brick

13   I Commenced Early this morning to work on the Brick from Mr Claibourne and I Had two hyred Hands, Cost 2.25 and John Cost 25 cts more.

14   Gen Wm H. Harrison is reported in to days Paper as Having Died on the 4th of April, ½ past 1 Oclock pm. To day I Have been quite Buisy geting Brick from Mr Parkers old Hotell, Cost of Hands to day, $3.12½.

15   Nothing New. We Hear to Day that a Declaration of War is anounced on the part of Ingland against the United States[4] — I am Quite Buisy at this time geting Brick from Mr Parkers old Ruins

16   Nothing New that I Know of. I Have been very Buisy

---

4 British-American relations were strained at this time over the McLeod case.

to day all day at work down at Mr Parkers geting out Brick. I paid Mr F L Claibourne to day $10 and I also paid another who Held an Execution against Mr Parker for $35 — I paid the 29 dollars and owes a Ballance of 6 Dollars on the Same — I paid it for Mr Parker, authorised by Mr Claibourne

17 Mr Saml. Davis returns from the North

19 Nothing new — I Commenced this morning again to work on the Brick

20 Nothing new that I Know of. Time are Dull — Mr Doniphan was called a Liar to day by Mr Sanaford Duffield — Mr Donniphan struck him over the Head with His stick They Both [*sic*] sent Him a challenge. Doniphan declined both and published [what] was said on the subject &c

21 Nothing new that I Know of

22 Nothing new that I Know. To Day it was that I opened my Baths for the 1st time this season. Nothing new — 7 Persons took Baths to day That is doing very good indeed for a Commencement

23 Nothing New that I Know of. To Day we Had a very Large turn out of all the Different Companies, Mock Funeral for Gen Harrison — I had 6 Baths To Day.

25 Nothing new. I went over to the Lake to day and Caught 17 fish, 8 of them was Cat fish — Mr Jackumine Caught 21 fish — Greate many persons fishing over thare

26 Buisness Dull. Nothing new

27 Nothing new that I Know of. I went up to the Auction Room to day a[nd] Bot of Mr Soria two small Lots belonging to the Estate of Mr Cochran and others. The Lots ran thus, 30 ft front, Each runing Back 100 ft, On a Credit of one, two and three years with 8 per ct interest — I wrode Down to the Shipping Comp and tryed very Hard to find where the Lot was that I Bot to Day but Could not, To night as I Came Home from super I Herd a fuss in the Tremont House Down stairs and it prooved to be Mr young Ephran Harrison in chace after Mr James Kidney He ran across the street and got into some French Ladies Room to Keep young Harrison from geting Hold off Him Young Harrison ran around the Back way and tryed thare to get in but could not get in Mr Kidney put out in the time and went home. He is a member of the Natchez Guards and to run in that maner does not become him — Bill Nix went to Concordia to fish in Company with Joseph Mesh and others Bill caught only thirteen Fish — Fire was seen to Break Out to night about 11 Oclock to night in the fine

Frame Building of Mr Philo Mitchell and Burned it up or nearly
so   The Engines were all Out and did well, very indeed   The
Building is Destroyed and used up

28   Maj A Miller Has been apointed Marshal for the Southern Destrict of Miss under Mr Tyler the President of the United
States — I wrode Down to the Shiping Company To Day and found
the Lots that I Bot and I Dont Like them   They are not as Levell
as they are represented to be by Mr Soria   I have some notion
of not taking them at all — Mr S S Prentess Gets Shaved twice
To Day — Something Out. I think I Know[5]

29   Nothing new that I Know of. Buisness only tolerable.
A Man belonging to the Harman Estate was murderd Last Night
in the Road. The Murderers tryed to Burn up the Corpse after
they Had murdered Him

30   To Day nothing new that I Know of   Buisness tolerable
good   I went into the swamp with Mr Tucker and we took guns
along and shot some Birds   He useed my Big Gun and I had my
small one — He Killed 1 Squirrell, 2 Snipe, 2 or three wood Peckers &c. I Killed 2 Snipes, 1 yellow Hamer, 2 or three wood Peckers
&c.

May 1   To day Buisness was pretty fair   I Took Kitty
Fisher down to the River and went over and took William Bucks
along with me and I think He caught near 2 doz Fish — the first time
that He Ever caught a fish in His Life — We Caught 4 doz & 8
between the two — I was some what Late in Getting across the
River and Had to Leave my Horse over thare at Wheelocks

2   Buisness Has not been very good to day — I went across
the River to day after Kity Fisher and then went down to the
Lake and caught 18 fish and came Home again

3   To Day is Quite a Dull Day   Nothing new that I Have
Herd — I Took a Boy by the name of Edmond from Mr N. Hoggatt to day to Lern the trade of Haircutting & shaving &c — Mr
George Snider Died Last night or Just before day Light this
morning

4   Nothing New that I Know of   To Day I went up to
McCarys Shop and told Him that I had two Little Boys and was
requested by Mr Hogatt to get situations for them to Learn a
trade of some Kind — He wanted One of them and I Gave Him
Choice of the two, Jefferson and William   He Liked the Look of

---

[5] This was almost a year before the marriage of Prentiss to Mary Jane Williams,
daughter of James C. Williams of Longwood. Adams County Marriage Records,
VI, 541; Dickey, *Seargent S. Prentiss*, 199.

Wm Best tho   Wm told Him that He wanted to Live with me so
Mc then said He would take the other — Accordingly I sent Jeff
up to Him this Evening

 5 Nothing New that I Know of Except that there will be no
United States Court this term Report Seys that the newly
apointed Marshal, Mr Anderson Miller, Has been arrested in Washington City, which will bring about a Defeat of the term

 7 I was Out to day in the Pasture Looking at Some Riffle
Shooting — Jackumine made a match of 100 yds Shooting to day
in 2 inches 1 q[ua]rter, off Hand

 10 Nothing New that I Know of. Buisness geting remarkable
Dull.

 11 I Bot a Keg of Lard and 56 lbs of Bacon at the Landing
this Evening It was very Good indeed

 12 This morning Shortly After Breakfast time The Boy
William ran off and Took with Him Jeff, His Brother, that I had
put with McCary They Both went Out Home. They are Boys
that were put with me by Mr N Hogatt William was the Cause in
Toto — From what I have seen of Him I am Inclined to think that
He is a Boy of no Kind of Energy — Young William Commenced
this Afternoon to Moove the Effects that He had in a Room Back
in my yard that He was to have paid me Eight Dollars per month
for — McCary got on His Horse To Day After those Boys Ranaway And tried to overtake them, but did not Cucceed

 13 I Bot a Small Barrell of Spanished Brown[6] from Young
Williams Allowed Him five Dollars for it in Rent, I was to day
puting up an arning down at the House — Forty four Persons
Served in my Shop to day, Three Baths. Wm Cannon & V. Boyer
Has a fight Cannon Gets the Best of the fight &c

 14 I am Nervous to Day And will have some fighting to do
before night I do Expect, Tho I hope not, Cincerely do I, and I
will try and Keep Cool — Very Singular that Steven ranaway to
day And the two Boys that ranaway the other day should have
returned at the same time Just as One ranaway two Came back
or one rarther, for One of Said Boys ranaway from Mc, the other
from me, I wrode Out this afternoon to the Forks of the Road to
try and swop Stephen off for Some One Else, But could find no one
that I would Like

 15 Buisness thus far Dull — Tax, Tax, Tax, Tax, Tax — I
paid my Tax To Day To Mr Baker, the Collector. The Amount

---

[6] The phrase "Spanish Brown" meant either paint or sugar. In this case Johnson
probably referred to paint.

of which was $61. I also paid a Tax for Charles which amounted to Eight Dollars, 50 cts. I am inclined to think that very Tall Taxation, Steven ran off to day about Dinner time, Had on clean clothes — Several things Occured To Day in town   Yes, Poor Micheal Weldon Died   This Has been a very Dull Day indeed   I was Over to Day at Messrs McAlister & Watson and I thare Bot Two Barrells of Roman Cement at $5.25 a Barrell. From thare I went over to Mess[r]s Thomsons & Co and there was a work Horse, a Black Horse, He was offered to the hiest Bider and I Bot Him, paid fifteen Dollars, 50 cts for Him — the Horse, Sadlle, and Bridle   The owner of the Horses name was Thorn — I am some what of the opinion that the man is not a good man from the fact of His swearing so much, He guaranteed the Title to be good — The Bill was Drawned out by Mr Pitcher and Signed before Him by Said Thorn who, when He was asked by Mr Pitcher where He Lived, He Said that He Lived out near Greenville or Shankston And that He Had only owned the Horse five days   The Said Horse was very Poor — I paid Mr Geo. Weldon to day Eleven Dollars on acct. and I will Soon pay the Ballance if I am Spared

     16   Buisness fair to day   John has a Pistol Taken from Him to day and Caps   He was making Preperation to Hunt, After being foiled in his opperations He got on Bourd of Steamer Constelation and went to New Orleans — Steven is runaway too at the present time

     17   Buisness has been very dull indeed   Nothing New that I Know of, Mr Hogatt was in town to day and we had a Little Chat about the Boys &c.

     18   Nothing new that I Know of   Buisness Dull.   A Mr B B. Rowan was taken up to Day by Young Withers as the murderer of an overseer in Wilkinson County some time ago. He had Just returned from Nashville

     20   Buisness Tolerable Good — I wrode up to the Shipping Comp this Evening and took my Short Rifle and Shot two matches   The First I Shot was 40 yds, 3 best in 5, and made the match in 3 inches ½, the other 3 best in 5, Same Distance, 2½ inches

     21   The Shooting Matches Came off To Day by the Companies   The Shooting was very good indeed.

     22   Nothing new that I Know of   Buisness Tolerable only

     23   Buisness was Only Tolerable. Nothing new that I Know of   I wrode Out this afternoon on my old Black Horse and thare I found a number of men playing at wicket   Some were shooting and some were playing — I Left thare and went down to the Shipping Company to Look for my Horses and I found them near the spring and the Gate nailed up by which they went in   I Could not get them Out.   My nag Kity I did not see at all

24   Nothing new that I Know of   I took my gun this afternoon and went out to the Bayou and shot several matches with Mc and I only Lost One Match out of four — To Day has been Dull some what, I Sent Winston down to the mill this Afternoon to get my Little mare and He brought Her up after a Long run

25   Nothing new that I Know of   I went up to Mcs to day and thare I found him Siting back in His Room

26   News of no Consequence to day

June 3   To Day has been One of Common place   Nothing new has transpired to day to my Knowledge that is worth attention

4   Buisness as usual, not very Lively nor very Brisk

6   Pheebe, the mother of William & Jeff, Children of Mr Wilford Hogatt, Came in together with Emeline & Misouri and Little January Hogat — they remained untill after Dinner and then Left Leaving Misouri and January to stay in town — The Boy is to stay with the girl as Company for Her, for a few days   Tis a good Idea.   But from the appearance of the Little Girl I am inclined to think she is stuborn and of Strong passions and not Easily managed — I am pretty shure that is the Case with her[7]

7   Buisness has been Dull for the time of year.   To Day the Capital offence Came of[f] before the Court, ie, the tryal of Isum

---

[7] The will of Wilford Hoggatt, dated August 28, 1840, and probated January 25, 1841, stated that on December 24, 1824, in St. Helena Parish, Louisiana, a Negro woman named "Febe" had paid him $550 for her freedom, and afterward, in Mississippi, had seven children: Jeffrey, William, Anthony, Gim, Abb, Emiline, Eliza. He directed that Febe be paid $600 in yearly installments of $50, that the seven children be freed, and that a mulatto child named Mary (four years of age) also be given her freedom. He further directed that the eight children be given "an equal portion of his Land [which he stated was 4,000 acres] Slaves Stock and household furniture." The girls were to receive their shares when they became sixteen, the boys at age twenty-one. The remainder of the estate was to be used for the support of the eight children. Nathaniel Hoggatt, Jr. (one of the executors appointed by the will and probably Wilford's nephew) arranged for the manumission of five of the above-named children—Jeffrey (or Jeff or Jefferson), William, Anthony, James, and Emily—and of January Hoggatt in Ohio in 1853 and 1855. See Adams County Will Books, II, 228–31; Adams County Deed Records, KK, 44–45, LL, 207–208. All of the five boys freed worked for Johnson at various times. For the marriages of January, Anthony, and James, 1855–58, see Adams County Marriage Records, VII, 351, 404, 554.

For other emancipations by this Adams County family of large-scale planters, see Adams County Will Books, II, 113, III, 19–20; Adams County Deed Records, KK, 42–43.

for the murder of Mr Wilford Hogatt — He was found Guilty.[8]
Several Gentleman on the Jury that I Am well acquainted with, Mr.
Robt Tinner Walker, [blank]

   8   Buisness this morning Early is very Good — Grows dull as
it Grows Late, To day the Trial of Mr John Barland Comes on
for the Murder of Fitzjeral and he will get clear of it as Easy as
possible[9]

   9   To day we had a very seviere wind from the west That
threatened the destruction of much Property   We had considerable rain with it. Blew away an arning that I had put up down at
my dwelling House — Did some mischief in the country, the Extent
of which I have not herd

   10   I wrode Down at the Landing this forenoon and found
Some men shooting at a target. I got in a talk with them and

   [8] The judgment of the Adams County Circuit Court (see Minutes, 1840–41, pp.
313, 333, 372) holding Isham, a slave, guilty of the murder of planter Wilford
Hoggatt was later reversed by the High Court of Errors and Appeals on the ground
that Isham's master, who was offered as a witness to prove an alibi for his slave,
was not permitted to testify. "In prosecutions for offences," said the higher court,
"negroes are to be treated as other persons." Counsel for the defense also pointed
out that Isham's confession had been obtained while he was "in great pain" from
his shackles and because he was in fear of the "blind fury" of an "excited
company," which would have lynched him but for "the moderation of Philip
Hoggatt, equally creditable to his heart and his head." Volney E. Howard,
*Reports of Cases Argued and Determined in the High Court of Errors and Appeals,
of the State of Mississippi* (Cincinnati, 1843), VI, 35, 39, 42.
   [9] The court minutes do not state whom John Barland was accused of murdering,
but merely record that he was indicted for murder and found not guilty. Adams
County Circuit Court Minutes, 1840–41, pp. 310, 331, 374. Johnson was on friendly
terms with John Barland: he lent Barland small sums of money, he sometimes
grazed his stock in Barland's pasture, and they went hunting together.
   John Barland was a free Negro, an acknowledged son of William Barland,
Adams County white planter who held three land grants from the Spanish government, and his slave Elizabeth. She and their twelve children (including John)
were freed by William Barland in 1815 after he had petitioned the Territorial
assembly for authority to emancipate them and his petition had been granted.
See Petition of William Barland, December, 1814, Petitions and Memorials, Series
D, No. 38; *Acts Passed at the Second Session of the Eighth General Assembly of
the Mississippi Territory* (Natchez, 1814), 40–41; Adams County Deed Records,
H, 369; Adams County Will Books, I, 132–38.
   Elizabeth Barland and her children inherited William Barland's property and
were sometimes listed in census and tax rolls as white, sometimes as free Negroes.
In 1839 and 1840, John Barland was listed on the tax rolls as white and in 1843
and 1849 as a free man of color. In 1844 he married "Mary E. Fitzgerrald." See
Auditor's Records, Tax Rolls, 1839, 1840, 1843, 1849, Adams County; Adams
County Marriage Records, VI, 653.
   For John Barland's signed acknowledgment that he was one of "the issue of the
said William Barland and Lisey his Wife who was a coloured Woman," see Petition
of Children of William Barland, *c.* 1830, Petitions and Memorials, Series I, No. 97.
For John's participation in the division of his father's estate, see Adams County
Deed Records, Z, 152.

found them to be the same men that Clossin was throwing Bricks and Drawing Gun Barrells on them. They However suied him before Esqr Perdue and bound him over to Court in the sum of three or four hundred Dollars for his appearance, To day has been Quite a Lively day and nothing new that I Know of. Winston I find has after the best admonitions that I have been able to give, will disobey my orders — I find him to day with a Pistol in his Pocket, This Pistol I find belongs to old Mr Bryley and that his own son stoled it from him and had sold it to Winston — Oh if I could only find some honest Person that I could trust in   My Kingdom for some one that is truly honest

11   I was this Afternoon in the Bayou this Evening Shooting with Mr Jaqumine for a pr of fine Shoes — The 1st Center would win — After Shooting the whole Evening, 27 or 28 Balls Each, we had to Leave off — a stand off

16   I set Charles several Lessons on the slate in Cyphering — he did very well indeed

17   I got three Little chickens to day from Mother as a Present, 2 of them was Freeslings — the whitish Rooster

19   Nothing new that I Know of   Buisness To Day was Good, Bathing and Shaving also

21   Nothing new this morning that is worth the attention of a smart man

22   The Trial of Bealy B. Rowan Came of[f]. The Case was not decided untill nearly 12 Oclock and He was aquited in a very few minutes — It was for the murder of Mr Martin whom report seys that B B Rowan Killed several years ago

23   Greate number of Citzens Left town to day for the north, Messr[s] Lambdin, Dick Carson & Family, Stewart

24   Nothing new that I Know of   I Commenced yesterday to put up a pump on the stand above the Barrell to force the water into the Barrells   A Carpenter put up my windlass on the Cistern, Charged $2 for it.

25   I went out this Evening a shooting in the Bayou with Jaqumine and Mc   We shot 19 matches, Mc won 8, Jacqumine 9 and I won Only 2. A Cigar was the Entrance   They were pool Shooting and not matches

26   Buisness is dull, Quite so   Nothing new — Sentence was passed on the Criminals. Judge Cage presided as Judge

27   Nothing new that I Know of — Several Gentleman down this morning from Vicksburg, Maj Miller, Mr Cox, Prentess &c.

30   I went Down in the Bayou this Evening and shot a good

many times with my old rifle   Made some very bad shoots a[t]
[one] Hundred yards   Shot only five times, Quit, and then went
to shooting twenty yards. Made bad Shooting at the onset but
towards the Last I shot tolerable well   This Shooting will, if I Continue to think as I do at present, do for my Last Shooting for
Several, Several Days Shure, ie, Riffle Shooting   I Lost ½ Dozen
Cigars with Mc this Evening on one shot with the Riffle. A Mr
Turner and Mr Miderhoff has a Scuffle — It Commenced in this
way, Turner Commenced on Miderhoff with a Cow hide, fell by
accident, at that time M Jumped on him but other was too Strong
for him. Miderhoff Jumped of[f] and ran away   Left his hat in
the fight. He fought prety well for a very Short time and at the
close of the fight he made a Splendid run   It was in very good
time that he made the Run

    30[*sic*]   To day Has been One of the dullest days we have had
for some time   I signed twelve notes of mine to day, Payable in
One, Two and Three years from Date. The notes were given in consideration of two Lots I Bot at Auction in April Last, $18.83 is the
Amount of Each note   They are all made Payable in the Commercial Bank to the order of the several Different owners as Follows, Commercial Bank, Mrs Cocharan, Mr A P. Merrell, Jefferson
Beaumont, &c.

    July 1   To day has been a very dull day in the way of Buisness
and nothing of Any interest has transpired   Mr Midderhoff's Card
in this morning papers, also in hand Bill form, it reads thus

To The Public

    I hereby denounce N E. Turner a base paltroon and an arrant
Coward   This Scoundrel made an assass[i]nlike attack upon me
night before Last at Dusk when I was unarmed & did not Expect
an attact — When yesterday a friend of mine Called on Him to
Cross the river, he basely sculked from responsibility by saying
that "he was not a fighting man."
Natchez July 1st 1841   J A T Midderhoff

    I had the big gate put up to day that Mr Raly gave me   The
Carpenter charged me $3.50 for putting up the same
    2   Buisness very dull, nothing a doing — I was around this
morning to Esqr Robatiles office   The Buisness I had theare was
only to see the man that was Beatten so by Mr Thoms Welldon,
The Particulars will be put down I presume.
    3   I gave Mr Weldon to day my note for two Hundred and
twenty Dollars — this was the amnt on a settlement that I owed

him — I also paid Mr Reynolds twenty Dollars on acct. I Loaned Mr Barland my big shot gun this day and He crossed the River and Killed a fine Buck with Her. Tis the First that she Ever Killed I Know

4   Nothing new that I Know of. Greate many persons are Frollicing to day, tho to morrow is the set day for the Celebration, and a Large parade is Expected, Good many of Our Citizens have gone over the River to take a Frollic. I ive [I've] since herd that it broke up without affording much pleasure to the Company — Mr N Hoggatt sent me a Cow & Calf by his Boy, Prince, to day

5   To day is the day the Citizens Celebrate for the 4th   The Cricket Club has a Dinner Out in the Capt Miner Pasture[10] — Several fights so I herd, Ive not herd particulars yet — The Little Black fellow Shedrac Murdered the Cook Ned at the Mansion House to day in a fight — it was supposed to be an old Grudge

6   There is nothing new that I Know of to day Except that the Boy Shedrack that murdered the Cook man Ned yesterday, the Fellow was tryed before Justice Robetile, Mr Vannerson in the behalf of the Prisner and no one in behalf of the State   He was cleared of Course

8   Nothing new — I went down in the Swamp to fish and I caught three Doz and 11 fish. Mr Walker, the Tinner, Caught Eighteen. Wins Caught Five [doz] and 5   I was Hunting part of the time or I would have Caught more, We fished in Dock Lake — Messrs. Wrigley, Barland, Paine was Down on a Deer Chase, tho they did not get One

9   Nothing new that I have herd

12   Thare is a report in town, that S. B. Withers was Dead, that He died at Memphis — The Nephew I herd is also quite Sick, sun Struck, Report Seys that Mr Rouley Met Mr Robt Dunbar to Day and Cursed Him and His wife for Every thing he could think of and Mr Dunbar stood it and did not resent it — Peter Little and R Bledsoe met under the Hill and had a fight, Old Peet Knocked Mr Bledsoe Down and hurt his Eye,   Bledsoe Started of[f] for a gun, a Pistol, seying, give me a gun, a Pistol, Shoot Peter Little, Look at my Eye, Gun, Pistol, &c

13   Nothing new that I Know, Little Gim Hoggatt Came in to day and tried to follow the man that Brot Him in out Home again

14   Buisness Quite dull indeed   Nothing new — R North, I

---

[10] The cricket club was still in existence the following April. See description of a match and a notice of a Saturday meeting in Natchez *Courier*, April 27, 30, 1842.

herd to day, Gave Judge Rawlings a Terrible Flogging with a Large
Lether Strap and the worst of it is that he stood and Took it and
remarked that he would do as Midderhoff did — I will Stand
and take it Like a man   It was a Day or two ago this happened   Charles made a run to night that was no way slow, the
City Guard was after him

    15   I paid a man $5 to day for years Subscription to the
Picaune Paper — from Feb, 1841, to Feb, 1842

    16   Nothing New that I have herd of

    17   Nothing new that I Know of. Shooting Match Came of [f]
To day at the Race tract. They Shot for Beef. Mr Pryor won 1
or 2 quarters, the hyde and Taller. Mr Jaqumine also won a
Quarter and Mr. Bassinet and Himself won a quarter &c. And I
have herd to day that a man was found near Washinton this
morning with his Brains Blown Out. They were travelling and
the man that Shot Him was in the Employ of the Deceased, Martin   The Fellow that Shot him was named Harwick or some
such a name[11]

    18   Nothing new that I Know of. To day about 11 oclock I
and Bill Winston went down into the swamp To fish. We fished
on the back of the Winn Lake   I caught 19 fish and Wince caught
9. Commining back we found a number [of] Gentlemen were on
the Bank of the River Drinking and Shooting &c. Mr Wrigley,
also Mr Barland, Mr Izod, Mr S Wood, Mr Strickland, Mr Collins
— I Came off and Left an umbrella — W. West handed me a Confession of those men that was hung on the 9th of July inst   I
Commenced on it to night and got through it at or near 1 Oclock
to night

    19   I paid Mr G. Weldon to day fifty Dollars on account of
my note that he holds, The Little Boy Gim of Mr Hoggats that I
had, wran away this morning and went Out Home And I Sent Out
William Winst and Edmond after him tho they did not find him.
Edmond then Kept On Out Home and has not returned yet and
it is now night

    20   Mr Owen gave me $75 in good money on the rent For
Mr. Staples. Two months Rent is due to 19th inst. Mr A Kenney
paid me thirty four on his rent. He Owes a Ballance of Eigty
Dollars, 50 cts. He gave me his note on demand for it, Edmond
Came home from Mr Hoggatts to day and did not bring Gim with
him. I Loaned Col Bingaman the pamphlet to day that Contains

---

[11] See short account in Natchez *Free Trader,* July 19, 1841.

the Confession of those four men that was hung at St. Louis on 9th inst. Mr I. Thomas read it through to day in the Shop.

21   Nothing very new. The dwelling House of Mr Samuel Woods was Burned Last night and was no doubt Set on Fire. The fire Commenced on the Kitchen side that was Occupied by Mr Howells Servants

22   There is nothing new to day. Buisness dull. Town healthy, with a few Gentlemen sick, Mr Saml Woods is Quite sick, was very Low Last night, Some what better, I Commenced this Evening Late to do some work Down at the House, Lathing up the under part of the Gallery for to make a Dining or Eating Room — Not one single Bath takin this day in my B. House, remarkable indeed, A mistake, it was Tuesday 20th

23   Nothing new that I Know of. Mr B. Peyton of New Orleans past up this Evening. Brought two Letters, the one for Messrs Postlewaite & Ernest, the other [for] Messrs Fox and Brasier. To day has been very dull in the way of Buisness — I went arround to Mr Jaqumine to day with him and He gave me a Puppy by his white Dog out of Flora

24   Nothing new that I Know of — Large Comp of Our Citizens went out to day in the Bayous in search of Runaway Negroes. Capt Ruffner & Mr McAlister, Mr Joseph Mesho and a number of Our Respectable Citizens was out — Mr R finds a fire Burning in the woods — Jo Mesho finds a Bucket of meat in a tree where the Runaways has been tho there was no Negroes Caught that has been Known — I had a Settlement to day with Mr Reynolds and I find to my surprise that instead of owing him about $20, when the Documents was Compaired he was in my debt 16 cents   Close fit it was[12]   To day has been the Beef Shooting at the Race tract and target shooting &c. Mc was Out and won $10 from the people

25   A young man on the other side of the River was Son struck — His name was Delamer

26   Buisness very Dull   Another shop opened around by the market House, a Duch Barber he is — report seys that he will shave three men for 1 Bit — Bull Beef — Bull Beef — &c. Big fight to day arround at the Kane Coffee House   Dimmit VS Geo. Evans. They wound up the fight by Demmetts Knocking P. Laurrence in the Head with a Brick bat &c.

27   Nothing new that I Know of

28   Buisness has been dull, very much So

[12] The account totaled $251.81.

29   This has been quite a dull day, so much so that I have been away all the Evening making a Shed in the yard

30   Just at or about Supper time we had a heavey Shower of Rain and a strong wind, So very Strong that I ran from where myself [and] Winston was at work plump into the Back House and Winston with me — It was very Cowardly to do so. And my Family up Stairs

31   Nothing new. I wrode Out to the race tract this Evening to See the Shooting for Beef — Col. Bingmen won the 1st Choice and Jaqumine won the 2 next Choice and Mr F. Weese won the other Choice.

August 1   Buisness very dull Indeed   Nothing new that I Know of   Charles Complains of being a little sick and Takes a Dose of Antimoral wine

2   I Know Several gents that put on there winter Cloths. I Saw no Sporpt [Sport] to day. Nothing in town, [A] $100 Mach was shot this Evening between Mr Prior and Mr Jaqumine. Mr P. with a rest, Mr J. off Hand, 60 yds to 100 yds rest. Mr Jaqumine won the mach Easy

3   Buisness much better which I am proud to see. Charles is some what better than he was yesterday   B. Savage sentenced to Peniteniary for one year in La for remaining in the State VS. Law.

4   To day there is nothing new that I Know of   Greate many Snakes in the Grass — tis dangerous to walk, tis indeed

5   I find Buisness very dull and Snakes are very thick Even in Our Amediate Streets

6   Nothing new that I Know of. The Courrier has an article in it this morning that eminated from the hands of Several; Signed many Citizens   I know what I Know. Nothing of any Importance going on to day   Buisness has been dull, very indeed, I am Sorry to See it indeed   Old Mrs Bingaman is very sick, Edd. Hoggatt is Sick also. Charles Has Just recovered from a Spell of Sickness, 3 days duration, Our Papers of to day announces to there readers that the *Yellow* Fever has made its appearance in New Orleans and that several Cases had terminated in Black vomit &c.

7   Large meeting was Intended to have been held in the City Hall tho I understand there was not a greate many thare[13]

---

[13] The Natchez *Courier*, August 7, 1841, announced the meeting: "FREE NEGROES AND SLAVES. A general meeting of the citizens of Adams County is requested at the Court House in Natchez at 5 o'clock in the afternoon of Saturday next, the 7th instant, to take into consideration the propriety of enforcing the 26th section of the Revised code of the laws of Mississippi, imposing a fine

9   Lynch, the City Guard, in talking and raving threw up his stick or the End of it and broke the Glass in a Large Frame and had, as I thought, no money to pay for it. Nothing of any interest has occured during the day

10   Another meeting was held this Evening in the City Hall, I hardly [know] for what perpose. To day the Courrier published the proceeding of the Last meeting. Every[thing] was well ment and nothing Out of Character Appeared in it. Judge Dunlap paid me on his acct. one Dollar and 25 cts to be put to his acct, A Mr —————— was caught in bed with Mr Parkers old Big Black woman Buster and a Mr [blank] was Caught in bed with old Lucy Brustie, Hard times indeed, when Such things Ocur

11   I wrode down this Evening to Mr Barland To put my Horses to pasture and I Bot a Cow from Mr Winn for 17 Dollars and Brot up another to take if I Chose, I put my two Horeses in Mr Barlands Pasture this Evening To grass

12   Considerable Humbugery going on in town and some men are on the List that I Know is too much the Gentleman to have any thing to do with it, Mrs C. C. Binghaman[14] Died Last night   Was Sick for Several days

13   Nothing of much interest Occured to day. Mr Oblemis is Sick. I wrode Out to his House this morning and cut his Hair, He was Telling Mr McGraw about some of the Citizens of Arkensaw taking the Life of twenty three men who He herd had Commited Roberrys and Counterfeiting &c. He Said that they Drowned 11 of them and shot the rest. Mrs C C Bingaman was Buried this Morning Out at Fatherland, the old Home Plantation   It was a very Large Funeral indeed   The Largest Ever Known in the place

14   Nothing new To day worth the attention of any Bond payer — Several hits at the Different papers relative to the Bond Discussion in Vicksburgg &c.

16   The City is at this time perfectly Healthy and nothing new thats interesting

17   All Sorts of Tryals going on   The different Offices has been full all day and they Continue to arrest Still — The Lord

---

on the owners of slaves who permit them to go at large and hire their time; and also of enforcing the 80th section of the same code, requiring free persons of color to remove from the State and to prevent their emigration into the state." The notice, dated August 6, was signed "By Many Citizens of Natchez."

14 This was Mrs. Charlotte C. Bingaman, widow of early settler Adam Bingaman and mother of Colonel Adam L. Bingaman. Her estate was valued at about $150,000. "Estate of Mrs. Charlotte C. Bingaman," Adams County Probate Records, File 84.

Knows how those things will terminate for I have no Conception myself[15]   Buisness is very dull indeed, nothing Lively in the way of my Profession at all

18   Nothing new that I Know of   The Horrows [horrors] of the Inquisition is going On still in this City, It Seems that Dr Merrell and the Jg [Judge] has a tryal this Evening   I have not herd any thing moore about it   The report of Harriet Cullen or Harriet Johnson[16] being in Jail is not true, She was not put in the Jail, Glad of it

19   Nothing new that I Know of. Buisness Cannot be worse I think than at present   The Tryal of Berry Came of[f] To Day and I have yet to Learn for I dont Know what the result was at all yet

20   Buisness Qu[i]te Dull and nothing new that I Know of   Steven is drunk to day or this Evening and gone on the town somewhere   Yesterday Ann Perkins that was Commited to Jail some 3 days ago was tryed under Habeas Copus — She prooved that She was of Indian Decent and Came of[f] Clear — Mr T. Armatt was her Council — Saunders & Thatcher V.S. Her — She was put in by a [two blanks] by the name of Sandy Parsons — His witness [was] Peter Lardence — Big Berry Duncan was Cleared at the same time and was Ordered to Leave the state in thirty Days. Fullman was also tryed at the same time and the result was the same as in the Case of Berry Duncan[17] — To day Big Francis and her Daughter was tryed I believe and was put in Jail for further notice, &c.

---

[15] On August 17, 1841, the Natchez *Courier* carried the following advertisement: "NOTICE. A Special meeting of the Board of Police will be held at the Court House, on Thursday the 26th inst., for the purpose of granting or recalling Free Negro licenses." The notice was signed by the president, Henry L. Conner.

[16] Harriet Johnson was a free mulatto woman, about thirty-four years of age in 1841, who had been freed (along with her infant son, Robert) by William Cullen of Wilkinson County in 1829 in consideration "of the truth and fidelity of the said yellow girl called Harriet, and also for the sum of five dollars to me in hand paid by her friend William Casey." Cullen had purchased her in 1826 for $500. In 1840 she had paid $620 for a lot at the corner of Franklin and Pine streets, and she therefore was among the small group of free Negro property holders in Natchez. See Adams County Deed Records, R, 419, BB, 321–22, 519–20; Adams County Court and Police Board Minutes, 1832–45, March, 1832.

[17] The Natchez *Courier*, August 28, 1841, printed a lengthy opinion by the Adams County Circuit Court to the effect that either the justices of peace or "the Conservators of the Peace" could require Berry Duncan, unlicensed free mulatto, and other unlicensed free Negroes to leave the state within sixty days.

Fullman was probably unlicensed Thomas Fullman, husband of Matilda Lieper, free woman of color who had a license to remain in the state. See Adams County Deed Records, X, 473.

21   Buisness To day has been very Dull, The meetings are
Still Going on in the Inquisitions Court, The Lord Only Knows the
result, Phill Came up from the Swamp this Evening. Seys they are
well. The Following Gentlemen Signed William's Petition To Day
— Col A L. Bingaman, Mr Duffield, Col Wilkins, Capt. J B. Nevitt,
I Confess there is Something about this Law that I do not understand, Report Seys that a Bond is required After the Lycences is
obtained   I Cannot understand the mater fully

22   To day I wrode down into the swamp and took Steven
with me and Left him at Mr Gregorys to work at the rates of 20
dollars per month — He had Just been Brot in from Mr Minors
Quarters and I had to pay 4 dollars for taking him up

24   Lotts of F. P. C. are running arround Town with Petitions
to have the Priveledge of rama[in]ing in the state, tis Laug[h]able
almost, Wellington[18] was Out into the Country this Evening to have
his Petition signed and He got the following Gentlemen on his
Paper — Dr Steven Duncan & Col A L Bingaman, Dr Calhoun, Col.
Wilkins, Mr R. C. Evans, Mr J Routh, Mr S. D. Elliotte — Those
Names are Enough to make any Common man Proud — Those
Names are an Ornament to Any Paper — Those are Gentlemen of
the 1st Order of Talents and Standing

25   Good deal of Excitement in town to day. The Safety Committee flying arround and Consulting with Each other on Every
Conner, To morrow being the Day that they are prepairing for

26   To day has arrived — this is and Exciting day with the
People of this place — that is, the People of Couleer and the Inquisition

27   To day has been a day of much interest to the Citizens of
this place. The Veto of the Bank Bill reached this place to day
and the Whigs are very much Disappointed whilst the Demmocrats are rejoiceing at the veto — The people have something to do
to day in the way of Talking Politicks

28   Nothing new that I Know of — The Democrats Last night
Set a Couple of Barrells of Tar on fire at the Bluff where the Log
Cabbin stood — I believe that was all that was done on the Ocasion
— The Sale of George Sniders Property Came off to day on a Credit

---

18 Wellington West, who occasionally worked for Johnson, was among the free
persons of color licensed to remain in the state in September, 1841. Adams County
Court and Police Board Minutes, 1832–45, September, 1841. During much of the
period 1837–65 he lived in New Orleans, where as late as 1845 he resided in the
home of James Miller, Johnson's brother-in-law. Orleans Parish Succession Records,
Second District Court, File No. 25,534.

of 6 months. He had a Large Quantity of things of One Kind or other — There were a great many Persons at the tract to day to Shoot Pigeons   They Shot at about Eigty of them and Killed 49 of them — Mr J Stockton and Mr Combay, both of them Killed a pigeon Every Shot   I paid Mr G. Weldon ten Dollars to day and did not take a Receipt for it

   29   In the afternoon I took my Horse and wrode down into the Swamp as far as Maj Tom Winns Plantation   I went down to take Steven as I found him in town to day and ½ Drunk. I made him Lead down the Sorril Horse for young Winslow Winn to wride in place of his Horse that is Lame. I wrote a Letter to day and Took it down to the Baton Rogue and when I got down thare I Knew no One on the Boat so I did not send it

   30   Nothing new. Buisness dull as Possebly Can be Imagined

   31   This has been Quite a warm Day and if we have many more such Days we will I think have Sickness of a Dangerous tipe

   September 1   Nothing of Any Interest Except that the Bankrupt Bill has passed and become a Law and will take Effect in the month of February next, 1842. I dont Expect any Benefit from it myself — Col. Bingaman Left to day on an Electioneering Campaigne through the State — I wish him all the Cuccess imaginable

   2   Nothing new that I Know of Except that old Mons Seash Living on Perl St was passing off Counterfeit two dollars Bills of New Orleans money under the Hill this morning. Pass[ed] One on West & 1 on Mr Rogan, 1 on Furst and passed 2 others down thare — They all Called on him and got there money and did nothing more — He aught [to] have been Erested right off — Big Deer Hunt over the River to day

   3   Maj J. Shields, One of Our noble, Generous and Gentlemanly young men Came to me and said if I wanted any assistance or if he could do anything for me to Let him Know. I promised to do so — Such men as he is, is an ornament to Society — I received a Letter to day from Mr Tucker at Louisville

   4   I got on my Horse this morning very Early and wrode down into the swamp. Left in the night quite Late, Messrs Rowley, Jdg Tenney, Mr Prentess, Gen Huston, Dr Pollard, Mr McWhorter, Mr Duffield — They are off to Arkensaw to fight a duel

   5   The accounts of the yellow fever in New Orleans by the Papers of to day seys that it is much worse — whilst this place is One of the healthiest places now that I Know of

   6   No Buisness a doing — Police Court in Session again to day trying the rirghts [writs] of Petitions   There were a greate many Petitions hand[ed] in to day and some of them was I understand regected by the Board — Old Dr Wren adressed the Bourd at Length — Mr H Conner Got tireed of the old Fellow and Ordered him to Hush and if, seys He, you say another word I have you put in Jail — and the old Fellow stoped off   I have seen a Greate many that was very Glad of the old Fellows defeat — His remarks was that old Nancy Kyle & Caroline Kept a House of ill fame, a House of asination, a whore House, &c. — but he could not Shine[19] — Mr Owen paid me to day for Mr Staples seventy five Dollars House rent for the month of August, 1841 — Mr T A. S. Doniphan and a Mr Stigells has a fist fight up on the Conner at Soria — They were parted   It was so good and so good — Stiggells got a Blow in the mouth and D got a Blow on the forehead raising a not for a short time

7   Buisness has been very dull so far. Nothing new that I Know of   We Shall hear by the first Boat Down the accts. of the Arkensaw Duel.

8   Mr Charles Gregory is up to day from the Swamp and I hired Phillip and his wife to him by the month at the rates of twenty five Dollars per month and he took them both down with him in the Skifft.

9   Buisness Just as dull a[s] can well be Imagined   Nothing new that I have herd of. Poor Andrew Leeper was, I understand, ordered off to day, and so was Dembo and Maryan Gibson[20]   They

---

[19] This was not the first time that the Board of Police had been petitioned to revoke the licenses (originally granted in 1832) of Nancy Kyle and her daughter, Caroline, granting them permission to remain in the state. In August, 1838, upon representation of "various persons, respected citizens of the City of Natchez" that the Kyles were "dangerous members of Society," they had been ordered to leave the state within ninety days; but in January, 1839, the order had been suspended. And in September, 1841, their licenses were officially renewed. In 1841, Nancy was at least sixty years of age, and Caroline about thirty-one; Nancy was a mulatto, and Caroline "of light complexion," and both were about five feet, eight inches in height. See Adams County Court and Police Board Minutes, 1832–45, March, 1832; August, 1838; January, 1839; September, 1841. The Kyles had been freed in 1825–27 by Christopher H. Kyle of Natchez, who had bequeathed $1,000 in his will to secure their freedom and a lot to Nancy. In 1850, Nancy and Caroline and a family of six other free Negroes were still in Natchez, and in 1860 Caroline was listed as the owner of one slave. See Adams County Will Books, I, 419; Adams County Deed Records, O, 343, 397, R, 29–32; U. S. Census Reports, 1850, Schedule I, Adams County, 30; Auditor's Records, Tax Rolls, 1860, Adams County.

[20] Dembo had been freed by direction of the will of Samuel Gibson, illiterate free man of color, who had been a Natchez property owner as early as 1823 and died in 1832. Samuel Gibson had left his estate "consisting in a house and Lot where I now reside and a vacant Lot near the Theatre" to "the issue of my Body begotten on free woman of color named Esther," whom he had already freed. He

are as far as I Know inocent and Harmless People And Have never done a Crime since they have been in the State that I have Herd of   I saw an article to day that Mary Leeper has a Bill of Sale for Andrew Leeper and it is nothing moore than an Article of agreement between Mr Lynch and Herself, which Binds her to pay him $200 on [or] before the first of March next and the date not put on it — It then went on in the form of a receipt, one for the sum of $85 and the other for One hundred and fourteen Dollars and 50 cts, the whole being 50 cts Less than the Amount she was to pay for him — and in another part He, Lynch, promises to Emancipate said Andrew at the Expense of Mary Leeper — I see very plainly that Lynch Can do as he pleases in the affair[21] — Oh what a Country we Live in

10   To day has been one of the Dullest days we have had for some time. I was pitching Cents yesterday And I won 8 Cigars from Him — Big Berry Duncan Left here to day and before he Left I understood he told J. Soria that Armsted Carter New or had something to do with his money and Mr Soria had Amsted arrested about it — So I am told

11   The Steam Boat [blank] Came down this Evening Late and brot the news of the Duel between Mr Rowley and Judge Tenney — Judge Tenny was Killed. He Died in about One minute after he fell — They fought with Riffles at 30 yards Distance — Mr S. S. Prentess was the Second for Mr Tenny, General F. Huston was the Second for Mr C N. Rowley — Nothing new that I have heard of. The Baton Rogue Came Down to day. Gen Huston Came Down on her — He Brot his riffle down with him   Mr Rowley

---

had also left his "personal Estate consisting of drays horses, mules, cattle, working utensils, &c &c and money in Bank" to be used for the education and support of his children. Dembo worked for the estate until 1835, when he was emancipated in Ohio; he was still in Natchez in 1843. Mary Ann Gibson was perhaps one of Samuel Gibson's children. See Adams County Deed Records, N, 38–39, W, 51, Z, 243; Adams County Will Books, II, 28; "Estate of Samuel Gibson," Adams County Probate Records, File 63; Auditor's Records, Tax Rolls, 1843, Adams County. See also this diary, entry for August 27, 1844.

21 The Liepers were a large free Negro family in Natchez. All of them probably stemmed from Robert Lieper, Sr., who in 1826 was emancipated, along with his wife and daughter, by Charles Lynch, governor of Mississippi, 1836–38. Lynch subsequently sold to Robert Lieper, Sr., his son Robert, Jr., and a Natchez lot. Robert Lieper, Sr., then emancipated Robert, Jr., another daughter, and a granddaughter (whom he had purchased), and in 1838 sailed for Liberia, accompanied by his daughter-in-law and her two children. According to the above entry in Johnson's diary, former Governor Lynch must have been still selling Lieper children to the free Liepers remaining in Natchez. See Adams County Deed Records, P, 485, Q, 635, R, 664, S, 62, 286, 516, T, 34, 387, AA, 63; Sydnor, *Slavery in Mississippi*, 224.

Came down also tho he got out at his plantation. Greate many persons went down to the Landing Expecting to see the Body of Judge Tenney, tho the Boat Said that the Judge was Buried up at Mr Turnbulls Plantation. Mr S S. Prentess and Mr Duffield got out at Vicksburg.[22] Charles was out at Sally Carys to day and Wellington acted the N—— with him strong whilst out thare

12 Nothing new that I Know of — I understood this morning Early that Steven was in town and I Knew if he was in town that he must have runaway from Mr Gregory where I had hired [him] to haul wood in the swamp. It was after Breakfast and I got on my Horse and wrode up the street and I found him in the Back St. near P. Bakers — Gave him a tap or two with my wriding whip and then Brot him to my shop and in a few minutes after I got to the shop Mr Vernon Came to inform me that Steven had took a watch from one of his men and that he had been seen to have it and that he had taken it yesterday as he passed there. I Commenced a Search on his person and I found it in his Coat Pocket   I gave it to Mr Vernon and was Glad that he Came So Soon for it. I then made him get on a horse and go on down to Mr Vernons place and there I made his Driver Give him a good Floging with his Big whip. I then took him down as far as Mr Fords Lane and Left him with Mr Gregory and he took him down and Set him to work   I Borrowed a Gun from young Mr Barland and I Gave my Little Gun to Winston and we went into the Lake. I killed 5 Large Snipe and 2 Squirrells and he Killed 1 Sparrow hawk and 6 Snipes — Justices office were full all day   J Soria was tring to recover his money that he Lost. They were trying a Boy [of] Mr Fields. The Boy was Sentenced to be whiped but was not. His master [entered] an apeal I herd

13 Buisness oh how very dull — nothing new. News of the death of Parson Winchester arrivd Last night   He died at N. York — Mr Stapples arrivd to day from the North

---

[22] A published letter, written in Natchez on September 5, 1841, described the preparations for this duel, which occurred between Judge Tenney and C. N. Rowley, both of Concordia Parish, Louisiana, as a result of a court decision by the judge which affected Rowley's property. Tenney's seconds were Seargent S. Prentiss, Mississippi Whig orator, and J. M. Duffield, editor of the Natchez *Courier*. Rowley's seconds were General Felix Huston, late commander of the Texas army who had nearly killed Albert Sidney Johnston in a Texas duel, and Lewis Saunders, "former States Attorney of Kentucky." The duel was to be fought on the Arkansas side of the Mississippi River. Each of the principals was to be armed with a rifle, a pair of dueling pistols, and a bowie knife. The rifles were to be discharged at a distance of thirty paces, and the combatants were then to advance until one or both fell. New Orleans *Weekly Picayune,* September 13, 1841.

15 Old Peetor Boiso arrived from Cincinnatti Bringing news of a Cincinnatti mob that had taken Place Just has [as] he Left He Says that 2 Darkies and 1 white man was quarrelling and the 2 Darkies Killed the white man and that the Citizens went to Take the 2 Ds and that the Ds. raised and retired to the Methodist church — The Citizens Serounds the Church to take them Prisoners The Ds. was armed and Fired at them Killing 14 or 15 white Citizens and that the Citizens then fired on them in church with 2 pieces of Cannon. No body Knows how many was Killed — George Hawkins has returned from above yesterday

16 Every body is inquiring about the Cincinanatti news — we have nothing very authentic from thare yet — There is a rumor in town to day that the yellow fever had made its appearance at Herrons old Buildings in the part occupied [by] Roberson the Baker The man was a Patient of Dr Lyles

17 Nothing new that I Know of Buisness dull, very dull and the only Consolation that I have that it is so with every body else in buisness — I was pitching Quoits with Jo Meshio to day and he Beat me Easy. I lost 5 15-cts worth Cigars at the Game

18 Buisness very dull Nothing new to day. Yellow Fever is still flourishing in New Orleans — Pigeon Shooting. I wrode out to the race tract to day to see this sport and Cant say that I Like it by Any means. There was a Greate number of Persons out there, Some Shooting with Riffles at the targets. I saw some shooting to day that Looked Like a Snap — The shooting was between Jackumine & Moose, Odell made the Bets They were with Mr. McCollor, $10 Each — He was well Satisfied that there was 2 pluck 1 in the Game

19 Nothing new. Buisness Dull. Charles wrode up to Maj Youngs this morning to see them all

20 To day buisness dull. Nothing new. The City in Good Health, never in bettr.

21 Nothing new To day. Buisness [h]as been unusually dull to day

22 The Free Trader of to day gives the names of the following men that is said to be wounded by the Cincinnatti fuss: Boyd badly wounded by a ball in the forehead, George Dewit Slightly wounded in arm & Side, Samuel Baldridge Slightly in the arm, Jones, a street paver dumb man, slightly, I Nickalson of Newport Mortally — Jas McCormick wounded on Thursday night Originating the mob — recovering Blitz very badley wounded — Said to have taken

place on 6th inst — Every acct. we have Lessens the number and I would not be Greatly Surprised to find it all a Lie

23 I think the City very Healthy indeed. This Mornings Papers brot forth the Veto No 2 — The Citizens has been Looking for it for Several Days and I Know of no one that is Disapointed by its arrival.[23] To day whilst Mr G Tyler and Mr Jeff Arlette was in a Little Buggy taking a wride out to see Mr Pulling Out at Mr Stutsons Residence the Horse that they had took fright and ran off with them near the Gravy yard   They Both Jumped out. Mr Arllette got his Leg Broke Just above the Ankle. The Horse ran with the team against the Rack of Mr McGraw. Broke the Concern all to pieces — He them [then] Came on down and ran against Mr McGowans Horse and Broke the spine of the Horses back and hurt his own shoulder very much   Put it out of place — N. O. Papers of 22d inst says that there is 551 sick in the Different Hospitals in N. O

24 Nothing new to day. We have news that Congress has ajourned, Said to have ajourned on the 13th inst — I was pitching Quoits a good part of to day with Jackomine, Meshio, Mr Rogers & Mr Antonia. I Came of[f] Even

25 Nothing new that I Know of. Pigeon shooting Out at Race tract. Our City is very healthy and not One single Case of yellow fever has made its appearance yet. I am Lear[n]ing to play the Guitarr by note   Mr K S. Robbins Died to day in New Orleans with yellow fever — He was 28 years old and from Acomac County, Virginia — this is Coppied from a paper dated 6th Oct inst

26 Nothing has transpired of Any interest — Mc and myself wrode Out this Evening towards Col Wilkens   We met Peter Bugg as usual

27 Nothing new. To day is the day that the trial of Mr McCleoud Comes off in Oneida County, New York, and I here predict that nothing at all will be done with him — They will Let him go to a moral Certainty, ie, they will not find him Guilty for the American people Cannot and will not Come to the Scratch — They have not the means, nor the Disposition Either to fight.[24] The Circus Company Came this Evening

28 A Mr [blank] McDowell Died Last night — tis Said with Congestive fever — Irishman

[23] Johnson referred to the second national bank bill passed at this session of Congress, which Tyler vetoed on September 9, 1841.
[24] Johnson was correct in his prediction on the McLeod case. The Canadian deputy sheriff proved an alibi and was acquitted.

29   Nothing new that I Know of. Buisness very dull   I have Lost time to day Pitching Quoits — 5 or 6 of us   I paid Mr Geo. Weldon to day twenty Dollars on account of my note that he holds yet — Two runaways, the One belonging to Mr Sevier, the other belonging to Mr Samuel Davis Esqr — They were found in the House of Mr Garnet Howell Esqr. Said to have been Kept thare by his boy in the absence of Mr Howell and Family

30   Buisness has been remarkable Dull. Oh did Any One Ever See Such times before in Our City — no never — The officers went in search of Mr G. Howells Boy to day, to have him up about his having those runaways in his House, but they Could not find Him — Mr Earnest is the agent for Mr Howell, and was very Angry at the Proceedings of those Gentlemen who arrested the Boys. I am taking a few Lessons on the Guitarr at present

October 1   Nothing new to day. I was pitching a Little this morning or Evening I should have said and was taking a Lesson on the Guitarr Also — Mr S H. Lambdin arrived to night from the north — Stephen Came up this morning from the residence of Mr Gregorys where he has been at work — He is sick — His month was up on the 23d ult Sept   I Told young Mr Wren to day that I could not Keep my Box in the Post office any Longer — buisness would not Justify the Expense

2   I took my Gun this morning very Early and went down in the Swamp and I took Winston along with me and he had my Little gun. I went down as far as Mosbey. I had my Large Shot Gun and I made a poor Hunt Considering the Game that I Saw — I Saw to day 3 deer, 2 Turkeys, 5 Ducks, 11 Squirrells, 13 Snipes and this is the amount of my Hunt. I Killed 2 Squirrells, 1 duck, 7 Pover, 1 Crow — Winston Killed 3 Plover only — My Old man Phill was a Little sick, the rest of the People down there were all well, There were a greate many persons out a Hunting to day in Different Direction   All frome Town

3   Nothing new to day worth attention   Buisness not at all Lively   Every thing unusualy dull

4   The Circus is agoing On in full blast, they are having Good Houses not withstanding money is so scarce

5   Buisness is remarkable dull for this month — I Give the Boys Several Lessons to day in reading and writing in there Room — I then Pitched Quoits a part of the afternoon and Lost 75 cts worth of Cigars with Mr Jaqumine   I then took him and we played against Mr Kenney and Meshio and they beat us Out of One Dozen Cigars — Charles Went to the Circus to night   He was perswaded to go by Bill Nix — Welling[ton] went also — I Gave all three of them a pass to go — Mr Thoms Kemps hand bill Came out this Evening Denouncing Mr Chas N. Rowley tho what the Document is I do not Know for I did not Get to see One of them. Mr Thomas Glasscock Died To night Down at his plantation

6   The City very healthy   Mr W. Gaunt Declines running for the office of Justice of the Peace, the public regretts it.

7   Buisness Continues dull — Our Editors are abuseing [each] other Daily as is usual with them, Natchez is not improving much Any One may See

8   I feel very bad this morning   I have head ache and a General Debilety — I am in fact Sick — Court is in Cession down at Woodville   To day the tryal of Web, the Horse thief, Comes on in that Court

9   Nothing new worth writing about — Col. Floyd is anounced in the papers of to day a Candidate for Constable, The Circus was in Performance and a Greate many of Our the first Familys were thare with there Children — Aristocracy with Beauty and intelegence a plenty was thare — This has been a Dull week with me for I Could not Collect any money from Any One. Oh what times   Here are the names of Several that owe me that I cant get any money from — Mrs. Beltzoover, Meshio, A Kinney, & Boyd, & Patterson &c.

10   Nothing new has taken place to day   Buisness has only been Tolerable to day. After work was over I went home and remained Home all the afternoon Except One small walk on the Bluff Late in the Afternoon — I walked up [to] the Mc Shop also — this is now a mistake altogether

11   Buisness Tolerable good. The walkes that is spoken of yesterday was to day. Buisness was much Better yesterday than it has been to day. Nothing new that I Know of

12   I Took my Big Gun this morning Early and made off for the Swamp Taking Ned along with my Little Gun and I also Took Steven Down to Mr Gregory to work again for He Came up on the 1st day of this month Sick and I Kept Him untill to day. His other month was up on the 23d Sept. Phill I found Sick when I went Down. I then went in the woods a Hunting — I wounded 2 Ducks the 1st Shot but Killed 1 Dead   There was 3 of them together — I got 2 of them and Lost one — I Killed 8 Large Plover, 1 Squirrell, 2 Beckeroach, 2 owls, 1 crane and 1 Rabbit — making

in all 17 heads   Edd Killed 4 Plover with the Little gun — Mr Gregory went in the Afternoon and Killd 4 Squirrells

13   Nothing new that I Know of to day. Judge Shadock[25] Spoke in Our Court House to day to a Tolerable Large Crowd, They Seemed to be very well pleased with His Language and maner. He is a Candidate for Governor and I may here remark that he will be Elected. Wellington went down the River To day on a Steam Boat. The Circus Company went on the Same Boat

14   Nothing new to day. Buisness has been Only Tolerable to day. I had a Little run to day after a Black Boy that Slapd my Little William. I got near Enough to give him a very seviere Kick on his but — I dont think He will attemp to runaway from me Soon — The Little rascal belongs to Mr Racy Parker. Mr J. D. Freeman[26] returned to the City this morning very Early from making a tour through the State, I wish him Success in his Ellections

15   Nothing New that I Know of, Whilst Standing on the Bluff this Evening nearly dark, I Saw 8 or 10 wild Irishman fighting all among One another   It was realy Laughable indeed — They Beat one man by the name of Rountree — a guard he is for the City. He Hallowd Like a Clever fellow — Then on the Hill at the 10 pin alley, McFarlands place, there was two moore fights   Carbine, 1 of them, got whiped — Folies wife struck him with a Brick Bat — Cut his head thrugh mistake &c. Just like such people

16   Some Little Shooting Out at the tract to day, Rifle &c. Steven ranaway this morning from fear of being Sold — Gregory Came up from the swamp to day And paid me twenty Dollar wages for Steven — Phill Came up from the Swamp to day Sick

17   Nothing new that I Know of — Several Small Fights Last

[25] David O. Shattuck, Methodist preacher, circuit judge, and lawyer, was the Whig candidate for governor. His speech was criticized in Natchez *Free Trader,* October 16, 1841.

[26] John D. Freeman, Democratic candidate for attorney general, supported repudiation of the Union Bank bonds. He was elected, and served until 1851. In the election campaign of 1840, Freeman had made a speech upholding President Van Buren for refusing to set aside a decision rendered in a Navy court-martial in which free Negro testimony was allowed. Freeman had argued that not only were free Negroes competent witnesses in all types of Federal cases, but that any law prohibiting their testimony would be unconstitutional. He had also pointed out that free Negroes were competent witnesses in Louisiana courts. This speech, which had been violently condemned by Mississippi Whig orators, had been noted with approval by William Johnson. The Democratic position on this question was one reason for Johnson's anti-Whig attitude. For Freeman's speech on the question of free Negro testimony, see Natchez *Free Trader,* August 27, 31, September 3, 10, 1840.

night in the Lower Town. Some of the Joness with the Assistance
of Some women Cut and Sliced a mans arm very badly — And
There was a man Killed out in the Country at Mr Riggs — he was
a Duchman by the name of D. O. Kirkwood. He was Shot by
Samuel H. Still with a pistol. Was Shot right through the forehead — Mc And myself wrode Down this Evening on the Bank of
the Creek and attempted to wride through into the Swamp — We
got Down I think about 2 miles and could get no farther on acct.
of the Thicket — We Left the Creek Considerbly on Our Left

  18   Nothing new. McCary and myself Started this Evening
And made another attempt to Get into the Swamp by the Creek
Bank   On Our way down I Saw 8 or 9 wild Turkeys   We got
Down about 1½ miles farther than we got yesterday — We went
altogether on the Bank of the Creek tho we Could get no Farther
and had to return. We had nothing but Pistols with us — We
Came around by the foot of the Bluff

  19   Nothing new   Mr M. Ruffners Effusions appeared in the
F—— Trader of this morning. Qs [Questions] to Dr Metcalf in
regard to His not Patronizing a Democratic mechanic &c. The
Gaile affair   I Sold my Black Horse for Thirty Dollars   I Sold
him to Middleton, payable in ten days or Less time. I hope so

  20   Buisness has not been as Good as it was yesterday. A very
Laughable Trial Took place this day at Esqr Perdues office between
old Mrs Buie and old Mrs Wade or Some of her Stock. It was
Rip VS Rip — I was up at McCarys to day and got my 2 weed
Cutters and I Cut some of them with it   The One I got of him
was very Dull indeed — I made a Swap with him, Mr Alfred Cox
was Buried yesterday in Vicksburg where He Died

  21   Nothing new that I Know of — The Contents of to Days
will be found over in the Next Page

  23   I got up very Early this morning and Got on my Horse
Taking Edd with me and went Down into the Swamp on a Small
Hunt, I took my Big Gun along and I Killed 6 Plover or Snipe
and two Large Blue Cranes, 3 Squirrills, 1 duck, and 1 owl — Edd
Killd 1 Snipe and 1 Summer Duck with my Little Gun

  24   The Quarnteen Law Abolished to day in this City — Sickness abating in N Orleans — Steven was taken this morning by Bill
Nix and Brot Home — When taken he had a hot Loaf of Bread
under his arm — Tomorrow is a week Since that He would have
been Out — no 5 days

  25   Nothing New. To Day there was a Large Meeting at the
Court House And Mr J. D. Freeman adressed the Meeting — It was

I understand a question in regard to paying the Bonds or not — Mr Freeman is a Strong Anti Bonder — He made a very Long Speech on the Subject So I am told — After he Spoke then Gen Quitman Spoke for a Short time, then Col Woods arrose and made a Speech also — after which the meeting adjourned[27]

26   Nothing New that I herd Except that the papers State to day that McCleoud Has been acquited. If so it was what I predicted some time ago — There was a Small Difficulty Last night between Mr D P Jackson and Mr H. Claibourne — It occured at the Race tract. Mr Jackson struck at Mr C and Mr Claibourne Drew a Pistol and [was] about to pop Him when he was prevented by the Croud — What Ever is, is right — I had a grate put up to day in my 3 story Building   It was put in by Mr Brick and it was very well done — I Bot them new at the Auction Store yesterday and gave 29 Dollars for the 2 Grates — Meshio and the old woman was quarreling to day — Meshio was drunk and Crying Like a Child because the old woman said that he owed her 7.50 and would not pay her — What a Childish Creature he is

27   All sorts of Candidates in the field and all Sorts Electioneering. Tis amusing to see this man, I. Warner, how he is a running arround the town in Every Direction Electioneering

28   Nothing new to day. Free Trader Calls Mr Duffield a Dirty Fellow about town and Demi John on Legs, a Bouie Knife Candidate

29   I got my Horse very Early this morning and Started for the Swamp with my Gun, wriding my valuable nag Kity Fisher. I Killed 1 Patridge at the foot of the Bluff, Killd 4 Ducks in the 1st big Lake   I then went on Down and was Lost for a Short time oposite the Cypress Bayou Lake — Killed 1 Black Squirrell — Came Back into Lake, Crossed Just below the Bayio, then turned Down the Lake and went Down as far as I Could well get with my Horse, Eate my Dinner, Left my Horse and took down the center of the Lake. Chased a turtle but Could not Stop him — I then got a Shot   Killed 2 malard Dks., then went on Still below and Shot & Killed 4 teal ducks, then [shot] again and Killd 3, after which I Started up for my Horse, mounted and wrode up to Mr Gregorys. Stoped a few minutes, Came on from thare to the Fords field, got a Shot at some Crows and Killed 3 of them, then Came on Home to town with a very Sick Head Ache — Thus my hunt was in numbers the following — 1 Patridge, 1 Squirrell, 13 Ducks, 3 Crows — 18 heads in all   I used my Big Gun

---

[27] The report of the Natchez *Free Trader*, October 26, 1841, was pro-Freeman.

30 My Bird Got Out of the Cage yesterday or was turned out by W. I found it to night under the Hill. Mr Ramsey had Bot it from Mr Sylver Gave him 1 dollar for it. I found him Out at the tract and he told me all about it, tho yesterday he said that he caught it up in Franklin St and that it had got away from him. This is what He told Charles — I am to find it and get it tomorrow morning Early — Good Luck is a Greate thing I do assure you — To day I paid Mr G. Weldon Sixty Six Dollars in Cash and then allowd him as cash his bill of $15 that he owed me, making in all $81 that I pay him to day, and tis the Last Cent that I owe him in the world and the Last Ballance on a note that he held of mine for Two Hundred and Twenty Dollars — To day when we settled he Could not find my note. He had Lost it he said so I took a receipt from him for it

31 We must have had Considerable rain Last night from appearances of things this morning Very Early this morning it Commenced to rain and has rain[ed] all the forenoon and of all the Rains I have Ever seen I think it was the hardest and it still Rains very hard now this Evening — The Damage Done by the water is very Considerable indeed — Bridges, Fences, roads have been much Injured indeed — Our new House Leeks very much from the rain

November 1 I hyreed Steven To Mr Raby to day for Eighteen Dollars per month. To Day the Election Comes on. All the Different State officers — Greate many Candidates Out.

2 Nothing new has turned up to day — Buisness is Tolerable fair. To day is the Last day of the Election and it is Quite a Close Election Among some of them — Report Seys that Mr Robt. W Wood and Mr Wm P. Mellen is Elected Justices of the Peace for the North Preceint of Natchez and Young Withers and Samuells are the Constables for the Same Distrct. The majoritys we will have to morrow I Expect — Mother pd me to day 25 dollars on the money that I Loaned Her to pay Mr Murchson with a Long time Ago

3 The returns of the Ellections will be in tomorrows paper as the[y] have Just Got through Counting of them to night at Supper time — Charles and Ned was painting a good deal to day in the State Street Store And I Rented it to a Mr Barbeare[28] to teach

---

[28] This was Joseph Barbiere, dancing master, who was in Natchez for a few months in late 1841 and early 1842. He paid Johnson $30 per month rent and probably occupied one or two rooms in the house on State Street. The remainder

dancing Scool &c.

4   Nothing new that I Know of   Buisness just Tolerable good

5   [At] ½ past 3 Oclock this morning I got up and got ready to go down in the Swamp with Mr Stutson on a Duck Hunt. We were off in a few momements after I was up and when we got Down to Mr Barlands place the Bridge and gate and part of his fence had fallen in the Bayou. This was Shortly after the Big rain that we had a few Days ago. We got across after a while Down below the old Crossing place and a short way below we found that the other Bridge was also gone and we had some trouble in finding the place to cross it. We got on however below Fords place before it was Day. The Lakes was very high and mudy and we got on Down to Cypress Bayou and Could get no farther. We Came Back and went arround the Lake and Down on the front side of it past Gregorys and went in Back of Dock Lake. Left our Horeses at the foot of Dock Lake And Crossed the ridge to Long Lake and went Down very near the Lower End of Long Lake   Mr Stutson Shot a Little white Shoate that had Just been run across the Lake and was backed up against a Large Cypress tree And as soon a[s] it saw us it ran right up after the Dog and Came right up in Length of our Guns. Mr Stutson Jumped Back and shot it tho I told him not — After it was shot we swang it up and I helpd him to skin it — we then took it up to our Horses and before we found our Horses Mr Stutson Killed a Little fawn, and found Our Horses. Young Winn Had made them fast and took some of our dinner. Our Hunt was as follows. He Killed 1 Squirrell & 3 Ducks, 1 Shoate & 1 Deer & I [killed] 2 Squirells & 3 duck — Fish ducks

6   The Elections news Comming in very slow indeed — Mr Winn was up from the Swamp to day, Took Dinner with me   Col Bingaman got Home from his Electioneering through the State to day — Looks fine

7   Nothing new   I felt very unwell in the night. Quite So indeed. Chill and a heavy fever all night   Sat. night I mean — Mrs Amie was down to See us to day and so was Mc [who] Stoped and took supper with me. Good many of the Citizens has arrived to day from the north, B. McAlister, A Britton, Pollock, &c.

8   Nothing new worth much Considerations of those that are not Concerned. Mrs Fuller, the Sister of Mrs Gemmell, was Burrid

---

of the house was occupied by Johnson's mother-in-law or the Johnson family, or both. Apparently Johnson accepted no other tenants in this building after Barbiere departed.

at 4 Oclock this Evening — Died with Consumption I herd   I Gave Lucinday a Good Floging this Evening for her Conduct on yesterday. She asked Leave to go to Church yesterday and in place of going to Church a[nd] rema[in]ing she went off in some private Room, the Little Strumpet

9   Buisness has been Tolerable fair   I find The people are willing to Bet that Judge Shadock will be Beaten by Mr Tucker,[29] Tho I am Sorry to think that. Col Bingaman, Tis thought, Cannot be Ellected   If he Could only Come it, I would be Glad, but alass he belongs to the wrong party to Come it.[30] I Got an order from Mr Kenney to Day on Mr Robertson for fifty Seven Dollars. Mr Robertson accepted the Same   The money Due Mr Kinney was work and Boot done Mr Sweny Deceased. Mr Robertson was the administrator of the Estate of that Gentleman — Mr W. Robertson has Kindly offer[ed] to pay me the Same this week — I Received a Box of Cologne to Day by Mr Lambdin from Boston — I Dont say from the appearance of the Cologne that I really Like it, however the Price will settle the matter beyond a Doubt

10   Buisness Tolerable fair   Nothing new. To Day Everything Seems to be going on fair, Mr Wm Robertson Came to day and paid me Fifty Seven Dollars, This being the amount of the order that I got from Mr A Kenney to him on yesterday — Election For Governor so far as is herd from to Day[31]

12[*sic*]   Col Bingamans vote in Twenty Six Counties is 10229, Dr Gwins vote in the same 26 Counties 10104 — Col. Bs majority 125 over Dr Gwin & His Majority over Judge Shattuck is 45 — thus he is a head of the field thus far — Judge S. is a Candidate for Gov.[32]

11   Two of my Cows have not been up for several days and I have sent Wince and Edd both to Look for them to day but neither

[29] According to J. F. H. Claiborne, Tilghman Mayfield Tucker was "illiterate, slow and prosy," but had "much shrewdness, a good deal of dry humor, a fund of smutty anecdote, and a certain popularity connected with his nick-name, old *Til-le-toba,* or the blacksmith, to which respectable craft he once belonged. And he was an earnest, sincere and honest man." See *Mississippi,* 433. As Democratic candidate favoring bond repudiation, he was elected governor.

[30] Bingaman, a Whig candidate for Congress, was defeated.

[31] Here followed an incomplete statement of the gubernatorial election returns, which the editors have deleted. Johnson copied his table of returns from Natchez *Free Trader,* November 10, 11, 1841. Tucker was elected over Shattuck by a popular vote of 19,059 to 16,773. See Rowland (ed.), *Official and Statistical Register of the State of Mississippi, 1924–1928,* 307.

[32] Dr. William McKendree Gwin had reorganized the Democratic party in Mississippi in 1841 and had persuaded T. M. Tucker to run for governor. Gwin and Jacob Thompson, an incumbent, defeated Albert G. Brown, the other incumbent, and Adam L. Bingaman, for seats in Congress.

Could find them — I went myself and Could not find them — To Day whilst at Dinner Mr A. Kenney Came in the shop, so I am informed by the Boys, Stating that he wanted to see me D——m bad and asked the Boys if they had herd anything about ——————, refering to the Little buisness between Himself, Mr Robertson and myself   They, I am told by them, Said no — He then said something about his Liking to see a man act right and fair &c. Mr S Davis Gin Burned Down to night at or about 9 or ten Oclock   There appeared to be a good deal of Cotton in from the way it appeared to burn from this side of the River

12   Nothing new. Mr Powell paid me $15 that the man Middleton owed me on the Black Horse that I sold Him. Mr Powell paid me also five Dollars on his own acct. I am in good Luck   To day my Two Cows have Came Home After an absent of 3 or four Days

13   Nothing new has turned up to day that I Know of. Dr Volney Metcalf Took the But of his whip, Flogged a Mr [blank], a Teacher. The man hallowed murder and ran — The young man had whiped the Dr[s] Nefphew — Lawyer Baker did not pay his bill at the City Hotell according to regulations and Mr McDonald had his room Locked up — Mr Baker then Got mad and slaped Mr McDonald['s] Cheek. I Bot a Cow to Day and Gave 9½ Dollars for her. I also Bot 30 yds of Carpeting to day at 7 Bits per yard

17   I remained at the Shop untill near ½ past One Oclock, then I went to the tract and the old Field to see the muster and the Race. I made several Bets and Came of[f] Home $4 winner on the Days sport

18   To day was the Last Day of the Races and it was the 3 best in 5 and there was 3 Entrys for the money — Chicopa, Powell and Vertner — Powell won the two first Heats tho Chicoppa won the 3 Last Heats and won the money. Vertner was Drawn Out on the 4th round

19   I went Out to the tract to day to see a Race, One mile Out. A Tennessee Mare VS. Mr Mardices Lizar Jones. The Tennessee Nag won the Race very Easy tho I Came off before the Race was ran — Mr N Staples paid me by my acct in the store $20 and by Cash fifty five Dollars making in all $75 that he has paid me in good funds   Equivelent to $100 in agricultural money. This Last payment is for the month of October 1841 to the 18th day

20   Nothing New that I Know of.

21   I had Started Down to Mr Mosbeys Tho it Look[ed] so much Like Rain that I Turned back and doing so my Horse got away from me and I had trouble before I could get her again — I Caught Her at the Bluff and then I wrode her pretty fast to pay for Her treatment to me. I wrode up on the old Quigless place, shot a Bird or two, then got as wet as water, in my Broad Cloth Sattin vest &c. I had my two Little Puppies with me, 1 of them was a pup by my Old Pollo and the other was a pup given to me by Jaqumine and by his Dog Schellum

23 The City Looks some what Lively Auction Houses selling off pretty fast. I Bot two Glass Cups to day at Mr Sorias Auction Room, Cost 1.12½. To day I paid my Taxes which amounted to Forty Seven Dollars and 5 Bits — It Reads thus — State Tax, 22.25, County Tax $11.12½, Bridge Tax $14.25. This is hard that a man has to pay so much for I may say Nothing. Greate many Pigeons in the woods now and I am so Lame that I Cannot Hunt. Oh what Luck. Mc was Out to hunt Pigeons & seys that he Killd a Dozen — Steven ranaway this morning from Mr Raby — Mr Rose Brought Steven to me this Evening Quite Drunk. I Took him Home and gave him about a Hundred then Let Him Go for Reasons

24 Nothing of importance to day Steven got up very Early this morning and ranaway. This morning Early Col. Bingamans Horses Started for New Orleans on the Embasador — My Little Richard was sick yesterday and Last night but is much Better to Day, Thank God

27 To day Has been a Day of Greate Trouble with me on acct of the Seviere illness of my Little Richard — He is very Sick and has had several Fitts or Spasems which So alarms me, I remained all the Evening at Home, Did not go to the Shop — Col Bingaman and Mr Elliotte and Several others Left for New Orleans this Evening Taking allong Bill Nix as Body Servant. I paid Bill for his month in full tho the month is not due untill the 1st of December.

28 My Little Richard very ill indeed — I didnot go to the shop this whole day and the Boys were very Buisy and not any One to help them

29 To day was a fine Day Tho one of Trouble with my Family — My Little Richard still very sick, Dangerously ill, having more of those Spasams or Cramps — Oh how the poor Little Fellow suffers God Grant that He may recover from this Dreadfull malady

30 To day I find Richard no better. Still Suffering As much as a poor Little Soul Can

December 1   To day buisness has been Good and nothing new — My Little Richard Suffering a greate deal indeed from His sickness — oh how the Poor Little Child pains

2   To day has been a good Day by work in the Shop tho I have been no Help to them for my Little Richard was too sick for me to Leave   Dr Davis still attending to him   Oh how weak the Poor Little Child has become from his sickness

3   To day the buisness has been good in the Shop tho the illness of my Little Richard prevents my working at it — no body to work but Charles and Winston

4   My poor Little Richard is so sick that I Cannot Injoy the day be it Ever so fine

5   I went up to my Shop this morning very Early and worked To the usual Closing time. Buisness was very Good — My Little Richard very Low. Poor Little Fellow, He suffers so much — McCary and Mrs Gibson Sat up with him to night all night — He was very ill Just before Day. His Cough was very Troubled about it ie the Child Could get no rest. Oh no One Knows how much the Poor Little Fellow Suffers at this very time — I got moore Sleep to night than I have had any One night sinse it was Taken

6   My Poor Little Richard is very sick yet. Dr Davis Comes very Regular to see him — The Poor child has had a very hard time of it. Poor Little Fellow. God Grant that He may soon recover from this Dreadfull sickness — McCary and Hester Commings has Came to night to set up with Him

7   My Little son Richard is still very sick and has been Restless, Quite so — Had 1 of those Spasms shortly after supper to night — I was at Auction to Day and Bot a Looking Glass — Cost of which was $11.50   Fair price I think — Mr McMurran told Judge Dunlap that if he was worth the notice of a Gentleman that he would cow hide Him — Judge Cage fined Mr McMurran $100 for Contempt of the Court — A Suite was settled to day or the other day in which the Planters Bank VS. Maj Miller for 4000 Dollars. Tis Said by Mr Pinkerton that the Maj Over Drew

8   Buisness is pretty fair to day And I [am] glad of it. And Thank God my Little son Richard is some Better

9   Mr John Williamson Got married this morning to a Young woman in Washington   She was a teacher of inteligence, Him a wine merchant of this City — Enough Said — My Little Richard has been very bad of[f] All of this Day. Had another Spasm to day. Oh what a time of it we have had — We have to set up Evry night with Him — Mother sit[s] up with Him to night, Mc untill

½ past 10 Oclock, then returns Home — Tis now at the time of my writing nearly 4 Oclock in the morning and I am now setting by the Bed Side of Richard who I thank God appears a Little Easy in his Sleep &c.

10   I Bot a red and white Cow to day from Mr Dashield for $25 and I paid Him the money Cash. I Borrowed Mc['s] Horse this Evening and wrode Him Out to hunt my two Cows that I Bot of Winn but I could not find them or Hear of them

11   Buisness was Tolerable fair to day, Myself, Charles and Winston working. I Bot to day at Auction 1 Barrell of Canrass Hams at 6 cents and One ½ Barrell of Mess Pork at 4.50. To day Mr Gregory paid me fifteen Dollars in part pay for Sylvias wages

12   Nothing new that I Know of. Buisness is Tolerable fair To day. I was to shave Dr Lawernce to day and it is the 4th time I have shaved Him since he was sick — I remain[ed] at Home all day. My Little Richard Something Better to day, tho still quite unwell and has to be set up with yet.

13   Buisness has not been so good to day as it has for several days — My Little Richard Quite ill. Dangeroully so. Very weak   Maj J. Surget and Mr Louis Bingaman Came up to night from New Orleans Races

14   To day would have been a very Cheerful day if my poor Richard was only Better tho I [was] sorry to see Him so much weaker to day. Middleton or Littleton paid me five Dollars which was Ballance due me on the Black Horse   It was To day or yesterday I dont know which, that Mr Dicks, the merchant, has Mr Thom Munce arrested for Brick Bating and breaking his window — The result of the tryal was that Mr Munce gave Bail for his appearance at the Criminal Court. This is pretty tight I think. A Bucket of water was thrown on Mr Munce whi[l]st in the street

15   I Sent Winston Down to the Mill for Kity Fisher and after Dinner I sent Him in search of my 2 Cows that I Lost A short time ago but He Could not find them. I walked Out Late this Evening on the Bluff and found a Cow that I Bot a few days ago from Mr Dashield — She has the following mark, upper and under Bit of Each Ear and has a white face and is a red and white Cow — Nothing new to day   Buisness has been pretty good to day — I Gave my Little William a very seviere whiping to day up at the Shop for his bad Conduct, Throwing Brick and so forth, and sent Him Down Home — oh I gave him what I thought was right in the Case — Mc Sat up with my Little Richard Last night for the Little Fellow was very sick in the afternoon and part of the Night —

Thank God, He is much Better to day. Would to God He was only well this day   Mc Buys a New Hat to day I believe — Mr Winn Started a day or two ago to New Orleans with Cattle for Sale

16   Bill Nix Came up from New Orleans this morning. Col. Bingaman, Mr Elliott also came up, yes, and Capt W J. Minor. They Came up on the Baton Rougue. Nothing new that I Have Herd off. Buisness has not been so good Quite to day. I sent Winston to day in Search of my Cows but He Could not find them. Judge Stone offers me his Rooms up Stairs for 12 Dollars per month, Choice of them — I dont Know yet whether I Shal Take them or not, My Little Richard is much better to day Thank God.

17   Judge Crawford Presides in Court To Day. Ju[d]ge Cage takes his in another District   Capt Cotten, not Knowing that Judge Crawford was inn, asked Mr Van Hosen How the Judge would do. He replyed that he would do very well if he would Keep sober. The Judge replied that he would try and do that — They were all of Course surprised & confused — We have by to days Papers full Confermation of the Capture of the Sant te fee [Santa Fe] Expedition.[33] Tis all right as Pope Seys.

18   To day has been only a Tolerable days work with me   Not so many Strangers in Town as I thought there would be. Nothing of any interest Going on — I Sent Winston to Look for my Cows to day and Let him take my Little Gun with him and He did not find the Cows but Killed 5 Birds ie. 2 Black, 1 Robbin, 2 Larks, and Two Raccoons. He went down as Low as Mr Fords Plantation. Seys that they are now Clearing back side of Fords Field

19   Buisness just Common Size. I remained Home all day to day and have nothing new that I know

20   Buisness not as Good as I thought it would be on acct. of the Ball, Quite a Light Days worke I thought, Nothing new has transpired to day

21   I got up this morning Early and I Cannot find my white puppy no where. I have made much inquirery for Him and have not herd of him yet — The Jury in Concordia Gave a Disission Last night in favor of Mr I. Watson in the Bank Suite

23   Nothing new   Buisness Quite dull

24   I got on my old Grey Horse this morning very Early and took my Gun and went into the swamp. I went down trough the

---

[33] Johnson referred to the so-called Santa Fe Expedition sent by President Mirabeau B. Lamar of the Republic of Texas to occupy part of New Mexico and divert its trade to Texas. The expedition was captured by the Mexicans. The Natchez *Free Trader*, December 24, 1841, mentioned the incident.

old Field and when I got down to the Creek I was affraid to attempt to Cross the Creek. I then went back to the foot of the Bluff and wrode on and took a Path by the Little Mounds and Came out at Mr Barlands place and I then took down the back of the fence and wrode all the way back of the Plantations. Found that Mr Ford had Cleared the Lower End of the Little Lake above Him. I made a very Poor Hunt. I Killed 1 Squirrell, 1 Woodcock, 1 thrush, 2 Sparrows, 1 Rice Bird, 3 Sap Suckers — Mr Tucker Came down after Breakfast on my Little mare and had my Little Gun. He went down as far as Mossbeys to Collect some money, $34 was the Amount. M. would not pay him any interest and wanted him to take Ilenois money at par and he would not do it and Came off

25 Buisness Dull, more so than I thot of. It is a sort of a dull Christmas I Kept the Shop oppen all day and the Boys Staid at Home, Edd Got Drunk at night, Quite so, on Whiskey.

26 I have one of the worst Kind of Colds, almost sick, and have had for several days.

27 I so unwell as not to be able to be at Shop but a very short time to day and The Boys made a very poor days work indeed, $3.62½, poor buisness. I got a Letter to day from Mr Miller by I Comming One of Col Bingamans Field Hands Cut a Mr Dickson in the face with a Knife. Cut him across the nose This was done Last night. He was before Justice to day. The result I dont know. Mc went down Second Creek with Capt Thrift and Cannady and Mc Killed 1 Goose, 2 Patridges, 1 Squirrell

28 Nothing new that I Know of, Buisness is very dull and money hard to Collect Edd wrode out Home this afternoon on the Little mare Kitty Fisher, Little Gim Came in Col Bingaman took his man Out with Him, Last night I Did not Learn what was done in the case

29 I did not go to the shop during the whole day. I was somewhat Sick with a Cold and had Taken some Thomsonian Medicine Last night. Buisness was dull, Quite So, in the Shop. Nothing new that I Know of

30 The mud very deep in the streets and buisness dull. Nothing of much interest going on — Antonio Bringgo was married to a Duch Girl to day, the One that gave Concerts here a short time ago — They were Living up at present in Mrs. Rieds House near Mc Shop in Main St. Jo Meshio paid me One Months Rent of the Shop to day. Pays up to the 1st of Oct., 1841.

31 Buisness was dull to day The Shop made only 4.50 to day — The Streets are very mudy and walking very unpleasant.

Nothing new that I have herd. Little Winn Came up from the Swamp this morning and from New Orleans Last night Late. He Left them all well when he Left. He had Taken down in a Flat Boat a Lot of Cattle, 22 head. He Said that he sold them very well and reported the market full too. I Learnd from Him that the amount of money that he got from Withers was $600 and I think he told me that he was to give 200 dollars for the use of it, Oh did Ever [a] man hear of Such Interest in private Buisness

1842

January 1   I Got up very Early this morning and went up to the shop and shaved this 1st man in it in 1842, he was a Stranger and I Got the Cash for it — I also Cut the 1st head of hair. It was a small Boys and I got the Cash for it, I went around to Dr Davis this morning Early and paid my Doctors bill, the amount of which was One Hundred Dollars — I paid it and then went to Breakfast, Nothing new that I Know of. I saw Mr Walsh, the officer, selling Mr Vernons Horse at Auction in the Streets and for Debt, I suppose

     2   Nothing new that I Know of. Buisness Dull   Dr Broom & Capt. Gaunt gets into a small Difficulty with some saillors: 1st place the Sailors wrides there Horses, 2nd place Dr Knocked 1 of them down with a Brick, 3d place Dr runs abourd of another Ship & Draws the Captains Pistols on the Sailors who were in persuite of Him, Shuts himself up in the Captains Room, Stays there untill a parcell of young men from town Came to his assistance & the Sailors are then put in Jail — The matter is Draped and the Sailors are Discharged

     3   Nothing new that I Know of. The Circus and Theatre are both in opperation at this time and both of them making a Little money[1]

     4   Buisness Tolerable good   Mr Hoggatt sent in Emeline and Mosouri to day from the Country and Little January also — They all went to the Theatre. This mornings papers Contains the result of the City Election.[2]

---

[1] The theater season of 1842 in Natchez was an exceptional one and included performances by James H. Hackett and the second Joseph Jefferson. The Natchez press devoted considerable space to the various actors and their programs.

[2] Among the city officials for 1842, as reported in Natchez *Courier*, January 4, 8, 1842, were: Samuel Cotton, president of the board of selectmen and city magistrate,

5 I wrote a Letter to day to send it by Isac Commings and the Black rascal went off and did not come for it, I Saw Little Winn to day and He Had Mosbeys negro man up with him to Sell him to rais money to pay Mr Withers. Buisness has only been Tolerable to day. Nothing new that I Know of Mr S H. Lamdin was married Last night to Miss Bisland and Left this morning in a Steam Boat for New Orleans They went in in the Embasador, I Took Emeline and Mosuri up to Miss Dowells to day for to Stay if they would suite; I Left them with her and Told them it would be well to stay thare untill Mr Hoggatt Came in Himself from the Country

6 Buisness Only Tolerable Nothing new The Governors Mesuage was Printed in Our papers of to day A Mr Wm Diamond got married To a Miss Bants, both of Washington, Miss. Mr Pain, the Carpenter, got married to Miss Morton

7 The Streets are mudy and unpleasant walking in them, Nothing new that I Know of Buisness dull. I took in Cash to day 6.37½ And Collected $29.50 Those times are very different from what they were 6 or seven years ago — The City is full of French and Duch Jews — trading mostly in Dry Goods, I got a Letter from Mrs Miller to day in which She mentions that George Britton, very Lately on a visit to New Orleans from Bayou Sarah, So Stoping at Mrs Williams Gratis. Got up Early in the morning and Stole a wach from Mrs Williams and Left the City, That is too bad for the Lady is quite Poor indeed

8 To marketing 1 Dollar as usual, Nothing New. Buisness dull for the Season, Quite so. The Circus Company Leaves to night. They have not met with much Encouragement this trip up here

9 Our Streets is very mudy. Buisness Quite dull Nothing new that I Know of. To day Mr Hoggatt sent me in a Cow by his man Prince with a red Heiffer Calf The Calf is Quite young. The Cow and Calf is both in very good order. Mc and myself wrode out or up in the neighbourhood of Capt Nevitts Swamp and the Shipping Company. We did not remain Long Down thare. Saw nothing new or instructing I Sent Rachel, a Cow belonging to Mr Hoggatt, Out to his House to day in place of the other he sent me, Meshio paid me to day $25 for Rent of the Fruite store on Main St. up to the 1st of November, 1841

10 Buisness has been so very dull and unpleasant day and nothing new Very Little money made these days at any price. I went under the Hill this Evening and Bot 2 Bales of Hay. The

and John R. Stockman and Robert Stewart, selectmen. The three men were elected from a field of fifteen contestants.

weight of Both were 737 lbs., at 1 Dollar per hundred. I got 1 sack of Oats, 75 cents

11   Nothing new to day. Mr Staples paid me to day $92 which is Equivelent to $123 in Agricultural money. This Sum pays his Rent for One year Ending 17th December, 1842. I was up at the Auction Room to day and I Bot A Little Bay Mare for $29.50   She was sold at Messrs Strickland & Co and was sent from the Livery stable and owned by a Mr Kelly — I wrode the nag Out to McCabes Store to try and Collect $3 from him that he held as stake money on a Race and when I Got Out thare I had to take 2 Barrells of Corn and 12 Bundles of Foder in part pay for the Debt. Why he must be a Greate Rascal   He owes me a Ballance yet of 1.37½   Mr C. Reynolds Take Little James Hoggatt to Learn the Brick Layers trade

12   Buisness Only so so. Greate deal of Furniture sold to day at Auction and sold at high prices I thought and Clothing sold well also. I saw Carroll to day and he wanted to Know if Evans, his old partner, had Ever paid the Last months rent of their old Store in State St — and I told him no. And I requested him to try and get Mr Evans to settle the Rent and he said he would do so

13   Nothing new that I Know of. Buisness has been Quite dull to day and money as usual scarce. I was up at Auction to day and I Bot some Clothing for Steven and 1 Bridle and martingale, and I was up at Mr Soria Auction Room and there they were selling a woman belonging to Mosbey and I at the request of Winn bid her in at 296 Dolls and I told him that if she suited my Family that I would Keep her and if not I would try and sell her for him, The officer Came down and I told him that I would be good for the woman when Ever he should want her and if I Liked her I would Keep Her, &c.

14   I Got [up] Just before Day and got ready and went to the swamp taking Winston with me, I wrode my new nag that I Bot the other Day and he wrode Kity Fisher. I stopd at Mr Fords and he was telling me about Mr Mosbys and young Winn and himself Falling Out &c. I then went on down to Mr. Gregorys, Thare I found himself, B. Winn and B Winns Son and 2 Negro men all at work with puting up wood for the S Boats — I was down at Mr Mosbeys to day and I wanted to inquire of him whether Pegy was Healthy and Sound &c. and found out by Inquiry that He was willing to warrant Her sound and did do so and told me that it was Only on acct of His being so much in debt that he was selling Her. I then agreed to Give him 296 Dollars for Her and sat down and wrote the Bill of Sale which reads $300 and he Signed it. I was to return to town and pay the Excecutions against him, which was 276.68 I think and he gave me $40 to pay Mr Tucker for Carpenters work, The Amount of his Claim was $34. He gave me $40 to pay the same with if I Could   Now for the Hunt   I Killed 1st Shot none but Broke the wings of 3 ducks, 2nd Shot I Killed One of them and got it Out, the other 2 I Lost   The next Shot I Killed a Large mallard Duck and Lost it. I then Killed 2 Squirrells and 1 Large Duck of Mallard, 4 heads   Winston Killed 1 Large Mallard only

15   I paid Mr Dillon, the officer, to day Two Hundred and Seventy Dollars and 57 cts this being the Amount of Executions against Mr Wm Mosbey I Took a Receipt from Mr Dillon as follows. Received of William Johnson the Sum of Two Hundred and Seventy Dollars, 57 cents in full of Executions against William Mosbey and all cost. Signed H. A. Dillon   I Also paid Mr Dillon $37.50 for a Judgement that Mr Josiah Tucker had against Mr Moseby, the true amount was $34 and the Cost was $3.50. I took a receipt from Mr Van Hosen for the amount paid but did not get Mosbeys Note for he said it would be all right and I told him that Mosbey Coold Call and get the Executions himself when he Came to town, Mr Mosbey Gave me a Document against the Capt of the Steam Boat Luda and wished me to send it Down to New Orleans to Mr Miller to see if he Could make anything out of it, The Case was to be before Judge Jackson. I took the document and gave it to Mr James Robertson who started for New Orleans to day with instruction to find out and if possible Collect the Claim, He promised to do so, and if he could not to Leave it with Mr Miller   To day has been a very dull day

16   Buisness dull. Nothing new. I took a wride Out in the afternoon with Mc   I wrode my new Horse or Filly. Mc wrode his Black Horse — We wrode out by the Scotts old Field and Came around by old Jones or Quigless Lands

17   I saw Mr A Kenney this morning on the way to my shop and he told me that he had Commenced to moove Out of my Shop on Saturday night and that he aught to have told me of the fact tho he did not &c and that he had been a tenant of mine near 4 years and that he hoped I would not be hard with him &c, We talked and was to meet again for a Settlement. He Owed me a Ballance on a note, $23.50, and Owed me for Rent, $79, in all $103.00   We had a Settlement as Follows. He pd in Cash $31.25 and gave me accts against those Gentlement. Capt. Minor $14.50,

Mr L R Marshal $10, Mr Barker $14.00, John Shanks $12.75, Mr Vernon $5.00, Mr Sheldon $7.00, R. W. Wood $5, Lyman Potter $3.50, Making in all $103.00   Hyrd Pegy to Mr Samuels to day

 18   I got up this morning very Early, Took a Light Breakfast in Company with Mc and we then started Down in the Swamp on a Hunt. I Stoped at Mr Fords and I asked him if he felt Liking Taking a Hunt for he had told me that he and Mr Gay would take a Hunt on to day. That was my Reason for Calling. He told me that he had seen Mr Lapiece go up on a Steam Boat and that he wanted to see him to get some money from him and that he had to go over the River to see him, I then went of[f] and in an hour or two after, I Saw him and his wife Down at Bailer Winns.[3] Now Why Was this Lye told, How much Better would it have been for him to have said that he did not want to go or did not feel Like going &c. Mc Killed 1 hawk, 5 Duck and 1 Owl, 7 heads, and I Killed 2 Duck and took One from a haw that I think [I] Killed, 3 owls, 1 sparrow hawk, 1 Ivory bill and Caught 3 possoms. Heads in all, 10 heads   Winston Killed 1 wood cock, 1 Log wood cock, 2 heads   Old Pollow would not Bring Out Ducks and I Beat him severely and said that he should not go with me again, My Little Pollow Died yesterday with Distemper, I Stoped at Mosbeys and gave him the Recept I got from Dillon, also the Bill and Cost of Tucker. I then Startd down in the swamp from his fence, Turned up and Came home &c. The Boy's only [made] $3.50 to day

 19   Nothing new. Mr Lamdin and Lady Came up from New Orleans yesterday Or On Monday Night, Seven dollars and twenty five cents is or was made in the Shop to day   Emeline and Mosouri went out home to day Just before the Rain and they were Caught in it no Doubt. They Came away from Miss Dowells night before Last — They were thare to Learn to sew but the old Lady was too Foul mouthed Intirely. It would not do[4] — Mr Winn is up to day and Stops at my House all night   Came up to settle that

---

 3 "Mr Ford" was Washington Ford, who had married Helen Winn. "Mr Lapiece" was Peter M. Lapice, executor and administrator of the estate of Helen's father, George Winn, a free Negro. (Lapice was one of a number of residents of Natchez who owned plantations across the Mississippi River in Concordia Parish, Louisiana.) "Bailer Winn" was Baylor Winn, who later was accused of killing William Johnson in a dispute which centered chiefly on the proper location of a land boundary. Both Ford and Baylor Winn had land and residences on the Mississippi River, south of Natchez. Johnson had had financial transactions with Baylor Winn as early as 1831.

 4 Emiline and Missouri were slaves under the control of planter Nathaniel Hoggatt, Jr.; Miss Dowell was the only woman in Natchez advertising as the owner of a store. Her advertisement offered her customers "Tuscan Braid," straw bonnets, shoes for children and ladies, and carpeting. Natchez *Courier*, December 28, 1841.

money Buisness with Withers — From what I Can Learn from him, Dick Ellis will get the two hundred 75 acres of Land belonging to Mosbey down Low in the Swamp. Mr Henderson is to advance the money for Dick Ellis

20   Nothing new. Buisness Only Tolerable, To day Richard Ellis or Chas Wilcott Gets the Mossbey Land and W. Winn Gets Back his note from young Withers. The Amount of the note was $780.00 I think. Mr Henderson paid the money for him and got the Land tho the Land was recorded in Wilcots name, Winn is now at my House sick — To day Kenney Brings the Key of my Shop that he has been renting for three or 4 years — He has moovd around to the Tremount House — I Came down at the House Late this Evening with Edd and Winston and we went to work at Diging and Mooving Dirt from the Cistern that Steven is now Diging in the yard

21   Mr L. Pitcher pd me Seven Dollars on acct. of Shaving and it pays his shaving bill up to 1st of Janry, 1842   Dr Geo. Pulling pays his acct for shaving in full up to date. The Amount was $20.88.   This was his acct. against me and we Just made a Swop of Our accounts to day — Buisness was only Tolerable. Some Small Collections was made   I Received a Letter from Mrs Miller to day informing me that she had Lost her youngest Child, a Daughter, a Beautifull Child & only Lived Eight Days

22   Buisness has been to day very good

23   Buisness only So so   Nothing new

24   Nothing much adoing   I mooved my Shop to day from Mr. Rogans House to that of Capt Cottons under the Hill   Andrew Evans was Burried to day   The Procession was Large, Quite So   He was a Grand son of old Col Marshalk[5]   The Boys Commenced to day to say thier Books again   I will try and Keep them at it for a time, if possible, Tho I Know my failing so well that I am doubtfull whether I will keep them at it Long

25   Mr Staples told me to day that he was agoing to moove in a few days from my House and he wantd to Let me Know so that I might get a tenant   He talks of mooving to the store owned by Dickson nearly in front of the City Hotel

26   Nothing new worth relating. Buisness Quite dull and has the appearance of being more so. I wrode Out this Evening Late on the Bluff near Mrs Linton. The Streets were very mudy. Wriding is unpleasent in such whether

---

[5] This was confirmed in Natchez *Courier*, January 25, 1842. He was a grandson of "Mr. A. Marschalk, the father of the Press in Mississippi."

27   Nothing new worth attention — Very Little done in the way of Buisness. Myself, Winston and Edd Came down after dinner this Ening and worked at the Diging of the Cistern   We had the old Grey Horse in the Cart, Hauling Dirt &c.

28   I got awake about 4 Oclock and soon afterwards sent for my Horses and started in the Swamp on a Hunt, taking Winston with me; Mc and Mr W K. Henry was along. Mr Vernon and Mr Bard we Saw down in the woods. They wrode Down a piece with me   Mr Henrys Boy Frank Had missd them with there Horses and I wrde Back to Look for Him. They found him. Mr Vernon & Bard wrode on to try and find Mr Doyal, Mr Wrigley, Collings & Capt Thrift who was Hunting with hounds. They Could not find them and returnd Killing nothing — We did not find them untill they Came along in the Afternoon and Capt Thrift Had Killed a find Buck, The rest of His Comp. Killed nothing, Mr Henry Killed 1 dove and 1 Sparrow Hawk and One Crow and One or two other Birds and 1 owl & 1 Lark, making 6 or 7 heads   Mc Killed 2 Large mallard Ducks and 1 Lark, in all 3 heads and I Killed 2 Large Wood Cock or Timber Ducks, 1 Sap Sucker, 8 Crows and 1 Rabbit, 12 heads in all   Winston Killed 1 yellow Hammer, 2 Sap Sucker, 1 Robin, 1 Little hawk, in all 5 Heads

29   Buisness only tolerable   Nothing new. I wrode Out to Maj. Chotards Residence this Evening and Cut Miss Mariahs Hair. A Passenger from off the Steam Boat Preemtion got Drowned to day at Our Landing & a Mans Hand was found wraped up in a Cloth of Some Kind to day in the old Livery Stable up at the head of Main Street. It was found in or under the Horse troft and the Stable is now Kept by Mr Chapman, the Ranger, Very Curious. The hand was taken off at the wrist; Supposed to be the Hand of a white man[6] — Mrs Warren and Mrs Barker Came in to day from the Country and Brot my Little Canary Bird and One female Bird for the use of Him. Mr B. was to have sent me a pair of young Birds for the use of him but did not do it. Miss Catharine Evans is not hardley Expected to Live the night out — She is very Sik   They Sent the Carriage for Mrs Battles to night and she went out Amediately to see Her and when she got Out she found her speechless and dyeing and the poor Lady Died at 11 Oclock to night. Good many of her friends was present at her Death

30   Mrs Battls is Out at the Miss Evans.

[6] On January 31, 1842, the editor of the Natchez *Courier* commented: "Every one who saw the hand must have concluded with us, that *foul and midnight* MURDER *had walked* abroad!"

31 Miss Kathrine Evans was Burried to day   Nothing new that I Know of   Buisness Dull and I fear is geting more so. I sorry to see it. Kenney, the Shoe maker, moved Out of my Property on the 19th inst. He has moved around the Corner to Dr McPheeters Room — the Calf got Out this Evening and ran off with its Mother. She is a Cow that I Borrowed from Mr Hoggatt. I Bot the Civil Code of Louisiana to day and I got it for 1.50 cts   It was an old volume, the Code of 1825. Little Dick was quite sick to night. We had to give Him a Dose of Oil

February 1 Ann is Quite sick to day. I sent for Dr Davis and He Came arround, made some few Inquirys and Left saying that if she did not feel Better by night to take 3 of Cooks pills — I have been down at the House nearly all day with Her and have worked at diging the Cistern a good part of the day or Evening. Mulbury, the Cow, that ran way Last Evening, Winston Brought her back to day about Dinner time. He started Out very soon this moring for her and had a good deal of trouble in getting her back again — the shop made $5 to day — the times are geting worse, I am sure
2 I was Quite Buisy to day working down at the House Diging Dirt from the Cistern, Nothing new that I Know of
3 I was at work diging the Cistern and Leveling the yard off &c.
4 I was up at Auction and Bot 3 Kegs of Lard, 2 Boxes of Candles, &c., and a Lot of Cannary Seed
5 Buisness Dull. Nothing new. I was a portion of to day buisy in diging the Cistern &c. Mr Staples mooved Out of my store to day
7 I wrode my Little mare down at the Barland place and there I found my Cow and she has no appearance of having a calf and I dont think she will have One for some time to come, My Little Richard is sick and has been very sick for 3 Days — Whilst I was down this afternoon I took a good Look at the Colier place and I think it would be a poor place for a person to have for Cultivation. I think it a very poor place indeed, takes but a Small rain to run all over it.
8 Nothing new that I Know of   Buisness Dull, I was at the House this Evening at work diging the Cistern   Edd was also at work and Steven. We got out Considerable dirt this Evening
9 Nothing new worth relating. The Courrier of to day has a well written Letter in it from Dr Ker. Tis a Splendid thing,[7] My

[7] The communication of Dr. John Ker of Adams County, published in the Natchez *Courier*, February 9, 1842, explained his actions as a member of the state senate

Little Richard is quite sick to day — I Rented Out the Shop formerly Occupied by Kenney to day for $20 per month to a Mr [blank] and He gave me five dollars on the Rent. I did very Little work in the Cistern to day. I Bot a Chair to day at Wemples Sale of Furniture and his Furniture Sold at a very hansome price.

10 Dr Young Came down to see Richard, who is not as well this Evening as he was this morning — Bankrupt news reached this place to day. The Bill to repeal it was Lost in the Senate by one vote. I Loaned A Mr Bryley to day ten Dollars to be returnd in a few Days

11 It has been a remarkable dull day in the way of Buisness. Nothing new that I Know of. If to day had have been a Clear day I think I would have been able to have nearly finished diging the Cistern, but so it is. It will have to be finished at Some other time, The Dr Came twice to day to see my Little Richard who has been Quite Sick all of to Day — There is a Mr Barbiere,[8] a Dancing man, who I Cannot bring myself to believe is a Gentleman in the full acceptation of the word, I dislike him considerabley. He owes me $90.00 and I am much affraid that he will not pay me, untill he [is] Compelled to pay me

12 I have not been well to day   Had a Cough that troubled me much, Buisness was Dulle to day, Quite So   Nothing new that I Know of

13 Nothing new. I took a Small wride this Evening on my Bay Filly. I went down to the Saw mill and theare I saw a Rabbit and I Shot it with a young mans Gun and gave it to him — Some One Broke open my Shop under the Hill

---

in 1841 in blocking an attempt made in the legislature to nullify the will of Captain Isaac Ross of Jefferson County, who died in 1836. This will contemplated that most of his 160 or 170 slaves and their offspring should be transported to Liberia under the auspices of the American Colonization Society. After tremendous financial and legal difficulties, between 235 and 300 Ross Negro emigrants (including some liberated by two children of Captain Ross) were shipped to Africa by 1849. Ker, as an agent of the American Colonization Society beginning in 1842, and Dr. Stephen Duncan, a wealthy resident of Natchez and president of the Mississippi Colonization Society, played prominent roles in the affair, which created considerable excitement in Mississippi. See Sydnor, *Slavery in Mississippi*, 224–30.

[8] Joseph Barbiere, a tenant of Johnson's, was probably the "Mons. Barbiere," who in the summer of 1840 had headed the dancing and music school and directed the band at Brandon Springs, the Mississippi watering place, some eighteen miles from Jackson. An advertisement in the Natchez *Courier*, July 1, 1840, stated that he was "too well known throughout the Union to require one word from us as to his merit." For advertisements of his Natchez school and "cotillion parties" given by him at the Mansion House hotel, see Natchez *Free Trader*, December 24, 1841; Natchez *Courier*, January 4, 27, February 1, 1842.

14 Buisness was dull. Nothing new. My old grey Horse had a Race to Day with Edd. Steven wrode the Horse and gave him 10 Steps and has to wheel his Horse, which he did, and then won the race by 6 ft. Distance, One Hundred yards

15 I was Out this Evening with Charles and Bill over by the old fort and they had [a] race with my old Grey Horse   Distance, 100 yds — the Horse to give them ten Steps,   They were off and the Horse won the Race by a Short Distance — Bill 2d and Charles Last, Steven wrode wing on the Race, [I won] 4 Barrells of Corn. Steven then wrode same Distance VS. Edd and gave Him 15 Steps and ran for a Frock Coat against Edds Calf and the old Horse won that Bad, very Easy — Nothing new that I Know of   Buisness dull &c. Mr J. Bunces Lyon died Last night or this morning   He was a very Large Dog. They Burried him Out in Capt Minors Pasture

16 Buisness Quite dull   Nothing new worth Talking about. Mr Mosbey was up to day and took dinner with me and told me that when he got his fence up that I might send down any stock that I wanted to free of any charge

17 Buisness dull and nothing new. I was down at the House a good part of to day diging on the Cistern and do Expect to finish it tomorrow

18 I hyred 2 hands to day to help dig the Cistern and we got threw with it to day or this Evening rarther, It is now ready for the Plasterer or Cement man. Courrier of to day gives greate Credit to Dr. Ker for the able Letter he has written or did write a short time ago.[9]

19 Nothing new. I wrode Down to Shipping Company this Evening and Fed my Cow. She seems to be prety forward with Calf   I fed Buxes Cow also — I was at Auction to day and Bot a suit of C[l]oaths for Richard, Cap &c. and a Barrell of Fish &c. Buisness to day dull. To day I Settled with Mrs Walker and Web the full amount of there acct. which was 27 dollars and Mr Web Owed me a Ballance of $21, so I paid him the difference which was $3. Enough Said   Mr Oblemis Commenced the arch to my Cistern to day and put it in.

20 Nothing new.   Buisness Quite dull   I wrote a Letter to day and sent it down by the S. Boat Baton Rogue to Mr Miller   I took a wride this Evening with Mc and I went Out near Eight miles and Came in by Washington. Tis the first time that I have

[9] Johnson's statement presented a correct interpretation of the newspaper account.

seen the Town for several years, and how bad it Looks. Diserted Completely. We were Quite Late in geting Back to town.

21   Nothing new that I Know of. Buisness dull, Quite So   I wrode down this Evening to see my Cow and I found Her near Mr Browns Mill. I fed her and then Came up. I fed Williams Little Cow too. I Saw Mons. Barbiere to day and he promised me to give me an Order on Maj Chotard to morrow for some money — I have my doubts about it now

22   Buisness has been pretty Good. Nothing new of Any Interest Only to day the Companies of this place all turned Out. The guards has the greatest number of them, I mean muskets.[10]

23   To night Mr Barbiere gave me and Order on Maj Shotard for Sixty dollars. This was for the Tuition of his Children. Mr Barbiere is still in my debt $30 to the 7th of Febuary, 1842 — I wrode Down to the Mill this Evening and found my Dashield Cow with a young Calf and I drove her Home, instantar

24   Buisness was Dull to day and nothing new that I Know of.

25   I was down under the Hill to day And Bot Twelve Bushells of Bran at 15 cents per Bushell. Hay is worth 1 doll and Corn 50 cts per Barrell, Buisness Getting Quite dull

26   Buisness Tolerable Considering the times   I was Out to day to the Race tract to see a race between Capt Minors Longwaist Filly VS. Mr Mardice Bay Stud Colt by Scarlet. Single Dash of a mile, They both got off in fine Stile and the Colt ran Down to the 1st Corner and threw the Boy over his head and Stoped. The other ran on and Came Out alone, wining the money, $100 aside — I saw several Races to day. They were Quite Amusing   I Came off Looser on the day 50 cts tho I subscribed a ten to the Jocky Clubb. I Loaned Mr Jo Riechlew to day or to night $3 to be paid in the morning

27   I Took a wride this afternoon with Mc and we wrode Out in the direction of Col. Wilkins, went past his House and then past the St. Cathrine Bridge tho not far beyond it, We then turned

---

[10] The Washington's Birthday celebration featured a morning parade by the city fire companies and an afternoon parade by the militia units. The firemen's companies included the Hook and Ladder Company, Achilles Engine, Neptune Engine, Protection Engine, Water Witch Hose Company, and Relief Hose—all of which apparently were divisions of the Phoenix Independent Fire Company, incorporated in 1836. The militia units included the Natchez Fencibles, Natchez Guards, Adams Light Guards, and the Natchez Hussars. In reporting the military parade the Natchez *Courier*, February 23, 1842, commented: "There evidently was new life in each soldier—with warm hearts and noble minds, each has a bearing peculiar to himself, but *all* marking their course in precise military style."

around and wrode back again. Got in after the usual supper time   Nothing new a Goin off that I Know off

28   I sent and got 3 Barrells of Corn at 5 Bits per Barrell. Nothing new what Ever. Dr Broom returns from a Hunt from the other side off the River. He seys he Killed a goose   Talks of having a good shot at a Deer, very Large Buck, drew blood &c. Mr. Duffield and Dempsey P. Jackson arrived this morning from Jackson Legislature. Mr D. spoke of his Coming near a fight with Dr Hagan for refusing to recognize the Dr as a gentleman   I have here made a mistake for they got here yesterday and not to day as I have stated above. Nothing new, only that the Banks are geting some what worse in New Orleans and is the cause of moneys getting so scarce. Corn is to day five Bits per Barrell. The money is the Cause off it.

March 1   The Jocky Club Races Commenced to day, 2 Entrys, Capt Minor and Col Bingaman, and Capt. Minors horse won the Race with Ease. Nothing new to day   Buisness Quite Dull.

2   I got on my Horse and wrode Out to the Race tract and saw the Race between Jim Bell and Celerity and Thetris, 2 Mile heats   The tract was very heavy, the mud nearly ancle deep. They got off in fine Stile and Gim Bell and Celerity had the Sport to themselves for Thetris was no where,   1st One was a head and then the other tho Gim Could have beaten her Every Jump tho he Suffered her to run a head sometimes. Thetris was more than distanced the 1st heat   Gim won Every heat with Ease and Could have Distanced Celerity Easy and I Know it — I Lost a pair of Shoes on the Race with Kenney[11] — Nothing new to day   Buisness was dull very, indeed

3   I was Out at the Race tract and got tolerable wet, To day a nag of Col Bingamans and One of Capt Minors ran the 3 best in 5. Col wone 1st heat, Cap 2d heat, Col won 3d heat and 4th heat. I made a greate many Bets One way or other and after all I came

11 Jim Bell was owned by Joseph G. Boswell of Lexington, Kentucky, who had "wintered his cavalry" at Natchez before entering the spring races at Natchez and New Orleans. Celerity belonged to Adam L. Bingaman, and Theatris to a Mr. Shy. On March 3 the editor of the Natchez *Courier* wrote that "Jim Bell, the nonpariel" is "the best three year old, we believe, in the country," a judgment shared by many racing critics. On March 19 in New Orleans, Sarah Bladen, the pride of Colonel Bingaman's stables, was beaten by Jim Bell in time very close to the American record. Johnson was in New Orleans at the time, but his diary entries for the trip were very sparse. See Natchez *Courier*, March 22, 23, 1842; New Orleans *Bee*, March 21, 1842; *American Turf Register and Sporting Magazine*, XIII (1842), 104, and Appendix, 7, 10; Brinley, *Life of William T. Porter*, 200.

home Thirty Dollars and 50 cts Looser on the day. I won a pair Shoes from Kenney. There was more money Bet on this Race than any race this week and the Race, if it had have been managed right, would have been the other way — Mr S S Prentess was married this morning to Miss Mary Jane Williams and has Left on the Sultana for New Orleans

4   John, the Boy of Mr N Hoggat, ran off and came to town yesterday and I sent for him yester Evening and made him stay at my House Last night and after Dinner to day I sent him Out Home to Mr Hoggatt by Edmond — both wrode my Old Grey Horse Out — Nothing new to day That I have herd, Mr Brown, the wheel right, Commenced this Evening to make the body to Col Bingamans Cart or Dearbon, ie. for him to Take to New Orleans with him &c.

5   Buisness dull. I was up at Auction to day and Bot Some Rose Bushes. Came home After Dinner, Mooved the wooden Cistern and planted the Rose Bushes &c.

6   I wrode out in the afternoon with Mc   We went out as far as the old former Residence of old Mr Guion and the Ruins of Mrs Norton &c. I met Edd Just Comming in on my Old Grey Horse from Out to Mr Hoggatts

7   Nothing new what Ever   Buisness as usual, quite dull, and giting to all Appearance more so — I made Out a List of the names of Gentlemen that Owed me or that I had Orders on from Mr Kenney. Said Orders I had Lost and I want to have them written Out again for me, He promised to do so for me &c.

8   Nothing new. I was down at the House to day assisting a Little in making the yard Levell &c. To day myself and Winston put One Course of Brickes on the Cistern Top and then put on the Top and Cut a hole through the Top for the pipe and planted a post for the Pipe to Rest on — Mr Walker, the Tiner, put up the pipe from House and Kitchen to the Cistern for which he Charged me $5.75 — Mr Jno Jaqumine Bot a woman to day at Auction for Two Hundred and [blank] Dollars — She was from the other side of the River at Harrisenburg, La

9   Blue Backs or Commercial money has Created a good deal of Excitement to day. Some Boat, up very Early this morning from New Orleans, Brot news that Commercial money was at 30 per ct discount in New Orleans and the People has been running Every way trying to get it off there hands &c. I had Ninety dollars of it and I Saw Mr Oblemis To day and wanted to Know of him how much he was agoing to Charge me for Building my Cistern, He did not tell me how much But Said I must try [to pay] what I Could have One made for Like it &c. I then paid him $90 on the Cistern and took no receipt for it — I paid him in Commercial money.¹²

10 Buisness has been Tolerable good Considering the times. I had a small Cannary Bird Taken up to the Jefferson Hotell to night to be sent by the mail to morrow morning down to the Coal Springs To Dr Buck   He is to give me $5 for it when He comes to Town &c. Commercial money Still very Doubtfull, Greate many persons refusing it for goods &c. I saw Little John Jourden to day and he was Out in the Street abusing His mother for Every thing that he Could Think off. She was Over at Our House and was telling how She had treated him &c. He had written a Letter to the school master abusing him for Every thing that he Could write about. The School master Came Down, caught John, gave him a whiping, John gets away, Bites his hand quite bad, then ran away across the Commons, Commenced abusing them all &c., Comes in at night, Begs parden, his mother Drives him of[f] &c.

11 Nothing new that I Know of. I allowed Jo. Meshio Twenty Dollars for his two Birds in Rent.

12 Buisness has been Dull in the way of Cash, good deal of Credit Buisness — The Commercial Blue Backs flying in Every direction to day. People all anxious To get rid of them — Mr Chapman, The Ranger, Died this morning — Said to be the Effects of Disapation — His wife was at the time of his Death up at Water Proof Landing — N Strictland went up after Her   I was down to day having Col Bingamans Little Bugy wagon fixed, the price of which $38.12½

13 Nothing new to day   Buisness tho, very Dull, I wrode out this Afternoon Towards Capt Nevitts. Saw the Funeral procession of Mr. Chapman as it past along this Evening — it was quite a Large One   The Fireman and The Fencibles and a good many other persons were present, Mc went down to the gravy yard also

14 Buisness very dull   Several Boats up to day tho nothing new, Tis thought that the Blue Back money will be some what better Shortley. The Blue Back money is still very doubtful — few merchants will take it to day — I Bot a Coat and a pants to day. The Cost was $26.00   Jo Meshio paid me to day $20 on his Rent   From all appearances we are agoing to have a very dull Summer, I Sent my old Grey Horse down to Mr Mossbeys to day by Winston   He took him down but the old Rascal will runaway I Expect

¹² See the account in Natchez *Courier*, March 10, 1842.

17   I was on the river this morning Early and got in the Port of New Orleans about 11 Oclock AM on Bourd of the Steam Boat Princess. She had a vesell in tow.

18   Will Bucks was Sick   Dr Mackie was doctor for him

21   Nothing new that I Know of

22   Nothing new that I Know of to day

April 2   Buisness was Dull I thoght   I Left New Orleans to day about ½ past 1 Oclock

3   I was all day to day on Bourd of Steam Boat Princess on my way up for Natchez.

7   I fixed the water Bucket on the windless to day, I went under the Hill to night to see if I Could see Kenney, The Boot Maker. I do this very night think him a mean Swindling Scoundrel, oh he is a Damed Damned Rascal in my honest belief

8   Nothing new worth writing about. I was arround to Arther Kenneys to day to get him to give me the orders that he promised me to write Out for me a month ago and he told me that he would have them for me to morrow

9   Nothing new to day   I was Out to Mr Pains this forenoon in Search of my Cow but had to return with Out her. Could not find Her &c. I met Gregory and had a Long talk with him &c.

10   Nothing new. McCary and myself took a wride Out in the Afternoon, My Cow had a Calf Thursday morning Out at Mr T. Pains plantation and I sent Winston After it to day, and himself and Stephen found them and drove them Home. The Cow Looks well, the Calf fine — Jack Wooshem and Joseph McAdams has a fight in the Street before the Door of the City Hotell with Sticks   McAdams got the worst of the fight

11   Nothing new, Only that a party of Texans or men from Tennessee Camped Out in a public Square in New Orleans — Could not get a House to Stay in. They were on there way to Texas[13]

12   Nothing New that I Know of — I was at Auction to day and Bot a good many things of One Kind or other, Pearce & Co. Deed of Trust Sale   Jake Riemer Beat the Duch Jew Myres to night and he stood it Like a puppy. Cryed Like a Child but would not fight.

---

[13] Early in 1842 the Mexicans invaded the Republic of Texas and took San Antonio and two other towns, but soon retired. Meetings in behalf of Texas were held in the Mississippi Valley river towns. The Natchez *Courier*, April 1, 1842, announced a Natchez meeting on the subject and also that some Mississippians had joined a body of 110 Tennessee riflemen who were calling themselves "The Texas Wolf Hunters." This was probably the group referred to in this entry.

13   Nothing new. I was at Auction to day and Bot some Little Mantle Ornaments and Oil of Orange and some Razors &c.

14   Nothing new worth Speaking of   I was at Auction to Day and Bot Some Boys pants Cheap — Dix a Scally, a dime per pair — I paid Mr Oblenis to day Thirty five Dollars which was the Ballance of the money I owed him for Building my Cistern, $125 was what he charged for Bui[l]ding the Same. I have paid him and dont owe him a cent. Steven walked Out this morning Saying that Mr Petter wanted to hyre him for the Day and I told [him] very well and he went off to go to work and has not returned to night to feed the Horses. My impression is that he has ran off to get drunk

15   Nothing new that I Know of — Buisness Quite Dull, yes unusually So to day — Mrs Samuels sent my woman Peggy Home to night   If She had have staid untill the day after to morrow, 17th inst, She would have been thare Just 3 months precisely — I Received a Letter to day and two news papers from New Orleans. The Christening Document of my Little William was in the Letter,[14] I told Arthur Kennys Brother to night that I should next week advertize the Orders that A Kenney gave me VS Several Gentlemen And I have a serious notion to do so — that is fact

16   Nothing new to day   Steven was Home twice to day and wranaway again   He was Drunk but will be Caught when he Dont think about it, Mr Rabbey had a race with a man today — 600 yds — Rabeys Horse won the race Easey by 40 feet — Won three Horses from the man — Broke him Easey. I paid Mr Edwards to Day for the Free Trader,· Six Dollars

17   Buisness of Every Kind Dull   I was at the office to day and paid old Dr Wren for Box rent, 3 dollars, up to the 1st of April, 1842. Also paid him for Postage up to the 1st of July, 1842   I told the old man Long since that I did not want the Box, And I told him so often and still the infernal old Rascal would Continue to put the papers in it — I am willing to swear that I wont take Another Box from him whilst I Live, D—— him   I Lost the Bird to Day that I Bot of Jo Meshio — It Died from Taking Cold by being Left in the window

18   Nothing new to day   Buisness dull, very dull

---

[14] Johnson referred to the baptismal certificate of his eldest son, William, Jr. With the exception of one child who died soon after birth, all of William Johnson's ten children were given Catholic baptisms in the "Cathedral and Parrochial Church of St. Louis" in New Orleans. Eight of the nine certificates of baptism are in the Johnson Papers; all of them testify that the children were legitimate offspring of free persons of color.

19   Mrs Wilcox Stop at my House nearly all day and Mc took Dinner with us also

20   Nothing new that I Know of. Business Dull, Quite so indeed   Mr T Rose Came in the shop to night and we began and ta[l]ked untill After ten Oclock — The Subjects, Banks & Banking — prospects of war — money Loaning — insolvent people. England and the English — Slavry — Texas & Mexico

21   Nothing new that I Know of   Buisness very dull — Aniversary of The Fencibles to day was Celebrated in Capt Minors pasture by the Fencibles[15]

22   Nothing new To day   Buisness Quite dull as usual. I marked the Piggs To day. I was at Auction to Day and bot 2 doors, the Cost was \$2.87½ but when I paid for them it was 3 Bits more added on the amount   It was at Stockmans. I say it was Rascally myself

23   Nothing new to day that I have herd, I Sold Mr James Paine a pair of small white Handle Razors and warrened [warranted] them for 6 months, price \$3.50 — William H. Perkins Died to day with Convulsions

24   Nothing new has transpired to day worth the attention &c. Mc and myself took a wride Out this Evening to the Scott old Fields and the Creek &c — There we read the Laws of Louisiana in pamphlet form &c.

25   Nothing New to Day. Buisness very dull — Mrs Battles Staid Out all night to Mrs Carys to Set up with Cary who is at the point of Death at this time — Mr Henry Patterson petioned his pocket to Buy a Mocking Bird — Mr Caleb Hurst Died to day at his Plantation on the River

26   We Heard this morning Very Early that Mr C S. Smith by accident Shot himself yesterday over in the Parrish of Concordia   Particulars are these as far as we have heard — Sexton Report for the Last Week Ending to day, Two Deaths — H. Perkins, April 23 and an infant Daughter [of] Henry Quarterman, April 26th, both with Convulsions

27   Nothing going on in the way of Buisness — The remains of Mr C S. Smith was Buried to day. The Guards went across the river for his remains — Brot Him Over and was Joined by the Free Masons near the City Hotell, Poor Milford Carey Died this morning about 3 Oclock and [was] Burried this Evening a[t] 4 or 5

---

15 See Natchez *Courier*, April 21, 22, 23, 1842. The issue of April 22 stated that Captain Minor's Hussars, Captain Page's Natchez Guards, and Captain Clark's Light Guards participated in the celebration.

Oclock   Poor Man, He sufferd so Long with illness &c. Has been a meare Child for the Last year Having Lost the use of His Hands [and] arms for more than year

28   Nothing new   Buisness has been Dull, very Dull — We Lost a Beautifull Little Cannary to day, One that we Raised — prety One   It got Out — Mrs Linton, Daughter &c. Left this Evening for the North on the Grey Eagle S B

29   The Fair at Washington took place to day[16] — I Bot to day of the Broker Fifty five Dollars, Blue Backs, and gave him thirty three Dollars N. O. Funds for it   I then Bot Fifteen Dollars N. O Funds and gave Him $14 in Specie for it — I had a Door Cut in the Back of the Lower Room in the dwelling House in State Street. Cost to be $20.00   This John Blake, that belongs to Mrs Wade, Str[u]ck Winston to night — Mr Tho Finney and Sandy Parsons has a fight to day Out at the fair and Finney Flogged him Easy, Easy

30   Nothing New worth relating. This Fellow John Blake Commenced again to night to Bully and dare Bill Nix when he was Comming from his supper

May 1   Nothing new in the City that I have herd of. Buisness Quite dull   I got Quite Blind to day soon as I was done my dinner — dimness Came over my vission Completly   Lasted for an hour or so — then Left me with a pain in my Eye which hurt me all the Evening more or Less — Mc and myself wrode Out this Evening Late and went down to the Creek. Mc tried to cetch a fish but had no Bait. Frank Marschalk, Hunting a Cow, went a Cross the Creek to Maj Surgets place &c.

2   Nothing new   I paid two notes of mine that was Due in the Commercial Bank to the order of J Beaumont, the One, and the other to the order of Dr Merrell as agent for Mrs Elzer Cocharan, Adminx of the Estate of Alfred Cochran, Decd — 18.20 was the amount of Each — I paid them in Good money — Dr Merrill promised that if I would pay them in good money that was due now that he would take Blue Backs for the Remain[i]ng 6 Notes that he held of mine &c.

3   Nothing new that I Know of — Buisness as usual very dull — Mrs Wilcox Took dinner with us to day and Left on the

---

16 This was one of three weekly agricultural exhibitions held at Washington during the early 1840's by the Jefferson College Agricultural Society. See Sydnor, *A Gentleman of the Old Natchez Region*, 152–63. This particular fair was announced and described in Natchez *Courier*, April 29, 1842; *Southern Planter*, I (1842), No. 4, pp. 13–19.

Princess soon After dinner — Jeffs Mother was in from the Country yesterday and Left town to day

4   Buisness dull. Nothing new. I Loaned the House of Messrs McAlister & Watson Two Hundred & Fifty Dollars to be returned in a week — I was under the Hill this Evening to try and get Blue Backs at 42 or three discount but Could not find any at all — Ductch Jew Bloome went up the River to Dogue [dodge] my debt for Shaving — Considerably — I spoke to Mr Samuel Davis to day for permission to make a small fence on a part of his Lot and he gave me Leave to do so. I thanked him and we parted

5   Nothing new that I Know of   My Little Richard is sick and has been for three days — Thank God he is much better this Evening — I Sold $16 Spiecie at five per cent Premium at Mr. Brittens Office to day And I sold $40 dito at Mr. Vaughn Office at 7 per cent Premium — thus I have made $3.60 on selling Specie — And I Bot of B. Walker $20 Blue Back Money at 42 cents discount on the dollar, gave him $11.60 for the twenty And I Bot $85 Blue Backs from Mr Griffin at 41 discount, paying him Only $50.15 for the 85 dollars, making $34.85 on the trade — Old Mr Bryley wran off from Natchez to day   His wife had Borrowed $5 from my wife and they were about to Leave and she sent down and made Out to get $2.50 of the money — the Ballance is gone   Mr T. Rose Left this Evening for England by the north &c. I waked down to Mr A Browns this Evening and Bot a dray Load of stuff for making fence with at $2 and he wanted me to give him Credit for the same on my Books, which I do

6   Nothing new that I Know of   Buisness very dull &c   I went down to Mr Brown Mill and got two Dollars worth of Lumber and Creditd his acct with the same, as he is owing me some money on an old acct   I had the stuff Brot up and Commenced to make a small fence on the Lot of Mr S Davis to put my Calves in &c, Edd and myself

7   I wrode Out to day to see the ballaon assend but the man did not attempt to put it up at all — told them that they would put it up to morrow and he Just took the Consern and put it in the Judges Stand — A Mob was soon raised and they tore it all to peices, Destroying Evry thing as they went and they were all then about to whip him but was prevented by the Entreaties of the Lady that they had in Company with them &c. The mob was Large, quite So

8   Nothing new that I Know of   Buisness dull, Quite so.

Mc and myself took Our Horses and wrode down on the Banks of St. Katharine Creek — took out Our Lines and began to fish — it was in the Afternoon. We fished untill dark. McCary Caught Eleven and I Caught Twent[y] four   They were all Small Fish

9   To day the Fencibles and Adams Light Guards Left this place for Port Gibson by Land. I Let Winston go up with the Company — He went up to Shave them and wrode a Horse belonging to Elward   They were a mery Set. William Perdue Esqr Died Last night with Cho[l]era of Morbus

10   Nothing New that I Know of. There was a fire Last night up on Pine Street. It was a frame Building belonging to old Mrs Beaty, the painters wife that use to be.   I dont Know that any body is very Sory about it — I was a good part of to day at work in the Sun puting up a fence around the Lot oposite my Dwelling House. I was making a Calf Lot

11   I was at work a Little to day with Edd making the fence for the Calf Lot. Nothing new that I Know of. Buisness Dull, very indeed, produce Low, Quite So — Money Scarce   McCary has been Building a Chimney, no a Kitchen I should have said — I have sold him 24 pounds of nails at 6 cts

12   Nothing new that I Know of   Buisness of Every Kind quite dull   I finished making the Calf Pen yesterday and to day I put the Calves in it — To day I Commenced to work by fencing in the Garden in the yard — I sent under the Hill and got Laths at two dollars a thousand to do it with — Charles wrode my Mare Out to see How Sally Cary was and found Her Crying and Hallowing, Falling down &c, on the road Side — She was on Her way to town She said to see Stewart, the Sexton, &c. Mother hyres the Girl belonging to Gimy Toolley Esqr

13   Nothing new to day   I have been at work to day making a Little garden fence in the yard — Edd was my help and Steven was to white wash

14   I Know of nothing new to day what Ever. The Fencibles and the Adams Light Guards Just returned this Evening from there visit to Port Gibson   They went up on Monday Last and Only returned this Evening — They Speak of some man being Shot up at Port Gibson by the Cannons going off to soon   Blew his arm off &c. And to day I was Quite Buisy in making the fence arround the few plants that are in the yard &c. Buisness is very dull indeed   I dont Know what to think of such times, I dont Sure

15   Buisness Quite dull   Nothing new what Ever — I remained all day at Home untill Late in the Evening and then I went out on the Bluff with Mc Just before supper time

16   Nothing new that I Know of. Buisness to day has been a Little Better than it has been for several days — Corn is worth Only three Bits a Barrell at the Landing, retail, and in Quantities it is only worth 31 cts   Oats 2½ Bits per Barrell — I Bot 6 Chickens to day, 3 of them was grown — got all for 10 Bits — Good deal of property sold to day at auction by the Sherriff — Some of J Beaumonts, some of Jno Smiths and some of McAlisters &c. The Bank Bot his, McAlisters

17   Nothing New to day what Ever — Mr Thomas Paine Died Last Night with [blank] and was Buried this Afternoon by the Masons — He was a good man and many, very many, Liked Him — I was to day Buying Corn for my Cows — I got ten or 11 Barrells — yesterday I got Oats, no it was to day

18   Nothing New what Ever   Buisness Dull. Money very scarce indeed. City very Healthy And the People Generally pretty Poor

19   To Day has been very warm and I Am Just about to prepare for Bath Buisness again — To day has been a very dull day in the way of Buisness   Nothing at all new, Now it is said that a number of the Banks below are paying Specie on there paper

20   Nothing New that I Know of   Buisness Quite dull — I sent Winston down to Mr Mosbey to day to get my old grey Horse and he Brought him up and the old Horse had been worked Hard, Quite So indeed, Strong Collar marks   Set Steven to work with the dray and he broke a shafft the 1st Load that he attempted to haul

21   Nothing new that I Know of   Buisness tolerable Brisk   Commenced to give Baths to day — Eight Persons took Baths. Half Credit

22   Nothing new of Any importance   The News from the Race of Boston & Fashion — Boston was Beaten as I thot, Shure   I took the Children William, Richard and Byron and my 3 small puppies and walked Out as far as the Pond near Mr Marshal gate or Pond &c.

23   Nothing new that I Know of — Buisness Only tolerable   Mr Seltzar, the Butcher, told me to day to give me 5 Dolls, Said he, and I will Bring up your Cow that you Lost some time ago — I promised to give Him $2.50 and He Brought Her up. It was the Brown Cow that I Bot of Winn. I then Bot a Cow from a Butcher to day that had a Large Calf. The amout

was fifteen Dollars that I was to give for Her   The Cow is poor and Looks as tho she would be a fine young Cow &c.

24   I Sent Mag. Miller the two young Birds that He Bot from me — I took a Bell and had it put on the Cow that the Butcher sent or Brot from where she has been Lost for some time   I had a talk with Mag Young to day and He surprised me very much when he told me that the Boy's [Charles's] time has been out for some time &c. After Considerable talk He wanted me to say what His Services is worth and what they were worth for the Last year & I wanted him to do the same but he would not   So I told him that I would settle the Amount of a Debt that He told me that he was dunnd for up at Mr J B Nights Store — It was agreed on and He then wantd to Know how much I would give for Him for the next year. I told him that a good part of the time there was Little or nothing doing, 6 months of the year that was very Little to be done, so that I Did not in reality want Any One. Well, seys he, suppose we make and avarrage of what you think. Say about fifteen dollars, and we agreed on the Same

25   Municipality money is now 25 per cent discount

26   Nothing New that I Know of — Mothers Cow has a fine Littl Calffie, had yesterday or last night sure

27   Nothing new to day at all — Last accts from New Orleans — Mrs Miller to day or yesterday wrote me a Letter &c. Two men were very well whiped for stealing a Coat or something to that Effect under the Hill on a Steam [boat]

28   Nothing New that I Know of — Buisness Tolerable Dull. Wrode Out this Evening, took my Little Girl with me wriding On my nag

29   Buisness has been uncommonly Dull to day. Several Baths to day, most of them on a Credit. Mc and myself wrode up this Evening in the hallow near the spring   We met a good number of Boys &c who had Been Fishing   They had Caught a good number of Fish — Mr Stockmans 2 servants and his sons Let my mare through the Gate and she ran off way down by Browns saw mill — I wrode Mcs Horse and Brot Her Back again

30   To day has been a dull, very dull day. Court is in Cession — Rownd tree, the Capt of the Watch, was ordered to Jail by Mr E C. Cage, the Judge — assalt and Battery was the charge VS him — I Gave Bill Nix ten Dollars on his wages to day

31   Report Seys that Gov. Dorr, the newly Elected Gov of Rhode Island, Has ranaway or hid himself. Fear of being put to

Jail by the Lawful Gov. King[17] — Mr Thornton Alexander, the Tavern Keeper, died this morning under the Hill — To day Winston Makes the Little wagon for My Child — It was well done

June 2 Lobstine, the Butcher, was up to see me about Buying my Lot under the Hill — This has been a Buisy day with the people who had uncurrent money. Brokers office has been full all day

3 Buisness Dull, very indeed

4 Nothing New. Buisness Continues very dull. Oh what times, what times. I Rented my House to Day, Conditionally that the Rent is to Commence on the 12th inst for twelve Dollars per month, payable monthly Mr [blank] gave me five Dollars on the 1st month — Jake Remer got his sentence to day and it was that he is to pay fifty dollars — He has been in Jail for several days — There was a number of others that was sentenced or fined — Rountree, the Guard, was also fined fifty Dollars — all for fighting — Reymer was put in for whiping One of those Dutch Jews — Poor old Sulivan and another man was put in for 6 days and fined One Hundred dollars each

5 Nothing new that I Know of — I Remained all the afternoon at Home, good part of the time asleep or nearly so

6 Nothing new that I Know of Except that some people on the other side of the River Caught One of those Runaway Slaves that helped Kill a man by the name Todd Living near Red River — They Burned Him up soon after he was taken   They Caught One moore of them and they Broght him to there Concordia Jail &c. They shot the other one but did [not] Kill Him

7 Nothing new what Ever

8 Nothing new that I Know of — I made preperations this Evening to go a gun on the morrow

9 I Got up very Early this morning and took my Good old Grey Horse with my Fishing Tackle and startd in the swamp and took Winston with me, wrode my Sorril Horse — We took Guns along with us   We Caught 44 or 5 fish. I Caught 3 or 4 more than Winston did tho He caught Larger Fish than I did — I made Him shoot at an aligator   He Shot Him in the Eye tho did not hurt him much I think   He wounded or Killed 1 Loon and shot One Black snake. I Only Shot my gun Once and I shot at a Puldo or duck and Killed it.

11 Nothing new. To day it was that I took Little Alfred,

---

[17] Johnson referred to Dorr's Rebellion in Rhode Island.

the Little Rascal, and gave him a floging for runing away — And He ranaway 3 or 4 times after that tho we made out to cetch him Every time — I Sent Mrs Miller 7 split Brooms this Evening by the Steam Boat Baton Rougue — Mr Jno Flemming sent me 4 hens for my wild goose that he got of me   One of the Hens he Lost before he Brought it to me — I sent Charles for it but he did not get it.

12   Nothing New — Buisness Quite dull — I walked Out into Minors pasture this Evening with Mc and His two sons, William and Robert, and I had my Little William along also — We had Each of us a pupy to give them Exercise — The pup that I had Could Out run Mcs puppy very Easy indeed — We Eat Black Burries for a while then Came around by the Cricket ground and Came Home

13   A Dull day in the way of Buisness — I went up in the afternoon to the Shellings Lake to cetch craw fish for my Birds but Could not find Any — Winston Caught a Greate many fish out of the draind pond of Mr Brown

14   Business Has been Dull, Quite Dull — Nothing New   This morning Early Young Kenney opened in my shop that was Formerly Occupied by his Brother — Here is a plain statement of the manner in which He has got into the House. A Mr Gromley Came to me and wanted to Rent my shop and I agreed to Let him have it at twelve dollars per month and he proposed to pay the months Rent in advance, which he did, and I gave Him a Receipt for One month up to 12th of July — He then told the Boys in my shop that he had Concluded to Rent or stay in the House that he was Living in, that the Owner had Reduced his Rent to 8 dollars per month and that he would now Let Mr Kenney have it if it would make no difference with me. I was not home at the time he Came and of Course had no say in the mater But when I Came Home at Night I found that He [and] Kenney had nearly finished mooving in — Now I wont put up with no such intrigue as this amounts to — Certain

14 [*sic*]   A very remarkable Dull Day   Nothing New has been discoved this Morning   A Duel was fought this Morning between A Mr Myres from Arkensaw and Mr Hatcher of this place   They fought with pistols at ten paces — Mr Hatcher was shot through the thigh at the 1st fire — there the matter Ended — Mr John A Hewitt was second to Mr Myres and Lawyer Baker second to Mr Hatcher — Mr Miderhoff and Irish John, a Hosler,

has a fight   I Bot a Lycences to day for One of my puppys — the No was 84

15   Nothing new that I Know of   Buisness unaccountably Dull — It has been near Eight weeks since we have had Any Rain   I never have seen such Dry times in sumer before I believe

16   Nothing New that I have herd of to day   Buisness very dull — Streets dusty and no money. I was Rolling or Slideing Dollars to day at five dollars per Game with Mr Jaqumine and I Quit Just five Dollars Looser — I wrode out to Maj Chotards Resedence this Evening and cut the Hair of three of his Children — I went out to Mr L. R Marshals Residence to day and found my Brown Cow   She had a young heiffer Calf of Red Color

18   Nothing new of Any persons Knowledge that I Know of. Mr Moris Came up the River from His plantation Bri[n]ging his children and he took them Out with Him to Mr Hoggatts   He took Edd out with Him — They are all alike Sure — Mother paid me $5 this Evening that I Loaned her the other day — Mrs Brustee went down to day on the Baton Rouge

19   Concordia Inteligencer Commenced the second number yesterday   I must try and make an arrangment with the Editor for it in trade[18] — Nothing new what Ever — Oh Buisness, Buisness, where have you flown — I gave Bill Nix ten Dollars on his wages

20   Buisness as dull as Can be Imagined — Nothing New. Peggy has Got a very bad foot   A Fish fin Stuck in it the other Day

21   I was up at auction to day and I [bought] two Berkshire Hogs, both of them Black Sows — they were young — I gave 1.62½ Each for them — Took them Home and marked them and put them in a pen — I Bot a dress or a Lot of Cercassion[19] to make One for Sarah — I paid Mr Elward two Dollars to day, Subscription for a Roman Catholic work and I owe him Still 1 dollar moore on it

22   Buisness as dull as Can be Amagined. Nothing new. I plaid a few Games at Shuffle Board with Mc to day and I Lost about a doz Cigars — together with what I Lost the other day I owe him Seventeen cigars — I Just believe that He can beat me and give me ten in thirty

---

[18] Johnson referred to the *Concordia Intelligencer*, published at Vidalia, Louisiana, across the Mississippi River from Natchez.

[19] Johnson probably meant either circassian, a variety of light cashmere, or circassienne, a twilled cotton-and-wool fabric.

23   Buisness tolerable thus far — The Sexton Reports 3
Deaths for the Last week Ending yesterday, 22d inst — June
16th, Mary Vanname, aged 23 years — 16th, infant child of James
Walsh, the Constable, aged [blank] — James Luckesbury, aged 5
years, Epelepsy

24   Nothing new worth writing about   Buisness dull and
Getting worse — I was playing at Shuffle Board to day and I Lost
1 doz cigars with Jaqmine and I paid them at that — Edd Returned from the Country to night   Has been Out thare a week
to night

25   Buisness is very dull indeed   Nothing New or Interesting   I was playing to day with Mc on the Shuffle Board and I
won 6 games at 2 Cigars Each — it was Just what I owed Him —
I feel Greatfull this Evening of Our Lord that I and all my Family
are well at present. Peggy is unwell with a Bad foot. Edward
Duffie died to day — I dont Know him   Edward Fry died of
abcess of the Liver

26   Nothing new that I Know of   Buisness is so very dull
I dont Know what to think. I had Peggy mooved up from my
House to the Shop for Mother to attend to Her — A Colord Child
died to day — I dont Know it   Old Mrs. Odam died of disentary,
aged 80 years

27   The Returns from my Shop below is net about as small
a sum as I could wish to see, paying Journeman Leave a Ballance
of $25.00   That is Hard Shure

28   Nothing new worth attention to day. Beky Fraizer, a
poor woman, Died yesterday or to day   I Am told that the Poor
woman has Left Six poor Helpless Children to Suffer in this wide
world, Poor Children. I am Sory for the woman   I hope it will
be in my power to render them some assistance

29   Nothing new that I Know of   Buisness a Shade Better
to day than it was yesterday, Mr McAlister man, Tailor, Found
Mothers Little Red Cow this Evening in the Bayou where she
has been for three Days a Starving   I helped to Get Her Out —
My Present Stock of Animals are as Follows, 1 old Grey Horse, 1
Sorril Horse, 1 Sorril mare, 1 Bay mare. Cows, Pink with Heiffer
Calf, Pide with Bull Calf, Polly Hopkins with Bull Calf, Chery
with Red Heiffer Calf   Hogs, Betts with two Barrer Pigs, 2
Birkshire Sows, Molly and Mugg, and 2 Little white Piggs, Sows.
Baker presents His acct VS City for Killing Thirty five Dogs —
Amount $35. The acct was allowed &c.

30   Buisness very Dull. Nothing New. I Had a small settle-

ment with Joseph Meshio to day and He paid me by An Order
on Mother for $12.12½ and my Own acct in Store of 3.50 and a
small Ballance in silver making the twenty Dollars in all which
pays for the Rent up to that date — He now Owes me for the
month of April, May and June and to morrow it will be four
months due

July 1   It was to day that Mrs Tainter wanted to See Bill
Nix about Having some Books that Jane Had taken from them
with Out Leave. The Books was taken by Jane and Given to Bill
Nix as a present   The American Songster is one, the Book of
James Hoyles Games and the Life of Gim Crow was the Books
that I saw that She presented to him   I asked where he got
Hoyles Games from and He told me that it belonged to his
Brother Andrew and that he got it out of his trunk and that he
has had it along time &c. The Concequince was that the Girl was
sent Home a Crying and she was Ruined   To day Maj Young
was in town and I Paid One Hundred Dollars in Dimes at 8
for the Dollar   The Maj did not Like to take it tho After Calling
severall times to see me about it He finly went off   I told him
that I had paid Charles Dr. Bill &c. which must have Amounted
to 30 or 35 dollars which I believe is strickly true

    2   Nothing new that I Know of   Buisness dull, Quite
So   Tis strange how very Dull Every thing is at present   The
Natchez Guards Left Here this Evening to go Out to Franklin
Depot. Charles went with them   They Left at 3 Oclock taking
all the Music that was [entry incomplete]

    3   Nothing new that I Know of   Buisness Quite dull   I
Remained at Home all day to day and did not go Out farther
then the pen, my Calf pen, and there to Read in the Latest dates
&c.

    4   Two of the Companies turned Out to day and of all the
Music that I Ever herd in my Life   Mr Sorias John and some
other Boy, oh it was dreadfull indeed, past Anything that I Ever
Herd in my Life

    5   Nothing new that I Know of. Buisness dull and we cant
help it at all — I had a conversation to day with Dr. [blank] and
he agreed to Give me Three Hundred and Fifty, $350, for my
House for the year, the Rent to Commence from the 25th of
July inst and I was to Extend the Fence to remoove the Privy or
have a small One made &c. To day the Natchez Guards Returned
from there visit to Franklin County. Charles was with them —
They had fine time whilst they were Out thare

6 Nothing new that I Know of Buisness Better than it was yesterday tho nothing to Bragg on as yet

7 Buisness Just So So — Nothing new what Ever. The Boys Charles & Winston was Laying of Brick all day to day down in the yard — They have a greate deal to Lay yet and it will take a Quantity of Brick — Yesterday I gave an officer an acct. vs Joe Meshio for Forty Dollars and it made Joe Angry, tho he told me if I would take it out of the officers hands that he would Agree to pay 1 dollar Evry day untill he shall hav paid up the Amount he owes and he owes me just 80 dollars to the 1st inst — and he Called to day and gave me 2 dollars.

8 Charles was at work to day down at the House making a pavement in the Yard

9 I Spoke to A. L. Willson the other day to procure me a passage on the Steam Boat, Maid of Arkensaw, which he promised to do and to day when the Boat Came I went down to see about it and I saw him and He told me that he had spoke to the Capt. and that he had Refused to Let a State Room, But that my wife Could have the whole of the Ladies Cabbin to Herself but it was a Rule on his Boat not to Let any Col persons have State Rooms on Her — I askd him to go with me on Bourd — He went on Board and showd me the Capt. and I asked him if could not spare a State Room and he told me that He Could not spare one that it was against the Rules of His Boat and that he had said it once and that was Enough and that he was a man of his word and Spoke of Prejudice of the Southern people, it was damd Foolish &c, and that he was a doing a Buisness for other people and was Compelld to adopt those Rules — I did not prevail by no means — He then said that I Could Have a State Room on Conditions which I told him would answer.

10 My Family Left for New Orleans yesterday — I was alone to day to dinner I Lay down in the afternoon, took a nap, After that took my Horse and my 3 puppies and wrode down with Mac to Capt Nevitts Lower fence on the River by Shipping Comp — Thare I threw Sticks in the River and my Puppys went in and brot them Out as well as an old and well trained dog would have done it and when we started for Home Rome took the Stick in his mouth and Brot it home in the yard before he put it down — I had my Little William with us

11 Winston and myself Commenced to dig in the yard of the new House to Lay a pavment with Brick — We Got along first rate. We would have got throug if it had not have Rained in the

Afternoon and we had to stop. One of Dr Cartwrights women, when Crossing the River to day in the Steam Fery Boat, Jumped over Bourd and was Drowned Amediately — Where is the natural instinct that he has written so much about — oh whare did you come from

12   Winston and myself was at work to day Laying Brick in a Kitchen to my new House — We got through with it and then Levelld the yard and dug a gutter, Coverd it up &c. Made a good days work of it — This Evening about 6 Oclock Mr S Wiswalls Little son, aged [blank], fell from [blank] and Fracterd his Head in such a manner as to Cause his Death about 9 Oclock tonight — Oh what distress to the parrents — Mr Wiswall himself was at Woodville and is thare now — Mr Wm Proud died to day I herd

13   Nothing new to day. I sent a Letter to New Orleans to day to my wife by the Steamer Mail — I have been hard at work all this day remooving and Stacking Brick in the yard — Steven and Winston was with me, My old grey Horse and the Sorril too was both in the corn field of Mrs Paine this Evening when I sent for them. What a Consumate old Scamp the old grey is

14   Buisness Like it was yesterday, very dull indeed and nothing new that I Know of — The Sexton Reports 4 deaths for the week Ending 10th as Follows — July 6th, 1 Col Child; 8th, F Yates, congestive Fever; 10th, Tom, Colard; 10th, Negro, not Dr Cartwrights woman   The City then pays T A S Doniphan for ½ years printing, $85; S. Cotton Esqr for 1 qr Sallery 300; R North Dito, $150; B Wade, for 12 days attendance $24; R. Parker do, $24; J. R. Stockman, $24; R. Stewart, $24; G I Dicks, $24; J W Sharp, $24, and then adjourned — Winston and myself and Steven did a greate deal of work to day — that of the hardest Kind — such a[s] mooving Brick, diging dirt, Laying Brick, Paving, &c.

15   Winston and myself was very Buissy to day. We had a hole Dug yesterday and we Bricked it up and to day we Built a House on it and finished it off in Stile — Beside we did considerable Fencing &c. We got the Brick all Out of the yard to day — what we did not Stack up — Gim had those Big Gates swung at lower End of my yard and the Fellow that put it up Charged me 1.50 and Gim charged me one dollar for the gates and a short time ago He gave the same to me and I Know it — Veni Vidi no Vici — Veni Vidi no Vici — Enough Said.

16   Nothing new that I Know of   I was very Buissy to day

at work in my yard making a fence and doing other things of some importance to a Family Residence &c. I paid my Tax, City Tax, to day and it amounted to Fifty Seven Dollars and fifty cents — I paid the Tax for Mother, the Amount was five Dollars and fifty cents. I paid the Tax for Maj Young for Charles — the Amount of Tax was Eight Dollars and fifty cts — Little Vivear mooved all his Effects Out of the Exchange Late, very Late to night, and has put them where they Cant be found—What will Dr McPheeters say when he finds it Out — He wont Like it sure

17 Nothing new that I Know of. Buisness to day was very dull indeed — I Remained at Home all day to day or untill very Late and then I went out on the Bluff and took along Will and the 3 Puppies and returned to supper soon — I Commenced this Afternoon to put my News papers in order to have them bound   I found but few and they were very much Out of Order

18 Nothing new to day that I have herd of. Buisness Quite dull — I went down to the [house] this afternoon in State St and Winston and myself Layd down a good many Bricks, paving the yard &c. I Loand my two Horses

19 Nothing new has transpired that I have Herd — Buisness is Quite Dull and I am affraid it will be no better   I was Out at my House to day and Hanah Fry son came to me to Let me Know my Little Cow was then On the Bluff and had Just had a Calf and that I aught to send Amediately and take Care of it for the Hogs was about to Eat it   Came very near Eating the Calf several times and was prevented by him — Tis Singular that a man with my team Haulling Corn met the Cow Only about and hour before Coming up from under the Hill and when He Returned from thare we were driving the Cow and Calf home   It was then about ½ hour or such a matter old

20 I have been unwell all day to day   Mr W. K. Henry Came to take a Bath to night and He was tolerable well in for it I assure you   Got very Sick and was sent Home in a Hack

21 I went down to the House this afternoon and Commenced to lay Brick and Layd a good many. There is Even now about 2 days work — I sent my Little Cow up to day to the shop to Have Her Broke and made tame — I was up to a Auction to day at Dan. Stevensons House, Lately Kept by Duck Williams, and I Bot 2 Pichers, 1 Doller Each, 1 wash Stand with Bason, 1 Center table, 2 Goblets — I Recevd a Letter to day from my wife in New Orleans. They were all well &c.

22 I was down in the yard to Lay Brick but Could do but Little for the Rain — Nothing new to day. I was alarmed at a small Circumstance which does not amount to anything these Hard times, that is, the Scarcety of Money

23 Nothing new has transpired of much Interest — The Officers was Buisy to day in search of stollen Goods They found a Considerable Quantity of Goods and Plunder in a Mrs Macens House and Celler — They have her in Custady now The Goods was in part Stollen by Moses Lee who belongs to Mrs Gemmell They have got Him and another Boy that was found also in the same House I am told there was upwards of three Loads of a Dray found thare

24 Nothing new of Importance to day that I Know of I Remaind at Home all day. William & Little Robert McCary took dinner with me to day and Mc to tea with me to night

25 Nothing new that I Know of Buisness as usual very dull. Wors than Ever I Knew it before — I was Engaged to day a while to pack up paper &c., News papers. Winston worked a Little while to day Laying Bricks in the yard My old Grey Horse was found this morning Out in Mrs Paynes Garden or Corn field — He was sentenced to imprisonment in the Stable for the Ballance of this week unless he can get some One to go his Bail — The City is Healthy, thank God

26 Buisness Extreamly Dull. Nothing New To day that I have heard of I Spent a good portion of to day in arranging my news papers to have them Bound. Greate many numbers are Lost.

27 I Saw Mr W Burns this Evening and had a Long talk with him about Winston. He wantd to Know how he was ageting along &c and I told him that He was doing very well tho I was not at this time Learning him much in the way of his Book. He wanted me to do so and he thought that Winston was now about Eighteen years old and that he wanted to have him Learn to Read and write, so that he might be able to Keep his Books or accts when he became older Enough to do Buisness for Himself He thought that wages was and Injury to a Boy, that it would give them Bad Habits, and that he did not want him to have any but to work along as Long as he was satisfied. We Could agree I thanked him. He Said that he thought that there would be something Left out of the Estate and that if he conducted himself well that he would give him a start some day — I told him that Winston was a very smart Boy and that I Liked him very much indeed[20]

28 Nothing new that I have herd — Buisness dull as it can possibly be. My Wife Came up to day on the Maid of Arkansas and had my three youngest Children on Bourd, Richard, Byron and Anna and Seva [servant] Lucinda. They Left here on the 9th inst and arrived here to day — Fifteen dollars for there passage and five for Wellington — I was quite sick to day and took a dose of medicine, 6 pills.

29 I went under the Hill to day and I Bot three Little Sows — gave five dollars for them   They are well grown pigs — I was sick yesterday but am up to day and on my feet   I Loaned Mr Jaqumine to day One Hundred and five dollars in dimes at 8 dimes to the dollar

30 To day is the fair at Washington and a Greate many persons have Gone Out to it and we have had Rain nearly all Day — It was a very disagreeable day for the fair[21]   I wrode Out this morning and took my Little Gun and My pup Romeio — I Shot 5 Birds, 4 of them wood peckers — I Shot 1 Jay Bird also — Romeo acted Like and old and well trained Dog Bringing Every Bird to me as I Killed it — Nothing new to day   Buisness has been a Little Better to day than it has for Several days past and I am glad of it — I gave Mr Charles Reynolds to day twenty Dollars in good Silver and he agrees to Build me a Cistern 12 by 20 ft deep — I am to furnish 1 hand to dig the Cistern and to furnish the Brick and him to build the Cistern for the sum of Eighty Dollars and it will be Recollected that I Loaned Him a short time ago twenty dollars so he has already Received Forty dollars of the money and the other Forty he wont ask for untill Christmas — With those Conditions we Closed the Bargain

31 Every Sunday seems to be Less Buisness a doing — Tis Strange. I never thought we would see such times as those

August 1 Mr Fitzchew Gave me a Couple of Little wild Summer Ducks — I wrode this morning Early and took my Little Gun

---

[20] It was customary to end the apprenticeship of free Negroes when they became eighteen, but William Winston (Negro barber who worked for Johnson) was not yet free. The will of Fountain Winston had directed that "Bill or William" should be freed when he was twenty-one years of age, had made provision for his support during his minority, and had left all property in the estate (amounting to more than $3,000 after certain deductions) to the executor to hold in trust for the young Negro. See Adams County Will Books, II, 81–83; "Estate of Fountain Winston," Adams County Probate Records, File 69.

[21] This fair is described in *Southern Planter*, I (1842), Nos. 7–8, pp. 1–2, 19–22.

and my pup Don — I shot 5 wood peckers and 2 Jay Birds — The pup did not perform as well as I thought He would — I wrode Out in the afternoon on a Horse that I Bot to day at Mr Stockmans Auction Room for twenty dollars — I shot 1 Bird, a wood pecker, on him and he Stood Still

2   Nothing new that is worth relating   Buissness as usual dull and I Remaind Home all day. My Little Rose Has troubled me a good deal. She wont go after and Bring game when I shoot it

3   Mr Boney Goins[22] of Vicksburgh passed down the River this morning with his Family. Has taken the Benefit of Bank Rupt Law and is now on his way down to New Orleans and seys that Buisness is worse than Ever Known before in Vicksburgh — I Got a Keg of Lard to day at 6 cts and a Bag of Shot and 79 pounds of Bacon

4   I got up Early this Morning and took my gun and went in the Swamp. I wrode my Bay mare and Winston wrode my Sorrill Horse and had my Little Gun — I took my three puppies down with me, Rome, Don & Rose   At the 1st fire in the morning I Killed a Rabbit and the pups soon found it — the next shot I Killd 1 duck and Broke the wing of a nother   The wounded One got away. The pups Brot me the dead One — the other they could not find   Here is what I Brot Home or Killd — 3 Summer ducks, 4 Beckroachs, 1 Grobeck, 1 Rabbit, 1 Small Snipe and 1 owl for the Hogs — 11 heads and Winston Killd 1 Duck, 3 Little Snipe and 1 Little Indian Hen. I went down to the Building below, Mr Mossbey at Wilcotts, then Came back to Mosbeys and Left my Little Rose to be trained to Bring Out ducks by Mr Wilcot — He will have a hard Job if He can Learn her to Bring ducks Out of water — The other pups does very well indeed   They Brot Out ducks and other game Just Like and old dog

5   Nothing new. I wrode Out to day to Mr Barlands place but did not see Him — He had Came to town — Buisness very dull   I dont Know what to thing of Such times

6   Nothing new. I wrode My Bob tail poney this Morning Out to see Mr Barland and I took William McCary along with me   We got Out thare and Mr John Barland and we wrode across by Dr Gustines Plantation, then by Mr Fosters, then by Mrs. Fosters and Mrs Woods and by Mr McIntosh, and all around by the creek and back again to the old Fields, Hunting for my Little Cow that I Bot at the Bradish Sale But Could not find Her

---

[22] Napoleon Goings, a free Negro, had been in the barber business at Vicksburg.

no where. It was a Long and tyresome wride which Gave me [a] Head ache and I did not Come Out on the town after I got Home during the day

7 I got Some Late papers this day from New Orleans and I Remained Home all the Evening reading the same tho there was nothing much in them Those papers was sent me by Bob Sperzin that I sold to my Brother in Law some years ago — Times are as dull as can be Imagind — nothing new at all — I must make a change in my Buisness shure for it is too dull

8 Nothing new that I have herd to day Buisness remained the same as Last week — God Knows what we will all do for I dont Know, Sure. I Remained at Home all Day, ie, I wrode my Little poney down in the afternoon to Capt Nevitts Spring in Company with William McCary — We made but a Short Stay. Robert Walker, Tinner, arrived this morning from a visit to Cincinnatti and Somewher Else I presume.

9 Buisness Continues dull and nothing has transpird to day worth attention that I Know of

10 Nothing new that I Know of Except Some Spouting in the News papers between Mr Farrar and Mr Brice — They made considerable talk in the papers

11 Nothing new To day, buissness has been dull Mr McCary and myself and Winston Got up Early this morning, Took a Light Breakfast and wrode into the Swamp. Mc and myself took Rifles and Winston took my Little Shot Gun — Mc Killed 1 Indian Hen, 1 Summer Duck, and 1 Snake And I wounded [one] Squirrell that I had Shot the nose off of it, and wounded Sligh[t]ly 1 darter and I Killed 1 Indian Hen, 3 Darters, 1 Rabbit, 1 Roseate Spoon Bill And Shot mortally the Squirrell that Mc Killd and I Caught 1 Soft Shell Turtle Winston Killd 1 Sqirrell and 1 Beck roach — We took dinner down at the popaws pach I had a flask of whiskey Mc had a Bottle of wine — Madrie

12 I Road Out to Mr Barlands this Morning to see him about my Cow that He Had found &c. I got Out Early and I saw the Cow but I told Mr Barland that I did not think that was my Cow unless She had Changed very much since I saw Her Last He Said that she had been sick and that she had altered very much and that he had no doubt but she was my Cow — I could not see myself that she resembled my cow at all, Only slightly about the Head and Hip — The Brand was altered and seemed to have been Latly done — in fact She seems to be too

white Every where for my Cow. After talking about the mater
for some time I gave him the $5 for taking her up and got him
to put my mark upon the Red and white Bull Calf, which is a
cross and under bit in the right Ear and a cross and Slit in the
Left Ear — I told him too that if Any One Should Call for that
Cow and Claim her to make them pay back the five dollars for I
told him that I would hate to swear to that Cow and so we parted
and it was agreed upon before we parted — The Cow Looks sick
and is no doubt sick now

    13   Nothing new that I Know of   Buisness still without any
Change for the better, [I] wrote a Letter to New Orleans to day
and sent it down on the Steamer Maid of Arkansaw — I had Last
night and this morning together several Quarrels with my
wife   She Commenced it of course   I did not have a great deal
to say — all amounts to nothing any how for I Cant say that I
said anything to Her to Hurt her feelings that I believd myself
whilst I was talking. I only did it in a Spirrit of Retalation —
that [is] all so Help me — All sorts of fights at the City Hotell
to night, Mr Geo Pulling and Thom Munce. Mr Munce got
whiped and there [were] several other fights that I dont hear
anything said about this Morning

    14   To day it was and Last night that I had a small fus with
my wife and it was to day that I wrote the Letter &c. instead of
yesterday — Tis the Last One I hope — Nothing new that I have
herd of to Day

    15   News Reached this place to day of the Late Mob in
Philadelphia   Particulars I have not herd yet. To day has been
Tolerable in the way of Buisness tho dull Compaired to former
times — I Remained at Home all day and took several Good naps
of Sleep during the Afternoon

    16   Nothing new   Buisness Quite dull. I Remained Home
untill Late in the Afternoon when I took a wride on my bay mare,
Little Will on the Poney and Little Robert McCary on his Black
Horse Charly — We were Looking for my Old Grey Horse and
the Sorril   We went Out as far as the old Quigless place but
could not find them and had to Return as we went. Got Home
After the usual supper time — There was a Good Deal of Property
sold to day by the Sheriff or Marshal — Mr Izods Lot sold for
Eleven Hundred Dollars And Jno Hodens place sold for $5 and
Mr Sisloffs Mill sold for six thousand dollars and was Bot in by
Capt Minor — good Lick — Mrs Battles wrode Out to Miss Evans
this Evening and came Back same way in Carriage — Took in

the Shop to day $2.12½   Mr Poindexter is very anxious to sell me a Bill of Exchange or an acceptance for $130. I told him that I had no money or that I had nothing but Gold and did not Like to part with it

17   I Loaned Mr Poindexter this Morning before I Eat my Breakfast One Hundred Dollars in Gold which [he] promised to return to me when He returns in the Norma S. Boat. I Loaned Mr Morris to day $12.00 in Specie to pay or for Passage Money. He has Just Got Home this Morning from Cincinnatti Bringing Edd, Emeline and Masourie²³ — Mother Gave Mr Poindexter the Black Slut Corah to day and he took her down this Morning on the Steam Boat Mail — She Gave trip away the other day also

. *18*   Buisness as usual not brisk — far from it — Nothing new to day — Mr Miller Came up from New Orleans this Morning Early — Came up on the Maid of Arkansas — We Spent nearly all day down at my Residence — took dinner about 2 Oclock, played the violin Some, Shuffle Bourd Some and wrode Out in the Evening up towards the or above the Cotton Press &c.

19   Nothing new that I Know of — Buisness dull, very dull indeed

20   This morning very Early Mr Miller and myself and Winston went into the Swamp to Hunt and Mr Miller wrode my poney and I wrode my Bay mare   Winston wrode my Sorril Horse. I Killed 1 Squirrell, about 24 Snipe and 1 duck, 2 wood Peckers, and Mr Miller and Winston Killed 24 Snipe between them

21   Nothing new   Buisness dull and geting worse   Mr Miller and myself got on the Steam Boat Mail and went up for Vicksburg

22   Buisness Dull. Nothing new. Mr Miller and myself arrivd this morning Shor[t]ly after sun up in Vicksburg.

23   I am in Vicksburg and I find it more the appearance of Buisness than it is in Natchez. I Left Vicksburg to day at 12 Oclock and I got Out at Grand Gulph and walked over the town a Little. We Stopd also at Rodney but I did no[t] go ashore at

---

²³ John W. Morris, attorney for Nathaniel Hoggatt, Jr., Adams County planter, arranged for the emancipation of Hoggatt's slave "Edward, being of the age of twelve years, of bright mulatto complexion," in Cincinnati on July 18, 1842. Adams County Deed Records, KK, 42–43. Edward Hoggatt had already begun to work for Johnson. Frequently mentioned by the diarist as "Ed" or "Edd," he was one of Johnson's barbers at the time Johnson died in 1851. In the next year, Edward Hoggatt married Margaret Lieper, member of a prominent free Negro family. Adams County Marriage Records, VII, 90. No record of the emancipation of Emiline and Missouri has been located.

that place at all — Both those Last named places appears to be very dull indeed and was told that nearly Every body in the place would take the Benefit of the Bank Rupt Law

24   Nothing New that I have herd

25   I Got up this morning quite Early in Company with Mr Miller and McCary and To[ok] Our guns and went into the Swamp on a Hunt. We Killd and Got as follows, Winston Killed 11 Snipe, Mr Miller Killd 10 Snipe, and Mr McCary Killed 12 Snipe and 1 Squirrel and I Killed 10 Snipe, 1 Rabbit and 1 Large Grobec and two Ducks and 1 Aligator which was a Small One — So I was the Captain On the Hunt. I had my puppy Rome along with me and Mc had his pup and his One Eyed Dog with him and they did not perform at all — We had Some fun Out of the One Eyed dog   He was affràid of Every thing almost

26   Buisness very dull   Nothing new that I Know of — Mr Cary and Mr Miller took dinner with me to day and we Sat prety Late at the table Drinking wine &c. Mr Miller Left this Evening at 5 Oclock on Bourd of S. B. Maid of Arkensaw for New Orleans — Mc and myself went down to see him off

27   Nothing new. I Remained Home all day or untill Evening and then wrode Out with McCary towards the Old Fields of Quigless Estate. We returnd and Mc took supper with me

29   Nothing new that I Know of   Buisness as usual, very dull. Considerable fuss to day in town about a duel that some people think will Come off between a Mr Downer and a Mr Wm Robertson of the Planters Bank   The thing will End without a fight and I am willing to bet all I Can Raise on it. I did Hard work to day for a few minutes down in the Cistern digging dirt   It was warm work. Made me very tyred indeed. Just as I predicted, I understood that the difficulty between Mr Robertson and Downer was settled and it was a missunderstanding   Arm-poop — am — armk poopem &c. [*sic*]

30   The Boys Commenced to Lay Brick in the new Cistern   Buisness Quite dull   Town Healthy and the people all Broke

31   Nothing new to day   Buisness dull, Quite So to day — This afternoon Perry Sells Came and wanted to hyre a Little Boy to Mother and he asked thirty dollars a year for Him and brot with him the Indentures of the Boy. I Read them and a part of them has been Destroyed, torn of[f] and Lost. He Said that the part torn off was of no Consequence to Him — Mother and him agreed on the price and She Calld on me to get twenty dollars

which I had not with me but I Loaned Her Seven dollars which She paid Him and the Boy was to stay a year at that price and Longer if he did not Come for him, at the Same Rates — Bill Nix went up to see the Mother of the boy Francis and She was very willing for the boy to Stay with Mother

September 1   Not Anything new. I Bot Joseph Meshio Gun to day and allowed him thirty Dollars for it and a half Dollar for the Powder horn — to be taken Out in Rent. I Loaned Mother Thirteen Dollars to day to pay Perry Sells for One years hyre of Francis   She paid him twenty dollars for the year in advance and took writings to that Effect. I then Bot his Indentures from Perry Sells for the sum of twelve Dollars in Cash and the Boys is to serve me untill he is twenty One years of Age   I also took writings to that Effect from him   We had the first Coat on the Bottom of the Cistern put on this Evening and the Cistern Built up as high as the Commencement of the arch   Mr Poindexter paid me to day One hundred Dollars that I Loaned him the 17th of August, 1842   The money I Loaned him was in Gold and he paid me Sixty Dollars in Gold and the other forty in Specie

2   Nothing new that I Know of   Buisness very dull. I have been Quite Buisy all day working in the yard haulling Dirt. The Arch was turned to day over the Cistern in my yard   I had the Canoe Brot down to the House this Afternoon to feed in — Wm Nix agrees to work at the Rates that Charles works for, 12.50 ct per mont[h] or at the Rates of One Hundred and fifty Dollars per year

3   We had one very Heavy Shower of Rain this Afternoon and the Rain Beat in Considerable On the Arch of the Cistern and wran down behind the Brick work — I worked Considerable at it — I was a Good Deal Bothered this morning about a black sow that I thought some One had stollen from me — I walked about for some time this morning Looking for her — The white Pig turns Over the Churn   We Lost the Butter — I greesd my puppy Rome all over with it. I had my pen mended and put the sow with the Young Piggs in it and she broke Out again in a very short time — Wellington Left this place to night on the Maid of Arkensaw for New Orleans Intending to run on the Boat but I dont believe him myself — Nothing new to day — I was a good plagued to day One way or other — Small perplexities &c.

4   Buisness dull and nothing new that I have herd of what

Ever   Yes there is too, for a party of Persons Shelverdereed[24]
Mr John Williamson Last night — They were Finally Stoped by
the Shirriff and Police officers — They have never had a chance
at him since He married before and this they Gave him because
he had made use of some Language that some men did not Like
when Mr Patterson was married — They were dressed in all
maner of Shapes   One was Dressed to Look in shape Like Mr
Williamson with a Large Corporation and another was Dressed
Like his wife with a behind as Large as they Could well make it
to Look   The thing went of[f] well I am told

5   Last night I was Frightend by the alarm of fire and the
Bells Ringing &c. I got up as soon as [I] Could and ran to find
Out where it was and it was in Franklin St on the Corner Occu-
pied by Flemming and Balwin, formely Mr Stockmans old Stand.
I saw nothing but a Desk that had been on fire on the inside and
had Burnd some papers. Report of this morning seys that the
window next to Stewarts Shop had been Broken Open and that
the Rogue or Rogues had tried to get in to the Iron Safe but
Could not — Old Mr Simon Moses died this Evening under the
Hill without any sickness

6   Buisness Quite dull and nothing new. I spent a good part
of to day in hard work a Loading the Cart with Dirt &c. Winston
and Frank was also at work with me. We did a good Days work
— Little Winn was up from the Swamp to day and Took Dinner
with me and my wife — Told me that Ford and his wife both had
been Sick, Quite Sick, and that they were On the mend again —
Little Morgan I herd was One of the men that Shifareed Mr
Williamson — Capt Page and Quigless, the Ice man, had a fight
this morning Early under the Hill on the warf Boat   Qui[g]less
got the Best of the fight or in other words he Gave the Capt a
whiping in very short order   He gouged him and Knocked him
too hard — Report Seys that the Ice man Whiped Easy — report
farther Seys that the fight Grew Out of Quigless Sueing Mc-
Michael and when McMichael sent for Ice, Quigless thr[e]w the
money at her and told her that McMicheal was a D—— Scoundrell and a D—— Rascal and agreat many other things and would
not sell her the Ice — Report seys that McMicheal went to the
Ice man to day and cursd him — I dont Know how it is

7   I have been at work all day, have the dirt remooved from
Out of the yard &c. Winston Commenced this morning and Tore

---

[24] Johnson was attempting to use the French word "charivari"; in the United
States usually called "chivaree," sometimes "callithumpian concert."

off some Old Shingles and put on five Hundred new Ones on the rooff of the Shoe makers Shop — Nothing new to day and buisness Little better yesterday — Some One Stole one of my Little Pigs   It was a fine Little Black One

8   I was at work to day in my yard Leveling and grading the yard in Order to make the water run of[f] in front   I work[ed] untill night and was so very tyred that I Could Hardly Sleep when I got to Bed. Steven & Winston and Frank and Will Buck and now and then Little Andrew [helped] — Mr Jas Tooley Came up to See me to day about Frank and he told me that he would see to having Frank Bound to me — He Showd me the Indentures that Perry Sells had or a Coppy of them &c.

9   Nothing new — I have been at work again all day Grading the yard to make the water Run Out in front of the [house] — Winston, Steven & Frank wer helping me. I am very tyred indeed but not so bad of[f] as I was Last night — My Little Byron was sick Last Evening with a Hot fever and we gave wine to drink which gave him some Relief, tho he was up this morning as is usual with him, playing, tho Late this Afternoon he has another fever — Buisness has been very dull Indeed to day — Soon after Supper time to night we herd the alarm of Fire and we ran up the street and found that it was in the building back of the Free Trader office   It was Set on fire th[e]re is not a doubt as they found a Pan that they must have fired it [with] — It was Soon put out

10   Buisness Quite dull   Nothing new. I have been at work all day in my yard Levelling and hauling &c. Wellington Came down from Vicksburg and brot me a Vickburg paper — He was on Steam B Maid of Arkansas

11   Buisness worse than I Ever Knew it I think for to day I only took in the shop 7 Bits — I Remaind Home all day, untill After the Rain. I then took my old Grey Horse and wrode Out towards Mrs Pains in search of my Horses and I found them Out in front of her House — Nothing new worth Relating — Mc took supper with me to night

12   Joe Meshio was handling a Pistol to day and it went of[f] acidently and shot a Ball right through the arm or Shoulder of Maretee. Dr Loyd Cut the ball Out. It past through the Fleshy part of his arm and Lodged in his back or shoulder Blade — The Ball was mashed Considerable

13   Nothing new that I Know of. I was at work during the whole day in my yard with dirt &c. An Irishman was taken before

Mr Woods for attempting to Beat to death a man down at Cole Springs the other day   He was tyed and taken Out of town on Horse Back — He was taken to Woodville in Wilkerson County

    14   Our Little white sow Betsy had Her pig to day after dinner in the Pen. She Had 9 hansome Pigs — namely, 5 Boars and four Sows — Buisness dull   I Spent an hour or so to day making a Ram Rod and wiping stick for my big shot gun

    15   Nothing new that I Know of   Buisness very dull indeed   Only took in 1.50 to day — Wilgus sits all day in my Shop talking — nearly all day &c.

    16   Buisness has been very dull To day and nothing new has transpired durring the day.

    17   I was up very soon this morning and took my Mare Out and had Frank put on with the saddle bags and she Broke off in a fast Gate or ran off and threw him off and threw the saddle bags off also but did not hurt him, the Boy   Poor thing, Her fate Here Ends, viz. Mr L David Came down very Early in the morning and we started down in the swamp to take a Hunt and to show Mr David the Lakes. We wrode down to Fords and he was said to be still in bed — We then went on[to] the back of his Field and went over to the first Lake — I thare Killd a black Squirrell   We then Came out and went down to the old Lake back of the Fie[l]d below. We thare went in to the Lake, turnd down the Lake and went across to the other Side   Went to the Lower End of the Lake and took a peep into the other Lake, Crossd the head of it and hunted up towards our Horses. I Killd a Grey Squirrell on the Ridge Just below the fie[l]d — had to Climb a tree for it — It got Loose from me   I Shot it again & Killed it. I then started for the Horses   When I got thare I found my Mare very sick, Swelld Conciderable — I or we started them off for Bailer Winns place and I found him on the River off at the wood packing place — Told him the Condition   We then Commencd to drench Her and Bleed Her which did no good. I then wrode Her away up the Lane, then turned of[f] and wrode up towards Mrs Mosbeys — Wrode down thare on Her but I Could no[t] make her Swet. I wrode up again and then gave her to Winn to work on and he tried his best but the poor thing died after being sick for prehaps 1 hour and a half — The Amount of my Hunt to day is this that I Killed 2 Squirrells, 2 Ducks, 9 Small Snipe, 1 Patridge and 1 of the Largest snakes that I have seen in the way of a Mocasin — I Killd 1 Sparrow Hawk. The number in all 16 heads — Mr David Killed 6 or 7 snipe and 3 doves and 1 King Fisher — 10 heads

18   Nothing new. Maj. Miller Came down to day — Mr Jno Fletcher Came Home for Another [blank]   Mothers Blue Sow had Piggs to day.

19   Mr Fletcher and Mr Rabey has Just arrived from up the Country — My Black sow Muggy had 4 Pigs and One of them was dead, So She has Only three Left   ——— ———, the daughter of old ——— ———, had a Child, a Boy Child. Old Mrs Bennett [midwife] was with Her. The Child, report Seys, is ——— ———s Old Grany ——— Like to have Died when She found that her ——— had a child instead of the Dropsey

20   Nothing new that I Know of   Buisness Continues as dull as usual — Oh for a Change for the better — The Plasterers are Sifting Sand to Commence to plaster my Cistern and will Commence very Like to morrow — William Potter was at our House To day and I wrote a Letter to Mrs Miller by Him   I was up to McCarys Shop yesterday and Saw a Spanish Saddle that young McDowell had made Mc a present of it — a young Man from Texas gave it to McDowell, The Cash Receipts of my shop to day is Only 1.75. Oh Good Heavens what times we are now Having — Peggy Came Home to day to work and it is the first work that She has done at Home Since the fish Bone stuck in her foot Some months ago — Steven Commenced to work with Mr Williams to day about 10 Oclck

21   Nothing new. Allexander was married to Miss Allexander — They were married under the Hill and a Large Party of men went Down to Shelvaree them and Just as they Got under way the Fellow Came Out and invited them in to Drink and after they Drank they Came away.   I took in cash $3.87½   Best days work for several days

22   Mr Morris Came very Early this Morning to [pay] for a months wages for Sylvia   He paid ten Dollars — I Got a Long Letter To Day from E Miller — the Suject Matter, Politics and Religion — Mr Mosbey was up to day to see me and ta[l]ked of Buying Pegy — Spoke of hyreing or Buying, on[e] or the other. I told him I was willing to do Either — I wrode out on my Poney this Afternoon to hunt old Spot and I found her in the Old Quigless field. Coming back again I saw Mr H Patterson in the Old Field shooting at Bull Bats or night hawks. I showed him some Patridges   He shot from of[f] my Poney but did not kill one — Mr Sharp and Miller Finished Plastering my Cistern to Day.

Wellington Came up to day on Steam B. Maid of Arkansas —
Reports them as being well &c. By Cash to day 4.87½   Best
day in this month

   23   Several travelers that has been away part of the Summer
have arrived — Mr Peck, Mr Duffield, Mr Waters — I wrode Out
this afternoon at 6 Oclock and tried to Kill some Bull Bats. I
only Killd 1 and was the first Shot and I then Shot four times
After with my Little Gun but did not hit with my Little Gun — I
wrode my Little Poney and took William Jun[ior] with me

   24   Buisness has been Dull and nothing new, I have been
doing very Little to day. Mc And myself played a good many
Games of Marbles this Evening and He won a good many more
Games than I did   He Can beat me Easy — Mr Henry Patterson
went across the River this morning and took a Hunt   He Killed
10 Squirrels, 2 Ducks and 1 grobeck. Pecans are Just Getting
Ripe

   25   Nothing new that I Know of — Buisness Quite dull

   27   Buisness has [been] Some what Better to day that it has
been any One day this week — Nothing new what Ever. I have
been geting Ready this Evening to take a hunt in the Swamp
in the morning

   28   Nothing new that I Know of. McCary and Mr Thomas
was at my Gate this morning by day Light or Just before day
Light waiting for me to go to the Swamps with them to Kill
Aligators   Mc took a Light Breakfast with me and we all Shoul-
dered Riffles and wrode into the Swamp

   29   Nothing new that I Know of   Yes there is news for Late
dates seys that on 11th San Antonia was taken by the Mexicans
— It Seys that Court was in session at the time that they were
all taken. Fifty odd Citizens were taken Prisoners, the Judge
among the rest — Tis Said that there were 1300 Mexicans   I dont
believe it

   30   Nothing new that I Know of   Buisness getting a Little
better — I dont feel as well as might, tis from the fatigue of my
hunt in the Aligator Lake &c.

   October 1   Nothing new of Consequence. Steven has been
at work at Mr Williams Black Smith Shop and he Left thare
yesterday after Breakfast and got some Liquor and Got drunk
and ranaway. Bill Nix went in persuit of him yesterday and After
Cetching him and geting near home with him Steven Struck Bill
or Shoved Bill over or down and Broke and ran off a second
time   I went Late in the Evening to see if I Could find him but

could not   I found my Poney Out at Hendesees Groceries with
the Martingale Broke   To day it was that Bill Nix and Joe
Meshio went out to the Camp Ground to Get Steven and they
found Him. Joe put him up behind him, made him wride in on
my Little poney   The[y] got in Just After supper time

2   Nothing new that I Know of   Buisness has been very Dull
to day. Great deal of Bustle about the streets, people geting ready
to go to Camp meeting — I got on my poney to day and wrode
Down to Mr Mosbeys. I Stoped at Mr Fords and Left Peggy with
him and he told me that he would take her. I passed on down to
Mr B Winns and he, they told me, had gone Out to Camp Meeting.
I Left him as a present 3 Cakes of Soap and a new Razor — I
then past on to Mr Mosbeys and there I Left Steven to work — to
Commence from to morrow. Winston and Frank went on down
to Charly Wilcotts to get my Little dog Rose and to find my
Little Sorrill Mare but they did not find Either of them — We
Left thare and we went across from the Lake to Cypress Bauyo,
up that Lake to the next, then on to 1st Lake   Thare we Stoped
and Winston and Frank Caught some fish   Frank Caught 1,
Winston Caught 10, and I Lost 2 of them before I got Home

3   Nothing new. The Sale of the Lands of Mr James Stockman was Sold to day at the Court House and there was several
of the slaves of Mr Stockman Sold   They were Bot by Mr S. H.
Lambdin. The Prices I do not Recollect but they were sold for
Planters Bank Money. The Lands were bot by Mr Lamdin also
at 1.25 per acre   I regret very much that I did not buy them
myself   The House and Lot was Bot by Mrs Martha Stockman
for 9900 Dollars So I herd. Tis more money than it would Bring
if it was sold for Cash now. To morrow if I live I will make
some Inquiry about the Land that was sold to day and I pray
the Lord that I may be Lucky Enough to make some good Investment

4   Nothing new that I have herd — Dr Broom Brought Home
my Pup Don this Evening — He has had him Out in the Country
to train Him — Caroline Baker went across the River this morning and got married to a Dr Jennings and they were not married
but half hour before she had Left him and Came back to this
side of the River again and the man has been in persuite of her
all day — Every body Laughing at the trick he plaid on her or
she on him, I dont Know which — Dr Broom has had the use of
my Sorril Horse Ever since Friday Evening and has him yet — I

have been in a terrible way all day about the Swamp Lands I
have been wanting to Buy

    5   Nothing new that I have herd of — Bill Nix and Jane &
Will Bucks goes to Camp meeting To day in a sort of a gig — Mc
Saw Mr Watt to day and asked him about some Land that he
had on the River. Mr. Watt began to talk about 10 dollars per
acre, then you Know, Enough was Said

    6   Nothing New that I Know of   Buisness dull, very dull I
think — I Came very near making a purchase as I thought to day
from Mr Lamdin   He asked me the sum of two Thousand Dollars for it. We Could not agree on the time — thus the trade
Ended apparrently — To day has been Quite a warm day and
to night after supper was over Mc and Myself went Out on the
Pine Ridge Road to Camp Meeting   We Staid thare an hour
or two then followed the Road Home. We Started on the Road,
then Came back and took the Horses that Charles and Bill wrode
and Led them to town

    7   Nothing new. The Boys of my Shop are in trouble to day
about the Horses that they think they Lost Last night

    8   Nothing new that I Know of   Mr Wilcott was up to day
and brot home my puppy Rose from down in the Swamp. William
Jun[ior] was ahead of Winston and Frank this afternoon, Took
in $2 in the Shop to day. Bad buisness Sure. I am in hopes it
will bee better Soon — Mc Sent Andrew Liepers Horse Home this
Evening   We Brot them in from the Camp ground

    9   A Miletary Company Came down this morning from Port
Gibson and stoped at the Residence of Mr Alexander on the other
side of the River and will be down to town in the morning — Buisness has been very dull to day, took in 1.12½   Oh what times

    10   Buisness very dull. Only took in my Shop $2.37½ in
dimes   I Received from Charles for 2 weeks work $24 in dimes,
8 to the Dollar — Mr Finney brot my Cistern top to day, new
and well made, and put it on this Evening Just as the Natchez
Fencibles & Natchezs Guards, Adams Guards and Claibourne
Guards was passing my shop — I was Out this Evening and took
a Look at them as they were parading on Our Bluffs &c.

    11   I Know of nothing new. Buisness Quite dull. Consider-
able marching about the town to day. The Fencibles, N. Guards,
Light Guards, Claibourn Guards, N. Houszors and all were Out
to day and they Looked very well indeed, I took in my Shop
$3.50, in dimes at that. The Following hunters went over the
River to day on a Hunt, Mr Izod, Mr S Woods, Ruffner, Wrigley,

Patterson & Collings — They Killd four deer, Mr Izod Killd 1, Ruffner 1, Collings 1, Wrigley 1

12 This has been a real Miletary Day. All the Companies turned Out and the Fencibles Gave a Dinner Out in Capt Wm Minors Pasture, It went of[f] well, very well indeed Some of the Party was Drunk of Course I had a talk with Mr Ford to day and he told me that Pegy Could not Keep up her Row — She had to [be] helpd up I am now of the belief that Ford is Small Potatoes for he had Bot Peggy of me fairly and now backs out

13 Buisness Only Tolerable to day. Nothing new. The Claibourne Guards Left here to day for there Homes — they have had a merry time of it Since they Came here. I made in the Shop to day $3.37½

14 I Got up on my Horse this morning Early and started in the Swamp and G. Brustee was with me, We went down back of Fords Lake, Crossed it, Came Out back of his fence. We then went down in the Lake, back side of the Lakes, to Cypress Buyou, Crossed it or the Lake and went down to the River Bank to B Winns place. Got a Circingle that I Left thare, then went down to Mossbeys And before I Left thare I sold him Peggy for three hundred and Fifty Dollars. He paid me Fifty Dollars in cash and I took his note payable the 1st Feb., 1843, and I took a note payable 1st of May, 1843. Each of the notes was for One hundred and fifty Dollars Each — We then Left Mossbeys and went down to the Lower End of his field and took out into the woods. I saw a doe, very fine deer, Jump and run through the woods and it Stoped and [I] took a Shot at it with my Gun. Had in Small Shot. It then ran right within twenty or 30 steps and I fired at it again and I [am] Certain that I Shot it both times that I fired at it. Oh if I had of had Large shot in my Gun — We Left thare and went over to Cypress Buyou and from thare to Mudy Lake. Thare we say [saw] Lots of Aligators And I also saw 3 Large Ducks of Mallard We both fired at the same time and we Killed 2 and wounded the other One bad — We then Left and Came up to Long Lake, took my Kiggs[25] and we Caught 2 Large turtles and 20 odd Fish — 10 fine Buffellos — We put them in the sacks and Came home.

15 Nothing new. Buisness has been good I took in to day 6.37½ in the shop. Nancy Jerrideau died to day — has been [sick] Only a few days

16 Nothing new. Buisness is Quite dull to day. I Remained

---

25 Johnson probably referred to a pronged fish spear called a gig.

home all day. My horse was on the Commons some where and I dont Know where Exactly, Mc Came down but I did not wride Out with him

17   Nothing new. A Yellow Boy was sold to day Out of Jail and was in the Name of Calamies. In a Horn for Stutson & Comp[any]

18   Nothing new that I have herd. Buisness Quite dull. Mr Harrison Miller paid me his acct. to day which was 9.50. Has been due for some time — My Sorrill Horse is Quite Lame. I had his shoes taken off, a nail was sticking in the Quick of his foot. I wrode Out this Afternoon to hunt my Little Poney and Could not find him — I took my Little Gun along and Shot Only One time and Killed a Sparrow Hawk.

19   Nothing new   Buisness dull — G Malin Davis Gets Married to night to Miss [blank], daughter of Old Mrs Dayton — Jaqumine has a daughter Born unto him Last night

20   Nothing new that I Know of   Buisness Quite dull.

21   Just before Day I got up and made for the Swamp and after I got Down to the Thom Winn place Mr F. Thomas and Mc Caught up with me. We then went down on the back Side of Fords place, wrode across upper Long Lake, Except Mc. He took down the right hand side of Long Lake. Thomas and I went the Left Bank of Long Lake, Crossed Over to Mudy Lake, Saw 2 Sand hill Cranes and a Large Flock of Mallard Ducks — They flew and we did not Get a shot, We then Crossed back to Long L. and went down to Cypress Buyou. Left Our Horses to the Old Cypress tree, went down on both Sides of the Lake to the End, then walked back, Met Mc on the River Side of the Lake   We then Crossd the Lake and went down Long Lake for a Considerable distance, Came to a Small Lake on Our Left. Here we found a very Large Aligator in the hole. Mc Shot at him 1st about 18 or 20 Steps and Missed him. I fired and put Out his Eye, then Thomas, and between us we Killed him   I Stucke my harpoon in him and had hard work to get it Out, had to Cut it Out with a Knife   We then Left and wrode down farther and I got off my horse and went into a Lake which was a part of Long Lake. I walked down a Short distance And there I Killd an Aligator that had a greate many young Ones All around her and had no water in the Hole   From thare I turned arround and took back up the Lake   Mcs Horse Came very near geting Bogged in the mud   Mc Fell off of him, gets a Lick of the horses head over his Left Eye — The Horse fell also but got out Safe   We then Came on up and

wrode into Cypress Buyou Lake, up it and Crossed over to the River.
Took Our dinner Just on the Bank above B Winns. Mc went up
the River Bank and Thomas and myself went over to Mudy Lake.
I tryd to cross it but Could not   Found 3 or 4 tarripins but did not
take them. We then went back to Long Lake, up it and to the 2d
pond in it and I thare Caught 4 Soft Shell turtles and 8 Bufflows
Fish and a parcel of Garrs — the garrs I Left where I Caught them
— Here is the total of what we Shot besides the Aligator. Mc Killd
1 Squirrell and Mr Thomas 2 Crows and I, 1 Black Bird — poor
Buisness — When I got home I found myself prety tight, Brustee
put up my tin guters to day

  22   Very dull day and Nothing new — I and Winston put up
the fence, Swung the Gate, dug the Gutter, made a prop to a
tin Spout &c. to day. It was for my new House — Took in yesterday 1.87½ and to day 1.75 — this is truly hard times

  23   I felt very sore and bad all day, pain in my back, sore-
ness in my Arms, Legs, head &c. I took a wride Out in the afternoon with Mc   We went up near Tom Purnells Residence, we
then returned. After I returned I felt much worse, took tea and'
went to Bed pretty Sick, took peper tea.

  24   Mr Ford was up to day and paid me five dollars for the
hyre of Peggy. He had her hyred for two weeks — I paid Mr
Abbott twelve dollars to day for One months Rent of Shop under
the Hill

  25   Nothing new that I Know of, Buisness very dull indeed.
Mrs Lintons Family & Dr Duncans & Maj. Chotards Families
Came Home from the North — No he [Major Chotard] is not
Come — We had Our Little Spotted Barrow Killed this Evening,
He was in fine Order and would weigh I think about 60 lbs and
is the 1st One that we have had Killed from Our Little Stock;
this was a pig from Betsey.

  26   Dr Calhound & family Came Home this Afternoon in the
S B Mount Vernon   They have been to the North

  27   Nothing new that I Know off. I had G Brustee to put up
my tin spout to day   He made a finish of it. He put up in all
near about eighty ft. of pipe besides Some Elbows &c. For the
puting up an[d] all He Charged me twenty Dollars and fifty
Cents, The bill is Reasonable One I think

  28   Buisness Quite dull. Nothing new. I sent Winston down
in the Swamp to day to get my Little Mare Kitty. He got her
down near or at Mr Mosbeys & she Looked Like she was in fold,
He said the cotton Looked very white in the fields and that they

were all very well and I now find that the Lakes are Dry, all of them down thare and many of them got fine Grass growing in them

    29   Buisness has been rarther dull than other wise   Nothing new. I walked Down under the Hill to day to see the Steam Boat Mosouri   She was Lyeing Oposite Wilsons Store, McCary was with me. The Boat is a tremendious Large One   After I Came On the Hill I wrote a Letter to Mrs Miller and Sent it down by Mr Wilcox — I wrode Out on my poney this afternoon and Winston wrode Kity Fisher. We were hunting for My old Grey & Sorril. I wrode along the Bluff as far as I Could go, I then took down the Bluff right where there is two Logs and I had to take off my Saddle to get along and after I got down in the Bottom I still found the Road much worse — I had the hardest work imaginable to get through. I dont think I will attempt to Come throug that way again for many days — After all I Could not find my Horses — I Came Out throug the old Quigless Field & Came Home. I Lost my Sturrep before I got Home — Mr Patterson went over to day to see the Lakes and Hunt. He Killed 4 Squirrell and 1 plover & Seven ducks, 4 of them were plover teal, 2 Summer and 1 mallard

    30   Nothing new that I Know of. I wrode down in the Swamp this Evening to take my nag Kitty Fisher to be Let go in the Swamp   I Let her go in the Lake and I shot a very Large Aligator with my Pistol. I shot him three times, I Left him Lying out in the Lake, Winston Caught a parcel of Garrs. We Left them or nearly all of them at Thom Winns plantation. I Borrowed a grey Horse from Mr F Fletcher. The Steam Boat North Alabama struck a Snag this Evening up by Browns Mill and was towed down to the Lower Landing where she sunk   She had a Load of Cotton on Bourd, near about 14 hundred Bales on her — It was nearly all goten Out of Her.

    31   Buisness was tolerable good today. I made five dollars in the shop — To day was the Meeting at the Court House to organize the Clay Club. Mr Matherson Spoke and Col Bingaman Spoke also

    November 1   Buisness has been a remarkable dull day in the way of my Buisness, made 1.87½ cts in Shop to day. Bill went Early to Catholic Church to Learn to sing to night — I Noyes Buys Stutsons Property 3 or 4 Days ago   He got it for twenty five Hundred dollars so I herd. Mr Ballard sells His plantation — I herd that Dixon the Carpenter has Bot the Quigless Plantations and the amount paid or to be paid is five thousand dollars   I Consider the Amount Quite Small for the place   Cheap, Cheap, Surre   And I also herd that Long Carpenter, the Yankey, has Bot Lancarshire at four thousand Dollars in Blue Back money — tis said that Lancarshire owed Carpenter most of the money

2   Nothing new that I Know of   Buisness is dull, quite dull indeed — I was under the Hill twice to day for a wonder.

3   Nothing new that I Know of   Times are very dull for the season   The French Barber mooved around to the City Hotell to day   Every shop on the Hill of the Kind is now on Main Street Excep a Dutchman that Keeps On Market Street and all of them has got on the south side of the street

4   We herd to day that Jake Sorias Daughter had married Little Mike Haglety in New Orleans

5   Buisness of Course has been very Dull, I had a barrell of Coffee sold yesterday at Auction And it Sold for $7.35. The wt. was 105 lbs, Commission was 55 cts, Leaving me a Ballance of $6.80   Report seys that the Steam Boat Maid of Arkansas took fire and Burned up at Carrolton the other day — I paid Mrs Battles $10 to night and it is the Last of the Borrowed money — I State this for my Recollection is bad

6   Buisness has been quite dull, Nothing new — After dinner I Got on my poney and wrode down to the Barland place or Collier place and I walked in to the Little Lake, then below   I went in and up a Small Buyou at the Corner of the fence, then Looked arround and Came Out to my Horse and wrode up to the Hill and Came up the Bluff. The Lake was dry at the foot of the Hill

7   Nothing new that I Know of   Buisness dull. I got up Early this morning and to[ok] my gun and Poney and started into the Swamp   I took all three of my pupys with me and old Pollo. I wrode Down right back of Fords Fence and took Out untill I Came to water, then followed the same untill I Came to a ridge and then I had water on both sides of me. I went down a mile and a half I suppose — I then Came Out and went down on the other Side of the Lake, next to the head of Mudy Lake, I then went down Mudy Lake to the hole that is in it and thare Just above it I Killed 6 Large ducks and wounded 1 that got a cross the Lake and I also Killed 4 Squirrels, 2 of the[m] Fox and 2 of them Black ones, making in all that I broght Home 12 heads. I also in the same Lake Killed 2 Little teal ducks — My Pup Don Stole my Hat whilst I was [at] Mudy Lake and took it

Out and pup it down,   Gave me a Greate deal of trouble, and at Last when I was about to give up the hunt Don went out into the woods and got it,   Charles pays 2 weeks work $35 this Evening — Mr Reynolds Boys was at work to day on my Little Building

8   Buisness something Better than it has been for several Days — I Bot a Cistern Bucket to day and had it put to the Chain and fastened it on to the winless and Drew out a Buckett of the first water, and took a Drink of it, that Ever was Caught in the Cistern — It was pleasent and good — Maj. Young Sends me 3 Bushels of Potatoes as a present   Good.

9   Buisness some what better than has been for several days — Nothing new. We had Our Little Spotted Shoat to day. This was the Last of Betsy 3 pigs   Two out of the Lot we got and one was Stolen and was Eaten over at Rabys Stable

10   Nothing new that I Know of   Buisness dull, Quite So — I had a Conversation to day with Mr Dix about his Land and he told me that Mr Jemison would soon be up here and any arrangment that I would make with him he would acceed to and he gave me to understand that it might be had for twenty five Hundred Dollars   I talked of Eighteen Hundred Dollars &c. so we have done nothing yet. I Shall now wait with patience to see and hear what Mr Jemmison will be willing to ask or take — If he will take Any thing in Reason I will be apt to be the purchaser

11   Buisness Quite dull. Nothing new to day. Mrs Richards sends to Know of me if I am accquainted with Jaqumine and whether he would be good for his Rent &c.

12   Nothing new that I Know of. Buisness is quite dull   I am now and have been for several days very anxkcious to Buy the old Collier plantation but I am affraid that I Cant Come it — I Compaired accounts with Joe Meshio to day and He owed me One Hundred and forty four dollars and he had an account against me for 64.12½ which Left him in my debt $79.87½ to the first of November, 1842. Mc Came from the tract this Evening or to Knight as Drunk as he Could be   He fell off from his Horse on his way Home

13   After I ate my Dinner I wrode down to the Collier place and gatherd some Cats tails or Cat tails, A Kind of weed that Looks Like Cotton. I Got my Game bag full of them And on my return Home Lost one of my Sturups from of[f] the Saddle

15   Mr Jacqumine Gave me a pupy from his dog Scillum and Venus   I croped his Ears and his tail soon as I got him

16   Buisness was dull, quite dull, and nothing new   I was buisy to day, Quite So, in cetching my Pigs and I Only got One Pig Out of nine that my two sows had   I also put up my seven Black Pigs by Hanah, One of them, a fine One two, has got her Back Broke by Some Rascal

17   Nothing new   Buisness Quite Dull

18   Mc and Myself got up Early this morning and started into the Swamp. Oh, but it was Cold — We wrode on down to Mudy Lake but before we got to Muddy Lake we went into Some Lakes right back of Fords Plantations and I asked Mc where he thought we were and he placed us about 3 miles below where we were. I then told him and we Started and wrode Out to Long Lake and we Came Out at the head of it, After we got down to Mudy Lake Our Horses got away and wran away. I Caught mine about 2 miles above and Mc never found his Horse untill about 5 Oclock in the afternoon — We Spent the day a hunting for him and we saw a greate many ducks in Aligator Lake but did not shoot at them, I Shot a Large turkey on the Ridge but did not get One. They [were] five in the Flock — Mc did not kill anything during the day and I only Killed 1 wood cock, 1 Ivory bill and 1 wood Duck — The 2 Walkers was along and young Collings and they did not Kill any thing at all

19   Buisness has been dull, Quite So. The Streets are quite mudy.

20   I remained home all Day untill Late in the Afternoon   I then took a walk On the Point below the old Fort with Mc   We herd some 4 Sailors down in Bayou talking about there voyages &c.

21   I got up Early this morning and Started down into the Swamp in Company with Mr Patterson to take a hunt   We traveled over a greate deal of Ground and made but a poor hunt at Last, I was Lower down in the Swamp to day than I have been yet — I was within 70 or 80 yds of Hendersons Salt Licks near Long Lake — We went down on Long Lake and we were on Aligator Lake, Gar Lake, Mudy Lake, &c. Mr Patterson Killed 2 Squirrells and I Killed 1 Squirrell and 4 Ducks — We Saw B. Winn in the Swamp with Gay   They were hunting

22   Buisness Dull yet. Nothing new thats worth relating

23   Nothing New. The Jocky Club Races Commenced to day and there were two Races Came off to day — I was on my way Out to the tract to day and I went in the Rail Road Cut and doing so my Horse fell into a Bridge or wooden Box and would

have died if it had not have been for some of Major Chotards men who Came and helped him Out of the place — I then went to the tract and Quit Even on the day — First Race 2 mile heats. Col Bingaman Enterd Sun Beam, Capt Minor Enterd Lady Jane Grey, Mr Kenner a dark Iron grey named [blank]   Capt Minors Nag won the Money with Ease — Sun Beam was distanced Easy — Second Race, Mr Kenner Entered Kate Aubry and Col Bingaman Entered Sandy Young   Mr McDonald Enterd a Brown Filly named [blank]   Col Bingamans Sandy Young won the Race Easy, Easy — Mile Heats   Time 1.57 — 1.57

24   I was Out to the Race to day and saw a 2 Mile Race — The Nags were George Kendall, Thom Marshall, Sarah Morton and Norma — It was a bursting Race. Sarah Morton won the Race Easy — Thom Marshall was the Last Horse in the Race — Mc won five Dollars for his neighbour   I Recivd a Letter from Mrs Miller on the Subject of a Lye that Elward told on me in Orleans

25   Buisness was dull, very dull. Nothing new   I Saw a Race to day between George Martin and Sandy Young — 3 Miles heats — George Martin won the Race by distancing Sandy Young in the First heate Easy, Easy

26   Buisness has been very Good to day for the times   I was Out to the Race tract to day and there I Saw a fine Race. The Nags was George Martin, Oraina, Mary Walton And Music, They were running the three best in five. George Martin was the favorite by Large odds VS the field. Music won Every heat and had to do her best to win   George Martin ran Close on her for the 1st two Heats and the next heat he was Only 3d best, Music wining the Race and Mary Walton Close On her, Mr Minors nag Last in the Race, There was a fight in the Afternoon between Collings, tavern Keeper under the Hill, And St. Clair, Collings Came of[f] best in the fight   He got St. down. There were several races in the Afternoon. R. Rabey won a fine Sadle in the Afternoon by beating 2 other Nags, Crizers Horse and a nag Called Fairly Fair, Mc Came Home from the tract five dollars winner.

27   Steven Came up from Mr Mosbeys bringing a note from Mr Mosbey dated 26 inst.

28   Buisness has been tolerable Only — The Circus Company has Arived and Performs to night for the first night, Nothing new in the City. Court Commences to day and Judge Cage presides — A report is in the City this Morning that two or three Dutchmen and One dutch woman was taken up and it was Supposed that they had Murderd Some One Last night as there were Blood found in and about the Duchmans house

29 Nothing new Except that Miss Wales ranaway to night with Young Jo. Winston and gets married to him on the other Side of the river. Mr Seth. Cox assisted him in the Snap

30 Nothing new of any importance, I Bot 2 Keggs of Lard to Day and I believe they are both taler Lard I paid 1½ ct per lb. Col. B. C. Wailes and Mr Seth Cox has a fight. They were sepperated amediately. Mr Cox was about Choaking him, had the Col. against the Banisters of the Court House yard

December 1 Buissness tolerable good, I was in Conversation with Mr Jemerson about the Collier Land and I Sent around to see if the Property was Still Owned by Collier &c. Transferred by Gerault to Lewis A Collier, in 1834, was Sold by Collier to John E Hunter for the Sum of Seven Thousand five Hundred Dollars in 1838, the Said Land Comprising Seven Hundred arpents — it was an absolute and unlimited Sale — The above is a Coppy of the note that I received I had a Conversation with Mr Jemmerson to day and He told me that he Could not tell me any thing about it at present tho it was Covered over with Mortgages and he wanted to Know of his Lawyer How they Stood and if they held the property — Why, he Said, he would not give a Picayune for it, tho he remarked that he thought he would be able to Let me Know by Saturday, Nothing New to day More than Lawyer Saunders and Lawyer Barrett has a small Fight — Saunders Choked the old man but would not Strike him

2 Nothing New. Children all went to the Circus to night I was walking about to day to see if I Could make a Proffitable talk with a Gentleman about Land to Day tho we had but few or no words on the Subject to day

3 I had a talk with Mr Jimmerson about the Colleer Land, and he told me that there was a talk that the heirs of Moore talked of sueing for that Land and if they did so there was a probability of its not being worth much, I saw a Small plat of it and it is shaped in the form of an L or nearly so, It Runs up on the Hill at One point near the Creek.

4 Nothing new, I took a wride in the Afternoon away down in the Lower part of the Collier tract and we did not get where we wanted to get, mistook Our way and Came Out near where we went in; we took a Look at Dixons Improovements and we found that he had made Rapid Change in the appearance of the place

5   Our Citizens are Looking Every hour for the arival of Mr Clay from Kentucky

6   To Day Our City was visited by the Hon. Henry Clay, he Came soon after breakfast, The reception was rarther Cold for a Community to have been so Long apprised of his near Approach to Our City, He was receivd by the Fencibles, this being the Only Company in town that turned Out, He was Escorted up in town by old Dr McCreary, Capt Minor & Mr S. Cotton, They all wrode up in the Same Carriage Drawn by 4 fine Horses. They Halted at the City Hotel. There Mr Lee Claibourne made or deliverd a Short but hansome Adress, after which Mr Clay arrose and made Answer to said adress and Spoke of [the] Citys Misfortune, meaning the tornado, and some other few remarks &c., then walked into the saloon of the Hotel and thence to the Drawing Room where he was visited by the Citizens Generally — After a Stay of an hour or so he was then taken Out in a Carriage drawn by a pr of fine Bay Horses to the Residence of Mr St John Elliotte where He Dined &c²⁶

7   The Streets are full of People and a greate many of them has came to town mearly to see the Hon. Henry Clay, He was in town again to day to receive visitors and a Greate Many was in to see him, Just before dinner he taken Out again to Mr St. J. Elliottes. Buisness has been tolerable good to day — I Saw Maj Young to day and he wanted to Know of me if I Could Let him have some money And I told him yes he Could have it, Nothing more past of Any Importance, Mr Remmington is now Lectureing on Intemperance to full Houses; he is a Smart man, Sure

8   I paid Maj Young to Day fifty Dollars as Charls wages. Nothing New. Buisness Only tolerable   Mr Seth. Cox and his brother whaled, So I am told, Roundtree, up at the Conner of the Agricultural Bank to Day about 2 Oclock

9   Buisness Only tolerable, Young Welding [will] finish working on my Little Shed to morrow, ie making the door &c, puting the Latch &c.

10   Buisness has been tolerable Good, Nothing New that I Know of To Day it was that Young Mr Barker pd me or Welsh in my Shop, twelve Dollars that he owed A Kenney and Kenney had given me an Order on Mr Barber for the Amount wich order together with Several others I Lost. Young Kenny pd me thirteen dollars in Cash and several small accts that he had V.S. me, mak-

²⁶ The residence of planter-philanthropist William St. John Elliott was D'Evereux.

ing in all the sum of thirty One Dollars, The 13th Day of this month he will owe me a Ballance of $17.00

11   I was Quite unwell with a head ache all day and when I went down to the House I remained all the Evening Home with out going abroad at all

12   Nothing New. Buisness tolerable Only — to[day] Beatings Estate was sold at the Court House and the House on Commerce St sold for fifteen Hundred Dollars and was bot by Mr Wadsworth on a Credit of twelve months, Mr Geo Welding Bot the Land, there was nearly 200 Acres of it, at $6.25 per Acre.   It was Situated 25 miles below this place on the River, &c.

13   Nothing new. Buisness tolerable fair, Court in Cession in Vadalia and in Natchez both at this time.

14   Nothing new. Buisness tolerably fair Only

15   Nothing new. Bill Nix Left for New Orleans this Morning in the Sultana, serving Mr Steven Elliotte — I paid him 9 dollars as wages for the time up to the 17th inst, and also gave him twenty Dollars to buy something for the shop

16   Buisness has been very Good to day. Myself and Winston working Only. Took in $7.25

17   Buisness Good. Took in to day $7.20   I made a bid on the Collier place to day but did not trade, I sent for a Barrell [of] Oysters to day by Wilcox

18   Myself & Winston worked alone in the shop from soon in the Morning untill about ½ past twelve Oclock without Eating Any breakfast at all, Mc has new Boots and new pants

19   Buisness good   Me and Winston at work alone in the Shop. Took in $5.00

20   My Second Daugter, that is the fifth Child, was born this morning some where between ½ past 2 and ½ past three Oclock — The Child was a very fine Large Child.[27] House belonging to Ried out near the forks of the Road burned Down and also burned the top of[f] of the Magazine.

22   Buisness has been dull to day. I wrode Out this Evening and took 15 shots with Mc Pistol and my own   Did not make good Shots by a Long ways — Nothing new to day worth attention

23   Buisness has been tolerable good — Nothing New that I

---

[27] Although her baptismal certificate was dated exactly one year later, internal evidence makes it very probable that this was Katharine Johnson (later known as Katharine G. Johnston), who died February 6, 1901. Adams County Probate Records, No. 1,682, File 237; Adams County Will Books, V, 305-306.

Know of   I went Out this Evening near Mrs Lintons and shot a
Mach With Mr Jaqumine, the 3 best in five, for One Barrell of
Oysters — I won them with Ease,   McCary went Out this morning
Early with some more Persons   They went down the Woodvill
Road — Mc Killed 4 Geese but could not find One of them but
his dogs brot 3 of them   He Came home in good time

24   Buisness has been tolerable Good, Nothing New that I
Know of, Lucas buys a Plantation for 27 thousand Dollars, payable
in nine years with Out Interest. He is to pay three thousand dollars
a year untill the sum is paid

25   Buisness was Good   Nothing New worth relating.

26   Buisness has been Quite fair to day. I drank Egg-nogg
this morning the 1st thing [when] I got [up] and I drank some
Last night and yesterday morning

27   Buisness has been good and Nothing New. Edd Hoggatt
Came in this Afternoon to work. He has been Out Ever since —
Capt. Barlow is Drunk to night and is Cutting up all Kind of shines,
hallowing and cursing at Dr Broom. Oh it is ridiculous to hear
him, Sure

28   Nothing new to day — I wrote a Short Letter to day and
sent two turkeys down to New Orleans by Steamer B. Rougue. Dr
Broom has Capt Barlow bound Over to Keep the peace

29   I was up to day at Auction and bot 2 grates for 4.50 And
I Also bot One Cask of Meat at Auction, Jowel they were — I went
around to day to pay my bill to the Doctors and I did So and the
Ammount of Dr Davis & Young Medical Bill was $30   Mr Addi-
son was married this Evening to [Miss] Jerault. They were married in the Presbyterian Church — Mr Geo Mandeville was also
Married to Miss Postlethwaite up At the Residence — There was
also a marriage, Mr [blank] to Becky Hunt. They then had a
Dance at old Cinty Greens

30   Nothing new. Buisness Quite dull to day — I settled to
Day with Mr Reynolds and paid him $8.50, this being a Ballance
due him on his bill against me, the amount of which was $113.50.
I also paid my doctors bill which was $30.00   I paid it to Dr
Young and Davis

31   Nothing new. Buisness Quite good to day. I Spent this
day at the Shop with a few Exceptions during the day

William Johnson's Natchez, a contemporary lithograph
Courtesy Mississippi State Department of Archives and History

Petition for manumission of William Johnson
Courtesy Mississippi State Department of Archives and History

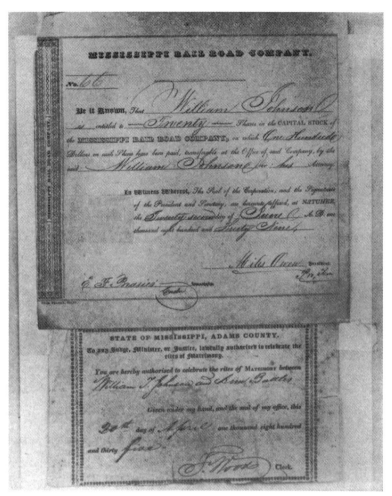

Stock certificate and marriage license
From the Johnson Collection

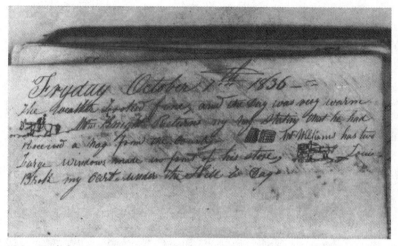

"Mr. Knight Returns my nag"
From the Johnson Collection

"Mr R. Bledsoe and Mr Hewit has a . . . fight"
From the Johnson Collection

Excerpt from account book, 1836–1837
From the Johnson Collection

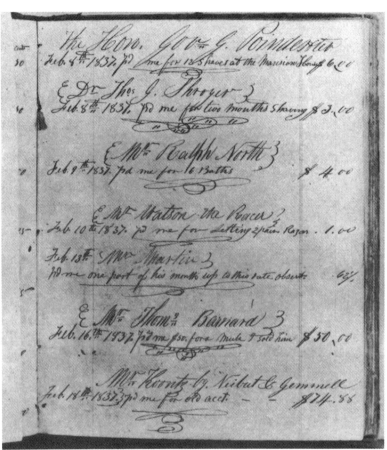

Excerpt from account book, 1837
From the Johnson Collection

"½ half mile race this evening"
From the Johnson Collection

1843

January 1   Nothing new to day — Mr McGraw and the two Weldons were down to day Looking a[t] Mr. Dix or Gimmerson Land — I was down to day under the Hill. I Saw Mr Barland and we talkd about the Land and from what he told me in regard to the Land I was much Less inclined to purchase than I was before I saw him, He said that he was informed that Mr Elick Moore intended to sue for it and the Cause was that the Land was not Legally sold — I have Nothing to remark moore than I have ate too much to day and to night also. I gave Steven & Lucinda a pass to night to go to a supper at Henry Adams and they have gone thare

2   Buisness has been tolerable Only, Joe Meshio paid me to day fourteen Dollars in full for the Month of December Ending the 1st of Janry, 1843 — The Election Came off to day and the result will be known in the Morning. Mr Bunting paid me to day Six Dollars, money that I Loaned him some time ago

3   In this mornings paper we have the City Election returns and they result as Follows —

For Selectmen

Mr John R. Stockman	422	John M Baldwin	253
Geo I Dicks	370	Andrew Donan	242
Peter G Crigier	299	Samuel Cotton	241
D L Rivers	296	Robert Stewart	227
John Duffield	293	Joseph Sharpe	191
Mr Breeden	283	William K Henry	161
E Profilet	271	Rhasa Parker	158
Mr J M Duffied Elected		Henry Tooley	110
Mayor		Alexander H. Parsons	30

For Treasurer	
Eli Montgomery	504
Geo Pulling not a Candidate	87
Collector	
Peter P. Baker	371
Levi G. Harrison	256
For Assessor	
Jacob Byers. No oppsition	593

Mr Samuel has been Elected Police Officer, Getting 4 votes — Mr Baker 3

4   Nothing new has Occurd to day worth attention. Buisness has been fair to day — Mr Dicks is in town to day and I should Like to make a bargain with him about his place if I Could

5   About Eleven Oclock Mr Jaqumine and myself Started down in the Swamp on a Hunt or to see if we could not get a Shot at a Deer that Mr Rigley and Ruffner might Start, We got down in behind the Goose pond Lake and Jaqumine got a Shot and Killed 1 Large duck and as they Flew over me I Shot and Killd 1 Large One also — They were flying very High — The Leaves are very dry tho we saw a good many Ducks — they are very wild   We Came home and took Egg nog, Oysters, Coffee &c.

6   I saw Mr Finney to day And He wanted me to Give him some information about the Mosbey Land, I think his object is to get the Land for Some One Else, tho I dont Know. He Seys That Mosbey wants 6000 dollars for his Land alone but would ask $7000 for the Land, A man & A woman, 160 head of Hogs and 30 head of Cattle and 2 Horses — I am much Surpised to find at this Season of the year that the lakes are nearly all Dry in the Swamp — Mr Gale pd $18.00, Mr Norris pd $4.50, Dr Leggett pd 1.37½ — Mr. Jaqumine pd fifteen Dollars money that I Loaned him

7   Nothing new. Buisness remarkable dull to day. Some small Collection. Mr Jno. G Taylor paid five dollars on acct — Mr D Mobley paid five dollars, the full Amount of his Acct   This was for Bathing. Mrs Jordan was taken very ill this Evening and is now very sick

8   Buisness dull I thought. I remained all the Afternoon and was Cleaning my Gun.

9   Nothing new to night or to day. Buisness dull to day, Quite So.

10   Nothing new. Eleven Oclock to day Mc and Myself wrode down in the Swamp   We went down to Mosbeys — I took my Riffle along and gave Mc my Little gun   I got 8 Rice Birds and nearly Killed or Quite Killed a Squirrell. Then Mc shot it with the Little Gun — I asked Mosebey to day what he was agoing to do — if he intended to sell his Land or not and he told me that he had no Idea of selling it what Ever

11   Nothing new more than the Selectmen Elected Mr Thomas Munce as Clerk — To day has been a dull day, quite so, And I have missed my Bunch of Keys and Can not think where or when I had them last — Mr Bunting, Pulling & Patterson, & you[n]g Britton was Over to day on the Iseland on a hunt Killing

Rabbits — Mr Patterson Killed 6, Britton 3, Bunting 1, Pulling none.

12   Mr Izod paid me ten dollars to day on his shaving bill

13   Nothing new to day. Mr Sam Woods paid his Acct. To day to 1st. inst — Great Rabbit Hunting on the Island — Mr Griffin is thare, Capt Thrift, Mr Patterson, Bunting, Britton and several others — Capt Thrift Killd 4, Mr Griffin 5

14   Nothing new. Buisness has been Only tolerable to day   Bill Nix sick all day yesterday and part of the day to day — Mr Patterson just from the Island to Day and Killd 7 Rabits, Mr Bunting 3.

15   Buisness was tolerable Only and nothing new worth attention. I took a wride Out in the afternoon with Mc,   We wrode Out by the Col Wilkins, wrode and Came in by old Jones — I Lost my Spur on the wride — A party of 4 in number Killd 28 Rabbits on the Island to day.

16   Buisness has been tolerable Only — Nothing new that I Know of.

17   Nothing New   Buisness rarther dull   Made in the shop to day $4.37½   Won on a Quarter Race $2. Spent at Auction $3.50 — also under the Hill $4.75   The Race to day was between a Stranger by the name of Denny, ran a Sorril Horse, and Mr Crizer Horse. The Stranger tis said won the Race by 10 feet.

18   I went Down in the Swamp this morning and Mc went with me and we got a Skiff at Mr Fords and went across the River to the Island and we had bad Luck for we Only got 5 Rabbits. Mc got 3 and I got 2. We found Dillon and big Fox over thare but they had good Luck. Dillon Killed 12 and big Fox Killd 2. Our old Cow Spot has got a young Calf   Steven drove her up this Evening

19   I went down to the Collier tract this Evening with Mr Gemmerson to Look at the Land but we did not trade at all — I offered him five Hundred dollars for 60 acres.

20   Buisness was dull for the season. Nothing new that I Know of. I offered Mr Gemmerson to day five Hundred and fifty dollars for 60 Acres of his Land that Fronts on the River, I bot a vest to day and One Dozen pairs of Shoes for the Children

21   Buisness has been dull, Quite so, I think   I have had several Conversations with Mr Gimmerson to day about his Land tho we made no trade after all, I think that it will be bot by Mr Weldon & Co

22   Nothing new. Young James Bisland had Dr Holt Stoped Just as he was in the acct of Going away with a Slave. Tis reported that the Slave belonged to the Bisland Estate. Young Bisland took the Slave out Home with Him, The tryal will Come of[f] this week, I took Will up behind me and I wrode Out through the old Quigless place and down through the Colier tract, then over the Quigless Hill   I found my Horses and Left them again in the old Field or woods

23   I wrode Out to the tract this Evening and saw a Race and Lost fourteen Dollars. It was a Race between R Rabees Horse and a Nag of Mr Grier. She won the Race by about 30 or 50 yds but the Judges decided that the boys wrode fould so away went my money. So much for So much, Judges on the Race was Capt Minor, L. Claibourne and B O. Smith — I wrode Out this Evening and found the remains of my Cherry Cow that I bought of Little Winn. She was on the Commons near Mr Howells Residence

24   Buisness has been Only tolerable to day   Mr William R. Johnson is Seven years old to day   I wrode Out to the fire this Evening. It was the House Out on the Hill Owned by Mrs Postleth-waite and was built by Mr R H Adams many years ago — I bot 14 Bushells of Oats to day at 13 cts per bushel

25   I Bot 21 Bushels of Oats to day and I got them at 13 cts per Bushel, very cheap I think   Nothing new to day. Buisness tolerable to day

26   To day was the greate day amoung the Bank Rupt Cases and oh what a Rascally Law this Bankrupt Law is — Here is a List of the Cases, Brown Cozens, Cooper, Gaultney, L. Robalite And Several others, which the Sale will be Continued to morrow at 11 Oclock — Steven ran away this morning after geting drunk. I will astonish him some of these days if he is not Careful, Winston went down to Mr Fords this Evening and got my Keys that I Lost some time ago — I had already thought that I would never have them again

27   Steven was in Jail this morning And I went and took him Out and Floged Him not a Little, He was taken up by a Duchman who had him before Esqr. Rivers and tryed to make it appear that he had Stollen some things from Dr Ogdens but Steven got up and Cleared his own self before the Jury in a minute

28   Buisness has been much better, Mr Robt McFadin Died Soon After Dinner to day and it is a Singular fact Just as he was Dying Midcalf and myself was trading for a note that I held of McFaddins and we had Closed the trade and taken a Drink and seperated when I herd that the Old man had died — $77.39 was the Amount of the Note with the interest but I agreed to take $60

in trade for it and it was agreed on by both parties. Midcalf was to have Came up to night and taken the note &c. but it is now ½ past 9 Oclock and he has not Came and will not I Expect — Therefore he is not a man of his word

29   Last night near about 6 Oclock I awoke and discovered a bright blaze through the window and On getting Out of bed Discoverd the property of Judge Quitman all on fire, i. e., it was a white Frame House standing on the Bluff   I wran thare and went to work and I never worked harder in all my Life at a fire than I did at that One, The Ingines were very slow in geting to the fire, I Consider that the adjoining Buildings were out of Danger before they Commenced to Opperate on them   It was well that the wind did not Blow that way or those buildings of Mr Rabees would have been Burned in spite of the People. The House in wich the fire Oringinated was burned and a new Stable along side of it also — the Loss was not much. Mr Midderhoff and Joe Meshio had a Small fight Last night at the Keno table, It was only a sort of a Grabing at Each other, It was about the Cards or tickets &c. Buisness has been dull, very indeed, Mr McFaddin will be burried to morrow morning — Offercers are getting very smart, taking up the people about town again

30   Tax, Tax, Taxes, Taxes, Taxes, Tax   I gave in my Tax List as Follows—

One Town Lot & 2 Houses, Value	5000
Five Slaves, value	1500

Mrs Amy Johnson Property —

Five Slaves, Value	800

Mrs Harriett Battles Property

One House & 1 Lot, Value	1900
2 Slave, Value	300

Buisness has been Quite dull to day and nothing new to day that I have herd of — To day I Gave Mr Midcalf my note that I held of Mr McFaddin for $77.39 on the following Conditions, i. e., if he will be allowed any thing for the note on Settlement he is to pay me according to our Contract which allows me $60 for the note and I am to take it out in trade

31   I Saw several Races to day, One was a Filly of Capt Minors against a Strangers Horse, ½ mile   The nag won the Race very Easy — I saw also a Race between Mr Crizers Horse and Mr

Rabees Horse, 1 mile Out   Mr Rabees Horse won very Easy, I Saw a 600 yard Race After dark. A man by the name of Lee ran his horse V. S. B Daugherty horse   The Dorhertys horse won Easy — I was under the Hill to day and was trying [to] Buy a Flat Boat top from a Flat Boatman &c.

February 1   Nothing new   Buisness dull   I was under the Hill to day and I bot a Lot of Corn for which I am to pay thirty five dollars, that is, I take it in Consideration of the McFaddin not[e] and I also took the Roof of the Boat and fals[e] floor at fifteen dollars — to be taken in the same way

2   Nothing new. I have been the whole of this day at work Geting Out Corn from the flat Boat and we got threw to night   Edd and myself has worked all day out and Late this Evening we Commenced to take of[f] the Roof — Bill Nix sick all day

3   I was out after my Horses this Evening and got them up and Steven Hauled one Load up with the Poney and old Grey — Gilbert Hauled 1 Load also

4   I was quite buisy to day in having Lumber hauled up — Steven hauled up five Loads and Guibert hauled 5   I got a bale of Hay to day   Nothing new to day

5   Nothing new. I wrode out in the afternoon, Mc and myself

6   Armsted Carter was sold today at the Court House for five years and was bought by Homes & Son for twenty five Dollars — Nothing new to day   Buisness good

7   Buisness very dull indeed, Twelve dollars and fifty cents, I paid for 6 framed Pictures to day   I wrode Out to the Race tract and Lost $3   Rabee Horse VS Kellys Horse   Kellys Horse won the race Easy — I got a Small Lot of Posts from Mr Sisloff and hauld them up with my Poney — they were 25 in number and was of Cypress wood and was of bad Quality

8   Bill Nix Came to work this Evening. Has been sick for Several days   I was haveing post set out to day to fence up the Lot owned by Mr Lapiece   We did not Quite finish Our work — Nothing new of any importance. Buisness Quite dull for the Season

9   Warners Card appeared in this mornings Courrier. I was fencing to day and will properly get throug fencing to morrow Evening. Nothing new of much importance

10   We Came very near finishing the fencing   We will proberly get throug to morrow if nothing hapens

11   Nothing new   Buisness has been dull to day   I have been nearly all day at work making a gate and fencing &c. We put up the gate, Winston and myself made it and we put it up, Mc and the Little Tinner went a goose hunting. There were four or five Out at the Same time   Mr Wrigley got 1, Capt Thrift 1, Mc 1. Mr Elward and Kenneday did not get Any at all

12   I took a walk in the Afternoon with Mc and we went down down arround by the Buyau and Came up in Wall St   Tis the first time that we have been in this Bayou for many years

13   Nothing new that I Know of   Buisness tolerable Only. I had a Small Fence made this Evening across the Lot and had made a Commencement to Clean the yard — We did not get through with it, There was a Race between Edd and Andrew this Evening and Andrew won the Race

15   Nothing new to day   McCary House took fire to day and Burned to the Ground. One of his other Houses took on fire but the Ingins Commenced on it and in short Order they had it Out   Tis supposed that Every thing was Lost as himself nor wife was at Home at the Commencement of the fire. I was never more buisey than I was at the fire and the fireman did wonders with the Ingine

16   Nothing new to day but there was several fights Last Evening and Last night, 1st Mr Ruffner and a Mr Crouly — They had a very Long fight before they were parted, Mr Crizer and Burl Vaughn had a fight. Mr Crizer floged him, tis Said, very Easy

17   Business Dull and nothing new

18   Nothing new what Ever

19   Mr H Clay arrived this morning from New Orleans on his way to Jackson, the Capitol of the State, During the Salutes that they were fireing this morning One of Mr Jaqumine young men, aged about 45, was at the Cannon when the other Greek man was at the vent. It Burnt him and he took his thumb of[f] when the gun discharged and Blew off his hand and Broke his arm

20   Nothing new that I Know of   Buisness tolerable good to day. Mr L. Pitcher paid me Seven Dollars, this being the full amount of His account, To day Winston and myself Commenced to work at the Shed or to make One

21   Nothing new that I Know of   Buisness Some what dull   I bot a Little Boy by the name of Anderson from Mr Thornton who signed his name as Agent for a Mr Covington, When Ever Mr Covington Calls and will make me title He will get his money, which is Two Hundred and ninety dollars

22   Buisness has been very good. Great many person has been in town to day and all the Companies turned Out and they

Loo[k]ed very well indeed   I never saw them Look better — I took in ten Dollars 50 cts to day in work   Greatest quntity of Persons to night at the ball that I have seen for a long time

23   Nothing new. Winston finishes his Shed this afternoon — good Job

24   Buisness has been uncomally dull — Steven ranaway to day And I caught him and whiped him and also whiped old Dicy for Leting him Loose   I was Out to the tract for a few munutes and I saw a Race between Cap Minors Norma and Col Bingamans Blue Dick and a nag of Mr Kellys. Norma won the Race Easy, 2 miles and repeat.[1]

25   Nothing new. Buisness dull, Quite So   I saw a Race to day between the McNulty Filly and Kelleys Mare and a Horse Colt of Dr Dubois   The Kelly Nag won the Race, time 1.52, 1.53 and [blank] — McNultys mare was distanced in the third heat

26   Nothing new — Myself and Winston wrode Out to Mr Jno Barlands to drive in the Cow and Calf. We found her in the old Field or pasture after we had Looked for her for some time in the Bayous   We had no trouble in driving her to town, The Calf is about two weeks old

27   Nothing has Occured to day — I paid Mr Thornton to day, On the boy Anderson, fifteen Dollars and I owe a Ballance of two hundred and $75 on him yet. I was cleaning up the yard to day next to me

28   Nothing new. I pd V. Boyers One Hundred Dollars this Evening on the Boy Anderson that I Bot from Mr Thornton as agent for a Mr Covington, Tax, Tax, Tax, Taxes — I paid Mr Boyer to day My Taxes for State and County which Amounted to $44.10, 3 town Lots valued at 5,500, On[e] gold watch $60. H Battles Tax, 1 Town Lot valued $2000, 2 Slaves, amount thirteen dollars — I also pd Mr Boyer twenty One Dollars for Lumber that I bot Ma[r]ch 12th, 1840 or 41

March 1   Mr Covington arrived to day and is the man that I am to pay for the Boy Anderson — Mr Ruffner is quick sick from cold and the fight he had at Mc fire and So is the man Crowley that faught with him

2   Nothing new. I understood to Day from Mr Rabee that Mr Covington was not agoing to make me a title until he Could

---

[1] The Pharsalia Course races of February 24–25, 1843, were reported in the *American Turf Register and Sporting Magazine*, XIV (1843), 234. On the first day William J. Minor's Norma won over Mary Bell owned by Miles Kelly and Dick Bluewater owned by Adam L. Bingaman.

Collect the hundred Dollars from Mr Thornton. I give him to understand that it was paid by me and believing too that I was paying the proper man, and that I Could not Loose it by no means

3   Buisness has been dull   Nothing new

4   I got On my Little Poney this morning Early and took my Gun and the Boy Anderson and took him out on the Woodville Road

5   Nothing new. Buisness Only tolerable to day

6   I paid a Mr James M. Covington to day by Mr Koontz One hundred and seventy five Dollars which was a Ballance on a sum of $290 that I was to pay for the Boy Anderson   I paid the money and he made me a Bill of Sale. This I[s] what I have been waiting for him to do for Several days

7   Dull day in the way of Buisness — Nothing new to day

8   Nothing new. Buisness dull. Joes Partner pays his Rent to day — $14.00

9   Buisness tolerable Only — Judge Turners Opinion was Delivered to day in regard to Certain things   Mr Wm Conner returning from town to day was taken with an Applectic fit and is not Expected to Live

10   After Breakfast this morning I wrode down in the Swamp and got a Shot at a flock of Ducks — I Killed 7 siting and 3 on the wing but could only find 9 of them   One of them got away in the woods — I then Shot 6 fine Large fish, Bufalow Fish   They were all fine and fat — Mr L. Harrison and Stedson was down   They Say that they got 30 between them, Mr David I have not seen yet, tho I am told he Killed 19 ducks and he caught 4 Fish.

11   Nothing new   Buisness Good — William Nix Left to day for New Orleans with Baron Elliotte &c. I paid Bill Nix Eighteen dollars to day

13   To day has been very Cold and unpleasant   It has been very Cold indeed, Nothing new — this Climate, this Climate, Enough said

14   I paid Maj Young to day fifty Dollars as wages for Charles — This makes one Hundred Dollars that I have paid him since he Commenced by the month — Mr Duffield is the man, the agitator, the Revelutionizer — very good

15   To day has been a very cold day and in the Evening it Grew very Cold indeed, Cloudy, and this wind blew very hard and after a short time Commenced sleeting and then Commenced snow-

ing and by 9 Oclock the whole face of the Country was white with
Snow and was some 2 or 3 inches deep

16   This morning Early Several Slays was running and the
City Look perfectly white with Snow and Citizens was throwing
Snow balls at Eeach other in Every direction about the Streets

17   Nothing new to day   Buisness Some what better than
yesterday

18   Buisness only tolerable   Nothing [new]   The Commet
Still visible at night

20   This has been a very Cold day indeed, the Coldest wether
Ever Known in March by the oldest Citizens   Nothing new —
Buisness dull, Quite So. The planet is not visible to night on
account of Clouds   I wrode Out this Evening and took William T.
Gur [Jr.] with me and I took my Long Gun, I mean the Joe Meshio
Gun and I Shot 9 Robbins

21   Buisness very dull. Nothing new — Great many Plover
all over the fields

23   This has been a very Cold and unpleasant day   Tis very
Cold indeed, No One here has Ever Seen Such wether in March
here   Greate many Plover in the fields in Every direction from
the City tho they are very Poor

24   Nothing new more than the Effects of Mr F Stanton in
Bank Ruptcy was Sold to day and a Short time after Dinner we
had the Snow to Commence falling and in the course of three Hours
the town was perfecty white   Then the Citizens Commenced to
throw Snow Balls

25   To day the Sun shone out very fine but did not melt all
the Snow that fell yesterday   Prety good Snow Balling to be had
to day in the Shade, Nothing new. Buisness tolerable Only —
Comet was visible to night.

26   I rode Out this Evening and took William with me. We
went down in through by the Colier track and Came around by old
Dicksons, through by Mrs Smith &c. I was in seach of my horses
— did not find them   I saw 1 Squirrell, 1 turkey, 2 Rabbits, 2
Ducks, 6 or 7 Plover and as many partriges, I had no gun   Joe
Meshio paid me twenty Dollars to day and Owes me now 49 Dollars
yet — To day Old man Guinea John was Drunk and at the time
was under the Hill and an Italian by the Name of Cariscino Commenced a beating the Old man with a Stick and Continued to do
so untill he was driven Clear over on the opposite Side of the Street,
Here the Italian was Just in the act of throwing Him Over the wall
where the perpendicular fall was I suppose about a hundred

feet   Just as John was about to fall, he drew a knife from his bosom and plunged it in Cariscino Just below the navle, Tis supposed that the nife has Cut a Gut — John was taken up a short time afterwards by Dillon and was committed to Jail by Rivers, the Justice of the peace

28   Two men were Robed Last night at Mrs. Alexanders Hotell by a Set of Rascals.

29   Buisness very Dull indeed, A report is now that Mr Graves, the Treasurer, has ran off and has Stollen, tis reported, One hundred and Eighty Thousand Dollars, The Gov. of this State has offered One Thousand Dollars for his Apprehension.[2] I took an order as it were on Mother from Joe, $16.98, that is, took the amount of her acct with him from my bill — I also Loaned Antonio Linch forty Dollars. He got it of Mr Britton and I then Let him have ten more out of my pocket, making in all fifty Dollars — With this money he bot out the interest of Joe Meshio — Joe got One Hundred and five Dollars for his Share of the Stock

30   Nothing new. Business dull. I Saw Joe Meshio yesterday and I told him I would sue him if he did [not] pay me the fourteen Dollars that he as good as Stole from me

31   Nothing new to day and business as dull as it can be and no prospects of a change for the better   Mrs Alexander sent up to Know what I would take for the Piano. I sent her word that I would take twenty five Dollars for it.   Joe Meshio Came past the shop this Evening and said he wanted me to pay him for a window, that he had taken down from thare at his shop

April 4   Col Bingaman and Barron Elliotte Came up from the New Orleans Races   They got up this morning

5   Nothing new. Buisness tolerable good   Another Spanish Barber has opened a Shop around by Mr Kanes in State Street — Mr Antonio paid me to day twenty Dollars and owes me Still thirty Dollars

6   News — that Gen Santa Ana had made a propsition to Texas to acknowledge her Independence upon Certain Conditions[3]

---

[2] Richard S. Graves, state treasurer, had embezzled over $150,000 of the state's funds, of which more than $40,000 was later recovered. See Rowland, *History of Mississippi*, I, 629–31; Rowland, *Encyclopedia of Mississippi History*, II, 824–26.

[3] The conditions included a provision that Texas was to acknowledge the sovereignty of Mexico. Although there was not the slightest chance that Texas would agree to this provision, President Sam Houston used the offer to secure an armistice between the Republic of Texas and Mexico. Joseph W. Schmitz, *Texan Statecraft, 1836–1845* (San Antonio, 1941) , 195–98.

&c. Another report Seys that President Boyer had fled from Port au Prince[4] — Cap Navet told me good news today — I am thus far pleased.

7   Nothing new. Buisness Dull to day. I was up at Auction to day and Bot 2 Drillen Coats, 5 Black Bombaset Roundabouts and a piece of Carpeting and a pair of Pair pants

8   I was Out to the Race tract this Evening and I saw a Race between Mr Crizers Horse Bill and a Large Grey Horse owned by Mr Chole. He was wrode by John Callatin who weys 130, the other a cetch   Mr Crizers Horse won the Race by 22 feet and I won Just $12.62½   Mr James Kenney paid me today thirteen dollars 50 cts and my bill in the store was 22.50 making in all Thirty Six Dollars which Sam pays for the months of January, 1842, Feb. and to 12th March, 1843.

9   Nothing new   I took a wride this Evening and my wife also and Mc was along   We wrode on the Point of the Bluff opposite the Lapiece Plantation and then wrode through by the Dickson Plantation and Came Home, meeting some poor but proud individuals

10   Bank Bill and Willis had there trial to day, was both Sentenced to receive thirty nine Lashes on there bear Backs which was done, Joe Meshio trial Came On. I had sued him and I got Judgment against him for the 14 dollars that he was as good as Stealing from me

11   Nothing new has transpired of much Interest to day. I bot 2 sets of Knives and Folks [forks] to day at auction and paid 9 bits per set for them — I took a Long wride this afternoon in search of my old Grey and Sorril Horse and found them Close at Home at last   I saw several turkeys this Afternoon and if I had a Riffle I might have got One — I saw some snipes also that I might have got but I had no Gun

12   Nothing new that I Know of   Buisness dull. Col Johnson arrived to night at a Late Hour and Came up to the City Hotell

13   Buisness tolerable good, Col R M Johnson Came Last night and this morning at 11 Oclock the Different Companies turned out and gave Him a Hearty welcome to our city — Col A L. Bingaman made him a beautiful Little address and afterwards the Old Col J. made an answer or speech of Considerable Length. The Company that turned Out was Large an[d] respectible   The Court House would not have held them all

---

[4] Jean Pierre Boyer, president of the Republic of Haiti after the gaining of its independence, fled the country during the insurrection of 1843.

14 I took Breakfast this morning at the usual Hour and a short time afterwards I had my Poney saddled and taking Anderson with me wrode down into the Swamp to try and Collect Some money from Mr Mosbey   I got down to his place, saw him. He told me how he was situated and that he had to give a forth Coming bond for a Hundred and ninety dollars and if he could do that he would then have a two years stay on the ballance which was near Eight hundred dollars — He said that young Winn and B. Winn had both promised to go on his Paper for the $290 but they returned and did not, which he thought hard of. During the time I was up at Mr Mos'y House I got him to go down with me to Little Winns and thare I got my Riffle which I Left at Mr Fords, Stating that if he wanted the gun he m[a]y take her by giving me a good Cow for the gun. I did not see him myself but Left the gun with young Winn — During my short stay that I made at Mr Winn I herd him remark that there was a Horse and wanted to Know of me if he Came down with me. I told him no. Mr Gay was there at the time and we all, after a short time, Came to the Conclusion that the Horse must have got off from some boat. We thought that the H. had fell overbourd from the S. B. Missouri which had Just passed but a short time before we discovered the Horse, Mr. W. took charge of the Horse and sent him to his Horse Lot by One of his Sons and remarked that he would be his Horse if no One would say anything about it. As far as I Know we made no promise to him about the Horse   I came off very soon after — During the trip I Killed 2 Squirrells and Left them at Mr Mosbys — I then Killed a Large Snake at the Barlands place

19 I Left Natchez this day about [blank] Oclock on bourd of the Steam Boat Embassador for New Orleans and had quite a pleasant trip down. There was several on bourd who I Knew, Mr W K. Henry, Jo. Ferriday, Bill Scott, and four or five others that I would not know for Less than a five

20 I got into New Orleans this Evening if I recollect a right

25 New Orleans — Nothing new. Today I was around to Col. Hunts and I told him that I had some Idea of going up to Byou Sarah or to Natchez and he told me that I had better remain in the City.

26 New Orleans — I was in New Orleans all day and after going to market and to the different Auctions I then went up in Company with Mers [Messrs] Miller, Capt Johnson, up to Mr Scotts to dine. I remained there untill about 20 minutes of 5 Oclock. I then bid them adieu and Left. We Left Mr McCananon up thare but he very shortly after Came On down to see me off tho I found Out soon that the Steam Boat Princess would not Leave until Late, and so I remained up at Mr Millers untill 7 or 8 Oclock and then I Left.

27   Nothing new. I was on bourd of the Steam Boat Princess on our way from N. Orleans

28   I was on the River nearly all day on Bourd of the Steam Boat Princess and we arrived in the City about 4 or 5 Oclock this Afternoon   In the forenoon we saw a drowned man floating along down the River, It had a shirt but no Coat on

29   The Natchez Guards Left here this Evening and Dr Winston went along as Barber to the Company

30   I wrode Out this Evening in Company with Mc   We took Little Dick along. We went up as far as Capt Nevitts Mill

May 1   Nothing new that I Know of   Buisness dull. Mosbey was up to day and his wife also and there Land was sold, that is Mosbeys Land, and it was bid in by his wife at 700 and 50 dollars I think, There was only One Hundred and 80 or 90 Acres of it sold and it was said to be all that He owns down in the Swamp. His property was sold under a judgment in favor of Mr Mobley. He also bonded another claim or Judgment of 270 odd dollars, payable at the November term. Mr Gay was at the sale and bid on the Property Once Only — He was much disappointed to see how Completely he was taken in, in regard to the maner of the sale &c. I Lost 3 months shaving to day with Mr Griffin   Dennys Grey Horse VS. Rabbes Horse   Sam brought in my mare today and I gave him two dollars and told to take her back to the tract or Plantation again, which he did I believe

2   Nothing new. Buisness tolerable   To day Mr Reynolds boys finished working on the Pavement below the gate

3   I wrode down to Mr Mosbey this Evening but Could do nothing worth an[y]thing

7   Charles wrode my Poney out to Maj Youngs this Evening

8   I was up at Auction to day and Bot a Large Looking Glass for $21.00   It was the sale of Mrs Bingamans Effects, Things Sold well I think, Nothing new that I Know of. Business dull, Quite So — I bot 2 Mocking Birds, 5 [and] 7   I took Mr Mosbeys note to day for three Hundred Dollars payable two years after date   The Conditions were that I took a deed of trust on his two Slaves and also his Stock. Mr Hewit was the trustee

9   Steven plowed a small part of the yard   I had a bench made for my Large glass.

10 	Nothing new. Buisness has been tolerable good to day. Charles got back this night from Maj. Youngs 	Steven plouged up the yard to day slightly. I had bench for the Smaller glass to day. Bot a Kegg of rice, 56 pounds, at 3½ cts, 24 wine glasses, 3 cts Each and I bot 7 Deep plates, 31 ct for the lot. I Saw Mr Vanhosen to day and he told me that it was in the power of his Client, as soon as he gets Judgment, to advance on the bid and make the amount of his claim, for he Knew a man that would give 4000 Dollars for the Land

11 	Nothing new. Buisness very dull to day. I planted some corn this Evening in the Lot. Charles got back this Evening from the Country and has been gone 3 days

12 	Nothing new. I finished planting in the Lot to day, Buisness has been dull all day

13 	Buisness good to day. Nothing new to day

14 	Nothing new. Buisness has been dull, quite so indeed — I took William and Richard and Byron this Evening Out to wride and we drove the Cows Home with us

15 	Buisness has been very dull 	Anothing 	Bank Rupt Sale took place to day at the Court House 	It was a sale of some notes & other Property belonging to Mr F Stanton

16 	Nothing new that I Know of. Buisness quite dull. I saw to day a sight as follows. Mr. McAlister had taken Mr. George Powell by the Collar with his Left hand and he had a Pistol in the other and Mr. Izod was holding the hand that he had the Pistol in, Several others was holding him at the time and all this time he was holding Mr. Powell fast by the Coat Collar and he was standing Peaceably tho trembling Considerbly. He stood in that way for several minutes to the gaze of the Public tho after a while he pulled away and ran down the street fast whilst Every body was standing astonished 	This was for One thousand dollars that Mr. P. had borrowed from Mr McAlister and now wont pay it — Soon after the run that Mr. P. made his younger brother Came arround to the Corner Just above the F. Drugg Store and took a Seat 	Mr. Mc saw him and went down to him and Commence to talk with him and in a minutes time I Looked around and they were fighting 	Young Powell was fighting very fast and the other was tring to get Out his Pistol 	The[y] were soon seperated and the Pistol was taken from Mr. Mc whilst the other after seting down a while, got up and went to take a Game of billiards. The People all say that P. had all the fight in his own way or in his Own hands. Houghf, the Auctioneer, Left the City

Last night. Tis said to keep from appearing against Perry Sells — Tis Said that Upsall Wade gave him One hundred and 40 dollars to go away with

17   Nothing new. I walked out this afternoon to find my Horses and I found them Out near Mr Powells Residence   Business has been dull

18   Business dull   Report seys that Mr Powell made another run again today for fear of Mr McAlister

19   Buisness has been dull, Quite So — I was up early this morning and was in Search of my Horse and at Last I found him Out by old Jones place. William J. was with me   We saw 2 turkeys, One of them had young Ones. We went down to Fords place and thare I got my Rifle and she was in Just Such order as I Left Her — Thare are Small potatoes Some where thare

20   Nothing new that I Knuow of   Big fight under the Hill between the big Drayman Burns and Crigley the Ice man — They had a Long fight, quite so

21   Buisness dull — very — Walked Out on the bluff in the afternoon, Began to rain and I Left — Mc was with me

22   Buisness tolerable good — Otto Molty wrides out at the tract — Nothing new — Court Commenced to day   Whig meeting to day also

23   The Grand Jury is siting to day   I was at the Court House to day and they were selling Property by the Sherriff — Petter Baker Bot the Seltzer Property   It Sold for $773 — Clarrange bot old Bob Larrence, $40 — he was Sold for the term of five years — Mrs Andrews Property, 2 old women and 1 Horse, Sold for $17. Was bot by young Andrews and I Loaned him $6 and he gave me his boy Matt and 3 horses as Colateral Security for the Payments of the same   A girl belonging to McFarren was sold for $465 — was bot by young Homes & Co   A Carriage with 2 Horses Sold for $95, bot by the Same — Bay mare & colt was sold for 19 dollars — 8 acres of Land belonging to B A Aldison was sold for $108 — bot by Dr. Otts   It was the Residence of Mrs Inge or old Mrs Farrar — Old Mrs Perkins was burried yesterday. She died with an appoplectic fit   Nothing new. Court in cession On both Sides of the River   Buisness tolerable Only

24   Nothing new — The Grand Jury found a good many bills this term, 1 VS. Perry Sells, 1 VS. Hough, 1 VS. McAlister

25   Nothing new to day that I Know of. Buisness as usual some what dull

26 Nothing new. Buisness has been dull for a Saturday I thing [think]

27 I Loaned John my horse to go Out to the Cols He was in town to mind Corn, a Boat Load, I took my Little William this afternoon and we wrode down the Brown Saw Mill Road and we went up to the Steam Boat Princess and thare I found Mr Wilcox shaking out the Carpets belonging to the Boat &c. She has Layed up for the Season We then went up in a part of the Punch Bolls[5] — got Some magnolias and Came Home — I gave Mrs A L. Wilson 1 and Miss Niebut 1 also

29 Court is in Session Judge Cage takes a Hold of the Criminal docket this day, I was buying some gears to day for Hauling water for my bath Buisness

30 Nothing new. Buisness has been quite so so today. I received a Letter from Mrs Miller on the 26 inst. I was to day some what buisy in tring to fix up the Bath tubs &c. and to have some water hauled up. Commenced with the Poney and the Grey Horse, the reason is the Sorril Horse has a very Sore back. I have a half notion to go to New Orleans in the Morning tho I am not sure that I will, Twenty seven dollars I paid to day for the Courrieres and N. Y. Enquirer. I paid for it nine years Subscription up to the time I Left off taking it — I wish I had have paid for it before now

31 Nothing new to day that I Know of I got on Bourd of the Steam Boat Buckeye this Evening and Started to New Orleans, We Left town at 5 Oclock Mr Murcherson was a pasenger and got Out at Baton Rougue

June 1 To day I was on Bourd of the Steam Boat Buck Eye on my way to New Orleans

2 Nothing new. I was on the River part of this day tho got in to New Orleans soon after Breakfast, if I mistake not, I found Every body well and doing quite well I thought

9 New Orleans — I Left New Orleans this Evening at 5 Oclock. Capt Johnson and Mr Miller was down to see me off

---

5 The "Devil's Punch Bowl" lies a mile or so north of Natchez, on what was in ante-bellum days a part of Clermont plantation. It "is a gigantic semi-circular pit somewhat cone shaped, as if a tremendous inverted cone had burrowed into the precipitous bluffs of Clermont. It covers many acres and slowly almost imperceptibly enlarges year by year. The center looks as if the bottom had suddenly dropped out of this portion of creation, and to its precipitous edges ancient forest trees perilously cling until disintegration slowly carries them down to the depths below." See Edith Wyatt Moore, "Devil's Punch Bowl on Clermont," Natchez *Democrat*, September 13, 1931.

10   Mississippi River — Mr Maxent went ashore Just below Bayou Baton Rougue — John Cooper Came on Bourd at Baton Rougue. He had with him the Chains & hand Cuffs &c. that he took down the Fellow Seaman Moore who had Killed Hardy Ellis — Moore is to work for the State for Seven years — good — An Officer from Barkers Settlement Came on Bourd at Bayou Sarah — he had taken down a man by the name of Brown who had Shot and Killed a man by the name of Estee or Epse — We herd to day that young Adams had Killed Dr Hagan at Vicksburg — had Shot him dead.

11   We arrived at Natchez this morning ½ past seven Oclock on S. B. Buck Eye

12   It would be right I think to set down this date for the Commencement of the N. Guards Rent at $10 per month

15   Large Lot of Citizens went over the River on a Hunt and will stay they think untill Saturday — they have plenty of good things with them to Last them a week

16   The River is now very high. Completely over Levy St at the Landing in many places — Buisness very dull on acct. of Rain — We were washing windows nearly all day

17   Nothing new   Buisness dull, 3 baths to day, all Cash — I paid the Collecter for the Free Trader Six Dollars   Tis all that is actuly due the other office

18   Nothing new. Buisness is quite dull, very. I took a wride to day with Mc and we went Out past Col Bingamans Plantation Just beyond the bridge, then returned and wrode down the Creek botom to the Woodville road and in passing through by the Creek I saw my nag Kitty Fisher and her Colt, They both Looked very well. My Little William was with us — The red spotted sow had Pigs to day — I believe she had ten of them, Beautiful Ones

19   Nothing new that I Know of, Wiswall & Patterson Spoke to me to Know if they Could by any way Collect $40 that Mouthers owed them for goods — a Longer then the Law would allow them — I told Mr Wiswall that I would see Her and asked her to settle it if She Could

20   Nothing new. Buisness dull.

21   Buisness dull and nothing new more than Some One Stole a $5 gold piece Out of the draw[er] in the Shop Some time Since yesterday Morning, Mr Jno G. Taylor paid me to day on acct. $10 and brot and old acct VS me for 2 Suits of Cloaths Amounting [to] 12 dollars — I Know well that those things has been paid for a Long time ago — He also had some old acct against

Mother for, as he Said, they are for things that were bot in 1836 and 1837 — I Took them of him to show Mother and Mother told me that she would not pay it

22   Nothing new To day. Buisness dull, Quite So. I was with Winston making a fence to day in the yard up at the Shop and I then helped make a pair or 2 of bars down at the House, Mrs McAlister Came Home to day   Her Husband Made her Leave with the Children, He has been a week or more on a sort of a [blank]   Yesterday Fred Warrance and Elward had a settlement of some small acct. When Warrance Called E. a Liar, soon after that E. Called W a Liar and Warrance hauled of[f] and struck him in the face and made his nose Bleed. So the fight Ended

23   I was at Auction to day and bought about 20 yds of Cotton for 6 bits and a Basket of Cordial, 7½ Bits, and a Ice Cream Freezer for $2 and a Barrell of Cranburys for 2 bits and a half — Cheap, Cheap — The River is very high and is still on the rise. I am told that it Raised ½ an inch Last night, The 2d One of my Little sow has got Pigs — She has got [blank] Pigs

24   Nothing new   Ben Walker Stood On the Street this Afternoon for Some time waiting to See Dr Ferguson Come Out   He was in at Mr Dumaxs and was affraid to Come Out. James Kenny went and Seen the Dr and from thare he went to the Mayor of the City and then to the Sherriff who Came down and Escorted the Dr up to the residence of old Mrs Tooleys where he Boards. The Dr was very much Frighten. The Poor fellow is no doubt a Coward.

25   I wrode Out this Evening with Mc and I to[ok] my William with us   We wrode out past Col Wilkins and got some very fine black Berrys — crossed in to Scotts old Field and Came through by old Joness and we had to wride fast and was Caught by rain bifore we got in — Mrs Brustee took supper with us — Two Sows had piggs to day

26   I was all day at home bothering with the sows and Pigs and they Gave me plenty of bother Certain, I was making pens for them, Winston and myself, with Steven, having Shavings brot for them and moving them from place to place and did not have them fixed at Last to Suite me — One of the Sows, the black and red Spoted, has now 9 Pgs   Lost 1 yesterday — The Pale Spoted had 10 and Lost One, the other had Eight ie the white and black Spoted One. I got home the Little Black Sow to day with 7 Ps and the cister had 4 — they are all of the Birkshire Breed — Buisness has been very dull to day indeed — nothing new

27   To day has been a dull day in the way of Buisness —
nothing new.

28   To day has been a Dull day, quite So   Nothing new. I
Loaned Mr V. Boyer to day thirty Dollars

29   Nothing new.   Buisness dull. S Gosin Leavs Col Bingaman this Morning and Came to town and thought that he would
never go back again to the place as a manager. I paid my City
Tax to day, $42.50 and I paid mothers which was four dollars

30   Buisness dull   Tooke in Only $2.50 in the Shop to day
— Nothing new. Obrine & Spring offers to Shoe Horses all around
for 75 cts, Too cheap, too cheap to Last

July 1   Nothing new. Buisness dull, 5 Baths to day — Dull
times

2   I remain[ed] at home the Entire day. Wm Nicks Left this
morning for New Orleans

3   Dull times. Nothing new

6   W Nix Came up from N Orleans and brot William & James
up with him   They Came up on the Harrison — Soon after they
Came up they took a wride and my Sorrill Horse threw Will Miller
off and has hurt his rist some tho he will be soon well of it. I dont
think him much hurt for he will be able tomorrow to play again

7   Nothing new — Buisness dull, Quite So.

8   Buisness very dull, Nothing new to day. A Kenney paid
$5 on the shop rent — Dr Jones paid me $29.00 to day for his rent
Ending June the 25th, 1843

9   Nothing new. Times are dull. I wrode Out in the afternoon
and took William and James Miller & my Little Wm   We were
Caught in the rain and went to an old House in the field owned
by Mrs Smith — Wm M got behind the saddle and Like to have
fallen off. We ate a fine chance of Black buries — they are ripe
and nice

10   Big Repeal meeting to night at the City Hall and was well
attended, particulars to morrow I Expect, James Kenney paid me
to day by accts VS. Mr Reynolds 17, by Wm Nicks 3.23, by Self
for Carpenters acct. 3.90

11   The Cow that I brot in from Mr Barland has ranaway
or been Stolen Since yesterday morning. She was a pale Ball face
Cow — her mark I dont recollect at present   Wince took the
Poney and went Out to Look for her but Could not find Her.

Nothing new to day   Buisness dull, Quite So. Legislature is in Cession, yesterday the 1st day.[6]

12   L. David Killed a Deer today on the Iseland on the other side of the river

13   The Man put up the Blinds this morning to the front windows — I made a Jump or 2 with the Boys this Evening and beat Bill Nix about 6 inches in a ½ hamon Jump — Nothing new to day what Ever — The river falling so fast that it is astonishing but it is now so high that a person Cant get into the Swamp on Horse back yet

14   Nothing new that I Know of   Will Miller Struck Frank with a Brick Bat on the side of his Head in a fight. Buisness dull &c.

15   Nothing new that I Know of   Buisness tolerable only

16   I took my Little Buggy and wrode Out through by old Jones and Came around through by the Scotts old Field   I had my old Sorril Horse in the Bugy. I had along with me Wm J. Junr, Little James Miller. They were on Horse back, Then in the Buggy was Mr Miller, Richard, Byron, Anna and Mary Jordan — all was along   We got some Black Burries &c.

17   Nothing new what Ever. Buisness dull, very dull, very indeed — Bill Nix was Sick yesterday all day

18   Buisness dull, very indeed. Several Cases of Enfluenza in the City

19   Nothing new — Buisness dull. I Jumped on bourd of the Steam Boat Buck Eye this morning and Started to New Orleans. We got of[f] at Eight Oclock in the morning — we made a good run for the times

20   Mississippi River — I arrivd at Lafayette this morning about ½ past 7 Oclock. I then got in the Omnibus and wrode down to the City and was there two Hours before the Boat got in. From what I Can hear the whole population of New Orleans has been more or Less affected with the Enflurenzy. Mrs Miller is Sick with it and Mr Miller has Just recoverd from the Complaint

21   I arrose this morning Early and took a walk to the market in Coppany with Mr Miller then back to Breakfast and then to the office &c. We then got in a Cab about 11 Oclock and wrode down to the Ponchetrain Rail Road   We got in the Car and went down to the Lake. We then went down to the Bath House and took a Bath in the Lake. I remained for Some time in the Lake tho Mr M. Came Out amediately   We then wrode back to the City in the Cars,

[6] This was a special session called by Governor Tucker to investigate the defalcation of Richard S. Graves, former state treasurer.

took dinner, and I Bot a few things before dinner and among the rest was a Scein to fish with   After I went back to the House I found that Mr Miller was Sick from going to Bathe in the Lake and I came of[f] and Left Him coverd up in the bed — I did not get off from the City untill I suppose 7 Oclock. We made rarther a Slow run for the Boat was Heavy Ladend

22   We were on the River and got up at Baton Rougue about ½ past 12 Oclock   The Boat put Out Considerable freight, Cement, Bricks, Slate. I took a walk nearly all over the town of Baton Rogue, then Bot 2 Razor strap and a Book of Songs — About 2 Oclok we got fast in backing Out and remaind untill Late at night, 10 or 11 Oclock   We were taken Out of the Difficulty by the Steam Boat Mount Vernon

23   I was On the River all day to day. We stoped at Bauyou Sarah to day and did not get up to Natchez untill Late in the night, Say about 2 Oclock

24   I arrivd about 2 Oclck Last night and Came up the Hill. I found all well and nothing new. Buisness dull

26   I went into the field this Evening and Cut a Considerable Quantity of Corn that had fallen down. We had a fine mess of Corn for dinner from the Same place. We also Sold Some to day — I Sent Some Corn to New Orleans to day And Some Butter Beans and Mother Sent Some 4 heads of Cabbage &c. Dr A Jones paid me to day One months Rent to the first of August, 1843, which according to Our agreement I was to take of[f] $50 and Let him have the House for 300 dollars per year, which was agreed to day by me

27   Nothing new. Buisness is very dull indeed, The Called Session of the Legislature adjourned yesterday

28   Buisness dull. Nothing new   Dr Wren and O Bemiss has Cards in to days paper in regard to the Lost hundred Dollars — they were Contradictory, very — Antonio the fruite man is Sick to day — Little Bob Robe and Will has a fight to day and Buck hit him with a Stick

29   Laurahan Brown died this morning. Dr Fox and Mr Dicks Left to day for the north. Buisness Seems to get worse Every day. I was Cutting Some Corn to day to make Fodder with

30   Buisness, oh very dull — Nothing new, Very Soon in the aternoon I wrode Out in the Buggy and took Wm Miller, Richard & Byron and Winston with me, James and Buck on Horse Back. We were Caught in a Heavy rain Just beyond Col. Wilkins   I made Will [and] James Let there Horses go And got them in to

the Bugy tho we were all well wet with Rain — Poor old Tree Willow Died to day and was put in a Coffin in about 2 hours afterwards and Sent Out alone to the Grave. No one Knew that he was Even very ill — poor old man — Our City and County Representatives have all got back from Jackson, Safe &c.

31 To day has been dull in the extream. I dont Know what to think of Such times   Mr George Pulling Died Last night at 9 Oclock   He was a good man

August 1 Nothing new what Ever — Mr Day gets the Contract for Building the Jail and Commenced this morning Early to pull down the old One, I believe he gets 11,000 Dollars for the building of it &c.   Mr George Pulling was Burried this Evening ½ past 3 Oclock. He was a good man &c. I Only took in 9 dimes to day   Every day I make Less — oh what times &c.

2 Old Mr Tree Willow was dug up this Evening by a party of men to see the Condition in which he was in and other matters respecting the singularity of his death &c. Nothing new to day   Buisness dull, quite so indeed   My wife sicke 3 days to day   Something better this Evening Thank God

3 Nothing new. I took my Sorril Horse this morning and my Mesho Gun and Started for the Swamp and took my William and Little James Miller   I went down as far as Mosbeys, wrode around his fence and Came up again   We fished for an Hour & a ½, I Suppose So — James Caught 4, my Wm 8 and myself 12 — I Killed 1 Large Rabit, 8 Black Birds and 6 Jack Snipe or Plover, and I Killed One of the Largest Kind of Snakes — Swamp Mockoson   I am told that it is the Opinion of Several persons who was Out at the Examination of the Corpse of Tree Wheeler, that it Looked as tho the print of Hands was on the throat and a Bruise on the Breast, tho they, to save trouble, they made a verdict to the Contrary — The Lakes at this time are much higher than I have Known them in this month for several years — they are all full away up in the woods

4 This has been another dull day and nothing at all worth relating. Private oppinion seems to think that Lancashire is a bad man, that he is a Rogue and worse — Two baths to day Only

5 Nothing new to day

6 I wrode Out this Evening in my Buggy and took Wm Miller, Little Robt McCary & Richard & Byron all in with me and Wm McCary, William Johnson & James Miller wrode on Horse back — We went Out as far as Mrs Paines fence and then Came back and Stopd, played ball a while &c. Buisness tolerable and nothing [new], A Dr Bradstreet murdered a man by the name of Ryan a few days ago on the Other Side of the River. I have not herd the particulars. The man has a family of 2 or 3 children and a wife — pity, pity — Shame

7   Henry Adams and wife was sold to day at the Court House   They brot 1600 dollars I am told,   6 months Credit — Bot for old Mrs Brabston, I am told

8   Nothing new   Buisness Only tolerable to day.

9   A man at Yates Stable was knocked down Last night and robed of $100 or so by some person or persons — Severl was arrested to day for it. Wellington brings a Mr Bird from Port Gibson to see me this morning

10   To day Like many others has been very dull and nothing New.

11   To day has been another day in wich the [work] of my Shop has been very Limited indeed — I got On my poney Early this morning and took the gun that I got of Pulling and Started for the Swamp and I took those Boys viz — William Miller, James Miller, Robt McCary and my Little Wm — We got F. poles at old Mrs Mahon place and took down with us. I found the water in the Swamp high. I went back of Fords plantation, up and arround the 1st Little Lake and Down behind Long Lake and thare I Commenced to Fish. We Fish[ed] for good while but did not Catch but a few and they were Quite Small Ones — I Shot 1 Snipe, 1 young Aligator, 1 wood Pecker, 1 King Fisher, 1 Black Bird and Caught 17 Fish   My Wm Caught 5, Wm & James Miller Caught 4 each and Robt 2

12   Nothing new that I Know of   Buisness Some what Better to day

13   I took the Boys Out in a Bugy and we had a wride Out as far as Mrs Pains place, The Boys wrode Out in the B and I wrode Out on Horse back. The time was agreeable to us all, only Wm & James had a fight Out in the Butchers House   William got the better of the fight   He Struck James in the Eye, made it Blood Shot

14   Nothing new. Buisness dull, very. Steven ranaway yesterday and was brot Home to day by Bill Nix. I gave him a floging and Let him go — no, I mistake, it was today that he ranaway

15   This morning Early I got up and took my Horse and put him in the Buggy and Started over the River and I took Wm & James Miller, Wm & Robert McCary, & my Little Wm and

Mc Started over Late, quite Late, Came over at 1 Oclock. I Caught 63 Fish, Mc 26, Wm Mc 32, my Wm 25, James 17, Robt 7, Wm. Miller 3 — Flavius Fletcher Killed Iccum belonging to Mrs McCray Last night. He was shot at Mr Amatt plantation, F has got out of the way — made himself Scarce

16 Nothing new. Buisness dull. Lambert was found dead in the new Sewer this morning — The Frenchman that Lived the next door from me in State Street Shot himself to day with a pistol in the Street. Killed himself Dead and I understand that he said that Lankershire had on some of his Cloaths on Sunday which the Frenchman said he knew was his — So I am told. This was told me by Mr P. I was over the River to day to fish and hunt Took my Little French Gun I Shot 1 black Squirrell and 31 plover and Caught 61 Fish and got Over the River Early. There were a very Large party of gentlemen over to day a Fishing and Amusing themselves tho did not go down Quite as Low as they were; 13 Horses and 3 Bugys Came Over to night in the Little Ferry Boat.

17 Poor C L Floyd Shot Himself and was found dead in his Room. He did it [with] his own Rifle. [Line drawn through the preceding entry.] Those few Lines are all a mistake Not having wrote in this Book for several days is the Cause.

20 In the Afternoon Late I wrode out as far as the pasture of Col. Bingaman to see my Little mare and Colt. I Saw them They Looked very well, the Colt was in fine Order indeed — Mc was with me. I wrote a Letter yesterday and Sent it to New Orleans — Little William & James Miller has both arrived Safe in New Orleans this Evening, having Left here yesterday at 12 Oclock.

21 Nothing new. Buisness dull. I worked alone to day and took in 20 Bitts. Winston worked below and took in Only 3 dimes. Poor Buisness truly — Inquest was held over the Body of C. L. Floyd to day who shot himself with his Rifle in his Room Out at a Mr Fords — The Boys was oever the River to day fishing and they Caught 39 Each, that is Bill and Charles. Poor set, Small potatoes. Walter and Dick was along

22 Buisness has really [been] dull to day and nothing new. I was a portion of to day, ie. this Evening, Cutting Corn to Stack and dry in the yard. I Loaned Mrs Battles Eight Dollars and 80 cts to buy Scrip with to pay tax with, which was $11.00 Greate many persons gone Over to fish to day the other side of the River — big Frollic is Expected, Quite so

23 Nothing new. Steven ranaway Monday and has not Come

Home yet. I herd of him several times to day. I have been a
good part of this day Ingaged in cuting or puting up my Corn,
Buisness is very dull indeed

24 Nothing new. Buisness dull, I Came very near Cetching Steven to night. He was in the Stable ajoin[in]g mine but he
Jumped out and ran into the weeds somewhere

25 I was at Home nearly all day attending to my Crop —
The Hogs has anoyed me very much by breaking in my fence

26 Nothing new. Buisness tolerable Only — The Quarrantine
Law was put in force to day — Gen Quitman makes a Long
Speech to night V.S. Repudiation[7]

27 Not much of Any Interest Occured to day more than one
of Mrs Lintons Black men by the name of Rolla beat Mr Preston
this afternoon up at Mrs Lintons Gate. It was Whilst he was
in Company with Some Ladies His Friend Fouler or Fuller or
Some Such name was with [him] and was prevented from assisting Mr Preston by Mrs Lintons Carriage Driver, who would seize
him when Ever he attemped to interfear. Considerable fuss about
it to night, 8 of the Guards Ordered Out. Greate times indeed —
Steven was over in the Kitchen of Mr Staples Last night to try
and get something to Eat but soon went off Charles was over
the River to day a fishing and came home Drunk — Wanted to
marry an old Black mans Daughter and told the old man to
Refer to Wheelock & Sayers, A L. Wilson, or Erhart & Foster if
he wanted to know about his character

28 Nothing New but the Out Rage Committed yesterday on
the Person of Mr Preston by a Black man belonging to Mrs
Linton. The Boy has ran off and is not to be found at all — there
has been a greate deal to say about it.

29 Nothing new. Buisness Dull. City healthy Quarrantine
is in force, Commenced yesterday The City pays A L. Wilson
two Hundred Dollars per month to attend to the various duties
of Health officer &c.

30 Nothing new Buisness dull, very. The City Healthy —
people poor, generally Speaking — Some Dissatisfaction about the
maner in which the Brick Layers are progressing with the Jail.
Old man Tooley threatens to resign as a member of the police
Court

31 The Planters are now in want of rain for there Crops of

---

[7] The repudiation issue was still a strong one in state politics although more
than a year had passed since the legislature had repudiated $5,000,000 of Union
Bank bonds.

Cotton &c. I received a Letter from New Orleans to day, report my friends all well and that the yellow fever is tolerable severe thare at present and will be worse in a week or two

September 1 I had my plough brought Home to day and the Handle was broke when it Came home new from the Shop — I paid 1.50 for it and will Send it back again. Nothing new today Buisness dull, very. I Commenced to plant Turnips this Evening in the yard. I hope they are good Ones, and had the good Luck to get a rain on them as soon as they were planted which will [be] good for them — Dr A A Jones pd twenty five dollars to day for Rent of Store. Mr S. Elliotte is Sick and has been very Sick for 4 or 5 days

2 The Large Frame building at the Landing Owned by the City was Burned down to day about 9 or 10 Oclock A M — I have not herd how it occured as yet. Mr Collingsworth the overseer of Judge Covington made the Driver take hold of One of his Boys to flog him and the Fellow stabbed the Driver and cut off the arm of Collingsworth and ranaway but has been Caught Since and is in Jail. This was in La.

3 Nothing new. Buisness very dull indeed, I remained at Home nearly all day, tho I took a Small ride in the afternoon and took the Boy with me

4 Nothing new. Buisness dull I started after Breakfast this morning and took with me my Little Wm and Frank and I went down in the Swamp. I got down as far as the Cypress Bayou, and we had severall very heavy showers of rain during the day which compelld me to come home sooner than I would have Come, I took with me the Pulling gun — I Shot 1 Large Plover, 15 Small Jack Snipes, 2 Loons, 1 Large White Crane, 2 Squirrells and One Partridge — The Lakes are high and I tryed to Cetch some fish but they would not bite at all — Mr Knight has his Boy Lenson whiped and he Confessed to have been stealing for some time from him, and he gave the names of Mrs Irvin Frank, Buckanans Grocery and Whites and Sam Magruder and several others that I have nearly forgoten, Moores was One that was suspected very strongly

5 Nothing new. To day Came off the tryal before Eskr Wood, Mr Preston VS. Mrs Lintons Servants Beverly was tried and Sentenced to thirty nine Lashes and the other, Rolla, was Comited to court. This offence was this that the black man Choked and beat Preston for striking or attempting to strike him

7 Young John Quigless is married to night to Miss McGraw,

Considerable Excitement in regard to the Election altho it does not take place untill November

8   Nothing new. Buisness quite dull, The Police Court decided to day that the work on the new Jail was Substantial and good

9   In the after part of the day there were very few persons Left in town unless it was those attending to Stores and Could not Leave. Out at the track there was to be a barbacue and Shooting of Different Kinds. Candidates were Out in a greate abundance, Frederick McCrarey Knocked down young Antony Hoggatt, in a small fight that they had about nothing   Capt Barlow wants to fight very much indeed, was pretty tight. Came near having a fight with Mr B. O. Smith and Mr Rowley &c. McCary was Out, I am told a meare Looker on in Venice

10   Buisness was truly dull to day and nothing new, Old Man Wilson Died Last night in his house, supposed to be an appoplictic fit as he was not very ill and had no Doctor — he was Dyer by trade and has tis said a Family in Charleston, S. Carolina. I sent down and had him shaved but would Charge nothing for it — I have a cold that I took a few days ago and I am not well — Mc and Mrs G Brustee took tea with us to night

11   Nothing new. Dr Lawrence paid his shaving bill in full, $2.50, and has Left for Water Proof Landing To Practice — Charles brot $19.37½ for two weeks work under the hill

12   The Election Came of[f] for Selectman. The Candidates were as Follow, viz — John M Ballwin, Noah Barlow, W. W. Wilkins, W P Mellen

13   Nothing new — to day the Election came of[f] for the Mayor of the City and the result was that Mr John M Stockman was Elected to the office — Mr Rivers was the opposing Candidate — The Citizens gave the H Mayor a Splendid Dinner at the City Hotell in the afternoon and it was well attended by the Citizens generally. It was Kept up untill a Late hour in the night. He will Leave the place in the morning for Jackson where he is to Enter upon the duties of his office, that of Supreme Clerk of the Courts

14   Buisness dull, Marshal Bertrand arrived in this City   Considerable respect was Shown him, fireing the Cannon a Greate number of times and all sorts of small guns was fired at the Same town [time], he Landing at the Quarrantine grown [ground] and came ashore. Wrode in the Carriage of Major Chotard, Drawnd by four hansome Horses — I met him and touchd my hat very gracefully and his Son nod[e]d and the old Gentleman touched his hat to me very respectfully and passed &c. A Dinner was Given to Mr Duffield yesterday by the public at the Mansnon House yesterday

15 Nothing new. Go[o]d deal of talk about the Ellection for Sherriff. Mr Boyers Friends are very Sanguine about it — $25 VS 2 Cows I bet with Mr Jaqumine to day Gave him Eighty votes and took Mr Newman VS. Mr Boyer. They are both men that I Like very well. I have no Choice at all

16 Buisness dull for Such a time of the year. To day it was that young Spraigue Came to me and wanted to Know if I did Loan money on watches Some time and I told him I did not now but used to do so, tho I Could not spare any money — He Said that McPherson had Loaned him thirty dollars on a watch that was worth 100 dollars and he wanted to get $30 from me so that he could redeem or sell the watch for $60. Barbacue Out at Washington to day, a good many person were present, Shooting matches are to be Every Saturday untill Election is over &c.

17 Nothing new. Buisness uncommonly dull to day. Late in the afternoon I wrode Out & Charles & Winston and my three Sons wrode Out in the Bugy — They had in my Old grey Horse, We got Some walnuts whilst we were Out. Mr Ramsey Died to night about 7 Oclock at his Residence under the Hill. He has very Lately came up from New Orleans.

18 Steven worked until Dinner time with Mr Reynolds to day and then I had him to plough a Little. We now have twenty three pigs in the Pen to Kill, when we please &c.

19 Buisness dull, took in to day 1 dollar in dimes and yesterday we only took in 6 dimes. Before, such times would Cause me to quit buisness — I was buisy a part of this day in plowing the yard Leading to the gate to make the water run of[f] free and I was taken with a very siviere headache in the afternoon, which gave me so much pain that I Could for a time Lay down. It Lasted untill in the night

20 The City is healthy tho over in Vadalia there is, I am told, a greate deal of Sickness — there are now 7 or Eight sick that I Know and report seys that there is a greate deal of sickness in various parts of Louisiana, particularly new places &c. The City is very dull, very

21 I got up this morning very Early and was about to Start in the Swamp but did not go down untill after Breakfast. I then Started down taking with me my William and I took Frank.

I went down by the Old Quigless place, then wrode through and I [had] difficulty in finding the way through to the River. I Came out right Opposite the Gin, I then started down and got into the wagon road behind Fords Field, there I saw three hounds Come towards me and made a turn and ran down on Long Lake and I past on and went down on the Lake away back next to the Creek I think. I Crossed over to Long Lake. I there saw Elexander He was Looking for Mr Walton and I herd him fire both barrells off at wonce and that was the Shot that Killed the Big Buck, the One that has been So Long about Dock Lake and has been Seen by So many persons and been Shot at by So many. He was very Large and wayd over 200 pds — I took the Meshio Gun and I wrode my poney. I Shot 1 Patridge, 3 Blacks that I got and 1 that I Could not find, 2 Wood Cocks, 2 fat Indian hens and 7 Squirrels, all in good order, and I Shot 1 very Large Mocasin Snake — The Lakes have Considerable water in them

    22   Mc and F Thomas went out to Hunt Squirells and Mc only got One and Thomas Killed 4 and got Sick and Came home They made a poor Out I thing [think]. To day was a quiet day. Robert Smith and his Hacks and Horses All Sold to day at Auction, and they were All struck of[f] to Brevoort Butler which I think from what Smith told me, that it was no Sale, Intended to deceive Somebody I think

    23   Buisness was prety dull to day and nothing new in the way of buisness. People are talking a Little about the Ellection. Thats about all, I was Engaged a part of this day in helping Winston making the small house in the back yard up at the Shop. We Came very near making a finish of it, We had Steven to dig it and we made a pretty good One Everything Considerd

    24   Nothing new that is worth relating, ie, in the political world, Near 11 Oclock to day Phill Came down Main St. Leading Steven who had gone up the Street and had got drunk, very drunk. I was Buisy at the time and Could not get out to see him, He managed to Slip away from Phill and got in Mrs Dumax yard, Phill caught him and brot him to the Shop and put him in Care for the minutes of Bill Nix who Let him Slip out and he broke a sash in the door or pane of Glass. He then ran off arround the Corner and the Boys took after him and I followed but Could not See him. They however Caught him Some where up town and brot him down When he found that I was not thare he cut up Greate Shines, got in a fight with one of the men, an Italian that Lives in a part of my House, Antonio Lynch is his name, He bit the Italians hand a Little and the fellow made more talk about it than Enough — All this was done whilst I was up the street and when I Came down they had put him in the Guard House, I walked out in the afternoon Late and Winston he went with me and I took Richard & Byron with me We found the Horses and got Some grapes, Muskadines &c. Just before we went Out Winston whiped Mrs Jordans Ann, He pelted her with his fist. She called him a Lyar the night before, &c.

25 Nothing has Occured very particular to day, I went to the guard House this morning after Breakfast and took Steven Out, tho not untill the Capt. Hanstable had given him thirty nine Lashes with a whip which the Italian Said he was satisfied When I took him home the fellow would not agree to have the hand cuffs on after he had Sliped one of his hands out, tho I whip him a Little No doubt will give more in time to Come He is Jailed up in my Corn Cribb. I intend to send him to New Orleans Soon, Mrs Fleming Woods is dead we herd this morning and the hearse went over for the Corps this Evening. It will arrive in the morning. I suppose she died over at the plantation

26 To market in Natchez I do not go. Nothing new. Buisness is dull in the Extreme. To day or this Evening rather Winston and Frank took my Calf or, not my Calves but two belonging to Mother, and Drove them out to Mr Barlands pasture

27 Large Bank-Rubt Sale at the Court House To day It was the notes and accts of Some Bank rubpt individuals I Call the Bank Rupt Law nothing short of Robing a man Bad Luck to all who take it, Buisness is very dull indeed There is nothing done in the way of buisness

28 Buisness dull, Quite So. Nothing new of importance Oh, to day it was that the Committee Decided that at a Large Meeting to that Mr Maxwell and Saml Cotton Should be the Candidates for the Legislature Mr Midderhoff is also runing on his own Hook — was mad because he was not Elected by the former meeting to be a Candidate and Some think that he will be Ellected yet, tho I am not One to think So, Certain — I am agoing to take a hunt in the morning if nothing happens

29 I got up this morning Early & Saddled up my Horses and took a Breakfast and took my Long Gun, Stck. Gun, and made for the Swamp in Comp with G. Brustee We got down and Left the Horses opposite Fords place and we hunted down as far as the Lower Field and from thare down as far nearly as Bayler Winns — It grew very cloudy and rained Some So we had to hurry back as Soon as possible to Our Horses — I Killed to day Sixteen Squirrells and a Loon, and Brustee did not Kill a single thing, came back to town Just as he went and did not Kill a thing. I never saw Just such another Hunter as he is   We did not go below Baylor Winns place to day but Just hunted up and down near the paupaw patch, The Lakes have Considerable water in them yet, too deep for the Large Grobecks to Light in them yet.

30   To day we had Some very hard rains and the wind blew very hard. Blew off the wharf Boat and Several Flat Boats, tho they were all Caught and Secured again, Nothing new — McDonald the Tavern Keeper has a Sort of fight to night with a Painter by the name of Ross — he struck Ross with a musket which cut his Head and then he Broke and ran, Leaving Ross with the Gun in his hand. Ross gave McDonald a Black Eye and he Said that he Knew McDonald well and that he Lived by him for 6 years in the City of Philadelphia and that he has seen a many a time the Father and Mother of this same McDonald Lying both of them on there floor and so Drunk that the one could not help the other — and many other things he Said &c

October 1   Buisness has been dull, very. Camp Meeting Commenced To day, no it was yesterday   William Nick went down to Martin Millers and hyred a Horse, a Cabb or Bugy, and Drove out to Camp meeting taking Dick and Charles with him and they Started from thare Early and Came in Slow, gave up the Horse and Left the Horse, tho [it] was driven pretty hard in going Out

2   The horse that Bill Nix hired from Duck Miller yesterday Died Last night in the night, and Duck Miller Came up very Soon this morning and got Nicks to go down and See him and got him also to promise to pay for him to day. The Price is to be fifty dollars and Sure Enough Miller Came up to day at the appointed time to get the money and I Brot up the fifty dollars and gave it [to] Mr. Nicks who paid it over at wonce and took a Bill of Sale for the dead Horse   So much for so much — Nothing new to day   Camps Meating

3   Buisness was dull and nothing new. I wrode Out on my poney this Evening and the children went in the Buggy with Dr Winston and Mrs Battles, and we went Out to the pecans tree and got some pecans and we then went to the walnut tree and got Some walnuts and Came in, Pecans are ripe now at the tree, Last night there were a Considerable Spree at the bar of the City Hotel, A watch maker by the name of Thom Welden and Thom

Munce had a fight and Thom Munce whiped him — the fellow was Foolish and after Saying a good many things beged Mr Munces pardon   The fellow then has a fight [with] Thom Clay and Thom Clay Knocked him down   I and many others had Left and did not see it — Bill Nix cuts Mr McAlisters Hair and he gave Bill five dollars, so he seys

4   Buisness has been dull in the Extreme to day — I Only took in 10 dimes in the Shop to day — I Learned this morning that the man Thom Welden, a Silver Smith, that he had Lost a Silver patent Lever watch belonging to me, the watch was given to him to do some repairs on it. Charles got him to make the repairs — He told me that he had Lost the watch in the fight he had with Thom Munce, before the City Hotel — I did not believe it of Course and went in Search of it Amediately. I got the number of the watch, which was No 11314, made by Tobias, Liverpool, This Welden had Just redeemd [it] from a Black man Icum, where he had pond it for $5.00. I then found Out that he had taken the watch and pond'd it to a Mr Davis for $43.00 and had got $10 in money and $33 in caurincy — I got it by taking Welch, and was Just in the act of geting a Search warrant for it when Welch Came in and Said that he had Seen Welden and that he told him that he had Seen Mr Davis and that he would give up the watch, and we went right up to the Jefferson Hotel and there we found him and he said that he had not seen Welden at all and after some talk which was very mild and gentlemany he gave me the watch and I gave him five dollars which I said I would give to recover my watch, We then Left and I gave Welch 1.50 for his trouble   I then went under the Hill and told old Frank Pandolph that he had better come up as soon as he Could and get his watch for I saw that same man trying to pond his watch   The old man then went right of[f] and found Wilden and got his watch from Yates, by promising to pay back the money that he pond her for, $6.75

5   Buisness dull, Extreamly So — Nothing new to day more than the yellow fever is Said to be very bad at this time at Rodney. Greate many are Said to be Sick at this time, A. G. Carpenter and Dr Benbrook started up to R. Last night for the relief of the Sick and Lizor Cotten and Nancy Kyle Left to day to go to Rodney to wait on the Sick, Mr Paterson was over the River yesterday and Killed 2 beck roachs, 3 Squirrells and 13 Wood Ducks — Mr L. David was over also and Killd 8 ducks — Mers Frantz and Moouse Clarraige and Joe Pomet was over to the other Side also. They

Killd 28 Squirrels and 2 Rabbits — Some Tolerable tight words past between Mr Crizer and Mr Robt. Patterson, Politics was the Cause of the remarks &c.   If Mr P. had have Said the Same thing again he would have been Knocked — I am Glad that it past off as it did — Some one Let out Janes Birds this Evening or to night

6   Nothing new to day that I have Herd. Bloom Came to See me to day to get me to take an Acct from Welch that was given W. by me for Collections, Good many of our Citizens are Still North &c.

7   This [morning] Early Mr Postlethwaite and Potter has a fight   Elick Postlethwaite was the first to make the attack, and I am told that if they had not been Seperated that Potter would have whipped him, and as far as the fight went Potter got the best of it for he gave P. a Black Eye and Scratched his face and neck prety smart. Postlethwaite bit Potters finger a Little — The fight was about the Settlement of Some Estate in which they acuse Each other of Swindling the Estate. They Said a good many Hard things of Each other — Mr Potter told him that he had Collected moneys belonging to the Estate and give it to Key, the merchant, to buy goods with and that what he asserted was facts and &c   Capt W J Minor arrived to day from the north. He brot 6 very fine mules with him   They were very Large Ones — Things are very quiet in regard to the Election, very indeed   I hear no talk about it — A Lot of Slaves Came to day tho I dont Know who they belong to

8   Nothing new to day. Buisness has been tolerable brisk to day

9   I got up this morning Early and Took my Pulling Gun and started into the Swamp on a Squirrell Hunt and I took my Son William with me   We went down as far as the old Field and then Left the Horses. I wrode my sorrel and he wrode his bay horse   I then hunted on down as far as the Lower End of Long Lake or nearly So. I then waded across Long Lake and Came up on the other Side of it and the Lake was Just up to the top of my Boots on the far side, I saw but One small Flock of Summer ducks — I Killed 1 wood Cock, 2 Hen Hawks, and thirteen Squirrels

10   Nothing new worth Relating more than we had a good deal of Speaking to day in the Court House. The Speakers was as follows — Gov. T. Tucker, then Mr Hamit, then after they had spoke genral Quitman then made a reply in a few words — then

Gen Hueston[8] made a speech then after Super Judge Winchester[9] made another which was of some Considerable Length — It will be recollected that Gov Tucker and Mr Hamit are repudiaters or anti Bonders — The Spaniard returned my buggy to day

11 Tis the Opinion of a good many person should the wether become warm and continue so far about a week, that we would have a yellow fever in the City and quite an Epidemic. There has been Several Deaths in the City within the Last few days — A. Kenney paid me five Dollars to day on his rent which pays his Rent to 13th of July, 1843

12 Nothing new. Several gentleman has gone over the other side of the River to fish with the Hook and Line and Some where over thare several went to Hunt.

13 Mc and myself Started down to the Swamp to day on a Squrrell Hunt. We Left our Horses at Fords Fence and walked down to Cypres Bauyou tho the wind blew so Hard that we did not have much luck — Mc had his brag shot gun and he Killed 5 Squirrels, 1 wood Cock and the dogs Caught 1 that we had both Shot a[t] a time or two — And he wounded a Large Grobeck — And I had my Little french gun and I Killed 8 Squrrells, 1 wood Cock, 1 Summer duck, 8 Snipe and 1 hen hawk — 19 heads   Thare is one Little dry place in the uper part of Cypress Byau which the grass has Commenced to grow on — the balance has got Considerable water in them

14 Buisness in the Streets appears to day to be Quite Lively tho not much in my Line   Mr Pryor returns this morning on the Steam Boat Rain Bow, bring[ing] with him the Horses, Ruffin and others that is fast — Shooting match and Riffle shooting and mule Racing out at the tract this Evening So I am told

15 Nothing new that I have herd, Only that some Infernal Rascal has stolen my Horses. They were taken I Expect on last Monday night or Tuesday the 9th inst — I have been in search of them yesterday a Little but Could not hear of them   I got a nag from Mr Rabey to day and I wrode her. I went out throgh the woods near Mr. L R Marshals then came out again and went out

---

8 Felix Huston was a prominent Natchez lawyer and former commander in chief of the army of the Republic of Texas.

9 George Winchester, prominent Natchez lawyer and judge, was an important Whig leader who was active in the campaign of 1840 and unsuccessful candidate for the United States Senate six years later. Reuben Davis paid him high tribute, calling Winchester "a text-book in pleading and the law." *Recollections of Mississippi and Mississippians*, 80.

past the Evens to the Bayou and took down the same and Came
out near the white Hors tavern.

16   Nothing new. I have been hunting my Horses Ever Since
ten Oclock A. M — I wrode through by Judge Quitmans and the
Mers Ogdens, Rouths, Williams, and then throug by the Mrs
Williams Smiths, the Old Fields, by Col Bingmans, Capt Surgets,
then down and through by old Jones, and came Home and Could not
find anything of them at all — I wrode MC's Horse. This Evening
there was some Considerable talk of a Duel between a Mr Duncan
of New Orleans and Capt Page. They all went accross the River
this Evening and was to fight in the morning but the thing did not
Come of[f]

17   I wrode a fine walking Sorril mare this Evening belonging
to Jno Jaqumine. I wrode Out as far as Smiths at the Lower Quarantine Ground. I was Looking for my Horses but Could not hear
a word of theme — Winston Came from on the other side of the
River this morning Late   He had gone over thare Last Evening
with the Dueling party. They Came over in the night and Left the
old Dr assleep — The parties that Settled the Difficulty was Judge
Quitman and Lacoste. The Seconds in the afair was for Duncan,
Izod & Griffin & for Page, J. Bunce & Downer.

18   Buisness Only tolerable. I herd a young man by the name
of Martin speak Last night on the Bond Question and I was much
pleased with his speech, his Looks and his General appearance and
after he had finished Speaking Col Bingaman got up and Spoke a
Short time and much to the delight of the audience

19   Two Barrell of Oysters Bill has for Sale for I F. Miller.
He sold them to day — Nothing new. Buisness dull, very indeed.
To day Dr Davis was met at the Post office by young Richard
Lawrence, who after making some remarks to Dr Davis, he then
Spit in the Doctors Face and abused him at the Same time, all of
which I have herd he, the Doctor, stood, tho the Dr did dare the
other to Strike him which was not done — Mr L. R. Marshall Lost
one of his sons who was taken sick down at Mr Mosbeys Scool
and died in 30 hours from the time he was taken, Mr Jno Shanks
arrived to day from Scotland &c. Gen. Quitman gave a pleasent
Colation to the Fencibles at his Residence &c.

20   Buisness is tolerable to day — Sickness is said to be worse
than it was a few days ago in New Orleans and the same is said
of Mobile and 2 or 3 new Casess of Fever at Rodney — Mr N.
Woods Little Daughter was Burried to day — She died yesterday

at the Plantation on the other side of the River — I hired Steven to Mr Stutson to day at $12.10 per month.

21   To day has been warm again   Such wether will, I am told, produce new cases of yellow fever in New Orleans. The yellow fever [is] a terable mallady: but if it is Gods will, why not? Slay Slay them. Buisness is tolerable Only — Nothing new — I herd Speech to night from Mr S. S. Prentess which was one of the best I have ever herd   It was on repudiation   Oh he was very Seviere indeed, He spoke from ½ past 7 untill ½ past 10 Oclock to a full House

22   Cleard off at 10 and I took a Horse that I got from the Mansion House Stable, Winston went with me and wrode a Horse of Jaqumines — We went down past old man Jones in to the Scots old Field, then back through by uper Moore field, then down through the Lower field to the Colier place, then back to the creek and up the other Lower field and up to the Hills and through by old Dicksons to the City and Could not hear of my Horses at all

23   Buisness has been dull, very indeed — Nothing new — I saw a man to day and by the name of Seymore and gave him a discription of my Horses that I have lost. He wants me to Look Out for him to Come and join me in a Hunt for them, This is two weeks this day, two weeks ago

24   Seymore brot my three Horses Home to day in about three hours after I had seen him and talked with him about them and I paid him $15.00 in Cash for Bringing them Home — He said that he found them in the Cane pasture of Capt F. Surget — So it is I have got them but it dont change my Opinion at all for I have no Doubt but that Black Rascal Jeff took them of[f] — Nothing new — To day buisness has been tolerable fair.

25   Nothing new has taken place to day that I have herd of. I cleaned my big gun this Evening for the perpose of going a Hunting in the morning

26   I got up this morning Early and after all the nesessary preperations mounted my Sorrill Horse and, Frank on the poney, started for the Swamp. I took my Stockman Gun and I took Don & Rome with me   I Killed 2 Large Malard Ducks & 8 Large Plover and on the back side of Long Lake I saw a fine Large Buck and as he was on the run I up and pulld away at him and Bursted, and he wheeld and I fired at him with the other Barrell and must have put some Considerable small shot in him — He ran off in a direction to Goose pond Ridge — I [saw] Smiths Sons and 2 men on Long Lake   They were a going to haul the cein — I Left there

and got to home to dinner and was very Cold and wet, very indeed
— The water in Lakes is about 8 inches deep, yes, a foot or more
in some of them

27   Nothing new to day — Buisness Like yesterday is very
dull, The quarrantine is done after to day tho Dr Lyle reports that
he has a Case of yellow fever under the Hill — tis true no doubt.

28   Canes Barbacue took place to day and there was a good
[many] at it. It was Given at Steeles Springs — The Candidates
were there in quantietes and were making a greate many speeches.
The following Gentlemen Spoke — Lee Claibourne, Maxwell, Miderhoff, Rabee, Murcherson, Bunce, Lacoste, Bledsoe, Farrish, Glass-
bourn, and one [or] two others, yes Col Bingarman. The day past
off in Stile and all in good Feeling and all sorts of spree took place
at night.

29   Nothing new. Dorse Kirk and John Munce has a fight or
Several fights during the night — it was so good &c. Greate many
drunk Last night

30   Nothing new to day   Buisness tolerable. The people
are very buissy in Electioneering, all hands are at it — Spree upon
Spree is agoing on through out the town. The Courrier was prety
tight this morning, I do asure you, on Mr Simon Murcherson, the
independant Candittate for the Legislature. It was mighty tight
and was signd, a Natchez Whig

31   Nothing new — Buisness tolerable good to day. I was up
at Auction and I Bot a Red and white Cow, The Rump of the cow
is white   She is a Large fine Looking Cow. $8.50 was what I paid
for Her — I then Bot a Sorril Horse with a very remarkable White
Spot on the Left thy behind — no other marks that I am aware
of   He was Slightly Lame in the right fore Leg — I gave $24.50
for him. I then Bot a Little Grey poney for $15.50   I got him
from Bill Nix — The Little fellow is a white Horse and Can rack
prety well — I paid fifteen Dollars to day for Licences to run a One
Horse vehickle for One year

November 1   To day is the 1st day of the Fair and there was
a great many persons Out thare — I Looked at the Cattle and the
Hogs & Horses. They were very fine indeed   I took my Little
William with me on the Little White poney that I Bot yesterday
and I wrode the Combey Horse

2   Buisness Only tolerable. Several familys arrived yesterday
from the north, Mr Samuel Davis and Family and Several others
that I dont Recollect at all — W A Britton and his Brother also
Came — To day is the Last day of the fair at Washington. The

Chimney of the House owned by Mrs Lacrose Caught a fire to night and Created quite a sensation.

3 Ruffner and Mr Hewet had Some words to day in regard to the piece that appeared in the papers VS. Mr Murcherson. Ruffner, I am told, was not so bold as formily

4 The people are very buisy Electioneering — Several speeches was made in the Court House to night, 1 by Mr Hewit and one by Gen Quitman and One by Col Sanders, tho there was not many Speaches made at the Court House this week on Repudiation, tho it is all the talk at this time   There was a race to day at the track and there was Considerable Small Betting — Clark, St Clair, and Obrins mare was the Horses that ran — Nothing new   Wince and me Finished the Small Stable for the Poney this Evening

5 I took a wride this Afternoon with Mc   We wrode arround by Mrs Scotts Old Field and Came Out by Col Wilkins   There is Considerable Electioneering a going on [in] the City to day and will be more to morrow

6 There were a greate many persons in Liquor to Day this being the 1st Day of the Election for the Different officers of the State. The Friends of Mr Boyer is in high Expectations of his being Elected, Tis [this] night that Bill acknoledged that he did Stay with a Black woman by the name of Lucinda that Belonged to the Gemmel Estate

7 The times are warm in the way of Election, I made a bet to night with Thom Weldon on the Election of Sherriffs   Election Closed this Evening at 4 Oclock — Mc Spoke to Bill for the Last time I do Expect.

8 Nothing new, more than the results of the Election and will be published tomorrow. Half Dozen reports to day that Potter would be Ellected but I for one thought not, To day the Horse that I Bot a few days ago Jumpd at me and bit me on the arm and then ran and I after him and I Caught him after a Little and whiped him well with a whip

9 In the Way of Buisness it has been tolerable fair   Nothing new in the City to day — The Election returns were printed in the papers of to day — I won two dimes from Jaqmine as well as two Cows and Calfs, tho he objected to paying the Calves. I will not Exact them unless he is willing to pay them over to me. Tis a astonishing how the parties managed the things Concerning the Election. They did it Brown — Mrs Wade and Her Son from Louisville is here and has been here for Several days

10 Nothing new. Buisness dull, very. I wrode out to Jaqu-

mines to day and got the 2 Cows that I won from him   He gave me 1 Calf and I told him to take the other which he did. The Cows I must notice to morrow and take a Direct Look at them, Jaqumine and myself made a bet to shoot this afternoon with Shot guns at 25 yds Distance, 3 Shots and the most shot in the papers should win — His Shots was as follows — 1st Shot 13, and the 2nd 6, and the 3d 10 — total 29, and mine was as follows — 1st 6, 2nd 10, 3d 8 — total 24, and he won 3 dollars from me and I paid him and we quit

12   Mrs. Wade from Louisvill, Ky, Started to night for New Orleans — She went on the Alexander Scott — Mrs Wads Son got off to night also — he went up the River on the Queen City

13   Nothing new worth your attention   Buisness only tolerable, Mr Newcomber now owes me up to the time of his Sending the Horse home, which was on Friday night, 26 Days at 25 cts per day — I Loaned Mr Oblemis ten dollars to be paid on Saturday inst — I Loaned Mother two dollars also

14   I have a Cold and have had for many days

15   Mr Wemple Died Last night on Board of the Steam Boat Hark Away Just this Side of Vicksburg — his Family was on Bourd and Mr Emerson, at the time of his Death. His remains was brot up on the Hill this morning — Judge Thatcher is now from the returns that I See in to days paper, which is from 16 Counties, 304 a head   He is Ellected Sure

16   Poor old Rachail Died Last night and was Burried to day — Wm Cotton died this Evening at the City Hotel. He was an old trader of Slaves and has made money by that Buisness — Old Frank Pandolph and another Frank has a fight to day under the Hill. The Small Frank got the best of the fight. The old one has been Sick   Mr McAlister is in One of his ways, Drinking and Cuting up

17   I Arrose very Early this morning and made some preperation to go a Hunting but did not Get of[f] untill after Breakfast, I then Started and when I got down as far the old Barland Field I found it full of water and there was a good many Ducks in it, but I did not get One. I Shot at 2 whilst they were Flying but did get One   I then went down on the River Side of Long Lake and Crossed the Bridge Bayou and went on down to Cypress Bayou, then Came up it and Crossed the Cypress Bayou Lake and went on down to Duck Lake, and then On Down to a Couple of Lakes beyond it and then up and back the Same way that I went. I got 2 teal and 3 wood Ducks, 6 Squirrells, 3 of which was Blacke and 3 Fox, and 1 Wood Cock, in all 12 Heads — I Saw Smiths 2 Sons &

Deckard. They were haulling the cein in Cypress Byou, but caught 2 or 3 Little gars   I Saw Baylor Winn and he was agoing down to the Lower part of Long Lake to Drag the cein   A Stranger and Gergory was with him

18   My Sorril Horse went of[f] yesterday and I am affraid is gone. I went out to the Race track and beyond it this morning but Could not hear of him at all

19   I Caught a Mocking Bird to day and after dinner I took my Horse and wrode Out by Col Wilkins, then through by Col Bingamans Pasture and then through by the Property of Mr L Marshals, thence over the old Field. Wm was with me and we were in search of a Little Grey poney and a sorril Horse that I Bot at auction, but I Could [not] find Either of them, Our Cows are all well, that is a Live and in the range — Daniel O. Connell is reported to have been arrested in Ireland — treason or Something Like it,[10] Mr Vaughn got his thigh Broke to day by a Horse running away and Coming in Contact with his Horse

20   Nothing new that I Know of, Wrote an adverticement to day for my Sorril Horse. Buisness has been dull to day, Quite So, I herd to day from my poney and he had Swam across some creek or small River some distance from the City, I Bot a Barrell of Sugar to day weighing 225 pds net at 6½ cts per pound, 14.62½, also 56 pds of Coffee at 9 cts @ pound, 5.04   This was charged to me as they owed me, This [was] got of the House of Mesrs McAlister & Watson — Nothing new to day

21   Business tolerable only — Good many persons are in the City at present   Circus company [and] Some Racing doings are about to go into operation

22   Nothing new   Buisness was fair. Greate Quantity of Cotton Came in to town to day — A Race came of[f] this morning betwen Capt Minors Grey Filly, Lady Jane Grey, and Mr Sam Loughmans Bay Mare, Buck Eye Bell, 1 mile out, with Cetchey on Each.[11] The Buck Eye Bell won the Race with Ease in 1.49 scts, the Bets were two to one against her. Browns or Greers Sorril Horse then wran a mile vs Honey Browns Bad Poney and Beat the Bad poney only 3 feet — I Bot a black frock Coat to day at Hewit & Coulsons and gave 19 dollars for it

23   I Sufferd Considerable in the night with a pain in my Back, I was to sick to work after Breakfast and went to bed and Lay thare

---

10 Johnson referred to Daniel O'Connell, Irish orator and political reformer.

11 Johnson probably meant that the horses were ridden "catchweight," that is, without weight handicaps.

all day—Mc writes Sarah & Lucinday a pass to go to John G. Tailors to a wedding of his Cook to Mr Browns E[n]gineer

24 I have done very Little work to day for I was unwell and Could not—Nothing new to day only I herd Brustee had been treating his wife very badly and that she was very Anxious to go home to her people—L David was in the swamp to day on a hunt and Killed 1 duck and 3 Squirrells only

25 Nothing new—Buisness only tolerable tho will [be] good next week I am in hopes—Mrs G Brustee[12] was at my House this morning and wanted me to go get her passage on the Princess to New Orleans—I saw her afwards and told her she had better remain at my house, that I would see Mr Brustee and things would turn Out right—She thankd me and we parted and I did not see her nor him more durring the day

26 Buisness dull, Quite So. I wrode out this afternoon and fed my cows. I have five Cows and all Dry at this time

27 Buisness was Some what dull to day and nothing new. I gave Welch an acct against this Bloome, a Duch Jew of the meanest Capasity, I asure the Public   Old man Sicles has his property sold to day at the Court House and it Sold for Seven Hundred and twenty Dollars and I am told that there are five arpents in the piece of Land   It adjoins the property of Mr Lillard on the One Left hand Side of the Road and runs up a Considerable Distance along the road. The River is a rising at this time very fast indeed, and Our City is as full as it Can be of Strangers and nearly all Sportsman

28 Buisness Some what dull. There [were] Several fights in town Last night   Wild Bill and Jaqumine had a fight. Wild Bill Bit his finger and must have had the best of said fight, A Mr. McIntire has a fight, no, he was not fighting but was for peace and was Cut a very Seviere Cut in the arm. Tis thought that L. More did it. It was all done a[t] Jaqumines House. Court Commenced yesterday and the Grand Jury is Siting at this time   I am told that the River is a Rising very fast. I Came very near Driving up an Estry Cow this Evening but Let her go &c. I wrode down below the Hill this afternoon and took a Look at four cows that Mr M has down thare and I, after talking for Some time about them, agreed to give him forty One Dollars for the four Cows and One Calf, and by the time that I got home or very soon after, he Came

[12] Gabriel Brustie, free man of color, was listed on the 1843 tax rolls. See Auditor's Records, Tax Rolls, 1843, Adams County. Gabriel Brustie was godfather at the baptism of three of Johnson's children in New Orleans, and Marie M. Brustie was godmother in one instance.

up and I paid him the forty One Dollars in Cash and took a receipt from Him. The cows was as follows, 1 white Cow and 1 pale red Cow and 1 Brindle Spotted and 1 Large Dun, making in all four, and 1 calf which belonged to the white Cow, He or we made this Bargain that he would pasture the Same for me and charge me nothing untill the Cows Should have calves.

29 The Races Commencd to day, Jocky Club. The mile day, the 1st Race of the season, came off to day and these four Entrys. I will here put them down as the race terminated. Col Bingamans Lucy Dashwood, Duboys Sorril Stud and the Jefferson County nag, 4th Capt Minors Horse Black Jack — time 1st heat 1.54, the 2d heat 1.56. The track was in very bad Order and not many persons Out thare, The bets were in favor of Lucy Dashwood VS. the field[13] — Nothing new to day

30 I was at the tract to day and saw a Race between Capt Minors Horse or Filly Norma and Vagrant and Anna Stewart, 2 mile Heats The Horse had many Friends but he proved to be the Last Horse in the Race I Lost 2 dollars with Bill Nix and I won 1 Dollar from Mr Collins — Norma won the Race very Easy — She is Some in a race, It was to day that the Cows came up and with them Came a Brown Cow with a Little Red Calf, heifer calf it was, and I had her drove in and will report her as an Estray

December 1 I Saw this Greate Horse Ruffin Barrow Run a three mile Race to day. The Contending nag was Sally Shannon She could not make him do his best He won both Heats very Easy and I won the Painting of three Doors from Mr Dillon, the painter — I bet him ten to 6 dollars worth of work and 1 bet Mr Walker 4 to 2 in One Bet and in another I bet him 8 to 1, so I won $3.00 from him — The Road is in very bad Condition indeed, tis mudy and wet, Very indeed — Antonio paid me Eleven Dollars for 1 months Rent of Fruit Store.

2 I was Out to the tract to day and Saw a Race, 3 best in five, between Capt Minors grey Filly Jane Grey and Mr Farlys soril mare Mily Rogers — Jane won the Race in 3 Strait heats. She Distanced the other with Ease — I won Something On the Race — Four Overseers on the other Side of the River Took Old Moses

---

13 The Pharsalia Course races, November 29–December 2, 1843, resulted just as Johnson reported: Adam L. Bingaman's Lucy Dashwood and Ruffin won on the first and third days and William J. Minor's Norma and Lady Jane on the second and fourth. One-half interest in Ruffin, "one of the best colts to come out this season," had been purchased early in 1843 by Colonel Bingaman from Joseph G. Boswell, known in racing circles as "the lucky Kentuckian." *American Turf Register and Sporting Magazine*, XIV (1843), 286; XV (1844), 63.

Out and beat him nearly to death to night. The names of the men were Buck, Keiger, Deputy and the Felow that got his arm Cut so at Judge Covington place

3   Nothing new. After I Closed up my Shop to day and took Dinner I wrode Out Taking Winston with me. We went Out to Mr Warrens, from thare to Isreal Leonards place, then back to Sam Leonards or the Moore place, now the Fisk Place, in Search of my Cow, which I Saw yesterday, but all my Hunting was in vain for I Could not find nor hear anything of her   Such is my Luck. When Ever I turn Out anything it is Lost to a Certainty. The Cow I Lost was a Large red and white Cow. She was white over the hips and in the front part of the head, white under the Belly &c. She was marked with a Cross and under bit in the Left Ear and a Cross and a Slit in the right One, with tolerable Large horns, no Brand that I recollect of. I Bot [her] at Auction from a Mc Somebody that I dont recollect now and he bot Her of Thos Rose who purchased her of Saml Leonard, and Leonard tis Said Bot her of Mrs Daton on the other Side of the River, I have Just made up my mind that She is gone to the Shades

4   McMurtry Died this Evening and I went Out to shave him and did So — he Died with Bilious pleuricy and Left 2 Children, poor things — A Great many Gamblers Left here to day for New Orleans — I Subscribed for the weekly Crescent City[14] to day

5   Buisness has been good To day and I have been prety Extravigant for I have bought 3 pair pants and 1 Coat & a bale of Hay and a Barrell of Irish Potatoes, and Several other things   The City is prety well fill with Strangers and a greate many has Left for New Orleans. Mr Fisks man Brot my Cow Home this Evening and I gave Him two Dollars for it

6   Buisness of Course has been dull [rain], and nothing new in the city that I have herd of, A few Days ago a Mr Forister was here and brot with him Mr Baily Paton and Wa[l]ter Guion and others for the purpose of figting a Duel with Col Ham. Claibourne,[15] but from what I heare of the mater the Col will not fight   Report seys that Col. Claibourne will go on and make Out his report as a Commissioner and when that is accomplished he will then fight Mr Forister, Mr Prentiss, Mr Gwinn or any body Else that wants to fight Him,   In a Horn

---

14 The New Orleans *Weekly Crescent City.*

15 John Francis Hamtramck Claiborne, congressman, editor and historian, was appointed president of the Board of Choctaw Commissioners in 1842. The board was appointed to adjudicate the claims of the Indians under the Treaty of Dancing Rabbit, which had resulted in considerable corrupt speculation and fraud.

7 Buisness has been very Good, I have done a good deal of work To day in my line, Nothing new. My children, all five of them, has at present a very bad coughf and I think it is the whooping coughf, I hope it will be Light with them, Yes to day has been a fine day for buisness — James Miller Came up on the Vicksburg and has Left [on] the Steamer Concordia, Nothing new has transpired To day. Mr Bailey Paton Letter appeard to day and it was and Expose of proceedings between Col Claibourne and a Mr Forrister, One would Suppose from the article that Col Claibourne would not fight unless he was cornered, The Crops will be Light this year   Greate Complaints are made all the time now about the rains &c.

8 I drove my two Cows down to Farmers this Evening. The Large Cow is white and red and more white than Red, has a Crop and a Slit in the right Ear and a Crop and Large Slope or under bit in the other   The other is a Cow that I bot at Auction, Was brought thare by Pat Lynch, together with 17 others, which P. McGraw Bot at $3 a Head. My Cow was Choice and was a Black and White One, a white Spot in her face most Like a heart, right hind Leg has a Black Spot on it near a Span Long on the Knee or hock, 2 Large Black Spots on her right side, Short and Low in her make, marked [blank], very Long tail. Several other marks that I dont recollect now but will notice more particular after a while if nothing Happens

9 There were Several Races to day at The Tract but I did not go Out to See them, Robertson Horse VS. Mardices Colt, $100 purse. Rs Horse won the Race   Clarks Horse VS Yates Jaqumine & Com. C's horse won it. Both of the Races was mile heats. Then there were Several other Smaller Races, Denny Horse and Some other, D's Horse won   Joe Winston Horse VS. Bob Stanton. Winstons Hors won Easy &c.

10 Myself and Winston went down to a Mr McCance after The white Cow and Her Calf that I bot of him   We found Her and put a Rope arround her Head and I had great trouble in geting Her Home   I did not get home untill a Late Supper time and then had the assistance of Several persons to help me pull her along. Young Tyler, Jim Dicky and 2 others that I Could not See well as it was dark, but I had my Own Trouble in geting Her up here, This Cost me when I bought her Eleven Dollars ie, her and her Calf

11 I bot two tons of Hay To day from Mr Walsh   I gave an acct. VS. Bloome for which I had Suid On and judement obtained VS him for the money   The ammount was $20 in all but the

Fellow Bloome Swore that I owed him 4 dollars for towels   This made his acct. Only 16 dollars   I then allowed Commissions On the Same, $2   This made only a total of $14. This with 8 dollars I bot the two tons of Hay with. I bot a Rat trap to day too, I got it from Walker the tinner   I pd him 2 Bits & a half and got a trap and 3 milk pans from Him.   This was for a debt of three dollars that I won from Him on a Race

12   I had the Hay hauled up this Evening that [I] Bot of Mr Welch, There were in all 9 Bales   They were hauled up by Mats team and the Boy that drove the team was very drunk — Buisness was good to day, Quite so, and I hope it will Continue so, Nothing new to day

13   Buisness Only Tolerable to day   Nothing new. Jim Welch and Oblenis has a fight in the Sheriffs Office They were Seperated by Newman and others, Welch got a bruise on his Chin and Oblenis got a Lick over the Head with a Stick &c. Thus the matter ended. I bot a Spanish Bridal & Sadle to day at Auction   Cost $4.50   I wrode out this Evening and Drove up the two Cows that I won from Jaqumine to feed them &c. Mc wrode Out this Evening to the Scots old Field to hunt geese and he did not get a Single Shot but had a good deal of trouble with his dog Rose who Caught a Calf. Mc fell down in the mud in runing after Said dog a time or two &c. I wrode Out this Evening and Brot the two Cows that I won of Jaqumine, One of them appears to be some what stif in her joints

14   The Jaqumine Cow that I got of him I found Lying Down this morning and was unable to get up at all, She has the Red waters, a Complaint that will Kill her no Doubt. I had her Raised up wonce or twice to day but She Could not Stand but a minute or two, Nothing new. Buisness Only So, So — Lawyer Baker Came to Natchez to day and has been absent for a Long time and I thought I would not see him Any more, Court is still in cession

15   A young man that is Some relation of the Jones was Struck with a Stick by Lyman Mour right over the Head, and Died, I herd, Last night. It was On Saturday night Last that he got the blow. It was done at Some house of ill fame, So I herd to day. Mour has not been arrested yet but will be I Expect, He has been in a good many fights Latly and this is what may be Expected of Quarrelsome men — Nothing new   Buisness dull on acct of the wether more than any thing Else. Mary had a Child a few nights ago, tis a Girl child and the daughter of Sam Joy. J. C Bond gave Lesons To day in Dancing in the Armory for the first time

16   Nothing new to day. Buisness Only Tolerable To day.

Bill Nicks Left for New Orleans, Small potatoes [sent] to Mr Elliotte, Lou Bingaman, Emerson & others, I paid him to day $25   I have not as yet Looked How we Stand — The man Mc-Cance Came up to day and told me that two of my Cows were off, had got Out of the pasture, Such is my Luck and To day it was that I had the Cow Bled that Came from Jaqumine and she Died. Albert Tyler & Jake Reemer both Drunk, Came up the street &c. I Sent Mrs Miller and Capt Johnson a turkey a piece for there Christmas dinner

17   I after Dinner started Down to McCance to Look after my Cows and I found that Three of them had ran away, viz., the Cow that I got of McCance by Auction, White and red Cow and the Brindle Red Cow and the Large Dun Cow. I Looked about for them for Some time and then Came up and Looked over the top of the Hill On the ridge and I found him up thare too, which made me think for a moment that the Cows were up on the Hill but we both Looked for them but Could not find them at all, I then Came On to town as it was getting Late, I think that there is Something wrong about it, Bill Nicks got off this morning instead of yesterday Evening.   Steven Came Home this Evening from Mr Woods and Stutsons plantation. He Looks well and promises to do better but I have no Confidence in Him, Young Stanton wrode his Horse the other day right under the Bridge near the tract and broke the poor Animals neck

18   I was very much frightened to night by the alarm of the Cry of Fire, Fire, by Elick Postlethwaite. I Jumped Out in an instant   I found that it [was] the kitchen occupied by Dr Jones cook and in a short time it was all in a Light blaze but by hard work by a Large number of Gentleman [the fire was put out]   Oh there were a greate many working and the way I was Frightened was Curious. I, for a time, thought there would be no Chance of Saving any of them but thank God we got the fire Out with the Loss of the two Small Houses that Stood in the rear of Dr A. A. Jones, I Loaned McCance my Horse to day to go to the Country to Look for my Cows that ranaway and he found them and drove them Home

19   Fight took place to day between Mr Murcherson and Mr Hewit. They were seperated by the sherriff and others, It was about some articles that appeared in the papers against Mr Murcherson and was written by Mr Hewit, Mr M. got H. down in the mud and the mud is Just about 6 or 8 inches deep   They were giving the Lye to Each other often, Neither was hurt tho M. got the better of the fight &c. Nothing new. Buisness to day was uncommonly dull,

Nothing new. N L Carpenter Commenced to day to put up the Kitchen that Burned up Last night &c. I was at the Book Auction to night and bot 2 books. Said auction is now about to Close for the Season, The Children are now much plaugued with Colds. I pray they may recover from it. The Races Commences to day in New Orleans. I am very proud that I escaped from So much Danger Last night, Oh what Greate Luck I had, Steven is drunk to day and is on the town but I herd of him around at Mr Brovert Butlers and I sent arround thare and had him brot Home and I have him now up in the garret fast and I will Sell him if I Can get Six Hundred Dollars for Him, I was offered 550 to day for him but would not take it. He must go for he will drink

    20   The streets are as one might suppose they would be after a months Rain, Soft and plyant, Nothing new what Ever to day more than N L. Carpenter finished the repairs on the Kitchen this Evening And I told Him to bring his bill for the repairs To morrow and I would pay him for it

    21   I herd from the mile Race in New Orleans This morning and Ruffin won the Race Easy, The time of the 1st heat was won in 2 minutes, the second in 2:19 seconds. The tract was all mud. The nag was Ann [blank], the beting was Largely in favor of Ruffin, To day a gentleman, a Brother of Col. Garrets, Came to my Shop and had a Beautifull setter Dog with Him and I asked him if his Dog was well broke and he Said he did not know for the Dog had followed him up the Hill to the City Hotel but would not Leave him for he had tried to make him Leave him but he would not, I told him that the Dog belonged to Harrison or Mr Izod and that he would be very glad to get him and if he would permit me I would make him fast untill I Could See Him, which I did.

    22   I wrode Out Late this Evening to John Holdens to Look at a Horse that I thought was mine but when I Saw the Horse I found in an instant that he was not mine, It was an old bob-tail Bay poney — I Came off   The Road was in a Condition that I had to go arround by Capt Minors Stables   Nothing new had transpired to day in the way of news — Mrs Titcher Came down from Cincinnati the Other Day. At this present time The Editor, Mr Prewit, and both of The pu[b]lishers of the Courrier have Started to New Orleans   Baldwind & Risk are the men. Mr Lev. Mathewson will be the Editor untill His return from New Orleans

    23   I paid N L. Carpenter to day $27.20 for making up my Kitchen and Fence &c. He then had an acct VS. Mr Dicks for $8.20 for his part of Said fence, pretty tight I think   I Loaned John Bar-

land this Evening Thirteen Dollars   Said he would pay it back on or about the first January, 1844; I hope they will be paid to me Certain

24   Buisness tolerable fair   Myself, Wince, and Frank working. After I closed the Shop On Sunday I wrode down to McCances place in the bottom and I took Some Corn with me and gave it to the Cows. He wanted me, as I was about to Come away, To Lend him five Dollars and promised to pay it in ten days or he would forfeit his Little Cow, ie, if he did not pay me back the money again in ten days that I should take the Cow — With that I pulled out the money and Let him have it, I Saw a poor Cow of Mr Stockmans down thare that had Layed down and could not get up again, Poor Cow, She will arise never again — The roads are in bad travling Order at present.

25   Nothing new. The City is full of overseerers at present Looking out for new Homes, Buisness. good

26   Nothing new has transpired to day that I Know of   Mc was down at the House Last night and whilst He was Here to See my Little Sick Child we had some Egg nog made and Drank three glasses, Each of us — it was good

27   Nothing new that I have herd of — Buisness fair.

28   Nothing new more than news Came up Last night that Ruffin was beaten very Easy by Bob Saartin, a Gelding Owned by Thom Kerkman and I have very Little Doubt but that Our Citizens has Lost a few Dimes, Mr George Fox gets married to night To a Miss McAlister, They were married Out at Mr Warrens. Both of there Heads are red and all the Little Foxes will be Red of Course, My Cow is Out at Mr Chamberlains field So I am told, Reid bought a Cow to day for Sixteen Dollars & 25 cts.

29   Nothing new to day that I Know of. Several Balls about town to night, An Irish ball or two, then there were Darkey Balls. I am told that at Dr Benbrooks there were One and part of his Family were there and there relations. Monroe Beck Came thare and got in a fuss with young Carkeet and Choked Him. Dr Benbrook hits him Over the Head with a stick. He runs, hides Himself & throws Brick Bats at them &c. Henry Postlethwaite and George Kenneday Has a fight this Evening; K. got the best of the fight   They fought in the mud and the mud was Deep &c. Officer Samuels told me to night that Some of my neighbours Had Complained to him that a Stove pipe was Sticking through the Roof of my Kitchen and that it was Dangerous as it stood &c.

30   Nothing new. Buisness Tolerable fair. I Expect from

what past between Mr Cannon and myself that he will take Steven
On Monday if Nothing Happens — And what is the Cause of my
parting with him, why it is nothing but Liquor, Liquor, His fondness for it. Nothing more, Poor Fellow. There are many worse
fellows than poor Steven is, God Bless Him. Tis his Own fault.
This day was Committed before Esqr Woods, Monroe Beck and a
young Fellow by the name of Mitchell   They were bound over
to Court at the May Term. They are both bad young men, Sure.

31   To day has been to me a very Sad Day; many tears was
in my Eyes to day On acct. of my Selling poor Steven. I went under
the hill this Evening to See him of[f] but the Boat did not Cross
over again and Steven got drunk in a few minutes and I took him
Home & made him Sleep in the garret and Kept him Safe

1844

January 1   I rested bad Last night. I had much Care On my
mind, the night appeared very Long — I got up this morning Early
and took Steven with me down to the Ferry Boat and gave him up
to the Overseer of Young & Cannon. Crawford was his name   I
gave Steven a pair [of] Suspenders and a pr of Socks and 2 Cigars,
Shook hands with him and see [him] go On Bourd for the Last
time   I felt hurt but Liquor is the Cause of his troubles; I would
not have parted with Him if he had Only have Let Liquor alone but
he Cannot do it I believe, I receved a check from Mr Cannon to day
On Mr Britton & Co for four Hundred dollars and a demand note
or due bill for two Hundred more, I will Speak more of it when I
See it again for I did not Examin it very Close this morning — To
day Came On the Election and there were a great number of fights
during the day with One or another &c.

2   Buisness was tolerable fair. Nothing new   Dillon, the
Painter, was put in Jail for fighting and was bailed Out by McAtee
and Some One Else. I bot a vest to day &c. P P. Baker was Elected
police Officer for this year and was also Elected Tax Collector

3   Nothing new that I Know of   Buisness Some what dull, I
Subscribed two Dollars to day towards Defraying the Expences of
a Delegate on to Washington City to try and get the Naval Depot

and Armory Here &c. Mc put down his name for 50 cts   I bot a Cooking Stove to day at Auction, price Six Dollars 50 cts   It will do for a Small Family — I wrode Out this Evening and Drove up my Cows. Gave them Salt, Corn &c.

4   Mr Parson Boyd gets married to night to Miss Raily   Tis a big Lick for him   Mr George [blank] belonging to Col Bingaman, gets married to Sally Cary, widow of Milford Cary[1] — Greate times there will be in a Horn — Young Sharp brought Home my Little Horse to day and I gave Him four Dollars for doing So. The Little Rascal has been wranaway for a month and more. Greate many persons are about to Leave to day On the Sultana to See the Race that will come of[f] On Saturday next. Norma and others are to run,[2] Mr Samuel Woods Eqr paid me for One years shaving, $20. Oh he is a Capt. Certain

5   The Black and white Slab has got 11 pigs and has Lost 2 of them   They got her Home with 9 pigs. Geo. Weldon brought me a note for two Hundred and twenty Dollars that I gave him in 1841 and hav paid a Long time ago. He had Lost it and had Just found it and he brot it to me for which I thank him, Phillips, a sportsman, Knocked Down this Fellow Bryant and his wife both, the other night. Esqr Potter required Bail in the Sum of $200, which was given and the man has Left

6   Nothing new of much importance   A trial Came of[f] before Esqr Woods to day and it was Parkhurst was tryed for Stealing a Darkey belonging to Fields. I herd that the man did belong [to] Parkhurst and to prevent his Creditors from geting him he gave Him to Wm Purnell and it appears that Purnell Sold the man to Fields and that PKT, thinking that he would get nothing for the man, He gives him a pass and tryes to get Him of[f] up the River and he was arrested in it Some way or other and the Justice Woods required bail in the Sum of One Thousand Dollars, in default of

---

[1] This apparently was an instance of a slave marrying a free woman of color. Both Milford and Sally Cary were illiterate free Negroes, but in 1838, Sally was able to pay $620 for a plot of land near Natchez on the Woodville road. Moreover, the term "Mr." was a very unusual one for Johnson to apply to a slave and may indicate that George was a highly respected servant. None of the three free Negroes reported as attached to his household in the census of 1840 by Adam L. Bingaman were of the proper age and sex to have been "Mr. George." Adams County Deed Records, BB, 218-19; U. S. Census Reports, 1840, Schedule I, Adams County, 34.

[2] On January 6, 1844, Thomas Kirkman's Peytona defeated Norma, owned by William J. Minor of Natchez, in two four-mile heats, before a large and fashionable crowd at the Louisiana Course, New Orleans. Peytona was not seriously extended by the Natchez entry. *American Turf Register and Sporting Magazine,* XV (1844), 123.

which Parkhurst was Commited to Jail untill Court, which is in May some time — Three or 4 or 5 days ago Mr Wm Cannon and his wife Lost a fine child, a week [old] or such a mater, The Spoted Sow that had 11 piggs has Only 3 now. Tis the bad wether that Kills them So

7   Nothing new. I Started after I shut up shop to day and wrode down to feed the Cows and I wrode Down through by Dicksons, then along the top of the Hill, then down by Indian Mounds, then through to the Barland Field, then up to McCants where I was feeding my Little Cow with Corn and She by Some means got Choked and I fear will Die from it. I and McCants did all that we could think of and then Left Her. Poor thing, but a few minutes ago She was well, tho what is to be, will be, Certain, Certain   Mr McCants paid me the five Dollars that I Loaned Him, Betts, the white Sow, had Eight Pigs and we got her Home with 7 of them. Mr McCants paid me to day five dollars that I Loaned Him

8   I got On my Horse Erly this morning and wrode Out to See if my Little Spotted Cow was Dead and I wrode Out and Saw her from the top of the Hill   She was Still alive and was walking about. I Could not tell how much She suffered tho greatly no doubt, poor thing, Mr Elliotte, Capt Minor, Mr L. Bingaman, W. B. Bradish, Mr Price, Mr Crizer, Mr Gocian, and a number of other gentlemen Come up to night. W Nicks Came up as Servant to Mr Elliott, They Came up on the Sultana, I recevd a Letter this Evening from New Orleans from Mrs Miller and Mother got One also and Adelia Sent up forty Dollars to her for Sharlotts wages. I herd this morning that Norma was beaten the other day in New Orleans very Easy by Platona and that Sartan was beaten by Patrick Gallaway, three mile Heats, The croud was Largly in favor [of] Bob Sartin. The time very good indeed — This is the night of the Grand Ball at the Manshion House, tis a dreadfull bad night indeed for it

9   Buisness Somewhat dull, William Nix Commences to work Again, got up from New Orleans Last Evening — I wrode Out this Evening Late and worked some time with my poor Sick Cow that was Choked on Sunday Evening, She wont recover from [it] I am Certain. She Suffers Imensely, I Bot the Children, Each of the Boys, a pair of Boots to day and they are very proud of them, very — Mr John Barland gave me to day ten Dollars and Still Owes me a Ballance of three Dollars — this was Loaned Money — The White Turpin Estate was Sold. The Land was bought by old Mrs. Turpin at $2 an Acre. Every thing was purchased by the Family.

10 Mr Henry L Conner has a fight to day at the City Hotel with Preston   They were parted. They had 2 Little turns at it. Report was that the fight would have been in Ps. favor   I was Out to See my Little Cow this Evning and she still Lives and Suffers grea[t]ly, greatly

11 Buisness was Some what Dull to day. I Suppose it is Owing in a measure to the roads being So bad, The Little Cow that I got Choked the other day Died Last night. She was a pretty Little Animal. McDonald of the City Hotel gives a Small Dancing Party to night, sort of a French Doings.

12 This Certainly is a very remarkable Season, we have had so much rain. River planters are already Saying that we will have very high water in the Spring. Sales at Auction to day has been very Small, few people in attendance   Nothing new to day. Buisness very dull, very.

13 Nothing new Going On   Buisness tolerable   Mr John Barland paid me to day four Dollars and 30 cts, this being remainder of a thirteen Dollar Loan that I made Him, The River is now falling at this point, My two Horses ran off yesterday and William Could not find them anywhere to day. I hope they are not Entirely Gone

14 Nothing new to day. Buisness dull to day, very — Peter Baker takes up a young Fellow by the name of Wells who was wanting to fight in the streets and put him in the Guard House. Young Barnard and young Collins was with him, They Got him Out Late in the afternoon, They were on a Small Spree

15 Buisness dull on account of the Condition of the roads &c. I Loaned John Barland two Dollars to day. Nothing of any importance transpired to day. The papers of to day anounce that Col Claibourne and a Mr Graves were Discharged from the Bourd of Commissioners, Indian doings

16 Winston went Out this morning after Breakfast and after a very Long and tedious wride found my Horses in the Dixon Field, He drove them Home, Old Mr Boyer Died this Morning, he was the Father of Valentine Boyer. Nothing new. Buisness Only Tolerable, Rondeau or Rondo is the Entire rage now. Old and young are to be Seen thare night after night, oh the Cruel people

17 Baylor Winn Brot up the three Servants belonging to Judge Boyd, He told me that he Caught them Down in the Woods Close to the mouth of St Catharine. He brot them up this morning, Young Gim Kenney has made His Escape. He was the Cause of their runing away. They were put in Jail. Rondo, Rondo — to night

P. Baker Came up on them when they were playing and took the man and all the money that was on the Table, and took the man off   I Suppose put him in [jail], The other Party down at Jaqumines were off in an instant and was not taken

18   Nothing new has transpired   Buisness of to day has been Only Tolerable   The Streets are in bad Order yet, Mr Jacob Soria was Elected Last Night as Harber Master to the City in place of Mr Lacey, Remooved. There were fifteen Candidates for the office and Soria was Elected on the 4th Balloting by 1 majority, I have herd several Express astonishment at the result, &c.

19   Nothing new. I bought a man by the name of Billy from a Mr Hanks to day. He was in Company with Mr Miderhoff at the time   Our agreement was that I was to pay One hundred and Seventy Dollars for Billy in Cash, and thirty Dollars more Mr Miderhoff agreed to take Out in Shaving &c. with me, This Conversation was had on the Bluff and then I went to his, Mr M'd office, and he drew of[f] the Bill of Sale and was Signed by Mr F. Hanks and witnessed by Mr Miderhoff, He Said that the title is good and they would guaretee the Same from Claim or Claims &c. I then paid the money and took the Bill of Sale and gave a Joint note for thirty Dollars payable six months after date, Mrs Mary Davis has a fine Son to day near dinner time, said to be Large and fine &c.

20   Nothing new   Briant and Winston Cleaned the Chimney This Evening, It was very foul indeed, He then worked on it and draws the smoke up fine indeed, Buisness was Somewhat dull. I gave W Nicks to day five Dollars and 6 Bits as wages. He paid a Dutch. the money.

21   Myself and my two Oldest Boys took a wride this Evening and we went dow[n] to where McCants and took a Look at the Cows. We found them all well and I fed them and Salted them also and then Leeft them and Came Home

22   Buisness Only Tolerable to day. Nothing New that I Know of.

23   Buisness was tolerable Only to day. Nothing new.

24   I Sent in an acct. to Dr A A Jones[3] of twenty five Dollars

---

[3] Since July, 1842, Dr. A. A. Jones had operated a "Botanic Medicine Store" in part of the Main Street brick building owned by William Johnson. About the time of the above entry in the diary, Dr. Jones was succeeded in this venture by Dr. J. R. Applewhite, who maintained his "Botanic Drug Store" in Johnson's building until the end of 1846. For an Applewhite advertisement, see Natchez *Free Trader,* February 13, 1845. Other Johnson tenants at this time included Arthur Kenney (for his advertisement as "Boot Maker," see Natchez *Courier,* November 28, 1838), and Antonio Lynch and Joseph Meshio, both of whom ran fruit stores.

for One months rent, due the first of Janry inst and he paid it Like a gentleman would, which I have no doubt but what he is — I presented an acct against A Kenney to day and he handed in a bill up to Last Saturday 20th, 1844. The full amount of his acct. to that date was $39.50 which Left a Ballance in my favor of thirty Seven Dollars 50 cts to the 20th instant

25 Nothing new. I had my Soril Horse put in the Dray to day and Hauled Several things from under the Hill, some Bacon, some Bran, some pork and a Barrell of Flour, I find that he works well Enough, better than I thought for. Prices at present, Flour 4.50, Corn 56 cts, pork 3½, Bacon 6 cts, &c. The Mrs Taylor that was tryed before Esqr Wood yesterday gave Bail in the Sum of One thousand Dollars, gave the money, I am told, to Mr. S. Cox and Stutson and also gave him five Hundred Dollars to attend to the Case for her   Tis generally thought that She will not return and if She does not Cox will get the money, So I am informed, and I am told also that Hard things are being thought of Mr Samuels in regard to the Case, I Bot a Coat at Auction to day and paid five Dols. and 50 cts for it

26 Nothing new   Buisness tolerable. I bot a cask of meet to day at Auction, 249 pds. at 3¼ cts — it was bacon

27 Buisness was prety fair to day. The Ohio Black Smith Spoke to night and So did his friend the Pump Bourer. They are Clay men Out and Out and they had Quite a Large Meeting to night, much Larger than the One we had Last night, After they were done Speaking Col Bingaman made a moove that there be a Collection made for them, which was done in an instant, tho I dont Know what was the amount given, The Performance of Legerdemain and vantriloquism &c. was performed up stairs at the Same time, I bot a Hat to night at Mr Gales for $4. I bot a Secratary to day at Auction for $10.25. I Like it much

28 Nothing new. I wrode Out in the afterno[o]n and took Wm. and Richard & Byron with me. We rode down to McCants and fed the cows, Came back and wrode Out through by Mrs Smiths and there I met Mc and we Came back together   Nothing new that I Know of.

29 Nothing new, Only that Mr Henry Clay of Kentucky has arrived in the City and is well, I was up at auction to day and I Bot 20 pairs of Boots @ 1.12½ per pair and out of the Lot I found 6 pairs that fit me very well indeed, I Loaned McCants to day five Dollars which he promises to return in a few Days. I Loaned Jno Barland One Dollar for a few days   I made a Bargain with Mrs

Amee to day at a distance ie. to hire old man Billy to her for ten Dollars per month, To Commence to morrow.

30   Nothing particularly new, Buisness Tolerable fair. Maj. Young Sent me a very fine Large Turky and had four more of Them for Sale and I Bot them, gave a Dollar a piece for them, Mr Henry Clay is in this place at present. A Ball will be Given To Him on Thursday night at the Mansion House &c. I Saw Maj. Chotard To day and I asked him if it would be convenient to pay me That Little Order from Barbiere and he told me yes at any time I chose to hand it over. Yes Sir, Yes Sir, Seys I.

31   Nothing New To Day. I Sent a Letter to New Orleans this Evening. Waker wanted to Know of me if I [k]new Lancarshires girl and whether she was Smart or Not and I made Some Inquiry about her and I told Him what I had Learned and he told me that he would have nothing to do with Her &c. Mr Izod and S. Woods arrived this Evening from the other Side of the River   They have been over 5 or 6 Days. Natchez Guards paid me nineteen Dollare and 75 cts. On there rent, which pays there Rent up to the 12th of August, 1844   A Mr Antonio Lynch paid me Eleven Dollars on his Rent &c.

February 1   Considerable Preperations are being made for the Clay Ball that is to be Given To night, Nothing New to day, much more than I got up Early this morning and Started to the Shop and Just as I got Opposite the Shop I Saw Bill, Charles, Dick a[nd] Winston all Just walking Out to market to take Coffee, and I called Winston back and I went in   Old Wilgus who I permitted to Lay on the Sofa all night was Just Geting up and I found that the Little Table had been moved and that the Boys had been playing Cards all night in my room. I made Some remarks and then told them that I would Keep the Key myself Hereafter, Just by way of Knowing how the Cat hop[p]ed. I gave Mr Officer $5 to day for a wheel Barrow, Clay Club met to day

2   Buisness has been dull, very indeed, and nothing new, Mr Meyres paid me 1.50 cts which pays his acct To the first instant, The Ball was very well attended Last night, a good many Ladies were present and them of the big Kind, Lawyer Baker this day has Gotten two dimes from me and as good [as] beged me for them; he is nearly in rags and is gone from the paths that he Once mooved in   How the mighty has fallen, but a Short time ago and he was a sworn persecutor of the Poor Friendless Colord. I saw Old Mr Thornberg to day and I asked him if a Large Dun Cow that he Sold Mr McCants was up thare at His place and he told yes that she was up thare and was Safe tho the moss or Grass in the range was very Scarce indeed &c.

3   Nothing New, Buisness was pretty fair to day. All 3 of the Companies Turned Out to day and was Shooting for a medal. A man by the name of Bogle was married to a young Lady in New Orleans Last Monday night and got up in the morning a[nd] Left and has not been herd of Since. Tis Strange   Mr L. R. Marshall Lost One of his children to day, whooping coughf.

4   Nothing new. Buisness Tolerable fair. I wrode Out and drove my Cows up this Evening and fed and Salted them   Mr Pattersons Calf was with them, The Cattle all Look thin Every where now. Mc and myself took a wride this Evening and we wrode Out by Col Bingamans and through by his field, in the bottom of the Scotts old Field, and then Home, Quite a pleasant wride   Mc and Mrs G. Brustee took Supper with us

5   Nothing new. Buisness was very dull indeed. I was at a Sale to day of Some of the Slaves of the Harmon Estate, 23 of them was Sold   They were Sold by the Sherriff Newman, A good part of them was Bot by Seth W Jones, the man for whom they were Sold, Quily Bot 2, Esdra Bot 2, Preston Bot Several, 8 or 9 I think. They were Sold at tolerable prices, I think, Young S. Davis arrived from Jackson Last night, where he has been Spending a week

6   Nothing New. Buisness fair. Very much of a Dancing party at the Mansion House given by Mr Bond, There were a greate many at it indeed, full House. The city is full of Amusements at this time, Concerts, Lectures, Dancing parties and Balls, &c.

7   Buisness has been Some what dull   Nothing new. I Bot a Barrouge[4] to day   It was Sold at Auction and was Bought by Mr Reed and I gave Reed forty dollars for it and he gave $31, So he made 9 Dollars on me   I then Bought a Horse and gave $25.50 for him and was not pleased with him at all, for when I wrode him I thought that He was Blind, or nearly so. Mr S. Stutson paid me to day thirty Six dollars, 12 Dollars was for his years Shaving and $24.00 was for the hyre of Steven for two months   The shaving is paid for to the 1st of Janry, 1844. Mr Stutson took a pair of my 9 Bits Boots and would have them a La Niap[5]   So the world goes, Mr J. Knight Lost a Likly Girl to day   Bill Nicks Shaved her head. She died in 4 hours afterwards with Brain fever.

---

[4] Johnson probably referred to a barouche, a carriage with a folding top over the back seat.

[5] "Niap" or "napa" was a contraction of the term "lagnappe" or "lagniappe." It meant any complimentary present from a seller to a purchaser. In Louisiana the term is still used, but with a much broader application.

8   Buisness was very dull indeed. A Ball is Given to night at the City Hotell, It will not be very well attended I think, A young man by the name, Buel I think him and an old man by the name of Buel was attempting to Rob Quigless. They were tried and the result I have not herd. I wrote to New Orleans the other day. I receved one doz Razors by Mr Potter, the Cost was $6 in New Orleans, Little Winn is up from the Swamp. Dr Wren wants to buy his Land Or a part of it, Winn asked him $15 per acre

9   Buisness was tolerable, Nothing new. I was under the Hill and got Six pices of Scantling from Mr Sisloff and had them hauled up on acct. I had my Dray Hauled Home this Evening from under the Hill where Green had taken it. I was at the Stable to day and was trying to get a swap for my Horse that I Bot at auction the other day but Could not Effect One. Dr Benbrook is Lecturing On mesmerism at the Court House, Commenced Last Night, Young Robertson and [blank] at the stable has a fight at McAtees   The Stable man whiped him So I am told.

10   Buisness is good and Nothing New. Considerable talk in town about the conduct of Mrs ——— &c. The City is Quite Lively at present and all Sort of Concerts, Lecturing and now and then a fight   A big fight took place to night at McAtees. Johnson, the Brick Layer and a Large man by the name of Tod. Johnson whipped him after a very Long fight. Tod was more drunk than Johnson was, So I am told, A Kenney paid ten Dollars on His rent this Evening.

11   Nothing new. After I ate my dinner I took my Horse and wrode down to McCants and took my Little William with me. I fed the Cows, salted them and then Left, He had Just returned from Dr Calhouns where he is at work.

12   Nothing new. Myself and Winston Commenced this afternoon and made a small Shed in the yard   We broke up the other old One to make this One, I put on a pair of new Boots to day; one of those that I got at Auction for 9 Bits a pair

13   Nothing New. Buisness has been good to day. Greate many Strangers in town   Considerable hair cuting done   The Cotten is Coming in very fast indeed   The Roads are in good Order

14   Buisness was very fair but not so good as it was yesterday. I walked Out this Evening with Mc to See Some of Hanchetts new guns. I Saw Several Shots that was made, distance 325 yds, They were not very good. And then I Saw Some at a Short distance and

I did not Like the guns at all, I Loaned Jno Barland ten dollars to day

15 Buisness Lively. Streets pretty dusty and nothing new. I took the deed To day, or not deed, it was the Bond that was Given to me when I purchased the 2 Lots of Merss A P Merril, Mrs A Cocharan, J Beaumont and Commercial Bank and Left it with Dr Merrils Clerk, Mr Mason, by order of Dr Merrill who Said that he wanted it to get a Better Discription of the 2 Lots that I Bot of them, Four hundred Dollars was the Amount of the Bond, The Dr Left me a Line or two to find Out, the date of the Order to Sell from the Probate Court and also the date of Sale. Told me to get it of Mr North and as Soon as he got back from New Orleans he would make me the title &c.[6] I pd. the Bone Setter, Dr Sweet, ten dollars for working on the child Phillips arm and wrist &c. I took my Bay Horse arround to the Stable to day to have him Sold if Possible and I Left Word to Sell or Swap. Either would suit me. So, I Expect Mr Chapease will do One or the other to day. I told him to give Boot if he Could Get a good Swap by it.

16 Nothing New, I was at the Stable to day at the Mansion House and tryed to Swap off my Bay Horse that is nearly Blind, but could not make a trade in any way. I Came within 2 Dollars of a trade to day and did the Same the other day — Winston and myself Commenced to paint the old Carriage and we did not get through with it.

17 I was tring Still to Swap Horses to day but Could not make One in the forenoon, I wrode Out to John Hodens Sale to day and bot a Small Spoted Cow with a Little Brown Calf and I gave thirteen dollars for her   Mr Jon Williamson Bot Another and gave twenty 2 dollars for her, She was a fine Looking Cow indeed   Several others were Bot by Mr Thompson, Cheap I thought. I also Bot a Sow and three pigs for two dollars and 25 cents and I Came off and Left the sow and pigs to be Broat in at Some other time. I Swaped off my Little Bay Horse this Evening after I Came home from Holdens and Gave forty Eight Dollars to Boot for a Large Sorril Horse. The Sorrel is fine Looking Horse, ie, he is a Strong Horse, Old man Jno Sickles Shot a young man this Evening by the name of Locke and it Killd him   He Died in a very Short time. Sickels was put in Jail to awaite His trial, on Mondy next

18 Nothing new   After I Closd up my Shop I wrode out towards the fort   There I Caught up with Mr Tm Rose and we wrode along together for Some Distance, ie, we wrode through by

6 See Adams County Deed Records, EE, 314, 394, KK, 246–47.

Farmers down in the Hallow and all about on the Mrs Mahons Land, then back again and through by Dixon to his new Bridge across the Bayou near his House   We then came Back to the Hills then all over the Hills untill I found my Cows, and then Home   We were together all the Evening. Wm Joson [Johnson] Junr was along with us too — We were a talking about Mahon place and we were talking of Buying it at One time &c.

19   Nothing New   Buisness tolerable only   I was up at the Wemple Auction to day and Bot five Boxes of Rose Soap at 2.37½ per, 6 Small Rocking Chairs and 4 Small Toy childrens chairs, 1 Small work Table

20   I was up to Esdra Sale to day and Bot 47 Volumes of Buffins Natural History, and Gave 28 cts for Each volume, making in all $13.16   They are in the French Language or I Should be very much pleased

21   Nothing New To day. Greate many persons Has Left this Morning for New Orleans to the Convention, Embasador Took them down — I paid my State & County Tax to day

22   We had a Beautiful Turn Out to day with the fire Companies, it was rich indeed, Tis Generally admited that Our Companies Looked better than those did from New Orleans. The James Gulick Company Came up and after a fine Turn Out with the Company of the fire departments, then in the afternoon the Military Companies Turnd Out and the[y] Looke[d] fine Certain   Judge Fletcher Delivered a fine Little Address at the Mansion House yard I believe it was, Very near 11 Oclock a fire Broke Out in a frame Building on Pine Street and Burned one or two of them up, as the inmates was not Home but was at a Ball, so I am told.

23   The Fire men had a Beautifull turn out this Evening throwing water with there Engines   The New Orleans Comp I herd threw the water fifteen ft. farther than Our Company did, After Supper there was a Beautiful turn Out with the Ingines and they had torch Lights. They Looked very well indeed as there were a greate many out. Our city has been very Lively all the week

24   Buisness has been Tolerable fair, Several Races Came off to day at the Tract   Capt Minors Colt beat Col Bingamans Filly, mile heats, $250 a side. Clarks Horse beat Wallers Horse, Single Dash of a mile, $100 a side. Mardice Colt, Ben Pryor, beat young Leonard Filly that Came from Stantons, ½ mile Race, and a good many others that I dont recollect   The Fireman Left here this Evening for New Orleans   This is the Comp. that Came from New

Orleans, I saw Maj Young at the Race tract and told him that he Could have money any time after Monday.

25 Nothing new. Buisness is tolerable   I wrode Out Late this afternoon on my New Horse and was very much pleased with his walking   I wrode down by the Saw Mill &c.

26 Nothing new. Buisness good To day. Estate of Wemple is being Sold to day: The Dry Goods &c. I was thare a good part of the day but did not buy Anything at all, Greate many persons present and things went high I thought, Considerable sly talking Throug Out the City about Mrs ——— ——— ——— and Little Dr ——— Plain doings. Too bad.

27 Buisness Tolerable fair   I was up at Wemples Sale to day and some articles brot more than you find them at many Stores at private Sales   Mr Antonio Lynch paid me on acct to day twenty five dollars and also paid me Eleven Dollars for One months rent of the fruit Store to date

28 Nothing new. I was at the Sale of Mr Wemple to day and I thought things went high, So Some of them did, I think, We had a Smart little fire Last Night Down at the Cotten press, It was some old Buildings in the Rear of the Cotton press. The Buildings were old and worth but a trifle, I went down to the fire and Came back Just at 12 Oclock

29 Nothing new. Buisness Only Tolerable. I was up at Auction Several times to day and made Quite a stay   I purchased Several Boxes or rarther two Large Boxes Suitable for Corn Or Anything. I gave $3.50 per Box   I Also Bot a Book Case at $16.50   This was sold at a moderate Sum I think. I was at the Wemple Store this Evening and I Saw Ellen sold, She was Bot in the name of Bridget, Her mother, and was struck off at 440 Dollars, I think, Mr Emerson made a Long speech in her behalf and Said Some soft things, ie, he made a good talk and a Gentlemany Kind of a talk, I thought very well of Him for it. Then James was put up and I bid on Him a time or two and then Stoped. I had got a Gentleman to bid for me So that Some individuals would not run him up on me two high, tho they did run him on me to $790 where he was then Knocked of[f] to me, through Mr Canon, Tis thought to be high tho I am very well pleased with him[7]

---

[7] The Johnson Papers contain a bill of sale, February 29, 1844, showing that Johnson paid, or agreed to pay, $790 to J. Hubbard Emerson, administrator of the estate of James Wemple, a deceased Natchez storekeeper, for "a certain male slave, named Jim, aged about nineteen years—a slave for life." Johnson often called this slave "Gim" in his diary.

March 1   Nothing New, I was at auction to day and Bot a Dress Pattern to Line a Coach [coat] with, I bot a vest also — The Sale was over yesterday at Mr Wemples and in the course of nine months from now there will be Some persons hard run To take up there paper

2   I paid young Stockman to day Six hundrd and thirteen Dollars, 50 cts by paying him five Hundred and 85 dollars 90 cts in Cash, ie, a deduction of 4½ per cent. This was for the Boy James. I then gave my note Indorsd by R McCary for two Hundred dollars. I gave James a pass to night to go to a party at the House of Mr Rose, Esqr.

3   I wrode out this Afternoon with Mc   We wrode Out the Woodville Road and came through by Col Bingamans. Mc wrode my new Sorril Horse part of the wride, He was pleasd with my Horse, Winston and my Little Richard went down to McCants to Look for the white Cow, Brown Cow, and Gustin, None was found by them

4   Nothing new. James Came Home this morning to work, Brot His things down in the forenoon   I Set him to work to clean Out the Corn House To put a Floor in it &c., which he did with the assistance of Winston, I wrode Out this Evening and took William with me and I found my Cows and brought them Home

5   Nothing new. James and Frank was at work at the Fence and gate &c. They made a good gate &c. A few days ago Mrs ———— and John ———— was Caught together. Report Seys it was One of the plainest Cases in the world. Her husband gave her a wonderfull whiping, &c.

6   I wrote a Letter to Mrs Miller in New Orleans to day and sent it by the Embasador. Col Bingaman went down on her to the Races

7   Jim and Frank Commenced to day to plough. They ploughed all over the yard or Lot

8   Judge Dunlaps House was Burned up this Morning Erly and I am inform that they Lost Everything they Had. They Barely had time to get Out of the House, oh what a pity. The Judge was not home when it Occured, Nothing new   Times are dull, quite dull. I planted my Little Crop of Corn to day &c. I Loaned young Swain my Big Horse to wride this morning. I Loaned Little John Clark my Bay Horse to go Out to Mr McCrarys the day before yesterday and he Just got back with him to day.

9   Nothing new, Buisness dull Somewhat, I was at Home a good part of the day doing Some planting &c., Puting Hay in the

Loft &c. and doing many other things about the yard with Jim to do the work

10   I wrode down in the afternoon to McCants and down through the field, and whilst I was down thare I found the red and Brindle Cow that was wonce McCants was mird fast in the Bayou Near the House or in the Spring   After working for Some time, three of us, we got Her Out after a Long time tho we worked very hard indeed

11   Lucinda was Eating Her Breakfast this morning and Swallowed a pin and She Complains Considerably of its hurting Her in the Breast

12   Nothing new, Lucinda, by taking a vomit, got the pin Out of Her throat that she Swallowed yesterday. She Took a vomit and threw it up, as good Luck would have it   Mr Dillon painted the three hours Oken[8] to day. This was done on acct of a Bet that we had and I won the Job of[f] Him, Jim was at work a part of to day in making an iner fence in the yard of Some stuff that I got down at Mr Sisloffs Mill, I paid One dollar for it and told him to charge me with the other dollar.

13   The Horse Ruffin I am told is beaten by the nag Peytona in New Orleans, distance they ran was [blank] — tis Said She won with Greate Ease   Jim made a fence yesterday across the Lot or yard   Nothing new To day   Buisness dull. Billy was Sick yesterday from 10 Oclock and is Sick to day, Took medicine &c. Col Dunbars Boat Sunk the other day and he Lost Some Stock Consisting of Calves, Hogs, Sheep &c. and he had Several Cows to runaway from Him after they had been Saved from the Boat, &c. I Loaned my old Soril Horse to Mr McCants young man to go down after McCants at the plantation of Dr. Colround for the Child was very Sick indeed. He Started in the rain about five Oclock and has fourteen miles to wride, poor Horse, &c.

14   Nothing has transpired new to day. I was down at the mill to day and I paid young Mr. Sisloff One dollar on Some stuff that I got from him the other day and I orderd Some post and some Scantling which I have not paid for yet   I also Sent Mr Thom Finney down to the mill to order Some Stuff to make a flooring in the store, I Received a Letter from Mrs Miller to day and She Spoke of the dark Clerke and requested me never to Send anything more by him again, a Rascal &c. Enough said.

15   I had Some Lumber hauled up this Evening for to build a

---

8 Johnson meant oak stain.

Cistern House, Mr Seth Cox Knocked Dan Downer Flat Last night at the City Hotel

16   Buisness is Somewhat dull. Nothing new   I paid Mr Sisloff 7.40 cts for Some Lumber and Shingles that I got, Mr Sparks came up this Evening to Collect two dollars for Lumber   Some Rascals oppened Charles Shop Last night and Stole all the Razors and his Coat, Boots and Shoes and Several other things. It was done by two men and two Little Boys — Some of the Razors was traded of[f] for Liquor.

17   To day Mr Walsh Brought the two Little Scoundrels that Broks into my Shop under the Hill and stole my Razors, &c. I had them in the Shop for Some time to day and they at first denied Every thing but After a while they admited that they were not Brothers and that they were both thieves and had been Stealing for Some time in New Orleans. They told me of a Greate many Roberies that they had Commited in the way of Stealing Chickens and Skiffs and Such things   I Kept them for a while to try and make them tell where the two men were that was with them, but they would not tell anything more than that there names were Bob and Jack and that One of them was a Bow Leged man, The Boys, the Largest One, Seys his name was Charles Lemoniere and the other George Butterfield or Potterfield, They were put into the Guard House until Late in the afternoon when I had them turned Out to go there ways. To day I was quite unwell with the head ache   I remaind at home all the Evening and did not take my wride as formaly. Nothing New to day, buisness Only tolerably. Wilgus Died this morning about 8 O'clock with consumption I believe

18   Nothing new to day. Buisness has been tolerable fair to day and I am in hopes they will Continue So. There are two Balls in the City to night, One at the City Hotel and the other at the Mansion House. Gerasdys at the City Hotel and Bonds at the M. H — both has a good Ball, They are Just as they Should be, Some Small Potatoes at the One and you know whats at the other — Old Man Nat Fagan died to day — poor old Fellow — Sevral persons were trying to get money to pay the Expense of the Funeral &c. Capt Grist died the other day down at his plantation on the other side of the River

19   Buisness Tolerable Nothing new that I know of, The Ball that was Given Last night at the Mansion House was as Large again as the One Given by Gerarda at the City Hotel, I have been taking French Lesons for a week or Such a mater

20   Nothing new. Buisness Only Tolerable, I gave Wesh an acct against A Kenney for Thirty Eight Dollars And fifty Cents which I hope he will be able to Collect from the Infernal Rascal, for I can Look upon him in no other lite

21 Nothing new, Buisness Only Tolerable. My Big Sorril Horse is at work with Joe Cornishs Dray.

22 Nothing new. Buisness Only tolerable Mrs Amie has a Suite with George Weldon and she got Judgment against Him for the amount of her Claim, which I believe was Somewhere about thirty dollars. She then Servd a notice on him that if he remained Longer in the House that he would have to pay thirty Dollars a month for it.

23 Nothing new Buisness dull, only tolerable so. I made a bet with Mr˙ Waller To day that he could not place the nags in the Race and he took it directly &c.

24 Nothing new. Buisness Only Tolerable After the Shop Shut up I took my Large Sorril Horse and wrode Out to hunt for my Cows and after a very Long hunt I found them, One of the Cows, a very fine One too, I found was dead. She had got in the myre, was the Cause I believe Pôor Cow, she was a very fine One and One that I bot of McCants, I took my three Sons with me when I went down, I paid Bill Nix ten dollars as wages.

25 Nothing new. Buisness dull. The Strap man is in town Selling Straps and is Selling them prety fast. I believe I Gave Mr A J. Postlewaite the deed that I got of Mrs Cochran or Dr Merrell, He was to Look at it and return it.

26 Nothing new in the City Buisness to day has been dull, quite so. I made a Bet with Jaqumine to day or proposed a Bet and we bet another bet which was 1.50 that he would back Out. That taken, he did back Out and refused to pay the 1.50. He must pay it or I Shall think hard of Him, and will get Even with him when it may be Convenient &c. I bot 3 doz tweezers to day for 18 cts per doz. Petter Boise took One of them and I Sold three at Auction, 4 of them for twenty cents, I Saw Mr Farmer to day and I bot of him 200 ft. wetherboading and 7 nine ft Posts &c.

27 Nothing new, more than that the Barber at Rodney is dead and the citizens wants another to Come up there, William Nicks is in a greate way to go up and take the Shop — I hope he may — St Clair, the Carpenter, is at work at my Cistern House in the yard. Mr V Boyer paid by his young man to me to day thirty Dollars that I Loaned him a good while ago — tis a Long time Since he got it — I gave the French teacher to day five Dollars for French Lessons for Wm Nicks and myself &c.

28   Nothing new. Buisness has been Tolerable fair to day. William Nix Left here this morning on the Concordia To open a Shop a[t] Rodney — in place of the Dead man, I hope he may do well, I Know he can if He will Only try, for there is money to be made up thare and I Know it, We have not had a regular Settlement for thirty three months He has had in that time Cash to the Ammount Five Hundred and ninety three [dollars and] 82 cts and it was understood by us Some Eighteen months ago that he was very willing to work for the Same per month that Charles worked for

29   I paid the Carpenter St. Clair, for Building the Cistern House, Ten Dollars was the price I paid for the Building of it

30   I was out to the track to day and Saw the race between Clarks Horse and Jaqumins and Wallers Horse   It was a close race between the Last two I do asure you tho I won as follows from Jaqumine. I Bet him five against five, $17.50 vs. 15 and twenty vs. 18 and five vs. four, and then I won a Coat from him, in the Bargain, It was cold and I Soon Left the ground, and came home. Mr Mourcherson and Mr McNeil has a fight this Evening and they were fighting with chairs and Knives, Mr Mourcherson got Several Sticks in the arm and side &c.

31   Nothing New. I Spent a part of the Evening in hunting for my Cows, and I found all but One   The old white One I did not See

April 1   Nothing new. Buisness has been only tolerably Fair to day, I Paid Maj. Young to One Hundred and fifty Dollars, This was for wages of Charles, I dont know how we Stand at the present moment tho I am prety sure that I dont owe him anything at all

2   Nothing New, Buisness tolerable fair   Mr Izod, Woods & Griffin went to fish the other Evening and they report that they Caught 30 or 40 fine fish. I doubt it.

3   Nothing new. There is a greate deell of talk at this time about Texas being anext to the United States. As for my own part I dont believe anything of the Kind for I dont want to see it myself

4   Nothing new More than the Rascally Fellow Morgan that has been in Jail for three years for murdering young Isler, is acquited   Did not Come to a tryal   The Statute of Limitation I Suppose, The River is high and Corn is Selling at 75 ct per Barrell.

5   I passed along from the shop to night and I herd Mr McAlister telling Old Esqr Carson to go to the Devel — he called him a Damd Old Fool, and told him Several times more to go to the Devil, Poor old man   I was Sorry for Him, but Such is the way of

the worl — I paid Mr Dunham for Eigteen Barrells of Coal that I got of him a short time ago — ten Barrells of it I paid as a Debt that I Lost with Mr. Saml Woods

6   There was to have been a quarter Race between Mr Crizers Horse Anna & Mr Coffeens Brown filly   They were all the Evening trying to get the Race off but they did not start at Last. Made a Crow Race of it

7   To Marketing as usual &c   I took a ride this Eving and I went through all the alod [old] Fields

8   Bill Nix is down from Rodney. Got down this morning a Little before day and Left again to day about 8 O'clock to day for Rodney again   Took up Robert Smiths Little Boy with Him

9   Nothing new, Ned King Esqr was bound over until Court on the other Side of the River   He has been whiping a couple of men that was Stealing his hogs, A Soyree is given at the City Hotel to night   A Mr Davis makes a Political Speech to night, He is a strong Whig

10   Nothing New. I paid $70 to day To Mr Finney for work done in my Brick Store   It was for Flooring the Same &c. I think it is a pretty High price notwithstanding the hard times   Old Dicy is Drunk to Night, and has been all Day I believe, Clark Sells Out his grocery at Auction to day

11   Nothing new. I received One Letter yesterday from Mr E. Miller and to day I receivd One from Mrs Miller, New Orleans   I have been Some what uneasey part of yesterday and all day, for I have Some fear that there is Some claim Coming against Lucinda, I herd that Miss Dart had some notion of Suing from Her

13   Several Races were wran this Evening at the tract, I Saw two of them, Mr Crizer Sorril Horse wran a mile Race VS. Mr Coffeens Tow Head Horse, The Crizer Sorril won the Race very Easy — he then wran his horse Bitty against Coffeens Brown mare, a quarter Race and he won that. He then made a half mile Race VS. Jackamines Bay Horse Joe Boy and Mr Crizer won that. Oh he was in Luck to day   I Sent twelve Dollars & 3 Bits to git Some Razors with   I Sent a Letter to Mrs Miller by Mr Potter   I Loaned Mr John Barland five dollars to day

14   I took my Horses and the Boys and wrode down to Mc-Cants. Saw my red Cow down there, then came up to the top of the Hill, then down to Smiths   Sat there a Little while and then Came up   Found my Old white Cow and She had her Lift Eye knocked out by Some One. Poor Creature, She Looked very well otherwise, Buisness to day has been quite Lively and Nothing new

15   Nothing new. To day the Sultana Left here with a great many passengers   Mr Saml. Davis Family Left on her, young Mr Sam Davis Left also, Wm K Henerys Family Left also — I Let Mr Stutson have a Razor to day in place of a Case that he Said was Lost here   He got a Box and Soap with Brush &c. I Bot a Sow with four Pigs from Gim, Foxes Gim, and gave her to Little Sisa   Jack Came to work at the trade this morning

16   Buisness was dull somewhat, Nothing new.

17   Nothing new, buisness only tolerable

18   Nothing new more than I believe that Some One has Stole my Little Grey Horse from off the Commons, as I Cant find Him this Evening at all, Clark and Waller has a Race this Morning, Waller ran a Bay mare belonging to Beyty, Clarks horse won the race very Easy   Five Hundred yard Race it was — Potter Brought me up two doz Razors from New Orleans, paid twelve Dollars for them

19   Buisness has been remarkably dull   Our Red and white Cow Pink Had a Calf Last Night and I drove her Home this Evening at Dark

20   Nothing new. Buisness tolerable fair, To day is the Aniversary of the Natchez Fencibles, They had there Dinner Out in Capt Minors Pasture, Capt Clay made a mistake on his way in and insulted the guards   Considerable Jaw about it to night, Clark and Mr Coffine has a mile Race this Evening and Clark won the Race very Easy   I Lost $7.50 on the Race, Clark had bet me a New Saddle Contra five Dollars — the[y] were 2 minutes in running the mile, I Bot a Horse to day [from] Mr Guillbert   Gave him thirty dollars for it

21   Buisness was tolerable fair, Shut Shop at 11 O'clock, took a nap of Sleep and after dinner Some time wrode out to the Hills   Cut Some Bandey, Sticks &c.

22   Nothing new   Buisness tolerable only, The wether is warm very, and I dont want to have Texas anexed to the United States, Certain

23   Nothing new — Buisness is very dull to day — I take a French Lesson now and then

24   Nothing new, Buisness tolerable, I dont Know of anything New to day at all, I Loaned Sam Willis I believe one Dollar to Knight   He is a milk Seller or was wonce, To day I had my Big Sorril Horse put in to Harness and worked in Joe Cornish Dray. He mooved of[f] quite well indeed, I also had my Sorrill Horse put in Bobs Porter Cart and he worked very well indeed. I am

very much pleased with Him, I went up to Mc House this Evening and I found him Sick in bed and has been Confined to his Bed for two days — it was a Cold that he was troubled with

25   Nothing new, Buisness today tolerable fair   I received a Letter from New Orleans to day and it inform me of Mr Miller having got a very Seviere fall by a Dog having ran between his Legs and threw him, Bruising him, he thought that his hip was Dislocated, then of the accident of Mr Scott, His Horse having Ran away with his Cab and throwing him out Breaking 2 of his Ribbs &c. I was up to See Mc twice to day for he was quite Sick   Dr Lyle bled him to day. I was Out to Maj Chotard to day and he had his Hair Cut and Miss Mary one of His Daughters. He then paid me the Sum of Sixty Dollars by an order on W Britton and Co. Oh the Major is a gentleman and no mistake, and Mrs Chotard is oh she is a Splendid Lady at home and abroad and Every where

26   To day is the 1st day of the Fair, Mr Britton &c paid me by order from Maj Chotard, Sixty Dollars.

27   Nothing New. To day is the Last day of the Fair, The streets are very Dusty. We have no rain for Some weeks past, Buisness tolerable Fair to day   Mr Crizer and Mr Clarks Horse has a Race this Evening   One mile Out, and Clarks horse won the Race in 1.56 prety Easy. Clarks horse can beat them all very Easy. Mc is Still quite unwell and has been all the week, Lindo is now Painting up the Armory in fine Stile, I took in Eight Dollars in the Shop to day by work alone

29   I Loaned Mr. Gregory fifteen Dollars to day to be paid in three weeks — Sure   Sure

30   Nothing new. Buisness only tolerable, Greate many Citizens Over the River to Fish To day, Mr Jno Barland paid me five Dollars to day that I Loaned Him, a Short time ago.

May 1   Buisness Only Tolerable, I was a part of this Evening Engaged in making a Fence Out at the Vacant House on the Commons, It is the Property of Dr. Atchersons, I believe

2   Nothing New. Buisness tolerable   I find Mc is still Sick. Kept his Bed all day. Bill Nix and Henrieta Stut was married this morning Early and Left for Rodney Early this morning on the Steam Boat Concordia.

3   Nothing new. Buisness Dull Some what   I was making preperations to Commence Bath Buisness. It was to day that I herd that Bill Nicks wife that he married yesterday had been once given to ———— and he made use of her. This it was Said was done for a

House & Lot and afterwards he would not give it — So Seys report Current. I was at Auction to day and Bot 3 table cloths, 1 Counterpane and two pieces of Dieper for towelling, &c. I took out Lycences to day for a One Horse Dray and paid for it

4   To day I Sold a Cow that I had up at old Mr Murnsburg   I Sold her and her young Calf to Mr Farmer for fifteen Dollars Cash   Maj Miller and Maj Dunn tis Said had a fight up at Vicksburg yesterday or the day before, Maj M. Said that Maj Dunn was a Humbug — So they Met and fought with Sticks and Maj D. was two Strong for Maj M. and Larraped him pretty Smartly. Tis Said they met again and fired Pistols at Each other without Effect

5   Nothing new. Buisness uncommonly dull, I wrote out as far as Mr Smiths Pasture near Mr Howells, Eat a few Black Berrys, remained there an hour or two, then came Home, Report Seys that Mr Robbins and a Mr Downs fought a Duell yesterday and that Mr Downs was shot through the Brest and brok a rib or two. They fought with Yagers [at] fifteen paces, Lucinday was taken very sick to day indeed.

6   Buisness Some what Dull. Yes quite so. I Loaned John Barland to day the Sum of twenty Dollars payable in two weeks, if Possible

7   Nothing new   Lucinda is quite sick to day with a very Seviere pain in the Head. I had her head Shaved this Evening as she suffers very much with it, Report Seys that Waller Hicky has Shot a man up at Vicksburgh in a Street fight, a man by the name of, oh I cant recollect the mans name tho it was Mc Something

8   Nothing New. Lucinda still very Sick from Eating Ice Cream, which Sarah and her have Denyed Eating up to this date, but have Just now this Evening Acknolowedged have Eat any untill this Evening

9   Nothing new. Commenced to white wash the shop to day, and to Paper also — also to do Some fixing of tin pipe doings — Dr Applewhite pays his Rent to day to the inst instant

11   I Commenced the Bath Buisness to day and Sold fourteen Baths. Good, Good I think

13   Mr R. Bledsoe was Buried this Evening. Mr Andrew Brown was Brot up from New Orleans and was Buried to day.

14   Nothing New. Mr. Hoggatt Sent to me [to] know if I Could fing [find] a Sort of a Cabb or Buggy to buy it for him   I Looked arround but Could not See any that I thought would Suit Him, Edd Came in. Mr. Patterson Gave me his Robins to put in the

Cage, Circus Company are now performing in this City. Commenced yesterday or by the Same Day.

15 Buisness to day has been very dull indeed, Sold but one Bath to day — I Sent Out this afternoon to have the fence closed up arround that place out on the Commons and it was done by Gim, who told me that the Butchers had put there cattle in it with Out Leave

16 A Carpenter is now at work at my Galery Stuff, to make a Cover to the Gallery

17 Buisness dull   Nothing New — Winston [and] my Little Willeam went Out to Mr. Barlands and Brought in my Little Cow & Calf   It was yesterday Evening that She Came up and not to day

18 Nothing new, Buisness dull &c.

19 I wrode down to McCants this afternoon to Look at my Cows and I found them both down in the hollow below his House, &c.

20 St Clair finished off the gallery this afternoon and I paid him twenty five Dollars for it — a Mr Shaw and himself done the work

23 Nothing new. Buisness very dull   The Boys, Winston Jack and William & Jim they were geting Black Berrys

24 The Boys are painting down at the House &c. The front of the Old still Broke and fell out this morning, and it was mended and Set to work Soon after

25 There was a Large Whig Meeting To day at the Court House, and the Speakers were as follows, Col Bingaman, Mr Js Shields, Mr Frost, Mr S. C. Cox, Mr Dubison, and at Night Judge Dubison, S. C. Cox & Juge Winchester, &c. The meeting in the forenoon was very Large but in the afternoon it was very Small — Nothing New more than Gov. Brown[9] arrived this Evening in our City and there [was] Considerable Firing of Cannon &c. I Loaned St Clair twenty Dollars to day on Conditions that he is to pay me on monday by 12 Oclock or he forfeits the grey mare to me, or in other words I am to take for the twenty Dollars, I paid Mr. John Larcrose five Dollars to day in part pay of twelve that I owe the office of the Free Trader, up to Some time in August, next

[9] Albert Gallatin Brown had served in the state House of Representatives, as judge of the circuit court, and as a representative in the Twenty-sixth Congress. He served as governor of Mississippi from 1844 to 1848, and later in both houses of Congress. Of him Reuben Davis wrote: "I knew him well, and am certain that I never heard him make an unkind remark about any one in his life, and no person was ever known to speak of him unkindly." *Recollections of Mississippi and Mississippians*, 164.

26　Nothing New. Buisness Dull, I wrode Out this afternoon and went by Mr. Howells — Saw my white Cow, picked Some Black berrys, Draped most of them on my way Home, got mad with my Cow, Whiped the poor Creature, and She was Sick at the time or Lookd so

27　To day was the day St Clair was to have paid me twenty Dollars by 12 Oclock or I Should have the grey mare that he owns — the time came around and nothing could I see of Him or the Horse. In the Afternoon I went up to See Old Mr Obrine who had taken from him the grey mare, I Borrowed a Saddle and wrode her home

28　I was out to Genrl Quitmans and found him very Sick, Dr Cartwrite was the ficitien [physician]　Some One I fear has Stolen my Horse　I fear tis the Large Sorril Horse　My Brown Cow is d[y]ing at my Back gate, poor thing　She was a fine Cow indeed — Nothing new

29　To day in the Court House there was a fight between Mr McClure and Col. Sanders　It Grew Out of Some Expression that Col Sanders made, and as Soon as he went Out of the Court Room in to the Passage, Mr McClure Knocked him Down and Jumpd on to him and was gouging Him in an instant, He was pulld off of him — Judge Cage Fined Him $200 and Sentenced Him to Jail for Four Days, Good many Persons was Surprised to find McClure So much of a Man, The Citizens Gave a Dinner to day to Gov Brown at the City Hotell, it was not well attended I am told, tho they were of Both Parties, Whig and Democrats　Some wanted Judge Cage to adjourn Court but he would not do it, Our Brown Cow Died Last night and was hauld off this morning. She was a very fine Cow — Jim, Frank & Winston was picking Black Berries this Evining

30　Nothing New　Buisness fair　I Bot two Shaving Shairs from the Little Frenchman Eugene, the Barber　I gave him Six Dollars for the two, I received a Letter to day from Mr. Miller informing me of the Birth of His Little Daughter. She was Born at 12 Oclock on the night of the 26th inst.

31　Nothing new that I Know of　Buisness tolerable Fair, To Day Little Eugean Closes his Shop to quit Buisness to Live in New Orleans, Jim and Frank Complets the fence in the yard and Commences to repair the Stable,　If nothing happens will have it done tomorrow

June 1　Buisness only Tolerable, Not much Buisness going On to day, of no Kind

2   Buisness was tolerable fair to day. Charles and myself Put the Saint Claire mare in Harness to day and she worked very well, I wrode Out by Mr Smiths Old Field and then arround by Col Bingamans taking Richard and Byron with me, We did not get Home untill Late, &c.

3   To day Has been a fine Buisness Day — we are Buisy quite So. ·Nothing new, The Boy Washington oppens a Shop in Wall Street yesterday, I wrode Out to Mrs Lillards to day and She told me a Lye about her Boy Having opened a Shop with Out her Leave at all, &c. Mrs Linton and Family, Mrs Fiske and Family, Mrs D Sanderson and Family, All left On the Sultana for the North, I took in to day in work to day over Eight Dollars

4   Litening struck Fits Patricks Shop

5   I Sent Lucinda to Orleans this morning on the Steam Boat Yazoo, Capt Brennen, Buisness only tolerable   I hope it will be Better Soon, At the time that I Sent Her down I wrote Out two Bills of Sale, 1 with the above date and the other with the date of the 1st inst. to Mrs Miller, Four hundred was the Sum spoke of in the Amount. One Headed New Orleans, the other Natchez

6   Buisness has been very dull to day, Nothing New, To day Mr Welsh paid me twenty Dollars and fifty Cents, on the acct of Mr A Kenney   The money was paid by Col Bingaman to Welsh and he paid it over to him, on to me and I had a Settlement with Mr Kenney and with the Moneys paid. He has pd his Rent up to the 13th of May and four Dolls over. That is the way we Stand at present — Jim and my Little William went to Mr Dicksons field, and Drove our Cow Gustin Home with a fine Heiffer Calf   She had it Last Evening. Shure

7   News from the Democratic Convention are that Mr Polk of Tenesee and Mr Wright of New York are the nomenees for President and vice President,[10] I got ½ Doz Good Roasting years Out of Our Garden to day for table use, They were fine and the 1st that we have had this year — And as for Greens we have [had] Some Every day for dinner for Several weeks back, we have also had Squashes and redishes &c.

8   I paid Mr Tainter to day $13.80 for 6 Doz Packs of Cards that I got from Him Some time ago — He paid me by my acct with Him $13.50 and ten Dollars and 25 cts, which pays his Rent up to 16th of June, inst.

9   After Dinner to day I wrode Out and took my Boys with

---

[10] George M. Dallas of Pennsylvania became Polk's running mate in 1844.

me, and we went through by Old Jones, then through by Col Bingaman but Could not see my mare and Colt at all

10　Nothing new has transpired New, not at all, I Saw this
morning the Convicts to the Penetentiary　Buel was the oldest of
the three, and he is put in for 12 years — the other two was put in
as follows viz [blank]　I Loaned Mr. McCants five Dollars To
day. Bill Nicks was down to day from Rodney — and went back
again to day

11　Nothing new　Buisness is Some what Dull, Last night
Mr Fleming was Married to Miss J. R. Stockman.

12　Nothing new. Buisness has been very dull, Jim Commenced to make a Shed Roof in the yard to day after Breakfast, I
Sent to the Mill and had the stuff hauled up.

13　I Bot ten Barrells Corn to day at fifty Cents per Barrel,
Ratification Meeting to day at the Court House and a Mr Davis
Spoke, Considerable Shooting of Cannon &c.

14　This has been a remarkable dull day and we are Likly to
have many more of the Same, I had my Large Sorril Horse Shod
all around to day Obrins Shop. This Job I won from Him, Mr
Reynolds paid me to day Six Barrells of Corn and owes me still a
Ballance of five Barrells

15　Buisness was dull and nothing new

16　Nothing new　The River still on the rise,　The Mousouri
River Still Rising　I had my Big Sorrill Horse put in harness　He
works very well. I drove him Out to day and nearly to the Woodville Bridge, then Came back, Near Col Wilkins Residence we
stoped and Cooled off, got Some Black Berrys, I had the Children
[and] Bub. Brustee with [me]

17　I Sent Jack and Winston Out to Pick Black Barrys to day
and they came back without any, Saying they Could not find any.
I went out and took Frank and Jim and my William and we got
two Baskets quite full, Those we got to make a Cordial with

21　To day has been a pleasant and Sort of a buisness day
with me. I Saw Mr Charles Gregory to day and I Bot four head of
Cattle from Him, and paid him Thirteen Dollars for them, ie for
the four, 1 Cow, 1 Bull and 2 young heiffers. The Conditions are
as follows [blank]

22　[It was] to day instead of yesterday that I Bot the Cattle
of Mr Gregory　So the Above is a mistake Certain

July 4　To day was a very remarkable warm day and the City
was unusually Gay

10   Old Mrs Minor[11] was Buried this Evening Out at her Home place   Nothing new, more than the River has Commenced Falling at this Point to day and will Continue I Expect to fall

11   Reports are in town that there is considerable Sickness in Vicksburg and that there was five Deaths the night before Last. Mrs Judge Martin was One that Died On that night   Mrs Levy the Jews wife Died under the Hill this morning. She Left a child only 5 days old. The Cause was a cheap midwife. A Mr. [blank] got married to a Miss [blank]   They wranaway and was married at City Hottel   She was out a[t] Phill Greens

14   I worked untill 12 O'clock, then closed and after Dinner I took All the children that I could well get in my Carriage and Drove Out in to Col Bingamans Pasture On the Woodville Road, I thare cut 3 water Mellons that I Bot or had in the Carriage, which was more than we could all Destroy.

15   Nothing new. Buisness dull quite so.

16   Buisness still very dull, and nothing New, Little Tho Mc-Cants Commences To Moove from his Residence Down in the Bottom at Mrs Mahans, My dray is mooving him and my Little William ran off down with the Drayman and Staid untill night, Mr Jordans Ellin is sick, was taken yesterday

17   News from Philadelphia is that there is another Out break in that City between the Native Americans and the Irish   Private Letters reports that Something Like an Hundred has been Killed. So be it   I was after Mr Cannon to day to pay me the two hundred dollars that he Owes me and he promised to pay me as soon as he could

18   Nothing new. Our Little Phillip Came Home, ie was Brought home very Sick.

19   Nothing new that I Know of, Buisness dull very — Little Phillip died to day a Little after 7 Oclock   Poor Little Child   He must be Harmless

20   Buisness very dull, Nothing new that I know of. The River is Still very high, but is reported to have Commenced falling a Little, Our Little Phillip was Burried this morning   God Bless Him

21   Buisness was dull, Yates takes a man up who he thinks was about to Steal his Horse, had him put in Jail, After Dinner this Evening I wrode Out to McCants old residence down in the swamp Like and wrode down as far as the Bridge, through the

---

[11] This was Mrs. Katherine Minor, widow of Stephen Minor and mother of William J. Minor. See Adams County Will Books, II, 279-82.

water, took my Little William a[nd] Bryon and Mcs Jhon with me, We got a Little wet

22   Nothing new has transpired to day. I was about to [go] on a hunt to day but give it Out   Mr Patterson and Dr Broom was agoing but none went. This has been a mighty dull day

23   Nothing new, Only the River is falling a Little at this point, and I am glad of it, &c.

24   Buisness is very dull indeed at present

25   Nothing new more than there was a Large Barbacue On Pine Ridge to day. There were Several Speakers on the Ocasion; Mr Geo. Yerger, Mr Ogden, Mr Shie[1]ds, Mr Jeff Green, Mr Thorp, Col Bingaman and several others, I did not get thare until Late and did not hear Some of them Speak, There were about 70 or 80 Ladies, and Gentlemen to the Amount of Proberly 400. The party was pleasent indeed very, no One Drunk   I wrode Out in my Buggy and took my Little William with me

26   Nothing new. Buisness Only Tolerable   I wrode down to Smiths this Evening and found my white Cow Dead and had a Hole through her head Just below the Eye   Seems to have been Shot by Some One, Thus it is that man Kind will act, thus it is &c

27   Democratic Meeting to day   Capt Johnson spoke,[12] The two Basonets got offended at Some remarks that was made, and has Join the whig Partee. (who cares)   Louis Hardwic undertakes to steal my white sow but could not shine. Mr Rose prevented him, made him Let her go, 1st Said that he got her from Dr Merrell and when he took her to the Dr he told the fellow that he never Sold him any Such Hog and made [him] let her go. I went down this Evening to the quarretine ground with Mr. Patterson to take a hunt and we got but very Little indeed, I Killed 2 Ducks, 1 indian hen, 1 Beckroach, 3 Snipe. Mr Patterson Killed 2 Beckroaces, 1 Small Snipe, [with] my Pulling Gun

28   I remain Home all day after 12 Oclock   Nothing new. Buisness dull, very indeed

29   I received a note from Mr McCant and I sent him twenty Dollars, ie is [the amount] I had Loaned him Some time ago and ten to day and he sells the Cow to me on these Conditions, ie that I could take choice of the Cows or take them both, and if I did not want them I could Sell them for him and pay myself Out of the money, &c and I went Out to Mr Farmers and got the two Cows, and Drove them Home, &c.

---

12 "Capt. Johnson of Jefferson" County discussed the tariff and Texas questions. See Natchez *Free Trader,* July 31, 1844.

30   Nothing new has transpired during the day. Buisness dull quite dull indeed, I got a Sack of Salt to day from Mr McAlister on acct. &c   Deer are very plentifull at present and I am told that there [three] were Killed by young Sayres and Drayman Gim & Boy Martin   Great times these are

31   Buisness very dull and nothing new

August 1   Nothing new.

2   I got up quite Early this morning And had my horses Saddled up and went to the Landing to Cross in Company with Mr L. David and Mr Mitchell   We went across the River and down on the other Side to Mr Bislands Plantation or Mr W. Smiths. We wrode out through the place into the Back Grounds where we were soon into the water. We first tried to wride and Hunt but we Soon found that would not do, we then went to the fence and made our Horses fast and took a Hunt on foot. We were not more than 3 Hours out before L David Killed a fine young Doe, He Killed this However in Mr Smiths field, We took a Bite to Eat and then Seperated to meet again about 2 Oclock and I went up in the field and then out into the back water and thare I got a shot at a Long Distance with my big gun, and accidently Killed a Large Doe, Only One Shot hit her and that took her Just back of the head and past down out of the mouth and broke out a tooth, She was with young   I Killed a Rabbit, 1 Patridge, 1 Beckeroach. David Killed 1 Small Deer, 1 Beckeroace. Michel Killed 1 Partridge and that was all

3   Buisness Only Tolerable dull   I was out to the tract to day and saw a Race between Black Jack a[nd] Rodolph. They were to have run a mile and repeat   The bet was $500 on Each mile. Of[f] the[y] went and black Jack won the first Heat very Easy and the Second he ran against the fence or fell against it   Broke it down. Killed himself &c. and Lost his Race so it was a draw race between them, Mr Kenney paid me this Evening five Dollars in money and a pr of Shoes per Jim 1.50   This was in part pay of Rent

4   Nothing new   Two Cases of yellow fever reported in New Orleans   Tis Said that the[y] Came from vera cruse [Vera Cruz], I dont believe it. I wrode Out this Evening to the Col. Bs Pasture and saw my Colt   He is nearly Large Enough to Break. Did not see the mare at all

5   Nothing new. Buisness tolerable   Money scarce, City Healthy &c   I was Schooling my Children

6   Nothing new   Buisness dull. City Healthy and no

fights　　Clay Party trying to get up a Strait Out party to be Composed of Mechanicks, I made a Bet to day with Mr Morgan of
twenty five Dollars viz. He bets me that those ten States viz. will
go for Mr. Clay as follows Massachusetts, Vermont, Connecticut,
Rhode Island, New Jersey, Deleware, Kentucky, Ohio, N. York,
Tennessee, and if One Single One of those did not he would Loose
the Bet &c　　Mc[s] Dick has been on the Loafing Orders to day
and has gone of[f] from him on the City Somwheres

　　7　　Buisness very dull, Nothing new that I know of. Old Mrs
Erheart Came to Our House yesterday with her Servant &c　　Bill
Nix down from Rodney, reports all well. The River has been Rising
for a day or two, and has risen above Considerably: the Like was
never known before I believe, Several reports in the City about 2
murders that was said to have been Committed at the Convention
in La. the other day. I Cant believe them myself

　　8　　Bill Nix Left this morning Early on some Boat for Rodney.
Dr. Applewhite and Moss his partner has a fight this Evining in
thare Store　　A. P. White was Beating him with his fist and Moss
was Saying in a very Low tone, dont, dont, oh dont! It was a quiet,
very quiet affair

　　9　　The Excitement is fast Commencing about the Election. I
care very Little who is Elected, Natchez Guards at there Armory
had a meeting and a marching and wound up thare meeting with a
fight. In the first place Shanks and the Capt. Page has a quarrell,
After a Little Capt Page and W W W. Woods has a fight　　Page
caught him around the necke and choked Him wonderfully: untill
he was Seperated. Great times, we have them, I bet Mr Jaqamine
to day 1 pr shoes that his young heiffer from the Cow that I won
of him would not have a calf in year from this date and I bet him
1 pr shoes that my Horse would out walk his &c.

　　10　　News from Mobile County to day in Alibama favorable to
the Demmocrats,　Two Meetings to night in the City — One Demoic
in the Court House, the other Whig Strait Outs in the City Hall,
There numbers were nearly equal　　Whig Speaker Seth Cox &
Valow, Democrats L Saunders and Sam Walker, N. Claibourne. As
Soon as the meeting was Over the Rain Commenced and raind untill
1 Oclock prety hard　　The rain was much wanted indeed. Cisterns
were nearly Out. Mc[s] Dick went home this morning after having
been Loafing about for 4 Days &c.

　　11　　James Tooley was Burried this Afternoon in the rain, for
it Commenced to rain and thunder very Soon after they Started
So they were all in it. He was a Free Mason, The wether was So

498

unpleasent to day that I remaind home all day. A Little Boy of Mr Leopole under the hill was Drowned yesterday Evening in the River   He was in to Swim with Franks Brother and Some other Boys.

12   To day has [been] a rainy day and a Dull very dull One. Nothing New. There are Some Election news in town to day in favor of the whigs   The young heifer from the Jaqumine Cow is now in the Spanish Bayou. She fell in there to day.

13   A Mr. Clark Came to me this fore noon, and brought me a Saddle and Bridle and [said] that St Clair Sent it and told him to get ten Dollars on it   I told him at Once that I could do no such thing but that I would Let him have Seven Dollars on it   Just what I told him and that I would give no more   I had told St Clair that I would give no more than that for the Saddle and Bridl. The man Clark then Said that he would take the Seven Dollars On it and that St Clair had told him to take it, and Said that he was fully authorized to Dispose of the Sadle or Leave it as a Collateral for the payment of the Seven Dollars, and I took a written statement of the fact from him &c   Some of Our Citizens are getting home from the North. To day I Loaned a Mr. M Gibert fifty Dollars and took his note for fifty five Dollars payable in Sixty Days after date. Indorsed by William Wren   I hope it will be paid thats all, Billy is Sick to day and takes Pills

14   We had some Little rain to day and most Everybody in the city thought it would Continue and prevent the big Barbacue that is to Come of[f] to morrow tho it Soon Stopd and cleared off   Buisness tolerable Only

15   Nothing new. To day is the day of the Democratic Barbacue   At an Early Hour the[y] assembled on the Bluff and marched up the Street and I think it was the Larges[t] procession that I have Ever Seen in this City on any Ocasion, and they were Joined by many others On the Road. I wrode Out in the afternoon and took a Look at them. Oh they were a great many indeed about I think 2000 persons — it all passed off in Beautifull Stile and so pleasent   Did not see a realy Drunkin man on the ground   Dempsey P. Jackson came near geting in a fight by offering to Bet rarther too Loud   Jim Eacon and Nob Strictland and Mr Rowley was Discoursing him. He soon stopd talking.

16   Thom. Purnell was Burried yesterday   He Died Out at his Residence, where he has been Confined to his Room for Six weeks, Drinking Whiskey: tis said that it was Liquor that took him, Grafton Baker another individual who Flourished here in the

way of the Inquisition a few years ago is now in the work house in
New Orleans for vagrancy. He was bare footed when I herd from
him Last   So mote it be, I have turned the horses in upon the
garden and will Soon Commence to plough it up for turnips

    17   Nothing new. Buisness tolerable Only. The city Healthy.
The wether fine — Some news from Kentucky and Moussoury and
Ilenois — all in favor of the whigs

    18   Reports were in circulation this morning that Mr Simon
Murcherson had beat his man Arther very Severely on Friday
night with a Picket that he pulld off of the fence and that the Picket
had a nail in it which Stuck in the Poor fellows head, and that
the man Arther had Died Last night. There was Considerable talk
about it. So much so that Several Persons had went to Esqr Woods
and he sat down and wrote a note to Mr Murcheson about it.
Murcheson wrote back a note Stating that he, the Esqr, could ask
Dr Lyle, but in the mean time he had him *Burried* or there would
have been an Inquest held on this Evening, over the Body — Reports Seys that he beat the Poor man from 9 Oclock to about 10
Oclock at night when he was herd to hallow no more. Plain
case   This has been a Dull Evening with me   I have remained
at home all day   Did not wride out — William and Charles wrode
out in the Evening

    19   Buisness has been dull, Chancery Sale took place to day
at the Court House. It was Property that was mortgaged by Mr
Barlow & Holton, York and Dick, John, Speed, and Several weomen
were Sold and so[me] more men, but I dont Know what they
Brought — I believe there was none brought more than $700. In-
quest was held on the Body of Arther belonging to Mr Murcheson   They were 14 in number. They Looked at the head, found
it very much Bruised. Did cut it Open   Did not strip him nor
Look at his back. No One, Says One of them, is authorized to
work without Pay and the Law Seys that a Dr shall have fifty
Dollars for Oppening the head &c and no One would say do it So
they closed the man up again and Said he Died with Congestion of
the Brain, Thus it was and thus it is, &c. Livine Mitchel VS. Davis
the gin wright for Harbouring her girl. Held to bail in $2000 for
Court. Twenty-five dollars, the guards paid rent up to the first of
Sept 1844

    20   Nothing new to day. Buisness has been as dull as One
could Expect it to be to day — Our City is healthy and that is about
all that we can Bost of at Present, Edward Paid me One Dollar

to day that he has owed for 3 week or 3 months. I believe I won it from him on a Race

21 No thing new. Buisness Dull quite so

23 The forenoon of to day was Bright and Suny tho the afternoon [was] quite Cloudy and Rained very hard for a time Thundered very Loud and the Catholic Church was Struck and a very Large hole made in it Was Struck away near top Knocking off Some of the Staging and doing Some Considerable Injury to the Base or portions of the Steple, Some portion of the thunder bolt poped Down on the tin guter on the South side of the House. Nothing new to day. I paid Mr Brown to day $5.25 for the repairs on my Dray that Billy Broke, &c. and Still owes a Small Ballance, Somthing Careless about it, I do assure you

25 Nothing new. Buisness is dull. The city quite Healthy, tho Considerable Sickness in the Country though not of a Serious nature, There was a Large Whig meeting in the Court House to night and a Long Speech from Mr McMurran He spoke Principly on the Bank and after he quit Valeauo, the Carriage maker, made I am told a very abusive Poor Speech, Subject Gen Jackson, Col Bingaman was at Kains Coffee House amoung Foureigners Speaking of the American Flag &c, playing Cards &c Bill Nixs wife has a child Last week So I am told

26 Nothing new After 12 Oclock I closed my Shop and wrode out in my Buggy taking my two Little Daugters and Bub Brustee, Mary Jorden, and 2 Little B Boys behind I went arround by Mrs Smiths and came arround by the Woodville Road, Winston was on my grey nag, I saw Mc and His William Out there in the old field

27 Nothing new to day, more than that the Jackson La. Convention[13] had adjourned untill the 12th of January where they are then to Sit in New Orleans, Poor Buisness that. I received a Letter to day from New Orleans from Mrs Miller. It was short and told me that she had hyred Out [blank] at ten Dollars a month, but did not say anything about the Difficulty between Mr Miller and Francios. She is Cunning, Some what, I Saw Judge Dubison to day and I wanted to Know of him what he would take for the Natchez Island, and he told me that he Could not tell what the Owner of it would take for it but would write to him and Let him send On the Instructions, titles, &c and would Let me Know, I Saw Judge Dunlap to day and I wanted to Know of him what he would take

---

[13] The Louisiana convention which drafted the Constitution of 1845 met first at Jackson and later moved to New Orleans.

for his Buggy and he Said he had been offered Sixty Dollars for it So I Said no more at the time   Buisness Dull Quite So, I rested Bad Last night, had bad Dreams, and was suffering with the Poison from Antonios bean for the Corns, &c   To day there was a tryal before Esqr Potter and the Parties were a Mr Gibson VS. the Daughter of Poor Old Sam Gibson who the world Knows to be free, but during the Inquisition She and her mother went Out to Stay with this Gibson and now he puts up a Claim to her, by Saying that Sam G. her father belonged to his Father and that he had went Out of the State and was set free and returned to it again. Thus he became the Property of Said Gibson under Some old Law passed so seys Potter in 1807 — Greate God, what a Country, The Suit went in favor of Gibson[14]

28   I gave my wife $20 this morning for use of the Children &c. Nothing new to day. Buisness only tolerable Kentucky news is not so favorable to the Whigs as was reported to be the other day. Big Discussion yesterday in the Street between Col Bingaman and Mr James Stockman. Poltics was runing high   Tariff was the topic

29   The City is reported healthy, and the River is falling very fast indeed, Nothing new at Present in the City. Buisness still dull. I am about tracting for Some Cold at 35 cts per Barrell, Margaretts very sick at her mothers; Mrs Amees two Little Daughters was down at my House, and I went home with [them]. N. O. Papers of 25th inst. reports One Death by yellow fever, Considerable Sickness in Woodville   I understand that Old Mr Jerry Watson Died a few days ago and old Maj. Mibblen also had Died, and Old Madam Sharlot that used to Live under the Hill was Dead   She died at Mr Rouths Plantation

30   Nothing new   Buisness tolerable Only.

31   To night Came of[f] the grand Torch Light or Strait Outs meeting. It was very Large indeed

September 1   Buisness has been tolerable Fair   Nothing new tho, I have not felt very well for Several Days past   I and Charles and my William wrode Down Late this Evening to the Gilbert Land and the water has Just past of[f] and the place is mudy and Smells bad, The grass has grown very high

---

[14] Samuel Gibson, free man of color of Natchez, died in 1832 (see "Estate of Samuel Gibson," Adams County Probate Records, File 63), but for a statement to the effect that he was still alive in 1844, see Carter G. Woodson, "Free Negro Owners of Slaves in the United States in 1830," *Journal of Negro History,* IX (1924), 42. According to Woodson, Gibson took his slaves to Cincinnati in 1844 and settled them on free territory.

2   This has been a Powefull warm Day, oh very very and a few more such days and we will have Sickness. I think tho Our City is at present one of the healthyest places I know of

3   Nothing new. Buisness only tolerable   The town is Some what Lively on acct of the Excitement that is being got up for the Barbacue on the 5th inst.

4   Our City is all Excitement in the way of Politics   Strangers are Coming from Every Direction to be ready for the Barbacue that is to Come off on to morow in Capt Minors Pasture, Buisness has been briske Some what to day

5   The whole City was on the walk. Everything Look brisk to day   I was as buisy as I could well be a part of the forenoon, and after the Long procession passed Out, and got Out to the Ground Some time I Started Out myself and Looked at them a while, There was Some four or five thousand Persons On the ground I have but Little [doubt], I allowed the Boys to close the Shop for a Short time in order for them to Hear the Speaking: all my children Except One was Out Looking On. I herd a part of Mr Mathewsons Speech and a part of Mr Wm Yergers, and a part of Mr Smylies and in the Afternoon a part of Mr Prentess

6   We had as much as we could do well in the Shop and did no bathing at all   We had not the time. The City Hotel and Mansion House is as full as they can well be

7   Our City is at this time Healthy and the weather is very warm and Our Streets are remarkable Dusty, and tis [my] Humble Opinion That we will Have Sickness here in less than 10 Days — it is now reported to be very unhealthy in Woodville, Miss. and tis Said to be fever

9   Our streets are very Dusty at present, Charles went up to Jefferson yesterday, wrode my Grey Nag. Winston Staid in Our Shop below. There are Several Sick Persons in Natchez from the Swamps on the other Side — Dr Gegan Died to day at his residence on the Other Side, His Death was very suden indeed, A man by the Name of Logan also Died to day under the Hill

10   Buisness has been tolerable Only. I do nearly all the work myself.

11   Nothing new. Buisness has been dull, I wrote a Letter to day and Sent it to New Orleans and also Sent very near two Bushells of Corn meal, Sickness Continues to be bad in a new place, ie Woodville   I had no idea that it would have been so as it is represented to be, The worms are said to be very bad in Cotton fields. I Can hear of them in Every Direction up and Down the River, yes

Every way. Charles Young got home this Evening from Jefferson County. He went up on Sunday. Democratic Meeting to night at the Court House. Judge Dunlap Spoke, and tis Said to be a very Cold affair indeed, Greate meny Left the Court House before he quit speaking. I am Sorry, I am Sorry for I Like the man, Miss Alexander Died yesterday Evening with Congestive fever I herd She is a neace of Mr Jno Alexander &c.

    12   Our streets as usual pretty Dusty and the City still remains in good Health Nothing new

    13   I took my gun Early this morning and went down to the swamp and On my way down I Shot 1 Squrrel on the Hills and went down in the Bottom and Shot twice at some grey Snipe or plover and got 11 of them Killed 1 more squrrell — Went on Down and found that the Cotten was perfectly Striped of all there Leaves in some places, and after Looking at it for some time I came to the Conclusion that instead of an Injury it was a Benefit to the Cotten Growers, for all the Lower Bolls would open and the worms did not affect none but the very smallest Kind of the young bolls and that the Cotton was not as subject to trash, as if Left in its natural state, and that the Hands will pick more than they Could if the worms had not have Eaten the Leaves, I then Went to Mr B. Winns Found them all well. I Stoped on the way and Caught some Fish just below the popaus [pawpaw] Patches, They bit very well. A young man Came to where myself and William was fishen by the name of Harrison Tibles, who was then Cutting wood from the Land of Mr Sargent.

    14   Nothing new. Buisness was somewhat Dull, tho not so much so as was yesterday, for in absence yesterday the Boys did not take in but 75 cts Quite a Slim afair indeed, Dr Cartwright to day made a speech on the Tarriff and declared himself in favor of Mr Clay and that he intended to vote for him, At night there was a speech to the Strait Outs by Judge Montgomery, and by Col Bingman, The meeting then adjourned. There was a good many present. Mr McCants took his Cow home this Morning. She was the Little Ball face Cow and wore a Bell on her neck &c. Jack and Winston had a quarrell to night. Winst struck him

    15   Buisness was dull, Jasper & Calvin Winn[15] Brot up my Cow from the Swamp It was the Cow I got of Mr Gregory. She was a sort of Red Brindle, with wide Horns

    16   Nothing new. The Poor Little french Boy that Died yes-

---

[15] Jasper and Calvin Winn were sons of Baylor Winn, who owned land on the Mississippi River, below Natchez. His daughters were Emeline, Sarah, and Mary.

terday from a Fall in the Botanic Store was Buried to day. He was about 3 years old I think

17 Nothing new. Five Counties herd from in the Vermont Ellection for State officers and the officers on the Whig Side has a majority of 121 votes   Late in the Evening or this Evening I took my Horse and the children and Jack and went up to the Lake above the mill and I fished for a few minutes and I caught 1 and William 1 and Jack 3 and we come home to Super, Bob. brought Home my Buggy this Afternoon from Browns work Shop. I paid him Seven Dollars for Bob. and took his receipt for the Same &c. Barney Kelly was married to night to a young Girl.

18 Our Streets are quite dusty again, Tho Our City is at Present Healthy. Judge Covington[16] Died To day near Dinner time, Winston went up to Shave him   The Poor Man was taken on Saturday Last and Died to day. I Sent a Sovergn to New Orleans to Day   It was One that Mrs Miller sent to me to get her Some Quinces, which I Could not get any no where, I did not mention that Some time Last week the Rats Eat up my Trubiale or Mexican Bird, I Bought Eight rat traps to day to Kill Rats with, to pay them with, for Eating up my Birds &c.

19 Nothing new. The wether is warm, very I think for the Season, Our City is still Considered Healthy tho the Yellow fever is said to be in Woodville very bad yet   We Aught to bee very thankfull for Our good Heath to Our Blessed Redeemer, I remained Home all the while &c. I Gave five Dollars and fifty cents to day for a Barrell of Flour at Capt Caradines

20 Our City Continues to be both Healthy and dull, and nothing appears new. Mr Jake Tospott Came up to day and reports all well below in New Orleans

21 The Papers dont Say anything about the Sickness in New Orleans but Several Gentlemen up from New Orleans Seys that it is Quite Sickly thare, Mr Eligha Smith Came and paid me twenty five Dollars this being the amount of a note that I Bot of Mrs Smiths

22 Buisness Tolerable, Nothing new that I Know of. I took my Horse after Dinner and wrode Out. Charles, Wm and Richard was along   We wrode down by Mrs Smiths old Field and Down by

---

16 Levin Covington, well-known plantation owner, had been president of the Adams County Board of Police. His will, dated the day of his death, left his property to be equally divided among his three children and wife, Grissilla Cassandra Covington, exclusive of her community-property rights in Louisiana. See Adams County Will Books, II, 287–88; Adams County Court and Police Board Minutes, 1832–1845, entries for 1834, 1835, 1838.

the creek and thorough to the river and up. I found they had been making a prety good Levee Down on the creek, the Land tho I think is too Low Ever to be worth Anything more than a Pasture, The Sick Man Mr Moody Died to day at Mr M. Lindos and Some people think with yellow fever

23   Mr Gregory told me this morning that my young cow in the Swamp was troubled with worms from a cut or Snag that she got in the Swamp and that I aught to try and Get her Out of it if I Could &c. Billy Gets my dray Harnes from the River and I paid a man One dollar for Geting it out. The River is still a Falling Rapidly I believe

24   I took my Horse this mornin about 11 Oclock And wrode down to Mr B. Winns   I did not See him. I returned to the House and Drove up my Little Heiffer that I got of Mr Gregory   I had my Little Wm with me and I had some Considerable Trouble to Drive her Home, tho we Got her safe Home, I took my Mesho Gun with me and Killd One Squirrell   Only Shot Once. My 3 dogs Don, Rome and Rose Caught a Rabbit on a fair run Down below Fords fence

25   Nothing new to day. Our City is still Healthy tho Buisness is dull. Bob. Rabee Leaves town with a Large Lot of Passengers to go to the Church Hill[17] Barbecue which is to take place to morrow.

26   This was or is the day that the Barbecue Comes of[f] at Church Hill. Mrs Miller Came up from New Orleans Last night and brought her five Daughters up with her and a Servant. The[y] Came up about 11 Oclock Last night On the Concordia, and all was well

27   Nothing new. Mr Rabes team Came in this Evening from the whig Barbecue at Church Hill and they were the wetest Set of People you Ever Saw almost. Fire has been very agreeable all this Day.

28   Nothing new   Buisness very dull, My old Shop chimney Caught on fire to day and was Burned out very well indeed — Mr A. Kenney paid me ten Dollars on his Rent to day. I bot a Satin vest and pr of Pants to day: Cost $8.50 in all.

29   Nothing new   Buisness Tolerable Dull, After I Closed my shop I Took a wride this Evening and I took my Horse and wrode out to Look for my Horse but I could not find him

30   Nothing new and buisness Dull, This Evening Waller and

---

[17] Church Hill, in Jefferson County, was a community some fourteen or fifteen miles northeast of Natchez.

Stewart had a Sort of a fight. Stewart took up a Brick to Strike him with and Waller Knocked him down with a stick or Struck him Several times with his stick   Bruised his face Considerable. They put him in Jail for want of Bail and Waller gave Bail in the Sum of one Hundred Dollars, Greate many persons in town to day. The city Looked Lively. A Bet, Play or Pay. To day Mrs Miller Bets Mr Jaqumine a ten Dollar pr of Boots Vs. a ten Dollar Bonet that Mr Polk would be Elected President of the United States.

October 1   Nothing new   Buisness Dull quite So.

2   Nothing new. Buisness Dull. Mr H Patterson and Mr Crizer went Down into the Swamp to day to take a hunt and they Came back with two Turkeys but neither will say which of them that did Kill the turkeys, They went Down as far as Cypress Bayou.

3   Nothing new.

4   Nothing new. Buisness Continues Dull. I Got Mr Scheling this Evening to tune the Piano that we Borrowed of Miss Fany Brustee

5   Nothing new   Buisness Continues very dull, tis strange   Greate Quantities of Goods are being receivd Every day by Our merchants

6   Nothing new. After I Closed the Shop this Evening I wrode Out with McCary. We took a short wride, This afternoon the Steam Boat J M. White passed Down with a Delegation that was going to Baton Rogue Barbecue. There were 40 I Suppose On Board. On Saturday night the Straight Outs[18] went Down with the Big Ball, the Humbug Ball[19]

7   Nothing new. To day has been an uncommon Dull Day, and there is no news to day what Ever

8   At the Present writings I am not prepared to Say what Sort of a day this has been.

9   No acct taken at the above date. None at all

19   I was Out to the race tract to day to See the Races   It was a Race between the Farmers Colts, The race was won by Mr McNultys Filly, It was a mile and a repeat   McNultys, Jno Flemmings, Mr Hoggatts and a Mr Fultons. After the 1st heat Mr Flemmings nag was the favorite and then there was few would takers at that. None in fact. Then there was a Fight between Capt Dempsey Jackson and Mr Elward. Mr Jackson was Considerably

---

18 A Henry Clay faction.

19 This Whig method of arousing party enthusiasm had been used in the campaign of 1840.

beaten by Mr Elward. Greate many thought that he was struck by Some One Else. He was severely beaten Sure   It was a Political Concern, Mrs Miller and Family went down this Evening On the Princess.

21   Buisness was dull very.

November 1   Nothing new. The city is Lively at present. Party Politics are runing high, very indeed. News that the Steam Boat Lucy Walker is reported to have blown up and Burned up too at the Same time and has taken the Lives of a good many persons

2   Nothing new. More than Ellick McDonnell, Brother to the City Hotell Keeper, has Sloped off with the stakes of Several Gentlemen to the amount of ten or fifteen Hundred Dollars — so seys report. To day I paid an acct to young Brown of forty two [dollars] 10 cts for Lumber that I have got thare from time to time   I had an acct. V.S. him of $25 which he Allowed and I paid him the Difference, $17.10. To day I agreed to Let Mr Odell have the ten dollars that we had bet on the Election, on Conditions that if I won the bet he was to pay it back to me again, but if I Lost he Could Keep it, The bet was that Mr Shunk would receive a majortity of 5000 votes   All Sort of Speeches made on both Sides of the question

3   Nothing new, Buisness Tolerable fair, I went Down in the Swamp after Shut up Shop and Winston went along and took my Pulling Gun and he shot 1 wood cock and One Large Plover

4   To day the Election Commences, and it will be a warm affair, for they are Challenging a greate many Fouriegners, making them Show there papers — go it. It is what I like to see

5   Nothing new

6   Buisness Only Tolerable. Nothing new, Election news is Comming in to day

7   Nothing new. Buisness Only Tolerable.

8   Nothing new. I Sold the Little white Poney that I bot the other Day, to a Mr Brown for $15.00   I made 3.50 cts on the trade, I had an Oyster Supper this Night to our selves   Parties present, Mc & Brusttee, Wilcox & Myself

10   Considerable to do about the Ellections. As far as has been herd from the Democrts are ahead — both parties are Scared, Greatly Scared. Gim found my two Horses to day and Drove them Home

14   Mr Crizer makes a bet with Mr Wrigly of twenty five dollars that Mr Polk would be the President

25   Nothing new — more than there [is] a report in town that

they are Contesting the vote of New York — I dont think that it will do them much good

26   Nothing new. Not ½ the talk to day as there were yesterday about the Contesting of the New York vote, We took in the Shop to day $9.00 which is a very fine days gathering

27   Andy Leeper was at my House very Erly this morning wanting to Borrow money, but Couldent Come it. Count Dorsey Leaves this morning and Could not pay a ten that I Loaned Him 25th inst, Welsh paid me to day $16.25   This was an acct VS. old Billy Adams, witness by N. Barlow

28   Buisness was Tolerable fair to day   I made a Bet with Mr Rabee to night to this Effect   I bet him that Patona would win the money in New Orleans the 4 mile day, I bet him my Little Jaqumine Cow against his spoted Cow — I had the Glass Frames moved out of the Brick Store Down to the House in State St. No it is a mistake. It was not to day it was farther along   I Saw a race to day between the Quarter horse Bull and another Horse from below, The Horse Bull gave 17½ ft to the other Horse, and beat him 21 ft.

29   Buisness Dull &c. Loaned Mother $3 to Buy a Barrell of Pinders[20] with

30   Nothing new   I wrote a Letter to New Orleans this Evening by St Boat Princess, I Saw a race to day between Bull, the Great race Horse, a quarter, and another mans Horse from Louisiana, Bull Beat the Race 21 ft. so I herd, I was not very well this week, by no means

December 1   I remained at Home all day.

2   I Bet Mr Rose $12 to day that Patona will Beat the Big Stake in New Orleans. I Bet 12 to 10 of it. No Staks up.

3   Nothing new. Buisness tolerable Fair — I made two Bets with Mr St Claire to day as Follows. I bet him fifteen Dollars to ten that Patona would win her money, Play or Pay VS the Field: the stake was put in my hand, I then Bet him five Dollars more Even that Patona would Beat the field[21]

4   I went up to day and paid my note that was due to day to the Wemple Estate which was two Hundred Dollars. I also Sold Mr

[20] Peanuts. The word, along with "goobers," was used principally in the South.
[21] Johnson won these bets on the "Great Four Mile Stake" run at the Metairie Course at New Orleans on December 3, 1844. Peytona defeated Blue Dick— owned by Colonel William R. Johnson, known as "the Napoleon of the Turf" —in a race that attracted a very large crowd. All other entries, including Colonel Bingaman's Ruffin, failed to start. *American Turf Register and Sporting Magazine,* XV (1844), 569, 707–10.

Cannons note, that I held for two hundred to Mr Coontz, for two hundred 8 dollars provided that he gets $216 for it but two hundred five any how, ie if he does not pay the whole of the Interest, I Gave Capt Page the note I held of McAlister and Watson for 250 with the Interest On the Same I presume, which had a Credit On the back of it of One hundred fifty Dollars — he promised to Look over the Books and Settle it — I then went under the Hill and Bought 6 Bales of Hay that was then in the River at 50 cts per Bale and then Bot fifteen Bales of another man, and Gave him twelve Dollars for the fifteen Bales — Bull ran to day and was to give the Little Horse 30 ft in a Race but was beat 7 ft Even, Causing Emerson and Farrar to Loose Every thing they had, Horses and all So I herd

5 To day has been a pleasant day untill Evening Late and then we had a Light Shower of rain, which wet Some Hay that I had Spred Out in the yard to Dry; Six Bales of it   I hope it will be a good Clear Day to morrow that I may to Dry it, Mr McAlister paid me through Capt Page One hundred and 20 [dollars and] 18 ct   This was a Ballance On two hundred Dollars that I Loaned the House, 1842. The Store Act. was taken Out and it Left the above Ballance in my favor

6 Nothing new   Buisness has been fair

8 I wrode Out this Evening in my new Buggy And it went very Easy   I drove old Trim in it, Went Out to Mrs Scotts old Field   Took Little Dick along with me   Met Mc Out thare

9 Nothing new that I know of, Mr. Crizers Horse Bill and a Horse they Called the old Horse, belonging to a Mr Tilman, wran a Quarter to day and the old Horse won the race prety Eazy. The 3 young Barnards was trying to Sell there Cotton to day and the Best price they Could Get for it was 4 cents   This is what I would Call Low indeed.

10 News up to night from New Orleans that Ruffins was the Last Horse in a Race where there was three Entrys. Four mile heats. Moth won the Race and Sally Shannon was 2d in the Race,[22] I Lost 2 dollars and 2 Cigars on the Same

11 Dr Broom has his Furniture Sold to day at Auction, I Bot

---

[22] On December 8, at the Eclipse Course at Carrollton, near New Orleans, Colonel Adam L. Bingaman's horse Ruffin (a 5-to-4 favorite) ran third in a race against Moth and Sally Shannon. *American Turf Register and Sporting Magazine*, XV (1844), 757. In the previous spring Ruffin's time in a New Orleans race had been considered by a New Orleans reporter the best ever run in the United States, in spite of the fact that many turfmen elsewhere were disdainful of such reports emanating from New Orleans because of the comparatively light weights carried by horses on the tracks there. *Ibid.*, XV (1844), 113, 306, 314.

his Piano $62.00 and Several Small things, My Hay is all up, safe and in good order, Mr W Gay and Healy went Down to Mr Mosbeys to day and offered him the whole Amount of money that the property Sold for and his Judgment making in all ·Some $900 and Mosbey told him that he had nothing to do with it that it was his wifes Property &c. I Loaned Mr McCants five Dollars, ie I handed it to Farmer for him, per Contract or promise

12 Nothing new. I Sold my tin Box to day for five Dollars and I gave $4.75 for a Barrell of Flour to Mr Caradine, I pd to day for those things that I Bot yesterday, at Auction

13 Nothing new, Mc And Brustee and Wilcox was at my House to night. Took a Late Supper

14 Anto[n]io Gave me a white Dog to day that the Frenchman Left to him   G Brustee Left for New Orleans this Evening On the Princess.

15 I was tolerable buissy to day, and nothing new has Occured to day that I Know of   I wrode down in the woods this Evening, went down by the Bluff, went down by the new Levy that Gilbert is making and find that he is making a new fence that will Extend nearly arround his Land, I find a new road is being cut behind the Waltern Field, when Completed will be much nearer. His Land is falling in the River very fast indeed, The whole of there Lands are not worth much, Winston was along and he had my Pulling Gun. I Shot her once at a Flying Flox of Geese but did not get One, The Swamp is very Low, and very mudy. Not much Game in the Swamp

17 Nothing new that I Know of

18 Big Auction Sale Commences to day. I intend to Buy Some articles before the Sale is over

21 Nothing new   Buisy tolerable fair. I wrote a Letter to New Orleans this morning for Mother. She wanted Some money to pay small Debts with &c.

22 I took a wride this Evening down as far as Mrs Walterns plantation with Mc   We were hunting Cows. We Came back by way of the creek, found a new fence On the Ground &c.

23 A greate many persons in town to day, I paid $11.11 for some Little articles at Auction   I got them On Saturday

25 There were Considerable mirth in the City

26 A Miss Harman gets married to night to a Mr Cordell

31 Nothing new. I worked a part of the day in the Shop and then about 11 Oclock I Started in the Swamp to take a Small Hunt to have a Duck for my New Years Dinner tomorrow, I wrode down by Mrs Waltern place and I went through by the Gin and I Shot at a Flock of Rice Birds thare and Killd 3 of them, I then wrode and took up the Swamp and wrode up to a Bayou, then I crossd it and Started out for a Lake and in about a hour walking gave it up and Started back to my Horses and I found them after a while and I wrod down to the goose pond Lake. And thare was a good many Ducks in it. I got a shot and Killd Only One and I then went to another Lake and I Killed another one and as I Came Home I shot 1 Sky Lark and this was all I Shot.

1845

January 1   Buisness was prety good. Thank God my Family is all well this day and all my relations in Orleans and I am very glad indeed,   The Princess Came up to night and brot news that Oblemis had Shot a mans Head nearly of[f]   Killed him dead in-stanttar and had sloped off,   He got up here in the 1st Boat for I Saw him to day — Mrs Miller Sends up twenty five Dollars this Evening as Sharlots wages in New Orleans

2   Nothing has transpired more than very near 3 Oclock this Morning my Little third Daughter was Born.[1] She is a very Large fine Looking child, Mr Price at Mr Gales paid me his bill to night: 1.50 to the first instant

3   Nothing new has transpired that I have herd of, Buisness fair, I Bot 4 Barrells of Oysters to day at 9 Bitts per Barrell

4   Buisness was fair. Nothing new   Mr A Kenney paid me fifteen Dollars On rent this Evening.

5   Buisness Tolerable fair. Nothing new. After the Shop was Closed or I should have Said after Dinner I wrode Out in my Buggy to the old Fields of Mrs Smith, and fed my Cattle   There [are] 7 of them, namely — Old Spot & her Calf, Jaqumine Cow & Calf, Little Rose, Gregory heifer, & the Rabee Cow. All of them had on there Bells   Richard & Byron was with me & Charles and William wrode on Horse back. Mc Came out and his William and we Came in together, Butcher Mack Came to me to day to Know if

---

[1] This was Eugenia Johnson, who married Juanito Garrus, August 23, 1873. Adams County Marriage Records (Colored), XXI, 279.

I would Sell my Cow that is in the Swamp and I told him no I did not want to sell her and he tolde me a Lye and Left.

6 To Day the City Election Comes of[f] &c.

7 Nothing new. Buisness tolerable fair, I was at Auction to Day and bot the One Horse harness and a Clock and a Large Basket. Mr Stockman was Elected mayor of the City to day.

8 Jim Ploughed up the Garden to day to Plant Oats in to day — I Bot Some Stove Pipe at Auction to day and a Coat, 2 Bells &c.

9 To day has been a day of Some Events in this City. Dr Davis & Dr Frank has a fight to day in at Dr Franks office, Dr Davis was On him Sort [of] Choking him whilst the other was pulling his Hair, Quite a fight   Poor Oblenis is in the Point Coupee Jail[2] with heavy Irons on him,   He Said, I have understood, that if he had not been taken so soon that he would have Killed Capt [blank] of the St Landry — he Said he would have done it in 20 minutes more, for insulting his wife

10 Nothing new   Buisness prety fair.   Concert to night   Ethiopians Singers in the City. To night Last night of performance — I pd Mrs Wilcox three Dollars for her passage of Lucinda up on the Steam Princess from New Orleans.

11 I pd Mr McAlister to day twenty four Dollars to day for 1 Barrell of sugar, 56 lbs Coffee, 1 Sack of Salt which was got in 1843. Buisness was good to day, After Supper Some time I went arround to the Tremont House to the Raffle of my watch   It was put up at $70 and the chain was the Property of Jn[o] G. Taylor, and after all was set they Commencd throwing and I won it at the No. 8 throw   I threw Forty One, which won it very Easy. The next higest throw was 40, thrown by Mr O Morgan for Collins the Tinner, I Bot Out the chance of Mr Prewit, gave him Two Dollars for it, and then he threw and only threw thirty three, I gave a treat of five Dollars to the crowd and Left, J. G. Taylor then Came arround and paid me with what I Collected $52   I may say tho he gave me Forty Only, and the Ballance he will proberbly Sink   However I am Lucky to get off so well

12 Nothing new that I Know of, Buisness was Only Tolerable, yes a Little more So. After 12 Oclock I wrode Out in my Buggy to Jno Barlands Place, to Look for a Cow that I Bot of McCants that Came from the Barnard Plantation. But I did not See her

13 I was at Auction to day and Bot some Blacking &c, 35 cts

2 Johnson referred to the Pointe Coupee Parish jail at New Roads, Louisiana.

a Dozen, Nothing new to day   Buisness Dull to day Quite so I thought.

   14   Nothing new. Buisness dull Quite so. I Bot from Stockman & Taintor at Auction to day

To 1 Boue Knife 14/1	1.81
To ½ Barrell Rice	.81
1 pr. flat Irons	.60
3 Shawls @ 5/	1.88
1 piece Silk 26 yds 36 cts per yd	9.36
total	$14.46

   17   The streets are very Mudy. Very indeed. Buisness was dull very Seys the Merchants, tho I am glad that I have not Seen it plainly yet, I receivd a Letter this morning from Mr David Barland[3] requesting me to Loan him four Hundred Dollars untill he makes another Crop. He wanted to give a Bill of Sale as Collateral Security for the payment of the Same, I could not come it and I wrote to him to that Effect, Mr Wilcox Gave me a fine Barrell of Oysters to day

   19   Buisness was Tolerable. Nothing new. I wrode out by myself this Evening and took a Look at my cows &c. I Loaned Mr Waller to day ten Dollars.

---

   [3] David Barland was one of the most successful of the twelve free Negro children of Adams County white planter William Barland and his slave Elizabeth. In 1840 a local newspaper referred to him as "David Barland, Esq."; he owned a 300-acre plantation on the Mississippi River below Natchez; and he sold 16 slaves, 75 head of cattle, 20 hogs, 2 yoke of oxen and an oxcart, and kitchen and household furniture for $12,000. See Natchez *Free Trader,* May 11, 1840; Adams County Deed Records, BB, 475. Although he was occasionally listed in tax rolls as white, the U. S. census of 1840 designated him as the head of a free Negro family of six and the owner of eighteen slaves. U. S. Census Reports, 1840, Schedule I, Adams County, 34.

   William Barland, his father, had secured three substantial grants from the Spanish government, including one which embraced a considerable portion of the original Natchez townsite. In 1814, William petitioned the territorial assembly for authority to free his slave, Elizabeth, and their twelve acknowledged children. The assembly passed a law granting his petition, and in 1815 he emancipated all of them. Furthermore, his property was bequeathed to Elizabeth and the children by his will, probated in 1816. Petition of William Barland, December, 1814, Petitions and Memorials, Series D, No. 38; *Acts of Mississippi Territory,* 8 Sess. (1814), 40–41; Adams County Deed Records, H, 369; Adams County Will Books, I, 132–38; "Estate of William Barland, Senior," Adams County Probate Records, File 2.

   For David Barland's signed acknowledgment that he was one of "the issue of the said William Barland and Lisey his Wife who was a coloured Woman," see Petition of Children of William Barland, c. 1830, Petitions and Memorials, Series I, No. 97. For David's participation in the devision of his father's estate, see Adams County Deed Records, M, 157.

20 Nothing new. Good many Strangers in the City to
day   Some in attendance to the Grand Lodge and others returning
from the Court at Jackson &c. I thank the Lord that we are at
present all well

21 Buisness was very Good, for I made $12 in the shop to
day   Tis the best days work that we have had for a many a day,
I was up at Auction to day a[nd] Bot a childs Carriage for nine
Bits, Poor A G. Carpenter Died at 3 Ocolck this morning and was
burried this Evening, by the Fencibles

22 Buisness is tolerable good   Good many Strangers still in
the City

24 I got up this morning about 20 minutes After 4 and made
some arrangements to [go] to the Swamps On [a] Hunt in Company with Mr Patterson, He Killed 1 Large Blue crane and nothing
Else and I Killed 1 Squirell, 1 crane, 3 Larks and woun[d]ed another Lark that I did not get   We went down to Mudy Lake.

25 Nothing new, Buisness fair.

26 Buisness was Tolerable fair, After I got through with
work, I took my Horse and wrode Out to Col Bingamans To Look
for my Mare Kity Fisher, but I did not See Her at Last, She was not
among His Horses at all that I Could See, My Colt they told me
was Dead and Had died Some 3 weeks ago.

27 Nothing new To day. Buisness has been quite fair to day.
The Goods in the store of Mr Bradley is now to day agoing around
to the Court House to be Sold I Presume.

28 To day has been some what rainy tho not so much as to
prevent Buisness, Nothing new that I have herd of, I was at Auction to day and I Bot One Doz Razor straps at 9 cts a piece.

29 Nothing new. Buisness Tolerable fair, To day the Race
Came off between Rodolph & the Little Kentucky mare   The bets
were in favor of the Kentucky mare, and she won the Race very
Easy. Big Davis won Considerable On the Race, and I won Eleven
Dollars and Collected five on the Same Race very Easy

30 Nothing new has transpired that I have herd of, Buisness
Only Tolerable. I had my Measure taken to day for a new Coat I
Bot   I did buy a Large One Horse Cart to day from Mr Fields, and
I Paid him fifteen Dollars for it, Cash — I took a chance to day
in Mr McMicheals watch, I am in hopes I shall win it

31 Nothing new. Buisness Only Tolerable, Wilcox Gave me
five Dollars to take a chance in McMichels watch, which I took and
the number was 13. I took a number for Charles and myself at 14,
and a number for myself at 8, and I threw 36 but it would not win,

Mr Thomas Clay threw 42 which won it very Easy, But I am wrong in Saying that it was to night, for it was Sat Feb 1st that it was raffled off

February 1 Nothing new. I was at a Raffle to night of Mc-Michel watch and I could not win it. I Only threw 36, that was all, Capt Clay threw 42 which won it very Easy — I threw a chance for Dr Lyle and Only got 24. That was too bad

2 Nothing new.

3 In the Afternoon I wrode Out to Mrs Smiths old Fields and oh what a rain Caught me and my William. It poour down Some

4 Capt Minor Cut the End off his finger with the nail, by striking his Hand VS the Lamp-Glass — Mrs Linton has a Large Party at Her House to night, Great many has gone from the City, Yesterday was the day that they were to Commence to work the Swamp road. I am Glad of it myself

5 Nothing new. Buisness was dull Quite So. I Loaned Mr Sesh to day Fifty Dollars On a Note of a Mr Myres, due 24th Feb. 1845, The Conditions of the trade was that he would pay it himself if Myres did not So I took it

6 Mr Gilbert from below wants to Borrow One Hundred Dollars. Did not have it to Loan, From what I can Lern the Butchers have Stolen my Dark Brindle Cow that I had in the Swamp, I Bot 5 Canary Birds to day and paid $12.50 for them.

7 I Bot 3 Cannary Birds to day and paid 6 Dollars for them, They are very fine ones indeed

8 Nothing new. Buisness Only Tolerable, and all is well

9 Nothing new. After I had the shop closed up I took a wride Out in the Old Fields of Mrs Smith, and McCants was along too, and we took a Long wride together. He was Looking for his Cow but did not find her, I wrode Down the new road this morning for the first time. Tis Something of an improovment, I believe

10 Nothing new.

11 Nothing new. Buisness Good. I Bot a red and white Cow to day from Mr Fred Bure and paid him fifteen Dollars for her, and the Calf. I Bot a Cannary Bird to day from the Bird man for $2.00 and Sold it to Mr Broughton, of Port Gibson.

12 Money is in Greate demand I have [had] Several Demands for money to day But I did not have any. Brustee wanted $50, Mr Izod and Woods wanted $500, Capt Page for use of the House $100, but did not have any to Loan.

13 Nothing new, Buisness Only tolerable. Greate deal of Cotton in, &c. I Bot 33 Bushels of Oats to day at 33 3/d cts per

Bushell from Gaw & C. at the Landing and I Could have gotten them cheaper from Another, any other man, Yates the Stable man ran off Last night

15   Nothing new   Buisness Tolerable fair

16   Nothing new has Occurd that I Know of — I was part of the day a Looking for My mare and Horse but Could not find them

17   Buisness is some what dull, Capt Nevitt paid me One Hundred dollars that I Loaned him the other day

18   Nothing new   Buisness Tolerable Only, Mr Chamberlain Came in this morning and Said he would Like to Know how old the mule was and said when he came to town again he would Let me Know wether it would work or not &c. Mr Sergent wanted [to] Know if Mr Ford would make him an offer for his Land on the other Side of the River &c.

19   Nothing new. Buisness dull &c. I Sent Out to Col Bingamans to day and got my Horse home that had ranaway from me, and went Out thare

20   I Bot a Bob. tail Poney from a Mr Thoms M Yates for forty Dollars and is to Pay him in the Morning for him

21   Nothing new. I paid Mr Yates Forty Dollars for a Rone Poney: ie I paid him twenty three Dollars and a months Shaving and Mr Boyer Paid him fifteen dollars for me On Acct, Farmer was shot in the Back part of the shoulder to day by a man by the name of Gadsbury It was down at McAtee's Coffee House

22   To day was the Firemens Procession   A Small speech was delivered by W. W. W. W. W. Woods in front of the City Hotell,[4] Mr Deputy got in a Fight to day at McAtees Coffee House with Gim Aiken   They had too fights Among the firemen and I am told that they Flogged Deputy but I did [not] See it, but the way he did get Out and run was Very Singular, and a Duckman ran after him But Could not see him, Oh how he ran was fast

23   Nothing that I Know of, Buisness only tolerable   I took the Boys and wrode Out but did not find all the Cattle, The Jackumine Cow I did not See at all, I had Both of Mcs And all of mine, We went Out by Old man Jones and Came around the Cols House, Young William Waker Died this morning about 7 Oclock   He had the Consumption. Poor Fellow

24   Nothing new agoing on that I have herd of

4 The order of the procession was as follows: Neptune Fire Engine, No. 1; Water with Hose Carriage; Achilles Fire Engine, No. 2; Protection Fire Engine, No. 3; Relief Hose Carriage; Natchez Fire Engine, No. 4; and Hook and Ladder Carriage. The address of the occasion was delivered by W. W. W. Wood in front of the City Hotel. Natchez *Free Trader*, February 22, 1845.

25   Nothing new.

26   Nothing new, Buisness Geting dull, Mr Myre Paid me to day Fifty Dollars, this being the full amount of a note that I Purchased of Mr Seshe, I received by the Princess to night One natural[5] for a Lady, Price Ten Dollars, I wrode out this Evening on my Big Horse, and Took the Boys along with me

27   I Loaned Mr Seshe Thirty Dollars To day and he Promises To return the Same in a Couple of Days, I wrode Out this Evening and Drove up my Cows. Took Richard & Byron & Bub. with me

28   I Loaned Mr Vanater Ten Dollars to night and he promises to pay the Same On Monday next.

March 1   I was up very Early this morning for the Simple Reason that I did not go to bed Last night at all, McCary & Brustee, Wilcox and myself were up the whole night   W. and myself Beat them ten Games, we were 30 and they were 20. Thus we Quit

2   Mr Farmer Died this morning near 3 Oclock from being shot by Gadsbury. On wriding Out to day I found Some of my Cattle tho not all of them   There were two that I did not find at all, I must Look again

3   To day has been a very rainy day and the mud is deep in the Streets, Buisness dull of Course, I sent my mare Kitty Fisher Out to Mr Barlands Pasture to day by Winston and I Sent Jim Out to Mr Chamberlains this Evening to see if he had determined on what he would do in the case of the Cows and the mule trade, Mr Seshe Paid me thirty Dollars to day that I Loaned him the other week

4   Mr. Jaqmine and myself wrode Out to Mr Barlands to Drive in a Bull that I had Out thare, which we did with the Assistance of Mr Barland

5   Nothing New. I sent Jack and Gim Out to Mr Barlands this morning very Early to get the Little Bull that myself and Jaqumine drove in yesterday Evening   The Boys got in by Breakfast time with him, And this Evening about 5 Oclock I took Gim and wrode Down to Mr Fords Place to see a Cow that was Said to be mine and when I got thare it was I believe an Old Cow that I Drove Out of the Swamp some time ago. She then belonged to McCants. Dr Applewhite paid me $25 for One months Rent of Store to 1st instan.

6   Nothing new. Buisness Tolerable fair. To day the Tract of

---

[5] A lady's wig.

Land belonging to the Clement Estate was Sold and was Purchased by [blank] at [blank] per Acre. The Irishman that Stole Mr Roses Darkey and McClures Horse, was Brought Home to day by Benbrook and Samuells. They Caught them down in the neighbourhood of Red River

7 I drove my Bull Out to Jaqumines this Evening and I Looked over his Place   He is fast improoving his place, The High Court has decided that the Injunction Stand Vs the Banks. Thus they have not the Power to Collect by Suit, any more, The Billy Goat fell in Our Cistern yesterday Evening and was not found untill this morning, drowned of Course, Jim Painted the Bugy to day and then Commenced to drain water Out of the cistern to clean it &c. Mr Chamberlain Sent the mule Home

8 I was at the tract to day and Saw a Race between Rodolph & Ben Pryor, ½ mile Race, Perfect throw of it was Shure. Good many Small Bets made, tho not many Big Ones, Rodolph won the Race Easy Enough

9 To Marketing as usual and nothing more   Buisness was Tolerable fair to day and nothing new. Whilst the Sportsman are in town Buisness is Good but if it was Confined to Our Own Citizens it would be a Dry affair, Shure. I found my old mule to[o] this Evening and drove her up in the lot

10 Nothing New. Several Fights about the Town Last night   Mr Cheetum Knocked McDonald down with a Decanter, Drew a Pistol and cut Several Shines. Little Red Head Davis and Bunting has a fight   Bunting Knockd him down So I am told

11 Nothing new. To day the Guns or at Least the Cannon was Fired a Good many times in Honor of the Anexation of Texas, I gave One Dollar myself towards it, I am always ready for Anything. I would have Given the Same Amount of money to have fired for the Defeat of the Texas Anexation, Bill Nix Came Down Last night and brought his wife with him so I am told, I Subscribd five Dollars to the Race tract &c. I Bot a Pump to day from Dr Merrill for my Cistern at $15.00

12 I wrode Out this Evening To Look for my Horses and my Cows, I found nearly all them, The mising Part of my Cattle is a Large Dark Brindle Cow Branded on The Hip, She was in fine Order and was Taken From Out of the Swamp, I Sold Mr. S S. Prentess a Cannary Bird To day for Five Dollars and I Sold him a Cage for 2 Dollars which Sum he paid Like a gentleman. To Day I had a Settlement with Mr A Kenny And he produced a receipt of mine which date way the 6th of June and was a Settle-

ment to the 13th of May 1844. After deducting the amount of Cash
Paid Since that time and his Bill together which was $71.50 in all,
it Left a Ballance of $27.50 in my Favor. I then agreed to take his
two Journeys Promise for the 25 Dollars and Mr. Kenny Promisd
to pay the remaining 2.50 in Cash. So I took a Due Bill from the
two young men Thomas S Clark & G. A. Rice for the 25 dollars
which they Promise to Pay as Soon as Possible &c.

13   I had my Poney put in a Cart to day and Hauled up 12
Bushels of Oats from under the Hill   He works very well indeed   I am pleased with him very much indeed, I was Out this
Evening to the Lot making up the fence and we fixed it up Some
&c. The River is Rising very fast indeed, at this time, Mr. Polks
adress was received and Published this Evening.[6]

14   Nothing new To day, Buisness is Only Tolerable, I had
The Lot Ploughed up to day. Jim plowed with the Big Sorril Horse,
Mr Vanneter paid me ten Dollars that I Loand Him, a short time
ago, I had Seven Barrells of Damaged Corn Brought up from the
Landing this Evening, for the Cows &c.

15   The Democracy of this City Celebrated this Day by the
Firing of Cannon and One or two Public speeches this being the
Birth Day of Gen. Andrew Jackson. He is now Seventy Eight years
Old, There was a turn Out among the Boys and men too. Gen
Quitman and Mr Vanhozen Spoke, The Menagery Came to town
To day. Buisness was very Good to day.

16   Nothing new. Buisness Tolerable fair to day   I wrode
Out in the old Field to day and Drove home my Horses and
Williams Heifer. She was troublesome to Drive. Very

17   Buisness has been Dull in the Evening but was very Good
in the forenoon, Jim was Laying Out the Garden To day, I Took
the Children to the Animal Show to night   I paid for the Following Children, My William, Richard, Byron, Anna Anderson, Mcs
William & Robert, and Elen and Mary Jorden &c.

18   Nothing new. Buisness Tolerable Fair, Maj Young was
in Town To day and I paid him One Hundred Dollars for Charles
wages   I wanted to Know of him how we stood and he Said that
he had Kept no acct. whatever and I told him that I had the acct
but had not Looked over my Books to See. I paid Mr Wadsworth
twenty five Dollars for the Painting [of] the Botanic Store &c.

19   Tis the first day of the Races   I was Out to day and
Saw a very fine Race   The Race was between Ruffin, Marco,
Norma & Cripple, and Ruffin won it very Easy. It was 2 mile

---

[6] See Richardson (ed.), *Messages and Papers of the Presidents*, IV, 373–82.

Heat. Marco was Drawn after the first heat and he was Second in it, but in the 2d Race Noma was 2d and Cripple was Distanced Easy. I Lost $2.50 with Bully Henderson, $2 with Waller, and $5 with Mr McCray — Nothing new to day

20 I was Out to the tract to day a[nd] made several Bets. I Bet 2 to 1 with L. Harrison and Lost 10 to 5 with Jones & Lost 1.50 to 1 with the Stable man, and 1 with a Sportsman and 10 with Mr Mardice, making in all $24.50 and I won $6 Leaving a Ballance vs me of Eig[h]teen Dollars 50 cts — Listillet was the nag I Bet on VS the field, Dr Jance Homes wanted to Borrow $25 this Evening. I did not have it at the Present time

21 Lucy Dashwood walked for the purse to day   Marco paid the Forfeit to her. Nothing new to day   Buisness dull

22 Nothing new. Buisness has been tolerable fair to day   I was Out to the tract to day and Saw the Race between the Cherokee Maid and Red Eagle, the Single dash of a mile and a $1000 a Side. Cherokee Maid won the Race very Easy, time 1.52. I won $2 from Waller on One Bet and I [won] $5 from him On another Bet, and $5 from Mr Vanhozen, and 1 dollar from a Sportsman and five Barrells of Corn from Mr Midcalf [blank] and on the 2d Race I won $5 from Mr Jarbon and $2.50 from Harrison, the Irishman

23 Nothing new that I Know of. I wrode Out Late in the afternoon and took a Look at my cattle and I got wet very Easy, myself and the children.

24 Nothing new   Buisness tolerable fair, Ole Bull gives a Concert to night at the City Hotell. He gave One Last Saturday Night at the Same Place &c.[7] I Loaned Mr. Vanater $5.00 to day. There was a Race to day between Rodolph and a Grey Horse belonging to Col Johnson, Rodolph won the Race, very Easy — I did not See it   Mrs. Miller paid me on acct. $5.25   I Loaned Mr. Vanater 5 dolls to Day — Mr. Red and white Boat Cow fell in the Bauyou to night and must Dye, I think

25 Nothing new to day   Buisness Tolerable fair. The River rising very slow, indeed, I Bot 15 pieces of Rope to day at Auction for 56 cts for the Lot. Cheap — I paid Mr Elward 2 dols that he won from me on the Race the other day

26 Nothing new. Buisness Good and Easy. Col Bingamans Stable of Horses Left Last night for New Orleans Races   There

---

[7] The Natchez *Free Trader*, March 22, 1845, had heralded Ole Bull's arrival: "This greatest living violinist arrived in our city on Thursday and will give a concert this evening. The mere announcement of this fact is sufficient to draw a large audience."

were Some good Ones among them, Ruffin, Lucy Dashwood, Betsy Coody, And Labarcant, and Something Else

27   Buisness has been prety Good. Mr. S. T. McAlister Left here to day for a Sea voyage, Good many of his friends went to See him off at the Landing — We were Planting Garden Seed To day in the Garden &c.

28   Nothing new Has Transpired To day of importance. Buisness has been Tolerable Good to day. Harman that belonged to Dr. Applewhite Died This Evening. Poor Fellow

29   Nothing Has transpired of much interest to day. Buisness thank God has been prety fair in my Line, I Loaned Capt Nevitt to day two Hundred Dollars   He promises to give it to me the first or second trip that the Paul Jones makes up from New Orleans — I gave Mr J. Barnard $12 for a Cow and Calf to day   She is a Red, Pale Red, and has a Red Calf

30   Nothing new   Buisness was Tolerable fair, I wrode Out this Evening and I found the Cow that I won from Mr. Rabeey and she was Dead and was Calving when she died. Thus she is dead, &c.

31   I Bot a Large Lot of Hay This morning at the Landing   It was the Bottom teer of a Flat Boat. I got Forty Eight Bales of Hay and Gave 5 Bits a Bale for it.

April 12   Steam Boat Luda On the Mississippi. Saturday morning I was On the river   Was at Several of The Large Plantations, & was at Baton Rogue and Bayou Sarah, &c. I Saw French William at Bayou Sarah to day, and had a Long Talk with him. He told me a good deal about his music &c

13   Nothing new   I arrived this morning from New Orleans on the Steam Boat Luda. My fare was very good — John Taylor was Head Stewart, Batiste 2d stewart. I wrode Out This Evening To Mr Jno Barlands To Look at my mare and her Colt that was Folded on Last Friday night and is a Filly by Jno R Grimes. I also Saw a Fine Looking Colt by Wood Pecker from a fine Large mare of Mr Barlands   The Colt is 8 or nine days old. To days Race in Orleans. Entries Jery Lancaster & Loubarchants. Four Mile Heats   Time 7.38 — 8.14. Jerry won the Race, $700 Purse — No this Race was on Saturday. Sure

14   Nothing new. Buisness was tolerable fair. I Loaned Mr. N. Carpenter to day Forty Dollars and took a Due Bill for it. The Boys took in whilst I was away the 12 days $61.12½   First rate I do assure you, After Comming from New Orleans Everything appears to be the Same tho dull

15   Our Little Rose, Pinks Heifer, had a Calf This Evening
way out on the Point, on the Jerault Land under a Pine Tree, &c.
Sundays Race was a good One   Entries 2 Mile Heats. Croton
2-1-1, D F Kenners Blue Bonners 1-2-2, Mr Baras Uncas — 3
Distances   Jon Turnbulls Morman 4th Drawn   P A Cocks Nau-
tive Drawn

16   I had the Points of my Cows Roses Horns Sawed off
to Prevent her from hurting Anyone

17   I commenced to work at the Hay, in moving it in to
McMurran Stable

18   The Light guards has a Anversity to day, Gav a Dinner
in Capt Minors Pasture, I Bot a Barrell of Beef to day which I
think is good

19   Mr Fords man Told me to day that he herd that the Boys
had found my Cows down in the Swamp. He though[t] — I Hope
it is true

20   Nothing new   Buisness Tolerable fair considing the
Season &c. After Dinner this Evening I wrode Out to Mr Jno
Barlands To See Kitty Fisher and her Colt. Tis a Pretty Little
thing indeed. Tis a Little Filly

21   To Day the Fencibles had there 21st Aniversity and partook of a Large and good Dinner in Capt Minors Pasture, It was
well Contested   Very indeed. The Shooting Match was Let and
the Prize was won this Evening by Jno Jaqmine, John McDanal and
Wash opens a Barber Shop in the City Hotell, Let them alone, To
day, I believe

22   Buisness has been very good, Quite a Large Milatary
Ball To night, I am Told   The Natchez Guards paid me To day
Sixty two Dollars which Sum pays there rent to the first of April
and Leaves them in my Debt Eight Dollars to the 1st instant, News
reached here to day of that tremendious Fire that took place in
Pittsburgh a few days ago

23   Buisness has been very Good to day in my Line &c. Mr J
Ross Wades Residence was Burned down on Monday night I herd
and Burned a child To Death of Mrs Richardson and Burned the
Lady Considerable but she was Saved by a Slave

24   Buisness is Tolerable fair, And I Glad of it, of course.
To night the Ball Comes of[f] at the City Hotell and the Last One
for the Season, I Bot the Little Buggy from Mrs McAlister To day
and gave Her $20 for it, with all the Harness &c. and will Send
and Get it On to marrow I think   Several Gentleman & Ladies
went on a Fishing trip this morning and Caught a good many

25   Nothing new. Buisness To day has been dull Quite So.

26   Buisness Only Tolerable. I Bot a Cow and Calf from the Butcher Mr. Zinser   She is a Brown Cow with mark and Brand

27   I was Quite unwell. Took a dose of Antomy wine and remain Home all Day. Nothing new to day — Buisness Only Tolerable. I Sent my mare up to Jefferson County by Charles to Mr Paines grey Horse to be put.

28   Nothing New   I sent my old mule down to the stable to try and sell Her but did not do it, Charls Little Puppy got run over this Evening & Killed Dead by old Minge Hackman — Charls is up in Jefferson County.

29   Buisness has been Quite mild, and I have been glad of it because I was unwell and did not Like to work. Charles has not returned from Jefferson County yet. He went on Sunday Evening Late.

30   Nothing new. Buisness to day good. I Bot 2 Dining Tables to day at auction and paid 9 dolars Each makeing $18.00 and also paid for the Tables Covers, 3 Bits Each — I also bot 4 shirtts, 4½ bits per shirt, and I also Bot from a Mr. Jery Barlow a Brown Horse about 6 or very near 6 years old. I gave $45 for the Little Horse, I Bot 2 Cover Lids to day at $5.81 for the two &c. This Horse was raised by the man that Sold him   So he Seys &c. Those articles that was Sold To day was the Property of Col. Fleming Woods, who is about to Leave this Place for Washington City

May 1   It was to day that I was in Conversation with Mr Ford and he then set in to tell me what was his Suspitions. He told me too that he strongly believed it. He told me that Mr. Mosbey and a Boy of his was Conspiring together to take his Life and that he had found a grave yard or that he had found a Grave in his Field that was dug by Fords Boy and he Supposed that then was done to Bury him in   The Plans are going rabid not [now], I tell you.[8] Ford has Mosbey up and he gave Bail in the Sum of five hundred Dollars — Tis bad tis Bad — Dr. Duncan pd his Shaving Bill to day which was $7 to 1st of May

3   Nothing New. Buisness To day was Fair.

4   Nothing new

6   Nothing new   Buisness Tolerable

8   Nothing new. Buisness to day has been dull, Pollo, my

---

[8] The men referred to were Washington Ford and William Mosbey, who had married daughters of George Winn, free Negro farmer. Both men believed that they had been wronged in the handling of Winn's estate.

good Faithfull Dog Died To day Between 11 and 12 Oclock, is about 13 years old   Several men tried to Break Jail To night, but did not Succeed. The Boys Papering Some Little to day & Painting also. Wm Mosbeys Note is due to day

   9   Nothing new. Buisness Quite dull — I Sent $10 to New Orleans by Potter to day to get me a Ladies wig — tis for Mrs Little   I Bought 25 Barrels Corn this Evening at 58 cts per Barrell.

   10   Nothing new   Buisness Only Tolerable

   11   Nothing new. Buisness Tolerable. After Dinner To Day I Took my Horses and my 3 Sons and wrode Out in Serch of my two Horses that has been missing for a Day or two and I found them Down in the Old Scotts Field not far from the Woodville Road, They have been wriden by Some One I presume, We Brot them Home Easy Enoughf, Ana Johnson paid me fifteen Dollars for the Red & white Cow Hester, which cow is now hers in fact. All said, This writing was made to day 12th inst. and I put it the 11th instant

   12   Buisness has been Tolerable Good to day, Took in Something over five, dollars in the Small Collections. Our Old Cow Gustine has Disappeared. I am afraid she has been Killed.

   13   Buisness Tolerable dull, I Sold a Hone to Capt Nevitt for two Dollars

   14   Nothing new has transpired of much Interest to Anyone, Large Party went to Fish to day On the other Side. Mr Newman & Family, Mr Koontz, and many others and it rained nearly all Day   They had no Luck of Course. I received a Braid from New Orleans this morning for Mrs Peter Little. She was much pleased with it.

   15   Nothing new that I have herd off. I was making Some arrangement to go a Fishing in the Morning &c.

   16   I got up this morning quite Early and took our Fishing tackle and my Brown Horse and old Carraige and Started over the river to Fish

   20   Nothing new has transpired Durring the day. I loaned Mr J. Crizer to day Fifty Dollars for a week &c

   21   Nothing new. Buisness Tolerable fair, $10.[9] I was down

---

[9] On May 24, 1845, the *Free Trader* reported the military holiday: *"Target Firing.*—The three Volunteer Infantry Companies of this city shot on Wednesday last for the Minor Medal, which was won by the Natchez Fencibles. The Light Guard with 21 men, each man shooting three times, put 40 balls in a target 30 inches across. The Fencibles with 18 men put in 39 balls. The Natchez Guard with 27 men put in 32 balls. Of course the Medal was awarded to the Natchez Fencibles." See also Natchez *Courier,* May 23, 1845.

to day to See Mr Mosbey and to try and Collect the money that he owed me but did not Get any thing, He showed me his Property but I did not get or did try to get any of it, he is a poor man indeed

22   Nothing new, Buisness has been tolerable fair, Three Baths to day, I bet five dollars with Mr Walker To day that Peytona would win her race VS Fashion, I saw Mr Baylor Winn to day and he was partly persuading me to take Mosbey's Property, I told him that I did not Like to distress a man in his situation &c.

23   Nothing new and buisness tolerable fair, Took in the Shop [$5]   Collected from Mr S Woods $13 and Collected from Mr Seshes $35. Great many persons went over to Fish to day on the other Side of the River. Charles & Winston Drove my Horse in a Buggy to the Lake and he Came home with the thumps very bad, They did not cetch many Fish at Last, from what I Saw of them, Billy & Jack & Jim Saw the Little Duch Gun Smith on a Cow that we Call Gustine to night about ½ past 9 Oclock. They went Out on him and he got up and Started up the Street and I took a Lantern and Followed him up and Looked him in the face & Saw him and Knew him to be the Gun Smith that Got his Leg Broke a Short time ago   By the Steammer Princess to night we get News that Patona had won the race very Easy in two strait Heats   Time 7.39¾ and 7.44¾. Tract heavy

25   Nothing new. Buisness only Tolerable, I wrode out with the children this Evening to the Plum trees and we Got Some fine Ones

26   Court is in Session. Judge Cage Presides, &c. Buisness Some what dull. Three Baths to day — Several officers who herd of the mans Killing the other and the 2 young weoman — when [went] in persuit of them

27   This has been a good day for me ie Tolerable good, Mr. G. Brustee Called and paid me the above Acct [$17.50] that I paid for him some time ago

31   Nothing new of much Moment. More than I have been very Mad nearly all Day   Tis about my Son William   It appears that he went out to Drive a calf to the Commons and it farther appears that 2 of Dr Jones children Got in a fuss with Him and what Ever name they Called Him he returned it and it then is Said by a man who I would Hate [to] believe on his Oath, I mean a Certain Horse Drover, by the Name Foreman

June 1   Nothing new.

2   I wrode out this Evening and took the children — oh no it was not to day, but was yesterday

3   Nothing new I believe

5   Nothing new. The Criminal Court is in Cession at present, Buisness only Tolerable, My spotted Jaqumine Cow has a fine young Calf this morning, Winston the negro Trader was tried and found Guilty of manslaughter in the 4th degree, so I herd

6   Nothing new. The Criminal Court is Still in Cession, and Gadsbury was tryed and found Guilty of Murder in 1st Degree

7   Buisness To day has been very fair considering the times, Mr Taintor paid me to day ten Dollars on His Shaving Bill, I received a Letter from Adelia Miller To day from New Orleans Informing [me] of the receipt of two Hundred Dollars that I Loaned Her, which Sum She Promises to pay as Soon as She can, She informed me also that E Millers of Vicksburg had his Property sold and it Sold for Only four Hundred Dollars. Tis a bad old chance for him Ever to get it Back again, I think

8   Alls well & nothing new. I wrode Out this Evening and took my Little Boys with me, We were Looking for two Horses that has Gone to the Fields. We got a plenty of black Berrys and have Eaten a plenty of them

9   Buisness rarther Dull for a Commencement, and nothing new that I Know of, Buisness Only Tolerable, I went up the Residence of Mr Burns this Evening and had a talk with Him about Winston and the Ammount of Our talk was that I would give him a Hundred & Fifty Dollars for him for a year, ie to the first of May next 1846, which was agreed upon, I promised to Learn him what Ever I could during the year, ie to spell and to read, & write also — if I could, Mr Mosbey was up to day and his trial was put off untill the next term of the Court, Poor Fellow I am sorry for him

11   A Scotchman by the name of Smith was Stabbd yesterday Evening at a Late Hour by a young man by the name of Swearagin from Amite County, Somthing about a 20 ct Hat was the Origin of the fuss

12   Young Sweargin was acquited to day for the murder of Smith. Tis too bad — this I Speark of was on the 11th insted of to day 12th

13   Buisness Only Tolerable

15   Jack Commences this fore noon to go to Mcs To Learn To read &c. My Little Richard & Byron Commences to Learn at the Shop, to day also

16   Nothing new in our poor Little Town, I was up at auction to day and bot Some wines &c.

527

17   Nothing new to Day that I Know of. James Pomet Died to day near 10 Oclock, He died at his Brother in Laws, L Davids.

18   Buisness Only Tolerable   Nothing new.

20   Nothing new — Buisness dull

21   Nothing new. I got On my Horse Early this morning and wrode down in the Swamp. I took the Mesho gun   I went Down as far as Mr Mosbeys and returnd in the heat of the day, with a Head Ache. I Shot 1 Black Squirrell, 1 Black Bird, 1 Patridge   The Reprieve of Gadsbury Came to the City this morning. It was brought by Mr Josep Hewit

22   Our City Seems to be dull Quite So. I Gave Winston this Amount [$22.50] — this being money that I had of his to Keep for him a Short time &c.

23   Nothing new has transpired. I Swaped my big Mule Away this afternoon for a very Small One and I Gave $5 to Boot.

24   Nothing new   Buisness Some what dull, Great many Persons are Leaving for the North, and our City is remarkable Dull. William Commenced to write to day

25   Our old Spot had a Calf this mornin and I Drove her to home this Evining

28   Nothing new to day   Mr Mosbey was in town to day and I Saw him in regard to Our trade, ie our Buisness and After talking Some time about it, I proposed to give the full Amount of my claim for what it Covered, ie for what I held the deed of trust On. He was very willing to do it I believe And he Said So. My Lawyer Said that it was no use to wait Any Longer and that I had better bring the Buisness to a Close, and the Only way I Could get a title to it was that it must be Sold at the Door of the Court House which was agreed on and then I got Mr Mosbey to waive the time to be Sold by Law and to have it Sold on the 7th July which was done accordingly

29   I wrode Out in the Afternoon Late; and did not get in untill greatr [quite] Late

30   Nothing new. It was to day that so many of Citizens Started north   They went On the Mariah. Mrs Linton & Family, Mrs Duncan & Family, Some of Dr Cers Family and Mrs Chaplain, Walter Brian, Col Clifton &c. and others

July 2   Mr Crizer paid me fifty Dolars that I Loaned him a Short time ago. Also pd me $5 for the use of it, I was up at Auction to day and Bot Several things that was very Little wanted

3   I was down near the Waltern Lake when it [rain] Commenced   Myself & Jack got very wet. We Left Our Guns at Mrs

Walterns Place,[10] with Mr Nickolson the Overseer. I had been down in the Swamp to See about Geting up the Cattle from Mr Mosbey   We drove them up and put them in his Pasture

4   Nothing new   I Got up very Early this morning and wrode down in the swamp and took Jack & Jim and my Little William with me to drive up Some stock out of the Swamp which we did with the assistance of Mr Stunp [Stump] & Johnson, We drove up fifteen Head of Cattle and there were in the Lot 7 Oxen

5   It was to day that the Deed of Trust Sale took Place and I Bot 13 head of Cattle and 2 Horses and the woman Peggy. I Loand Mr Seshes to day forty five dollars and took his note, payable 29th July.

6   Nothing new   I was Out at the Pasture this Evening and was taking Some notice of the stock, in writing, which I have to date, Paid Winston 12½ dollars for One months work Ending 4th July, inst

7   Buisness worst to day than Ever — I was out nearly all day Hunting for my Cattle and found them in Scotts old Field or near it.

8   I Started I think this morning Early To Drive Some Stock Down in the Swamp. There were Sixteen Head in all, My object is to Keep them in the Swamp and Let them Get in Good Order   Myself & Jeff & my two oldest Sons and Jim was along — We drove down as Follows, One red & white Steer, One Large White & red Steer, One Red Steer, One Large white Jawed tho he is a white and Red Steer.

1846

June 1   Gim & Billy was up from the Swamp but did [not] go down because of the rain. My Corn in my Garden is Considerably Blown down, by the wind of Last night, The Requisition from the Gov Came to day, So Our Soldiers are Buissy, Quite So — They will Soon be off I presume,   I find buisness dull, Quite So — This is the Effect of the Mexican War. So much for So much, I Comme[n]ce this night to read the Bible through, Once more.

10 "Mrs. Walterns Place" referred to the plantation of Mrs. Parke Walton, on the Mississippi River below Natchez.

2   The Soldiers are Still recruiting for Texas   Nothing new to day. Buisness Dull. Gim & Billy took down a few pea Seed to plant to day; I have Sent for more

3   Buisness Quite Dull. I Started in the Swamp Late this afternoon   I took Byron with me. Rome Caught a large Possum On Our way down. He is a good dog.

4   I was up Early this morning and I collected a Lot of Peas and Started to have them planted

6   Nothing new,   Billy & Jim both up from Hard Scrabble[1] this Evening   They report all well &c.

7   Nothing new. Buisness Only Tolerable

8   Nothing new. I find the City very dull indeed at present. I started into the Swamp this Evening with Frank — To work.

9   Nothing New. I was in the Swamp this Evening, in fact all day, Frank too, We were very Buisy to day in Cutting and Haulling House Logs. We Commencd yesterday   We got as [many as] we wanted and then Quit and [I] then set Billy & Jim to Haulling fire wood, no it was to day that we Commencd to work at the Logs

10   We were at Hard Scrable Cuting Logs for a Hen House &c. We got through Erly this Evening, and [I] made Billy Haul Fire wood &c. I started Home. My Corn in both Fields is Commen[c]ing to tasel, Peas have Came up very fine   They look well, Mr Winn paid me One of his notes to day with the interest, amounting in all to $57.50

11   Nothing new. Buisness dull.

12   Nothing new.

13   Nothing new. A Tenessee Company was down this morning and was shot by One of thiere Own party — his name was Snead, He was Buried with the Honnors of war on the Grown — Jeff & Billy and Gim was up from the Swamp

14   Nothing New. Buisness dull   I remaind at Home all day   Late in the Evening walked Out with the Children, a Little showr of rain drove us in, a few drops Only

15   Buisness Only tolerable. Nothing New, Billy and Gim at work in the Garden

---

[1] "Hard Scrabble" was the designation given to a tract of land situated on the Mississippi River and purchased by Johnson from Winslow Winn for $600 in August, 1845. The tract was supposed to contain 120 acres, but a survey revealed less acreage. In a suit for the deficiency, Johnson was subsequently awarded $146. See Adams County Deed Records, FF, 81–82, and Johnson's diary entry for December 3, 1846. Hard Scrabble was the southern part of Johnson's principal farming and timber tract, all of which was in Sections 5 and 9, Township 6, Range 4, West.

16   Nothing new. Buisness Tolerable

17   The Natchez Fencibles arrivd from Vicksburg this morning   Regected   They hold a meeting in the Court House, pass Resolutions, Disband &c.[2] Winston goes into the Swamp to Build a Small House   Buisness Good to day

18   The Fencibles Disbanded to day I believe   That is the Texas Fencibles

20   I was at the Landing to day and Bot of Mr Metcalf a Lot [of] Corn and then a Flat Boat. The Corn and Boat I paid $43 for   I then sent the Boat with the Corn down to Mr Winns place, I have agreed to Let him Have the One Half at Cost, I was at Auction to day and Bot Some Pantaloons, News of the Elections Came to day, Jeff. Davis Ellected Col., Capt. McClung Lieut. Col[3]

21   Nothing new. I went down in the Swamp to See about the Boat that I Bot. I found her at Mr B. Winns, He had taken out his Shair of Corn and the Boat was ready for me. I took her down in Company with Winns George, Ca[l]vin Winn, Jeff & Ephraim — We got her down very Easy indeed. Mr Gay passed us this Evening with Mr Winns daugher under His arm   Jasper had a Tennessee gal and all Hands were marching along up the Road.

22   I was in the Swamp this morning and Commenced Erly to take out the Corn that was in the Boat and strip Her — I was sick before we got through with it. My force at the Commencement was as follows — my Son Wm. & Jeff, Billy, Gim, Zora & Sam. We were all pretty Buisy at work, untill we got through

23   To day I was unwell, quite so indeed   Mr Wilcott & myself had the 2 Little Studds cut that was in the Swamp. Mr Spangler altered them for us. I had my roated Corn to dry and it raind prety Likely. I sold my Boat to Little Winn[4] payable in 30 days for $35.00

24   Nothing new. Samuels has closed up Antonio's[5] store. He wants money, thats all, for the use of Frank under the Hill,

---

[2] Mississippi's quota of troops had been fixed at one regiment of infantrymen or riflemen. Under the order of Governor Brown only those companies first organized were to be accepted for service. The Natchez Fencibles had failed to qualify because of a numerical deficiency of a few men. See Rowland, *History of Mississippi*, I, 658–59.

[3] Jefferson Davis, then a member of Congress, was elected colonel and Alexander Keith McClung lieutenant colonel of the First Mississippi Regiment when it was organized at Vicksburg.

[4] "Little Winn" was Winslow Winn, a free Negro.

[5] Antonio Lynch operated a fruit store in part of one of Johnson's Main Street buildings.

Buisness tolerable good to day. Old Jones sent his woman up to Cincinnatti & children too. Nancy Kyle[6] went also

    25   Buisness dull — I was out on the Commons this Evening [and] saw a Scoundrel running my Horses on different parts of the old field, but found that he was after cetching McAttees Black Horse; which he did not get at Last

    26   I left town this Evening   Took Jack & Robert & Sam with me. This is to see my Corn and things all put away in good order, Gim and Billy had put the Corn all up, had made 3 shelves in the new House, and put some under a shed for Amediate use, besides a Box that was in the Room, George Smith is accused of trying to kill a man to day or something — and has wran away

    27   Buisness is very dull indeed   I· was in the Swamp and was ingaged in work remooving the False Floor from the flat Boat that I sold to Mr Winn; we got through with it and Mosbey took it down to his yard with him to Load with wood, at $30   He takn the Boat, I Keeping all the Loose Lumber — I Left there this Evening with the Boys   I shot 2 Duckes to day with the Meshio gun. Jack shot a Squirrell near my corn field.

    28   News from the Oregon Question has been receivd to day confirming the ratification of the Question,[7] I remaind Home untill Late in the Evening, when I wrode out to Salt my Horses on the Commons.

    29   Carpenter has the Zink taken off and Shingles put on instead there of   I made Out a Bill this Evening to Antonio for Rent   He owes me $40 for 5 months rent — to the 1st of July — the River is falling very fast.

    30   Buisness tolerable fair, I gave Rachael Winston[8] my note for One Hundred Dollars for value received.

    July 1   Buisness is dull very. I paid Winston Eighty Seven dollars and a Half for seven months wages to the 4th of July inst. and Gave him as a present $10, ie, to get him cloathes with it.

    2   Nothing new   Winston started up the River to night late in the night   He went on the Uncle Sam. Severell Gentlemen from the City Left also.

    3   Nothing like Buisness done to day at all. I paid Maj

    6 Nancy Kyle was a free woman of color.

    7 The Oregon boundary treaty with Great Britain had been signed on June 15, 1846.

    8 Rachel Winston was the mother of William Winston, one of Johnson's barbers. Both mother and son were free by 1850.

Young $50 to day   According to the Last record that I have this will pay to the 1st of Aprill 1846.

4   I was at the Race track to day and saw the Race between Mr Crizers Josephine & Mr Rabeys Horse & Winstons Bay Mare Ellen True and the Bird of the world   The horse Blue Dick paid the forfeit   The Race Came off just as they are put down in 1.56   Track was in good order, not much Betting. I won $28 in all and Came Home

5   I started down in the Swamp this Evening. I Saw Mr Gay away up by the paupaw Patch Locked arm with B Winns Eldest Daughter

6   I was in the Swamp all Day to day and I wrode down very near to St Catharine Creek, then came back and took a Bee Hive and put them in a Barrel near the Horse Lot. I Flogged Zora this morning for neglect &c.

7   Gen Duffields article Came out this morning. The governors Came out the other day. They are strong. Little Sam is sick. Dr. Stone Came to See Him to day. We used Leeches on him and gave medicine.

9   Nothing new. Buisness dull

10   I Had the Antonio Lynch Store Sold out to day. The amount of the Shop was Some 61 dollars, that is what My Bill was, tho there was Some other things Sold that did not Amount to much. Tho I believe I Bot a 43 Sheep to day with $45   I got them of Mr Shwab at the forks of the Road and drove them in this Evening.

11   I started in the Swamp this morning with the Sheep that I Bot yesterday, 43 of them. Mcs William and My William drove them down, they got them all down Safe. I wrode down myself and Came Home with them at night. I collectd fifty seven Dollars from Mr W. Winn this Evening   This is for a note that I held of his for money Loaned.

12   Buisness dull, &c.

13   Nothing new   Buisness quite dull

14   Three of Our Calves fell Down the Bluff. They were the Calves of Patsy Mosbey & Francis Wren and Rody Patterson   They were Evidently Driven over the Bluff by some bad person.

15   Mr Miller and myself wrode down to Hard Scrabble to day. We wrode down and staid a short time, took Dinner and remaind but a short time and then started up again.

18   We, Mr Miller, McCary and myself and my William, went over the river to fish   I caught 4, Mr Miller 2, Mr C 17, My

Wm. none. I wrode my old Black Horse. Mr Miller wrode my Horse Bob. Wm. wrode Billy. I Cookd the Fish and we Had a good Mess.

19   I wrode Out with Mr Miller and Mr C   We wrode out by Col Bingamans and Came in by his House. Dr. Applewhite pd me twenty five Dollars for One months Rent up to 1st of July, inst., no it was not to day.

20   Mr Miller and myself took a small wride up by Waymouths and back.

21   Nothing new   Buisness Dull. Mr Miller and myself wrode Out   He wrode my Horse Bob and I wrode my Horse Dick. We wrode out by Mrs Minors Gate beyond Mrs Bondurants and returnd and passed threw by Capt Minors Residence and Came out into the Washington wrode, then Came in threw the City, down by the institute, Home — it was a pleasant wride. Mr McCrey Left for Memphis the other Day.

22   Paul Jones — Mr Miller Left on the above Boat this Evening — took with him Lots of Peaches some meal & other things   We wrode to the Landing together   Mr Koonts & Lady, Mr Williamson & Lady and others Left on the same Boat for New Orleans — and watering Places. Twenty three dollars and some cents Cash by Charles to day.

23   Buisness quite dull   I wrode down into the Swamp this morning and before I went I tryed very hard to take Kity Fisher with me and her colt, but the colt would not go one step beyond certain spots — So I had to Leave the mare and colt and go on. They were pulling Fodder down at Hard Scrabble. I Commenced to pull and toward night I got very sick and Left   Did not get up untill near 11 Oclocke at night, Billy, Phillip, and Johnson and myself   Sarah was taken sick this morning and did not work to day. I took Dinner at Mr Wilcott. Mr Wilcott is now pulling Fodder. Mr Bailer Winn is also Pulling Fodder.

24   Charles and Jim went down into the Swamp — to Pull Fodder — they wrode Bob & Dick.

25   R. Parkers Daughter both told some Lies on my Children this Evening and has Caused me to whip them. It was wrong in me to do it tho I whipt them   Billy, Phill and Gim Came up this Evening from H. S., yes and Charles too   They were Pulling and Stacking Fodder. They put up One Stack of Fodder in the Lower Field   In regard to our children, R. Parker stated that my children had Brick bated his Children and that One of them had insulted his wife and Daughter, &c, which information I find his wife tells

and Daughter tells him, also — I have only to add that God Knows that what they have stated is not the truth. I bot a Cask of shoul[d]ar's to day at Auction. They weiged 908 pounds, ½ cent a pound.

26   Buisness very dull indeed. I remaind all day at Home the wether being too Hot to be out.

27   I sent out to Col Bingamans to get my Bull, he was in the Pasture   I gave Jack $10.

28   F. Vinegerhotz Selling out at Auction. I gave in Property to the City, no the State and County

One Hundred and twenty acre $300
9 Slaves 2000
2 town Lots 3000
1 Piano 50
1 watch 50

Billy, Gim, Frank, Phill in the Swamp Pulling Fodder

29   I started in the Swamp, took Byron with me, We took down Kitty Fisher and her Colt   We did not get down until night, I got two Bunches of Shingles to day to put on my old House, 3.80

30   I was in the Swamp all day and was ingaged at work with the Fodder   We put up One Stack and then went to pulling Fodder in the Back Field

31   I was Engaged in pulling Fodder and we got it very wet. We got through with the Back Field. I fear that I will Loose the Fodder by its getting so wet. Myself, Mr Johnson,[9] Billy & Phill was a pulling

August 1   I left my place ½ past 6 Oclock   Got in town after 9 Oclock. Billy and Phill were all puting up a Shed in the Horse Lot and Johnson too   To day Johnson and Billy Got Done with theres but Phill did not get through with his. I paid Johnson off to day, $5.50 for Eleven Days work. Mr Torris Mooves in my house next door to day at $8 per month

2   Nothing new   Buisness quite dull indeed.

3   I Sold Burly Johnson my Little Spanish Horse to day for twenty five Dollars and he paid me twenty two Dollars and owes me a Ballance of three Dollars, on the Horse   He then Came and Borrowd six Dollars from me, thus he owes me $9. Johnson then Got Drunk and wrode arround the streets and the Horse threw him and got away   I had him caught for him and he started of[f] quite drunk. Mr. Finney Finishd a closet to day for me on my

_____
9 "Mr Johnson" was a white laborer who was not related to the diarist.

galery. Margaret Lieper goes up to Rodney this morning on the Paul Jones. I got a Letter from Mrs. Miller; She had her old Billy Sold on a years credit for $500.

4   I went to the Swamp this Evening Late. Phill was sick yesterday. Johnson was at work yesterday — Billy was haulling in the Logs that he cut for Corn Cribb — I took my Meshio Gun with me. I Shot 2 Partriges at 1 shot on my way down.

5   I was in the Swamp all Day. Started Late in the Evening for Natchez — got up near ½ past 9 Oclock p.m. I Saw Kity Fisher to day and she has got the Glanders or Distemper — I Left them in the Pasture together. I shot 4 Crows to day. Johnson shot a wood Pecker. I had a Long talk to day with Mr Mo[s]bey to day about his Land, we could not trade   He wanted to give me 50 acres for what he owd me, said He would not do any better. We Left without a trade.

6   Jeff wrode down in the Swamp to day   They were hauling off Logs to build a Corn Cribb with. Cloud has a Calf to night — a Little Bull Calf.

7   Jeff was Down at Hard Scrabble to day and brought up Kity Fisher and Left her young Colt   We thought She was Sick   I paid Maj Young fifty Dollars to day for Charles wages up to the 1st of August inst   He allowed the bill of clothing which was $12.25.

8   I got in the Swamp this morning at an Erly Hour. I spent nearly all this Day in talking with Mr Mosbey about his Swamp Land, but did not Effect.

9   Buisness is very dull indeed. Nothing new. Volunteers arriving in New Orleans Every Day   They are generally in good Health, report Some Sickness among the Indianans, not to any Greate Extent However

10   Billy & Phill goes down this morning taking 1 showlder of Bacon, ½ Bushell meal, cross cut Saw to Saw off Blocks to Make Corn Cribb

11   The Catapillers is said to have made there appearance already on some plantations, Antonio Lynch comes to take or Claim the Counter. I pays Winston acct. and the One that he held VS me for the Counter &c. He said my Bill was near 7 dollars and the Counter making all $10. So we settled it in full of all Demands.

12   Jeff and Frank and Jack was shingles or shingling the old part of the House in part. I hired 2 Loafers and discharged them at Breakfast time. They were geting drunk. Sam Woods returns

from Pass Christian   Army worm is commencing on the Cotton in this Neighbourhood.

13   Jeff went in the Swamp to day to See how the Corn Crib Comes on, ie, they were Building it.

14   Jeff & Gim, Billy & Phill all in the Swamp trying to Build a Corn Crib for me   They came up to night   Report that they got up the Logs to the Higth [incomplete], then stopd. Jeff & Gim Came to town to night.

15   Billy & Phill are up to night. One hundred thirty five dollars I paid to Brown for the repairs on my Buggy to day and then took a wride in it, &c.

16   Bill Eastern returns from Mexico this morning   Looks bad, has been sick

17   I made the hands commence to day to turn F[odder] down in the Lower Field   Finished about 11 Oclock   Then Commenced to pull the Fodder in the Winston Field and turned it down as we went   The Crows had nearly ruined it   We then Commenced on the back field and turnd it down and pulled the top fodder as we went on. I Killed 1 Patridge, 1 Duck, 2 Squirells as I went down to day

18   I was in the Swamp — I started my force this morning Erly to turning down the Corn in the uper Field. We got done by Breakfast time, Billy got the dray & Hauled Logs down as Johnson & Gim Sawed them off   Phill getting out the Rafters for the Corn Crib

19   Several of the volunteers got back from Mexico to day: Elick McGowan, Hy Postlethaite, Haliday and others   I got up very Erly this morning and started to town, got up about Breakfast. Mr Mc and my Wm and Gim came up with me. The Boys were shooting for 2 Days and Killd nothing but a few Birds

20   I received a Letter from Winston to day   He is in Cincinnati — dated 18th July — Volunteers came up to day.

21   I had my Small Buggy Brought Home to day from the Shop. New shaft-hound &c was the repairs on it.

22   This has been a very Dull Day in the way of Buisness and no news of importance. Phill & Bills report that they have sawed all the Log up and Hauld it down to the House and then commencd to make the Bourds &c   Had shockd up the Fodder

23   Nothing new   Buisness Dull. I remained Home all Day until Late in the Evening   I then went to the Bluff with Richard, Robert, McC, Jim, Byron, Anna, &c.

24   The city Looked a Little Lively to day. Gim Pilmore

Came Home to day from the seat of war. Nothing new. Jeff & Frank & Gim was shingling to day on the old House   William unwell to day but is, I thank God, better to night   I was at auction to day, Bot spoons & towells, Hatchets, &c.

25   Nothing new. I was at Auction to day and Bot 2 Barrels of Bacon Hams, wighing 532 pounds. I sold 53 pds of the same to Dr. Miller, Leaving 479 lbs net. Twelve dollars and twenty five cents was the Cost   Gim Drove Mothers 2 Calves into the Swamp to day.

26   Nothing new. Buisness very dull indeed, The wether is delightfull at present, I dont hear much about the worms in the Cotton.

27   Nothing new   I started in the Swamp this morning Quite Erly with my Little Black Buggy, and I brok down in it very Easy, but tyed it up so that I made Out to get down in it   The men finished one side of the Corn House to day ie the Roof   Gim and Frank Brought up Cloud Parker and Her Calf, the Calf was Calved on the 7th of August 1846. They Brot up Blackey Fields at the Same time with her Calf which is a month or two old.

28   I started from the Swamp this morning at 6 Oclock and arrived at Natchez at 10 Oclock   I drove the old Roan Horse up   Brot a Barrell [of] Corn, 3 pumpkins, 4 Kershaws[10] — This is the First of my Crop.

29   Nothing new   Buisness Dull, very. Mansion House Stable on Fire to night and I was awfully alarmed but thanks to providence I Escaped without Loss   The Engines was very active indeed very   They soon got it out. I thank them very much indeed. Mr. Sheldon paid me Eight dolls for Cloud and calf in money and his Cow to Boot.

30   I was trying to drive the Sheldon Cow on the Commons this Evening but could not so I Left Her Home   Celia's Calf died this Evening on the Commons near Smiths Pasture. It fell I suppose into the Bayou

31   Buisness dull. Jim found Bob and the Roan Horse down by the old Barland field

September 1   I Started in the Swamp this forenoon to drive Dicy Young and Cloudy Paneson or Cloud Sheldon   We got them down in the Afternoon, then worked on the House ie puting up the Lining Business

10 The cushaw, a long-necked squash grown in the southern United States.

2   I got up Erly this morning and went to work at the House stoping up the cracks and Laying the Floor in the upper part after which we Commencd and hauled in the Fodder that was shockd   We hauled in five shocks of it in 4 Loads of the Small Buggy and put it up in the Corn House   It was in Bad order, We then Commenced to stack up the Logs that was in the yard   We then went down to the field and pulld 3 Barrells of Corn and 9 pumpkins, [and] Kershaws. Mr. Gregory Bot the Mosbey Property Last Monday. So I herd to day tho I dont know how true it is — He is to pay three Thousand Dollars for it. So I dont know, yes and is to get the money in Eight Days from Monday Last. I hope he will not raise the money. No harm ment.

3   Buisness only tolerable. The worms are very bad at Present on the Cotton   They seems to have made a Fresh start on it — H. Stump told me to day that Mr Mosbey told me a Lye when He Said He had not Sold his Land to Mr Gregory for he Said that Mr Gregory told him that he had bot it and had Eight Days to pay for it in — tis very strange how man will act at times   Very indeed.

4   Nothing new. Buisness only tolerable. To day I paid Mr Haugton $10 for the Vicksburg Expositor or Sentinnel[11] — and ordered it Stopd Entirely. Some time ago. So I hope to Hear no more of it.

5   Nothing new. Buisness tolerable Dull for the Season. Mr. Font & Son was about To Leave here very Suden when they were garnsiheed and ther Property Seized and Hauled to the Court House, It was at the instance of W. K. Henry or others, I am Sorry that it tis so for I Lost two Customers by them, I whiped old Anderson this Evening for Striking a Little Boy in the Head with a Brick Bat. I gave him 5 Lashes for it   The worms are Sweeping the Cotton at present in Every Direction Down at Mr Waterns and Fords, B Winns &c   William wrode up the Little Jim Miller Horse   Tis the first time that he has been wrode since he has been up here — The Stack of Fodder in the Lower Field was put up in the House for winter

6   Buisness Tolerable fair. Nothing new. City Dull. I remain at Home, yes untill Late in the afternoon, then I wrode out To Look up The Cows — $22   Charles paid by the shop below the above amount. The young man Ch. Craig Brot me up Some Razors to day and Sed that he paid all the money that was given to him to Buy them and that was 7 Dollars 80 cents when at the Same time the Bill only Called for $5.00. Shure there is Something

---

[11] Johnson referred to the Vicksburg *Sentinel and Expositor.*

rotten in Demmark   Billy goes down to day with 6 geese, Some few chickens, and some meal

7   I find nothing new worth relating — Buisness dull for the Season.

8   I started to my place this Evening at 5 Oclock   I Stopd at Mr Mosbeys untill Late talking about Land and we did not trade at Least   Some One Stole his Skifft while we were talking on the Galery   It was that Jacky that Broke Jail I Expect.

9   I was in the Swamp this Morning Erly and I Commenced to work at the Fodder and I put in the Loft 628 Bundles of fodder in the 4 rows that I put up—viz, 161, 161, 136, 150, and Left Considerable below to be put up   Old Phill Made the Doors to the Corn House and Billy Cut away the Stump between the Houses — Samuels was in the Swamp to day Looking for Runaways, did not get them. Yesterday I Bot an old Sorril Horse at N. Bunce Auction for $13.00. To Day I Left him with Mr Mosbey untill I want to use him.

10   Buisness very Dull indeed. Nothing new whatever. I Loand Mr Farris 14 Dollars to day to be paid on Monday shure

11   Buisness quite dull   Nothing new   I mended my Buggy this Evening   And I Bot a two Horse waggon from Mr Brown to day for $12.50   This was a wagon that belongd to Mr McMurran at one time and he Swaped to Mr Brown.

12   Nothing new. Buisness tolerable only — Nothing new again — Zora Came out of the Swamp this Evening and She Came in the Buggy. Phill Brot 2 Barrells of Corn. They had Commenced on the shed to the Corn House on the off side, Next the woods

13   Nothing new. Buisness has been only tolerable.

14   I wrode down in the Swamp   I did not get there untill Late. Billy and Phill was pulling Corn in the Lower field   I was talking to day or to night with Mr Mosbey about his Land this Night, but did not offer him Anything at all. I received two Letters from Orleans this morning which gave me a greate Deal of pleasure indeed   They were On Buisness of Course.

15   To Day I was in the Swamp very near all day, And I had a talk with Mr Mosbey about his Land, And after a Long Confab about it He offered it to me for $3000 payable in fifteen or on these Conditions, that if I did not raise the money in the Course of the Stated Time that I would then take fifty Acres for my Claim against him. Thus we parted. On my way up I was Looking for my big Sorrel Horse and Could not find him at all.

16 My William has been Sick for Several Days, was Taken Sick on Sunday Morning Last, and was Some what unwell on Saturday. I Sent Gim into the Swamp to day to Look for my Keys and the Large Sorrel Horse that I Left in the Swamp and He found both. Keys & Horse — Reports Billy & Phill as having done the Lower field of Corn.

17 My Wm. is still unwell and Dr Stone was to See him to day and prescribed for Him

18 I am Greatfull to Our Maker that our Wm. is better This Evening. Yes I think much better The fever brok off to day and I am greatly in hopes that he will recover from his illness fast. Nothing New. Marerro was married Last night to a Daughter of Mr Sweysey — tis a mighty Hot night — ah tis

19 Mr Baker paid Mother fifteen Dolls for Patseys finding his money, which was Some 917.14. So Said his advertisment Billy and Phill is up to night and they Have not Done Pulling Corn yet So I am told

20 Nothing new Buisness only tolerable, tho the day has been So agreeable — Mr Miller Came up from New Orleans this morning. Reports all well and nothing New in the City.

21 Nothing New. Buisness Quite Dull. I got on my Horse to Day and wrode Down in the Swamp I Saw Mr Mosbey and wife and after Some talk I Promisd to Call to Morrow and pay him Cash for his place, which $3000 for the Land and 100 dollars Cash for his Stock of Every Kind and Farming utensils, Corn, Fodder and all.

22 I had a Deed made Out to day to the Mosbey Land And Esqr Woods, Mr. Miller and Mr Jaqamine And myself all went in the Swamp to Day and I Bot Mr and Mrs Mosbey Land and paid him by his Note that I held for $953.70 and for ten monts wages for Peggy, 60 Dollars, and bill of tax $24, and acct that I pd Mr Gay 7.50, so that he owed me the Sum of 1045.70 I paid him three thousand Dollars for the Land and One hundred Dollars for his Corn & stock of Hogs & Cattle, farming utensils and Everything that He had about the Primises This being Done we Soon Left for Hard Scrabble[12] There we got Something to Eat and Drink and then returnd Home

[12] The deed records reveal that on September 22, 1846, William Mosbey and wife sold Johnson 242.14½ acres of Adams County land on the Mississippi River for $3,000. All of this land was in Sections 5 and 9, Township 6, Range 4, West, and was adjacent to Hard Scrabble, to the south, which Johnson had purchased in the previous year. These two purchases were to constitute Johnson's principal farming and timber tract.

23   Buisness Only Tolerable   I was at Home to day all day. I paid $240 for recording the Deed for the Mosbey Land sold to me yesterday in Presence of Justice Wood. Mr James Miller & Mr Jaqmine, Mr Winn & Mr Mosbey & Mr Miller started this Day at 12 Oclock for New Orleans on the Steam Boat Paul Jones   He took with him Patsey and &c.

24   I started into the Swamp this morning after Breakfast and I found Everything Straight   I saw Capt Barlow in the Swamp to day   He was in Serch of Money from Mr Mosbey — He did not get any I believe, not a cent.

25   I was in the Swamp this morning Erly. I Staid all night in the Swamp. I wrode up this morning to Mr Mosbeys and took Breakfast with him, I then wrode down to Mr Wilcotts and took Dinner. Mr Gregory & B Winn was Down thare   After Dinner I Came up to my place then went to work with my Corn. We were Haulling in Corn from the field above the House. Mr Mosbey and his wife with three children Left This Evening for the uper Country. I hope they may do well — Robt. Ellis went Last week to Jessy Davis, to Learn the Barbers Buisness

26   Elick Johnson was at Mosbeys to day Taking away the things that I Bot or the things that he Said he got from Mr Mosbey   I objected to a part then and I now think that I will Let them Take them all for I Dont Like them to think that I would take them after they were given to them. Far from it

27   Nothing New. Buisness Dull, I remained all Day at Home all day ie after Shop shut up

28   Nothing New. I had a Mortgage Drawn out to day in favor of Mr James Miller of New Orleans[13]   Mr Gregory was up to day   Wanted to see me to rent my Mosbey wood yard Plantation, I [will] see about it

29   Nothing New   Buisness Some what Dull, I sent the Morgage by Wellington to Mr Miller this Evening by S B. Embassador.

30   Nothing New. Buisness Dull. I wrote a Letter to Mrs Miller to day and Sent a Bag of Peas by [the] Paul Jones. Gim is up from the Hard Scrable Place with 3 doz ½ Eggs, 1 Bushel Potatoes, 1 Bag of Peas, 2 Barrels of Corn, &c. I wrode down in the Swamp this Evening and rented my wood yard Place to Mr Gregory for One Hundred Dollars per year

---

[13] This referred to the mortgage of Johnson's 242.14½ acre "Mosbey" tract for $1,700 to his brother-in-law, James Miller. See Adams County Deed Records, FF, 454–55.

October 1 I caught a Large Possum Last Night Coming from the Swamp. Mr. D. Richardson was married in Esqr Woods office to a Miss Blue from Tensaw Parrish, La., to day

2 Nothing new. I got my Gun, The Meshio Gun, and started in[to] the Swamp [at] 6 Oclock in the Evening and with McCary We got down to Hard Scrabble on or about ½ past 8. Our Caluculations was to hunt Squirrels in the morning. We start Erly in the morning. We found Everything tolerable fair. Nothing new.

3 Nothing new. Buisness Dull. Quite So. I got up this morning Erly and started into the Swamp. Mc was with me. We walked up and down in the woods and we took a tremendious walk. We were after Squirrells and Mc Killed 1 Coon & 7 Squirrels and I Killd 1 Coon and 10 Squirrels. We hunted from my place up as high as the Sarjent Land. Finished Pulling Corn and hauling it in, that is from my own Land. I brot up about 2½ pounds of Butter from below to day

5 Nothing new. Oh how Dull was buisness to day — oh awfull indeed

6 Nothing New. Buisness Dull Billy & Phill went down to day and so did Gim to Pull Corn in the Mosbey Field. They Commenced this morning

7 Gim returns from the Swamp this Evening. Reports them done Pulling Corn in the Mosbey Field and I got on my Horse Cuff and wrode in the Swamp, So that we Commence in the morning to haul it

8 Nothing new I Commenced to Haul Corn in the Mosbey Field. We hauld 5 Loads to day and Al Johnson Hauled 4 do — We hauled 12 Baskets at a Load And he hauls 20 Baskets.

9 I was prety buisy Having Corn Hauld in. We got through this Evening and the amount Stood thus. I got 91 Barrels, which was 14 Barrels more than Came to my share for 231 Baskets was the Amount of all that was gatherd, thus 77 Baskets was Each mans shair but I paid Alx Johnson $5.25 for the 14 Baskets. Buisness Dull. I bot a Set of wagon Harness for two Horses to day at Mr Dicks, paid him Sixteen Dollars for them in Cash. And I Sent Gim Down in the Swamp to bring up some Corn

10 I find Buisness only Tolerable. I wrote a Letter this Evening to Mrs Miller by Wilcox, S B Princess — Jim Came up from Hard Scrabble this Evening bringing 4 Baskets of Corn, 50 Bundles of Fodder, 1 Bushell Potatoes, 9 Eggs from Mosbey Place and 2½ pds of Butter, Bag of Peas, 1 doz and 7 Eggs from Mosbey Place, and the 9 was from H. A. Scrabble.

11   Nothing New, buisness some what Dull. I remaind Home all day untill Late in the Evening, then took a walk with my 3 sons on the Commons & the streets are very Dusty indeed at present.

12   Buisness Tolerable Only, $24 by Charles under the Hill. Hauld ½ Cord of Blocks up with Cuff & Bob in the waggon. To Day it was that Phill & Billy drove down Sally Wren and Calf, Bellar & Calf, & Patients — into the Swamp.

13   Nothing new   Buisness only Tolerable, fair   I got a Game Bag and Shot Pouch from Mr Odell to day and told him if he would Stock my gun well that I would take those things and Consider us square up to the 1st Day of January 1847, which was agreed on by him &c. Jack and Jim went in the Swamp this Evening driving Cuff and Bob in the waggon.

14   Nothing new. Jim and Jack Came up from Hard Scrabble this Evening bringing Zorah & her Bull Calf & Dinah with her heifer Calf   There Calves are a Little old at Present.   Jim broght up a Load of Hay from the Mosbey Place, 8 Eggs dito and 6 from H D Scrabble, 1 Pd. of Butter from dito, & ½ Bushel Potatoes from the Mosbey place

15   Nothing new   Gim & Frank went in the Swamp this morning and brought a Load of Hay Each, the One Driving the 2 Horse wagon, the other the 1 Horse Buggy. They report all well at Hard Scrabble. The Hay Came from the Mosbey Place — Capt Barlow gave me a Bull Calf to day from his Cow that went dry — I recevd 2 Letters from New Orleans to day & Some News papers.

16   Nothing New. Buisness Dull or Tolerably so. Gim & Frank went into the Swamp to day and brought a Load of Hay Each, and Some Fodder and Some Pumpkins and a bag of Peas from Hard Scrabble.

18   Nothing new. I was at Home all day to day.

19   Nothing new. Buisness is dull   I wrode down in the Swamp to day to See How things Looked down there & I found Billy & Phill & Peggy were Pulling Grass at the Mosbey place   I was at Home at Hard Scrabble and Pulling Peas — Gim & myself was Picking Peas.

20   Nothing new. I Slept in the Swamp Last night and I got up Erly this morning and went to picking Peas. I Picked untill Breakfast time and then Started to town   I wrode to town smartly under two Hours on Cuff. I sent Frank down this Evening with the Buggy to Pick peas   He took Sam with him. Maj Young Sent me a Lot of S Potatoes as a Present to day. The River is very low at the Present time, very indeed. I sent a mattress down to day by Frank.

21   Nothing new   Buisness tolerable Only. I was at Auction to day and bot some trifling things thare. Dutch Miller went down to Hard Scrable to day to Commence to work to make rails &c. Mr Austin Williams was Burried to day. He died at his Plantation, Hank Watson was Buried also to day. He died at the Hospital and Burried from Mrs Dalias   I received $25 to day from Dr Aplewhite for one months rent of store to 1st instant.

22   I received $8 from Mr. Torris to day for rent to the 1st inst, I received a Letter from Mr Miller to day & he remarked that I had rented my Land too cheap.

23   Nothing new. Buisness only tolerable, There was a Drill of officers on the Bluff. Tomorrow will be the Genr Muster, Tis very Strange, I Bot of Mr F. Marschalk a sorril mare to day and gave him $30 in Cash and my Buggy and Harness for his mare and He took the money and the mare and wrode off said he would send the mare up as soon as he got down under the Hill, which he did not, but Borrowed the other and wrode out and crossed the River. Forman would not give up the nag because he, F Marschalk, had not paid his bill — Tis a little strange to me — I bot a Cow from Mr Barlow this morning for 9 Dollars and a Bushel of Potatoes, $5 I paid him the Cash for & owes him 4 Dollars yet.

24   To Marketing as usual and the times are only tolerable. Gim is up from Hard Scrable to day and bring 19 Bundles of Fodder and 16 Bushells of Peas and a few Pumpkins all from Hard Scrabble, 1 doz and 3 Eggs also — I sent a Bushell of Peas to day, ½ for Capt Johnson and ½ for Mrs Miller and Family. Tis to day I believe that the Frenchmans rent commences — I had some shingles put on the House to day by Mr Roses Boys.

25   Nothing new   Buisness quite So-So. Mr Ford has arrived from the North, got Home this Evening. I had my Wm. and Richard with me this Evening and we Drove the Cow that I bot of Caps Barlow down as far as Mr. Walterns place — to be driven farther to morrow.

26   Nothing new. Buisness only tolerable fair. Bily & Phill startd down to day in the wagon to drive to Hd. S & they

took 50 ct sugar, 50 ct Coffee', 1 Shoulder Bacon, 1 Ham, 1½ Bushell of Meal, 1 Paper of Coffee also.

27   I was having Frank Pave the yard a part of the day to day

28   Nothing new. I had 1 Buggy Load of wood Hauld and 1 waggon Load also from the wood that I bot of Mr Waltern   I dont know how much there is but I suppose 4 or 5 Cords. Sam Winston and Mr Martin the District Etorney has a fight this Evening   S Winston Bit Martins Finger pretty smartley — they were Seperated by the Croud, Gim Brot up 3 Bushells of Peas and seys they are the Last down thare, and that they done picking of them, and he hauld up a Load of Hay from the Mosbey place and brot up a shoat, the first one that has been Killd at Hard Scrabble. It weighd 39 lbs.

30   I made a trade this Evening for a Little waggon and Harness and a Little Sorill mare, gave sixty five dollars for the Concern

31   Buisness dull   Gim took the old Barlow Cow & Calf down as far as the Mosbey Field

November 1   Nothing new. Buisness only tolerable   I took a wride this Afternoon with my 2 youngest Sons   I wrode old Charlie and Richard and Byron wrode the two sorril mares — We wrode Considerable over the Hills &c. Dr Duncans Family & young Davis &c has returnd from the North

3   Nothing New. Buisness Some what dull   Circuit Court is in Session at present. Commenced yesterday. Mr. Laneare Came to me to day to Know if I would Let a Mr Higgins to moove in in the Mosbey House to remain but a short time that he was agoing to Liece a piece of ground from Mr B. Winn, and he wanted to get my Consent to allow Mr Higgins to remain in the House untill he could Build a House on Mr Winns Land. I told him that I had rented the place to Mr Gregory and that I wanted Possession of the place on the 15th or the 20th or in fifteen or twenty Days. So He promised to give full and Entire posession at that time so I Left, and Came to town   I Commenced yesterday to Pull or dig the Sweet Potatoes out of the Lower patch — I am Some what Late with them

4   Nothing new. Court in Cession at Present, Judge Posey Presiding. I Commenced this morning to have potatoes Dug at the Mosbey place — Phill & Billy was Digging them.

5   I receid a Letter from Mr Miller to day — Gim went to the Swamp to day, drove old Charlie and Trim, brot up 14 Bushes of Sweet potatoes from the Mosbey Place

6   To day has been a very pleasent and agreeable Day and nothing new — I Bot a Cow & a calf to day at auction, $8. They belonged to Soria

7   Nothing new. I was at Home all Day to day   Gim brot up 5 Bushells of Corn and 13 Bushells of Potatoes, the Corn from Hard Scrabble, Potatoes from Mosbey P

8   To day has been a pleasent day very and nothing new. Buisness only tolerable. I drove a Cow down to day as far as the Pasture of Mrs Watern with her Calf, a Heifer Calf   I Bot them at the Soria Sale at S. & Taintors — pd 8 Dollars for Her

9   Nothing new. I was at auction to day, the School Land Sales, and I bot 403.10 Hundredths acres of Land at 1.25 per acre for it.[14] There was a good deal Sold to day and some at a Good Price — Gim was up from the Mosbey place to day and brot 15 Bushels of Potatoes, and Some Hay and Alfred a Load of Hay — both in 2 Horse waggons

10   Nothing new   Buisness Tolerable fair   Gim & Alfred Came up this Evening from Hard Scrable bringing by Gims wagon 7 Bushels of S. Potatoes, 20 Bushells of Corn, 60 or 80 Bundles of Fodder, 5 pumpkins — Alfred Brot a good Load of Hay — the Hay and Potatoes Came from the Mosbey Place, the Corn from Hard Scrable, Mr Galbrath was in the shop to night and I had a Long talk with him about Land &c., the Swamps &c. Alfred Commenced this morning to work by the month for me.

11   Nothing new   Buisness tolerable fair. The wether is very warm indeed   This has been the Prettiest spell of wether I Ever saw. So mild, So warm, pleasant, So fine for agricultural Pursuits. Gim and Alfred returns from the Swamp with a Load of Hay and Foder, reports Billy and Phill Digging Potatoes down at Hard Scrabble   Bungin the Murderer was cleard to Night for Killing Mr Sessions Servant

12   Gim and Alfred brings up two Loads of Fodder and stuff from Mosbey Place — Mr Dick paid me five dollars on acct.

13   Nothing new — I wrode into the Swamp after Breakfast this morning. Robert went with me, I went down to my place   They were Just about to Finishing the Diging of the Potatoes, in the uper Field   This now is the Last that we have

---

[14] Johnson's ninety-nine-year lease of 403.1 acres of school land, Section 3, Township 6, Range 4, West, for $500 was recorded in Adams County Deed Records, II, 427.

to Dig on the Place. Mr Forshey was down this Several days runing out the Lines between Mr Henderson and Little Winn and Willcot   The Land fell far short of the amount I am told so I believe that Little Winn agreed to Lett the Loss be mutial between the two, which I think Leaves a Ballance only of 206 acres to Each man, and then he has the ten acres from the Lower End of my tract Surveyed off and I dont think it ought to have been done without my being thare to see it — Alfred Came up with a Load of Fodder &c. from the Mosbey place

    14   Nothing new. Buisness tolerable fair. Alfred made 3 Loads of wood from Mrs Waterns to day. Frank & Gim with the other wagon made 2 and Wm with the Buggy made two. I wrote a Letter to day to Mr Miller and sent a Bag of Meal, 1 Bushell   Billy and Phill walked up this Evening from the Place below.

    15   Nothing new. I wrode down to Mrs Waltern this Evening. My Wm was with me   We were Looking for the Cow Zora

    16   Nothing new   Races commenced to day and Scintila of Mr Kenner[15] vs. Capt Minors Bay Filly. Mr Kenner won the Race very Easy — and I won 3 dollars — Easy

    17   We had rain to day which made the mud prety Heavy and two Races was run to day. Capt Minor won the 1st Race and Col Bingaman won the other by walking for it. And Mr Turnbull was the winner. Nothing new   I won $6.50 to day on the Race.

    18   I was out at the Races to day and Capt Minor galloped for the money — He gave Col Bingaman ½ not to run   The other Race was won by Capt Minor   It was the Mr. Hoggatts Black Dick vs Col Bingamans Bets Bounce and Mr. Kenners Night Breeze. She was the Last in the Race. I won $3.50 on the Race, and came Home in due time, the Race was a good one & the Col won one heat but could not win.

    19   Nothing new. I was at the tract to day to see a Race &c.

    20   Nothing new. I was at the Race tract to day and saw a Race or two.

    21   Heavy Racing to day at the tract. Several Nags Enterd. 1 mile Heats.

    22   Nothing new   Buisness quite dull. Considering the

---

15 Duncan F. Kenner, Louisiana sugar planter and later a Confederate agent in Europe, was at this time a prominent turfman. His mother was a daughter of Stephen Minor, father of William J. Minor of Natchez.

time of year. I wrode down in the Swamp this Evening and took with me Cuff and the Sorrile Filly and Left them there, I was Surprised to find that Mr W. Winn had sold his Land to Mr Gregory ie he told me that he had promised to do it and the ten Acres which he supposed that he had in the tract that he sold me — We talked some time about it and then we Separated for the Night.

23   Nothing new. Buisness tolerable fair   I was in the Swamp this Morning and Came up with Little Winn, Mr Gay and my Son, Wm.   Shortly after we got up Mr Gregory Came up with his Brother Charles from the Swamp. We went to the recorders office to day and thare Examined all the deed given by the clerk of the Court

24   Buisness only tolerable   Nothing new. I was out to Dr. Smiths this morning to try and get him to go Down to Survey the 120 and a fraction of acres that Little Winn sold me and He told me that he regrettd very much that he could do it as he was then ready to start up the River to survey for Mr Jno Ruth and was compelld to start this very morning — which was the truth — I then started and went to see Brewerton and I found him up the River doing some surveying for Capt Nevitt, so I Came Home and Could do no more

25   They were working the Road to day in the Swamp, and my hands did not work. I did not get a chance to tell them   Col. Bingaman, Mary Ellen, Sends Mr Miller 3 Barrels of Potatoes, pinders [and] walnuts. Capt. Nevitt is having surveying done up in his Swamp by Mr Brewerton

26   I wrode down to Mr Fords to see Mr Gregory about my not working the Road and to offer his Brothers a Situation on the Com. Bank Plantations — The Government wants 9 Regments more to fight, &c.

27   I saw Mr. Brewerton this day and he promised me to go with me into the Swamp to morrow morning to Commence the Survey. I was at the Probate Office to day and on Looking over the map of the Swamp I found that the Entreyes made by P. Andrews were as Follows, 321 [and] 60 Hundredths of an Acre   This is the Land now in the Possesion of Bailor Winn. The next 176.40   This is the Land that Mosbey sold me; so in 1815 the above was the amount it containd, tho [in] 1841 or 2 it was found to Contain 111 acres, and some Fractions   The Next was 236 acres [in] 1815 but [in] 1841 or 2 it was found to Contain two tracts of 130 acres Each, making you See 160 [260]

acres and some Fractions   The next 58 Acres [was] then [in]
a tract Enterd by G Winn of 280 acres

28   I was up this morning, yes before day, and was making
preperations to go into the Swamp with Mr Brewerton to have
him Survey the tract of Land that I Bot of Little Winn, We got
off prety Erly in the morning and got down there and found some
opposition in the Survey by Disenterested men as they Called
themselves, that was the two Mr Gregorys and Mr Ford. The
truth is that Mr Jas Gregory had Conditionally purchased W.
Winns Land and had put him up to refuse to have the Survey
made, Saying that he had had his ten acres ran off and was satisfied with it and that if I wanted the other Survey that I could
do it but he did not want his ten Acres as he call it ran off, and
it was Some time before he would agree to have it ran off and at
Last he Consented and after runing the Line it turns out to have
only a fraction over Eighty acres in it instead of 130, and a
Fraction, tis strange very strange. Bot the 3 Cows & calves that
Came in from Mr Ruckers to day whilst I was in the swamp, paid
$10.50 Each for them. They were a white Cow & a Brown & a
Red one, all 3 Said to be good Ones.

29   Nothing new has transpired during the day — I took a
Long walk this Evening with Mc   Walked around the town
nearly, then up to or beyond Mrs Lintens. Took a view of Mr
Browns Premises, &c.

30   The Swamp Delegation was up this Evening and Mr
Ford offered me $6000 for the whole of my interest in the front
Land in the Swamp — which I did not agree to take

December 1   Buisness tolerable. Mr Torris paid $8 [to]
me for one months rent Ending 1st November. Dr. Applewhite
has been away for Some Days to Arkensaw, his Family wants to
see him.

2   Nothing new. Buisness Tolerable to day   Little Winn
came up from the Swamp with the two Gregorys and is about
Closing off all the Land that he owns together with the ten acres
that belonged to the tract that I own at present

3   This morning Erly I was up and writing or about to
write, After Breakfast I got out a Garneshee vs Mr Gregory for
the money that Winslow Winn owed me   The amount was 76
Dollars including the Interest on Money Loaned &c and 75 Dollars
on acct of the Deficientcy of the Land, that he Sold me, So Mr
Gregory paid me or the officers $146 — So our dispute is over and
done with I hope.

4 Nothing new. Today Gim and Bottle drove into the Swamp Mr Dicks Martha and her Calf, Mcs Kate & her calf, Browny had no Calf &c. 5 heads

5 Nothing New. Buisness tolerable, only. To day it was that Mr Gregory was up to day and I had the Lise drawn for One year on the Mosbey Property, that is the part that is improved and none other, only the privilidge of Cuting Rail Timber, Enough to do the Fencing of the place during the year, and that he is to give up the Possession quietly at the End of the year, the Liese to Commence from the first of January 1847, and to End 1848, and the Consideration to be $100 — I then had a talk with Elick Johnson and he rented the place of his present Residence for the term of One year for fifty Dollars and is to take Care of my stock, &c.

6 Nothing new. Buisness only tolerable, I remaind home all day

7 Nothing new. I Came very near Loosing my School Land to day by my [not] knowing that the Board of Commissioners were to meet. I Came very near not hearing of the fact at all, but Mr Clay was Sent arround by Mr Lacoste Just in time to have me get there before the Board adjourned; I Came in in a Hurry, full of Excitement, so as to make the whole of the Gentlemen Laughf. Dr. Metcalf wanted to Know what I was a going to do. I made Out to tell Him that I would give notes and a good indorser, that was McCary, which was agreed on. I then took a paper and took it to Mr C. Lacoste and Left it with him. Gim Came up from the swamp this Evening and brought a Hog, weight 75 lbs. Tis one of our raising — I Sent him down this morning Erly with the waggon, Mr Gregory Sends his hands Down Erly this Morning to my Mosbey Place to work

8 Nothing new. Buisness dull, I Sent Gim down into the Swamp this morning to Moove the Corn from the Mosbey place down to Hard Scrabble   I wanted all of them to Haul. I sent them to haul all the Chickens, and Everything Else

9 Mary Ellen and Jack Left for New Orleans to night on S. B. Natchez — I requested Mr Whitehurst to day to Let me Know how much Land there was in the School [Land] Sec. No. 3, Township No 6, Range 4 west, and have [it] Bounded &c. I wrote a petition this Evening requesting the Consideration of the Selectmen to a certain Tax on a town Lot, &c. Gim is up with 6 Barrells of Corn this Evening

10 I was at Home all day to day, and buisness Some what dull.

1847

January 1   Buisness Tolerable fair. Mr Raily paid me The full amount of his shaving Bill $4.50 up to the 1st of January inst. Mr Peter Jordan paid me Sixteen Dollars in full for two months Rent of Store On Main St. to the 1st inst — Mr White paid me One Dollar which paid his Shaving bill up to the 1st inst — Mr Lyons paid me two Dollars and a half yesterday which Sum paid his Acct. to the 1st inst   I paid Maj Young fifty Dollars yesterday for Charles up to the 1st inst and took out fifteen Dollars for Clothing &c. This was yesterday   Mr Benum removes the remainder of the things that Dr Applewhite Left in the Botanic Store, I had the fence repaired to day and the yard cleaned that the Dr Left — Old Billy is hauling shucks to day from a Flat Boat at the Landing — I Loaned young Babbit two Dollars to night to Go to the Concert

2   Nothing new. The Candidates are very buissy Electioneering night and Day.

4   I got On my Little Horse Dick and wrode down into the Swamp   I Stoped at B. Winns and Lookd at the Jno Fletcher Map — I Looked at it and then went down to my uper Line and wrode Out On it 1600 yards untill I Came to the Lake, Long Lake I think — I crossed 2 Small Lakes which I wrode over. I Came on back and went on to Hard Scrable   I there went to Wilcotts to See Stump — Made him an offer, then Came back, took dinner, then Lookd at them work awhile   They were cuting down the trees   I ordered them to go to work and pile up the trask to Burn it.

10   William wrode up fome the Swamp this morning in the Cold   I was Just prepairing to go down as he Came up so as to take my Gun and take a Hunt. But did not Go.

11   Buisness Only Tolerable. Mr Barton up from the Swamp to day. Told me that a number of men were cuting timber and wood back in the Swam and that he was at it too   Him and Mr Everen — B Winn was Cuting near my school section

12   Gim Came up from the Swamp to day and reports the Gregory heifer and Gustin as having Calves and Pink too. He Said that he Could not find 6 of the Sheep &c. One of the Slabbs had Piggs and one or two of the other Sows also

13   Buisness Dull to day as I was not at Home. I Got On

my Horse this Morning Erly and went to the Swamp   I took my Son Wm with me and Claiborn to try and find the Conners of my School Land, and I found according to my Calculation that it Connerd over on the other Side of Long Lake where I took and marked Some Percimon trees. This was On the Side of the Lake, I then Started and went an East Course untill I Came to a willow place which was all Lengths of the Rope which was 28 yds Long, Distance 308 yds   I then turnd around and went back and took a north Course and went twenty five Lengths of the Rope ie Seven Hundred yards   Here I Struck Mudy Lake and the course appeard to run up thru the Head of Mudy Lake   I in the first place measured 62 Lengths of the Rope which was a mile and Conered over on the Hills Side or North Side of Long Lake   In going along accross by Cypress Byou I found that the Flat Road that B. Winn had cut was on a part of My School Land, He has got a Lot of men in thare Cuting of Timber   B. Everen and Barton & others are thare Cuting of[f] timber also   I paid Dr Stone my doctors bill today   It [was] Sixteen dollars and 2 dollars of this was for Charles

14   Nothing new. Buisness Tolerable Only

15   It was to day that I wrode Out to the tract to See the Fight Between Lilly and Burchell at the Race tract.

17   Buisness Only Tolerable. Myself and Wm took a Lacky wride this Evening Out by Mr Marshalls and by Mrs Smiths to Mrs Scotts Field &c. We were Looking for the Jacqumine Cow but Could not find Her at all

18   Gim and Alfred and Billy & Phill went down to day   I Sent Some trees down by them, 22 of them in all, 6 of them was Peach trees, the Ballance China — They report that they are now working up above the House in the field — Mrs Meeks Mooves in to day next door to us in State St. She has bot the Property. I paid Collecter Britton $6.55 for Crigier & Wilson to day for Mothers acct. Mr Merret Williams arrivd this morning from Kentucky. Looks well   Has not been here for a great many years, 8 or 9 I think — Shoe Maker rents a Shop above me this day at 8 per month. Payable monthly

19   Gim is still in the Swamp   The old Brown Cow that we bot of the Ruckers died to night near Mr Sultzer.

20   Nothing new. Buisness oh how dull Very indeed   Yesterday was more so. Plenty of Ice to day Every where. Good many hunting ducks   This wether for ducks. I Shot a malard duck about a week ago with my Little Gun and a Squirrell too.

Gim is still in the Swamp. Aught to have been up to day　Stump was up to day to See me and I Promised to go to the Swamp in the morning and See him about it. Pink & Gustin and Gregory hiefer & Mosby hiefer and Phillis Rose all of them have had Calves

　　21　Gim Came up from the Swamp this forenoon and I went down with Claibourn and took a Long hunt for my Sheep and Could not find them　Stump was with me. I Shot 1 duck of Malard with my Little Gun down near St Catharine Creek.

　　22　I was in the Swamp to day and was helping to make a road at the foot of the field for Stock to go around in. Stump Commencd this morning to work and our bargain is that he is to have one third of what is made on the ground and one third of the Proffit that may arise from wood that may be Cut by Billy, Phill and Peggy and he to find his own Family and I to find my force &c. I Left there near 1 Oclock and hunted my way up past Fords Field and back of Mrs Walterns, and Came up by the creek and Came through the fence there by and out to the Road &c.

　　23　Gim & William Started down to day to Look for the Sheep. They having all of them ranaway — I found 5 of them On the back of the Lake and one of them had a young Lamb with her — Billy and Phill Came up this Evening from the Swamp　They report the Pasture Fence up once more. Gim and William up this Evening from Swamp and had found Seventeen Sheep and the Jackamine Heifer with a young Calf — they were all driven Home to the House　Twenty six Sheep Lost as yet

　　24　Nothing new. Buisness Only Tolerable. After dinner I Took my new Horse and wrode him Out and took Jeff along with me　We wrode down in the Swamp back of Mrs Walterns　We wrode on the Creek Bank down as far as the Swamp would Let us go. I suppose we went a mile and a ½　We then turned off to the right and wrode up a white Oak ridge which Led to Mrs Walterns Farm House or Gin — we were Looking for Some Sheep that had ranaway from my place — We Saw much Sign on the Creek Bank but Could not find them, Tis not more than a mile I think from Mrs Walterns place back to the Creek. Bailor Winn is at this time Got a Large force in the Swamp at work Cuting Out wood and Cypress timber, to run it to Orleans

　　25　Nothing new　Buisness dull, Billy & Phill went down Last night Late with the dray and Harness to have the Rails Hauled, and Logs to Build Phills House &c. To day I made Out an acct. VS Mr. D. Mobley for shaving for 5 years　I took off for absent time &c the sum of $40 and that Left a Ballance of

$46. I then took out the Bill that he had VS Charles which was
$12.75 I then deducted my bill from said acct which was $12.80.
This then Left him still in my debt $20 and some cents This
some [sum] I promised to take out in the store as I want &c.

26 Nothing new Buisness only tolerable Gim and Claibourne has been in the swamp Ever since Monday or yesterday
morning — they went down to hunt sheep &c. The River is high
for this Season Corn 75 cts, Hay $12 a ton, Bacon Hog rounds
4½ cts, Potatoes per Barrel 1.50, Flour 5 [to] 6.25, Cotton
11 cts

29 Buisness only tolerable Dull day

30 Nothing new. Buisness has been very Good to day.
Good deal of work in the way of Hair cuting — Gim brought up
3 of the Mosbey Stock of Hogs, Good Large Shoates. This is the
4th One that I have Got of that Lot of Hogs that I bot of him,
Also brought up 3 Cows and there Calves Viz Gustine & calf, Rose
and do, Phillis & Calf, and reports the House Built for Filly &
Phill On the Ridge opposite the House, Mr Q Claibourne Came
up to day. Mrs Wilcott moves up to day to my House

31 Nothing new. Buisness Only Tolerable. I remaind at
home I took a walk with Mc to the old Fort and back Home
After dinner again

February 1 Produce High at present. Cotton too. Mr S
Murcherson died this morning a Little After Eight Oclock at his
Residence in the City. Jim went down to day and took with him
meal, Coffee, Sugar &c and Some clothing for Petty and Zorah in the
wagon. Mr Delshamer Mooves or is prepairing to moove into my
new House as it is Called at $25 per month Cheap rent I
think tho there is Considerable to do in it before he mooves in it.

2 Nothing new to day Mr Murcherson was Burried this
morning and it rained all the time

3 A L. Wilsons wharf Boat Sunk this morning Just before
Day at the Landing with all her Goods on her — Gim in the
Swamp still. Mother Sent 6 hens to Mrs Miller On The S. B.
Natchez. Old Pink and her calf died the day in the swamp

4 I had my Iron Steps Hauled up to the Store this Evening to put up — Gim Came up this Evening from Hard Scrabble
— Brought Nothing. Corn 1 dollar, Coal 75 cts, Hay $20 per ton

8 After Breakfast I went down into the Swamp and Took
Claib with me. After dinner I wrode down with Mr Stump to
work, no to Look for a Sheep with her young One, and Stump

found her and drove her up　　I took my Little Gun with me and Killed one teal duck as I went down.

9　　I was down in the Swamp and I got up very Erly in the morning and went to work in the Lower field and was Burning Brush　We Burnt Considerable of it. I Left after 3 Oclock this Evening and on my way up Killd 2 ducks, 1 Mallard and 1 Diving duck

10　　Nothing new. Buisness only Tolerable　Gim Goes into the Swamp this Evening to remain untill Saturday — Phill is burning Brush

12　　Mr Torris paid me twenty four dollars rent for the Shop he now Occupies　This pays his rent up to the First of Feb inst

13　　Nothing new

14　　To day we have nothing New and buisness Quite as usual　I See no Change.

15　　Nothing new.

16　　This has been a Good day in the way of work and The Cause, in part, of that, is the Grand Lodge is in Cession at present, and is very well attended, I weighed myself to day and I weigh 135 pounds with Coat, Shoes, Hat, watch &c on.

17　　Corn is worth a dollar and a half per Barrel, Meal 1.50 per Bushell & Potatoes 2.25 per Barrell. I Sent Alfred down this Evening with two plows and a Bushell of Meal and a Corn Mill and a Barrell of Potatoes to plant. The Shoe Maker Byrne Left To day and all I got from him was One pr of Boots at 7 dollars, and that is more than I thought I would Get

18　　It was to day instead of yesterday I Sent Alfred down to my place &c. and he went down in the Skift with a Mr Williams,　The Rain of Last night is said To have Caused the creek to raise higher than it has been Known to rise in the recollection of Some of the oldest in the neighbourhood — Mr E. Dixon told me this Evening that it was 3 ft. higher than he had Ever Seen it before, Mr Dixon told me this Evening that he had my Sheldon Cow out at his House and was milking her and that She had Lost her Calf &c. John Grant was tried to day for Stealing Whiskey, Flour &c. and was held to Prison to await his trial at Court

19　　Nothing new. Buisness not Quite So Good as it has been for the Last 4 or 5 days — Hay is Selling at Our Landing at Our Landing at $25 per ton, Corn 1.50 a Barrell, Oats 60 cts per Bushell, Corn meal 1.50 a Bushell, potatoes 2.25 lb [barrel], Pork is very High, meats of all description are up &c. Mr Stanwood the assessor told me to day that my Estimate ($28.50) was too Low   I told him then to bring a man by 12 Oclok to give me as much and he promised to do So but he never Came at all. I tharefore think the Estimate will Stand Good — Mr C. Railey will Lecture to night at the institute Schooll &c. First time, Mr. Rose Gave a Ball Last night at his Residence, And it was a Darkey Ball So I am told, and the Following Per[s]ons were present, to wit, Wm Nicks, Andrew Lieper, his Brother, Jeff Hoggatt & Wm, Mr Hoggatt, Frank & Claibourne, Wm Burns, Randolph B[urns][1]

20   Wm wrides Big Jeff to day down to H. Scrabble   Nancy Ragan VS James C Jones, Her Husband — 9th Judicial district Court term, 26th Jany 1847. I See that She is for dissoving the matrimony debts &c. The Lower Land

21   I paid Miller this morning fifteen dollars on acct. of his work &c. Phill Came up this morning   He was Compell by the rain to Stop at Mr Walterns Last night. Billy he came on up Last night through the rain and it was a tremendious rain Last night. The Streets Look as clean this morning as you please, Nothing new this morning. Buisness Only tolerable, After 12 Oclock to day McCary and myself took a walk together and went Out by the Spanish Bayou, and there we found Some Boys playing Cards — We got Mooles to Load up his Gun and Hallow at them and Shoot at the Same time which he did and oh what runing you never Saw. They Left a Knife and 50 cts and there Cards, which Jeff went down thare and got when they ran off — We went Out to the Pond and there we past off and hour I Suppose in Sailing Little Boats accross the pond to amuse the Small Boys and ourselves too. My Boat out Sailed Mcs untill he found Out That I had a rudder on mine and then his Boat Out Saild mine being Larger than mine — Wm Came up from H. Scrable and States that Stump had Killd two of my Mosbey Lot of Hogs and that A Johnson had Killd One of his that was in the Same Gang — He

1 William Nix, Andrew Lieper and his brother, Frank Burns, Claiborne Burns, and Randolph Burns were free Negroes. The Burns family, headed by mulatto Rachel Burns, had been freed by William Burns of Jackson and Natchez, Mississippi, in 1840. See Adams County Deed Records, II, 557; U. S. Census Reports, 1850, Schedule I, Adams County, 11. Jefferson Hoggatt and William Hoggatt were still technically slaves (see Adams County Deed Records, KK, 44–45, LL, 207–208), but were treated like free Negroes. The two Hoggatts and Frank and Claiborne Burns were apprentices in Johnson's barbershop at this time.

For a reference to Thomas Rose as the "kind and gentlemanly host of the Natchez Guards" at a militia meet at his residence, "two miles from town," see Natchez *Free Trader*, May 24, 1845.

Said that one of them was a very Large Hog but was not very fat at the time &c.

22　I Sent Jim down to day with the wagon and two plows and a sack of damaged Corn and One doz peach trees and two double Trees to plough with — I have not Commenced to plow yet

23　Nothing new. Several Girls that was in a fight yesterday was whiped to day. The[y] Got fifteen Lashes Each　Three of them, the Gibson girl and Bety Dumat and a Girl of Mrs La-Crose. Thom Rose & L David was on the Jury — Gim is in the Swamp　Went down yesterday. I paid Mr B. Wade Thirty dollars to day for five months Rent of the Shop at the Landing which Sum paid the rent up to the 1st of Feb inst according to his receipt but I think it is not due untill about the 24th inst. if I recollect aright — I paid Mr Newman To day my ⸜State and County Tax which was twenty five dollars and fifty three cents, ie by paying $5.63 for Mosbeys Tax. I indorsed a note to day I think it was for Mr Torras to the Amount of $43 payable in forty days after date

24　I started down with Some Cattle to the Swamp. It was The old Brown Soria Cow, the red & wite Sided Shelden Cow, the two Rucker Cows, the 1 a white the other a red Cow, Fany and her calf, the red Calf Ben, the Brown Cow Mariah and her calf Polly, Francis & the old Black & white Cow from Dr Stone with her Calf red and white — in all 12 head of them　Gim Came up this morning and brought me Some Corn [and] 2 Shoats of the Mosbey Lot of Hogs

25　My Force Commenced to plough this morning for the first time this season and I think they Commenced below the House in the old Ground. Sent Gim down with the Buggy to take down the Plough that he brought up with him yesterday and to drive down the Stock that I Started with yeserdaty — Claibourn went with him

26　After dinner to day I wrode down to Hard Scrabble and took Mc Wm with me & My Wm also.

27　I got up Erly this Morning and took my Mesho Gun and wrode down from Hd. Scrble to near the Creek, and I Shot a duck of Mallard, then Came back and went up and found Our Cow Fanny Dead in the Cane, but what could have Killed her is more than I can tell, The old Cow Sally is also dead. She was found in the cane dead　I Sent Phill to Skin them both which he did

28   Buisness has been tolerable fair to day   Nothing new. Corn $2 a Barrell at the Landing, Hay $30 a ton.

March 1   Nothing new.

8   I Got up before day Light this morning and went on foot in Search of my Horses Bob. & Cuff. and After walking all the morning returned without them — tho Gim found them while I was away

11   I Got on my Horse this morning and I wrode into The Swamp this morning on my Horse Cuff and I took my Little gun and I Shot 1 Squirrell on my way down, I went on the S B. Princess who was wooding at Wilcotts and She told me that she had ran over a flat boat the night before   She was Laden with Corn. I worked at rolling of Logs &c. Mr Stump was out in the woods and Came in with three Hogs — two of them He brought Home and the 3d One was One of mine and that was Left at Elick Johnson for I found it thare as I went Out to Hunt in the Evening — Now this I do not Like it — at all — This Evening I went out and we only Caught a Possum

14   Nothing new. Buisness Tolerable Only — The River is Still On the rise at this point and is Quite High

15   Nothing new   Buisness Only Tolerable

16   Buisness Only So So — Sent Gim to the Swamp

17   The water is Geting high. The river is Still rising — and is Only about 3 ft below the water of 1844

18   I Started to the Swamp this morning about 10 Oclock   I found the river geting very high but no water between the House & the Quarters, but the Ground begins to Look damp

19   I was in the Swamp this morning and had Claib. with me, and we worked untill Breakfast time piling Brush — We then took Breakfast and then went to Look for Stock &c. and after a Long hunt we found and Drove up a Lot of my Hogs that was on the Hurricane Ridge — they were about 26 or 8 of them in all. We marked 7 or 8 of the young Ones and turned them all into the Pasture; there was only 30 Sheep that I Could find up and 1 at Wilcotts — I Started Home in the Afternoon and brot Some Corn up in the Buggy. The Little Sorril mare was in it. The Blaunch Heifer died to day — the Small One I mean

20   The river is very high at present and is On the rise still. Corn is worth 10 bits per Barrell. I have not planted much more than half my Ground as yet

21   Nothing new. I sailed Boats this Evening with Mc and the Boys and Mc Boat Beat the old Shark at Last. It was a new One that he made

22   Nothing new. Buisness Quite dull indeed — I Saw Alecx Johnson to day and He wanted to Sell me his Black Horse which I told him I would like to get if I had the money to Spare &c. His wife and himself had Fallen Out and he told me he was off for the uper Country to Leave her, Wilcox took dinner with me to day — he was passenger on the Natchez. Mr Sargent told me that he would take the Oxen that I bot the other day at $50, wagon an all

23   Nothing new. Buisness Tolerable Only   I Sent Gim in the Swamp this morning [to] See what he could [find] of the Stock, and report to me tomorrow when he comes up — Little Winn up to day And wrode my Horse Jeff — whod gave him the permission is more than I Can tell, The River is very high at present and Still rising at this point.

24   Buisness Tolerable fair To day — This morning I Aught have Sent the Oxen to Mr Sargent but could not get a chance to do So but will On to morrow if I Can   Sure as Fate, I Made a Contract with Hommer To take them up To Pittsfield. Mr Mobley paid me by 6 Shirts Six dollars   The Shirts are for Charles

25   I Sent the Oxen up this morning to Mr Sargent by the man Henry — The River is Quite high at present and Looks very much Like an over Flow. Gim Came up yesterday Evening and reports the River very high and that Considerable of my Stock was still out in the Swamp and Could not be found — The mother of the 9 months Heifer has a Calf

26   Nothing new. Buisness Only Tolerable   I about 10 Oclock To day wrode my horse Bob into the Swamp Taking Byron with me on the Marshchalk Filly, I worked awhile in Burning Brush, then returned, wriding Wms Roan mare and Byron Little Billy — I Saw about 28 of the Sheep and 20 head of the Cattle, Calves and all. The water is so high that we have to cross in the Skift from the House to the Quarter — The Cattle I saw to day as Follows — Sheldon C[o]w, Sallys Calf, Savanah & Calf, Favors & Calf, Ruffin, Gustine, H. Pinks Bull, Patients old Brown Cow, two Mosbeys Cows with ther 4 calves, Prety, Hester, Black hed Steer, Redd, Francis — 20 Head, and there was 21 Head that I recollect that I did not See at all, Alex Johnson Came back to his wife this Evening She having Came to town After him when he had Left her, and whiped her &c.

27   Nothing new. Buisness Tolerable, &c. No it was today that I went in to the Swamp and not yesterday

29   Nothing new. The River is still on the Rise and is very high — I Bot an old woman to day from Mrs Mix   Her name was Rose: She was very old and I paid $35 in cash and the Judge Dunlap paid So he said $15. So that was the Consideration, $50 the Judge was owing me. So I now Say that we are Square &c. I pd Mr Hackett $11 for the Hay that I bot of him a Short time ago, &c.

30   Nothing new. Buisness Only tolerable. Charles paid $28 to day. This was taken in the Shop below. I took a Dose of Medicine Last night and I feell week this morning from it

April 1   I Started in the Swamp this morning Late to Look at the State of things and I found my Little Sorril mare very sore and Stiff and has been Severely Hurt as she now Shows it plainly — they Say by Geting Boged in the Levy up at the head of the field — Considerable of the Ground is not plowed nor planted yet, We have been Slow at work in Consequence of water

2   Nothing new. I was in the Swamp this Morning and I Started to drive up Some of My Cattle and Some of them I Could not Get up — they were too Sick and weak &c. Mariah, She got down near B Winns And Could not Get up. So did the Sheldon Cow that I Got of him. So we had to Leave them there to Dye. Old Bellar, She died a few Days ago just above The Duch Joe Shanty   Yesterday we were all at work at the Cattle ie Mr Stump, Bily, Gim, myself & Willaim — We got up to the City with those Only — Dunn Mosbey & Calf, Brown Zinzer & Calf, Pretty Boman & calf, Young Parker Heifer, the Red Steer Jerry, Hester & Calf, Savanah & Heifer, Parker C. & Calf, Pink Bull, Parker red Side Cow, Spted Heifer, Martha Dick, Polly & Sallys Calf

3   The River Still on the Rise as far as this place   Over the Bank on the other Side, Oposite the Jail

4   The water is very high and is still rising at this point

5   This week I want to be able to plow and plant The uper part of the new Grownd that we are clearing, at Least I hope so.

6   Buisness pretty Good to day. Rose that I bot of Mrs Micks Came home to my possession — She is a Smart old woman, I think

7   Nothing new. I wrote a Letter to Mr Miller This Evening by S. B. Natchez. We want rain very much at present, Good many are planting Cotton at present. The River is So high that

it is unsafe to try to Go down in the Swamp at present   The Land is so Low near Bailer Winns The Bank is Caving pretty Smartly. I bot Some Books to day   Some of them was Robt Pattersons Estate. I Agreed to Shave Dr Broom 1 month for a Bible — Holy — The River is Still rising at this Point

    8   I Sent Gim down to the Swamp this morning to see how the water Looks — Buisness dull to day and I am Afraid will be So all day — River is Still on the Rise yet at this Point, Tho it is presumed it will take a fall in a day or two, Gim returned to night and or this Evening and reports the Shelden Cow as having died on the Bank by B. Winns and that the other Cow Mariah was also down and would die he thought before morning.

    9   To day we had a fine Light Shower of Rain which Lasted for a Short time and it Came in Good time for the city was all dust and the planters wants it very much indeed. The River is still rising at this point and is very high — Jackumines old Joe Bogs was out to day Pestering my mares very much. The Rascal, I wish he would Keep him up

    11   Nothing new. Buisness Quite dull to day   I was prety much alone to day, ie the Afternoon, for I Took my 3 Small Boats and went Out to the Pond of Mr John Johnson and Sailed my Boats alone to see which was the fastest, The Long Boat Rough & Ready beat the party Easy Enough. Good many Scotchmen was present, old Hardy, Hamilton Johnson and a good many others.

    12   Nothing new. I very Soon after Breakfast this morning Got on my Horse big Jeff and wrode into the Swamp and took Claib. with me on the big Sorril mare   After I Got down thare it was with Greate fear that I crossed the water by B. Winns for it was very deep and Dangerous, I Looked for Stock nearly all day and did not find any at that worth Speaking of   I found Some few Hogs but no cattle. They were Just plowing in the new Ground on the ridge, The Winston Field. Stump he was Kniting a fish net   In the Afternoon we wrode up behind the Mosbey Field and there we found twelve young pigs or Shoats and we Caught 3 of them and Killd them and a Rabbit and a Possum &c. I had a very bad Head Ache indeed — very

    13   Nothing new. I Started Some time After Breakfast this morning to Come to town from out of the Swamp   We first took a Look for Cattle then Came Home, I found Several of them to day which I was Affraid was Lost. Jasper Winn was up to day from the Swamp, Tate, B. Winns wife and Tates wife &c. Very

Green   Locked arm   Came up to see the Show of Animals and they were a Show themselves for Sure — B. Winn is Just Building his new House.

14   Nothing new. Buisness Tolerable   The River is Still riseing up here, ie at this point, and Some Seys that the Rivers are all a rising above   If true it is bad &c. I Sent Williams Roan mare to Mr Boyers Wood Pecker To day and I Sent Kity Fisher to him also — this is the first time too

16   Nothing new   I was in the Swamp the day before yesterday and I found The Following Cattle Only, viz

Redd	1	did not see those	
Thom	1	York	1
Ruffin	2	Henrietta	1
Blck head Steer	1	White B. heiffer	1
Rachel & Calf	1	Mosbey yerling	1
Abigal & Calf	1	Mosbey heifer & calf	2
Dinahs Calf	2	Brouney Mosbey	1
Bloss Mosbey	2	Mosbey hevers	2
Kate & Calf	1		—
Francis	1		9
Mosbey yerling	1		
Bellars calf	1		

This Lot Dead I Suppose, viz. Certain

Ben	1
Fany & calf	2
Dr Stone cow & Calf	2
Soria Cow	1
& Calf	1
Blaunchs hefer & calf	2
Mosbeys white Back hefer	1
& her calf	1
Shelden Cow	1

17   Some what Buissey One [day] with me for I was a Good portion of this day down at the Quarrantine Ground and at Mrs Walterns at work at Some Corn That I had bot from the Flat Boat that had Sunk   I got 20 Sacks at 25 cts per Sack from Mr Fields who had bot the Ballance or nearly all; Tis night and I am very tired indeed from working &c.

18   Nothing new of much importance but I Discovered Some very Singular Conduct on the part of a Dutch Family on the Commons: they have from what appearances would indicate that they had thrown a Cow of mine down in the Byou and hid her down thare.

    19   Nothing new, It was to day that I was Out with Mr Dillon to have a Cow dug up that was Buried in the Buyou by the dutch. We found the hide and Enterals &c. but the Infernal Rascal had Stolen the meat and burred the hide, head &c. I am Satisfied in my own mind in regard to the matter — This Cow was Jane, She was owned by Mrs Neibut Last year, and she Sold her to the Fields who Traded her To me or I bought her and two others, The Dutch Family that Lives On the Commons must have Known all about it for the old wife was Said to have been at work all the Evening on Saturday and this was the time that The Cow was Slaughtered, and the Beef made use of or taken away, and a Butcher that Popkins had minding his Cattle was there all the Evening also, who said that he herd the cow fall Down the Buyou and that when She fell he used these words, that we went down and turned her over and her neck was Broke, and we Left thare and Came out, He then Said that two negro men were taking her out the Last he Saw of them; Oh for a good witness in this Case, Popkins Said that the Fellow told him that it was a Large red Cow and a young Calf that fell in and that the both went in together. So much for So much

    21   Charles Started this Evening to Jefferson and wrode my Big Horse Jeff

    22   I had a Settlement with Maj Young this morning — I paid him fifty Dollars for Charles wages up to the 1st of April inst. He allowed my acct. VS. Charles for 6 Shirts at — — — 6.00

                 And a Coat at — —   4.00

                 ————

         Thus the Cash I paid was $40 & the bill   10.00

I Then had a Settlement with Mr Dalsheimer And I Allowed his Wadsworths Bill of   6.00

And the Carpenters bill of $17   C. Stietenroth   17.00

and the Painters & Glazers bill   8.60

My own bill of — — —   11.25

                 ————

                                 42.85

And he owed Me $60 and paid me the difference $17.15   This paid me the full Amount of his rent to the 1st of April 1847 — Kitty And the Roan Mare was both Sent to day to Wood Pecker. The R. Mare refused him — this is the 2d time

    23   Nothing new. Miller Came up from the Swamp To day

and reported that he had to back out, that the water was Getting too high for to work. So he Said that he had Cut Fifty Cords of wood at 68¾ cts per cord   34.34 cts   And 30 do at 75 cts per Cord — 22.50 cts   And 2500 Rails at 68¾ per Hund — And 1500 do @ 75 per do — By his acct. I have paid him Forty dollars And I paid him twenty To day which is 60.00

    24   Nothing new   Busness So So

    25   Nothing new. Buisness Only Tolerable. After I Shut the Shop I Took a Skift that I Bot and Started down to my place and I took my Son Wm with me and I Took my Little Gun and I Killed 3 ducks and 5 Plovers on my way down and I went to the Iseland and it was nearly coverd   Only a Little Spot on the uper End was bare and a very Little it was too. Some Hog sign on it tho very Little. Some Rabbit do but I Saw no Rabbits — Down at Hard Scrabble the water is runing Over, Just above where Elick Johnson Lives and Down below between me and the Gregory place it is runing over very fast — you Can Hear it roar — The Levee has broke Late this Evening at Mr Zenos on the other Side of the River. River Commences to Fall this Evening Late[2]

    26   I was In the Swamp this morning and I got up prety Erly this morning and went up to the Mosbey field To Shoot ducks &c. but did not Get One   After Breakfast Stump and me went Out to Look for Stock and found Only fifteen Head out in the cane, We fed The Hogs and I thought we Got the Site of Some of The Mosbey Hogs, tho I am not Shure, Claib. Came down and we Started up to town in the Skift and Hunted up and I Killed 3 Ducks and 6 Plover on my way up — The water was running over above and below B. Winns Place and he is Still at work yet with the timber   I was out this morning Looking at the wood that Mr Miller Cut out Side of the Pasture, and it was 20 Cords

    27   Nothing new. Buisness Only Tolerable

    28   Buisness Only Tolerable. Nothing new. Miss Jane Rabee was married this Evening to Mr Poindexter and they Left this Evening in an hour after the marriage on the S. B. Natchez[3] — I went down this Evening to Mrs Watern. I went down with Mr Patterson, Mr Jaqumine & Wm McCary   We Killed as Follows, I Killed 11 Snip or Plover, Mr Jaqumine 10 dito, Wm 7 do,

---

2 See Natchez *Courier,* April 30, 1847.

3 William L. Poindexter, a lawyer of Concordia Parish, Louisiana, married Jane Ann Rabe of Natchez. Adams County Marriage Records, VI, 819; Natchez *Courier,* April 30, 1847.

Mr Patterson 2 Ducks, We went down Late in the afternoon and Got back in time for Supper

29   Nothing has transpired of interest To day — Ann is Still Confined to her Bed and is not quite as well as she was a day or two, Burk and Several other Hands that B. Winn had, Left him the other day — they were Engaged in Rafting timber from the Swamp, part of cypress and the other ash

30   Nothing new. Buisness dull — The River is Said to be falling a Little at this point,[4] Ellen Barnard fell down in the Dutchmans field, but through the Kindness of Mr Hall, he told me in time to Save her — Three and one-half feet Bank on the Tensaw River, and the Back water rising very fast indeed — Mr. V. Boyer Knocked a man down the other day about some liberties he took with his wife or in other words tryd to insult her — I Got a Letter from Winston this Evening

May 1   This was to have been a Big turn out with the children at the institute. They did turn out Late and a very Large turn out it was   They partook of Some Little refreshments at the City Hotell And then went to the City Hall to dance[5]   I Loaned W. H. Stump twenty Dollars to day, The River is Still falling & has fell about 5 inches to this date &c.

2   Nothing new — Buisness Quite dull to day — This Evening it was that I wrode out and found my Little Cow Known as the Seven months heifer, She was away down in the Big Bayou Dead   She had went thare to have her Calf and was thrown down by Some means or other, and was instantly Killd. My Poor old Mare Kitty Fisher was found this Evening on the Commons with her Eye Knockd out by Some Outrageous Rascal. Oh if I Knew him — Mr Robertson paid by a young Horse ten dollars fifty cents. This was at the Bank Sale — Some infernal Thief Stole my Skift the other night that I Borrowed from Mr Stump

3   It was to day and not yesterday that the Bank Sale took place — and I bot The Little Poney that is Spoken of above.

---

[4] On April 30, 1847, the Natchez *Courier* reported: "The Mississippi. At length, to our great joy, the 'Big Drink' begins to show undeniable signs of retrocession. . . . The river has been between one or two inches of the great flood of 1844." For additional details, see Monette, "The Mississippi Floods," *loc. cit.,* 465–67.

[5] On April 30, 1847, the Natchez *Courier* had announced the May Day picnic: "Tomorrow, the fete of flowers comes off at Minor's Grove under the auspices of the seven hundred pupils of the Natchez Institute. Parents, teachers and students will all fill that delightful grove, and should the day prove fair, joyous thousands may be present to mingle in the festive scene, each giving and receiving pleasure. All are invited from city and country."

4   The River is Still falling and we are Glad of it. The Grand Jury is Sitting at present and found a true Bill VS. Young Cosens to day for obtaining money by False Pretences, So mutch for so mutch.

5   The River is Still Falling and we are Glad of it — tis not off of the natural Bank yet by Several inches. Old Dr Richard Harden Died the other Day at Baton Rougue, poor old Man

6   The River is still Falling at this point and we are Glad of it as the water has been runing over us for some time, Mr Williams pd me 3 dollars worth of Sugar for a Sugar Crusher.

7   Nothing new. This day 7 years ago the Tornado Swept this City. The River is falling prety fast but has not fell more than 2 feet I think up to this date, B. Winn is up this morning from the Swamp and he is the first man That has crossed since The water has fell on Horse back, He Thinks there is some danger Still in crossing &c

8   Nothing new to day. Buisness has only been tolerable To day. I am in hopes it will be better in a day or two. Mr Lyons was Burried to day. He died yesterday. Phill, Billy & Alfred all up this Evening from the swamp. They report alls well and that the old Cow Dicy had died about a week ago. They were plowing and replanting Last week where the water had Left.

9   Buisness only Tolerable. The River has fallen tis thought about 4 feet at this point, and is Still Falling — I Started up   No I Started down in the Swamp this Evening. I wrode Wm Mare & Wm wrode Kitty Fisher — We took down three Colts, Kitys 2 and Fanys 1

10   Nothing new. I was in the Swamp This morning and my Wm   We Staid untill after Breakfast and then Started up   Byrons Little mare with Her young Colt was Brot up this morning by William & I wrode up big Jeff. This Morning I Got Erly in the Swamp and found Eight or 9 of my Hogs Laying Dead. They Seems to being dying from Poison of Some Kind — tis very Strange indeed. I am afraid I Shall Loose many more of them.

11   Mr Pitts, Mr McDonald, F. Dominique, Mr Smith, Monkey Jack, all are in Jail   They were all put in to day. Mr McDonald & Pitts were Bail out. Mr Cozens was found Guilty to day by the Jury. Tis awfull. Shure Shure. Judge Posey is in the chair & Mr Martin, District Atorney

12   Nothing new. Buisness Dull. Quite So. I Sent Gim in the Swamp Erly this morning to Look at the Sheep & Hogs   The

Hogs were ding very fast when I Left the other day. He was to put them into the Pasture & to Salt them &c. The River is Still Falling   He took down a Bushel of Salt for the Hogs and wrode big Jeff. B. Winns Daughter Came down to H. Scrabble without Shoes   She had Just Escaped from Irons that her father had chained her in to Keep her from Geting Married to a Mr Burk the wood chopper, and the young One tried also to Escape but She did n^' So Stands the afair

13   Nothing new   Buisness Quite dull, Gim returns from the Swamp and brings a Small Shoat, one that we have had in our pen   on Corn, He brings the Following acct that the white Poney is Proberlly Dround as he was yesterday seen behind Mr Fords Field in Swiming water, and that old Sorril Horse Charly Could not be found any where   Tis very Droll indeed, He reports 15 Hogs dead. Found the r[e]mains of 2 of my cows, ie Browney Mosby & the Rucker Cow — He reports also that B. Winns Daughter had Left him and Gone Down below to Tates. So he seys

14   Nothing new, Buisness dull. I Sent my William down this Evening to H Scrabble To take Some Seed Corn to replant with or rarther to plant in the Sloughs with, The River is Still falling and has fell about 6 ft. I think, Miss Emeline Winn was married to day to Mr Burke, tis Said on the other Side of the River, &c.

15   The nights are very cool at present. Tis not doing much good for the Cotton, The court ajourned at a Late Hour to night   Gim & Hanah is about to Seperate with mutial Consent, I believe.

16   Nothing new. Buisness dull. Hanah Came to me this morning and made her Statement in regard to her visits to Certain places &c. She Said that She had went thare twice and she went thare on buisness for her Cozen Mary and that the man had never Said a Dispectfull word to her in his Life, This She repeated. So then this Mary Spoke up and Said that She Had Sent Her and if She was H. She would not care a cent, Gim might Go, for [all] her &c. I remaind all the Evening at Home   No I did go out to the Commons and Got Some Mulburys with the Boys

17   I Sent Sam down this morning to the Swamp And Rose also who is to cook for Mr Gregory at $7 per month. Phill went down in the Skift and Claibourne also to pull it back. I Sent 50 wt of Hams, ½ Bushell of Peas, 50 cts of Sugar, 2 Bushells of Corn meal, by the Same trip — Prices, 87½ ct per Bushell for meal, 5 cts for Hames and they not Good — I Sent The Long mare to Wood Pecker To day again and she Took Him

18   Nothing new has transpired   Considerable number of Swampers up here at Court to day for Stealing timber from Government down at Dead Mans bend — for want of proof tho they have all Gotten clear, Oh they are not honest. Gim Sends Hanahs Ring back to her. She refused to accept it but returns it to him, They are variance because Jdg. ——— tis Said has taken the 1st chances, Mr Rose is down Looking at the Bank plantation in Wilkerson County.

19   Buisness I fear will be dull — I was quite unwell yesterday Evening with head Ache &c. The River Still Continues to fall here, and we have not had a rain in about 3 weeks

20   About 9 Oclock To day I wrode down On my Little Horse Dick and wrode up my Sorril Hatcher Mare and I have Some notion of putting her to The Horse Wood Pecker, Byrons Little Bay mare and colt and Wm Roan colt made for the Swamp. I Left them down To Mr Fords — B. Winn is plowing and Fencing up his new grown and at work at his new House, We are not quite finished Planting yet in the Swamp   The water has not quite Left yet, There is a good deal of water in the Sloos yet and they march up and plant as fast as the water will Let them   My Corn is a Great many different highths and different ages. The Cotton in the Gregory field Looks better than any cotten in the Swamp that I have Seen, Burk and his new wife is down at C Wilcotts. Hurah for Hurah, I find that Mrs Waltern intends to rais Corn Entirely this year. She has plowed up all the Cotten — Shure

21   Nothing new. Buisness Some what dull

22   Nothing new. The Paper Free Trader Gave a Greate Puff to Lieut. S. Scott, who has Just return from the Seat of war — Very Sudden Death   A Mr Bunting, who was a Brother of Mrs Lyons took Sick and Died at the Breakfast Table — tis Strange, very Strange — The young man fell dead from the Table, I had a Large Bay Horse that took Sick to day and must have had the Botts for he died very Suddenly   He died Out by Mr Howells Residence. I bot two Skift Loads of Damagd Corn and pd 1.00 for it and Sent it down to the Place by Jeffn & Claib — they Got down Safe with it All hands Came up from below this Evening

23   Nothing new. Buisness dull, Quite So — I did intend to go into the Swamp to day after 12 Oclock and waited all the Evening for Mc To Come and Go with me and he did not Come

at all — So I did not Go but remaind home all the Evening   Yes I wrode out to the Commons in the Evening Late but was Gone but a very Short time indeed, I had the Bay horse that I bot of Bunce thrown over into the Bayou this morning. He died near Mr Howells Residence with the Botts, Tremendious Large Funeral this Evening — The Bunting Funeral

24   Billy, Alfred & Phill wrode down Cuff, Dick & Bob down in the Swamp. I don't feell well to day   Gim is Sick to day. Claib. went to the island to day to get Due Burries

25   Gim wrides the Marshalk Mare in the Swamp, takes Coffee, Peas, a dress a piece for Zora & Peggy, a Bonnet apiece for all 3 of the women, Shoes for Zora, Returns, reports Some few Deaths among the Hogs and Some 5 or 6 head of Cattle in the Bog on the bar near St. Catharine Creek, 1 of them mine, 1 Cozens and others, The[y] were Got out tho — Reports Zora in the field and Peggy Cooking, &c.

26   After breakfast I wrode down in the Swamp And on my way down I found Gregorys Grey Horse, B. Winns Colt and Pearce old Bay Horse. They were on the Hills near Robersons Gate and I drove them in the Swamp — Went down in the Swamp and Pulld Mr Cozens yearling Calf out of the Bog on the Sand bar, Branded the 3 Mosbey Calves and marked 2 of them &c. Gim was along.

27   I was in the Swamp this morning Erly and I mounted my Horse and Came up by Breakfast time and I wrode Cuff. They are Still plan[t]ing a Little Corn where Ever the water will Let them; Gregory Corn is about 3 to 4 inches high — his Cotton 7 or 8 inches H — B. Winns Corn is high as ones head and Some Little young Corn, The Goats were all Killd this week. To [in] the Swamp — I have not One at present.

28   Nothing new. Buisness Only Tolerable.

29   Buissness only Tolerable To day   I am very much affraid that we are agoing to have a very dull summer — I Sent Jeff down this Evening to bring up my Scein To Loan Col Bingaman, to haul in the creek   Gim Came up to day bringing Some Eggs [and] a Small Shoat.

30   Nothing new.

31   Nothing new, It was this Evening that I Took the old mare that I had out to Lands of Mrs Smith And Gave her to the old Man Moses — I made her a present to him, I got a few Black Burrys and then Came Home and on my way I Kill a Large Snake and Byron brought it Home with me &c.

June 1   Nothing new, Mrs Cory Sent me the Following Lines this morning Viz — Mr Johnson, Capt Taylor wants Claibourn to go with him on the Boat again and I, Claiburn wants to go with him and I want Some money very much myself for I am not able to work myself. Mr H. Mandeville buried his Second child to day ie, the 2d one that he has Lost this week[6]

2   Buisness Commences very dull this morning — Bacon is Selling very high, this present writings, 10 cents for all Kinds nearly, tho I got 6 Shoulders at 5 cts yesterday   Not the best tho — I Sent Gim in the Swamp to day with 2 Shoulders of Bacon &c. He wrode Cuff Down, Claibourne Leaves the Trade to day To Take a Birth on a Steam Boat. Mr Dalshiemer paid me $20 for a months Rent to day and I Gave him a receipt for four months rent he having Lost or mislayd a receipt that I Gave him some time ago for 3 months. His rent is now paid to the 1st inst.

3   Mr Benbrook finds out to day that it was his own Girl in the Kitchen that was a Brick-bating his House all this time, and he puts her in Jail to try and find out about it, She Confessed it — I Sent Gim in the Swamp yesterday and he has not Came up yet   He went down to Sheer the Sheep — he aught to have done by this time, He wrode Cuff

5   I Got up Early This Morning and Got On my Horse Bob. and wrode Down to the Swamp   I Got there about Breakfast time   Mr Stump was out in the Lower part of the Swamp   Gim and Alfred wriding up to B Wins to Look for a cow & did not Get her, Gim and others Sheered the Sheep yesterday and the wight of the Fleece I do not Know but they Got a Box full and Something over four Barrells of wool from them   They Sheered 3 of the young Ones. Gim reports 41 of the old ones and fifteen of the young ones, 56 in all. They are in pretty Good Order at present, Ellen Jorden is thirteen years old to day 5th of June 1847.

6   Nothing new. Buisness Quite dull for the Season   Richard and Byron Drives Mr Cozens Calves Home this Evening, 3 of them   One was Left on the way out and I whipd them both for doing So. Phill and Rose Came up this Evening. Billy was Home Sick &c.

7   Nothing new   Buisness Dull. I remained at Home all day Except very Late in the Afternoon I wrode out by Mr Howells to Look for a Colt that has Left the Commons about a week ago

---

6 See Natchez *Courier*, June 1, 1847.

And Gone I Know not where. Certain — Pinks Bull and a calf of the Niebut Cow is also misen at the present time

8   The River is rising at this point at present, Commenced the other day. Phill, Rose & Gim went to the Swamp this morning — I Sent 50 cts worth of Sugar And a Bushell of meal, 75 cts, a Moqueto Bar to Zora, pr of Shoes to Phill, pr pants to Phill.

9   Buisness Dull,   Capt Barlow was Burried to day   He Died Last night about 12 Oclock   Poor Man, He Jumped or fell from the uper Stairs parts of his House, and was very much Bruised   Mr Myres paid Me for One Months Shaving to day, 1 dollar. Charles Paid twenty three Dollars to day by the Shop, ie he pd $18 for Razors and the Ballance in money — I Gave him two Dollars 50 cts of the Same

10   Gim is up to day from the Swamp and reports all well and that they had not Commencd to work on the Road as I thought they would have done. They Commence to morrow morning I Believe very Erly — He, Billy, has been Sick Some 4 or 5 working Days — Just got up to work again yesterday &c. Gim took 11 pounds Bacon, 1 Shouldar and 9 pds [blank], 1 midleing, ie 2 pieces in all &c. I Loaned Mr N L. Carpenter thirty dollars to day.

11   Mr Dalhgreen paid me five Dollars on an old acctt, owes a Ballance of $3 yet. This has been of a Long Standing. Miss Ferriday Died yesterday Evening at 5 Oclock in the Country. To day it was that Judge Dunlap told me that He had Just Sold the two Little Girls and got $650 for them, and that they were Sold to a man who lived only a very Short Distance from where they Formerly Lived. So they want now to Sell the old woman Fanny. They want $350 for Her, Poor creatures I am Sorry for them

12   Buisness Commences very dull indeed, I very much fear such times — My Health is not very Good at present   Gim is up this morning from the Swamp

15   Everything is full of Excitement, Mirth &c. The volunteers of Mississippi have arived and The Citizens have all turned Out En-masse to welcome them   They are to dine on the Bluff. A Speech was made them by Col Bingaman and another in reply to Col Bingamans was Made by Col Davis and Lieut McClung &c. They were well done very indeed and much applauded too, They Sat down to a Dinner then Given to the volunteers and Late in the afternoon the[y] Left on the S B. Natchez

& St Mary.[7] I was in the Swamp this morning and got on Bob. Horse and Got in town before the Boats Got up that was to bring the volunteers &c. My Little Dick was with me too &c. Mrs Rabee Sent of[f] her Servants this Evening, Viz Betsy Pleas and another

    16   Nothing new. Buisness Quite dull   I Sent Gim down this Evening with a Bushell of meal and 50 cts worth of Shugar, Some tobacco. Bunch, the Deputy Dog Killer, Killed our Rose this morning in the street

    17   There was a rain Last night Out at the Race tract but did not reach the City at all, Gim is in the Swamp to day   He wrode big Jeff down Last Evening

    18   Gim returnd from Hard Scrabbe this Evening and reports the Road as finished, that they had done it, and that all was well &c.

    19   Buisness Quite Dull. Mr McNulty died yesterday about 3 Oclock and was Burried to day at 4 Oclock. Mr Wm Walton died   Last night about 12 Oclock and was Burried to day — poor young man   I Knew him well

    20   Nothing new. Billy and Phill Came up this morning Erly from the Swamp, Mr Stump Gave them the day on acct. of working well &c. Billy wrode old roan and I find that he was rubed very much with chains and his Eye very near Out. I Suppose that he must have had a Lick in it Some way whilst he was at Mr Gregorys for he had the use of him for a week

    21   Buisness Only tolerable

    22   Nothing new   To day Louis Hardwick brought up the twelve Cows and Calves that I bought of him on Saturday and Mr Winn was to have half of them, We according to an arrangment that we made, Drew for our Cows   That is the way we Divided them and it fell to my Lot to get the worst of the Bargain. We in the first place made out the names of the Cows and Color &c. with the No from 1 to 12 — put them in a Hat and Drew them Out and I Drew as Follows — No 3, a Bob-tail old Cow, Redish Color, Branded E A   No 4, a Ball face old red Cow, very old, Same Brand as above   No. 6, a white Cow with Flesh Colord, Blue Spots, Branded as above &c. No 7, Red sided or Frosted in appearance, Rachel, Brd as abve   No 10, Polly, a Muly Cow, Red Color, Brande EA Marked, Formily belonged to

---

[7] The First Mississippi Rifles were returning from the War with Mexico. See Natchez *Courier*, June 15, 1847. For the war record of this regiment, see Rowland, *Encyclopedia of Mississippi History*, II, 229-31.

a Mr Alnut on Byou Mason, High Lands, I Sent Gim down to the Swamp this morning to take a piece of Bacon, wt. 10 pounds and to take Coffee also — He Came back this Evening   Reports all well but the Slab Sow — She had died — Nothing new below, Reports Smart Size water Mellons — none ripe yet. Gim & Wm., Richard & Byron all took the Following Cattle into the Swamp or nearly so — Mary, Parker, Patuna, Polly, old Spots Heiffer & Calf, young Spotted Hieffer & young red & white Steer, Adeline and calf, old Brown Cow & calf, Gims old Bull, Ellen, Jenny, Savanahs Heffer, 15 in all   Mr Winn Buys a Grey Horse from Mr Gay to day   Paid him fifty Dollars for the Horse &c. Mrs Ann Johnson[8] Buys a Light dun colord Cow from Mr Winn to day at $12.50

    23   Nothing new. Buisness Only tolerable   Phill & Billy Still Diging On the Pond Out On the Commons   Little Winns Cow Gets her horn Broken off Some way tho I cant Get no clue to the thing at all. I Came up out of the Swamp this morning   I Started at a very Erly Breakfast. Byron was with me

    24   Nothing new. Buisness Dull, I am still at work at the Pond on the Commons

    25   Phill & Billy still at work at the Pond — Ann Johnson Buys Mr Winns Cow   Pd him to day for her &c.

    26   Mr Ford was showing Quite a Large Bole of Cotton to day   It was a pretty Large One, Little Winn Goes out to the Forks of the Road to Look at Cattle and did not Like them   Returns with out Buying Any — Mr. Torras paid me $24 to day for 3 months Rent and nearly Owes 2 months more; Billy & Phill got done with the Pond to day about dinner time   Anderson Brot the dun colt from down at Fields Pasture, Delta has a article in it about Mrs Miller asaulting a Dutch man by the name of Hannagan. She is bound in the Sum of $500 for Her appearance to Court &c.

    27   Nothing new. I went Down in the swamp this Evening and Wm McCary went with me   I wrode Jeff — We Got down Late in the afternoon   We Saw Some Stock &c.

    28   Nothing new. The Effects of Mr S T McAlister was Sold to day at auction   They were but few attended the Sale and the whole Concern Sold Low — House Furniture in particular, as no one would bid against Her — Buisness Tolerable Fair — Mr Fields Came to See if Mr Winn was agoing to Commence to

    [8] The diarist's wife.

Butcher Cattle &c. His advise was for him to not try it at all —
The River is still on the rise and will be very mudy and Discolord
for Some time I think, I paid Mrs Mix Sixty five Dollars for her
Little Boy John. He only has One Eye, poor Little Fellow   She
warrented the title to be a good One &c. and the old man She made
me a present of, which I acceptd and will try and take Care of
Him if I can

 29 Nothing new. Buisness Only Tolerable &c.

 July 1 I wrode my Sorril mare to day out to Mrs Brabston
to where there was to be a Sale, but it rained and very few was
in attendance so the sale was postponed and I wrode in with Deal
and we Got very wet. We stopd out at a Mr Martins and waited
for the rain to cease — Popkins was thare too — I Loand Mrs
Jorden twelve Dollars this morning and took a watch in pledge
for the Same. She promisces to pay next week   I paid Mr B.
Wade to day thirty dollars for five months Rent of the shop under
the Hill to 1st day of July 1847 — Charles pd me $19 to day by
the Shop

 2 Buisness only Tolerable. Nothing new, I find my pond
dont whole water very well. It seems to Leak Out prety fast   Reports are that the cotton worm has made its appearance in the
Fields of Mr Davis, Maj Chotard and Mr Lapiece and another
report Seys that Mr Deal has Just taken a Lot of catterpillars
and put them in Some cotton Leaves and they wound them selves
up on the Same and he shows them to the Editor &c.

 3 Nothing new   Buisness Only Tolerable to day — there
were a Greate many persons in the City this day and Mr Stump
was in town to day and I Loaned him $20. He Said that he was
agoing to Get himself Some provisions, Mess Pork &c. I Loand
young Marshal 50 cts and I Bot wood, $2.50 and Shugar [$]1 for
the House, 50 cts for Swamp &c. Billy was up this Evening with
the wagon Bringing Some Eggs, Some Beets and Corn to cook and
Corn for the Horses, also Beans, Tomattos, Fodder, &c.

 4 Nothing going on very Lively to day altho tis the
4th   Old Roan and the Sorril mare wran off from the Commons
to day Some time

 5 Nothing new, I Sent Phill & Billy & Alfred to work at
the Pond this morning to fix the place where it Gave way — I
have had the horses wrode to day Considerable a hunting for the
old Roan Horse and the Sorril mare   I have herd from the old
roan but have not herd from the Sorril mare yet. I bot 2 shoulders

of meat to day, 6½, to go in the Swamp — Fords Jim Said that he turned my Roan Horse below his gate this morning

6   Nothing new to day   Dr Winston returns from Cincinnatti this morning in Good Health[9] — Greate many persons went to Fish to day. Amsted Carters Hack turnd over this morning with his Family in it but none of them Got Hurt. A Good Many Gentlemen from the City went also to fish   Bill Burns Came very near geting drowned   Was Saved by Martin and Sandy — I am told Came very near it indeed, I Sent Billy and Gim Down to day and Gim was to bring up my Horse Cuff   He returns and does not bring any news of my Sorril mare, They went down in the wagon taking down two whiskey Barrells &c., two cross cut Saws and a Axe for Alfred to cut wood with

7   Nothing new — Winston Goes under the Hill to day to work   Gim has been out for the Sorrill mare all this day and returns and Seys that he Can not find Her at all

8   Nothing new. Buisness Only Tolerable &c. I paid Mr Winn to day $14 on three Cows and I owe him now 16 dol more on them, Gen. Tax $28.24, The School Tax $27.66   The Last tax was to be paid in Specie — I also paid Mothers which was $15.20, of this Amount $4.80 and the School Tax $10.40. Thus when I add up my own Expense it amounts to $55.90 And Mothers in all was 15.20, making the sum of $71.10

9   Winston, Jeff &c. bot a Sorril mare from a Mr Bole. Paid him twenty One Dollars and Seventy five cents for the mare and the mare he warranted her Sound, She was Branded On the shoulder with a Single Letter D. The mare appears to be very much Jaded — I was in treaty to day with Mr Cozens to Get Post for a fence to be made on a Lot of Mr Brills — I Bot 6 Bottles of Sweet oil to day at the Grasons And Lum Sale, 46 cts per Bottle, 4 Razors for 80 cts

10   To marketing as usual and buisness quite dull and Nothing new. Grasons & Lum selling Out at Auction, Credit untill 1st December &c. Billy and Phill up to night. Reports the Corn being Smartly Eaten by the Coons &c. Not much a doing down thare this week.

---

[9] The manumission of a number of Natchez free Negroes was legally accomplished in Cincinnati. Since William Winston, who worked for Johnson, had reached the age stipulated for his emancipation by the will of Fountain Winston, it is possible that the trip mentioned here was for that purpose. In any event, both he and his mother were listed as free in the census of 1850. U. S. Census Reports, 1850, Schedule I, Adams County, 31.

11 I Took Winston Down in the Swamp with me He wrode Cuff and was Leading a Little Sorril mare that Himself and Jeff Bot The other day. I had her turned into the Pasture, The water was a perfect Sheet from The Briars near the Mounds clear down To Mrs Walterns Field and about Knee deep at that, I found all the Crops Looking very well, Mr Ford & Mr Winn Has had a Falling Out Graareled [quarreled] about the Road.

12 I was in the Swamp this morning very Erly The water Stands in the Swamp Just Like it did in the time of high water, Winston Gave Me $5 to Keep for him and Jeff gave me $10 to Keep for him. Mr N. L Carpenter paid me Eleven Dollars on Some Borrowed Money which Leave a Ballance of ten dollars on that acct, The Road that was worked the other day is very much washed out again and will Soon need more work on it, We Cut two very Large watter Mellons to day in the Swamp I Weighd One of them that weighd Thirty two pounds, i e the ½ weighd 16 pounds very Easy — I met Billy and Phill Just doing down They were near the Lower End of Mr Fords Field. Our Little Sam was missen to day for a Long time and he was out Some where at the Folks [Forks] of the Road &c. Phill [and] Billy takes down One Bushell of meal and 50 cts worth of sugar &c.

13 To day I was Knocking about getting Lumber at the mills I Got I think thirty Six Post of Mr Cossens and I got a full Load of Plank of Mr Brown for which he charged me four Dollars Only — I had them hauld up to the yard and by Wm Rose team and it Broke down just as he Startd to Drive off with it from my Gate. Nothing new and the time Quite dull. I Commenced to day to Dig the Post holes to make The Fence on Mr Brills Land for a calf Pen &c.

14 I sent 4 young Geese to Lavinia Miller this Evening by the Natchez, Mr Rabee Left on this Boat for N. Orleans — Mrs Mix and Judge Dunlap Left On the Same Boat. They are agoing to Urope [Europe] by the way of New Orleans, Winston and Jim was making Fence to day on the Lot on the Hill Mr Brills Lot. They Commencd to day to work — Mr Winn Sends his Horse to Mr Dixon Pasture.

15 I was buisy to day putting up the Fence on the Brill Lot. About ½ done with it

16 Nothing new. I was at work to day at the mill geting Some Lumber to make the calf Pasture Mrs Miller and Daughters came up this Evening On the St Mary, Lavinia, and Octavia,

Emer, Dilia, Mama Oker, and Little Albert, with Servants Moses and Patsy

17   Nothing new. Visitors to day, Miss F Brustee &c.

18   Nothing new. Buisness very dull indeed — I remaind at Home all day Only walking out in the afternoon to the Fort with 3 of my sisters children and 2 of mine, visitors Mrs Anie [Amie] and daughters[10]

19   To marketing as usual &c. To day has been Quite warm and nothing new. Buisness is at this time very dull indeed — Gim Goes down in the Swamp this Evening and returns bringing back the wagon with 6 Large water Mellons, On[e] of them weiging 43 pounds net.

20   Nothing new. Buisness Quite dul

21   I sent Mr Miller the Large water mellon that I Raised Down in the Swamp — it weighed 43 pounds — I Sent by Lee on the Natchez

22   Gim Brings in the Sheep from Mrs Henrys, 29 of them and 10 of them young Lambs and 19 grown Sheep   Frank went with him

23   The children all Got into the waggon and the Horses turned it Over Hurting Anna a Little &c. I Saw Mr Hunter to day and paid him for the twenty nine Sheep that I bot from Mrs Henry trorgh [through] Gim. I paid him $33.19 in all for the 29 — They were 19 grown Sheep and 10 Small Ones — Gim took them down this day   Moses and Sam went with him   He took the wagon down — We have not Commencd to pull Fodder yet but we hope to Commence on Monday if the Lords willing. Mr A Britton paid me 18.75 to day this being a Ballance on fifteen months Shaving

24   To Marketing as usual

26   We commenced to Pull Fodder in the Swamp — Alfred Sick and in town. Phill Sick and in town

27   To day Alfred & Phill went down to work   They went to work to Pully Fodder

30   Mrs Miller And Family are up to see us

August 1   Nothing new. Buisness dull, quite so indeed

2   After Dinner to day I wrode down in to the Swamp and

---

[10] Mrs. Amie and her daughters apparently lived in New Orleans, although she had controlled property in Natchez in 1844. They were probably free Negroes with a strong admixture of white blood. See Lavinia Miller to Mrs. William Johnson, December 2, 1848; Mrs. Lavinia (Miller) McCary to Mrs. William Johnson, October 26, 1852, Johnson Papers.

took Brustie with me — He wrode my Horse Bob. I wrode the Sorril Filly. Forks Road. We got down Late in the afternoon and remained all night, Alfred was sick, Rose was Sick also

3 I was up in the Swamp very Erly this morning and went to pull Fodder untill Breakfast time. The Foder that had been [pulled] before was all Spoild and was in the yard, We Left and got to town about 12 Oclock to day

4 It was to day that I Settled with Mr Winn in full and he thout that he would get off this Evening and he Left two orders with me to Collect, One for $5 on Mr Nickolson, the other on Calvin Winn for $5. The Money had been Loand in both Cases &c.

5 Buisness Only tolerable. Jeff & Gim Came up this day about 1 Oclock from the Swamp where they had been pulling Fodder — they stated that they had Finished or nearly so — He reported the Force all well   He Stated Rose was at work again for Mr Gregory

6 Nothing new. Buisness dull, Quite so   Winston & Jeff Bot a Little old Grey Horse this Evening for Eight dollars from Mr Farris — he was an old Stray Horse, and tis a bad trade that they have made shure I think — I Let Winston have 4 dollars to pay for the Horse. Jeff I Let have the Same and for the same purpose &c.

7 The Quarrantine Law was put in force To day, The yellow fever having Commencd in New Orleans, The City is very dull at present and there is nothing new in the city, Buisness is quite dull and I have a bad cold at present, tho I hope I will soon get the better of it. Colds are very prevelent among the children, Billy & Phill & Alfred are all up from below this Evening and they report that they had put up Three Stacks of Fodder which was all that was Left from the Pulling, &c.

8 Our City Quite Healthy at present, Charles Goes out to Washington and returns again to day — Old Mrs Jeredore was at the Landing and Quarantined. Will be up to day, Mrs Maxent is down also

9 Nothing new, I Sent Alfred down with the Buggy this morning and he took 1½ Bushells of Corn and three shoulders of Bacon, 35 lbs at 7 cts, $2.45.

10 I Bot a One Horse Cart from Dr Blackburn To day   [I paid] $8 for it and what Harness I could find about it and I now give him Creddit for the Same &c.

11 Nothing new. Our child is very sick — Buisness very dull indeed

12 Nothing new. Buisness Dull. Our Quarrantine Law is in force at present I Sent my Small Sorril mare to Wood Pecker To day. This is the Second time that She has Taken him. I Sent her Some time ago and was Supp[r]ised to find that She is not with or in Fold

13 Buisness Only Tolerable, I Wrode Down into the Swamp this morning and remained there Some hour or two then wrode back again I wrode my Small Sorril mare, I found them all up and about. Stump on the Gallery as usual and the hands at work Cutting wood, They have made very Little Head way indeed at wood cutting

14 We had a Little Shower of Rain Just as Capt Clark was Leaving with the Company of recruits, I was at the Landing when they Left. Among them was H Cobler, Abb Mardis, Talt Mardis, young Branch, young Perkins, Theodore Harmon, that I knew and others that I dont now Recollect, They were all pretty Drunk when they went on Bourd — I had a settlment to day with Mr Lacoste for Alfreds wages and I paid him Forty nine Dollars and fifty Cents for the four months & a ½ that I had him.

15 Mrs Miller and Family is up here now from New Orleans. I remained Home all this Evening and only wrode out to Mr Howells and then to the pawpaw Ridge & with young Howell Several of our children has got the whooping Coff very bad at present.

16 Nothing new. Buisness dull very indeed.

17 Nothing new. Yellow Fever in New Orleans very bad at present Alfred is at work at my pond that I am having dug this Evening, at the Brill Lot He told me that He was hired to Crone up the St and that he would Commence on tomorrow morning up thare, I Bot to day at the Court House a Bay mare and a Cold for twenty three & a half Dollars — Col Saunders Buys a Grey Colt at the Same Sale at $17 I Bot a Corn mill from Mr Howell this morning, no this Evning Fifteen dollars is what I paid for it.

18 Nothing new. Miss Mary Stanton Died Last Night. She was a Sister of F. & W. and D Stanton. Mrs. Newman & Family that Lives next door to us in State Street Mooves Out to the Country this morning. Billy Came up to day from the Swamp with a Load of water Mellons, 45 of them in all. He Gave 1 to Speer Pearce and 1 to Wm Ford

19   Our City is very Healthy at present   The Sexton reports not a Single Death for the Last week. Thus we have beyond doubt a Healthy City and [at] this very time there is Lots of People dying in New Orleans at the present writings, Good many Ladies at our House Last Night, old Mrs Brustee, old Miss F. and young Miss F., Mrs Amie & two daughters, Miss Henrietta, Some other Miss of Jerman Extraction, Mr Brustee and all our own children   They Kept up the sport until 11 Oclock

20   Our city is Healthy and dull, Mr Bob. Walker of this City is in the City having Just arrive from St Louis or above &c.

21   Nothing new and buisness Dull. I was at auction to day and I bot a Cask of Bacon at 3¼ cts per lb. and Let Mr McGraw have ½ of it   So So   I got to my part 29 Shoulders and the weight was 485 lbs and Mr McGraw got 400 wt. at cost $13 and my own Cost me $16.25

22   Nothing new. Buisness Only tolerable. I remaind at Home nearly all day — Took a walk in the Afternoon Late with Mr Brustie to the Fort. Took a view with the Spy Glass &c.

26   I Got up this morning very Erly and Started down into the Swamp. We had two Carriages and we had a good Lot in them. I wrode my Horse Cuff. All was along, my wife, Adelia, Lavinia, Emer, Anna, Little Delia, my Baby, Varina, Mr Brustee, Frank & Gim

27   Nothing new. Winston Drives the Horses down into the Swamp in the big waggon, My Wm wrides the Bay Mare that I Bot the other day and her Colt. Mr Galbreath thinks he owes me about 10 Months Shaving

28   Nothing new. Buisness dull, Mr Winn paid his Board up to this date, 28th inst. and Commenced by the Month again.

29   I remaind at Home untill Late in the Evening   I before closing my Shop for the day Sat down and wrote a Long Letter To Mr N. Hoggatt in regard to Jeff — This was about his Late Engagement with a Mr Beltzoover to go to Mexico as a Body Servant   I found that his time was not out with me by about 7 or 8 months. I therefore wrote the Letter in which I made Several Statements that was news to Mr Hoggatt and He thankd me for the information.

30   To day it was That I started down into the Swamp with a Lot of Cattle, Cows, Calves and [in] all there were Seventeen of them, viz, Pinks Bull No. 1, Phillis & calf No 3, The old Ball Face Red Cow, Mrs Hardwick with Bull calf No 5, Cloa Hardwick & Calf   She is a Bobtail Red Cow No 7 — Cintha

Fields with a Red Bull Calf No 9, Patsy & her Calf No 11, One Horn & Calf No 13, Jane Winn with H calf No 15, Pink Hardwick & calf No 17. Ther were Several Fights on our way down. The Tensas Stag whiped George Bull & Buffin whipd George too. Quite Easy — I took a very Long wride to day and went to the St Catharine creek and up its Banks Some distance, then up through the Swamp to I may Say to Natchez. I was Looking for 2 Horses, old Charly and Sway Back, and could not find them at all — Something wrong — I think Lavinia Miller was very Sick to day.

31   I Hear of Nothing new this morning what Ever

September 1   Nothing new. Buisness quite dull

2   Nothing new. Buisness Quite dull. Mr Brustee and Miss Henrietta Camp took dinner with us and we took a walk at night to the Bluff, then up to Mrs B House   We fenced in the Garden this Evening and planted it with turnip Seed. We Commencd yesterday and finished to day — We did a good deal of work in the Affair I do assure you

3   Nothing new. We Swung the Gate this morning and made Some other improovments. Then went out to Mr Howells and undertook to Haul in the Mill that I bot of Him with my old Roan Horse but could not and we had to Leave [it] in the Road — Late in the Afternoon.

4   Nothing new. Yes News that Gen Scott has Surrounded the City of Mexico and Can March in if he thinks Proper &c. Extras are Out &c. to that Effect.[11]

5   I Sent Gim into the Swamp to day and returns and reports that the Bay Horse Sway Back has Died   Was Boged on the Bar — This is the Last of 3 nags that I Bot Some time Ago from Mr N Bunce &c.

6   Nothing new   The yellow Fever is very bad indeed at this time in Orleans[12] —.Miss Henrietta Camp and Mr Brustee Left to night after 11 Oclock for New Orleans — They have been Several weeks in the City &c. Col Bingamans Big Bull died yesterday — He was the Thom Hall Bull, Betzoover — Mr Uri Bennet was married to night to Miss Leakin

7   Gim [and] Frank all day Looking for the Cow & calf that I Sold Mrs Miller &c. and finds her this Evening — I Spent

[11] See Natchez *Courier,* September 7, 1847.

[12] The Natchez press occasionally published reports concerning the yellow-fever situation in New Orleans.

a part of this Evening in cutting down weeds in the Calf Pasture &c.

8   Mr John Hoge Died Last night and Mr Blinkin Died near day Light this morning — I Sent Down the Four Pigs that mother gave me by Gim this Evening in the wagon &c.

9   To day has passed and I Can Hardly Say that I recollect Anything that has Happened. Yes this morning Erly I wrode down into the the Swamp and Sold Seventeen Sheep to Mr Rozette at $2.50 Each Head — the Amount $42.50   This is the first Lot that I have Ever Sold. I Lost a Quoung [young] Sheep to day that died from Sickness — I have I think up to this date 62 Sheep on the place and this is Leaving Out the One that died to day — Those that I Sold to day were wethers and Rams — those that I have now are yews & Lambs &c.

10   Nothing new   I Got up this morning and wrode down to the field of Mrs Walterns and Caught Some Fish and two Large Loggy Head turtles and brot them up in a cart. I by Some means to day Lost my Keys from my desk

11   Nothing new.

12   Nothing new   Buisness very dull indeed

13   To day is dull and Nothing new. Our Streets are very dusty indeed.

14   Nothing new. Buisness Quite Dull

16   Nothing new   Buisness is Quite Dull at present   I Started down in the Swamp this morning or about 12 Oclock   After Getting down in the Swamp I Commenced to work at the cleaning off of a place to make a Turnip patch, We pull the Corn and in the Small place there was nearly a Cart Load of Corn and in the Same Space there was 170, Some Large, odd pumpkings which was a mighty yield I thing [think] for One Crop of ground of that Size   It was to day that I rented a Shop to a Frenchman and told him that he could have it for 1 mon[th] if He would repair it which he Said he would do and that he wanted it for a year   So he took the Key this morning, 16 inst

17   Nothing new. There was a Shooting match to day out at Washington[13]   I was in the Swamp and did not See it. I Got up very erly this morning and went to work to clean of[f] a Little Turnip Patch which we did. We Got through with it about 10 Oclock. We then pulled Some Grass and Left for town bringing about 100 Bundles of Grass and 1 Barrell of Corn and 12 pump-

---

13 See Natchez *Courier*, September 17, 1847.

kins, 1 Peck of S. Potatoes, Mr Henderson Sends his work Stock into the Swamp a few Days ago and Sends a Jack with them. Wrong, wrong, Shure

18   Nothing new   Buisness is dull, Quite So indeed

19   The Streets are very dusty. Everything in the way of Produce is very High indeed — Lard is 20 cts a pound — We did intend this morning to Commence to pull Corn this morning but Billy & Phill both was Sick and we did not Commence at all — So Gim he Came up again — He took Down 2 Shoulders of meat and 2 ox yokes for the yaks, $4.00, and he took ½ Bushel of meal — Mr Gregory Bot 8 yoke of Oxen and 6 Cows & Calves — paid 400 and Some odd dollars for them. Expense of to day — Marketing 1.00, to paper for Lavinia 25, to Medicine for Marmys Millers Foot 50, to do for Billy & Phill, 25, to B & P .25, to Bergamot 10 cts

20   I find Buisness Quite dull indeed   Nothing new.

23   Mrs Miller and Family Left this Evening on the S B. Natchez   The Children, Lavinia, Emer, Adelia, Octavia, Varina & Albert, 2 servants Mosses & Patsy.

24   I Started down into the Swamp and we Commencd to pull Corn.

25   I was up by times in morning and went to work in the field Pulling Corn

26   I was very Buisy to day haulling Corn, We numbered as Follows, Mr Stump, myself, Wm McCary, Robt McCary, My Wm & Gim, Phill & Billy, yes & Frank, Richard & Byron

27   I was up this morning Quite Erly and was up at work at my Shop &c.

28   I was up this morning Quite Erly at work and after working in the Shop for Some time took my Horse and wrode down into the Swamp and went to work at the Pulling of the Corn   We workd very hard to day

29   Nothing new   Still at work Pulling of Corn in the upper Field; we numberd Mr Stump, myself, Frank, Phill, Billy, Gim & Anderson, 7 in number — I was down in the Swamp a trying to get in my Little Crop and was very hard at work. I wrote a Letter to day from the Swamp to Mrs Miller in Orleans. I Sent it to town by Anderson, on old Charley

30   Nothing new   Buisness Only Tolerable. I was Still in the Swamp Hard at work.

October 7   Nothing New   Buisness Fair   Jeff in the Country and has been for Several Days.

8   No News from Mexico. Gim Came up from H. Scrable this Evening bringing about 2 Barrels of Corn and twenty Pumpkins   They were Good Ones &c.

9   Nothing New. I wrode Out past the Race tract this Evening on Bob VS Col Bingamans Horse Coon Mardis and Bob Just Walked right away from him, with Ease &c. A Meeting was Out thare to day and Some Public Speaking was Out thare between Col Cooper & Mr Jones Stewart Esqr. They are both Candidates for the Senate for this district and One or two other Counties &c   Jeff went Out to take Dr Winstons mare and he has not Come back yet   Has been Out four days at Least — I sold old Charley[14] to day to Mr Dorsey for thirty Dollars to be paid On the first of January, 1848 — He Gave me [a] note to that Effect with His mark on it &c.

10   Nothing new   Buisness Only Tolerable. Jeff Still Out in the Country. Charles [paid] $20.00 by Cash to day, Expense $5.50, this was shoes and a Hat for himself and I gave him about 2.50

11   Nothing New from the Seat of War, not a word, Buisness Tolerable fair. I Received two Letters from New Orleans to day and One was from Mr Miller, the other from His wife. Mr Miller writes me that he Received the One Hundred and twenty dollars that I sent him by Mr Lee on the Natchez and Stated that Mrs Miller Had not paid the One dollars over to Him that She Promised me to pay over, and that She had said nothing to him about it &c and in her Letter she spoke of the money She owed me and promised me that as Soon as she Collected Some money that was due Her she would send it to me and &c. Winston and Gim was a Shingling to day On the top of the Old House and did not get through with it at that. They [will] get through with it to morrow I Expect. Jeff still Out in the Country and has been a week I believe to day or to morrow,

Still Out in the Country

My beautiful mountain home

Give me thy seclusion

12   Nothing New. Winston & Gim Finished Shingleing the House this Evening. Gim makes a top to Cistern Top in the Old Parker Lot by order of Koontz   I was under the Hill to day

---

14 Old Charley was a horse.

and Bot 2 Cows and there Calves from Mr Higgins — I Gave him Fifteen Dollars in money and the Eight Dollars in an acct. that He Owed me for the hire of my Oxen, thus I may say that it was $23 that he got for the two Cows &c   Corn is worth 75 cts a Barrel and Oats 35 cts a Bushell, I Got a Draft [for] $116.90 To night from Mr A. H. Marschalk for Collection   It was VS the U S Mint at New Orleans, I Gave him a Receipt for the Same, I intend to Send it Down by the S. B. Natchez on to morrow Evening

13   I spent nearly the whole of this Fore noon Looking for the two Cows that I Bot yesterday from Mr Higgins and at Last did not find them, Tho they were found by Anderson Late in the afternoon in Dixons Pasture   I started Down with nine Cows and Calves this morning and Drove them Down as far as Mrs Walterns Pasture and there Left them, to Drive to morrow. I shall Start down I hope to-morrow with the two Cows that I Bot yesterday, I wrote a Letter to day to Mrs Miller and Sent a Draft in on the U S Mint, for $116.90 and requested her to give the same to Mr Miller to Collect, This was in favor of A. H. Marschalk   The two Cows that I had refference to above was found by Anderson this Evening.

14   Nothing new. I started down with 5 Cows and 5 Calves, with Jenette, and Drove them down to Mrs Walterns where I Left the Cattle on yesterday. Myself and Stump & My William Drove them Down. We had in all as Follows — The Cows Calves in all

No. 1. Gustin with a B. calf		—	2
No. 2. Rose — a Hfr. — do		—	2
No. 3. Blaunch Mosbey & a Hfr.	— do —	2
No. 4. Hester Buie & a Hfr. — do		—	2
No. 5. Jaqumine Cow & a B — do		—	2
No. 6. Brindle McCouley & a B	— do —	2
No. 7. Mary Hardwick & a Hfr.	— do —	2
No. 8. Muley Hardwick & a Hfr.	— do —	2
No. 9. Lizette Hardwick [& a] Hfr.	— do —	2
No. 10. Tidey Higgins [& a] B	— do —	2
No. 11. Julia Higgins [& a] B	— do —	2

15   Nothing new   Buisness only tolerable. I was in the Swamp to day   I Left there this Evening   Frank drove the waggon up, Brot 27 Pumpkins &c 1 Doz & 10 Eggs — I Swapt a Little Red Cow to day with Mr Gregory for a Broken Horned Ox, which he says must work or tis no trade — I started up about

1 Oclock — Got up Near or after Supper time. Roan & Joe worked up in the waggon. Jeff Came in yesterday. Princess was down to day I think, 1st trip this Season

16   Nothing new. Buisness good   Gim brot up a Lot of Corn & 7 Pumpkins — And I Sent down as Follows to Mr. Stump, 6 Pound of Shot [and] 1 Box Caps 60 cts & 50 cts worth of Powder, 1 Bag of Salt $2.25 — Mrs Waltern makes on the Plantation below Natchez 160 wagon Loads of Corn. The wagons that it was hauled in held 35 Bls [and] 25 Bls — Hauld most in the Large one

17   Buisness Tolerable fair   Nothing New. The Poor sick Woman Mrs John Chapallier who lived in my House with Her Husband was Taken Sick Thursday Evening I think and Died Last night or This Morning about 4 Oclock. Poor woman   She was a Friendless woman and a stranger in our City, Peace be with Her — Gen. Quitman is now the acting Governor of Mexico — The accounts we have in full[15] — Our city is Healthy Even at this time. Thank Heaven

18   Nothing New. Buisness has been Quite fair to day. I Receivd a Letter to Day from Mr. Miller   It Contain a Hundred Dollar Bill and He Stated that He had Kept the 16 Dollars as I directed Him to do which sum paid the Entire Interest of the Money that I owed Him — The money that I Elude to is [the] sum that Belongs to A. H. Marshalk. It was a Draft that He Gave me to Collect from the US Mint at New Orleans. I Left town Late this Evening and went to the Swamp and I Drove   Bot a Cow without a Calf, Her Calf died a short time ago — Mr Gregory Bot a Ox Cart to day [for] $35   He has not pulled his Corn yet nor has Mr Ford. They were both Buisy Picking Cotton. I saw as I went down the Following Stock — Rose & Calf, Gustin & Calf, White Nose & Calf, Old Mary & Calf, Jaqumine & Calf   Mr Stump Commences to Haul wood to day for the 1st time.

19   Nothing new, the wether quite warm   I was in the Swamp and got up very Erly this morning and was Looking around for the Stock. I Saw about Eighty Hogs Little and big in the field, 3 of the Sows has Pigs But I could find none — I then Commenced to Look for Cattle but Saw but few of them in my Rambles. See Stock Book of to days Entry. I Left Erly this

---

15 George W. Kendall, war correspondent and editor of the New Orleans *Picayune,* called it "a most excellent appointment." Natchez *Courier,* October 19, 1847.

Evening and Had my new gun. I Killed 1 Duck & 1 Squirrel. I
Came up back of the Lakes — I paid over $116.90 to Day to
A. H. Marschalk. This was a Draft that he gave me for Collection on the U S Mint at Orleans. On my way Home to day I
found B. Winn out on Black Hog Lake and we wrode together
as far as the back part of his Field or Dwelling House. He Spoke
of Having the Swampers up for Living in Adultry Down thare,
that it was a Shame &c.

    20   Nothing New. Buisness Dull to day and nothing new.
Several of our Citizens Left to day for New Orleans, Lansnester
& Hammet and others that has been waiting to go down, Morgan,
Wilkins White, S. S. Prentiss, and others — This is the first time
that they have ventured Down Since the fever Commenced in
Orleans   The Little Frenchman John Chapallier sold out his
Shop to Signaigo for thirty Dollars. I wrote the Receipt myself,
for the Money — I paid Mr Brill two Dollars on the Lot that I
got of him on a Liece of two years from the 1st of August Last
1847 — Mr Cannon Left to day, owes me for two months Shaving
$2.00

    21   My Health is not Good   I have a bad Cold. Tho
thank God I am still able to be up and about   Nothing has
transpired of interest to day. I have been some what buisy to
day Fixing a closet under the steps, Gim was the Carpenter, Mr
S. Woods [was] at the Shop this Evening and I Gave Him a List
of the names of the voters as I thought that was in the Swamp —
as Follows.

O. K. Fields	W. Ford	B. Winn	Jas Gregory
Greaves	Pearce	Jasp. Winn	Alk Johnson
H. Stump	C. Wolcott	Joe	Williams
Chas Gregory	Wm. Wolcott		Marks
Smiley	H Burk		

    They are all Living in the Swamp at Present and I believe
those are all.

    22   This has been a pleasent day and nothing new. Gen
Stanton & Mr S. Wood went to the Swamp to day to see the
Swampers. I Sent Down a Bottle of Good Brandy and a Bottle
of Clarret wine and Something to Eat in the way of Beef &c.

    23   Now we may Look for rain and Cold and the Article
of Coal will be high for it is worth a Dollar a Barrell now. I
played a game of Dominos to day with Jaqumine and won his
Roundabout from him   I played $3 VS. it. Gim was not up this

Evening from the Swamp as I thought, nor did any of the rest of them [come]

24   Gim was in the Swamp and did not Come up untill this morning   He brought up some Fodder, 120 Bundles, and about 1 Barrell of Corn, Pumpkins near a dozen of them, Phill Came up Last Night   Gim Said that he Saw a good Deal of the Stock, &c.

25   Several of Our Citizens of the County arrived this Morning, viz, Dr. Duncan & Family, L. R. Marshall & Family, S Davis & Family, Cochran & Family. To day it was that F. Mc-Creyry told me that he Gave me as a Hint that he did not wish me to say any thing about the Election for a greate many would think that what I would say would have a greate Effect   I promised him that I would not but at the Same time I dont care anything about it — I had the shop white washed to night by way of a change, Mr Guiger the overseer on the other side of the River Died and was Burried to day by the Masons

26   Nothing new. Buisness only so so. I was at Auction to day and bot Severall things, 2 pr pants &c   The Boys were Painting Some Little to day in the Shop, on the windows &c.

27   Nothing new. Buisness rarther dull &c. I wrode my Horse Bob down into the Swamp   Gim & Wm went down with the waggons   I found 5 of the Cows that I bot of Louis Hardwich to day on the Hills in the Dixon Pasture — I drove them back in the Swamp again

28   I was in the Swamp this morning very Erly for [I] slept here last night, Mr Stump was Engaged when I got down yesterday in diging Potatoes. They had dug One Patch and was very near geting through with the other. I saw 3 deer to day when I was away down back of Gregorys and ought to have Got a shot at them but was not quick Enough for them, I had my Pulling gun with me and on my way Home the Dogs caucht a Larg Black Possum and on my way I shot 2 Squirrels & a Coon.

29   Nothing new. Buisness only tolerable   I was up at Auction to day and bot 8 pairs of Shoes @ 45 cts per pair — I also Bot a Little Stove at 3.25. I made the Following Bets to Night, 1st I bet that Mr Wood would beat both of his opponents, with Mr. Odell, 5.00   Then $25 that he would, same way, 25.00   I then bet $10 with Winston, same way, 10.00

30   Nothing new. Buisness only tolerable. Boys Finished Painting or nearly so in the Shop to Day. Gim returns from the

Swamp & Seys that Byrons Little Cows Calf Died the other day. It was a fine Calf I thought

31   Nothing new. Buisness only tolerable. Some Excitement in the way of Elections to day. I made some few bets on the Elections to day. They were small Ones, viz. 1 Bushell Potatoes   I Bet Stump 1 Bag of Shot that Lacost would not get 70 majority over B an that Glasburn would Beat Stanton 50 votes &c.

November 1   Nothing new. Buisness only So, So — To day the Election Commences and there is Considerable Betting in a Small way

2   This has been a Beautifull day and Nothing new. Plenty of Excitement to day on the Election &c. I have made Several Bets on the Election to day and to night and some of them Pretty wild ones, I do think — I have made so many Bets on this Election that I cannot now Recollect them all

3   Nothing new. Buisness only tolerable   I made Several Bets to day on the Election and will win some of them I think

4   Nothing new. I got in the dutc[h]mans Buggy this morning after Breakfast and went down to the Swamp, turnd off from the River and went out to Cypress Byou, then down it some distance and I found one or two Flocks of Ducks and I got 3 shots and Killed 1 Duck, it was a Large Mallard drake, and 1 Squirrel and I had my Pulling Gun. I Saw 15 Squirrels to day but did not get but the 1. The acorns is Falling very fast indeed, so viz the Leaves, The Lakes are geting Dry Pretty fast. Roam caught a Possum on the way up.

5   Nothing new, We have news to day from Franklin County that Mr Coopers Majority was only 16 in that County, which if true will Elect Stewart by 4 votes   Mr Darling paid me the stake that we won from Mr Odell of Franklin County. We bet it in this way — 1st that $5 that Cs majority would be under 50 & $5 that it would be nearle 40 than 50 & $5 that it would be nearer 44 than 50 & Jeff then Bet him $5 that he would Loose one of the Bets — thus there was $40 put up by us all &c. Gim reports some Red Calf as Dead in the Swamp of mine. I was much surprised to find one whole pen of Pumpkins was all fed out to the Hogs &c.

6   Winston Came up from the Swamp this Evening and wrode Cuff — Killed One Squirrel. Phill Came up to night   We have news to day that Judge Sharkey will be Elected by a Large

Majority over Jud[g]e Wilkerson,[16]   Good   Good   Certain —
Old Bectill has Came back to the Swamp to Live, arrived to day
— I am not Glad

7   Judge Sharkey is Elected Shure — Now I am Glad of
that. Honesty is the best Policy — McCary took supper with me
to night and we talked of Election returns &c. Phill is up to night
ie he Came up last night.

8   Nothing new. Buisness Only Tolerable. I started into
the Swamp this morning soon after Breakfast   Wrode my H.
Bob. Wm. wrode Little Dick — We drove Roan & Fanny down
with us — After geting down there we wrode Out Down by the
Back of Some of the Ridges and went down as far as the Gregory
Land, then turned in. We were Looking for the Mares & Colts.
We did not find them. We saw no stock, Scarsly. Old Billy &
Fill was Cutting wood back on the Ridge and doing very Little
at that. Stump he was Complaining and was doing nothing — I
wrode out on the Line of my Land. Tate, that married old Bec-
tills daughter, is in the Swamp again.

9   I was in the Swamp this morning and I got up very
Erly and ordered ten of the Largest of my Barrows put up to
Fatten and I had the Ballance turned out. Except the sows &
Pigs. Those I wanted to be Kept up in the Fields. I Saw very
few of the Cattle indeed — I Saw all the sheep that was in the
Pasture, 56. I Slept in the swamp Last night and not one of the
Shop Boys Came a near the House at night to Sleep. So I am
told on my return Home. Yesterday I met several of Mrs Waterns
teams Haulling Corn and some other things. The Boys only took
in the draw 2.62 and yesterday $2.75. Judge Sharkey is Elected
by a Large Majority — Good.

10   Gim wrode my Horse Bob Down in the swamp to day
and broght up the Buggy, with 4 Pumpkins and a Bag of Turnips; He reports all well. The River is on the Rise: Coal is selling
at 60 cts   Col. Bingamans Horse Black Dick beat Capt Minors
Mare Jenny Linn — I Lost 2.50 by it   Mile Heats — tract Heavy
— I wrote a Letter to New Orleans this Evening by the SB.
Natchez — I Loaned Jack ten Dollars to day and he promises to
pay me again on Saturday Evening next   Paid   Charles pays
over this Evening $24.50 and I Gave him $2.50 of it for himself
&c.

16 In 1847, William L. Sharkey was re-elected to the High Court of Errors
and Appeals.

11 Col Bingaman won the 2 mile Race to day   Dandy Gim vs. Capt Miners Trabatoni — there was not many Persons out there and tis the 1st time that I have been out this Season — I paid Winston thirteen Dollars to day that he won from me on the Race to day

12 Nothing new. Buisness only tolerable. The Race to day between Veryfier and Bundle & Jo — 3 miles heats   Verryfier won the 2d & 3d Heat there by wining the money — And I Lost On the day $17.50.

13 I was out at the Race track, Betting away money Like it was nothing, on the Horse Black Dick VS Capt Minors Jenny Linn, and I Lost Every Bet that I made. I will here Charge myself with the Bets as Well as I can recollect them —

> 1st I bet young Burns $7 VS 5 that Black Dick would win the Race
>
> 2nd with Winston that Black 25 VS 5 Dick would win 1 heat
>
> 3d with Nott. that Black 10 VS 5 Dick would win
> 4th with Dr Broom   10 VS 5 Dick would win
> 5th F. Thomas   5   5   do do
> 6th with Horse trader   10 V. S. 5   do
> 7th with Denny   5 VS 5   do do

14 Nothing new. Buisness only tolerable, Stump was up to day from the Swamp and brought me $24. I Kept $16 and gave him Eight. He Said that he Sold 12 cords of wood, at 2 dollars per cord — Peggy Came home to Day from Mr. Fords

15 Nothing new. I wrode down into the Swamp this Evening, and I find Billy is Haulling wood and had in a Borrowed Oxen from Mr Gregory. Phill was assisting him. There was Something Like 7 or 8 Cords on the Bank when I past. Stump had been cording wood a little during the week and had been helping Mr Gregory to raise a House. We Drove in the Swamp to Day Corah & Matilda and we found Muly & Calf, Red Neck & Calf & Mrs Millers Cow & Calf and I Bot or swaped with Mr Rosett my Cow Cela for a cow & Calf

16 I was in the Swamp and got up very Erly this morning and worked untill Breakfast time with Bily and Phill — After Breakfast I wrode in to the Swamp and found my steer and Drove him up for Billy to work. I Left there about 1 Oclock and Came up by way of the Lakes & I had my Little Gun with me and Killd 5 Large Ploves & 4 small Snipe, & 1 Partridge. Four men back in the Cypress at work on or near the Creek

17   Buisness only tolerable, Circus Company Performing in the City at Present. The Boys all went to Night to Circus. Mrs Stump & Daughter and others were up to Night to the Circus — no it was Last Night. Mr White & Dr. Benbrooks Family & Mr Frost all Left for Orleans to Live   S B Natchez took them Down — We Got a Barrell of Flour this Evening for the Family.

18   There was a Muster to day and the Swampers came up. Mr Stump reports the sale of 6 Cords of Wood at $2.50 per cord — He Said that he thought they had cheated him a Little. He gave me $16 and I gave him 5.33 as his share — this makes in all 18 cords that he has acctd for.

19   The tryal of Mr Kelly Came off this Evening and the Jury Brot in a verdict of Not Guilty — tis strange, very strange, for this was a Downright wilfull Murder, The Jury was as Follows as near as I Can recollect, Mr. Whitmare, John Johnson, Ira Carpenter, W. W. Wilkins, Young Leonard, Rchd. Elwood, & two of the Fords — I Got an Order from Mr M. Miller to day to Mr Lyle for fifteen Barrells of Coal and the amount to be placed to his acct. Coal is worth now 60 cts a Barrell, Greate many strangers in town at present   The Circus Company is here too

20   Nothing new. Buis good — Stump was up to Muster to day & A Johnson was up on my Little Horse Dick — too smart — Billy is up to night   Pd Little Winn for Stump this Evening five dollars

21   Buisness only Tolerable, and nothing new. After 12 Oclock I started Down in the Swamp and took Wm & Winston with me   We went down to Long Lake and then over to Mudy Lake and back home again this Evening — Winston had my Little gun and Killed a Crow, he had my Little Gun with him — I Commenced to day to Build a Shed for the Mill — as regards the shed tis a mistake for to day is Sunday

22   It was this morning that I commenced to build a shed for the Corn Mill and we only Built a Temporary one for the present. I got a Letter to day from Mr Miller and he states that his wife is on the mend but is still Confined to her Bed. She is under the treatment of a French Dr.

23   Buisness Tolerable fair. Nothing new — I took my Pulling Gun and I wrode my Bob Horse and I took Little Dick with me   He wrode the Little Boy poney. Byron wrode in the wagon with Gim. Pone & Fany in the wagon. I Shot 1 Large Hawk, 1 Squirrell, 1 Spoon Bill Duck & 1 Large mallard drake. I did not get Down untill Late.

24   I was in the Swamp this morning   Got up very Erly this morning and was out when Billy was Hauling in the Miller wood. The Road was in bad order and He Commenced to haul them from the Pasture to the Bank in Front of the House. Gim & I started up with a Barrell or so of Corn & 117 turnips. They were for the S. B. Natchez, I then started up and wrode Cuff, Dick wrode Dick & we went out to the Hurry Cane Lake   There I found the Mosbey Hogs that I Bot of Him. I saw about 20-5 and I got a Shot at a Sow, a red spoted one and Killed Her. She was in Good order — This is the 2d one that I have gotten of that Lot. When I bot them I was told they numberd 60. Mr. Stump came out and Brot it Home, we Cleand it, and I Left at 5 Oclock pm.

25   Gim went down to the Swamp & Brot up the Hog that I Killed yesterday. Thanks Given to day, the 1st Day of the Kind that was Ever Set Apart for this Ocasion — The Day was Generally observed by all but a few Jews — Frank took my Little Gun and Killed 1 Sparrow Hawk, Winston Killd with Mesho Gun 2 Larks, 4 Rice Birds. Sixteen Hogs Mrs Waltern has brot from her plantation This Evening — they were Killed — Old Mrs Stump was sick and Peggy was Cooking

26   [At] 3 Oclock this Evening I wrode Cuff Down to Mrs Walterns to Kill Larks, but I never got a Shot at them   I killed 1 sparrow, Pulling gun, Winston Killed 1 sparrow Hawk also. He wrode Little Dick. Dr Broom & Gay was along and I dont know what they got   The number was small shure. Mrs Waltern is having Her Hogs Killed and brot up from the swamp to her Residence. She Has a good many of them, Mc and myself has a game of ucher and I beat him very Easy indeed, Wilcox & Carter did not Come Up.

27   Gen. Quitman arrived Last night or Just before Day this morning   He surprised the people smartly for they were in weight for him   William wrode Little Dick in the Swamp this Evening. Mr. Stump killed two of the Mosbey Lot of Hogs to day in the Swamp

28   Nothing new. Buisness tolerable fair   I remained at Home all day to day, only took a walk to the Old Fort and to the Bluff. Mc took supper with us to night   I Read the Great Speech of Henry Clay this Evening — it was a Long Document and a Strong one too[17]

---

[17] See Natchez *Courier,* November 30, 1847, for the copy of the Lexington (Ky.) *Observer* version of the text.

29   To day has been a Beautifull day and the Biggest Sort of a Day at that. Gen Quitman was Glorifyed to day — in fine state. A very Large Procession of the different Companies, Masons &c. A Fine Speech from Mr Martin, and was replyd to by Gen. Quitman. The Concourse was Large.[18] Mc Came up from the swamp to day about 11 Oclock. His Gustin Heifer has got a Calf.

30   Nothing new. Buisness only Tolerable Fair — Corn is worth Five Bits at present only — Circus is here, Spalding a performing to full Houses. They are said to be good which I dont doubt, as I wont see them, I was at Hoffners Sale to day and bot 6 pair of Pants, paid $6.35 for them.

December 1   I wrode Down into the Swamp this Evening and took my Wm. with me and he wrode Little Dick and I wrode Cuff   I took my Pulling Gun. I did not kill anything on my way Down, I went down this Evening that I might take a Hog Hunt on to morrow.

2   We started from Hard Scrable to take the Hunt, and we numberd as Follows, B. Winn, 2 Gregorys, C Wolcot, Calvin Winn, Stump & Myself, William & Gim, and after wriding all day we got nothing — We could not find any Hogs at all — I shot 3 crows Late in the afternoon — Wilcox left us in the day and on his return Home Killed 2 Large Hogs   One of them I saw the other I did not see at all, and it was the Last One that he got in too. This morning it was skined and salted away. As we made so poorly out to day we intend to try it again tomorrow, Provided all is willing.

3   Nothing new. I was in the Swamp this morning and direcly after Break fast we started into the woods on the Hog Hunt. We went out by the Heavy cane and then went up through it, but could not find them   We then found 2 of the tame Mosbey sows and drove them up to the House   We then started out and I went back of the Heavy cane again and there I shot a white Shoate, I soon after that found the Rest of the Hunters and they had started nothing at all, but very soon after that we herd old man Winn and he had Killed 2 of my Large Sows   We then sent them Home and started out after the rest of the gang, and

---

[18] For a complete account of the parade, Quitman's speech in front of the City Hotel, and the celebration dinner, see Natchez *Courier*, November 30, 1847. One of the volunteer toasts at the dinner was given by James C. Cox, First Captain of the Fencibles: "When the American cannon and rifle, on the afternoon of September 13th, roared at the gate of the city, Mexico cried out, 'Who's dat knocking at the door,' the answer was, 'John A. Quitman, a Natchez Fencible.' "

Late in the Evening we found them. Mr Winn shot a Barrar[19] of his and a wild shoate and a wild sow, and He caught a Shoate — 6 head — Stump shot a Boar of Mr Winns and a Barrar of mine and a sow of mine — 3   Mr C Walcot shot a Large Wild Sow, 1 head, and wounded another that was Lost Entirely — I shot a Large sow and wild Boar and they both fell together and I caught a 'Shoat and then shot a Barrar, in all 5 head of them   Thus we got 16 head of them all together and I bot the wild sow from Wolcott   Left 2 dollars for it. I got eleven of them and Mr Winn 5 of them, So We Left Several of them in the woods and yes 7 or eight of them intending to send for them in the waggon to morrow morning Erly — We number as Follows to day — B Winn, myself, Little Washington, Stump, C Winn, & Gim, C Wolcot & Wm

 4   I was in the Swamp this Morning and Commenced to weigh and have the Hogs Salted away that we Killed yesterday. We got through in Good time and I Came to town.

 6   Nothing new. Buisness only tolerable.

 7   I started from the Swamp to day and wrode up big Jeff, tho I started on Cuff. I Left him at the wood yard with Stump, This morning in front of my Gate Mr. C. & James Gregory was out there & Mr Stump. The talk turnd on the Murder that was Commited down at the Creek by Jacob Marks — Stump Said that he was told that Johnson was Severely beaten by Marks on Saturday Last a week ago, this would be 27th of November, and that he was very Low from the Beating that he received, up to Last Sat 4th December. He said that Tate had told him so, and remarked that He, Tate, Said that Mark had beat him with a Cotten wood stick until it had worn out and he Said he gave him [a] Large stick or hoe Handle which he Said when he struck him a time or two with that. It done Johnson some good — Mr C Gregory said then as regards the statement about Johnsons being Confined to his Bed a week from the Beating that Mark gave him was not so, for he said that he saw Johnson on Saturday 4th inst in Natchez and that he was killed on Saturday night and there was no doubt of it. He said also that John Williams was talking with Johnson at the time he saw Johnson in the street — They, all of us that was present, agreed that it was a greate outrage and that it aught be taken notice of and that it was the Buisness of any Person to take Notice of it. We very shortly Separated after

---

[19] Barrow.

the Conversation and it appeared from what I understood of the talk that they all thout it was done by several of them, that was John Williams, Tate, A Johnson & this Mark. They were all present when the murder was Commited. I Bot 5½ Bushels of Potatoes from Mr Stump to day at 30 ct a Bushell   This Amounted to 1.65 which I place to his credit. $53.62½   This was for 78 Barrells of Corn I Bot of Mr. Stump at 5 Bits & a ½ a Barrell.

8   Nothing new. Buisness very dull today on account of the wether I suppose. I took a chance in Mr Seth Cox nag to day   She was put up at $130 and there was thirteen chances at $10 a chance. Jeff & Winston took a ½ chance with me, thus my Loss was $5 and I found Out too a good Deal by this Raffle. Small Potatoes in abundance, Abundance, S. W. — I will allways Know by the Initials, shure. Gim Came up yesterday Evening with me and brot up a good chance of Potaotes an Several Barrells of Corn. I had my Big Gun and Only Shot her Once and Killed a Squirrel and shot Once at a Mark and made a Good Shot. I Find that the Slut Sharp has got Puppys

9   Buisness has been very dull indeed. The wether tho I I suppose is part of the Cause &c. This has been a gloomy day, very — The names of the Men who took Chances in that Raffle yesterday was Thom Rose, N. Bunce, Hatcher, Thos Clay, Mobley, Sam Woods, myself, R. Smith, Holoway, Crizer, George Evans, Mark Izod, young Massey — that was all — Shure — Bill Nix is now in Orleans a waiting on Col. Bingaman, Mary Ellen &c.[20]

20 In connection with this reference, the following data has come to the attention of the editors: (1) In 1844 a free woman of color named Mary Ellen Williams and her children were licensed to remain in Mississippi. See Adams County Court and Police Board Minutes, 1832–45, May, 1844; Natchez *Free Trader*, November 22, 1859. (2) In 1856, Colonel Adam L. Bingaman wrote a letter requesting a close friend to arrange that the Mississippi legislature pass a special law permitting Mary Ellen Williams and her children to remain in the state and hold property there, stating that a similar law in their behalf had already been passed by the Louisiana legislature and listing her four children including Charlotte, aged eighteen, and Eleanora, aged five. Adam L. Bingaman to A. K. Farrar, January 16, 1856, Alexander K. Farrar Papers (Louisiana State University Department of Archives). (3) In 1860 a woman who signed herself M. E. Bingaman wrote from New Orleans to Mrs. William Johnson stating that her daughter, Charlotte Bingaman, would soon be married in St. Louis Cathedral in New Orleans. M. E. Bingaman to Mrs. Johnson, April 21, 1860, Johnson Papers. (4) In 1865 Adam L. Bingaman acknowledged James A. Bingaman and Elenora [*sic*] Lucille Bingaman as his "natural Children," and in a will written at New Orleans, August 10, 1869, left all his property to Elenora Lucille Bingaman, "my son Jas. A. Bingaman having died." See Adams County Will Books, IV, 576–78; Adams County Probate Court Records, No. 1,174, File 224; Orleans Parish Second District Court Succession Records, No. 20,292.

10　Nothing new. Buisness Fair. Wm wrode Jeff in the Swamp this Evening & wrode Bob up — He said that he saw Rachel to day in Mrs Walterns Pasture. He reports all well　Billy was up to night and said yesterday they did not do much but sawed a couple of Blocks to cut Sauceridge on,[21] and shucked some corn and to day they were Cutting House Logs and had Cut about 40 of them. I was at Auction to day and Bot nearly $7 worth of toys and nonsense.

12　I helped get a cow out of the Sewer. She had fell in up at the upper part of the Sewer and Floted down and Fell in to this Cispool　I got hold of her 1st　Maj Bennett and Oar and one or two others helpd get her out.

13　I wrode down in the swamp to day. Started near 10 Oclock. Gim Drove down the wagon and brot up some Corn and a Block for Saucridge Meat, Billy & Phill was hauling Logs to make a Smoke House with. Stump was out a Hunting and I did not see him at all, I had my Little French Gun along and Killed 2 squirrells and a teal duck, 3 Head. Mr Ford is Killing his Hogs to day — So I am told　He has 28 in the Pen, Bailor Winn was up to day and C Gregory and I herd that he got out a writ for Marks who Killd Johnson. On my way up this Evening I Saw Alx Johnson and told him that I wanted to Get some wood choppers as Soon as Could and that I would like to have the House that he Lived in for them to Live in as I did not want them Among my people and that I would Like have it about the 1st of Janary — he said he would.

14　Nothing new. I was at auction to day and bot some few toys and one Dozen Shawls at 1.15 per doz　At 22¢, this was for some 6 Boxes of toys, &c. Mr. Levi Harrisons Daughter was Burried this Evening. She Died Last night, On my return from the Swamp Last night I found that Anderson was Drunk and I Floged him for Getting in that Situation

15　Nothing new, buisness only Tolerable.　I Learned to day that the officers Benbrook & Dillon brought up the Following Men from the Swamp　Tate, Alexander Johnson & John William on a charge of having some Knowledge of Killing Indian Johnson. They were put in Jail

16　Nothing new. Buisness only tolerable, Stump said to day that Marks was down the River at work about 30 miles below the city, ie cutting wood at a wood yard, and said that he would

---

[21] Johnson referred to a sausage block.

go in if the rest of the people in the swamp was willing to raise money, to pay an officer to go after him and take him   I then told him that I did not want to have anything to do with them at all, but for the sake of getting those men out and of getting the right one I would be willing to throw in something; I told him that I was sorry that they were in thare if they Knew nothing of the matter and then nothing more was said about it. Mr Winslow Winn told me that he herd Alx Johnson say that I was cutting a greate many shines in Coming by his House Calling my Hogs and Gim was in the habbit of doing the same and that he intended to [give] me a real niger Beating and that he would Beat me to death and that he would whip Gim the 1st time he came along thare calling of my Hogs. I Listen to his remarks and did not say anthing in reply. He told me too that at the time he herd Alx Johnson make these threts he Johnson was a Cording of[f] wood in front of the Mosbey Field, I saw Mr Dillon to day and he told me that Charles Wilcott was very angry at what Charles Gregory had said in regard to seeing Indian Johnson in town on Saturday Last and that C. G. had told a Dam Lye and he could prove it

17   Nothing new. Buisness tolerable, To day it was that Tate, John Williams & Marks was to have there tryal. They Came Out to the office and But for want of a witness by the name of Simpson the trial was put off untill next Thursday. No tis to-morrow They are to have there trial. I was in the Swamp to day. Mr Stump Sold 11 Cord of wood the other day to a Boat — $27.50   His part was $9.12½, which I paid him.

18   Nothing new   Buisness Only tolerable   I had a settle-ment with Mr Stump yesterday, and I owed him $75.02 and he owed me seventy-nine & 75 cts, thus he fell in my Debt on Settle-ment $4.73

19   Poor old Man Jessy Died to day nearabout ½ past One Oclock — He died very Easy.   Poor old man, he was Burried this Evening.   May the Lord Have Mercy upon him — Charles & Gim went out to the Funeral — I hope He will be Better off.

20   Nothing new. Buisness good. Mr Sterling paid me the full amount of his shaving bill up to the 1st of January, 1848, $15.00   Mr Galbrath paid me fifteen dollars to day which sum pays his Shaving Bill up to the 1st of January, 1848, tho I think his bill is not quite so much. I will Look and See what it was. I Bot a 8 Dollar Coat to day for winter use — I got Old Zora a pr of shoes to day for 1.25 at Mr Dalshimers. Gim and Jeff went to the swamp to day to drive up two cows if they can find them with their calves

21 Jeff went down yesterday Evening and Came up this morning bringing with him two cows, Abigail & Hef Calf & Peggys Second Daughter with her B calf. Gim came up also with my waggen and Brought Corn and a fine Hog, 1 that I had in the Pen to fatten, it was a fine one indeed. Mother bought one from Helms man at 8 cts, it weighed 170 wt. — Gim Drove the wagon Down to the Cotten Press a[nd] Got 300 ft of Lumber from Jno. Newcomer at 1.12½ per hundred, The Boys reports Billy Sick in the Swamp

22 Gen. Taylor was Received to day and There was Considerable Excitement The reception was a warm and Enthusiastic, he was addressed by the Mayor of the City and the General replyed to him in a short adress that He made[22] Mr Stump Came up from the swamp this evening and will remain all night.

23 Gen Taylor Left this City this Evening on the Elhambra; There was Considerable shooting this Evening with the canon &c. The trial of Tate, Alx Johnson & Williams Came off to day and they made a short Buisness of it for there was no witness against them and they were discharged, and this is the way that they were Punished for the murder of Poor Johnson

24 Nothing new. Buisness Only Tolerable, Mc & Wilcox VS Carter & myself We beat them a Little

25 Nothing new. This has been a rarther a Dull Christmas There was a 800 yds Race to day, J. Mardis vs Gim Norman, The Mardis won the Race Easy Enoughf Mother Left this Evening for New Orleans, to see Adelia who is sick — I Bot Wm & Robert McCary a pr of Boots Each to day & I got a pr for myself also — I got Billy & Phill a Coat Each to day Cost $7.50.

26 Nothing new. I Let Gim go out to day to Mr Ferridays Planatation to see his Friends

27 Nothing new. I was in Company a Good Part of this day with Mr Stump, and was trying to make a Bargain with him to stay another year I offerd him fifteen Dollars per month and he Said that he Could not think of staying for Less than twenty Dollars per month. So I told him that I could not give it, and remarked at the same time that if he Could get more he was doing very wrong to stay. So Ended the matter and no more

---

22 The Natchez *Courier*, December 24, 1847, closed its article describing the celebration for the "old general" with the words: "all was enthusiasm, all was joy, all was gladness."

was Said on the subject in the afternoon However. I wrode down as Low as Mrs Walterns with him and had no farther talk more than he asked me if I was coming down soon or when would I be down thare, I told him on One Day in next week, or this week I should have said. Paid Mr. Burns for Funeral Expense of Jessey, $10. Gim was home Erly this Evening from Mr Ferridays where he went on [a] visit yesterday &c.

28 Buisness tolerable Good, Mesrs Louis Bingaman, Thomas Carneal, Water Bradish, and Judge Veasey were all drunk to night driving a team of oxen up the Main St., Mr L. Claibourne & Mr McCouller wrode Down this day to Mrs Walterns to Look at it. They are wanting to Purchase I think if they can cheap

29 Nothing new has transpired to day, I wrote a Letter to day and did [not] write it in time to send it on the Natchez

30 Buisy has been tolerable fair I received a Letter from Mrs Miller and She is a Little better than she was — The Princess Just Got up to Night when she aught to have been up here this morning very Erly. I paid old Sandy to day ten Dollars for Mother on a Hog that she Bot of him and it Left a Ballance of 3.60 due him, Zora and Billy Came up from the Swamp this Evening in the Waggon. They Brot up some Corn and Potatoes, a turkey &c.

31 Buisness Only So, So. I pd Mr Denny ten Dollars that he won of me Dandy Gim VS Tratatoni, Orleans Races — I bought 833 lbs of Bacon at Auction to day. It was sides @ 4 cts It amounded to $33.32

1848

January 1 I Sent a Hog to New Orleans to day to Mrs Miller and it weighed about 65 lbs and I sent one to the Princess that weighed 67 lbs. — I wrote a Letter to Mrs Miller to day also — Mr S Davis paid me twenty Dollars to day on Shaving acct, Sharlott pays three Dollars for her wages &c.

2 After I shut up the Shop I wrode down in the swamp as far as Mrs Walterns to Look at her Hogs and then returned again, Winston & Wm. went with me

3 Buisness only Tolerable Today the Election Came off

for City officers and I won $15.00 from Winston and I paid him
ten Dollars in Cash which makes $25.00, ie, paid him to day and
told him to have his bill in the store charged to me which is $4
and something   I will find out in a Day or two

 4   Nothing new. This mornings Papers has the result of the
Election in it, which is as Follows: For Mayor   Messrs Stockman
[and] Vanhosen   For Selectmen   Mr Boyer, Steward, Rose,
Walworth, Walker, Pendelton, Elwood, Parker, I got on my horse
after Breakfast this morning and wrode Down into the swamp to
see after things in general. I got Down in fair time and and after
Eating my Dinner took a Fresh Start in to the Swamp to drive
out my Cattle that was reported to be in Danger. Stump was with
me and I found 4 or 5 head of them, and started them out, and
away down on the Ridge I found any quantity of timber, ash, cut
by Winn and Wade to Float out   It was Cut on that Bank
Land. So goes the world. I made a Bargain to Day with Mr
Stump to stay and work for me at fifteen Dollars per month by
the year in my arrangement. I told him that I would put those
hands aside &c.

 5   Nothing new   Buisness tolerable Fair for the times
&c. Mr Inge paid fifteen Dollars on shaving bill yesterday, I
shall Look how we stand shortly.

 6   Nothing new, Buisness good, I Loaned Jno. Mardis $25
to day and he called and paid it this Evning, I Loaned Mr Winslow Winn thirty four dollars this Evening and he took his watch
and gave it to me to Keep untill he pays the same, I Redeemed
it from Hatcher & Co for him,   Mr. Wheelock pd me his acct in
full to date. $6

 7   Nothing new. Buisness dull to day — I went around to
the clerks office [and] Probate office to Look at the Maps, and I
thought them very imperfect for I noticed a tract of Land put
Down as Mr Walterns which according to the map would make
it appear as tho it was ajoing the Lands of Jessy Bell in Dead
Mans Bend — I then went up to Mr Maxwells office and I saw
the Patents that he [had] for the heirs of Jonathan Thomson and
the Lands amounted to 1100 and odd acres — I find also that
Ford has 1100 and odd acres in his two tracts, The Lands belonging to the Thomson Estate must be behind Mrs Walterns Land

 8   Nothing new, buisness dull. Mr R. Walker paid me for
one years shaving to first inst. fifteen dollars — I paid Dr. Davis
fourteen dollars and his partner Dr Kellog $6 making in all $20
for Last years Doctors bill. I paid Mrss Walker & Collins to day

fourteen Dollars 30 cts for their tin bill for Last year — up to date. Jeff Started to New Orleans this Evening on the Princess and is to be back again on the same Boat. I Sent him to see how Mrs Miller was Getting. Buisness to day has been Prety Good.

9   Nothing new, buisness good. Louis Wiley came up from New Orleans to day and says that Mrs Miller is very Low indeed and that I aught to go down and see her as soon as Possible

10   This has been a very bad night, ie Last night, very indeed, and tis hardly day Light now and is very Cold indeed. I am up and in wait for the first Boat that will come along that is bound Down the River. Mr Chas. Williamson paid me to day four Dollars & 50 cts. for the acct of his shaving bill. This pays the amount in full to date. I got off for N. Orleans this day on S. B. Riogrand.

11   I am on the River this morning and will get to New Orleans this Evening on the S Boat Riogrand, I did arrive this Evening about 4 or 5 Oclock and Started to the Residence of Mr Miller where I Exspected to find My Poor Dear Sister alive, but on geting near the House Patsy told me that she was Dead.[1] Oh, Mercifull Father. Have Mercy on me — Oh my Greate God. When I Got to the House and Saw in all its Rooms no trace of my Poor Much Loved Sister. She was Burried on yesterday — Oh mercifull Father Have Mercy on me, and Grant oh Mercifull God that She is Happy — How Glad I am Oh God that I hear that she said that she was Prepared to die and that she felt resigned to Leave this world

12   New Orleans. I Got up very Erly this morning and started down to the Lower Markets and walked about in them a short time and then went to the shop and there I found a young Frenchman, ie he came in a very short time after me, and I Got Him to go with me to the Grave of My Dear Dear Sister, who Died on Sunday the 9th of January, 1848, in the City of Orleans, [At] 3 Oclock this Evening I started from the Levee in Orleans on the S. B. York Town and brot Wm Miller up with me; I find them all very clever indeed on the Boat. Capt. Holdeman is a good man, the Barber, Minor, is Kind and clever indeed.

13   Nothing new. I was on the S Boat York town on my way to Natchez — We were on the River all day.

Oh how sad, how very sad I feel to night. The future seems all dark. No ray of light illumins its dark unpenetrable

[1] Johnson's sister, Mrs. James (Adelia) Miller, had died on January 9.

gloom   Truly most truly, Sin brings its own reward, that of an-
guish, and remorse. And I have sined most grevously, by giving
vent to a passionate temper, In allowing my Lips to give utterence
to angry words. O, the misery that is entailed on one by an ungovernable temper. Would that I could blot out from memory
the past week, which has indeed been one of Unhappiness to
me. But alas it is folly to mourn over the past, the relentless
past, which all my sighs can never recall. On the future lies my
only hope of happiness. In the future I may at least, in part atone
for the past by a strict adhesan to duty, by endevoring to become
more amiable, And by striving thus to Emulate the good I may
at last enjoy at least a semillance of that Joy and contentment
which they Say only the good can enjoy, But can I hope to attain
that degree [of] excellence and goodness that will insure happiness   I can but try, and if I fail — *try again*[2]

14   I arrived safe at Home about 12 Oclock to day with
William Miller and a Horse that I brought up with me — I had a
very pleasant Passage up indeed, there was a Good many Passengers on the Boat — The Barbers name was Minor Munce, Head
Stewart, Thom Wakefield — Capt. Holdeman.

15   Nothing new, buisness fair. Bill Nix Commenced to run
on the Steam Boat Princess as Barber, I wrote out a Bill of Sale
to day of Sharlott and sent it to New Orleans, together with a
Letter, to Mr. Miller, This I did because it was the request of
mother that I should do so. She sold her for Seven Hundred 50
Dollars. I then took and Proffered to pay the acct of my sister
which was I think about $38.50 and then send him the Ballance
to make up the fifty Dollars. And then I requested him to credit
my note with the Hundred Dollars that my sister owed me, So
that the $750 and the 150 would make 900 Dollars that I wished
him to credit on the back of my note, which I hope He will do.
Mr. Gaws Girl I saw on the Boat too agoing down

16   After I closed up Shop and took Dinner I took the new
Horse and wrode Down to Mrs Walterns with Mr Bradley as he
wanted to Look at the Place and Rent it, We wrode down together and He was pleased with the place, Mr Miller & Mr Mc-
Cary & Robt. all wrode out this Evening together, &c.

17   Nothing new   I was up at Auction to day and Bot Six
Head of Horses and a white mule, all for the Sum of $51.50   They
were a Lot of Stock that was sold from Mr Lapieces sale. There

---

2 This section was apparently added a few days later.

were in the Lot a[s] Follows: One Large Bay Horse, One Large
Bay Mare, One Small Bay Mare, One Old Brown Horse and two
sorrils, one of them had a Broken Ear, and One Small Grey Mule
— I Started Down in the Swamp after Dinner time. I took An-
derson down to the Swamp to work and I worked some in wriding
Down on the New Horses

18   I was in the Swamp Last night and I Got up before day
this morning and made a fire and waited untill Day Light. I
measured the Wood that Miller Had Cut for me and I found that
it would only measure about 71 Cords   This I thought strange
indeed, I helped Billy do some work in Hauling wood. I then
went up to the Mosbey Field and Commenced to pull Cotton
stocks [stalks] for the 1st time, Phill, Peggy, Zora, Anderson,
and Myself,   I turned some stock in the Field to day. Dr.
Saunderson purchased Maj Shields Plantation.

19   Nothing new. Winston wrode in the Swamp this Evening. Said he was agoing to work some. Mr Oblemis pd me ten
Dollars that I Loaned him some time ago. Mr Waymouth pd me
$2 that I Loaned him. Mr Winslow Winn pd me forty one Dollars
that I had Loaned him on his watch.

20   Nothing new. Mother Came up from New Orleans on
the S. B. Princess. I had a Barrell of Sugar, wt. 238 @ 5 [ct]
11.90 & a Sack of Coffee, 167 lbs [@] 7½ $12.52   In all
$24.55   Mr Dalshimer paid me to day One hundred and forty
Dollars for seven months rent to 1st of January, 1848, ie he Paid
me by his acct vs me in store [which] was $121.00, thus he owed
me $19 on Settlement which He paid — I gave Mother my note
to day for Seven hundred & fifty Dollars for value Received. Mr
Miller Sent me a receipt to day for nine Hundred Dollars that
he received by Cash and by Slave Sharlott which made the
amount   He told me that he gave me credit on the back of my
note for the nine Hundred Dollars. This will Leave me in his
Debt $800.00

21   Nothing new. I have been in buisness to day. I bought
a Lot of Corn meal & Corn from Mr Norton, in all 102½ Bushels.
Winston came up from the Swamp Last night and found 2 of my
new nags that I bot Monday and to day I found Andrew Lieper
with One of them that he said had been up here Ever since Wednesday Last. I sold Winston One of the Horses that I Bot on
Monday Last, Just for $2.

22   After Breakfast to day I wrode down to the Swamp
on my Horse Fiddler and Mr Wren wrode down with me and

took a Look at my Place, His object was to Look and See for himself and to crop it with me this year if we could agree on the terms. The Proposition that I made him was that he should put on an Eaqual Quantity of Hands with me and divide the Proffit by an Eaqual and fair Division of the Crop and then the Hands to go on and chop wood and the Proffits to be Eaqually Divided too as in the first place, and He to pay an Eaqual Shaire of the Expense from the Commencement and to pay the half of Mr Stumps wages. I was Down in the Swamp to day and did not see Stump the whole time I was thare, but I found out by Mr Samuels that he was out on a Hunt with Mr Winn & others, I bot Some Hay to day or this Evening

23   Nothing new. Buisness only so, so. I remained Home all to day. Wm & Robt, Jack & Wm Miller all wrode out this Evening

24   My William is twelve years old to night

25   Nothing new. Buisness some what dull, on account of the weather.

26   Buisness rarther Dull than otherwise, Nothing new. I wrode Down in the Swamp this Evening on the Fidler Horse, and Pulled stocks a while then wrode Down to the Lower Place to stay all night. Miller is cutting wood & Billy is Haulling wood, Phill, Zora & Anderson is Cleaning up or Pulling up the stocks

27   I was in the Swamp this morning and Got up very Erly, took Breakfast and went up to the Mosbey Field to work, and we pulled cotton stocks all Day. Mr Stump worked all Day to day. Myself, Phill, Anderson & Zora, we made a tolerable fair days work

28   I was in the Swamp Erly this morning and after Breakfast I started up to town, Left about as much Cotton Stock to Pull as would Keep the Hands at work untill night, no untill 3 or 4 Oclock. Gim Brot up the Four Ploughs from the swamp this Evening to be mended &c. Mr Gregory Paid me One Hundred Dollars for the rent of the Mosbey Place Due 1st inst.

29   Nothing new. Buisness dull. I was at work in the shop to day myself and Jeff was in the Swamp, and was trying to put up a Smoke House at the Mosbey place, but it Rained so they could Hardly get the Logs up as High as they wanted them. Phill was up to night and wrode up one of the new Horses that I Bot at the sale a week ago &c.

30   Nothing new. Buisness quite dull — I was at Home all the Evening untill Late, Then walked out with McCary to the

Horse Lot and the Horses Got away and ran off and did not get One untill Late Supper time.

31   I was quite buisy to day in geting some ploughs to work the farm with, I bot 3 of them, 2 at Mr Dicks, price $9.75 for both and one at Little & Baker at 6.00. I bot 250 ft of Lumber this Evening from Gaw & Darling and some Hay. Hay is worth $20 a ton at this time. Peggy died to day from Fields giving Her the Ever greens to Eat which Killed Her in an Hour or two.

February 1   Nothing new, buisness rarther dull. I was Having my ploughs mended to day — To day Mr Gerault offers Some of his land at Auction but did not get a bid for it more than a $5 bid that I made &c. Gim was unwell this Evening, was Bleeding at the Lungs. Dr. Blauckburn was Called in

2   Buisness very dull. I pd out about $28.50 to day for One thing or other.

I pd Mr Gale for 1 pr Boots & 5 prs shoes for the Boys 5.70
I pd Mr Dick [for] 4 Bridles 6 chains 4 prs harness   8.90
I pd Mr Boger [for] repairs on ploughs & 2 Double
                                trees, 2 Single do   6.00
I pd Mr Crizer for 2 Double, 3 Single trees, sharpening
                                  2 ploughs   5.00
Yes and for other work   2.25

And Winston & me painted them ploughs at night. I wrote a Letter this Evening to Mr Miller

3   Nothing new, buisness dull. I started Down in the Swamp this Evening and took William Miller[3] with me, and we Got Down Late in the Evening, found Billy was Hauling Fire wood to the uper place and a Little Corn also. Anderson Had Just Came in   Mr Stump had him out with him a Hunting. Zora & Phill and Billy had been at work cutting up some Logs and rolling Cotton Stocks Just before I got down.

4   We got up Erly this morning in the swamp   Staid untill Breakfast then wrode up to the uper Place and went to work a roling of Cotton stock, and we worked very hard untill 4 Oclock. When we got through with the Cotton Stocks, Myself, Mr Stump, Phill & Bill, Wm Miller & Anderson, Zora was cuting grass in the fence conners. And we Came Home at night very

---

[3] William Miller was Johnson's nephew and a son of James Miller of New Orleans. Less than three years later Johnson was referring to him as "Capt. Wm. Miller."

tyred indeed. One old Sheep and two young ones was found dead, and we threw them in the River,   Winstons old Horse died Last night, with old age I believe, Mr Stump paid me thirty dollars to day for thirteen and half cords of wood that he sold for me. It was the Miller wood

    5   Nothing new, Buisness doing so so — Winston went down in the swamp this morning and took down a Bushell of meal and Came up at night and wrode my Grimes colt up   To day is the first time that she Ever had a Bridle on — Bill & Phill both came up to night — My Little Wm went down yesterday and Came up with them to night.

    6   Nothing new. I remaind at Home all day and walked up around by Browns Saw mill with Mc in the afternoon. $8.45   Mr Stump was up from the Swamp this Evening and wrode Bob — I paid him the above Sum of money as his Part of Peggys Hire to Mr Ford. He Said that she only worked two months and 16 Days and he paid me $25.37½ for the time. Mr Stump said that she went up to work at Mr Fords 14th of August and Commenced to work on the 16th and she came home on the 14th of November, 1847. It would then be 3 months insted of two and 16 days — Charles was taken Sick this Evening.

    7   Gim went down in the swamp and took down in the wagon 6½ Pints of Coffee and 4 Quarts of Shugar to Mr Stump &c.

    8   Gim came up to day from the Swamp — Brot 3 Bushels of Potatoes. He reported that there was 23 Bushells of them in all, He put them up in Peggys House &c. Reports them cleaning up the Corn Ground on the Mosbey place, Gim Said that there was in all 23 Bushells in the Heap — I wrode Down to Capt Nevitts Spring this Evening — Took a drink out of it.

    9   Nothing new, buisness is dull I think for the Season of the year. I wrode down to Mrs Walterns this Evening to try and buy some of Her Hogs, but I could not see the overseer. This is about 4 times that I have wrode down thare to see about those Hogs, and yet I have not made a Purchase. John Mardice Caught the Dutchman that Struck his Father to day and beat him smartly in at Steers Coffee House, Some impudent Fellow Kicked Wm Miller to night on the street. The New Boy Joe was telling me about the fight.

    10   Buisness dull. The remains of Col Atchison that died down at the Bay Last Fall was brot up on this Princess Last Night and was Burried by the Mason & Citizens to day — I saw

Mr Waller to day Collect some Int [interest] and Dollars from D. P. Jackson to day, and I went after as Soon as I could and he owes me $35, and I could not Get a Single cent from him and he had the Money in his Pocket at the time. So much for so much. I saw Dr Williams to day and I wanted to find out how much he wanted for his Land and he did not say but at the same time wanted me to make him an offer for it, which I did not do.

11 Nothing new Miller[4] Came up from the swamp this Evening to Get Provisions for himself I Bot a Lot of Light Lumber from Mr Brown this Evening for $5.40

12 Buisness so so. I was away from the shop the most of to day in fixing of the Fence in the garden &c. This I done with a Lot of stuff that came from Mr Browns Mill — Charles sends me word that he dont like to Keep this Joe in the shop Wants me to take him up at my shop. Says that he is Lazy &c. Phill Came up this Evening from the Swamp and He says that they have done Burning Corn Stocks and &c but have not Commenced on the cotton stocks yet and that they were moving the Fence some in the Front and says that Mr Stumps Family moved up from the Lower Place to day.

13 Buisness Good to day — Nothing new. I was at Home untill Quite Late in the afternoon I then went Down to the fort and took the children with me and came around by the Road up the Hill.

14 Nothing new, buisness tolerable fair. I was at the Landing to day and Bot a Flat Boat from Mr Wm Eaheart. Gave him Cash $42 and two months shaving for it. It had Some Little Corn in it which I Got with the Boat and whilst I was under the Hill Jeff went Out Home without Saying a single word to me about his going Well now he can do Just as he pleases for I have no more use for any Such a Fellow Gim Came up from the Swamp this Evening and brot up my Bob Horse. I hired my sorrill mare Fanny to Mr Earheart to day for 5 Bits a Day

15 I got up this morning and started into the swamp, by way of the River I took Down a Flat Boat that I bot yesterday It had in it 20 or thirty Bushells of Corn and about 26 Bushells of Irish Potatoes and a Barrell & about a ½ of Onions in a Damaged State. Those were to plant, Near 700 Oak 6 ft Boards and some other Light Lumber. We Got Her down in

---

4 This "Miller" was evidently a white man, not related to Johnson's brother-in-law, James Miller.

safety. She is about 50 ft Long, 16 Breadth — Joe & Gim and Byron & Richard was on Board.

16   I was in the swamp this morning and commenced to take of[f] the Lumber that was on the Boat. There was about 800 ft of wether Boarding besides some other stuff for fencing &c. We got threw in the Evening and took the Boat down to the Lower place and there we Left Her, Gim & Joe I sent to town Erly this morning in the wagon, and my William Brot it down again

17   Nothing new. Buisness so so. I was still in the swamp. We were Planting onions to day and did some Plowing to plant them   I commenced by Plowing Old Roan and the Old Lapiece mare, then Jeff. The Blind mare would not work Good &c.

18   To day it was that I was Planting Potatoes and Onions. Wm. Miller was down doing a Little work.

19   This was the day that Mr Prentiss and Irwin was to fight, Mr Stump at work some to day with the Horse shed that he Put up, he was putting on the Rafters &c to day.

20   Nothing new. Buisness good to day — I walked out with Mc to the Fort in the afternoon &c.

21   Nothing new. To day it was that I sent down a Lot of Small trees to be set out at the Mosbey Place. There must have been 60 or 70 of them in all, most of them Peach trees, We set some of them out this Evening and will set the Ballance out to morrow if I can

22   To day we had some rain in the morning which Prevented us from Planting Potatoes tho I was buisy in Setting out my Little Trees. I got up before it was day and dug 18 holes to plant trees in by the time it was day — Mr Stump coverd the Horse Shed this Evening and I Built with the help of Zora and Anderson the fence on the uper side of the Lane, to divide the Places. Billy was Hauling Rails from Elick Johnsons House, I was out hunting Possums to night. Mr Stump [and] Mr Anderson was along   We did cetch one

23   I got up this morning before day and started to town and got up ½ past 8. And to day has been dull   I Loaned Mr N. L. Carpenter fifty dollars this Evening — is to pay on Friday

24   Poor James Miller Jun Died to night.

25   Nothing new. Buisness some what dull, Wm came up this night and brot up the Buggy with Some Potatoes & Some Peas & 2 Pumpkins — seys all is well, the Lane was Finished and the Stable Shed and Rack trough, &c.

26   William Miller Came up to day to the Shop and got ready to go to New Orleans this Evening on the Princess and Left.

27   It was this morning Erly that I received the Funeral ticket of Poor Young James Miller who died on Thursday night Last   Poor Poor James, he was a good young man and Promised to be a very smart and usefull one. Oh how' soon it is that he has Followd his Poor Mother, my only sister

28   This has been a Lovely day indeed   I got up this morning Erly and went to the River and Bot 2 Plows from a Flat Boatman at $3 Each   They were for working Corn with — I Sent Jim down this morning after Breakfast with a Plow and 2 Collars, trace chains, &c. and a Dutchman to work by the year for One Hundred and 25 dollars, and I to find his Provision. Old Mrs Bectill went down in the Buggy also   She Came to town to Look for Her Husband that it appears has gone up the Country some where. Gim took down also 2 gallons of mollasses, 6 pounds of Coffee, 9 pound of Shugar — Gim Came back to night and Brot back news that Miller wanted me to take up his wood and that he wanted to go to Mexico to drive a team, I paid Mr Myers to day $38.50 for goods that Mrs Miller got of Him — I paid dito $7.25 that Jack got of Him.

29   Nothing new. Buisness Has been rarther dull. I got on my Horse and took Richard with me and went down into the Swamp. I met the Dutchman that I hired the other Evening Comming back to town. He got drunk when he went down, and that was the Reason that he did not stay. I wrode down to the Lower place and put up some Fence, then return to the uper place and Marked Some Hogs, and then went back in the Evening and marked Something Like 20 odd of them. Miller Left the Swamp yesterday

March 1   I got up this morning and went to plowing and I plowed untill about 4 Oclock. Richard wrode and I plowed Joe and the Big bay mare. I then started up home. We Got up Quite Late. I Brot up the Big sorril mare. Mrs Mariah West and Mr. Miller, Emer, Octvia, Varina & Albert Miller Came up on this Princess this morning

2   Nothing new. Buisness Only Tolerable.   I Started Jim in the Swamp. I sent him down this Evening that He may plow tomorrow

3   I got up quite Erly this morning and Started to plow,

yes to Shave for it is a mistake for Jim it was that went down yesterday and not me.

4   Nothing new. Buisness only So So

11   Nothing new. Buisness Only Tolerable. Gim, Phill and Andrson came up to night from the Swamp. They report all well and that they would have Goten done p[l]owing the Mosbey Lower field if it had not have rain the other day — so they will be about two days more I suppose before they get throug[h] with it. They have Broken 3 plows this week and brot 2 of them up to be repaired   He reports the Sale of Some wood but I dont Know how much

12   Nothing new. Buisness fair. I remaind Home all the Evening.

13   Nothing new.[5] Buisness Only Tolerable &c. It was to day that I bot Mrs Walterns Hogs from Mr Hall her overseer — Mr Pearson Commenced to work for me this morning at $125.00 the year — I was to Furnish his Shoes & Provisions

14   Poor Dinah was Burried to day — God have Mercy on Her, I Pray

15   Mr Miller Left for New Orleans — S B Natchez, L M. Patterson Sells out at Auction to day — Jim went down in the Swamp this morning and took Richard with Him in the wagon — they took down a trundle Bed and a Small Bed stead — It was this Morning that Mr Winn Commenced to Plant Corn and it was this Evening that I Commenced to plant in the uper Mosbey Field — Gim was down and I was at the Shop

16   Nothing new   Buisness Only tolerable.

19   Nothing new. Buisness So So

20   I went under the Hill this morning and Bot two new Ploughs, One a Common Plow, the other a Sweep — the 1st I paid $3.50, the other $5.00   They were both new Ones — I Sent One of them Down by Billy, 2 Bushells of meal and One Barrel Seed Corn from the Flat Boat. Mr Dalshimer paid me forty dollars for two months Rent up to the 1st inst

21   Rarther dull and nothing new   I Bot Mr Winslow Winns watch. I paid $43 for it or in other words I paid $40 in cash and a pr Boots, ½ Bushell of peas — I paid 2.25 for a Load of wood for mother.

---

[5] Johnson ignored the second visit of Tom Thumb to Natchez, on this date, as he had the first visit in 1847. See Natchez *Courier*, March 10, 1848; Diary of Bee Mandeville, 1848, entry for March 13, Mandeville Papers. Tom Thumb also visited Natchez in 1850. See Natchez *Free Trader*, February 27, 1850.

22   Nothing new. Buisness So So

23   Nothing new. It was this Evening that I went to the Swamp and found them planting in the Lower Mosbey Field — It was this Evening or to day 11 Oclock that we got threw p[l]anting the Lower Mosbey Field

24   I went to the Swamp, oh no I got down the Evening before this, i. e. , yesterday, no I am not right yet for it was on Wednesday that I got Down here and went to work and planted Corn in the Lower Field, Mosbey Field — McCary Came Down to night with my Wm   They [came] down about Supper time.

25   I paid Mr. Stump twenty four dollars towards his wages this Evening.

27   Phill went down and took 2 Bushells meal and 1 new Sweep plow and another that I Had Sharpened, to work with. Common plow

28   I wrode down as Low a[s] Mrs Waltons and found that Mr. [blank] had Just Commenced to day to plough for the first to make a Crop — Wm Lost my Shot Pouch full of Shot — Mr Stump Came up to day — Staid all day. I Sent down ten Pints of Coffee by him, 1 Bottle Mustard, 1 Paper of Beet Seed, 1 Paper Peas &c.

29   Nothing new. Busness Only Tolerable and nothing new.

31   Nothing new. Buisness Only So So

April 1   Nothing new. Buisness Only So So.

2   Nothing new. Buisness Only tolerable.

8   This day I was up and about tho not a doing much, for I have been Sick for the Last week

10   Nothing new, or Strange. Mr Carter took Dinner with me to day and after Dinner we wrode down into the Swamp. Wm McCary went down with us. We got down about 6 Oclock in the Afternoon.

11   Nothing new. Buisness Only Tolerable   I was in the Swamp this morning Erly and was up by the Crack of day or Just before and was Out. Went Down to the Stable and Fed the Horses

13   Mr Jordan gets married to Mr Bailor Winns Daughter Mary to night — In the Swamp the River is very High at present and is Still On the Rise

May 1   Nothing new. Buisness good to day   This has been the First day of Court, Jasper Winn Has Left his Father and came to town — He wants an overseers Birth

2   Nothing new. Court is in Cession and buisness Only So — I wrode out to Col Bingamans this Evening on Byrons Filly   I went out with Mr Miller & my Wm

3   Mr Miller Left this Evening on the Natchez. Mrs Jerry Bunce Left, also Capt Hicky and his Father   They are Gone to Texas — The Natchez I am Told had Quite a Large number of Pasengers and I could not Get off to See when She Left. My Health is very Bad and has been — Dr Blackburn prescribes for Lavinia — She has the Rheumatm

4   My Big Sorril Mare Had a colt to day at about 10 minites after 11 Oclock — it was a Horse colt. I think it is a Sorril   She had it near the back Gait. I saw her geting through with the Jobb   Tis a fine colt.

5   Nothing new. Buisness Only so so

6   Nothing new — I was at auction to day and Bot 8 cersingles, 2 pairs of Pants and 3 Books, 1 chair, 1 Stool. I paid Maj Young fifty dollars for Charles wages to 1st April inst

7   Nothing new. Bnisness Only so so. I took a wride in the Afternoon with the children   Wm wrode his Bay Horse colt this Evening, the 1st time out of the yard — Charles disgraced Himself this Morning by Marrying Mrs Littles Servant Girl Mary Known to the City as being a Buster.

8   Nothing new. Buisness Only so so

9   Nothing new. Buisness Only Tolerable, It was about to day that I think Mr Teas is Puting me out 25 Barrells of Corn down a[t] the Mosbey Place

11   Nothing new   Buisness Fair   Nothing new or Strange in the City

12   Nothing new. Buisness Declining a Little, Court being nearly Over. From the City I Started into the Swamp this Evening and Took with me as Follows, Wm who wrode His Roan Colt, Richard wrode the Bay Colt And Byron wrode the old Bell mares Colt And I wrode Byrons Filly — thus we all wrode Colts in a manner

13   I was in the Swamp Erly this Morning and I wrde down To Hard Scrable Erly in the morning And returned to Breakfast at the other Place. Old Mrs Stump wanted me to Buy her Turkeys and a Bedstead that She owns And Says too that She intends Leaving and going Down to Her Daughters who has Just had a Baby a night or two ago — They have Just Finished or will Finish the Evening Plowing the Little Winn Place. This is the first working that it has had Since it was Planted

14   Nothing new. Buisness so so — I paid Winston five Dollars to day. He wrode out to Mr Hoggatts to Bring in Wms mare that was put to his Horse

15   Nothing new. Winston Came in this morning, no it was to night from Mr Hoggatts with Williams Roan mare

16   I Saw Bill Dorsey to day and he paid me twenty Dollars on a note I held vs him for the old Horse Charley that I Sold him.

17   I Got up very Erly this morning and it was then Raining and we have up to this date a very fine shower which was very much needed indeed both in town and in the Country. Winston takes Fany to Ruffin this morning — I Left town this Afternoon with Young Robt McCary for the Swamp. We got down about Supper time. We Met Mr. B. Winn, had a long talk in the Road &c.

18   I was in the Swamp this Morning and Commenced to Sheer the Sheep — Gim Came Down with the Buggy for the purpose of taking up the wool, We did not Get through with Sheering   Stump was Sick or Got Sick After Sheering a Little while and did not work any more to day   Gim and Pearson was helping at the Same time.

19   Nothing new. Buisness Only So, So. Gim Started up to town in the Buggy this day about 12 Oclock with what wool we had Sheered from the Sheep — He drove Bob. up in the city and Drove Fany back, ie, Wm did. Mr Pearson is plowing in the upper field. This the Last time that he is going over it before he Lays it aside

22   Nothing new. Buisness Only Tolerable   Frank by Some Calculation or other Seys that His time of Apprenticeship is up with me yesterday and that he is now Eighteen years of age — I Received a note from his mother On the Subject. I Saw his mother. She told me that any arrangment that I Could make with Frank she would be Satisfied with. Accordingly I Saw Frank and he agreed to take $100 for the next year or for this year and I promised to find his shoes also — Charles Sent me thirty five Dollars to day for work under the Hill &c.

23   Nothing new. Buisness rarther Dull. I wish now that I had my Potatoes all Planted or Set Out. The First Irish Potatoes that we have for our table use from the Place we had on yesterday or the day before. We had about 2 Bushells Brot up. Now this is from the 23d that I Commence to take notice of the

Receips &c. Dr McPheeters has a fit To night and Died instantly
I am told; if true tis Strange

 24 Gim and Wm went in the Swamp this morning To Set
out Some Sweet Potatoes Plants. I Got them from Lanier — I Bot
a Big Bay Horse at auction to day, $7. Cheap Cheap

 25 Nothing new Buisness is so so Only

 27 Nothing new. Buisness good to day. I was in the Swamp
this morning and after some time Pulling weeds out of the Potato
Patch I wrode down to Hard Scrabble with Mr Stump And Took
a Look at the Corn &c. It was Growing very fine and was Rarther
a Bad Stand. Mr Stump Just Finished the other day working or
Plowing in the upper Field, and intends to Commence this week
Comming on the Lower Field to plow it.

 28 Stump was up from the Swamp and in the Afternoon
I and Mr Miller wrode Down in the Swamp with him Stump
and Mr Miller took it turn about and wrode in my Cab. and New
Horse Bully Boyd, We Got Down in two hours ten minutes. I
wrode Little Dick, Stump big Jeff

 29 This morning we were in the Swamp And Got up Quite
Erly and The Plowman Started to Plow in the Lower Mosbey
Field which is Entirely Contrary to my Judgment for the Corn is
all about Tassaling and Some Silking. The vines are runing
ve[r]y Beautfully and they of Course are torn all to Pieces B.
Winn has Left his. Mr Ford has quit his Corn and Laid it bye,
but Stump is Still at work at it. I have no Peas Planted yet and
tis full Late I think, Mr Miller and myself wrode out this morning
After Breakfast and wrode nearly over the whole of my Land.
We wrode over the back Line, or very near it, and this Evening
we Started up Dr[i]ving Crop Lapiece in the Cabb. He performed
very well indeed Mr Ford Lost One of his men this Evening

 30 Mr Miller[6] Left here in the night for New Orleans. His
Children mooved down here this Evening from Mothers where
they have been for Some weeks — they were Lavinia, Emer, Oc-
tavia, Varina, Albert, and two Servants, Martha & Patsey. Wm
& Robt McCary and Miss MacNiel was down to the House this
Evening. Staid untill Late &c.

 31 Mr McCouller informs me that the Brindle Cow that I
Bot of Him has returned to his Place and has a Calf She had
[it] this morning I think he told me

 June 1 Gim is up from the Swamp. He went Down yes-

---

 [6] James Miller was Johnson's brother-in-law.

terday. His Report is that the Peas was Planted on yesterday and the day before, and that they are now Plowing down at the Lower Place, Commenced this morning I Suppose, He brot up near about 2 Bushels of Potatoes, This is Lot No 2. I Shall Only remark that my Corn is Something Smaller than my neighbours. I cant tell the Reason, Mr Hamilton Came to See me to day and told me that he would give an order on me for about ten dollars   I told him that I would accept it so we parted &c.

    2   Nothing new. Buisness Dull, Quite So. Gim & myself was a Painting the Buggy a good Part of the Day, yes and the Irish waggon too, Paints Cost a Dollar to day for the two waggons. It was to day that Mr Lemly Came to Know if I Except this order of Mr Hamiltons for $10 which I did

    5   Nothing new. Mr Gloadin of Orleans went up to the Jail with me to See after his Boy Simon who had Left him, and he found the Boy here in Jail. He went through the usual forms and Took him out of Jail and after dinner he got of[f] for New Orleans. I find him a Gentleman   The Planters Bank was Selling Some Property to day[7] and I came near Buying some Property that She owns in Arkensaw, 1407 acrs I think, It all sold for 105 dollars and I did not get it. Mr Wm Hall Bot it for Mr Walworth as he had the Only claim VS it — There were a Lot of Yazoo[8] Lots Sold and they were Bot by Mr Withers cheap — 10 & 15 dollars per Lot

    6   Nothing new   Buisness So — Mr Koontz paid 2.50 this Evening which pays his acct. to first inst — I went under the Hill this Evening and paid for two Barrells of Lard at 4 cts per pound — that is I paid $16.50 for the two Barrells. I herd to day that Bailor Winn & Wade had Bot the Bank Land. Thus they Own it all now[9]

    8   I got up Erly this morning and Started into the Swamp. Got there at a Late Breakfast and found that the People were all down at the Hard Scrable Place, It appears that they Commencd with the Hoes on Monday morning, Mr Stump, Violet & Anderson and a part of the time Pearson   They had only got down below the House a Little over ½ way down the Front Ridge — I Commenced with theme and we Soon Got of[f] the Front Ridge and Finishd the Small back Ridge also this Evening

    9   To day we Commenced to work in the Back Ridge above

---

[7] For the announcement of the sale, see Natchez *Courier*, June 2, 1848.
[8] Johnson probably referred to Yazoo City, Mississippi.
[9] See Natchez *Courier*, June 2, 1848.

Phills House and we did Some 80 odd Rows and was Stoped by the Rain or we would have gotten through or near it

    10   Anderson was up to day with Some Cucumbers and Cabbages. He wrode Crop & Billy came up afterwards wriding my Big Bay Horse, he Brot up a small tin Bucket of Butter and Some things, Snaps &c. for himself — now when I Left the Swamp there was not Quite a Days work to be done in the Hard Scrabble Field.

    11   I paid Mr Wade $36 for 6 months Rent of Shop under the Hill to 1st inst — I Paid Winston Eleven Dollars to day, ie I am to Pay Dalshimer for him. Winston went to the Swamp this morning to work No it was not to day that Winson went down.

    12   It was to day that Some Rascal Knockd one of my Shoates in the Head and I had her Killd and cleaned. It was Only yesterday that I found One of the Large Size ones Dead over by Johnsons stable — Winston went down Erly this morning to work. Took down 1 dollars worth of Sugar & 15 cts of Beef, 1 Paper of Cabbage — Mr Finney Gave me a fine Shoate to day   It was a young Stock Hog

    13   Nothing new more than a full Confermation of the Nomination of Mesrs Gen. Tailor and Mr. Philmore of New York,[10] To day it was that Mr Pearson Came up and I had a Settlment with Him. He admited that he had Lost three weeks which I deducted from his wages So I paid him in Cash $15.50 and paid 9.25 cts in Dalshimers Store for him also — this being the Amount that I owed him for work from 13th of March to 13th of June, which was two months and 1 week   He Bot Some Medicine and then went down. He wrode Crop &c. I wrote a Letter to Mr Miller to day   Told him that I would Send Some Potatoes the next trip of the Natchez for I have not dug them up yet, We had a very hard Rain this Evening and wind with it which blew down Our China tree in the yard. It fell on the Cistern House — Mr Pearson Seys that he thought that Mr Stump was Having the weeds cut in the Sloughs to day

    14   Nothing new to day — Winston Came up from the Swamp this Evening. He reports that they had Gone down to the Lower Place to finish the Field. This I thought would have been Done on Monday Morning — but we have had a Greate deal of Rain this week

---

10 *Ibid.*, June 16, 1848.

15   Ellen Phill got the Ends of two of Her Fingers Ground off in the Corn Mill to day. I Cut the End of One of them off with my Knife, Four or 5 of the Runaways that was in Jail Broke out Last [night] and ran off.[11] The Sultana has I Learnd ran into the Grey Eagle and Caused her to Brak her Connection Pipe and Burst Her Boilers and has Cause the Death of 16 or 20 Persons. It was done up the River — I Bot 12 Barrels to day to Put Potatoes in

16   Nothing new   Buisness dull, Quite So. Phill is up to night and reports all well. They had cut the weeds down in the sloughs and had Commenced on the Ridges & he Seys that they were making some Preperations to chop wood, Mr [blank] was to see [me] to day to Know if I wantd any work done — I told him that I wanted to have some wood choped &c. I wanted to have 100 Cords cut if I Could make the arrangment. Phill reports the whole of the Potatoes as Planted &c. I Loaned Mr Mardis two dollars this Evening to be paid next Saturday, I Loaned mother three Dollars this Evening to Pay Cooper. Mr W. Fords Corn is very much Burnt, or Fired as they termed it

17   Nothing new   Buisness Only Tolerable   I remaine[d] at Home a part of the day and in the afternoon I wrode out to Col Bingam[an]s and brought Home my Little Grimes Filly and cannot see that She has improved Any Since She went out

18   Nothing new. Buisness Some what dull.. I wrode down in the Swamp this morning and my Wm went with me   We took down with us Byrons mare and Colt, the Bell mares Colt, the Roan Colt, the Dun Colt and Thom Denny and the Abigaile cow — I went to work To day To dig Potatoes and we got one Patch Dug and the yield was Small tho the Potatoes was Large. Twenty-seven Bushells was got from it

19   I Commenced this morning to dig Potatoes in the other Patch on the Hill or Ridge and the Produce of this Patch was Better than the other   Mr Pearson Commenced to work yesterday, the 1st work Since Our Settlement. I won $10 from Mr Stump to day on a Bet about Potatoes

20   Nothing new. Buisness Tolerable fair

21   I was in the Swamp at work, the hands, where was they. Oh they were at work in the Fields choping down weeds &c.

---

[11] The Natchez *Courier* carried an advertisement for the runaways on June 20: "$100 Reward. The State of Mississippi, Adams County. Five Negro Slaves confined as runaways, escaped from the jail of this county on the night of the 15th instant."

And the Forenoon of to day I had them all down in the Slough Planting a Little Corn that I had in the Bottoms of the Sloughs   They get through with that in an hour or So, then went to the uper Place to Choping weeds again. My Wm and Myself did the Last Planting this Evening and then Started to the City. Got home Late at night

22   To day it was that I went to the Landing and Bot 8 Barrells Corn from Welsh at 25 ct per Barrell, It was damaged. I then Bot a Lot from a Mr Carter and I am to Give him Seventeen Dollars for the Lot. He thought there was about a 100 barrells or more. Mr Stump won five dollars from me to day on the Race between Wm Roan mare and Cuff   They wran 300 yds and the Horse won [by] 4 feet. Hard work at that

23   I was Down to the River Several times during the day to Look at the Boat. I Bot 15 Barrells to put up Potatoes in   I intend to Send them down in the Flat Boat. I paid Mr Shelling $5 to tune the Piano

24   Old Anderson was up to day and reports 4 Sick, 2 children and Billy and Peggy. Billy was taken Sick Last Tuesday night and Sick yet — I Bot Some Medicine to day and Sent it down by Anderson and he took the waggon down and run it over the Hill Side and I had Some trouble in geting it up again   Mr Delome came along and helped me to get it up again   We got it up and Left Anderson to go on down — Five of Delomes hands was Sick this week — I was out to Mr Smiths this Evening and got my Big mare that has been thare for a week or morre

25   I Started this morning Erly into the Swamp   I went under the Hill in the first place and Bot 14 Barrells to take into the Swamp and I Put them in a Flat Boat that I had a Lot of Hog Corn in and I also put in a Corn mill that I had to take down. I Bot the Corn of a Mr Carter. We Commenced to take it out After dinner and before we got through with it Mr Gay Came down and Summons Mr Carter to Come to town on a debt of Metcalfs for $32 and Some cents — I Loaned him my Little Horse Dick

26   We were drying the Corn in the Stable yard and if I recolect aright we had Some rain in the afternoon and my corn got wet again, so we had to Let it remain Longer — Seventeen dollars is what I paid for the Corn and I think there was about 100 Barrells of it in all — Varener Falls from the gallery, 3 doctors in to See her — Davis, Blackburn & Thornton. Mr Bunting Commencd yesterday to Build his Shed for the ten Pin ally

27   After Breakfast we Starte[d] to clear off the Ridge between my two Places. Mr Stump, Pearson, Phill And Anderson was at work and Myself — We did Some work, then after dinner we Commenced and Put the Corn up in the House. It was not dry but I was affraid of more Rain and we did have a very heavy one after the Corn was up

28   After Breakfast time I went down with the Rest to work. We Commenced to cut down trees as usual   I staid to work untill the Evening about 4 Oclock   I then Started Home in my Buggy with Dick & Byron with me — We did not get home untill Supper — Old Mrs Wilcott Came up to day and got some of her things and returned to her daughters in the afternoon

29   Nothing new, Buisness dull and nothing going of importance, I Left them in the swamp to continue the clearing of the Ridge.

30   Nothing new   Buisness Only So So

July 1   Phill Came up Last night bringing a Small Bucket of Butter and nothing Else   He Seys that Mrs Wilcott had mooved Down to her Daughters on Saturday and that She took her Bedds and all with her, Now I hope She will remain Just as they are

2   I was Sick and was up a good Part of the night. I had taken 4 Pills Last night and they Sortr took me Just as it was Raining hard. I Recollect that fact because I had to take of my Draws I notice, Mr Miller Sent me twenty five Dollars in cash and Mrs Battles is to Pay for the other five dollars thus making $30 that I Receivd by this Boat for 14 Barrells of Potatoes, He wrote me that he Sold 10 Barrels and 4 of them He Could not Sell at the Present writings, I Bot Louis Bingamans Buggy to day at Constables Sale for $11.75 and then on my way back I Lost from my Pocket twenty five Dollars During the Evening, a 20 Dollar & a 5 dollar Bill. God Knows whether I will Ever find it again   Winston Drove up the Cow I Sold my Sister. My Wm & Gim helped bring her in from Mr McCoullars to night with her Calf — Several Persons got drowned this Evening on the Wharf

B   This is Monday the 3d of July insted of the 2d as I Stated yesterday

4   I went out to the tract[12] and made Several Bets on the

---

[12] The Natchez *Courier*, July 4, 1848, announced: "Pharsalia Race Track. We understand some fine racing will be had at the Pharsalia Race Track, to-day, commencing at 1 o'clock. Some of the best nags in the country will run. Fine

Race   Three horses wran as Follows and they Came out as Follows, Mardices Mare, Clarks Horse, McCoullers Horse. I Bet $5 with Gay, $5 with Henderson & 5 with Waller and $2 with Mardice

5   Nothing new. Buisness dull for to day. I was at the Landing to day   I saw Mr Glaudin on his way to New Orleans, had been to Natchez and to Vicksburgh to Look for his runaway Boy Simon. He did not get him   He had gone to St. Louis Jail — A Mr Webb and Potter Came up to See us and Sat untill after the usual Dinner time   They Declined Eating &c.

6   Nothing new. I Sent Gim into the Swamp this Evening 1 Bushel Meal, ½ B. Potatoes and 1 Large Middling of Bacon

7   Nothing new. Buisness Dull, I Got up Very Erly this morning and Started into the Swamp in my Cabb and I Got Down a Little after 9 Oclock to work, They were Just finishing Some Little chopping on the Ridge. I took my hoe and went to work at Some young Corn that I had Planted in the Slough — I worked untill Dinner and then went up to the House. After dinner we Commencd to work on the Pea Patch and we got throug with [it] by night — Gim was Sick in the Swamp to day and so was Billy

8   Nothing new. I was in the Swamp this morning and we Commencd work in the Garden this Morning Erly and workd the new mellon Patch over by Breakfast. We then went down [to] Hard Scrabble to work the young Corn   This we done by dinner time, We returnd and After dinner Some time we Knockd off   We Brot up in Gims wagon 14 water melons, a Lot of tomatoes and Small Lot Cucumbers and about 2 pounds of Butter — We got up about Supper time, My William Came up too.

9   Nothing new, Buisness Only So So

10   Nothing new and buisness Dull

11   I went down in to the Swamp this morning to Pull Fodder And went [when] I got thare I found Anderson Sick, Billy dito, and I went to work and during the day Claib Came Down and we went Strong to work   Pearson was at work too.

12   Nothing new. Buisness Some what dull. I was Still Pulling Fodder and Pearson got Sick to day and so did Claibourne. They had Chills & Fever

14   I was in the Swamp this morning and arose very Erly

sport is anticipated. Capt. Clark will provide a sumptuous dinner for the occasion, and will be prepared to serve all his friends with the best of eatables and drinkables, which is peculiarly *his* characteristic."

and went to work in the Field Pulling Fodder — Here is our Strength to day in the Field, Mr Stump, Myself, Richard

15   To day we were To work in the Corn Field, We were Gathering Foder and Stacking it up. To day we Put One Stack up in the Lower Field and Better than half   Put up One in the Pea Patch and we got near a half of a Stack wet Slitghtly   We got throgh and we had a Smart Shower of Rain. I Came Past Mr Winns and he had pulled 227 Rows. I have up to this date about 3 stacks Pulld.

17   Nothing new. I Remained at the Shop and Frank and Gim went to the Swamp to Pull Fodder.

18   Frank & Gim is below in the Swamp.

19   Mr Miller Left this Evening On the Natchez,   I Sold him my watch this Evening for Seventy five Dollars and He Gave it his Daughter Lavinia — I told him that I would be owing him Money, interest money, and that it would be all right — William Came up from the Swamp this Morning. He brot up Some water Melons. He went down yesterday and took Sylvia in the Buggy with him — I paid to a Dutch Fellow by the name of Solloman $6 for taking my horse out of the Bog under the Hill, He is a Rascal. This is all I have to say

20   To day we had a Smart Little Shower of Rain and Comming at this time it Spoils Foder, They are Pulling Foder down near the House, Billy Came up this day from below and Claibourne went Down to Pull Fodder   To day Dr Rusell has his trial and is held to Bail in the sum of 1000 Dollars —He wont be able to Give it I think[13]   Report sey that Some Fellow Stole $100 from George Dyer Last night under the Hill at Franks Coffee House. Dr Broom and others Hung the Dutchman for a Little while to make him tell the truth but they Could Not Come it.

21   I am Just about ½ done Pulling Fodder at this time — I Presume that Mr Stump & Phill, Frank & Gim & Claib., Zora & Violet are all at work to day. Yes and Sylvia & Mary

22   Gim Brot up the wagon this Evening and Frank & Claibourne Came up in it   They have been Pulling Fodder and have Left a greate deal of it down on the Ground wet.

23   Nothing new. I started after Breakfast this morning and went down into the Swamp and I found that there was a

---

13 The Natchez *Courier,* July 21, 1848, reported that Dr. J. G. Russell had been expelled from a local I. O. O. F. lodge for "gross immoral conduct."

Greate deal of Foder on the Ground. We did nothing with it to day.

24   Nothing new. Buisness Only tolerable. I was in the Shop this morning Erly and we commencd to Pull Fodder in the Lower Field. My Force Consisted to day of the Following names, Philip, Zoora, Sylvia, Gim, Violet, Claibourne, Mr Stump, myself, Robert, my 2 Sons, Mitchell & George

25   To day again we were all in full Blast and Mary was at work too to day. Thus we got along a Little Better. We then Commenced to turn down the Corn in the uper Field and this we work[ed] at untill dinner and then Quit and went to Pull Fodder again

26   Nothing new. I was still in the Swamp to day at work with my Fodder.

27   To day has been a Buissy day with us — Mitchel was Sick and Zora was Sick also tho we Pulld a good deal of Foder to day.

28   To day has been another very Buisy day with us. A part of the day we were Stacking and a part of the day we were Pulling and tying up Fodder.

29   Nothing new. We were very Buisy to day and we Finished the Pulling of the Mosbey Field and then we Commenced to Stack up and we Put up 3 Stacks to day, 2 in the Lot and One in the uper Field, This makes the 10th Stack of Fodder that I have Pulld and Leaves a Ballance of ½ a Stack in the Shed, Slitely Damp — I Came up to night to the City and Robt., Richard & Byron & Wm Miller & George all Came up.

30   Nothing new. I remain at Home all day to day, that is After the Shop Shut up

I paid George to day for One week's work —   5.25
I paid Mitchel also —   5.25
and gave them Each 25 cts.

31   Nothing new. I remained all day at the Shop and about it. I Sent Gim & Winston Out to Mr McCoullers to get the Brindle Cow & Her Calf   They returnd and Brot her in   Gim & Doctor repares the old waggon this Evening   Will Miller Shoots at My Hat 10 Paces for a Hat   I won it. He then Shoots 5 Paces for do   I won that, for he never touch the Hat.

August 1   This day I aught to be at work at Hard Scrable Pulling Fooder. I Paid Mr Stump to day twenty Dollars on wages. Mr Joseph Shields is about ½ Done Pulling Fodder to this date — Jack Sent in to day for the Grey mule, and I Sent it out to him

2   I was in the city ½ of this day and in the Afternoon I Startd down into the Swamp — Gim & Andrew went down this Evening to Pull Fodder

3   Nothing new. I was in the swamp this morning Erly and we Commencd to Pull Fodder on the Hard Scrable Place.

4   I am in the Swamp this morning and am still agoing a head on the Fodder

5   I was in the Swamp Erly this morning and Commencd to tye up Fodder. We got through about 10 Oclock.

6   Nothing new.

8   William Miller Left for New Orleans this Evening on the Steamer Natchez, Gim & Anderson Came up this morning from the Swamp   They brot up the Buggy: We worked the Road to day that is our Part of it

9   Nothing new   It was to day that Will Miller went to Orleans and it was to day that Gim And Anderson Came up instead of yesterday.

10   Nothing new. Buisness dull to day. It was this day that Frank Left by my Order. I found that it was his intention to Leave from what was Said by Mother, I then told him to Leave as Soon as Possible and for two cents I would have taken his Jaw — a Buster

11   I got up very Erly this morning and Harnessed up the Horses and went to the Swamp taking my wife & Lavinia, Emer, & my children, 3 Boys   We got down thare Erly After Breakfast   After diner we wrode down to Hard Scr[a]ble and it Raind whilst we were thare, and On our way Back We Caught 2 wild shoats.

12   Nothing new   Buisness dull. I was in the Swamp, the Family also. We spent the day very agreeable to day in deed and in the Afternoon we Started up and had the good fortune to Get up without any Loss or misfortune. Thank God. McCary was along   He Came down this Morning Erly

13   Nothing new   Buisness rarther dull   Myself, Winston & Gim at work

14   I paid Frank ten dollars & 38 cts to day for wages and this was the Last that I Expect to pay any Such a Scamp — I Shall recollect him — It was to day that I Receivd 100 Guny Bags at 10 cts Each — Winston went in the Swamp to day.

15   Nothing new. Buisness Some what dull

16   I Started into the swamp this Evening — I found a Mr Miller trying to get off his Raft of Timber from the Bar

17   I hired a Mr Blackburn to work by the month at $10 per month, We made a Commencement Late in the Afternoon but done very Little at it, I Sent Violet Home this Morning with her two children & Paid Mr Hamilton $11.60 for her wages.

18   To day or at Least before Day I got on my Horse and Started for the City and by So doing I Escaped the rain.

19   The Buggy Came up from the Swamp with Mrs Bakers two old Men in it   They were Said to be Sick, Miller the raft man Left one of his men yesterday at my house in the swamp   He was sick.

21   I Receivd a Letter from Mr Miller and a Small Box with a wig &c. Anderson Came up to day and Seys that the man Blackburn & the Raftsman is both Sick — he Came for medicine for Him

September 1   I Got up quite Erly this morning and Started Down in the Swamp and Took my Richard with me. I wrode down behind the Field and in doing So I missed Seeing The Big Soldier Blackburn that was To have Commenced to chop wood for me two weeks ago. He Left To day. He was Pretending all this time that he was Sick   Miller that has Just returned from Mexico Left the other Day and went Down to Mr Gregorys to work. This I did not think of him but Alass Butter will Run   I found Phill at work down in the woods, Barking the Polls that is to make the Corn House, Mr Stump is unwell and has been for more than a week, Anderson is Sick and is at town, Billy also. Thus it is there is no one to work but Zora and Phill, She was cleaning Out a Place for a Turnip Patch, I helped Phill a Little while   I was at Hard Scrable to day and I found the Foder or corn that was Lately Cut was Drying fast and was in the House, Mr B. Winn was down at the House for Some time this afternoon a chating, Tis now Several weeks Since I Quit Pulling Fodder and I have not had no wood cut yet. Not at all, I Stacked up a Little Grass that Zora cut to day in the melon Patch, Mr Stockman Gets the Barlow Cow to day and has his choice to hire or Buy.

2   Nothing new. Buisness Dull, I Got [up] Erly this morning and went to work and cleaned my Little Gun and Started out to take a Little Hunt and I Killed One Squrrile and Came home to Breakfast. After Breakfast I went to work with Phill,

We were hauling House Logs on the Dray with old Roan and the old Soril Horse Charly — we hauld Severl Loads with them, I Sufferd with the head ache Considerable to day. Mr Stump Caught another One of those Little Wild Boars to day and alterd him and marked him and Put him in the Pen, We Caught him in the Front Lane

3 Nothing new. They have not put the Quaratine Law in the force, no they have not taken up the warf Boat yet. The Hackman Frank Ray was Burried this morning. He was Drowned on Thursday night Last by attempting to Jump from One Boat to the other, Charles was Sick this morning and is not able to work. He Sent the Key and I Sent Gim down to work in his Place

4 Mr Stockman pd me two dollars for a months shaving up to the 1st inst, It was to day that I Got this Book from Maj Elward, Price $5. This was One of the Books that I won from Him [on] the Election of Asseser

5 Nothing new. To day has been quite a Buissy day for I have been alone nearly all day — Charls was Sick & Gim had to take his Place under the Hill and Winston was Sick, So was my William and my Richard. Thus I was by myself and did not get my Breakfast untill 1 Oclock, Thus we See how beholding man is. Everything depends on our Health

6 Nothing new. Buisness decidedly dull   I Bot a ½ Barrell of Flour, $3.00 and I Bot 616 ft. of Lumber at 1 dollar per hundred   This I intend to Cover the Shed with before Long if nothing Happens. Flour is worth 5.25 cts per Barrell at Present. The River is on the Rise, I Sent Anderson Down to day to See what was wanted, He Came back this Evening and Seys that Coffee & Sugar, Meal and meat is wanted. Charles is Sick still   Was taken Last Saturday night.

7 Nothing new   Our City is Considered Healthy at Present but I think we have a Good many Billous Cases — Mr S Woods called to See if I would not go in with Several of them in a $500 bet, ie for me to go in $100. I did not Consent Exactly but told him that I would Like to go in about $30. So we did not Say any more.

8 Nothing new. Buisness dull   The City Considered Healthy tho there is to my Opinion a Good deal of Sicknes about in town, I went under the Hill to day and Bot Lumber to the Amount of $7.90 from Mr Cozens to repair the Stables &c. and I hired two men to Cover the Shed. I have been for a week now

Anxious to Pull my Corn but Cannot get at it yet and the Article is worth a Dollar per Barrell.

9   There is a Good deal of Light Cases of Sicknes in the city, The new Princes arrived this Evening and this is her first trip down — She Brings Down a Good Freight. My William Came up from the Swamp with Phill to Night and they attempted to Come up with a Load from the Swamp and Broke Down the wagon near Mr Fords House and had to Leav it and reports that Anderson Broke the Shafft of the Buggy when he took it Down So it appears that most Evey time that I am not along my self Something of this Kind Happens — Democratic Meeting to day & Gen. Quitman Spoke and at Night Judge Veazy & young Duncan Spoke

10   Nothing new. After I closed the Shop this day I Started Down into the Swamp with my Buggy. I got down in the afternoon and I went down to Hard Scrabble   Took a Look at things in General. The Potatoes or vines had Lots of Grass in the field and very few Pumpkins and they are not generally Large; the Sheep dont Look well. They appear thin, I have not Commenced to Pull Corn yet   I discover tho that Mr Ford has been Pulling for Several Days and So has Mr Winn   I have no House to Put my Corn in at Present So I must Past the Present time

11   Nothing new. Buisness very dull. I was in the Swamp and this morning Erly I Got up and whiped Anderson about the Breaking the Buggy   By Breakfast he reports himself Sick and did not get to work, Phill was at work making Oak Boards to Cover the Corn House with. I Started this Evening with my cab with Bob. in it and Billy had in 2 Horses in the wagon, Anderson had Crop in the Buggy with Grass &c. Bill Brot up Some Corn, abot 2 Barrells, Some Fodder and Seven Pumpkins — We had a greate deal of trouble indeed in getting up the hill   It was raining all the while and the ground was Slipery in deed — The Hound of the wagon Broke Down and we had a Broken Shaft on the Buggy — We got up tho it was 11 Oclock when we got up.

12   A Good many casses of Light Sickness in the City — I was under the Hill this Evening and bot a Corn Sheller from Mr Gaw for $12 and paid him for it. I bot 1000 Shingles to day at 2.50 cts and Billy hauled them up — I was at Mr Crizers to day and was having my carts repaired and the Horses Shod. This Cost me 2.75 cts   I paid 3 dimes for making a Screw driver,

People are Getting alarmed for fear of Fever[14]   Anderson is Still Sick and has a fever, the Doctor prescribed for him this Evening — Greate many Pecans on that tree of mine in the Field

13   Nothing new. Still Some reports of Fever in town, which Some Doubts, A man by the name of [blank] was burryd from the House of Mr Meyers on Main St to day — I sent Billy down to day with a Load of Shingles, 2000, and Winston he took down the Bugy with Some Little Lumber in for the Dr to Build a repository in the Swamp — They report Phill is still trying to get out the Bourds for the wonderfull Corn House that is to be, I Bot Col Robertsons Tilbury or Cab this Evening and agrees to Deduct $40 from his acct. for the Same

14   Considerable Talk about the yellow Fever in the City and the People are devided in the oppinion about the Disease. Some think that the Fever is here whilst others do not believe it and I for One is very much inclined to doubt it, A Mr Brewer Died Last night and was Buried at Washington To day — To day Mr Jas Stockman Buys the Barlow Cow at $15, and wants to Know if he gives me the Calf if I will Pasture the Cow when She Goes Dry. I told him yes, sir — To day or this morning that I Loaned Mr James Mitchell my revolver. He and his Daughter was a Going over to Her Plantations, It is out of order and I have no Confidence in it. I gave him Some Balls and Some Caps — Winston Seys that Mr Stump went to work to day at the Boards and that to morrow He intends to Get up the Oxen to haul the Logs for the Corn House, Winston & William Put up the repository To day but did not Shingle it, having no nails

15   We had a Little Shower of Rain which made the Air pure and I think it is Calculated to make the City Healthy. Mr Stockman Bot the bob tail Barlow Cow from me yesterday. She is a good Cow.

16   Nothing new. Sickness in the City is Some what abating I think, Judge Winchester Spoke to day at Length, a Good Speech[15] — I Got the Cab home to day that I Bot of Col Robertson, Tis a very heavy thing on a Horse I think, Phill is up to night. He wrde up big Jeff — Lawyer Crab Killed Mr Jenkins

---

[14] The city quarantine law had been put into effect early in the month. See Natchez *Courier*, September 5, 1848.

[15] Judge George Winchester spoke before the Rough and Ready Club of Adams County. See Natchez *Courier*, September 19, 1848.

yesterday in Vickburg by Shooting him in a fight[16] — Sold a Big Pumpkin to day for 25 cents to Mr B. Roach

30   I Got up Quite Erly this morning and went to work On the Shed that we Commenced yesterday and I worked untill Breakfast time, then I Stopt and Started to town and I took Byron And Richard to drive the Buggy and Fanny was in it. They Brot up Some Corn whilst Wm and Anderson help me drive up the two Higgins Cows and there young Calves. We Got up to the City Erly. Billy also Came up Driving the 2 Horse Waggon   He also brot Corn and Some Hay,   The Shop took in to day 3.90 cts, the Bag for 5 days, 14.25

October 1   Nothing new. Buisness dull, Quite So — I was in town to day at work and when I Got through I Left the City and Started down into the Swamp and I had Bot 3 Sheep Just before I Started and got them very cheap indeed   I gave Only 2.50 cts for three of them, and I drove them down before me. They got down in Safty. Robert Mc went down with me.

2   Nothing new. Buisness still Quite dull   I am in the Swamp at work at the Shed that I and the old man Phill Comm[e]nced on Friday Last, Mr. Miller Came up to day from New Orleans   This Eveng he Came down where we were at work and did Some work himself. Mr Stump did Some work too this Evening

3   Nothing new. I Started up from the Swamp this morning after Breakfast.

6   Winston was down in the Swamp a Shelling Corn &c. Now the above is a Mistake for it is in November instead of the above date.

7   My Wm Came up for medicine for Peggy. She was Quite Sick — Nothing new   Buisness Dull to day. The above is a mistake for it is in Novemb I intend to write about.

29   I Came up from the Swamp yesterday and brot up the Family with me   Sarah Came up from the Swamp to day and is very Sick. Was taken in the Swamp — Mitchell Brot her up in the Buggy

30   To day Mr Stump & Billy was Haulling Pumpkins — I Commencd to Shell a Little Corn this Evening Late for the First time with the Corn Sheller

[16] The brief article in Natchez *Courier*, September 19, 1848, was headed: "Rencontre in Vicksburg."

31   To day Mr Robert, no Stump, was Hauling Pumpings in Hard Scrable

November 1   I was down in the Swamp to day and was Shelling & Sacking Corn   To day Robert & my Wm & Anderson was at work at it, Richard & Byron also — Mr Stump, Billy & Phill haulling Pumpkins

2   Nothing new   I Came up from the Swamp to day and Brot up Some corne in the wagon and Robert and Judge Came up, and Byron & Richard. I paid $12 to Robert and the Same to Judge for work   They have been thare Ever Since I Commencd to pull Corn, I finished Pulling, no Sacking, 37 Bushells of Corn yesterday. I put up 17 Sacks of it and Left 5 whole 3 Bushels Barrells which would make 50 Bushells that we Shelld out.

3   Winston went Down in the Swamp yesterday afternoon in the 2 Horse wagon — Mr Robt Dunbar Died to day before Dinner, Young Ludorf was Burried to day. Mrs Wadsworth was Burried to day

4   Wm Came up from the Swamp for medicine for Peggy who he Seys is Quite Sick

5   After Dinner I and Robert wrode down in the Swamp and I wrode down to Hard Scrabble to See how things Looked and I found that all Look well.

6   I went down to Hard Scrable and we Sacked out 19 Sacks of Corn which made 50 Sacks that we had Put up

7   Nothing new. This is Ellection day and a Good number of People were in town to day — Mr Stump was up to day and I Paid him Fifteen Dollars   He went Home this Evening

8   I went under the Hill to day and paid Mr Gaw $4.70 for Bacon that I Bot of him a short time ago — I Bot 30 Gunny Bags of Mr Wilson to day, 15 cts Each, $4.50 was the Amount. I also bot about 27 or 8 old Sacks from Mr Little for 1.50 cts for the Lot. Wm. Richard & Byron all went down in the Swamp this Evening   They drove Bob in the Buggy — I paid Mother $4 to day for a Bird that Lavinia got. She is to send the money up Shortly, I went to the Shop and remained there all the Evening.

9   I wrode Down in the Swamp to day and On my way down I met Mr Winn and he told me about his Son Calvins haveing Left him the night before or Last night and that if he should meet him he intended to cowhide him and would do it where Ever and when Ever he Could find Him. We talked about the Election Some and before we Left we bet a Hat on the Election   He bet me that Cass would Get a Majority of 2000 over Gen Taylor in the State of Mississippi. I then went on down and went to work in the Potatoe Patch   We had dug about a hundred Bushells I think   We Put up a 70 or 80 Bushels of them, and I Put up 30 Bushells of them in sacks, and will Send them to New Orleans by the Princess No. 3.

10   I [was] Sacking Corn at times and Shelling &c. Nothing new   I made Several Bets to day On the Ellection with Mr Stump when we were in the Potato Patch, they were on this State

11   Rain in the Afternoon on the Corn that I had hauled in Sacks to Ship on the Steamer No. 3. She Came along at night and I Put 81 Sacks on Board of her of Corn and Eight of them held 2½ Bush. Making in all One hundred 66 Bushels Corn and I Sent twenty Sacks, ½ Bushells Each of S. Potatoes, 30 Bushels in all

12   Nothing new — Anderson Came up to day from the Swamp and Brot up 3 Barrels Corn And Some Hay, near 3 Bushells of Potatoes &c.

13   Nothing new. I Sent down to day by Anderson 5 Hogs, all Spotted Ones — I Paid a note to day in at Mr Brittons & C of Seventy Seven Dollars 60 cts. It was due C A Lacoste or the county treasury for School Land that I Bot two years ago of them and was indorsed by Robt McCary   Winston went to the Swamp to day   He wrode Cuff down

15   Nothing new. Buisness dull and I Some what unwell   Confind to my Room. To day the Races Commences. Three Entrys to day — Mardice Little Mare, Col Bingam[an]s Sunbeam Filly, a[nd] a red River nag. Red R. nag won the Race. Nothing new from the Ellection to day, not a word. Winston Came up to day from the Swamp, reports all well.

16   Some Firing on the other Side of the River. News from Alabama.

17   William Johnson Jun. Came up from the Swamp this Evening   He wrode Jeff — He Seys that they had finished digging all the Potatoes and that there were 3 stacks of them, He reports the Potatoes that I Got of Voilet was only 3 Bushells.

20   I went to the Landing this morning and I Got a Paper from the Boat. I Got a Letter from Mr Miller. He Sent me word that he had Sold my Corn at 45 cts per Bushell and that he had Sold 14 Sack of Potatoes at 1 dollar per Bushell and ahalf — I Bot a Lot of Bacon to day from Mr Gaw that Amounted to $5.06 and I Bot a Lot from Mr Wilson Amounting to 3.25 ct and an

ox yoke. This to gether with 6 Hogs I Sent down into the Swamp   Mr W. Winn Came down to day in the Chancelon. He is from Iindiana.

     21   Nothing new   Buisness tolerable   I Drew a bet this Evening with Mr Lacock where I had bet him that Gen Cass would Get a Majority of 1000 votes over Gen Taylor by Giving 2.50 cts credit on his acct. and I thought he was Glad to do it. I Let Winston have fifteen dollars to night on his acct. He Got it to try and Bet on the Election yesterday. The John Holden Property that used to be was sold and was bot by Allen Davis at 1000 dollars — cheap I think

     22   Nothing new   Buisness Good. Wm Came up to night and Leaves the wagon on the Road   He had a Lot of Hay — The Sides of the wagon Broke down and He Left the Hay. He also Seys that one of my Oxen had Just Died Last night — They Could not find out what was the mater with him   It was the ox that I got of Mr Gregory in a Swap — I made a bet to day that Mr Cass would not beat Gen Taylor in this State over Seven Hundred votes, $2 was the bet. I Gave mother on acct. to day $2.50. I Gave Wellington $12.50 to Get me 100 Guny Sacks in Orleans — I also Loaned big Bob. five Dollars and he Promised to pay it as Soon as he Came up the Hill. Paid a week after Appointment [later]

     24   Nothing new   Buisnes Only Tolerable. We have not anything Positive How the States have all voted yet. Wm wrode Bob Down into the Swamp this Evening to come up tomarrow with Corn if nothing Happens. The River is Rising very fast indeed. Must have risen a foot Last night from reports about it

     25   Buisnes Only Tolerable   Jeff. Came in Late this Evenuing from Out Home and wants work. I have not made up my mind about it yet. William & Anderson Came up to day and brot up about 3 Barrells of Corn and Some Potatoes, and old Phill Came up at night and wrode up the Big old Bay Horse

     26   Nothing new. Buisness Only So. I after dinner to day wrod down to Mrs Walterns Place to the Creek and returnd home again before night   Robert, Richard & Byron & William all was along

     27   Nothing new   The Election for Justice of the Peace Came of[f] to day & Mr Charles Marshall and Mr C Coffin were the Candidates. Mr Coffin was Elected by a small Majority it was[17] — Jeff is Still at work with me to day and I have as yet

---

[17] The election was mentioned in Natchez *Courier*, November 28, 1848.

made no arrangment with him about work   Tax   Taxes — I
Paid My Taxes to day as Follows,

for Mrs Battles

I paid Her General Tax	$ 9.00	
School Tax	5.40	14.40

&

Pomet Lot that I hold

Geneal Tax	3.00	
School do	1.80	4.50

A Johnson

General Tax	3.60	
School Tax	7.80	11.40

My own do

Geneal Tax	26.60	
School Tax	23.29	49.89

Total $80.29

I receivd to day the act. of Sales of 80 Sacks Corn, 8639 lbs
or 155 Bushells @ 45 cts   69.75

Charges —

Brokerage	1.55	
2½% Commission,	1.68	3.23

66.52

New Orleans 23d Novm 1848   Norment Cooper & Co
I sent also 20 Sacks of Potatoes, 30 Bushells   For this I Got $14.
They were Sold by Mr Miller — So I Only got in Cash today
$80.00

28   Nothing new. Buisness dull for the Season. I was up
at the Auction to day And I Bought two mules. They Came from
Mr Lapiece Plantation   I paid $14.25 for One & Seventeen dol-
lars for the other One, Making 31.25 cts for the two. The One
a Mare mule the other a horse Mule — They were both of a
Brownish Color. Those that I bot I thought them the best that
was Sold. I made an arrangement with Jeff to Commence from
yesterday to work for One Hundred & twenty five for a year.
This I Promise to give him Shoes also — I hope he will be as
Good as his word

29   Buisnes Only So So — I paid Mr G. Lancaster to day
2 dollars that he won from me on the Election on this State. I
Bot Richard a Saddle & Bridle to day, four dollars

30   Nothing new has Happend that I Know of   Report

634

Seys to day that Capt Minor has won his Race or verrified   I
Shoul[d] Like to Know how they have made it with the other 2
Horses in the Race — To Night Mr John Ker was married to
Miss Ruth   She is a daughter of Mr Frank Rouths. Report Seys
that the S B. Marengo had Sunk below Red River

December 1   The Body of One of the men was brot up
from off the Steam Boat Marengo this morning   He was Killed
by the Boat in Some maner
    2   Nothing new. Buisness Tolerable fair, Good many pur-
sons in to day from the country. Wm Came up this Evening and
brot up a Little Corn and Some Hay and two Quarters from two
Hogs that was Killed yesterday, They were Some of the Mosbey
Stock of Hogs   They were in fine Order, Hester Cummings was
to the Shop to see me to day and wanted me to pay her tax for
her   She Left Enough to pay her tax Except $2.10 which Sum
I am to Loan her, Wm Seys that they have put up Eigteen Sacks
of Corn, 2½ B. in Each
    3   Nothing new. Buisness Tolerable fair. The Circus Left
here this morning to go below[18] — Sons of Temperance turnd out
to day   It was a Large Procession, no it was not to day, it is tomorrow they turn out. I wrode out this Evening and Edd & Jeff
went along. They run Fanny VS Winston Mare. Winston mare
won the Race Easy
    4   Nothing new. Buisness Pretty Good. It was to day that
the Temperance men turned out   It was Large and fine Procession.[19]   I Loand Young Wm Stanton five Dollars And I Loaned
Mr McCants five dollars also — Mr McCants has paid. [later]
    5   I was in the Swamp to day and tis the first time that
I have been down for Several weeks. I wrode down from the
House to Hard Scrabble and found them at work Shelling Corn,
They have now 18 Sacks in Sacks Ready to Ship — I was very
much Surprised to day when I got down into the swamp to hear
from Mr Stump that Mr Ford had Said that he would give me a
Damed thrashing on the first Sight — I told Mr Stump that I was

[18] Rockwell and Company's Circus appeared in Natchez on December 1 and 2,
1848. Included in the entertainment were trained-dog and horse acts, clown,
slack-rope and slack-wire performances, vaulting, and a "Spanish Bull Fight"—
all to the accompaniment of "the Queen City Brass Band."
[19] A description of the procession was published in Natchez *Courier*, December
5, 1848. A modern historian describes such processions: "Other temperance enthusi-
asts made a specialty of joyous processions of the 'cold water army,' and the Sons
of Temperance, with ritual, regalia, and banners, gave a martial touch to
thousands of communities." Nevins, *Ordeal of the Union*, I, 125.

Greatly astonished to hear Anything of that Kind for I Knew very well that I had never Said anything disrespectfull of Mr Ford and I thought it very Strange indeed that he should have made such th[r]eats. I told him that I have nothing in the world against Mr Ford and I have never Said anything about [him] that Could Lead to Such talk on his part, and I told him I thought may be he was Just talking for to be a talking for I did not think it Possible that he would do it for Nothing. Edd. Hoggatt & my Son Wm & Richard went a long with me. The Boys drove down 2 Cows an One Calf. Now in regard to what Mr. Stump told me to day I have not Said half that he told me off [of]

    6   Billy went down with the wagon, I did not Send down anything in it. Stickneys Circus is now Performing — Commenced yesterday night,[20] I Loand Winslow Winn $6 to day and took his due Bill for $10.50. I had Loaned him 4 dollars and fifty cents before, I Give Winston $10 to day to go and bet Mr Jones on the Election and I Loaned him two dollars this morning for the Same purpose, Hester Cummings Gave me Sixty dollars to Keep for her — She owes me $2.10 that I Loaned Her to pay her Taxes

    7   Nothing new   Buisness rarther dull, The Democratic Majority of this State is set down at 734 To day[21] — Charles paid me thirteen dollars 70 cts and I am Certain that I am at a Loss with that Shop — I Gave him two dollars for himself   I Let Winston have ten dollars yesterday to bet And to day he gave it back   He made a Bet with Mr Jones of the Money but it was not put up

    8   Nothing New — After dinner to day I went down in the Swamp — Wm went with me. Mr Stump I found has made a New Little Stable for the Horse Cuff. We Rubed him up a Little. Yesterday he was put up in his Stable the first time, He is fat and Looks well

    9   I was in the Swamp this morning and we were Shelling Corn and Sacked a Little, and had Shelld out not much. They are Geting along very Slow indeed, Billy Brot up Some Corn, abot 2 or three Barrells of it — I Bot 3 Sacks of Oats for Cuff   I Gave 3 dollars for them

---

    [20] The Stickney New Orleans Circus, accompanied by the New Orleans Brass Band, appeared in Natchez on December 5–9, 1848. Two years earlier the Clinton *Louisiana Floridian*, November 28, 1846, had claimed that the organization was "the largest and most extensive establishment in America."

    [21] The Democrats polled 26,537 votes while the Whigs polled 25,922 votes. See Rowland (ed.), *Official and Statistical Register of the State of Mississippi, 1924–1928*, 311.

10   I Remaind Home all day and Slept Some part of the Evening — Nothing new. Buisness Dull, oh no the Buisness was Good To day — I am told that the Circus fell down on the Spectators, ie the Curtain did[22]

12   Nothing new   Buisness Only tolerable

13   Nothing new. Buisness So, So. Myself and William wrode down in the Swamp this Evening. There was a Poor Brown Horse in the myre Down by the Gate in the Bottom And we tryed to Get him off or Out of the mud but we Could not. We Got down in the Swamp and I found that a Little or nothing had been done Since I Left. There was very Little done, I find the River is Rising very fast indeed, more So than I Ever Knew before.

14   Buisness Dull for the Season   I was in the Swamp this morning Erly and I was up before day and Built a Pen arround a Fodder Stack   This I done before day — and on getting up and wriding around I found that Some Dog or Dogs has Killed 5 of my Large Sheep and had Left them Wher they Killd them in the Road. I would Like to Know who did   Mr Stump was out the other day with Mr Gregory and Mr Wilcott and they Killd 4 Hogs. Mr Gregory Got 3 of them and Mr Wilcott got One

15   Nothing new   Buisness rarther Dull for the season   I Left the Swamp this morning and wrode up Jeff — The River is Rising very fast indeed. I Saw Mr Delome to day and made a Proposition to him to cut wood and it was this, that I would find the hands and Give ½ for the other, and he Said that he could not do it for he wantd Some Cash and he was Compelld to have it. I Even agreed to find the hands myself — he Said he could do it

16   Wm Came up from the Swamp bringing up the Little wagon with 3 Barrells of Corn and a Small Lot of Potatoes, Phill and Anderson he reports was Sacking Corn down at Hard Scrable, Wm Seys they found 3 Sheep to day and One dead up behind Mr Winns Field. It was to day I am told that Mr Winns hands went over the Land marks and Cut wood on my Land

17   Nothing new   Buisness So So. I remaind at Home untill Late to day then in the afternoon I wrode Out to Jacumines   Wm was with me   We all wrode Out and took a Brush with our Horses ie Big Jeff & his Horse   He Beat Jeff off Pretty

---

[22] The center pole broke during a high wind. There were no injuries. Natchez *Courier,* December 12, 1848.

Easy and then Pulld up. I was Just trying Jeff to See How he would run &c. McCary and Wilcox was at my House to night   They Staid Some time &c.   I have made an arrangment with Mr Delome to have Some wood Cut and I hope I shall be able to get through with it

18   Nothing new. I think it was to day that I Started down into the Swamp   I found but very Little done indeed   They were Shelling or Sacking a Little to day   Mr Delorme Came down to day and I wrode arround and Showd him the Land and wood as it stood &c. Nothing new. I was in the Swamp today and there was not much done. I had the Corn Sheller Hauld up this Evening Late from Hard Scrabble to the House for I intend to Shell up there After this

19   I was having Some Corn Hauld to day from below to the uper Place and afterward I had two Killns of S Potatoes opened and I found that they had rotted very much indeed. I had the Little House Coverd and the Potatoes were put into it to dry them, We hauld one Killn at 1 Load and the other two Loads it took to haul it   Old Billy was up a Little while to day but did not Stay Longer than Late this Evening — Little Winn is at my House and has been for Several days. Poor creature I Pitty him very much indeed — I am Sorry that he drink So much — I had 63 Sacks all Shelled out and Sowed up and we Shelld out about 25 Bushels more to day and I think it is no hard matter to Shell out 50 Bushells a day with that machine &c.

20   I Left the Swamp to day After Breakfast and Got up to the city about ½ past ten. I met Mr Winn and had a talk with him and I Met Mr Ford and did not speak at all — Miss Mary Winston was married to night to Mr Thorn Hill

22   Nothing new   Buisness Only tolerable. Mr Liga Smith Paid me three dollars 25 cts for three Months Shaving to day — To day Charles Paid me twenty Six dollars for work below in the Shop

23   Nothing new. I paid Mr Wade to day thirty Six dollars for Six months Rent of Shop under the Hill. The Cholera is Said to be making Havoc in New Orleans at Present.[23]

24   Mr Stump Came up this morning Erly and brot up Cuff to run the Race, We took Cuff and gave him a Little Run, Jaqumine Lookd at him when he was runing and was pleased

25   Nothing new. Buisness Quite Good, After diner to

---

[23] The Natchez *Courier*, December 22, 1848, reported that while the cholera was severe in New Orleans, it had not reached epidemic proportions.

day I Started out to the tract with Cuff and a Short time Afterwards Mr Hoggatt Came Out also. Edd., we and others soon got
off and had a hard Race, and we Lost it by 3 feet. We had a
Race with B. Jeff and a Large Sorry Horse and ½ mile   Jeff
won the Race very Easy. Then the Winston mare Beat the Same
Horse 3 hundred yds — Mr Jn Mardice wrode to my William and
William on [won] the Race by a foot or two, After the first Race
was Over Mr Hoggatt Left for Home and took Edd with him and
Several other Boys — I paid Edd. his ten Dollars and he Left for
home, Winston did not put his money and I Let him have $2.50
out at the tract to Bet on the Race — Jeff did not put up any
money Either, So we fell in his debt $10 — Well he then made a
Race vs Big Jeff and we won that which was five dollars   So
that Left us five dollars in Jeffs debt. With Winston I Lost ten
dollars and won thirteen So he fell in my debt $3.

    26   Nothing new   I Paid Mr Stump to day ten dollars at
One time and at Another time five dollars, making in all fifteen
dollars that I have Let him have to day — I Gave Clemment Miller
a due Bill for Sixty dollars to day   This is for Money that he
Left with me to Keep for him — Jeff Started out Home to get 2
hounds for Mr Sargent. Was to have Came home this Evening
but has not done it — Phill Came up this Evening and brot Mrs
Calcotes Carriage up the hills from Dixons for Mr Delome — Mr
Henderson Gave me five dollars to pay Winston and I paid him
over the money to day

    27   Buisness Tolerable fair. Jeff & Gim both of them are
away today — Gim went Out to Mr Ferridays & Jeff went Out to
Gen Stantons or to Mr Hoggatt.

    28   Nothing new. Buisness is quite dull   I Paid Maj
Young fifty Dollars to day   He allowed fifteen Dollars that
Charles had Paid out for clothing and Medicine — He was Down
on Charles about Getting married against his Orders — He told
me that Charles Should have to give up that wife or Remain a
Slave all his Life — On Our Settlement I told him that the Doctors
bill was not Paid over yet and would not be untill he Returnd
from Kentucky.

    29   To marketing as usual. Nothing new   The streets are
oh very mudy indeed and will be worse before it will be better,
Mr Clay of Kentucky and Dr Blackburn Came down this Evening
from Kentucky — Mr David Ker paid me $5 that he owd me on
acct.

    30   Nothing new. Buisness tolerable fair. Wm went in the

Swamp this Evening   He drove the mule and Fanny in the wagon   They went along very well, I worked on the Big Hill this Evening by myself Smartly — Robt Woods is Out to day for Mayor of the City

31   Nothing new, I worked at the Shop untill about 11 Oclock and then I took Richard & Byron and wrode Down into the Swamp. I met my Son Wm on his way up with the wagon with Some Corn and Fodder, Potatoes &c. and old Billy who had the whole week been acting the Rascal   Mr S. Flogged him this morning and Sent him up — In wriding behind the field I found old Joe tyed fast with a Rope Starving to Death. He was put thare by old Billy who I have Just found Out to be a Drunkin old Rascal. I am Sorry to find it out. On my way up I Stopd on the Road and had a Long talk with old man Winn about Love &c. I Stopd a few moments at Delomes and had a Small talk — I think he had been drinking &c.

1849

January 1   Nothing new. The Election Came of[f] to day for officers of the City,[1] and it was to day that I wran big Jeff vs Jacks Sorril mare, a ½ mile and Jeff won the Race Easy — Wm Ran the Winston mare VS the Tips mare and another Horse and the Little W[in]ston mare won the Race. She also beat her a 3 Hundrd yard Reace then run a mile Race and made a dead Heat. We then run it over and She Beat my Little mare 30 yards I do Expect. Streets are very mudy.

2   Nothing new. Sale of the Rail Road took Place to day and all the Slaves belonging to it and other things   Some went cheap, others high — The Sales I dont Recollect at Present   Three mules were Sold also[2]

3   Nothing new. Buisness Only Tolerable. Mr Delorme told me to day that he could not come up to his Contract about hiring me his hands   He had changed his mind and will Come to town to work at his trade, I paid my Doctors bill to day to

---

[1] For results, see Natchez *Courier*, January 2, 1849.

[2] This was probably the Mississippi Rail Road Company, which had been in financial difficulties since 1840. See Adams County Deed Records, CC, 627–34; *Laws of Mississippi*, 24 Sess. (1840), 28; 26 Sess. (1842), 75; 28 Sess. (1844), 138, 146.

Dr Davis   It was Sixteen Dollars — ten dollars of the amount
was my Bill and $6 was for Mr Millers Family — I Bot 270 ft
Lumber to day. Will haul it up tomorrow. Mr Delorme talks of
Renting a Shop from me,   I Shall see it after a while, as man
is uncertain. I Shall not think more about it, Winston paid me
$24.50 to day. This was money that I Loaned him Lately

    4   Nothing new. I wrode down into the Swamp to day and
returnd   Anderson drove up the waggon with Foder and Potatoes
and Corn, Commenced to day to clean up the Corn Ground. I
find there is Scarcly anything down thare done when I am not
thare, I found Mr Stump and Little Winn going down the Road
when I Came down this mor[n]ing

    5   Nothing new. Buisness Only Tolerable   I was at Auc-
tion to day and bot 2 doz Socks at 1.10 cts per Doz — Cholera is
on the Decline — I Glad of it. My Health is not very Good — I
Sent Anderson Down to day with a Barrell of old Salt for the
Hogs — The River is falling tis Said — Mrs Newman who is a
daugter of old Mr Melvin was Married a few nights ago to old
Mr Chandler, the Plasterer, Mr Dalshimer Presented his acct. to
day — the Amount of which is $74.00 — This Imbraced the acct
of Winston & Jeff both — I bet 5 Vs 2.50 ct to night that Jacks
Nag would not Beat My Horse Jeff 50 ft. in the Mile Race

    6   This morning about Day break Gim Came in a fast run
to run for me and the Doctor that My Mother was very Sick. I
ran with all my might and found Her in Bed and oh My God
How changed She Seemed. She had fainted from weakness but
She felt Better. She told me that She had drank a Glass of Molases & water when She went to bed and that she Had taken Sick
in the night and was up and down often in the Course of the night
and that She had Got very weak   The Doctor, Blackburn, came
in a few Minutes and Gave Medicine and we commencd to treat
for cholera by Rubing and mustard Pla[s]ters but her Stomache
would not bear the medicine. She Commen[c]ed to Sink Gradualy
and with all we could do or think of she Continued to Sink untill
twenty minutes of 3 oclock when we Lost Her for Ever — oh My
Poor Dear Mother is no more

    7   To day has been a [day] of Great trouble to me and all
of my Family. The Remains of My Poor Mother was Burried,
oh my God. My Loss is too Greate. Oh my Poor Belovd Mother
is Losst to me forever in this world

    8   I sent Gim down into the Swamp to bring up Some
food for the Horses and he did not come back as I thought he

would   Mr Stump & Little Winn went down yesterday — They Came up on Saturday Morning, oh yes it was to day that they went down and I promisd to Send Gim down to marrow to haul up Horse food &c. Mr J Abott gets married to night to Miss Benbrook. She is the daughter of the City Constable.

9   Gim went down to day and was to have been up this Evening but did not Come, I was at work a while this Evening a cleaning up the yard at the Shop yard &c. Mr Samuel Winston paid me his acct to day of 2.50 to date — Old Delorme backs Out from taking my House on main Street.

10   Nothing new   Buisness tolerable fair. River Rising Slowly   Corn Selling at 45 cts per Barrell at retail, Coal 60 cts   I Sent two Letters Down to Orleans this Evening informing Mr Miller & Lavinia of the death of My Mother, oh my God it Seems even now that it is a Dream but alas My Lord it is too true, [I paid] $2 to Hackman this Evening for Funeral wride. Winston pays me back 10 Dollars that I Loand him to bet on Friday night Last on the Race.

11   Nothing new. Buisness Dull, I was not at the Shop very much to day. Mr Stump was up from the Swamp this morning And Came for a Settlement I think and Said that he thought of Quiting Down thare, I Paid Him the amount that was due him. I had Paid him at Sundry times the amount of $87. Then

2 Hogs that was Sold to Isler wich was cash	11.72
Cash On Election	14.00
Cash in hand to day	70.00
	———
	182.72

Thus I have Paid him $182.72 this being the Last Dollar that I owe him, in fact I think he now owes me a Little on the Race that we had a Short time ago, Cuff vs. Edds Hoggats Horse. Mrs J. C. Wilkins Died the other day — Mr Bunting Paid me to day twenty Dollars on Rent of the ten Pin Ally — He pays a Rent of five Dollars per month.

12   Jim & Mitchel went Down in the Swamp to Kill 3 Hogs. They went Down and Killd them and returned this Evening. They were very fine Hogs, all Pretty Large, Mr Stump Shot them in the Pen for them   Mr Railey Paid me to day thirteen Dollars which Sum Pays his acct to the 1st of January — or I may Say to date, Estate of Mr L. Robetile Paid me to day five Dollars for Shaving his Corpse. Estate of Mr J. Reddy Paid me five Dollars for Shaving his Corpse — I Paid Robert Smiths Hacks

Account for Mothers Funeral ten Dollars   This was for five Hacks. There were two others that I paid for the other Day — Mrs Dr Merrell Died yesterday morning @ 4 Oclock

    13   I Sold George Isler a Hog To day that weighed One Hundred Seventy pounds at 4 cts and I Sold Mr Jaqumine the ½ of a Hog Excepting the Head that I Kept   The ½ weiged 77 lbs. at 4 cts   I went in market this morning & it is the first time that I have been in market in ten or Eleven years as well as I Can Recollect, The Pork I Sold to day amounted to $9.88. I Sent MCary a Spare Rib and a Large Shoulder — Corn is worth Only 45 cts at Present, Potatoes 1 dollar per Barrell, Poor H Cabler Died Last night about 7 Oclock and was Burried to day — Young Conner whips Mr Alvord to day up the Street, it was Something about an acct. Maj Elward is out in an article vs. Mr Adams to day in the Free Trader

    14   The Streets are very mudy, indeed   Nothing new. Buisness Quite dull, I remained at Home all day Except Going to the Gravy yard and to the Bluff

    15   Nothing new. Buisness dull   I After Breakfast this morning wrode the Horse Fiddler under the Hill   I mean in the Swamp. I found the Bank was Caving Considerably by Mr Winns and by my House too. I went down as Low as Mr Gregorys and he Bought a Hundred Barrells of Corn from me and is to Come up and get it Shortly at 50 cts per Barrell. I found the hands haulling wood for House use

    16   I wrode Out in the woods with Mr Stump and Came in about Dinner time. We came up by Mr Gregorys Place, I had a talk with Mr Stump about Staying another year with me, but he decline under the Circumstances So I Came away. After dinner Mr Winns chopers are Cuting wood over my Land and I requested the Little Irishman not to cut any more, He Promisd not to do so tho he Said Mr Winn had told him that was the Line.

    17   I went under the hill to day and bot a Barrell of Potatoes for 1 dollar and One Barrell of Apples at a Dollar. They were very fine Ones. Potatoes were Selling a few days ago at 75 cts per Barrell, but I did not Hapen to See them at the time, I went to Mr Walshs House and Bot ten Barrells at One Dollar and fifteen cts per Barrell, Paid for them And Left them to haul After a while.

    18   Mr Partlow Died about 25 minutes of 4 Oclock this morning. He was alone when he died, but his woman Cloea, He Died in the back of the next yard to us in State Street, up stares, in a Little 2 story Brick Building — I Bot twenty four Barrells @ 10 ct to day and I Bot Seven more of them at the Same Price

19   I Sent money down to the Landing to Pay for 10 Barrells of Potatoes that I have had hauld in to Charles Shop at 1.15 cts per Barrell — I paid Mr Myres ten Dollars for Winston to day and $10 that mother owed him

20   The Streets are very Muddy indeed, I walked down under the Hill to day and went from the One End of the Landing to the other in seacrch of Potatoes and they are Selling for 1.25 pr [per] Barrell to 1.50 or 50 ct the Single Bushell — Corn is worth 50 cts per Barrell, Shipman, the Gin wright was Burried to day

21   I Remaind at Home all day Except going to the Bluff   Mc took Supper with us to night. Wm and Byron wrode down to the Place this Evening to bring up old Joe and to see how things Looks in General

22   Nothing new. Buisness very dull indeed, I paid Clay & Griffin two Dollars 75 ct to day for Mother   To day I Bot 3 Horse Collars and 2 old Blind Bridles from Mr Delorme for 1 Dollar and I Bot 2 Sweeps and One Halls Plough, 2 trace chains, 3 pr Haims, 2 Double trees, 1 Single tree and 5 hoes from young Delorme for $11.50   I think them cheap. I pd the amount over to Mr Dunham for him, I Drove under the Hill this Evening to hauld up my Potatoes and the mud was so deep that the two teames Only hauld One Barrell. After Supper to night I Stepd head first into the cellar and Came near breaking my Neck as well as cutting my chin very much

23   Nothing new. I Remaind at Home all day to [day]. Layed up from Falling into the cellar — Gim And Anderson is Haulling Some Corn from Mrs Watterns Place for Dr Blackburn — the Corn was Purchased from Mr Delorm, The[y] Commencd to haul it yesterday, Old Mrs Milliken Died yesterday and was Burried to day. Large Funeral

24   Old Madam Lear Knox was Buried this Evening. She is Happy I have no doubt for She was a Good old woman — Gim & Anderson hauld 1 Load a Piece to day for Dr Blackburn, and he Said that he did not want Any more for the Corn was not good — I Remaind at home all day to day. This was from the Fall that I had in the cellar, I feell much better to day than I did yesterday

25   Nothing New. Gim & Anderson Left for the Swamp this morning. Orders were to repair Fences &c. Gen. Tailor Past

up To day. I was on Bourd but did [not] See him   I saw His
white Horse and took a hair from his tail, A Large Piece of the
Bluff fell down in the Road this day and it was thought that
Firing the Cannon for Gen Tailor was the cause, It was on the
Middle Road as you go to Cozzens Mill[3]

26   Nothing new. Buisness dull. The S. Boat Saladin wran
into a Flat Boat Ladened with Hay belonging [to] John Sparks
& Gim Diky, Agent   They have not made a Settlement as yet   I
was at Auction to day at the Sale of Clay & Griffins things and
I bot as Follow[s]

2 Casks of Bacon, 392 lbs., 2½ cts per pound	$9.82
10 Plow Lines	.80
1 oven & Skilet	88
2 Pots, 2½	62½
1 Lot old Bridles or piecs	80

27   Nothing new. Buisness So So — I was away from the
Shop most all day. I was under the Hill a Part of the Day and
was at a Sale of a Hay Boat that was Sunk a few nights ago
by the Saladin — the Boat Sold for $40 and the top Sold for $41.
Both was Bot by Mr Heveran. Gim and Phill came up to Night
from below, One Brot Corn, the other brot Potatoes; both wagons
Came up — Gim Brot up a Part of two Barrells of Apples from
the Swamp that Mr Winn traded Potatoes for   Even Swap. Gim
Seys the Jackomine Heiffer has Got a Calf, and is up to the House
with it

28   Nothing new   Buisness Only Tolerable — I remaind
at home all day to day &c.

29   Nothing new. I Started down in the Swamp to day and
did not get down untill Late; Little Maj Winn was on the Place.
Nothing much a doing. They were not done choping down the
Stalks, quite.

30   To day I was in the Swamp and I Commenced to Haul
Some Planks and Pumpkins from the Lower Place, for I Rented
it to day to Mr Gregory for $50 for this year.

31   Nothing new   Buisness Only So So   I was still in
the Swamp and Commencd to Haul wood from the Swamp to the
R. Bank for fear that the River would take it

February 5   Nothing new. I had a Settlemet to day with
Mr Dalshimer and I allowed an acct. of 76.65 that he had against

---

3 The Natchez *Courier*, January 26, 1849, reported that the incident was "without any known 'just cause or provocation.' "

me and the Boys together, and he paid me Eight months Rent at 20 dollars per Month which was 160 dollars. So he paid me in Cash $83.35   Thus we are Square to the 1st of Febuary 1849 — Mr Inge Paid me to day fifteen dollars for the years Shaving up to the 1st of January 1849 — Mr. Sterling Paid me Eight dollars which Sum pays his acct in full to the 1st of March inst — Mr Jas Stockman paid his acct to the 1st inst — 1.25

6   I Started Down into the Swamp To. day   It was Late. Mr G. Gregory went Down at the Same time; I took Little Sam Down with me   Gim went down also in the wagon and my Wm went down too. The River is Very High at Present and Still a Rising   It Looks very much Like an Over flow indeed — Anderson was Haulling wood to day with the Oxen. He made 4 Loads from the Elick Johnson House to the wood Pile

7   Nothing new. Buisness dull.

8   I think it was to day that I Shipd by the Gen Lane 100 Sacks of Corn and 6 Sacks of Potatoes, and She Chargd me 20 cts per Sack for them. She took 18 cord of wood from me at 2.25 ct per Cord.

9   Dr Broom & Mr Gay Came Down to day and was Hunting Game — They Both took dinner with me   To day I Shot A wild Boar and I found that he was marked in Mr Wolcotts mark and I sent him word Amediatly about it and he Said it made no difference, and I Shot also a Shoat of mine

10   I was very Buissy to day Haulling of Shucks & Fodder from Hard Scrablle Place,   We were Quite Late before we got through with them, in fact we have more to Haul yet   I Bot five Shoats from Ellick Johnson to day And Gave him five dollars for them. They [were] a Lot of Shoats that was always about the trap or about the House, so I Bot them from them.

11   Nothing new. Buisness dull. I Started up very Erly this morning from the Swamp to Come to town and the water was very High and I Brot Jim up untill he crossd the water and I Followed him. He went back and I Came on to town to Breakfast.

12   Nothing New more than there is Some Little talk about Small Pox in the City — Mr Patterson asking me about a note of Hand that he Held of Mothers for 30 or 40 dollars. I told him that I though[t] I Could find nothing that I Knew of to Justify Such a claim for as well as I Can Recollect She had made a full settlement with that Store, I was under the hill to day and bot a

Skift at the Landing for five dollars — I Bot the Skift of Mr Higgins.

13 Nothing new. Buisness very dull, I was under the Hill to day to Look at my Skifft and found it Sunk   I Bailed it Out. It is now ready for use, The River is Still Rising and will Continue so I think; Some few Cases of Small Pox in the City at Present. There was One Brought in a few Days above me to day and I made a report and he was taken Out to the Pest House. He was Bar Keeper to Micheal Johnson — I Started down into the Swamp this Evening in a Skifft and took Mary and he[r] two children with me   We did not Get down untill Late, near Eight Oclock at night, tho we got down without much trouble, I have not as yet Done Any Plowing nor cleaned up the Ground, nor yet Even Put up my Fences

16 To day I was in the Swamp and was a Hunting, I was out with Several men, Stump, Johnson, Williams & B. Wolcott, We Killed 6 Small Hogs.

17 I was Still in the Swamp and went Out to Hunt and I Killed 4 young Hogs and Gim Hauld them in with the wood Cart.

18 I Got in a Canoe and two Little Irishman went with me and we went out back of Some of the Ridges and then Came in again and I was So cold, oh me   The Ice was thick   The Ground was Coverd with Sleety Ice — It was Freezing nearly all day. Gim Caught a Hog to day and marked him, and Put him in the Pen

19 I Started to the City this morning and I Got up as high as Mr Winds and could not Get over the water; and had to turn back to Get On the Steam Boat Natchez, and Wm and myself Came up on the Boat, Gim was Still Haulling wood and will Finish to day I think

20 The River is Still Rising at this Point   The River is very high indeed

March 1 I was in the Swamp To day and I made a Bargain to hire Mr Saml. Clark to work by the month for me at $12 per month. Farming work of all Kinds

2 Nothing new. Buisness Kind of Dullish &c. I was in the Swamp I believe.

4 I Remained at Home all Day untill Evening Late and then took a walk with Mc On the Bluff

5 Mrs Dennys Hands commenced to chop wood To day, 8 or 9 of them, I went down in the Swamp to day and found all hands at work &c. I took Down a Little Ferry Flat and Wm a skift and we took down Seven Barrells of Potatoes with me and a Corn Mill.

6   To day we were Plowing on the Ridge   Clark, Myself, Wm., Phill & Anderson

7   To day we had Considerable Rain which Lasted near all Day and made the wood choppers Loose a Cord of wood Each, My Force was at the Fences.

8   To day we were Fixing the Lot Fence arround the Stable &c.

9   Nothing New   Buisness Only Tolerable, I was in the Swamp to day and was work[ing] making up the yard Fence around the Corn crib &c. The women was doing the Same

10   I was in the Swamp to day at work. We put the Oxen in the yoke this Evening and hauled out the Logs from the Lower End of the Mosbey Field, Mrs Dennys Hands cut there task this week, Except the day that it Raind, Wednesday, and they Lost a cord Each   Griffin was taken Sick and went Home the other day — Elick was Sick a Day or two in this week. He was Mr Zenos Hand — This Evening Cat Galbreath, W T. Bradish, Elick Sterling, Maj. Haladay & John Lacroze and Richard Chotard all made a Start for California, tho tis Said that R. Chotard will not Go farther than N. Orleans

12   Nothing new   Buisness Tolerable fair, I paid Hester Commings To day fifty Dollars   This was money that She Gave me to take care of for her   My Wife also Gave me ten dollars to day which Hester Commings Left with her for to be Given to me. I paid Mr Gaw $2.50 for ten Bushels of Corn this Evening that Gim Got whilst I was in the Swamp.   The River is Reported to have Risen Some to day, This is the 2nd Rise and we may Look out for this Rise to a certainty. Tis said that the waters are all ariseing above

13   City Tax City ASSESSMENT.

I Filld Out my List to day as Follows

Houses & Lots	2	2800
Watches	1	50
Piano	1	40
Slaves	6	1800.00
Mrs B[attles] in State Street		1700.00

I took that acct. $5 I had VS. the Estate of Dr A McPheeters and Ballancd the Auction acct vs. me and Paid the Difference which was 30 cts — the River is on the Rise Still.

14 Left the City about 10 Oclock, Came down in the Skft with Williams — Brot down 6 pounds of Shot, 2 pounds of Powder, 1 dollars worth of nails, 2 Curry Combs, 1 Bottle [of] No. 6, 1 Bottle of Turpintine, one Bottle Caster Oil, 50 ct of Rice, 20 ct of Candles, 50 ct Tobaco, 1 Small 20 ct Basket, Small Lot of Red Pepper, 2 Bottles of Cayane Dito, Commenced this Evening after Dinner to Plant Potatoes in the Lower Field, Anderson was Hauling wood this Evening, I and Mary and Violet was planting, Phill Plowing, Dr Winn and Mr Clark Cuting Potatoes, Sam Carrying &c. I Brot 1 Shoe makers Knife to Battice, Zora & Billy Sick — One of the young Cows Broke off her Horns by a Chopper Falling a tree on her head — I wrode down to Alx Johnsons to get Dr Harpers Perscription. River very High & Rising — Mr Henderson Has Lost 3 of his Hands of Cholera and has taken them all From Mr Wolcotts   I also brot a pr Shoes to Violet, cost 1.25

[Dr Harper's prescription:] Apply a Blister to the pit of the Stomache   Give Every hour a quarter of a Grain of mophine and 2 Grains of Calomel till the vomiting Stops or till 20 Grains of Calomel have been taken   Apply Large mustard Plaster to the Legs and inside of the thighs   If the Purging Continues Give an Injection of ½ tea cup full of thin Gruel and 40 drops of Laudanum — to be Kept from pasing away as Long as Possible   Dr Harper

15 To day was a Clear day and all went on right   Mr de Armon Came over to see the wood   We Only took a Partial Look at it because it was not all Corded up, tho we made the Calculation for one week and 3 days up to Last night and the Calculation was 99½ Cords that they had Cut — the wood of to day was not put in at all — I was cutting and planting Potatoes assisted by Mary, Violet, Phill & Anderson and Wm

16 [At] 9 Oclock Jackson Came in Sick and did not work today any more — We Commenced to day to take up the Mrs Dennys H[and]s wood. We did not get through with it, as far as we went tho we took up 88 [and] 1 qrter Cords — to-morrow night they will have worked 12 Days, ie, they Commecd on the 5th of March

17[4]   Nothing New. Buisness Only Tolerable   Not as yet Any Fall in the River. I was in the Swamp this morning and has been nearly all Day in Taking up the wood of the wood Choppers, and did not Get through with it at Last, and after all in Sending

---

[4] This and the two following entries are composites of entries found in Johnson's diary and in his pocket notebook.

my acct to Mr De Armond I made a mistake for Insted of 132 as was the true acct. I Sent word that it was 146 Cords

   18   I was in the Swamp and during a part of the day Mr Winn and myself was down in the woods Taking up the wood that was Cut by Davy & Ned and Elderage, We got through and did not take the wood of Pompey for he did [not] put up his wood and was sick and Gone Home

   19   I was in the Swamp and Commencd to Plow On the Front Ridge below the Corn House   Phill was Sick and Anderson got Sick also After Breakfast, Violet Plowed in his place untill Dinner. Mary & Little Sam took the Lower Fodder Stack and Violet Hauld it up in the Buggy — It was put in the Loft of the stable, Myself and William Plowed untill Late in the Afternoon   The hands of Mr De Armond Came over Last Evening and the full amount of there wood Cut up to Saturday night was 132 cords and they have worked 12 days — The Capt Zeno Hands have Cut 159 Cords up to Saturday night. This is Leaving out the work of Pompey for it is not been taken up yet, Now this is the true acct unless I have had the Sticks turned on me whilst taking acct

   20   Nothing new More than Gim Came Down from town this morning after me to Come up to the City, that Silvia & Rose both were Sick with the Small Pox, I was Plowing at the time and I Quit and went to the House, Made Jim take me up in a Skift to the wood yard, then Go back to Plowing and I went on to the City. I found Every thing Going On Smoothe and that Silvia & Rose both were Confined in their Beds with Small Pox; I Left Phill Quite Sick in the Swamp with Fever at times &c. Gim On his Return to the Place to Plant Potatoes. Mr Pearce Brot down this morning 6 Barrells of Potatoes that I have had to the Shop in town for Several Days   They were to Plant this Evening

   April 6   To day we took the plows and Started to work in the Lower field, 3 plows and I with the Harrow and we went On so until after dinner when Anderson took the Harrow and Commenced with me, We did the Front anyhow — ie the front ridge &c.

   7   Anderson and my self Commencd to Harrow in the Lower Field on the back Ridge and we worked up to 20 or 30 yards above the Chiny tree by 11 Oclock   We then started after 12 Oclock and Joind in with Mr Strong & Gim and we Finished the uper Field by 6 Oclock on the Same Day. That is work. Now I am under the opinion that 4 Plows can go over the whol Entire place in the Course of 3 days. That is my Candid opinion

8 Nothing new. Buisness Dull for the Season. I was in the Swamp Erly this morning and I Got On my Horse and wrode up to the City Gim was with me and wrode up the big Sorril mare, The water was High and Crossing at this time is dangerous. Quite So — I worked at the Shop to day and after 12 Oclock went Home and Slept the Ballance of 2 hours to dinner and took Another nap in the Afternoon, then took a walk out to the Pasture to Look at the Colt ie my Grimes mare Colt and Wms Mares Colt ie the old Roan mares Colt She had on Tuesday night. No it was Monday night Last that She had it. The other Grims Fillys Colt is 4 or 5 days older than the other, and the Little Grey mares Colt is a few Days older than Both of the rest

9 I was in the City all day and nothing new. I was at the Landing this Evening and bot a Dray Load of Plank & Post. The River is very high at Present and is Falling, To day Mr Strong is to Commence to Plant the upper Field in Corn &c. Charls paid me Some money to day, 25 dollars I think, more or Less, and I gave him 5 dollars of the money for himself &c.

10 Nothing new Buisness Quite dull indeed, Gim was at work at the fence On the St[ate] Street and I was not much at the Shop to day, was at Home a Good part of the Day, and at Browns Mill and I think I Shall Buy Some Lumber from him, The River is high but is falling and has fallen about 8 inches, not more I think. I Suppose by this time that my Corn must all be planted in the upper field, Mr Winn Started the other Day to New Orleans with a Raft of timber that was Cut up the creek — I am under the belief that he is Cutting timber in Every Direction without any regard to Lines or anything Else So Any man that will do that Kind of Buisness is not an Honorable Man — I wrode out to Dixons Pasture to day and found that old mule Britt Had ran off and was up at his Gate I turnd him through and he is now at Home

12 I was wriding Several times to the Landing to day to See if Mr Browns Lumber B was ready to Start for I had 3500 feet of Lumber and 22 Scanling — I paid $35 for the Lumber I Left the City ½ past 5 Oclock and got down about 8 Oclock, We Got out the Lumber in Good order — I Had the Lot Planted with Oats this morning in Natchez, I Swaped off Old Brit to day for a Little Black mule and gave $10 to Boot.

13 We Commencd this morning after Breakfast to finish Planting Corn in the uper Field. Now this is a Job that I thought was Done on Monday & Tuesday but Mr Strong was Sick & Anderson was Hunting Horses — thus things Go — We finished the Planting of the Corn & then Came Down and Stacked up the Lumber, then went to work in the Potato Patch & it Raind in the Evening and we had to Leave it.

14 The Ground too wet to work So Mr Strong Commencd to make a Room on the Gallery & I Commencd to make a Fence, upper Side of the House. I Sent Down a Statement of Wood Cut for the 2 weeks Ending to night and it was 96 Cords   I pd Elick 1 dollar & Isack 1 dollar

15 [The] Harry Hill, at Hard Scrabble, was run in to by [the] Gen. Worth at day Light   H. H. did not get off untill Late this Evening, with One Wheel — I took a wride Down to Look at the wood this Evening and it Looks Like it will be a Greate Job to Haul it out from there

16 Nothing new. I was at work all Day making a Plant fence arround the House in the Swamp   Mr Strong Came down from town near 10 Oclock   He went up Last night, Mary & Zora & Phill was at work at the Potatoes, Eldrige was sent home Sick to day — Pompey was Sick   Isack was at town with Capt Zeno. Elick took Elderage Home

17 Ground wet   River High & Rising   I Commencd with Mr Strong to plough the Potatoes after Breakfast this morning and we got through ½ past 12 — After Dinner we took Corn and replanted 75 Rows below the Corn House, Anderson was with us, Phill, Mary & Mosoury was Hoeing Potatoes

18 Mr Strong & Anderson, myself & Sam replanting Corn in the Lower Field, We Finished the front Ridge and right Smart distance up on the back Rge — Phill, Mary & Zora Still working the Potatoes, no part of the Corn has as yet been worked over, Mag. Winn Bot Some meat off Flat Boat and it was not good — He gave away his Stick to a Dr Somebody

19 Nothing New. Mr S. and myself Commencd to plow over on the Little Ridge & the Ground was too wet. Anderson & Phill Commencd to Harrow in the upper Field

20 Anderson & myself was haulling Rails from up the fence Down to make a fence arround the Potatoe Patch   We moovd Several Rails from the front fence — Phill was Harrowing in the uper field by himself

21 Nothing new. Mr S. and myself went Down in the

woods to Get Some Stakes to Fence in the Corn Field [and] Potatoe patch, We got Some and hauled them up and we Commencd to work on the fence but we did not get it done   At Last we got the front Line Done and Quit, Anderson Hauld Some New Rails got in the Bogg with the wagon, or cart

    22   Left town about 10 Ock   Got in the Swamp at Dinner — Hoed Corn all the Evening — Gim, Wm & Hubert was plowing — I Let Mary & Sam go to town this Evening to see Sam who was very Sick — the River is falling a Little — Huburt Commencd to work

    23   Buisness has been Quite Dull, I was in the City all day and Gim was out Hunting for my Oxen   Returnd and herd nothing of them — He went out as far as the Harman Plantation — I Choked Down the Little mule that yesterday throwd Gim Down   I used him bad — I did that, Phill did not Get up or off untill Qu[i]te Late Breakfast   To day Fanny was run off — this has been a Day of Some vexations to me. I Flogged Sarah, Dicy and the Little mule all to day; Saturday Jeff went off to wait upon Gen Stanton, They went up to Jackson in this state

    24   I got a Letter from Mr Mosbey to day and a Letter for Amlia Ellis to my Care

    25   Nothing new   I Received a Due Bill to day or a note from Mr Merrero for Sixteen Dollars. This is money I stood Good for Phillip Smith, I wrote On the back of the note that the Amount be paid to Mr Benbrook — I had my Little Mule Put in the Dray this After noon to work and Sandy hauld me up 2 Cords of wood from the Landing with him And others. Oh he is as wild as a Buck and untameable I think, I Sent down the Letter to Amelia Ellis that was Dirrected to my Care by Pearce. I Sent a Letter to Mr Mosbey to day and One to Mr Miller of New Orleans

    26   Nothing new — I Sent Down 67 lbs of Bacon to day by Mr Burke, 5½ cts is what I Paid. I got it at Mr Wilson

    27   The River very high

    May 1   Hired or Set Ellick to work to day in the Field

    2   I was in the Swamp at work Ploughing the Lower field and the Hoes were following

    3   I was plowing to day and Anderson too. The wrest was hoeing — Still in the Lower Field

    4   I was in the Swamp to day and we Finished working the Lower field this Evening and then went to work in the Potatoes. We commencd to Plow them and had to Stop On acct of Rain

   5   We were at work at Fencing up the Potatoe Garden, We did not get through with the Rails untill Late

   10   Nothing new. I Saw Mr Bradly this Morning and Bot his Dun Horse for twenty Dollars, five in Cash and fifteen in January and I must Go to morrow or Send and Get him — The River is Falling very fast at Present but has not Got within her Banks — Will Miller is in the Swamp and has been for more than a week, Court is in cession at Present and has been Ever Since Monday Last   I Bot a Little Skift to day from young Lindor under the Hill   Gave him $3.50 for it

   11   Nothing new. Buisness Tolerable fair to day   I Bot or Got the Horse to day that I bot of Joe Bradly   He is a Dun Horse and tolerable Old — My Little mule that Rascal John Saunders Bruised up so Died Last night 11 Oclok and was Hauled off this morning, I Paid Jeff two Dollars and a half this Evening for to Pay for Shoes that he had made, I Bot 2 Coats at Auction to day and Sold Mr McGraw One for Cost which was 1.95 cts Each   Court is in Cession and The River is falling very fast, I Bot a table to day at 30 cts, cheap, I think   William wrode Jeff Down this Evening after School was out, I showed Gerge Evens the map of my Land this Evening to Convince him that the Sargent Land had a front on the Mississippi which he did not at the time think &c.

   12   Nothing new. Maj Young was in the City to day And I paid him fifty Dollars which Sum according to Receipt pays Charles wages up to the first of April 1849 — Mr C Nickels was to See me to day And I Gave him my Due Bill for One Hundred and Twenty three Dollars for the cuting of One hundred and Sixty four Cords of wood. This is the Amount that W Winn Reports. The Rascally negro that Killed my mule Lost his own mule to day for it Died from the Same Drive — Phill is up to night and reports that they finished Plowing Out the Potatoes and Finished hauling the rails to make the garden fence, then went in to the upper field to work and that he had but very Little Done. Mozora was Sick all the week

   13   Nothing new   Buisness So So. After The Shop was Closed I took a walk On the Bluff with Anna & Katharine, I Sat on the Bluff and read a Small Book ½ through, Came home to Dinner and in the Afternoon To a wride and Met William Com-

ming out of the Swamp — he wrode Jeff and reports old Gustine
and Mary both Dead, both of them milk Cows

14   Nothing new. Buisness Tolerable fair to day. Yesterday we had reports in town about the Imense Loss by Cholera of
Mr I. Millers Hands up at Water Proof. Tis said that he has Lost
all but One On his Place. Oh it was Dreadfull indeed. Some Say
39, others Say 40 odd, So we dont Know how it is yet.[5] Court is
Still in Cession and the Court in Louisiana has adjourned. They
had but a very Short term this Cession, The water is Falling very
fast and Down as Low as Orleans tis awfully high   Runing over
Lafayette. Citizens are very much alarmd at it, The Crivasse
Cannot be stoped it appears down thare, I wrode out this Evening
and went below the Big Hill on the Dun Horse, Wm &c. went
down this morning to Drive up the Cows and Calves or Some of
them, I think $4.70 was the amount of money that I Gave
Charles. He gave me to day in his walet in all about $50.00 but
Said there was more at the time   Thouht there was Sixty odd,
but it was a mistake Shure

15   Wm and Gim Came up from the Swamp to day and
brot up a Lot of Cows & Calves — Several of the Mares and colts
— they were all very very Poor indeed, The River is still on
the fall at this Place, Two old calves and 3 Dry Cows were brot
up viz. Rhody, Savanah & Rose, and there were others that gave
Milk, Blaunch, Rebecca, Bets, Henrietta, white Hardwick Cow

June 9   I was in the Swamp and was very buissy Plowing
The Slough in the Lower Field   Wm & Anderson, Gim and Matt
we were all at work, and we Got through with the cut, had Some
Potatoes Dug and Some Corn Shelled and Gim & Matt Started
for town in the Skift and they brought Mr Clark and his things.
He Came to town to go to the North, Wm and myself Came up
by Land   Phill Starts up in the Buggy with Some Corn and we
did not get up any higher than Mr Winns where we Left the
Buggy and Corn &c.

10   Nothing new. Buisness Only Tolerable   I Paid Mr
Clark ninety Eight Dollars to day in cash   He has Cut according
to what Little Winn Seys 109 Cords of wood, and Said that our
agreement was that I was to Pay him 1 Dollar per Corde for all
the wood that he cut for me in Gum and 7 bits for the other
Kinds of wood, Nineteen and one half Cords of wood was cut by
Him in the uper field, I paid him but at the Same time I have

[5] See article in Natchez *Courier,* May 15, 1849.

no Idea that we had any Such a bargain, I am Certain that he is [a] prety Smart Rascal

11   Nothing new. I paid Mr Wade thirty Dollars for 6 Months Rent of Shop under the Hill to day which Sum pays his Rent up to the First of June inst, I pay him 5 dolls per Month at Present. Yesterday Lanier Beat Mrs Smiths Daughter Martha for her trying to Keep him from whiping Pugg. Gim and Matt went Down to day in the Skift. Bot a Piece of Meat &c.

12   Nothing new, I was not very well to day tho I have been at work all day — Gim is in the Swamp and Jeff up to Jackson — I think that Gim must be nearly done Ploughing to Plant by this time

21   The Little Thom Denney Horse was Killed the other Evening by that Horse of Mr Wilkotts — I am sorry to Loose him

24   I paid Winston ten Dollars to day on acct of wages

25   Nothing new. Buisness Quite Dull — News of the Death of Mr Wm Blackburn in Frankford, Ky. Was Killed in a Street fight — Report Seys that Cashus M. Clay was Mortally wounded also in Some fight too[6] — To day I Started Down in the Swamp. Wm & Anderson & Matt. Started Down also. We took Down all the Mares & Colts and the One yoke of Oxen and the 2 waggons, We took Down the old Roan Mare & her colt, Byrons mare & her colt, the Grimes Mare & her colt, the Grey Mare & colt, the Spanish Mare & her colt & old Ned — yes and Wm Roan 3 years old and the Bell mares colt, 13 head of them I believe   After Geting Down we found there was no meal so Matt & Anderson Ground meal and I and Wm was hoeing Down in a Little cut of Corn below the Corn House where we had ploughed.

26   There Came a heavy Shower of Rain in the Afternoon So I could not Plough   We then put in Some Potatoe Slips

30   I was in the Swamp

July 1   Nothing new. I came up this morning from the Swamp and Wm Came up — Matt Drove up the Buggy and brot up Some Irish Potatoes and Some Corn, 1½ Barrels of it.

3   Nothing new   I was in the Swamp to day and was at work in Sacking Corn &c.

6 The Natchez *Courier*, June 29, 1849, reported that W. E. Blackburn had been killed by Thomas Steel in Woodford County, Kentucky, and that as a result of a fight with bowie knives between Cassius M. Clay and Cyrus Turner at Foxtown, Kentucky, the latter was not expected to live. The rumor regarding Clay was false, for he lived until 1903; Turner died of his wounds. For a succinct account of antislavery leader Clay's game fight, see J. Winston Coleman, Jr., *Slavery Times in Kentucky* (Chapel Hill, 1940), 315–16.

4   I Started from the Swamp this morning Early and Got in the City to Brekfast   The Buggy and the waggon both came up this morning. One of them Brot up 6 Bags of Corn, the other 2 Sacks — in all 16 Bushells — I Sent Dr Blackburn 7 Sacks — 14 Bushells — I was out to the Race tract to day and Saw the Race between the Mardice Fily and Dorkertys Filly & Waking Wilson & Colliers Horse. The Mardice Filly won Easy in 1.51   The Saddle Race was won by Dorkertys Colt in 1.54. Dorkertys colt won the money

5   Buisness Rarther dull for the Season, Nothing new — I was trying to Sell Some Corn to day to Mr Henderson to feed on and Some to Mr T. to Sell on the Coast below — Mr Langfor went Down Late to day — Drunk   He Came up yesterday to the Race

6   To day After Breakfast I Started down in to the Swamp with Mr Leas   He was Looking at my Corn   I Remaind and he Came on to the city. I went right to work to Shucking Corn with nearly all my force

7   We were Still Shucking Corn and did so all day — Mr Burk and Matt & Anderson were Plowing Down in the young Corn at the Lower End of the field — have about 2 hours more of Plowing in the Cut

10   I was at the Mill To day and Bot of Mr Cozzons 2 pieces of Timber 30 ft. Long, 14 by 14, at 2 cts 180 ft., cash $19.60 and I gave Mr Linders son 1 dollar To take The timber down with a Skift of mine that he has had for some time   He Took it down as far as Mr Fords. There we met him and took the timber Down. Young Delorme is quite Sick To day and Dr Blackburn is at Mr Fords to See Delorme

11   We Commencd to day and put the Roof on the Corn House, We were Still Shucking Corn and have been for a week, Billy Wolcott gave us Some help

12   We are Still Shucking Corn in the Shed Roof — Mrs Bectill Died to day — Gave Birth to a Little Boy child before Her Death an hour or such a matter — Mrs Burke has taken the Poor Little Motherless child to Raise it — Mr Langford made the Coffin for the old Lady   My Wm & Mr Langfords Mrs Came Down from town and brot 2 pieces of Bacon & Some Flour[7]

13   We Commencd to day to haul out the timber that I Brot Down a few Days ago — We got it out and hauld it up to

---

[7] Johnson forgot to transfer the above sentence from his pocket notebook to his diary.

the House Lot with the Oxen   Mr Langford is Sick. Only workd One day in this week — took Pills to night.

14   We have been Shucking Corn all day and will not be through for Several Days yet

15   I Came up from the Swamp this morning and Matt Brot up the Buggy & a Barrell of Corn

16   Mr Shaw Pays $30 that I won from Mr Black and others by my Horse Cuff

17   I was in the Swamp to day and Nothing new, Buisness Quite Dull

18   Nothing new and buisness Quite Dull, I had Some Corn Shelld out this Evening to Send to town   I pd Mr Burk One Hundred Dollars in Brandon money that he won from me on corn Shucking   We got done with Corn Shucking this Evening

19   I was in the Swamp to day and we made an Attempt to put up the timbers to the Corn Mill — After we had got it within ½ inch of up where it was wanting it fell down so we had to go to work and put it up again

20   After dinner I started with the waggon and other things to town with Corn and got as far as the big Hill and there we Broke Down or in other words got Stalded and the rain poured down   We had to unload the waggon Intirely and change the horses in such a manner that we got up at Last

21   I Remaind at home all day Except a walk to the Bluff with Mr McCary in the Evening Late   Mr Koontz pd to day 1.25

22   I went under the Hill this morning and Bot 250 lbs of Bacon Sides at 4¾ c   This I Bot of Marriner — I then went to Mr Browns Mill and Bot 150 ft of Plank and Eight Pieces of Scantling, 2½ by 6, 14 ft Long   The Plank I Bot for Mr Langford — Mr Isack Dunbar Died Last night at Washington

23   I was in the Swamp to day at work Shelling Corn &c.

25   I was in the Swamp at work

26   I was in the Swamp this morning at work   We were Puting up the mill   We worked at it untill Dinner then Mr Langford Got Drunk and did no more work, This was his Last Job — The hands were at work prepairing the ground to Dig the Potatoes

27   We were diging Potatos to day and I Sold 4 Bushels of Potatoes to day in the Patch, Mr Miller Left for New Orleans this Evening   Has been up here for Several months — Mr Langford & Son Left to day — I hauld them up in my Buggy to the

City by Matt

29 To day My fifth Daughter and Eighth child was Born a Little after One Oclock.

30 Matt. went Down to day and took 2 pieces of meat with [him], ie Bacon — I want them to Continue to Dig Potatoes which I hope they will do for me

31 I was quite buisy to day Diging Potatoes and getting them in order for the S. B. Natchez My Potatoes are Small, Quite So — I Commencd to day to Save a Little Grass — I have Pulld no Fodder as yet and I am affraid I am too Late to Commence to do it.

August 1 I was in the Swamp to day Prepairing to Sell a Lot of Potatoes or to prepairing them for the S. B. Natchez, She Came Down in the afternoon and I Shippd Seventy One Sacks of Corn and Seventeen Sacks of Potatoes on her — Good many Passengers on her from Natchez, Mesrs Jno Hunter, Jm Mardis, Miller, Stone, Canady and Dalshimers Brother in Law and others that I dont Recollect &c. After they were put on Bourd I Started to Natchz on Cuff — the Moon Shone Bright and Beautiful. Mr Winn has the hands at work on the Road, Commenced on Monday — Matt. & Anderson worked on it, Anderson 1 Day, Matt 2 Days — They work on the Big Hill

2 Nothing new I was in town all day — I Bet Louis Winston twenty Dollars that Mr Boyer would Beat Mr D Stanton for the Office of Treasurer — I Bet Mr Jones $25 VS a Season from Mons Bertrand that Mr Boyer would Beat the 2 Candida[tes], that is, Mr Stanton & Dick by twenty 5 votes

3 I went down in the Swamp to day to work Richard & Byron went Down with me — we werre cleaning off the Grass from the Potatoe Patch to Dig Potatoes

4 Nothing new. Buisness only So So

5 Nothing new. I started from the Swamp this morning at or before day Light and Got to town to Erly Breakfast

6 Buisness Tolerable fair. Winston is Out to Mr Hoggatts Place. Started out yesterday — The wagon went down this morning And took down Mary & 2 children and Silvia and her Bed, Mr Langfords trunk & Box Mr Langfords Son remaind in town Sick He goes down to work on Conditions, that is, he is to take no more Sprees If he does we are to Settle forthwith

7 I believe I Started down in the Swamp To day.

9 I Sacked out a Little Corn to day tho not much.

10   In the Afternoon I took the force and went up to work on the Road. We workd untill night on the End of the Road next to Mr Winn

11   Workd in the forenoon on the Road close to the House. We workd down to the Lower End of the field

12   Nothing new &c. I Receivd a Letter from Mr Miller to day and in [it] containd the accts of Sales of my Corn that I Sent down to Orleans in Feb Last as well as a Lot of Corn that I Just Sent down   The net Proceeds of the Corn was as is Stated in the first Place, $92 and some cents   I dont Recollect at Pr[e]sent

17   Anderson and Matt. Came up from the Swamp and brot up a Load of Corn   I Sent Doctor Blackburn [blank] Sacks and Sent Mr Hudson [blank] Sacks.

19   Nothing new, I Received a Letter to day from Mr Whitehurst at Washington in regard to a request that I Made of Him, ie, I have Spoken to Him To write a [letter] To the Surveyor Genr To Get the Old Field Notes of The Swamp Lands — This is a Coppy of the Letter word for word

Natchez Miss   August 20th 1849

To the Surveyor Genr
South of Tennessee
Jackson Miss —
Sir

Be So Kind as To Send me by the return mail a Coppy of the Field Notes made in the Survey of Sec. 3, 4, 5, 6, 7, 8, 9, 10 & 11 of Township 6, Range 4 West. The Register office of this Destrict has but One plat in his office of this Township. It is a Plat of the first Survey Made upwards of 40 years Since   I presume it is the Only Survey Ever made, Otherwise a Plat of the Same would Have been Returned to the Registers office, It is a matter of the Greatest Importance to me to Get the Information asked with as Little Delay as Possible

Very Respectfully

Coppy of the Town Plat   Your Obednt Servt
William Johnson

20   The S. B. Natchez Came up this morning and Brot up Fifty Sacks of Corn from my Place to Maj Jas. Surgets Spit Head Plantation at One Dollar per Sack and the Sack to be returned, She Passed on up with it. I was Quite unwell and has been for Several days   Therefore did not go to the Landing — My Wm

660

went Down in the Swamp to day in the Buggy. Byron Came up on the Winston mare, Reports all well Except Violet, who he Seys Had a Still Born child Last night or night before   I forget which at Present. Said it was a Boy child. Cash Sent to Genr Bradford $10.00 To Get a Coppy of the old Field notes of the Survey of Sec 3, 4, 5, 6, 7, 8, 9, 10, 11 of Township 6, Range 4 West

21   Anderson is up to day with a Load of Corn, Wm also. They Brot up 12 Sacks of Corn with them

22   William went Out To Col Bingamans Last Evening and brot Home My big Sorril mare and Colt after Paying Fiddler his usual Fee &c. Mr Koontz pd me three Dollars for 3 Sacks of Corn, I Sent R. McCary two Sacks Corn to Day — I Sent Mr C Rayley 3 Sacks, Dr [debtor] $3.00

23   Nothing new. William & Anderson Came up from the Swamp. Three Sacks of Corn & seven Sacks of Potatoes, and Sold as Follows, 1 Sack Potatoes to Mr Bunting, 1 To Mr Micheal Johnson, 1 To Mrs Marshall as a Present, Sold 2 Sacks To Italian, Cash, and I Sent My Friend McCary One Sack and the other I Kept Home, I Loaned Randolph five Dollars to day to be paid on Saturday Coming

24   Nothing new has transpired To day

25   Buisness good for the Season, Frank Left this place this Evening to go to N Orleans to get a Situation On Some Boat, Last Night Luke Oconner & his wife has a rumpus fight &c. The Partees to the fuss was arrested to day. Richard & Byron went in the Swamp and Took with them my big Sorril Mare & Colt. I Sold Maj. Elward three Sacks of [corn], Dr $3.00

September 10   Nothing new. Charles went Down to work yesterday under the Hill. Has been up there Severall Days on acct of my Lame hand. Wm went to the Swamp this morning and took Mary Down in the Porter Cart with him — also took 7 pieces of Meat Bacon Down. Mr A Browns Poor old Sam Joy Died and was Burried To day

11   I Gave my Note to Capt M Zeno to Day Payable on the first Day January 1850 For Two Hundred and Eighty Dollars for and in Consideration of a Lot of wood That was Cut in Co-partnership by his Hands   We think about 300 Cords

12   Nothing new. Buisness Only Tolerable, Maj Surget Returns my 50 Sacks that I Sold him Corn in

13   Nothing new. After breakfast this morning I wrode Down into the Swamp and found them all at work at Cutting

Grass   I helped them for a few minutes and then Left. Wrode Down and took Dinner and then wrode Down and took a Look at the Line between Mr Winn & myself — Mr Langford went with me and He remarked that he had been Sick Ever Since He had been Down or nearly so and that he had not Done but 14½ days work Since he Came Down &c. In Sec 6 Mr Wade & B. Winn Claims by deed 324 Acres & 162 do. The Last is Aldriges Entry

     14   Nothing new. Maj James Surget paid me Fifty Dollars for One Hundred Bushells of Corn that was Sent to his Spit Head Plantation, I was under the Hill this Evening and gave a Dollar for 3 pieces of Oak timber

     15   Nothing New. Buisness Tolerable fair to day — I wrote a Letter to day to Mr Miller by S B Princess — I paid Mr Dott for Mr Andrew Brown $22.50 for a Lot of Lumber that he Sent Down to my Place 2 or 3 weeks ago — I paid Mr Burke fifteen Dollars to day as wages — To day Mr Dicks Draws a House & Lot at Water Proof worth 2000 dollars and Rents for 300 Dollars per year

     16   Nothing new and Buisness Dull, very to day — I Remained at Home all day to day

     17   I Saw Mr Winn to day and I told him that I was now Ready to have the Land Surveyed that we were in dispute about. He thought it was not quite Dry Enough in the Swamp yet

     18   Nothing new. Buisness Only Tolerable. J S B. Thatcher vindicates his Character in to days Paper[8] — Wm Came up from the Swamp. Brot up a Bucket of Butter, a Lot of Fodder, 2 jegs of vinegar, 2 or three Emty dito and a Sack of Potatoes — Anderson Came up Sick   Sam Came up also   Mr Burke & Phill Commences to Haul wood to day — Mr H L. Conner Died Last night at his residence.

     19   Mrs J D Henderson Died Last Night in childs-Bed — very Suden Death indeed

     20   Nothing new. Buisness Some what dull   Col Bingamans is Quite Sick at Present and has been for Several Days

     21   Nothing new. Col Bingaman was very Sick Last night and to day

     22   Nothing New. Buisness Dull, quite So for the Season   Leopole Dalshimer Left with his Family this Evening for New Orleans to Live thare, It was Last Evening that I gave Mr Kenny, the Surveyor, The Old Fields Notes to Look at &c. I wrote a Letter to William Miller this Evening, The wagon Came

---

[8] See Natchez *Courier*, September 18, 1849.

up this Evening full of New Corn in the year and so did the Buggy — William & Richard Drove them up   Antony Came up also — They have been Hauling wood this week. Phill Laid up Sick

23   Nothing New. I Remained at Home all day untill Evening   I then took a walk in the afternoon and took the children with me

24   Nothing new   I Saw Mr Winn to day & askd him if he was willing to wave the 10 days notice and have Our Lines resurveyd — He to my Greate Surprise refuse to agree to have the Lines run Out after having told me to write to Jackson and get the old Field Notes, Now they have Came He turns around and refuses to have the Lines run out and Mr Wade told me to day that I could have the Lines run out and that he thought there Could be no Difficulty about it and aded that I Could See Mr Winn. So I did See Mr Winn and After a Long talk I could Come to no terms and so the matter Stands, I went around to See Mr North and he told me that he would see Mr Winn and Mr Wade, and see what they are willing to do in the Primices   Mr Winn and Mr Gay was both up in my House to day Looking at the old Field notes.

25   Nothing new   Buisness Tolerable fair — Wm Came up from the Swamp to day and Brot up 4 Sacks of Corn, a Little Hay — He reports that the Bank in front of Mr Fords Place has made a tremendious cave down below the china trees, He Drove up Bob.

26   Nothing new. I got up Erly this morning and went to market and Found a Dr Wright cutting up and Swearing and Defying all the officers of the Place to take him to the Guard House   He cursed Mr Benbrook in Particular and threatnd to cow Hide Him &c. He cleared all of the officers out for none of them would tuch him — I Bot a pair [of] Brichen from Mr Dicks to day, Price $6, and had it charged to my acct. as he is in my Debt at Present. William Drove down in the Swamp this Evening to Come up to morrow with Some Corn — I Showed Mr North my Deeds to day and he told me that he Could See no Reason why I should not Survey and Seemed to think it Strange that Mr Wade and Winn Should object to the Survey — L. Wyley gets a Sack of Corn, Dr 90 cts

27   Nothing New   Wm & Anderson & Sam Came up this Evening   Brought up Corn   They had the 2 wagons and the Buggy — They Brot Some peas and a Bucket of Butter. They

brot up Corn in the Ears — Mr Clark Came Last Night from the North &c. Sold Mr Lemly 1 Sack of Corn to day, Cash 90 cts   Sold Mosses 1 Sack of Corn, Dr — 90

     28   I have not been well, Wm, Anderson & Sam went Down this morning Early with there wagons &c. Mr Clark went Down with them also — They took Down a Barrell of Flour and Some Bacon for him   He is Just a going to make a Commencment to work for Mr Wade & Winn, I sold 1 Sack of Corn to Mr Somebody, Cash, by Mosses, 90 cts, 1 to R Lieper, 90 cts cr & 1 to Mr Henderson, 90 cts crd

     29   Nothing new   I Sat Down Last night and wrote a Long Letter to Mr Mosbey and to Mr. W Winn — I Sent a Letter to Mr Miller this Evening and a Bag of Sweet Potatoes. I Sent them in Care of Mr Charles Williams on Princess No 3 — Wm Came up from the Swamp this Evening. Brot up 1 Sack of Potatoes, 1 Sack of Corn, 1 Bucket of Butter and Some Fodder — Reports Antony Sick yesterday Evening and old Phill Sick all the week and all Last week

     30   No news, Anthony Came up this Morning and Reports Himself Sick & Seys that Phill and Peggy & Little Cela are all Sick, thus I may Calculate with Safty that there is not much to be done for this is the Report too often from thare   Byron Came up this morning also

     October 1   Nothing new. Buisness To day very dull indeed and a Greate many Persons in town for the Police Court was in Cession and the Scool Commissioners was also in Session, and not withstanding, buisness was Extreamly Dull, Anthony Came up yesterday Morning and was Sick   Had a fever and is unwell to day. Mr Hoggat was in town to day with his waggon. I wrote a Small note to Edd Hoggat and made him Banter that Cuff Could Beate his Horse or Grey Colt, for $1000 in Brandon Money or a Much Less Sum in good Money   I Sold 3 Barrels Corn to Mr Tho Henderson to day @ 180 cts per Barrell and one Barrell to Lemly, 80 cts, And Six do to Mr Bully Henderson for 75 cts   This was all on a cridit — Matt. paid me One to night that I Loaned a Short time ago — Mr Allen Mardice writes from California that he was offered 300 Dollars per month to Clerk and he refused and was agoing to the mines

     2   Nothing very new more than The Republic of St. Domingo has changed her Destinnys very much for the worse by Proclaiming Her President Emperor, So Seys the report, but I hope tis not true, Soluke is a very Dark man, a Black Man, and has a wife and one Daughter to this date,[9] I Bot a Buggy from Mr Jaqumine the other day and got it Home yesterday, price $25, five Dollars to be paid in Shaving. I hired the Same to Mr Stump and W. Wilcott to[o] for 6 Dollars per month Commencing from to day — They had Fish in market this morning very Erly, for the first time they have hauled this Season. William Drove Down Dandy in the other Bugy of mine to day   He is agoing to haul wood for a few Days   Anthony[10] went home this morning and wrode Fidder — I paid him to day 1.50 cts on his wages   He Quit on Saturday Last or Friday — I took a Long walk this Evening up above Mr Browns Mill and through it and was very weak when I Got back, and when I Came to Supper Winston was telling about the Shop Bells both ringing by them Selves and that he Saw them. Mr. Theodore Harman was in the Shop at the Same time and herd them also   Bot for Mr Langford One Coat, 4.50, One pr Pants, 2.50, Dr to Dalsimer for these — I Sent Down by William that went down to day Some Pills & 2 Doses of Calomel, One for Cela, the other for Mary, and a Bottle Containing the Medicine that I had put up for Chills & Fevers — Mr Henderson pd me for 6 Barrells Corn @ 6 Bits pr Barrell which sum is $4.50 — Moses pd me for 1 Sack, Dito 90 cts

     3   Nothing new. Buisness Some what Dull — After Dinner to day I Started Down in the Swamp and did not get down thare untill night or nearly So and the weomen was pretending to work at pulling grass — Old Phill has been Laid up for 2 weeks — Cela & Sam both Complain[in]g. Sam was not Sick but Cela was, Old Man Langford was making a Body to a waggon, a Small one, and was making a wheel too. Mrs McCafferry Died this Evening.

     4   I was in the Swamp and I Got up this morning as I thout and wrode Down to the Lower End of the Swamp on the bar   I was Looking for my Little Grey Mare but did not find her   I got back to Mr Stumps, there I took Breakfast and we wrode back but did not find Her then, so we wrode on up. Set a while, & then went to work to pull Corn, ie a Load or too for Customers, I Got 2 Small waggon Loads and a Buggy Load too,

   9 See article headed "A New Empire—Island of Hayti," in Natchez *Courier*, October 2, 1849. Johnson referred to Faustin Soulouque, a captain of the palace guard who became president of Haiti in 1847. In 1849 he had himself made emperor under the name of Faustin I, created an extensive nobility, and held the reins of government for the next ten years.

   10 "Anthony" was probably Antony (or Anthony) Hoggatt, who was freed in 1852 by Nathaniel Hoggatt, Jr., executor of the will of Wilford Hoggatt.

also Brot up a Sack of Potatoes, a Bucket of Butter, Some Butter Beans, 1 Sack of wool &c. It was to day that I Sold Mr Stump my old Bay Horse for Eigteen dollars and he agrees to Sell Him back to me for Six Dollars After he Quits fishing which he Said would be about Christmast, Mrs Lee, who was Formily a miss Ross, Died this Evening at the Mansion House

5   Nothing new. Mrs McCaffery was Buried this Evening — it was yesterday that She Died. Mrs Lee Died this Evening at the Mansion House — She was formerly a Miss Weir. I Saw a Small Flock of Geese to day on the Bar near the creek, no it was yesterday — Some Tar was taken Down in a Bucket by Anderson

6   Richard, Sam and Dan Coleman went to the Swamp this morning in the Buggy   They Drove Bob in it — Geo Chase paid 1 dollar that I Loand him a short time ago — I have not gatherd my Corn yet — Anderson, Phill & Mary and Sylvia Came up to night and Little Mary Jane — They brot up 2 Small wagon Loads of Corn & a Small Sack of meal

7   William & Richard both Came up this Evening from the Swamp in the Buggy. Brot up Some Peas & Some Fodder. Old Ned mule runs of[f] to night and goes for the Harman place

8   Mr Allen Davis Brings in word that old Ned had got out to his House & He brot in a Boy, Giles, for me to Look at to Learn the trade. I told him that I thought him a Little too Small at Present — Wigs nominated Mr Farrer to day for County Representative

9   Buisness I thought a Little Dull. I was at the mill to day and Bot $4 worth of Lumber and paid 50 cts for Hauling it up. Anderson Came up and brot the Small wagon with Some Corn and I Sold it to day as soon as it Came. Anderson reports that the Hands were Cording wood under the Bank — Mr Burk was haulling. Anderson Brot up a wheel to have the tyre put on it

10   Nothing new   Some Report about Some Steam Boats Burning up at N. Orleans, 4 or 5 of them,[11] Anderson was up to day and brot 5 Sacks of Corn and 2½ Barrells in Ears. Phill & Same Came up to Night & brot Corn, [blank] Barrells. He Drove the mules up

11   Nothing New. Buisness at the Shop very dull indeed — Phill Came up again this foernoon with a Load of Corn that He Got of Anderson who he met at Mr Fords — Anderson then took his team and went on Down and returnd this Evening with

---

[11] The Natchez *Courier* reported the incident on October 12, 1849.

a Load and Sam also with a Buggy Load of Corn, Those 3 Last Loads have all been of the old Crop — William Langford Came up to day and I Put Him to Live with Mr Winston for $2.00 per month and his Cloathes, Bourding &c. So He Commencd this Evening — Young Rountree Gets Married to day to Miss Mary McAlister. She is about 14,[12] Dr Clagget Pulls out Cellas tooth. Cash 1 dollar

12 Wm and myself both unwell to day. Phill Came up to day with Fany & Roan bringing a Load of old Corn, Anderson and Sam went Down this Morning with Buggy and waggon. Phill goes Down this Evening

13 Nothing new Buisness Good, Greate many Persons in the City to day. Jersey Burns Died On Tuesday Last in Jackson, It was to day that Phill, Anderson & Sam Came up and brot up Corn, 2 waggons & the Buggy — This was all New Corn

14 I was at the Shop untill 12 Oclk I then Came to the House and went in Seach of Big Jeff & Fiddler. Did not find them. Came back to Dinner and went to take a Nap of Sleep Old man Langford sent for me. I then Got up and went Down and we had but a very few words before I told him that I had no farther use for Him and that I wanted to Settle with Him, which I did, and I paid him for One month and fifteen Days tho his Own acct. Only made 1 month 14 Days, tho I told him I did not Care for a Day or two, So I had paid him in all $21.50 and I paid the Amount that he claimd, ie, in plain words $22.50 was the amount & $21.50 he had Receivd So I only owed him One Dollar which I paid him and Gave him One Dollar over. I then took my Horse and Startd towards the Swamp to Look for Fiddler & Jeff — I herd of them Down at Mrs Walterns place. I followd on and went to the Swamp and about 10 Oclock Rain Commencd Mr Langford Said a good many things that He Said [were] Spoken by Burke and his wife and when I got Down thare I wanted to Know if Such was the facts and they both Denied it and Said they had never Said any such things

15 Dr Young & Jeff got to town to Night Came Down on S B Memphis — Frank & Claibourne Came up the River — they stopd in town too

16 I got on my Horse Bob very Erly this morning and Startd to town and the Banks was very Rapidly Caving in and when I came up to the Walton Place the 2 hands that was then

---

[12] James O. Roundtree was from Shreveport, Louisiana. See account in Natchez *Courier,* October 12, 1849.

at work told me that they had Lost 100 cord of wood by the Caving Bank and was still Caving — I Came to town and Sent her word. She returnd her thanks but Could Send no help   I Left word for all hands to pull Corn this morning untill there was a finish made of it — Antony went Down this Evening Late. He Came up on Saturday. Charles Wolcott and Little Winn both Came Down Last night from Indiana

    17   Mr A. Brown paid by Davy for Corn in full for or up to this date, Eight Dollars, Nothing new   Buisness Tolerable, J. S. B. Thatchers Card is Out this Evening in regard to his Election   I Broke up a meeting to night in my Shop Composed of Winston, Jeff, Frank & Claibourne

    18   Nothing new. Mr Butler was Married to Night to Miss Ker, Jasper Winn was up this morning from the Swamp with Fish, Said that he had to Let Down the Fence at the Walton place to pass, the Bank had Caved So much, I Bot a Coat and pr pants to day from Dalshimer, $8 for the Coat, $3.50 pants. I paid $6.00 and owes him $5.50 Ballance, I Bot a pr Shoes for Byron, Cash 75 cts

    19   Nothing new. Buisness Tolerable   The Boys Paperd the Shop to day with wall Paper I Bot a[t] Liddells Store — Wm Came up to day from the Swamp and brot up the trunk and Chest of Mr Langford and Left it at Mrs Paynes Place where He was — Wm also brot up a Sack of Meal and a Buckt of Butter, He reports Little Winn as being in the Swamp at my House, They are Still Pulling Corn Down in the Swamp in the upper Field, I paid Winston fifteen Dollars to night and He Bet it with Esqr R. Woods On the Election in Franklin County as Follows, 1st that Jude Thatcher would beat Judge Smith in Frankelin, Even Bet $5 — 2d Bet that Judge Smith would not beat Jdg Thatcher 50 votes, 3d that Jdge Smith would not beat Jdg Thatcher 100 votes in Franklin. So we Shall Se what we Shall See, I Since writing the above having gone ½ in the Bets with Winston

    20   Great many Persons in the City to day, and a Greate many at the Race tract at the General Muster.[13] Mr Billy Newman on the review of the Soldiers gets thrown from his horse, Colt Show at the tract. Several Premiums were Taken by Col Nat. Hoggatt. Democratic meeting at the tract, Great Effort was made to try and Get Gen. Stanton to Run for County Representitive But he would not agree under no Circumstances   Mr Amos Alexander was nominated and will Run — I paid Jeff three & a ½

13 *Ibid.*, October 19, 1849.

Dollars to day &c. I owe him 5.50 cts on old acct. I paid Mr
Burke five Dollars to day on his wages   He was up to muster
to day. I Bet Mr Swaine a pr Boots this Evening Even that Jude
Smith would beat Judge Thatcher   I also Bet Mr Chisolm that
Jude Smith would beat Jude Thatcher in Jasper County, 1 dollar
— I also made a Bet of a pr of Moscovy ducks that Judge
Thatcher would not Beat Judge Smith 200 votes in this County
and I Bet him that Judge Thatcher would not Beat Jdge Smith
over 150 votes in this County

    21   Nothing new. Richard & Antony Came up this morning
and brot up my Little Grey mare & her Colt. She has got a toch
of the Big Head — tis for Reason I wanted her brot up &c. They
Report that they have Pulled and Hauled all the Corn out of the
Field above the House, After Dinner I took my Horse & Winston
wrode the other Hs. and we went down on the East Side of Long
Lake as far as Mr B. Winns Residence, and it was night when
we got back. This was Shortly after the Rain and I find it has
fulld the whole back Swamp with mud and water. Long Lake is
also full which Prevents the Fishing Buisness.

    22   Nothing new   I Sent Down the Buggy this morning
by Winston & Sam. They took down 4 Large Middlings, 1 Jug
molases, 1 broom, 1 Stake, 50 cts of Coffee, 50 ct of Sugar — Now
we will See how they will Last, Winston is to Leave the Swamp
and return in the morning — Mr Hudson paid me $12 for 12 Sacks
of Corn that I Sold him a Short time ago

    23   Nothing new more than Dr Bar wran off Last night in
Debt to a good many of citizens. They were in Search of him
but Could not find him — Winston Came up from the Swamp to
night with Sam. He brot up Fodder, 2 sacks of Corn and a Bucket
of Butter, Reports Little Winn having Killed 5 Squirrells yesterday & 2 this morning. Winston Killed 2 yesterday, Wm McCary
is talking of going up Cincinnatti to work with S Morris — The
Hands in the Swamp were Pulling Corn in the Lower Field on
the back ridge. I Gave Gim Permission to Marry this Evening
in note to Mr & Mrs Hunter

    24   Nothing new, To day a very Severe article appeared
in The Free Trader against Judge Thatcher in regard to the Hand
Bill that appeared VS. Jdg Walker. This Looks very much Like
Jdg Thatcher wrote it Himself   I was at auction to day and Bot
as Follows

        17 Books   30 cts for the Lot
        2 Boxes of Tea   3.72 at 31 cts, 12 pounds

4 pr Specticles	40
8 hair Brushes	1.92 at 24 cts Each
½ Barrell of Beef	1.63
3½ Barrells of Fish	1.95 at 65 Each

25   Nothing new. Buisness Tolerable, Jim gets married
to night To a girl named [blank] Belonging to Jno Hunter —
quite a Croud was Present. Yes indeed there was a Lot of them
I am told, The Last Hand Bill vs. Jdge Thatcher Seems to be
doing him a greate Harm. I am Confident now that He will be
Beaten,[14] Athony is up this Evening and reports that they were
hauling The Last Load of Corn in when he Left and that they
did not then have ½ of the big Crib of Corn in all, That is Certainly the worst Crop that was Ever Made upon that Ground,
Well I Cannot Help it, I Received a Letter from Mr Miller this
Evening and it was a regular Built Dun for Some money that I
o[w]e him, He Spoke of Some of his tenants being behind hand
with him, Corn is worth a Dollar a Barrell at Present and Scarce
at that

26   Nothing new Changes are Going on Smartly in favor
of Judge Smith   Bets are Still in favor of Judge Smith vs Jdg
Thatcher   No other Candidates Spoken of at all, Dancing man
Stewart Gives Ball to night at the City Hotell, William Langford
Leaves Winstin by order of his Father and Goes Down in the
Swamp to Mrs Paynes Place   It was Formily Mrs Walterns,
Antony went Down this morning After Breakfast and Sam went
Down also and took the Buggy & a Small Lot of Fish, ½ Barrell,
and a Lot of Bricks. I Bet 20 cts with Mr Miller in Cigars that
Jdge Smith would be Elected

27   Nothing new   Judge Thatchers Final appeal appeared
this morning And I don't think it will do any Good to his Cause
at all[15] Mrs Fanny Brustee and Anna and Her Little Girl, I forget
her name, went Down this Evening on the S B. Magnolia, Com
Giles, Clerk, Capt Thomaston, Commander, I also paid 75 cts for
3 Sack of Sweet ptatoes that I Sent to Mr Miller from the Place.
The Steam Boat Princess No 3 was to have Stoped and Got Fifteen Sacks of Corn to be Left at Hutchens Landing for Mr James
Mitchell, This was Sold for 80 cts per Sack, Charles Gave me
twenty or thirty odd Dollars to day — His acct was what was

[14] Joseph S. B. Thacher was a judge of the High Court of Errors and Appeals
and was running for re-election. He was defeated by the Whig candidate, Cotes-
worth P. Smith.
[15] Thacher's article was headed "A Final Appeal to the People." See Natchez
Courier, October 30, 1849.

taken in, was 40 odd Dollars   Jeff Gave me 2 Small Rolls of
Silver money to Keep for him   I dont Know how much for I
did [not] Count it — Phill Came up to night wriding the Harman
Horse

   28   I was Down the Street this Evening and I found a
number of People at the Globe Hotell Looking at a Lot of Cattle
that a man Had for Sale and the man was very anxious to Sell
them. I bot 1 Cow from Him. After I made the Purchase Mr Gay
then Laugfed and told me that the man had no right to Sell and
that the man who owns the Cattle Could Come on, take away all
the Stock that was Sold by this Cow Driver   I remarked that I
was Sorry for it, and that if I had have Known it I would not
have bot for no Consideration, and that I would not Buy again
at any price, so I Left and had no more to Say to him about
it, Those are Persons that Bot of Him, Michel Johnson, Wm Gay,
Mr Nickolson, Mr Orr and Michel Hail & young Steer — They
Bot Thirty Three Head of Cattle, at 3.50 cts a head — They made
The Purchase after night and Drove them off by Moon Light,
Now it is a Clear Case they Knew before they made the Purchase that The man McDaniel had not a Shadow of a title to the
Cattle, and that they wer Satisfied that this McDaniel was only
Imployed by a Mr Jacob Paine to Drive His Cattle Down to his
Plantation on the Coast, and that the man McDaniel Had started
with 104 Head of them and a man belonging to Mr Paine assisted
by a young Lad, and that the young Lad had became so Disgusted
at the Conduct of the Said McDaniel that he got on his Horse
and Left   This he done on Saturday morning 27 inst, I had a
Talk with The Black man and he told me that he belonged to a
Mr Jacob Payne of Yazoo &c. and that his master had Employed
this man McDaniel to Drive his stock Down to the Coast where
he has 1 or 2 Plantations, and that he had been Drinking Ever
Since he Left and that He had been Selling the Cattle all the
way and that he had been gambling with a Horse Drover and had
Lost over a hundred Dollars in Cash, and he Said also that the
man had tryd to Sell him for 300 Dollars, I then told Mr Johnson
that he would be doing a Greate Kindness to The true owner if
he would Only Keep the man and the Cattle too untill the owner
Came for them, and he Said he Knew he would but he did not
Like to interfere with the Buisness at all, I then went off from
thare and went to See if I Could See Judge Montgomery who the
B. M [Black Man] Said Knew his master and young Mr B Roach
was very intimate with [his] Master and that they Lived Close

to Each other up on Big Black — I Could not find Jdg. Montgomery nor yet Mr Roach, So I went to Esqr R. Woods and
to[ld] him in Private the whole story and requested him to write
to the Sherrif a Small note of the facts in the Case which he
Promised to do amediately for I told him unless Something was
done instantly the Fellow would Sell all of the Cattle and Horses
and Prehaps Run the man off too before morning — So he Startd
up in his Room for the purpose of writing and Left, I am Convinced from what I Saw this Evening that the Globe Hotell is a
money Making House and so are One of its intimates, Enough
Said. Anthony and Anderson Drove up 2 young Cows to day from
the Swam[p], viz, Sally & Calf, the Broken Horn young Mosbey
Heiffer and Calf, Anderson & Phill goes back again this Evening
Late   This should have been 2 pages over but for a mistake.
Anderson reports that the Princess No 3 did not Stop and get the
fifteen Sacks of Corn that I had out on the Bank for Her. I Sold
the Corn to Mr Mitchel at Hutchens Landing but he was on
Board himself and if he did not Choose to have the Boat Stoped
I Cannot help it, The Corn got wet this morning some, Said Mr
Burke was agoing to Look for the Oxen to work tomorrow

    29   Nothing new, Buisness oh very dull day, Mr Dillen
Puts the Cow man McDaniel in Jail and the Boy also that he had
in charge; and after he done that I proposed to take the Horses
on Pasturage and they were Given to me by Mr Dillen to take
Down and I started down with them and I made an arrangment
with Mr Hudson to take his mules on Pasturage at 1 dollar per
month per head, and He wrode out with me untill we Came to
them and he turned back and then his mule Driver took them
down. Winston and Wm went along. There were 23 of them all
together, 12 mules I think among the Lot — There was 5 head of
Horses belonging to Mr Payne Viz one Bay mare & Colt, One
Bay Horse Blind, One Sorril Horse Blind, and a Little Creole
Poney — Antony went down after Breakfast this morning — Came
up yesterday   News this morning that Cotton has advanced
Pretty Sharply — Mr Wheelock, Mr Henry Duncan & wife, Dr
Mercer, Miss Lizar Young had returned from the North, Bill
Nix and Coleman, attendants in a Small way

    30   Nothing new   Good Deal of Excitement about the
Ellection. I mean the Judicial Election, From appearances Judge
Thatcher is Gaining Ground, Anderson & Sam Came up with
waggon & Buggy. Brot up Corn & Shucks, Some Potatoes and
Turnips and a few Pumpkins and Fodder, The Boys on there

way Down yesterday met Mr Winn, and he Said that he intended if he Caught Any of those mules out Side of my Field, that he would run them out of the Swamp, Very well, we will See what we Shall See,   I Sent Anderson back to haul wo[o]d, The River is on the rise and I have got a Lot of wo[o]d on the Bank that is [in] Danger of Falling in

31   Nothing new, Considerable Talk about the Election of the Judges, Tis thought that Judge Thatcher is gaining a Little all the while, Still I think that Jdg Smith will be Elected, I made a Bet to night that Judge Thatcher would get this County   I bet $5 VS. 1. The Hecla Promises to Call for the Corn that is to go to Mr Mitchel at Hutchens Landing, I paid Mr Crizer 2.50 for work that he thinks his shop has Done for me but I Dont recollect it very well as yet, and he paid me for 7 Barrells of Corn that I Sold him a short time ago. Corn is very Scarce and worth 1 dollar per Barrell easy — Mr Hudson Sent Down thirteen head of mules to day and had then put in the Field with the 23 that was taken the other Day

November 1   Nothing new   Buisness Tolerable fair. Mr Jacob Payne Came up to day from New Orleans and I told him at once that I had bot One of the Cows and that She was in my Lot and that his Horses was all Safe in my Pasture, and when Ever he wanted them To Let me Know and I would have them Driven up   He appeared very Glad to hear that I had the mare Safe for him, I gave him a List of The people that Purchased Cattle of his man McDaniel, He Said that he would not make use of my name in the affair, William and Sam Came up this Evening Driving the Harman Horse and when he got to the big Hill he fell down and broke the Shaft of the Buggy, I had to Send Gim to help Get up the Buggy, They brot up a few Pumpings, Some Potatoes and a Lot of Fodder and Some Turnips — I got a Letter from Mr Miller To day and he Spoke of Anna's arrival in the City and he appeared to rejoice to See her, Dr Mercer & Frank Surget got up from New Orleans Last night on there return from the North   Bill Nix and Peet Coleman were the Domestics &c. I paid Mr Fields 8.10 cts for ten Barrells of Corn that I Bot of him to day for Joe Bontura — William reports the Sale of 6 Cords of wood by Some Boat the other day — Good

2   Nothing new   Buisness Tolerable fair, I wrode out to the tract to day and Saw a Race between Jno Mardices mare, Lizar Beman & Walking Wilson, Odds was Largely in favor of the mare, and I Lost ten Dollars, for the Horse won the race

Easy, about 30 ft or more. Distance 1000 yards, Purse 100 Dollars — After I Left Joe Boggs run vs. Mr Robersons mare, One mile   Joe won the Race. It was a Close one, I received a notice to day to pay another one of my School Land notes, Due 9th & 12th inst   Mr Paine Came to day to Let me Know that He wanted his Horses that I had in my Pasture. I paid the clerk of the Wilson House $3 for my Daugters Pasage to N Orleans on Magnolia

   3   Nothing new. Buisness To day has been very good. The best days work by the Shop for a many a day — Mr J[acob] Payne paid me to day three dollars, 65 cts for a Bale of Hay and Hauling the Same — Also $2.35 for Pasturage of his Horses. I Bot this Evening for the young man as Follows

3 lbs Butter Crackers		.30
3 do water Buiscuit		30
10 do Cheese		1.25
6 do Smoked Beef		60

Mr Payne then Left Fifty five Dollars in Money to be given to the young man in The morning when he is Ready to Start — Said money I have counted and find it Correct, Received of J[acob] Payne by the hands of Wm Johnson fifty five Dollars to be used to defray the Expenses of his Cattle & horses what has engaged me to assist in Carrying to his plantation on the Bayou Beouff in the State of Louisiana   Natchez Nov. 3d 1849

   4   Nothing new   Buisness good — Good deal of talk about the Election at present with some beting — I wrode out this Evening after work was over   Took Wm & Byron. We went Down to St Katharine back of Dicksons — did not find my cows at all   Theopelas Fontenot & Billy both Started this morning to take Mr Paynes Cattle Down. The[y] Left with 47 head, for McDanald got one, and they Left a Calf that they thought would be unable to travel; this was a Little Red Bull calf

   5   Nothing new. Buisness prety fair to Day — To day the Election Commences and thus far the Election goes on Smooth and no fuss what Ever. Circus Commences to Night also — Several of the Candidates viz. Judge Smith, Judge Thatcher, Judge Dubison, Mr Hicks, Mr Mervin, besids our Local Candidates, I Swapt my Little Sorrel mare to Wm for his Roan Filly and is to give 5 dollars to boot. I Bot 20 Barrells Corn to day @ 7 Bits per Bl, $17.50

   6   The Election passed off to day very Calm indeed — Nothing new. Circus is Performing at Present, Mr Burke Came up this morning and voted for P. Smith & Boyer & Merwin & Dubison — I dont recolect the Rest. I paid him ten Dollars to day on his wages and he brot me up $32 from the Sale of wood   He reported 10 cords in 1 boat, 4 to another, Anderson Came up to day and brot a Load of Corn in the Shuck.

7   Nothing new, Good many Persons in the city at Present and there is greate Doubt as yet who is Elected of The 2 canadidates for Supreeme Judge   Tis thought tho that Judge Smith is the Lucky man[16]

8   I went out to the Race tract to day and did feel well by no means, and I Came quite unwell   Had a chill at night. Won a 1.50 on the Race   There was very Little Betting to day. This was a Race between Genny Breeze and a Ruffin Colt, 2 mile heats, and the Betting was in favor of the mare but the Horse won the Race Easy, Slow time[17]

10   There is a greate number of Persons in town at Present. To day Ends the Races for this Season and I am Sick and Confined to my Room and Cannot See them, Col. Bingamans Temtation galloped over the tract, Walking Wilson, Toleedo, Lizar Bemman and Something Else, Lizar Beman threw the wrider and ran off   W. Wilson won the race Easy. Jeff was out to See it and old Doctor was at the Shop and was unwell he said

11   Buisness is dull, The River is falling a Little at this Point and Corn is Scarce and is very ready Sale at 1 Dollar per Barrell

12   Anthony went Down this morning and Phill went Down after Breakfast   Took Down Fifty wt. of Bacon with him — I paid my note to day in the Bank, $74.57   This was a Joint note given by myself & McCary in 1846 and was Given for School Lands I Purchased of the State, this being the 3d note that I gave and is due to day. My Son William went up and paid it to day with my orders &c. I sent to the [steamboat] Hecla to Know what She did with 3 sacks of Potatoes that She had to take to Mr Miller and She Sent me word that She used them Herself — Good, She is responsible

13   William & Sam went in the Swamp this Morning and

---

16 See article headed "Mississippi Election Returns" in Natchez *Courier,* November 16, 1849.

17 This was the second day of the three-day fall racing meet of the Adams County Jockey Club. The time made by Ruffin's unnamed colt (Adam L. Bingaman, owner) in the race against Jenny Breeze was 1:46–1:49 in two one-mile heats. Contrary to Johnson's statement, this was reported as "most excellent time." New Orleans *Picayune,* November 13, 1849.

took with [them] from here Several Cows and Calves, Cherry and her Hf. Calf, Red Color, The white Cow Called Sook & her Hf. Calf, Bett with her Bull Calf also, Jenny Linn & a Red Bull Calf I got of Mr Payne and Patsys white back Hf Calf   Mr Stump is up this morning and I gave him an acct. against Mr Chas Wolcot in favor of Dr V. Metcalf for $25.00 and Mr Stump told me that it was all right and that it would be paid. A Mr Hamerton Fell Dead to day up the Street and was in good Health up to his death. The Poor man has a Family of Some 3 children   Winston has been Sick 4 days

  14   Buisness Fair and nothing new. We have News to day that Judge Smith is Surely Elected beyond a Doubt. I wrode Down to the Wattern Place to day with a Mr Mills and Dr Branum. Mr M. wanted to See the Place, I met William & Sam and they had 3 Sacks of Potatoes, 1 Sack of turnips, a Little Butter and ½ Barrell of Corn. Wm Seys that they hauled 6 Loads of wood Each to day. Well I hope So. I wanted [it] hauled very much indeed, I was Looking at the Plot of Land this Evening of Mrs Watern and I find it Calls for 716½ acres of Land

  15   Nothing new, We have not got the full returns from the Election yet tho I Supose we will have them Complete in the next number of Our Paper, I got a Letter to day from Indiana from Mrs Rachal Johnson, It was directed to me tho intended for Mr Stump,[18] In the Letter she requested me to read it to Mr Stump, The River is falling at Present and Corn is worth a Dollar a Barrell and none in market, William McCary Came up from New Orleans this morning on the S. B. Princess No 3. Brot up a Letter from Lavinia   William and Sam went down in the swamp to day to get meal, They did not get back to night

  16   Nothing new   Philo Mitchels Furniture was sold to day and he intends to moove to New Orleans   He starts in the Boat to morrow, The Furniture Sold very High indeed, Election news comes in Slow, 8 Counties to hear from yet. Judge Smiths Majority 1262, Wm Came up to day and Brot up 1 Sack Potatoes, 2 Sack of Meal, a Little Fodder, Reports all well,   Winston Came to the Shop this [morning] to work

  17   Richard and William wrote their first Letter to day

---

[18] Rachel Johnson was the wife of Alexander Johnson, who had formerly been the occupant of one of the houses on land purchased by William Johnson. She presently returned to the Swamp. "Alex" (or "Elick") Johnson and wife were probably not related to William Johnson. W. H. Stump was an overseer on Johnson's farm.

that they Ever wrote. William wrote to Lavinia Miller and Richard wrote to His Sister Anna Johnson   They Sent down a Barrell of Potatoes and a Bag of meal and Some Homely [hominy], in Care of young Robt McCary who is now making his first trip to New Orleans On bourd of The S B. Princess No. 3. Mrs Morris is On bourd also, Buisness has been Fair To day and nothing new to day in the Political world   I Notice that the California news is not so favorable as formily and that there are greate numbers of People backing Out that did intend going, I wrote a Letter to day To Rachel Johnson for Mr Stump and Direc[t]ed it to Indiana, Hanover Co.

18   After Dinner I wrode Out to Col Bingamans to See my Sorril mare and Colt and they Looked very well, I think I Saw a Flock of Wild Pigeons to day near Col Bingamans Place — Wm & Richard was along.

19   There was a few wild Pegeons in market, They have Just Came and but few. Very little game has Came as yet, very few ducks. Steam Boat Louisiana Exploded her Boilers the other day in Orleans, and has Killed a great number of People   Killed & misen about 150 and the Killed, wounded & missen 250, Oh it is Dreadfull.[19] Young John Deary was Killed who is nephew of Jno Watts, William took in the Swamp to day, Sugar & Coffee and my old Riffle, He goes to tell them about Commencing to dig Potatoes, I find that Mr Ford has not Dug his Potatoes yet

20   I was under the Hill this Evening and Bot 220 ft. Plank and paid 3.30 cts for it, I bot 3 Shoulders of Bacon, wt. 24 lbs, 5½ cts. Mr Stewart is buying a Large quanty of Pop'lar Lumber, Mr Odell was at the Shop to night and made several Bets with the Boys on the Reported Majority for Judge Smith and it appears that he Knew at the time what the Majority was and he Bet them $30 VS 20 that he Could guess within 30 votes of the true majority. The bets were all Closed and I am Satisfied that he Knew at the time he made the Bets — as Follows. Here is the way the Bets was made, 1st as above Stated and 2d that he Bet Jeff 10 VS 5 that he would win the Bet he made with Winston, then 5 VS 2.50 more with Winston Same way and 5 VS $2.50 with Jeff Same way — Mr Bunting pd me to day twenty Dollars on acct. of House Rent

21   Nothing new to day   Buisness Some what Dull, I am having my Potatoes dug at Present. Judge Smith is in the City at Present and on his way to Jackson — S. B. Hecla pd me three

19 The Natchez *Courier*, November 20, 1849, carried an account of the disaster.

Dollars for 3 Sacks of Potatoes that She used on her Pasengers   Mr Wilsons Safe was broken last night and $800 taken and 2 gold watches Stole from it

22   Nothing new. Buisness Some what dull. I Lost two Dollars to day on a bet with Mr Jones & Raicker by a mistake of Winston. S B. Natchez Past down last night on her first trip. She is a new Boat, She has lost by not geting Out Sooner, I Saw Mr Stump to day and he reports all well in the Swamp and Seys that Mr Winn is Cutting away on the timber with a Lot of hands, perfectly regardless of Lines   Mr Stump mails a Letter to day to Mrs Rachel Johnson, Jefferson Co, Indiana. My Wm has been in the Swamp for Several days to help Dig Potatoes &c. To day L Wyley hauls me up Some 220 ft plank, 33 in number and Some One Stole 5 of the Plank for there were 38 in all

23   Buisness Some what dull. Nothing new, Gen R M Gaines pd me $10 and owes a Small Ballance of $2.25 Still

24   Col Bingaman and a number of others Leaves to night for N'Orleans For the Races, Mr J. Mardice, Mr Henderson, Mr Elliotte and a number of others   Richard & Byron wrode down in the Swamp to Drive Mr Stockmans Cow. They Got Down Safe with her I am told   Phill & Sylvia Came up to night and brot Corn & a Little Fodder, and they Got oh Dreadfull wet, very indeed. Phill gets Drunk. Mr Erheart gave him a Dram   Col Robertson from Jackson Last night. Been absent 8 or 10 days

25   Nothing new. I remained at home all day Except a Small walk I took with the Children To the Bluff, Buisness I find a Little dull   Corn is very high and worth a Dollar per Barrell and very Scarce at that

26   Nothing new   Buisness Tolerable fair, We had quite a Cold day, a fine Frost Last night which I think will do up the Sweet Potatoes, Phill & Sylvia went down to day and hauled the Potatoes in to the yard or garden to put them up for the winter, and from what I Can Learn They have turned out very Poor indeed. So much for So much   Little Winn Said to night that he thought my teams had hauled about 300 Cords or prehaps 350. I Even doubt it Sharply — He Came up to night and brot Ducks and wrode my Horse Cuff. So there must be an End of that Kind of Sport, News about the Election is very Contradictory for To day Judge Smiths majority is 1556 and it was Only the other day that the Same was reported to have been 1734, and money was bet on it by the Boys VS Mr Odell, It was to day that I made a bet with Mr Waller, for I 1st made a bet of 12.50

cts that Voucher would beat the field, 2d that Error would beat Verrifier in the four mild Post Stake, This we bet $12.50 on as we did in the Case above, December 2d I Learn that Voucher wran instead of Verrifier, New Natchez up to night, first trip she has made up

27   Nothing new   Buisness Only So So — After Breakfast this morning I Got on my Horse and Richar[d] with me and we drove down Rose & Patsy Higgins — I Left Richard to take them down from the foot of Fords Field and I went Down and went accross the Byou on the other Side of Long Lake, and took Down the Lake in the Float Road made by B. Winn, and I got away down behind Long Lake or Hurricane Lake and had to turn back and go again into the Float Road which took me down to the creek to Winns Shanty. I then took down Same Road and Came around the foot of Long L. and Came up to the House   Considerable wood to haul yet. They have not got much more then ½ out yet. Very Little Corn in my Crib, Almost no Crib of Corn at all — Phill was Just puting up the Potatoes as I Came along and there was a very Small Quantity of them indeed. Oh I have had bad Luck this year in the way of Croping, very indeed — I took my Little Pulling Gun along and I Killed 3 Ducks and a Pigeon.

28   We had new[s] to night or this Evening that Capt Minors Horse Voucher had won his Race VS Doubloon, John Black & I think Rigadoon, 2 miles heats[20]   Natchez No. 2 was for Orleans to night   Abundance of People down to See her, She is a fine Looking Boat. Genr Scott & Oregon both up to night. Brot news from the Race 1st day — I won a dollar from old Claiboun that the Scott would get here before the Origon by 100 yds   Won it Easy

29   Nothing New. Buisness Tolerable Fair, I was at the tract this Evening and Saw 2 Races and Came home 2.50 cts winer. I had a Small Race with Jack, Bill Stiths Poney vs Jacks Poney, Princess No 3 did not Come up this morning. No news

30   Nothing new   Buisness Tolerable Only. Corn One Dollar a Barrell and none in market, William wrode down in the Swamp To day to bring up meal and Potatoes, Jasper Winn Came

---

20 On November 27, 1849, the first day of the fall races at the Metairie Course in New Orleans, William J. Minor's horse Voucher won the "Minor Stake" over Doubloon, the favorite, and Rigadoon. Two other horses, including John Black, paid forfeits and did not start. Voucher also won "the great post stake" on December 1 at the same meet. Voucher was "by Wagner," one of the leading horses of the period, "out of Britannia," imported by Minor from Great Britain. New Orleans *Picayune*, November 27, 28, December 2, 1849.

up with fish and has been Drunk all day in Town and was here to night Dancing at M Johnson. Stump was up with fish also this morning — Lavinia writes to Wm this mornings Boat. John Kyle was Bailed Out of Jail this morning by Mr Rose. Was put in Jail on charge of Stealing Horse feed from Millers Stable[21]

December 1   Very little buisness a doing. We Sent a Letter & Some Cabbage Down on the S. Boat

2   Nothing new. Buisness Tolerable fair — I remained at Home all day after I closed up the Shop, No news. Wm is in the Swamp and aught to have been up before this.

3   No news. Jno Mardice, Ricorr, Bully Henderson and others Came up from N. O. this morning — S B. Natchez No 2 — Buck Woods Came from Colidge yesterday and was Dissmissed, Expelled — Voucher won the 4 mile day beating Error Easy, Mr Waller now owes me the Sum of $37.50

4   Jasper Winn is in town, His Father has driven him off — This was the Effect of a Spree, Several Corn Boats in this morning. Corn Still a Dollar — William Came up from the Swamp to day and brot the Buggy, 2 Sacks of Potatoes, 2 of Turnips and Some Fodder, Mr. Burke Sent up 8 ducks by Stump   Such work as that is the way my wood is hauled Out So Slow, I Saw Mr Crowley to day and he told me that he brot the remains of Mr Brown up   He died Down at Mr Surgets place, Another man Died down thare too

5   Nothing new   Buisness Good To day, Thank Heaven

---

[21] While Johnson was greatly interested in the regulations of free Negroes, he made no mention of the following item which appeared in the Natchez *Courier*, November 30, 1849: "Of Public Interest. We have been requested by several gentlemen to publish the fourth and fifth sections of a law to be found on page 948 of Hutchinson's Digest, the existence of which they incline to believe has been entirely forgotten by those who should have in it most frequent remembrance. We cheerfully publish it for the satisfaction of our friends in particular and the information of the community in general.

"4. Not Lawful for Slaves or Free Persons of Color, to keep House of Entertainment. Also unlawful to vend any goods, wares, merchandise, or spirituous liquors, and the offender, upon conviction before a Justice of Peace, may receive not less than twenty nor more than fifty lashes for every offence, to be inflicted by constable of beat or district.

"5. Duty of Justices of Peace and Constables. Such officers to search into and prosecute every violation of this act, and failing to do so, wilfully or knowingly, are liable to be presented or indicted before the Circuit Court, and upon conviction pay a fine not exceeding fifty dollars."

For the complete text of sections 4 and 5, see A. Hutchinson, *Code of Mississippi: Being an Analytical Compilation of the Public and General Statutes for the Territory and State, with Tabular References to the Local and Private Acts, from 1798 to 1848* (Jackson, 1848), 948–49.

for it. Frank Opened Shop again This morning in his old Stand near the Mansion House, William went down in the Swamp this Evening with the Buggy to bring up the meal that he forgot the other day — He took down 50 cts in Sugar & 50 ct in Coffee — 25 cts in Shot for Mr Burke, Dr Broom returned from the North, arrived Last Evening. Brot 2 Ladies with him, relations of his

6   Nothing new   Buisness rarther dull to day, I took a ride this Evening to a Stock Boat up by Browns mill, did not Buy any Stock, William Came up this Evening And brot up Some meal & Turnips, 2 Sack, and a Barrell of Corn, Reports Burke as Sick, has been for Several days, Ever Since Monday

7   I went out to Look at the Shooting in the Byou this Evening and Lost $5 by the operation, Easy Enough   Things went on well Enough, and at church I went after night, and Listened to the Preachers   They Preached & Prayed mightyly, I Sent my Buggy down to Mr C. Nickols to get Phillip to make up a Body for it, Jasper Winn wants to get a Horse from me. Cant Come it — Shure, Winston gave 5 d. to day and 5 d. that I held as a Stake VS Mr Odell. Makes the ten Dollars that I gave a Short time ago

8   Buisness has been very Good to day in my line and I am glad of it, To day Duch Phillip Smith Sold me a Buggy for fourteen Dollars 50 cts, tis not much worth [it] I think   Greate many Preachers in the City at Present of the Methodist order,[22] Phillip Smith Sells 1 yoke of Steers to Capt Nevitt to day, Mr Waters is down from Cincinnatti to attend Court at Woodville, on the Commercial Bank — I Gave Sam a Smart Floging this Evening about Breaking a Bottle of Cordial

9   Old Phill Came up Last night wriding Little Dick and Seys that they have 67 Cords of wood on the Bank. Antony Came up this Evening, He wrode of Jeff

10   Phill goes down this morning, wrode Jeff and Left Antony without a Horse all day and he did not go down to day at all, Buisness very dull to day — indeed

11   It was Only to day that Antony went down in the Swamp. Wm went down also. I See plainly that I will not be able to get out my wood by Christmast, I Sent down 1 midaling of meat and 2 Shoulders of Bacon and Kept the Same amount of meat up here, Corn is worth 75 ct and Coal worth 62½ per Bar-

---

22 The occasion was the meeting of the Mississippi Conference of the Methodist Episcopal Church. See Natchez *Courier*, December 7, 8, 1849.

rell, Hay $18 per ton, I won Jeffs Rule & Lantern both this Evening

12   After breakfast I Took my horse Cuff and wrode down into the Swamp and when I got down thare it was about 11 Oclock   I went on and found the women at work at Knocking down stalks   They Said that the Oxen was all Out and had been Ever Since Sunday. I then went on to hunt for them. Anderson & William was both Out And returned with Only One Ox, Red   I was Out in the woods and Killed 9 Pigeons and 1 Swamp wood Cock — I was down in the Cane below the house   Not much Game, Some Pigeons about — Phill and Antony was hauling   Bruke was Laid up and has been for a week   So goes things, Not much wood out nor they wont begin to get it out by Christmast   Burke Killed 2 or 3 Small Hogs yesterday in the woods   He Said they were wild —I did not See him nor William whilst I was down thare

13   Buisness Dull, I felt bad from my ride yesterday. Was in bed Part of the time to day. Robt McCary came up from Orleans this morning on Princess 3

14   Buisness some what dull, I wrode out to Col Bingamans this Evening to Look for my horse Dick, Did not find him nor hear of him   I Bot in Perfumery to day, &c., $10.16

15   The Streets are very mudy at present and will be for Several days to Come, Richard & Byron went down in the Swamp this Evening. Both wrode Cuff   Billy Wolcott told me to day about a Large Sow of mine in the Cane shot through the head by Some One and he give me to understand that She was Killed by Bailor Winn — and yester[day] Gim Gregory was Out and Killd 3 hogs and amoung them B. W. Said was a Large Barrow of B. Winns. Promised to Send B Winn half &c. Mr Bontura pd me $12.15 for 15 Barrells of Corn I Sold him Some time ago

16   I went under the Hill to day After Dinner To Look at the Body of a man that had been found drowned in the River   He had been Drowned Only a few hours and was a young Irishman and his name was John Whelen, Was found by Charles, a Fisherman   Was fast on a Hook — Tis Singular indeed, This Evening Late Richard & Byron Came up from the Swamp and reports the Oxen Still Lost. Have been gone a week to day — Now if that is not Enoughf to make a man Sin — Oh what management, My Country, Mr Burke, he Sent me 1 duck & 1 Squirell.

17   I wrode Out to the race tract this Evening to Look at Some Mexican Horses and mules. They were Poor and Small.

The Horses Mr Adams had taken away below with him

18   Nothing New, Buisness Only Tolerable to day — William was and is in the Swamp Still and I presume not doing much. I made a Fair Bet to Night with Mr Odell on the Ellection of City Treasure, Mr Dicks vs. Mr Shrimp Harrison — $5.00   And Mr Carpenter was present & he then backed Out & Said that if any One took him to be a Gentleman they were Damably Fooled, Enough Said, shure

19   To day was The Day in which the Sale of Land Took Place, and I got Bluffed off at the 50 cts per acre and would go no farther   It was the Land owned by Pitcher Lacoste &c. I was rarther in a hurry and I bid 45 cts and the gentleman, a Mr Lee, bot the Land.

20   Nothing New. Buisness Tolerable fair taking the times in Consideration   I was at the Court House to day and there was a Lot of Land Sold to day in Different Parts of The State, It was all Bot I believe by a Mr Lee who, I think, is an agent for The Banks below — They sold a Lot of Land which was and [an] Island near Vicksburg   It was Bought by Mr Lea. Jdg Montgomery was biding on the Same, It was 34 hundred acres and Brot $5000. I Sory that I did not take a view of things. A Large Quantity of Land, Say 1700 Acres was Purchased by A Dunnan in Warren County to day at 21 cts per Acre. Mr Collins Gave me a Puppy to day from his Terrier Slut. Well, from Mr Stump [I] Learned this Morning that they had not found my Oxen yet, Oh what Buisness, Good Heaven

21   Buisness Only Tolerable — Mr Burke was up to day and hauled up in the Buggy by Anderson Some Turnips & a Lot of Sweet Potatoes & Eggs &c. Oxen not found yet, Considerable wood yet to haul, I paid Mr Burke to day ten Dollars on his wages — Last night a man by the name of Josh Smith cut Charly Brogen with a Bouie Knife Pretty Severely   Brogen run and Jumped Down in the Bar Room through a Hole and the other, a Mr Sterling Smith, Jerked a Door off the hinges and Sprung out of the window   I tell you they Left in Short Order — Smith has Left for the Swamps Some Where — Zora was up to day. Came up with Anderson   Anderson went down this Evening Just before dinner and Took Down with him 50 cts Coffee, 50 cts Sugar and a Jug of Molasses, and 1 gallon Lamp Oil, The Last Call I hope They will make this year   Charles paid me to day thirty nine Dollars or there about, Reports Expendures To the Amout of 6.00 for 1 pr Boots, 3 pr Draws, 2 under Shirts

22   Nothing New Buisness So So. I paid Maj Young to day fifty Dollars for the Cervices of Charles up to 1st of December instant and he paid me 6 Dollars that Charles got Clothing with — I paid Mr Wade thirty Dollars to day for Rent due 1st inst

23   No News of importance

24   Nothing new. Buisness Tolerable fair   Great many Persons in the City to day — I paid Mr Odell this Evening thirty five Dollars for Jeff & Winston   This was a Bet that they had made with him on Judge Smith Election, 12.50 cts was for Winston and 22.50 cts was for Jeff. Several of my hands are up to day from the Swamp, old Phill & Sylvia, Mary & Zora & Sam   They are all well at Present. Mr Wm Weldon pd me this Evening ten Dollars on acct and [o]wes a Ballance of 2 to the first of January 1850. Old Mary wrode up old Dun and Antony old Prince and reports that old Anderson is hauling wood with the Oxen. We Shall See what he does — Mr S Powers paid me two Dollars on his bill which Sum pays his acct up to 1st Janry 1850 — Mr Wm Weldon Paid to day ten Dollars on his acct and owes a Ballance of two Dollars to the first of January 1850

25   Nothing new. After the Buisness of the day was prety much over I wrode Out to the race tract and there I had 2 Races   I won a Race on Bill Slitts Poney VS. Little Dick, 4 Hrd yards, and then Bob. McCarys Grey Horse, Peet VS. Bill Slitts Poney, ½ mile — Bill Slitts P. won Easy

A Coppy of a Letter I Received from Mr William Mosbey To day the 28th of December 1849 [But inserted here by Johnson]

Madison Jefferson Co, Indiana

Dear Sir

We are all well at Present but I are Sorry to Learn of your Trouble from Sickness. In regard to the Dispute about the Survey and Lines, all I have to say is this   I never was Satisfied with Forsheys Survey but I Knew well that if I got into a Contention with B. Winn about it he would buy false witnesses to proove the Conner to be not Cut down but which I Knew to be the fact   So on the whole I Concluded to Leave the State and have nothing to do with them — Every honest man Knows B. Winn to be a Black Hearted wretch & those in Co with him no better.

With due respect

William Mosbey

November 28th 1849[23]

[23] The original of this letter is in the Johnson Papers. Johnson's rendition here

684

26   Nothing new   Times are Tolerable Dull and Corn worth 75 cts per Barrell and not much in market at that, Great Many Persons in the City, The Boys are in the Swamp To day   William & Richard & Byron & Edd went down in the Buggy. They will be hunting all the time I do Expect, The River is rising fast at Present, Produce Some what high. I Loaned Mr Sargent my Violin this Evening and it is to be returned To morrow. I had a greate notion to trade this Evening For an old mule that Mr Hudson has

27   I find Buisness only Tolerable   I Saw Mr Burke up this morning and he Came to inform me that Mr B Winn had Commenced to haul the wood away   Is at the foot of my Field and he Knows that he do not own a foot of it. I went to See Mr North who told me that my Only Course was to Sue him and that it would be better to have a talk with Mr Wade about it before Sueing him. I Sat down and wrote a Note to Mr Winn to day and in it I requested him to Let the wood alone untill I could have the Land Surveyd &c. This note I Showd to Mr Inge and then gave it to Mr Burke to take down, Now it is a strange thing to me that Mr Wade & Winn should act in this way, very indeed, Now the truth of the Buisness is that old man Winn is an overbearring old Colord Gentleman, and it will be found out So before Long if he fools much with me, for I Know him too well,[24] A very Large [sale] took Place to day at the Court House   It was the Slaves belonging to Alexander Dunbar, at the instance of Capt Frank Surget and they all Sold very high and was nearly all Bot by the Captain, Tis not more than a week ago that he Bot the Plantations of Jessy Guice, Thom Gilbert & Mrs Denny. They were all ajoining Each other on the River in Louisiana — Mr Burke was up and told me to settle with Dr Volney Metcalf, $15 for him, which I Promised to do. Jim has a Pass to go to Dr. Broom's to night and Lucinda has a Pass to Dr Duncans to night & So has Sam — Greate Many Persons in to day to the Dunbar Sale

28   I was up very Erly this morning and was ready to work

---

is substantially correct except that the original stated that "he would by false witnesses prove" instead of "he would buy false witnesses to proove."

[24] Baylor Winn, who lived in the Swamp, and Benjamin Wade, Natchez banker and landowner, were joint owners of land adjoining Johnson's. The extended trial of Baylor Winn for the murder of William Johnson was to be decided on the question of Baylor Winn's alleged Negro blood. Ralph North was one of Johnson's lawyers.

but things looks rarther dull to open with, I Bot a Country Bale of Hay To day for 1.50 ct. I wrode out this Evening To the Tract to See a fight of Chickens and I saw 3 fights and Lost 2.50 and it is a Sport that is to me Disgusting in the Extream, I Shall not go to See any more I Promise, Phill Came up To day in the Buggy from below — The Boys are all Down thare at Present Hunting

    29   Some Little news from The Newly Elected Speaker in Congress   Reports Seys this morning that Mr Cobb of Georgia is the Man, Some doubt yet as to the truth[25] — Mr W. Burns relation, 2 of them, Came Down   Mr Jackson Last Night and Mr Duffield Came as there Attorney, Tis Strange that there has been no will found, no not a Particle. I am very Sorry To Learn that the children will all Proberbly be Sold   Oh what a Country, what a climate &c.

    30   Mc Staid and took Supper with me.

    31   We did not Get the Presidents Mesage untill To day and it Came Out in to days Free Trader which has Just Came Down street and mooved into the Tremont House — Edd, Richard & Byron all Came up from the Swamp this Evening — Phill, Silvia, Mary & Zora went down to day To work — To day Mr Dickerson McCreyry gave me an order to Mason & Metcalf for Seven Dollars & a half in Payment of his acct. of Long standing with me

1850

    January 1   I was after Mr Conchey, the Surveyor to day to Know if he had Given the Notices about the intended Survey that I want to have him make for me, He then told me that he intended to do it To night and that he [had] written a note to Mr Ford for information in regard to the Land — I Saw Mr North also and he told me that he had not Seen Mr Wade yet but that he would See him to day if he Could — I Saw Mr B. Winn This evening and I asked him about the wood that I herd his teams was a hauling away and he told me that he would not have Commenced to haul any of it if my teams had not to have

---

[25] The Natchez *Courier* of January 1, 1850, confirmed the report that Howell Cobb of Georgia had been elected speaker of the House of Representatives.

Commened on it first and I told him if they did it was not my orders and I did not Know that they had done so — And he Said that what wood he hauled was up at the head of the field to it self to be Seen at any time, I then told him that we would have it Surveyed as soon as we Could do it Lawfully — He Spoke of holding me to my Lines, and Said that I Could not Go beyond my Lines and so we parted. Mrs Henrys Hands was hyred out to day at Auction for One year   She hired them all Herself, Three of them went for 262 Dollars. Cheap I thought. Mr Grilo pd me 1.50 ct. on a Bet. Mr Wm Weldon pd in full to date, $2.00

    2   Nothing new. Buisness rarther dull to day — Mr Konchee told me this Evening that he had notified Mr Wade about the Survey and that he, Mr Wade, would himself notify Mr Winn — It was to day that Mr Dalshimer gave me his acct to Look over   It amounted to $119. This imbraced the acct of Jeff which was $35 and of Winston of $13.75   I Shall attend to it in due time — I hired my Buggy to a gentleman this Evening for 15 ct per day

    3   Nothing new. I went down to Mr Hendersons To day and borrowed his map of the Swamp, T-6 R. 4 W., and I find by it that the Land I have is 8 chs 45 L. ie the Land in Sec 5. Tis plain case that Every map that I have Seen shows pretty plain that is the trac[e] Distance, William went down this morning to see if They have found the Oxen which Billy Wolcot Seys has been out now for several days — I paid Dr Vol Metcalfe fifteen dollars by order of Mr Burke which was due to Dr M. from Mr Burke

    4   Nothing new   Buisness Only Tolerable. Buisness in Cotton Square Seems to be Good, I went out this Evening To Mr Perows and bot 32 Bushells of meal from him And Gave him 3 bits per bushell amounting $12.00   This was hauled home by my old mule, Hudson — Gim hauled it all [in] 3 Loads with Said mule — I also got a Barrell of Peas for 1.50. A Little Thespian Performance to night Out at Judge Boyds and Lawyer Maxwell Took Winston out as Valet de Charmber   The remains of Mr S B. Stutson was brot over from the Swamp yesterday Evening and Buried. He Died with Neumonia at Dr Doniphans House — Old Mrs Lillard Got married Last night to a man by the name of Brown; Desparity a Plenty, Mr Konchee Bot young Brewertons Maps &c. of Mississippi & Louisiana   He got them all for 40 Dollars   Cheap I think. Jack brings Home Mr Buntings Horse from Training

5   Nothing new. I paid Mr Dalshimer to day One hundred and nineteen Dollars & 24 cts, This being the Amount of money Due on His Books vs me including Jeffs bill of Thirty five Dollars & Winston bill of Thirteen Dollars & seventy five cents — I also Paid Mr Signaio & G. F. Brano four Dollars   This was for a Lamp and Some repairs &c. & They Paid me for Fourteen months rent up to the 5th instant at 6 Dollars per month. Eighty four dollars was the amount they paid me   Mesrs Signaio paid me for Eleven months rent up to the first of January, 1850, The amount of which was Two hundred & twenty Dollars — The fine and Gentlemany Dr Ker was to have been brot over To day — He Died yesterday at his Plantation with 5 hours Sickness — a Disease of the Heart — William Came up on Saturday morning, ie this morning, and reports the Sale of 36 Cords of wood at $2.25.

6   After Dinner I went under the Hill and bot a Lot of Hay as Follows,

1st Lot of 2 Bales	540 wt. at 30 cts	1.62½
Lot No 2 was 2 Bales	490 ... at 30	1.47
Lot No. 3 was 2 Bales	300 do	.90
Lot No. 4 was 1 Bale	200	60
	1530 wt.	3.59

This Hay I Left under the hill and the hogs tore it all apart and it Got very wet indeed.

7   To day has been a Beautifull day and Just as warm as a Summers day. We had a very heavy rain Last night and the Loudest and Longest Peals of Thunder I have heard for many a Day. Oh and the Lightning was vivd Long — Some hale fell too and about ½ past 2 or 3 there was a Hurry cane or Tornado past near and through Washington and the Dweling House of Mr Robt McCoulough was Blown apart and He was Killed by the falling of a Brick or Bricks — Oh he was a man that Every body that Knew him had much Respect for.[1] Dr Ker was brot over to this side of The River and Buried To day. He was a Gentleman that I Liked very much, This day 1 year ago was a Sad day to me for my Loss was indeed Great. Poor Dear Mother   We had a Letter to day from New Orleans and all is well & thanks To The Allmighty Ruler of the Un[i]verse that we are all well at Present, I Sent Gim under the hill to day and he hauled up The Hay that I bot yesterday, with Bob. Mr Charles Wolcott Promises

---

[1] The Natchez *Courier* of January 8, 1850, carried an account of the storm in an article entitled "Dreadful Tornado—Mournful Loss."

me to stop at my Place and Leave me a 1000 ft of Boat top Lumber this Evening at 1 per Hundred.

8 Nothing new.   Mr McCoulough was Buried to day   Large Funeral, Mrs Murcherson gets married to night to a Mr [blank] Buck.   Mr Gregory was in town to day and he Called to See me and paid Fifty Dollars for the rent of Hard Scrable for the year Ending January 1st 1850. To day I was up to Mr W. K. Henry to pay my Bill[2]   I paid Mr G. Mandeville $.50 for a Barrell of Flour that I was told by him that it was got by mother on the 6th of July 1848;   I then paid him $6.00 for a Barrell of Flour that I got Oct. 11th 1849, and 91 cts for a Ballance on Bacon Got Same time, also November 26th, $4.92 for 68 lbs Bacon Sides, 6½ cts, Coffee 4, Janry 8th 1850 for 1 Bag of Buckwheat, 1.00   This I paid to day in full and I am shure that I paid for that Barrell of Flour that was charged to mother Long Since — Mr G Mandeville paid me to day four Dollars fifty cents, this being the full Amount of his acct. up to this day, 8th of Jan. 1850

9 Nothing new   Mr Lenier Called To See me This Evening, He Said, To inform me That Mr Bailor Winn had Said in his Presence and in the Presence of Mr Jno Olive That if I Came in the Swamp to Survey or attempt to run the Lines On Land, that we are now in Dispute about that he wood Shoot me, I Thanked him very Kindly indeed and told him that I thought it his way of Talking and that I did not think he would do it. I Saw [him] again in the Evening and requested him if he was not too buissy on that day to Go along with us as we would want chain bearrers. He told me he thought he would be thare &c. Messrs Wheelock & Co Presented a Bill to day to me for a Cashmeere Dress Pattern, Cost 4.00, and a pr of Boots, cost 1.50   Got his [he] said, by my Girl in Oct 30th and in November 13th 1849. I told him I did not Know anything about it but that I would Pay it and if any thing was wrong it should be made Good — which was agreed to [by] both of us — I took Cinda arround with me and I found out that She had Got the things thare for herself and that she had told me a Lie and I Sent her home and told her She had better Settle the matter as Soon as Possible   I found that when I went home She had Gone and got my money back. I Shall find out more about it after a while

---

2 For advertisements of W. K. Henry's mercantile establishment, see Natchez *Courier*, August 13, 1838, November 14, 1846, March 16, 1852, and intervening issues.

10   Nothing new. Buisness Some what dull. Mr Konchee told me that I was in the right for Contending for the Land in the first place and in the next place Mr Ford had told him that he thought I was wrong for Contending for more than was in the Survey made by Mr Forshey which was done I think wrong. Mr Tho Rowan Gets returns from 60 Bales of Cotton to day Sold at 10⅝ whilst Mr Jas Rowan gets 11¼ cts up here — Corn is worth 75 at Present, Pork $9.50 per Barrell, I Bet this Evening with Mr Bunting that the mare Ann Huese would beat his Horse John Anderson. Money up.

11   Nothing new. I went up at Auction to day and Bot 9 vest, 6 of them 52½ cts and 3 of them 1 Doll. per vest   Mr Jas Mitchell paid me twelve Dollars to day for fifteen Sacks of Corn that I Shipped to him a Short time ago.

12   Nothing new   There was Several Races to day at the tract. I was thare too and Saw them. The first One was a race between Mr Bunting & VS. the Sorril mare Anne Huges belonging to Mr Turner, It was [a] mile race. Mr Buntings Horse John Anderson won the Race Easy and I Lost 1.75 with Winston, 3.50 with George Lancaster, 10.00 with John Mardice and 1 with Capt Stricland, 5.00 with Jack, 4.00 with Winston and that was all I Lost. I then won 1 Dollar On the race that Toledo would beat Joe Boggs, and then I won on the Hockett Colts Beating Dick Blue Water, 10.00 from Mr Jones, 5 from a Kentuckan, 25 cts from T. Mardice & 1.50 from Mr Jaqumine, 2 dimes from big Bob. Mr Burke was up to day and brot me up The Money from 6 woodings that he had sold   Phill Came up to night and Seys that the Joshua Larrence stoped and took 38 Cords of wood this morning at 2.25 per Cord.

13   Nothing new — I wrode out with Wm & Edd this Evening as far as Mr McDonalds Place and then returned to Supper or near that time, Mc was down this Evening or to night   Sat a while &c.

14   Nothing new that I think worth speaking of,   I wrode out to the Tract this Evening and I run a race this Evening   Big Jeff Vs B. Stiths Colt, ½ a mile for $10. My Wm wrode to Little Billy and Jeff won the race by a few feet, We then had a race, Stiths Poney VS. Mr Dillons Poney for 5.50 ct   This I won very Easy   This was a ½ mile Race also, This is what I have won, $10 from B. Stith, $2 from Mr Carrouthers, $5.50 from Mr Jaqumine, I Sent down by Phill this morning 1 Bag of meal, 1 Jug of Molasses, 1.25 worth of nails, 1 Dollars worth of Sugar

15 Nothing New   Buisness has been dull to day and was more So yesterday. Richard Came up to day and has been down Ever Since Saturday Morning and I was affraid very much that he was Sick and so he was. He reported Three Boats that wooded down thare Since I had the Last Settlement with Mr Burke, Joshua Laurence 38 cds & the Hiram Powers 16 cds, Talerand 12 cds   He reports all well at Present Down Thare, Mr Hamilton was with or Came up with Richard, He Came To See me to day and This is the arrangement That we made & a Faithful Coppy of the article, Viz —

Natchez January 15th 1850

Received of William Johnson ten Dollars in advance for or on account of two Servants that I agree to hire to said Johnson for the term of One year — Wages to commance from the 10th inst — Said Johnson agrees to pay the Sum of One hundred and Forty Dollars for the hire of the 2 Servants Viz. Violet & Peeter for the year Ending 10th January 1851 — Said Johnson agrees to find them there Clothing & Medical Bill for the year.

Jessee Hamilton

W. Johnson

It will be remembered that he Promises to Send the man Peter Down, who is now at Rodney, by the first Packet

William started down this morning to See why Richard did not Come up and Richard got up here before W. got into the Swamp

16 Buisness very dull indeed. Nothing new. Mr L M. Day Esqr has not Sent me the Mississippian yet and I gave him five Dollars to pay for it when he Left here for Jackson, Mr Farrer the County representative, will Leave this Evening to go up to Jackson and requested him to State that to Mr Day for me &c. I Learn to day that Dr James Metcalf has bot The Hutchens Landing Plantation from Mr James Railey at either 57 or 65 Dollars per Acre, which is a tall Price I think, Tho I dont Know how many acres there are in the tract, Dr L P Blackburn[3] handed me in his Medical Bill To day as Follows —

1848	Amy Johnson	
Feb. 18th	To Visit & Venesee (woman)	3.00
March 9th	To ” & ” ”	2.00

---

[3] Dr. Luke Pryor Blackburn, a medical graduate of Transylvania University, performed medical services for Johnson's family, apprentices, and slaves from 1848 to 1851. Blackburn and the Negro barber were on very friendly terms and occasionally did each other favors. Blackburn was Johnson's medical attendant at

[March 9th]	To Jnes (Boy)			1.00
" "	To Dressing Finger "			2.00
August 1st	To Visit & pres. "			2.00
October 29th	To visit & pres. (Negro Sarah)			2.00
" "	To visit & pres. " "			2.00
" 30eth	To 2 visits & pres " "			4.00
" 31st	To " " " "			4.00
Novem. 1st	To " " " "			4.00
" 2d	To " " " "			4.00
" 3d	To " " " "			4.00
" 4th	To " " " "			4.00
" 5th	To " " " "			4.00
" 6th	To " " " "			2.00
" 8th	To " " " "			2.00
" 10th	To " " " "			2.00
" "	To one visit (Mother in Law)			2.00
" "	To " " (Self)			2.00

52.00

1848	Johnson		
	To L. P. Blackburn	Dr	
Feb 1st	To visit & pres (Jim)	"	2.00
" 2d	To " & (child)	"	2.00
" 8th	To two visits (Charles)	"	4.00
" 9th	To visit & pres.	"	2.00
April 3d	To (Self) "	"	2.00
" 4th	To two visits (self)	"	4.00
May 1st	To visit & pres (Niece)	"	2.00
" 5	To " "	"	2.00
" "	To " "	"	2.00

the time of his death and signed the bond required to guarantee the proper administration of Johnson's estate by his widow. The doctor's social position is suggested by his captaincy of the Natchez Fencibles, the town's leading militia organization. Natchez *Courier*, July 7, 1847.

In the late 1840's, Dr. Blackburn began medical work that was "to make him known to the entire nation." He took a strong interest in the control of epidemics, concerning which he developed "profound knowledge" and during which he often served without compensation. During the yellow-fever epidemic of 1848 he established and served a hospital at Natchez to accommodate sick persons aboard boats who were not allowed to enter the town because of quarantine regulations. *Ibid.*, September 19, 1848. He eventually persuaded Congress to erect other marine hospitals and secured favorable action by the Louisiana legislature and later by Congress on his proposal to establish a quarantine station below New Orleans. He later became governor of Kentucky, 1879–83. See E. Merton Coulter, "Luke Pryor Blackburn," *Dictionary of American Biography*, II (New York, 1929), 317.

,, 30	To ,, ,,	,,	2.00
June 29th	To two visits Venes &		
	Enema (Niece)	,,	6.00
Sept 3d	To visit & pres (Charles)	,,	2.00
,, 4th	To two visits ,,	,,	4.00
,, 5 ,,	,, one ,, ,,	,,	2.00
,, 5th	To ,, ,, (Charles)	,,	2.00
,, 6th	To Two visits ,,	,,	4.00
,, 7th	To visit & pres ,,	,,	2.00
,, 15th	To pres ,, ,,	,,	2.00

$48.00

1849	Johnson	
	To L P Blackburn Dr.	
	For Medical Attendance Viz —	
January 6th	To Attendance upon Mother	5.00
August 12th	To visit & pres — Self	2.00
,, 18th	To visit & pres. Self	2.00
,, 31st	To Lancing Abcess (Jim)	1.00
Sept. 6th	To visit & pres Self	2.00
October ,,	To ,, & ,, Son	2.00

$ 14.00

17 Mr Francis Lewis is to be burried to morrow at Washington, I was under the Hill To day and bought three Hundred & fifty 8 lbs of Bulk Pork at 4 cts, $14.32 I got it of the Dutchman near Charles Shop I was again under the Hill by Mr Browns Mill and Looked a[t] Some Cattle in a Boat

18 I have been nearly all day away from the Shop — in the first place this morning Quite Erly I got on big Jeff and wrode Down to the Flat Boat up by Mr Browns mill and Got two Little red Cows Gave $15 in Indiana Money for them, Only One Calf, for the other Died before we Left the Boat. They were young, both of them, I then went under the hill and bot 125 five ft Cypress Boards at 2.50 ct per hundred, I then went To Mr Gaws and bot 7½ Bushels of Shelled Corn at 37½ per Bushell — I Received a Letter from Mr Miller to day and it had a $50 Bill in it which he requested me to take the bill and take it to the Brokers and see what it was worth and if it was Good to Sell it for what I Could Get for it, and send him the proceeds of it, I went to Mr Brittons[4] to day with the Bill and he said he did not Buy that Kind of money and did not Know what it was worth, tho[u]ght that Mr Cockran would Give more for it than any body Else. Corn is worth 75 cts per Barrell and Some talk of a further rise. River is Quite high at Present and Still a riseing. To night Winston put $3.50 up that Mr Crizers Horse wins the race to morrow — Capt Jones paid me five Dollars that I Loaned about a week ago

    19   Nothing new   Buisness quite dull to day. To day I took the fifty Dollar bill that I got in a Letter from Mr Miller and got it Exchanged for $42.00 in good money and I Enclosed it in a Letter and Sent it by Mr Morris to Mr Miller, I Saw a race to day   Mr Crizers Horse VS a Kytey or Stranger. I Lossed $5.00 with a Stranger, $3 with Winston & 2.50 Same way and $5.00 also with Winston &c. I sent Mr Miller $42.50 in a Letter to day   This was money that he Sent me to Exchange for him   Mr Hamilton Sends his Peter Down Princess. Sold Dr V Metcalfe a Razor to day, crdit Dr 1.50 cts   Mr Burke Came up to day and so did William   A very Dirty article appeared in the Free Trader to day   Mr Burke brot up accts of 3 woodings viz

S. B. Talerand 16 cds at 2.25 ct $ 36.00
”   ”   Hiram Powers 11 cord 2.25 ct   24.75
       Joshua Lawrence 38 cds 2.25   85.50

    20   Anderson & Anthony Came up to day from the Swamp   Seys all are well. I paid Anthony twelve Dollars to day on his wages   I paid old Anderson $2.50 for 5 days work during the holidays. Antony wrode up the Bay Colt Billy and Anderson wrode up big Jim

    21   Nothing new. I went under the Hill to day and bot 243 six ft Pickets at 2.50 cts per hundred and I also got 6 pieces of 3 x 4 Scan[t]ling amounting to $2.60 from Mr Scofield. I then Got 464 ft of 16 ft Plank amounting to $4.80 (this Lumber was for Dalshimers fence)   I then Got Louis Wyley to haul them up. I Got a Letter from Mr Miller to day and they were all well, He spoke of Mariah and that he did not want her, and that he thought the title to her was not a good One

    22   Nothing new.   Buisness Tolerable fair. I wrode Out to the tract this Evening and The race I started to see was over before

---

    [4] As early as February 25, 1839, W. A. Britton had advertised his "Lottery and Exchange Office." Thereafter he occasionally advertised as an "Exchange Broker." See Natchez *Courier*, February 25, 1839, and following issues.

I got thare   It was a Bay mare VS a Grey Horse. Bay mare won the race by 4½ ft   I Saw a race between a Sorril Horse and a roan   The Sorrill Horse won the race Easy. I won a dollar on it and 3 dolls On the first race, I wrode under the Hill this Evening and Baled Out a Skift that I bot of Mr Marriner the other day and then I Bot a Bale of Hay, wt 358, $3.20   Corn is worth 6 Bit a Barrell. Chs Gregory Came up this morning   Has been below with a Boat Load of staves for Mr Hamilton. Said he had not been in the Swamp Since about the 5th inst — Mr Konche went down or Said that he was agoing Down to day to Look at the Land that he was agoing to Survey to morrow, This he wanted to do alone, i e, he wanted to See it alone, I did not Like it so well

23   Nothing new. Buisness Only Tolerable, I wrode Down into the Swamp To day and I thought to have the Sectional Line run out and Mr Khonke made the Commencement when Mr Winn wrode up and put a stop to the Survey. He Just told Khonke that he had no rirght to make the Survey and that I had no right to order the Survey to be made, and talked and Humbuged the mater over untill it Grew So Late that Khonke posponed the Survey untill Tuesday next. Here was present to day the Following Persons, Viz, Mr Jas. Gregory and Mr Charles Gregory, Mr Burke, Mr Chas Wolcott and Mr Calvin Winn and a Stranger, Antony & William & Peter, Here was Calvin with a Double Barrell Gun & the old man with his revolver and he talked very Large. Spoke of what he would do if I made a mark on his Land, he would put a mark on me & I never Said any thing but Just Told him that no man would put a mark on me   I was not affraid of it at all — I was Siting on the fence at the time and I thought from his maner of wriding up to me, that he intended to Strike me but if he had — Enough Said — Shure as you are born — Well on Tuesday next the Survey will Commence again — It was Outrageous Conduct on the Part of the old man Winn

24   Nothing new. To day I was Discoursing prety sharply On the Conduct of B Winn and Our atempt to Survey, Public Opinion very much against him   We are to have the Survey on Tuesday if Gods willing   To Day Mr Odell and myself Swaped accts. Thus we are Square untill the 1st Janry 1850

25   I went under the Hill this afternoon and paid $5.00 for two Hundred Pickets for Mr McCary and they were hauled up to him in order, I Saw Lawyer Martin to day & he told me That I had better Take an officer Down with me if I apprehended any Interfearance from Mr. Winn So as to take Charge of him. I

Told him that I thought he would Think better of it and would not attempt to act as badly as he had done before, He told me about the Law in regard to cutting Down of Certain timber or trees &c. and that it would be best to try and have the Survey made On Tuesday and if They Continued to Cut wood thare why Then it was best to Get out an injunction and restrain them from any further waste &c. Now I am in hopes that I will be able to proceed with Out Any further Interruption from Mr Winn   I Know I shall not attempt to do anything that will Cause a Difficulty, Peace to the old Gentleman   I have no ill will vs. him, I Bot to day 4 vest @ 35 cts per vest & 4 prs pants at $2.00 per pair & 1 pr dito @ 40 cts and 1 Barrell of Sugar @ 4 cts & wt. 237 lbs., 9.48, and 10 plows at 1 dollar per plough, $10. I Sold 2 of the Ploughs for 4 dollars. Mr J Fox, Dr to 1 Plough, $2.00

26   Nothing new to day   Buisness of Course Dull from the rain &c. I Saw Mr. Martin This Evening and I Gave him a Discription of The Situation of that Land in the Swamp as well as I Could, I told him that from what I Could Learn in regard To this Survey that we Only wanted to run Out a Sectional Line, that I had Every reason to believe Divided My Land from the Land of Mr Winn and that I wanted to run out the [line] So as to divide it & that he had objected to the Surveying of the Land and that he wanted to hold me to a Survey that was made by Mr Forshey and such a Survey as he made was never made there before   Therefore I doubted the Correctness of the Survey &c. I also Told him that I was Shure that the Land That I Bot really Contained more acres that was Deeded to me and it was all Done through a Mistaken Survey that Mr Forshey made, and that Mr Ford owned The Land 1st and that it was no Doubt his full Intention to have Conveyed all the Land that he had in those two Sections, yet through a Mistake of the Surveyor he had not done so Tho he had acknowledged to me Several times he had Sold all the Land to Mosbey and to Winslow Winn that he had, without making any reservation at all   He then told me, i e Mr Martin did, that if Such was the Case that the Court would appoint a Surveyor and have the Land or Proper Boundaries Established and would have all Such Lands Imbraced in my deed as was intended to have been Imbraced by the vendor, Mr Ford, in the first Place &c. So I Promised him that I would bring around my Deeds in the Course of the day on Monday next and Let him See them &c. I paid Mr Hamilton this Evening ten Dollars On the

wages of Violet and Peter — and took his receipt for the Same in
Franks Shop

27   This morning Early I Sent down by Petter about 2½
or 3 Bushels of meal and 1 dollars worth of Coffee and [a] Jug
of Molasses and 9 or ten pds of Sugar. This was taken down in
a Skift, Mr Hamilton went Down also with Peter, who but for
him I would have waited untill tomorrow morning. Phill also
Started down this Evening and Took down with him a couple of
Sacks of meal and Some Tar, I gave Mr Cole & Co five Dollars
in advance for Beef this morning as he has Just made a Commencement in that Buisness.

28   Mr Winn is up to day and saw Mr Koncke and gave
him Some instructions how he Should Proceed in the Survey about
taking Depositions &c. and to Observe old Land marks &c. Mr
Winn has Said that I Cannot go beyond The marks of Land that
I Purchased to — This He told Mr Lanere — Very well we Shall
see

29   I got up this morning Erly and made ready To go down
into the Swamp To See Mr Concke run out The Sectional Lines
between Mr Winn & myself and I got Mr E. Cole To go along
with me and we all went together, and we did not get Down thare
untill Late, and then Mr Koncke made a Commennt tho not untill
he had taken the Deposition of Mr James Gregory and Mr
Charles Gregory, who as well as I recollect, Swore that the Box
Alder Tree in question now Standing on the Bank of the River
Some 2 chs and 50 links or there about was always as far back
as they recollected Said tree, Considered to be on the Sectional
Line runing East and West and a witness tree to the true Corner
of the intersections of Sections 9 & 10   Well then Mr Koncke
made a Commencemt and run the Line East and West and
found the true Corner to be one chain and 33 Links from the Box
Alder tree, Now at the Commencement of this Line runing East
& west or in other words at the Corner Stake Mr Koncke Started
On the North Line and at the Commencement of the Line between
Mr Wade & Winn & myself. Mr Winn Cursed and tore around
at a wonderfull rate, Cursing me at times and then the Boys that
was to help clear the way,   [Through] all this I done nothing
Nor did I Say anything but Suffered him to go on untill he got
tired or ashamed I dont Know which   Well we went on but did
not get but a Short Distance before we had to Stop for want of
Light   Mr Koncke & Mr Cole both went up to town and Left
the chain Bearrer Snider to stay all night   They did not Com-

menc this Survey untill very near dinner time — Those were the
Persons where we Commenced the Survey   Mr James Gregory,
Mr Charles Wolcott, Chas. Gregory, Mr B Winn, Calvin Winn,
Jno Barnes, Mr E. Cole, Mr H Burke & Mr Snider and Several
Boys of my own[5]

30   Nothing new   I was in the Swamp to day because I
Staid here Last Night and this morning when I got [up] I Commenced to work on a Little Levy above the House and worked at
it untill ½ past Eleven Oclock, At this time Mr Koncke Came
down and we all then started down to make the Survey   This we
Commenced rarther Late and we Got along very slow indeed. I
noticed at the Edge of the Second Slough Blazed a Hack-Berry
tree fore & aft. This tree is nearly Opposite a Large Cotton wood
tree that has a hole near the Ground, South Side of the tree,
thence a Locust tree nearly fore & aft, a Hackberry — Side Line.
Here he Spoke of a 21½   This was at the Edge of a Slough and
the Line run between two Cotton wood trees, twin trees, in about
ten steps of a twin. He cut 2 chops on a Small Hack Berry 3 ft
from the Line, 7 ft to a Small Ash tree that is Blazed, then 6
ft to Dead Locust, quite a Small tree, Mr. Chas Gregory & Mr
Winn was Present when the Surveyor Stopd and we then wrode
from this Point to the back Lines and then up to the uper Line
then Down to the Line between Sec. 9 & 5 and then Home again.

31   Nothing new   Corn is worth a dollar per Barrell, Hay
1 dollar at retail. I went to Mr Koncke to night and got the Plat
& Field notes &c. that I gave him for insite

February 1   I went under the Hill this morning and Bot
22½ Bushels of Corn, Shelled Corn, This I Bot of Mesrs Walsh
& Co at 50 cts per Bushels   This amounted to $11.25   I then
after dinner went up To Mr Marriners and bot 6 Bushells & a
½ at 36 cts per Bushell   I then got 1 Barrell Ear Corn, 40 cts
Damaged. Yes and I Sent Down five Barrells Corn this morning
by Mr Stump at 90 cts per Barrell. I Gave Mr Martin to day the
Field notes and a plat of the Brewerton Survey made in 1846
and also the Depsitions of Mr Jas Gregory & Chs Wolcott Taken
by Mr Koncke on Tuesday Last inst — Little W. Winn Came up
Last evening and to day I Gave him a pr Shoes 1.25 & a pr of

---

[5] Gregory and Wolcott were owners of land tracts to the south of Johnson and
Wade-Winn holdings. Calvin Winn was a son of Baylor Winn. Burke was a
former overseer for William Johnson but now a son-in-law of Baylor Winn. Two
depositions, dated January 12, 1850, state that H. A. Kohncke was county surveyor of Adams County. Johnson Papers.

Pants worth 2.75 and a vest worth 1.25 and he went down Home this morning with Mr Stump. I sent a Broom down also

2   Nothing new   Buisness Only Tolerable fair   I wrote to New Orleans to day to Mr Miller. Mr Martin told me to day that He thought that there Could be No Difficulty about the Land for it appears to all be right, and that the Court would Set it all right. Winston Sick all day to day and I gave him his F. Papers to day

3   I remained all day at Home Except Going to the Bluff   This I done in the afternoon. Mr T Weldon and Bill Gay had a fight This Afternoon Down at the Globe, The Cause was that 2 of his Boys Followed Georg Weldon Down there to try and Get him to go Home and B Gay Knockd him Down and also Struck another Boy of his. The Boy went of[f] and told T Weldon who Came and very Soon a fight took Place, and they had Sever[al] Blows to pass before Mr T Weldon got a hold of his throat and got him Down and Beat him Prety Smartly, when they were Separated. Report Seys that he would have Killed him if he had been Left alone, So much for so much

4   Greate many Persons in the City to day. Grand Lodge in Cession at Present.[6] Buisness prety Good to day.

5   Buisness has been fair to day, Greate many Strangers in the City. Grand Lodge in Cession — Nothing new — Some Scattering Cases of Cholera in the Country and at St Joseph and Tensaw Parrishes, Marsh & Pendleton Buys the Large House that Mrs Barfield Lives in of the Commercial Bank, $5000.00   Mr Gray takes his mules out of the Lot to day. Mr [blank], I Sent to him and got my Buggy to day — he has had it for Some time. I Loaned Mr N. L. Carpenter to day Sixty Dollars to be paid in a week or ten days.

6   Nothing New. City very Healthy and a good many Strangers in it at Present and the River very High   Buisness Some what Brisk. Hester Comings told me to take out 7.37½ that She owes me & then I did so. She Seys Now I owe her $12.62½   Mr Burke Came up this Evening and brot the Money for two S. Boats Wooding. Viz the

S Boat Violet 9 cords at 2.25   20.25
S Boat Saint Paul 8 cords 2.25   18.00

7   Nothing New. Buisness nothing Like as Good as it was Yesterday. Mr Burk still in town up to Dinner time to day   His

---

6 The Grand Masonic Lodge of the State of Mississippi was holding its annual convention. See Natchez *Courier*, February 5, 1850.

wife & Mrs Jorden Took Dinner with me to day and Angeline also. C Wolcott was in market this morning and I paid him $5 for Some Lumber I got of him   Mr Stump pd me two Dollars which was a Ballance on the old Bay Horse that I hired to him — Burke is, I think, begining to Drink a Little too much for my Interest, It wont do at all, no Sir — I wrode down to Mrs Walterns this Evening in Seach of my old mule but could not find him   Fords Jim gave me 2 small Ducks & 1 Large Dito Mrs Jno Quigless — R C Jones is an old Gentleman who has Lost a Horse by a Fellow who Calls his name Atkinson & was on or about a Flat Boat. Dr Blackburn wants me to see what Mr Whitcom will take for the Gilbert Place

   8   I Loaned Mr William Weldon ten Dollars to day — Reports to day that Mr Ogg. McCray has Died and fourteen of his hands with Cholera   They Died at a new Place that they have rented On the Tensaw. I went to see Mr Whitcomb to day and he told me that Mr Gilbert had rented his Land to Mr Field for 2 years and has gone to Calefornia and he did not Know when he would return, and that he Could not Sell the Land untill he Came back again

   9   Buisness has been Tolerable fair, and nothing new. I went up to the Auction Room to day and Bot a Sorril Horse for thirteen Dollars. He was Sent in from Mr Chamberlains Plantation, He was Struck of[f] to a Mr Elderige and he Let me have him for his bid — Mr Walker has Just Came over from his Place On Black River, reports all well and that he Commenced to Plow on Tuesday Last at his Place, Dr Blackburn & Dr Fox wrides down to the Waltern Plantation to Look at it, They Came back and Dr B. told me that he would give four Thousand Dollars for it, i e $2000 in Cash and the other in One and two years — I am agoing to make the offer for them for I should Like them to get it, I Sent $6 to Lavinia Miller this Evening to Pay for Anners Schooling, This I think will pay nearly 2 months or more to Come, Richard & Byron and Dan goes Down to Mrs Pains Place to Look for my old mule and William went with them and he was to Keep On and try and bring my Big mare up from my Place with him

   10   Buisness So So. After the shop Closed or after Dinner I wrode Down to the Waltern place To day and Took a good Look for my old mule but Could not find him any whare Down thare, I fear he has Gone Clear off   As for my Red Cow that I got of Mr Pain, She is a clear Loss.

11   The River still on the rise. Corn is worth 90 cts and Hay 1 dollar per Hundred, Some few Cases of Cholera over in the Swamps, La. — I had my new Horse put in the Buggy this morning and William Drove him about a while and he appears Like he will work very well — William hauled One Load of Corn with him and the 2d One, When Jim Drove him he refused to pull and was taken and Fiddler pulled up the Load — I Bot 16 Bushells of Corn to day of Mr Marriner at 40 ct and a Bale of Hay from Mr Gaw, $3.62. I Bot 1 doz Razors to day at $3 from the Little man, Mr [blank], who comes Every year, to trade, Antony went Down after Breakfast this morning, He Came up yesterday Evening and brot up my Big Sorril and her Colt and I was Surprised to find that She is not with fold, tis strange indeed, Mr Ford is in town to day and tells Dr Blackburn that the Waltern Place is no maner a Count, and the Dr Listens at him and never Let on to him anything about it and an hour or two afterwards Dr told Mr Inge that He would Give $4000 for it, whilst Mr Ford Seys that he will Give as much for it as any [one] Else will

12   Wm and myself took a wride this fore noon in the Buggy. We drove the new Horse. We drove Out as far as Dixons Field and the Bluff   I Looked for the old Hudson mule but Could not find him at all, Stolen to a moral Certainty, Nine Barrells of Corn I Sent down by Mr Burke this morning. This I got of Mr Teas & Teaford, I Sent it down in the new Skift that I agreed to Buy from H Stump, Wilcott reports a Lot of my Cattle Down on The Creek Bank where they will be Lost I think   I Sent down a sack of meal to day to swamp

13   Buisness Dull to day for tis Cold, Nothing new. We Learn that the Mes[s]rs McCreys has Lost 17 of there People and Mr Ogg McCrey is 18 that have Died up thare Since they have rented that place, Dr McGoun is up thare at $50 per Day, and 2 others thare at 2 dollars per day, Several Days Since this man has Gone up thare   His name is Wary

14   Nothing new   Buisness Only Tolerable. I went under the Hill this Evening and bot I think about 400 four ft Cypres Boards and put them On board of a Flat Boat to Send Them in the Swamp

15   Buisness Some what Dull. Corn is Still Selling at 90 cts per Barrell   The river still on the Rise and is Only about 10 inches from The high water mark of Last year, I was to day under the Hill and I find that Mr Teas is not quite ready to

Leave with his Boat, Mr Gregory was up to day and Promises to take Fifty Barrells of Corn from the Boat

　16　I Sent by William McCary To day Two Hundred Dollars to Mr Miller in Payment of a Debt that I owe him, I think I owe him about 600 Dollars To this date　I also Sent down a Hog in Good Order and a Bucket of Sausage and a Bundle &c. Mr Burke Came up to night and brot returns from the Sale of the Following Boats —

Buenevista	16 Cords @ 2.25 cts per Cord
Magnolia	32 do at 2.25 per Cord
St Paul	28 do at 2.25 do
Not the Names	10 do do 2.25 cord

　17　I went to the Landing before breakfast this morning and Started Down home on a Flat Boat that had Corn in it and I Bot as follows, 9 Barrells that was Sent Down by the Skift and 5 Barrells that I took out at town at the Price of 85 cts per Barrell　We then went on Down to the Place　There I had 66 Barrells taken out and this in all was Eighty Barrells that I Bot of him　The Last 10 Barrells of Corn I got of him at 80 cts per Barrell, Thus $67.50 was The Amount that the Corn Came to — I had it all put away in the Small Room — I then went on Down to Mr Gregorys and he Bot 40 Barrells of Corn at 85 cts per B. I then wrode home to the House. Richard & Byron was along on the Boat when we went Down — Mr Teas was the owner of the Boat and he was taking about 600 Barrells of Corn to Mr Mc-Cowen, The River is very high and rising.

　18　I was in the Swamp this morning and I got up Erly and Stored away the 400 Pickets that I took down on the Boat, i e with the Hands on the Place after Breakfast. I got into my skift and went down with Mr Burk to the Creek to try and Get off Some Cattle of mine that was thare　We had a good deal of trouble in doing so for in the 1st place we wanted them to Swim the Creek, but Could not make them so we Drove them up through the Swamp　This we done with some trouble　I had 8 head of mine thare and there was nearly twenty head of Mr Wolcotts and Mr Gregorys & 1 of old man Winns, After we got the Cattle up I took my Gun and went Down the Ridge and shot 4 wild Hogs　They were in good Order. Mr Burke shot Several times and did not Kill any that I now recolect of at Present　I made a Bet to day of $10 with Mr Burke that we did not have in all 185 Cords of wood. This I won

　19　To day I was up the Swamp and I got up Prety Erly

702

this morning and I Started out to take a hunt and William Killed 4 hogs with my Pulling Gun and I Killed 1 Wild Boar. Mr Burke did not Kill any. I Caught 2 wild Pigs. The hands they were not doing much at c[l]eaning up Stalks

    20   I was in the Swamp to day and was up very Erly this morning and all hands went to work to Cording of wood and we made a Good days work. All hands, Little and big, was at worke — Some hawling & Some Cording &c. Nothing new. They Lack about One days Plowing to Finish the back Ridge in the Lower field — It was to day that the Childe Harrold took 12 cds of wood at 2.25 ct and pd me $27 for it

    21   To day we Commenced as usual and made a Good days work a Cording of wood   We got through in good time this Evening and hauld a Load of. wood a Peace with the wagons to the house and there was in all 163 cords of my wood, 1 Cord of Phills, C Wolcott Sold out all his wood to day, Mr Gregory has Considerable yet.

    22   The River is quite High and rising — Antony & Anderson hauls up the 3 ft Boards from Hard Scrable, Wm and me went to the woods and Mr Burke   I Killd 1 Wild Hog and got a Shot at 3 deers that I Saw on the Ridge but did not Kill one — And we Caught a Small One with dogs

    23   This morning I wrode down to Mr Gregorys to see if he wanted to rent the Hard Scrable Place and he Declinded and I was glad for I did not Care to rent it — Wm and myself and Mr Burke Drove up across the high water near Mr Winns 30 head of Cattle and got them Safe to town, We also Drove the Little Spanish mare with her Colt up too

    24   I remained at home after Shop was closd untill after dinner then the Boys Wm, Richard, Byron, Dan, all of us went down to Look for the mare and Colt   We found her and all was right &c.

    25   Buisness only So So. I paid $67.50 To Mr Teaford and Teas to day for the 80 Barrells of Corn that I Bot of them a week ago

    26   Buisness Some what dull, Reports are that there are a Greate many Cases of Cholera in Trinity On Black River   Mr W Snider Died Last Night   He Took Sick on the trip from Trinity, He Died with cholera. William Started Down into the swamp this morning to Drive up some Cattle and Colts, Old man Winn Drove Some Cattle up accross the Break water to day, I find by a Calculation That I make to night that there has been Sold by Mrs Burke acct. 315 Cords of wood to this Date

    27   Buisness Tolerable fair, I was at auction to day at the Sale of Mr Philomel Greens, 20 Hands. They were sold at the Court House in Lots or Families   Mr McGraw Bot One Lot, 4 I think in all, and Col Robertson bot another and I think a Lot was Purchased by Mr Cox, Son in Law of Mr Green, Deceased. They were Sold at the instance of the Commercial Bank. I Bot an old man by the name of Ned for Only fifteen Dollars, and I am told there is another Brother who is Sick and has been for a Long time, This man was Sold with other Brother, His name is [blank]. Gim Started Down in the Swamp This morning to help Drive up Some Cattle and The Colts. I Bot a Large Sorril Horse from Mr Bunting for forty five Dollars and This Amount I was to give him Credit for the amount on rents &c.

    28   Buisness Only So So, in fact it was quite dull, This morning Erly I got on my Horse Cuff and went under the hill and I Sent a Small Bag of meal Down in the Swamp by Mr Stump & Wilcott, I Started down in a Skift with them and went to Jordens and Bot a Small Skift from Him for $4. I Started down in it and went as far as Mrs Walterns and there I met the Boys Coming up with The Cattle. They Had 22 head of them in all and Several of the Colts. I closed a Race On Jeffs Beating Mr Wolcotts Billy John, $10 — Jim Drove the old Horse [and] new Horse down to get a Load of Saw dust. I then Sent him after a Bale of Hay and One Hundred wt of Bran   The Bran was Selling for 1 dollar per hundred, Corn at 90 cts, Hay 1 dollar per hundred — Mr Burke reports 3 Boats that wooded at my Place Since I was Down. River is very high and is still rising, tis Frightfully high, one or 2 Deaths of Cholera To day under the Hill. My wife was taken very Sick to night Late, was Bled and took medicine — Winston Called on the Dr Blackburn to night. Mr N L. Carpenter paid 20 on $60 that I Loaned him.

    March 1   Mr Burke and William Came up this Evening and brot up The Bay Colt Billy and the Paint Colt and He also brot returns of Three woodings, Viz S. B. Knoxville, 25 cords, $56.25, S. B. Empire, 15 Cords, $33.75, S. B. Montgomery, 20 cds, $45.00   The full Amount, 60 Cords, $135. My wife Thank God is a good deal Better [to] night than she was Last night or this morning — Mrs Mary Morris has a fine Daughter Last night. She got married 24th May 1849. Thus it is 9 months and 5 days

2 Buisness Only Tolerable, yes I must Say prety fair — I Let Mr Burke have five Dollars to day in town and $5 at the tract and then I paid $12.50 for him On the Crizer Race. Then when he Came to town I Let him have Eight Dollars more, thus in all he has Got to day $30.50, and Last Saturday I won $10 from him on the wood Buisness, thus it makes $40 that he has had this time. I won $10 from Mr Stump on the Race on One bet and $2.50 on another Bet. This was on a Race between Big Jeff & Billy John, A Race to day between Mr Crizers Horse & a Kentuckians Sorril Horse The Little Sorril Hs won the Race Easy by 30 or 40 yds

3 Buisness Only Tolerable. I remained at Home all day to day Except going down under the Hill to See Phill & Anderson and Sylvia get off in the Skift. They took down with them as follows 50 ct of Coffee, 50 cts of Tea and about 1 dollars worth of Sugar. River Still very high and rising, Corn worth 90 ct To day, Hay 1 Dollar, Bran 1 Dollar, Oats 75 ct per Bushell.

4 Mr Wm Winston has his face Lanced by Dr Blackburn, ugly Job of it — To day there was a Race between Walking Wilson and a Roan Horse from Kentucky, 600 yds W. Wilson won the Race by 29 feet. I Lost $7.50 on the Same with Mr Jaqumine

5 I was under the hill and bot 8 Barrells of Damaged Corn at 35 cts per Barrell, I also Bot the False Bottom in a Flat Boat and took it out. This I wanted to take Down But they thought that they would not be able to stop at my place and make there own Landing So I took it out. Charles pays over to day $40

6 Buisness rarther Dull I had two Loads Hauld by Mr Wilsons Drayman to day and One by Rob Jones This I will place to there Credit. The Flouring that I Bot of the Boat, this Boat was bought to go to Nelsons place but the Fellow thought that he Could not make my Landing. I got in the skift this morning and went down to the place and I found Burke up at the Point Fishing, him and Little Winn, and when he Saw me he started down from the Point and went to the house and Got the hoe and went to work on the Levy before the Door Oh what Rascally Conduct for a man that pretends to do Buisness, I found Phill, Anderson, & Mary, Sylvia & Zora all Down at Hard Scrable a Pottering with the Fence, I made them Leave thare and Come up and work On the Ridge. Peter & Antony Plowing in the uper field

7   I got up very Erly this morning and started down to work on the old Field and we made a good days work Cleaning up the Ground   The S. B. James Town Took 12 Cords of wood @ 2.25   The Dewit Clinton 20 Cords.

8   I was at work by times this morning and all hands and we made another very goods days work   We are at work on the Ridge and S. B. Concordia Came in about day Light this morning and took 26 Cords of wood at 2.25 ct per cord, and the Charles Hammond Came in to night and took 11 Cords and I Came up to Natchez On her and She [charged] me One Dollar Passage up to the City — very moderate I think. Mr Job Wiliams was abourd also. Now I Recollect that I did not see but 10 young sheep whilst I was down this trip

9   Buisness Tolerable good to day. I Sent down One Hundred Dollars to day by Julia Elliotte to be handed over to Mr Miller when She arrives in Port, I was under the hill this Evening when the Princess Left. Col Bingaman & Mr Elliotte and others went Down to the City to See the Races. The Cols Horses went Down about a week ago. Mr Miller of the Swamp Came up to Know if [I] would Let him Live for a short time in the Ellick Johnson old House. I told him yes that he Could do so untill the water fell. Old Dr Winston went Down with him to my Place.

10   Mr Burke Came up This morning and Petter Came up also and Took Down a Bag of meal, 2 Bushell, Mr Burke brot up a Lot of Fish with him to Market, Three Gentlemen he Said had went Down thare from Natchez to hunt   They Staid all night and was to hunt to morrow — After Dinner this Evening I took a Horse and Started Down to Look for my Cattle &c., Some few of them being down at the Pain place   Wm Richard & Byron & Jim was all along. We worked a while at Mr Fords old Sorril Horse but Could not get him up from where he was Laying, The River is about 3 inches higher Than it was Last year and is now rarther on the fall, but report Seys that there is another rise a Comeing in the Ohio;   Corn is Worth One Dollar per Barrell at present at the Landing

11   The City and County Representatives Came home this morning from the Capital of the State, Mr William Weldon paid me five Dollars and still owes me $5. This was money that I Loaned him on Saturday Last. Mr George Weldon paid me to day five Dollars on acct   This will pay his acct in full to date. To day I made Out my List of Assesable Property as Follows—

Taxable Property.

Houses and Lots	2	$ 2500
Watches	1	40
Pianos	1	40
Slaves under 60 years	4	1,500
Poll or House Holder		
for Mrs Battles	1	mm
1 House and Lot	1	1,700

The Circus arrives to day and puts up there Circus tent &c.[7]

12   Buisness Just So So. Reports of a Tremendious rise in the Rivers above   All are Said to bee rising very fast in deed but The water is on the fall at this place, My Poor old Rome Died to day under the Table whilst we were at Dinner   He Came in and Died in a minute or two after he Layd Down without a Kick or a strugle, Poor old Fellow. I understand that Poor old man George, The Ox Driver, Died yesterday with cholera Down at Mr Winns   He was a faithfull old Servant, Poor old man, I understand That a number of Places are under water and are still getting under Every day, I have planted no Corn as yet and I am in Dout Kow [now] whether I shall or not

13   The River is very high and thought to be on a Stand to day but the Swamps is rising very fast and greate number of Plantations are already under water and they are a mooving there hands off there places and Some there stocks. A Mr Buel Came Down this Evening On the Natchez with Stock and Hands and So did a Mr Moore, There was a number of Planters on Board, Some Cholera on Gen Sparrows place. Has Lost two of his hands and 2 more very Sick, I was at the Circus to night and tis the Best Performance of the Kind that I have seen for a Long time if Ever. Buisness Quite dull and The Rondo Tables are all Stoped and buisness I think Dull from the fact,[8] Winston in the Swamp and has been for a week, I wrote a Letter this Evening to Mr Miller and told him One Hundred Dollars that I Sent to him by Julia Eliotte On the Princess Last trip

14   Buisness Only Tolerable, There was a Day Circus To day for The Benefit of The Asylum, very Generous in them indeed,[9] The River is Falling at this Point and a greate many Per-

---

[7] On March 8, 1850, the Natchez *Courier* announced the coming of the "Mammoth Double Circus."

[8] An act of the state legislature prohibited the playing of rondo, pool, keno, and similar gambling games. See Natchez *Courier*, March 12, 1850.

[9] The performance was for the benefit of the St. Mary's Orphan Asylum.

sons are overflown already, A Poor Fellow that belonged to Mr McNiel Died to day very Sudenly under the Hill. He Droped Dead in the Street   His Life was Insured I am told, This morning Got a Letter from Mr Miller which informd of The One Hundred Dollars That he receivd Said money I Sent to him by Miss Julia Eliotte   It was to day that Mr Henderson Hired my big Sorril Horse. He got him this Evening. This I Consider the first ½ day at 37½ per day

     15   River has fallen about 5 or 6 inches in all   The Circus Company is here and geting Crouded Houses in the old Parker Lot

     16   Buisness pretty fair To day and none at work but myself, Gim & Jeff — We were prety Buisny all day. This Evening Mr Burke and Little Winn and Anderson, yes and Winston, all Came up to day to the Circus I suppose   Winston he was Sick and The Doctor was sent for as soon as he Came. Dr Blackburn Came

     17   After I Closed up shop or after Dinner I took my Horse Cuff and wrode Out through Col Binamans fields and I Saw Cuff, no Little Dick, and my Sorril mare and her Colt. The Colt Looks very well and is Growing finly I think   We were all Out a Hunting Cattle &c. but did not find The Cowse that we were in Serch of   Gim Came through thare and Brot Little Dick

     18   I was Quite unwell, had a chill and was sick all the Evening, Old Winston was quite sick to day and the Dr Came up to see him and prescribed for him   He saw me but did not prescribe, Mr Waller Came to see me to day and to Look at The fence where I wanted him to Build a Small House, We talked it over and he Left, I remained all The Evening at Home

     19   Buisness very dull to day. Nothing new   The River appears to be On the fall, Corn is worth 1 dollar a Barrell, Edd Hoggatt is in town This Evening, Gim has Driven up Patsy Higgins & her Calf about 2 weeks old, prehaps 3 weeks, and also Driven up Abigail and her Calf That She has Proberbly had it this morning, Mr N. L. Carpenter paid this Evening forty dollars this being the Ballance on Sixty dollars that I Loand him Several weeks ago

     20   Buisness Quite Brisk to day. Dr Levi Baker Came To Borrow $20. I promised to Lend him ten and would hand it to the Brother Sam Baker   I wrode down To Browns Mill and Bot 30 pieces of Scantling 20 ft Long and 2 pieces 16 ft, 4 by 6, and

2 dito 20 ft, 4 by 6, but did not pay for the Same untill I get
Some more   The Amount of the Bill was $11.16

     21   I was under the Hill at Mr Browns mill   This was to
get Some Lumber and I got as Follows.

22 Scanling	3x4	20 ft	440 — 1½	6.60
2 Post	4x6	20 ft	80 — 1½	1.20
2 Dito	4x6	16 ft	64 — 1½	0 96
16 Pieces	3x9	16 ft	576 — 1½	8 64
2 pieces	4x6	30 ft	120 — 1½	1 80
588 ft W. Boarding			588 — 2	11.76

                                               $ 30.96

     22   Charls is Sick this morning and Sends the Key of the
Shop and I Sent Winston To work in his Place, & he made 4
dollars very Easy indeed by work, No the above is now a mistake for it was not to day that Charles was Sick

     23   Nothing new   Buisness rarther dull

     24   I worked in the Shop untill The usual hour and Then
Closed up and after Dinner I wrode Out in Search of my Cattle
and we did not find them all

     25   Buisness very dull indeed and nothing new, Mr Pearce
Came up this morning and Paid me twenty Dollars for two months
wages of Peggy up to the 24th inst. and he brought Peggy home
with him, Reports all well, The water is still very high and is
falling a Little at this Point. It has fallen in all about 10 inches
at this Place   Mr Burk was up to day and brot $27 for 12 Cord
of wood that the S. B. Griffin Yaterman took. This I Recollect
was 13 Cords that I Left thare and he reported Only 12. This is
strange I think and I dont Like it, He reports the Corn as having
Came up and Looks Like it is a good Stand. I was under the Hill
to day and Bot 12½ Bushells of Corn at Mr Marriners   It was
good Corn, Ed Hoggatt went Out home to day and he Promised
to Come in and Live with me One year to finish his trade, I Sent
down 2 ploughs this Evening by Mr Burk and 2 Axes also

     26   I sent under the Hill to day and bot as Follows

1 ps	5x6	30 ft	1½	1.13
1	2½x10:21	40 ft.	2 cts	80
300 ft	Com W. Boarding		1½	4.50

                                               6.43

2 Painted tubs	75
1 Doz Plates	35
1 " Cordial	3 75

4.85

I Spoke to Mr Waller to get him to Commence my work to morrow morning & he promised to do so — This morning Peter Came
up and has worked about the yard all day. I went Down to the
Stable to day and Swaped away my old Sorril Horse Samson and
gave $12 to Boot for a Little Sorril mare That Tip. use to own   I
Swaped with a Mr [blank]   Peter Seys that they have planted
the uper field and has Plowed the uper part of the Hard Scrable
Field but had not Planted it yet and spoke of its being very wet,
too wet he thought for Plowing

27   This has been very Cold and wet. The Snow fell to
day in abundance. It snowed for several hours and it fell in and
on the City for Several hours and the Ground became quite
white   It thawed Considerably in the afternoon. Oh it was a
very heavy Snow[10] — Considerable snow Balling in the streets
among the Boys — River is falling very Little at present, Say ½
inch in 24 hours

28   To day has been a much pleasenter day than yesterday
was, and nothing new   Buisness was better than yesterday — the
River Falling Little [as] yet, Mr Waller Commences to day at
a Late hour to put up the Little Frame house in the yard, Isum
also Commences to put up the gallery Post up a[t] the Dalshimer
Store, Jeff goes down in Country to Shave Mr W. Stanton

29   Buisness has been dull, very indeed, I had three Loads
of Lumber hauled up this Evening from Mr Browns Mill Consisting of Scantling, Joice & Flooring   Commenced to day to
wether Bourd the back Building. Mr Y. Raily Paid 2 Dollars to
night for Shaving acct. Mr Martin informs me that that Portion
of the Land that Lay in next to me was not included in the Land
of Mess[rs] Stockman & Fletcher at the time that the Planters
Bank had a mortgage on the Same for Mr Newman when he made
the sceizure on Stoman & Fletcher Land   He did not have it in
Said mortgage, but that he thought that the Land was still in
there Possession   Any how Mr Withers did not Sell that Portion
of it to Wade & Winn — but that it has Since been Sold to them.

30   Buisness very Good. To day good   The River is still

---

[10] The Natchez *Courier*, March 29, 1850, stated that it was the heaviest snow-
storm within the memory of the oldest citizens.

falling at this Point. Mr Waller was at work to day a Little while at the Building in the yard   I wrode under the Hill to day and paid for three Cedar Post which amounted to 3.15 cts and the[n] I paid Mr Baker 7.50 cents for 5 windows Sash at 10 cts and I paid Isum $4 for his work a Puting up of The Gallery Post in the Dalshimer House — Charles is Still Sick and Winston is Keeping the shop under The Hill

31   I Saw Mr Wolcott To day and he Came up for the Purpose of Going up the River to Indiana   After Dinner I Took a wride out to Col Bingamans and I Took my Big Sorrill mare and The Bob Tail mare That I got of Mr Wickersham. I had The Small mare put to Ruffin and the Big Sorril mare put to Grimes and I Brought my Lame mare away with her Colt. I want to wean her if I Can. I met Jack on my way in and I told him that I gave him a perfect Clearance on my Books which he Seemed very glad of — I met Capt Nevit to day and gave him $80 for a check on the Brittons & Co at Sight. Antony has been Sick all this week

April 1   Buisness quite dull. The Carpenter was at work to day at my Building on State St. The River is at a Stand at Present and has been for Several days. Winston took my two mares Out to Col Bingamans to the Stalions Grimes and Ruffin — They both Took — Mr C Wolcott Started up the River this forenoon to Indiana and he gave me twenty Dollars to pay Doctor Vol Metcalfe and he gave me 2.75 ct to pay his Taxes with and his taxes was 3.80 ct and I paid it and he paid me the Difference before he Left. The Mesrs Brittons paid Capt Nevitts Check for $80 to day — I wrote a Letter to day to Mr Mosbey and sent it by Mr Wolcott, I Saw Mr Ford to day and he told me that He had Mr George Winns Receipts for all the Land that he had at his Death and that he would Show me the Certificates at any time that I would Call and see him, But that it was nesesary that he should Keep the Certifficates to Show his authority to Sell The Land

2   Mr Waller finished Wether Bourding and then Commenced and Finished Puting on the shingles, I wrode Out this Evening On Richards Colt for the first time I Ever wrode Him, Williams old Roan Mare had a Colt To day about 9 Oclock. Tis a Little Filly with a white Place in its forehead, The Little Brown Heiffer of old Francis was brot up this Evening with a Calf about 3 or 4 days old I think

711

3 Mr Waller was at work To day at the Building in the Yard and will no Doubt make a Finish To-morrow. Col Binga-mans Horses arrived the morning from below, River Rose 2 inches L. Nt [last night] I pd Mr Brown to day Forty Eight Dollars, fifty five cts for Lumber

4 Mr Waller Finished to day working On my Frame House in the yard. The old Bob tail Cow fell to day and was unable to get up untill Late this Evening

5 I Paid Mr Waller to day Seventy five Dollars for The Building of my Frame House in the yard, This was for the work alone. The Materials I Paid for myself and they are near $130. I was Surprised to think how things runs up to an Amount, I had my Little Sorril Filly wrode to day for the first time by Peter and afterwards by Richard — The Paint Colt Threw Richard yester-day Evening and ran off and This Evening he threw Peter, Mr Waller paid me $37.50 that he has owed me for a Long time, Gim & Peter was to day making a Fence.

6 The River Still Falling and The Lord be thanked for it. The article of Corn is worth a Dollar and Oats to day 50 cts Maj. Young was in town To day and we had a Settlement To The First inst. as Follows, Charls Medicall Bill, Dr Blackburn, for 1848 & 49.

The Drs Bill was	$20.00
Two undershirts & 2 prs Draws	3.50
6 Shirts	12.00
One pr Pants	3.50
This part Maj. pd me, Say 39 dolls, &	
8 Dollars I paid The Maj in Cash	11.00
	$50.00

Mr Martin Miller pd me to day on acct five Dollars & Left for N. O A Mr Finn pays me to day a Ballance of Rent $2. Our News Papers are in morning for Mr J C. Calhoun

7 Buisness to day has been good, Gim and Peter was to day Laying Brick in the yard, Old Bob tail Cow had a Calf Just before day this morning and the Little white Heifer, old Sooks Yearling, has a Calf to day — River is falling near One inch in the Last 24 Hours. After The Shop Shut up to day & after Dinner I took a Horse and wrode out to See for Stock and I went Out to Col Bingamans and I saw old Sarah Bladen with a Colt about 48 hours old by Ruffin and I Saw old Ariline with her Colt Folded On Wednesday Last, and it was a very Large One indeed, Rich-

ard Byron & Peter was a Long And on going Dow[n] in the
Pasture The Paint Colt wran off with Peter and Threw him a
Heavy fall &c.

    8   Buisness Tolerable fair   Gim & Peter was at work Down
at the House paving The yard

    9   Buisness rarther midling. After Breakfast I went under
the Hill and got in the Skift with Mr Pearce & Pearson and went
Down in the swamp   We stoped at Jordens awhile and then at
The Wade & Winn wood yard and Pearce had a paper of some
Kind of Medicine to John Barns, We did not remain Long Thare
but went on Down and got to my Place 7 or 8 minutes of ten
Oclock. I then went out and took a Look at the Corn which ap-
peared to be a very Good Stand both in the uper and in the
Lower Field. On the back ridge found Burke a plowing with
Danny and the Hands at work with there hoes, I then past On
Down and went to Hard Scrable   This I found Only The back
ridge ploughed and the fence Down in several Places, The front
Ridge being too wet to plough. I then Came on up and took
Dinner and afterwards made Anderson take the old Bill Horse
and wride before me to pilot me across the water, I wrode Fany.
We got over prety Easy tho it was Dangerous   I then Came on
to town and I met Mr Ford and had a Long talk with [him], in
his Lane near the midle or Lower End of it. Subjects was as
Follows: Certifficates of my Land, Transfers of Philo Andrews
having never been recorded, His Finding a Cedar Post as his true
Line above his Field, Mosbey Plot with his Boy John, Punish-
ment to John, Js Confession, Little Winn with trecherous ways,
Promises to Come to town and bring me the Duplicates on the
Certifficates That he has of the Land That I Bot of Mosbey and
Winnslow Winn, The Irishman takes old Jeff to day through
mistake and works him in a Cart but could not Drive him, Poor
Little John gets his thigh Broken to day by a piece of Timber
that fell On it in the yard. Dr Blackburn put in Splints and at
night I put it in a Box to Keep it Straite, William takes his old
R. mare to Grimes 1st time

    10   The Boys, ie the two Peter and Gim, was white wash-
ing inside of the new House and did not get through at that. Buisness some what dull for the Season, and nothing new

    11   A Mr Patison is married to night To Miss Helm. He
resides in Orleans, Peter and Gim is or was at work to day at
the House white washing   They made a Sort of a Finish of it
in the new House and then gave the Kitchen a Coat. Little John

has his Leg put in the Box by me the other night is doing very well, The Letter from N. Orleans to day states that my Little Anna did not make her Speech at the Examinatun as was Expected She would,   Thus I am Disappointed

    12   Nothing new Has transpired to day worth attention. Peter and Gim are still white washing in the yard &c. Mr Ford was in town to day and He Brought up 3 Certificates to show me that Mr George Winn did own The Land that he, Mr Ford, Sold to William Mosbey & wife and To Winslow Winn, and The Following is a Correct Coppy of the Certificate That I Coppied, The uper Line of The Certificate was written in Pencil writing, ie, The words, Give a Certificate of West Part.

NO 925½   Receivers office Washington Miss. Class No 1 —
                per act of 2d March 1821, May 25th 1829. Received of George Winn a fre P c. of Adams County The Sum of Forty five Dollars, [blank] Cents in Cash, [blank] Dollars and Cents in forfeited Land stock which with the Discount herein after Stated and allowed at the rate of 37½ per cent under the act 21st of March 1828, is in fee of the Ballance Due or to become due for the Purchase money of the Fractional Sec No. 9 in Township No. 6 of Range 4 West Containing 236 acres at $2 per acres, Purchased 15th Oct. 1815 (Contains 236 instead of 200 acres) Viz,

Cash paid as per above $45.00
Discount On $72.00 at the rate of 37½ per Cent,   27.00
                                            ———————

                      Total Ballance   72.00
         A Wm Daniel, Receivere

I wrode under the hill this Evening and bot 5 Barrells Corn and Then went to a Glass Boat and Bot ½ Doz of ink and 6 hoes and returned and went to the Commons and found Only 29 head of my Cattle, Out of 52 of them.

    13   Buisness fair, I had Gim and Peter white washing To day. I wrode under the Hill this Evening and bot 2 gallons of Peach Brandy at 1.25 cts per gallon and I Bot 70 cts worth of writing Paper and 3 mugs for the Boys and I went to day To Mr Dick and got a Bridle and had it charged to me @ 1.50 cts   Peter wrides the paint Colt this Evening and Dan wrode the Little Sorril Filly out for the First time that she was Ever wrode out of The yard

    14   Buisness rarther dull. After the Shop was Closed or after Dinner I took a wride Out by Col Bingamans to See my

Tip mare, but I did not See her. Jeff was along and wrode Dicks Colt and the Colt Could not throw him at all — William & Richard & Dan was along and Dn wrode my Little Grimes Colt

15 The River is Falling a Little and Corn has wrisen to 1 dollar & 25 cts per Barrell. The Sorril Horse, big Jim, Fell in to the Byou To day I Suppose and myself, Wm, Peter & Gim got him out again — The Little Cow that I got of the Pock marked Butcher up the Hollar, has a Calf to day in Mr Marshals Pasture, Edd Hoggatt was in town yesterday Evening and Staid all night and went home this Evening. Came in for to use Ruffin. Gim & Petter at worke at the Shed Fence to day. I got to day 70 ct worth of Nails at Mr Barkers, nails that he Furnished as his Part. I Bot Bacon Hams to day at 6½ ct. and I got 87 pds of it and I Bot 8 Poplar Scantling @ 1½ cts per ft. — I Consented to day to Let Edd Hoggatt in Our race with young Ruffin Colts   He is to run a Colt from The Grey mare that is now about 2 weeks old. The Entry is $50, forfeit $25.00

16 Gim and Peter puting up The Fence between me and the Turner Lot and was doing a Little white washing also, We Commenced to work in the Garden, Planted a few Cabage Seed, Removed a few Brick &c. Spoke to Mr Waller To make me a pair of Steps to Building at the House, $18 in Cash and he is to do it for $20.00   Corn is worth 1.25 per B. and meal 1.00 per Bushell — Mr Garnett Howell Died to day at his Residence on the Lake

17 Buisness has been prety fair To day. I went under the Hill to day and bot 30 Slats 12 ft Long at 1 cent the runing foot, amounting to 3.60 cts, and I bot a Canoe from Young Lindar at 25 ct, then I went to the Lower Landing and bot a Bale of Hay, pd $2.15 for it, wt 175 pds — William takes the big Sorril mare out to Grimes this morning and Wm Drives The Abigale Heifer up this Evening with a fine young Bull Calf, She had it to day, Gim and Peter Dug out the Privy to day and was all Day in cleaning it out. Corn is worth 1.25 per B., Hay 1.25 cts per hd., meal 1.25 per Bsh., Bran 1.25 per Bushell, &c

18 Buisness very dull to day   Gim And Peter at work about the yard making a Cross Fence &c. Mr Garnet Howell was Burried yesterday, He died the day before — Bill Nix brought up a Ladies wig for Mrs Little   Cost 15.00

19 The Boys Gim & Peter Commenced the wash House &c. River nearly at a Stand, Nothing new   Corn worth 1.25 per B, Hay 1.25 per Hd, Bran 1.25 per hd

20 Buisness Tolerable fair, William Commences to Break his Little Filly by the Bell mare. He took his old Roan mare Out to Col Bingamans to Grimes, The River is Falling a Little at present, Mr Benbook pd five Dollars I Loaned him the other day — Mr S Cox Came Down this Morning with his Family

21 Buisness So So. I remained at Home all day, ie, I wrode out in the afternoon and went to Col Bingamans Pasture To Look at The two mares and they were both doing very well, Sam, The Stock Driver, was wriding Little Dick and has been wriding him for a week or more, Mr Burke was up this morning and took Down Eight Barrells of Corn at 1.25 per Barrell, Anderson was up with him, They both got Home Safe & Drunk

22 After Breakfast this morning I Started down in the Swamp in Mr Pearce Skift, We got down to the Place Erly and went right to work to plant a Small Cut of Corn in the Lower field, which we did. Burke I found away down the fence takeing a Bee hive and was prety Drunk, He took the plough and went to work Laying of[f] Corn rows, We got through with the Planting and then Commenced to work on the 1st Cut of Corn on the Back ridge and Came within a rowe or 2 of finishing it wich was a tall days work Gim & Peter got down and Commenced to work after Dinner, Peter was Plowing with Mr Burk, Gim, Phill, Anderson, Zora, Silvia & myself was hoeing, Antony was Plowing in the uper field, Mary & Peggy both on the Sick List, Wm Brot in the Bell Mare Filly with a young Hs Colt. Had it this Morning.

23 We Commenced on the 1st Cut that we Left off yesterday and made a Finish of it and Started on the Second Cut in the Lower field and did a short row or so

24 We were up by times this morning and went to work in the Lower field and got nearly half done when a rain Came Down and we had to Leave, We then went to the House for a few minutes, We then turned out and had a few rows plowed in the Cabbage Patch. We then Set out I think about 7 Rowes of Cabbage. We then had the Irish Potatoes Plowd and then Commencd to work them. We got through Just at night — Myself, Gim, Antony, Anderson, Phill, Silvy, Mary & Zory & Byron.

25 I was in the Swamp & Erly in The morning I got up and Set the Hands to work to put out Potato Slips. We put 5 Roes of Them out in Short order — I then wrode out in the Cane with Anthony, Came home & Staid untill Dinner, Then after

Dinner started to town on Cuff — Jim & Anderson in the Skift   I
Drove up The old Black Horse & The orphan Boy   We brought
up a Small Lot of Cabbage Plants, We set them out in the Garden   Reports are that The River is rising above all of them, Mc
Glazer mooved in my Shop to day at $5 per Month.

26   I Started Anderson Down This morning with 1½ Bush-
ells of Meal and 1 Barrell Seed Corn, 6 pds of Tobaco for the
wemen, 4 hoes. To day I paid Mr Gaw ten Dollars for Eight
Barrells of Corn That I Sent Down Last Sunday morning by Mr
Burk & Anderson, I sent Down a Sifter to day — I pd Mr Tea-
ford $1.25 to Day for 2 Barrells of Corn that was Goten by the
Boys 27th of March 1850   Mrs Little Pd $15.50 for a wig I
Sent her the other day

27   It was to day that Mr Bunting ran his Horse John
Anderson VS. a Bay mare that Mr Jaqumine Claims as his. They
ran a ½ mile and The mare won the race very Easy. Their was
Considerable beting on the race and The Parties [that] were beting and wining was Messrs Al. Davis, John Mardice, Mr S. Cox.
Bets got at the Close ran $100 to 20 &c. I Lost with Mr Waller
$2.50 on the race and 1 dollar with Jack   This was on
time   They made it in 52½ Seconds, I won a Dollar bet from
Mr Purnell, a Dollar Bet from Maj Elward and a Dollar bet from
Mr Mackey of Jefferson, 2 Dollars from Mr Bontura. This was
a regular Bite for the proper name of the nag was Ularlee and
she formerly belonged to Capt Minor and was Sold to Mr Prior
and was put in the hands of Mr Jaquemine as a Bite. Mr R.
McCary went to New Orleans this Evening on the Princess and I
wanted him to bring up my Daughter with him — He promised
to do so

28   Buisness Only So So. I wrode Down in the Bottom
This Evening and sent [blank] in the Swamp to await my Orders. Phill and Anderson went to the Swamp

29   Buisness Only Tolerable, Reports are that The uper
Rivers are all very high and are Still rising. The river is Rising
at this Point also. Mr Dillon was Shot to day and hurt by a run
away belonging to Mr Stanton whilst Dillon was in pursuit of
him, William Nelson was brot up and put into Jail this Evening
for a charge against him about writing a pass for a Servant of
Mr Elick Henderson. He was tryed before Esqr Coffin and held
to Bail in the Sum of 2000 dollars for his appearance to Court,
but he did not give it and was Commited, The Partner of Nelson
I understand has run off and Left his Boat   This would Look a

goodeal Like he was Guilty of some offence, A Mr Baird was Elected Road Inspector to day by the Board of Police, Salery 1500 Dollars

30   Buisness Tolerable fair. The City very Healthy. Corn 1.25 per Bl, Hay 1.25 a Hd   The River nearly upon a stand. Mrs Spruel and One of Her Sons Came around to tell that Mr Nelson had Sent around for me to Come and See him at the Jail. He wanted me to go his Bail and Keep him out of Jail untill Court. I of Course, Explained my self, with Satisfaction to my-self, I Sent the Bell mare Filly to Wood Pecker To day for the first time.

May 1   Buisness Tolerable fair, This has been a gay day indeed for hundreds of children are perading the streets. Several fairs agoing On. Wm Nelson sent for me to day to go On his bail and take him Out of Jail   I told him very promptly that I was not in a situation to do anything in that way at present, for I was and am at present under a Pledge to not go Security for any One at all for no shape nor maner, and I told him from what I had herd in regard to his Case that they would not be able to Convict him at all, and he Said he thought not himself but that he wanted to get out very much to prepare himself for tryal. He then requested me to go and See Lawyer Sanders and to tell him to Come around and See him. I did so and Col Sanders Said that he would attend to him in a ½ hour and that he was at that time drawing up or doing some writing for Mr and Mrs Sigmond who was agoing off to Urope, I find out to day that Mr Waller cheated me Sharply in Selling me the Sofa yesterday. It has but 3 Legs   Very well, I must get Even with him if I Can — Our Poor old Bob tail Cow died to day and was hauld off — The remains of Dr Benbrook was brot up this morning on the S Boat Lounds

2   McCary Came up from New Orleans on the Princess and did not bring up my Daughter Anna as I requested him to do. He said She was unwilling to Come up untill her cousins Comes up — He brot no news. Jeff wrode out home this Evening on the Horse that Edd wrode in, The River is falling a Little at present and The Cause is owing to the breaks in The Levees up about Mrs Lees and Milligen bend

3   Buisness to day Quite Dull, Jeff is Out in the Coun-try. Anderson Came up To day to Get Corn   He seys they are Out. He Seys they have goten through with Planting Hard Scrable Back ridge but they had not Plowed or planted The front ridge at all, and he told me about Mr Burkes having made some re-marks about Tobacco. So it is all well, Reports him as being Drunk yesterday a Good Part of the Day, Little Winn Came up with Anderson. I Sent Down Five Barrels of Corn at 1.25 cts per B and I Sent two Bushells of meal at 1 Dollar per Bushel and I Sent a new plow Line. Alx. Johnsons wife went Down in the Skift with her 2 children. I Loaned Mrs Dallia Three Dollars this morning. The river is very high & in the Swamps the water is 3 inches higher than it has been this Season

4   Buisness has been very Dull   In Consequence of it Corn is selling at 1 Dollar & 25 ct per Barrell, Hay is worth 1.25 per hd. Dr Broom Sells at auction to day a poor woman and her 3 children that was Set Free by a Mr ——— who was the Father of her children. Seventeen hundred Dollars was what they Sold for. Purchased by Mr Yorke

5   Buisness was Tolerable fair Only   I wrode out After Dinner the Woodville Road as far as Col Bingamans. I tryed The Big Sorril Mare to Grimes and She refused him. I Saw the big bob tail mare and She needed the Horse very much. I Left orders to have her taken up to the Horse

6   My young Roan mare Lost her Colt this morning   It was a splendid Large Filly. I am sorry that She has Lost it for it was So Large. It was marked very much Like its mother, Wil-liam Lost his Puppy this Morning   He was stollen from him, Buisness is good to day. Anderson & Petter Came up to day on the Skift to work out a short time, They having workd the Corn over, Circuit Court Commences this morning. Mr W. Martin Canes old Mr Stockwell in the Street on acct of his abuse &c.

7   It was To Day that I bot The young Black Filly from Mr Henderson. I gave him Thirty Dollars in Cash and my acct. VS. him for the hire of my Big Bunting Horse, which [I] find to be 9 days hire at 3 Bits per day. It was To day that I met Mr Lewis and pd him for The Bedsted and the mattress which amountd to 1.75 cts. It was all this forenoon that I was in Doubt about wether Mr Henderson had my Horse 1 week and a few Days or 2 weeks which I thought was the true time — Tho it always turns out wrong for me for I find out that it was 9 work-ing Days, Court is in Cession   Considerable Buisness, Dr Mc-Intosh Williams Died This morning of Inflamation of The Bow-ells. He was Supposed to have had the cholera at first

8   Dr I McWillams Died yesterday and was buried To day out at his Family Burriel ground — Greate many Persons thare

at the Funeral — My William was out this morning a Looking for my big Sorril Mare and her Colt, Fidler and his old dun horse and Little Dick. Tis stranger than I Cannot see in it — Wm Returns this Evening and found the Horses in Scotts old Field. Mr Wm W Cochran gets married to night to Mrs Campell. She is Daugh[t]er of Dr Ogdon, I Sent 50 cts of Sugar & 50 ct Coffee & 1 gallon Mollases to the Swamp

9 Buisness Only So So. Old Mr Congo gets a verdict in the Case or Suite VS Mr Fisk. He got allowed him by the Court $1200.00 It was for Cutting Timber from the Land of Mr Congo. I Sent The Bell mare Filly arround to Wood Pecker yesterday Evening. This makes the Second time. Peter & Anderson at work in town yet — River is thought to be on a stand Corn is 1.25 per Barrell, Hay per hd. 1.25, Oats 65 ct a Bsh. Gim is Down in the Swamp and it was to day that Mr Caradine Called me and told me that it was all Settled, ie that I Could Send for Gim and have him home I thanked him and Said I would do. Mr L. Bingaman was at the Corner at the time and some other Gentlemen.

10 Court is in Cession Still. To day The Court Decided VS. Mr Rhasa Parker. This is what might have been Expected for it what [was] a suit brought VS Mr Pullem or Pullin for a Slave Woman that Mr Parker Bot of him some 10 years ago and then Suffered about 7 years to Elapse before he Brought Suit. Very Large Party To night at Mrs Austin Williams. Greate many are invited and will be thare. I was at Auction to day and Bot a Carriage for $30. It Formmerly belonged to Mr Forman. It was cheap I think, Two of Mrs Minors old Carriages was Sold thare also to day, 1 for 53 dollars to Mr P. Smith, the other 28 Dolls for [to] Dunham.

12 Mr Waller Puts up The Gallery Post This Evening or to day — I Saw Mr Martin this Evening and he told me That The Court had Ordered The Survery and appointed Mr Tho Kenney To make the Survey — Judge Thatcher was The Attorney for Mr Wade The Judge was in favor of Geting Mr J L. C. Davis To make the Survery but at the Susjestion of Mr Martin, Mr Kenney was appointed, I am very glad to here that for I think that he will do Justice to both Parties, Gim and Anthony Came up this Evening and They reported my Sorril Horse Bill Dead which I am very Sorry to hear indeed, They Say that the Corn is on the back Ridge about waist high, They Say The Corn is clean and They have Just Commenced to Plow it over To day, Old Phill, The old

Scamp, has got up an old Sow and Feeding away my Corn, Anderson and Peter Came up to night from working under the Hill and brot up only $5.70 for the week, This I consider ve[r]y Poor work. This may Pass but next week I will make The arrangements myself, Dr McGoun Paid me to day ten dollars on his years bill for Shaving &c. His year is up I think in May inst., Court has ajourned untill Monday next

    13   Buisness not very Brish for Court times — After Closing The Shop this day or after Dinner I Took a wride out with the Boys. I wrode Dicks Ball Petter, Wm wrode The Roan Filly, Richard, Mariah Henderson, Byron, Virginia Burns, Dan, Alice Gray — I wr[o]de out by Mrs Danolds, then through by Mr Marshalls, then back Home, We met the young Marshalls and Talked awhile Then we Left and got a few Mulbuerys, They are wripe now. About a quarter past 6 Oclock This morning Fanny Hatcher had a Little Horse Colt, She had it in the yard, It resembles Dicks Horse Ball Peter

    14   I went under the Hill to day and Bot 10 Sacks of Corn and The Weight of it was 1270 lbs. The first five Sacks weighed 654 and the 2nd 615. This was at 75 cts per Bushell and The amount was $16.87½   I Then Bot 200 ft of Pine stuff at 1½ ct per ft. and I then Bot of Mr Wash 110 lbs Bacon @ 5½ cts. I then Bot of him 216 ft of Plank @ 1¼ — Then a Barrell of Flour, $6.00   Mr Shatts Sold me 108 Hogs Heads for $5. Mr Burke was up to day and I paid him $2.00 in Cash and I Sent 2 Bushells of meal Down, a Bucket of Tar

    15   Several indictments for Playing at Rondo to day by the Court, Yesterday John, the Poor Boy, or "Homer", was found Guilty of Grand Larceny   This was for Stealing a few St[r]ips of Plank from The Church Building On Pearl St, N L Carpenter was the informer, Gim has been at work all day to day at the House Making a couple of Gates. Winston and him Built me a Little Carriage House yesterday. I Sent my Little Roan mare to Limber John This Evening For the first time, I Sent Mr R. McCary My Red neck Cow with a young Calf that she had this morning on the Pine Point — My Horses are all Out at Present   I have taken them out of Lanieres Pasture, Mr Boyer has got a Great many in thare, Peter Came home Sick this Evening. I gave him Pepper & Brandy. Mrs Battles was Sick Last [night]   Sent Jeff & Cinda for Dr Davis

    16   I got up Erly this morning and went to the Shop and Saw that the shop was opened. I then Took an Erly Breakfast and then Started Down in the Swamp with Mr Pearce in his Skift. I took Down about ½ Bushell of Pease To Plant and I took Down 1 Dollars worth of Sugar and 50 cts worth of Coffee, I took Down Anderson with me and Set him to Plowing. I then Commenced to Plant Peas in the Cut below the Potatoe Patch. We did not make quite a finish of this Cut. Burke & Anderson Plowing and I Draped Pease & Hoed. Phill, Sylvia, Mary, Peggy with Hoes — The Court tryed Mr Conners man Buisness rarther dull for Court to be in Cession yet Such is a fact   I was in the Swamp this morning and I went to work to Planting a few more Pease in the Lower Field for we were at work in the Lower Cut in the field next to the woods, I worked all day to day with the hoes and I think we got about 1⅓ of it done. Myself, Phill & Anderson, Sylvia & Peggy at the hoes — and Mr Burke Plowing, Mary Sick. Violet Caught a red Slut to day in the Field. I suppose that She has fallen off Some Boat.

17   Court in Cession. To Day they tryed Gen. Stantons man for Shooting Mr Dillon. He was accquited very Easly

18   Buisness not very Good for Saturday; I thought very few Strangers &c. Mr York Buys Out the Interst of Mr Edwards in the Concordia Intilegencer. The River is near upon a Stand   I was under The hill to day and Bot a Bale of 160 lbs, $2.05, and a Sack of Oats, 1.45 ct   I then Bot a Sack of wry, 2 Bushells and 12 lbs, 85 ct per Bushell — 1.80   This I think I will plant in the fall — Mr D. P. Jackson Brot down his work Stock from his Plantation to day, Oxen & Mules & Horses — Mr Burke & wife Came up to night and so did Anderson and Brought up Violet & Sylvia and they Brot up 8 Sacks of wool in the Skift, This was of the Last cuting from the Sheep — Now I was fully of the opinion that The work that I Left them to do in the Lower cut would have been Done in a single day after I Left, ie on Friday and now it is Saturday night and They have not done it yet, Well I have my own trouble, That I do. Maj Young Came in to day and wanted to Borrow Some money. I declined on acct. of having a good deal to pay out very Shortly. Peter pd his wages to night & Anderson. They only worked in all 5¼ which was for Both, 3.95

19   I Sent down 2 shoulders of Bacon and 4 Jowls or Hogs heads, Cost 1.35 cts, ½ Bushel of meal 50 cts, and a Bushell of meal that I think Burke got at Shatts. This I had paid for. After Dinner I took a wride Out, William & Robert, Byron, Richard & Dan was with me   We went down in the Waltern field. Mr Tyson had Just Bot it and was moving into it with his Hands &c.

20   Buisness has been quite Brisk — Nothing new. Court
Still in Cession   Criminall Court is over. Sever[al] Sentanced
to the Peneteniary   Antony Came in to day from Mr Hoggatts.
He has been out thare 8 or [9] days — He will go down in the
Swamp To morrow Some time, Large Partee to night down at
Dr Jenkens and a great number has gone down to it, Jeff Cut 5
of my Little Bulls and the Larges Calld the Heggins Bull is
Bleeding wonderfully and will Die I am affraid

21   Buisness not so good as it was yesterday, Nothing
new. I find The Higgins Bull will die so I traded him off for five
Dollars To Gorge Isler — He Came and Killd him in my yard —
Anthony went down to day to work   Has been Out home 9 days
— River is still rising a Little at this Point, Everything high in
the way of Provisions &c.

22   I would Call this rarther a Dull Day in the way of
Buisness — I Sent The Roan Filly To day to Limber John   This
is The 2nd time she has been to him, I had Fanny & the old
Black Horse put in the Carriage this Evening and Dick wrode in
it up to Mr Boyers Shop to have the Axil tree straitened

23   Buisness quite dull I think for the season — Court Ad-
journd this Evening Late, I wrode under The Hill this Evening
and was about to make Some arrangement to Buy Some Corn &
Some Hay and Send it Down by his Boat, I then wrode up to
Mr Malerys and Bot 10 sacks of meal at 1 dollar Each. I paid
him for them and will Send for them tomorrow I think, I took
a Long wride on Richards Colt. I Consider him Broke now, The
River is not Falling any as yet, but we Expect a fall Shortly as
it is falling above prety Smartly; Roasting Ears very small   Was
in market this morning from Mr Lapiece Garden, 1st of The
Season

24   I was a good part of To day in Looking up Winstons
acct. with me and I did not find all untill 1 Oclock at night or
after, This is the Last days work that he has done in the shop
for he Leaves to morrow morning with Mr Cox for the North, I
find by Looking over his acct. that I have paid him $170.00 and
I owed him for 2 years and ten months work, at $12.50 per month
— Fany St to Limber John to day, also Roan Filly

25   Streets very dusty, The River Said to be on a stand, I
made a Settlement to day with Winston and paid him as Follows
— To wit — I had paid him up to date The Sum of One hundred
& 70 Dollars 25 cts in Cash and I then agreed to pay Mr Dalshimer $14.75 and I paid Jeff for Winston 10.00

Thus I have paid him	170.25
And Cash to day	100
and assumed Dalshimers Debt of	14.75
and Jeffs Debt that I paid to day	10.00
	———
	295.00

And I owed him for two years and ten months work for me which together with Eighty 7 dollars that he gave me to Keep for him makes   512.00

here Subtract what I have pd him   295.00

                                    ———

which Ballance I gave him my note for $217.00

Mrs Erheart gave me to day to Keep for her a note of Messrs Walker & Collins note for 5 hd dollars   Edward Hoggatt gave me in cash to day fifty five to Keep for him   Little Bell mare Filly refuses Wood Pecker to day

    26   Our Streets are very dusty indeed, We need a Little rain very much indeed, After the Shop was closed or in the afternoon I took a wride On my Horse Billy and I found The Young Red Sides had a Caft Last night or this morni[n]g and So did the Little Black Heiffer. She had it in the yard — We had Radishes for Breakfast The other morning and a few this morning   The[y] are the first that we have had

    27   The River is not Falling nor rising and is quite high — wrode out this Evening to Dixon' and Brot home Richards Little Bull. Mr Fields Gets my old mule up and set him to work to day in the Brick yard, I Saw quite a Large house was Floating pass the City

    28   Buisness only So So. I Saw Dicks Cow on the Commons near Mr Robsens and She had a Calf about ½ past 6 Oclock this Evening and it is a Bull Calf, a red One   I Saw all the Horses Except The old Black and the Orphan Boy — Jeff went out to Maj Chotard and cut a Little Girls hair

    29   After Breakfast This morning myself and Wm Took my Little Skift and Started into the Swamp   We went by the Island and got a few Dew Burrys, Then got home in Good time, I found them at work in the Lower Field in The lower Cut in the Front ridge, I set in and Planted a Lot of Peas and Some Pumpkins Seed. I find that the Corn in The front ridge is rarther Small and Pale and a bad Stand, Greate deal of water in the Slough and has some appearance of rising   The River has risen within a few Days Several inches, I Found Sylvia Laid up Sick and Mary, She did not work the Day Out   Bet She Laid up too.

  30   To day I was in the Swamp and worked all day — I was awakened about 1 Oclock last night by the Noise of the Steamer Princess. She had Came up and was Puting off Four Bales of Hay and five Sacks of Corn, I intended to have went up to town on her but she was off before I Could get out to the gate — The River is very high and is rising a Little tis Said   The Corn was Broken Down Considerably from the wind we had and rain we had the other day

  31   After working in the Corn fields we then stoped and went to Seting Out Potatoes slips and we Finished all Except One Roe — I also Planted a number of Cabbage Seed — 3 papers of them, We worked a part of the time in the garden spot next to the House and it was yesterday that we plantd or Set out the Slips. We went to Killing Rats This morning and we Killed in the Smoke House and Corn crib together 19 Rats. I Left before day this morning and tryed to get up to the City by Pulling the skift up but I could not and I had to return and went to bed again, I worked about down thare untill after Dinner and then I Started up again in the other Skift and Anderson and Wm Pulling — We got up about Dusk or before, Jasper Winn I See is at Mr Fords about to oversee for him — I Brot up 5 Sacks of wool this Evening

  June 1   Things are Growing very fast now for we had a fine rain On Friday night, I paid M. Chas Williams two Dollars and 8 cts for a Ballance on the Bill that he brot me from New Orleans for Corn and Hay — Last Saturday I Sent by him for the above and gave him $30 to pay for it and I find that the 5 Sacks of Corn Amountd to $15.89   This I paid but Sent back the ammount or the Bill and told him to See the clerk of the House and rectify the Small mistake. From what I can understand very Little work was done in the Swamp   They worked a Little while in the garden Scraping Potatoes &c. The Roan Filly was taken to the Horse to day and still takes him

  2   Buisness good to day. Phill and Antony Came up Last night and Anderson Came up this morning before Light and Phill and Anderson went Down this Evening and Left Anthony up here, Common report Seys that Gim Gregory Keeps Rachel Johnson who is the wife of Elick Johnson in the Swamp. They are an awfull Set down thare, Byrons mare had a Colt very Erly this morning

3   Papers State that the Cuba Expidetion has made a Dead Failure, and Gen Lopez is now at Mobile.[11] The Bell Mare Filly refuses Wood Pecker This Evening — 2d time she has done it, Mr Finney Sends his man to do a Little Patch work on the Roof of The Paint Shop this morning, and he did a Little work on Mr Dalshimers House also — Several of Williams Colts has got the Distemper   I Took my big Sorril mare and her Colt Down yesterday to the Tison Pasture, and I took big Gim Down also, Mr Tyson has 23 head of his Cattle Driven Over to day and Sent Down to his Place   Mr Ford & wife Left yesterday for the North on The S. B. Hungarian

4   The River is Said to have fallen a Little Last night but the fall is thought that the Break in the Levy Down at Mr Hendersons is the Cause of the Suden fall, S. B. St. Louis has Bursted her Boilers near St Louis & has Killed 20 & wounded about 40.[12] We again need a Small Shower of Rain, I Sent an Order to Mr. Marriner this Evening To Let Mr Higgins have the 30 Dollar Flat Boat and I would pay him for the Same

5   Buisness rarther Dull for the Season. This morning After Breakfast I Got in a Skift with Miller and Took my Richard with me and we went into the swamp   We Got Down thare Quite Erly in the Day and I found That Burke was sick and that the Hands were all well and had Gone Down to Hard Scrabble to work. I went down thare and found them on the back Ridge and that they had Just Commencd to replant and work the ½ Stand of Corn   I orderd them to go on and replant and not to stop to work the Corn which we did and when we got thr[e]w we Commencd and worked back again to where they first Started, To day we got down as far as about 8 Small Rowes of a Finish on the back Ridge. This we Left untill morrow morning when we shall begin it again

6   We were Still at work on the Ridge and Cannot finish to day   Anthony & Anderson were plowing on the front Ridge at Hard Scrabble, Miller the Dutchman is about to give up the fishing Buisness. The Rain of this Evening prevented us front [from] Doing some Wo[r]ke, Burke is still sick and doing no work. Jeny Winston has a Colt this morning, a Little Filly it is

---

[11] This was the second expedition of Narciso López against Cuba. See article in Natchez *Courier*, June 5, 1850.

[12] An account of the disaster appeared in Natchez *Courier*, June 12, 1850.

7 We were at work at Hard Scrabble, and Anthony & Anderson Finished plowing on the first Ridge, and we did not get through with the cut on the ridge untill about 4 Oclock   The Plows Came over and plowed up the middle on Small Ridge this Evening — the hands after they Left here and went up and Dug Potatoes. They are very good Ones But I planted very few of them indeed — The Coons are very bad indeed   They pull up the Corn nerly as fast as we planted it — Mr Burke was Still doing nothing   Seys he is Sick, very well, At the time we got up to the House and dug Potatoes the Supper was nearly ready and I then waited for Mr Winn to get his Fish ready and it was about 10 Oclock before we got off and we did not reach the city untill nearly 3 Oclock and I will not I think try this mode of travelling. Anderson and the Maj. Winn pulld up the Skift.

8   Byron Sent his mare to Montgomery. She Took him to day; It was this afternoon that Mr. Williams Called and paid me $8.25   This was a Ballance on the 5 Sacks of Corn that the Boat brot up for before this Last trip, at 70 cts per Bushell

9   Buisness rarther dull. After shop closed or after dinner, I took the Boys and went down in Bottom to the Tison Place   I Gave Edd five Dollars of his money yester Evening To [give] Bowen The man that Kept Wood Pecker. Mr Bunting was Taped Last night by Dr Chapalier   Nearly five Gallons of water taken from him, Capt Clay arived To day from New Orleans, Looks bad, I was a Reading O. Ka. Chublee, which is a tisue of Lies from beginning to Ending[13]

10   Clemment Miller Came up to the shop and presented me a Due bill of mine for Sixty Dollars dated Feb 26th, 1848. This I paid and he presented me another acct or Due bill for $70 dollars   This I dont Recollect at Present. Yes, yes, I do   It was money that he Left with me when he went To Mexico, This amount I paid him in Cash — He Told me that he will soon be off for the upper Country. William went into the Swamp Last Evening and returns this morning with Richard who I Left in the swamp Friday Last

11   Buisness is very Dull indeed and in the Afternoon I took a wride in Pasture of Mrs Marshall and Got Some Black Berrys. They were very fine, Wm, Richard & Byron & Dan and Several of Mr Marshalls Little Boys   We all Picked together

---

[13] Johnson probably referred to Lewis Leonidas Allen, *A Thrilling Sketch of the Life of the Distinguished Chief Okah Tubbee, Alias William Chubbee* (New York, 1848).

and Got a fine chance of them, Mr Spain was shot I herd to day by Some man by the Name of Furguson and was Shot Dead — No Provication to Justify it I am told[14] — It was to day that I paid Mr Newman Hester Cummings[15] Tax which was four Dollars and fifty cents. I gave my mare a Light Brush this Evening for 250 yds, I suppose, with Little Dick and the Black mare, and The Littl Sorril mare out run them the first heat and the Black mare beat the Last heat Easy

12   The Natchez brot down the remains of Mr. Spain that was shot up at Water Proof by Ferguson — I had a Race This Evening with Mr Jaqumine, 300 yds — a Little Sorril mare Eliza Parsons Vs The Paint Horse, Casooks, for $2.50   I won the Race Easy, Fielding Culling & Edd Hoggatt was the Judges, The mare won the Race by 15 ft but I think it near about 27 ft,   Gim Came up this morning from the Swamp, and reports all well, Anderson Came up also and brot up the Skift and brot up a Plough To be repaired and wanted as follows, Sugar and Coffee and Molases and Corn, and I sent Down five Barrells of yellow Corn that that I Bot of Mr Walsh at 1.25 per Barrell and I Bot 2 pieces of Meat at 6 ct, Sides, 45 pounds, and 50 ct of Sugar & 50 cts of Coffee, and 50 ct Molases. They are now a Breaking up a Piece of Land in the Slough Just Back of The House from the Levy Down, Saturday they hoed a piece of Corn back of the field next to the China tree, They then worked in the uper Cut in the field, This they Got through with and Commenced on the young Corn near the Oak Field Tree, Thus things stands up to yesterday the 11th inst

13   Buisness openes rarther Dull and I am affraid will Continue So during The Day, Yes it did for we had a heavy rain in the afternoon & Drisled on untill night, Two of my Calves fell in The Sewer to day and was washed Down some distance   One of them went Over The Precipice and Came out Safe. Tis a Calf of a Little Black Cow, The other was a Calf of Patsy Higgings. I got it by the Ear and held on untill I Got Some help   Gim Came with a Rope and we got it arround the neck and we Pulld it out. Tis Strange that we did so well, tis indeed, Edd treats to 6 Bits worth of Ice Cream on the Woodville Road &c.

14   The City has been very dull indeed, Nothing new. After Dinner I Took a Look for My Little Sorrill Mare, and after

---

[14] The shooting took place at Waterproof, Louisiana. See Natchez *Courier*, June 19, 1850.

[15] A free woman of color and friend of the Johnson family.

Taking a wonderfull Long wride and found The mare Just above
The Foundry. I met a Stock Driver of Mr James and he told me
The Little Mare was name Fanny — My Young Black Mare I
did not find at all

15   I was at Auction to day and Bot an old Beareau or 2d
hand One — I paid $4.00 for it and 25 cts for a Small Matress. It
was To day That I Sent William to pay Mr Welsh 6.25 for five
Barrells of Corn that I Sent into The Swamp The other day by
Anderson, Court is Just over in Woodville; very Short term, I
Sent The Roan Filly To the Horse This Evening, I Sent up and
got a Barrell of Lime at Mr Henrys this Evening and will pay
for it when I see The Book Keeper — price 2.25 cts

16   I find buisness Only Tolerable fair. I wrode Down in
The Flat this Evening after Dinner To Look up my stock and I
found Fiddler, Jeff & Mariah Henderson out in Dicksons Pasture, I Left Little Fanny Parsons in the Bottom with my Big
Sorrill mare and Colt

17   To day some time I Started Down in the Skift with
Anderson & Little Winn and Edd Hoggatt went Down with me
and we went to Jordens and I Bot a Large Cypress Log from him
and had Considerable work to Get it out from the Byou. It was
on ground, and Just as we got it ready to start we were Caught in
a heavy Shower of Rain and we got Quite wet, I took Down to
day 12 Jowels or Hogs heads and 2 Large Middlings and 50 ct
Coffee, 50 cts Sugar, 25 ct of Rice and a Large Cypress Log That
I Bot of Jorden at $5. This I took Down and Left at the foot of
the field, The hands were all well Except Mary and she was
sick. They had Just returned from replanting at Hard Scrable
and was working out a piece of Corn on the Ridge at the foot field
and then fininishd a piece of Corn right below the Corn Crib —
This I planted in Peas, myself & Edd And Anderson

18   I was Still in the Swamp   I worked The hands untill
Breakfast time in the Potatoes, and after Breakfast I Started them
Down to Hard Scrable and Planted the Winston Ridge and then
Crossed over and Planted the front Ridge as far down as the
Corn Crib and then night Came on and we Left for home

19   I had them at worke again in the P. Patch untill Break-
fast and then went down and made a finish of the Hard Scrabble
Field, ie, Planting of it   We got through with it about 10
Oclock   Edd Hogatt helped us. We then got thrugh with this
and went up and after dinner we made a Commencement on the
Large Corn Near the China tree, This we hoed 20 Roes — The

Plowing to day was Done all this Evening by Burke, Antony & my William who Came down to day to bring me some Ho[r]ses, They did not get through with this cut   They Plowed very Slow indeed, and I Started up in the night Late to go to the City and took William with me

20   William went down again this morning and took 2 horses for Edd & himself to wride up on, They must be done with the 1st Cut of Corn now and into the 2nd cut on the back Ridge. I got up to town this morning Just after day Light — The children Came up from N. Orleans this Evening on the Princess

21   Buisness rarther Dull To day. The River is Falling very fast at Present and has been falling all this week   Col Robertson Paid me to day The full Amount of his account which was Two Hundred Dollars. We deducted The amount he had Previously Paid which was ninety Dollars. Thus he paid me in Cash to day One Hundred and Ten Dollars. This shows Conclusively That he is a Gentleman in every Respect, for I was Perfectly willing To Take $50 but he Said no The $200 was right and Thus we Settled, Mr Jno G. Tayler paid me yesterday five Dollars On his account, William, Edd are still in The Swamp. I thought They would have been up to day, but I Suppose They are at work, I hope They are. I wrode under the Hill This Evening and Paid Mr A L. Wilson Two Hundred cents or two Dollars. This was for a Cotten Rope that Mr Winslow Winn got from thare on Monday Last for which I Promised to pay for, Mr Edd Cole Told me to day that Mr Chonke and himself was yesterday Surveying The Wattern Lands, now Mr Tysons, and That the Watern Land ran up a Good Distance in Maj. Surgets Field

22   Edd., William & Antony Came up This Evening from The Swamp   The[y] Got up Erly   They Left about 2 Oclok and the[y] report that they got through with both Cuts in the Lower field, ie a Plowing, and that The Plows were in the cut opposite The House   The hoes are Just into the Lower Cut on the back Ridge and God Knows when they will get through with it, for I dont. They report that Burk and Anderson will be up to night with Fish &c. Greate times these are indeed. I am the Sufferer for Lost time, I am that. This will Learn me Something, Peter did not make any returns for this weeks work

23   Greate many of Our Citizens were at The Landing waiting To Get off on The Origon, and The Boat Came up Late in the afternon. Col W Robertson & St. Jno Elliotte, Dr Mercer and a number of others that I Dont recollect, I was under the hill to

try and get Some Corn This Evening but Could not for all the
Houses were Closed up. Anderson & Peter was thare and Sam to
go Down.

24 I Got up Quite Erly this morning and went under The
Hill to start in the swamp and I went To Mr Gaws and bought 3
Barrells of Corn in The Ears and 3 Sacks That Contained 7½
Bushells at 85 cts per Bushell, and 50 ct of Sugar of Mr Wilson
— We started and got Down in the Swamp about ½ past 9
Oclock I had Peter, Anderson & Sam, yes, and Antony, When
I got Down I found Burke a Ploughing in the Potatoe Patch, and
I recollect That he told me yesterday that he had Done The
Ploughing in the Potatoe Patch on Saturday — I found him
Drunk He Got through with That and went in the Corn, and
the very 20 Rows that was Left there when Edd Came away was
still thare untouched, He then Commen[ce]d to work on the Corn
and after working thare untill Anthony had plowed 13 Rows with
the mules runing 3 furrows in Each a Breaking up. I went over
thare and found that Peter and him Both was not doing much. I
then had that cut Left and went to the uper part of the field and
had them to Lay off and I Commenced Planting it. This we did
not Get ½ through with before a tremendious wind and Rain Came
Down and we Left it — We were unable to do any more for we
had Considerable rain with the wind It was a Light Storm We
planted Peas in the [u]per Corn to day — Smith and Andrews &
Billy Wolcott took dinner with me to day They were very wett.

25 I found it best to take the hands down and mend the
Fences at Hard Scrabble and this we did. We put up the fence in
the Slough next to Mr Gregory and Then we put the fence in the
uper part of the Slough at the Levy The water was very deep
here, up to arm pits, Burke & Anderson did the wading, Peter,
Phill and Peggy and Zory and Sylvia all we[re] hoing the Corn,
yes, and Sam too — Burke was again to day tolerably Drunk, still
he was able to work some. The Rain Came On and we had to
Leave about 12 Oclock. We got very wett, all of us, We got up
to the House and after dinner we made Several attempts to work
in the Potatoes but we were often Driven in and got Quite wet
Several times, We put up 4 roes of Potatoes in the Irish Pt. Patch,
and Dug about 4½ Bushells of Potatoes, and had them washed
and Sacked up to take to town

26 We workd a good part of the day in the rain, Ditching,
mending fence &c. My Corn is very much firerd from Plowing the
other Day after having goten wet Several times To day about

5 Oclock in the afternoon I wrode ole Gim towards town and got up after Supper a Little   Mr Prentice is very ill indeed, I hope he may Get well

27   Anderson & Little Winn Came up Last night and I sent Down by the Skift to day One Barrell Mess Pork, Cost $12, and 2½ Bushels of meal, Cost $2.12 and 50 cts of Sugar. He brot up from the Place nearly 5 Bushell of Potatos Last night

28   I was Out this Evening to pick Black Berrys with the Girls, They wrode in my Carriage. We got a good many of them in a short time, Lavinia, Emer, Julia, Margarett, Anna, Octavia, Byron & Wm was along.

29   Buisness has been Only Tolerable To day and nothing new, Jeff makes a bet with Mr Mardice of $30 that The Jaqumine Mare, Goose, would beat his mare Elizar Beeman, I held the Stake and is to put up Jeffs Part of it, Mr Mardice wants to bet me 20, 30 or 50 Dollars if want that his mare wins the money, and I would not Stand it And I am right too   Capt Strickland did the Same in a Small way — I refused too — It was to day that I Loaned Mr Waller Ten Dollars which he promises to pay me On the 4th of July. I wrote to Mr Miller This Evening by the Princess, I Bot Wm Some Clothing to day at Mr Dalshimers on a credit as Follows, 1 pr pants, 2.50 & 1 pr, 1.90 ct, 1 Coat 4.50 ct and a Hat for myself at 3.00   Those articles I did not Pay for, I Bet $5 to day that The Mardice mare would Beat the Jaqumine mare, This Bet I made with Jeff, I have now all my Back Land near the Oak tree to Plow and Plant And all the Slough, which I think is about ½ of the Land under fence

30   After Dinner I Took Richard & Byron and Started Down in the Swamp   I Left about 4 Oclock and got Down thare before Sunset   I took a ride down to Hard Scrabble and the Corn was doing Tolerable well Tho the Horse had bin in thare and Eat up Corn and Broke Considerable of it down

July 1   We were Planting Corn in the uper cut of Corn, but did not Get through, We Stopd Planting to Let the Plows Break up the Ground   We then went Down and Plowed and Planted a piece back of the House in the Slough   Then the rain Came on so thick and fast that we had to Leave

2   Mr S. S. Prentis was Buried   He Died Last Evening Late between 6 & 7 Oclock. He was Gentleman and a Schollar, and Public Loss — Peace, Peace to his [re]maines. Mrs Furguson Died this Evening, Poor Lady — The Effects of Wm Norton was Sold to day.

3 Our City is very healthy at Present thanks To Heaven for it. Mr Lucioni paid me five Dollars to day for the Rent of his Paint Shop, Richard & Byron went Down to the Place this Evening

4 After Buisness was prety much Over to day I wrode Out to the Race Tract and there was a Large Amount of Persons Out thare To witness The Races   The first Race was between Mr Jaqumine Horse or Filly Known as Ulilte Ularlee or Goose, against Mr Mardice mare Lisar Beeman. This was a mile Race between those 2 and it was a Good Race too, Done in 148¾ Scd   The Jaqumine mare won the Race Easy 1 thought, whilst the other was the favorite at no odds. I made Several Bets to day On the Race and the Bets Stands as Follows as well as I Can recollect

Dollars cents

5.00	with Jeff that Elizar Beeman would winn.
1.00	Stranger, Dr Branums Horse VS. The Field
1.00	New Combs Same way
5.00	Cash with Mr Icum Winn

12.00

I won a Bet of Mr Mardice of	5.00
and one Mr Cal Collins	5.00
& One of Jeff	2.50
& One of Bob	.25
& One of Jack	50
& 1 of Capt Pomp ½ Bl Sugar	4.00

16.75

5 Buisness rarther dull to day — nothing new — Anthony went Down to day to work. He Came up the other Evening to Spend the 4th   Edd. Gave me ten Dollars to Keep for him. Edd Gave me $2.50 that Mr Waller paid him on the Race, This is to Keep for him

6 There was a Small Race this Evening betwen Mr Mc-Coulers Bay Ruffin Colt a[nd] Mr Covingtens Grey horse and the Colt won the Race Easy. It was a mile Race, and Bets wer[e] all in favor of the Colt. Nothing new to Day. Buisness Tolerable to day

7 Buisness Some what Dull. I wrode Out in the afternoon by self down below the Bluff On the River front and Came up by Mrs Mahons old Place   Jim wrode out Col Bingamans and Brot in my bob tail mare. She Looks well   I intend I think to Keep her home for a Day or two

    8   Buisness quite Dull I think   Hester had Calf to Day in Mr Marshalls Pasture. Tis a fine Bull Calf   To day Jim found my Little Parsons mare. She was out on the Washington Road Some Distance

    14   I came from the Swamp Last Evening and I feell Some what worsted by the trip, ie tyred.

    15   Buisness quite Dull and nothing new   My Skift was up and I Sent Down as Follows,

7 pieces of Jowels or heads	
2 Sides — wt 77 lbs @ 6½	4.95
½ gallon vinegar	15
1 gallon molasses	35
5 Barrells of Corn at 1.50 per Bl.	7.50
12 yds of Cotton at 10 cts	1.20
1½ Bushels of Meal, 80 ct	1.29
2 pr of Pants	1.60
To tobacco for Mr Burk	25
To Antony, Cash	20
To Petter	10

I wrode Down in the swamp This morning and I got thare not Long after the Boys got thare in the Skift. I found them out about there work To day and I Commenced at it myself   I found my William Down thare and I made him Commence to work with me and we made a very Good Days work   We were to day Cuting Grass for the Purpose of Plowing and Planting Corn, Tis very Late indeed but I will try what Can and will be Done by nature &c. Mrs Burke and Dan wrode up to town to day and Dan Lost her Shawl and $4 that was in it.

    16   To day I was in the Swamp, and was hard at work Cuting Grass with the hoes and doing Some Plowing at the same time   This we were a Doing in the Lower field

    17   I was in the Swamp To day hard at work and all my force, We were Still at the Plow and hoe trying to clear a piece of the Grass to Plant.

    18   I am still in the Swamp and at work Plowing a Little, hoeing & Planting — We are Killing a Greate many Snakes to day in the the grass and some of them very Large indeed

    19   We are still at work in the swamp and in the Lower field, and are planting Some Little to day, but I See we Cannot get th[r]ough this week.

20   I Got up very Erly this morning and am unwell, very much so indeed — tho I will try and Keep on my feet and work a Little to day — we were all at work to day but Could not get through by night, so from what was undone I Judge that it will be about Monday Night before they get Done Plowing it, Peter has been Sick for 2 Days

22   The Skift was up this morning — She brot up 4, yes 5, water melons, a few Bundles of Fodder that I pulled myself, and a Large Sack of Potatoes — Mr Waller pd me $20 that I Loaned him yesterday   I Loaned Mr Kenney $10 to day — I Sent down to day as Follows

1½ Bushells of meal	1.75
And 4 Barrels of Corn Welsh crd	6.00
" 76 lbs of Bacon @ 6½	
30 lbs of Flour	1.00
To Bread for Phill, Anderson and all	.30
Edd Cash	25.00
to tobacco for Mr Burk	20

23   Yesterday I Drove Byrons Mare & Colt, Mrs Genny Winston & Colt, Virginia Burns, Big Jeff & Billy & Billy mule Down as far as the 2d Gate

24   Buisness Only So, So. I took a wride This Evening and Thought to find my old Black Horse & Mare but Could not, Jim went out at Dinner time to hunt also — I think by this time they have Pulled Fodder in the Swamp or have Commenced to do So — William McCary Commenced the Gum Sucking again. Just got out from a Spell of Sickness

25   Mr Miller Came up from New Orleans This Morning   Looks very well indeed. We wrode out this afternoon and Drove up the Horses — Mr B Walker Died This Evening.

26   Mr Benj. Walker was Buried this Evening and The Procession was a very Large One   Odd Fellows, Masons & Temperance Cocietys turned Out. Mr Miller & Mc & myself took a walk to the Bluff this Evening

27   Buisness Only So So — William, Richard & Byron Started Down this morning with a Lot of Cattle and a few Horses to take them into the swamp   They took a Little meal with them

TAXABLE PROPERTY

1 Watch	50
1 Clock	8
20 Head of Cattle	120
1 Piano	40

8 Slaves   2000
2 Town Lots   2600
800 acres of Land   850
Mary & Sylvia Came up this Evening. They have pulled The
Fodder on the back ridge. They Commenced on Tuesday, A very
Small weeks work indeed, but what Can I Expect? Young Mr
John McCreyry Died Last night and was buried this Evening   Procession Came throug the City. I had no rain in the
Swamp this week I am told up to today. Glad on acct of Fodder
     28   Buisness So, So. I remained at home all day   Late in
the afternoon took a walk with Mr Miller & McCary. We went up
above Mr Lums on the Bluff. I paid Edd $5 at 12 Oclock to day
and about 5 Oclock in the afternoon I paid him $10 more. This
was a few Dollars more than I owed him, the Deposit that he
made with me
     29   Buisness Only tolerable thus far   The old Black Horse
& Black mare that has been gone for a week Came in yesterday
and Last night I turned them out and they have Gone off again
for Gim Could not find them in Long hunt this morning — I Sent
Down this morning by Anderson in the Skift 4 Sides of meat
$4.20   I Sent Down also Sugar 50 cts, Coffee, 50 cts, Molasses,
½ gallon, 17 ct and Meal, 1½ Bushells. They are Pulling Fodder
now in the Swamp and are Pulling in the uper Field. Mr Reef
Lewis Got Married Erly this morning To Miss Stockman. She
is a Daughter of James Stkm   Young Lewis went up the River
amediatly and Left his Lady for a few hours, Strange I think
     30   My Little Grey Filly Alice ran off or was stolen Last
Night — Wm Hoggatt Came in to day and wrode there Paint
Horse   They Commenced to Pull Fodder at his house a Little
on Saturday Last
     31   I wrode Down in the Swamp this morning and took
Down The Black Filly Mariah Henderson and Wm wrode the old
Black Horse. I found the hands at work in the Lower Field   They
had pulled a Lot of Fodder on the Front and a Little on the
middle Ridge. I wrode on Down and took Dinner with Mr Stump
and then I wrode on Down to Mr Gregorys Lower Field and
Looked at his Corn.   Came on back and a Shower of Rain overtook me and I Jumped into the Field and went to Pulling Fodder,
no, to Shocking it, but it got wet tho not to hurt it much, After
diner they Packed all the Foder that was in the Lower Shocks up
to the Stable and Corn House and we went Down and tyed up a
Small Lot of green fodder that was thare and then we went to

the uper Field and Pulled a Lot of Fodder Down and then Packd out a Little of it.

August 1 I Got up this morning before Day and wrode Down in and through Hd Scrablee and day broke whilst I was thare, I was Looking after the Hogs that I thought was in thare of mine They have Done a good Deal of harm in thare, I was back to Breakfast and they Commencd to tye up the Fodder that they had Pulled near the crib. This they Packed up to the House, We then Pulled Down Some Fodder in the upper Cut in the Field and Packd up Some Shocks that was thare that did not Look very well. We then Knockd of[f] for dinner and after dinner we then went to work with the Ploughs — Peter & Antony Plowd and we Followd with the hoes. We then went to work on Some Corn that was Planted On the fourth day of July and we got through with 3 Little Cuts of it, 1 being in Each Slough We then return after Finishing it at 6 oclok and put up all the Fodder that we had pulled down in the forenoon by Breakfast, but Left it thare.

2 Richard & Byron went down after breakfast this morning and took down Some meal. And in the afternoon Wm Came up and Seys that they were working in the cut opposite the House in the forenoon and that after Dinner they had Commenced and was at work on the uper End of the field in the young Corn and will work on Down through it.

3 Mr James Miller Left here this Evening and before He Left I paid him One Hundred Dollars on acct of Some money that I Borrowed of him, and in writing the Receipt for me he wrote it thus.

Recd New Orleans Aug 3d 1850
of William Johnson One Hundred Dollars
On account
$100.00   J. Miller

I remarked to him that he made a mistake for he had writen New Orleans insted of Natchez in the receipt. He offered to write another and I told him that it make no Difference at all and thus it is — McCary and myself went Down to the Landing to See him off — he went Down on the Princess — Mr Mandeville went down with his family this Evening He goes thare to Live[16]

4 The Skift Came up this morning Violet & Anderson

---

[16] Johnson was incorrect in this instance. The Mandeville family continued to reside in Natchez throughout the 1850's.

Came up   Brot up water melons   Phill Came up also yesterday Evening and wrode The old Black Horse, Zora walked up — Fred Cabler Shot a Mr More to day in at Jaqumines. Killd him instatly.[17] Mr Gegans Died to night in a fit.

5   The Skift went down this morning and I Sent down 60 lbs of Bacon Sides, a Basket of Peas, 50 cts of Coffee, 50 cts of Sugar, 1 dollar Dress for Violet, 1 gallon vinegar, 1 gallon of molasses, 3 and a half Bushells of meal

6   Buisness Dull   Late in the afternoon I wrode Down into the Swamp. The roads are in very bad Condition. They have not been worked on yet   I Got Down and found that the hands were at work in the Slough near the old oak tree, Peter & Antony Ploughing and the hoe hands Close up to them, I did not get Down thare untill night

7   The hands workd out all the Corn in the uper field, i e the Phill Slough and the young Corn in the Slough next to the House. This we Got Done Late this afternoon

8   We Commenced this morning Erly and went to work at the young Corn at the Cross Fence in the Lower Field and we did Considerable worke Geting Done after or at Dinner time to day — Tho I have made mistake for it was yesterday morning that we Commenced in the Lower field and this morning Erly we pulld a Lot of Fodder that was in the uper field   This we Done by Breakfast time and after we ate Breakfast we went to work where we Left off in the Lower Field; and as I before Stated we got through about ½ past 11 Oclock, We then made Small road Down to the River for the Stock to Drink, Then after Dinner we startd Down to Hard Scrable and Commencd to work in the uper End of the fie[l]d and we did Considerable work on it. Got Down as far as the Corn House in front but did work it back the full width of the Ridge.

10   We startd up in the field this morning and Took up 200 Bundles of Fodder   This was what we pulld yesterday morning   We brot it to the house and put it in the mill Lot House & after Breakfast we started Down to Hard Scrable and we worked it out by night. We Stopd I Suppose 2½ hours durring the Afternoon. Now this shows that we Commenced after Dinner yesterday and did not Commence until near 9 Oclock to day and we worked all over the Front and the Winston ridge, I may Say Something Less than 1½ days

11   I got on my Horse Jeff very Erly this morning and

[17] The incident was mentioned in Natchez *Courier*, August 7, 1850.

started to town and on my way up I found One of my Red Cows at B Winns and he had Marked and Branded her   A man told me that they had Done it through a mistake

12   Jeff wrode down in the swamp to day and he told me they had got through with Pulling the Fodder that the hands Comm[enc]ed on in the back Ridge at hard Scrable, and that they had Commen[c]ed to work on the uper Cut of the Corn in the head of the field, Mr Baird was in the Swamp to day wriding with old man Winn and I am told that Mr Bard had Laid out the road in Such a manner as to give me about 3 miles of Road, which I am not disposed to work at all, I Shall see to it

13   I Saw Mr Kenney to day and I promised him that I would see Mr Martin and Get The papers from him in regard to the Land and he could See them, I See that he is in favor of making the Survey in Septm. and I am opposed to it very much.

14   I was up Quite Erly this morning and went to work on the road, The hands Commenced yesterday Morning Erly, No I think it was this morning That they Commenced it.

15   I arose very Erly this morning and Commenced on the road after prepairng a Little Turnip Patch, Yes I Sowed a few of them, The road as it is Layed out at Present, I work from my Corn Crib up to Mr Wades wood yard Levee

16   I started up this morning to make a finish of my part of the road and did so about 11 Oclock to day   I then started to dig up the Potatoes. We got through all to ½ a roe   After this was done I Left the hands to Continue to work on the Patch and make it fit for turnips   I then had some Corn Pulled and Put in the Buggy and Peter Drove Bob up in it, We Came the Back way and Left at 6 Oclock and got up at 9 which was good time, No One has workd the road as yet but myself and I finished to day.

17   To day old Bailor Winn, the Cow Marker, gave a fish Fry, Several went down from town to it — I Sent Down the Buggy this morning 1st time this Season, 2 Sides of Bacon, 49½ lbs, and 2 hams, 1 gallon Molasses, 1 gallon Lamp oil.

18   Antony Came up out of the Swamp this morning and I Let him have ten Dollars on his wages, I remaind at home untill quite Late and then I wrode Jeff out in the Dixon Pasture. Reports that Peggy is quite Sick   Edd and Richard went out to Mr Hoggatts this Evening and will return again to morrow

19   I was up by times this morning and wrode out to Dixon Pasture and Started to Drive Down The Harman Ox Lamb, We

Drove him Down as far as the Brick yard in the Bottom, Left A. to Drive him

20　To day nothing new. Buisness quite Dull

21　I was in the Swamp Erly this morning and was doing a Little in the way of Puting dirt to the Corn, or in it, that the worms have attacked and a part of the time Seeing to the geting of Some Lumber out for to build a shed for Stock. Antony Sick. Mr Burk Sick — Peggy Sick. Mary Jane also — and old Phill Laid up for a Little thorn Sticking in his finger

22　I was puting up Forks &c. for a shed in the Lot. All the force that I had was Peter, Anderson & Mary, Zory and Sylvia — All the rest Sick. I was made quite so.

23　Buisness Only So, So — Considerable preperations on foot to Celebrate The Osequities of Gen Taylor, This was Done in the Court House yard. I was at the Residence of Gen Gains to day, and I wanted to get the Map of the Land that I Sent to Was[h]ington for, and I Could not get it for he said he did not [have] it nor the field notes Either amongnst the Papers that I Gave Lawyer Martin to take Care of

24　Considerable Persons in town to day　The Mock funeral of Gen. Taylor Came of[f] to day and there were a greate many Persons in the City to day. Prayer by some one I know not, a Sermen by Parson Drake, Oration by Mr North, All past off very well indeed[18]　Mr Burke was up to day and I paid him $12.00 as wages — Peter Came up to day and brot the Buggy. Mary Jane brot up Sick in it. Sam Came up too. Wm wrode up my big Sorrill Mare.

25　I remained at home all day　No in the Evening, I wrode out to Col Bingamans to See if my big mare was done with the Horse and She proovd to have Done the Same

26　I Sent Gim Down in the Swamp with Peter this morning and I Sent Down a Rope for a fishing Line and 3 Doz Hooks and Some twine.

27　Gen Gains Gave Mr Kenney to day the field notes and he wrote out the notices to day and gave Judge Thatcher, there attorney, the notice for the attorneys[19]

---

[18] President Taylor had died on July 9, 1850. For the program of the "mock funeral" held in Natchez, see Natchez *Courier*, August 21, 1850.

[19] On this date Thomas Kenney, surveyor, gave notice to attorneys for both plaintiff and defendant that he would survey "the premises in Controversy" in the case of "William Johnson vs Benjamin Wade & Baylor Winn." His survey was to be in pursuance of an order issued to him by the Adams County Circuit Court in the previous May. The notice to Johnson's attorneys was addressed to "Gaines

28   We again had a fine Shower of Rain this afternoon which makes the Ground Just right to Plant Turnips, Antony went down this morning to work. This has been a week that he has been sick. Anderson Came up to day and Brought Mary up   She is Quite Sick and has taken medicine to day   The wind of yesterday Blew Down the Shed that was Just put up and One Side of it was Coverd and the other was not and besides that it Blew Down a good deal of Corn in Evry Direction at both of my places — those that have [we] may Loose, This we Cannot help. Judge Smith & Col Saunders went over to the Lake to fish to day — did very well

29   Buisness very dull indeed. Dr Blackburn was to see Mary this morning, She is Quite Sick, I am unwell myself to day and have taken a Dose of Blue Mass — I Sat Down This Evening and wrote a Letter to Mr Jessee Hamilton & Directed it to Port Gibson, Woodlawn Plantation

30   I was at the office of Gen Gains to day and he gave me the Plot of the Land that Came from the Land Office, which I want as Soon as I Can to show it to Mr Kenney, The Surveyor, Maj B Winn of the Swamp was in town to day and Called on the Surveyor to See him in regard to the Swamp Survey — I wrode Jeff up to the McCaffery Shop and had his Shoes on, 75 ct for the Job, Cash by Charles twenty Eight Dollars

31   Mr Luccioni paid me for One months rent of Shou up to date. Mr Waller paid me ten Dollars that I Loaned him a Short time ago — I Loaned Wm Nicks 12 Dollars to day and it is to be paid next Saturday by Promise

September 1   Buisness Only Tolerable, The past week has been very dull indeed — My Shop was Robed this Evening by Some One of about ½ Doz Razors. They I Suppose Entered the window, Something Strange about it

2   My wagon goes down this morning with as follows

30 lbs. of Flour, Cost	1.00
79 lbs of Bacon	4.80
3 Bushells of Corn meal	2.40

& Martin & Ralph North." Johnson Papers. Richard M. Gaines, referred to in this diary as "Gen R M Gaines" and "Gen Gains," had been attorney general of Mississippi in 1830–34; and Will T. Martin (as he signed his name in the Johnson Papers) was later Confederate Major General William T. Martin. Joseph S. B. Thacher, attorney for the defendant, had been a judge of the High Court of Errors and Appeals, 1843–49.

741

1 Keg Tar from the House
To Bran for old Jeff   .05
To Sugar   50
To Taller to greese the Carriage with   10
Sylvia and Phill went Down together   Sam went Down to day
and brot up my big Sorril mare and Colt. Fany Hatcher was
Driven Down by Wm in the Buggy with orders to bring up Bob.
& the Sorril Mare. Mr Kenney to day told me that he saw Mr
Winn and he wanted him to run back to the Town Ship Line,
which he told Mr. Winn that he was not authorised to do so by
the Court and that he was Only instructed by the Court to Survey
the Land in Controversy and no more &c. I Sold Mr Bly. Henderson a Barrell of Corn and tis the first One that I have Sold this
year at 1.35

    3   I was at auction to day and Bot 1 doz pr Socks, 1 piece
Maddrass Hank, 2 Table Cloths. Anderson & Wm Came up and
brot up Fanny in the Buggy and Corn & Fodder, and Wm Brot
up old Dun and The Old Black Horse and the Bob Tail Mare,
Tiffener Wickersham.

    4   Buisness quite Dull, Dr Donaphan Died the other Day
in the Swamp, La, The People are geting back from the Springs
or Cooperes Well and the Springs, Maj Young was in town to day
and I was buisy and we did not have a Settlement, and I am much
pleasd to find on refering to my Books that instead of owing him
a hundred Dollars I Only owe him fifty Dollars

    5   After we had Taken Breakfast we all made a Start in
to the Swamp   We had a Carriage and 2 buggys and I was On
Horse back — Here is a List of all in Company to day — Myself
& wife & William, Richard, Byron, Annie, Katharine, Eugenia,
Allice & Josphine, Lavinia, Emmer, Octavia, Varrener, Abort
(Millers)   Servants, Jim, Sarah, Patsy & Sam — And Sylvia I
met at the hill and took her back, which makes 20 heads in all

    6   I was in the Swamp and was assisting to get Out a Log
that we wanted to make Bourds of. We did get out 5 Cuts off from
it. Wm put Billy in the waggon to day and worked him Easy —
They hauled wood with him — At this time Mary is in town Sick
and Zora is a Little unwell also

    7   I wrode up from the Swamp this morning and got here
to Breakfast. Was about 2 hours 20 minutes in the trip. Mr
Burke Came up this morning and I pd him five Dollars in Cash
as wages

8   Buisness Only So, So. My family is all in the Swamp at present, and So are all my nieces, &c.

9   Buisness Only Tolerable, tho I was not in town after Breakfast Long, for I Started in the Swamp to See the Survey made by Mr Kenney, He went down in my Carriage and I wrode on horse back. He took a Little Nephpew with him, Soon after we past Mr Winns we herd him Shoot off his revolver. Six Barrells was Shot   He then mounted and Came Down and Jasper was with him. The old man had a Large Stick & Jasper a Overseers whip. We went on Down and very shortly after we got down to Mr Gregorys we Saw the Commencment made   Mr Wolcott and Mr Tate was the Chain Bearers   Mr James Gregory was along, Well I believe that Every One present was under the Impression that The true Corner is near the Box Elder Tree, 1 Chain 33 Links East of it, We then Started from the corner and wran out the Eighty chains North and then started west and Came to the River in Just the Quantity of Chains as is expressd in the Field notes and in the map and the fact of all the Corroberative proof   The old man Winn was not Convinced of the Same or he pretended that he was not, We then started and ran up to the other Sectional Line and then back to the river, This then aught to have Convinced any body of the incorrectness of all former Surveys

10   After Breakfast this morning we made a Start at the Corner of Sections 5 & 6 and ran North to the Intersection of 5 & 4, This Line we ran to the River and it appears that One hundred and fifty yards has fallen off in to the River — This is not impossible nor Improberble. No we did not Strike the River   We make a Corner and then we Startd from thare and made to the River and I think there was 7 or 8 chains Short of the Complimet

11   Jeff was at the Shop Several times to day and was passing about.

12   Buisness very Good. My Force at Present in the shop is myself, Edd and Jim, for Jeff has Left and taken the Shop on the S. B. Natchez and she is now about starting for New Orleans — She made a Start and broke Something about her Connection pipe and will not Get off untill tomorrow. I was to See Mr North this afternoon and I told him about the Survey — and I am now in this mood at present. I [am] not very willing to Come to a Compromise at all — but Let it Rip

13   Buisness Only Tolerable   Edd was Sick all day. Wm

Came up from the Swamp to day   Seys Anderson and Mr Burke are both Sick   Antony was up walking about, has been Sick Several Days — I Saw Mr Kenney to day and he told me that he Saw Mr North to day and he told him what he thought about it, i e the Survey. Mr Tyson was telling me to day that he would hold the piece of Land that Mr Ford was Claiming up thare behind him and that he was now Cuting wood on it and would Continue to do so — My Family are all in the Swamp   I Sent a Letter Down to day to Mr Winn that Lawyer Hewit Gave me to hand to him or Send to him. I gave it to his Brother in Law Cooney — To Day Friday 13th 1850, we got news in regard to the Passage of Several very Important Bills — The Texas Boundry Bill, The California admited into the union, the fugitive slave Bill[20] and the Death of the King of France[21]

     14   Buisness Tolerable fair   Myself and Jim worked prety much alone. Edd was Sick. Old Bailor Winn Goes Out to day to the Land Office and I Dont Know what was his buisness

     15   After or about 12 Oclok I Started Down in the Swamp and wrode my Little Horse Billy — I got Down thare about 2 Oclock, found all well and nothing new. Wm went to day and Took Margarett in the Buggy with him

     16   Buisness Tolerable fair, It was to day that Mr Dicksons Bull Hooked my steer, a young steer   He was out at Dicksons and Gim took the Butcher out to See him and Sold the Calf to him for $5.00   Emer went this Evening   Gim and he brot the Horse back

     17   Buisness Only so, so   Gim had to wride Down back this morning to look for trace that   he Left on the road some where. As he Came up this morning He found it on the road Some where, Mr Fields pd me to day for the muley steer and the pale red one too. Gave me twenty Dollars and is to give me 2 more as soon as he Can find him — Anderson Came up to day and brot up Some Corn and Fodder

     18   It was to day that we bought Mrs. Wolcotts old Cow for $15. She has a Calf with her. William and Richard & Byron Drove her up — They Drove the Cow I Sold to Mr Bennet (Matilda) for twenty Dollars

     19   Buisness Only Tolerable   Mr Stump Came up from

---

    [20] On September 18, 1850, the Natchez *Courier* carried this announcement: "The day has come at last! Passage of California bill, Texas boundary act, New Mexico territorial bill without Wilmot proviso, and the Fugitive Slave Bill."
    [21] Louis Philippe died on August 26, 1850.

New Orleans the other morning and he wrode Fiddler up this morning and I wrode Down this Evening with him and we had Considerable talk on the way — And he then Told me that he had herd Mr Winn Say that I Should not have the 2 Cows that he had Taken up and that I was a Lyar, that I had never Seen them Cows untill I Saw them at his House &c. I then told him that I had bot them and all about it, so that on old man Winns part I thought it very wrong in him indeed, I also told him that I was much Surprisd at his pretending to Claim them, Mr Wolcott and Mr Stump was up in the Swamp and played Cards a while, then went home   Maj Bennett paid twenty Dollars for the Cow Matilda and her Calf that I Sold him — I am glad that he is So much pleased with her

    20   I was in the Swamp this morning Erly and I got on my Horse Cuff and Came to town to Breakfast. They are pulling Corn or pretending to do so — has been at it all the week — Oh what a time my Country — Willam, Margarett, Jener and Antony Came up to[o] this Evening Late. Wm drove up Bob in the Little Buggy and brot up my Little Geener and Margarett Lieper. She had been Down on a visit, I had a Conversation To day with Patterson and Mr. J Rosette about those Cows of mine that Mr. Winn is Claiming and they both recollets the Cows Directly and They were the 1st that told me about the Cows being for Sale on the Boat where I got them

    21   Antony went down this morning after Breakfast   He Came up yesterday with William &c

    22   Nothing new   After the Shuting of the Shop I wrode Down into the Swamp found them all well Except old Anderson and he had been Sick all the week, and has not done any work, Trifling Fellow Shure, I wrode On Down to Hard Scrable and I found that the Horses and the crows has Eaten up the Entire crop or nearly So. The Pumpkings was the Same, Wm McCary Came up yesterday Evening Late and returned directly after the shop was Closed to the Swamp again, Antony has been Sick nearly all the week, Cannot work, Mr Burke he has been Layed up also with Boils &c. Has done a Little or nothing. Mr Wattern P Smith Sent over to day and got his Large Black Dog and the Boys that Came after him brot a hound Slut and 2 Cur Puppys and Left them, Peter Came up with wagon and brot up Load of Corn & Fodder and returned again this Evening

    23   Very Large Meeting to day at the Court house. A Rally for the Union, Judge Veasy Spoke. Joe Shield and Col

Bingaman, They all made Good Speeches indeed, I am told[22] —
Antony was Sick to day in town

    24   Nothing New. I Sent Gim Down to day to Drive up the
Two Little Red Cows That I Bot out of a Flat Boat on Friday
18th of January, 1850. Mr Rosette went Down also and Drove
them up, I had Sold them to him for $16 which Sum he paid me
before he started after them, Mr Stump was up to day and I
Told him about them, Gim and Mr Rosette got the 2 Cows and
brot them up, They got up Late this Evening with them both, Mr
Dickson Bot the above 2 Cows the Same Day that I Sold them
to Rosette for $18.00

    25   Nothing New   Buisness dull or So, So, I Sent Wil-
liam and Jim Down this Evening to bring up the Family. They
are all in the Swamp and have been for Some time, and I told
them to Drive Down any of my stock that they might See on there
way, going Down, I was up at Mrs Caradine Sale of Furniture
and I bot 1 Glass, a Toilet Glass, and a Mattrass and 2 Buckets,
3 Pans, 1 Coffee Pot, 1 Strainer, 2 Dish Covers, &c.

    26   My Family Came up from the Swamp to day, a Car-
riage & 2 Buggy Loads of them and there Plunder, They report
all well, and that they are Cutting Grass at Present, and that they
are Done Putting Grass on the Front Ridge and have Commenced to Pull on the back Ridge.

    27   Young Jno Gains shot a Black man that had ranaway
from Mr Hutcheons This morning and Killed him Dead. This was
done in woods, I went under the Hill to Day. Paid Mr Ray for
a Keg of Lard that I got of him a short time ago. When I sent
Wm for it and I also paid him for 96 lbs I think it was of Bacon
at 6 cts   I also went up to the auction Room and bot as Follows
below,

To 1 violin	20
To ½ Doz Tumblers	50
To 1 Lamp	1 25
11 Razors 20 ct	2.20
2 Brushes 35 cts	.70
4 Bottle of Cologne water 50 ct pd	2.00
10 Yds of Prints	75
4 Linnen Bosom Shirts 70 ct	2.80
To Soda and Apples, Cigars &c.	25
To Shot 3 lbs	25

[22] For a report of the meeting, see Natchez *Courier*, September 25, 1850.

to Dito 3 lbs	25
To a Sythe Stone	20
To 3 balls of twine per Mr. Burke	.15

28 I was out to the tract to Day and Saw the Race be-
tween the Following Horses, viz, Mr Robersons grey Filly, Mr
Covintons grey Horse, Mr Wrigleys Bay Mare, Mr Crizers Sorrill
mare, and Mr Hendersons Sorril Colt, and Mr Pickens grey
Mare   The Race Terminated Just as I have Enterd there Names
Down Here

29 Nothing new   Buisness Some what Dull, I Sent Gim
in the Swamp this Evening To Take Mary Down   He Drove
Fanny in the Buggy. Mary has been up for Some time Sick
&c. The whole of this is a Misstake for it was to day that Richard
& Dan Coleman Came up and Anderson too. They Came up on
Horse back. Reports that they are Pulling Grass in the Swamp,
and all are well

30 It was to day that Jim went Down with the Buggy
with Mary and Mary Jane

To City or General Tax	21.40
To School Tax	16.70
To Mrs Battles City tax	8.50
To School Tax	5.10

October 1 Nothing New   Buisness rarther Dull for Season, To day it was that Mr Grillo paid Me five Dollars that he
has owed me Ever Since the Election of Judge Thatcher, He Said
he would have paid it before but that he was hard run &c.

2 Buisness Getting a Little Better, I saw Jeff This Evening and paid him fifteen Dollars on the amount that I owe
him   I owe him now a ballance of Twenty Dollars   Last Night
my Grey Mare Alice Grey and Richards Colt got out and wran
of[f] to the Swamp I Expect, Gim Met Mr Cole To day and he
told G. that he herd Mr Winn Say that he intended To get out
a warrant for Gim Rosestt for Driving out the 2 Red Cows that
I sold him, Why dident he do it whilst he was in the City, It
was to Night That Mr Micheal Johnson was telling me about his
Coming very near Getting into a Difficulty with two of the Brothers in Law of Jasper Winns wife   He said that the one of them
said that any man that would take the part of a Colord Man
Marying a white woman was a Damed Rascal. At that Johnson
Call him a Lyar, When The Man Struck him across the arm with
a Stick and He then Knockd the man down and if he had have
gotten a hold of a stick or Pitcher, he would have Killd

him, Thus the thing Ended. This was done the day before yesterday, I Saw Mr Kenney To day and he informed me that he
believed that he would have to Survey The Land again, That
Judge Thatcher had been after him several times To Know why
he did not go back to the Township Line to Commence,   I remarked that I Could not See the use of it for it was a thing Fully
Established, that the true Conner was where we started from, and
that we were all Satisfyed that it was the true Conner, and besides you were fully Convinced I believe that Such was the
fact. He Said yes, that was true, that he was Still under the belief that it was true, but that Judge Thatcher had asked him
Several times why he did not Commence at Township Line — I
told him that I would Like him to See Mr North and Lawyer
Martin before he Proceeded to do Any thing in the Case. I told
him too that I was So Situated that I could not witness a Survey
at Present for One of my hands had Left me and I Could not
take the time, I went around and Saw Mr North amediately and
Told him about it

   3   Buisness Some what Dull for the Season, Mrs Burke
Came up this Evening and brot Sam with her. Reports all well
Except Peter who was Taken Sick To day, She Seys also that
they have Commenced to work at Hard Scrabble To pull
Corn, The[y] Commenced to day   Mrs Dallia owes me now
The Sum of $7.75 with what I Let her have to day

   5   To day I was at the tract and Saw the Race between
Mr Wrigleys Mare and Mr Crizer Mare and the Covington
Horse, a ½ Mile, and the Horse won the Race Very Easy in-
deed, Wrigley Mare Lost in the Race   Charles paid To day
Twenty Seven Dollars from the under the Hill Shop, I Saw Mr
Martin To day and I Told him about The Survey and He Told me
not to pay Any attention To them but To Let them go a head
and Survey and to hold them to the Survey that he made be-
fore, Phill is up to night with 7 Pumpkings and a Lot [of] Corn
& Potatoes & Peas

   6   Buisness Only Tolerable, After the Shop Closed to day
I Took Some Dinner and got on my Horse and wrode Down into
the Swamp, Dan Coleman went with me   I went Down The
Back of Long Lake near The Goose Pond, This I found very
near dry   Long Lake is quite Shallow and in some places The
water has Left and in others very Shallow, I went down To The
Cypress Byou and the Lake has very Little water in it   The
uper End there is none and is growing quite full of young wil-

lows   I wrode over to Muddy Lake and I found it had Considerable water in it, Great many Fish I thought, I Came back and Cross Cypress Bauyou Lake and Came Out behind Mr Winns Lower Field. I then wrode on Down to my house and went on down To Mr Gregorys   Thare I saw him and had a Talk with him   This being over we started for my House, Stopd and Took Supper, and after Supper Started to Town   Gim I brot along for he had gone Down by water and Took with him 3 Canoes That I Bot of Mr Gim Harris under the hill, Three Stacks of Hay up and Little more Cut. I Left orders for them to go to Pulling Fodder in the Morning, Richard and Byron Came Down to day also, Peter is Sick and has been for Several Days

    7   Mr Wilsons wharf Boat Sunk This Morning and Destroyed Considerable Things and Damaged goods — Mr Kenney Called This Evening and requested me to give him the notice That he gave me a few Days ago of his intened Survey that he was to make on the 18th of the Present month, Gave it to him and he tore it up and remarked that he had Seen Mr. Martin and had a Talk with him and he Said that he would not make another Survey and that he had done all he could do in the affair, Mr LaNeer was present at the time

    8   Nothing New. Buisness Quite Dull To day. I understood this Evening That Mr F. Surgets Quarters Burned Down To Day, Those were Just Built I am Told on the Place That he Got of Maj Chotard, Mr Patterson was over to day On a Hunt and Killed 4 Ducks, 4 Squerrills, 1 Becroch and 1 Posum, This is a Prety Good Hunt for the Season, Mr B. Wolcott Came up from the Swamp and reports that my Field had a Parcel of Horses in it as he Came up This Morning, Richard and Byron Came up to day and Seys that instead of Pulling Fodder That they are Cutting Down young Corn To shock up

    9   Buisness So, So. Streets are very Dusty indeed, Judge S S Boyd arrived This Evening from the North, Came Down The River, Richard went down This morning and took Down Jeff, Cuff & Billy. I Made Swap This Evening with Mr S Semore, and gave my old Black Horse, Known as The Edd Hoggatt Horse, for a wild and unbroke Spanish Mare of a Dunish Color, We make an Even Swap, As My Horse is not home I, if Nothing hapens, will Deliver him in the morning, Mr Ray paid me back 1 Dollar that he Took too much in my Last Bacon Bill

    10   This Morning Byrons wrides The Spanish Mare Kitty Semore 1st and Dan Next, Mr Semore Came and got the Old

Black Horse so the Swap is Confirmed, Gov. Quitman Left To day for Jackson. Several Guns were Fired This Morning when he Left, Gardner Lindar Makes a Commencment to work for me at $5 per Month   He agreese to do anything in The Shape of work, I Sent him Down on Little Dick, The Hands were at the Last accounts Shocking Corn   That was False [f]or not likly to produce anything, B McC. Commenced the Gum Sucking again — has got well again

    11   Richard Came up To day and wrode Little Dick and wanted to get Some Sperrits Turpintine and Tobacco, Powder and Shot &c. This I Sent down by him   He reports all well, I Sent him back in the afternoon and Dan went with him, and wrode Down the old Spanish Mare That I got of Mr S Semore, We Swap for my old Black Horse

    12   Buisness Only Tolerable. Nothing New. I was out to the tract to day and Saw a Race between Mardice Mare and Mr Philbricks Mare, 600 yds, and the Mardice mare won the Race very easy indeed. Richard and Dan Came up to day and I whiped [Richard] for Not bringing up the Mare I Told him to bring up. She was a mare of Mr Hoggatts. I won to day 2.50 and a Bag of Shot on The Race, Tis now after ten Oclock and Them infernal fools are Seting in the Parlor — Oh What fools — for God Sake, I Mean the Gum Sucker & Lavinia

    13   Peter Drove up the Mules in the wagon and brot up Corn and Fodder and a few Pumpkins, They report all well below, I was Some what uneasy after hearing That Mr Berk had so much of My young Corn Cut Down, Contrary To my orders. I remained at home all Day and did not go out on acct of The Dust, I Sent the Boys Down this Evening to Drive up Some Milk Cows

    14   Gim brot up a Buggy Load of Corn and Hay This morning and William and Richard and Byron and Guardner brot up Mary and Calf, Adeline Heifer and Calf, young Mulely and Calf, old Cherry Wolcott and Calf — I think it was to day that Antony went to work with Mr Rose, This was his first Day

    15   Buisness Some what Dull, Lavinea, Emer, and William went to Mrs Smiths To Night to tea, This was Williams First visit.[23] Gardner wrode Down this morning after Breakfast To work he having Came up yesterday with the Cows from the Swamp

---

[23] Mrs. Robert (perhaps Phoebe) Smith was the wife of a free Negro; Lavinia and Emma Miller were nieces of the diarist; and William was his fourteen-year-old son.

16   Buisness Dull, Oh No it was Good to day, I paid Jeff five Dollars to day, I Bot me a Suit of clothes to day and paid forteen Dollars for them at Mr Winston Store, Mr Ford Came home yesterday and To day he Came in and Jasper Winn[24] was in at the Same time   He told me that he would Take his hands and go Out and put up the Houses that Mr Tyson pulld Down, and said if Mr Tyson Came about Thare he would shoot him full of shot, That he had got advice on the Subject and That he would Killed him if he Came to interupt him, and Said that he told Mr Cole So. He farther remarked That they had No Kind of right to the Land and That he would show them Something This Evening   He would show them how it was to Take forcible Possission, He Said old Mrs Tyson, a Damed old Rip, had Came out thare with a Gun and she being a woman he Left, but Said that she had not Better Come out thare again This Evening, Mr Thom Bradford Gets Married To Night To Miss Bisland[25]

17   Buisness Only Tolerable, William Miller[26] Came up from N Orleans   The Boys [came up from] the swamp This Evening and brot a Buggy Load of Corn &c. Reports all well And that Burk Does not do any work at all, but always Hunting — The Boys Took Down Some Cows and Calves, and as they went Down They Saw old Bailer Winn, and he Told them that I was always Driving Down Some Poor Cows, and That if I did not Mark & Brand them he would. All this I Shall pay no attention to but Let him do it   I Saw Mr Martin this morning and he wanted me to see what Proof I Can of the Partnership of B. Wade & Winn   He told me to Look on some of the Steam Boats and see, I Told him I would, Capt Wm Miller Came up to day from New Orleans, and reports all well, He Came up for his Sisters, They Talk of Going down on Saturday on the Princess, Young James Gustine, The Son of Dr Lem. Gustine, Died up the River The other day, was Brot Down, and Burried To day at This Place in the Family grounds, I presume

18   Buisness Only Tolerable   I Saw Mr Newman cominging from The Swamp To day and I Called him and I found out through him That he had Sommons [for] The following Persons, Viz, Mr Ford, Mr James Gregory and Mr Stump in behalf of Mr

[24] Jasper Winn, twenty-five years of age at this time, was Washington Ford's overseer. U. S. Census Reports, 1850, Schedule I, Adams County, 37.

[25] Mt. Repose, the home of the Bisland family, was several miles northeast of Natchez.

[26] Johnson referred to his nephew, William Miller, son of James Miller of New Orleans.

B Wade & B Winn — Mr Ford I find has imployed Mr Martin
in the Case between Mr Tyson and himself, Harah for the Swamp
and its inhabitants, Some of them will be ashamed of there Proceedings before The Court is over, We Shall See, what we shall
see, My Family was up at Mr Myres to night   Lavinia & Emer
played on the Pianos up thare, for they had Several up thare for
Sale

    19   Mr Burks Came up to day and informed me that he
was offered Good Wages by Mr Winn to work in the swamp and
that he was agoing to work for him. I told him that was all right,
I had no objection at all, I gave him five Dollars on his wages.

    20   I paid Antony To day four Dollars on his wages

    21   Buisness Only Tolerable, I was in the Swamp this
Morning and after Breakfast I Took a wride Down to Mr Gregorys & I thare found him below on the Road and I hired him 4
hands To pull his Corn, Viz, Phill, Sylvia, Anderson & Mary — he
is to Give $2.00 per day and find them, We then took a wride to
Look for the Aash Corner. This tree we found and then we
tracked up the Line west untill it Came to the River   This is
the Line on which the Box Alder tree, Called a Station tree, on
the East & West Line. We Saw old Blazes on this Line besides
the marks made by Mr Forshey. This prooves to my mind that
Mr Forshey did mark off the Lines   I Came on to town and
met B. Wolcott and told him that I would Like to hire him for
One Month. He Said that he woud Come, I saw Mr C. Wolcott
to day   He has Just Got back from the North, or from Indiana,
and brot his daughter with him   This Morning Mr Burkes Came
up and we had a settlement and our Settlement went as follows, He had Commenced To work for me 20th of June 1849
and has been up to this date Sixteen months. He Said that he
had Lost About two Months, So that I then was in his Debt fourteen Months at $15.00 per Month, 210 dollars — I had paid in
Cash to date $157.50   I then paid him to day in Cash fifty two
Dollars 50 ct   Thus we are square to this date, and I Expect to
Keep So

    22   Buisness Only So, So. Nothing New, It was to day
that I had the Settlement with Mr Burke instead of yesterday.
Thus I will state it As Follows — I had paid him $157.50 in Cash
During the year past, To Mr Burkes as a Cash Ballance Due
him $52.50   To Day I hired Mr B. Wilcott to oversee for me
for one Month. He is to Take Possesion in the Morning Erly

    23   Buisness Tolerable fair. Old Dr Winston Came to

Natchez to Day from up the River   He has been waiting On Mr Seth Cox, &c. I was at Mr Kenneys this Evening, and saw the field notes that Mr Winn got from Jackson, So he Seys, And I was Surprised to See how Little to the purpose they were, They Gave No Satisfaction to Mr Winn, He Left them with Mr Kenney, And requested him to give him A Coppy of My Notes, Mrs. Kenny told Me So, I was under the Hill to day and bot 168 lbs of Bacon Sides at 6½ ct Amounting to 10.92, And I Sent 4 of the 9 pieces into the Swamp by Peter who Came up with the waggon and brot up Corn and Fodder and Some Moss, The Moss I gave to Mrs Kenneys at her request.

    24   Major Winn Came up out of the Swamp yesterday   Reports that Burkes was drunk the night before he left and had abused him very much and for no Cause, Tis Strange what a Man he is, tis indeed, The four hands that hired to Mr Gregory the other day has I presume finished Pulling of his corn to day — Peter took down the waggon yesterday Evening and Took down also 4 Sides of meat and an Emty Barrell for Purposus on the place

    25   The Cisterns all over our City is Out or nearly So. Several Citizens got home Last Night or this Morning. Mr Batterson and Mr Elliotte, Mr Fisk, both of Them. Maj Winn went Down into the Swamp to day and I bot for him to day before he Started Several articles, viz. a Hat, a Vest, a pair of Pants, and 2 under Shirts, The amount of which was $9.25   I was up to day at Auction and bot Several articles, a Couple of Coats or Cotees and 2 pair pants, The Amount of Which was $9.25   The above amount was Charged to me at Dalshimers Store but the Last was at Auction and was Cash, Winston went into the Swamp This Morning to take a Hunt, He wrode my old Horse Bunting. Winston Gave me to day to Keep for him $[blank] and a paper of Some Kind that I did not read, for I threw it in a Drawer, and will Read it to morrow.

    26   I Saw Mr Martin to day and he told me that Mr Ford Came in to Town the other day, and he was in the Country and did not See him, So he did Not Know wether he brot the papers in regard to my Land or not, He Mentioned Somthing about The Quanty of Land that Mr Wade & Winn had, and that they had Taken notes of the Same, &c. I Saw Mr Maxwell to day and I got him to Lend me a map of Township 6, R. 4 west, Together with the field notes

    27   Buisness Only Tolerable, After the Shop was Closed

or after dinner I wrode my Little Grey mare into the Swamp This Evening & Williams wrode old Roan

28   Buisness Dull, I got on my Horse Alice Grey and wrode to Natchez after Breakfast this morning — S. Boat Natchez Layed at the head of my feeld all Night And So did The Bunkerhill No 3   The Fog was very heavy indeed, The Tryal of Land, or the right of Possession did not Come of[f] to day between Mrs Ford and Tyson   It was put off untill next Wednesday a Week, I am Told

29   Buisness So, So. Mr Martin Miller paid me today $5.00 On his Acct. William Came up this morning and brot up my Buggy or Cab and Sack of meal and Bag of Potatoes, Yesterday Mr Wolcott had the hands at work Digging Potatoes, Winston ahunting and Killd 8 Squirrells in the Swamp yesterday, and My William Killed 2 Ducks, It was to day I got a Letter from the Brokers office on a Notice to pay soon, pay one of My School Land Notes, $71.50

30   Buisness Tolerable Only, The Land Case that was to Come off to day between Mr Tyson & Mr Ford prooved a failure   Mr Ford had The Suit Dismissed at his Own Cost, and I understand he intends to Bring his Suit in Chancery, This was for a tract of Land back of the Walern tract, Winston Sends up 3 Squirrells and 3 Ducks to day and yesterday he sent 5 Squirrells. This is Good hunting.

31   I find buisness Tolerable Good To day. Mr Hyram Baldwin Gets married Last Night To Miss Mary Bradley and This morning ½ 8 Oclock Mr Samuel Winston got Marreed To Miss C McCrarey, both Natives of Our County. I Saw Mr Martin to day and asked him if Mr Ford had brot him any Documents at all in regard to the Land   He Said that he had not and That Mr Ford had told him that he, Mr Ford, had the Lines run out in That way and that he had the Deeds made out according to the old Survey

November 1   I Wrode in the Swamp in the afternoon — Found all well And That they had nearly put up all the Potatoes, There was 5 rows of them remai[ni]ng Still & that there was a Parcell of young Corn Just pulled that I think will be a total Loss for it is Green. Winston and my William was both in the Swamp and they reported that they Branded 14 head of Cattle to day. As for the sheep they report that there is but 47 of them as yet found and the Ballance is in the woods some where & 1 died about a week ago. Mr Wades teams are haulling away my wood, Burks and a Black Fellow was Driving the Same, This wood They were Hauling from The Lower End of the Field.

   2   I got up Erly This morning and took a wride out to Dock Lake and here I found 2 ducks and got them by the Dog Bull &c. They had been wounded by some [one] the Day before, I wrode for the purpose of Seeing if I Could find the Conner of Secs. 3, 4, 6 & 7 from South west Conner of which There is a Marked Locust tree, R. 4 W. 7, 6 or Some Such a Mark. Mr B Willcott was along. We returnd to breakfast and after Brkst we wrode Down to Mr James Gregorys and found him at the mill a Grinding away with all his might. The object I had for Seeing was this, I only wished to See about The Field Notes that I had written for him and also to give him a Small map that I had Coppyed for him, Mr Wolcott and myself wrode arround The Line and he Showed me Some old Blazes that he Said was George Winns, which was intirely out Side of Any Line that Mr Wade or Winn[27] Could Claim or in other words was far from the Line by which he wants to hold me to, I then Came on up and took Dinner. Gim Roset was at my house and wrode back to the City with me in the afternoon — I fear that I Shall, having been down in the swamp and did not See Any of the Men that I wanted to See, have Some trouble in geting them to appear at Court, William and Winston both in the swamp to day hunting Ducks and Cattle &c. Mathew, The Tailer, Shoves Down the old Lucconio and cuts his head. Lcc. Charges him with Killing his Parrott and it was all a Mistake. L. Called him Boger, Saucey man, nasty man, poor man, Tailor, Son of a Beachee &c.

   3   Nothing New or very interesting. Yes there is Some thing New too, That is, Mc Received a Letter from his William and The Contents of it was that he had got the Consent of Mr Miller to Marry his Daughter Lavinia and that he Mr Miller was agoing to Set him up in Buisness, So Mout it be, I am affraid that both of the young Ones are Small Potatoes, I feel So. Cant help it[28]

---

  [27] George Winn, free Negro who died in 1831, had been the owner of part of Johnson's farm property. "Mr Wade or Winn" referred to Benjamin Wade, Natchez banker and landowner, and Baylor Winn, who was later tried for the murder of Johnson. Wade and Winn were joint owners of land adjacent to one of Johnson's tracts.

  [28] Johnson was discussing the prospective marriage of William McCary, son of his close friend Robert McCary, to Lavinia Miller, daughter of his brother-in-law, James Miller. During this period Johnson was disparaging in his remarks about William, whom he called "the Gum Sucker" or "the Natchez Gum Sucker." The

4   Buisness So, So   To day is the first Commencement of the Court. The Docket is a Light One, I did not do much To day for it is the Commencment of the Court and I am not prepaired to go to tryal yet in the Land Case, I Started Down in the Swamp This Evening and Mr Wm Wolcott went down this Evening with me, I started Down wth a view To get Some wittnesses to go with me to ascertain the amount of the Trespass Commited by Messrs Wade & Winn, I Got Mr James Gregory, Mr Wm Wolcott and Mr Stump and myself, We Started and went to the back Line and Commen[c]ed and we found that there was 10 Trees Cut near the Corner, East Corner in Section 9, and Then we found also That There were 6 trees Cut on the west Side of The 4 chain Line Near the Fence and 101 Trees On the West Side of The Kenney Line, Thus making in all 116 Trees, I parted from them and we Started for Home. I Came On to town and I Saw Mr Ford as I Came up   He was having his House rebuilt that was pulld Down by Mr Tyson. He remarked that he was building up again, and he Showed me his map of the Land, &c. I then Commenced about my own Land, I then told him that of Course he Could have no interest in trying to Keep me from geting all the Land that belonged to Sections 5 & 9, and Said No he had No interest in it, but Said that he Sold Only to the Survey or Lines of Forshey for he Said that he did not Know at the time but what he was Selling all the Land in Section 5, and Said he had never had it Surveyed and did not Know but what he was Selling to the Sectional Corners &c. I then Came on to town and went Out to the tract and Saw the race between Col Bingamans Colt, Gov. Greaves & Mr Turnbulls Filly, Feliceana, 2 mile heats   The Colt won the Race Easy. I won a Barrell of Flour to day from Capt Pomp. and $7.50 from Mr. W. Boyer & 2.50 cts from Mr Isam Winn, and I Lost $5 with Mr Marriner

5   I have writen on the other Side Some things in regard to having Counted The Stumps and Trees on The Land That Mr Wade & Winn Tresspassed On of mine and I now find that it is mistake about it being yesterday, for it was This Morning That we Made The Search and not yesterdy. Also there was The Race that I Spoke of it Came of[f] to day instead of yesterday[29]

6   The Swampers are all up to day, Except Burke who was too mean to Come up. Very well, I See it all

marriage took place on January 6, 1851, in New Orleans. In 1874, during the Reconstruction period, William McCary was sheriff of Adams County.

[29] This "match race" was run before the opening of the Pharsalia Course for the November meet.

7   Buisness Only So, So, Court is in Session and The Races Coming off at The Same time, Mr W Wilcott Came up this Morning To Court but as the tryal did not Come off he returned again. I went out to the tract To day and I Saw a race between Fanny G. and Folly, and it was a 2 mile race and Fanny G. won the race very Easy. Jasper Winn made a race This Evening VS me for $25.00   He ran a Horse that they have Lately bot, and I ran a Grey Colt of Mr Hoggatts, Distance 400 yds., and the Colt won the race very Easy — He then ran against Jacksons Horse, and Js. horse beat him too. So I think That he must have Lost 50 or Sixty Dollars   There Horse is not fast, Dr F. Stanton Came On from the North Last Night & Looks very well indeed.

8   Buisness tolerable fair to day. I was at the Race tract To day and I Saw a 3 Mile Race between Error & a Little Sorril Mare, Evira Mills I think. Error won the Race very Easy. Mr Jno Hunter & Horrace Hunter and young Officer Came home Last night from California — Jno Hunter Looks thin

9   I was Out to the tract to day and Saw a race between Fany G. & Goose & Lizar Beeman, 3 best in 5. Fany G. won The race. Goose took 1st heat and I Lost on it a Little and I Saw H Chotards Horse ran VS. Bonturars Roan & Chotard Horse won. I Lost on it Sharply & Saw Nash Horse Beat Sulton 1 Mile, and I Lost on all of them Smartly. I am under the impression that There is Something done in the way of Swindling out there at times

10   Buisness Only so. Peter brot up the waggon and a Load of Hay & Corn, Wm Sent up 6 Squirrells by the Waggon To day — Lizar Rowen Came here to day in the Worth. She came from Vicksburg and Orleans.

11   Buisness Good to day.   Greate many Persons in town, The criminal Docket was taken up to day, My Land Suit has not come off yet, Mr Ford told me to day that Mr Winn Could not go beyound the sectional Corner & that he would be bound to Stop thare &c. Wm & Richard brot up Henrietta & Calf, Jenny & Calf & his Little Bull.

12   Buisness tolerable dull, Court in Cession yet. I Took My field notes yesterday and Loaned them to Koncke To refresh his memory; and he, I feel confident, took a Coppy of them for he Started down the river this Morning to Make a Survey for Mr Winn, This I Call the meanest trick that has been Served me for Some time. I was under the Hill to day and Mr Cole told me about Mr Conkees having Gone to Survev Those Lines for Mr

Winn & Wade, Mr Cole told Mr Wilson that he wanted 100 hands to Cut wood. Mr Wilson Said that he Expected that you [they] are agoing to Cut all the wood off of the Land and then Complain of the Title. Yes, Mr Cole Said they would Cut off all the wood and then make a Squable about the title, The[y] both Laughed, but I was thinking all the time that there would be truth in it when pay day Came around. Mr Cole then told me that I was bound to Gain that Land, but that he was in doubt wether I Could make him pay for the trespass, as he would plead Ignorence of the Line &c. I paid my note [of] $71.55 to day in Mr Brittons & Co. This was Given for School Land and the note was indorsd by Robt. McCary 4 years ago. Mr Jas. Gregory remarked this morning in presence of Judge Posey that Mr Nelson was agoing to proove by Smith that Smith was thare at the time that Mr Nelson bot the Negro and that the Boy was of a different name from the One they charge him of Selling, and I remarked that I thought that would make no Difference when it was proven that he was one and the Same person

13 Konche is Down in the Swamp Still Surveying. Court is in Cession and to day The Jury finds Mr Conners man guilty and he will be hung.[30] Mr Nelsons tryal will come off to morrow Some time in the day. Mr Odell told me to place five dollars that he won of Wm & me to his Credit — be it So   Wm Makes a Stall in the Stable for his Colt   I paid Jeff for Winston to day four Dollars and 50 cts. Ch. Wolcott brot up 30 ducks to market.

14 Buisness Some what fair. A Large Partey to night a[t] Mr Railys in the Country and a Wedding Out at Mrs McCoullers, Miss Perkins to a Mr [blank]. The State vs. Mr. Nelson to[o] on a charge of Stealing and Selling a Slave, He was aquited. Sanders & Miderhoff VS. Mr Hicks & Martin. He is to be tryed again to morrow on another charge wher Mr Henderson is the Prosecutor   Mr Wm Wolcot is up to day and remained all day in town

15 Court is still in Session, & They have been all day ingaged in trying Criminals or Liquor Cases in part, and in the other case, [at] 3 Oclock They Commenced on the Nelsons Case. This is his second tryal, Pero was found Guilty for Trading with Slaves to day, This morning there came to tryal as follows, Mr Ford, Mr Cole, C Wolcot, B. Wolcott, H Stump, H Burke, J Gregory, who was already in town, Mr Konchee. Mr Konchee

[30] See account in Natchez *Courier,* November 27, 1850.

told me to day that he had been Surveying down in the Swamp for Mr Winn and that he had wran around The Sectional Line and had did 6 miles of Surveying, and I believe found nothing to Justify him in Swearing Possitivly to the incorrectness of Mr Kennys Survey, or in other ways in Swearing that Mr Kenney did Survey The Lines wrong, This I find is what the opposite Counsil whiches him to do in order to get an Order for a New Survey. To day Mr Pomp Strickland paid me a Bag of Shot and a Barrell of Flour that I won from him On a Race a Short time ago

    16   Court is in Session and The tryal of Mr Nelson was Going on to day and it was quite an Exciting time, I assure you, and he Got Clear of the Charges.

    17   I went down to the Globe Hotell to night after the Shop Closed and Saw Mr Jas. Gregory who was Sick at the time & I spoke of his health &c. He Commenced to tell me about Mr Midderhoff abusing him So; and he said if he had have been in Court he would have been apt to have Broken his head with a Stick as Soon as he Came Out, Tis true that he Said too much Intirely   A gentleman would not talked So seviere, Mr Midderhoff had better Look out.

    18   This Morning My Case in Law Came up and was turned over for to morrow, when I hope it will Come off. At Present There are Several witnesses that are Sick, Viz, Mr Harrison Stump & Mr Jas Gregory   Old man Winn was in town to day and he was making a greate deal to do in the way of Talking

    19   To day My Law Case Came up and Judge Thatcher On the Part of Wade & Winn, made a Strong Effort to pospone the tryal, which he Succeeded in. The Judge Granted The request and it was Laid over to the next May term, I would have been Glad to have had the Case Gone off. I was Glad to see it. I was that. Mr Tate did not Show himself at all Since morning — Mr Stump did not Come up at all yesterday nor to day. Mr Jas Gregory is Sick and at the Globe Hotell

    20   Just an hour or two to day light this morning I herd the alarm of Fire or the Bell of the Church a ringing and on geting on my Horse Cuff I Soon found that it was up town, and on riding up town, Discovered it was Some Little Buildings in the rear of Mr Koontz Residence. He Lost his Horse and Carriage and a calf, His Kitchen was Burned and Several other Small Houses, His winter wood was and so was his Coal all Burned, It was accidental I Suppose, My waggon Came up this Evening and brot up Shucks & Potatoes, The 2 mules in the waggon, Old Mr Hamilton Lost One of his men this Evening with Cholera.

21   Buisness rarther Dull, Court ajourned Last Evening after having gotten through with a good deal of Buisness. Peter went Down This morning taking with him 1 Bushell of meal and a Empty Barrell, Loaf Bread, Beef stake, &c, 2 mules in the waggon, 1 dollars worth of nails.

22   Senetor Foot[31] arrived this Evening and there was Some Shooting of Cannon on the Occasion, Mr Foote stops at the Mansion House, Mr Marriner paid me the One Hundred wt of Bran that I won of him a short time ago.

23   Gen. Foote adressed the Citizens of this place to day   Made a Long Speech and at Night made another adress To them,[32] I have not seen a Larger meeting in the Court House for a Long time if Ever, Mr Martin made a speech also and Mr Hillier he made a very fine speech   Was much applauded. Cesesion & the union was the Subject, Col R M. Johnson[33] Died a few days ago at Louisville & Maj Miller Died a Day or two ago at Alexandria

24   Buisness has been Good in the shop to day. After Dinner to day I Started Down into the Swamp   I wrode the Wickersham Filly. Richard & Byron both wrode on the Fiddler Horse, I wrode down as far as Hard Scrable, or Mr Wolcotts   I Saw Mr C. Wolcott. I Came on back to the House to Supper. Philis & Bett both have young Calves. The Fields are all oppen at Present. I found all well. Mrs Ford Lost her Child Last Night, Still Born

25   I was in the Swamp this morning and we commenced to make a Lane fence. We did not Finish it Quite before I Left. I Set the Grass on fire this morning and it Burned Some of my Fence, Mr Ford Came near Loosing Some of his fence by fire, We drove up 3 cows & there calves Viz, Philis & her calfe, Bets & calfe, young Patsy & calf. Some Fellow Knocked Winston Down to night and beat [him] near my front Gate & Left, Winston did not find Out who it was, (Calld his name Gim Thomson.)

---

[31] Senator Henry Stuart Foote was a senatorial colleague of Jefferson Davis. He was elected governor in the famous election of 1851, defeating Davis, the Democratic candidate. According to historian Dunbar Rowland, Foote's majority over Davis was .999 votes. *Encyclopedia of Mississippi History*, I, 717.

[32] For the account of Henry S. Foote's speech on Unionism and in support of the Compromise of 1850, see Natchez *Courier*, November 27, 1850.

[33] Richard M. Johnson, the former Vice-President, died at Frankfort, Kentucky, on November 19, 1850.

26 William and that Little Fellow Charley Drove Down Abigail & her calf & Ellen & calf — Winston gave me forty five dollars to day to Keep for him. He is sick to day. Some Fellow Beat him Last Night.

27 Winston Commencd to work   Winston gave me five Dollars to Keep for him. This Makes fifty that I have of his to Keep   I Sent Emer Miller five Dollars by Jeff for her Sow that Mother Gave her; I Sent Down 55 lbs. of Bacon to day by Mr Pearce. William Came up this Evening from the Swamp & reports all well & seys that the Hands are making a fence to Extend to the yard Fence, Mr Odell bought the Caradine Store from Col Robertson a few days ago. Price $4,500

28 Buisness only So, So. Yes I Say it was dull

29 Buisness dull. We have news to day that The man that murdered old Mr Buckner was Caught yesterday near Bayou Sarah[34] by Some Owner of a wood yard, The reward is $1500. A pretty good Lift for him, Peter Came up to day and brot the wagon and 4 Broken wheels to be repaired, He reports that They had pulled Down the Elick Johnson House & had hauled up a part [of] it to rebuild it[35]

30 Nothing new more than we have herd to day that Georgia has voted for the union by a Majority of 30,000, and that the vote of 23 countys. The Secessionist had got Only 2 countys and they Only by a majority of 200.[36] William Came up to night from the Swamp and brot 2 Pigeons and 3 Squirrells that he Killed this Evening, He Seys that they are haulling up the Logs from the Ellick Johnson House and that they had Got up the Oxen. William Saw One of my Oxen (Lamb) in Mr Fords teams. I Loaned Mr Kenney five Dollars. I Loaned Mr Waller five Dollars, and I Loaned Mr Jones 2 Dollars. Peter Came up this Evening and brot up a Load of Corn, Maj. Winn went down in the swamp this morning. Has been here Ever Since Court week.

December 1   I wrode out by Col Bingamans   Took Richard & Byron with me   I wrode the Grey Filly, R. Wrode Black Filly, B. the ticky Filly.

[34] See Natchez *Courier*, December 4, 1850. The town of Bayou Sara (also Bayou Sarah) was the Mississippi River port of St. Francisville, West Feliciana Parish, Louisiana.

[35] This house was on land previously purchased by Johnson.

[36] In its article of December 4, 1850, the Natchez *Courier* stated that "disunionism, secessionism, and Quitmanism are put down in Georgia by the emphatic voice of the people."

2   Buisness Some what dull   Mr S Davis got his Gin
Burned Down Last Night with Considerable Cotton it in.[37]   It
was burned down Erly in the Night in the absence of Young Mr
Alford Davis & Mr Vidal, I wran my Black Filly this Evening
VS Bub. Smiths Wood Pecker Colt, and the B. Filly beat
him   They wran two Races and She beat them both, I Saw Wm
McCary this morning and he (Gum Sucker) came on the
Natchez   He reports them all well below & tis the fi[r]st time
that he has been up since The Girls went Down   Julas told me
to day that he had turned out my Ox Lamb which is the same
Ox that he has worked of mine for a week, Mrs Cory, Franks
mother Died this morning, Poor woman — Charles paid me about
30 dollars to day. Louisville Journal of the 18th is hot, hot on
Col Saunders, Maj. Elward, & Capt Nevitt. Oh, it was awfull,
indeed

3   Buisness to day has been very dull indeed   Report Seys
that the Cholera is very bad in Orleans at present. Several valuable men have Died in the city,[38] Winston bets Mr Carter five
Dollars that Error will beat Rory O'More in the race that is to
Come off in Orleans.

4   William McCary, The Gum Sucker, went Down this
Evening on The Natchez. Oh what a green Creature he must
be. I Loaned him $14 To day   He told me that his father told
him to Come to me and ask the favor, I told him that I had a
Large amount of money to pay this month and Could not Spare
any more, Jeff Bet me $5 vs 5 that Error would beat both of his
compeditors Viz Rory O'More & Heiddleston, in the 2 mile Race,
& he bet me 2.50 the Same way, He Bet Winsten his Blind mare
Same way vs Five Dollars. Peter came up to night   Brot up
the wagon with a Load of Fodder & 2 Good Size Shoats or Small
Hogs

5   Buisness dull, To day Just before Dinner I wrode Down
into the Swamp   Took William with me. I wrode Bob. He wrode
Grey Filly Alice, We got down thare Late in the afternoon   Found the hands doing nothing, as is usual.

6   Got up this morning Erly and after Breakfast Started
out into the woods to take a hunt   My William & Wolctt was
along   We Soon Startd up a few hogs and I Shot a Large Spoted

---

[37] Samuel Davis, a planter living near Vidalia, Louisiana, lost 100 bales of cotton.
Ibid., December 4, 1850.

[38] *Ibid.*, December 11, 1850, reported on the New Orleans cholera epidemic.

Barrow 1st, then Shot a Large Spottd Wild Sow & then a Spoted young Wild Sow. William & Wolcott did not Shoot at all

    7   Mr J. Gregory, C Wolcott, Elick Johnson, W. Wolcott & my William & myself all was along   We went out to take a Hog Hunt and Mr J Gregory Killd 2 Hogs & Mr C. Wolcot Killed 1 Wild Sow & 3 Large Barrows and with my orders Killed my big Mosbey Sow. After these were all taken Home I & Wiliam started to town and we got up after 8 oclock or So

    8   The Remains of Mr J. B. Maxwill was Discovered this morning in the River below the City. It was found by John Ivy, The Fisherman   After the usual Formalitys it was brot up to the City and was put in his office

    9   The[y] Buried Mr Maxwell this Evening at ½ past 2 Oclok   Nothing New. Buisness good. Charles Sick to day   Gim went down in the shop. Peter and Sam Came up to night and brot a Load of Hay and 2 Hogs, a few Eggs. Mr Wolcott Came up also, I paid him $2 to night

    10   Buisness good   Peter and Sam went down this morning   Peter took down a Sack of Salt. Mr Wolcott took up at Mr Dalshimers to day in Clothing to the amount of Eighteen Dollars

    11   Circus Company, 2 of them in full Opperation at present, and all the town & Country are agoing   I paid Jeff Seven & half Dollars to day on a Bet on a Race between Error VS. Rorry O More & Heidleston   Rory did not run Tho I paid the bet, Tho I did not Loose it for I did not want any hard thoughts about it

    12   Circus Company Plays to day & to night and Leaves the place, Maj Young is in town to day and I paid him One hundred Dollars for 6 months Services of Charls, Deducting $12.75 for Clothing, Making a Cash payment of Eighty Seven Dollars 25 cts   This he Gave me a Receipt for. I paid Mr Barker five Dollars for Winston to day on a Race in Orleans   The wagon is up to night and brings Corn & the Waggon Brings Hay, Petter & Anderson, Drivers   I Bot 2 hounds this evening from Phillip Smith for 2 Dollars. He had 3 of them but had Lost one before I bot of him. Young Mr Abet Davis was in the Shop at the time I Bot them & So was Mr Pipes, who herd the trade   Young Mr Hall was also present, who made Scriptoral quotations Wm wrode Cuff Down in the Swamp to day & is to bring up Dick

    13   I got up Erly this morning and wrode down in the swamp and Looked around about an hour and had a pair of Bars made to Save the Corn in the House, &c. The Hands working in the Field Choping Stalks &c Mazora Sick, Things Looks bad and I have a Strong Notion not to Cultivate the place the Coming year, I wrode Down The Little Sorril mare and wrode up Cuff — got up Soon After Dinner; went out on the Commons in the Afternoon and Brushed the Horses, ie. the Black Filly. I find that Mr Tyson is still making and repairing his fences

    14   Buisness Only So, So today. After Dinner to day I ran the Black Filly Vs. Dick 2 hundred yds for a bet of $5 vs Wms Colt. Wm won the race by about 8 or 10 inches — We then run a Race for $2.50 with the Same horses and The mare won the Race Easy by about 10 feet. Mr Cole & Tyson has Seperated I am told. Mr. Cole & Winn I think are after Geting in on the Thomson Land by Some trickery or other, Tho we shall See about it in time, The Little pup Hunter ran of[f] to day and is Lost, I am Sorry for it.

    15   I remained at home all day after work was over. Dan Coleman Gives to Richard his Little Dog. Byron finds The Little puppy Hunter that ran off yesterday

    16   Very Little talk of the cholera in Orleans Now. Glad of it, to day the big Sale was to have Came off — I mean the Bisland Estate, It did Not Come of[f] because The Land did not bring The amount of its appraisment, So it was Laid over and I dont Know now when it will be Sold, I wrode out this Evening and took with me the 2 hounds and Hunter and all the Small Boys, We went out to the Dixon field, I Shot a Little Sparrow for Kate

    17   Buisness Only very dull. Nothing new. Maj Jas. Surget is puting a stop to the wood chopping by Mr Tyson On his Land — Antony Goes to Darkey Party to night, Birds of a Feather &c

    18   Buisness rarther dull, I find that Antony & Jeff was at a Darky Ball. Ferdinand Burns was thare   H Lee was thare too. It was Some where up at Sam Cottons, Oh what a Set. We had Rain to Night. Maj Winn is up to night and reports that Violet has Lost her child. It Died on Monday, Mr H Patterson wants me to take a hunt in the morning. Young R McCary & Winston has a Quarrell. Winston abused him and wanted to fight   Mr Henderson Rents the Volialia House.

    19   Buisness dull on account of the wether   William went down in the Swamp this morning with Little Winn who came up Last Night with Game, (16 Squirrells, 1 Pigeon)   He reports that Mr Wolcott Killed 4 wild Hogs The other day

    20   Buisness rarther dull, yes Quite So, indeed, I made

Several Bets with Winston To day on the Race of to day—
Young Mr Wren Came in to night, got his hair Cut and then paid
me 2.50 that he Said that he won from me Several years ago on
an Ellection and he Said that he thought that it was wrong to
have money that he did not work for. I refused to take it untill
he insisted On it   I then took it, Gave him change for a ten
dollar Bill, This is strange I think, very indeed, I Loaned Mrs
Kenney $2.00 to day. She Sent her Little Boy for it, and as well
as I Can Recollect this makes $22.00 that I have Loaned them,
up to this date

    21   I saw a race to day between a mare of Mr Crizers & a
Horse belong to a Mr Busby or Mr Grey—It was for $50 aside,
3 qrtrs of a mile—The Mare won the Race very Easy indeed
and I Lost the Following bets on it

A Bet with Mr Henderson	2.50
the old mare	10.00
a Bet with Dito of a Mare worth	10.00
a Bet with Winston of	5.00
a Dito with Dito of	2 50
a Dito with Dito of Franks Debt	5.00
a Dito of Randolps Debt	2.50
a Dito Bill Dorseys Debt	10.00
a Dito Jeff of	10.00

Altho I made those bets in town I found that when I got to the
tract that I could not get a Bet the other way at all, So I was
Compelld to Loose them. There is a Considerable bite in the
afair I think, Grey Lookd to me as tho he did not want to win
bad—It was to day that I took back a $10.00 bill that Mr Sam
Wren put off on to me Last night & he took it back. It was
thought to be a Counterfeit. It will be Recolected that I fell in
debt to Winston $15.00 which Sum I Keep for him

    22   Buisness only So. I wrode down in the Swamp [this]
Evening and I took my Pulling Gun along and Broke the Leg of a
Sand Hill Crane as he flew Near Cypress Bayou and I Killed 1
Squirrell as I went down

    23   B. Wolcott and myself went out to take a hunt and Wm
& Richard was along and we had our hounds along, and we
Started Some hogs and an old Sow of mine Cut 1 of the hounds
in the Ear. Thus we did not start any more hogs so we then Left
for home, and as I started Home I Shot 7 Squirrells and after
dinner we all went Out to take another hunt for them, and Mr

Wolcott Killd 8. I Killd 7, William 3, Richard 1, & this is the first Squerrell Ever Richard Killd in his Life

24   Buisness Only Tolerable. I was still in the Swamp   I got up Erly this morning and all of us Started out on a Squirrell hunt and I Killd 3, Mr Wolcott 3, William 3 and Richard 1.

25   Buisness Only So. I paid Jeff 10 Dollars that he won from me and $5 for Winston   He won it from Winston on a Race.

26   Buisness has been tolerable fair, Mr Wolcott was up to day & Peter went down to day to bring up a Load of Fodder &c

27   We did not take in a 1.75 the whole day, This is not usual for this time of Year, Steven Masengill is over here and has been for Several days. He Looks a Little old

28   Buisness rather dull and the river is still a rising. Corn is worth 1.25 ct, Coal 75 ct   Our Streets are very muddy   The waggon went down to day and Mary and Peter and Mary Jane went down in it, Lizar Rowan Leaves this Evening on the Princess, Anna and Kate goes to the 1st Concert to night with Edd

29   Buisness Quite dull, I remained at home all day to day, Miss F Brustee came around this Evening and So did Mary Morris & McCary.

30   Buisness Only So, So. Nothing New, More than old Baylor Winn & Bill Gay have both Gone up to Jackson for some Rascality I presume, We Shall See what we Shall See, Peter Came up in the waggon this Evening   Brot up Fodder & corn. Anderson Came up with him.

31   Maj Winn is up from the Swamp with game for the market. Mr Hamilton is Down to Night and whishes to Leave with his hands to morrow, Viz, Peter & Violet, 2 children   The waggon went down to day and took Down Phill, Sylvia, Anderson & Petter

1851

January 1   Good many Persons in town to day. City was Some what Gay. I Loaned Mr Jessie Hamilton my Horse Cuff to wride Down in the Swamp to see about his hands, Violet & Peter, They Came up in the waggon and I paid Mr Hamilton $110.00 and $30 that I paid Some time ago makes the One hun-

dred & forty Dollars. That was the amount that I was to pay
for the hire of Violet & Peter for the year. I was Satisfied & so
was he, I wrote a Letter to day to Wm Miller and stated to him
that I Could not spare The favor that he requested of me, Viz to
Loane him fifty or Sixty Dollars, Jeff. Left with me 100 Dollars
and 2 gold pieces worth I think about 8 or 9 Dollars. This money
I was to Keep for him on Deposit, William went Down in the
Swamp this morning. He wrode Fanny. I Received a Notice to
day from Mr Winns Surveyor, Mr Konche, Stating that he would
proceed to Survey Township 6, Range 4 west, and re-mark the
Same on the 21st of January 1851. This Mr Collins and Dr
Blackburn Saw, I Run the Black Mare and Billy 200 yds., and
the Black Mare Beat him

    2   The City Looks Quite Livly Tho There is not much
buisness a doing, It was to day that Mr R. Inge paid me $30.00
his account in full for two years Shaving To the First of January
1851, and I paid him $2 for Some writing that has been done in
the time. I paid Messrs Walker & Collins to day there bill which
amountd to Eleven Dollars & 88 cts for the year 1850. Mr Hamilton got off this morning taking Violet & Peter and the 2 children, He took them up to Grand Gulph. I was at Auction to day
and bot a Coil of Rope at 2 cts per lb. and a trunk & Contents
at 1.55 and 5 pr Boots at 1.15 cts per pr. Anderson went Down
with the wagon this morning and he took Down Sam with him
and a Sack of Salt, William is in the Swamp   He went yesterday
I think.

    3   Buisness Tolerable. We had Large Gunnell put Down to
day near My Shop. I Paid Mr D Dalshimer To day The full
amount of his acct. VS. me and what I assumed for Jeff, Edd &
Winston, The full amount of which was $141.05   Winston acct
was $14.75, Edds was $8.35   This was Winston old acct which

    31   Maj Winn is up from the Swamp with game for the
I Settld with him Some time ago — and his new acct is $13.00   Jeffs
ole acct. was $13. This I paid to day also — Mr Dalshimers Gave
me a Puppy which I shall Call Cezar, Yes and I pd Billy Wolcotts
bill which [was] $18.00

    4   I Took a Hunt to day on the Natchez Island and did
not Kill any thing down on the Island but a Logahead Turtle and
a Goose that I Killed on the wing as we Crossed the River. It
was a Beautifull Shot. Mr Paterson was along and he Killd 4
ducks, Bill Spillers Pulld the Skift up here, so did another man
by the name of Billy — William Came up from the Swamp to

night and brot a Load of Corn and Fodder

5   To day has been a very Buisy Day at the Shop, Bill Nix was up at the Shop and Robert went to New Orleans in his Place on the Boat. Considerable Electioneering among the candidats for Mayor and other Officers, William went Down with the wagon this morning   Little Winn went down with him. He brot up a Lot of Squirrells, 14 in number

6   Buisness quite Good to day, This being Election day. I Collected to day of Messrs Signio & F Bernero Seventy two Dollars for One years Rent of Fruit shop to 5th inst or to 1st instant,

CITY ELECTION[1]

FOR MAYOR

B. Pendelton	208	G Dick	185	P. over Dick	23
Isack Lum	21	Dr Wren	5	Lm. over Wren	16

FOR SELECTMAN

Wm Ray	315	T C Pollock	310	I C Coulson	293
Walworth	282	Tho. Rose	241	G. L C. Davis	227
R Walker	207	T. A. S. Doniphan	206	R. Stewart	204

FOR ASSESSOR

S. F. Power	210	S. E. Baker	138	C. Wesell	67

FOR COLLECTOR

H Patterson 136   V Boyer 120   Jon. Hunter 107   Lo. Weeks 59

7   William & Little Winn Came up Last Evening and Brot a Load Hay and Fodder. They report all well, They had 3 Squirells and a Rabit. Wm Sold them in market, and they went Down in The Waggon after Breakfast. They report my skift as Lost, Sunk, &c. The city is quiet and nothing new

8   William & Byron Came up this Evening from the Swamp and brot up a Load of Hay and 2 plows to be repaired. Mr Gregory was in town to day and I sent a Letter to Mr Stump. It Came from Ohio. I also paid Mr Gregory for 6 Turkys at 75 ct a piece — William reports that Zora & Anderson are unwell. It was to day that Jeff Left the Sum of $30 With me to Keep for him, Thirty dollars was the Amount

9   Buisness not so Good as yesterday. William, Byron & Charley went down this morning   They took the wagon with

---

[1] For published results of the election, see Natchez *Courier*, January 8, 1851.

them & Billy Horse, To day young Robt. McCary and Bill Burns Came from New Orleans   They have been to Lavinia & Wm Mc-Carys wedding which took place On Monday Evening Last.[2] Hutchens of the Livery Stable has Built a Cock Pit at his Stable, and I Suppose intends having Sport thare

    10   I got up very Erly this morning and after market was over got my Breakfast and wrode into the Swamp   I took my Little Puling Gun with me, I wrode down to the House and then wrode on down to Mr Gregorys   Sat a while thare and then he got On his horse and wrode down in the woods with me and Showed me a Line that he Discoverd which is the toun Ship Line, We wrode out on the Line Some Distance and we found that Mr Konke had ran a Line that Came in Just below the Ash Corner, and they then started and ran from the Ash Conner to the Box alder   This Line they also ran On inside of the old Lines & Blazes. I observed to Mr Wolcott that if he started to resurvey the Land to Compell Mr Konke to Start On the Lower Side of the ash next to the Slough, He Said that he would see to that, We did not Get to the House untill Night, They were working at the Lower End of the Field Clearing a Little piece of land down thare.

    11   I was in the Swamp this morning and I Saw a good many Ducks at the Lower End of the field but I did not get a shot   I Took Breakfast and then started to town and I got Several Shots On my way up and Killd Several ducks and Could not get them, I shot 2 Larks, 1 Partridge that I got & 1 or 2 that fell in the Bayou that I did not stop to Get, I Came on to town and went to the tract and Saw a Race between H. Chotards Horse & Robertsons Mare and she fell with the Boy and Broke her Back or spine in some way and was Left to die, Poor animal. The Next Race was between H Chotards Horse a[nd] a one Eyed Sorril Horse, 300 yds, and H. C. Horse won the R. and then ran VS a grey Horse belonging to the Same man, and beat that Race too. So I Lost in the Races in all $13.50   I then Came home   I saw 2 chickens fight also, The wagon brot up a Load of Hay this Evening &c. Mr L. David Kills a Deer in the Swamp to day I am told.

    12   Buisness Quite fair. William Drove up Dr Blackburns Cow & Calf from the Swamp.

---

  [2] Robert McCary, Jr., son of Johnson's friend, had attended the wedding of his brother, William. William Burns was a member of the free Negro family headed by Rachel Burns. See Adams County Deed Records, II, 464; U. S. Census Reports, 1850, Schedule I, Adams County, 11.

13   It Gives me pleasure to think it has been a Good day for Buisness   Nothing New. Mr Geo. Stanwood returnd to day from Calafornia, where he has been for a year or two, McCarys wife came up to day from New Orleans On the S. B. Natchez, I was Looking for My Richard to Come up too but he did not Come up, William wrode Cuff a Race this Evening VS my Black Mare, 2 Races for a pr Shoes Each, and the Black mare won the Races Each time, Sam wrode old Fiddler Down this morning, Took Down Coffee & Sugar, I Saw Mr Thom. B. Lee of New Orleans to day and I asked him how much he would take for his Land in the Swamp, and I found that he would take five Hundred Dollars for it, and I told him I would See him again, and it was agreed on that I should See him again   I Saw my Friend Col Robertson in the Evening and I told my wishes and he Said he would See Mr Lee for me. I thanked him for his Kindness

14   Buisness very Good, City Healthy, River Falling, Corn worth 80 ct per Bushell & 1.25 cts per Barrell, Col Robertson Saw Mr Lee and he refuses to take anything Less than $500 for the Land, I have a Greate Minde to Buy it any how, I Shall See to morrow, I think, if the Lord is Willing, Gim & the 2 Little Butcher Boys Came up and brot Fifty two head of my Sheep for Mr Field. He is to pay me $2 per head for them

15   I find Buisness Only Tolerable To day. I Saw Mr Lee To day and spoke to him about his Land in the Swamp, and he proposed to me to wride Down with him and Take a Look at it with him, and he Got a Horse and I Got my Horse Cuff and I wrode Down with him   We went Down behind Mr Fords Plantation and then behind Long Lake as far as where his Land Commences which was near Cypress Bayou   Here we stoped and Turned back, and he after some Little Talk agreed to take cost and interest for their Land, and Said that I Could pay for it when I pleased at 7 per cent interest   This I agreeded to do. So On Coming to Natchez I told him that I would pay Him Fifty Dollars and Give Him my note for the Ballance   When we Got to town He Came around to the shop and we went around to Mr Inges office to See if The Deeds Had been recorded to him & his Partner, which He found to be the Case. He then Said that he would go to New Orleans and would there make the Tittle. So I paid him Fifty Dollars and he gave me This Document as Follows Viz —

Natchez 15th 1851

We have This day agreed to Sell Wm Johnson all the Land we

Own in Township 6, R 3 West & Township 6, four West it being
one third interest in 1720 acres of Land on the St. Cathrine Swamp
in Adams County, on acct. of which I have received Fifty Dollars. The amt of the price agreed on between us is Three Hundred
& twenty five Dollars, the balance to be on interest @ 7 per cent
in one year from date

Thos B Lee

for Mott & Lee

I Saw Maj Young this Evening and he told me that he wantd to
do something for Charles and that he wishd to Give him a start
in a shop to hisself. I told him very well, and he spoke of Seting
him Free &c. and that if he did he thought it would be attened
with Some Difficulty in regard to his Comming back here again,
&c. He remarkd that he Came to See me in order that I should
provide myself for the Ocation, Telegraffic Dispatch to day is
that Dillon Came Down on a Red River Boat and that it was
thought that he had Robed a Passenger of Some money & a fine
Gold watch, The orders were for him to be arrestd as soon as
he arrivd. Officer Benbrook did not make the Serch untill this
morning Some time after he had got home, He found Nothing to
Justify the Charge vs Mr Dillon, Five dollars, This is a Ballance
on Mr Odells years Shaving to 1st Janry 1851. Twenty or 25
dollars, I dont recollect which, that Jeff Gave me to keep for him
to day

    16   Buisness Tolerable fair, Good many persons in the City
to day and nothing new. Buisness in the merchantile point of
view Good — I Saw Col Robertson this Evening and I told him
that I wanted him to do me the favor to write to New Orleans
To the firm of Messrs Mott & Lee To send me a tittle for the
Lands I purchased of them, which he was Kind Enough To agree
to do for me, He is a Gentleman, every inch of Him

    17   Col Robertson Came around this Evening and informed
me that he had written 3 Letters to Gentlemen in Orleans in regard to the Land that I Bot of Mesrs. Mott & Lee, One of them
to Mr Lee & One to Mr Saul & C. The Object of the Inquiry
was to Know Something in regard to the 2/3 portion of the Land
ownd by Pitcher Lacost & Co I do hope that it will be attended
to Amediatly. I was in favor of the Sending my Note Down this
Evening, for the Amount agreed on by us

    18   Col Robertson to day Sent my Letters to New Or-
leans. I hope they will be attended to, This has been a day of
very Little Proffit to me for I went out to the Race tract, Saw

771

Several Races and Lossed Every bet that I made Except 3 Small Ones — one with Mr Jas Roberson, $5 VS 3, & 1 with Mr Gay 1 VS. 50 cts, in all 3.50   I paid Winston Cash to day at tract $5, and he won from me to day on Races $8, So I fell in his debt $3.

 19   Mr Wolcott & Winn goes down to the Place this morning   Wm Goes Down this Evening   The Butchers Rosett & others brot up 1 Sheep of mine for Mr Fields and 17 They Bot of Mr. B Winn. They pd him $2.25 Each for them

 20   S. B. Natchez brings up news that the St. Charles Hotell is Burned up and Parson Clapps Church and the Methodist church and other Buildings are all Burned   Dreadfull news it is, and they report the fire Still Burning when they Left.[3] My Richard Came up this morning On the S B. Natchez. The Capt would take pay for his Passage, Wm Brot up a wagon Load of Corn & Fodder.

 21   Buisness a Little Dull, I was at the tract to day and saw a Race between a Bay Stud and Goose, & Goose won, 1 qrter for $50, Easy, by 23 ft., and there were Several other Races & Chicken fights &c. Little Alice Cow has a calf the other day in the swamp. Maj Winn Drives the waggon Down this Evening — They brot up a Load of Corn & Fodder yesterday, Jeff gave ten Dollars to Keep for him

 22   Buisness very dull, I got on my Horse after Breakfast and wrode Down into the Swamp to See the Survey that I herd Mr Winn was to have made or Commenced to make, On going Down However I met Mr Cole who told me that they had Surveyed the Lines in Section 9 and find no room for Controversy, that in runing in from the back Line to the River he only missed Mr Kenneys Line 2 Links, which Shows that Mr Kennys Line was correct. I got down thare and found the hands all Shucking Corn for it rained nearly all the time, Cattle are geting Boggd very much indeed

 23   I wrode down to Mr Gregorys this forenoon and had a talk with him and found that they had Surveyed about in the Swamp, and that they would not prehaps do any more at present, On my way up I Saw Mr Burke who told me that he thought

---

[3] The fire occurred on the night of January 18. More than twenty buildings were destroyed, including the St. Charles Hotel and the Presbyterian and Methodist churches. The loss was estimated at between $500,000 and $1,000,000. New Orleans *Daily Delta*, January 19, 1851; New Orleans *Daily Crescent*, January 19, 1851; New Orleans *Commercial Bulletin*, January 20, 1851; Natchez *Courier*, January 22, 1851.

Mr Winn would not do any more Surveying at present   So I Came On to town, and So the matter Stands.

    24   Buisness in the street Seemed Quite dull   I Notice that there was no Surveying a going On at all in the Swamp, as was thought to have Came off — I was down to the Bank to day to See if Col Robertson had herd Anything from below, and he had Gone up to Vicksburgh On buisness So I have not anything to do or Can I do anything untill I See him again, When I write this I am Speaking of my Purchase of the Swamp Property, Yes, I then went arround to the Clerks office and I could not hear of any thing that was going On thare wrong, ie any Sale &c. Mr W Wolcott came up this Evening and brot up Billy Horse for to run tomorrow VS the Black Filly

    25   Buisness rarther dull, I was out to the tract to day and I made a bet with Mr Wolcott of $2.50 that I won and 1 Dollar with Jack I won — and I Lost $3 with Mr Samuel & $2.50 with Winston   This was On Mosouri Lucy vs. Goose. The Black mare wran vs Billy to day and Beat Easy,   Mr Wolcot Lost $20, I believe, with William, $2.50 with me and $3 with Winston, and I pd him in Cash $2 to pay his rider with

    26   Buisness rarther dull, After Dinner I wrode my Horse Jeff in the Swamp and Richard & Byron went along wriding the Black mare & Cuff, Found all well, Col Robertson returns from Jackson and brot me word that Mr Mott was a Pasenger up with me and that he had receivd the Letters that the Col had written to him in regard to the Land that I had Bot &c, and that it would all be right as I desired it — I Gave him my thanks and we parted

    27   Buisness dull, I was in the Swamp this morning Erly and run the Black Mare Vs. Billy & She Beat him Easy. I paid Mr Wolcott to day $10 to pay Mr Gregory with,   I then started up to the City and Got up ½ past 9 Oclock, Sugar I Sent in the swamp to day was from the House, They Commence with 2 plows to day in the Swamp, Anna & Kathrine Commences to go to School to day.

    28   I Saw Mr Konke to day and he told me that he intended to Go down in the Swamp to Survey for Mr Winn to day and that he would be Several Days, I told him that I Should Like to be Present a part of the time, He told me that he intended to make a Commencement at the Ash Corner & run up the Township Line, He Said that Mr Winn did not have his compliment Quite

    29   I was in Conversation to day with Dr Smith, Mr Sargent & Mr D Williams about the Thomson Land, and it appeared to me that Neither of them was willing To take the responsibility on themselves of Selling the Land, In the mean time Mr Cole came up and I herd him offer $2.25 per acre for it. Such is the way that Prices are obtained, Jeff gave me thirty Dollars to day to keep for him untill Called for. I bot 4 chairs to day at auction, 3 Bits per chair

31   I was in the swamp to day and Mr Winn has Mr Konke Surveying down in, I Saw them run the Line from The Oak Corner. I mean by this the Corner of Sections 8, 9, 10, 11   They ran west from Said Conner to the River, The 1st Out is about 2 steps from a Small ash in a Slough, 2d out, 3d out, 4th out, 5th Out, 6 out was on the East Margin of a Slough near a Cotton wood Stump, and 7th out nearly in the Center of a big Slough, 8th out 1 chain 38½ Lks. Now I dont Know Exactly what I intended this for because I See in my notes that the ½ Sectional Cor [corner] of 9 [and] 10 is 3 chains 3 Links from Box Alder Tree, Mr James Gregory was along and so was Mr Wolcott, Mr Tate & Calvin Winn Chain bearrers — They then wran up my Front in Section 9. Here night overtook them and They all Left for the night

February 1   I was in the Swamp this morning and after Brakfast I went Down to See them Commence the Survey, and they made a Commencment at the Corner of Sections 8, 9, 10, 11   They did not Start at the 80 chains, as was measured from the Ash Conner, but Started 25 Lks west of it where it appears that the Sectional Corner is Crossed by the North & South Lines. The 1st out on the N. Course from Oak Corner, 2d out, 3d out, 4th out, 5th out is near a big Red Oak in the Switch Cane, 6th & 13 Lks to Larg Sickamore tree, 7th out on the margin of a Lake or Greens Slough, 8th out is the ½ Mile   This is a Small Slough near the Harry Can, or Cane break — the Stake was Driven near a Log that has a Small Chop in it, west Side of the Stake

2   I was in the Swamp this morning and did not get to town untill this morning after 9 Oclock

3   I Gave Col Robertson twenty Dollars to day to Send To Mr Mott & Lee for them to make me there tittle to The Tax title of the Barnard Pitcher Land which is 2 thirds of Said Lands, and at the Same time I told them through him that I would as soon pay the whole of the money as not, provided they Send me the titles &c

4 I requested Col Robertson to do the favor for me that I spoke to him about. He promised to do So. Winston gave me twenty five dollars to Keep for him. This is Some money that he won from Mr Jaqumine & Roberson on the Race, Bay Stud vs St Catharine

5 Buisness tolerable fair Great many Masons in town. Grand Lodge in Session at present.[4] Gen. Quitman arrived this Evening Late and Left again this Evening on the S. B. Bell Creole, Greate Many Pasengers on the Boat & on the Natchez too Gen Brandon & Col. Bingaman went on the Natchez, Col Robertson Left on the York Town Erly this Evening — I hope he will attend to the Geting of my Deeds for me. Jeff Gave me five Dollars to day to Buy a Chance for him in The McMicheal Piano. Jeff Gave me twenty Dollars to Keep for him this Evening

6 I Started down in the Swamp This Morning and took Richard with me, He wrode the Little Grey Filly and we were Over taken by Mr Konke, and he was On his way to Survey for Mr Winn. I past the house and they Soon Got ready and Came On Down and we made a Commencement on the East Side of Dock Lake at the waters Edge and Continued our Line North untill we Came to the Corner of Sections 3, 4, 6, 7

7 Late this Evening I Started to the City and Got in about ½ past 8 Oclock

8 I went to work in the Shop and there were several Calls On me to day for Small Loans Here is a List of them, 1st was Fiddler this morning — wanted 1 Dollar I Let him have it Mr Fords man I Loaned him $2.50, then he got that. Then Mr Gilbert wanted $25. This he got. Then Mr Jones 1 Dollar This he Got, and So it has been all day with me

9 Little Major Winn Came up yesterday Evening and intended to go Down to day but the rain prevented him from going Down, I remained at home all day after shop hours, Nothing new. Col Robertson Came up from New Orleans this morning & brought me two Deeds for the Swamp Lands that I Bot of Messrs Mott & Lee of N. Orleans. Oh he is a Gentleman, Every inch of him, I feel very Greatfull indeed to Col R. for his Kindness in this Buisness.[5]

10 Buisness was rarther dull to day. This Morning I

---

[4] See article in Natchez *Courier,* February 5, 1851, headed "Masonic Grand Lodge of Mississippi."

[5] See Adams County Deed Records, HH, 342, II, 428; and variants of same deeds in Johnson Papers.

Took The two Deeds and Showed them to Col Robertson, and he Said that he thought that he believed that it was writen right for it was not a Guarantee title or warrantee. They Said that it was Just the Same for it was The title that Messrs Mott & Lee obtained from Mr Henderson as Trustee, I took The Deeds around to the Probate office to have them recorded   I Left them at the office, I Sent Down to day by the wagon 2 ploughs and 1 axe, 2 New Collars and a grass Line to plough with, &c. William Miller Came up this morning from New Orleans on the Steam Boat Natchez, My William, Maj Winn & Sam went into the Swamp This morning in the wagon,   I paid The Tax $5.65, to day on the Land I bot the other week, & I paid Seventy five Dollars to Col Robertson to day and gave him my note to Messr Mott & Lee for two Hundred Dollars, payable 12 months after date at 7 per cent interest

    11   Buisness rarther Dull to day. Jenny Lind Sang in New Orleans Last Night, 1st time

    12   Buisness only Tolerable, The waggon Came up and brot a Load of Corn & Fodder, To day The Lottery Came off for the Piano That Mr McMicheal put up at $500 and it was won by Mr E. K. Chaplain.

    13   I went Out with Maj Winn & William, and we had a very [hard rain] on us and I Got wet and I then thought I would Keep on down in the Swamp, which I did, and we did not get Down untill in the night, after or about Late Super time   The hands they had been at work in clearing out Some Small trees and Brush at the upper End of The field

    14   We were at work at the uper End of the field Clearing the Land, I Commencd to day and made A[n]derson run the plow all around the river Bank in front to prevent the River Bank from washing in so much. I think it will have a good Effect.

    15.   Buisness Dull, I Came up from the Swamp this morning Erly and the Road was bad indeed for the water was up from 200 yds below the brick Kiln to the Mounds or Just below them

    16   The Methodist Church or chapell was on fire this Morning, and it was Some time before they would permit the door to be opened, The Fire Ingines were Greatly out of order and could not be brot to action amediately, tho after so Long a time they put Out the fire, &c. Mc was Down this Evening. He Sat a while

    17   Buisness rarther dull. Good many Citizens Got back this morning from New Orleans from Seeing Jeny Lind. I went under the Hill to day and bot a Lot of Spare Ribs, 287 lbs [@]

1½ cents. I Bot a Middling of Pork, Cost $2 at 7½ cts   Every thing is hig[h] in the way of Eatables, or Horse feed Either

18   I Met Mr Chas. Wolcott this Morning and he presented me with his attendants as a wittness in My Suit VS. Wade & Winn. This was for a $11.20   This I paid as Soon as I Learned that it was usual to pay Such dues before the Suit is terminated, He remarked that it made No Difference, that he would not attend at the next term of the Court, & that it was a Sufficient Excuse for his non attendace   I very Soon told him that it should be paid & that amediatly, but told him at the Same time that I did not think it was Just for the 1.50 ct per day that he Came for, though it was his wish to [have] Justice done, &c. Mrs B Winn is very sick at present   Has Sent to town Several times during the day for Doctors.

19   William Miller Left this Evening for New Orleans. He Borrowed a five from me this Evening before He Left. He went down on the Natchez, Mr E. Postlethwaite was Maried to night to Miss Browder, She is a relation of Mr Henderson,[6] Mr Ayres Merrell was Married to Miss Jane Surget yesterday at the Residence of Maj Shields, Parents were not present at the time

20   Buisness rarther Dull, I Sent a Spade Down to my place to day   It was One of those Long Ones to Ditch with. Mr Stump took it down

21   After breakfast this Morning I wrode Down into the Swamp and took William with me and Robt Fitzhue. At Least they came Down shortly after I did. I wrode Down with Dr. Blackburn, who was on his way to See Mrs Winn & Mrs Burke who are both Sick at this time, When I got Down into the Swamp I found that Sam & Sylvia was Sick and the rest was Down in the Lower End of the Field at work clearing up and fencing in a small piece of Ground Down thare. I saw a good many Pigeons this Evening and I went out after Dinner to hunt them and I Killd 8 of them and William Killed 3 & a Sqirrel and Robt Fitshue Kild 4, with what I gave him

22   I Got up Erly this morning and took a Small hunt and I Killed 14 Pigeons & a Sqirrell and William Killd 10 and Robt Killd 5, with 2 that Willcott Gave him, & 1 Robin   Yes and I killed a fine wild Shoate besides — Thus we brot 3 squirrells & 44 pigeons with us to the city

23   Little John Killd a poor Little Puppy to day Just for

---

[6] Johnson referred to the marriage of A. J. Postlethwaite to Miss M. E. Browder. Natchez *Courier,* February 26, 1851.

mischief, and I gave him a good Flogging for the Same, Nothing new. Buisness Only Tolerable   I am very well at Present, thank God.

24   I got out my Horse this morning Erly and wrode down into the Swamp and took with me a Large or long Handle Spade to Ditch with, and William went down also and brot my Pulling Gun with him, We went Out to hunt Pigeons & I Killed & Brot home, I am shure, 32, and William Killed 19 which makes 51 Pigeons, and we Killed 1 Squirrell Each. When I get thare I went to work at the Skift and I had it Pulld out and turned over, This was near 10 oclock & Mr Wolcott had not Came up from a Mr Jordans Flat Boat where he had Staid all night, I notice too that the Corn House Door was broken open by Some one, I think on Saturday night   Some thing about that I dont Like, Sam has been Layed up for 4 or 5 days.

25   I got up quite Erly this morning and we mounted horses and took a hunt for Hogs and we did not Get any. I shot the old hound and stung him Smartly. We came home and I killd 8 Pigeons and 1 Squirrell, and Wm Killd 3 pigeons, 1 Squrrell, Mr Wolcott 2 duck, 1 Pigeon,   We then went to work at the Ditch and worked untill night. We Dug 57 steps of it, Mr Wolcott Put up Post for Bars.

26   I Got up Erly before day Light this morning and started to town, Got thare Some time before Breakfast, I Sent Jim Down to Cork a skift   Wm came up with the Mule team. Brot Corn, Peas & hay & Potatoes

27   Buisness very Good. Greate deal of Hair cutting to day — Wm and Jim & Dan went into the Swamp to Drive up the Cows to milk. Gim was to haul some wood out of the Field too, Before he Came up. News from Jenny Lind this Evening that She will Come up and sing in this place and will do so in the Methodist Church

28   Buisness only So, So

March 2   I am sick to day and did not go to the shop at all. Very bad cold with very Seviere pains in the my Limbs generally.

3   I am Sick to day and cannot work at the Shop   Oregon Bursted her Boillers and Burned up Just above Vicksburg. Killed 40 or 50. Scalded Johnson, & his wife was on Bourd at the time

4   I am Still Confined to the house and not able to work at the shop.

5   William Came up this Evening and brot up 4 squirrells

778

that he Killed. Moose was Down thare too and he Killd 11 Pigeons, Wm Seys that Wolcott had planted nearly all the Corn that he had to plant.

    6   Buisness Dull of course, in Consequence of the wether, Nothing new.

    7   A Race to day between a Dun Mare and the Bontura Roan Horse, Winston Lost with Delany $7.50 & with Lucas $5, with me $3.50, with Jaqumine $2.50 & with Some One Else $2.50   I Received $178 of Mr Fields to day for stock that I sold him a short time ago. Richard, Byron & Andrew went in the swamp this Evening to hunt

    8   Buisness Only Tolerable, Greate many persons in toun at Present, I paid Winston twenty five Dollars to day. That is I paid Edd the amount for him by his Order, I Sent Down to day by Pearce 2 plows that has been Laid and Sharpened, Some Coffee & Sugar, Some beef & Onions, 3 pounds of Buck Shot, 2 Loaves of Bread

    9   Buisness So So. After the shop shut I wrode Down in to the Swamp and found that not much had been done. Wilcott was Out in the Swamp hunting Oxen with Mr Gregory. B Winn & Mr Dillon & Gay was out Hunting Hogs, They Killed 19 head of them I am told. I met his man with 3 shoats that they Killd Down on Greens Slough, and I believe that they were my Pigs. Thus it is that men play the game So fine. I wrode Down to Mr Gregory and talkd with him a short time and then told him about my Buying the interest of the Commercial Bank in that Land, Viz Pitcher, Lacost & Barnards, and I made a pro[po]sition to him and he Promised to Come up and see me about it

    10   I was in the Swamp Erly this morning and I got On My Horse and Got up to town to Breakfast   A Greate many Person in town to day. Buisness was pretty Good, Edd took out Mr Hoggatts women that was put in Jail this morning

    11   Our city is full of strangers   Came to See Jenny Lind.[7] They have Came from the Country and The ajoining

---

[7] The Natchez *Courier* gave excellent coverage to Jenny Lind's visit to Natchez. See issues of March 5, 11, 14, April 9, 1851. It reported that 790 seats in the Methodist Church had sold for $6,643. On March 14 the editor wrote enthusiastic praise of the singer's concert before "a numerous and brilliant audience," but by April 9 he found it necessary to deny the rumor that she gave $1,000 to charity in Natchez. The trustees of the Methodist Church had acknowledged that they received from the local committee of arrangements only $946.30, which was all that remained after the $5,000 guarantee and expenses had been paid to the artist's manager, P. T. Barnum. The editor added: "They did not even give or spend a cent in this city."

Counties. Buisness is very brisk. I Like to See Such very much indeed. The Shop took in to day $13.60　This is Good.

12　Buisness has fallen off very much since yesterday　The Concert Excitment is all Over, and the People wants and has Left for ther Homes. William wrode in the Swamp this Evening to bring up Some Corn.

13　I got up very Erly this Morning and went to the Swamp　The River is still arising here, I found when I got down in the Swamp that they were at work at the uper Cut in the Lower Field, I got to work after a wrid to the Creek, then I Commencd to help them fininish planting the cut next to the woods. Drove up Baunch & young Calf & a Black & white Cow with her Calf. She is a Stray Cow, Wm brot up a Load of Corn to day from the Swamp

14　Mr Wolcott Marked & Branded 6 or 7 head of the Calves and turned them out again, I was having the Ditch made to Convey the water into the big Dich in the slough, We finished this Evening in planting the cut of Corn below the Corn house on the Front Ridge. Mary Sick & Laid up

15　Buisness Only Tolerable. Old Winston was out to the tract to See the Race between Dun Mare & Roan Horse. They did not run. Bully Henderson Colt ran VS Roan Horse and beat him Some 20 ft or more, William & Sam Came up this Evening and brot up a Load of Corn　Said that the hands were making a Small Levy up at the uper End of the field, and that Fill had Laid up.

16　Buisness Only so, so. I remained at home all day, Only walking out in the afternoon with Richard. Wm went down this Evening with the Waggon

17　After Breakfast this morning I started Down in the swamp and found all well. The hands was cl[e]aning up in the new ground　To day Mr Coburns month is up and I hired him for 2 weeks Longer. He was still at work at the big ditch in the field.

18　Mr C Gregory hired the hard Scrabble place from me to day at 35 dollars for the year, The hands and myself were up in the clearing at work at Logs &c. Mr Cobourn was at work at the ditch up at the End of the Field　My Fields are both dry up to this date. Coburn is at work at the uper End of the Field still making a trench to Lead the water off.

19　I got up this morning in the Swamp and found that the water had Came up Green Slough and got into the field, We then

Got to work at it and tryed to stop it with a Small Levee, We then made another Levee at the other Slough and then a Small One at the End of the Field. Cobourn, Wolcott and William made it, And then in the afternoon William and myself Startd to town. We did a Good Days work before We Startd up — To day Mr Postlethwait Bot the Oct [*sic*] Mill Property under the Hill at $260 and is to make me a good title to my 2 Lotts that I had up thare

    24   Buisness So, So. I am having The Pond Dug out on the Commons   Commenced yesterday and will Finish To Morrow

    26   To day has been a pleasent day tho not very brisk in the way of Buisness, I Finished The Digging of My Pond This Evening On the Commons, Wm, Gim & old Gim Dug it   The River is Still Rising here yet, Mr McDonald Sells a good many Things at auction to day belonging to his tavern

    27   Buisness rarther dull for the Season, Nothing New. I Got in a Skift this morning and with Elick Johnson and went into the Swamp, and I found the hands Just returning from Hard Scrable where they had been to work for Mr Chas Gregory by my Contract with him, Phill, he had the plow   This I did not agree to Send, for I had Only promised him that I would help him roll his Logs out of the way, So all hands were Down thare, I find that The Corn is prety well up all over the Lower field and that the Stand is rarther a bad one, I Started the hands to re-planting and they did not get through with it, nor wont before ½ the day tomorrow, The River is still rising and is about 9 inches below high water Mark, I find that very Little has been done Since I Left more than was Done by Mr Coburn the Ditcher

    28   I had the Levy workd on to day, ie at the foot of the field, and a Pen made Down on the ridge to try and Cetch my unmarkd Pigs   This I think rarther a poor arrangment for it was not made in such a maner as to do any Good for the Door is too Small. The hands are replanting Corn that The Birds have Destroyd, I after Diner went out in the Harry Cane and the Dogs Caught 6 Pigs that we Marked, 5 of them Boars and 1 Sow Pig   There were Several of My Sows and 1 of Mr Wolcotts. Mr Wolcott Said that he thought his Brothers Sow had 9 Pigs. Well we passd them and when we went down on the other Ridge at the foot of the field I or we found The Sow and She had 9 un-marked Pigs with her   I was very Glad to See that for I was affraid that I might have Caught one of his Pigs. Wm Wolcott Marked them all   I Mean all 6 of the Pigs that was Caught from my Sow, I find that is the reason that I have always been so unlucky in the raising of my hogs, I never Marked them in time.

29   Buisness pretty Good to day, Dr McGoun paid me his years Shaving to day, $15.00, to the [blank] of May, Ead returnd from Vicksburge this Evening   He went up thare in place of B. Nicks. There is a great deal of Rascality a going On at present amoung a Certain Crowd, and I am a Looker On in Venice. Closely, I Shall be a match for any Set of Rascals that may make me unhappy, Journeymen & Barbers &c

30   Buisness Dull, I think. Anderson Came up yesterday Evening and brot up 1 Bushell meal, 1 Bushell Potatoes, 1½ of Peas &c. All is well   The River is very high and rising, Only Short of high water Mark about 6 inches, I think, After Dinner to day I took a walk over with Robt Smith to Look at his young Horses & Carriages &c. I wrode out this Evening as far a[s] Dixons to Look for my Horses

31   We had a very fine Rain To day and I got my Pond full of water for the 1st time it has rain Since I had it Dug. I am in hopes it will Keep the water in it. Mr James Girault Died On the 24th inst. in Jackson, Miss. The River is falling above and is rising here at this Point, Col Robertson Came around to Let me Know that Mr Mott has got The Deeds that I Sent to him and Mr Mott thinks that there is no use for a Deed or transfer for The Land from Mr Saul, the Commisioner, as Mr Saul has Long Since Given up his Commissions in the institution and transfer his right intirely to Mr Alling, the Present President, and I thought from his maner of Speaking about it that there is Some Doubt of his making me any better tittle than I have already Gotten from them, Tho Col Robertson Said that Mr Mott would attend to it for me and Send me the Papers, for which I thanked Col R. for his attention &c. Mr Wm Rey was Buried This Evening. He Died yesterday, in The Morning — Charles paid me about Sixty Dollars to day and I Gave him ten Dollars for himself — Mr Stockman Buys My Cow & Calf Blaunch, and he promises to pay me for his bill and the Cow The Sum of Thirty Dollars.

April 1   Buisness Extremly Dull to day, Charles Came around this morning and Gave up the Key of the Shop under the Hill and I Sent Gim Down in place of him, I went under the Hill and Bot Some Paper to paper the Shop with, out of a Glass Boat as they are So Called

2   Buisness Tolerable fair to day. Winston is Sick   Taken this Evening. Jeff Gave me Thirty Dollars to Keep for him to day   Mrs Erhart brot me Mesrs Walker & Collins note to day to Keep for her, Gim is at work to day in papering The Shop under the Hill. Mr William Cobourn Came up to day from the Swamp and I paid him for One Month & a halfs work, besides the Cutting of 3 Cords & a ½ of wood, This amounted to as follows.

One Month at $12.00	12.00
½ Month at $8	8.00
and 3½ Cords of wood at 6 Bits per Cord	2.25
To 1 Axe 1. and a Coffee Mill 50 cts	1.50
	————
This Sum I paid him in Cash.	$ 23.75

I deducted 1.25 for Cash I pd him before
    3   Mrs Woods Died to day of Apoplexy, was taken yesterday, Was very much of a Lady. Gim makes 1.50 cts to day below and the uper Shop 2.90 ct   The River is On a Stand tis thought to day.
    4   Buisness has been Something better to day than yesterday, The Lower Shop took in to day $2.05. This is geting a Little Better, I now See how I have been Humbuged. I Notice that Charles Can Get under the Hill now as Soon as Any One, Thus I find out Considerable in taking a Little notice, To day Col Robertson handed me my Buget of Papers that Came from New Orleans, ie, The Deed to Swamp Land from Mr Alling the President of the Commercial Bank of La, and I paid The Postage On the Same 20 ct and the fee for writing the Same $10.00[8]   Winston has been Sick for two Days.
    5   Some few to day reports that The River has fallen a Little, ½ inch or Such a mater, They all Say that it is on a Stand, Mr Mahoney Came up to night in the skift with Anderson & Phill and Richard, They Drove up Some Horses with them, I hope to See them tomorrow if Possible   Mr Mahoney reports that he has Cut Fifty five Cords of wood and has made 2000 Rails. For the Rails I paid him $10.00 and for the wood I paid him $30.00   He was also paid 1 Dollar for 2 days work on the Building & he paid me as follows 1.50 for the Wolcott Axe & 85 cts for Peggys washing for him, He Leaves the place to

---

[8] See duplicate deed in Johnson Papers, and Adams County Deed Records, GG, 480. This was a title to two thirds of nearly 2,400 acres in the Swamp, but apparently it was defective. See *ibid.*, II, 597, KK, 127, HHH, 720.

day and I think will go up the River. I Got a Letter to day from Mr Mosbey and he reports all well, To day Mr Jas. Stockman paid me thirty Dollars for the Cow & Calf Blaunch and his shaving Bill up to the first of the Present Month.

6   I Came near having a fuss with a young man to day about Cuting his hair, We had pretty Sharp words. I bot 2 hens today from Mr Hays and I paid him $5 for the two, Phill & Anderson went Down this Evening late and I Sent Down 10 hog heads by them at 20 ct Each.

7   We had Considerable Rain in the Afternoon, which made buisness very dull indeed   This Evening the Shop was not Lit up in time and Mr Boyd did not get Shavd. Edd in the Corner a Sleep, Winston over at Franks, This is the way.

8   Buisness So, So. The River Falling a Little here

9   River Still Falling a Little here. Young Jersey Gilbert was Married to Night to Miss Fany Byers.

10   Buisness Fair & Edd Sick & we were very Buisy to day in painting and fiting up The old Shop. So we were Last Night untill 11 Oclock or Near it, Gim only makes 60 cts in the Shop to day. Poor Buisness that, Mr Gilbert Buys about 40 acres of wood Land from Mr Dixon on the Road as we go Down in the Swamp.

11   Nothing new more than the River is still falling here and has fallen near 8 inches, and was falling yesterday at Pitsburg, but the Ohio River was again Rising, I paid Maj Young to day Fifty Dollars for Charles wages up to the first of April inst. This is the Last time prehaps that we Shall have A Settlement for this Life &c. Gave Mr North my Deed to Look at &c.

12   Buisness Tolerable fair, We hear to Day that Poor old Mr Bracket Got Drowned on his way back from California. Poor old Gentleman

13   The River is Still falling and has fallen about 12 or 14 inches

16   Nothing New more than report Seys that half of Grand Gulf[9] has Burned Down with heavy Loss to Several, The River is Still Rising. Edd went to New Orleans this Evening   Winston Buys a Horse this Eveinng from young Hawings at $30 and I paid for him. Jeff Gave me twenty Dollars this Evening. I Gave

---

[9] Grand Gulf was a river port some fifty miles north of Natchez. It served as the shipping point for Port Gibson and for the area comprising Copiah, Hinds, and Claiborne counties.

Cinda & Dicy both a Flogging this Evening about her Conduct to her husband Last Night

    17   The River nearly On a Stand today, and a rise is reported at Vicksburg. News by the boat today informs me that I have Lost $10.00 On Rigadoon VS Louis D'Or & Charmer on the 4 mile Race, I had again to Flog Cinda about Fighting her husband in the Street, Wm Wolcott Sends for meat today. They are Out of meat.

    18   Business Just Tolerable. The River is thought to be On a stand at present   Greate Quantities of Corn are being receivd Every day by the Merchants & it will be much Cheaper Soon   Sixty five cents is what it Sells for today.

    19   Myself, Winston & William were at work in the shop all day and we were very buissy all day and we made $13.00 in the Shop today alone by work. Bless the day, it has been a Benefit indeed,   We did a greate deal of Hair Cutting today

    20   The river thought to be On a Stand

    21   Edd. Came up from New Orleans this morning and brot the Children Some Bananahs & a Box of Orrenges. Reports all well below, This Evening I wran my Horse Little Dick VS Mr Hutchens Little Black Horse for $10, Distance about 250 yds, and my Horse won the Race very Easy. We then ran the Same Distance for $2.50 and I won that, and then we had a Race On Winstons Horse VS old Jeff, And Jeff Beat him and we made that Race over again & Jeff won that. I think that was run over too, & Jeff won that too, then he ran his horse vs Little Dick and Dick won the Race Easy.

    22   Buisness Quite dull, I went under the Hill today and bot 11 Bushells of Oats at 50 cts per Bushell, & Wm Bot 100 wt of Bran & Some ¼ Barrell of Corn, & I think Winston Got some 100 hd wt. of Bran also

    23   Dr Brenum Cash in advance for Shaving, five dolls

    24   Buisness rarther dull I think, Nothing new. River Falling a Little here   I am Glad of it. I think it was today that Mr Hutchens, myself and Winston made agreement to run our Colts or Poneys 1 quarter of a mile, $5 Entrance. Mr Pickens will run his Poney too I expect, Mr Thom. Henderson Calld today to inform me that he had been offered Seven Hundred Dollars for the adjoining Lot to me and he promised me the refusal of it, I thanked him for it Kindly   I must See to morrow what I Can as towards making The Purchase of it.

    25   It was today I saw Mr Henderson and bot The Pomet

Lot from him that ajoins me in State Street, The Price agreed on is Seven Hundred & fifty Dollars, This Purchase I made opposite Old Commercial Bank in Presence of Col Robertson and I was or am to pay for The transfer & Deed & Taxes &c.[10]

26   Buisness Dull to what it was Last Saturday, I wrode out to the tract this Evening and had a Race. I wran Little Dick V. S. Winstons Horse, and I ran The Little Fields mare in the Same Race and Gave him 10 feet. I won $10 from him, I then ran Little Dick VS The Hutcheons Horse and gave 10 feet & Winston did the Same. I beat them all more than 10 ft. and Hutchens Hs beat Winston Horse Even Race — $2 Entrance. I Gave up the Stake as he thought it was not Quite 10 ft.   So I pd Dr Elaerich 1 Doll for Winston, 4.50 Dolls in Cash, which makes Just $15 that I won from him or let him have today.

27   Buisness has been Tolerable Good. Nothing new. Anderson Came up yesterday Evening a[nd] brot up 2 plows to be mended, and he brot up Some Corn, Sylvia came up also. Reports Peggy Sick. When the Skift went Down this Eve[n]ing I Sent Down 75 lbs of Bacon by the Skift, and I Sent down a man also to Chop wood.

29   I Saw the old man This Evening that I Sent Down to the place On Sunday, and he told me that he had Cut 1 Cord of wood, and that I paid him for it. He Complained of being unwell, Poor old man, I Sent Down the 2 plows that Came up the other day to be mended, Mr. Nelsons Skift took them Down, Mr Thoms Henderson brot me the Deeds today for the Corner Lot.

30   I was at auction to day and bot a Curtain and a Oven & a matt for the Shop under the Hill, I saw Mr North this morning and I told him that he Could propose a Compromise to Mr Wade if he was a mind to and told him the Conditions &c. I Saw Martin and told him the Same, He told me that he would See Mr Wade and talk to him &c. I Saw Mr McMurran to day and I wanted to know of him if he Considered the Pomet tittles good to the Lot and he told me that he did &c. The Little Bay Mare or Bell Mare Filly has a Little Colt Last night or this morning   Tis by Wood Pecker

---

[10] The purchase of this lot was completed by Johnson's estate after his death. Thomas Henderson was acting as trustee and attorney for the estate of Leonard Pomet, deceased. The lot was located on the corner of State and Canal streets, extending 162 feet along the south side of State and 101 feet along Canal. Adams County Deed Records, HH, 526–27; and Henderson's receipt for final payment, November 1, 1851, Johnson Papers.

May 1   Nothing new to day   Buisness Only tolerable

2   I paid Mr Thomas Henderson five hundred Dollars today and gave him my note for Two hundred & fifty for the remainder of the Purchase Money of the Lot I bot of him the other day — Mrs Battles Gave me two hundred Dollars of the money — The River is falling fast and there is a Good deal of Corn at the Landing at present & is Selling for 55 cts per Bushell   This is a true Coppy of a Proposition that I Shall make To Morrow To Mr Wade & Winn, Viz

Natchez May 2d 1851

Messrs. Wade & Winn

Gentlemen   For an amicable Settlement & Compromise of the Controversy now Subsisting between us, I propose that the Sectional lines between Our respective lands as retraced by Mr Kenny & Certified to the Circuit Court Shall hereafter be taken and regarded our true Boundaries, and that any & all Lands at any time Claimed or Occupied by you which according to Kennys Survey are included in lands belonging to me, Shall be abandoned by you, as Justly belonging to me, and further that I Shall release my Claim To Danages against you and Dismiss my Suite, upon terms that you Shall pay The Cost of your Own Witnesses & the Cost of the officers of the Court and that I Shall pay The Cost of my Witnesses, and that you Shall pay for the wood Which was Cut & Corded by me on my Said Lands & afterwards Converted or disposed of by you, Estimated by me to be 12 or fifteen Cords, This Proposal is made at the request of Mr Wade Communicated by Mr Martin, An Erly reply is requested.

Respectfully
Your Obt Servt,
William Johnson

3   Oh what a Lovely rain we have had today. Several Beautifull Showers. Just the rain that was so much wanted by Every Planter as well as Merchant. Thank God, for this favor. Mr Wade Esqr. Called on me this morning and stated that he & Mr Winn would acceed to my proposition, and that I Could have my Suite Dismissed, I then saw him and requested him to Sign Their names to my propositions which he, Mr Wade, told me that it would be done to a certainty, Mr North Calld this Evening and told me that they had Complied with my request and that he had Dismissd the Suit &c. The river is still falling and Gives pleasure to many Persons

4   Nothing new more than The Dreadfull account of the

Burning of the Steam Boat Webster, and some 30 persons Burned to death On her,[11] I found my Colt of the old Bell Mares Tilly in the big Bayou and I wont be able to get it out in a Day or two

5 Court Commences to day and a fine young Daughter, Miss Anna Stone, was Buried to day. She Died yesterday morning I believe, Very Large Funeral indeed

6 This was the day for my Suite to have Came On between myself & Mesrs. Wade & Winn

7 Today is the aniversary of the Tonado, Today Mr Wolcott Came up To Court and I paid him five Dollars On Acct. This Evening I get my Colt Out of the Bayou, It has been down there Ever Since Saturday Evening — Jeff gave me twenty Dollars to Keep for him this Evening

8 Buisness tolerable fair   Bill Nix works in the shop today in place of Edd. who went to Vicksburg in his place

9 Court is Still in Cession   Mr Ford is in treaty to buy Mr Tysons Land, Maj Farrar Seys that in the Event of a Sale he would not Substitute Mr Tysons Paper for Mr Fords, I went to See both of my Lawyers today To Know what they would Charge me in my Case and I did not See but One of them & he told me he had not made up his mind what he would Charge me and that he would See the other and would Let me Know. I Could not See what was the witness Fees because the papers were in the Court.

10 Good Many Persons startd for the North today, and Some to Urope — Mr F Surget & Wife &c

11 After the Shop was closed today I wrode 'Down into the Swamp. Winston & Wm went with me. We got Down to my place Late in the Evening, and I then wrode farther and went On Down as far as Mr Jas Gregorys   I met him on his Horse and I Sat and talked with him untill near Supper time, I then Left him and wrode up to the House. Winston was with me, I Looked at my Corn and thot that was in the Lower field Looked very well, but the Corn that was in the uper field was rarther Small Potatoes, and was greatly in need of work   It wanted plowing very much indeed. They will Commence On it tomorrow Morning. I find that The River has fallen about 8 or 10 ft and The back water is falling fast in the Swamps. I find that Mr Winn has got a Good Deal of Large Cypress timber Floated out to the yard   I find that The Road has been worked in part since I was

---

[11] The steamboat burned about 100 miles north of Vicksburg. Some twenty persons were reported lost. Natchez *Courier*, May 7, 1851.

Down in the Swamp the Last time, I [found] my old Horse Rigadoon The old Spanish mare Down at Mr Tysons place, but I Could not Get them to town, Burke I find has movd into his house in the old Field and Tate has Left and gone away Some where, William Sells his old Bay Horse This Evening to Mr Mc-Cants for $25.00

12   I Sent William under the Hill today and he bot a Barrell of Corn @ 90 cts and a Bale of Hay from Mr Gaw, The amount of which was 4.45 cts — My Young Roan Mare had a Colt this morning about 9 Oclock. She had it On the Hill opposite Mr Robersons in Mr Marshalls Pasture, Tis a Little Filly Sired by Limber John

13   Cou[r]t is Still in Session here. I Saw Mr North this Evening and paid him thirty five Dollars   This was his fee for attending to my Suite VS Wade & Winn, I then went up to Mr Henrys Store and paid 1.25 cts for a Bit of a Bacon ham, which I Lost on Lady Sulfolk VS Roanoak, at New Orleans, I then went to Mr Izods Store and paid him a Bill of $21.74 that was made Janry 20eth 1851. This was for a Barrell of Flour & a 100 lbs of Sugar at 7 cs and a Keg of Lard @ 9 cts and 2 Barrells of Potatoes which is put Down at 6 Dollars.

14   Buisness So, So. I wrote a Letter to Mr Miller today and Sent it by Jeff.

15   I Saw Mr Martin To day quite erly and paid him $35. This was his Fee in the Suite VS. Wade & Winn

16   I was up before 4 Oclock this morning and my wife Gave Birth to a fine Large Boy Child,[12] and this is Our ninth Child & 4th Son, He was born 2 minutes before 4 Oclock this morning, Mrs Bennett was in attendance

17   Buisness Only Tolerable. Court adjourned to day and there was not much Buisness done this term, Mr James paid me to day 1.50 ct for a Razor that I Sold him a Short time ago

18   After the Shop was closed up I wrode Down in the Bottom near the River and tryd to Get up my old Spanish mare and old Rigadoon, but we Could not Drive them up. We had to Leave them, Edd and Richard & Byron was along   We got a

---

[12] This was Clarence Johnson (christened Gabriel Clarence Johnson), who was later known as Clarence R. ("Man") Johnston while he operated a Natchez blacksmith shop. He was the diarist's tenth child and fifth son, if one child deceased in 1844 is counted. He married Catharine Lynch, sister of John R. Lynch of Natchez, who was born a slave and became a member of Congress from Mississippi (1873), fourth auditor of the United States Treasury, and author of *The Facts of Reconstruction* (New York, 1913).

Lot of Black & Dew Berrys a[n]d Eat them Down thare, Shop below made $10.25 this week

19   I went under the hill today and bot a Lot of Irish Potatoes, and hauled a part of them up the Hill and a Part of them I put in the Shop under the Hill. I was also a part of the Day hauling a Lot of Corn that I bot with the Potatoes, I also bot in the first place 8 Barrells of Corn from G. Harris at the uper Landing at 25 cts per Barrell   This Corn was Sunk in a Boat a few Days ago & the Lot of Corn and Potatoes that I got of Mr Marriner I paid him $6 in Cash and am to give him 3 months shaving for

20   Ned was hauling Corn a part of the day. I hired a Large Skift this Evening from Adams and Loaded it with Potatoes and startd down in the Swamp with them, We did not get thare untill after 9 Oclock at night, We then took out a part of them and put them in Wolcotts Flat Boat   I took Down, too, 3 Shoulders of meat 40 lbs, at 7 ct, 2.80

21   I was in the Swamp Erly this morning and Commenced to plant the Irish Potatoes that I took Down Last night & we got them planted by 4 Oclock in the Afternoon, which was a good Days work, I think. I then Startd to town with Richard & Left William to Come up in the morning in the Skift

22   Ellen is quite sick to day.

23   Byron Drove up his mare with a young Colt the other day   It was by Montgomery.

24   Buisness not quite as Good as we Sometimes have it, To day Bully Henderson ran his colt against a Bay Horse a q[ua]rter of a mile, and he got beat 1 foot. I paid Winston twenty five Dollars to day — He Got it, he Said, to bet on Mr Hendersons Colt. Our Little Ellen is very Sick at present, Sylvia, her mother, Came up yesterday morning to Stay with her, Judge P. Smith made a Speech tonight at the Court House and was very Cold and slow in his Speech. You Must Know that it was Dry, When he Said the next morning that he would not have made it for a $1000. The Subject was Secession or Disunionism

25   Wm, Richard, Byron, Winston & myself wrode down in the flat this Evening

26   Buisness Some what Dull. Poor Little Ellen is very Sick and Dr Blackburn thinks there is no chance of her recovery

27   Sarah is taken quite Sick this morning   Simtoms very much Like Cholera. Dr Blackburn attends her.

28   Buisness fair   Mr Dutch Miller paid five Dollars to

day for Shaving — Jeff gave me to day twenty Dollars to Keep for him, Our Little Ellen is Still Quite Sick. Very indeed

29   I went under the Hill to day and Bot 87 lbs of Bacon, 7 pieces, and Sent them in the Swamp, and I Sent Some Flour, Some Salt Beef, Sugar & Coffee and a plug of tobacco for Maj Winn, I wrode out on the Commons this Evening and Give old Jeff a Small run and was Leading Telgraph, and my Pocket Broke out and I Lost $75.95   At Least I found that much and I Espect that I did not find it all.

30   Buisness Only Tolerable, To day about 12 Oclock, our Poor Little Ellen Died with Something Like Consumption, She will be better off in another world No doubt

31   Our Poor Little Ellen was Burried to day. She was the Daughter of Phillip & Sylvia

June 1   The River rising Tolerably fast. Mr James Currys Son was Drowned Yesterday Evening at The Landing   He fell off a log

2   Buisness rarther Dull

9   Robert McCary Came up this morning from New Orleans   He went Down in Jeffs Place on the Boat as Barber &c

10   I was up at auction to day and Bot a Barrell or ½ pipe of Gin at 30 cts per Gallon

11   Buisness Only So So. I had my Black mare Shod all over, ie all around This Evening — William had his Little Sorril mare shod Day before yesterday at Mr Crizers shop.

12   I wrode out to day with the children and Got a Lot of Black Berrys — Mr. Fords & Winns hands are working the Road in the Dixon Pasture

13   Buisness Extreamly dull

14   Buisness very dull indeed but nothing Like as dull as was yesterday. I Cannot find two of my Horses to day, Jeff & Fiddler — Something wrong I think, for they were Driven out of Lanieres yesterday Evening — Mr Hamilton paid me thirteen dollars for William. This was for his Horse that he Sold to Mr McCants & Hamilton

Index